UNDERSTANDING BANKRUPTCY

LexisNexis Law School Publishing
Advisory Board

UNDERSTANDING BANKRUPTCY

Third Edition

Jeff Ferriell
Professor of Law
Capital University Law School

Edward J. Janger
David M. Barse Professor of Law
Brooklyn Law School

ISBN: 978–0–7698–5920–0
ISBN:978-0-3271-8286-3 (ebook)

Library of Congress Cataloging-in-Publication Data

Ferriell, Jeffrey Thomas, 1953-
Understanding bankruptcy / Jeff Ferriell, Professor of Law, Capital University Law School ; Edward J. Janger,
Professor of Law, Brooklyn Law School. -- Third edition.
pages cm.
Includes index.
ISBN 978-0-7698-5920-0
1. Bankruptcy--United States. I. Janger, Edward J. II. Title.
KF1524.F47 2013
346.7307'8--dc23

2012043384

NOTE TO USERS
To ensure that you are using the latest materials available in this area, please be
sure to periodically check the LexisNexis Law School web site for downloadable
updates and supplements at www.lexisnexis.com/lawschool.

Editorial Offices
121 Chanlon Rd., New Providence, NJ 07974 (908) 464-6800
201 Mission St., San Francisco, CA 94105-1831 (415) 908-3200
www.lexisnexis.com

MATTHEW◆BENDER

PREFACE

This book is designed to provide a basic introduction to bankruptcy and related state debtor-creditor law. It will be useful for students taking an introductory course in Creditors' Rights that emphasizes bankruptcy, a course in Basic Bankruptcy, or an advanced course in Chapter 11 Reorganization. It attempts to provide students with a reasonably detailed discussion of the issues most likely to arise in these courses. It is as up-to-date as possible, given the fast-changing nature of the law it examines. This edition incorporates reported decisions interpreting the Bankruptcy Code through the end of June, 2012.

The primary goal of this book is to bring order and clarity to a body of law for those who are newcomers to bankruptcy law. In addition, it provides a basic explanation of much of the commercial and debtor-creditor law that operates in the background of bankruptcy cases.

We hope it provides a useful supplement to primary materials: the Bankruptcy Code, the Bankruptcy Rules, and cases decided under them. Students using this book will still need to study these fundamental materials in detail. In many situations they will find it useful to put this book down, pick up the Bankruptcy Code, and read the relevant statutory provision carefully. A full understanding requires facility with the Code, the Rules, and the cases.

In the last three and a half decades, bankruptcy has evolved from a somewhat obscure specialty to one of the dominant bodies of American law. Traditionally, the bankruptcy bar was divided into two groups — the rather small group that did consumer and small business bankruptcy, and the tiny group that worked on larger business reorganizations. Many bankruptcy practitioners retain a degree of nostalgia for the days when insolvency lawyers, if somewhat isolated from the profession as a whole, enjoyed (in much of the country at least) the kind of camaraderie that is usually associated with lawyers in a small town.

Much of this has changed. Bankruptcy has become a boom area of practice, one of interest to a growing number of large firms. The annual rate of bankruptcy filings grew rapidly in the late 1990s and early 2000s, reaching a peak of over 1.5 million. That number declined after the Code was substantially amended in 2005, but rebounded to well over one million in the wake of the financial crisis of 2008. The administrative and judicial structure of bankruptcy has become elaborate and formalized; the scope of bankruptcy has grown in unexpected directions. Bankruptcy is now a serious matter not only for commercial and insolvency lawyers, but also for tax lawyers, domestic relations lawyers, environmental lawyers, intellectual property lawyers, and labor lawyers, as well as those involved in business and personal injury litigation generally.

There are many reasons for this transformation. On the consumer side some say the change is attributable to the fact that bankruptcy no longer carries with it a stigma of failure and dishonesty. Others attribute this shift to changes in the consumer credit industry, especially the advent of subprime lending and lenders who can lend profitably to much riskier borrowers. On the business side, some alternatives to bankruptcy, especially state insolvency proceedings, have withered away or are ineffective in the face of national and multinational business enterprises. The Bankruptcy Code itself is in part responsible; it contains a number of legal devices that permit people and companies to achieve — or at least to try to achieve — goals that are simply not achievable under any other body of law. For example, bankruptcy is practically the only method of dealing with "mass torts" in a single consolidated proceeding.

Along with the explosion of bankruptcy litigation has come a parallel explosion of academic interest in bankruptcy. Not long ago, most law schools had little more in their curriculum than a single course in Creditor's Rights, only part of which was taken up by bankruptcy law. Today, many schools have several courses, covering not only basic bankruptcy but reorganization bankruptcy, bankruptcy tax, partnership bankruptcy, bankruptcy environmental law, and the like. Similarly, for many years there was only one important secondary source — Collier on Bankruptcy — a venerable treatise first published in 1898 (the 16th edition of which is still the leading authority).[1] Now there are many sources. Of special interest to the law school community are the multiple law reviews that specialize in bankruptcy law, and the many articles on bankruptcy published in non-specialist law journals. We have tried to include a fair sampling of these other sources, to which students should turn for further discussion when they find themselves excited by a particular topic.[2]

Bankruptcy has also become a hot topic among legal theorists. Nothing that touches so large a part of the American economy and American society can exist for long without triggering efforts to fit it within larger structures of economic and political thinking. While this book is primarily aimed at giving a basic overview of bankruptcy, it also introduces the reader to the most important theoretical perspectives. Bankruptcy is an area in which there is often little separation between theory and practice, not least because Congress is constantly returning to basic principles as it writes and rewrites the Bankruptcy Code.

Bankruptcy law in this country is federal law. The substantive parts are found almost entirely in the Bankruptcy Code (Title 11 of the United States Code). Procedural rules are found mainly in the Federal Rules of Bankruptcy Procedure and in various parts of Title 28 of the United States Code (the "judicial code"). A few provisions are in Title 18 of the United States Code (the federal criminal code"). Although some state law is directly incorporated into the Code, and other state law indirectly affects rights in bankruptcy, most of the conflicts between state law and bankruptcy law is resolved in favor of the latter.

One of the features of federal law is the wealth of legislative history that underlies it. Insofar as the Bankruptcy Code is concerned, the primary sources of that history are the House and Senate Reports that accompanied its original enactment. There was also extensive floor debate on some provisions; and most of the subsequent amendments to the Code are supported by similar reports and debates. The weight to be given these sources is today controversial. Several members of the Supreme Court, most noticeably Justice Antonin Scalia, largely reject the use of legislative history in statutory

---

[1] Not coincidentally, Collier's is a Matthew Bender publication.

[2] The suggestion that one might find bankruptcy law interesting and exciting brings to mind the teenage daughter of one of your author's friends. She found her father's amateur radio hobby both interesting and exciting, but when she passed her FCC amateur radio licensing exam, and thus became a "ham radio" operator, she made her father (W8HI) and his law professor friend (K8ZDA) promise not to tell any of her peers.

PREFACE

interpretation and sometimes seems to use the bankruptcy code as a laboratory to test out his theories of statutory interpretation.

We end by suggesting one final reason why we think you will find this one of the most exciting courses you will take in law school. In a practical, if not technical legal sense, bankruptcy is the court of last resort. In virtually every bankruptcy, there are far more claims than there are assets. Not only is there no free lunch; there is not enough lunch to feed everybody. In bankruptcy there is only so much to go around; it is not sufficient; yet it is all there is or will ever be. This means that bankruptcy law must make choices that are both unsatisfactory and final. How should the limited pool be divided up? How do we and how should we decide between the claim of the mortgage holder to whom the debtor owes money on a loan and the maimed victim of the debtor's intentional tort? How do we also fit in the tax collector, the utility company, the credit card company, the debtor's doctor and the debtor's unpaid housekeeper? Bankruptcy law again and again forces us to make the hard disagreeable choices that are otherwise too often ignored. You may agree or disagree with the choices that have been made, but you should understand them; you should also understand that a choice is unavoidable.

With all this said, we hope you will find your study of bankruptcy exciting and intriguing. We hope as well you will find this book a helpful guide. Good luck!

Jeff Ferriell, Columbus, Ohio & Oak Bluffs, Massachusetts
Ted Janger, Brooklyn, New York & West Tisbury, Massachusetts

ACKNOWLEDGEMENTS

Our first debt of gratitude must be to Rev. Michael J. Herbert of the Roman Catholic Diocese of Richmond, Virginia. Father Herbert provided the authors with no direct spiritual assistance, at least none that we know of. Instead, he provided us with the benefit of the considerable expertise in bankruptcy and related commercial law he acquired, prior to his ordination, while he was a member of the University of Richmond Law School faculty, and as the sole author of the first edition of this book. Although his ecclesiastical duties made it necessary for him to decline to be named as a third co-author of subsequent editions of Understanding Bankruptcy, its basic structure, format, and indeed many of its passages reflect work he did in the early 1990's. Without the benefit of his earlier work, our task would have been much harder. Any mistakes, of course, are ours alone.

Thanks are also owed to Deans Joan Wexler, Michael Gerber, and Nick Allard, the Dean's research fund at Brooklyn Law School, as well as to Capital University Law School Deans Jack Guttenberg and Rich Simpson, and Capital University Law School research funds. Our able research assistants on the second edition Mary Daugherty and Carla Cheung, and Eric Coss, Erin Porta, Noam Weiss and Colleen Connelly, as well as Keith Moore at Lexis-Nexis and Matthew Bender have provided necessary encouragement and patient research and editorial work.

We also owe a debt of gratitude to those who first introduced us to bankruptcy law, Profs. Gary Neustadter and former Prof. Sheridan Downey of Santa Clara University, former University of Illinois Prof. Jonathan Landers, and Prof. Douglas Baird of the University of Chicago. This work also benefitted considerably from our past students who suffered through many of our early efforts to explain bankruptcy law, and whose puzzled looks and thoughtful questions are responsible for inducing us to develop many of the better explanations that appear in this book.

Finally, thanks are also owed, in connection with both this work and every aspect of our lives, to our parents, Merlin and Frances Ferriell and Inez and Allen Janger, as well to our wives, Cheryl Hacker and Victoria Eastus.

TABLE OF CONTENTS

TABLE OF CONTENTS

TABLE OF CONTENTS

TABLE OF CONTENTS

TABLE OF CONTENTS

TABLE OF CONTENTS

TABLE OF CONTENTS

TABLE OF CONTENTS

TABLE OF CONTENTS

TABLE OF CONTENTS

TABLE OF CONTENTS

TABLE OF CONTENTS

TABLE OF CONTENTS

TABLE OF CONTENTS

TABLE OF CONTENTS

TABLE OF CONTENTS

TABLE OF CONTENTS

TABLE OF CONTENTS

TABLE OF CONTENTS

TABLE OF CONTENTS

TABLE OF CONTENTS

TABLE OF CONTENTS

TABLE OF CONTENTS

TABLE OF CONTENTS

TABLE OF CONTENTS

TABLE OF CONTENTS

TABLE OF CONTENTS

TABLE OF CONTENTS

Chapter 1

GENERAL PRINCIPLES UNDERLYING INSOLVENCY LAW

§ 1.01 THE NATURE OF INSOLVENCY LAW

[A] Introduction: Fresh Start for Individual Debtors & Fair Treatment of Creditors

Bankruptcy law generally seeks to advance two goals with regard to individual (human) debtors. The first is to provide honest but unfortunate debtors with a fresh start. If debtors are treated too leniently, they might incur debt too liberally and freely waste assets they have accumulated, without using them to pay their creditors.

On the other hand, if debtors are treated too harshly, people might generally be discouraged from taking what otherwise might be economically efficient risks that would produce wealth for society as a whole. Further, people who are saddled with staggering debts, with no hope of enjoying the benefit of their future labors — other than paying their creditors — are discouraged from working hard. If relieved from their obligations, and able to reap the benefits of their future endeavors, they are more likely to be productive citizens. Similar goals and concerns also apply to businesses that seek to reorganize, though it should be noted that corporations that liquidate do need, or get, a fresh start. They simply cease to exist.

The second goal of bankruptcy is to treat creditors fairly, even though they will not be paid in full. This involves, in turn, the debate over how to maximize the value of the assets that are to be dismembered, and the struggle over which creditors should be given the best crack at those assets, and which creditors may retain their rights against them.

The bankruptcy code employs several mechanisms that result in better treatment to some creditors than others, including enforcing secured creditors' liens, giving priority to certain classes of unsecured creditors, and making certain specified debts non-dischargeable. Over the years, Congress has given favored treatment to an amazing variety of creditor groups, including, among others, labor unions, retirees, those injured by drunk (or drugged) drivers, those who make or guarantee student loans, consumers who buy on lay-away plans, spouses and former spouses, children, landlords, shopping mall operators, farmers, and the Federal Reserve Bank. Many times Congress has made a judgment that certain claimants — children, for example, may be particularly harmed and are therefore more deserving, At other times, there is little coherent logic, other than raw political power, involved in the determination of who qualifies for a favorable position.

Both the scope of the debtor's fresh start and issues of priority among creditors must be judged against their effect on credit markets. If the scope of the bankruptcy discharge is too broad, or too easily obtained, the effect may be to constrain the availability or raise the cost of credit for honest and creditworthy borrowers. If competitions between creditors are resolved unfairly, incentives for creditors to make loans may be skewed in ways that make certain types of credit too easy to obtain while making other types of credit too expensive.

Against this backdrop it is perhaps remarkable that bankruptcy law succeeds so well at (1) providing a way out of trouble for hopelessly swamped individual debtors while also providing an efficient means to adjust creditors' competing claims; and (2) providing a mechanism where business debtors can either readjust their capital structure, or efficiently liquidate their assets. Nonetheless, what for debtors viewed as an escape from personal tragedy, or the rescue of a troubled business, is often regarded by creditors as a swindle. By the same token, creditors' efficient collection may be the debtor's peonage.

[B] Bankruptcy as a Debtor's Remedy: Fresh Start for Honest Debtors[1]

The historic concept of the "fresh start" for honest but unfortunate debtors is central to modern bankruptcy law.[2] In the simplest form of bankruptcy, a debtor surrenders assets that are not essential for basic living to his or her creditors, and in exchange is released from those debts with a second chance for financial success.

The individual "consumer" debtor's fresh start is provided by two principal mechanisms: a discharge from liability on preexisting debts and the ability to retain limited "exempt" property that is regarded as necessary for life in modern society. For consumers, the discharge is the most important feature of bankruptcy. Eligible debtors are released from nearly all of their debts, or to put it another way, creditors are prohibited from collecting on discharged debts.[3] Freed from their past obligations, debtors have a renewed incentive to engage in economically

---

[1] See Katherine Porter & Deborah Thorne, *The Failure of Bankruptcy's Fresh Start*, 92 Cornell L. Rev. 67, 88 (2006) (indicating that 35% of families who sought protection under Chapter 7 regarded their financial difficulties as the same or worse one year after bankruptcy).

[2] *See* Charles G. Hallinan, *The "Fresh Start" Policy in Consumer Bankruptcy: A Historical Inventory and an Interpretative Theory*, 21 U. Rich. L. Rev. 49 (1986); Margaret Howard, *A Theory of Discharge in Consumer Bankruptcy*, 48 Ohio St. L.J. 1047 (1987); Thomas H. Jackson, *The Fresh-Start Policy in Bankruptcy Law*, 98 Harv. L. Rev. 1393 (1985); Charles Jordan Tabb, *The Scope of the Fresh Start in Bankruptcy: Collateral Conversions and the Dischargeability Debate*, 59 Geo. Wash. L. Rev. 56 (1990) (reviewing the literature).

The term "fresh start" is derived from *Local Loan Co. v. Hunt*, 292 U.S. 234, 244 (1934), where the Court indicated that bankruptcy gives "the honest but unfortunate debtor who surrenders for distribution the property which he owns at the time of bankruptcy, a new opportunity in life and a clear field for future effort, unhampered by the pressure and discouragement of preexisting debt." *See also* Williams v. United States Fid. & Guar. Co., 236 U.S. 549, 554-55 (1915).

[3] Bankruptcy Code § 524. *See infra* Chapter 13 — Discharge.

productive activity knowing that they will be able to retain the fruits of their efforts.

The second key feature of bankruptcy for consumer debtors is the ability to retain certain types of property, such as clothing, furniture, household appliances, a car, and certain accumulated retirement savings, as "exempt" from the claims of creditors.[4] Exemptions enhance the effect of the discharge by providing debtors with the tools they need to continue in life.

However, this fresh start is only available to the "honest but unfortunate debtor." This limitation reflects a moralistic strain in fresh start analysis that cannot be ignored. It is embodied in many existing provisions in the Bankruptcy Code. For example, a debtor who has engaged in dishonest conduct, such as hiding assets, or lying to the court or creditors, may be denied a discharge.[5] Similarly, certain debts that were indurred dishonesty may not be discharged.[6] Moreover, recent amendments to the Bankruptcy Code seek to restrict the availability of the fresh start, based on the assumption that many debtors were using the Bankruptcy system dishonestly to avoid paying debts that they could actually have repaid. Most of the major amendments to the current Bankruptcy Code, since its original enactment in 1978,[7] have been broadly pro-creditor,[8] though sometimes they favored one type of creditor at the expense of another.[9] Although there have been cries, in the wake of the financial crisis that began in 2007, for Congress to swing the pendulum in the opposite direction, as of the summer of 2012, no siginficant revision has occurred.

Whether limiting access to Bankruptcy, or raising its costs, is good policy depends largely on one's assumptions. If a substantial number of bankrupts actually have the capacity to pay their debts, then the recent changes to the Code will lead to more repayment of legitimate debts.[10] Conversely, debtors are, for the most part, truly unable to pay, keeping them out of bankruptcy court does not, by itself, put dollars in creditors' pockets.[11] Limiting access to bankruptcy discharge

---

[4] Bankruptcy Code § 522. *See infra* § 12.02 Exemptions in Bankruptcy, *infra;* William J. Woodward, Jr., *Exemptions, Opting Out, and Bankruptcy Reform,* 43 Ohio St. L.J. 335 (1982).

[5] Bankruptcy Code § 727(a). *See infra* § 13.02[B] Denial of Discharge in Chapter 7.

[6] Bankruptcy Code § 523(a)(2). *See infra* § 13.03[B][2] Debts Fraudulently Incurred.

[7] In 1979 the Bankruptcy Act of 1878 was repealed and replaced with what started out as a pro-debtor statute, the current Bankruptcy Code. The new statute considerably streamlined the consumer bankruptcy process.

[8] A notable exception is the 1986 enactment of Chapter 12, which is decidedly pro-family farmer debtor. Bankruptcy Code §§ 1201-1231. *See infra Chapter* 20 — Family Farmer and Family Fisherman Reorganization under Chapter 12.

[9] Paul M. Black & Michael J. Herbert, *Bankcard's Revenge: A Critique of the 1984 Consumer Credit Amendments to the Bankruptcy Code,* 19 U. Rich. L. Rev. 845 (1985).

[10] *E.g.,* Todd J. Zywicki, *An Economic Analysis of the Consumer Bankruptcy Crisis,* 99 Nw. U.L. Rev. 1463 (2005).

[11] Gordon Bermant & Ed Flynn, *Incomes, Debts, and Repayment Capacities of Recently Discharged Chapter 7 Debtors, Executive Office for U.S. Trustees,* U.S. Dept. Justice (Jan. 1999); Marianne B. Culhane & Michaela M. White, *Taking the New Consumer Bankruptcy Model for a Test Drive: Means-Testing Real Chapter 7 Debtors,* 7 Am. Bankr. Inst. L. Rev. 27 (1999); but see, Ernst & Young, *Chapter 7 Bankruptcy Petitioners' Ability to Repay: The National Perspective, Policy Economics and*

may only encourage creditors to engage in costly and fruitless efforts to collect. Indeed, even where creditors take no action to collect, the crushing overhang of debt may destroy any incentives debtors have to invest whatever available resources they have to improve their financial condition and return to economic productivity. In this way, restricting relief may impose costs on society without a corresponding return in increased collections from overextended debtors.

Even when bankruptcy is available, it does not provide debtors with completely new slate. The fact of a bankruptcy filing may be retained in a debtor's credit report for 10 years.[12] Lenders may deny credit to bankrupt debtors or charge them higher fees and interest, or insist on collateral. Bankruptcy is thus by no means cost-free, even to debtors who have few assets to lose in the bankruptcy process.

[C] Business Bankruptcy — Breathing Room and Maximizing Value

Bankruptcy is not just for people. Business entities can also file for bankruptcy. Many of the mechanisms and legal principles are the same, but the emphasis is different. An individual debtor who files for bankruptcy lives on after his assets have been liquidated. This is the nature of the fresh start. A corporation that has been liquidated cases to exist and does not need a fresh start. Sometimes, however, a business may be worth more as a going concern — if it continues to operate — than if sold off piecemeal. When this is the case, a business (and its creditors) may benefit from a discharge as well.

The Bankruptcy Code also provides a mechanism for business debtors and their staeholders to determine whether liquidation or reorganization will produce a higher return. Chapter 11 of the Bankruptcy Code provides a judicially supervised process through which business debtors and their creditors can negotiate over the fate of the business; should they liquidate or reorganize; how best should the assets be bundled for sale; how best might the business be repaired; and how should the value be distributed.

To accomplish this, bankruptcy holds creditors' collecton efforts at bay while the financially troubled business attempts to solve the problems that led to its financial difficulties in the first place. While creditors' collection efforts are restrained, the debtor has breathing room to negotiate with creditors as a group over how to restructure its businesses to provide the highest possible return to creditors on their investment. The reorganization provisions of the Bankruptcy Code seek to prevent the losses that everyone that would suffer if a potentially successful debtor simply liquidated.

Quantitative Analysis Group (March 1998); Ernst & Young, *Chapter 7 Bankruptcy Petitioners' Ability to Repay: Additional Evidence from Bankruptcy Petition Files, Policy Economics and Quantitative Analysis Group* (Feb. 1998); Ernst & Young, *Chapter 7 Bankruptcy Petitioners' Repayment Ability Under H.R. 833: The National Perspective, Policy Economics and Quantitative Analysis Group* (March 1999).

[12] Fair Credit Reporting Act § 605(a)(1), 15 U.S.C. § 1681c(a)(1)(2006).

[D] Bankruptcy as a Creditor's Remedy

It should be recognized that long before there was a "federal" law of bankruptcy, states had their own laws to provide for the collection of debts. These laws still exist,[13] and are only partially supplanted by bankruptcy law. Indeed, the early history of federal bankruptcy law is replete with the tension between the proponents of federal bankruptcy law as a more effective method for collecting debts (particularly for national banks who were met with resistence in local courts), and bankruptcy law as debt relief. Since the enactment of the Bankruptcy Act of 1898, bankruptcy law has served both as a collection device for creditors and as a means for debtors to obtain relief from their debts. Even when bankruptcy law supplied no redemption for debtors, it was designed to provide an efficient and orderly system to collect and distribute an insolvent debtor's assets among competing creditors. These purposes remain intact today. Bankruptcy procedures are designed to maximize the value of a consumer or business debtor's assets and to divide them equitably among creditors.

[1] Maximizing Value

Although few consumer debtors have substantial assets, financially troubled business debtors usually have some property available for at least some of their creditors. Some debtors may only partially repay even their secured creditors. Others may have enough assets to pay creditors in full, even though they are experiencing cash flow difficulties that make them unable to make regular payments as their debts become due.[14] Some businesses may be solvent or not, depending on whether they are valued as a "going concern," based on the income the business produces, or based on the total value that their assets would have generated if they were sold item by item at a liquidating auction. When debtors hold valuable assets, bankruptcy seeks to provide an orderly procedure to maximize the value of those assets and distribute their value in a way that maximizes the distribution to creditors. For debtors whose business is destined to fail, maximizing the value available for creditors may require piecemeal liquidation of the debtor's property. For debtors with viable businesses, but more debt than its cash flow can sustain, keeping the business in operation may produce greater payment to creditors than closing its doors and selling the assets at a fire sale. In many modern business bankruptcy cases, keeping the doors open may also be a way of facilitating a sale of the business's assets, as a going concern or at a higher price than could have been obtained for the assets themselves.

The state law debt collection system is characterized by a race among creditors where the spoils go to the swift. Individual creditors focus on grabbing assets rather than preserving value for other creditors who may have lagged behind in their efforts to collect or who have different collection rights. The first vulture to arrive on the scene of a fresh carcass cares little about later arrivals.[15] This so-called "race

---

[13] *See infra*, Chapter 2, Creditors' Collection Rights.

[14] In the equine community this is known as being "horse poor." A person may own several valuable horses, but lack the income to pay for their keep.

[15] Douglas G. Baird, *A World Without Bankruptcy*, 50 Law & Contemp. Probs. 173 (1987).

of diligence" may cause creditors to overreact to a debtor's precarious financial condition. Forbearance and negotiation are risky when other creditors are rushing to collect. Restructuring is difficult under state law, and bankruptcy law seems to remedy this problem. Bankruptcy procedures thus seek to preserve the value of a financially troubled debtor and help ensure that the highest possible proportion of a debtor's total obligations is paid from the available resources.

[2] Equal Treatment of Creditors

Bankruptcy serves the interests of creditors not only by preserving the debtor's financial value, but by ensuring that creditors share whatever value remains, in an equitable fashion. Thus, a frequently articulated goal of bankruptcy is to ensure "equal treatment of creditors of the same class."[16] This distinguishes bankruptcy from the state collection system which, because of its "race to the courthouse" approach, usually results in better treatment of creditors who act quickly to collect, leaving those who are inclined to permit the debtor to attempt to resolve its financial difficulties, largely in a lurch. The equal treatment policy also helps maximize the debtor's value by discouraging overly aggressive collection efforts that might lead to a debtor's premature financial demise.

The equal treatment policy is reflected in numerous key provisions of the Bankruptcy Code. In liquidation proceedings, § 726(b) requires creditors' claims to be paid "pro rata among claims of the [same] kind."[17] In reorganization proceedings, § 1123 requires a Chapter 11 plan to "provide the same treatment for each claim or interest of a particular class, unless the holder . . . agrees to a less favorable treatment,"[18] and § 1129 prevents a plan from discriminating unfairly among classes of creditors who have not agreed to the terms of the plan.[19] Provisions in Chapters 12 and 13 impose similar requirements. Moreover, the bankruptcy trustee's ability to recover certain pre-bankruptcy payments and other kinds of property transfers to creditors that would disrupt the equal treatment policy apply in both liquidation and reorganization proceedings.[20] Not surprisingly, though, most of the complications in bankruptcy law arise from rules designed to determine which creditors are in the same class, and from those that create exceptions to the "equal treatment" policy.

---

[16] Thomas H. Jackson, The Logic and Limits of Bankruptcy Law 2-4 (1986); Elizabeth Warren, *A Principled Approach to Consumer Bankruptcy*, 71 Am. Bankr. L.J. 483, 483 (1997). *See* Howard Delivery Service, Inc. v. Zurich American Ins. Co., 547 U.S. 651, 669 (2006); Alan N. Resnick, *The Future of the Doctrine of Necessity and Critical-Vendor Payments in Chapter 11 Cases*, 47 B.C. L. Rev. 183, 184 (2005); H.R. Rep. No. 95-595, at 177-78 (1978), *reprinted in* 1978 U.S.C.C.A.N. 5787, 5963, 6137-39.

[17] Bankruptcy Code § 726(b).

[18] Bankruptcy Code § 1123(a)(4).

[19] Bankruptcy Code § 1129(b)(1).

[20] Bankruptcy Code § 547. *See generally infra* Chapter 15 Avoidable Preferences.

§ 1.02   MODERN THEORIES OF INSOLVENCY LAW[21]

For many years, bankruptcy law existed without much theoretical context. There was only one broadly recognized history of bankruptcy law: Charles Warren's "Bankruptcy in United States History," published in 1935.[22] This masked a sporadic and informal theoretical literature that was found spread across numerous cases, articles, and speeches. Although studies were made from the perspective of other disciplines, formal efforts to draw together the disparate strands of bankruptcy thinking, at least as far as lawyers were concerned, were rare.

This is no longer true. There has also been a renewed interest in bankruptcy history,[23] and a new effort to gather empirical data about bankruptcy practice and the substantive impact of bankruptcy law on real-world behavior.[24] For the theorist, the historian, and the pragmatist, there is now a wealth of material tackling bankruptcy from almost every conceivable perspective and nearly every mode of legal writing, from the philosophical to the statistical to the qualitative.[25]

It is impossible to summarize the full range of this literature here. Instead, we will briefly describe the two most influential strains of bankruptcy theory. These two principal strains, characterized in the first edition of this work as "economic" and "social," have since become more widely known as "proceduralist" and "traditionalist" views.[26] Both strains currently influence courts' decisions and congressional

---

[21]   Douglas G. Baird, *Bankruptcy's Uncontested Axioms*, 108 Yale L.J. 573 (1998).

[22]   Charles Warren, Bankruptcy in United States History (1935).

[23]   Bruce H. Mann, Republic of Debtors: Bankruptcy in the Age of American Independence (2003); David A. Skeel, Jr., Debt's Dominion: A History of Bankruptcy Law in America (2003); Vern Countryman, *A History of American Bankruptcy Law*, 81 Com. L. J. 226, 226-32 (1976); Rhett Frimet, *The Birth of Bankruptcy in the United States*, 96 Com. L.J. 160, 163-63 (1991); Nathalie Martin, *The Role of History and Culture in Developing Bankruptcy and Insolvency Systems: The Perils of Legal Transplantation*, 28 B.C. Int'l & Comp. L. Rev. 1, 20-25 (2005); Charles Jordan Tabb, *The History of the Bankruptcy Laws in the United States*, 3 Am. Bankr. Inst. L. Rev. 5 (1995).

For just a few of the many articles that have blended historical review with analysis of contemporary bankruptcy problems, see John C. McCoid, II, *Pendency Interest in Bankruptcy*, 68 Am. Bankr. L.J. 1 (1994); John C. McCoid, II, *Setoff: Why Bankruptcy Priority?*, 75 Va. L. Rev. 15 (1989); Thomas E. Plank, *The Constitutional Limits of Bankruptcy*, 63 Tenn. L. Rev. 487, 500-17 (1996) (discussing the development of bankruptcy law in England); Charles Jordan Tabb, *Rethinking Preferences*, 43 S.C. L. Rev. 981 (1992).

[24]   For a few of the most recent efforts in this regard, *see* Teresa A. Sullivan, Elizabeth Warren & Jay Lawrence Westbrook, *The Persistence of Local Legal Culture: Twenty Years of Evidence From the Bankruptcy Courts*, 17 Harv. J. L. & Pub. Pol'y 801 (1994); Paul B. Lackey, *An Empirical Survey and Proposed Bankruptcy Code Section Concerning the Propriety of Bidding Incentives in a Bankruptcy Sale of Assets*, 93 Colum. L. Rev. 720 (1993); and Ian Domowitz & Thomas L. Eovaldi, *The Impact of the Bankruptcy Reform Act of 1978 on Consumer Bankruptcy*, 36 J. Law & Econ. 803 (1993). *See also* Teresa A. Sullivan, Elizabeth Warren & Jay Lawrence Westbrook, As We Forgive Our Debtors: Bankruptcy and Consumer Credit in America (1989).

[25]   For an example of a work that contains both the statistics and their dramatization, see Teresa A. Sullivan, Elizabeth Warren & Jay Lawrence Westbrook, As We Forgive Our Debtors: Bankruptcy and Consumer Credit in America (1989). *See also* Elizabeth Warren & Amelia Warren Tyagi, The Two-Income Trap: Why Middle-Class Mothers and Fathers Are Going Broke (2003).

[26]   This taxonomy can be traced to Douglas G. Baird, *Bankruptcy's Uncontested Axioms*, 108 Yale L.J. 573, 576-79 (1998). *See also* Edward J. Janger, *Crystals and Mud in Bankruptcy Law: Judicial Competence and Statutory Design*, 43 Ariz. L. Rev. 559, 566 (2001); Charles W. Mooney, Jr., *A Normative*

enactments.[27]

[A] "Proceduralist" Theories of Bankruptcy[28]

Proceduralist scholars advance the view that bankruptcy law is and should be merely a bunch of civil procedure. Bankruptcy law should not create or disturb existing entitlements. As they see it, bankruptcy specific entitlements will lead to forum shopping into bankruptcy.[29] They further contend that creditors, rather than bankruptcy judges, are in the best position to distinguish between debtors who are likely to be rehabilitated from those who are likely to fail, and that as a general proposition, "rehabilitation" is not an independent goal of bankruptcy.[30]

Therefore, bankruptcy should do nothing more than preserve value for creditors by seeking to eliminate the inefficiencies that are inherent in atomistic state collection proceedings. When an individual creditor sues a debtor, that creditor's only interest is maximizing its own recovery, regardless of whether this is consonant with the greatest possible recovery for creditors as a whole. However, if creditors act collectively, proceduralists argue, they become concerned about overall recovery. Proceduralists are not altruists. Quite to the contrary, they simply believe that over time it makes more sense for creditors to share evenly in larger pools of assets from many debtors than to take their chances at being able to seize a disproportionate number of assets from an occasional, smaller pool of assets owned by a few debtors.

For example, imagine creditors A, B, and C, who are each owed $1,000 by three debtors, X, Y, Z. The value of each debtor's total assets depends on the way those assets are handled. The value is only $1,000 each if the debtors are liquidated in a piecemeal fashion, but it is $2,000 if the debtors are either liquidated in an orderly fashion or reorganized to preserve their ongoing concern value.

If creditors A, B, and C act independently each will attempt to seize all available assets of each debtor. This will cause a disorderly liquidation that will limit the value of the assets to $1,000 per debtor. Independent action makes it impossible for the debtors to reorganize or to conduct an orderly liquidation. This reduces the value of each debtor's assets, which in turn reduces the total payout to the creditors as a whole.

To further illustrate, suppose A gets lucky in its independent action against X and collects the entire $1,000 X owes to A. X's assets will have been completely consumed in satisfaction of A's claim; B and C will receive nothing from their

---

Theory of Bankruptcy Law: Bankruptcy as (Is) Civil Procedure, 61 Wash. & Lee L. Rev. 931 (2004).

[27] Mark Bradshaw, Comment, *The Role of Politics and Economics in Early American Bankruptcy Law*, 18 Whittier L. Rev. 739 (1997).

[28] Thomas H. Jackson, The Logic and Limits of Bankruptcy Law (1986); Douglas G. Baird, *A World Without Bankruptcy*, 50 Law & Contemp. Probs. 173 (1987); Douglas G. Baird, *Bankruptcy's Uncontested Axioms*, 108 Yale L.J. 573, 578 (1998); Charles W. Mooney, Jr., *A Normative Theory of Bankruptcy Law: Bankruptcy As (Is) Civil Procedure*, 61 Wash. & Lee L. Rev. 931 (2004).

[29] Thomas H. Jackson, The Logic and Limits of Bankruptcy Law (1986).

[30] *See* Edward J. Janger, *Crystals and Mud in Bankruptcy Law: Judicial Competence and Statutory Design*, 43 Ariz. L. Rev. 559, 566 (2001).

efforts to collect. A has obtained full payment on one debt, and if it gets equally lucky in its actions against Y and Z, it will be paid in full on all three of its debts. The corollary of this is that if A is three times lucky, B and C get nothing at all from X, Y, or Z.

In the example given, it is easy to see why B and C would prefer orderly liquidations, but why would A? The reason is that A has no guarantee that it will be lucky once, let alone three times in a row. Assuming B and C are equally situated, A's chance of getting lucky in any action is 1 in 3; its chance of getting lucky in all (and thus being paid in full) is only 1 in 9. There is a 2/3 chance, that it will get nothing at all.

By contrast, assume collective action of the three creditors would permit the debtors to reorganize or liquidate in an orderly fashion and thereby increase the value of each debtor's assets to $2,000. Moreover, assume the $2,000 would be equally divided among the three creditors. In that case, each creditor would receive two-thirds of its claims. This would directly benefit the creditors, who would exchange a remote chance of full payment and a real chance of no payment for a certainty of substantial payment. It would indirectly benefit the rest of the economy: the risk and uncertainty faced by lenders would be reduced, and they would in turn be able to make better (and cheaper) decisions about their lending.

For practical reasons, the three creditors acting on their own outside of a coordinated bankruptcy proceeding are likely to find it difficult, if not impossible, to cooperate. Bankruptcy fills this gap by making the choice for them. It leaves them with their existing rights, but forces them to exercise those rights in a manner that in every case benefits the group, and the expected value of their claims (in the example above, from 33 cents to 66 cents on the dollar. This model, which proceduralists support, is often called the "creditor's bargain," because it is the deal creditors would have been willing to agree to at the time they initiated the credit, if all creditors had been gathered at the inception of the debtor's business and asked to agree on a regime to govern the debtor's insolvency. This bargain is imposed because of the insuperable practical barriers to their making it for themselves.[31]

[B] "Traditionalist" Theories of Bankruptcy[32]

Both proceduralist and traditionalist bankruptcy scholars would want bankruptcy to be used to avoid a piecemeal liquidation of a debtor if rehabilitation or an orderly liquidation could double the value that could be retrieved from the business.[33] A key difference between the proceduralists and the traditionalists

---

[31] Thomas H. Jackson, *Bankruptcy, Non-bankruptcy Entitlements, and the Creditors' Bargain*, 91 Yale L.J. 857 (1982). *See also* Barry E. Adler, *Bankruptcy and Risk Allocation*, 77 Cornell L. Rev. 439 (1992); Douglas G. Baird, *Loss Distribution, Forum Shopping, and Bankruptcy: A Reply to Warren*, 54 U. Chi. L. Rev. 815 (1987); Thomas H. Jackson & Robert E. Scott, *On the Nature of Bankruptcy: An Essay on Bankruptcy Sharing and the Creditors' Bargain*, 75 Va. L. Rev. 155 (1989).

[32] Elizabeth Warren, *Bankruptcy Policy*, 54 U.Chi. L. Rev. 775 (1987).

[33] Thomas H. Jackson, *Bankruptcy, Non-bankruptcy Entitlements, and the Creditors' Bargain*, 91 Yale L.J. 857, 861-68 (1982).

concerns whether bankruptcy should be used to advance goals of stakeholders other than creditors.

Traditionalists point out that there are positive social benefits to the continued operation, for example, of a factory in a small city. They therefore approve of rules that protect other non-creditor groups who are likely to have been harmed by the debtor's financial failure but who might not be entitled to any of the debtor's value under normal collection rules. These groups might include current and retired employees, customers, suppliers, and other members of the community,[34] even though they do not have substantive legal rights that are protected by the state law collection system. Traditionalist scholars view bankruptcy as carrying out a "deliberate distributional policy in favor of all those whom a business failure would have hurt."[35]

Imagine, under the previous example, that the debtor was faced with a choice among three options: (1) piecemeal liquidation, yielding a value of $1000 and a distribution of 33¢ on the dollar; (2) a reorganization of the company that would yield a value of $2000, and a distribution of 66¢ on the dollar; and (3) a going concern sale of the company's assets for $2000 and a distribution of 66¢ on the dollar.

Both the proceduralist and the traditionalist would agree that options 2 and 3 are preferable to piecemeal liquidation. However, imagine that under the "sale" option, the purchaser plans to close down the factory and 300 people will lose their jobs, while under the "reorganization" approach those jobs would be saved. A traditionalist might prefer the reorganization approach, while the proceduralist would leave the choice to the creditors. Traditionalists prefer rehabilitation to avoid these additional losses (what economists would call "negative externalities") to those indirectly affected by the debtor's financial difficulties.

Traditionalists would also provide bankruptcy judges with considerable leeway to determine whether a debtor should be given time and leeway to pursue a going concern reorganization, while proceduralists do not think that bankruptcy judges are competent to do this.[36]

---

[34] Ted Janger, *Crystals and Mud in Bankruptcy Law: Judicial Competence and Statutory Design*, 43 Ariz. L. Rev. 559, 566 (2001). *See generally* Karen Gross, *Failure and Forgiveness: Rebalancing the Bankruptcy System* (1997); Donald R. Korobkin, *Rehabilitating Values: A Jurisprudence of Bankruptcy*, 91 Colum. L. Rev. 717 (1991); Elizabeth Warren, *Bankruptcy Policy*, 54 U. Chi. L. Rev. 775 (1987); Elizabeth Warren & Jay Lawrence Westbrook, *Searching for Reorganization Realities*, 72 Wash. U. L.Q. 1257 (1994); Janis Sarra, Creditor Rights and the Public Interest: Restructuring Insolvent Corporations (University of Toronto Press 2003); Karen Gross, Failure and Forgiveness: Rebalancing the Bankruptcy System (Yale University Press 1997).

[35] Elizabeth Warren, *Bankruptcy Policy Making in an Imperfect World*, 92 Mich. L. Rev. 336, 355 (1993).

[36] Ted Janger, *Crystals and Mud in Bankruptcy Law: Judicial Competence and Statutory Design*, 43 Ariz. L. Rev. 559, 574-75 (2001).

§ 1.03   INTERPRETATION OF THE BANKRUPTCY CODE

For several generations, it was a commonplace view that the traditional rules of statutory interpretation had outlived their usefulness.[37] Chief among these is what has commonly been known as the "plain meaning" rule of statutory construction. If the text of a statute had a plain, unambiguous meaning the court should not consider other sources such as committee reports, floor debate, and other legislative history, unless the meaning would produce an absurd result. It is analogous to a strict "four corners" application of the parol evidence rule in the law of contracts.

Innumerable studies have attacked the plain meaning rule as unworkable or incoherent if for no other reason that no English word or phrase is without ambiguity. The great majority of academic commentary on the rule has, historically, been hostile.[38] Federal courts, which, unlike most state courts, have abundant legislative history available, had at one time, largely rejected the plain meaning rule. In the specific context of bankruptcy, the plain meaning rule has been seen as an obstacle to the rational development of bankruptcy law, because of the difficulty of turning to Congress at every bend in the road, in an effort to obtain greater clarity. Thus, there was a long stadning tradition of paying only as much heed to the statute as necessary and maximum attention to perceived bankruptcy policy.

Over the past two-and-a-half decades, however, the plain meaning rule has been revitalized[39] In bankruptcy cases, this "new textualism" has been reflected in particular by Judges like Antonin Scalia and Frank Easterbrook with strong academic reputations. With an occasional exception,[40] the Supreme Court's bankruptcy decisions have insisted, with mixed results, on the primacy of enacted text to determine what bankruptcy law is.[41] Lower bankruptcy courts now regularly pay heed, or at least lip service, to its importance. Over the past eight years of bankruptcy courts' efforts to interpret the cumbersome prose of the 2005 Bankruptcy Code Amendments, adherence to the plain meaning approach to statutory construction has proven challenging at best.[42]

---

[37] Adrian Vermeule, Judging Under Uncertainty (2005). *See* Antonin Scalia, A Matter of Interpretation (1997).

[38] Lee Dembart & Bruce A. Markell, *Alive at 25? A Short Review of the Supreme Court's Bankruptcy Jurisprudence, 1979-2004*, 78 Am. Bankr. L.J. 373, 386, 390-91 (2004); Walter A. Effross, *Grammarians at the Gate: The Rehnquist Court's Evolving "Plain Meaning" Approach to Bankruptcy Jurisprudence*, 23 Seton Hall L. Rev. 1636 (1993); Robert M. Lawless, *Legisprudence Through a Bankruptcy Lens: A Study in the Supreme Court's Bankruptcy Cases*, 47 Syracuse L. Rev.1, 106-07 (1996); Robert K. Rasmussen, *A Study of the Costs and Benefits of Textualism: The Supreme Court's Bankruptcy Cases*, 71 Wash. U. L.Q. 535 (1993); Alan Schwartz, *The New Textualism and the Rule of Law Subtext in the Supreme Court's Bankruptcy Jurisprudence*, 45 N.Y.L. Sch. L. Rev. 149, 151 (2000-2001); Charles Jordan Tabb & Robert M. Lawless, *Of Commas, Gerunds, and Conjunctions: The Bankruptcy Jurisprudence of the Rehnquist Court*, 42 Syracuse L. Rev. 823 (1991); Ned Waxman, *Judicial Follies: Ignoring the Plain Meaning of Bankruptcy Code § 109(g)(2)*, 48 Ariz. L. Rev. 149 (2006).

[39] *E.g.*,William N. Eskridge, Jr., *The New Textualism*, 37 UCLA L. Rev. 621 (1990).

[40] *See* Dewsnup v. Timm, 502 U.S. 410 (1992), in which the Court used a "settled" preexisting practice to justify making a complete hash of the phrase "allowed secured claim."

[41] *See* Taylor v. Freeland & Kronz, 503 U.S. 638 (1992); Patterson v. Shumate,504 U.S. 753 (1992); Toibb v. Radloff, 501 U.S. 157 (1991); United States v. Ron Pair Enter., 489 U.S. 235 (1989).

[42] For an example of the current hypertróphy of the plain meaning canon of interpretation, see *Enron*

§ 1.04   CONSTITUTIONAL LIMITS ON BANKRUPTCY LAW[43]

For all of the significance of bankruptcy law, there is surprisingly little delineation of its constitutional boundaries. In a way, this is surprising. The power given by the Constitution to Congress to enact uniform laws on the subject of bankruptcy carries with it potential powers nearly as broad as those contained in the Commerce Clause. However, this is not a power without limits. Most significantly, the same Constitution that permits bankruptcy also protects property rights.[44] At some point substantive bankruptcy law may impermissibly disturb creditors' property rights.[45] Courts have generally tried to dodge the constitutional issue, however, by interpreting the statutory language in a way that avoids the problem.

The general assumption is that Congress may do virtually anything under its Bankruptcy Power that is reasonably related to dealing with insolvents, provided it acts prospectively. Congress may even deviate from its longstanding tradition of protecting certain property interests in bankruptcy, provided it does so only with regard to subsequently arising property rights. A constitutional problem might arise, however, if Congress were to enact a bankruptcy law that seriously impaired pre-existing property rights. Similarly, constitutional questions have recently been raised concerning the validity of bankruptcy specific state exemption statutes that some states have adopted.[46]

Most recently, a constitutional question has arisen with regard to the power of Bankruptcy courts to adjudicate state law causes of action that might be asserted by the estate. In *Stern v. Marshall*, the Supreme Court held that a bankruptcy court did not have the constitutional power to "hear and determine" a purely state law counterclaim because the defendant was entitled to have the case decided by an Article III court. The effect of this ruling is primarily procedural, but it may have important consequences for how bankruptcy cases are administered in the future.

Creditors Recovery Corp. v. Alfa, S.A.B. De C.V., 651 F.3d 329 (2d Cir. 2011) and consider Judge Koeltl's dissent.

[43] Jonathan C. Lipson, *Debt and Democracy: Towards a Constitutional Theory of Bankruptcy*, 83 Notre Dame L. Rev. 605 (2008); Kurt Nadelmann, *On the Origin of the Bankruptcy Clause*, 1 Am. J. Legal Hist. 215 (1957); Thomas E. Plank, *The Constitutional Limits of Bankruptcy*, 63 Tenn. L. Rev. 487 (1996); James S. Rogers, *The Impairment of Secured Creditors' Rights in Reorganization: A Study of the Relationship Between the Fifth Amendment and the Bankruptcy Clause*, 96 Harv. L. Rev. 973 (1983).

[44] U.S. Const. amend V.

[45] *E.g.*, Louisville Joint Stock Land Bank v. Radford, 295 U.S. 555, 591-92, 601-02 (1935); James Steven Rogers, *The Impairment of Secured Creditors' Rights in Reorganization: A Study of the Relationship Between the Fifth Amendment and the Bankruptcy Clause*, 96 Harv. L. Rev. 973 (1983); Francis F. Gecker, Comment, *The Recovery of Opportunity Costs as Just Compensation: a Takings Analysis of Adequate Protection*, 81 Nw. U. L. Rev. 953 (1987).

[46] *See* In re Schafer 455 B.R. 590 (B.A.P. 6th Cir. 2011); In re Applebaum, 422 B.R. 684 (B.A.P. 9th Cir. 2009).

Chapter 2

CREDITORS' COLLECTION RIGHTS

§ 2.01 SOURCE OF CREDITORS' COLLECTION RIGHTS[1]

The law of creditors' and debtors' rights is largely state law. The basic procedures used by private creditors to collect debts owed to them, and the priorities they establish, are established by state law. These procedures are derived from the common law writs, but they are codified in state codes of civil procedures, usually listed under "enforcement of judgments."[2]

Despite this, Federal Law casts a long shadow over these state procedures and represents an obvious intrusion of federal power into creditors' rights.[3] In recent decades, this intrusion has become more pronounced as state collection procedures have been subjected to federal consumer protection legislation. The most obvious examples of these federal interventions are the Fair Debt Collection Practices Act,[4] the Fair Credit Reporting Act,[5] and Federal Restrictions on Wage Garnishment,[6] all of which are parts of the Consumer Credit Protection Act. The new Federal Consumer Finance Protection Bureau, created in 2011, has jurisdiction to regulate unfair and deceptive or abusive acts or practices related to consumer financial products. How the agency will choose to regulate debt collection practices remains to be seen.

It is hard to fully understand bankruptcy law without a basic grasp of state debt collection procedures. Creditors' rights can be divided into three broad categories, each of which gives the creditor the right to satisfy the debt by selling the debtor's property. These property interests are collectively referred to as liens. There are three basic types of liens: consensual liens, judicial liens, and statutory liens.[7] These different types of liens are created in different ways, are enforced through different procedures, and are accorded different priorities.

---

[1] Arthur A. Leff, *Injury, Ignorance and Spite — The Dynamics of Coercive Collection*, 80 Yale L.J. 1 (1970).

[2] "The forms of action we have buried, but they still rule us from their graves." Frederic William Maitland, The Forms of Action at Common Law 1 (Cambridge ed. 1962).

[3] Richard M. Hynes, *Why (Consumer) Bankruptcy?*, 56 Ala. L. Rev. 121 (2004).

[4] *See infra* § 2.14[C]Fair Debt Collection Practices Act.

[5] *See infra* § 2.14[D] The Fair Credit Reporting Act.

[6] *See infra* § 2.11[A][4][a] Federal Restrictions on Wage Garnishment.

[7] *See* Justice v. Valley National Bank, 849 F.2d 1078, 1085 n.7 (8th Cir. 1988) (distinguishing judicial liens, statutory liens, and consensual liens).

The first category deals with property rights creditors obtain by contract. These rights include mortgages, deeds of trust, and security interests under Article 9 of the Uniform Commercial Code.[8] This chapter covers these laws in only cursory fashion, leaving their comprehensive treatment to other materials that focus more directly on real estate transactions and security interests.

The second category deals with creditors' property rights that are created by law, usually when the creditor has obtained a judgment in court and executed on specific property, rather than by contract. These are sometimes referred to as "involuntary" property rights, in the sense that the debtor did not explicitly grant them to the creditor. If a borrower fails to make a payment on a loan or a party to a contract fails to perform, the plaintiff may recover a judgment for damages and obtain a judicial lien on the judgment debtor's property and have the property sold to satisfy the judgment. Or, the creditor might garnish the debtor's wages or bank accounts. In other circumstances, involuntary judgment liens and garnishments arise as a result of the debtor's tortious actions, such as an auto accident, a barroom brawl, or a violation of someone's civil rights. But, of course, the substantive rights that give rise to these judgment liens cover the entire range of American, Foreign, and International Law.

§ 2.02 CONSENSUAL LIENS; LEASES

Consensual liens are created by the agreement of the person granting the lien. The most familiar examples are home mortgages and purchase money security interests in new automobiles. A mortgage grants the lender an interest in real property to secure payment of a debt — often for the purchase price of the land. If the borrower does not repay the debt, the lender can foreclose on the property. Similarly, if a borrower defaults on a loan secured by her car, the lender can repossess the car and sell it in satisfaction of the debt.

Consensual liens come in many forms, however. A business borrower may grant a lien on its inventory, equipment, accounts, and other types of contract rights. In these transactions, the debtor voluntarily grants the creditor a contractual lien, usually in exchange for a loan, or perhaps in connection with a sale on credit. The lien enhances the likelihood that the debtor will voluntarily pay, and gives the creditor an interest in property that can be sold to pay the debt if the borrower defaults.

---

[8] Comprehensive treatment of U.C.C. Article 9 is beyond the scope of this book. *See* William H. Lawrence, William H. Henning, & R. Wilson Freyermuth, Understanding Secured Transacitons (LexisNexis 4th ed. 2007).

[A]　Real Estate Mortgages and Deeds of Trust

[1]　Basic Operation of Mortgages and Deeds of Trust

[a]　Mortgages

Generally speaking, interests in real estate collateral are established either through a mortgage or a deed of trust. Originally, a mortgage was nothing more than a fee simple on condition subsequent. The borrower conveyed a deed to the lender and the lender's deed was subject to a condition subsequent that would revest ownership (or "seisin") in the borrower upon repayment of the debt. The borrower's right of repayment operated to defeat the lender's title only if the borrower made the required payment on "law day." If the borrower paid the debt, the lender's interest would terminate and title in fee simple absolute would revert to the borrower. However, the borrower's failure to make the payment due on law day destroyed the contingency on the lender's title and irretrievably vested title in fee simple absolute in the lender. But, it is often said that "equity abhors a forfeiture" and that the potential unfairness of this outcome led seventeenth century English chancery courts to permit a borrower who had defaulted on law day to redeem the property from the lender by paying the balance of the obligation due, despite the default. This avoided a loss of both the property and the payments that had previously been made. Eventually, procedures were developed to permit the lender to petition the chancery court to "foreclose" the equity of redemption by putting the property up for sale, with the buyer's rights invulnerable to attack by the borrower.[9]

In a traditional mortgage transaction, the borrower (the "mortgagor") transfers a property interest (a "mortgage") in her land to the creditor (the "mortgagee"). Upon default by the mortgagor, the mortgagee has the right to obtain a judgment in court that will result in the property being sold by the county sheriff. The money received from the sale will be used to satisfy the mortgagor's debt.

If the property is sold for less than the debt, the lender can usually obtain a personal judgment against the borrower for the amount of the deficiency; though some states have adopted anti-deficiency statutes which protect homeowners from this type of liability.[10] Very, very rarely (in a parallel universe somewhere), collateral is sold for more than the amount of the debt. If this happens, the "surplus" is paid first to any junior lienholders, and then to the mortgagor. [11]

---

[9] Marshall E. Tracht, *Renegotiation and Secured Credit: Explaining the Equity of Redemption*, 52 Vand. L. Rev. 599 (1999). *See* Grant S. Nelson & Dale A. Whitman, Real Estate Finance Law 7-8 (4th ed. 2001).

[10] *E.g.*, Cal. Civ. Proc. Code § 580b (West 1976). *See generally* Robert M. Washburn, *The Judicial and Legislative Response to Price Inadequacy in Mortgage Foreclosure Sales*, 53 S. Cal. L. Rev. 843 (1980). Anti-deficiency statutes also sometimes apply with respect to security interests in consumer goods. *See, e.g.*, Unif. Consumer Credit Code § 1.106 (1974); Ind. Code Ann. § 24-4.5-5-103(2) (West 2006).

[11] Grant S. Nelson & Dale A. Whitman, Real Estate Finance Law 7-8 (4th ed. 2001).

[b]   Deeds of Trust[12]

In many states, deeds of trust are commonly used, instead of mortgages. This mechanism only works in jurisdictions where it is validated by statute. Deeds of trust operate similarly to mortgages, except that no judicial action is necessary to complete the foreclosure process. Unlike a mortgage, a deed of trust involves three parties: the borrower, the lender, and a trustee. In broad outline, the borrower deeds an interest in the land involved to a trustee, with the lender named as the trust's beneficiary. The trustee holds a "power of sale" which permits it to sell the property if the borrower defaults. Upon default, the trustee sells the property and remits the proceeds of the sale, to the extent necessary to pay the debt, to the lender.[13] As with a mortgage, any surplus resulting from the sale is paid first to junior lienholders and then to the borrower.[14] If the money obtained from the sale is insufficient to pay the debt in full, the creditor can go to court to obtain a judgment for the unpaid balance due.

The procedures for enforcing deeds of trust are detailed by statute in the jurisdictions where they are available. These procedures are more streamlined than those used in judicial foreclosure actions. Nevertheless, they still ensure that the borrower has adequate notice of the nature of her default, the time and place of the sale, the amounts received from the sale, and how these amounts were distributed. They also frequently establish waiting periods and advertising requirements that must be followed when conducting the sale.

[c]   Installment Land Contracts

Another variation on this theme is an installment land contract, sometimes called a "contract for deed."[15] In an installment land contract, the buyer takes possession of the land and makes regular monthly installment payments to the seller, over a set period of time. The seller retains title until the payments are complete, and then she delivers a deed to the buyer. Traditionally, the contract for deed gave the seller an exceptionally generous remedy: if the buyer (sometimes still referred to as the "vendee") missed a payment, the seller (the "vendor") could keep all payments made and retain title to the property.

This resulted in a forfeiture of the payments the buyer made before her default. However, as in connection with the law of mortgages, "equity abhors a forfeiture"[16] and this devastating outcome has been whittled away by legislative actions and court decisions,[17] that protect the borrower from losing the equity she has built

---

[12] Grant S. Nelson & Dale A. Whitman, *Reforming Foreclosure: The Uniform Nonjudicial Foreclosure Act*, 53 Duke L.J. 1399 (2004).

[13] *E.g.*, In re Krohn, 52 P.3d 774 (Ariz. 2002).

[14] Grant S. Nelson & Dale A. Whitman, Real Estate Finance Law 11 (4th ed. 2001).

[15] Grant S. Nelson, *The Contract for Deed as a Mortgage: The Case for the Restatement Approach*, 1998 BYU L. Rev. 1111 (1998); Grant S. Nelson & Dale A. Whitman, Real Estate Finance Law 70-71 (4th ed. 2001).

[16] *E.g.*, Fugate v. Rice, 815 S.W.2d 466 (Mo. Ct. App. 1991).

[17] *See* Grant S. Nelson & Dale A Whitman, Real Estate Finance Law 70-124 (4th ed. 2001); Restatement (Third) of Property (Mortgages) § 3.4 (1997).

through her payments.

[2]   Two Step Process: Agreement and Recordation

Mortgages, deeds of trust, and other similar mechanisms nearly always involve a two-step process. The first step is execution and delivery of the document containing the parties' agreement, that establishes rights to the property between the lender and the borrower. In most cases, a second step — proper recording of the document or the taking of possession — is required to establish the creditor's rights against third parties, including most subsequent buyers[18] of the property, holders of any consensual or non-consensual liens,[19] and the bankruptcy trustee in any bankruptcy case filed by the borrower.[20]

Ordinarily, the mortgage or deed of trust document itself must be recorded in the real estate records of the county in which the real property is located. If the mortgage is not recorded, or is recorded improperly, the creditor's interest in the property remains vulnerable to the rights of a good faith purchaser for value. It also remains vulnerable to the rights of a subsequent mortgagee or to a creditor who obtains a judicial lien on the property. Likewise, it remains subject to "avoidance" in a bankruptcy proceeding by the bankruptcy trustee.[21]

[3]   Priority of Mortgages and Deeds of Trust

Priorities among competing mortgage holders are generally established on a first-in-time, first-in-right basis. Who is first-in-time is determined by the state's recording statute. Interests in the property that are recorded first are generally given first priority. But, this is a broad generalization with many variations. For example, depending on the jurisdiction, a person who has notice of a previous unrecorded mortgage might take subject to that mortgage, even though it was never recorded.[22]

Insofar as protection against a bankruptcy trustee is concerned, recording of the transfer is a virtual necessity. The bankruptcy trustee has the power to avoid any interest in realty of which a bona fide purchaser *could* take free.[23] Therefore, the bankruptcy trustee's actual knowledge is irrelevant.

Mortgages are sometimes subordinate to state real estate tax liens. However, even this rule is subject to variation, as in some jurisdictions, purchase money

---

[18] In colloquial language, "purchaser" is usually understood as a synonym of "buyer." In commercial law, it refers to anyone who obtains a voluntarily created interest in the property. *See* U.C.C. § 1-201(b)(32), (33) (2010). In this technical sense, both buyers and secured lenders are purchasers. *E.g.*, In re Arlco, Inc., 239 B.R. 261, 268-69 (Bankr. S.D.N.Y. 1999).

[19] *See generally* 14 Richard R. Powell & Michael Allan Wolf, Powell on Real Property §§ 82.01-82.04 (2000).

[20] *See infra* § 14.02[C] Trustee as Bona Fide Purchaser.

[21] *See infra* § 14.02 Strong-Arm Power.

[22] *See generally* 14 Richard R. Powell & Michael Allan Wolf, Powell on Real Property §§ 82.02[1] (2000).

[23] Bankruptcy Code § 544(a)(3). See *infra* § 14.02 Strong-Arm Power.

mortgages retain their priority even over real estate taxes.[24]

[B] Security Interests in Personal Property

The system for creating and recording consensual liens in personal property is different from the system used for real estate mortgages. Personal property, unlike real estate, tends to move around, making the location of the collateral far less important. Moreover, many types of personal property, such as accounts, intellectual property, and other intangible rights, have no corporeal existence and thus no physical location. In the United States, consensual liens in all types of personal property are governed by Article 9 of the Uniform Commercial Code, which has been adopted in all American jurisdictions.

[1] Article 9 of the Uniform Commercial Code[25]

[a] Scope of Article 9

Most aspects of the law regarding security interests in personal property and fixtures are governed by Article 9 of the Uniform Commercial Code (U.C.C.). The scope of Article 9 is determined by the economic substance of the underlying transaction rather than by the label the parties attach to it. Article 9 governs if the interest is granted in order to secure payment or performance of an obligation (usually a money debt),[26] even if the transaction is characterized as some other type of deal, such as a lease.[27] Article 9 also applies to most outright sales of accounts, chattel paper, payment intangibles, and promissory notes, even when the transfer is not made to secure an obligation.[28] It also governs certain "consignments," statutory "agricultural liens," and security interests arising under other articles of the Uniform Commercial Code.[29]

[b] Attachment of Security Interests

The basic enforceability of a security agreement between the parties is referred to as "attachment." In most situations, attachment involves three elements. There must be (1) an authenticated security agreement between the debtor and the

---

[24] *E.g.*, Am. Gen'l Fin. Serv. Inc. v. Carter, 184 P.3d 273 (Kan. Ct. App. 2008).

[25] Note that the discussion of Article 9 security interests is more extensive than that of other liens; this is because many bankruptcy casebooks use more cases and questions drawn from Article 9 than from other bodies of state law creditors' rights. For a far more detailed discussion of Article 9, see William H. Lawrence, William H. Henning & R. Wilson Freyermuth, Understanding Secured Transactions (LexisNexis 4th ed. 2007).

[26] U.C.C. § 1-201(b)(35) (2010). The obligation is not always a money debt. One of your authors recalls examining an agreement entered into between a pet breeder and one of its customers. The agreement specified that the customer was not permitted to have the kitten "declawed," and that the seller retained the right to retake possession of the cat if the buyer breached this promise. The obligation was to preserve the claws of the cat intact.

[27] *See generally* Corinne Cooper, *Identifying a Personal Property Lease Under the UCC*, 49 Ohio St. L.J. 195 (1988).

[28] U.C.C. § 9-109(a)(3) (2010).

[29] U.C.C. § 9-109(a) (2010).

creditor; (2) the secured party must give value (usually a loan) to the debtor;[30] and (3) the debtor must have rights in the collateral that it has the power to convey to the creditor.[31]

The authenticated agreement must contain an adequate description of the collateral.[32] The security agreement might provide for the security interest to attach to "after-acquired" property, that the debtor does not acquire until after the security agreement is signed.[33] The security agreement might also provide that the agreement also secures future advances that are made to the debtor, after the security agreement is signed.[34] Thus, a single security agreement can cover any number of loans made by the lender at different times, and these loans may be secured by collateral acquired by the debtor at different times.

Attachment fixes the rights of the secured party against the debtor. Most importantly, it establishes the secured party's right to repossess the property if the debtor defaults and to resell it to satisfy the amount of the debt, or in the case of a sale of receivables subject to Article 9, to collect the receivables directly from the obligor.[35]

[c]   Perfection of Security Interests

Attachment, while sufficient to provide the creditor with rights against the collateral, does not usually protect the secured party's rights against competing claims to the property that might be made by the debtor's other creditors or by buyers of the collateral. Nor will it protect the secured lender from the avoiding powers of a bankruptcy trustee.

To gain priority over these third parties, a secured party must "perfect" its security interest. Perfection can be accomplished in a variety of ways, depending on the nature of the transaction and the type of collateral involved. In a few circumstances, perfection occurs "automatically" when the security interest attaches.[36] However, in most types of secured transactions, perfection requires additional steps, such as "possession," "control," "filing" a "financing statement," or notation of the security interest on a certificate of title covering the goods.[37] These further steps are designed to give notice to third parties of the existence of the security interest and thus to avoid the possibility that subsequent lenders or purchasers might be misled by the debtor's apparent ownership of the collateral.[38]

---

[30] U.C.C. § 9-203(1)(b) (2010).

[31] U.C.C. § 9-203(a) (2010).

[32] U.C.C. § 9-203(b)(3)(A) (2010).

[33] U.C.C. § 9-204(1) (2010).

[34] U.C.C. § 9-204(3) (2010).

[35] U.C.C. §§ 9-607 & 9-609 (2010).

[36] U.C.C. § 9-302(1)(d) (2010).

[37] *See* U.C.C. § 9-310 (2010).

[38] In this respect in particular, Article 9 and its public notice filing procedures are closely related to the law of fraudulent conveyances.

[d]   Priority Rules under U.C.C. Article 9

Article 9's detailed priority rules are far too complex for treatment here, however, they generally give priority to whomever is the first to put third parties on notice by filing a financing statement covering the collateral or perfecting by some other means. Insofar as bankruptcy is concerned, the most crucial priority rule in Article 9 is that contained in U.C.C. § 9-317(a)(2). In most situations, it makes an *unperfected* security interest subordinate to the rights of "a person who becomes a lien creditor before . . . the security interest . . . is perfected."[39] As will be seen in greater detail elsewhere, the bankruptcy trustee enjoys all of the same rights as a judicial lien creditor as of the moment of the filing of the bankruptcy petition.[40] This means that an unperfected security interest can be avoided by the bankruptcy trustee. Other priority rules, such as those favoring purchase money security interests, those protecting certain buyers, those limiting the priority of future advances, and those in favor of certain statutory liens are beyond the scope of a book on bankruptcy law.

[e]   Enforcement of Security Interests

An Article 9 security interest gives the secured party something that unsecured or "general" creditors do not enjoy: a property interest in the debtor's assets. This property interest coexists with the interest held by the debtor. The debtor is usually in possession of the property and is free to use it in the ordinary course of its business or financial affairs. However, if the debtor defaults, the secured party may seize and sell the property. Most of the time, no court action is required to establish or enforce the secured party's rights to the collateral. Instead, it may be taken by self-help, as long as there is no breach of the peace in the process of repossession.[41]

In a bankruptcy case, a creditor with a perfected security interest has an even more valuable right. Although the secured creditor is by no means unaffected by the bankruptcy case and has no certainty of receiving payment in full, it is almost certain to obtain a much greater payout than is received by unsecured creditors. In Chapter 7 liquidation proceedings, secured creditors are frequently able, after obtaining permission from the bankruptcy court, to repossess and sell their collateral just as if the bankruptcy case had not been filed.[42] Even if not permitted to sell the collateral on its own, a secured party is entitled to receive the proceeds from the bankruptcy trustee's sale of the collateral up to the amount necessary to satisfy the secured debt. However, if the results of the sale are inadequate to pay the claim in full, the creditor's claim for the deficiency is unsecured. Secured

---

[39] U.C.C. § 9-317(a)(2) (2010).

[40] *See infra* 14.02 Strong-Arm Power.

[41] U.C.C. § 9-609 (2010). If self-help cannot be accomplished peaceably, the secured party must resort to judicial action, generally by seeking the remedy of replevin or detinue.

[42] The filing of a bankruptcy case operates as an "automatic stay" against virtually every type of creditor action, including repossession and sale by a secured creditor. Thus, even where secured creditors have the right to foreclose, they are required to obtain permission from the bankruptcy court, in the form of "relief from the automatic stay." *See infra* § 8.06[B] Relief From the Stay on Request of a Party.

parties are also entitled to "adequate protection" of their property interests while the case is pending and are entitled to receive payment, under the terms of the debtor's plan, in an amount equal to the amount of their secured claims.

[2] Superseding Federal Law

There are several federal statutes that deal with consensual security interests in personal property. Some of them work in conjunction with Article 9; others operate independently of it.

Federal maritime law governs security interests in registered vessels. In order for a preferred ship mortgage to have priority over the bankruptcy trustee, it must satisfy a number of formalities that are alien to Article 9.

Other federal laws only partially preempt Article 9. Security interests in aircraft, for example, are largely covered by the U.C.C., but perfection is governed by federal law, which requires notice of the security interest to be recorded in the F.A.A. registry in Oklahoma City.

The law governing perfection of security interests in various forms of intellectual property is particularly uncertain and complex: filing under Article 9 is sufficient to perfect a security interest in a trademark;[43] filing with the Copyright Office appears to be necessary to perfect a security interest in a registered copyright;[44] while filing under Article 9 may be required to perfect a security interest in an unregistered copyright,[45] though under an earlier decision it had been held to be neither necessary nor sufficient.[46] Dual filings under both Article 9 and with the Patent and Trademark Office may be necessary to fully protect a security interest in a patent against both the bankruptcy trustee and a subsequent purchaser of the patent.[47]

[C] Leases

[1] Real Estate Leases

Generally, long-term leases of real estate must be recorded to protect the rights of the lessee against third partes. Short-term leases need not be recorded. For example, in New York leases of three years or more must be recorded to be effective against a subsequent purchaser of the property.[48] In most other states, the cut-off is one year.

---

[43] Matter of Roman Cleanser Co., 43 B.R. 940 (Bankr. E.D. Mich. 1984), *affirmed*, 802 F.2d 207 (6th Cir. 1986).

[44] *See* In re Peregrine Entm't, 116 BR. 194 (C.D. Cal. 1990).

[45] In re World Auxiliary Power Co., 303 F.3d 1120 (9th Cir. 2002).

[46] In re Avalon Software, Inc., 209 B.R. 517 (Bankr. D. Ariz. 1997).

[47] *Compare* In re Cybernetic Serv., Inc., 252 F.3d 1039 (9th Cir. 2001) (filing under Article 9 sufficient for protection against a lien creditor and thus arguably against the bankruptcy trustee); *with* City Bank & Trust Co. v. Otto Fabric, Inc., 83 B.R. 780 (D. Kan. 1988) (filing with the Patent and Trademark Office required for protection against a subsequent purchaser of the patent).

[48] N.Y. Real Prop. Law Ann. § 291-c (McKinney 2006). *See generally* 14 Richard R. Powell & Michael Allan Wolf, Powell on Real Property § 82.02[3][a][I] (2000).

In general, the rights of both the lessor and the lessee are determined on a "first in time, first in right" basis. Rights acquired first have seniority. Rights acquired later are subordinate. Thus, if after the lease is made, creditors of the lessor obtain a lien on the leased property, the lien is subject to the rights of the lessee.

If a long-term lease is not recorded, the rights of the lessee may be subject to the rights of a later bona fide purchaser for value. The lease will also be avoided in bankruptcy.[49] Even if it is recorded, the Bankruptcy Code has a complex set of rules that deal with the ability of a bankrupt lessee to retain possession of the property leased.[50]

[2] Personal Property Leases

Article 2A of the U.C.C. governs leases of personal property,[51] and addresses the competing rights of the lessor and the lessee's creditors in the leased goods. Of primary importance, at least to the lessor, is that lessors do not need to "file" a UCC financing statement under U.C.C. Article 9, to be protected from claims to the goods that might be made by the lessee's creditors. So long as the lease is a "true lease" and not a disguised security interest, recording is not necessary.[52] Whether a lease will be treated as a security interest is a fact-specific inquiry, but the basic question is whether the lessor retains a meaningful interest in reacquiring the property at the conclusion of the lease.[53] Thus, the typical personal property lease is a one-step transaction. If the lease is enforceable between the lessor and the lessee, no additional steps are required to protect the lessor's rights against the rights of the lessee's creditors.[54]

§ 2.03 JUDGMENTS

A creditor who does not have a consensual lien does not have any right to claim the debtor's property. To obtain such an interest, the creditor must follow a two-step process. First, the creditor must obtain a judgment. Obtaining a judgment is the first step a creditor usually must take in attempting to use the courts to collect a debt. As most law students discover in Civil Procedure, a judgment may be obtained in several ways, involving varying degrees of time, expense, and complexity.[55] But

---

[49] Bankruptcy Code § 544(a)(3). *See, e.g.*, in re Huffman, 369 F.3d 972 (6th Cir. 2004).

[50] *See infra* § Chapter 11 Executory Contracts and Unexpired Leases.

[51] U.C.C. §§ 2A-102 & 2A-103(1)(j) (2010). As of August 1, 2012, forty-nine states, the District of Columbia, and the U.S. Virgin Islands have adopted Article 2A. It has not been adopted in Louisiana or Puerto Rico.

[52] U.C.C. § 2A-307 (2010).

[53] U.C.C. § 1-203 (2010).

[54] The only significant exception to this deals with a lease of goods that become fixtures. U.C.C. § 2A-309 (2010).

[55] At early common law, enforcement of a judgment was limited to one of several writs: *fieri facias*, which directed the sheriff to seize the judgment debtor's goods and to sell them to satisfy the judgment; *levari facias*, which ordered the sheriff to seize both the debtor's goods and profits from his land (but not the land itself); *elegit*, which ordered delivery of the debtor's goods to the creditor at an appraised value in satisfaction of the debt, and if necessary to further satisfy the debt, gave the creditor possession of (but

even this does not give the creditor a right to the debtor's property. A second step is required. The creditor must take whatever steps are necessary under state law to obtain a lien on particular property.

[A] Obtaining a Judgment

[1] Default Judgments

If the defendant fails to answer the plaintiff's complaint within the time allowed by the court's rules,[56] the plaintiff can obtain a judgment by "default."[57] This usually requires compliance with the Federal "Servicemembers Civil Relief Act," which prohibits default judgments against members of the armed forces who are on duty away from home, where they might not receive actual notice of the suit, and even with notice, where they might find it difficult to make arrangements to defend against the creditor's claim.[58]

[2] Summary Judgment

If the defendant files an answer to the complaint, summary judgment may be entered without a trial if no material fact is in dispute, and if the plaintiff is entitled to judgment as a matter of law.[59] In collection cases, where the debtor is in default and usually has no defense, summary judgment is commonly available. In most collection cases, there are no disputed facts: the debtor borrowed the money and failed to pay. In these circumstances, the creditor is entitled to judgment as a matter of law, and no trial is necessary.

[3] Consent Judgments

Judgment also may be entered by consent. This frequently occurs as a result of settlement negotiations between the parties while the case is pending but before a trial is complete.

---

not title to) one half of the debtor's lands until the judgment was paid; or of *capias ad satisfaciendum*, which imprisoned the debtor until the debt was paid. The writs of fieri facias and levari facias have mostly been codified, today, as writs of execution. *See* Thomas E. Plank, *The Constitutional Limits of Bankruptcy*, 63 Tenn. L. Rev. 487, 515 (1996); William Blackstone, 3 Commentaries on the Laws of England *414, *417-19 (1979).

[56] The Federal Rules of Civil Procedure give defendants 21 days to "serve" an answer. Fed. R. Civ. P. 12(a). The time may be longer in state court, where collection actions are usually brought. *E.g.*, Ohio R. Civ. P. 12(a) (28 days).

[57] Federal Rule of Civil Procedure 55(a) provides: "When a party against whom a judgment for affirmative relief is sought has failed to plead or otherwise defend, and that failure is shown by affidavit or otherwise, the clerk must enter the party's default." Fed. R. Civ. P. 55(a).

[58] Servicemembers Civil Relief Act, 2003, Pub. L. No. 108-189, § 1, 117 Stat. 2835 (2003) (codified at 50 U.S.C.S. app. §§ 501-596) (LexisNexis Supp. 2006) (formerly known as the Soldiers' and Sailors' Relief Act). *See* George C. Thompson, *The Servicemembers Civil Relief Act*, 48 Res Gestae 13 (Sept. 2004); Roger M. Baron, *Staying Power of the Soldiers' and Sailors' Civil Relief Act*, 32 Santa Clara L. Rev. 137 (1992).

[59] *See* Fed. R. Civ. P. 56.

[4] Judgment by Confession (Cognovit Judgments)

In some situations, a creditor may be permitted, without filing a complaint against the debtor, to enter a confessed or "cognovit" judgment against the debtor pursuant to the debtor's prior written consent. Judgment by confession is an ancient device[60] by which the debtor agrees in advance to permit the creditor to obtain a judgment against the debtor without formal notice or a hearing, sometimes through an attorney designated by the creditor, who purportedly acts on the debtor's behalf.[61] This was described by one court as "the written authority of the debtor and his direction . . . to enter judgment against him."[62]

The facts in a famous confession of judgment case, *D.H. Overmeyer Co. v. Frick*,[63] explain how judgment by confession works. After the debtor fell into default on its obligation on a promissory note to Frick, the parties entered into settlement negotiations, which resulted in the execution of a new promissory note. The new note contained a "confession of judgment" provision:

> The undersigned hereby authorize any attorney designated by the Holder hereof to appear in any court of record in the State of Ohio, and waive this [sic] issuance and service of process, and confess a judgment against the undersigned in favor of the Holder of this Note, for the principal of this Note plus interest if the undersigned defaults in any payment of principal and interest and if said default shall continue for the period of fifteen (15) days.[64]

When their relationship fell apart and litigation began, Frick engaged a lawyer to make an appearance on behalf of Overmeyer[65] " 'by virtue of the warranty of attorney' in the second note." The lawyer waived the issuance and service of process and confessed a judgment in Frick's favor, for the amount of the note. Overmeyer was completely unacquainted with the lawyer who was acting solely on the authority of the above-quoted language in the promissory note that Overmeyer had previously signed.[66]

The Supreme Court ruled in favor of Frick, holding that the cognovit provision was sufficient as a knowing and intelligent waiver of Overmeyer's constitutional rights to due process.[67] Although the Court indicated that cognovit provisions "may

---

[60] *See* William. Blackstone, Commentaries on the Laws of England *397 (1979); Don Hopson, Jr., *Cognovit Judgments: An Ignored Problem of Due Process and Full Faith and Credit*, 29 U. Chi. L. Rev. 111 (1961); Robert M. Hunter, *The Warrant of Attorney to Confess Judgment*, 8 Ohio St. L.J. 1 (1941).

[61] D.H. Overmeyer Co. v. Frick, 405 U.S. 174, 176 (1972).

[62] Blott v. Blott, 290 N.W. 74, 76 (Iowa 1940).

[63] 405 U.S. 174 (1972).

[64] 405 U.S. at 180-81.

[65] That's right, the creditor, Overmeyer. One party is permitted to act on its own to enter a judgment against the other.

[66] 405 U.S. at 181.

[67] The confession of judgment provision was specifically negotiated between the parties, Overmeyer was represented by counsel in the negotiation of the provision, Overmeyer was aware of the meaning and significance of the provision, both parties were merchants, and the provision was included in the wake of an earlier default by Overmeyer.

well serve a proper and useful purpose in the commercial world," it cautioned that the procedure might not be constitutional "where the contract is one of adhesion, where there is great disparity in bargaining power, and where the debtor receives nothing for the cognovit provision."[68] However, in the commercial setting presented by the parties, the judgment entered against Frick was valid, despite the absence of prior notice or an opportunity to be heard.

Judgment by confession has been eliminated by statute in many states.[69] Other states prohibit its use in consumer transactions.[70] The federal Consumer Credit Protection Act prohibits use of a cognovit provision without specific disclosures to the consumer.[71] And, a Federal Trade Commission rule makes their use an unfair trade practice in a variety of consumer transactions.[72] Where they are still used, cognovit judgments are subject to a variety of disclosure requirements and provisions for prompt notice from the court after the judgment has been entered.[73]

Debtors may usually take action to reopen the judgment through the same mechanisms used to reopen other types of judgments.[74] In many states, judgments entered by confession are easier to reverse than other judgments, sometimes merely upon a showing that there was a meritorious defense.[75] Thus, although a judgment might be easily obtained by confession, a debtor with a defense usually has the means to have the merits of his defense heard and resolved.[76]

[5] Judgment after Trial

Judgment also may be entered after trial.[77] This may take anywhere from several hours to several days, weeks or months. In extreme cases, where extended discovery may be necessary, it may take several years, even for a trial to commence.[78]

Most of the time, collection efforts can begin while any appeals are pending. For example, the Chapter 11 bankruptcy case of petroleum giant Texaco was precipitated by an $11 billion[79] jury verdict in favor of Pennzoil for intentional interference

---

[68] 405 U.S. at 188.

[69] *E.g.*, Fla. Stat. Ann. § 55.05 (West 2006).

[70] *See, e.g.*, N.Y.C.P.R. 3201 (McKinney 2005) (consumer goods); Ohio Rev. Code Ann. § 2323.13(E) (LexisNexis 2005) (consumer transactions).

[71] *See, e.g.*, McCoy v. Harriman Util. Bd., 790 F.2d 493 (6th Cir. 1986); Goldberg v. Del. Olds, Inc., 670 F. Supp. 125 (D. Del. 1987).

[72] 16 C.F.R. § 429.1 (2004) (door-to-door sales); 16 C.F.R. § 444.2(a)(1) (2004) (retail installment sales).

[73] Ohio Rev. Code Ann. § 2323.13(E) (LexisNexis 2005).

[74] *See* Fed. R. Civ. Pro. 60.

[75] *E.g.*, Bates v. Midland Title of Ashtabula County, Inc., 2004 Ohio App. LEXIS 5782 (Ohio Ct. App. Nov. 26, 2004); Advanced Clinical Mgmt., Inc. v. Salem Chiropractic Ctr., Inc., 2004 Ohio App. LEXIS 113 (Ohio Ct. App., Jan. 12, 2004).

[76] *See, e.g.*, 25400 Euclid Ave., L.L.C. v. Univ'l Rest. Holdings, L.L.C., 2009-Ohio-6467, 2009 Ohio App. LEXIS 5420 (Ohio Ct. App. 2009).

[77] *See* Fed. R. Civ. P. 54.

[78] Charles Dickens, Bleak House (Penguin Books 1971).

[79] This is not a typographical error — it was 11 billion dollars. Although the authenticity of the

with Pennzoil's merger agreement with Getty Oil Co.,[80] when Texaco could not afford to file a bond to enjoin Pennzoil from filing liens against Texaco's assets while Texaco appealed Pennzoil's judgment.[81]

[B] Dormancy, Renewal, and Revival of Judgments

Once obtained, a judgment does not last forever. States impose limits, similar to statutes of limitation, on the durability of judgments.[82] A creditor who has obtained a judgment must take steps to ensure that it remains viable. Otherwise, efforts to use the judgment to seize the debtor's assets may be fruitless, or even tortious. Once this time period has passed, the judgment may not be enforced.[83]

Traditionally, a judgment became dormant if the creditor failed to make an effort to collect, through a writ of execution, within a year and a day of the time the judgment was issued.[84] Once a judgment became dormant, it had to be "revived" through a court order, before a new writ of execution could be issued.[85]

Further, the statute of limitations on the judgment itself might expire. Creditors must bring an action to "renew" the judgment before this longer limitations period ends, or lose their right to enforce the judgment.

The effect of dormancy on a judgment lien varies tremendously from one state to the next. Some states permit continuation of the lien with its original priority intact if the judgment is revived; others extinguish the lien, its priority, or both, when the judgment upon which it is based becomes dormant.[86] Renewal may either extend the priority of the original lien (or more likely) result in a new judgment lien with priority based on the time the second judgment is docketed or recorded.

---

quotation has been disputed, United States Senator Everett Dirkson reputedly once quipped: "A billion here, a billion there, and pretty soon you're talking real money." http://www.dirksencenter.org/print_emd_billionhere.htm (last viewed July 5, 2011).

[80] Texaco Inc. v. Pennzoil Co., 729 S.W.2d 768, 784 (Tex. Ct. App. 1987).

[81] *See* Pennzoil Co. v. Texaco, Inc., 481 U.S. 1 (1987); In re Texaco Inc., 76 B.R. 322 (Bankr. S.D.N.Y. 1987); Thomas Petzinger, Oil & Honor: The Texaco-Pennzoil Wars 414-26 (1987).

[82] *See generally* Stefan A. Riesenfeld, Creditors' Rights and Debtors' Protection 59 (4th ed. 1987).

[83] *E.g.*, Hazel v. Van Beek, 954 P.2d 1301, 1307 (Wash. 1998) (10 years); Wyo. Stat. Ann. § 1-16-503 (LexisNexis 2005) (10 years with longer periods if the plaintiff is a minor or if the judgment involved is for child support).

[84] *See* Stefan A. Riesenfeld, *Collection of Money Judgments in American Law — A Historical Inventory and a Prospectus*, 42 Iowa L. Rev. 155, 172 (1957).

[85] *E.g.*, Leroy Jenkins Evangelistic Ass'n., Inc. v. Equities Diversified, Inc., 580 N.E.2d 812 (Ohio Ct. App. 1989) (explaining Ohio procedure to revive a dormant judgment).

[86] *E.g.*, Aetna Fin. Co. v. Schmitz, 849 P.2d 1083 (Okla. 1993).

[C]   Enforcing Judgments from Other Jurisdictions

[1]   Judgments from Sister States

A judgments can be enforced only in the state where it was rendered. To enforce a judgment in another state, a creditor must establish the validity of its judgment in that other state, usually one where the debtor's assets are located.[87]

This process is facilitated by the Full Faith and Credit Clause of the United States Constitution: "Full Faith and Credit shall be given in each State to the public Acts, Records, and judicial Proceedings of every other State."[88] Thus, states are constitutionally required to enforce the valid judgments of their sister states.[89]

The normal method to enforce a judgment obtained in one state is to "domesticate" the judgment in the second state where it is to be enforced. This involves filing a lawsuit in the second state, alleging that a judgment was obtained against the defendant in the first state. Proving that the judgment was obtained is usually easy, requiring little more than attaching a copy of the judgment to the plaintiff's complaint. Unless the judgment was invalid in the state in which it was originally obtained and thus subject to collateral attack (such as due to lack of personal jurisdiction over the defendant), the defendant will have no defenses and the court in the second state will be obliged to enter a second judgment against the defendant based on the original judgment. Once this second judgment is obtained, it can be enforced in the same manner as other judgments obtained in the courts of the second state.

Forty-seven states, the District of Columbia, and the U.S. Virgin Islands have adopted the Uniform Enforcement of Foreign Judgments Act.[90] It provides a system for the "registration" of judgments which makes it unnecessary to obtain a second judgment simply to enforce the first in another state.[91] Courts consistently rule that judgment debtors may not re-litigate the merits of a sister-state judgment when enforcement is sought under the UEFJA.[92]

[2]   Foreign Judgments

Enforcement of judgments obtained in foreign countries varies more widely from state to state. The creditor with the foreign judgment must bring an action in the United States, and the American court will determine whether to give effect to the foreign judgment. Many states have enacted another uniform statute, the Uniform

---

[87]   *See, e.g.*, Keeton v. Hustler Magazine, Inc., 815 F.2d 957 (2d Cir. 1987).

[88]   U.S. Const. art. IV, § 1.

[89]   *See* Restatement (Second) of Contract of Laws § 100 (1981).

[90]   Only California, Massachusetts, and Vermont had not adopted it, as of mid-2012. *See* http:// uniformlaws.org/LegislativeFactSheet.aspx?title=Enforcement%20of%20Foreign%20Judgments% 20Act (last viewed, July 31, 2012).

[91]   *See* Unif. Enforcement of Foreign Judgments Act § 2 (1964).

[92]   Sara L. Johnson, Annotation, *Validity, Construction and Application of Uniform Enforcement of Judgments Act*, 31 A.L.R.4th 762 (1984). *E.g.*, Canon Fin. Serv. Inc. v. Nat'l Voting Rights Museum & Inst. 57 So. 3d 766 (Ala. Civ. App. 2010).

Foreign-Money Judgments Recognition Act.[93] Its 2005 replacement, the Uniform Foreign-Country Money Judgments Recognition Act, has been adopted in 17 states and the District of Columbia, and, as of mid-2012, was under consideration in three additional states.[94] It generally requires recognition of a foreign judgment, but permits a state to refuse enforcement if the foreign country lacked personal jurisdiction over the defendant, lacked subject matter jurisdiction over the dispute, or if the country which issued the judgment had a judicial system that "does not provide impartial tribunals or procedures compatible with the requirements of due process of law . . . ."[95] Likewise, the American court need not recognize the foreign judgment if, among other reasons, the defendant did not receive sufficient notice of the action, if the judgment was obtained by fraud, or if either the judgment or the underlying claim for relief "is repugnant to the public policy of [the] state or of the United States."[96]

§ 2.04   JUDICIAL LIENS[97]

Obtaining a judgment provides the creditor with no assurance that the judgment will be paid. It usually creates no property rights, in an of itself, and is merely a piece of paper, suitable for framing. The effect of obtaining a judgment is twofold. First, it liquidates the debt, making it certain in amount. Second it is a ticket to the various judicial remedies available for enfocement. Of course, if the judgment debtor has insurance, such as in many auto accident cases, the debtor's insurance carrier may simply write a check to satisfy the judgment in full. If the debtor is not insured, the creditor may on its own, or through a collection agency, begin sending a barrage of letters and making a multitude of phone calls to the debtor, trying to elicit voluntary payment.

If the judgment debtor owns valuable property but remains unwilling to pay, a judgment creditor may take additional steps to obtain a judicial lien on the debtor's property and then foreclose on the lien to obtain payment. Judicial liens are involuntary liens that are available to creditors who have obtained a judgment against a debtor. They are involuntary because they are imposed without the debtor's consent. Sometimes this is the only recourse for a creditor faced with a recalcitrant debtor. On other occasions, the threat or actual imposition of a lien induces the debtor to pay voluntarily, without the necessity of incurring the expense of obtaining or enforcing a lien.

---

[93] Uniform Foreign-Country Money Judgments Recognition Act (1962), 13 (pt 2) U.L.A. 149 (1986) available online at http://www.law.upenn.edu/bll/archives/ulc/ufmjra/2005final.htm (last viewed July 18, 2012).

[94] Uniform Foreign-Country Judgments Recognition Act (2005), 13 (pt. 2) U.L.A. 43 (Supp. 2006) available online at http://www.law.upenn.edu/bll/ulc/ufmjra/2005final.htm (last viewed July 18, 2012).

[95] Uniform Foreign-Country Judgments Recognition Act § 4 (2005).

[96] *Id.*

[97] Stefan A. Riesenfeld, *Collection of Money Judgments in American Law*, 42 Iowa L. Rev. 155 (1957). *See* Stefan A. Riesenfeld, *Enforcement of Money Judgments in Early American History*, 71 Mich. L. Rev. 691, 694 (1973); Clinton W. Francis, *Practice, Strategy, and Institution: Debt Collection in the English Common-law Courts, 1740-1840*, 80 Nw. U. L. Rev. 807 (1987).

There are numerous subtle features to the rules governing judicial liens, which vary considerably from state to state. In most jurisdictions, a lien on real property is obtained by docketing or recording the judgment in the county where the debtor's land is located. A judicial lien on tangible personal property is usually obtained by having the local sheriff's department physically seize the asset pursuant to a court order. Acquiring a judicial lien on intangible property through "garnishment" is more complicated and may require the initiation of an ancillary lawsuit against a person who owes money to the judgment debtor.

State laws vary on these procedures, and law students taking a course in basic debtor-creditor law only rarely delve into the details of these procedures, even with respect to the law in their own state.[98] Accordingly, the following section merely identifies the most frequently encountered issues and sketches the most common rules.

[A] Judgment Liens on Real Estate[99]

A judicial or "judgment" lien[100] on real estate is established in one of two ways, depending on the jurisdiction: 1) by "docketing" the judgment, or 2) by recording the judgment in the county where the real estate is located.[101] In most states, formal entry of the judgment on the court's records alone is sufficient for the judgment to operate as a lien on the real estate located in the county where the judgment was obtained.[102] However, many states require the creditor to record notice of the judgment in the county real estate records, much in the same way a creditor would record a mortgage on the debtor's land. Docketing or recording the judgment puts third parties on constructive notice of the creditor's lien.

If the debtor owns land in several counties, the judgment must be recorded in each county in which the debtor's land is located. Assume, for example, that Merchant's Bank has a $300,000 judgment against Titanic Industries and that Titanic owns land in both Jefferson County, where the judgment was obtained, and another parcel in Madison County, in the same state. To obtain a judgment lien on the Jefferson County property, Merchant's Bank will usually find it necessary to docket the judgment with the Jefferson County courts, or to record it in the real estate records in Jefferson County. To obtain a judgment lien on the debtor's Madison County land, Merchant's Bank will have to record the judgment in Madison' County's real estate records.

Judgments obtained in federal court become liens on the debtor's real estate in a similar way. When a creditor obtains a judgment in federal district court, it operates as a lien on the debtor's property located in that state "to the same extent

---

[98] Collection lawyers, on the other hand, become thoroughly familiar with them.

[99] David Gray Carlson, *Critique of Money Judgment Part One: Liens on New York Real Property*, 82 St. John's L. Rev. 1291 (2008).

[100] Judgment liens were known to the common law as the writ of "elegit."

[101] *See, e.g.*, Cal. Civ. Proc. Code § 674 (West Supp. 2006).

[102] *See, e.g.*, N.Y. C.P.L.R. § 5018 (McKinney 1992). *See generally* In re Peterson, 80 B.R. 167, 169 (Bankr. D.N.D. 1987).

and under the same conditions as a judgment of a court of general jurisdiction in such state . . . ."[103]

Judgment liens on real estate normally have priority over later interests in the land, and are subordinate to previously recorded interests, other than ownership interests of the judgment debtor herself. Existing interests may or may not include the interests of a person who has an unrecorded interest but is in possession of the property, though as with most features of collection law, this varies somewhat from state to state.

Whether a judicial lien extends to real estate acquired by the debtor after the lien was recorded — to "after-acquired" property — also varies from state to state, with most states permitting a judgment lien recorded in a county's real estate records to encumber land that the debtor subsequently acquires in the same county where the judgment is recorded.[104] However, the lien may not enjoy seniority over subsequently recorded judgment liens, that are also recorded before the debtor obtains the new property. In most states, the competing judgment lien is entitled to pro-rata priority with respect to such after-acquired land.

Assume, for example, that as of May 2013, Franklin Manufacturing, Inc. owns Blackacre, which is located in Wood County. If in June 2013, Peninsula Bank obtains and records a judgment in Wood County, the lien will apply to Blackacre. If in September, 2013 Merchant's Finance Co. obtains and records a judgment against Franklin in Wood County, Merchant's will also have a lien on Blackacre, but it will be subordinate in priority to Peninsula Bank's lien, which was recorded first. But, if in November, Franklin acquires Redacre, which is also located in Wood County, Peninsula Bank and Merchant's Finance will in some states, share equal priority over the newly acquired land. Other states, however, would preserve Peninsula's priority in Redacre, based on the time its judgment was originally recorded.

Insofar as bankruptcy is concerned, a judicial lien on real property has the same status as most other kinds of liens. If the judgment is recorded before the bankruptcy case is filed, and the debtor has equity in the property, the judgment creditor will have a secured claim in the bankruptcy proceeding. But, if the lien was not properly recorded, or was not obtained until the last ninety days before the debtor's bankruptcy petition, it will likely be set aside by the bankruptcy trustee, pursuant to one of the trustee's avoiding powers.

[B] Judicial Liens on Tangible Personal Property[105]

Imposing a judicial lien on tangible personal property usually requires several steps beyond obtaining and docketing a judgment. Recording the judgment in the county where the debtor's goods are located, or even where the debtor resides,

---

[103] 28 U.S.C. § 1962 (2006).

[104] *See* Zink v. James River Nat'l Bank, 224 N.W. 901 (N.D. 1929); Estate of Robbins, 346 N.Y.S.2d 86 (N.Y. Sur. 1973).

[105] David Gray Carlson, *Critique of Money Judgment Part Two: Liens on New York Personal Property*, 83 St. John's L. Rev. 43 (2009).

usually means nothing with respect to this type of property.[106] Instead, a judgment creditor must "levy" or "execute" on the items, most often through physical seizure of them by the local sheriff pursuant to a court order.

Historically, a debtor's property could be seized by the sheriff and sold to satisfy a judgment pursuant to a writ of *fieri facias*, which is still commonly abbreviated and known colloquially in states where it is used as a "fi fa."[107] The procedure involved to obtain a modern "writ of attachment" or "writ of execution" on a judgment debtor's goods is not appreciably different from that used to obtain a fi fa. After judgment, the creditor requests an order from the court, or the clerk of courts, directing the sheriff to locate and seize the debtor's property. Issuance of a writ of execution is a ministerial act, which gives effect to the court's judgment.[108]

After the writ is delivered to the sheriff, deputies are dispatched to comply with the instructions contained in the writ. Naturally, the more information the judgment creditor supplies to the sheriff's department, the more likely that the deputies assigned to the task will be able to successfully locate and seize the debtor's property. The debtor, of course, can be expected to resist the sheriff's efforts, though usually through stealth rather than force.[109]

In most states, the sheriff must physically take possession of the judgment debtor's property. However, in some jurisdictions, the seizure may be merely symbolic. It might be accomplished by attaching some sort of official notice to the property, indicating that the property has been seized by the sheriff's department. Some states do not even require this minimal form of seizure. In California, a judicial lien on personal property can be obtained by recording the judgment in the state's U.C.C. filing system. Other states treat the property as having been sufficiently attached if it came within the "view and control" of the sheriff.[110]

Thus, in *Credit Bureau of Broken Bow v. Moninger*,[111] a truck was successfully levied on when a duly authorized deputy " 'grabbed ahold of the pickup' and stated: 'I execute on the pickup for the County of Custer,' " even though he did not either take the vehicle into his possession or even acquire a set of keys to it. However, as indicated above, in most states, the sheriff must place the property under her physical control, and hold on to it.

---

[106] *E.g.*, In re Tropicana Graphics, Inc., 24 B.R. 381 (Bankr. C.D. Cal. 1982) ("Unlike real property, a judgment lien has no analogue that reaches personal property.").

[107] Del. Code Ann. tit. 10, § 5041 (1999). *See* United States v. Crittenden, 563 F.2d 678 (5th Cir. 1977) (the court jokingly noted that the facts did not require the court to determine whether the judgment debtor, the FHA, "could have attacked Crittenden's fi. fa. with a fo fum or whether the result would be different if Crittenden had English blood."). *Id.* at 680 n.4. *See also* http://www.gwinnettcountysheriff. com/index.php/divisions/first-division-title/writ-of-fieri-facias-fi-fa-personal-property-levy/ (last viewed, January 11, 2012).

[108] Coonts v. Potts, 316 F.3d 745, 751 n. 4 (8th Cir. 2003). *Cf.* State v. Robb, 723 N.E.2d 1019 (Ohio 2000) (authorizing "execution" pursuant to a the death penalty).

[109] *See, e.g.*, Hickey v. Couchman, 797 S.W.2d 103 (Tex. Ct. App. 1990) (illustrating the debtor's delaying tactics).

[110] *But see* Socony Mobil Oil Co. v. Wayne County Produce Co., 196 N.Y.S.2d 729 (N.Y. Sup. Ct. 1959) (property viewed through a window, but not under the sheriff's dominion and control).

[111] 284 N.W.2d 855 (Neb. 1979).

If the sheriff fails to make a successful levy, there are several potential consequences. Most importantly, the creditor is deprived of the priority it would have achieved over subsequent creditors who obtain a statutory, judicial, or consensual lien on property the sheriff might have attached.[112] Second, if the failure was because the sheriff's department did not perform its statutory duties, the judgment creditor might be able to recover the amount of its judgment from the sheriff in an "amercement" action.[113] Sheriff's departments are usually bonded against liability for this type of mistake. Still, the rate a Sheriff pays for her performance bond are likely to increase if her failure to fulfill her statutory duties results in claims against the bond.

In most states, a judgment creditor's priority over other creditors dates from the time the debtor's property was physically seized.[114] This provides the greatest possible protection for good faith purchasers and other creditors, who otherwise might be misled by the debtor's apparent unfettered ownership of the property subject to the lien. On the other hand, unless the sheriff has a duty to execute writs in the order in which she has received them,[115] it might make priority dependent upon the order in which assignments are made in the sheriff's department. This could lead to abuse due to political favoritism, or even bribery.

In other jurisdictions, priority relates back to the time the writ was delivered to the sheriff,[116] or possibly back to the time the writ was issued by the court.[117] These procedures prevent manipulation by the sheriff's office but may result in the imposition of secret liens in the period between the date the writ is delivered to the sheriff, but before the property is actually seized.

A few states take a completely different approach to the matter. California, for example, permits a judgment creditor to obtain a judicial lien on the business debtor's personal property, both tangible and intangible, by filing notice of the judgment with the state Secretary of State, where records of contractual security interests are also usually recorded. This system works much in the same way that other states' systems for recording liens on a debtor's real estate operate, except notice of the judgment is filed centrally, with the Secretary of State instead of the county recorder's office.[118] The property still must be seized in order to be sold, but the creditor's priority over competing claims is determined by the date of filing.

---

[112] *See* U.C.C. § 9-317(a)(2) (2010) (security interest); Illi, Inc. v. Margolis, 296 A.2d 412 (Md. Ct. App. 1972) (competing fi fa).

[113] Ryan v. Carter, 621 N.E.2d 399 (Ohio 1993); Vitale v. Hotel Cal., Inc., 446 A.2d 880 (N.J. Super. Ct.), *aff'd*, 455 A.2d 508 (N.J. App. Div. 1982). *See* Frank B. Wyatt, *Amercement of Sheriffs*, 10 Wake Forest L. Rev. 237 (1974).

[114] *E.g.*, Cal. Civ. Proc. Code § 697.710 (West 2005). *See generally* D.E. Murray, *Execution Lien Creditors Versus Bona Fide Purchasers, Lenders and Other Execution Lien Creditors: Charles II and the Uniform Commercial Code*, 85 Com. L.J. 485 (1980).

[115] *E.g.*, Ohio Rev. Code Ann. § 2329.10 (LexisNexis 2005).

[116] *E.g.*, N.Y. C.P.L.R. 5234(b) (McKinney Supp. 2005); 735 Ill. Comp. Stat. Ann. 5/12-111 (West 2003).

[117] Tenn. Code Ann. § 26-1-109 (LexisNexis 2000).

[118] *See* Cal. Civ. Proc. Code. Ann. § 697.510 (West 1987).

[C] Garnishment of Property Under the Control of Third Parties[119]

Property under the control of third parties is generally acquired by the creditor through garnishment.[120] This property usually consists of money owed to the judgment debtor, such as wages, bank accounts, and less frequently, accounts receivable. Although courts sometimes suggest that garnishment is purely a creature of statute and a stranger to the common law,[121] it had its origin in European cities during the middle ages in a procedure then known as "foreign attachment."[122]

Garnishment is usually initiated through service of a court order on a person in control of the debtor's property, directing that person to deliver the debtor's property to the creditor, to the extent necessary to satisfy the creditor's judgment.[123] In this respect, garnishment sometimes resembles a lawsuit within a lawsuit. The garnishment suit is brought against a third party, such as a bank, alleging that it owes money (or some other form of property) to the judgment debtor.

Wage garnishment is the most common type of garnishment. In wage garnishment, the judgment creditor brings an ancillary action against the judgment debtor's employer. The creditor alleges that the judgment debtor is an employee of the defendant, who is usually referred to as the "garnishee,"[124] and that the employer owes money to the judgment debtor. The garnishment requires the employer to pay the wages owed to the employee to the employee's creditor, instead of paying them to the employee.

The employer may defend the action the way any defendant might — by denying the allegations of the complaint, such as where the judgment debtor is no longer employed by the defendant and owes the debtor no wages.

Federal law imposes significant limits on the percentage of a person's wages that are subject to garnishment. The Consumer Credit Protection Act generally prevents judgment creditors from garnishing more than 25% of a person's

---

[119] Jonathan Glusman, Note, *Garnishment of Receivables in Chinese Law*, 3 Wash. U. Global Stud. L. Rev. 455 (2004).

[120] Garnishment can also be used to recover tangible property in the hands of a third party, but it is most commonly used to recover amounts owed to the judgment debtor by a third party.

[121] *E.g.*, Western v. Hodgson, 494 F.2d 379 (4th Cir. 1974).

[122] *See* Ownbey v. Morgan, 256 U.S. 94, 104-05 (1905); Stefan A. Riesenfeld, Creditors' Remedies and Debtors Protection 240 (4th ed. 1987). *See* Nathan Levy, Jr., *Attachment, Garnishment and Garnishment Execution,*, 5 Conn. L. Rev. 399, 405 (1972).

[123] Peggy Coleman, Warren Ross & John P. Finan, Note, *Creditor's Rights in Ohio: An Extensive Revision (Introduction)*, 16 Akron L. Rev. 487 (1983).

[124] "Garnishee" is a noun, which refers to the person against whom the garnishment action is brought — in a wage garnishment proceeding, the employer. "Garnishee" is frequently misused by those uneducated in the law of creditors' rights, as if it were a verb referring to the act of garnishment itself. The proper verb in this setting is "garnish." Black's Law Dictionary 702 (8th ed. 2004). Properly speaking, a person's wages are "garnished"; they are not "garnisheed." "Garnisheed" is not a word.

wages.[125] In addition, states may impose their own additional limits on wage garnishment.

Garnishment proceedings are also frequently brought to recover funds on deposit in a judgment debtor's bank account. As with a wage garnishment proceeding, the bank, as garnishee, has the opportunity to defend the lawsuit by denying allegations that it has any of the judgment debtor's funds on deposit.

Bank accounts are attractive targets for creditors hoping to enforce a judgment. Unlike real estate or tangible personal property, funds in a bank account are highly liquid. Moreover, a bank that fails to properly respond to a garnishment proceeding may find itself liable to the judgment creditor for the entire debt its banking customer owes to the creditor.[126] Banks tend to pay their debts.

Judgment creditors sometimes find that the bank in which a debtor's funds are deposited is one of the judgment debtor's other creditors. In this case, an effort to garnish the debtor's bank account is likely to precipitate the bank's exercise of its right of setoff against the debtor's account. Assume, for example, that Titanic Industries is indebted to both Island Bank and to Merchant's Finance Co., and keeps its cash in an account at Island Bank. If Merchant's Finance tries to garnish Titanic's account at Island Bank, the bank might set off the debt owed by Titanic against the money in Titanic's account, effectively cleaning out Titanic's bank account, leaving no funds for Merchant's to garnish. This inevitably raises questions about the propriety of the bank's exercise of its right of setoff and of the relative priority of a garnishing judgment creditor and the bank's equitable or statutory right of setoff.[127] Most of the time, the bank's right of setoff wins.[128]

§ 2.05 STATUTORY, COMMON LAW, AND EQUITABLE LIENS

Statutory, common law, and equitable liens arise without court action.[129] They are imposed automatically by operation of law, usually as a result of the nature of the transaction involved between the debtor and the creditor. The most common example is a statutory construction lien (frequently called a "mechanic's lien"), which operates for the benefit of someone who has supplied goods or services in connection with improvements to the debtor's land. Other examples include artisan's liens in favor of individuals who perform repairs on motor vehicles and other personal property, landlords liens, veterinarians liens, and even common law "charging liens" in favor of attorneys, which are sometimes imposed on the proceeds of successful litigation in which the attorneys have engaged. These various

---

[125] 15 U.S.C. §§ 1671-1677 (2006). *See infra* § 2.11[A][4][a] Federal Restrictions on Wage Garnishment; *infra* § 12.03[D][1] Wage Exemptions.

[126] *E.g.*, Tenn. Code Ann. § 26-2-209 (LexisNexis 2000). *See generally* Robert Laurence, *The Supreme Court and the Defaulting Garnishee: An Essay on* Metal Processing, Inc. v. Plastic & Reconstructive Associates, Ltd. *and a Few of its Predecessors*, 40 Ark. L. Rev. 1 (1986).

[127] *See infra* § 2.06 Setoff of Mutual Debts.

[128] *See infra* § 2.06 Setoff of Mutual Debts.

[129] *See In re* Speciality Prop. Dev. Inc., 399 B.R. 857 (Bankr. M.D. Fla. 2009) (garnishment lien, obtained through judicial action and not solely due to a specific statute, was not a "statutory lien.").

statutory and common law liens provide leverage to the creditor who may use the lien to obtain voluntary payment, and if necessary, to ensure the availability of a source of payment.

Another important example is the tax lien, granted by the government in favor of itself, to enhance its ability to collect taxes owed by the debtor.[130] Because financially troubled debtors are usually in arrears on their taxes, especially withholding, sales, and other "trust fund" taxes, tax liens are especially important.

Except for construction liens on real estate and tax liens, most statutory liens are "possessory," that is, the lien holder must have physical possession of the property subject to the lien. A creditor who relinquishes possession of the goods waives its lien. In most other respects, the details of these statutory and common law liens vary tremendously from state to state, making generalizations about these details extraordinarily difficult. Nevertheless, some common patterns exist.

[A]   Construction or "Mechanic's" Liens

A "mechanic's lien" (also sometimes known as a "construction lien," a "materialman's lien," or a "laborer's lien") is a statutory lien designed to protect those who supply goods and services in connection with a construction project from the risk of non-payment by the landowner, or default by the prime contractor. Protection provided to these suppliers is thought to reduce the cost of construction by eliminating some of the credit risk that the parties otherwise face.[131] They protect against unjust enrichment by ensuring that the landowner will pay the subcontractor for the benefit conferred by the subcontractor's labor.

In most construction projects, the construction process is managed by a "general" or "prime" contractor who is responsible for completing the building or other improvement for the owner. Usually this prime contractor is the only person who deals directly with and who is in contractual privity with the owner of the land. The prime contractor parcels out portions of the job to various subcontractors and material suppliers. For example, one subcontractor will do the plumbing, another the electrical work, a third the interior design. The actual goods used in the project will be acquired from building supply companies. Since the plumber, the electrician, the designer, and the supply company do not have a direct contract with the owner of the project, they cannot sue the owner directly if they are not paid by the prime contractor. Mechanic's lien laws protect these parties by giving them liens on the improved real estate for the goods and services they have provided to the owner in connection with the improvements. Typically, these liens arise when construction begins. The lien is generally perfected by a system of notice to both the public and to the owner, generally involving the recording of notice of the lien in real property records and making personal service on the owners.

Construction liens are neither limited to the amount required to be paid by the owner to the prime contractor nor affected by payments from the owner to the

---

[130] *See* 26 U.S.C. § 6321 (2006).

[131] *See* Chesebro-Whitman Co. v. Edenboro Apartments, Inc., 207 A.2d 186, 188 (N.J. Super. Ct. 1965).

prime contractor who is supervising the overall project. Thus, owners incur a serious risk of having to pay twice for the same work if they pay the prime contractor without obtaining some sort of protection against the risk that the prime contractor has not remitted payment to others who have contributed to the project. This protection is normally secured either by obtaining a payment bond from the prime contractor or by obtaining lien waivers from the subcontractors and suppliers, before or at the time payment is made.

It is usually necessary for the lien holder to record notice of the lien in the real estate records in the county where the land is located.[132] Notice may also be required to be published in a newspaper or served on the owner.[133] State laws vary widely on the priority date for mechanic's liens. Once recorded, priority may relate back to the time the overall construction project began,[134] or to the time when the work was done.[135]

[B]   Repair or "Artisan's" Liens

Repair liens operate in favor of persons who have repaired personal property, such as an automobile, and who have not been paid. They operate similarly to mechanic's liens, except they are designed to protect service providers from the risk of non-payment by the owner rather than from default by a prime contractor. Such liens are also referred to as "mechanics" or "artisans" liens but they should not be confused with construction liens which also sometimes frequently bear the former label. They might arise under the common law or rules of equity but today are nearly always statutory. Accordingly, both their scope and priority depend upon the provisions of the state statute under which they arise. As with most aspects of state collection law, they vary widely from state to state.

Repair liens almost always require the lien holder to remain in possession of the repaired property.[136] An auto repair shop that relinquishes possession of the car it has worked on usually loses its lien on the vehicle. Repair shops rarely relinquish possession of goods they have repaired without being paid, but it has been known to occur.

The most commonly recurring priority issue deals with conflicts between a creditor with a statutory lien and a competing creditor with an Article 9 security interest in the same property. Under U.C.C. § 9-333, a creditor with a "possessory lien" in goods that secures payment of an obligation for services or materials supplied to the debtor in the ordinary course has priority over a conflicting security interest in the same goods, unless the state statute that created the possessory lien provides otherwise. Loss of possession by the lien holder results in loss of this priority.[137]

---

[132] *See generally* Grant S. Nelson & Dale A. Whitman, Real Estate Finance Law 979 (4th ed. 2001).

[133] *See generally* Grant S. Nelson & Dale A. Whitman, Real Estate Finance Law 979 (4th ed. 2001).

[134] *E.g.*, Mich. Comp. Laws Ann. § 570.1119 (West 1996).

[135] *E.g.*, Nw. Nat'l Bank v. Metro Ctr., Inc., 303 N.W.2d 395, 398 (Iowa 1981).

[136] *See, e.g.*, In re Borden, 361 B.R. 489 (B.A.P. 8th Cir. 2007).

[137] U.C.C. § 9-330 (2010).

Some states have statutory "agricultural liens" that are imposed by the legislature to secure payment to those who provide agricultural supplies to farmers, to assist them in growing crops or raising livestock.[138] Article 9 of the U.C.C. provides a set of special rules to resolve priority disputes.

In addition, the federal Perishable Agricultural Commodities Act,[139] provides some protection to farmers or claims they have against buyers of agricultural products, without making payment.[140] It imposes a "statutory trust" in favor of sellers and other suppliers of perishable agricultural commodities, many of whom are farmers. This trust operates in the same manner as a lien, which has priority over those who extend credit to the buyer of those commodities. It applies any time the buyer is a "dealer" or "broker." The term dealer has been held to include not just farm commodity middlemen, but also supermarkets, cruise lines, and restaurant chains who purchase in wholesale quantities.[141]

[C] Common Law Liens[142]

Although most of the liens discussed in this section are found in state statutes, a few common law liens persist. Like statutory liens, they usually operate in favor of a creditor based on his or her status as a landlord, an auctioneer,[143] carrier, or a warehouseman. They usually arise to prevent unjust enrichment of the debtor whose property has been improved as a result of the efforts of the creditor for whose benefit the lien operates.[144] As with statutory repair liens, they nearly always depend on the lien holder's continued possession of the goods subject to the lien.[145]

---

[138] E.g., Mont. Code. Ann. § 71-3-901 (2008). *See generally* Donald W. Baker, *Some Thoughts on Agricultural Liens Under the New U.C.C. Article 9*, 51 Ala. L. Rev. 1417 (2000); Keith G. Meyer, *A Garden Variety of UCC Issues Dealing with Agriculture*, 58 U. Kan. L. Rev. 1119 (2010).

[139] 7 U.S.C. §§ 499a-499t (2006).

[140] Mark Duedall, *The Perishable Agricultural Commodities Act and Its Effect on Secret Liens (Emerging Trends in Commercial Law: Surviving Tomorrow's Challenges)*, 2 DePaul Bus. & Com. L.J. 707 (2004); Michael D. Sousa, *Are You Your Produce Vendor's Keeper? The Perishable Agricultural Commodities Act and § 523(a)(4) of the Code*, 15 J. Bankr. L. & Prac. 6 (2006).

[141] *See* In re Old Fashioned Enters., Inc., 236 F.3d 422 (8th Cir. 2001) (restaurant); Foods Co. Inc. v. RJR Holdings, Inc., aka T.G.I. Fridays, 252 F.3d 1102, 1107 (9th Cir. 2001) (restaurant); Red's Mkt. v. Cape Canaveral Cruise Line, Inc., 181 F. Supp. 2d 1339 (M.D. Fla. 2002) (cruise line). *But see* In re Italian Oven, Inc., 207 B.R. 839 (Bankr. W.D. Pa. 1997) (restaurants not dealers).

[142] Ray Andrews Brown, The Law of Personal Property § 107 at 512 (2d ed. 1955). *See* Richard L. Barne, *UCC Article Nine Revised: Priorities, Preferences, and Liens Effective Only in Bankruptcy*, 82 Neb. L. Rev. 607, 627 (2004).

[143] *E.g.*, Thoroughbred Horsemen's Ass'n of Tex. Inc. v. Dyer, 905 S.W.2d 752 (Tex. Ct. App. 1995) (common law auctioneer's lien).

[144] *E.g.*, Burns v. Miller, 714 P.2d 1190 (Wash. Ct. App. 1986), *rev'd in part* 733 P.2d 522 (Wash. 1987).

[145] *E.g.*, Cent. Contractors Serv., Inc. v. Ohio County Stone Co., 255 S.W.2d 17 (Ky. 1952).

[D] Equitable Liens

Equitable liens are sometimes imposed when an unpaid creditor has no adequate remedy at law.[146] They are usually awarded only when there is specific property to which the creditor's claim is related. For example, in *Palm Beach Savings. & Loan Ass'n v. Fishbein*,[147] the court granted an equitable lien to a bank whose mortgage was invalid because the debtor's former husband forged her signature on the loan documents. She benefitted from the loans when the original mortgage was paid, so the court concluded that imposing a lien on her property was not unfair to her. However, the lien was limited to the extent the proceeds of the bank's loan were used to satisfy a preexisting mortgage and taxes on the property, for which the wife had been liable.

As *Fishbein* illustrates, equitable liens tend to be imposed in situations where there was an unsuccessful attempt to obtain a consensual lien, and where the denial of relief would result in the debtor's unjust enrichment at the creditor's expense.[148]

Most jurisdictions disfavor equitable liens because they are inherently secret. The debtor retains possession of the collateral and nothing is filed on the public record to give other creditors notice of the lien. Indeed, the existence of the lien may not be established until the court rules. Thus, equitable liens present a serious risk for other creditors who may be misled into believing that the debtor's property is unencumbered. Given the ease of obtaining a security interest in personal property, the drafters of Article 9 of the U.C.C. attempted to eliminate equitable liens.[149] However, their efforts have not been completely successful, and courts still sometimes impose them.[150]

[E] Seller's Right of Reclamation

In some cases, sellers have a right to reclaim goods delivered to an insolvent buyer. U.C.C. § 2-702(2) gives sellers a limited right to reclaim goods from the buyer, if they were sold on credit, and the buyer failed to pay. Section 2-507 gives sellers a similar right, where payment was supposed to have been made in cash upon delivery, but where payment was not completed, usually because the buyer's check bounced.

---

[146] *See, e.g.*, In re Broadview Lumber Co., Inc., 118 F.3d 1246, 1253 (8th Cir. 1997).

[147] 619 So. 2d 267 (Fla. 1993).

[148] *E.g.*, Wash. Metro. Area Transit Auth. v. Reid, 666 A.2d 41 (D.C. 1995) (employers who paid workers compensation benefits to employee entitled to equitable lien against employee's tort recovery to prevent unjust enrichment of the employee).

[149] U.C.C. § 9-203 cmt. 5 (2010) ("Since this Article reduces formal requisites to a minimum, the doctrine [of equitable liens] is no longer necessary or useful. More harm than good would result from allowing creditors to establish a secured status by parol evidence after they have neglected the simple formality of obtaining a signed writing.").

[150] *E.g.*, Davis v. Guaranty Bank and Trust Co., 58 So. 3d 1233 (Miss. Ct. App. 2011); In re Carpenter, 252 B.R. 905 (E.D.Va. 2000); In re Czebotar, 5 Bankr. 379 (B.A.P. 9th Cir. 1980).

[1] Reclamation in Credit Sales

U.C.C. Article 2 gives sellers who have delivered goods on credit to an insolvent buyer a limited right to reclaim them. U.C.C. § 2-702 gives a seller the right to reclaim the goods if:

- the goods were sold to the buyer on credit;

- the debtor was insolvent when it received the goods; and

- the seller demands return of the goods within ten days after the buyer received them.[151]

Section 2-702's right of reclamation only applies if the goods were sold on credit. It limits the right of reclamation to situations where the buyer is insolvent at the time it received the goods. If the buyer was solvent at the time the goods were delivered, but later became insolvent, § 2-702 provides no protection for the unpaid seller.

In most cases, the seller must assert its right to reclaim the goods within ten days after the buyer received them. However, § 2-702 imposes no time limit if the buyer gave the seller a written misrepresentation of his financial condition during the three-month period before the goods were delivered.[152] When the buyer is bankrupt, however, the bankruptcy code imposes its own restrictions on the seller's reclamation rights.[153]

[2] Reclamation in Cash Sales

In cash transactions, § 2-507 gives the seller a similar right to reclaim the goods, where the seller had not anticipated delivering the goods on credit. It provides: "Where payment is due and demanded on the delivery to the buyer of goods or documents of title, his right as against the seller to retain or dispose of them is conditional upon his making the payment due."[154]

Section 2-507 does not require the buyer to be insolvent. Further, although its language does not require the seller to demand return of the goods within any time period, some courts have applied § 2-702(2)'s ten-day limit by analogy.[155] However, the Code's official comments, which originally suggested that § 2-702's time limit should be applied under § 2-507, were later changed by the Code's drafters to indicate that no such limit should be imposed in a cash sale.[156]

---

[151] U.C.C. § 2-702(2) (2010).

[152] U.C.C. § 2-702(2) (2010).

[153] Bankruptcy Code § 546. *See infra* § 14.08[C] Limits on Seller's Reclamation Rights.

[154] U.C.C. § 2-507(2) (2010).

[155] *Compare* Szabo v. Vinton Motors, 630 F.2d 1 (1st Cir. 1980) (ten-day limit imposed by analogy), *with* Burk v. Emmick, 637 F.2d 1172 (8th Cir. 1980) (no limit).

[156] The proposed revisions to Article 2, if adopted anywhere, would make the rights of reclamation in §§ 2-507 and 2-207(2) identical, requiring the seller to assert its right to reclaim the goods within a reasonable time.

[3] Priority of Right of Reclamation

This right of reclamation is not as useful as it first might appear to be. This is because the seller's right is subordinate to the competing claims of third parties who obtain an interest in the goods. Competing claimants might include a buyer in the ordinary course, who purchased them from the buyer[157] or another purchaser from the buyer, such as a creditor with a security interest in the buyer's existing and after-acquired inventory.[158] Although § 2-507 makes no mention of a purchaser's superior rights, most courts addressing the issue have ruled that the buyer's secured lender prevails over the seller's right of reclamation.[159] Moreover, Bankruptcy Code § 546(c) expressly makes a reclaiming seller's rights subject to the "prior rights of a holder of a security interest in such goods or the proceeds thereof."[160]

[4] Bankruptcy Code Limits on Seller's Right of Reclamation

A seller's right of reclamation is also subject to limits imposed by the Bankruptcy Code. Since nearly all reclamations occur in the context of a buyer who has become insolvent, there is a strong likelihood that the buyer will be a debtor in a bankruptcy case and therefore that the seller's rights will be subject to any restrictions imposed by the Bankruptcy Code.[161]

Bankruptcy Code § 546(c) broadly validates a seller's right to reclaim, but adds a further requirement that the seller's demand for the return of the goods be made in writing. In addition, it limits the seller's right of reclamation to goods the buyer received within forty-five days before commencement of the buyer's bankruptcy case.[162] Further, as explained in more detail elsewhere,[163] § 546(c) also imposes limits on the timing of the seller's demand for the return of the goods, requiring the demand to be made within forty-five days of the time the buyer receives the goods or, if the bankruptcy case commences before expiration of this forty-five day period, within twenty days of the commencement of the case.[164]

The 2005 Bankruptcy Code Amendments eliminated § 546(c)'s reference to "any statutory or common law right" and instead created a 45-day reclamation period.

---

[157] In re Coast Trading Co., Inc., 31 B.R. 663 (Bankr. D. Or. 1982).

[158] *E.g.*, In re M. Paolella & Sons, Inc., 161 B.R. 107 (E.D. Pa. 1993); In re Arlco, Inc., 239 B.R. 261 (Bankr. S.D.N.Y. 1999).

[159] *E.g.*, In re Dairy Mart Convenience Stores, Inc., 302 B.R. 128, 134-36 (Bankr. S.D.N.Y. 2003); Genesee Merchants Bank & Trust Co. v. Tucker Motor Sales, 372 N.W.2d 546 (Mich. Ct. App. 1985). *See also* In re Samuels & Co., 510 F.2d 139 (5th Cir. 1975), *rev'd en banc*, 526 F.2d 1238 (1976).

[160] Bankruptcy Code § 546(c)(1). *See* Simon & Schuster, Inc. v. Advanced Marketing Services, Inc. (In re Advanced Marketing Services, Inc.), No. 06-11480 (CSS), Adv. Proc. No. 07-50004 (CSS), 2007 Bankr. LEXIS 135 (Bankr. D. Del. 2007).

[161] *See, e.g.*, Paramount Home Entertainment, Inc. v. Circuit City Stores, Inc., 445 B.R. 521 (E.D. Va. 2010).

[162] Bankruptcy Code § 546(c)(1).

[163] *See infra* § 14.08[C] Limits on Sellers' Reclamation Rights.

[164] Bankruptcy Code § 546(C)(1)(A)-(B).

Thus, it is now unclear whether it establishes an independent reclamation right or whether unpaid sellers must still rely on state law to establish a right of reclamation.[165]

Section 546(c)'s limits, together with those imposed by the U.C.C. make it extraordinarily difficult for a seller to successfully negotiate the statutory restrictions and successfully recover the goods through reclamation. Sellers concerned about payment should insist on a cashier's check upon delivery, or obtain a purchase money security interest in the goods and take the steps necessary to ensure priority over a conflicting inventory lender.

[5]   Seller's Administrative Priority in Bankruptcy

Bankruptcy Code § 503(b)(9) gives unpaid sellers an administrative priority claim for deliveries made to the debtor within twenty days before the debtor's bankruptcy petition.[166] This accords unpaid sellers one of the highest priorities among unsecured creditors who participate in the debtor's bankruptcy case. A post-petition supplier has an ordinary administrative expense priority under § 503(b)(2).

[F]   Tax Liens[167]

An important area of creditors' rights law is the power of government to attach and foreclose on property for unpaid taxes. Tax liens, particularly federal tax liens, are of great concern to those who own or who have extended credit to financially troubled businesses. As one might expect, governments tend to award themselves sweeping rights that can even be superior to those of existing private-sector creditors.

Although individuals who get into financial trouble frequently have unpaid income tax debts, unpaid income taxes are not usually a problem for a financially troubled business. Financially troubled businesses typically suffer from too little income and too many deductible expenses, rather than unpaid income tax.[168] The tax problems encountered by failing businesses more commonly arise from unpaid payroll and sales taxes. Collecting but failing to remit payroll taxes is a serious problem for financially troubled business debtors. These unpaid taxes, and the priority they sometimes have over other creditors, is a concern not just for the taxpayer, but also for its other creditors. Also, failure to remit payroll taxes provides a basis for piercing the corporate veil and may give rise to personal liability for shareholders, officers, and directors.

---

[165] *E.g.*, In re Dana Corp., 367 B.R. 409 (Bankr. S.D.N.Y. 2007).

[166] Bankruptcy Code § 503(b)(9).

[167] William T. Plumb, Federal Tax Liens (1972).

[168] Businesses end up in financial difficulty as a result of selling goods and services below what the goods and services cost to provide. As many bankrupt businesses quickly discover, this is a problem that cannot be solved but is in fact exacerbated by increased sales. For a business engaged in this tactic, expanded sales of the holiday season accelerate the decline into insolvency.

[1]   Federal Tax Liens[169]

The law governing federal tax liens is codified in the Federal Tax Lien Act, a part of the Internal Revenue Code.[170] Tax liens, like most other liens, are imposed through a two-step process. The first step establishes the government's rights against the taxpayer; the second step establishes the government's priority over other creditors.

The first step involves the assessment of a tax — the formal method to determine the IRS' claim that the taxpayer has not paid all taxes due. Once a tax has been assessed, the lien attaches to the taxpayer's property.[171] At this initial stage, the lien is enforceable only against the taxpayer. It remains a secret to the rest of the world, and thus vulnerable to losing priority to the taxpayer's other creditors.

The second step, which addresses this problem, is filing a public notice of the lien. As is true of other filing requirements, the public notice is designed to alert buyers and creditors to the existence of the lien and thus of the IRS' interest in the taxpayer's property. Notice of the lien is filed on a statewide basis, at a place usually determined by state law.[172]

When imposed, federal tax liens apply to every imaginable type of property interest held by the delinquent taxpayer. Moreover, although subject to previously perfected liens of all types, a properly filed tax lien usually has priority over all subsequently arising liens including many of those on after-acquired collateral and those which secure advances made after notice of the tax lien has been filed.

This priority creates headaches for existing creditors. Article 9 of the U.C.C. generally permits a security interest to attach to after-acquired property, and gives secured creditors who properly perfect priority over these subsequently acquired assets.[173] However, if the debtor acquires property after notice of a federal tax lien has been filed, the tax lien usually has priority over after-acquired collateral, even though the Article 9 creditor filed its financing statement before the tax lien arose.[174] Similar rules protect the IRS from security interests that increase in amount as a result of subsequent advances of credit from the Article 9 lender.[175]

---

[169] William H. Baker, Drye *and* Craft — *How Two Wrongs Can Make a Property Right*, 64 U. Pitt. L. Rev. 745 (2003); Peter F. Coogan, *The Effect of the Federal Tax Lien Act of 1966 Upon Security Interests Created Under the Uniform Commercial Code*, 81 Harv. L. Rev. 1369 (1968); Lance Staricha, *Giving and Taking Notice: The Relative Priority and Enforceability of the Federal General Tax Lien Versus the State's Specific Real Property Tax Lien*, 21 Hamline L. Rev. 469 (1998); Timothy R. Zinnecker, *Resolving Priority Disputes Between the IRS and the Secured Creditor under Revised U.C.C. Article 9: and the Winner Is . . . ?*, 34 Ariz. St. L.J. 921 (2002); Timothy R. Zinnecker, *When Worlds Collide: Resolving Priority Disputes Between the IRS and the Article Nine Secured Creditor*, 63 Tenn. L. Rev. 585 (1996).

[170] I.R.C. §§ 6321-6323 (2006).

[171] I.R.C. § 6321 (2006).

[172] I.R.C. § 6323(f) (2006).

[173] U.C.C. § 9-204 (2010).

[174] I.R.C. § 6323(c)-(d) (2006).

[175] I.R.C. § 6323(c)-(d) (2006).

For example, suppose that as of June 1, Shady Dealings, Inc. owed River Bank $100,000 for a loan it made a year earlier, and that River Bank has an Article 9 security interest in all of Shady Dealing's existing and after-acquired equipment as collateral for the debt. On July 10, of the same year, the IRS filed notice of its federal tax lien against Shady Dealing's property. A few days later, on July 15, Shady paid cash for and acquired a new machine to use in its factory. Afterwards, on July 20, River Bank loaned Shady an additional $30,000 for working capital. This advance was secured under an optional future advance clause in the parties' original security agreement.

River Bank has priority for the entire $130,000, but only in the equipment that Shady owned before the IRS filed notice of its lien. If that equipment is only worth $90,000, River Bank will not be able to use the value of the new machine acquired by Shady on July 15 to satisfy the unpaid balance. Instead, the IRS will have priority over the new machine because it was acquired after the IRS filed its notice.[176]

There are some additional variations to how these rules operate, depending on the nature of the collateral. These complex provisions give significant protection to creditors like River Bank who have security interests in after-acquired inventory and receivables. However, even those rules give priority to the IRS over collateral acquired by the taxpayer more than forty-five days after notice of the tax lien was filed and with respect to advances made by the lender after that period. A detailed examination of their provisions is beyond the scope of this book.[177]

In a bankruptcy case, a federal tax lien's priority depends first on whether the IRS has filed notice of its lien. Filing establishes the IRS's rights against third parties and thus indirectly against the bankruptcy trustee. If notice of the tax lien was not filed before bankruptcy, the IRS is left with an unsecured claim. Its unsecured claim may be entitled to priority[178] and may be non-dischargeable, but it will not be secured.

[2] State and Local Tax Liens

State and local tax laws also provide for the imposition of liens on a taxpayer's property for overdue taxes. All states have the authority to impose a tax lien on a taxpayer's land for unpaid state real estate taxes.[179] States also impose tax liens for unpaid income, franchise, withholding, sales and use taxes. Most of these laws are less sweeping than an IRS tax lien. In many states, for example, only real property is subject to the lien. As with state construction and repair liens, many variations exist from state to state regarding the scope and priority of these liens.

---

[176] Treas. Reg. §§ 301.6321-1 to 301.6323 (2006).

[177] The Treasury Regulations accompanying the Tax Lien Act provide an exhaustive (and exhausting) explanation of the operation of the priority rules in the Act. Treas. Reg. §§ 301.6321-1 to 301.6323 (2006).

[178] *See infra* 10.04[A][8] Tax Claims.

[179] *See* Frank S. Alexander, *Tax Liens, Tax Sales, and Due Process*, 75 Ind. L.J. 747 (2000).

§ 2.06 SETOFF OF MUTUAL DEBTS[180]

[A] Creditors' Right of Setoff

There may be no right of creditors that is more obvious or ancient than the right of setoff. This historic right is rooted in Roman law, where it was based on the obvious notion that if debtors are obligated to one another, each should be permitted to reduce the obligation it owes by the obligation it is owed.[181] For example, if Max owes Roberta $25 and Roberta owes Max $10, the right of setoff permits Max to offset Roberta's $10 debt to him and pay Roberta only the $15 balance.

In a commercial context, the exercise of a creditor's right of setoff can have a dramatic impact on a debtor's business. As a practical matter, it has the same effect as a security interest in the debtor's property. Assume, For example, that Franklin Manufacturing owes $60,000 to Peninsula Bank. At the same time, Franklin has an account at the bank containing a balance of $100,000. The bank's right of setoff effectively makes it a secured creditor, with the funds in the account as the collateral. Peninsula can exercise its right of setoff against the $100,000 in Franklin's account debiting the account in the amount of Peninsula's $60,000 claim. This setoff will eliminate the debt Franklin owes and reduce the size of Franklin's bank account to $40,000. If Franklin needed the $100,000 in its account to meet its payroll, its inability to do so would have a devastating effect on its ability to stay in business.

As the foregoing example illustrates, the right of setoff permits parties who owe money to one another to net out their mutual debts.[182] Setoff is routinely used in a cooperative way between merchants who regularly buy and sell from one another, and between financial institutions that transfer funds to one another on a daily basis. In the context of debt collection, it has its most important application when exercised by a bank against funds held on deposit by one of its loan customers.[183]

---

[180] See Barkley Clark, *Bank Exercise of Setoff: Avoiding the Pitfalls*, 98 Banking L.J. 196 (1981); Randal Lawson Dunn, *Banker's Lien and Equitable Setoff: Constitutional and Policy Considerations for Protecting Bank Customers*, 27 Stan. L. Rev. 1149 (1975); Lawrence Kalevitch, *Setoff and Bankruptcy*, 41 Clev. St. L. Rev. 599 (1993); Alan M. Keeffe, *Setoffs and Security Interests in Deposit Accounts*, 17 Colo. Law. 2107 (1988); William H. Loyd, *The Development of Set-off*, 64 U Pa. L. Rev. 541 (1916); John C. McCoid II, *Setoff: Why Bankruptcy Priority?*, 75 Va. L. Rev. 15 (1989); D.E. Murray, *Banks Versus Creditors of Their Customers: Set-offs Against Customers' Accounts*, 82 Com. L.J. 449, 463 (1977); Stephen L. Sepinuck, *The Problems with Setoff: a Proposed Legislative Solution*, 30 Wm. & Mary L. Rev. 51 (1988); John Teshelle, *Banker's Right of Setoff — Banker Beware*, 34 Okla. L. Rev. 40 (1981).

[181] William H. Loyd, *The Development of Set-Off*, 64 U. Pa. L. Rev. 541, 541 (1916); Michael E. Tigar, Comment, *Automatic Extinction of Cross-Demands: Compensation from Rome to California*, 53 Calif. L. Rev. 224, 229-230 (1965).

[182] *E.g.*, Minnesota Voyageur Houseboats, Inc. v. Las Vegas Marine Supply, Inc., 708 N.W.2d 521 (Minn. 2006). *See generally* 2 Barkley Clark & Barbara Clark, The Law of Bank Deposits, Collections and Credit Cards, ¶ 18.01, at 18-2 (Rev. ed. 2006); Barkley Clark, *Bank Exercise of Setoff: Avoiding the Pitfalls*, 98 Banking L.J. 196 (1981).

[183] Steven Walt, *After Article 9: Security Interests and Bank Setoffs in Consumer Deposit Accounts*, 125 Banking L.J. 224 (2008).

Funds on deposit with a bank represent a debt owed by the bank to its customer.[184] If the customer borrows money from a bank and then defaults, the bank is likely to seek to exercise its right of setoff against funds it holds on deposit for the customer.[185] This right is derived from the contract between the depositor and the bank. Setoff is such a useful right that banks sometimes require borrowers to keep a minimum amount on deposit as a form of additional security.[186]

The most important limitations on the right of setoff are the dual requirements that the debts be both "mutual" and "matured." In addition, setoff may be limited either by statute or based on an express or implied agreement between the parties.

[1]   Setoff Limited to Mutual Debts

Only mutual debts may be offset. For debts to be mutual, they must be owed "in the same right and between the same parties, standing in the same capacity, and [of the] same kind or quality."[187] In the context of setoff by a bank, the debt owed by the bank's customer must be owed in the same capacity in which the customer holds her account with the bank. For example, if Dora Darrow owes $10,000 to Merchant's Bank, arising from Dora's use of her personal credit card, funds Dora holds on deposit with the bank as trustee for her nephew are not owed to Dora in the same capacity as that in which Dora's personal debt to the bank is owed. These are not "mutual" debts, and the bank has no right of setoff against the trust account.[188]

There are other circumstances where the mutuality requirement limits a bank's right to any setoff. It sometimes imposes a barrier to setoff when the debt is owed by one of the bank's customers and the account involved is owned by two customers, jointly.[189] The mutuality requirement also prevents setoff against a deposit that the bank knows is dedicated to some special purpose, such as for paying taxes, meeting payroll, or making payments to an employee's retirement fund.[190] Thus, in the

---

[184] We sometimes discuss money we have deposited in a bank account as if it is still "our money," subject to some sort of bailment with the bank as the bailee — like goods stored at a warehouse. This, of course, is mistaken. Money loaned to a bank as part of a deposit transaction belongs to the bank. The deposit is really a loan to the bank, accompanied by the bank's corresponding obligation to repay the loan. All the depositor owns is a right to have this loan repaid. *E.g.*, Crocker-Citizens Nat'l Bank v. Control Metals Corp., 566 F.2d 631, 637 (9th Cir. 1977).

[185] Lawrence Kalevitch, *Setoff and Bankruptcy*, 41 Clev. St. L. Rev. 599 (1993); Gary D. Spivey, Annotation, *Bank's Right of Setoff, Based on Debt of One Depositor, against Funds in Account Standing in Names of Debtor and Another*, 68 A.L.R.3d 192 (1976).

[186] *E.g.*, First Nat'l City Bank v. Herpel (In re Multiponics, Inc.), 622 F.2d 725 (5th Cir. 1980). Such a requirement also raises the effective rate of interest on the loan, by permitting the bank to earn interest on the amount required to be kept on deposit with the bank.

[187] Boston & Maine Corp. v. Chicago Pac. Corp., 785 F.2d 562, 566 (7th Cir. 1986). *See* In re Hal, Inc., 196 B.R. 159 (B.A.P. 9th Cir. 1996). *See generally* Barkely Clark, *Bank Exercise of Setoff: Avoiding the Pitfalls*, 98 Bank. L.J. 191 (1981); Stephen L. Sepinuck, *The Problems with Setoff: A Proposed Legislative Solution*, 30 Wm. & Mary L. Rev. 51, 71 (1988).

[188] *But see* Pope v. First of Am., 699 N.E.2d 178 (Ill. App. Ct. 1998).

[189] *See* Gary D. Spivey. Annotation, *Bank's Right of Setoff, Based on Debt of One Depositor, Against Funds in Account Standing in Names of Debtor and Another*, 68 A.L.R.3d 192 (1976).

[190] *See, e.g.*, Nationsbank v. Ames Sav. & Loan Ass'n (In re First Am. Mortgage Co., Inc.), 212 B.R. 479 (Bankr. D. Md. 1997).

example used earlier, Peninsula Bank might not be permitted to offset its $60,000 claim against Franklin Manufacturing's $100,000 account at Peninsula, if the bank knew that it was a special account, designated to be used to pay Franklin's employees at the end of the month.[191]

[2] Setoff of Matured Debts

It is also necessary for both debts to be "matured" when they are set off against one another. A debt is matured when it is currently due. Thus, a creditor may not exercise its right of setoff on behalf of a debt that is not yet due from the debtor.[192]

Assume, for example, that Industrial Supply Co. has $120,000 on deposit with Citizen's Bank and owes $80,000 on a promissory note to the bank, which does not become due until March 15, 2020. Citizen's Bank may not set off the promissory note against the account until March 15, 2020 — the date the note matures. If the due date of the note is subject to acceleration and Citizen's Bank properly accelerates the note, making it due immediately,[193] the obligation represented by the note will have matured and it may be set off against Industrial Supply's deposit.[194] On the other hand, if the note had been payable on demand instead of at a definite time, the bank could exercise its right of setoff at anytime, because a demand note matures anytime after it has been issued, upon the creditor's demand for payment.[195]

[3] Statutory Restrictions on Setoff

Federal and state consumer protection statutes impose limits on a bank's right of setoff. For example, the Federal Fair Credit Billing Act prevents a bank from setting off debts arising from use of a credit card against a consumer's deposit account.[196] Some state statutes restrict setoff against consumer accounts in similar ways.[197]

---

[191] In re Applied Logic Corp., 576 F.2d 952, 958 (2d Cir. 1978).

[192] *See* Wenneker v. Physicians MultiSpeciality Group, Inc., 814 S.W. 294 (Mo. 1991).

[193] Promissory notes and other obligations may be accelerated, if provided for in the parties' agreement, at any time the creditor in good faith deems itself insecure. *See* U.C.C. § 1-309 (2010).

[194] *See* Boyle v. Am. Sec. Bank, 531 A.2d 1258 (D.C. Ct. App. 1987); Minnesota Voyageur Houseboats, Inc. v. Las Vegas Marine Supply, Inc., 708 N.W.2d 521 (Minn. 2006).

[195] Marion Ins. Agency, Inc. v. Fahey Banking Co., 572 N.E.2d 124 (Ohio Ct. App. 1988) (formal demand not required to trigger maturity of a "demand" note prior to exercising setoff); Allied Sheet Metal Fabricators, Inc. v. People's Nat'l Bank, 518 P.2d 734 (Wash. Ct. App. 1974) (right of action against maker of demand note arises immediately upon delivery, and no express demand is required to mature the note).

[196] 15 U.S.C. § 1666h (2006).

[197] *See generally* 2 Barkley Clark & Barbara Clark, The Law of Bank Deposits, Collections and Credit Cards, ¶ 18.02, at 18-3 to 180-5 (Rev. ed. 2006).

[B]   Priority of Right of Setoff[198]

A creditor's right of setoff is nearly always senior to the rights of competing creditors. A bank's right of setoff thus defeats a claim of a the payee of a check drawn on the account that had not been finally paid when the setoff was exercised.[199] Setoff also usually defeats a competing judgment creditor of the customer who serves a writ of garnishment on the bank in an attempt to obtain the funds in the customer's account.[200] Likewise, the bank's right of setoff is usually senior to a creditor with a competing security interest in the account.[201] The principal exception to this priority involves competing claims of the IRS and other tax authorities, which are usually governed by express statutory authority that gives priority to the government.[202]

Setoff rights are largely preserved under the Bankruptcy Code, although the exercise of those rights may be postponed by the automatic stay.[203] The Bankruptcy Code treats setoff rights as if they were secured claims.

In addition, setoff that permits the offsetting creditor to improve in its secured position during the last ninety days before the debtor's bankruptcy petition was filed is avoidable under Bankruptcy Code § 553 to the extent of the improvement in position.[204]

§ 2.07   FORECLOSURE PROCEEDINGS[205]

Foreclosure is the primary method used by various types of secured creditors to enforce their rights against the debtor's collateral. Methods of foreclosure vary depending on the type of collateral and the jurisdiction. However, at its most basic level, the pattern of lien foreclosure is the same in one key respect: the collateral is sold and the proceeds are used to pay the secured debt.

A wide variety of mechanisms are used to ensure that the sale pays as much of the debt as possible. The debtor and others with an interest in the collateral, such as junior lien holders, are entitled to notice of the sale. The sale must usually be advertised and the method of sale is usually regulated.

---

[198] Stuart D. Albea, Commentary, *Security Interests in Deposit Accounts and the Banking Industry's Use of Setoff*, 54 Ala. L. Rev. 147 (2002); John C. McCoid II, *Setoff: Why Bankruptcy Priority?*, 75 Va. L. Rev. 15 (1989).

[199] U.C.C. § 4-303 (2010) (setoff priority vis-a-vis checks presented against account).

[200] *E.g.*, Wenneker v. Physicians MultiSpeciality Group, Inc., 814 S.W. 2d 294 (Mo. 1991).

[201] U.C.C. § 9-340 (2010). However, the bank's right of setoff is subordinate to the competing secured creditor's interest, if the secured creditor has obtained "control" of the deposit account by becoming the "customer" on the account. U.C.C. § 9-340(c) & cmt. 2 (2010).

[202] United States v. Cache Valley Bank, 866 F.2d 1242 (10th Cir. 1989); Peoples Nat'l Bank v. United States, 777 F.2d 459 (9th Cir. 1985) (unexecuted right of setoff does not defeat tax lien).

[203] Bankruptcy Code § 553. *See infra* § 8.02[F] Setoff.

[204] Bankruptcy Code § 553. *See infra* § 15.06 Setoff Preferences.

[205] Debra Pogrund Stark, *Facing the Facts: An Empirical Study of the Fairness and Efficiency of Foreclosures and a Proposal for Reform*, 30 U. Mich. J.L. Ref. 639 (1997).

Any surplus resulting from the sale is paid to any junior lien-holders and, if any funds remain, to the debtor. If the sale of the collateral does not produce enough money to pay the secured lender in full, the debtor is usually liable for this "deficiency."

[A] Real Estate Foreclosure[206]

There are three primary methods of foreclosure on real estate: judicial foreclosure, private foreclosure under a power of sale, and strict foreclosure. As the name suggests, judicial foreclosure is initiated by filing a complaint, proceeding to judgment, and obtaining a court order for the sale of the land. Private foreclosure is accomplished without judicial action, under a power of sale, or under the terms of a deed of trust which permit the trustee to sell the property for the benefit of the creditor. Strict foreclosure, which is rarely permitted, allows the creditor to simply keep the property in satisfaction of the debt, without holding a sale.

[1] Judicial Foreclosure[207]

Judicial foreclosure is the most common of these three methods.[208] Foreclosure, especially home foreclosure, is nearly always a disaster for everyone involved.[209] Families are displaced from their homes, neighborhoods are broken up,[210] and both borrowers and lenders lose capital.[211] Nevertheless, when financial difficulties push families and businesses to the breaking point, foreclosure is nearly inevitable.

As with many creditors' remedies, the details of real estate foreclosure procedures vary considerably from state to state. Despite differences in the details, foreclosure procedures adhere to a common pattern.[212] The process involves judicial action culminating in an auction sale of the encumbered property and distribution of the proceeds from the sale to the foreclosing creditor in an amount sufficient to satisfy the secured debt.

---

[206] Steven Wechsler, *Through the Looking Glass: Foreclosure by Sale as De Facto Strict Foreclosure — An Empirical Study of Mortgage Foreclosure and Subsequent Resale*, 70 Cornell L. Rev. 850 (1985).

[207] Debra Pogrund Stark, *Facing the Facts: An Empirical Study of the Fairness and Efficiency of Foreclosures and a Proposal for Reform*, 30 U. Mich. J.L. Ref. 639 (1997).

[208] Harold L. Levine, *A Day in the Life of a Residential Mortgage Defendant*, 36 J. Marshall L. Rev. 687 (2003).

[209] Lorna Fox, *Re-Possessing Home: A Re-Analysis of Gender, Homeownership and Debtor Default for Feminist Legal Theory*, 14 Wm. & Mary J. Women & L. 423 (2008).

[210] A house next door to one of your author's homes is currently in foreclosure. It seems like the house will be vacant for months, and perhaps years.

[211] Adam J. Levitin, *Resolving the Foreclosure Crisis: Modification of Mortgages in Bankruptcy*, 2009 Wis. L. Rev. 565, 565-571 (2009).

[212] *See generally* Debra Pogrund Stark, *Facing the Facts: An Empirical Study of the Fairness and Efficiency of Foreclosures and a Proposal for Reform*, 30 U. Mich. J.L. Reform 639, 644 (1997); Grant S. Nelson & Dale A. Whitman, *Reforming Foreclosure: The Uniform Nonjudicial Foreclosure Act*, 53 Duke L.J. 1399, 1403 (2004); Section of Real Property, Probate and Trust Law, American Bar Association, Foreclosure Law & Related Remedies: A State-By-State Digest (Sidney A. Keyles ed., 1995) (summarizing the foreclosure laws and processes in every state).

Foreclosure is initiated in the same way as any other lawsuit: by filing a complaint and serving process on anyone with an interest in the land who will be affected by the foreclosure. The debtor, any co-owner of the property, and anyone with a junior lien on the property must usually be joined. Junior lien holders might be creditors with second mortgages, judicial lien holders, or creditors with statutory or common law liens against the property. These parties have the opportunity to raise defenses, but it is rare for them to have one. Judgment is frequently entered by default, or, if an answer is filed, in response to the creditor's motion for summary judgment.[213]

Once a foreclosure judgment has been entered, a time and place for a sale of the encumbered property is scheduled. The procedures that govern the time, place, and manner of the sale are statutory; they usually require the property to be sold via public auction conducted by the county sheriff's department. The sale is usually required to be held at a public place, sometimes on the courthouse steps.[214] Notice of the time and place of the sale must be given to the debtor and to anyone else with an interest of record in the real estate that will be affected by the sale. Typically, the time and place of the sale must be advertised.[215]

Between the time of the foreclosure judgment and the time of the sale, and in many jurisdictions for some period afterward, the debtor has a right to redeem the property by paying the entire obligation owed to the foreclosing creditor, in a lump sum. This right to redeem the property from the mortgage is what is actually being "foreclosed" in what is habitually (and imprecisely) described as a "mortgage foreclosure" action.[216] The right to pay the mortgage after default — the debtor's "equity of redemption" — was routinely recognized by early English chancery courts to avoid the risk that the debtor would forfeit the value of the property above the amount of the debt.[217]

Sale of mortgaged property vests the buyer with whatever title the debtor had the power to convey. The buyer usually receives a "sheriff's deed" that reflects the purchase. The foreclosure judgment and sale cuts off the rights of the debtor, as

---

[213] Adam J. Levitin & Tara Twomey, *Mortgage Servicing*, 28 Yale J. on Reg. 1, 31 (2011); Andrea Kupfer Schneider & Natalie C. Fleury, *There's No Place like Home: Applying Dispute Systems Design Theory to Create a Foreclosure Mediation System*, 11 Nev. L.J. 368, 385-86 (2011); Andrew J. Kazakes, Comment, *Protecting Absent Stakeholders in Foreclosure Litigation: The Foreclosure Crisis, Mortgage Modification, and State Court Responses*, 43 Loy. L.A. L. Rev. 1383, 1341 (2010).

[214] *E.g.*, Tex. Prop. Code Ann. § 51.002(a) (Vernon 2000). *See* Alex M. Johnson, Jr., *Critiquing the Foreclosure Process: An Economic Approach Based on the Paradigmatic Norms of Bankruptcy*, 79 Va. L. Rev. 959, 973 n. 46 (1993); Basil H. Mattingly, *The Shift from Power to Process: A Functional Approach to Foreclosure Law*, 80 Marq. L. Rev. 77, 87 (1996).

[215] *E.g.*, Ohio Rev. Code Ann. § 2329.26, 2329.27 (LexisNexis 2006); Tex. Prop. Code Ann, § 51.002(b) (Vernon 2000).

[216] Marshall E. Tracht, *Renegotiation and Secured Credit: Explaining the Equity of Redemption*, 52 Vand. L. Rev. 599, 607 n.22 (1999). *See* Black's Law Dictionary 646 (6th ed. 1990).

[217] Grant S. Nelson & Dale A. Whitman, Real Estate Finance Law § 1.4 at 8-10 (4th ed. 2001); *e.g.*, Perry v. Miller, 112 N.E.2d 805 (1953). *See generally* Abraham Bell & Gideon Parchomovsky, *A Theory of Property*, 90 Cornell L. Rev. 531, 609-611 (2005); Trauner v. Lowrey, 369 So. 2d 531, 534 (Ala. 1979) ("Execution of a mortgage passes legal title to the mortgagee. . . . The mortgagor is left with an equity of redemption, but upon payment of the debt, legal title revests in the mortgagor.").

well as the rights of any creditor whose interest is junior to that of the foreclosing creditor (provided, of course, that they were notified of the foreclosure action in the first place).

Assume, for example, that Citizen's Bank holds a senior mortgage on land owned by Franklin Manufacturing, Inc. and that the land is also subject to a junior mortgage in favor of Merchant's Finance Co. If Citizen's Bank brings a foreclosure action to enforce its senior mortgage, and the property is sold to Global Industries, Inc., the sale cuts off both Franklin's title to the land and Merchant's junior lien. Global Industries acquires clear title.

Foreclosure sales by junior lenders are rare, but in the unusual instance of foreclosure by a junior mortgagee, senior liens on the property remain, and the buyer takes subject to the senior lien. Thus, if Merchant's Finance Co. conducted a foreclosure sale to enforce its junior mortgage on Franklin Manufacturing's land, a sale of the land to Global Industries would not foreclose Citizen Bank's senior mortgage. Of course the existence of the senior mortgage would reduce the price Global would likely be willing to pay for the land. Thus, if the land were worth $350,000 and Citizen Bank's senior mortgage secured a $200,000 debt, no sensible person with knowledge of Citizen Bank's lien would pay more than $150,000 for the land at a foreclosure sale conducted by a junior mortgagee like Merchant's Finance Co.[218] This is because, to take clear title to the land, it will be necessary to satisfy Citizen Bank's lien.

In most instances, the foreclosing creditor will purchase the property at its own foreclosure sale. The foreclosing creditor has several distinct advantages over other prospective buyers. First, it is likely to be more familiar with the property than other bidders. Second, and more importantly, the foreclosing creditor can pay for the property by making a "credit bid" — bidding the amount of the mortgage debt owed to the creditor, without having to pay cash.[219] Other bidders must have ready cash.

Foreclosure sale procedures are time consuming and expensive.[220] Moreover, they rarely yield the price that could be expected to be obtained from a conventional sale of the property on the broader real estate market, facilitated by a real estate broker.[221] This is not surprising. Most buyers of residential real estate do not look for a new home by combing the newspaper for property scheduled to be sold at upcoming foreclosure sales. The market of prospective buyers of property in

---

[218] Further, because of the risk that the senior mortgage debt would increase, due to accumulating interest, collection costs, late fees, and other charges, the amount someone would be willing to pay would likely be even less.

[219] *See* Grant S. Nelson & Dale A. Whitman, *Reforming Foreclosure: The Uniform Nonjudicial Foreclosure Act*, 53 Duke L.J. 1399, 1423 (2004).

[220] *See generally* Grant S. Nelson & Dale A. Whitman, Real Estate Finance Law § 7.11 (4th ed. 2001); Comment, *Cost and Time Factors in Foreclosure of Mortgages*, 3 Real Prop. Prob. & Tr. J. 413 (1968).

[221] *See* Grant S. Nelson & Dale A. Whitman, *Reforming Foreclosure: The Uniform Nonjudicial Foreclosure Act*, 53 Duke L.J. 1399, 1419-22 (2004); Marshall E. Tracht, *Renegotiation and Secured Credit: Explaining the Equity of Redemption*, 52 Vand. L. Rev. 599, 607 (1999); Steven Wechsler, *Through the Looking Glass: Foreclosure by Sale as De Facto Strict Foreclosure — An Empirical Study of Mortgage Foreclosure and Subsequent Resale*, 70 Cornell L. Rev. 850, 853 (1985).

foreclosure is smaller than the market of interested real estate buyers in general. Moreover, buyers who are willing to consider buying property at a foreclosure sale may have difficulty making arrangements to view the house, which is usually still occupied by the debtor. A professional inspection of the premises is nearly always out of the question. Further, debtors who are unable to make their regular monthly mortgage payments may not have kept the property in good repair, making the transaction even more risky for prospective buyers, who face the very real possibility that the structure is laden with hidden defects. Moreover, the terms of the sale are frequently "as is," with no warranties of title and no recourse for the buyer when these problems are eventually discovered. These factors make buying property at foreclosure too risky for most prospective homeowners to tolerate.[222]

Various mechanisms are imposed by state statutes in an effort to ensure that foreclosure does not deprive residential owners of any financial equity in their homes.[223] These include prescribed methods of advertising the sale to the public;[224] giving the debtor a temporary right to "cure" its default, de-accelerate the obligation, and reinstate the mortgage debt according to its original terms;[225] extending delays between the time of a foreclosure judgment and the time of a sale; and requiring the sale to be "confirmed" by the court.[226] Some states require a court to establish a minimum or "upset price" based on an appraisal of the property, imposing a floor below which the property may not be sold.[227]

In some states, the debtor and junior lien holders have an additional statutory period of redemption, during which they may purchase the property from the person who bought it at the foreclosure sale by paying the purchaser the amount it paid at the sale.[228] Although this right was designed to protect homeowners from buyers who might pay too little for the property, it can easily drive down foreclosure sale prices by subjecting buyers to the risk that they will lose the property.[229]

---

[222] Grant S. Nelson & Dale A. Whitman, *Reforming Foreclosure: The Uniform Nonjudicial Foreclosure Act*, 53 Duke L.J. 1399, 1421-22 (2004). *See* Carteret Sav. & Loan Ass'n v. Davis, 521 A.2d 831, 835 (N.J. 1987).

[223] Patrick B. Bauer, *Judicial Foreclosure and Statutory Redemption: The Soundness of Iowa's Traditional Preference for Protection over Credit*, 71 Iowa L. Rev. 1 (1985); J. Douglass Poteat, *State Legislative Relief for the Mortgage Debtor During the Depression*, 5 Law & Contemp. Probs. 517 (1938); Michael H. Schill, *An Economic Analysis of Mortgagor Protection Laws*, 77 Va. L. Rev. 489 (1991); James B. Hughes, Jr., *Taking Personal Responsibility: A Different View of Mortgage Antideficiency and Redemption Statutes*, 39 Ariz. L. Rev. 117 (1997).

[224] *E.g.*, N.Y. Real Propr. Acts. § 231(2) (McKinney Supp. 2006).

[225] *E.g.*, Or. Rev. Stat. § 86.753 (2006) (debtor may cure up to 5 days before the sale); 41 Pa. Cons. Stat. Ann. § 404 (West 1999) (debtor may cure until one hour before sale of residential property). *See* Unif. Nonjudicial Foreclosure Act § 202(c) (2002), *available at* http://www.law.upenn.edu/bll/ulc/uFBPOSA/2002final.pdf (last visited July 18, 2012).

[226] *E.g.*, Hazel v. Van Beek, 954 P.2d 1301, 1307 (Wash. 1998).

[227] *E.g.*, Wash. Rev. Code Ann. § 61.12.060 (West 2004).

[228] *E.,g.*, Cal. Civ. Proc. Code §§ 729.010-090, 726(e) (West Supp. 2006). *See generally* 4 Richard R. Powell & Michael Allan Wolf, Powell on Real Property § 37.46 (2006); Patrick B. Bauer, *Judicial Foreclosure and Statutory Redemption: The Soundness of Iowa's Traditional Preference for Protection over Credit*, 71 Iowa L. Rev. 1 (1985).

[229] Edgar Noble Durfee & Delmar W. Doddridge, *Redemption From Foreclosure Sale — The Uniform Mortgage Act*, 23 Mich. L. Rev. 825, 841 n.51 (1925); Grant S. Nelson & Dale A. Whitman,

If the amount received from the foreclosure sale is insufficient to fully satisfy the debt, the mortgagee usually has the right to recover the unpaid balance as a "deficiency." Some states, in an effort to protect mortgagors from low foreclosure sale prices, have enacted anti-deficiency legislation, which prohibits mortgagees from recovering deficiencies in certain types of transactions, particularly residential mortgages.[230]

[2]   Private Foreclosure Under a Power of Sale[231]

In roughly half of the states, where deeds of trust are customarily used instead of traditional mortgages, foreclosure is accomplished without going to court.[232] In these transactions, a deed of trust or mortgage agreement grants the creditor a "power of sale," permitting a third person, acting as a trustee, to sell the property and pay the proceeds from the sale to the creditor in satisfaction of the debt. Just as in a traditional judicial foreclosure proceeding, any surplus from the sale is paid to the debtor. Likewise, the debtor usually remains liable for any deficiency, although she may be protected from this by an anti-deficiency rule.

Though it does not require judicial action, a power of sale foreclosure is subject to the possibility of judicial review. A debtor who believes that she has a legal defense, justifying her default, can either seek to enjoin the sale or wait until after the sale and use her defense to resist being ejected from possession of the property.[233]

Power of sale foreclosure laws require notice to the mortgagor of its default,[234] and they frequently provide the debtor with an opportunity to cure its default and reinstate the debt according to its original terms. The trustee usually conducts an auction sale of the property, and provides the buyer with a trustee's deed. This deed is similar to the sheriff's deed that the buyer would obtain following a traditional judicial foreclosure sale. Although the sale does not have to be confirmed by a court, there is usually a short period for the debtor to object to the sale. Thus, private foreclosure pursuant to a power of sale bears a close resemblance to judicial foreclosure, but it does not require the initiation of a court proceeding, and often proceeds much more quickly.

Reforming Foreclosure: The Uniform Nonjudicial Foreclosure Act, 53 Duke L.J. 1399, 1439 (2004); Robert M. Washburn, *The Judicial and Legislative Response to Price Inadequacy in Mortgage Foreclosure Sales*, 53 S. Cal. L. Rev. 843, 931 (1980).

[230] J. Douglass Poteat, *State Legislative Relief for the Mortgage Debtor During the Depression*, 5 Law & Contemp. Probs. 517 (1938); Marshall E. Tracht, *Renegotiation and Secured Credit: Explaining the Equity of Redemption*, 52 Vand. L. Rev. 599, 609 (1999); Robert M. Washburn, *The Judicial and Legislative Response to Price Inadequacy in Mortgage Foreclosure Sales*, 53 S. Cal. L. Rev. 843 (1980); *e.g.*, Cal. Civ. Proc. Code § 580b (West Supp. 2006) (dwelling of up to four families occupied by purchaser); Fla. Stat. Ann. § 702.06 (West 1994) (purchase money mortgage).

[231] Grant S. Nelson & Dale A. Whitman, *Reforming Foreclosure: The Uniform Nonjudicial Foreclosure Act*, 53 Duke L.J. 1399 (2004).

[232] Grant S. Nelson & Dale A. Whitman, Real Estate Finance Law 581-82 (4th ed. 2001).

[233] Grant S. Nelson & Dale A. Whitman, Real Estate Finance Law 605-608 (4th ed. 2001).

[234] *See generally* Grant S. Nelson & Dale A. Whitman, Real Estate Finance Law 581-585, 615-620 (4th ed. 2001).

[3] Strict Foreclosure[235]

At one time, the debtor's right to redeem the property from a mortgage was terminated simply by the establishment of a deadline after which the debtor's equity of redemption was "foreclosed." This vested indefeasible title in the mortgagee.[236] This became known as "strict foreclosure" and was distinguishable from conventional foreclosure because the creditor is not required to conduct a sale of the mortgaged property.

Strict foreclosure persists in a few states,[237] but it is both highly regulated and strictly limited, particularly with respect to debtors' homes.[238] It is also preserved in Article 9 of the U.C.C., with respect to personal property. Under Article 9, the debtor must be given notice of the secured party's proposal to retain the collateral in satisfaction of the debt, and has the right to compel the secured party to conduct a sale.[239]

[B] Self-Help Repossession of Goods[240]

Both Article 2A and Article 9 of the U.C.C. permit self-help repossession of goods, without court action. Article 2A gives a lessor the right to seize leased goods upon the lessee's default.[241] Likewise, Article 9 permits a secured party to take possession of the collateral anytime after a debtor's default,[242] though a few states have limited or eliminated this right with respect to many consumer goods, other than motor vehicles.[243]

"Self-help" means that repossession may be accomplished without notice, a hearing, a court order, a bond, the sheriff, or any immediate post-seizure judicial review. Because no state action is involved in self-help, it does not run afoul of the Fourteenth Amendment's Due Process Clause.[244]

---

[235] James Geoffery Durham, *In Defense of Strict Foreclosure: A Legal and Economic Analysis of Mortgage Foreclosure*, 36 S.C. L. Rev. 461 (1985); Sheldon Tefft, *The Myth of Strict Foreclosure*, 4 U. Chi. L. Rev. 575 (1937).

[236] *See generally* Grant S. Nelson & Dale A. Whitman, Real Estate Finance Law 581-585, 554-558 (4th ed. 2001); 4 Richard R. Powell & Michael Allan Wolf, Powell on Real Property § 37.46 (2006).

[237] *See* Abacus Mortgage Ins. Co. v. Whitewood Hills Dev. Corp., 479 A.2d 1231 (Conn. Ct. App. 1984); Great Lakes Mortgage. Corp. v. Collymore, 302 N.E.2d 248 (Ill. App. Ct. 1973); Stowe Ctr., Inc. v. Burlington Sav. Bank, 451 A.2d 114 (Vt. 1982).

[238] *See* Grant S. Nelson & Dale A. Whitman, Real Estate Finance Law 555-558 (4th ed. 2001).

[239] U.C.C. § 9-620 (2010).

[240] Jean Braucher, *The Repo Code: A Study of Adjustment to Uncertainty in Commercial Law*, 74 Wash. U.L.Q. 549 (1997); William C. Whitford & Harold Laufer, *The Impact of Denying Self-Help Repossession of Automobiles: A Case Study of the Wisconsin Consumer Act*, 1975 Wis. L. Rev. 607.

[241] U.C.C. § 2A-525(2), (3) (2010).

[242] U.C.C. § 9-609 (2010).

[243] *See, e.g.*, Ohio Rev. Code Ann. § 1317.13 (LexisNexis 2002) (prohibiting repossession of consumer goods, other than motor vehicles and mobile homes, if the debtor has paid 75% of the cash price of the goods).

[244] *See, e.g.*, Adams v. So. Cal. First Nat'l Bank, 492 F.2d 324 (9th Cir. 1973); Alan R. Madry, *State Action and the Due Process of Self-help; Flagg Bros. Redux*, 62 U. Pitt. L. Rev. 1 (2000); *Cf.* Flagg Bros.,

There is one key statutory limitation on self-help: the creditor must not commit a breach of the peace.[245] This restriction has engendered volumes of decisions dealing with the parameters of the conduct in which a repossessing party may engage without breaching the peace. Broadly speaking, a secured party may neither engage in nor threaten any type of violence.[246] It may not enter the debtor's house or closed garage without permission, and it must discontinue its efforts to repossess if the debtor resists or verbally objects.[247] The secured party must not take any illegal action,[248] break into a locked area,[249] or continue an immediate attempt to repossess after someone resists.

In general, the debtor can prevent a self-help repossession simply by telling the creditor attempting to repossess (the "repo man") to "go away." However, if there is no verbal resistance, the repossession may go forward, even if the debtor successfully blocked the creditor's earlier attempt to take the collateral.[250]

If self-help repossession cannot be accomplished without a breach of the peace, then the secured party or lessor must use judicial means to obtain possession — usually replevin.[251] Failure to cease and desist, when a breach of the peace is on the verge of occurring, exposes the repossessing creditor to liability to the debtor.[252] It may also prevent the creditor from obtaining a judgment for any deficiency.[253] In extreme cases, punitive damages may be awarded for an improper self-help repossession.[254]

Inc. v. Brooks, 436 U.S. 149 (1978) (imposition of statutory warehouseman's lien not state action). *See also* Shia Mentschikoff, *Peaceful Repossession Under the Uniform Commercial Code: A Constitutional and Economic Analysis*, 14 Wm. & Mary L. Rev. 767 (1973); Robert E. Scott, *Constitutional Regulation of Provisional Creditor Remedies: The Cost of Procedural Due Process*, 61 Va. L. Rev. 807 (1975); James J. White, *The Abolition of Self-Help Repossession: The Poor Pay Even More*, 1973 Wis. L. Rev. 503 (1973). *See generally* Gary D. Spivey, Annotation, *Validity, Under Federal Constitution and Laws, of Self-Help Repossession Provision of Sec. 9-503 of Uniform Commercial Code*, 29 A.L.R. Fed. 418 (1976).

[245] U.C.C. §§ 2A-525(3), 9-609 (2010).

[246] Morris v. First Nat'l Bank & Trust Co., 254 N.E.2d 683 (Ohio 1970) (creditor's representatives surrounded the debtor's son, making him fearful of being beaten).

[247] Over a period of years, Prof. Ferriell's father made himself quite popular with hourly employees at the factory where he worked, by walking out to the parking lot under his office window to express his objection to any attempted repossession of any of the other employee's vehicles parked in the company lot.

[248] *See* Morris v First Nat'l Bank & Trust Co., 254 N.E.2d 683 (Ohio 1970).

[249] *E.g.*, Laurel Coal Co. v. Walter E. Heller & Co., 539 F. Supp. 1006 (W.D. Pa. 1982).

[250] *See, e.g.*, Wade v. Ford Motor Credit Co., 668 P.2d 183 (Kan. Ct. App. 1983) (debtor, who was armed at the time, told repo man that if she saw him near her car again she would "leave him laying right where she saw him." The car was later repossessed without incident during the middle of the night, and the court found that there was no breach of the peace).

[251] *See infra* § 2.07[C] Replevin.

[252] U.C.C. § 9-625 (2010).

[253] U.C.C. § 9-626 (2010).

[254] *See* Big Three Motors, Inc. v. Rutherford, 432 So. 2d 483 (Ala. 1983).

[C]   Replevin

The common law writ of replevin (and, in a few states, detinue, sequestration, or "claim and delivery") is a long-established method to obtain possession of property that is wrongfully detained by the defendant. In the context of state creditors' rights, its primary significance is as a judicial alternative to self-help repossession of goods that are subject to a security interest. Historically, replevin was an action to recover possession of the goods themselves; the related writ of detinue was an action to recover either the goods or their value.[255] Because of the expense involved in a replevin action and the risk of mistakes in following the statutory procedures, creditors with security interests usually prefer to repossess goods through self-help. They resort to replevin only when self-help is either impossible without a breach of the peace or statutorily prohibited.

Once a creditor obtains possession through a judgment of replevin or one of its common law or statutory cousins, the creditor is usually required to sell the property in accordance with the procedures detailed in Article 9.

[D]   Sales of Collateral under U.C.C. Article 9

Under Article 9, collateral is ordinarily sold by the secured party rather than by the sheriff. Article 9 specifies: "After default, a secured party may sell, lease, license, or otherwise dispose of any or all of the collateral"[256] The sale may be by either "public" auction or a "private" sale.[257] Every aspect of the sale must be accomplished in a commercially reasonable manner.[258] In nearly all cases, the secured party must supply advance notice to the debtor (the owner of the collateral) and to any secondary obligor, and in some cases to competing secured parties whose rights may be affected by the sale.[259]

The proceeds of the sale are distributed first to cover the costs of the repossession and sale, second to satisfy the secured debt, and third to satisfy any junior debts secured by the collateral, in their order of priority.[260] In rare cases where a surplus remains, it must be paid to the debtor.[261] More commonly, the collateral sells for less than the amount of the outstanding debt, leaving the debtor personally liable for a deficiency.[262]

---

[255] Frederic William Maitland, The Forms of Action at Common Law: A Course of Lectures (A.H. Chaytore & W.J. Whitaker eds., 1968). *See* Roy Ryden Anderson, *Of Hidden Agendas, Naked Emperors, and a Few Good Soldiers: The Conference's Breach of Promise . . . Regarding Article 2 Damage Remedies*, 54 SMU L. Rev. 795, 838 (2001); George Lee Flint, Jr. & Marie Juliet Alfaro, *Secured Transactions History: The First Chattel Mortgage Acts in the Anglo-American World*, 30 Wm. Mitchell L. Rev. 1403 (2004).

[256] U.C.C. § 9-610(a) (2010).

[257] U.C.C. § 9-610(b) & cmt. 7 (2010).

[258] U.C.C. § 9-610(b) & cmt. 2 (2010).

[259] U.C.C. § 9-611 (2010).

[260] U.C.C. § 9-615 (2010).

[261] U.C.C. § 9-615 (2010).

[262] U.C.C. § 9-615 (2010).

In rare cases, a secured party may propose to strictly foreclose and keep the property in full satisfaction of the debt, while giving up the right to a deficiency.[263] The debtor always has the right to receive advance notice of the secured party's proposal to strictly foreclose and may require the secured party to sell the collateral.[264]

Debtors have a limited right to redeem the collateral by paying the secured debt anytime before the secured party has either disposed of the collateral, entered into a contract to dispose of the collateral, or discharged the secured debt through strict foreclosure.[265] To redeem, the debtor must tender full payment of the outstanding obligation, together with any accrued interest; all of the reasonable expenses the secured party incurred as a result of the default; and any agreed reasonable attorney's fees and legal expenses.[266] This right to redeem may be waived, but only in a writing executed after the debtor defaulted. Any attempted waiver of redemption rights contained in the original security agreement is unenforceable.[267]

The requirement that the debtor pay the entire debt, plus the creditor's expenses, and in many cases, legal fees in a single lump sum, is almost always an insurmountable barrier. As is true in real estate mortgage foreclosure proceedings, debtors who have access to that much cash rarely default in the first place. Moreover, to redeem, the debtor may have to pay much more than the goods are worth. As will be described elsewhere, the Bankruptcy Code provides a considerably more favorable form of redemption, if the debtor can afford to redeem the property at all.[268]

Creditors who fail to adhere to the foreclosure procedures specified in Article 9 may find themselves precluded from recovering a deficiency judgment from the debtor. Many states have common law or non-uniform statutory rules that prohibit secured creditors who fail to follow the rules from recovering a deficiency.[269] Some states take a more lenient approach to defective foreclosures and permit the debtor to offset against the outstanding balance any additional amount for which the collateral would have sold if the foreclosure had been conducted properly.[270] In other states, and in cases not involving consumer goods, creditors who fail to comply with the foreclosure procedures outlined in Article 9 are denied a deficiency unless they are able to prove that the property would have sold for the same

---

[263] U.C.C. § 9-620 (2010).

[264] U.C.C. § 9-620 (2010).

[265] U.C.C. § 9-623 (2010).

[266] U.C.C. § 9-623 (2010).

[267] U.C.C. § 9-624(c) (2010).

[268] Bankruptcy Code § 722. *See infra* § 12.08[A] Lump Sum Redemption by Debtor.

[269] Herman Ford-Mercury, Inc. v. Betts, 251 N.W.2d 492 (Iowa 1977); Aimonetto v. Keepes, 501 P.2d 1017, 1019 (Wyo. 1972).

[270] *E.g.*, Greene v. Associates (In re Greene), 248 B.R. 583 (Bankr. N.D. Ala. 2000); Chapman v. Field, 105, 602 P.2d 481, 486 (Ariz. 1979). *See generally* Robert M. Lloyd, *The Absolute Bar Rule in U.C.C. Foreclosure Sales: A Prescription for Waste*, 40 UCLA L. Rev. 695, 699 (1993).

amount, even if they had followed the prescribed statutory procedures.[271] This "rebuttable presumption" rule presumes that the property would have sold for an amount sufficient to satisfy the entire debt if the sale had been conducted properly, but it gives the creditor the right to prove otherwise. In many cases, particularly those involving foreclosure sales of motor vehicles, the creditor will find it relatively easy to prove that any technical deficiencies in the foreclosure process had no effect on the price for which the property sold.

Where consumer debtors are involved, Article 9 does not specify a special remedy for an improperly conducted foreclosure sale. The remedy is determined by non-uniform state law. Many jurisdictions use the "rebuttable presumption" rule as a matter of common law, but other jurisdictions use the "irrebuttable presumption" rule that conclusively presumes that the debt would have been paid in full had the foreclosure been conducted properly.

§ 2.08 PRE-JUDGMENT SEIZURE[272]

Unsecured creditors are not usually permitted to seize a debtor's property before obtaining a judgment. However, creditors are sometimes justifiably fearful that a debtor's assets many be squandered, hidden, or transferred to others before a judgment can be obtained. They would like to seize the debtor's assets or at least block the debtor from transferring them, while a lawsuit against the debtor grinds toward the award of a judgment.

In extraordinary circumstances, pre-judgment seizure may be available. Not surprisingly, the Due Process Clause of the Fourteenth Amendment imposes constitutional restrictions on any effort to use the court system to seize a debtor's property prior to judgment. This section reviews the patterns found in modern pre-judgment seizure statutes and explains how the Due Process Clause imposes limits on these procedures and their use.

[A] Pre-Judgment Seizure Procedures

[1] Attachment

Attachment is a pre-judgment remedy that deprives the debtor of possession of its property to preserve it while the creditor's lawsuit is pending. It has also been used to acquire *in rem* or *quasi-in-rem* jurisdiction over non-resident defendants by attaching an object owned by the defendant and located in the forum state by a resident of the forum state.[273]

---

[271] U.C.C. § 9-696 (2010).

[272] *See generally* Steve H. Nickles, *Creditors' Provisional Remedies and Debtors' Due Process Rights: Attachment and Garnishment in Arkansas*, 31 Ark. L. Rev. 607 (1978); Doug Rendleman, *The New Due Process: Rights and Remedies*, 63 Ky. L.J. 531 (1975); Robert E. Scott, *Constitutional Regulation of Provisional Creditor Remedies: The Cost of Procedural Due Process*, 61 Va. L. Rev. 807 (1975).

[273] *See* Pennoyer v. Neff, 95 U.S. 714 (1878); Harris v. Balk, 198 U.S. 215 (1905). The utility of this use of attachment was, of course, seriously limited by the Supreme Court's decision in *Shaffer v. Heitner*, 433

Modern pre-judgment attachment procedures closely resemble post-judgment execution procedures. Like execution procedures, the mechanics of pre-judgment attachment statutes vary considerably from state to state but share many common features. They usually supply a set of statutory grounds to justify the seizure; mandate a court-ordered writ of attachment that directs the sheriff to seize a defendant's property and preserve it pending the outcome of the suit; and specify procedures for the debtor to post a bond to recover possession of the property.

[a]   Grounds for Attachment

The statutory grounds to obtain a writ of attachment vary but are usually targeted at circumstances that create a risk that the debtor's assets might be dissipated while the underlying suit progresses through the courts. Thus, it is common for attachment to be available if the creditor can show that the debtor's departure from the state is imminent, or that she will likely transfer, remove, or conceal her property in an effort to defraud her creditors.

Ohio's statute supplies a good example. It specifies that a plaintiff may obtain a writ of attachment if, among other things:

> [t]he defendant has absconded with the intent to defraud creditors; . . . the defendant has left the county of the defendant's residence to avoid the service of a summons; . . . the defendant is about to remove property, in whole or part, out of the jurisdiction of the court, with the intent to defraud creditors; the defendant is about to convert property, in whole or part, into money, for the purpose of placing it beyond the reach of creditors; the defendant has property or rights in action, which the defendant conceals; the defendant has assigned, removed, disposed of, or is about to dispose of, property, in whole or part, with the intent to defraud creditors; the defendant has fraudulently or criminally contracted the debt, or incurred the obligations for which suit is about to be or has been brought; or . . . [incongruously] that the claim is for work or labor.[274]

Further, to obtain attachment without giving prior notice to the defendant, the plaintiff must demonstrate that the plaintiff will suffer "irreparable injury" if the attachment is delayed until after the defendant has had the opportunity for a hearing. If this showing is made and a writ of attachment is issued, the court must immediately notify the defendant of the issuance of the writ, and, upon request, the court must provide the defendant with the opportunity for a hearing.[275] In addition, like most states, Ohio requires the plaintiff to post a bond to protect the defendant against any loss that may be caused due to wrongful attachment.[276]

U.S. 186 (1977). The discussion here will be limited to the use of attachment to preserve the availability of assets for the creditor to foreclose upon once a judgment is obtained.

[274] Ohio Rev. Code Ann. § 2715.01 (LexisNexis 1999).

[275] Ohio Rev. Code Ann. § 2715.042 (LexisNexis 1999).

[276] Ohio Rev. Code Ann. § 2715.044 (LexisNexis 1999) (twice the amount of the value of the property to be seized); e.g., Fla. Stat. Ann. § 76.12 (LexisNexis 2004).

[b]   Seizure of the Defendant's Property

Following issuance of a writ of attachment, the sheriff levies on the defendant's property, much as it would pursuant to a post-judgment writ of execution. Naturally, the sheriff will want to be sure that she operates within the strict requirements of the state's attachment procedure; she will also want to make sure that she only seizes property that belongs to the defendant. Wrongful seizure of someone else's property exposes the sheriff to liability for wrongful seizure.

Following physical seizure of the property, the sheriff must preserve it pending the outcome of the underlying litigation.[277] The sheriff is also usually required to supply the court with a "return" — a report that contains information regarding the results of the seizure, usually including a descriptive "inventory" of the property that was seized.[278]

[c]   Release of the Property from Attachment

The defendant may recover possession of her property by posting a bond sufficient to cover its value.[279] Alternatively, the debtor might demonstrate that the statutory grounds for attachment were not met.[280] In addition, the defendant is usually permitted to show that the seized assets are exempt and should be released from the attachment.[281]

[d]   Liability for Wrongful Attachment

The plaintiff may find itself liable to the defendant if pre-judgment attachment was wrongful. Liability may accrue due to the plaintiff's failure to subsequently obtain a judgment against the defendant, the inadequacy of the plaintiff's motion or bond, seizure of property that is exempt under the state's exemption statute,[282] seizure of more property than was necessary to satisfy the plaintiff's claim,[283] or any number of common tort claims, including trespass, conversion, abuse of process, or more simply "wrongful attachment."[284]

If attachment is undertaken pursuant to an unconstitutional state attachment statute, the creditor may be liable for violating the defendant's civil rights.[285] Moreover, the Supreme Court has ruled that private parties who invoke a pre-judgment seizure procedure that is subsequently held unconstitutional are not entitled to qualified immunity from liability for offending the defendant's civil

---

[277] *E.g.*, N.Y. C.P.L.R. 6218 (McKinney 1980).

[278] *E.g.*, Ohio Rev. Code Ann. § 2715.18 (LexisNexis 1999); Cal. Civ. Proc. Code § 488.130(b) (West Supp. 2006). *See also* Rodrigue v. Biron, 510 A.2d 1321 (Vt. 1986) (attachment defective due to failure of sheriff to include list of property seized in the return to the court).

[279] Ohio Rev. Code Ann. § 2715.26 (LexisNexis 1999).

[280] *E.g.*, Mitchell v. Lavigne, 770 A.2d 109 (Me. 2001).

[281] *See infra* § 2.11 Property Beyond the Reach of Creditors.

[282] *See infra* § 2.11 Property Beyond the Reach of Creditors.

[283] *E.g.*, White Lighting Co. v. Wolfson, 438 P.2d 345 (Cal. 1968) (abuse of process).

[284] *E.g.*, Neri v. J.I. Case Co., 566 N.E.2d 16 (Ill. App. Ct. 1991).

[285] Guzman v. W. State Bank of Devil's Lake, 540 F.2d 948 (8th Cir. 1976).

rights.[286] Thus, creditors who utilize their state's pre-judgment attachment statute will want to assess the constitutionality of its procedures, to ensure that it meets established requirements. Making creditors liable in this way, should make them strong advocates for legislative enactments that meet constitutional muster.

[2] Lis Pendens

A lis pendens is a recorded document that gives constructive notice about a pending lawsuit that may affect title or the right to possession to real estate. A lis pendens is recorded to place subsequent buyers or lenders on notice that their interest in the property will be subject to the outcome of the pending litigation.[287] Traditionally, the mere filing of a lawsuit affecting real property was sufficient to provide constructive notice to subsequent purchasers regarding land located in the county where the lawsuit was pending. However, most modern lis pendens statutes operate only when formal notice of the litigation is recorded in the real estate records in the county where the land is located.[288]

In this respect, lis pendens is similar to pre-judgment attachment, but it is available only in lawsuits over the right to ownership or possession of real property. As one court explained:

> Lis pendens is a legal doctrine — literally "a pending lawsuit." It means that the filing of a lawsuit concerning specific property gives notice to others of the claim alleged in the lawsuit and that a purchaser of the property may take the property subject to the outcome of the lawsuit.
>
> Lis pendens is not a substantive right. It does not create a lien, but "charges the purchaser with notice of the pending action." . . . If applicable, it does not prevent persons from transacting an interest in the property subject to litigation. Any conveyed interest, however, becomes subject to the outcome of the pending litigation. The purpose of lis pendens is to protect the plaintiff's interest in the subject property. Under the doctrine, "no interest can be acquired by third persons in the subject of the action, as against the plaintiff's title."[289]

Although lis pendens developed as a common law doctrine, today it is largely statutory.[290] It is distinguishable from a writ of attachment in that it provides no mechanism to liquidate the plaintiff's claim; it merely preserves the priority of the plaintiff's interest in the disputed property.

Lis pendens, like attachment, serves three purposes: it protects the plaintiff by protecting its claim to the property against bona fide purchasers; it protects third parties, such as buyers and lenders, by alerting them to the pendency of litigation that might affect any rights they acquire; and, it preserves the court's jurisdiction

---

[286] Lugar v. Edmondson Oil Co., 504 U.S. 158 (1992).

[287] *See, e.g.*, La Paglia v. Super. Ct., 264 Cal. Rptr. 63, 66 (Cal. Ct. App. 1989).

[288] *Id.*

[289] Cincinnati ex rel. Ritter v. Cincinnati Reds, L.L.C., 782 N.E.2d 1225 (Ohio Ct. App. 2002).

[290] *See, e.g.*, Minn. Stat. § 557.02 (West 2000); Ill. Comp. Stat. Ann. 5/2-1901 (U.C.C. § 9-623) (West 2003).

over the affected property. Despite it's obvious potential impact on the value of real estate, state lis pendens statutes have consistently been upheld against constitutional challenges.[291]

[B] Constitutional Limits on Pre-Judgment Seizure

At one time, pre-judgment seizures of a debtor's property were permitted with scant due process protection against unwarranted seizures.[292] In 1969, the Supreme Court's decision in *Sniadach v. Family Finance*[293] led to a series of decisions that imposed considerable limits on the practice of pre-judgment seizure.

Sniadach was a wage garnishment case. The state statute permitted a plaintiff to garnish a defendant's wages before judgment without a hearing or even notice to the defendant about the impending seizure. The debtor could be reimbursed for her garnished wages only after prevailing at trial on the creditor's underlying claim.[294] The Court's decision emphasized the unfairness of this procedure, as well as the devastating impact that wage garnishment would have on a family that was living, as most families are, from paycheck to paycheck.[295] In a famous passage, Justice William O. Douglas, who taught the law of creditor's rights early in his career, indicated that wage garnishments could "drive a wage-earning family to the wall."[296] The Court's emphasis on this aspect of the case raised questions about whether a creditor could ever seize a debtor's wages before judgment. It also raised questions about other pre-judgment seizure, including replevin by a secured creditor.

Three years later, in *Fuentes v. Shevin*, the Court expanded the scope of the protection against pre-judgment seizures in replevin actions.[297] The replevin statutes in *Fuentes* allowed secured creditors to have the sheriff seize their collateral without prior notice to the debtor. Finding this unconstitutional, the Court emphasized that the replevin statutes involved did not provide an opportunity for a meaningful hearing before the debtor's property was seized. The fact that the debtor could retrieve his or her property by posting a bond did not rescue the procedure from this defect.

---

[291] *See, e.g.*, Bartlett v. Williams, 189 Conn. 471, 457 A.2d 290, appeal dismissed for want of a substantial federal question, 464 U.S. 801, 801 (1983); Debral Realty Inc. v. DiChiara, 420 N.E.2d 343, 348 (Mass. 1981). *See* Connecticut v. Doehr, 501 U.S. 1, 28 (Rehnquist, C.J., concurring).

[292] *See, e.g.*, McKay v. McInnes, 279 U.S. 820 (1929).

[293] 395 U.S. 337 (1969).

[294] Former Wis. Stat. § 267.18(2)(a). *See* Sniadach v. Family Fin. Co., 395 U.S. 337, 340 (1969).

[295] *See generally* Elizabeth Warren & Amelia Warren Tyagi, The Two-Income Trap: Why Middle-Class Mothers and Fathers Are Going Broke (2003).

[296] 395 U.S. at 341. Although he is most widely known for his decisions about citizens' civil rights, before he was appointed to the Court, Justice Douglas was the principal author of what we now know as Chapter 11 of the Bankruptcy Code. Before becoming Chairman of the Securities Exchange Commission, he was a professor at Yale Law School where he taught commercial law and bankruptcy. *See* http://lawhighereducation.com/255-william-o-douglas.html (last visited on July 20, 2012).

[297] 407 U.S. 67 (1972).

After *Fuentes*, it seemed that pre-judgment seizure procedures that lacked any notice to or opportunity for the debtor to be heard before the seizure were all constitutional defective.[298] However, this impression was dispelled two years later by the Court's decision in *Mitchell v. W.T. Grant Co.*[299] *Mitchell* involved a Louisiana sequestration procedure that permitted a secured creditor[300] to have its collateral seized by the sheriff without prior notice or a hearing if the creditor posted a bond with the court and supplied a sworn affidavit, specifying the alleged facts that entitled it to possession. The Court ruled that this affidavit, together with the requirement that a judge rather than a court clerk issue the writ, and the fact that the debtor was entitled to both an immediate post-seizure hearing and to damages if the property was improperly seized, provided enough protections to justify the pre-judgment seizure.[301] In reaching its decision, the Court noted that the debtor was not the only one with a property interest at stake, and that the risk of loss of creditor's rights in the collateral needed to be balanced against the property rights of the debtor.[302]

After *Mitchell*, it seemed that a pre-judgment seizure statute for secured creditors would satisfy the requirements of the Fourteenth Amendment if it contained the procedural protections that had saved the Louisiana sequestration statute.[303] First, the statute must require a judge to issue the writ, not a mere clerk. Second, the plaintiff must supply a sworn affidavit, detailing the circumstances that gave it a right to possession of the debtor's property. Third, the creditor must post a bond to ensure payment of any damages caused by an improper seizure. Finally, there must be an opportunity for an immediate post-seizure hearing regarding the propriety of the seizure.

The final decision in the series,[304] *North Georgia Finishing Co. v. Di-Chem*,[305] involved an attempted pre-judgment garnishment of a commercial debtor's bank account. *Di-Chem* ratified the protections that had sustained the pre-judgment

---

[298] *E.g.*, Barkley Clark & Jonathan M. Landers, *Sniadach, Fuentes and Beyond: The Creditor Meets the Constitution*, 59 Va. L. Rev. 335 (1973).

[299] 416 U.S. 600 (1974).

[300] At the time, Louisiana had not yet adopted Article 9 of the U.C.C. The creditor retained a common law "seller's lien" on property it had sold to the debtor on credit.

[301] 416 U.S. 600, 605-06 (1974). A majority of the Court seemed to announce that *Fuentes*, which had been a 4-3 decision by an incomplete Court, was overruled. Justices Rehnquist and Powell had only recently been appointed to the Court at the time of the *Fuentes* decision, and took no part in it. They joined with the three Justices who had dissented in *Fuentes* to form the majority in *Mitchell*. The concurring decision of Justice Powell, 416 U.S. at 623, the dissenting opinion of Justice Stewart, which was joined by Justices Marshall and Douglas, 416 U.S. at 635, and the dissenting opinion of Justice Brennan, 416 U.S. at 636, expressed the notion that *Fuentes* stood overruled. (Stewart, J., dissenting). Thus, a full majority of the Court indicated that *Fuentes* had been overruled.

[302] 416 U.S. at 604.

[303] Steinheimer, *Summary Prejudgment Creditors' Remedies and Due Process of Law; Continuing Uncertainty After* Mitchell v. W.T. Grant Co., 32 Wash & Lee L. Rev. 79 (1975); *The Supreme Court, 1973 Term*, 88 Harv. L. Rev. 41 (1974).

[304] These four cases used to be a staple of law school courses in debtor-creditor law. Because they were also sometimes assigned in courses on civil procedure and constitutional law, they were, for a time, some of the most widely studied cases in the law school curriculum.

[305] 419 U.S. 601 (1975).

seizure in *Mitchell*. The Court distinguished the Georgia garnishment statute before it from the Louisiana procedure in *Mitchell*, explaining:

> The writ of garnishment is issuable on the affidavit of the creditor or his attorney, and the latter need not have personal knowledge of the facts . . . . The affidavit, like the one filed in this case, need contain only conclusory allegations. The writ is issuable, as this one was, by the court clerk, without participation by a judge. Upon service of the writ, the debtor is deprived of the use of the property in the hands of the garnishee. Here, a sizable bank account was frozen, and the only method discernible on the face of the statute to dissolve the garnishment was to file a bond to protect the plaintiff creditor. There is no provision for an early hearing at which the creditor would be required to demonstrate at least probable cause for the garnishment. Indeed, it would appear that without the filing of a bond the defendant debtor's challenge to the garnishment will not be entertained, whatever the grounds may be.[306]

In the wake of *Sniadach, Fuentes, Mitchell, and Di-Chem*, most states amended their pre-judgment seizure statutes to meet these requirements. Many of these statutes now also require the creditor to show that there is some unusual risk that the debtor's property will be lost unless it is seized prior to judgment. Moreover, as a result of legislative responses to the strong language in *Sniadach*, pre-judgment wage garnishment is largely a thing of the past.

These changes to state statutes left the issue dormant for many years. The Court did not revisit the issue directly until its 1991 decision in *Connecticut v. Doehr*.[307] *Doehr* involved facts that were distinguishable from the circumstances in *Fuentes* and *Mitchell*, both of which involved seizure by a creditor with a pre-existing security interest in the property it sought to have seized. In this regard, *Doehr* more closely resembled the pre-judgement garnishment statutes in *Sniadach* and *Di-Chem*. However, it was unlike any of the Court's previously decided cases in that the creditor merely sought to obtain a pre-judgment attachment lien on the debtor's home, without depriving the debtor of either possession or use of the property while the underlying action progressed.

In *Doehr*, the Court applied a balancing test based on its 1976 decision in *Mathews v. Eldridge*,[308] where the Court had permitted the government to terminate state disability benefits without an evidentiary hearing. This balancing test weighed the interest of the creditor in obtaining an immediate provisional remedy against the risk that the defendant would be wrongly deprived of his or her property rights. In particular, the court examined: (1) the private interests of both parties that would be affected by the prejudgment remedy; (2) the risk that the defendant's interests would be erroneously deprived as a result of the procedures involved in the provisional remedy, together with the relative value of additional or alternative safeguards that might be employed; and (3) the ancillary interest the

---

[306] 419 U.S. at 607.

[307] 501 U.S. 1 (1991). *See generally* Linda Beale, Note, Connecticut v. Doehr *and Procedural Due Process Values: The* Sniadach *Tetrad Revisited*, 79 Cornell L. Rev. 1603 (1994).

[308] 424 U.S. 319 (1976).

government may have in making the provisional remedy available and avoiding the added burdens of additional protections for the defendant.[309]

Applying the first factor, the Court explained that the defendant's interests were considerable, even though he was not deprived of possession of his land while the case was pending. It explained, "[a]ttachment ordinarily clouds title; impairs the ability to sell or otherwise alienate the property; taints any credit rating; reduces the chance of obtaining a home equity loan or additional mortgage; and can even place an existing mortgage in technical default where there is an insecurity clause."[310]

With respect to the second factor, the Court emphasized that a trial judge could not meaningfully evaluate the plaintiff's likelihood of success on the underlying merits of his claim, supported merely by the "one-sided, self-serving, and conclusory submissions" on which the plaintiff's request for the provisional remedy was based. Even if pre-judgment attachment required "a detailed affidavit, [this] would give only the plaintiff's version of the [facts on which liability was based]."[311]

Moreover, the statute's procedural safeguards did not adequately guard against the risk of erroneous attachment. The attachment statute in question provided for a prompt post-seizure hearing, an opportunity for an interlocutory appeal of the results of the hearing, and double damages if the underlying suit had been commenced without probable cause; but, it did not require the plaintiff to post a bond to ensure that any damages assessed as a result of an erroneous seizure would be paid. The Court also explained that the pre-judgment sequestration procedure in *Mitchell*, where similar procedures had been found adequate, involved a situation unlike the one in *Doehr*, in which the creditor had a property interest in the sequestered property. In addition, the nature of the underlying tort action in *Doehr* did not lend itself to resolution by the type of documentary evidence that would frequently be dispositive in cases like *Mitchell*, which involved missed installment payments.

Finally, the Court explained that any substantive interests the state has in protecting the plaintiff's rights did not outweigh the defendant's property rights.[312] This conclusion distinguishes the pre-judgment attachment involved in *Doehr* from emergency seizure procedures provided in statutes, like the ones the Court had mentioned favorably in *Fuentes*, that apply in disputes where public health or safety is at stake.[313]

The *Doehr* decision leaves many issues unresolved. Most significantly, it leaves undecided whether additional protections for the defendant, such as requiring the plaintiff to post an indemnity bond or limiting the availability of the seizure to exigent circumstances, would have saved the statute. Justice White's opinion indicated that he would not sustain a pre-judgment seizure hearing unless it

---

[309] *Doehr*, 501 U.S. at 11.

[310] *Doehr*, 501 U.S. at 11.

[311] *Doehr*, 501 U.S. at 12.

[312] *Doehr*, 501 U.S. at 16.

[313] Fuentes v. Shevin, 407 U.S. 67, 90-92 (1971).

required the plaintiff to post a bond, was limited to situations involving exigent circumstances that necessitated an immediate seizure, and provided for an immediate post-seizure hearing.[314] However, only three other Justices joined in this part of the opinion,[315] leaving the issue open for subsequent resolution.

The other major issue left unresolved by *Doehr* is the extent to which pre-judgment attachment is permitted in cases where the defendant's liability might be resolved by documentary evidence that can be examined by the court on an ex parte basis before authorizing the seizure. The *Doehr* Court specified that the difficulty of resolving factual issues on an ex parte basis in an intentional tort claim was one of the factors that contributed to the likelihood of an erroneous seizure. Moreover, the balancing test used in *Doehr* was based on the Court's earlier decision in *Mathews v. Eldridge*, where the Court had permitted a pre-hearing termination of social security disability payments, in part because of the relative ease of using documentary evidence to determine the defendant's right to continue receiving the benefits in question.[316]

Since *Doehr*, lower courts have upheld the constitutionality of lis pendens[317] and construction liens,[318] both of which might be imposed without an advance hearing. However, in *Grupo Mexicano de Desarrollo, S.A. v. Alliance Bond Fund, Inc.*,[319] the Supreme Court struck down a pre-judgment procedure that permitted use of a preliminary injunction to "freeze" a debtor's assets pending trial. However, the Court's reasoning did not turn on the adequacy of the process, but whether a federal court's equity power extended to the procedures at issue.

---

[314] *Doehr*, 501 U.S. at 18-23.

[315] Even though the judgment of the Court was unanimous, only Justices O'Connor, Stevens, and Marhsall joined in Part IV of Justice White's opinion, dealing with the impact of these additional protections. Because most states' pre-judgment seizure statutes require a bond and an immediate post-seizure hearing and are limited to situations involving exigent circumstances, resolution of this issue is not imminent.

[316] Mathews v. Eldridge, 424 U.S. 319, 345 (1976). Termination of the benefits had been based on agency review of documentary information supplied by the patient and his treating physicians.

[317] New Destiny Dev. Corp. v. Piccione, 802 F. Supp. 692 (D. Conn. 1992) (lis pendens); *cf.* Aronson v. City of Akron, 116 F.3d 804, 811 (6th Cir. 1997) (criminal corrupt activity forfeiture proceeding). *See generally* Janice Gregg Levy, *Lis Pendens and Procedural Due Process: A Closer Look After Connecticut v. Doehr*, 51 Md. L. Rev. 1054 (1992).

[318] *E.g.*, Gem Plumbing & Heating Co., Inc. v. Rossi, 867 A.2d 796 (R.I. 2005); Conn. Natural Gas Corp. v. Miller, 684 A.2d 1173 (Conn. 1996); Haimbaugh Landscaping, Inc. v. Jegen, 653 N.E.2d 95 (Ind. Ct. App. 1995). Indeed, the *Doehr* opinion itself indicated that mechanics liens are not unconstitutional. *Doehr*, 501 U.S. at 11-13.

[319] 527 U.S. 308 (1999).

§ 2.09　STATE INSOLVENCY PROCEEDINGS[320]

Although federal bankruptcy cases are the most important proceedings that attempt to resolve the claims of multiple creditors in the same forum, state collective insolvency proceedings are also available.[321] The principal distinguishing feature of federal bankruptcy is the availability of a discharge for the debtor, though other less significant differences abound. The two most important types of state insolvency proceedings are assignments for the benefit of creditors and state court receiverships. In addition, state statutes frequently provide for regulatory receiverships of insurance companies and similar financial institutions that are beyond the scope of the Bankruptcy Code. And, of course, federal laws other than the Bankruptcy Code regulate the rehabilitation of federally insured banks through the Federal Deposit Insurance Corporation (FDIC).

[A]　Assignments for Benefit of Creditors[322]

An assignment for the benefit of creditors (an "ABC") is a debtor's voluntary transfer of all of its nonexempt property in trust to an assignee, who liquidates the debtor's assets and distributes the proceeds to creditors in accordance with their relative priorities.[323] The debtor's property is efficiently liquidated, but the debtor receives no discharge (though if the debtor is a corporation, the discharge may not be necessary).[324] In many states, procedures for ABCs are statutory.[325]

Some states have attempted to use assignments for the benefit of creditors to provide debtors with a fresh start by limiting creditors' right to participate in the distribution of the debtor's assets unless they enter into a binding agreement to waive any remaining claims against the debtor. If creditors are unwilling to supply the waiver, they do not receive a share of the debtor's assets and remain free to

---

[320] Geoffrey L. Berman & Catherine E. Vance, *Relief without a Petition: Non-Bankruptcy Alternatives Model Statute for General Assignments for the Benefit of Creditors: The Genesis of Change*, 17 Am. Bankr. Inst. L. Rev. 33 (2009).

[321] Interpleader is in many respects similar to bankruptcy and other insolvency proceedings. Both rule and statutory interpleader involve competing claims to a limited fund.

[322] James A. Chatz & Joy E. Levy, *Alternatives to Bankruptcy*, 17 Norton J. Bankr. L. & Prac. 149, 153 (2008); Melanie Rovner Cohen & Joanna L. Challacombe, *Assignment for Benefit of Creditors: A Contemporary Alternative for Corporations*, 2 De Paul Bus. L.J. 269 (1990); Robert Richards & Nancy Ross, *Relief Without a Petition: Non-Bankruptcy Alternatives Practical Issues in Assignments for the Benefit of Creditors*, 17 Am. Bankr. Inst. L. Rev. 5 (2009) (listing citations to state assignment for benefit of creditors statutes); Joel B. Weinberg, *California General Assignments: Still Alive, Kicking and Useful*, 29 Cal. Bankr. J. 293 (2007).

[323] *E.g.*, Compagnia Distribuzione Calzature, S.R.L. v. PSF Shoes, Ltd., 613 N.Y.S.2d 931 (A.D.2d 1994).

[324] *See* Internat'l Shoe v. Pinkus, 278 U.S. 261 (1929) ("The power of Congress to establish uniform laws on the subject of bankruptcies throughout the United States is unrestricted and paramount.").

[325] *See* O.C.G.A. §§ 18-2-40 to -59 (2007); Ala. Code § 7-9-301 (1999) (lien creditor); Ala. Code § 8-9-4 (1999) (fraudulent transfers); Ala. Code § 19-3-28 (1999) (notifying creditors); Ala. Code § 35-4-57 (1999) (recording the assignment); Fla. Stat. Ch. 727.101 to 727.116 (1999); Ky. Rev. Stat. Ann. §§ 379.010 to 379.170 (1999); Miss. Code Ann. §§ 85-1-1 to 85-1-19 (2000); N.C. Gen. Stat. §§ 23-1 to 23-48 (1999); Tenn. Code Ann. §§ 47-13-101 to 47-13-120 (1999); S.C. Code Ann. §§ 27-25-10 to 27-25-160 (1998).

pursue the debtor and any assets she subsequently acquires through the normal collection process.

Another alternative for creditors who are uninterested in cooperating with an assignment for the benefit of creditors is to initiate an involuntary bankruptcy proceeding against the debtor. Under Bankruptcy Code § 303(b)(2), the appointment of a custodian, trustee, or agent with authority to take charge of all of the debtor's assets, provides creditors with grounds to impose a bankruptcy proceeding on an unwilling debtor.[326]

Today, most assignments for the benefit of creditors are governed by state statute;[327] however, where statutory procedures are not available, an assignment can still be made using ordinary trust principles.[328]

Assignments for the benefit of creditors were once prevalent, but they fell into disuse for many years before experiencing a recent modest revival.[329] They can be an effective means to liquidate a debtor's assets in an orderly manner, without the added expense of bankruptcy. This is particularly true for corporate debtors for whom receiving a discharge is less important.[330]

[B] Equitable and Statutory Receiverships[331]

State court receiverships operate in a manner similar to assignments for the benefit of creditors, except that they are involuntary. Today, though possibly initiated by creditors, either acting alone or in concert with one another, they frequently involve the consent of the debtor.

Receiverships were originally equitable proceedings designed to prevent a debtor's property from being dissipated. These "equity receiverships" were initiated by creditors when the normal legal remedy of executing against the debtor's assets was at risk because of the debtor's mishandling, destruction, concealment, or dissipation of its assets. Receiverships are now largely statutory, though they remain viable as equitable remedies in some states.

Equity receiverships can be used for a single parcel of property, small businesses, or large corporations. In railroad cases, at the turn of the century, a combination of equity receiverships and voting trusts were used to reorganize

---

[326] Bankruptcy Code § 303(h)(2). *See infra* § 6.03 Commencement of Involuntary Cases.

[327] *See* Ohio Rev. Code Ann. §§ 1313.01-1313.59 (LexisNexis 2002) (designated as "Voluntary Assignments") (assignment to be filed with the probate court).

[328] *See, e.g.*, Tribune Co. v. Canger Floral Co., 37 N.E.2d 906 (Ill. App. Ct. 1941).

[329] *E.g.*, Consol. Pipe & Supply Co., Inc. v. Rovanco Corp., 897 F. Supp. 364 (N.D. Ill. 1995). *See generally* Melanie Rovner Cohen & Joanna L. Challacombe, *Assignment for Benefit of Creditors: A Contemporary Alternative for Corporations*, 2 DePaul Bus. L.J. 269 (1990).

[330] *See infra* § 13.02[B][1] Eligibility for Discharge — Individual Debtors.

[331] Bruce A. Markell, *Owners, Auctions, and Absolute Priority in Bankruptcy Reorganizations*, 44 Stan. L. Rev. 69, 74-87 (1991); E. Merrick Dodd, Jr., *Reorganization Through Bankruptcy: A Remedy for What?*, 48 Harv. L. Rev. 1100, 1100-10 (1935); Roger S. Foster, *Conflicting Ideals for Reorganization*, 44 Yale L.J. 923 (1935); James N. Rosenberg, *A New Scheme of Reorganization*, 17 Colum. L. Rev. 523 (1917).

financially troubled railroads as a going concern. This technique was an early precursor to modern Chapter 11 bankruptcy reorganization. Before the early 1930s and the enactment of the original reorganization provisions of the Bankruptcy Act,[332] equity receiverships were the primary mechanism to reorganize large complicated businesses, such as railroads, with diverse assets stretched across a broad range of territory.[333] However, they are rarely used in this way today.[334]

[C]   Regulatory Receiverships

By contrast to ordinary equitable receiverships, state and federal regulatory receiverships are common. However, they are largely unaffected by bankruptcy law. By long tradition, many financial institutions, especially insurance companies, have been regulated by state rather than federal authorities. Other financial institutions, such as FDIC-insured banks, are subject to a separate set of federal insolvency laws. Insurance companies and FDIC-insured financial institutions are not permitted to file bankruptcy. Those companies must be liquidated or reorganized under the relevant state or federal regulatory laws.

Title II of the recently enacted Dodd-Frank Act creates an Orderly Liquidation Authority to handle the liquidation of Systematically Important Financial Institutions — or SIFIs. Those receiverships would be administered by the FDIC, under rules that are somewhat different from other regulatory receiverships.[335]

§ 2.10   COMPOSITIONS AND WORKOUTS[336]

Workouts and contractual compositions are methods of dealing with debt that are negotiated in the shadow of default and bankruptcy. The term "workout" refers to an agreement between the debtor and a single creditor or, more likely, a group of creditors. A distinction is sometimes made between an agreement among creditors that reduces the amount the debtor owes, referred to as a "composition," and an agreement that lengthens the time for the debtor to repay the debt, called an "extension." These terms, however, have no precise legal significance and are not used consistently. The key to these mechanisms is not the terminology but the legal

---

[332] Bankruptcy Act of March 3, 1933, ch. 204, § 77, 47 Stat. 1467, 1474 (1933); Bankruptcy Act of June 7, 1934, ch. 424, § 77B, 48 Stat. 911, 912 (1934).

[333] Bruce A. Markell, *Owners, Auctions, and Absolute Priority in Bankruptcy Reorganizations*, 44 Stan. L. Rev. 69, 75-84 (1991); David A. Skeel, Debt's Dominion: A History of Bankruptcy Law in America 57-60 (2001).

[334] Indeed, these remedies have fallen into such disuse that some trial court judges have refused to allow their use. *See* First Nat'l State Bank v. Kron, 464 A.2d 1146 (N.J. Super Ct. App. Div. 1983) (trial court judge gave, as one reason for refusal to appoint a receiver, that the receivership statute had been forgotten and was no longer viable).

[335] Patricia McCoy & Kathleen Engel, *The Subprime Virus: Reckless Credit, Regulatory Failure, and Next Steps* (2011) (available at http://papers.ssrn.com/sol3/papers.cfm?abstract_id=1762869) (last viewed on July 23, 2012).

[336] Winton E. Williams, *Resolving the Creditor's Dilemma: An Elementary Game-Theoretic Analysis of the Causes and Cures of Counterproductive Practices in the Collection of Consumer Debt*, 48 Fla. L. Rev. 607 (1996).

substance, which is a contract that extends or partially discharges one or more of a debtor's obligations.

Historically, there have been two major conceptual problems with workouts: the common law doctrine of consideration, and the effect of these agreements on third parties. First, consider a bilateral workout between a debtor, Titanic Industries, and one of its principal creditors, Atlantic Consulting Corp. Assume that Titanic has been receiving consulting and repair services from Atlantic on 30 day open account credit and now owes Atlantic a total of $50,000. Of this amount, $40,000 is overdue, and the remaining $10,000 will become due within 30 days. Titanic proposes that Atlantic agree to reduce the amount of the total debt to $35,000, and Titanic will make a $10,000 cash payment to Atlantic within the next month and pay the $25,000 balance in monthly $1,000 installments over several years. Titanic agrees to pay for any future services in cash at the time the services are rendered.

While Titanic may be financially capable of performing this agreement, the two-party deal may be unenforceable due to lack of consideration. Atlantic has modified its rights, but Titanic has promised to do nothing more than perform a portion of its pre-existing duties. This appears to run afoul of the so-called "pre-existing duty rule."[337]

A few adjustments to the terms of the workout could supply the necessary element of exchange. If Titanic agreed to give Atlantic an increased interest rate, prepayment of principal, or some collateral in exchange for Atlantic's forbearance from requiring immediate payment of the full amount, such as a second mortgage on its warehouse and office buildings or a security interest in its inventory or accounts receivable, the necessary element of a bargain would be present and the agreement would be enforceable.

Another concern about agreements negotiated in the shadow of bankruptcy is that any payments, mortgages or security interests would be vulnerable to avoidance as a preference if Titanic filed a bankruptcy petition within the ninety day period after the transfer.[338] This would ultimately deprive Atlantic of the principal benefit of the bargain. To deal with this, many workout agreements do not release the debtor from its full obligations until 90 days after the last payment or transfer is made under the agreement.

Negotiating a composition agreement between a debtor and its creditors is more difficult. Some of the creditors are bound to be secured while others are unsecured. These creditors are likely to be distrustful of both the debtor and of each other. And their suspicions may be warranted. After all, the debtor may be an important customer of some creditors, who will be facing their own financial difficulties if the debtor's business fails. Likewise, some creditors may be key suppliers to the debtor's business, without whose cooperation the debtor would be doomed. Unsecured creditors may be skeptical about the value placed on the collateral claimed by a secured creditor and worried that secured creditors should be making greater sacrifices, since they face less risk if the debtor falls into bankruptcy. This mixture

---

[337] Alaska Packers' Assoc. v. Domenico, 117 F. 99 (9th Cir. 1902). *See* Jeff Ferriell, Understanding Contracts § 3.07 (LexisNexis 2009).

[338] *See infra* Chapter 15 — Avoidable Preferences.

of factors leads to conflicts among the participants.

One thing should be clear: when creditors make agreements with one another, consideration is not a problem. When one creditor agrees to reduce the amount of his claim, in exchange for another creditor's agreement to do the same, the necessary element of a bargain is present; the promise is enforceable, with the debtor as a third-party beneficiary of the deal.

Thus, the principal drawback is the practical difficulty of obtaining all of the creditors' consent. Holdouts, who have greater bargaining leverage over the debtor, might demand a larger payment than the debtor can afford. In addition, the agreement may provide that it is not enforceable against any of the parties unless everyone's agreement is obtained. Even without this provision, one key holdout, who is doubtful of the debtor's ability to pay, may disrupt everyone else's plans by continuing to pursue the debtor for the entire debt and by eventually seizing assets that the debtor needs to keep its business running. This holdout problem is one of the key weaknesses of workouts as a solution to a debtor's general default on all of its debts.

Although Chapter 11 of the Bankruptcy Code includes mechanisms to deal with these dissenters, as well as ways to evaluate the value of the debtor's assets, workouts retain important potential advantages over Chapter 11. Most importantly, the costs of a composition agreement are usually much lower than those of a Chapter 11 bankruptcy case. Further, in Chapter 11, details of the debtor's financial difficulties are likely to be revealed to the general public. Moreover, a composition agreement is not subject to the kind of court or regulatory scrutiny that is involved in Chapter 11.

Workouts and bankruptcy reorganizations are not mutually exclusive. In some cases the debtor and the requisite majorities[339] of creditors agree to all or most of the reorganization plan before the debtor files its bankruptcy petition; the pre-negotiated plan is then presented to the court and the other creditors for confirmation.[340] These are sometimes called "prepackaged" plans of reorganization or "pre-packs."[341] In the right circumstances, a Chapter 11 plan, which is usually in the nature of a composition agreement, can be worked out in advance and taken to bankruptcy court for relatively swift approval.[342]

---

[339] Bankruptcy Code § 1126.

[340] *See infra* § 19.09[E] Pre-Packaged Plans.

[341] Or, in the terminology used by the cognoscenti, a "prepak." *See* Tashjian et al., *Prepaks: An Empirical Analysis of Prepackaged Bankruptcies*, 40 J. Fin. Econ. 135 (1996).

[342] Ronald Barliant, Dimitri G. Karcazes & Anne M. Sherry, *From Free-Fall to Free-For-All: The Rise of Pre-Packaged Asbestos Bankruptcies*, 12 Am. Bankr. Inst. L. Rev. 441 (2004); *e.g.*, United Artists Theatre Co. v. Walton, 315 F.3d 217, 224 n.5 (3d Cir. 2003).

§ 2.11   PROPERTY BEYOND THE REACH OF CREDITORS

Not all property is subject to creditors' claims. In some cases, state law defines the types of property that are subject to levy and execution by the sheriff. For example, in *Network Solutions, Inc. v. Umbro Int'l, Inc.*[343] the Virginaia sheriff was unable to levy on (or garnish) internet domain names because the domain registration agreement was deemed non-property under Virginia law.

Similar issues arise with regard to governmental licenses which may be non-transferable as a matter of law[344] and in connection with licensing agreements where the contract rights may be non-assignable.[345] These issues frequently bedevil creditors and bankruptcy courts.

Where individual debtors are involved, there is a substantial body of state law that limits the power of a creditor to seize the consumer debtor's property. The popular image of a destitute debtor, left with nothing but an empty barrel held up by a pair of ratty suspenders, is pure hyperbole. All states have exemption statutes that provide a list of assets that are beyond the reach of creditors, unless the debtor has voluntarily encumbered them with a mortgage or a security interest. Further, some assets are immune even from security interests unless the security interest was granted as part of the deal that enabled the debtor to acquire the asset in the first place. Finally, limited types of assets are held in a form, such as a tenancy by the entirety or a valid spendthrift trust, that places them beyond the reach of even the debtor to encumber them.

The theory is that the debtor should not be left dressed only in a barrel held up by ratty suspenders. However, the scope of exemptions vary wildly from state to state, and with the type of creditor involved.

[A]   Exemptions[346]

State law permits even the most impecunious debtor to retain some assets. These assets are "exempt" from attachment or execution; unsecured creditors seeking to enforce a judgment may not seize them. The fundamental reason for exemptions is the belief that even the most hopelessly insolvent debtors should not be deprived of the basic necessities of life. To do this would only make them wards of the state. This non-bankruptcy policy is respected by the Bankruptcy Code,

---

[343] Network Solutions, Inc. v. Umbro International, Inc., 529 S.E.2d 80 (Va. 2000).

[344] *Compare* In re. Tak Commc'ns, Inc., 138 B.r. 568 (W.D. Wis. 1992), *with* Ridgley Commc'ns, Inc., 139 B.R. 374 (Bankr. D. Md. 1992), *and* In re Chris-Don, Inc., 367 F. Supp. 2d 696 (D.N.J. 2005).

[345] In re. SRJ Enterprises, Inc., 150 B.R. 933 (N.D. Ill. 1993).

[346] Wells M. Engledow, *Cleaning up the Pigsty: Approaching a Consensus on Exemption Laws*, 74 Am. Bankr. L.J. 275 (2000); Delmar Karlen, *Exemptions From Execution*, 22 Bus. Law. 1167 (1967); Marjorie Dick Rombauer, *Debtors' Exemption Statutes — Revision Ideas*, 36 Wash L. Rev. 484, 485 (1961); William T. Vukowich, *Debtors' Exemption Rights*, 62 Geo. L.J. 779 (1974); William T. Vukowich, *Debtors' Exemption Rights Under the Bankruptcy Reform Act of 1978*, 58 N.C. L. Rev. 769, 800-04 (1980); William J. Woodward, Jr., *Exemptions, Opting Out, and Bankruptcy Reform*, 43 Ohio St. L.J. 335 (1982); Richard C. Christenson, Comment, *Personal Property Exemptions and the Uniform Exemptions Act*, 1978 BYU L. Rev. 462, 466-67.

which also permits debtors to retain property that state laws exempt from execution.[347]

For many years, the exemption laws preserved a picture of nineteenth century rural American life. A debtor was allowed to keep cows, a few pigs, a spinning wheel, and a dozen or more dishes "for *himself, his* wife and *their* children." In recent years, largely as a result of the influence of the 1978 overhaul of the Bankruptcy Code, which contains an optional "modern" set of exemptions,[348] exemptions have become more realistic: cars have replaced horses and pension rights have replaced acres of farm land.

Exemptions fall into three broad categories: the homestead exemption for residential real estate; exemptions for items of tangible personal property, such as motor vehicles, household goods, and tools; and exemptions for various sources of current or future income. There are several key limits on these exemption rights, which are explained below.

[1]   Limitations on Exemptions

[a]   Exemption in Debtor's Equity

The most important limit on a debtor's exemption rights is that they apply only to a debtor's unencumbered property. Exemptions do not affect artisans or mechanics liens, or consensual liens, but apply only to the debtor's equity in her property.[349] For example, a debtor who owns a home worth $150,000 that is subject to an outstanding $150,000 mortgage will not be able to claim an exemption for the home because she has no equity in it. Neither will the debtor's unsecured creditors be able to levy on the house, because all of the value would be eaten up by the secured creditor's claim. If the mortgage were $145,000, and the state homesteead statute allowed, the debtor could claim an exemption of the $5,000 in equity. Again, there would be no value available to unsecured creditors. Moreover, if the mortgage debt were $130,000 and the state's homestead exemption were for only $8,000, the debtor could exempt just the $8,000 statutory amount. However, because the debtor's $20,000 in equity exceeds the amount of the available exemption, the unsecured creditors would be able to levy on the property and capture the excess $12,000 in equity. Thus, exemptions protect a limited amount of property from judicial liens, but they do not protect property from consensual liens

---

[347] Bankruptcy Code § 522(b). In some states, debtors may choose between the exemptions provided by their home state's exemption statute or a set of uniform exemptions in the Bankruptcy Code. *See* Bankruptcy Code § 523(d). Pursuant to authority delegated by Congress, most states have "opted-out" of this election, and left their residents with only the schedule of property exempted by the state exemption statute. Not surprisingly, most of the states that have opted out of the uniform federal exemptions are those with exemption statutes that are less generous toward debtors than those contained in the Bankruptcy Code. *See infra* § 12.02 Exemptions in Bankruptcy.

[348] Bankruptcy Code § 522(d).

[349] *See* In re Galvan, 110 B.R. 446 (B.A.P. 9th Cir. 1990); In re Rodriguez, 140 B.R. 562 (Bankr. D. Kan. 1992); Jungkunz v. Fifth-Third Bank, 650 N.E.2d 134 (Ohio Ct. App. 1994); Russell G. Donaldson, Annotation, *Avoidance under § 522(f)(1) of Bankruptcy Code of 1978 of Judicial Lien on Debtor's Exempt Personal Property*, 124 A.L.R. Fed. 465, § (1995).

like mortgages and security interests, or from statutory liens, like construction and repairmen's liens.[350]

As explained in more detail elsewhere, a bankrupt debtor may be able to set aside certain non-purchase money security interests that otherwise might impair her exemption in certain types of exempt property.[351] However, this ability to avoid security interests that impair an exemption applies only to debtors who are eligible for and can afford to file a bankruptcy case — an increasingly limited number of debtors.[352]

[b] Limited Categories

Exemption rights are usually limited to very specific categories of property, such as "real or personal property used as the debtor's principal residence"; "one motor vehicle"; or "wearing apparel and household furnishings." Thus, the debtor's property must fit into one of the categories of property that qualify for an exemption.

Determining whether a particular item fits within a specified category is sometimes difficult. For example, some state exemption statutes place an aggregate limit on the total value of "household furnishings" and "appliances" that may be exempted, but impose no limit on "wearing apparel." This may lead a debtor to claim that her mp3 music player, which can be worn as a wristwatch, is wearing apparel. The same sort of problem has arisen in connection with items that might be characterized either as "jewelry," which is usually subject to a more stringent restriction, or as "wearing apparel" for which most exemption statutes provide more liberal protection.[353] For example, in *In re Leva*,[354] the debtor's Rolex brand wristwatch qualified for a wearing apparel exemption, but his diamond "pinky ring" and gold bracelet did not.

Some states provide what has been characterized as a "wildcard" exemption, that permits the debtor to exempt any property, usually up to a specific dollar limit.[355] Following the example supplied by § 522(d)(5) of the Bankruptcy Code, the dollar limit of some of these wildcard provisions varies, depending on the extent to which a debtor has used any available homestead exemption.[356]

---

[350] The Internal Revenue Code has its own set of exemption provisions, which provide debtors with very limited protection from a statutory federal tax lien. I.R.C. § 6334 (2006).

[351] Bankruptcy Code § 522(f). *See infra* § 12.07 Avoiding Liens on Exempt Property.

[352] *See infra* § 6.02[B][2] Eligibility for Relief Under Chapter 7 — Liquidation.

[353] *E.g.*, In re Fernandez, 855 F.2d 218 (5th Cir. 1988) (jewelry exempt as "clothing" under Texas exemption statute).

[354] 96 B.R. 723 (Bankr. W.D. Tex. 1989) (Texas has long been viewed as a debtor's haven).

[355] *E.g.*, Ohio Rev. Code Ann. § 2329.66(A)(18) (LexisNexis Supp. 2006) ($400 "in any property"); 735 Ill. Comp. Stat. Ann. 5/12-1001(b) (West 2003) ($2000 "in any other property"); Mo. Stat. Ann. § 513.430(3) (West Supp. 2006) ($400 in "any other property of any kind").

[356] Stephen F. Yunker, Comment, *The General Exemption of Section 522(d)(5) of the 1978 Bankruptcy Code*, 49 U. Chi. L. Rev. 564 (1982).

[c]   Value Limits

Exemptions are nearly always limited in value. This limit may be imposed on each individual item, on categories of items, or on the total amount of property that a debtor may claim as exempt. For example, the Ohio exemption statute limits the value of each item of a debtor's "wearing apparel" that may be claimed as exempt to $200 per item, but the statute imposes no overall limit on the value of the debtor's total portfolio of these items.[357] The debtor may exempt as many $199 scarves as she wants — though an aggressive creditor may inquire into whether the debtor actually "wears" each scarf and thus question whether all of them fit the category.[358] Another portion of this illustrative statute permits debtors to protect individual items of "household furnishings" but limits the aggregate of such items that are exempt to $2,000.[359]

Value limitations supply another example of the omnipresent issue in debtor-creditor and bankruptcy law: valuation. The only real way to determine the value of an asset is to sell it. But selling the asset would frustrate the purpose of an exemption statute, which is to permit the debtor to keep the property, so long as it is fully exempt. Thus, the value of exempt property sometimes must be determined by appraisal testimony.[360] When the value of exempt property is contested, which sometimes happens in bankruptcy, fair market value is the governing standard, typically without any reduction for the amount that would have been consumed by the costs of the sale.[361] If the exempt asset is an intangible right, such as a cause of action, valuation may be particularly difficult.[362]

As a practical matter, bankruptcy trustees develop a fairly good sense of what common household items are likely to be worth. Most of the time they are worth very little — imagine the amount of cash you would expect to produce from a garage sale of all of your wearing apparel and furniture.[363] The value of motor vehicles are readily determined from the automobile bluebook, commonly used by automobile dealers.[364] In many cases, the debtor's home is the only asset that

---

[357] The potential folly of this type of limitation was illustrated by the original bankruptcy code, which permitted debtors to keep an unlimited number of "household goods," so long as each item was worth no more than $200. In re Wahl, 14 B.R. 153 (Bankr. E. D. Wis. 1981). After several debtors exempted thousands of dollars of sets of silverware, each item of which was worth approximately $180, Congress amended the law to impose a ceiling on the total value of items of household goods that could be exempted. *See* In re Siegle, 257 B.R. 591 (Bankr. D. Mont. 2001); Margaret Howard, *A Theory of Discharge in Consumer Bankruptcy*, 48 Ohio St. L.J. 1047, 1078 n.212 (1987).

[358] *See* In re Hazelhurst, 228 B.R. 199 (Bankr. E.D. Tenn. 1998) (engagement ring the debtor no longer wore was not reasonably necessary wearing apparel).

[359] Ohio Rev. Code Ann. § 2329.66(A)(4) (LexisNexis Supp. 2006).

[360] *E.g.*, In re Smith, 267 B.R. 568 (Bankr. S.D. Ohio 2001).

[361] *See* In re Sumerell, 194 B.R. 818 (Bankr. E.D. Tenn. 1996); In re Mitchell, 103 B.R. 819 (Bankr. W.D. Tex. 1989).

[362] *E.g.*, In re Ball, 201 B.R. 210 (Bankr. N.D. Ill. 1996).

[363] Items of upholstered furniture, for example, are virtually worthless unless they are antiques.

[364] *See* Kelly Blue Book *available at* http://kbb.com/ (last visited July 29, 2012) (the "Kelly Bluebook," also sometimes known as "the bluebook," has nothing to do with The Uniform System of Citation published by the Harvard Law Review Association).

might require a professional appraisal to determine its value. The value supplied by the debtor in the schedules she files with her bankruptcy petition will usually be relied on and may be dispositive in the absence of conflicting evidence.

Alternatively, the value of some items can be indirectly limited by restricting the exemption to items that are "reasonably necessary for the support of the debtor."[365] For example, in *In re Sydlowski*, the court held that the married debtors could each exempt one TV and one VCR as reasonably necessary, that a video game and library of video tapes were reasonably necessary for a custodial parent, but that a third TV and a lawn "edge trimmer" were not reasonably necessary and thus not entitled to an exemption for "household goods."[366] Another court ruled that a television and a VCR were reasonably necessary because of their customary usage in the home, but that "recreational equipment" not used inside the home such as "bowling balls, golf clubs, fishing equipment, [and] camping equipment" did not qualify for the exemption.[367]

Some particularly important items are sometimes exempt without regard to their value. The most obvious example is the exemption provided in most jurisdictions for "medically prescribed or medically necessary health aids."[368] The principal limitation here is that they must be "professionally prescribed" or "medically necessary."[369]

Categories of exempt property that contain no value limit are subject to potential abuse. In *In re Freelander*,[370] the debtor was permitted to exempt his $640,000 thoroughbred race horse, under an archaic exemption statute that had been well suited to an agrarian lifestyle, permitting debtors to exempt "a horse." And, before there was an aggregate limit on the value of household items, some debtors exempted extensive collections of silverware, with each individual knife, fork, and spoon, worth no more than the $200 "per item" limit.

Married debtors, who jointly own most of their property, are usually able to

---

[365] *E.g.*, In re Walsh, 5 B.R. 239 (Bankr. D. Colo. 1980); Michael G. Hillinger, *How Fresh a Start?: What Are "Household Goods" For Purposes of Section 522(f)(1)(B)(I) Lien Avoidance?*, 15 Bank. Dev. J. 1 (1999); John D. Perovich, Annotation, *What Is "Necessary" Furniture Entitled to Exemption from Seizure for Debt*, 41 A.L.R.3d 607 (1972 & Supp. 1999).

[366] 186 B.R. 907 (Bankr. N.D. Ohio 1995).

[367] In re Biancavilla, 173 B.R. 930 (Bankr. D. Idaho 1994). Apparently, gear necessary for sedentary forms of recreation are reasonably necessary, but items necessary for more active types of recreation are not. *See also* In re Davis, 134 B.R. 34 (Bankr. W. D. Okla. 1991). Some states explicitly exempt various types of sporting goods. *E.g.*, Tex. Prop. Code § 42.002(3)(E) (Vernon 2000). Guns are sometimes explicitly exempt. *E.g.*, Tex. Prop. Code Ann. § 42.002(a)(7) (Vernon 2000); Idaho Rev. Code Ann. 11-605(7) (2004); *but see* In re Barnes, 117 B.R. 842 Bankr. D. Md. 1990) (firearms were sporting goods normally used outside and away from home and were not reasonably necessary for day-to-day existence of people in context of their homes, and thus not "household goods").

[368] *E.g.*, Ohio Rev. Code Ann. § 2329.66(A)(7) (LexisNexis Supp. 2006); Bankruptcy Code § 522(d)(8) ("professionally prescribed health aids for the debtor or a dependent of the debtor").

[369] *See* In re McCashen, 339 B.R. 907 (Bankr. N.D. Ohio 2006) (unmodified van that could accommodate debtor's physical size was neither professionally prescribed nor medically necessary); In re Hellen, 329 B.R. 678 (Bankr. N.D. Ill. 2005) (modifications to van made to accommodate disability were medically necessary).

[370] 93 B.R. 446, 450 (Bankr. E.D. Va. 1988).

double the value limits imposed on exemptions. This is because most exemption statutes exempt "the debtor's interest" in the property.[371] If property is jointly owned, each owner has an interest in it that can be exempted. Thus, a state statute that exempts up to $1,000 of an individual's interest in one motor vehicle could be used by a married couple who jointly own the car to exempt up to $2,000 equity in it.

This feature is particularly useful in connection with homestead exemptions on a debtor's home, especially where the debtors have not consumed the entire value of their house through the use of an "equity credit line." It is also frequently useful in connection with exemptions for household items that might be worth more than the meager amount protected by the exemption statute. Of course, some valuable items, such as engagement rings, might not be jointly owned and thus are eligible for exemption only by the spouse who owns the item.[372]

There has been a great deal of controversy over the effect of exemption laws. According to some scholars, generous exemption laws ought to lead to an increase in bankruptcies, because debtors will be able to shed debt without losing assets.[373] However, the available empirical evidence provides scant support for this hypothesis.[374] Instead, it appears that relatively few debtors are influenced by the amount of property they can retain in a bankruptcy proceeding.[375] The most likely explanation for this counter-intuitive phenomenon is that most debtors do not have enough unencumbered property for this to have an effect on their decision-making.[376]

[2] Homestead Exemptions on Residential Real Estate

As suggested by its name, the homestead exemption protects some or all of a debtor's equity in her home.[377] In many states, the amount of the homestead exemption is too small to permit the debtor to keep her home. Instead, the limited

---

[371] *See, e.g.*, Ariz. Rev. Stat. Ann. § 33-1121.01 (West 2000).

[372] *Cf.* In re Gregorchik, 311 B.R. 52 (Bankr. W.D. Pa. 2004) (engagement ring not entireties property).

[373] *See* Michelle J. White, *Why It Pays to File for Bankruptcy: A Critical Look at Incentives Under US Bankruptcy Laws and a Proposal for Change*, 65 U. Chi. L. Rev. 685 (1998); Michelle J. White, *Why Don't More Households File for Bankruptcy?*, 14 J.L. Econ. & Org. 205 (1998); Reint Gropp, John Karl Scholz & Michelle White, *Personal Bankruptcy and Credit Supply and Demand*, 112 Q.J. Econ. 217 (1997).

[374] Susan Block-Lieb & Edward J. Janger, *The Myth of the Rational Borrower*, 85 Texas L. Rev. 1481, 1522-23 (collecting studies); Teresa Sullivan, Elizabeth Warren & Jay Lawrence Westbrook, As We Forgive Our Debtors: Bankruptcy and Consumer Credit in America 241-42 (1989); W.J. Woodward, Jr, *Exemptions as an Incentive to Voluntary Bankruptcy: An Empirical Study*, 88 Com. L.J. 309 (1983).

[375] Teresa Sullivan, Elizabeth Warren & Jay Lawrence Westbrook, As We Forgive Our Debtors: Bankruptcy and Consumer Credit in America 241-42 (1989); Susan Block-Lieb & Edward J. Janger, *The Myth of the Rational Borrower: Rationality, Behavioralism, and the Misguided "Reform" of Bankruptcy Law*, 84 Tex. L. Rev. 1481, 1523-24 & 1523 n.172 (2006).

[376] Richard M. Hynes, *Personal Bankruptcy in the 21st Century: Emerging Trends and New Challenges: Credit Markets, Exemptions, and Households with Nothing to Exempt*, 7 Theoretical Inquiries L. 493 (2006).

[377] The homestead exemption reputedly began in Texas. *See* United States. v. Johnson, 160 F.3d 1061

amount permits a debtor to keep a portion of the proceeds from the sale of the asset, assuming it can be sold for its full market value. Tennessee, with one of the smallest homestead exemptions in the country, protects only $5,000 of a debtor's equity in "real property which is owned by the individual and used by the individual or the individual's spouse or dependent, as a principal place of residence."[378] With the $156,000 median selling price of a house in Nashville, Tennessee, in 2011, $5,000 does not even cover the amount necessary for a 10% down payment. The amount of the homestead exemption varies widely from a mere $5,000 in Tennessee, to an unlimited amount in Texas,[379] and a few but growing number of other states where the extent of the exemption is measured in acres rather than dollars.

In a few states, to be eligible for a homestead exemption, debtors must file a "declaration of homestead" much in the way a creditor would file a mortgage.[380] In other states, the exemption is not available to protect a debtor from some sorts of claims. It would not be surprising to find, for example, that the exemption could not be used by a "deadbeat dad" to protect his home from a claim for unpaid support.

The homestead exemption is usually only available for property used as the principal residence of the debtor or one of the debtor's dependents.[381] In most states, the exemption now applies to both personal property and real estate used as a residence, permitting mobile homes, trailers, co-op apartments, and houseboats to quality for the protection. In rare circumstances,[382] a standard motor vehicle might qualify, though questions would arise regarding the debtor's ability to "stack" her motor vehicle exemption on top of her homestead exemption, and claim two exemptions for the car, one as a homestead and the other as a motor vehicle.

[3] Personal Property Exemptions[383]

A wide variety of items of personal property are usually protected by a state's exemption statute. There are many common themes, but the detailed differences from one state to the next are staggering. In some states, a debtor's interest in her

---

(5th Cir. 1998); 3 Laws of the Republic of Tex. 113 (1839). Indeed, along with a few other states, Texas has long been regarded as a debtor's haven. *See* Jean Braucher, *The Repo Code: A Study of Adjustment to Uncertainty in Commercial Law*, 75 Wash. U. L.Q. 549, 570 (1997); Julie B. Schroeder, Comment, *Perspectives on Urban Homestead Exemptions — Texas Amends Article XVI, Section 51*, 15 St. Mary's L.J. 603, 614-17 & 614 n.67 (1984) (referring to McKnight, *Protection of the Family Home from Seizure by Creditors: The Sources and Evolution of a Legal Principle*, 37 S.W. Hist. Quart. 369, 369-83 (1983), as outlining the early history and reputation of Texas in this regard).

[378] Tenn. Code Ann. § 26-2-301 (2010) ($7500 if jointly owned by co-debtors).

[379] Tex. Prop. Code Ann. § 41.002 (Vernon 2002) (10 acres of urban land, or up 200 acres in a rural area for a "family").

[380] *See, e.g.*, Va. Code Ann. § 34-14 (LexisNexis 2005); Zimmerman v. Morgan, 689 F.2d 471 (4th Cir. 1982) (debtor who failed to record notice of homestead exemption could not assert exemption in bankruptcy).

[381] *See* Holden v. Cribb, 561 S.E.2d 634 (S.C. Ct. App. 2002) (incarcerated debtor was not deprived of his homestead where he had been involuntarily removed from his residence and intended to return upon his release).

[382] A friend of one of your co-authors once lived in his long-haul truck cab.

[383] Michael G. Hillinger, *How Fresh a Start?: What Are "Household Goods" for Purposes of Section 522(f)(1)(B)(i) Lien Avoidance?*, 15 Bankr. Dev. J. 1 (1998).

"seat or pew in any church or place of public worship" is exempt, while specific exemptions for firearms and livestock are more common in western states. In other states, exemptions are available for quantities of firewood;[384] assorted livestock, including sheep, cows, swine, and chickens;[385] and in at least one state, a liquor license.[386] In Louisiana, an exemption is available for "musical instruments played or practiced on by [the debtor] or a member of his family" apparently without regard to its value and regardless of whether it is used to generate income.[387]

The most common exemptions for goods are those for household furnishings, wearing apparel, household appliances, motor vehicles, a limited amount of jewelry, and "tools of a debtor's trade or business." As explained above, exemptions for these categories of property are usually subject to limits. These limits are sometimes expressed as a limit on the value of individual items, as an aggregate limit, or more ambiguously as a limit to whatever is "reasonably necessary."

[4] Exemptions for Sources of Income[388]

Wage garnishment exemptions protect a portion of most debtors' earnings from being garnished. Federal restrictions on wage garnishment establish an absolute limit on the extent of wages that states may permit creditors to seize. In addition, many states provide additional protection from wage garnishment, beyond the limits imposed by federal law.

Most states' exemption statutes protect a wide variety of sources of income, such as retirement funds, workers' compensation benefits, personal injury awards, disability benefits, veterans' benefits, alimony and support, unemployment insurance payments, and life insurance benefits. Such exemptions may be limited to the amount reasonably necessary for the support of the debtor and the debtor's dependents.

[a] Federal Restrictions on Wage Garnishment

The Consumer Credit Protection Act imposes limits on the amount of wages that states may permit creditors to garnish.[389] It provides:

> The maximum part of the aggregate disposable earnings of an individual for any workweek which is subject to garnishment may not exceed
>
> (1) 25 per centum of his disposable earnings for that week, or

---

[384] Me. Rev. Stat. Ann. tit. 14 § 4422(6)(c) (West 2003) ("10 cords of wood, 5 tons of coal, 1000 gallons of petroleum products or its equivalent").

[385] Mich Comp. Laws. Ann. § 600.6023(1)(d) (West 2000) (10 sheep, 2 cows, 5 swine, 100 hens, and 5 roosters); Mass. Ann. Laws ch. 235 § 34 (West 2000) (12 sheep, 2 cows, 2 swine, no mention of hens or roosters).

[386] Idaho Code Ann. § 23-514 (LexisNexis 2001).

[387] La. Rev. State Ann. § 13:3881(A)(4)(d) (West Supp. 2006).

[388] Sherwin P. Simmus, *Pension Plan Loans and Bankruptcy: The Great Debate and a New View*, 18 Bank. Dev. J. 373 (2002).

[389] 15 U.S.C. §§ 1671-1677 (2006). The restrictions apply to garnishment or any other type of proceeding used to seize wages for payment of a debt. 15 U.S.C. § 1672(c) (2006).

(2) the amount by which his disposable earnings for that week exceed thirty times the Federal minimum hourly wage prescribed by section 6(a)(1) of the Fair Labor Standards Act of 1938 in effect at the time the earnings are payable,

whichever is less.[390]

For most employees, the maximum that may be garnished under this formula is 25% of weekly disposable income. However, if the employee's weekly disposable earnings are less than $290,[391] then only the amount that exceeds $217.50 (thirty times the current federal minimum wage of $7.25 per hour)[392] can be garnished. These numbers change when Congress and the President see fit to raise the federal minimum wage.

A couple of simple examples illustrate how these rules apply. First, consider an employee whose weekly disposable earnings are $1,000. Twenty-five percent (25%) of $1,000 is $250. $1,000 of disposable earnings exceeds $217.50 (30 times the current minimum wage of $7.25) by $782.50. The maximum amount subject to garnishment is *the lesser of* $782.50 or $250. Even those who became lawyers to avoid math know which of these two amounts is less. Consider an employee who earns $7.50 per hour, but who works only thirty-five hours per week. Her total gross earnings would be $262.50, but her disposable earnings, after deducting federal, state and local income taxes, and social security taxes required by law to be withheld, might be only $240. Although 25% of $240 is $60, $240 of weekly disposable earnings exceeds $217.50 (30 times the $7.25 minimum wage) by only $22.50. The lower of these two amounts, $22.50, is the maximum weekly amount that can be garnished.

These maximum amounts apply to weekly earnings. The Department of Labor has promulgated regulations that adapt these formulas with respect to employees who are paid on a biweekly or monthly basis.[393]

This 25% restriction does not apply to court-ordered support, state or federal taxes, or wage withholding orders in chapter 13 bankruptcy cases.[394] Further, the 25% maximum is raised to varying amounts, up to 65% of an employee's disposable earnings for creditors whose wage garnishment orders are for unpaid support obligations. A support claimant can garnish 50% of an employee's disposable earnings if the employee has dependents other than those who are garnishing her

---

[390] 15 U.S.C. § 1673(a) (2006).

[391] This is a meager $15,080 per year, assuming a work week of 50 weeks with 2 weeks of paid vacation. One of your author's remembers the day in the early 1960s, when his parents went out to dinner to celebrate his father's raise. His new annual salary was $10,000, an amount that as a college student immediately after World War II, he could not have imagined earning. As a "farm hand" before the war, he always said that he had been lucky to earn $1 a day. At the time he reached the $10,000 mark, he was a college educated chemist, working in a plastics factory.

[392] As of this writing, in July of 2012, the federal minimum wage was still $7.25 per hour. This amounts to $14,500 per year for someone who works 40 hours per week for 50 weeks. 29 U.S.C. § 206 (2006 & Supp. IV 2010).

[393] 29 C.F.R. § 870.10(c).

[394] 15 U.S.C. § 1673(b)(1) (2006).

wages to recover support, and 60% if the employee has no other dependents.[395] These amounts are increased to 55% and 65% for support obligations that are more than twelve weeks overdue.[396] On the other hand, the maximum amount that may be administratively withheld from a debtor's wages to satisfy a federally guaranteed student loan is only 15%.[397]

As suggested above, an employee's "disposable earnings" are less than all of her gross earnings. Disposable earnings are " 'that part of the earnings of any individual remaining after the deduction from those earnings of any amounts required by law to be withheld.' "[398] Amounts required by law to be withheld include deductions for federal, state, and local income taxes, social security, medicare, and any applicable unemployment insurance taxes.

Deductions for health or life insurance, retirement benefits, and union dues are not "required by law to be withheld" and are part of an employee's disposable earnings.[399] Likewise, amounts withheld pursuant to a court-ordered wage assignment, made as part of a divorce decree, are not required by law to be withheld within the meaning of the statute.[400] However, such decrees are generally regarded as separate garnishments.[401] Otherwise, a judgment debtor whose wages are already subject to a court-ordered support decree might be left with very little income for her own living expenses.

[b]   State Restrictions on Wage Garnishment

State wage garnishment statutes rarely run afoul of the federal limits.[402] Some states simply conform to the federal limits and go no further.[403] Other states protect a larger percentage of wages from garnishment[404] or restrict wage garnishment claims to limited types of claims, such as those for support.[405]

---

[395] 15 U.S.C. § 1673(b)(2) (2006).

[396] 15 U.S.C. § 1673(b)(2) (2006).

[397] 20 U.S.C. § 1095a (2006).

[398] 15 U.S.C. § 1672(b) (2006).

[399] Marshall v. Dist. Court, 444 F. Supp. 1110 (E.D. Mich. 1978).

[400] *E.g.*, Marshall v. Dist. Court, 444 F. Supp. 1110 (E.D. Mich. 1978).

[401] Long Island Trust Co. v. United States Postal Serv., 647 F.2d 336 (2d Cir. 1981); Marshall v. Dist. Court, 444 F. Supp. 1110 (E.D. Mich. 1978).

[402] *But see* Hodgson v. Hamilton Mun. Court, 349 F. Supp. 1125 (S.D. Ohio 1972). Ohio subsequently amended its statute to conform to federal law.

[403] *E.g.*, N.Y. C.P.L.R. § 5295(d) (McKinney Supp. 2006) (90% exempt); Ohio Rev. Code Ann. § 2329.66(A)(13) (LexisNexis Supp. 2006) (75% exempt).

[404] *E.g.*, 735 Ill. Comp. Stat. 5/12-803 (West Supp. 2006) (15% maximum).

[405] *E.g.*, 42 Pa. Cons. Stat. Ann. § 8127 (West Supp. 2006) (support, limited "board," some actions brought by a landlord, for taxes, some retirement payments, union dues and health insurance premiums); Tex. Const.Ann. art. 16, § 28 (Vernon Supp. 2005) (only for child and spousal support).

[c]   Exemptions for Other Sources of Income

Many state exemption statutes protect a wide variety of sources of income from garnishment. These include support payments, workers compensation benefits, unemployment compensation insurance benefits, welfare benefits, and disability benefits.[406] Likewise, funds received due to a claim for lost wages due to personal injury or by a dependent of a decedent for her wrongful death are frequently exempt, though sometimes only to the extent necessary for the debtor's support.[407] Annuities and life insurance policies are also frequently exempt.[408]

Various types of pension benefits are usually exempt, at least to some extent.[409] And, under federal law, employees' ERISA pension funds are not generally subject to garnishment,[410] even for claims brought by the debtor's employer based on the employee's fraud.[411] Not surprisingly, though, pension and other retirement income remains subject to garnishment to pay support.[412]

Individual retirement accounts, on the other hand, are not widely protected by state exemption statutes.[413] However, in 2005 the Supreme Court resolved a dispute over whether funds in an Individual Retirement Account were covered by the exemption in § 522(d)(10) of the Bankruptcy Code, for bankrupt debtors. The decision in *Rousey v. Jacoway*[414] disappointed bankruptcy trustees who routinely invaded IRA funds to satisfy the claims of a bankrupt debtor's creditors. This decision is of limited applicability because most states have "opted out" of the federal exemptions contained in § 522(d), though notably New York State recently opted in. Furthermore, because state legislatures retain the right to prevent debtors in their state from using the Bankruptcy Code's exemption scheme, the *Jacoway* decision does not prevent state exemption statutes from taking a different and more limited approach, though it may yet have an influence on state exemption statues that use language similar to that in § 522(d)(10)(E).[415] In 2005, Congress amended the Bankruptcy Code expanding bankruptcy protection for funds in an IRA,[416] for debtors whose states have opted out of the federal scheme of bankruptcy exemptions.

---

[406] *E.g.*, Ohio Rev. Code Ann. § 2329.66(A)(9) (LexisNexis Supp. 2006); Bankruptcy Code § 522(d)(10).

[407] *E.g.*, Ohio Rev. Code § 2329.66(A)(12) (LexisNexis Supp. 2006); Bankruptcy Code § 522(d)(11).

[408] *E.g.*, Ohio Rev. Code § 2329.66(A)(6) (LexisNexis Supp. 2006); Bankruptcy Code § 522(d)(7) (any unmatured life insurance contract owned by a debtor, other than a credit life insurance contract).

[409] *E.g.*, Ohio Rev. Code Ann. § 2329.66(A)(10) (LexisNexis Supp. 2006); Bankruptcy Code § 522(d)(10)(E); Darrell Dunjam, *Pensions and Other Funds in Individual Bankruptcy Cases*, 4 Bankr. Dev. J. 293 (1987).

[410] General Motors Corp. v. Buha, 623 F.2d 455 (6th Cir. 1980). *See also* Patterson v. Shumate, 504 U.S. 753 (1992) (ERISA funds are not part of a debtor's bankruptcy estate).

[411] Guidry v. Sheet Metal Workers Nat'l Pension Fund, 493 U.S. 365 (1990).

[412] *See* 29 U.S.C. § 1056(d)(3) (2006).

[413] *But see* Ohio Rev. Code Ann. 2329.66(A)(10)(e) (LexisNexis Supp. 2006); In re Diguilio, 303 B.R. 144 (Bankr. N.D. Ohio, 2003).

[414] Rousey v. Jacoway, 544 U.S. 320 (2005).

[415] *See* Farrar v. McKown (In re McKown), 203 F.3d 1188, 1189-1190 & 1189 n.5 (9th Cir. 2000).

[416] *See infra* § 12.03[D][3] Retirement Funds.

[5]   Tracing Exemptions

A key issue with respect to exemptions is the extent to which a debtor may trace an exemption in property after it is converted into another form.[417] Without the ability to trace exemptions, a large share of the protection provided by exemption statutes might be lost. For example, if a debtor sold her exempt homestead so that she could purchase a smaller house, with a more affordable mortgage, tracing would advance the policy of the homestead exemption. On the other hand, once the debtor has converted exempt property into a form not deemed by the legislature to be necessary for financially troubled debtors, the reasons for protecting the property from seizure may dissipate.

Exemptions for wages supply the most obvious example of this problem. On the one hand, if the 75% of a debtor's wages that are exempt from garnishment under the Consumer Credit Protection Act lose their exemption after an employee deposits them into her bank account, the protection provided by the Act loses most of its force. On the other hand, if wages remain exempt regardless of the form in which the debtor holds them, 75% of all of a debtor's assets might remain exempt forever, effectively negating the effect of other limitations on the types of property that a debtor may exempt from her creditors.

Consider, for example, a debtor whose disposable earnings are $1,000 per week. The most a creditor could garnish from her employer is $250. The remaining $750 is exempt. If a creditor could seize the $750 from the debtor's bank account, and thus deprive the debtor of the ability to use them to meet her current living expenses, the principal benefit of the exemption will be lost: the debtor will not have the funds she needs to live. It seems clear that the wage exemption needs to be preserved, even after the debtor's wages have been deposited into a bank account, if the purpose of the wage exemption is to be fulfilled.

However, the value tracing cannot last indefinitely. If the debtor's wages remain exempt, after they have been used to purchase $750 of jewelry, worth more than the amount of the state's $250 jewelry exemption, the state's limit on the exempt amount of jewelry would lose its meaning. If the wage exemption were extended to these assets, the legislative purpose to limit exempt property to items reasonably necessary for the debtor to get along in life will have been frustrated.

Concern that the underlying purpose of wage exemption statutes would be frustrated if debtors were not permitted to trace their exemption after the property had been converted into an alternative form has led many courts to conclude that exempt wages do not lose their exempt status after they have been deposited into a bank account or some other liquid form in which they remain available for the debtor's ordinary living expenses. In *Daugherty v. Central Trust Co.*,[418] one state supreme court explained:

---

[417] The related issue, whether debtors should be permitted to convert non-exempt property into an exempt form on the eve of bankruptcy or attachment is discussed elsewhere. *See infra* § 12.02[E] Exemption Planning.

[418] 504 N.E.2d 1100 (Ohio 1986).

[t]he legislature's purpose, in exempting certain property from court action brought by creditors, was to protect funds intended primarily for maintenance and support of the debtor's family. . . . This legislative intent would be frustrated if exempt funds were automatically deprived of their statutory immunity when deposited in a checking account which a depositor commonly maintains in order to pay by check those regular subsistence expenses he incurs.[419]

However, in *In re Schoonover*,[420] another court denied a debtor the right to exempt $80,000 deposited in a bank account that was traceable to Social Security benefits. There, the court said:

[The state exemption statute] exempts "the debtor's right to receive" public benefits; it has nothing to do with funds on deposit long after their receipt and commingling with the debtor's other assets. Like the anti-alienation clauses in the federal benefits statutes themselves, this law ensures that recipients enjoy the minimum monthly income provided by the benefits laws; it does not entitle recipients to shield hoards of cash.[421]

As these decisions reflect, there is little consistency in the approaches taken by states. As with many other aspects of state debt collection law, decisions in individual states need to be closely examined before one can draw any conclusions about the governing principles in that state.

[B]   Other Property Immune from Creditors' Claims[422]

Apart from property declared by the legislature as exempt, some types of property are, by there very nature, immune from creditors. Usually this is due to restrictions imposed by state law on the free transferability of the assets in question.[423] If the debtor is not free to transfer the property, her creditors are unable to seize it. Such assets primarily include spendthrift trusts and property held in a tenancy by the entirety.

[1]   Spendthrift Trusts[424]

A spendthrift trust is a trust in which the beneficiary cannot transfer the corpus (or "res") of the trust, or her right to future payments of income from the trust. This non-transferability is accomplished through language in the documents that create the trust, which manifest the intent of the person who originally contributed funds to the trust.[425] Because the beneficiary lacks the power to transfer these rights,

---

[419] 504 N.E.2d at 1103.

[420] 331 F.3d 575 (7th Cir. 2003).

[421] 331 F.3d at 577.

[422] Edward C. Halbach, Jr., *Creditors' Rights in Future Interests*, 43 Minn. L. Rev. 217 (1958); William T. Plumb, *The Recommendations of the Commission on the Bankruptcy Laws: Exempt and Immune Property*, 61 Va. L. Rev. 1, 77 (1975).

[423] *E.g.*, N.Y. Civ. Prac. Law § 5201 (McKinney Supp. 2006).

[424] Note, *Creditors' Rights Against Trust Assets*, 22 Real Prop., Prob. and Tr. J. 735 (1987).

[425] *E.g.*, McColgan v. Walter Magee, Inc., 155 P. 995, 997 (1916) ("[T]he donor has the right to give

they cannot be reached by the beneficiary's creditors.

Once the trustee has distributed funds from the trust to the beneficiary and the beneficiary acquires the full right to transfer the funds she has received, they become vulnerable to creditors' claims, unless, of course, they fit into an exempt category.

This immunity does not usually extend to funds contributed to the trust by the trust's beneficiary. Most state laws do not generally recognize the enforceability of transfer restrictions on what are called "self-settled" trusts.[426] Accordingly, "self-settled trusts" usually remain vulnerable to the claims of creditors.[427] This is not surprising. If it were otherwise, debtors could protect their assets from seizure by their creditors through the simple expedient of transferring the assets to a trust maintained for the debtor's own benefit. Funds transferred to a spendthrift trust by the debtor's rich relative are protected, but funds the debtor deposits herself are not. Despite this general rule, a handful of states have enacted spendthrift trust statutes that permit the settlor to also be a beneficiary, without depriving the trust of its spendthrift characteristics.[428] Whether these trusts will stand up to a challenge in bankruptcy remains to be seen.

There is an exception to this restriction on the immunity of self-settled trusts. Most pension plans are designed to qualify for favorable tax treatment under the federal Employee Retirement Income Security Act (ERISA).[429] ERISA-qualified pension plans frequently contain funds that were contributed by the employees for whose benefit the pension trusts were created. If the normal state rules regarding self-settled trusts applied, these retirement funds would be vulnerable to the claims of an employee's creditors. However, ERISA's preemptive effect makes the anti-alienation provisions of an ERISA qualified pension trust[430] immune from the claims of creditors, despite the limitations of state law that otherwise would render them vulnerable to those claims.

The full impact of ERISA's pre-emptive effect was recognized in *Patterson v. Shumate*,[431] where the Supreme Court ruled that the spendthrift trust restrictions in an ERISA-qualified pension plan prevented funds in such a plan from becoming part of the employee's bankruptcy estate. *Patterson*'s holding, as well as the ERISA preemption of state law restrictions on self-settled trusts upon which it was based, depends on the retirement plan's compliance with ERISA's strict restrictions.[432] Funds contained in retirement plans that fall outside the scope of ERISA's protection remain vulnerable to the claims of creditors, except to the extent they are

---

his property to another upon any conditions which he sees fit to impose.").

[426] *E.g.*, In re Spenlinhauer, 182 B.R. 361 (Bankr. D. Me. 1995).

[427] *See, e.g.*, Cal. Civ. Proc. Code § 704.115 (West Supp. 2006).

[428] *See*, Stewart E. Sterk, *Asset Protection Trusts: Trust Law's Race to the Bottom?*, 85 Cornell L. Rev. 1035, 1042 (2000).

[429] 29 U.S.C. §§ 1001-1461 (2006).

[430] 29 U.S.C. § 1056(d)(1) (2006).

[431] 504 U.S. 753 (1992).

[432] The details of ERISA's requirements are far outside the scope of this work. *See generally* Charles E. Falk, Patterson v. Shumate: *A Five Year Legacy*, 9 BNA's Bankr. L. Rptr. 743 (1997).

protected by an express exemption statute.

[2] Tenancies by the Entirety[433]

As a general rule, property held in common by two or more people is just as vulnerable to the claims of creditors as any other type of property. An important exception to this general rule protects property owned by married couples in a "tenancy by the entirety."[434] Only about twenty-five states continue to recognize tenancies by the entirety, but those that do generally prevent a creditor of only one spouse from reaching that spouse's share in property jointly owned with the other spouse in a tenancy by the entirety.[435] This result is due to the legal fiction that a husband and wife, as a couple, are one person, distinct from either spouse individually.[436] Because the property is owned by the couple as a single entity, it is vulnerable only to claims of creditors of both spouses.

Thus, entireties property owned by Dave and Kathy Morris may not be taken to satisfy a claim of a creditor of only Dave. If Dave owes a debt for which Kathy is not liable, neither the entireties property as a whole, nor either of their interests in the entireties property is vulnerable to the creditor's claim. This effectively makes the property exempt from everyone except creditors to whom Dave and Kathy are jointly liable. If Dave and Kathy were both responsible for the debt, the entireties property could be taken to satisfy the creditor's claim.

Most lenders, in states that respect tenancy by the entirety, know about this rule, and will not advance funds to either Dave or Kathy without getting both of them to agree to repay the debt, at least where there are significant joint assets. But, unsophisticated lenders, like family members, might not realize the need to do this. And tort claimants, who don't have the opportunity to negotiate the terms of their claims, might also find themselves unable to seize any of the couple's joint assets that are held as entireties property.

Federal tax liens are an important exception to this rule. The Federal Tax Lien Act imposes a federal tax lien "upon all property and rights to property, whether real or personal, belonging to [the taxpayer]."[437] The United States Supreme Court has interpreted this language to make an interest in entireties property subject to a tax lien imposed on the property, even though one spouse was not liable for the

---

[433] Patrick J. Concannon, Note, *Bankruptcy and the Tenancy by the Entirety Property: Its Treatment under the Code and in the Courts*, 58 UMKC L. Rev. 501 (1990). *See* Steven R. Johnson, *After Drye: The Likely Attachment of the Federal Tax Lien to Tenancy-by-the-Entireties Interests*, 75 Ind. L.J. 1163 (2000);William H. Baker, *Drye and Craft — How Two Wrongs Can Make a Property Right*, 64 U. Pitt. L. Rev. 745 (2003); Lawrence Kalevitch, *Some Thoughts on Entireties in Bankruptcy*, 60 Am. Bankr. L.J. 141 (1986); Benjamin C. Ackerly, *Tenants by the Entirety Property and the Bankruptcy Reform Act*, 21 Wm. & Mary L. Rev. 701 (1980).

[434] 7 Richard R. Powell & Michael Allan Wolf, Powell on Real Property § 52.03[3] (2006).

[435] *E.g.,* In re Hutchins, 306 B.R. 82 (Bankr. D. Vt. 2004); In re Cross, 255 B.R. 25 (Bankr. N.D. Ind. 2000).

[436] *See* John V. Orth, *Tenancy by the Entirety: The Strange Career of the Common-Law Marital Estate*, 1997 B.Y.U. L. Rev. 35; William Blackstone, 2 Commentaries *179.

[437] 26 U.S.C. § 6321 (2006).

unpaid tax.[438] In other words, the preemptive effect of federal law trumps the traditional limitation on the exposure of entireties property to creditors' claims. Using the above example, if Dave owed a federal tax for which Kathy was not liable, his interest in the entireties property would be subject to a federal tax lien imposed on his property. Kathy's interest in the property could not be taken, but the government could recover the tax from Dave's interest just as it could recover any undivided interest in property held by joint tenants or tenants in common.

§ 2.12 SURETYSHIP

A "surety" is someone who is obligated to pay a debt incurred by someone else.[439] For example, if when their son Hunter borrows money to buy a car on credit from Hybrid Motors, and his parents, Scott and Cindy promise Hybrid that they will pay Hunter's debt if Hunter doesn't pay, Scott and Cindy are sureties for Hunter's debt.[440] A surety is sometimes called a "guarantor,"[441] a "secondary obligor," or "an accommodation party,"[442] or more colloquially (and less precisely), a "cosigner." Obtaining a surety is an alternative method to ensure payment, which can supplement or substitute for a consensual lien on the debtor's property.

In a business context, the owners of a corporation might guarantee a debt owed by the company they operate.[443] Or, a commercial surety, who is in the business of providing guarantees in exchange for a fee, may provide a payment or performance bond.[444] Such bonds are customarily supplied in the construction industry. These commercial sureties act, in effect, as insurers.

---

[438] United States v. Craft, 535 U.S. 274 (2002).

[439] Laurence P. Simpson, Handbook on the Law of Suretyship § 4 (1950). *See* Restatement (Third) of Suretyship and Guaranty § 1(a) (1996).

[440] Federal Trade Commission rules requires certain disclosures be made to consumer sureties. Michael J. Herbert, *Straining the Gnat: A Critique of the 1984 Federal Trade Commission Consumer Credit Regulations*, 38 S.C. L. Rev. 329, 355-59 (1987).

[441] Much has been made of the difference between a "surety" and a "guarantor." Although the terms are often used interchangeably, a surety is usually jointly and severally liable with the principal obligor, while a guarantor's liability is not usually triggered until the principal obligor has defaulted. Restatement (Third) of Suretyship and Guaranty § 1 cmt. c (1996).

[442] *See* U.C.C. § 3-419 (2010).

[443] *E.g.*, State Bank v. Owens, 502 P.2d 965 (Colo. Ct. App. 1972).

[444] For example, as part of the inducement by a general contractor to persuade the owner to agree to hire the contractor to build a structure that the owner wishes to erect on his property, the contractor might pay a fee to a surety company who will agree to pay all of the subcontractors and suppliers who contribute to the project, in the event the general contractor fails to pay them. This type of "payment bond" protects the owner against the risk that payments she makes to the contractor will not be distributed to these participants in the project. In this situation, the surety company is a secondary obligor on the general's contractual duty to pay the subcontractors and suppliers. *See* Restatement (Third) of Suretyship and Guaranty § 1 illus. 1 (1996).

[A] Basic Suretyship Principles

Suretyship transactions involve three parties: the principal debtor, the creditor, and the surety. Assume, for example, that Titanic Industries, Inc. borrowed $100,000 from North Atlantic Finance Co. Assume further that Harland Wolff, the sole shareholder of Titanic Industries, guaranteed payment by the corporation. Titanic Industries is the principal debtor, North Atlantic Finance Co. is the creditor, and Harland Wolff is the surety. Similarly, when Scott and Cindy guaranteed Hunter's debt to Hybrid Motors, Hunter was the principal debtor, Hybrid Motors was the creditor, and Scott and Cindy were the sureties.

Suretyship transactions involve several separate contracts. The first contract is the one between the creditor and the principal debtor; it is sometimes referred to as the "underlying obligation."[445] This is illustrated by Titanic Industries' agreement with North Atlantic Finance and Hunter's agreement with Hybrid Motors.

The second contract is between the surety and the creditor: Scott & Cindy's promise to Hybrid Motors, and Harland Wolff's promise to North Atlantic Finance. This is the suretyship contract, in which the surety makes a promise directly *to the creditor* to satisfy the principal debtor's obligation.

The suretyship agreement may take one of several forms. For example, the surety may "cosign" the agreement entered into between the creditor and the principal debtor, agreeing to perform the same obligation as that of the principal debtor. Alternatively, the surety might enter into a separate suretyship agreement with the creditor, promising performance if the principal debtor fails to perform the underlying obligation.[446] Under most versions of the statute of frauds, the surety's promise to the creditor must be in writing.[447]

The third contract is the express or implied promise of the principal debtor to reimburse the surety for any amounts that the surety pays to the creditor.[448] The surety's right of reimbursement makes the surety a contingent creditor of the principal debtor, even before the surety has been called upon to perform its obligation. Thus, a shareholder who has guaranteed a debt owed by the corporation has a contingent claim against the corporation. And, Scott & Cindy, if they want to, have the right to recover from Hunter for any amounts they pay to Hybrid Motors. In the principal debtor's bankruptcy case, this contingent obligation is a "claim" against the debtor's estate.[449]

There are several varieties of agreements a surety might make. The normal obligation of a surety is to "guaranty payment." If the suretyship contract uses the word "guaranty" without any further limitation, the contract is normally construed to be a guaranty of payment. This means the creditor may pursue the guarantor as

---

[445] *See* Restatement (Third) of Suretyship and Guaranty § 1 cmt. d (1996).

[446] *See* Restatement (Third) of Suretyship and Guaranty § 1 cmt. g (1996).

[447] *E.g.*, Carey & Assoc. v. Ernst, 810 N.Y.S.2d 475 (N.Y. App. Div. 2006) (adult child's oral promise to pay parent's legal fees).

[448] Restatement (Third) of Suretyship and Guaranty § 22 (1996).

[449] Bankruptcy Code § 101(5).

soon as the obligation is due, without having to first obtain a judgment against the principal.[450] Alternatively, a surety may merely "guaranty collection." When collection is guaranteed, the creditor in most cases must sue the principal and attempt to collect the debt from the principal's assets before pursuing the surety.[451] Finally, a surety may become an "accommodation party," within the meaning of the Uniform Commercial Code,[452] by signing a promissory note or other negotiable instrument, made by the debtor, usually either as a co-maker or as an endorser of the note. An accommodation maker's contract is much like that of a guarantor of payment. If the debt is not paid when due, the accommodation maker may be sued immediately, without any prior recourse against the principal.[453] If the surety signs as an accommodation endorser, he will be liable only after the note is presented to and dishonored by the principal debtor as maker of the note.

In any event, it is important to stress that in each of these situations, the surety has a claim for full reimbursement from the principal. By contrast, the principal has no right of contribution or indemnification against the surety. The principal was supposed to pay the debt; if the principal does not do so, and the surety pays, the surety is entitled to attempt to collect the debt it has paid, from the principal debtor.[454]

In addition, a surety who pays the creditor obtains whatever rights the creditor originally had against the principal debtor under the doctrine of "equitable subrogation."[455] If the creditor held a security interest in the principal debtor's property and the surety pays the debt to the creditor, the surety is subrogated to the creditor's rights in the collateral. Thus, the surety's right to reimbursement will be secured to the same extent as the claim of the original creditor.

[B] Suretyship Defenses

Sureties have a variety of potential defenses. They are usually based on the creditor's conduct either in its dealings with the principal debtor or with any collateral for the debt.

[1] Surety's Use of Principal's Defenses

A surety can assert most of the defenses that the principal debtor could have raised against the creditor. The most important exceptions are debtor's incapacity or discharge of the principal debtor in bankruptcy.[456] Since incapacity and discharge in bankruptcy are among the risks that led the creditor to obtain a surety

---

[450] Laurence P. Simpson, Handbook on the Law of Suretyship § 6 (1950).

[451] Laurence P. Simpson, Handbook on the Law of Suretyship § 6 (1950).

[452] U.C.C. § 3-419(a) (2010).

[453] U.C.C. §§ 3-419(b), 3-412 (2010).

[454] Laurence P. Simpson, Handbook on the Law of Suretyship §§ 47-48 (1950).

[455] Restatement (Third) of Suretyship and Guaranty § 27 (1996); Laurence P. Simpson, Handbook on the Law of Suretyship § 47 (1950). See, e.g., In re Modern Textile, Inc., 900 F.2d 1184 (8th Cir. 1990).

[456] See U.C.C. § 3-305(d) (2010).

in the first place, a surety may not use the incapacity or bankruptcy of the principal debtor as a defense.[457] Thus, if Scott and Cindy promise Hybrid Motors that they will pay Hunter's debt in the event of his default, they cannot assert Hunter's status as a minor or his discharge in bankruptcy as a defense, even though these defenses are available to Hunter.

[2] Creditor's Impairment of the Collateral

If the guaranteed debt is secured, any action of the creditor that impairs the collateral discharges the surety to the extent of the impairment.[458] Collateral may be impaired in several ways, including failing to perfect or maintain the perfection of the security interest, releasing the collateral from the security interest without acquiring an adequate substitute, or acting negligently in any other way that reduces the value of the collateral.[459]

Discharging the surety makes sense in these situations, particularly when considered in light of the surety's right of subrogation to the creditor's rights. If the creditor impairs the value of collateral supplied by the principal debtor, the surety's right to be subrogated to the creditor's security interest in the collateral would be prejudiced. This would expose the surety to a risk he thought he had avoided when he agreed to become a surety.

Consider, an agreement by Kathy & Dave to serve as sureties for Friendly Finance Company's auto loan made to their son, Isaac. When the loan is made, Friendly Finance obtains a purchase money security interest in Isaac's new car but fails to take all of the steps necessary to perfect it. If Isaac defaults and files a bankruptcy petition, Friendly Finance would normally be able to recover the amount of the unpaid balance from Kathy and Dave. In turn, Kathy and Dave would normally be able to assert their right of subrogation and enforce the finance company's security interest in the car. But, because the security interest is unperfected, Isaac's bankruptcy trustee will be able to avoid the security interest and recover the non-exempt value of the car for the benefit of all of Isaac's creditors. The finance company's failure to perfect its security interest leaves Kathy and Dave with no recourse. Isaac's debt to them was discharged in bankruptcy, and the security interest in his car was avoided by the trustee. As a result, Kathy and Dave are relieved of their liability to the finance company, at least to the extent of the value of the car.[460]

---

[457] *E.g.*, Murphy v. Bank of Dahlonega, 259 S.E.2d 670 (Ga. Ct. App. 1979).

[458] Restatement (Third) of Suretyship and Guaranty § 42 (1996). *See* U.C.C. § 3-605(d) & cmt. 7 (2010).

[459] Restatement (Third) of Suretyship and Guaranty § 42 (1996). *See* U.C.C. § 3-605(d) & cmt. 7 (2010).

[460] *See* Restatement (Third) of Suretyship And Guaranty § 42 (1996); U.C.C. § 3-605(d) (2010).

[3] Release of the Principal Debtor

A creditor may find it useful to enter into a composition or other agreement that releases the principal debtor from all or part of the outstanding balance of a debt.[461] The debtor may offer to make a partial or early payment of the creditor's claim, in exchange for release from the remainder of his liability. The creditor, concerned about the likelihood of receiving any payment from the debtor, is likely to agree to the proposed compromise.

The traditional rule was that a creditor's release of the principal debtor had an effect similar to the creditor's impairment of the collateral: the surety was discharged. However, savvy creditors could avoid discharge of the surety by following a strict set of rules that permitted them to "reserve the rights" of the surety against the principal debtor and thus avoid losing their own right to recover from the surety any portion of the debt left unpaid by the principal debtor.

However, these rules are now in transition. It has been recognized that little was achieved by insisting on the formal requirements of "reserving rights." Institutional creditors nearly always take the steps necessary to avoid discharge of the surety, leaving only inexperienced lenders — usually family members — to be tripped up by their willingness to enter into compromise agreements with the principal debtor. Today, a creditor's release of the principal debtor discharges the surety's obligation to the same extent that the principal debtor's obligation was discharged.[462]

Thus, if Commerce Bank enters into an agreement with Titanic Industries, Inc., releasing Titanic from $20,000 of its $100,000 debt in exchange for an immediate cash payment of $10,000 and an increase in the interest rate on the remaining $70,000, the guarantor of the company's debt, Harland Wolff, will also be released from $20,000 of his liability. Of course, Commerce Bank might refuse to release Titanic unless Wolff agrees to waive his right to be released, but whether the bank is able to elicit this agreement will depend on how desperate it is to receive the $10,000 cash payment and the increase in the applicable interest rate that Titanic is offering.

[4] Time Extension

The effect of a creditor's agreement to extend the due date of the principal debtor's obligation is somewhat different from the effect of the creditor's release of the principal debtor. A time extension may harm the surety, such as where the debtor is solvent at the time of the extension but later becomes insolvent. However, the most common reason for creditors to grant a debtor additional time is that the debtor is already unable to pay, but anticipates a better financial condition in the future. If this is the case, granting an extension to the debtor would have no adverse effect on the surety's likelihood of recovery from the debtor.

Because of this, time extensions granted to the principal debtor discharge a surety only if the surety is able to prove that the extension caused the surety to

---

[461] *See supra* § 2.10 Compositions and Workouts.

[462] Restatement (Third) of Suretyship and Guaranty § 39(b) (1996); U.C.C. § 3-605(a)(2) & cmt. 4 (2010).

suffer a loss.[463] The burden of proof lies with the surety. On the other hand, if the principal debtor receives a time extension, the surety also enjoys the benefit of the extension and is not obligated to pay the debt until the extended due date.[464]

[5] Other Modifications

Other modifications, apart from releases, time extensions, and impairments of the collateral, such as changes in the interest rate, modifications of the conditions of default, or alterations of the schedule of payments (other than the ultimate date of maturity), also discharge the surety to the extent the surety can prove that the modification of the terms binding the principal debtor resulted in a loss to the surety.[465] As with time extensions, the surety's obligation is modified to the same extent as the principal debtor's obligation.[466]

[C] Suretyship Issues in Bankruptcy

There are several important suretyship issues in bankruptcy. The first regards creditors' rights against bankrupt sureties. Ordinarily, a claim of a creditor against a bankrupt surety will be a general unsecured claim. However, if the surety has supplied its own collateral for the obligation, the creditor's claim against the surety is secured to the extent of the value of the collateral. Rules discharging the surety due to the creditor's impairment of collateral supplied by someone against whom the surety has a claim of reimbursement do not apply when it was the surety who provided the collateral.

Second, because of their right of reimbursement, sureties who have paid the principal debtor's obligation have claims against the estate of a bankrupt principal debtor. Ordinarily the surety's claim for indemnification against a bankrupt principal enjoys the same status as the creditor's claim. If the creditor's claim was a general unsecured claim, the surety's claim is unsecured. If the creditor had a security interest in the debtor's property, the surety is subrogated to the creditor's security interest and has a secured claim to the extent the creditor's claim was secured.

Third, a potential problem arises when the surety has not yet satisfied the creditor's claim when the debtor's bankruptcy petition is filed. In that case, the surety's claim remains "contingent." It is contingent on the surety's actual satisfaction of the creditor's claim. Placing a value on contingent claims, particularly for the purposes of voting on a Chapter 11 plan, is sometimes difficult.[467]

Finally, questions sometimes arise regarding the extent of protection that should be provided to sureties while the principal debtor's bankruptcy case is pending. As a general rule, the bankruptcy of the principal debtor has no effect on

---

[463] Restatement (Third) of Suretyship and Guaranty § 40 (1996); U.C.C. § 3-605(b) & cmt. 5 (2010).

[464] Restatement (Third) of Suretyship and Guaranty § 40 (1996); U.C.C. § 3-605(b)(1) & cmt. 5 (2010).

[465] Restatement (Third) of Suretyship and Guaranty § 41 (1996); U.C.C. § 3-605(c) & cmt. 6 (2010).

[466] Restatement (Third) of Suretyship and Guaranty § 41 (1996); U.C.C. § 3-605(c) & cmt. 6 (2010).

[467] *See infra* § 10.02[C][4] Contingent & Unliquidated Claims.

the right of the creditor to sue the surety. Indeed, bankruptcy is one of the reasons why the creditor required a surety in the first place. However, in Chapter 12 and 13 cases, actions against some sureties are automatically stayed while the bankruptcy case is pending.[468] The court has some discretion to order a similar injunction when these automatic stay rules do not apply.[469] For example, in reorganization cases an injunction can sometimes be obtained restraining the creditor from pursuing a surety for payment until after the debtor's Chapter 11 plan has been confirmed and the case has been closed. Once confirmed, the plan itself might also affect creditor's rights to collect from those who have served as sureties for the principal debtor.[470]

§ 2.13   SUPPLEMENTAL COLLECTION PROCEEDINGS

[A]   Discovery: Examination of a Judgment Debtor

Before a creditor obtains a judgment on the underlying merits of its claim, information about the debtor's assets is usually beyond the permissible scope of discovery. However, once a judgment is obtained, discovery of this information becomes fair game.

State laws permit a judgment creditor to depose the debtor. Such a deposition is usually referred to as a "debtor's exam" or an "examination of a judgment debtor."[471] One such statute provides:

> A judgment creditor shall be entitled to an order for the examination of a judgment debtor concerning his property, income, or other means of satisfying the judgment upon proof by affidavit that such judgment is unpaid in whole or in part. Such order shall be issued by a probate judge or a judge of the court of common pleas in the county in which the judgment was rendered or in which the debtor resides, requiring such debtor to appear and answer concerning his property before such judge, or a referee appointed by him, at a time and place within the county to be specified in the order.[472]

A recalcitrant debtor may be compelled to provide sworn testimony about the nature, extent, and location of her assets.[473] The examination is under oath, and debtors who lie about their assets may be prosecuted for perjury. Even though

---

[468] *E.g.*, Bankruptcy Code § 1302.

[469] Bankruptcy Code §§ 1201 & 1301. *See infra* § 8.04 Co-Debtor Stay in Chapters 12 and 13.

[470] *See infra* § 8.05 Discretionary Stays.

[471] The word "examination" is not completely misleading. Sometimes debtors have the same difficulty in remembering what assets they own as students have in remembering, when questioned by their teachers, the material they were supposed to have studied the night before.

[472] *E.g.*, Ohio Rev. Code Ann. § 2333.09 (LexisNexis 2005); NY. C.P.L.R. § 5223 (McKinney 1997); Cal Civ Proc. Code § 708.020 (West 2006) (written interrogatories); Cal. Civ. Proc. Code § 708.110 (West. Supp. 2006) (oral debtor's exam).

[473] *See* Byron Originals, Inc. v. Iron Bay Model Co., 2006 U.S. Dist. LEXIS 35545 (N.D. W. Va. April 12, 2006) (providing a detailed list of questions commonly asked at a judgment debtor's exam).

prosecutions are extremely rare, the implied threat of jail induces most debtors to tell the truth.[474]

Upon disclosure of the existence and location of the debtor's assets, it may be possible to seize them immediately. Your authors have heard of one young lawyer who was told by his supervising partner: "Ask the debtor 'how did you get to the court?' When he answers 'In my car,' ask the judge to order him to hand over the keys."[475] However, most of the time, creditors use information they obtain from the debtor through this process to facilitate collection through the normal mechanisms of attachment and garnishment. Procedures also exist for obtaining the testimony of third persons who are in possession of the debtor's property[476] or who may have information regarding the nature and location of the debtor's property.[477]

[B]   Contempt Sanctions

Debtors who fail to cooperate with court ordered proceedings to locate their assets may be held in contempt for failing to obey the court's instructions. For example, Article 9 security agreements commonly require a defaulting debtor to assist the secured party in assembling the collateral.[478] If the debtor refuses to comply, the secured party may be able to get a court order for specific performance of the debtor's promise. Further refusal then becomes civil contempt; a court may order the debtor to pay a fine. If the debtor commits criminal contempt, she may go to jail. Imprisonment for contempt does not violate prohibitions against imprisonment for debt, because the imprisonment is not on account of the unpaid debt, but for contemptuous refusal to obey the court's order.

§ 2.14   COMMON LAW AND STATUTORY RESTRICTIONS ON CREDITORS' COLLECTION EFFORTS

Overly aggressive creditors can be liable to the debtor as a result of belligerent actions. Creditors have been liable to debtors from whom they were trying to collect for committing a number of garden-variety torts, such as fraud, defamation, intentional infliction of emotional distress, or invasion of privacy. In addition, several "lender-liability" cases have held creditors liable for taking precipitous action to accelerate a debt or to terminate a line of credit that the debtor was relying on to operate its business. Some states have enacted legislation directed at creditors'

---

[474] The creditor conducting the examination must, of course, ask the right questions. Professors Lynn LoPucki and Elizabeth Warren describe the story of a defendant with $10,000 cash in his pocket who truthfully denied having any cash available in his house, his car, his office, the bank, or with his broker, and walked out of the debtor's exam having never been asked: "How much cash do you have with you here today?" Lynn M. LoPucki & Elizabeth Warren, Secured Credit: A Systems Approach 13-14 (4th ed. 2003).

[475] The practical utility of this maneuver depends on whether the auto is already encumbered by the claim of a secured creditor and the extent to which the debtor's equity is exempt. Moreover, the keys will not be nearly so helpful as the certificate of title to the car.

[476] Cal. Civ. Proc. Code § 708.120 (West Supp. 2006).

[477] Cal. Civ. Proc. Code § 708.130 (West 1987).

[478] See U.C.C. § 9-609(c) (2010).

overly aggressive out-of-court collection tactics. Likewise, there are federal restrictions on some of the most egregious activities of debt collectors, and on the activities of credit-reporting agencies and their customers.

[A]   Common Law Tort Liability[479]

Creditors naturally have the right to take reasonable action to pursue debtors and collect the debts they owe.[480] However, creditors' informal collection methods sometimes go beyond the bounds of reason. When this happens, the roles of the parties can reverse, with the debtor obtaining a judgment against the creditor for its out-of-bounds conduct. For example, in *Household Credit Services, Inc. v. Driscoll*,[481] a collection agency, acting as the creditor's agent, persistently called the debtor at home, frequently at odd hours, used abusive language including "f***" and "b**ch," told her that he had "put a contract out" on her, and called in bomb threats to her employer. In her claim against the creditor, for "unreasonable debt collection, gross negligence, intentional infliction of emotional distress, invasion of privacy" and for violations of the Fair Debt Collection Practice Act, the jury awarded her $11,697,059.35, less the $2875 in principal and interest that she owed the creditor on her unpaid VISA Account. Still, as described below, debtors face considerable hurdles in trying to find creditors liable for traditional tort claims, based on their informal efforts to collect, without going to court.

[1]   Invasion of Privacy[482]

Courts sometimes impose liability on creditors for invading a debtor's privacy.[483] To establish a claim for invasion of privacy, a debtor must show that the creditor went beyond the reasonable steps that a creditor may take to persuade the debtor to pay. Creditors' attempts to collect may result in some intrusion on the debtor's privacy;[484] liability attaches only if the intrusions were unreasonable.

Unreasonable intrusion occurs as a result of harassing phone calls, particularly when made frequently, at all hours of the day and night, or to the debtor's friends,

---

[479] Michael M. Greenfield, *Coercive Collection Tactics — An Analysis of the Interests and the Remedies*, 1972 Wash U. L.Q. 1; Charles E. Hurt, *Debt Collection Torts*, 67 W. Va. L. Rev. 201 (1965); Arthur Allen Leff, *Injury, Ignorance and Spite — The Dynamics of Coercive Collection*, 80 Yale L.J. 1 (1970); Robert E. Scott, *Rethinking the Regulation of Coercive Creditor Remedies*, 89 Colum. L. Rev. 730 (1989); Myron M. Sheinfeld, *Current Trends in the Restriction of Creditors' Collection Activities*, 9 Hous. L. Rev. 615 (1972); William C. Whitford, *A Critique of the Consumer Credit Collection System*, 1979 Wis. L. Rev. 1047.

[480] *E.g.*, Housh v. Peth, 133 N.E.2d 340, 340-41 (Ohio 1956); Jacksonville State Bank v. Barnwell, 481 So. 2d 863, 865-66 (Ala. 1985).

[481] 989 S.W.2d 72 (Tex. Ct. App. 1998).

[482] *See generally* Samuel D. Warren & Louis D. Brandeis, *The Right to Privacy*, 4 Harv. L. Rev. 193 (1890).

[483] *See* Jeffrey F. Ghent, Annotation, *Unsolicited Mailing, Distribution, House Call, or Telephone Call as Invasion of Privacy*, 56 A.L.R.3d 457 (1974); J.L. Litwin, Annotation, *Public Disclosure of Person's Indebtedness as Invasion of Privacy*, 33 A.L.R.3d 154 (1970).

[484] *E.g.*, Sears, Roebuck & Co. v. Moten, 558 P.2d 954 (Ariz. 1976); Household Finance Corp. v. Bridge, 250 A.2d 878 (Md. 1969); Gouldman Taber Pontiac, Inc. v. Zerbst, 100 S.E.2d 881 (Ga. 1957).

relatives, neighbors, or employer.[485] For example, in *Jacksonville State Bank v. Barnwell*,[486] a creditor who made several dozen phone calls to both the debtor's home and to his place of employment was characterized as having engaged in a "'systematic campaign of harassment,'" which, when combined with its use of "unequivocally coarse, inflammatory, malicious, and threatening language" at the debtor's place of employment, left the creditor liable for invading the debtor's privacy.[487]

In addition, creditors may become liable due to their unreasonable disclosure of private information about the debtor or regarding their claim against him.[488] For example, in *Biederman's of Springfield, Inc. v. Wright*, a creditor was liable for invasion of the debtor's privacy because one of its agents complained loudly in a public restaurant about the debtor's failure to pay.[489] Similarly, in *Mason v. Williams Discount Center, Inc.*, a publicly posted list of customers from whom the creditor would not accept checks was actionable as an invasion of the debtor's privacy.[490] In *Voneye v. Turner*,[491] the creditor, a debt collector acting before enactment of the Fair Debt Collection Practices Act (FDCPA), went further, but escaped liability for invasion of privacy. One of its representatives called the debtor's employer to disclose the status of the debt. Although the court pointed out that public disclosure of a private fact may constitute invasion of the right to privacy, it found that communications from a debt collector to an employer are acceptable disclosures; people who do not pay their debts are protected only from undue or oppressive publicity. Decisions like *Voneye* are among those that prompted Congress to enact the FDCPA.

---

[485] Malcom E. Calkins, Comment, *The Debtor v. Creditor Dilemma: When Does a Creditor's Communication With the Debtor Employer Result in an Actionable Invasion of Privacy?*, 10 Tulsa L.J. 231 (1974).

[486] 481 So. 2d 863 (Ala. 1985).

[487] *See also* Fernandez v. United Acceptance Corp., 610 P.2d 461 (Ariz. Ct. App. 1980) (creditor's agent threatened repossession without lawful right to do so and placed large number of telephone calls to debtor's place of employment and to debtor's neighbors); Housh v. Peth, 135 N.E.2d 440 (Ohio Ct. App.), *affirmed* 133 N.E.2d 340 (Ohio 1956) (systematic campaign of harassment, involving phone calls at all hours of the day and night to the debtor and to her employer).

[488] A convenience store, where your co-authors have sometimes stopped for refreshment in the middle of a veloconference (bike ride), regularly posts notices in the window with the names of several customers advising them to "come in and pick up your bounced checks." However, because neither of us has a license to practice law in the jurisdiction in which these signs appear, and we do not wish to wear out our welcome in this establishment, we have refrained from offering unsolicited legal advice about the potential liability associated with the sign. *See* Restatement (Second) of Torts § 652D, illus. 2 (1977).

[489] 322 S.W.2d 892 (Mo. 1959).

[490] 639 S.W.2d 836 (Mo. Ct. App. 1982). *See also* Brents v. Morgan, 299 S.W. 967 (Ky. 1927) (store listed debtors on a 5' × 8' sign in the window).

[491] 240 S.W.2d 588 (Ky. 1951).

[2] Intentional Infliction of Emotional Distress[492]

Creditors' overly aggressive conduct may result in liability under a theory of intentional infliction of emotional distress,[493] also sometimes called "outrage."[494] To establish a claim of intentional infliction of emotional distress, the debtor must establish four elements: (1) the conduct of defendant must be intentional or in reckless disregard of the plaintiff; (2) the conduct must be extreme and outrageous; (3) there must be a causal connection between defendant's conduct and plaintiff's mental distress; and (4) plaintiff's mental distress must be extreme and severe.[495]

Creditors' persistent efforts to persuade debtors to make additional payments are sometimes annoying, but they rarely rise to the level necessary either to constitute extreme and outrageous behavior[496] or to result in the type of extreme and severe emotional distress that the debtor must suffer from to have a claim for intentional infliction of emotional distress.

[3] Fraud

Creditors sometimes lie to a debtor as part of their efforts to persuade him to pay. Creditors who threaten action that they do not intend to take may be liable for fraud.[497] And, not surprisingly, creditors who unilaterally alter the language of their agreement with the debtor, in an attempt to remedy deficiencies in the documents memorializing their contract, are also liable for fraud.[498] Needless to say, attorneys who advance collection strategies based on this type of dishonorable behavior, with the knowledge of their client's dishonest conduct, run the risk of professional sanction, and also of committing violations of the Federal Fair Debt Collection Practices Act which exposes them to their own personal liability.[499]

---

[492] Michael M. Greenfield, *Coercive Collection Tactics — An Analysis of the Interests and Remedies*, 1972 Wash. U. L.Q. 1, 23; A.J.C., Comment, *Intentional Infliction of Mental Stress Within Debtor-Creditor Relationships*, 37 Alb. L. Rev. 797 (1973); Allan E. Korpela, Annotation, *Recovery for Emotional Distress or its Physical Consequences Caused by Attempts to Collect Debt Owed by Third Party*, 46 A.L.R.3d 772 (1972); Joel E. Smith, Annotation, *Recovery By Debtor, Under Tort of Intentional or Reckless Infliction of Emotional Distress, for Damages Resulting from Debt Collection Methods*, 87 A.L.R.3d 201 (1978).

[493] *See* Restatement (Second) of Torts § 46 & cmt. 3 (1976). *See, e.g.*, Champlin v. Wash. Trust Co., 478. A.2d 985 (R.I. 1984); Hamilton v. Ford Motor Credit Co., 502 A.2d 1057 (Md. Ct. Spec. App. 1986); Sherman v. Field Clinic, 392 N.E.2d 154 (Ill. App. Ct. 1979).

[494] *E.g.*, Snyder v. Med. Serv. Corp. 35 P.3d 1158 (Wash. 2001).

[495] *See* Restatement (Second) of Torts § 46 (1965). *E.g.*, Caputo v. Professional Recovery Services, Inc., 261 F. Supp. 2d 1249 (D. Kan. 2003).

[496] *E.g.*, Public Finance Corp. v. Davis, 360 N.E.2d 765 (Ill. 1976).

[497] Third-party debt collection agencies and other "debt collectors" who engage in this type of dishonest behavior also violate the Fair Debt Collection Practices Act.

[498] Jacksonville State Bank v. Barnwell, 481 So. 2d 863, 865-66 (Ala. 1985).

[499] *See infra* § 2.14[C] Fair Debt Collection Practices Act.

[4]   Intentional Interference with Contractual Relations.

If the creditor's collection efforts interfere with the debtor's contractual relationship with a third person, the creditor may be held liable for intentional interference with a contractual relationship.[500] This might occur if the debtor loses her job as a result of the creditor's actions, or if one of the debtor's suppliers refuses to continue dealing with the debtor, in breach of an existing contract, because of the creditor's intentional actions. For example, in *Long v. Newby*,[501] a collection agent for one hospital, who happened to be a member of the board of trustees of another hospital where the debtor worked, induced the rest of the board to pass a resolution that required the debtor to be terminated from his employment if he did not repay the other hospital to which he was indebted. The employer hospital followed through on its resolution and fired the debtor when he failed to satisfy the other hospital's claim.[502] The creditor interfered with the debtor's contract with his employer, and was held responsible for the resulting harm.

Liability depends on the existence of the debtor's contract with the other party, the creditor's knowledge of the contract, his intent to induce a breach of the contract and a resulting breach.[503] Thus, discharge of a debtor who is an "at will" employee is insufficient; this is not regarded as a breach of the employment contract.[504]

Even if the creditor has intentionally interfered with a contract of the debtor, the creditor is not liable if the creditor's actions were justified by his otherwise legal pursuit of his legitimate interests. Thus, a creditor's legitimate collection efforts, that cause the debtor to default on its other obligations, do not give rise to liability under this theory.

[5]   Abuse of Process[505]

Creditors who improperly use the judicial system in their collection efforts can be liable for abuse of process.[506] A claim for abuse of process arises when a person has an ulterior motive to pursue some claim and commits a willful act in the use of the process that is not proper in the regular conduct of the proceedings.[507]

---

[500] *See* Restatement (Second) of Torts §§ 766-766B (1977). *See, e.g.,* Long v. Newby, 488 P.2d 719 (Alaska 1971).

[501] 488 P.2d 719 (Alaska 1971).

[502] Troy v. Interfinancial Inc, 320 S.E.2d 872 (Ga. Ct. App. 1984) (plaintiff was terminated by his employer when defendant told him he "could never expect to get anything out of this company again"); Hill Grocery Co. v. Carroll, 136 So. 789, 792 (1931) (employee discharged after creditor threatened debtor's new employer with loss of business if employer failed to either induce payment or fire debtor).

[503] Restatement (Second) of Torts § 766 (1979).

[504] *See* Frank J. Cavico, *Tortious Interference with Contract in the At-Will Employment Context*, 79 U. Det. Mercy L. Rev. 503 (2002).

[505] Dean Gloster, Comment, *Abuse of Process and Attachment: Toward a Balance of Power*, 30 UCLA L. Rev. 1218 (1983).

[506] Restatement (Second) of Torts § 682 (1977).

[507] Restatement (Second) of Torts § 682 (1977). *See* A.S. Klein, *Use of Criminal Process to Collect Debt as Abuse of Process*, 27 A.L.R.3d 1202 (1969); *e.g.,* Brown v. Kennard, 113 Cal. Rptr. 2d 891 (Cal. Ct. App. 2001).

In the context of creditors' efforts to collect, claims for abuse have been successful where the creditor's wrongful actions consisted of wrongful attachment, either by levying on property that did not belong to the debtor or that was protected by an exemption, or by seizing more property than was necessary to satisfy the judgment.[508] This obviously goes beyond basic use of the courts to collect a debt.

[6] Defamation

Creditors who disseminate false information about a debtor may incur liability for defamation if the false information damages the debtor's reputation or otherwise causes him harm.[509] A creditor who mischaracterizes the debtor's financial condition, or publishes a false credit report regarding the debtor will be liable for harm the debtor suffers as a result.[510] Truth, of course, is a complete defense. In addition, the law of libel and defamation recognizes a mercantile privilege for credit reports, which requires the debtor to prove malice in order to be able to recover. This privilege virtually immunizes credit reporting agencies from liability, but may leave an individual creditor liable where it can be shown that it has some intent to harm the debtor.[511] Moreover, provisions of the Federal Fair Credit Reporting Act have been held to preempt state law claims for defamation, invasion of privacy, and negligence, against those who report false information to a credit reporting agency.[512]

[B] Lender Liability[513]

Loan agreements frequently give lenders some degree of discretion over the terms of the loan. For example, a creditor might have the right to insist on additional collateral, to raise the interest rate, to accelerate the due date, or to terminate or reduce a line of credit. This discretion is accompanied by an implied duty of good faith. A creditor who exercises its discretion in bad faith can be held liable for the harm suffered by the debtor as a result.[514]

---

[508] Dean Gloster, Comment, *Abuse of Process and Attachment: Toward a Balance of Power*, 30 UCLA L. Rev. 1218, 1228 (1983).

[509] Restatement (Second) of Torts § 559 (1977).

[510] Dun & Bradstreet, Inc. v. Greenmoss Builders, Inc., 472 U.S. 749, 757-63 (1985).

[511] Roger D. Blair & Virginia Maurer, *Statute Law and Common Law: The Fair Credit Reporting Act*, 49 Mo. L. Rev. 289, 297-300 (1984); Note, *Protecting The Subjects of Credit Reports*, 80 Yale L.J. 1035 (1971).

[512] Purcell v. Bank of Am., 659 F.3d 622 (7th Cir. 2011).

[513] Werner F. Ebke & James R. Griffin, *Lender Liability to Debtors: Toward a Conceptual Framework*, 40 Sw. L.J. 775, 795-98 (1986); Werner F. Ebke & James R. Griffin, *Good Faith and Fair Dealing in Commercial Lending Transactions: From Covenant to Duty and Beyond*, 49 Ohio St. L.J. 1237, 1241 (1989); Daniel R. Fischel, *The Economics of Lender Liability*, 99 Yale L.J. 131(1989); Frances E. Freund et. al., *Special Project, Lender Liability: A Survey of Common-Law Theories*, 42 Vand. L. Rev. 855 (1989); Troy H. Gott & William L. Townsley, Note, *Lender Liability: A Survey of Theories, Thoughts and Trends*, 28 Washburn L.J. (1988).

[514] *See generally* Steven J. Burton, *Breach of Contract and the Common Law Duty to Perform in Good Faith*, 94 Harv. L. Rev. 369 (1980); E. Allan Farnsworth, *Good Faith Performance and Commercial Reasonableness Under the Uniform Commercial Code*, 30 U. Chi. L. Rev. 666, 669 (1963).

K.M.C. Co., Inc. v. Irving Trust Co., is the most famous example of a lender being held liable for breaching its duty of good faith because of an exercise of its contractual discretion.[515] The court held that Irving Trust breached its duty of good faith when it refused to advance funds under a discretionary line of credit it had previously supplied to the borrower. At the time it refused the draw, the line was oversecured, and the debtor alleged that the reason for the denial arose out of a personality conflict between the debtor and the loan officer. The court ruled that under these circumstances, declining the draw without notice violated the implied duty of good faith.[516]

Bankers were aghast! They argued that it would restrict the very discretion they had bargained for, and would lead to increased interest rates,[517] and other limits on the availability of credit. The decision elicited considerable backlash.[518] Other courts have held that it cannot be a breach of good faith to take an action that is specifically permitted by the terms of the loan agreement. For example, in *Kham & Nate's Shoes No. 2, Inc. v. First Bank of Whiting* the court rejected the premise of *K.M.C. Co. v. Irving Trust* and ruled that:

> Firms that have negotiated contracts are entitled to enforce them to the letter, even to the great discomfort of their trading partners, without being mulcted for lack of "good faith." . . . When the contract is silent, principles of good faith . . . fill the gap. They do not block use of terms that actually appear in the contract.[519]

Lenders who take action as part of an effort to harm their borrowers may be held liable for the consequences of their actions, but otherwise creditors have no obligation to act in the best interests of their borrowers.[520]

[C]   Federal Fair Debt Collection Practices Act[521]

In 1978, the inadequacy of existing common law restraints on the worst conduct of collection agencies led Congress to adopt the Fair Debt Collection Practices Act (FDCPA).[522] The FDCPA "prohibits debt collectors from making false or misleading representations and from engaging in various abusive and unfair

---

[515]   K.M.C. Co. v. Irving Trust Co., 757 F.2d 752 (6th Cir. 1985).

[516]   757 F.2d at (6th Cir. 1985). *See also* Brown v. Avemco Invest. Corp., 603 F.2d 1367 (9th Cir. 1979).

[517]   *See generally* Daniel R. Fischel, *The Economics of Lender Liability*, 99 Yale L.J. 131 (1989).

[518]   A. Brooke Overby, *Bondage, Domination, and the Art of the Deal: An Assessment of Judicial Strategies in Lender Liability Good Faith Litigation*, 61 Fordham L. Rev. 963, 997 & 1002 (1993).

[519]   Kham & Nate's Shoes No. 2, Inc. v. First Bank of Whiting, 908 F.2d 1351, 1357 (7th Cir. 1990). *See also* In re Clark Pipe and Supply Co., 893 F.2d 693, 702 (5th Cir. 1990) (noting that creditors have no fiduciary obligation borrowers or to other creditors of the debtor with respect to efforts to collect the creditor's claim).

[520]   *See generally* Teri J. Dobbins, *Losing Faith: Extracting the Implied Covenant of Good Faith from (Some) Contracts*, 84 Or. L. Rev. 227, 251-62 (2005).

[521]   Elwin Griffith, *Fair Debt Collection Practices Act: Some Problems In Interpretation*, 27 Willamette L. Rev. 237 (1991); Scott J. Burnham, *What Attorneys Should Know about the Fair Debt Collection Practices Act, Or, the 2 Do's and the 200 Don'ts of Debt Collection*, 59 Mont. L. Rev. 179 (1998).

[522]   15 U.S.C. § 1692-1692o (2006).

practices."[523] It applies primarily to collection agencies and lawyers, but has also had a significant impact on state courts' interpretations of state unfair and deceptive trade practices statutes and debt collection statutes.

[1] Scope of the FDCPA: Debt Collectors

The FDCPA restricts the conduct of debt collectors. A "debt collector" is defined in the statute as a person "who uses any instrumentality of interstate commerce or the mails in any business the principal purpose of which is the collection of any debts."[524] This language makes it applicable primarily to collection agencies, whose principal purpose is to collect debts.

The Act also applies to "any person who regularly collects or attempts to collect, directly or indirectly, debts owed or due or asserted to be owed or due another."[525] The key word in this definition is "another." The Act only applies to businesses who regularly try to collect debts that are owed to someone else. It does not apply to the efforts of the corner drugstore to collect unpaid bills from its own customers. Nor does it apply to efforts by large department stores to collect charges made to the store's proprietary credit card. However, it would apply if one of these businesses decided to expand its operations to collect debts owed to other businesses in town. Thus, the retailing giant Wal-Mart is not a debt collector if its collection efforts are limited to attempts to collect debts owed to Wal-Mart. But if it expands to include a division that "regularly" attempts to collect debts owed to other businesses, it would fit within the definition and be restricted by the act.

Although "debt collector" does not ordinarily include creditors who try to collect debts owed to themselves, it includes creditors who use other names in collecting debts that indicate that a third person is collecting or attempting to collect such debts.[526] For example, in *Taylor v. Perrin, Landry, deLaunay & Durand,*[527] a lender fell within the definition of "debt collector," even though it was collecting its own debt, because it used a lawyer's letterhead and facsimile signature on the collection letters it sent to its borrower. The letters gave the impression that a third person was collecting the unpaid debt. Thus, if one in the direct employ of Corner Drugstore contacts the debtor using the name "City Revenue," the Act applies, even though Corner Drugstore is only attempting to collect debts owed by its own customers.

When originally adopted in 1978, the FDCPA contained an express exemption that insulated attorneys from the scope of the Act.[528] This exemption was removed in 1986.[529] Thus, attorneys whose principal practice consists of collection work are unquestionably subject to the Act's restrictions. In addition, attorneys who "regu-

---

[523] Heintz v. Jenkins, 514 U.S. 291 (1995).

[524] 15 U.S.C. § 1692a(6) (2006).

[525] 15 U.S.C. § 1692a(6) (2006).

[526] 15 U.S.C. § 1692a(6) (2006).

[527] 103 F.3d 1232 (5th Cir. 1997).

[528] Pub. L. No. 95-109, § 803(6)(F), 91 Stat. 874, 875 (1978).

[529] Pub. L. No. 99-361, 100 Stat. 768 (1986).

larly" engage in collection work for their clients are likewise covered by the act.[530]

The Supreme Court's 1996 decision in *Heintz v. Jenkins*[531] concluded that attorneys who regularly attempt to collect debts "through litigation" are equally subject to the law.[532] The attorney in *Heintz* regularly engaged in traditional collection litigation, including sending pre-litigation collection letters to its client's loan customers, in an effort to collect the claim prior to the initiation of suit. In addition, lawyers who regularly engage in attempts to collect unpaid rent owed to landlords are within the scope of the Act.[533]

The Act excludes some third parties from its scope, including officers or employees of the creditor when they are attempting to collect for the creditor and using the creditor's name;[534] entities who are related by common ownership or affiliated control, so long as they only collect claims owed to an affiliated creditor and if their principal business is something other than the collection of debts;[535] governmental employees acting within the scope of their governmental authority;[536] process servers;[537] and non-profit consumer counseling agencies.[538]

[2] Debt Collectors' Communications with Debtor and Others

The FDCPA imposes a variety of restrictions on the timing and manner of a debt collector's communications with either the debtor or third parties, such as the debtor's employer, her relatives, or her neighbors. It generally prohibits debt collectors from engaging in communications with persons other than the debtor, except to learn information about the debtor's location or to implement a post-judgment judicial remedy, such as garnishment.[539] In contacting the debtor's

---

[530] *See* Fox v. Citicorp Credit Serv. Inc., 15 F.3d 1507, 1513 (9th Cir. 1994).

[531] 514 U.S. 291 (1995).

[532] *See also* Goldstein v. Hutton, Ingram, Yuzek, Gainen, Carroll & Bertolotti, 155 F. Supp. 2d 60 (S.D.N.Y. 2001) (firm whose income from collections was only 0.5% of its total annual gross revenue was not a debt collector within the FDCPA). *Compare* Fox v. Citicorp Credit Serv., Inc., 15 F.3d 1507 (9th Cir. 1994) (attorney who generated 70% of his legal fees from debt collection was a debt collector); Ditty v. CheckRite, Ltd., Inc., 973 F. Supp. 1320 (D. Utah 1997) (one-third to one-half was regular), *and* Blakemore v. Pekay, 895 F. Supp. 972, 977 n.2 (N.D. Ill. 1995) (attorney who filed over 1,200 collection actions in the last year and was elected to Illinois Creditors Bar Association was a debt collector), *with* Nance v. Petty, Livingston, Dawson & Devening, 881 F. Supp. 223 (W.D. Va. 1994) (0.61% of partner's practice and 1.07% of firm's cases not sufficient to bring lawyer within scope of the act), *and* Mertes v. Devitt, 734 F. Supp. 872 (W.D.Wis. 1990) (attorney who averaged two collection matters per year which represented less than one percent of his practice was not a debt collector).

[533] Romea v. Heiberger & Assocs., 988 F. Supp. 715 (S.D.N.Y. 1998). *See* Scott J. Burnham, *What Attorneys Should Know about the Fair Debt Collection Practices Act, Or, the 2 Do's and the 200 Don'ts of Debt Collection*, 59 Mont. L. Rev. 179 (1998).

[534] 15 U.S.C. § 1692a(6)(A) (2006).

[535] 15 U.S.C. § 1692a(6)(B) (2006).

[536] 15 U.S.C. § 1692a(6)(B) (2006).

[537] 15 U.S.C. § 1692a(6)(B) (2006).

[538] 15 U.S.C. § 1692a(6)(B) (2006).

[539] 15 U.S.C. § 1692c(b) (2006).

employer, neighbors, relatives, or others, debt collectors are prohibited from volunteering the reason for their efforts to get in touch with the debtor.[540] They are also prohibited from contacting third parties more than once.[541]

Moreover, letters sent to a third party must not contain information on the outside of the envelope that would reveal the nature of the debt collector's business, as this might reveal the debtor's financial woes to the mail carrier or others.[542] Postcards are thus prohibited. And, after the debt collector knows that the debtor is represented by counsel in connection with the debt and has information about how to contact that attorney, the creditor is prohibited from engaging in further efforts to communicate with third parties, at least until efforts to communicate with the debtor's attorney fail to elicit a response.[543]

Once the debt collector locates the debtor, its communications with the debtor must not occur at "any unusual time or place."[544] However, communications with the debtor after 8 a.m. or before 9 p.m. are presumed convenient.[545] Moreover, the debt collector must not communicate with the debtor at his place of employment if the debt collector has reason to know that the debtor is prohibited by his employer from receiving personal communications.[546] If the debt collector knows the debtor is represented by an attorney in connection with the debt, the debt collector is required to direct its communications regarding the debt to the debtor's attorney. After the debtor notifies the debt collector in writing, either that he is unwilling to pay the debt or that he wants the debt collector to cease its communications with the debtor, the debt collector is required, with a few exceptions,[547] to end its stream of communications with the debtor.[548]

[3] Harassment or Abuse

The FDCPA prohibits debt collectors from engaging in any conduct that would have the natural consequence of harassing, oppressing, or abusing the debtor or any other persons, such as members of the debtor's family.[549] Specifically prohibited are threats of any crime or violence, obscene or profane language, publication or advertisement of lists of debtors who refuse to pay debts, incessant phone calls with

---

[540] 15 U.S.C. § 1692b (2006).

[541] 15 U.S.C. § 1692b(3) (2006).

[542] *See* 15 U.S.C. § 1692b (2006). Communication by postcard is absolutely prohibited. *Id.* § 1692b(4). Further, the outside of any envelope used by the debt collector must not "use any language or symbol . . . that indicates that the debt collector is in the debt collection business or that the communication relates to the collection of a debt." 15 U.S.C. § 1692b(5).

[543] *See* 15 U.S.C. § 1692b(6) (2006).

[544] *See* 15 U.S.C. § 1692c(a)(1) (2006).

[545] *See* 15 U.S.C. § 1692c(a)(1) (2006).

[546] *See* 15 U.S.C. § 1692c(a)(3) (2006).

[547] *See* Tinsley v. Integrity Fin. Partners, Inc., 634 F.3d 416 (7th Cir. 2011) (okay for creditor to contact debtor's attorney).

[548] *See* 15 U.S.C. § 1692c(c) (2006). *See, e.g.,* Herbert v. Monterey Fin. Servs., Inc., 863 F. Supp. 76 (D. Conn. 1994) (phone call made after receiving a letter from the consumer's attorney stating consumer refused to pay the debt).

[549] *See* 15 U.S.C. § 1692d (2006).

the intent to annoy the debtor, or phone calls without full disclosure of the caller's identity.[550] These of course are all activities that many collection agencies routinely used before the Act was adopted.

[4] False or Misleading Representations

Debt collectors are prohibited from making false, deceptive, or misleading representations when attempting to recover an unpaid debt.[551] Among the specific potentially misleading actions they may not take are:

- misrepresenting the "character, amount, or legal status of any debt;"[552]

- misrepresenting the amount or recoverability of fees in connection with its efforts to recover the debt;[553]

- representing or even implying that failure to pay the debt will result in the debtor's arrest or imprisonment;

- representing or implying that they will take any action that the creditor is legally prohibited from taking;[554]

- communicating or threatening to communicate to any third person information that is known to be false;[555]

- implying that any transfer of the claim against the debtor will result in the debtor's loss of any defense which he otherwise might have;[556]

- falsely implying that the debtor has committed any crime or other conduct that would disgrace the debtor.[557]

Moreover, the debt collector may not threaten legal action that it does not intend to take. This precludes false threats to file suit,[558] particularly if the debt collector's past practice of never actually filing suit belies its threats to do so,[559] or if the debt collector delays filing suit for a much longer time than the threat suggests.[560]

---

[550] *See* 15 U.S.C. § 1692d (2006). *See, e.g.*, Grassley v. Debt Collectors, Inc., 1992 U.S. Dist. LEXIS 22782 (D. Or. Dec. 14, 1992) (threat to have debtor "picked up").

[551] 15 U.S.C. § 1692e (2006). *But see* O'Rourke v. Palisades Acquisition XVI, LLC, 635 F.3d 938 (7th Cir. 2011) (false statement to judge in litigation not within scope of act).

[552] 15 U.S.C. § 1692e(2)(A) (2006). Debt collectors therefore must be certain that they have accurate information about the amount owed by the debtor.

[553] 15 U.S.C. § 1692e(2)(B) (2006).

[554] 15 U.S.C. § 1692e(4) (2006).

[555] 15 U.S.C. § 1692e(8) (2006).

[556] 15 U.S.C. § 1692e)(7) (2006).

[557] 15 U.S.C. § 1692e)(7) (2006).

[558] 15 U.S.C. § 1692e(5) (2006); *e.g.*, Edwards v. National Business Factors, Inc., 897 F. Supp. 455 (D. Nev. 1995) (creditor had not yet authorized collection agency to bring suit).

[559] *Compare* United States v. National Financial Services, Inc., 820 F. Supp. 228 (D. Md. 1993), *affirmed*, 98 F.3d 131 (4th Cir. 1996) (attorney who threatened suit had not brought a single suit in collection matter in the past seven years), *with* Higgins v. Capitol Credit Services, Inc., 762 F. Supp. 1128, 1136-1137 (D. Del. 1991) (where attorney had filed suit on regular occasions).

[560] *E.g.*, Trans World Accounts, Inc. v. FTC, 594 F.2d 212 (9th Cir. 1979).

However, communications falling short of a direct threat to initiate suit but indicating that the creditor may "consider" legal action have passed muster under the Act.[561]

In addition, debt collectors must accurately reveal their identity and the purpose for their call.[562] They must not falsely imply that they are affiliated with a governmental agency[563] or that documents they provide to the debtor were issued or authorized by a court or other governmental body.[564] This rule prohibits them from using badges or uniforms that might indicate that the debt collector is a police officer or other public official.[565] They must also avoid representing that the communication is from an attorney, if it is not.[566] They may not falsely claim that any documents they provide to the debtor are "legal process."[567] They may not falsely represent that they are employed by a credit reporting agency.[568] Finally, debt collectors are affirmatively required to disclose, in their initial communication with the debtor, that they are "attempting to collect a debt and that any information obtained will be used for that purpose."[569]

[5] Unfair Practices

The FDCPA also prohibits any "unfair or unconscionable means to collect or to attempt to collect any debt."[570] Among the actions specifically restricted under this broad prohibition are:

- collecting any amount unless it is both authorized by the agreement with the debtor and permitted by law;[571]

- accepting a check from the debtor or anyone else that is post-dated by more than five days, without supplying that person with written notice of the debt collector's intent to deposit the check three to ten days before the deposit;[572]

- soliciting a post-dated check to subsequently threaten or institute a criminal prosecution should the check later be dishonored;[573]

---

[561] *E.g.*, Knowles v. Credit Bureau of Rochester, Div. of Rochester Credit Ctr., Inc., 1992 U.S. Dist. LEXIS 8349 (W.D.N.Y. May 27, 1992).

[562] 15 U.S.C. § 1692e(14) (2006).

[563] 15 U.S.C. § 1692e(1) (2006).

[564] 15 U.S.C. § 1692e(9) (2006).

[565] 15 U.S.C. § 1692e(1) (2006).

[566] 15 U.S.C. § 1692e(3) (2006). *E.g.*, Russey v. Rankin, 911 F. Supp. 1449 (D.N.M. 1995).

[567] 15 U.S.C. § 1692e(13) (2006).

[568] 15 U.S.C. § 1692e(16) (2006).

[569] 15 U.S.C. § 1692e(11) (2006).

[570] 15 U.S.C. § 1592f (2006).

[571] 15 U.S.C. § 1592f(1) (2006).

[572] 15 U.S.C. § 1592f(2) (2006).

[573] 15 U.S.C. § 1592f(3) (2006).

- depositing or threatening to deposit any post-dated check before the date stated on the instrument;[574]

- causing any kind of charge to be made to any person for communications by concealing the purpose of the communications, such as by making a "collect" call to the debtor;[575]

- threatening to use self-help to take possession of the debtor's property, if there is no right to possession, no intent to take possession, or if the property involved is exempt;[576]

- communicating with the debtor via post card;[577]

- using any language or a symbol on an envelope or telegram that reveals the nature of the debt collector's business.[578]

It should be noted that the express statutory prohibitions are not an exclusive listing of the actions that may be held to be "unfair or unconscionable."

[6]   Debt Validation

The FDCPA provides consumer debtors with the right to have a debt claimed to be owed by the debt collector, validated.[579] Although it seems unimaginable to those of us with tendencies toward obsessive-compulsive behavior, others are not surprised that consumer debtors sometimes lose track of debts they owe. Moreover, the frequent assignment of obligations from one creditor to another might make it difficult for debtors to keep track of the current owners of their obligations. Accordingly, within five days after any initial communication with a debtor in connection with the collection of a debt, the debt collector is required to send the consumer a written notification, containing (1) the amount of the debt, (2) the name of the creditor to whom the debt is owed, (3) a statement advising the debtor that the debt collector will assume that the debt is valid unless the debtor disputes its validity within thirty days; (4) a statement advising the debtor that if it disputes the debt within thirty days that the debt collector will obtain and mail to the debtor a verification of the debt; and (5) a statement that upon request within the thirty day period, that the debt collector will supply the debtor with the name and address of the original creditor, if that person is different from the current creditor.[580]

Although debt collectors are permitted to continue efforts to collect from the debtors during this thirty day period,[581] their efforts must not "overshadow" the debtor's right during this period to have the obligation verified.[582] For example, in

---

[574] 15 U.S.C. § 1592f(4) (2006).

[575] 15 U.S.C. § 1592f(5)(2006).

[576] 15 U.S.C. § 1592f(6) (2006).

[577] 15 U.S.C. § 1592f(7) (2006).

[578] 15 U.S.C. § 1592f(8) (2006).

[579] Pub L. No. 95-109, 91 Stat 874 (1977).

[580] 15 U.S.C. § 1692g (2006).

[581] *E.g.*, Sprouse v. City Credits Co., 126 F. Supp. 2d 1083 (S.D. Ohio 2000).

[582] *E.g.*, Johnson v. Revenue Mgmt. Corp., 169 F.3d 1057 (7th Cir. 1999); Rhoades v. West Virginia

Rabideau v. Management Adjustment Bureau, the court held that a statement in a communication from the debt collector asserting that "immediate payment would avoid further contact" from the collection agency, operated to contradict the validation notice because it implied that making payment was the only way to avoid subsequent contact from the collection agency.[583] It misled the debtor, who could have prevented subsequent contact from the collection agency, at least until verification of the debt was provided, by giving notice that it disputed the debt.

[7] Bona Fide Error Defense

Debt collectors, including lawyers, who run afoul of these restrictions may seek refuge from liability if their violation was not intentional and resulted from a "bona fide error notwithstanding the maintenance of procedures reasonably adapted to avoid any such error."[584] This defense will protect debt collectors who, for example, miscalculate the amount the debtor owes based on information supplied to them by the lender, despite reasonable procedures to ensure the accuracy of information obtained from the lender.[585] However, it does not protect debt collectors from liability for violations that resulted from a mistake of law about the act's prohibitions.[586]

[8] FDCPA Remedies

Violations of the FDCPA permit the debtor to recover any actual damages it suffers as a result of the violations.[587] However, in many cases, actual damages are likely to be minimal or difficult to calculate. Therefore, the court has discretion to assess up to $1,000 in additional damages,[588] depending on the frequency and persistence of the debt collector's violations, the nature of its violations, and the extent to which its violations were intentional, negligent, or inadvertent.[589] Additional damages are available in class actions.[590] However, a debt collector is completely shielded from liability if it shows, by a preponderance of the evidence, "that the violation was not intentional and resulted from a bona fide error notwithstanding the [debt collector's] maintenance of procedures reasonably adapted to avoid any such error."[591]

Credit Bureau Reporting Servs., 96 F. Supp. 2d 528, 532 (S.D. W. Va. 2000).

[583] 805 F. Supp. 1086 (W.D.N.Y. 1992).

[584] 15 U.S.C. § 1692k(c) (2006).

[585] Peeples v. Hasenmiller, No. 00-C-7028, 2004 U.S. Dist. LEXIS 19715 (N.D. Ill. Sept. 30, 2004).

[586] Jerman v. Carlisle, McNellie, Rini, Karmer & Ulrich, L.P.A., 130 S. Ct. 1605 (2010). *See generally* Shauna Cully Wagner, Annotation, *Construction and Application of Fair Debt Collection Practices Act (FDCPA) Bona Fide Error Defense,*14 A.L.R. Fed. 2d 207 (2006).

[587] 15 U.S.C. § 1692k(a)(1) (2006).

[588] 15 U.S.C. § 1692k(a)(2)(A) (2006).

[589] 15 U.S.C. § 1692k(b)(1) (2006).

[590] 15 U.S.C. § 1692k(a)(2)(B) (2006).

[591] 15 U.S.C. § 1692k(c) (2006).

In addition, the Federal Trade Commission may administratively enforce violations of the Act as violations of the Federal Trade Commission Act.[592] Administrative enforcement usually results in a "'consent decree," which operates as an agreement by the debt collector not to engage in specific acts or practices that are spelled out in the order. The consent decree does not usually indicate that the respondent admitted any wrongdoing; this, of course, deprives it of any collateral estoppel effect in a private enforcement action; and, it limits its formal precedential effect. At the same time, the decree does provide a good indication of the position likely to be taken by the full Commission regarding the actions the respondent has agreed not to take in the future. Therefore, such consent decrees are a useful guide to the position of the FTC.

[D] Federal Fair Credit Reporting Act

Credit-reporting agencies collect, assemble, and report information concerning consumers, to lenders, employers, landlords, insurers, and other businesses. The Fair Credit Reporting Act (FCRA)[593] regulates the activities of these agencies. It also regulates the conduct of their customers who receive credit reports, as well as the actions of those who supply information about consumers to credit-reporting agencies. In addition, the FCRA provides consumers with various rights that are designed to enable them to detect and correct inaccurate or outdated information that concerns them and their credit history.

The Act attempts to ensure that consumers have access to information contained in their credit reports by giving them the right, upon request, to one free copy of their credit report each year,[594] as well as to additional copies for a modest fee.[595] This facilitates consumers' detection of potentially inaccurate information in their credit reports by requiring creditors, employers, and others who take "adverse action" with respect to a consumer that is at least partially based on information contained in a consumer credit report, to advise the affected consumer of the adverse action, the name and contact information of the credit reporting agency from whom the information was obtained, and the consumer's right to acquire a copy of the credit report on which the adverse decision was based.[596] After such an adverse decision, the consumer has a right to a free copy of the report that was supplied to the creditor, employer, insurer, or other person who took the adverse information.[597]

Upon receipt of a copy of his or her report, a consumer has the right to contest the accuracy of any information contained in the report and to compel the credit-reporting agency involved to conduct an "investigation" of the accuracy of the contested information.[598] The entity that supplied the contested information must

---

[592] 15 U.S.C. § 1692l(a) (2006).

[593] 15 U.S.C. §§ 1681-1691v (2006).

[594] 15 U.S.C. § 1681j(c) (2006).

[595] 15 U.S.C. § 1681j(a) (2006).

[596] 15 U.S.C. § 1681m (2006).

[597] 15 U.S.C. § 1681j(b) (2006).

[598] 15 U.S.C. § 1681i (2006).

participate in the agency's investigation.[599] If the contested information is inaccurate or cannot be verified, the credit-reporting agency is required to report the results of its investigation to the person who took adverse action against the consumer based on information contained in the report. Thus, if a prospective creditor denies credit to the debtor after receiving a report about the debtor and, after an investigation, the information in the credit report cannot be verified, the credit reporting agency must notify the creditor that the information it had previously provided could not be verified.

Of course, this investigation may or may not result in a reversal of the creditor's adverse action. A prospective creditor or employer may have had reasons for taking the adverse action that were not based on the inaccurate information in the credit report. Likewise, a prospective employer who used the credit report may have filled the available position in the meantime by hiring a different applicant; and, a landlord who received the incorrect credit report may have already rented the premises to someone else.

The extent to which these and other mechanisms in the Fair Credit Reporting Act provide consumers with meaningful relief from inaccurate information that might be contained in their credit reports remains open to question. In particular, the mechanisms to resolve disputes about the accuracy of information contained in consumer credit reports have been subject to severe criticism. Moreover, they preempt state law claims for defamation, invasion of privacy, and negligence, against those who report information to consumer credit reporting agencies.[600]

[E] State Consumer Protection Statutes[601]

A variety of state statutes exist to regulate the debt collection process. Foremost among them are the "Unfair and Deceptive Trade Practices" statutes, or "little FTC" acts, which many states have adopted, and which emulate the Federal Trade Commission Act's prohibition of "unfair and deceptive trade practices."[602]

In addition, a few states have adopted more specific statutes that emulate the Fair Debt Collection Practices Act, except they frequently govern not only collection agencies and other similar debt collectors, but also creditors themselves.[603]

Further, a few states have adopted the Uniform Consumer Creditor Code (UCCC), which prohibits creditors from engaging in "unconscionable conduct in

[599] 15 U.S.C. § 1681s-2 (2006).

[600] See Purcell v. Bank of Am., 659 F.3d 622 (7th Cir. 2011) (Fair Credit Reporting Act preempts state-law claims for defamation, invasion of privacy, and negligence against those who report information to consumer credit reporting agencies).

[601] 2 Howard J. Alperin & Roland F. Chase, Consumer Law 3560 (1986); Joel E. Smith, Annotation, *Validity, Construction, and Application of State Statutes Prohibiting Abusive or Coercive Debt Collection Practices*, 87 A.L.R.3d 786 (1978).

[602] See Federal Trade Commission Act § 5, 15 U.S.C. § 45 (2006); Debtor-Creditor Law § 8.09[3][a] (Theodore Eisenberg ed. 2006).

[603] E.g., Iowa Debt Collections Practices Act, Iowa Code § 537.7101 (West 1998); Cal. Civ. Code §§ 1788-1788.32 (West Supp. 2006).

collecting a [consumer] debt."[604] The UCCC defines unconscionable conduct to include a wide variety of tactics that the federal Fair Debt Collection Practices Act precludes collection agencies from deploying.[605]

Finally, states that have adopted the Uniform Consumer Sales Practices Act[606] have applied its prohibition against "unfair or deceptive acts or practices" and "unconscionable acts or practices" to prohibit creditors from engaging in the type of collection strategies that would violate the Fair Debt Collection Practices Act if engaged in by a third-party debt collector.[607]

The overall impact of these state statutes is to make actions by creditors that would violate the Fair Debt Collection Practices Act if engaged in by a third-party debt collector, a violation of the state statute. Debtors are usually provided with the right to recover actual damages[608] or rescind the transaction,[609] and also may be permitted to recover punitive damages.[610]

---

[604] Unif. Consumer Credit Code § 5.108(2) (1974).

[605] *See* Unif. Consumer Credit Code § 5.108(5) (1974).

[606] Unif. Consumer. Sales Practices Act (1970); *e.g.*, Ohio Rev. Code Ann. § 1345.01-1345.13 (LexisNexis 2002).

[607] *E.g.*, Liggins v. May Company, 373 N.E.2d 404 (Ohio Ct. Com. Pleas 1977).

[608] *E.g.*, Ohio Rev. Code Ann. § 1345.09(A) (LexisNexis 2002).

[609] *E.g.*, Ohio Rev. Code Ann. § 1345.09(A) (LexisNexis 2002).

[610] *E.g.*, Ohio Rev. Code Ann. § 1345.09(B) (LexisNexis 2002).

Chapter 3

A BRIEF HISTORY OF BANKRUPTCY[1]

§ 3.01 THE BANKRUPTCY CLAUSE[2]

Among the powers bestowed on the national government by the Constitution is the power to enact "uniform laws on the subject of bankruptcies throughout the United States."[3] Like many of the other powers granted to the federal government in 1787, the Bankruptcy Power remained largely dormant through most of the nineteenth century. And, like the commerce power and the police power, it came into its own in the twentieth. Although it is the Commerce Clause that has been the primary vehicle for the expansion of federal power over trade and credit, the Bankruptcy Clause has played a substantial secondary role. To a large and growing degree, the law of debtors and creditors, not to mention "secured" credit, has been federalized; Congress' power over bankruptcies is a major reason why.

§ 3.02 BANKRUPTCY LAW PRIOR TO 1898[4]

During the nineteenth century, Congress exercised its bankruptcy power sporadically to meet the periodic crises of a growing market economy. Federal bankruptcy legislation was used as a temporary emergency measure, appropriate only to deal with the aftermath of economic downturn. Temporary federal bankruptcy laws were in force from 1800 to 1803,[5] from 1841 to 1843,[6] and again from 1867 to 1878.[7]

---

[1] David A. Skeel, Jr., Debt's Dominion: A History of Bankruptcy Law in America (2001); Charles Warren, Bankruptcy in United States History (1935); Vern Countryman, *A History of American Bankruptcy Law*, 81 Com. L.J. 226 (1976).

[2] Kurt H. Nadelman, *On the Origin of the Bankruptcy Clause*, 1 Am. J. Legal Hist. 215 (1957).

[3] U.S. Const. art I, § 8, cl. 4.

[4] Peter J. Coleman, Debtors and Creditors in America: Insolvency, Imprisonment for Debt, and Bankruptcy 1607-1900 (1974); Vern Countryman, *A History of American Bankruptcy Law*, 81 Com. L.J. 226 (1976).

Regarding the history of English bankruptcy law, on which ours is predicated, see Jay Cohen, *The History of Imprisonment for Debt and its Relation to the Development of Discharge in Bankruptcy*, 3 J. Leg. Hist. 153 (1982); Ian P. Duffy, *English Bankrupts, 1571-1861*, 24 Am. J. Leg. Hist. 283 (1980); Louis E. Levinthal, *The Early History of English Bankruptcy*, 67 U. Pa. L. Rev. 1 (1919).

[5] Bankruptcy Act of 1800, ch. 19, 2 Stat. 19 (repealed 1803). This Act was a near copy of the English statute.

[6] Bankruptcy Act of 1841, 5 Stat. 440 (repealed 1843).

[7] Bankruptcy Act of 1867, 14 Stat. 517 (repealed 1878).

In ordinary times, state creditors' rights law was viewed as sufficient to deal with the problems of debtor default. In the absence of federal legislation, bankruptcy relief was left to the states. This state law was limited by the inability to grant debtors a discharge.[8] Relief was also provided through federal equity receiverships, which dealt primarily with the large railroad insolvencies of the late nineteenth century.[9] The latter, combined with added protections to protect dissenting creditors, served as the basis for many of the features of a modern Chapter 11 reorganization.[10]

§ 3.03 THE BANKRUPTCY ACT OF 1898[11]

The first permanent bankruptcy law in the United States was the Bankruptcy Act of 1898. Enacted in the aftermath of the crash of 1893, it endured for more than 80 years with only one major set of amendments. These amendments occurred in 1938 in the wake of the Great Depression of the first-half of the twentieth century.

During the depression that followed the crash of 1893, two different groups pressed Congress for a bankruptcy law. Once sought debt relief. The other sought enhanced federal power to collect. Debtors, especially farmers who had been hit hard by the depression, wanted a voluntary act that would relieve debtors from creditor pressure. Creditors, especially commercial creditors, wanted an involuntary act that could be initiated by creditors and used to pry assets out of recalcitrant deadbeats. The resulting law represented an uneasy compromise between these two factions. The law permitted both voluntary and involuntary forms of bankruptcy (but protected farmers from the latter), provided both a fresh start for debtors and new collection tools for lenders, and became the basis for a body of substantive and procedural law that is far more important today than the Congress at the time could have imagined.

Although there were many amendments to the Act over the years (indeed, the first amendments were enacted just a couple of years after the Act was passed), the core of it remained intact until 1979, when the current Bankruptcy Code became law. In response to the Great Depression, the Chandler Act of 1938 added several chapters to the Act to deal with business and individual reorganization. The business reorganization chapters were denoted Chapter X, Chapter XI, and Chapter XII. Only the first two were of much significance, Chapter XII dealt with the adjustment of individual debts secured by real property. It was not used much until it was determined that real estate limited partnerships were eligible. Chapter X was designed for the reorganization of large, publicly owned companies. Chapter XI was designed for reorganizing small, closely-held corporations.

---

[8] Sturges v. Crowninshield, 17 U.S. (4 Wheat.) 122 (1819).

[9] Stephen J. Lubben, *Railroad Receiverships and Modern Bankruptcy Theory*, 89 Cornell L. Rev. 1420, 1474 (2004).

[10] *See* Charles Jordan Tabb, *The History of the Bankruptcy Laws in the United States*, 3 Am. Bankr. Inst. L. Rev. 5, 21-23 (1995).

[11] David A. Skeel, Jr., *The Genius of the 1898 Bankruptcy Act*, 15 Bankr. Dev. J. 321 (1999).

From at least the 1960s onward, there was growing dissatisfaction with the Act. Complaints were many and varied, including those about the opaque language of the statute, which had been so glossed by court decision and scholarly interpretation that the actual words of the Act were frequently ignored. The division of business reorganizations into two separate proceedings was viewed as cumbersome and inefficient. Chapter XIII, which provided a method for individual wage earners to reorganize, seemed to be a failure in all but a few districts, mostly in the southeast, where it became part of the local legal culture. Moreover, the court system was clumsy, with jurisdictional provisions that defied rational justification.

Against this background, Congress established the "National Bankruptcy Review Commission" to review and make recommendations for changes to the existing system. Although many of its recommendations did not survive the legislative process, they nevertheless served as the framework for Congress's eventual action.[12]

After much legislative wrangling over both the substance of the Code and its sweeping jurisdictional provisions, the Bankruptcy Reform Act of 1978, which included both the Bankruptcy Code and a number of related procedural and jurisdictional rules, was enacted.[13] The Bankruptcy Reform Act provides the framework for the current bankruptcy law.

§ 3.04   THE BANKRUPTCY CODE[14]

Few laws that do not involve taxes have been greeted with as much anticipation as the Bankruptcy Code. During the final months of the Act, bankruptcy filings dwindled as lawyers waited to take advantage of the new law. A burst of pent-up bankruptcy petitions greeted the Code as soon as it went into effect. The most influential treatise in the field, *Collier on Bankruptcy*, was issued in a new (fifteenth) edition, specifically to deal with the new law.

The Code became effective on October 1, 1979,[15] and almost immediately became the subject of much debate and many calls for revision. The loudest complaints came from the consumer credit industry, which decried the Code as a charter for deadbeats. It may seem odd that so much of the furor centered on consumer bankruptcy, as the monetary stakes in the typical consumer bankruptcy are negligible. However, consumer creditors were concerned not by any particular bankruptcy, but by the overall effect they saw on consumer borrowers' willingness to repay. It was not the fear of losing $100 that spooked creditors, but the fear of losing $100, a million times over. If indeed the Bankruptcy Code reduced the cost of a fresh start, then bad debts would rise, profits would fall, the price of credit

---

[12] Report of the Commission on the Bankruptcy Laws of the United States, Rep. No. 93-137, pts I and II (1973).

[13] Bankruptcy Reform Act of 1978, Pub. L. No. 95-598, 92 Stat. 2549 (1978). *See* Kenneth N. Klee, *Legislative History of the New Bankruptcy Law*, 28 DePaul L. Rev. 941 (1979).

[14] David A. Moss & Gibbs A. Johnson, *The Rise of Consumer Bankruptcy: Evolution, Revolution, or Both?*, 73 Am. Bankr. L.J. 311 (1999).

[15] Bankruptcy Reform Act of 1978, Pub. L. No. 95-598, tit. IV, § 402(a), 92 Stat. 2549, 2682 (1978).

would be pushed up, and the specter of government intervention to impose limits on interests rates would loom.

Whether the Bankruptcy Code, or changes in the market for consumer credit are to blame, the effective date of the new law marked the beginning of a long period of generally rising bankruptcy filings. The years 1979 through 1982 included a period of considerable economic stress, with a burst of high inflation, followed by what was, up until then, the worst recession since World War II. With greater prosperity in the mid-1980s, bankruptcy rates stabilized and then fell, although admittedly not to their pre-1979 levels. More economic trouble in the late 1980s and early 1990s led to another surge in bankruptcy petitions. The improvement in the economy after 1991 coincided with another plateau, and by 1994 filing rates were markedly down. In the decade between 1994 and 2004, filings almost doubled from 832,339 in 1994 to 1,597,462. even increasing during the years of the "dot.com" boom of 1995-2000.[16] The filing rate dropped precipitously on October 17, 2005, when the new set of amendments considerably reduced the relief available to consumers. Filings fell dramatically immediately after the effective date, and began to rebound slowly after that. The national financial crises that began in 2007 and peaked in 2008, also prompted a large number of filings, peaking in early 2011 at an annual rate of 1 ½ million. Since then, the rate has started to decline.

It might seem that the bankruptcy filing rate is linked to the general state of the economy, but the recent story is not so simple. Filings have increased in good times (1995-2000) and declined when the economy was not clearly improving. According to a study conducted by Ronald Mann, prior to the 2005 Amendments, the best predictor of the bankruptcy filing rate is the amount of consumer credit outstanding.[17] The increase in consumer bankruptcy may therefore reflect the staggering increase in consumer debt in the past 30 years, indicative of a change in lenders' attitudes toward extending credit.

In any event, the initial struggle over the original version of the Bankruptcy Code came to a head in 1982. To the surprise of most observers, the United States Supreme Court held that the jurisdictional provisions of the Bankruptcy Reform Act were unconstitutional.[18] Suddenly, the country was faced with the possibility that there would be no bankruptcy system at all.

For two years, while the bankruptcy courts labored under a jury-rigged system of possibly unconstitutional jurisdictional rules, Congress fought over revision of the Code. One of the main struggles concerned consumer bankruptcy. Many efforts were made to scale back the relief afforded to consumers, even to force some consumers to reorganize under Chapter 13 rather than to liquidate under Chapter 7.

The most draconian creditor proposals were defeated, at least for another two decades. However, the Bankruptcy Amendments and Federal Judgeship Act of 1984

---

[16] The filing rate in 2005 peaked at over 2 million, but this spike is generally attributed to the large number of debtors rushing to file before the effective date of the 2005 Amendments.

[17] Ronald Mann, Charging Ahead: The Growth and Regulation of Payment Card Markets (2006).

[18] N. Pipeline Constr. Co. v. Marathon Pipe Line Co., 458 U.S. 50 (1982), judgment stayed, 459 U.S. 813 (1982). See infra § 5.02[B] History of Bankruptcy Jurisdiction.

("BAFJA")[19] made several important changes, including an amendment to § 707, which permitted dismissal of a Chapter 7 petition to consumer debtors if providing relief would constitute "substantial abuse."[20] Of greater significance, at the time, was a new and highly complicated jurisdictional structure that seemed to herald a return to the cumbersome and inefficient jurisdictional rules that reigned under the old Bankruptcy Act.[21]

Almost two years later, Congress sprang yet another October surprise. In 1986, the Bankruptcy Judges, United States Trustees and Family Farmer Bankruptcy Act of 1986 went into effect.[22] The two most important provisions in these amendments were the establishment of the previously experimental United States Trustee program on a nationwide basis, and the enactment (subject to a sunset provision) of Chapter 12 of the Bankruptcy Code to facilitate the reorganization of family farms.[23]

There were still many complaints about, and much tinkering with the Code. Dissatisfaction did not decrease. Instead, it increasingly focused on business rather than consumer bankruptcy. The hot issues from the mid 1980s through the early 1990s were the propriety of creative uses of bankruptcy to deal with mass torts, labor disputes, and declining real estate markets.

A number of ambitious proposals were made to revamp and even to jettison the Code. In the last days of the 103rd Congress, the Bankruptcy Reform Act of 1994 enacted an assortment of minor amendments.[24] It overturned a few controversial court cases,[25] strengthened the position of secured creditors on a variety of fronts,[26] and provided some assistance to institutional lenders.[27] However, despite the raw number of changes, the 1994 amendments did not have the sweep of the 1978 Act, 1984's BAFJA, or even the 1986 Amendments.

---

[19] Bankruptcy Amendments and Federal Judgeship Act of 1984, Pub. L. No. 98-353, tit. III, §§ 306, 453, 98 Stat. 353, 375 (1984).

[20] *See infra* § 17.03[B][3] Abuse under the Discretionary Standard. *See, e.g.,* In re Walton, 866 F.2d 981, 984 (9th Cir. 1989) (debtor's "ability to pay" is the "crucial" factor in determining whether relief would be a substantial abuse). *See* Paul M. Black & Michael J. Herbert, *Bankcard's Revenge: A Critique of the 1984 Consumer Credit Amendments to the Bankruptcy Code*, 19 U. Rich. L. Rev. 845 (1985).

[21] *See* Charles Jordan Tabb, *The History of the Bankruptcy Laws in the United States*, 3 Am. Bankr. Inst. L. Rev. 5, 38-40 (1995).

[22] Pub. L. No. 99-554, 100 Stat. 3088 (1986).

[23] *See infra* Chapter 20 Family Farmer and Family Fisherman Reorganization.

[24] Bankruptcy Reform Act of 1994, Pub. L. No. 103-394, 108 Stat. 4106 (1994). *See generally* Robin E. Phelan, Richard E. Coulson, Stacey Jernigan & Alvin C. Harrell, *1994 Consumer Bankruptcy Developments: The Bankruptcy Reform Act of 1994*, 50 Bus. Law. 1193 (1995); Ned Waxman, *The Bankruptcy Reform Act of 1994*, 11 Bankr. Dev. J. 311 (1995).

[25] *See* Timothy R. Zinnecker, *Purchase Money Security Interests in the Preference Zone: Questions Answered and Questions Raised by the 1994 Amendments to Bankruptcy Code § 547*, 62 Mo. L. Rev. 47 (1997).

[26] *See* Kathryn R. Heidt, *The Effect of the 1994 Amendments on Commercial Secured Creditors*, Am. Bankr. L.J. 395 (1995).

[27] *See* Charles Jordan Tabb, *The History of the Bankruptcy Laws in the United States*, 3 Am. Bankr. Inst. L. Rev. 5, 42-44 (1995).

The 1994 Amendments provided for one potentially significant change: it created a new Bankruptcy Commission to study the Code and make recommendations.[28] The legislative history called upon the Commission to be cautious, by explaining that "the Commission should be aware that Congress is generally satisfied with the basic framework established in the current Bankruptcy Code." The report eventually promulgated by this new Commission[29] was controversial and, at least where consumer bankruptcy aws concerned, did not form the basis for enacting subsequent legislation.[30]

In the mid 1990s, advocates for restricting consumer debtors' access to bankruptcy proposed legislation that in various ways restricted access, increased the cost, and reduced the scope of the bankruptcy discharge.[31] The impetus for these new restrictions originated in an empirical study of consumer debtors financed by the consumer credit industry, which concluded that approximately one-third of consumer debtors could pay a substantial part of their debts if all their income above the poverty level was applied to their debts over a five-year period.[32] To respond to this, they proposed a "means test" for access to Chapter 7. After eight years of Presidential vetoes and legislative setbacks, this proposal was finally enacted, together with a variety of additional changes, as the "Bankruptcy Abuse Prevention and Consumer Protection Act of 2005" or "BAPCPA."[33] Most of its provisions went into effect on October 17, 2005.

The 2005 legislation implemented controversial but sweeping changes in the role that bankruptcy will play in the lives of consumer debtors.[34] Most significantly, it imposes a mechanical "means test," which limits access to chapter 7 liquidation

---

[28] Pub. L. No. 103-394, tit. VI, §§ 601-610, 108 Stat 4147 (1994).

[29] The commission's report was issued in 1997, Nat'l Bankr. Review Comm'n, Bankruptcy: The Next Twenty Years, Final Report (Oct. 20, 1997). http://govinfo.library.unt.edu/nbrc/reporttitlepg.html (last visited July 21, 2012).

[30] Gary Neustadter, *A Consumer Bankruptcy Odyssey*, 39 Creighton L. Rev. 225, 230 & n.5 (2006).

[31] H.R. 3150, 105th Cong. § 101(4) (1995). *See* Marianne B. Culhane & Michaela M. White, *Taking the New Consumer Bankruptcy Model for a Test Drive: Means-Testing for Chapter 7 Debtors*, 7 Am. Bankr. Inst. L. Rev. 27, 28 n.8 (1999). *See also* General Accounting Office, Personal Bankruptcy: The Credit Research Center Report on Debtors' Ability to Pay, GAO/GGD-98-47 (1998); General Accounting Office, Personal Bankruptcy: The Credit Research Center and Ernst & Young Reports on Debtors' Ability to Pay, GAO/T-GGD-98-79 (1998).

[32] Credit Research Ctr., Krannert Graduate Sch. of Mgmt., Purdue Univ., Monograph No. 23, Consumers' Right To Bankruptcy: Origins And Effects, Consumer Bankruptcy Study Vol. I (1982); Credit Research Ctr., Krannert Graduate Sch. of Mgmt., Purdue Univ., Monograph No. 24, Personal Bankruptcy: Causes, Costs And Benefits, Consumer Bankruptcy Study Vol. II (1982). *See also* Teresa A. Sullivan, Elizabeth Warren & Jay Lawrence Westbrook, *Limiting Access to Bankruptcy Discharge: An Analysis of the Creditors' Data*, 1983 Wis. L. Rev. 1091; Charlene Sullivan, *Reply: Limiting Access to Bankruptcy Discharge*, 1984 Wis. L. Rev. 1069; Teresa A. Sullivan, Elizabeth Warren & Jay Lawrence Westbrook, *Rejoinder: Limiting Access to Bankruptcy Discharge*, 1984 Wis. L. Rev. 1087.

[33] Pub. L. No. 109-8, 119 Stat. 23 (2005). *See generally* Susan Jensen, *A Legislative History of the Bankruptcy Abuse Prevention and Consumer Protection Act of 2005*, 79 Am. Bankr. L.J. 485 (2005); Jonathan C. Lipson, *Debt and Democracy: Towards a Constitutional Theory of Bankruptcy*, 83 Notre Dame L. Rev. 605, 688-89 (2008); Gary Neustadter, *A Consumer Bankruptcy Odyssey*, 39 Creighton L. Rev. 225, 228 n.2 (2006); Angela Littwin, *The Affordability Paradox: How Consumer Bankruptcy's Greatest Weakness May Account for its Surprising Success*, 52 Wm. & Mary L. Rev. 1933 (2011).

[34] Melissa B. Jacoby, *Ripple or Revolution? The Indeterminacy of Statutory Bankruptcy Reform*, 79

bankruptcy for consumers whose incomes are above their home states' medians and have disposable income. This test, which has been heavily criticized as inconsistent and ineffective,[35] forces some debtors into Chapter 13 rehabilitation plans, if they are to receive relief from their debts at all. At the same time, it uses this same means test to determine the amounts that must be paid to creditors under Chapter 13. It also mandates consumer credit counseling for consumer debtors as a condition of filing and prior to obtaining relief from their debts. The 2005 legislation had a marked impact on bankruptcy filing rates as well as on the availability of bankruptcy counsel. At least initially, the new statute drove many lawyers from the field. It also gave bankruptcy courts numerous opportunities to construe the statute. Sometimes, courts have used the "plain meaning" approach the current Supreme Court appears to prefer. At other times, courts have tried to make sense of provisions that are, to say the least, inartfully drafted.[36] Jurisprudentially, it is not clear which approach is better, but the inconsistency has led to deep divisions among the courts. Whether the legislative changes it made are desirable or not, largely depends on one's perspective.[37]

Since 2005, there have been many calls for further revision of the Code, particularly with respect to its treatment of home mortgages. However, despite millions of home foreclosures, and substantial evidence that lax underwriting contributed to the financial crisis, efforts to amend the Code to provide further avenues of relief to homeowners have not been successful.[38]

Am. Bankr. L.J. 169 (2005); Richard M. Hynes, *Non-Procrustean Bankruptcy*, 2004 U. Ill. L. Rev. 301, 361 (2004).

[35] Robert M. Lawless, Angela K. Littwin, Katherine M. Porter, John A. E. Pottow, Deborah K. Thorne & Elizabeth Warren, *Did Bankruptcy Reform Fail? An Empirical Study of Consumer Debtors*, 82 Am. Bankr. L.J. 349, 387-98 (2008); Rafael I. Pardo, *Failing to Answer Whether Bankruptcy Reform Failed: A Critique of the First Report from the 2007 Consumer Bankruptcy Project*, 83 Am. Bankr. L.J. 27 (2009).

[36] Jean Braucher, *A Guide to Interpretation of the 2005 Bankruptcy Law*, 16 Am. Bankr. Inst. L. Rev. 349 (2008).

[37] Robert M. Lawless et al., *Did Bankruptcy Reform Fail? An Empirical Study of Consumer Debtors*, 82 Am. Bankr. L.J. 349 (2008); Ronald J. Mann, *Bankruptcy Reform and the "Sweat Box" of Credit Card Debt*, 2007 U. Ill. L. Rev. 375, 378-79.

[38] Adam J. Levitin, *Resolving the Foreclosure Crisis: Modification of Mortgages in Bankruptcy*, 2009 Wis. L. Rev. 565 (2009); Mark S. Scarberry, *A Critique of Congressional Proposals to Permit Modification of Home Mortgages in Chapter 13 Bankruptcy*, 37 Pepp. L. Rev. 635 (2010).

Chapter 4

PARTIES AND OTHER PARTICIPANTS IN BANKRUPTCY CASES

§ 4.01 PARTIES AND OTHER PARTICIPANTS IN THE BANKRUPTCY PROCESS

Bankruptcy cases always involve the debtor and several creditors — sometimes many creditors. Their number and role vary with the size and nature of the case. The parties to the case administer and negotiate over the fate of the "bankruptcy estate." The estate, in any given case, consists of "all of the debtor's legal or equitable interest in property" at the time he or she filed the bankruptcy petition — in short, everything the debtor owns on the petition date. This estate is administered by a court-appointed bankruptcy trustee, unless, as frequently happens in Chapter 11 cases, the debtor remains "in possession" of the estate, and administers it for the benefit of the various stakeholders.

A trustee in bankruptcy (or "TIB") is always appointed in Chapter 7 liquidation cases, to collect and administer the debtor's property. However, because the overwhelming majority of consumer liquidation cases involve no assets for distribution to creditors, the case trustee's role is frequently limited to reviewing the paperwork submitted by the debtor in an effort to detect hidden assets or circumstances that would make the debtor ineligible due to "abuse."[1]

In rehabilitation cases under Chapters 12 and 13, a trustee is involved, but he or she does not take control of all the debtor's property. Instead, the trustee reviews the debtor's rehabilitation plan and receives and distributes payments the debtor makes pursuant to the terms of the debtor's court-approved payment plan.

In Chapter 11 cases, the debtor's estate is usually managed by the debtor itself, who remains in control of the bankruptcy estate's assets and is referred to as the "debtor-in-possession." This is true, even where the debtor is liquidating in Chapter 11 rather than reorganizing. The intuition, in both reorganizations and cases liquidated in Chapter 11, is that incumbent management of the debtor is in the best position to maximize the value of the debtor's business, either by continuing the business operations, or by selling off the assets. Of course, these are the same people who steered the debtor into bankruptcy, so the intuition may not always be correct. Where this is the case, the creditors may seek appointment of a trustee. This is rare, but occurs when creditors have lost confidence in the debtor's corporate managers and can either show that they have engaged in some kind of wrongful conduct, that they have "grossly mismanaged" the debtor's business, or that a

---

[1] *See infra* § 17.03[B] Dismissal of Consumer Cases Due to Abuse.

trustee is otherwise in the best interests of the creditors. In other cases, an "examiner" might be appointed to investigate the financial affairs of the debtor, and provide information to its creditors. This might occur where the management suspected of wrongdoing has already been replaced, or in other cases where a trustee is not desired, but a second set of eyes would be helpful.

In reorganization cases, the United States Trustee typically appoints a "creditors' committee," consisting of large creditors with an interest in monitoring the case. The purpose of the Committee is to represent the interest of similarly situated creditors. Sometimes the Committee will support a debtor's effort to reorganize, sometimes they may seek liquidation or a sale of assets. Likewise, when a Chapter 11 debtor is a partnership or a corporation, owners of the bankrupt business (known as "interest" or "equity interest" holders) might form into "equity committees." Given that litigation is expensive, and that many stakeholders will receive a small distribution if any, these representative committees can be quite important in monitoring the progress of a case.

Several governmental officials might also become involved in a case. The United States Trustee is an administrative agency charged with monitoring bankruptcy cases on behalf of the United States government. This helps to maintain the financial integrity of a system that might otherwise be administered completely by the private parties who have a financial stake in the outcome of the case. In big reorganizations involving publicly held securities, the Securities Exchange Commission might also be involved, though its role is now less important than it was in the past. And, of course, the bankruptcy court system will become involved in the case, with a full array of clerks, courtrooms, and judges.

§ 4.02   DEBTORS AND DEBTORS IN POSSESSION

In most cases, the "debtor" is the one who initiates the case by filing a bankruptcy petition,[2] although creditors might also get the ball rolling by filing an involuntary petition.[3] In rehabilitation cases under Chapters 11, 12, and 13, where the debtor retains possession of the bankruptcy estate's property, the debtor morphs, for most purposes, into the "debtor-in-possession," though the term is usually reserved for use in Chapter 11 cases. The Code makes it clear, however, that where an estate is managed by a debtor-in-possession or "DIP," that the DIP has all the statutory powers of a case trustee.[4]

[A]   Debtor

The "debtor" is the subject of the bankruptcy case. In liquidation cases, the debtor has a limited role once the case is filed. After filing his or her petition, together with the accompanying paperwork about the debtor's financial affairs,[5] the debtor's only real role in the case is to turn over his or her non-exempt

---

[2] *See infra* § 6.01[A] Voluntary Cases.

[3] *See infra* § 6.01[B] Involuntary Cases.

[4] Bankruptcy Code § 1107.

[5] *See infra* § 6.02[C] Petition and Schedules; Statement of Debtor's Affairs.

property if any exists, and to receive a discharge of debts. There are occasional exceptions. For example, the case may involve litigation over the dischargeability of one of the debtor's particular debts[6] or over whether the debtor should be granted a discharge at all.[7] However, especially in consumer cases, where there are few debts, fewer assets, and little likelihood of serious misconduct by the debtor, such litigation is relatively rare.

In addition to filing the necessary paperwork, debtors must cooperate with the trustee and appear at any examinations or hearings involved in the case.[8] Section 341 also requires the debtor to appear at a meeting of creditors. The meeting is convened under the authority of the United States Trustee, and usually presided over by the trustee appointed to administer the case.[9] This meeting is frequently referred to as the "341 meeting." No judge is present, and in consumer cases, it is usually not even really a "meeting" in the normal sense of the word, as creditors rarely appear. When they do, they rarely hold anything that anyone would recognize as a meeting. Instead, the event serves primarily as an opportunity for the trustee to ask the debtor a few questions about his or her financial affairs. This "examination" of the debtor serves much the same function as a state law judgment debtor's examination.[10] The trustee takes the opportunity to probe for the existence and location of the debtor's assets and into other matters such as fraudulent conveyances,[11] preferences,[12] and the like,[13] that might lead to additional assets that the trustee might recover and use to pay creditors' claims.

The debtor is required to appear at the meeting and to answer the trustee's questions under oath.[14] The debtor may also be questioned by creditors, any indenture trustee, an examiner, if one has been appointed, or the United States Trustee.[15] The scope of the examination encompasses the debtor's "acts, conduct, or property, or to the liabilities and financial condition of the debtor, or to any matter which may affect the administration of the debtor's estate, or to the debtor's right to a discharge."[16]

In reorganization cases, the examination will likely be more elaborate. It may:

> [R]elate to the operation of any business and the desirability of its continuance, the source of any money or property acquired or to be acquired by the debtor for purposes of consummating a plan, and the

---

[6] *See infra* § 12.03 Non-Dischargeable Debts.

[7] *See infra* § 12.02 Denial of Discharge.

[8] Bankruptcy Code § 521. *See infra* § 6.02[C] Petition, Schedules, Statements, Certificates and Disclosures.

[9] Bankruptcy Code § 341; Fed. R. Bankr. P. 2003.

[10] *See supra* § 2.13[A] Discovery: Examination of a Judgment Debtor.

[11] *See infra* Chapter 16 Fraudulent Transfers.

[12] *See infra* Chapter 15 Avoidable Preferences.

[13] *See infra* Chapter 14 Trustee's General Avoiding Powers; Limits on Avoiding Powers.

[14] Bankruptcy Code § 343; Fed. R. Bankr. P. 2004.

[15] Bankruptcy Code § 343; Fed. R. Bankr. P. 2004.

[16] Fed. R. Bank. P. 2004(b). *See* H.R. Rep. No. 95-595, at 332 (1977), *reprinted in* 1978 U.S.C.C.A.N 5963, 6288.

consideration given or offered to those who supplied these funds, and any other matter relevant to the case or to the formulation of a plan.[17]

Thus, the examination must concern matters that are relevant to the bankruptcy case itself. The debtor also may be ordered to surrender books and records relating to his or her financial condition to the trustee at the 341 meeting.[18]

A debtor who has committed crimes might naturally be reluctant to reveal information that would expose him to prosecution. Filing a bankruptcy petition does not operate as a waiver of a person's constitutional privilege against self incrimination. However, immunity from prosecution may be granted. If it is, the debtor must testify or run the risk of being held in contempt or denied a discharge.[19]

A consumer debtor must also file a statement of his or her or her intentions regarding encumbered property indicating whether the debtor intends to retain the property, surrender the property, claim the property as exempt, redeem the property, or reaffirm the debt that is secured by the property.[20]

[B] Debtor-in-Possession

In cases under Chapters 11, 12, or 13, if no trustee is appointed, the debtor remains in possession of the estate, and is referred to as the "debtor-in-possession" (DIP). In Chapter 11 cases, in particular, there is normally no case trustee appointed to administer the property of the estate. Instead, the incumbent officers and directors remain responsible for managing the estate's financial affairs while the case is pending.

For example, when Titanic Industries, Inc. files a Chapter 11 case, its successor in the bankruptcy case is Titanic Industries, Inc., Debtor-in-Possession. But, when people refer to the DIP they may be referring to Harland Wolff, the president of Titanic Industries, and the Corporation's board of directors who continue to operate the debtor post-petition.

In Chapter 11 cases, the DIP has most of the powers and functions granted by the statute to the trustee.[21] This includes the power to operate the debtor's business, to sell and use property of the estate, and to borrow money. To the extent that these activities are in the "ordinary course of business," the debtor may act without seeking court authorization. The DIP may also propose extraordinary actions, such as sales of a division, or even all of the debtor's assets, or negotiating a post-petition financing facility to fund the debtor's operations. These actions are subject to court approval after notice and a hearing. The DIP may also seek to assume or reject executory contracts, seek to avoid prepetition transactions, and to formulate and seek confirmation of a plan of reorganization. Its activities may include bringing lawsuits to recover property for the benefit of the estate, possibly

---

[17] Fed. R. Bank. P. 2004(b).

[18] Fed. R. Bankr. P. 2004(c).

[19] Bankruptcy Code § 344.

[20] Bankruptcy Code § 521(a)(2)(A). *See infra* § 6.02[C] Petition, Lists, Schedules, Statements, Certificates & Disclosures.

[21] Bankruptcy Code §§ 1107, 1203, 1303.

including actions against officers, directors, shareholders, and other insiders of a corporate debtor who might have received preferential transfers or fraudulent conveyances before the bankruptcy case began.[22]

§ 4.03 THE ESTATE[23]

When a bankruptcy case is filed, an estate is created.[24] The estate consists of all of the debtor's property.[25] The debtor no longer "owns" the property, instead it is under the jurisdiction of the court. In this respect, the filing of a bankruptcy petition has some of the same legal effects as a person's death. The filing of the petition, like death, creates an estate and transfers all of the debtor's property to that estate.[26] The debtor's estate is comprised of whatever property the debtor owned at the time the bankruptcy case was filed, together with whatever additional income that property produces while the case is pending,[27] as well as any assets that the trustee recovers pursuant to her avoiding powers.[28]

The value of the estate's property is the baseline for what creditors will be paid. In liquidation cases, the creditors receive either the estate's property or its value. In reorganization cases, the creditors are entitled to receive at least the value of the property that would have been distributed to creditors in a Chapter 7 case involving the debtor.[29]

§ 4.04 CREDITORS AND CREDITORS' COMMITTEES

Creditors may participate in bankruptcy cases on their own. But, in Chapter 11 cases, they may organize themselves into one or more committees. A duly constituted creditors' committee is entitled to have its expenses, including its attorney fees, reimbursed from the debtor's estate, thus sharing the expenses with all creditors from funds that would otherwise be paid to creditors on a pro-rata basis.

[A] Role of Creditors in Bankruptcy Cases

Nearly all individual bankruptcy cases involve consumer debtors with few or no assets. Accordingly, creditors generally play a passive role. Apart from receiving notice of the case and perhaps receiving a small distribution, the typical creditor pays little heed to what transpires in a consumer debtor's bankruptcy case. In most

---

[22] *See infra* § 15.02[E] Preference Period: 90 Days or 1 Year (for Insiders) Before Bankruptcy.

[23] *See infra* Chapter 7 Property of the Estate.

[24] Bankruptcy Code § 541(a)(1). *See infra* § 7.01 Creation of the Debtor's Estate.

[25] Bankruptcy Code § 541(a)(1).

[26] Richard H.W. Maloy, *"She'll Be Able to Keep Her Home Won't She?" — The Plight of a Homeowner in Bankruptcy*, 2003 Mich. St. DCL L. Rev. 315, 320 n. 16 (2003).

[27] Bankruptcy Code § 541(a). *See infra* Chapter 7 Property of the Estate.

[28] Bankruptcy Code § 541(a)(3).

[29] *See* Bankruptcy Code §§ 1129(a)(7)(A)(ii), 1225(a)(4), 1325(a)(4). *See infra* § 18.08[E][1] Best Interests of Creditors.

cases, creditors do not even bother filing a simple proof of claim form.[30]

The reason for this is found in simple economics. The bankruptcy value of creditors' claims are negligible. In the vast majority of consumer cases, unsecured creditors' claims are worthless — the debtor has nothing and creditors receive nothing. In some business cases, this may be different. If the debtor remains in business, creditors may have the opportunity for some meaningful payment from the debtor as part of or after the reorganization process is complete.

Creditors usually learn that the debtor has filed a bankruptcy case either directly from the debtor or in an official notice sent by bankruptcy court's clerk's office.[31] In most consumer cases, this notice will advise the creditor that the debtor has no assets and that there is no reason for the creditor to file a "proof of claim" form.[32] In an unusual case, in which payment of a "dividend" to creditors seems likely, the notice sent to creditors includes a simple proof of claim form that the creditor must submit to establish its right to a share of the debtor's assets.[33] In Chapter 11 cases, the schedules filed with the debtor's petition establish the prima facie validity of listed creditors' claims, and creditors need not file a proof of claim if they agree with the amount and character of the claim as scheduled by the debtor.[34] If the creditor disagrees, it must file a proof of claim. This simple step establishes the validity of the claim absent some further objection by the debtor or someone else with a stake in the case, like another creditor.[35]

In reorganization cases, creditors also have the opportunity to object to many decisions a debtor may make during the case, including sales outside the ordinary course of business, debtor-in-possession financing, the assumption or rejection of contracts, and the debtor's proposed plan of reorganization.[36] Creditors with large claims actively participate in the case, either individually or as members of an official creditors' committee.

[B] Creditors' Committees[37]

In Chapter 11 cases, creditors' committees sometimes play a significant role in charting the course of a case. Creditors' committees are also occasionally used in complex Chapter 7 liquidation cases.[38]

---

[30] *See infra* § 11.02 Claims of Creditors.

[31] Fed. R. Bankr. P. 2002(a).

[32] *See* Fed. R. Bankr. P. 2002(e).

[33] Bankruptcy Code § 502; Fed. R. Bankr. P. 3002(a).

[34] Fed. R. Bankr. P. 3003(b). The same is true in a chapter 9 case involving a "municipality."

[35] Bankruptcy Code § 502(a).

[36] *See infra* § 19.12 Acceptance of Plan by Holders of Claims & Interests: Voting.

[37] Daniel J. Bussel, *Coalition-Building Through Bankruptcy Creditors' Committees*, 43 UCLA L. Rev. 1547 (1996); Andrew DeNatale, *The Creditors' Committee Under the Bankruptcy Code — A Primer*, 55 Am. Bankr. L.J. 43 (1981); Kenneth N. Klee & K. John Shaffer, *Creditors' Committees Under Chapter 11 of the Bankruptcy Code*, 44 S.C. L. Rev. 995 (1993); Lynn M. LoPucki, *The Debtor in Full Control — Systems Failure Under Chapter 11 of the Bankruptcy Code? (pts. 1 & 2)*, 57 Am. Bankr. L.J. 99, 247 (1983).

[38] *See infra* § 17.07 Creditors' Committees in Chapter 7 Cases.

The legal and other expenses of a creditors' committee are paid for, after approval by the court, from the debtor's estate. Thus, a large creditor might choose to participate in a case through membership on a creditors' committee rather than by taking an active individual role, which would make it necessary for the creditor to pay whatever expenses were involved, out of its own pocket. However, this may be a double edged sword. A creditor who joins the committee acts in a fiduciary capacity when sitting on the committee, and may sometime have to recuse him or herself when there is a conflict of interest. Also, in modern Chapter 11 cases, many claims are owned by creditors who are in the business of trading claims, either to realize on the value of those claims, to enhance their leverage in the case, or even to gain control of the debtor. Creditors' commitee members (or other creditors) may find themselves in possession of inside information, and may therefore be unable to trade.[39]

§ 4.05 TRUSTEES AND EXAMINERS[40]

The appointment and role of a trustee or an examiner varies, depending on the type of bankruptcy case involved. In Chapter 7 liquidation cases, a trustee is appointed to handle, or "administer," the debtor's estate. In Chapter 12 cases involving family farmers and family fishermen, and Chapter 13 cases involving individuals with regular income, a trustee is appointed, but has a more limited role. In Chapter 11 reorganization cases, a trustee is appointed only "for cause," such as pre- or post-petition misbehavior of officers or directors, or where it can be shown that a trustee is in the best interests of the creditors, usually because the creditors have lost faith in incumbent management. In less extreme cases, the court may appoint an independent "examiner" to inquire into the debtor's financial condition and to report the results of its investigation to creditors and the court, even though no trustee is appointed.

[A] Case Trustees

[1] Case Trustee in Chapter 7 Cases

In Chapter 7 liquidation cases, the debtor's estate is administered by a court appointed trustee.[41] These "case trustees" are also referred to as "panel" trustees, because they are appointed from a panel of individuals who have previously qualified to serve. In nearly all cases, the "interim trustee" appointed at the outset of a Chapter 7 case from among those on the panel of qualified trustees serves throughout the case as the permanent trustee. Creditors may elect a different person to serve as a case trustee, but it is extraordinarily rare for creditors to elect a different person to serve in this role. Nor is it common for the interim trustee to lose his or her qualification or decline to serve, necessitating the appointment of

---

[39] *See* In re Washington Mutual, Inc., 461 B.R. 200 (Bankr. D. Del. 2011).

[40] Hon. Steven Rhodes, *The Fiduciary and Institutional Obligations of a Chapter 7 Bankruptcy Trustee*, 80 Am. Bankr. L.J. 147 (2006).

[41] Bankruptcy Code § 701.

another trustee.[42] Although it is not necessary for a case trustee to be a lawyer,[43] most panel trustees are lawyers with substantial experience in bankruptcy cases.

A case trustee is generally responsible for locating, assembling, and liquidating the debtor's non-exempt assets.[44] Case trustees are also expected to pursue recovery of avoidable preferences, fraudulent transfers, and other questionable transactions involving the debtor's property, in an effort to increase the amount of property available for creditors generally. Likewise, the trustee is to examine the debtor and appropriately challenge the debtor's claim of exemptions[45] and his or her right to a discharge of his debts.[46] Case trustees may also seek to dismiss a debtor's Chapter 7 liquidation case due to "abuse."[47]

In the vast majority of consumer liquidation cases, in which no assets are available to distribute to creditors, trustees are compensated with a portion[48] of the debtor's filing fee.[49] When assets are available, the trustee's compensation is based on the size of the estate and the complexity of the trustee's duties in administering the estate.[50]

[2] Trustee in Chapter 11 Cases

As noted above, there is no trustee in most reorganization cases. Instead, the debtor's estate is administered by the debtor-in-possession, who has all of the same rights, powers, and duties of a trustee.[51] A trustee is appointed only for cause which includes "fraud, dishonesty, incompetence, or gross mismanagement" of the debtor or its assets, or if the court determines that the appointment of a trustee is "in the interests of creditors."[52]

[3] Standing Trustees in Chapter 12 and 13 Cases

Trustees in Chapter 12 and 13 cases have a different role than trustees in Chapter 7 liquidation cases or those appointed for cause in Chapter 11 reorganization cases. In Chapters 12 and 13, the debtor nearly always remains in possession and control of the estate's property. Most Chapter 12 family farmers keep control of and continue to operate their family farms.[53] Family fishermen keep possession of the boats, nets, and other gear used in their fishing operations and use them to operate their fishing business. Similarly, Chapter 13 debtors remain in possession

---

[42] Bankruptcy Code § 701(c).

[43] In re Clemmons, 151 B.R. 860, 862 n.1 (Bankr. M.D. Tenn. 1993).

[44] Bankruptcy Code § 704(1). *See infra* § 17.05[B] Duties of the Trustee.

[45] Bankruptcy Code § 522(l); Fed. R. Bankr. P. 4003(b)(2).

[46] *See infra* § 17.09 Distribution of Estate Property.

[47] *See infra* § 17.05 Role of a Chapter 7 Trustee.

[48] Bankruptcy Code § 330(b)(1).

[49] 28 U.S.C. § 1930 (2006).

[50] Bankruptcy Code § 330.

[51] Bankruptcy Code § 1107.

[52] Bankruptcy Code § 1104(a). *See infra* § 19.05 Appointment of Trustee or Examiner.

[53] *See infra* § 20.03[A] Chapter 12 Debtor-in-Possession.

of their personal and business assets.[54] Because of the nature of these cases, which do not involve a liquidation and distribution of the estate's property, there is no need for a trustee to collect and sell the debtor's property.

Instead, debtors in these cases develop a plan to make regular payments from the debtor's earnings to the standing trustee.[55] The trustee is responsible for collecting and distributing these payments to creditors, in accordance with the debtor's plan. The trustee can object to the debtor's plan when it does not meet the statutory standards for court approval ("confirmation"). The trustee, like her counterpart under Chapter 7, might also bring actions to recover property from others to augment the debtor's estate. Moreover, the trustee has the right to object to claims filed by creditors, and if necessary, to seek dismissal of the debtor's case or for its conversion to a liquidation proceeding under Chapter 7.

[4] Eligibility, Qualification, and Role of Standing and Case Trustees

To be eligible as trustee, an individual must be competent to perform the trustee's duties.[56] In cases under Chapter 7, 12, or 13, the trustee must reside in or have an office in either the district in which the case is pending or in an adjacent district.[57] A person who has served as an examiner[58] in the case may not serve as trustee.[59] Finally, the United States Trustee may serve as a case trustee only "if necessary," such as where no one else is qualified or willing to serve.[60]

A case trustee must "qualify" to serve. To qualify, the person designated as trustee must obtain a sufficient bond,[61] must neither have nor represent any interests that are adverse to the interests of the estate or its creditors, and must be a "disinterested person."[62] Once qualified and appointed, the trustee is the representative of the debtor's estate,[63] and has a fiduciary duty to act in the best interests of the estate. In the typical liquidation case, this means to obtain the maximum amount, sometimes referred to as a "dividend," for creditors.

---

[54] *See infra* § 18.05[A] Role of a Chapter 13 Debtor.

[55] Bankruptcy Code § 1122(a)(1). *See infra* § 19.06[A] Submission of Sufficient Income to Fund the Plan.

[56] Bankruptcy Code § 321(a)(1).

[57] Bankruptcy Code § 321(a)(1).

[58] *See infra* § 19.05 Appointment of Trustee or Examiner.

[59] Bankruptcy Code § 321(b).

[60] Bankruptcy Code § 321(c). *See* In re Tyrone F. Conner Corp., Inc., 140 B.R. 771 (Bankr. C.D. Cal. 1992).

[61] Bankruptcy Code § 322.

[62] *See* Bankruptcy Code § 101(14). *See generally infra* Chapter 21 Role of Professionals in Bankruptcy Cases.

[63] Bankruptcy Code § 323(a).

[B] Examiners

In Chapter 11 cases, an examiner may be appointed as a less intrusive alternative to the appointment of a trustee.[64] When appointed, an examiner is normally charged with responsibility to investigate some or all of the debtor's financial affairs, and to report its findings to the court and to parties with an interest in the case, such as the members of a creditors' committee. An examiner might also be appointed to assist a debtor-in-possession to administer the estate or to fulfill other functions under more direct court supervision.

Although appointment of an examiner is normally within the sound discretion of the court, if the case involves more than $5 million in unsecured claims, appointment is mandatory upon the request of either a party in interest or the United States Trustee.[65]

As with other officials such as the trustee and professionals engaged by the estate, an examiner must be a "disinterested person" within the meaning of § 101(14). Thus, the examiner may not be a creditor, an equity security holder, or an insider. In addition, he or she may not be have served as a director, officer, or employee of the debtor within two years before the date of the petition. Likewise, the examiner may not have, either directly or indirectly, "an interest materially adverse to the interest of the estate or of any class of creditors or equity security holders."[66]

[C] The United States Trustee

The United States Trustee is another official who may become directly involved in specific bankruptcy cases. Care must be taken to distinguish between the case or standing trustee on the one hand and the United States Trustee on the other. The former is assigned to serve in an administrative function in specific bankruptcy cases; the latter is an agency of the United States government that is part of the United States Department of Justice, that is responsible for supervising case trustees and other aspects of the bankruptcy system.

Before 1979, bankruptcy courts had only a rudimentary administrative structure. Basic issues, such as the appointment and supervision of trustees and creditors' committees, were dealt with by bankruptcy judges, sometimes haphazardly.[67] In this earlier era, it was not uncommon for judges to wear several hats, sometimes serving as a judicial officer in resolving disputes, sometimes dispensing patronage in appointing trustees, and sometimes dispensing ex parte

---

[64] Bankruptcy Code § 1104(c).

[65] Bankruptcy Code § 1104(c)(2).

[66] Bankruptcy Code § 101(14).

[67] *See* Ted Janger, *Crystals and Mud in Bankruptcy Law: Judicial Competence and Statutory Design*, 43 Ariz. L. Rev. 559, 586-88 (2001); Harvey R. Miller, *The Changing Face of Chapter 11: A Reemergence of the Bankruptcy Judge as Producer, Director, and Sometimes Star of the Reorganization Passion Play*, 69 Am. Bankr. L.J. 431 (1995); Stephen A. Stripp, *An Analysis of the Role of the Bankruptcy Judge and the Use of Judicial Time*, 23 Seton Hall L. Rev. 1329 (1993).

advice to attorneys and parties alike.[68] Although there was little evidence that these diverse roles led to outright corruption or systematic abuse, the inherent conflict in these functions was one reason for the subordinate status of bankruptcy judges, and was among the problems Congress was determined to address when the current Bankruptcy Code was adopted.

The congressional solution was to significantly limit the role of bankruptcy judges in case management, and to limit their role to resolving disputes. At the same time, the office of the United States Trustee was created to take over the administrative functions that judges had performed.[69] Originally a pilot program for only a few districts, the U.S. Trustee program went nationwide after the 1986 Bankruptcy Code amendments.[70]

The United States Trustee for a geographic region is appointed by the United States Attorney General for a term of five years, subject to removal at any time, with or without cause.[71] The United States Trustee thus serves at the pleasure of the Attorney General.[72]

The powers of the U.S. Trustee are broad. Its duties include:

- appointing interim Chapter 7 trustees and establishing panels of trustees available to serve in individual bankruptcy cases;

- approving non-profit consumer counseling agencies to provide consumer counseling education programs to consumer debtors;[73]

- supervising the administration of bankruptcy cases and trustees;[74]

- monitoring and commenting on applications for attorney fees and other professional compensation;[75]

- interviewing small business debtors in Chapter 11 cases;[76]

- moving to dismiss consumer Chapter 7 liquidation proceedings on the ground that the filing is a substantial abuse of the Bankruptcy Code;[77] and,

---

[68] Harvey R. Miller, *The Changing Face of Chapter 11: A Reemergence of the Bankruptcy Judge as Producer, Director, and Sometimes Star of the Reorganization Passion Play*, 69 Am. Bankr. L.J. 431 (1995); Thomas E. Plank, *Why Bankruptcy Judges Need Not and Should Not Be Article III Judges*, 72 Am. Bankr. L.J. 567 (1998).

[69] 28 U.S.C. § 581 (2006).

[70] Michael J. Herbert, *Once More Unto the Breach, Dear Friends: The 1986 Reforms of the Reformed Bankruptcy Reform Act*, 16 Cap. U.L. Rev. 325 (1987). There is no United States Trustee in Alabama and North Carolina. There, "court administrators" perform the U.S. Trustee's functions.

[71] 28 U.S.C. § 581(b), (c) (2006).

[72] 28 U.S.C. § 582(a), (b) (2006).

[73] Bankruptcy Code § 1111(b).

[74] 28 U.S.C. § 586(a)(3) (2006).

[75] For a discussion of professional compensation under the Bankruptcy Code, see *infra* § 21.03 Fees for Professionals.

[76] 28 U.S.C. § 586(a)(7) (2006).

[77] *See* Bankruptcy Code § 707(b). *See infra* § 17.03[B] Dismissal of Consumer Cases Due to Abuse.

- making various reports to the Attorney General regarding administration of the bankruptcy system.[78]

The United States Trustee program was initially controversial.[79] The efficiency of having a tax-supported public official monitor cases that might otherwise be monitored by the creditors whose dollars are at stake has been questioned.[80] However, the Trustee's office has been expanded from an initial pilot program in a few districts to an almost nationwide system for governmental oversight of bankruptcy cases.[81] It now plays a significant role in monitoring consumer bankruptcy cases and ensuring that case trustees are fulfilling their statutory duties.

§ 4.06 BANKRUPTCY COURTS AND BANKRUPTCY JUDGES[82]

For most of the history of bankruptcy law in the United States, the bankruptcy system lacked its own independent court system. Its decision-makers were called "referees," rather than judges. While many of the referees were of outstanding ability, they were branded with second, if not third-class status.

Today, the bankruptcy court is a largely autonomous adjunct of the federal district court.[83] It has its own judges, courtrooms, clerks, and dockets. Its pleadings, orders, and other documents are captioned with the designation "United States Bankruptcy Court." However, its jurisdiction is derivative of the district court's jurisdiction[84] and the district court may at any time withdraw part or all of any case from it.[85] The fact that such withdrawals are rare reflects only the practical reality that district court judges are usually not much interested in bankruptcy and are overwhelmed with other litigation.[86] Bankruptcy judges, unlike district judges, are not appointed by the President and do not have lifetime tenure. Rather, they are appointed by the judges of the relevant federal Circuit Court of Appeals for terms

---

[78] 28 U.S.C. § 586(a)(7) (2006).

[79] Hon. Steven W. Rhodes, *Eight Statutory Causes Of Delay And Expense In Chapter 11 Bankruptcy Cases*, 67 Am. Bankr. L.J. 287 (1993).

[80] *See* Thomas D. Buckle, *The Untapped Power of Bankruptcy's Wild Card: The United States Trustee*, 6 J. Bankr. L. & Prac. 249 (1997); Christopher W. Fros, *The Theory, Reality and Pragmatism of Corporate Governance in Bankruptcy Reorganizations*, 72 Am. Bankr. L.J. 103, 153 (1998).

[81] Bankruptcy cases in Alabama and North Carolina are not currently within the jurisdiction of the United States Trustee Program.

[82] Thomas E. Plank, *Why Bankruptcy Judges Need Not and Should Not Be Article III Judges*, 72 Am. Bankr. L.J. 567 (1998).

[83] *See infra* § 5.02[C] Bankruptcy Jurisdiction of Federal Courts.

[84] 28 U.S.C. § 1334 (2006).

[85] 28 U.S.C. § 157(d) (2006).

[86] The relationship between district judges and bankruptcy judges is similar to that which one of your authors had with his immediate boss when they both served as church janitors. When questioned about why he never cleaned the bathrooms, the boss replied: "If I had wanted to do that, I wouldn't have hired you." Most federal district judges feel much the same way about becoming involved in bankruptcy matters.

of 14 years.[87] These appointments can be, and often are, renewed. Bankruptcy judges may be removed during the term by the circuit court judges.[88] By contrast, federal district judges, whose appointments are made pursuant to Article III of the Constitution, can only be removed by impeachment in the House of Representatives and conviction by the Senate.[89] The division of labor between bankruptcy and district courts was recently thrown into question by the Supreme Court's decision in *Stern v. Marshall.*[90] In that case, the Supreme Court found that bankruptcy courts do not have the constitutional power to adjudicate a purely state law tort claim, even when it arises in the context of a bankruptcy case because bankruptcy judges are not Article III judges. How far this restriction may extend is still uncertain.

§ 4.07 LAWYERS AND OTHER PROFESSIONALS

Lawyers dominate bankruptcy proceedings. The trustee is usually a lawyer, and she is sometimes represented by another lawyer. Although pro se proceedings are permitted, debtors usually have a lawyer. Creditors' committees engage their own attorneys, paid for at the expense of the debtor's estate, and individual creditors are likely to be independently represented. In large cases, there are a great many lawyers, with correspondingly large fees; the largest business bankruptcies have fees in the tens of millions of dollars.

Other professionals may also be hired. These include accountants, actuaries, investment bankers, real estate brokers, and in rare cases, business consultants. Their fees too may be very high. Indeed, a perception exists that some cases, particularly some protracted Chapter 11 cases, serve mainly to provide lawyers with large fees at the expense of creditors.[91]

To avoid conflicts of interest that may result in harm to creditors, and in order to restrict fees that might otherwise impair the efficient administration of the debtor's estate, the hiring and compensation of these professionals is regulated by

---

[87] 28 U.S.C. § 152(a)(1) (2006). If a majority of the circuit judges cannot agree on an appointment, the bankruptcy judge is appointed by the chief judge of the circuit. *Id.* § 152(a)(3). In United States Territories, the district judges serve as bankruptcy judges, unless Congress authorizes the appointment of bankruptcy judges, in which case they are appointed by the Circuit Court within which the territorial district is located. *Id.* § 152(a)(4).

[88] The grounds for removal, however, are limited, and there are procedural protections:

> A bankruptcy judge may be removed during the term for which such bankruptcy judge is appointed, only for incompetence, misconduct, neglect of duty, or physical or mental disability and only by the judicial council of the circuit in which the judge's official duty station is located. Removal may not occur unless a majority of all the judges of such council concur in the order of removal.

28 U.S.C. § 152(e) (2006).

[89] Note, however, that bankruptcy judges are "judicial officers of the United States district court established under Article III of the Constitution." 28 U.S.C. § 152(a)(1) (2006).

[90] 131 S. Ct. 2594 (2011).

[91] *See generally* Lynn Lopucki, Courting Failure: How Competition for Big Cases Is Corrupting the Bankruptcy Courts (2005); Sol Stein, A Feast for Lawyers (1989).

the court.[92] The specific rules dealing with appointment and compensation of lawyers and other professionals are discussed elsewhere.[93]

---

[92] Bankruptcy Code §§ 327, 328.

[93] *See infra* Chapter 21 Role of Professionals in Bankruptcy Cases.

Chapter 5

BANKRUPTCY PROCEDURE, JURISDICTION, AND VENUE

§ 5.01 PROCEDURE IN BANKRUPTCY CASES[1]

Bankruptcy is body of both substantive and procedural law, with its own specialized court system and its own rules of procedure,[2] jurisdiction,[3] and venue.[4]

The Federal Rules of Bankruptcy Procedure govern most aspects of a bankruptcy case, such as the filing of petitions, bankruptcy trustees and others who will be involved in administering a case, claims of creditors, responsibilities of the debtor, bankruptcy courts and the clerk's function, collection and liquidation of the debtor's property, adversary litigation, appeals, and other general matters.

Original and exclusive jurisdiction over bankruptcy cases is vested in federal district courts.[5] However, district judges have greater expertise in other matters, and have not, historically been particularly interested in handling bankruptcy cases. Also, given the expedited nature of many bankruptcy cases, and the havoc this would wreak on a federal court's general docket, each federal judicial district court has delegated responsibility for bankruptcy cases to the bankruptcy court for its district.[6] District courts also have original, but not exclusive jurisdiction over litigation that arises in connection with bankruptcy cases, but, as with bankruptcy cases themselves, authority over these disputes is routinely delegated to bankruptcy courts.

Bankruptcy judges are neither appointed by the President nor confirmed by the Senate, and thus, as "legislative judges," or "Article I judges," they have limited powers.[7] As a constitutional matter, some causes of action must be handled by an Article III judge. Thus, although many matters relating to bankruptcy cases may

---

[1] Stephen E. Snyder & Lawrence Ponoroff, Commercial Bankruptcy Litigation (1989); Thomas J. Salerno & Jordan A. Kroop, Bankruptcy Litigation and Practice: A Practitioner's Guide (Aspen 3d ed. 2005); Michael Cook, Bankruptcy Litigation Manual (Aspen 2004).

[2] *See* 28 U.S.C. § 2075 (2006) (authorizing the Supreme Court to promulgate rules of bankruptcy procedure).

[3] Provisions regarding the bankruptcy jurisdiction of federal district courts are at 28 U.S.C. § 1334 (2006). Authorization for bankruptcy courts to exercise this jurisdiction is contained in 28 U.S.C. § 157 (2006).

[4] 28 U.S.C. §§ 1408-1410, 1412 (2006).

[5] 28 U.S.C. § 1334 (2006). *See infra* § 5.02[C][1] Bankruptcy Jurisdiction of the District Court.

[6] 28 U.S.C. § 157(a) (2006). *See infra* § 5.02[C][2] Referral to the Bankruptcy Court.

[7] *See supra* § 5.02[B] History of Bankruptcy Jurisdiction.

be fully resolved in bankruptcy court, some disputes must be handled in federal district court, or state court. As this edition is being written, the dividing line between matters that can be handled by a Bankruptcy Judge, and those that must be handled by the District Court has been rendered uncertain by the Supreme Court's recent decision in *Stern v. Marshall.*[8] That case held that a purely state court tort claim had to be heard by an Article III judge, notwithstanding the Bankruptcy Code's grant of jurisdiction over the matter.

In addition, the judicial code provides venue rules to determine the district in which a bankruptcy case may be filed and the district in which any litigation connected to a bankruptcy case may be pursued.[9] Other procedural issues sometimes loom large in bankruptcy cases, such as the extent to which the parties may be entitled to a jury trial,[10] whether states are entitled to sovereign immunity,[11] and whether arbitration agreements are enforceable in bankruptcy.[12]

[A] Rules of Bankruptcy Procedure[13]

Many of the procedural aspects of bankruptcy are addressed by the Federal Rules of Bankruptcy Procedure and the accompanying official Bankruptcy Forms. These rules were originally adopted in 1983 pursuant to the Supreme Court's authority to "prescribe by general rules, the forms of process, writs, pleadings, and motions, and the practice and procedure in cases under [the Bankruptcy Code]."[14]

The Bankruptcy Rules may be informally divided into three broad groups. The first group deals with administrative matters that arise in the course of various types of bankruptcy proceedings, such as bankruptcy petitions, creditor's claims, the estate's property, and debtors' reorganization plans.[15] The second group deals with litigation connected to a pending bankruptcy case, referred to as "adversary proceedings."[16] These rules are modeled closely on the Federal Rules of Civil Procedure. The third group of rules deals with bankruptcy appeals.[17] In addition, the Supreme Court has adopted an extensive set of official bankruptcy forms for such things as bankruptcy petitions, financial information about the debtor and its

---

[8] 131 S. Ct. 2594 (2011).

[9] *See infra* § 5.03 Bankruptcy Venue.

[10] *See infra* § 5.02[E] Jury Trials in Bankruptcy Court.

[11] *See infra* § 5.05 Sovereign Immunity.

[12] *See infra* § 5.06 Arbitration Clauses in Bankruptcy.

[13] Lawrence King, *The History and Development of the Bankruptcy Rules*, 70 Am. Bankr. L.J. 217 (1996); Kenneth N. Klee, *The Future of the Bankruptcy Rules*, 70 Am. Bankr. L.J. 277 (1996); James J. Barta, *The Impact of Technology on the Bankruptcy Rules*, 70 Am. Bankr. L.J. 287 (1996).

[14] 28 U.S.C.S. § 2075 (2006). The rules are not permitted to "abridge, enlarge, or modify any substantive right." *Id.*

[15] *See generally* Jennie D. Latta, *"What You Don't Know May Hurt You" — Time Limits under the Bankruptcy Code and Rules*, 28 U. Mem. L. Rev. 911 (1988).

[16] Fed. R. Bankr. P. 7001-7087.

[17] Fed. R. Bankr. P. 8001-8020.

creditors, proofs of claim, and the like.[18] Moreover, each federal judicial district has its own set of local rules that govern various detailed aspects of bankruptcy cases in that district. Beyond these rules are innumerable local customs and traditions, sometimes dictated by the standard operating practices of local standing trustees.[19] Despite the constitutional mandate for a uniform law on bankruptcy, there are wide variations from district to district in the actual application of bankruptcy law.[20]

[B]   Trial Process in Bankruptcy Litigation

With over a million cases filed each year, bankruptcy is one of the most common types of federal litigation.[21] Many of these cases spawn ancillary disputes that must be handled by the court. These disputes arise in one of two forms: "contested matters," which are initiated by motion,[22] or "adversary proceedings," which begin with the filing of a complaint.[23]

Although many of these disputes require discovery or even a full-blown trial, it is common for bankruptcy litigation to proceed more quickly than litigation in other courts. Bankruptcy judges and bankruptcy litigants are sensitive to the risk of depleting a financially troubled debtor's limited assets, and things tend to move along more quickly than in state and federal trial courts. In other respects, the litigation process in bankruptcy court operates in much the same manner as in other courts, with pleadings,[24] discovery,[25] status conferences,[26] the opportunity for summary judgment,[27] and enforcement of any judgment obtained.[28] Where there is a constitutional right to a jury trial, either party can seek to have the case removed to the District Court. Nontheles, the Bankrupty Code and Rules grant bankruptcy judges the power to conduct jury trials where both parties consent.

---

[18] 28 U.S.C. § 2075 (2006). *See* http://www.uscourts.gov/FormsAndFees/Forms/BankruptcyForms. aspx (last viewed August 4, 2012).

[19] For example, Mr. Frank Pees, the Chapter 13 Standing Trustee in Columbus, Ohio, has long required chapter 13 debtors to participate in a debtor education program as a condition of receiving a discharge. In 2005, this requirement was incorporated into the Bankruptcy Code.

[20] Jean Braucher, *Lawyers and Consumer Bankruptcy: One Code, Many Cultures*, 67 Am. Bankr. L.J. 501 (1993).

[21] In 2011, only about 294,336 federal civil cases were filed in federal district courts. *See* U.S. District Court — Judicial Caseload Profile available at http://www.uscourts.gov/Viewer.aspx?doc=/uscourts/ Statistics/FederalJudicialCaseloadStatistics/2011/tables/C00Mar11.pdf (last visited on February 3, 2012) During the same year, over 1.5 million bankruptcy cases were filed, with about 40,000 more filed in 2011 than 2010.

     http://www.uscourts.gov/Viewer.aspx?doc=/uscourts/Statistics/ FederalJudicialCaseloadStatistics/2011/tables/F00Mar11.pdf (last visited on February 3, 2012).

[22] Fed. R. Bankr. P. 9014.

[23] Fed. R. Bankr. P. 7003; Fed. R. Civ. P. 3.

[24] Fed. R. Bankr. P. 7003-7015.

[25] Fed R. Bankr. P. 7026-7037.

[26] Bankruptcy Code § 105(d).

[27] Fed. R. Bankr. P. 7056.

[28] Fed. R. Bankr. P. 7069.

Jury trials, though, remain rare in bankruptcy courts.[29]

[C] Appellate Process in Bankruptcy Litigation[30]

Bankruptcy appeals are routed either to the District Court, or, in circuits where they exist and the parties do not object,[31] to a Bankruptcy Appellate Panel[32] comprised of bankruptcy judges from districts other than the one in which the case arose.[33] Although Bankruptcy Appellate Panels are "inferior" to District Courts, they are not bound by district court decisions in districts other than the one in which the case arose.[34] Curiously, some courts have held that, as a result of the 2005 BAPCPA legislation,[35] decisions of Bankruptcy Appellate Panels do not have stare decisis effect on bankruptcy judges in the circuit in which they are issued, but are effective only on the parties involved in the case in the appeal involved.[36]

The normal rule that appeals may ordinarily be taken only from final judgments, orders, and decrees, also applies in bankruptcy.[37] Interlocutory orders or decrees may generally be appealed only with leave of court.[38] The principal exception to this is an order that reduces or expands the period during which a Chapter 11 debtor has the exclusive right to propose a plan of reorganization.[39]

In rare circumstances, a direct appeal may now also be made to the United States Circuit Court of Appeals, but only if the circuit court permits the usual procedure to be bypassed.[40] This may be done only because of the absence of controlling authority regarding the issue, the public importance of the issue, the existence of conflicting decisions regarding the issue, or the likelihood that a direct appeal will materially advance the progress of the case or proceeding involved in

---

[29] *See infra* § 5.02[E] Jury Trials in Bankruptcy Court.

[30] Paul M. Baisier & David G. Epstein, *Resolving Still Unresolved Issues of Bankruptcy Law: A Fence or An Ambulance*, 69 Am. Bankr. L.J. 525 (1995); Lissa Lamkin Broome, *Bankruptcy Appeals: The Wheel is Come Full Circle*, 69 Am. Bankr. L.J. 541 (1995).

[31] Bankruptcy Appellate Panels have been established in the First, Sixth, Eighth, Ninth, and Tenth Circuits. 6 Collier Bankruptcy Practice Guide § 117.02[2], at 117 n.24 (Asa S. Herzog & Lawrence P. King eds., 2010).

[32] 28 U.S.C.S. § 158(c) (2006). The election to have the appeal heard by the district court must be made via "a statement of election contained in a separate writing filed within the [30 day] time [period]" prescribed by 28 U.S.C. § 158(c)(1) (2006). Fed. R. Bankr. P. 8001(e).

[33] 28 U.S.C. § 158(b)(5) (2006).

[34] In re Silverman, 616 F.3d 1001 (9th Cir. 2010).

[35] *See* 28 U.S.C. § 158(d)(2) (2006).

[36] *E.g.*, In re Rinard, 451 B.R. 12 (Bankr. C.D. Cal. 2011).

[37] 28 U.S.C. § 158(a)(1) (2006). *See* DeLauro v. Porto (In re Porto), 645 F.3d 1294 (11th Cir. 2011); John P. Hennigan, Jr., *Toward Regularizing Appealability in Bankruptcy*, 12 Bank. Dev. J. 583 (1996); Charles J. Tabb, *Lender Preference Clauses and the Destruction of Appealability and Finality: Resolving a Chapter 11 Dilemma*, 50 Ohio St. L.J. 109 (1989).

[38] 28 U.S.C. § 158(a)(3) (2006). *See* Judy Beckner Sloan, *Appellate Jurisdiction of Interlocutory Appeals in Bankruptcy 28 U.S.C. § 158(d): A Case of Lapsus Calami.*, 40 Cath. U.L. Rev. 265 (1991).

[39] 28 U.S.C. § 158(a)(2) (2006).

[40] *See* Laura B. Bartell, *The Appeal of Direct Appeal — Use of the New 28 U.S.C. § 158(d)(2)*, 84 Am. Bankr. L.J. 145 (2010).

the appeal.[41] The final level of appellate review is to United States Supreme Court, nearly always via a petition for a writ of certiorari.

§ 5.02   BANKRUPTCY JURISDICTION OF FEDERAL COURTS[42]

The subject matter jurisdiction of bankruptcy courts has long been one of the most vexing problems in bankruptcy law. For generations, lawyers, judges, and academics (not to mention bewildered law students) have complained about jurisdictional rules that are at best prolix and complicated.

[A]   Article I Status of Bankruptcy Judges

Some serious questions about bankruptcy jurisdiction persist and have never been fully addressed. Most of these problems can be traced to Congress's unwillingness to grant life-tenured status for bankruptcy judges under Article III of the Constitution.[43]

The United States Constitution permits two kinds of federal judges: full-fledged Article III judges, who are appointed by the President and confirmed by the Senate, and continue to serve "during good behavior"; and more limited "Article I" judges, who serve either at will or more commonly, for a term of years. Bankruptcy judges are Article I judges, appointed by the Judicial Council for each Circuit for fourteen year terms.[44]

As legislative officers, bankruptcy judges' powers are limited.[45] Article III district, circuit, and Supreme Court judges are vested with broad authority to exercise the judicial power of the United States. Broadly speaking, Article I judges may resolve disputes involving "public rights" — those created by Congress — but may not adjudicate "private rights," that usually arise under state law.[46] Fortunately, the Bankruptcy Code, and the right to seek relief from creditors' claims, is a creature of Congress, so matters surrounding the allowance or disallowance of creditors' claims are deemed "public." But, disputes over a debtor's private rights sometimes arise in the course of a bankruptcy case. When this happens, and unless the parties consent to the bankruptcy judge's authority, this

---

[41] 28 U.S.C. § 157(d)(2) (2006).

[42] Ralph Brubaker, *On the Nature of Federal Bankruptcy Jurisdiction: A General Statutory and Constitutional Theory*, 41 Wm. & Mary L. Rev. 743 (2000); Ralph Brubaker, *One Hundred Years of Federal Bankruptcy Law and Still Clinging to an in Rem Model of Bankruptcy Jurisdiction*, 15 Bankr. Dev. J. 261 (1999).

[43] *Compare* Susan Block-Lieb, *The Costs of a Non-Article III Bankruptcy Court System*, 72 Am. Bank. L.J. 529 (1998), *with* Thomas E. Plank, *Why Bankruptcy Judges Need Not and Should Not Be Article III Judges*, 72 Am. Bankr. L.J. 567 (1998).

[44] 28 U.S.C. § 152 (2006).

[45] James E. Pfander, *Article I Tribunals, Article III Courts, and the Judicial Power of the United States*, 118 Harv. L. Rev. 643 (2004). *See also* Alan M. Ahern, *The Limited Scope of Implied Powers of a Bankruptcy Judge: A Statutory Court of Bankruptcy, Not a Court of Equity*, 79 Am. Bank. L.J. 1 (2005).

[46] Stern v. Marshall, 131 S. Ct. 2594 (2011).

litigation may have to be resolved either on the more deliberate docket of a Federal District Court or a state court. As will be discussed below, the line between "public rights" and "private rights" after *Stern v. Marshall* is one that will be litigated for a while.

[B]   History of Bankruptcy Jurisdiction[47]

The Bankruptcy Act of 1898[48] designated district courts as "courts of bankruptcy," but permitted the judges of each district to appoint bankruptcy referees to assist them with their duties.[49] Referee's decisions were subject to review by the district judge.[50] Under this system, the bankruptcy court's power ultimately depended on a hoary distinction between "summary" and "plenary" jurisdiction.[51] Bankruptcy referees handled summary matters, which were limited primarily to administrative matters in connection with the case,[52] resolving disputes over property that was already in the actual or constructive possession of the court,[53] and deciding plenary matters where the parties provided their consent.[54] Bankruptcy courts were otherwise unable to handle other "plenary" matters.

The 1978 Bankruptcy Reform Act sought to eliminate this cumbersome distinction between summary and plenary jurisdiction, by vesting jurisdiction over all matters even related to a bankruptcy case, with the bankruptcy court. Unfortunately, the Supreme Court declared this new system unconstitutional.[55] In *Northern Pipeline Construction Co. v. Marathon Pipe Line Co.*,[56] the Court determined that a grant of authority to legislative courts, over disputes involving "private rights," arising solely under state law, violated Article III of the Constitution. The private right involved in *Marathon Pipeline* involved a simple contract dispute between a Chapter 11 debtor and a third party with whom it had

---

[47] *See* Ralph Brubaker, *One Hundred Years of Federal Bankruptcy Law and Still Clinging to an in Rem Model of Bankruptcy Jurisdiction*, 15 Bankr. Dev. J. 261 (1999); Jeffrey T. Ferriell, *The Constitutionality of the Bankruptcy Amendments and Federal Judgeship Act of 1984*, 63 Am. Bankr. L.J. 109, 113-121 (1989); Robert G. Skelton & Donald F. Harris, *Bankruptcy Jurisdiction and Jury Trials: The Constitutional Nightmare Continues*, 8 Bankr. Dev. J. 469, 473-476 (1991). An elaborate version of this history is recounted in *In re Marshall*, 600 F.3d 1037 (9th Cir. 2010).

[48] 30 Stat. 544 (repealed 1979).

[49] Bankruptcy Act of 1898 §§ 1-2, 33-43.

[50] Id. § 38.

[51] *See* James E. Pfander, *Article I Tribunals, Article III Courts, and the Judicial Power of the United States*, 118 Harv. L. Rev. 643, 719-721 (2004).

[52] Bankruptcy Act of 1898 §§ 2, 38. *See, e.g.*, U.S. Fidelity & Guaranty Co. v. Bray, 225 U.S. 205, 218 (1912).

[53] Bankruptcy Act of 1898 §§ 2, 38. *See, e.g.*, Thompson v. Magnolia Petroleum Co., 309 U.S. 478, 481 (1940).

[54] Bankruptcy Act of 1898 § 23b; MacDonald v. Plymouth County Trust Co., 286 U.S. 263, 266-67 (1932).

[55] Geraldine Mund, *A Look Behind the Ruling: The Supreme Court and the Unconstitutionality of the Bankruptcy Act of 1978*, 78 Am. Bankr. L.J. 401 (2004); Martin H. Redish, *Legislative Courts, Administrative Agencies, and the Northern Pipeline Decision*, 1983 Duke L.J. 197.

[56] 458 U.S. 50 (1982), *judgment stayed*, 459 U.S. 813 (1982).

a construction contract. By giving bankruptcy courts jurisdiction over disputes regarding private rights, that did not directly involve issues in the bankruptcy case, Congress had improperly granted a portion of the "judicial power" of the United States to an Article I court.

It took Congress two years to resolve the crisis that the *Marathon Pipeline* decision precipitated. The Bankruptcy Amendments and Federal Judgeship Act,[57] popularly known as "BAFJA," granted jurisdiction over bankruptcy cases to the district courts, but permitted the district courts to refer many bankruptcy matters to the bankruptcy judges for the district, in a manner that is reminiscent of the older distinction between summary and plenary jurisdiction that prevailed under the Bankruptcy Act, but with a few added elements designed to buttress the constitutionality of the new jurisdictional regime.

[C] Bankruptcy Jurisdiction

The current jurisdictional scheme, adopted in BAFJA, assigns jurisdiction over all bankruptcy matters to district courts,[58] but permits each district court to refer most bankruptcy matters to the bankruptcy court for the district.[59] District judges are free to hold on to authority over bankruptcy cases and have the power to withdraw bankruptcy cases that have been referred to the bankruptcy court at any time. Thus, bankruptcy judges remain under the supervision of the district court, even though district judges only rarely act to exercise their supervisory authority.[60]

[1] Bankruptcy Jurisdiction of the District Court

Bankruptcy jurisdiction is initially vested in federal district courts. Their authority extends to bankruptcy cases,[61] to civil proceedings connected to a bankruptcy case,[62] and to "in rem" jurisdiction over property involved in a bankruptcy case.[63]

The district court's jurisdiction over bankruptcy cases themselves is exclusive. Bankruptcy cases may not be filed in state court.

District courts have original, but not exclusive jurisdiction over civil proceedings arising "under [the bankruptcy code], arising in a bankruptcy case, and related to

---

[57] The Bankruptcy Amendments and Federal Judgeship Act of 1984, Pub. L. 98-353, 98 Stat. 341 (1984).

[58] 28 U.S.C. § 1334 (2006).

[59] 28 U.S.C. § 157(a) (2006).

[60] One notable exception is the general withdrawal of the reference by the District of Delaware. *See* Order of the United States Court for the District of Delaware (Jan. 23, 1997) (Farnan, C.J.) (withdrawing reference from Delaware bankruptcy courts); Leif Clark, *Crossing the Delaware*, Am. Bankr. Inst. J., March, 1997, at 34-35.

[61] 28 U.S.C. § 1334(a) (2006).

[62] 28 U.S.C. § 1334(b) (2006).

[63] 28 U.S.C. § 1334(e) (2006).

a bankruptcy case."[64] And, consistent their jurisdiction over bankruptcy cases themselves, their jurisdiction over property that belongs to a bankruptcy estate or to a debtor who is involved in a bankruptcy case, is exclusive.[65]

[2]   Referral of Jurisdiction to the Bankruptcy Court

Despite this broad grant of authority, district courts do not ordinarily assume direct day-to-day control over bankruptcy cases and their attendant litigation. Instead, bankruptcy matters are routinely delegated to the bankruptcy court pursuant to a general order of reference, entered in each district, generally referring nearly all matters within the district court's bankruptcy jurisdiction to the district's bankruptcy court.[66] The district court retains the power to withdraw this reference, in whole or in part, either on its own motion or the motion of any party.[67]

In some limited circumstances, withdrawal is mandatory.[68] The relevant statutory language provides: "The district court shall, on timely motion of a party, so withdraw a proceeding if the court determines that resolution of the proceeding requires consideration of both [the Bankruptcy Code] and other laws of the United States regulating organizations or activities affecting interstate commerce."[69] Most courts apply this language to make withdrawal mandatory only if the dispute involves "substantial and material consideration" of federal law other than the Bankruptcy Code,[70] even though the case may also require consideration of a Bankruptcy Code issue.[71]

Thus, either under the discretionary or mandatory withdrawal provisions, the district court retains nominal power over bankruptcy cases despite their referral to the bankruptcy court. However, because this power is rarely exercised,[72] it is almost always bankruptcy judges who decide disputes arising in bankruptcy cases.

---

[64] 28 U.S.C. § 1334(b) (2006).

[65] 28 U.S.C. § 1334(e) (2006).

[66] 28 U.S.C. § 157(a) (2006) provides: "Each district court may provide that any or all cases under title 11 and any or all proceedings arising under title 11 or arising in or related to a case under title 11 shall be referred to the bankruptcy judge for the district." All federal district courts took advantage of this language and entered an general order of reference as soon as possible after the ink was dry on the legislation granting them this authority.

[67] 28 U.S.C. § 157(d) (2006).

[68] 28 U.S.C. § 157(d) (2006). See Erich D. Anderson, Comment, *Closing the Escape Hatch in the Mandatory Withdrawal Provision of 28 U.S.C. § 157(d)*, 36 UCLA L. Rev. 417 (1988).

[69] 28 U.S.C. § 157(d) (2006). See Erich D. Anderson, Comment, *Closing the Escape Hatch in the Mandatory Withdrawal Provision of 28 U.S.C. § 157(d)*, 36 UCLA L. Rev. 417 (1988).

[70] *See, e.g.*, United States v. Delfasco, Inc., 409 B.R. 704 (D. Del. 2009) (proceeding required substantial interpretation of federal environmental laws).

[71] *E.g.*, In re Vicars Ins. Agency, Inc., 96 F.3d 949 (7th Cir. 1996).

[72] Withdrawal seems most appropriate when a jury trial is required. *E.g.*, Lars, Inc. v. Taber Partners (In re Lars, Inc.), 290 B.R. 467 (D.P.R. 2003).

[3]   Bankruptcy Court Authority Over "Bankruptcy Cases" and "Core Proceedings"[73]

Upon referral, "[b]ankruptcy judges may *hear and determine* all cases under title 11 and all *core proceedings* arising under title 11, or arising in a case under title 11 . . . subject to [appellate review]."[74] Thus, the bankruptcy court has full authority over bankruptcy cases,[75] and over all "core proceedings" that arise either under title 11 or in a case under title 11.[76] The court's authority over other disputes that are not "core proceedings" is more limited. This makes the scope of "core proceedings" of critical importance.

Core proceedings[77] include most routine matters likely to arise in a bankruptcy case, specifically including those dealing with:

- administration of the estate;

- allowance of claims;

- counterclaims against persons who file claims against the estate;

- turnover of estate property;

- the use, sale, or lease of estate property;

- the trustee's avoiding powers;

- dischargeability of debts and objections to discharge;

- the validity, extent, and priority of liens;

- the automatic stay; and

- confirmation of plans.

Thus, roughly speaking, a core proceeding is one that fundamentally involves bankruptcy law and the management of the debtor's estate, even though other law may be secondarily involved.

---

[73] Jeffrey T. Ferriell, *Core Proceedings in Bankruptcy Court*, Jeffrey T. Ferriell, 56 UMKC L. Rev. 47 (1987); Thomas S. Marrion, *Core Proceedings and the "New" Bankruptcy Jurisdiction*, 35 DePaul L. Rev. 675 (1986).

[74] 28 U.S.C. § 157(b)(1) (2006) (emphasis added).

[75] In re Shemonsky, No. 11–1227, 2011 U.S. App. LEXIS 16076 (3d Cir. August 03, 2011).

[76] 28 U.S.C. § 157(b)(1) (2006). *See generally* Wood v. Wood (In re Wood), 825 F.2d 90 (5th Cir. 1987). It is entirely unclear what is supposed to happen in a matter that is not a "core proceeding" that "arises under" or "arises in" a bankruptcy case, or whether it is even theoretically possible for such a thing to exist.

[77] *See* 28 U.S.C. § 157(b) (2006).

[a]   Personal Injury & Wrongful Death Claims Excluded

Despite this broad array of jurisdiction over "core proceedings," bankruptcy courts are specifically prevented from hearing "personal injury and wrongful death claims against the debtor's estate."[78] Absent the consent of the parties, these claims must be tried by the district court, unless it abstains and permits them to be heard in state court. This provision is particularly important in cases involving mass tort claims, such as those involving producers of asbestos or other harmful consumer products which have caused injuries to a large number of people.[79]

[b]   Counterclaims Against Creditors

The meaning of § 157(b)(2)(C), with respect to counterclaims brought by the estate against a creditor was addressed by the Supreme Court in *Stern v. Marshall*.[80] There, the debtor's stepson filed a proof of claim for defamation in the debtor's Chapter 11 case, accompanied by a complaint to have the debt declared nondischargeable under § 523(a)(6). The debtor responded with a counterclaim against the stepson for tortious interference with a $300 million inter-vivos gift from her deceased husband, the stepson's father. The Supreme Court ruled that § 157(b)(2)(C) extended the court's jurisdiction over the debtor's counterclaim, but that the statutory grant of jurisdiction was unconstitutional under Article III of the Constitution as interpreted by *Northern Pipeline Construction Co v. Marathon Pipe Line Co*.[81] The court explained that the debtor's counterclaim for tortious interference, like the debtor's breach of contract claim in *Marathon Pipeline*, arose purely under state law and was not affected by the son's claim against the estate for defamation, even though it arose from the same transaction and was properly characterized as "compulsory."[82] Because the debtor's counterclaim raised issues of law that were completely different from those involved in the claimant's defamation proceeding, the factual overlap between the two claims did not justify Congress in granting jurisdiction to an Article I court over the counterclaim.[83] The court held that "Article III of the Constitution [restricts the authority of a bankruptcy court] to enter a final judgment on a state law counterclaim that is not resolved in the process of ruling on a creditor's proof of claim."[84]

While *Stern v. Marshall* does not limit the jurisdiction of the district court (since district courts are Article III courts) like *Marathon Pipeline*, it threatens the ability of bankruptcy courts to operate as a central forum that can adjudicate all matters that are likely to have an impact on a debtor's bankruptcy estate. The necessity of litigating a debtor's counterclaim against a creditor in the district court may diminish the ability of the bankruptcy court to promptly and efficiently

---

[78] 28 U.S.C. § 157(c)(2)(B) (2006).

[79] *See infra* § 23.02 Mass Torts.

[80] 131 S. Ct. 2594 (2011).

[81] 458 U.S. 50 (1982).

[82] 131 S. Ct. 2594, 2617 (2011).

[83] *Id.*

[84] 131 S. Ct. at 2620.

administer the debtor's bankruptcy case, and make a full and final distribution of assets to creditors. In some cases, where the debtor's counterclaim against a creditor is a significant estate asset, this limit on the court's jurisdiction may impair the entire bankruptcy process.

Further, although Justice Roberts' opinion indicated that the Court's decision "does not change all that much," commentators and lower courts have raised serious questions about whether its reasoning might extend to restrict bankruptcy courts' jurisdiction over a wider range of administrative matters, including actions to avoid pre-bankruptcy transfers as preferences, fraudulent transfers, or otherwise,[85] and other matters previously considered as central parts of the administration of a bankruptcy case.[86]

Stern's rationale continues to permit bankruptcy courts to assert jurisdiction over matters involving "public rights," such as actions based on a creditor's violation of the automatic stay, but Justice Scalia's concurring opinion raises question about whether the "public rights doctrine" on which *Marathon Pipeline* had been based, is quite as broad as previously thought.[87] Serious questions have been raised, for example, over whether it permits the bankruptcy court to entertain actions to recover fraudulent conveyances.[88] Although fraudulent conveyance proceedings are the stuff of which bankruptcy proceedings are made of, they are squarely within the scope of the type of " 'the traditional actions at common law [that were] tried by the courts at Westminster in 1789' " that Justice Roberts' opinion indicated were outside the scope of "public rights."[89] Indeed, it might be that a different result would be reached when a trustee seeks to avoid a fraudulent conveyance under state law pursuant to Section 544 of the Bankruptcy Code, as opposed to when avoidance is sought under the Bankruptcy Code's own avoidance power for fraudulent conveyances — Section 548.

Likewise, *Stern* seems to permit bankruptcy courts to resolve counterclaims against a creditor where the counterclaim is so inextricably intertwined with the allowability of the creditor's claim, that the counterclaim has to be resolved as part of the process of determining the enforceability of the creditor's claim.[90]

---

[85] *Compare* Meoli v. Huntington Nat'l Bank (In re Teleservices Group, Inc.), 456 B.R. 318 (Bankr. W.D. Mich. 2011), *and* Yellow Sign, Inc. v. Freeway Foods, Inc. (In re Freeway Foods of Greensboro, Inc.), 466 B.R. 750 (Bankr. M.D.N.C. 2012) (no jurisdiction over fraudulent transfer action), *with* In re Direct Response Media, Inc., 466 B.R. 626 (Bankr. D. Del. 2012) (bankruptcy court could determine action to recover fraudulent transfer).

[86] George Kunney, Stern v. Marshall: *A Likely Return to the Bankruptcy Act's Summary/Plenary Distinction in Article III Terms*, 21 J. Bankr. L. & Prac. 1 Art. 1 (2011); Eric G. Behrens, Stern v. Marshall: *The Supreme Court's Continuing Erosion of Bankruptcy Court Jurisdiction and Article I Courts*, 85 Am. Bankr. L.J. 387 (2011).

[87] Justice Scalia takes a limited view of the public rights doctrine, believing that with limited exceptions, an "Article III judge is required in all federal adjudications." 131 S. Ct. at 2621 (Scalia, J., concurring).

[88] *See* In re Bellingham Ins. Agency, Inc., 661 F.3d 476 (9th Cir. 2011) (inviting supplemental briefs by amicus curiae on bankruptcy court's jurisdiction over fraudulent conveyance action).

[89] 131 S. Ct. at 2609 (quoting *Northern Pipeline*, 458 U.S., at 90 (Rehnquist, J., concurring)).

[90] In re Salander O'Reilly Galleries, 453 B.R. 106 (Bankr. S.D.N.Y. 2011); Tibble v. Wells Fargo Bank, N.A. (In re Hudson), 455 B.R. 648, 657 (Bankr. W.D. Mich. 2011).

Beyond this, little is certain, as the nation's bankruptcy court system struggles to decipher whether Justice Roberts' statement that *Stern v. Marshall* "does not change all that much," is an accurate assessment of the decision's effect.

[4]   Non-Core Proceedings — Civil Proceedings "Related to" a Bankruptcy Case

Conspicuously missing from the list of "core proceedings" that are fully delegated to the bankruptcy court are "civil proceedings *related to* a case under title 11."[91] These are included among the disputes that can be referred to the bankruptcy court, but the bankruptcy court does not have full authority to resolve them, without the parties' consent.

A proceeding is related to a bankruptcy case if is not "arising under the bankruptcy code" and is not "arising in a bankruptcy case" but nevertheless "could conceivably have [an] effect on the [bankruptcy] estate . . . ."[92] Thus, a proceeding is related to a bankruptcy case even though it might not involve a claim against either the debtor or the debtor's property. It is enough if the outcome of the matter "could alter the debtor's rights, liabilities, options, or freedom of action (either positively or negatively), and in any way impacts upon the handling and administration of the bankrupt estate."[93]

Examples of actions that are not core proceedings that are merely related to a bankruptcy case those brought by the estate to collect pre-petition accounts receivable,[94] the debtor's pre-petition personal injury claims against third-parties, and other actions based on private rights, similar to those involved in *Marathon Pipeline* and *Stern v. Marshall* that arise completely under state law. Successful pursuit of all of these types of actions would enhance the size of the debtor's estate and thus would have an impact on the debtor's estate and distributions to creditors, but are outside the scope of the bankruptcy court's authority, and their resolution outside bankruptcy court might delay full administration of a debtor's estate.

Sensitive to this concern, the Judicial Code specifies that cases which are merely "related to" a bankruptcy case or that are otherwise not within the definition of "core proceedings" may be *heard* by the bankruptcy court, but not *finally determined* without the participation of a district judge. Unless the parties consent to the bankruptcy court's entry of a final order, the bankruptcy judge is permitted to conduct any necessary evidentiary hearing and prepare a set of proposed findings of fact and conclusions of law for de novo review by the district court.[95] In most

---

[91] 28 U.S.C. § 157(c)(1) (2006) (emphasis added).

[92] Pacor, Inc. v. Higgins, 743 F.2d 984, 994 (3d Cir. 1984).

[93] Pacor, Inc. v. Higgins, 743 F.2d 984, 994 (3d Cir. 1984). *See also* Celotex Corp. v. Edwards, 514 U.S. 300, 308 n.6 (1994) (citing *Pacor* with approval).

[94] Orion Pictures Corp. v. Showtime Networks, Inc. (In re Orion Pictures Corp.), 4 F.3d 1095, 1102 (2d Cir. 1993). *See generally* Jeffrey T. Ferriell, *Actions to Collect Accounts Receivable in Bankruptcy Court*, 26 Houston L. Rev. 603 (1989).

[95] Orion Pictures Corp. v. Showtime Networks, Inc. (In re Orion Pictures Corp.), 4 F.3d 1095, 1102 (2d Cir. 1993).

cases, the district judge is likely to agree with the bankruptcy judge's recommended ruling.

Despite this limitation on the bankruptcy judge's authority, if no one makes a "timely and specific" objection to the bankruptcy judge's proposed ruling, the district judge may approve the bankruptcy judge's findings without reviewing them. Moreover, the parties may give their consent to the bankruptcy court's authority to finally resolve these matters.[96]

[5]   Disputes Beyond the Court's Statutory Jurisdiction

[a]   Disputes Not "Related To" a Bankruptcy Case

The district and bankruptcy court's limited authority over disputes that are "related to" a bankruptcy case raises a further issue regarding the outside limits of the court's jurisdiction. Some disputes are not even "related to" a bankruptcy case and are thus outside the bankruptcy court's statutory jurisdiction. The usual test to determine whether a dispute is related to a bankruptcy case is whether "the outcome could alter the debtor's rights, liabilities, options, or freedom of action (either positively or negatively) and which in a way impacts upon the handling and administration of the bankruptcy estate."[97] The United States Supreme Court has indicated that this might include "suits between third parties if the outcome will have an effect on the bankruptcy estate."[98] However, if the dispute will have no effect on the bankruptcy estate, it does not fall within the court's "related to" jurisdiction and, absent some other source of federal jurisdiction, might have to be handled in state court.

[b]   Probate Exception

The rule that federal courts may neither probate a will nor administer a decedent's estate is long established,[99] though it is not always clear whether this is for constitutional or prudential reasons.[100] And, although it's scope has been uncertain, the Supreme Court's decision in *Marshall v. Marshall*[101] (an earlier decision in the jurisdictional saga that culminated in *Stern v. Marshall*, which held that the traditional exception did not prevent the bankruptcy court from exercising jurisdiction over a widow's claim that her stepson tortiously interfered with her expectancy of inheritance or gift from her deceased husband), makes it clear that its ambit is narrow, particularly in a bankruptcy context. Although a later decision ruled that the bankruptcy court lacked constitutional authority to resolve the

---

[96]   28 U.S.C. § 157(c)(2) (2006).

[97]   Pacor v. Higgins (In re Pacor), 743 F.2d 984, 994 (1984).

[98]   Celotex v. Edwards (In re Celotex), 514 U.S. 300, 307 n. 5 (1995). *See also* In re Dow Corning Corp., 86 F.3d 482 (1996).

[99]   Waterman v. Canal-La. Bank & Trust Co., 215 U.S. 33, 43-45 (1909).

[100]   David B. Young, *The Intersection of Bankruptcy and Probate*, 49 S. Tex. L. Rev. 351, 354 (2007).

[101]   547 U.S. 293 (2006). This is the same "Marshall" involved in the Court's 2011 bankruptcy jurisdiction decision in *Marshall v. Stern*. Ms. Marshall is also known as Anna Nicole Smith, the 1993 Playboy Playmate of the Year.

dispute,[102] the Court left no doubt that the scope of the probate exception did not prevent federal courts from hearing disputes by or against a decedent's estate's administrator, or from resolving claims against an estate's beneficiaries or its creditors. The probate exception was limited to probating a will, administering an estate, or to assert purely in rem jurisdiction over a probate estate's property.[103]

[6] Jurisdiction over Jurisdictional Determinations

As is generally true with matters of jurisdiction, the bankruptcy court has authority to make an initial determination regarding its own authority to handle the dispute. On the judge's own motion or on the motion of a party, the bankruptcy judge can determine whether a proceeding is a core proceeding.

[D] Abstention[104]

Even when it has jurisdiction over a dispute, a bankruptcy court may elect to abstain from exercising power over the proceeding. If the court abstains, the matter will probably be resolved in state court, or, if there are other grounds for federal jurisdiction, in federal district court.

[1] Permissive Abstention[105]

The district court — and thus the bankruptcy court — is authorized to permissively abstain from hearing civil proceedings that "arise under," "arise in," or are "related to" a bankruptcy case. The court is permitted to abstain whenever abstention is "in the interest of justice, or in the interest of comity with State courts, or [out of] respect for State law."[106] Of course, this authority does not extend to the court's jurisdiction over a bankruptcy case itself, over which the court has exclusive jurisdiction.

Permissive abstention is rare. However, it commonly occurs with respect to family law matters that might arise in the course of a bankruptcy case such as divorce, dissolution, custody, or support.[107] In *In re Fussell*,[108] the bankruptcy court even abstained from determining whether the debtor's post-divorce, pre-petition credit card obligations were in the nature of alimony, support, or maintenance, and thus non-dischargeable under the Bankruptcy Code, because of the strong connection between the bankruptcy dischargeability issue and questions of state law arising from the debtor's divorce decree. On the other hand, in *In re Causa*,[109] the

---

[102] Marshall v. Stern, 131 S. Ct. 2594 (2011).

[103] Marshall v. Marshall, 547 U.S. 293, 311-312 (2006).

[104] Patrick M. Birney, *Reawakening Section 1334: Resolving the Conflict Between Bankruptcy and Arbitration Through an Abstention Analysis*, 16 Am. Bankr. Inst. L. Rev. 619 (2008).

[105] Andrew S. Atkin, Comment, *Permissive Withdrawal of Bankruptcy Proceedings under 28 U.S.C. Section 157(d)*, 11 Bankr. Dev. J. 447 (1995).

[106] 28 U.S.C. § 1334(c)(1) (2006).

[107] *See, e.g.*, In re Kriss, 217 B.R. 147 (Bankr. S.D.N.Y. 1998).

[108] 303 B.R. 539 (Bankr. S.D. Ga. 2003).

[109] 93 B.R. 409 (Bankr. E.D. Pa. 1988).

court decided that it need not abstain from resolving questions of the "equitable distribution" of marital assets between the debtor and his spouse, even though these questions involved issues of domestic relations law that are normally relegated to state court.

Likewise, it might be appropriate for the court to abstain from resolving disputes "involving unsettled questions of state property law."[110] Bankruptcy cases frequently involve questions of state property law, and if the underlying state property law is unclear, it makes sense for the dispute to be handled by an appropriate state tribunal. For example, in *Koken v. Reliance Group Holdings, Inc.*,[111] the court abstained from resolving a matter dealing partially with routine state contract and property law issues because it also required an intricate interpretation of the Pennsylvania Insurance Company Holding Act. And in *Allied Signal Recovery Trust v. Allied Signal, Inc.*,[112] the court determined abstention was appropriate in an action that, like the dispute in *Marathon Pipeline*, involved a debtor's cause of action based on state law but also involved related claims arising under the Bankruptcy Code.

[2] Mandatory Abstention

In limited circumstances, abstention is mandatory. The court is required to abstain when *all* of the following circumstances apply:

- the proceeding is based on a state law claim or a state law cause of action;
- the claim is merely "related to" a bankruptcy case;
- there are no other grounds for federal jurisdiction;
- an action has already been commenced in state court; and
- the state court action can be timely adjudicated.[113]

Thus, mandatory abstention never applies to civil proceedings "arising under" the Bankruptcy Code or "arising in" a bankruptcy case. The dispute must be at the outside fringe of bankruptcy jurisdiction.

Further, for abstention to be mandatory, there must be no independent ground for the district court to assert federal jurisdiction, such as federal question or diversity jurisdiction. If the proceeding is based on a federal antitrust claim, abstention is not mandatory because the case falls within the court's federal question jurisdiction.[114] Similarly, if the parties are from different states and the amount in controversy is sufficient, abstention is not mandatory because the case is

---

[110] *See* Thompson v. Magnolia Petroleum, 309 U.S. 478, 484 (1940); Orion Pictures Corp. v. Showtime Networks, Inc. (In re Orion Pictures Corp.), 4 F.3d 1095 (2d Cir. 1993).

[111] Koken v. Reliance Group Holdings, Inc. (In re Reliance Group Holdings, Inc.), 273 B.R. 374, 384 (Bankr. E.D. Pa. 2002).

[112] 298 F.3d 263 (3d Cir. 2002).

[113] 28 U.S.C. § 1334(c) (2006).

[114] 28 U.S.C. § 1331 (2006). Here, the district court may be required to withdraw the reference of the matter to the bankruptcy court and handle the case itself. *See supra* § 5.02[C][2] Referral to the Bankruptcy Court.

within the district court's diversity jurisdiction.[115] Of course, in these cases, the court may nevertheless abstain pursuant to its permissive abstention authority, or the district court may withdraw the reference and resolve the matter without the assistance of the bankruptcy court.

Finally, most courts have mandated abstention only when a state court proceeding is already underway.[116] Abstention is not mandated where a state court proceeding could be commenced and would expeditiously resolve the dispute, but where it has not yet begun. Likewise, abstention is not mandated simply because a state proceeding is already pending, if its disposition would significantly delay the liquidation or reorganization of the estate.[117]

A key exception to mandatory abstention is a proceeding to determine or estimate "a contingent or unliquidated personal injury tort or wrongful death claims against the estate." Such claims are reserved for special treatment. As claims against the estate, they would ordinarily be regarded as "core proceedings" within the bankruptcy court's authority. But, an exception is carved out for these cases, preventing them from being resolved in bankruptcy court.[118] Section 157(d) provides a further special rule, preventing the district court from abstaining from hearing such disputes, which are instead to be "tried in the district court in which the bankruptcy case is pending, or in the district court in the district in which the claim arose, as determined by the district court in which the bankruptcy case is pending."[119]

Thus, if the debtor is in bankruptcy because it impaired the health of thousands of women to whom it sold a defective contraceptive device, the central issues of the case are not core proceedings[120] and may not be resolved by the bankruptcy court without the parties' consent. But, because abstention is not mandatory, they need not be sent to state courts for resolution, and instead are to be tried either in the district court where the bankruptcy case is pending or in the district in which the claim arose.[121]

---

[115] 28 U.S.C. § 1332 (2006).

[116] *E.g.*, Walker v. Bryans (In re Walker), 224 B.R. 239 (Bankr. M.D. Ga. 1998); W. Coast Video Enter. v. Owens (In re W. Coast Video Enter., Inc.), 145 B.R. 484 (Bankr. E.D. Pa. 1992).

[117] 28 U.S.C. § 1334(c)(2) (2006).

[118] 28 U.S.C. § 157(b)(2)(B) (2006).

[119] 28 U.S.C. § 157(b)(5) (2006).

[120] *See* Georgene Vairo, *Mass Torts Bankruptcies: The Who, the Why and the How*, 78 Am. Bankr. L.J. 93 (2004).

[121] These claims may still be the subject of voluntary abstention. The Code does not prohibit them from being tried in state court. Moreover, the rule does not apply to tort claims brought by the estate against someone else; it only applies to tort claims brought by a creditor against the estate. A personal injury claim by the estate may be subject to mandatory abstention. Although there is ambiguity in the wording of the relevant statutory provisions, it appears that § 157(b)(5), which requires personal injury cases to be tried in district court, applies only if the district court has not voluntarily abstained from hearing the proceeding.

[3]   Appeal of Abstention Determinations

A district court's decision to abstain from a case is virtually unreviewable by a higher court. Section 1334(d) specifies, "[a]ny decision to abstain or not to abstain made under [§ 1334(c)] . . . is not reviewable by appeal or otherwise by the court of appeals . . . or by the Supreme Court of the United States." Thus, a bankruptcy judge's decision regarding abstention is appealable to the district court or to the appropriate bankruptcy appellate panel, but not beyond.[122] The only exception to this broad rule permits appeal of a decision *not* to abstain under the mandatory abstention rule.[123] Despite the seemingly unequivocal language of § 1334(d) on this point, some courts have permitted limited review of all mandatory abstention decisions, at least for the purposes of ensuring that the statutory requirements for mandatory abstention have been met.[124]

[E]   Jury Trials in Bankruptcy Court[125]

For many years, civil proceedings arising in the course of a bankruptcy case were regarded as equitable matters in which the parties had no right to a jury.[126] Significantly, bankruptcy court courtrooms did not have a jury box.

However, in 1989, the Supreme Court's decision in *Granfinanciera, S.A. v. Nordberg*, ruled that "a person who has not submitted a claim against a bankruptcy estate . . . [is entitled] to a jury trial when sued by the trustee in bankruptcy to recover an allegedly fraudulent monetary transfer."[127] *Granfinaciera* raised questions about how far the right to a jury trial in bankruptcy proceedings extended, as well as whether bankruptcy courts had statutory or constitutional authority to conduct jury trials where one was required.[128]

The latter issue was at least partially addressed by Congress in its 1994 Bankruptcy Legislation. Section 157(e) of the federal judicial code now provides:

---

[122] *See supra* § 5.01[C] Appellate Process in Bankruptcy Litigation.

[123] 28 U.S.C. § 1334(d) (2006).

[124] *E.g.*, S.G. Phillips Constructors, Inc. v. City of Burlington (In re S.G. Phillips Constructors, Inc.), 45 F.3d 702 (2d Cir. 1995). *See also* Lindsey v. Dow Chem. Co. (In re Dow Corning Corp.), 113 F.3d 565, 569 (6th Cir. 1997) (permitting mandamus).

[125] S. Elizabeth Gibson, *Jury Trials in Bankruptcy: Obeying the Commands of Article III and the Seventh Amendment*, 72 Minn. L. Rev. 967 (1988); John C. McCoid, II, *Right to Jury Trial in Bankruptcy:* Granfinanciera, S.A. v. Nordberg, 65 Am. Bankr. L.J. 15, 28-37 (1991); G. Ray Warner, Katchen *Up in Bankruptcy: The New Jury Trial Right*, 63 Am. Bankr. L.J. 1 (1989); Symposium, *Jury Trials in Bankruptcy Courts*, 65 Am. Bankr. L.J. 1 (1991).

[126] Katchen v. Landy, 382 U.S. 323, 336-37 (1966) ("as the [summary] proceedings of bankruptcy courts are inherently proceedings in equity, there is no Seventh Amendment right to a jury trial."). *See* In re Global Int'l Airways Corp., 81 B.R. 541, 543-44 (W.D. Mo. 1988).

[127] Granfinanciera, S.A. v. Nordberg, 492 U.S. 33, 36 (1989).

[128] S. Elizabeth Gibson, *Jury Trials And Core Proceedings: The Bankruptcy Judge's Uncertain Authority*, 65 Am. Bankr. L.J. 143 (1991); Ned W. Wasman, *Jury Trials After Granfinanciera: Three Proposals for Reform*, 52 Ohio St. L.J. 705 (1991).

There was also a practical problem. Unlike most other courtrooms, most bankruptcy courts were constructed without a jury box or a jury room.

> If the right to a jury trial applies in a proceeding that may be heard under this section by a bankruptcy judge, the bankruptcy judge may conduct the jury trial if specially designated to exercise such jurisdiction by the district court and with the express consent of all the parties.[129]

If the right to a jury trial applies in a proceeding that may be heard under this section, § 157(e) permits bankruptcy judges to conduct jury trials, but only if authorized by the district court and only if all of the parties in the case have given their consent. The necessity of obtaining the parties' consent puts aside the constitutional question of whether Article I bankruptcy judges may conduct jury trials. However, not all jurisdictions have adopted local rules permitting jury trials, and even where they are permitted, jury trials in bankruptcy courts remain rare.

In many cases, a party who otherwise might prefer to have a jury trial will have waived its right to a jury. In *Langenkamp v. Culp*, the Supreme Court ruled that filing a claim against the estate amounts to a waiver of the right to a jury trial, not only with respect to the creditor's right to receive a distribution from the estate on account of its claim, but also with respect to any counterclaim the estate may have against the creditor that arises from the same circumstances as those that gave rise to the creditor's claim.[130] The Court indicated that by filing a claim against a bankruptcy estate, the creditor triggers the process of "allowance and disallowance of claims," thereby subjecting himself to the bankruptcy court's equitable power. If the trustee responds to the creditor's proof of claim with an action to recover a preference, that action becomes part of the claims-allowance process which is triable only in equity.[131] In other words, the creditor's claim and the ensuing preference action by the trustee become integral to the restructuring of the debtor-creditor relationship through the bankruptcy court's equity jurisdiction. As such, there is no Seventh Amendment right to a jury trial.[132]

Whether filing a claim operates as a waiver of the right to a jury trial on causes of action arising from separate transactions between the parties remains open to debate.[133] Of course, a creditor who has not filed a proof of claim has not waived any right to a jury trial in an action brought against it by the estate.[134] And, after *Stern v. Marshall*, bankruptcy courts may not determine counterclaims brought against a creditor simply because the creditor has filed a claim against the estate, unless resolution of the counterclaim is necessary to determine the allowability of the creditor's claim.[135]

---

[129] 28 U.S.C. § 157(e) (2006). *See* In re Vigh, 85 F.3d 630 (6th Cir. 1996).

[130] Langenkamp v. Culp, 498 U.S. 42 (1990).

[131] This assumes, of course, that the counterclaim can be pursued in bankruptcy court at all, under the Supreme Court's ruling in *Stern v. Marshall*, 131 S. Ct. 2594 (2011). *See generally supra* § 5.02[C][3][b] Counterclaims Against Creditors.

[132] *Id.* at 44-45.

[133] *See* Official Employment-Related Issues Comm. of Enron Corp. v. Lavorato (In re Enron Corp.), 319 B.R. 122 (Bankr. S.D. Tex. 2004).

[134] Heater v. Household Realty Corp. (In re Heater), 261 B.R. 145 (Bankr. W.D. Pa. 2001).

[135] Stern v. Marshall, 131 S. Ct. 2594 (2011).

§ 5.03   BANKRUPTCY VENUE[136]

There are two key questions of venue in connection with bankruptcy cases. The first is where the bankruptcy case itself may be filed. The second is where litigation connected to the bankruptcy case may be brought.

[A]   Venue of Bankruptcy Cases[137]

Bankruptcy cases may be filed in the district in which the debtor is located. In most cases, this is any district where the debtor's "domicile, residence, principal place of business in the United States, or principal assets in the United States" are located during the 180 days immediately preceding the commencement of the case.[138] When an individual debtor has resided in multiple places during the 180 days immediately before filing her petition, venue is proper in the district in which the debtor was located "for a longer portion" of this 180 days.[139] For most individual debtors, there is only one possible venue.

For example, if Ted lived in Columbus, Ohio from January through April of 2013 before moving to Brooklyn, New York in May of that year, proper venue for a case he files in July, 2013 would be the Southern District of Ohio, where he resided for the bulk of the 180 days before filing his petition. If he wants to file his case close to his new home, he will have to wait until August, when he will have lived in New York for a majority of the 180 days prior to his petition.[140] The answer might be more complicated, however, if from January through April, he kept apartments in both cities, and commuted for work to New York three days each week.

For purposes of bankruptcy venue, a corporate debtor is regarded as being domiciled where it is incorporated. It may file either where it is incorporated, where its principal place of business in the United States is located, or where it owns significant assets.

Corporate debtors with affiliates in multiple districts have more flexibility with respect to venue. A debtor who is affiliated with another debtor[141] that is located in a different district may file in the district in which the affiliate's bankruptcy case is pending. Thus, a New York corporation owned by a parent corporation in California may file its petition in California, if that is where the parent's case is already pending. Likewise, the California parent may file its petition in the appropriate district in New York if the New York subsidiary's case is pending in New York.

---

[136] Frank Kennedy, *The Bankruptcy Court Under the New Bankruptcy Law: Its Structure, Jurisdiction, Venue and Procedure*, 11 St. Mary's L.J. 251, (1979); Charles Seligson & Lawrence P. King, *Jurisdiction and Venue in Bankruptcy*, 36 J. Nat'l Ass'n Ref. in Bankr. 36 (1962).

[137] Lynn M. LoPucki & William C. Whitford, *Venue Choice and Forum Shopping in the Bankruptcy Reorganization of Large, Publicly Held Companies*, 1991 Wis. L. Rev. 11.

[138] 28 U.S.C. § 1408 (2006).

[139] 28 U.S.C. § 1408 (2006).

[140] Even then, he may find the New York court reluctant to permit him to take advantage of New York's more generous exemption statute. *See* In re Coplan, 156 B.R. 88 (Bankr. M.D. Fla. 1993) (homestead exemption of debtor who moved from Wisconsin to Florida before filing petition limited to value of homestead protected by Wisconsin exemption statute).

[141] Bankruptcy Code § 101(2) ("affiliate").

Corporate debtors with affiliates in many jurisdictions have virtually unlimited choices of where to file.[142]

Similarly, general partners may file in the same district in which a case involving either their other partners or their partnership is pending. Thus, Nancy, who resides in Las Vegas, Nevada and is in partnership with Doug, who resides in San Diego, California, may file in either in the District of Nevada or, if Doug already has a case pending in San Diego, in the Southern District of California.[143]

The familiar doctrine of forum non conveniens applies to bankruptcy in largely the same manner that it applies to other types of cases. The court has the power to transfer a case to another district, even though it was filed in the proper district, if transfer is warranted "in the interest of justice or for the convenience of the parties."[144] Transfer depends on a variety of factors, including the location of the debtor and its assets, the location of the debtor's creditors, the location of witnesses whose testimony is necessary for administration of the estate, and the relative expense to the estate to handle the case where it was initially filed or to transfer it to another district.[145] Cases are only transferred under this discretionary rule. On the other hand, if venue was improper in the first place, the court in which the case was filed has the authority to transfer it to a district where venue is proper.[146]

[B]   Venue of Civil Proceedings

Normally, civil proceedings connected to a bankruptcy case may be brought only in the district in which the bankruptcy case is pending.[147] This rule facilitates the efficient administration of the estate by permitting all litigation connected to the case to be conducted in one place, under the supervision of a judge who is familiar with the debtor's circumstances.

Venue in another district is proper in only three limited situations. First, where the trustee brings an action as a "successor to the debtor or creditors under section[s] 541 or 544(b) [of the bankruptcy code] . . . venue is also proper in the district in which the proceeding might have been brought by the debtor or creditors who could have brought the action if the bankruptcy case had not been filed."[148] The most obvious example of this is a trustee's action to recover a fraudulent conveyance, brought under state law pursuant to § 544(b), asserting the right that one of the debtor's unsecured creditors would have had to recover the

---

[142] Lynn M. LoPucki & William C. Whitford, *Venue Choice and Forum Shopping in the Bankruptcy Reorganization of Large, Publicly Held Companies*, 1991 Wis. L. Rev. 11.

[143] 28 U.S.C. § 1408(2) (2006).

[144] 28 U.S.C. § 1412 (2006).

[145] *See* In re Commonwealth Oil Ref. Co., 596 F.2d 1239, 1247-48 (5th Cir. 1979); In re Enron Corp., 274 B.R. 327, 343 (Bankr. S.D.N.Y. 2002).

[146] 28 U.S.C. § 1477(a) (2006).

[147] 28 U.S.C. § 1409(a) (2006).

[148] 28 U.S.C. § 1409(c) (2006).

fraudulent transfer.[149]

Second, venue of actions brought to recover small amounts may only be brought in the "district in which the defendant resides." This rule applies to actions "to recover a money judgment of or property worth less than $1,000," to those to recover a "consumer debt of less than $15,000," or to recover "a debt (excluding a consumer debt) against a noninsider of less than $10,000."[150] This rule protects defendants in what are essentially small claims actions from having to defend in a distant geographic forum.

Third, actions initiated by the trustee that are based on claims arising "after commencement of [the] case from the operation of the business of the debtor" may be brought only in a district where venue would have been proper if the case was not pending.[151] Thus, the general federal venue statute applies to actions sought to be initiated by the trustee or the debtor in possession that are based on transactions that occur while the case is pending.[152] Actions against the estate that are based on such post-petition dealings may be brought where the bankruptcy case is pending, or in the district where they might have been brought under otherwise applicable venue rules.[153]

As with venue of the underlying bankruptcy case, venue of civil proceedings connected to a bankruptcy case can be transferred to another district "in the interest of justice or for the convenience of the parties."[154]

§ 5.04 NATIONWIDE SERVICE OF PROCESS IN BANKRUPTCY[155]

The broad "home court" venue rule, which permits most bankruptcy litigation to occur in the same district as the one in which the debtor's bankruptcy case is pending, is facilitated by Federal Rule of Bankruptcy Procedure 7004. Rule 7004 permits nationwide service of process in adversary litigation connected to a bankruptcy case. Rule 7004(d) provides: "The summons and complaint and all other process except a subpoena may be served anywhere in the United States."[156] This, of course, is quite different from the normal rule applicable to cases brought in federal court through the district court's federal question or diversity of citizenship jurisdiction, which requires that service on an out-of-state resident must be made

---

[149] *See infra* § 14.03 Power to Exercise Avoiding Powers of Actual Unsecured Creditors.

[150] 28 U.S.C. § 1409(c) (2006).

[151] 28 U.S.C. § 1409(d) (2006).

[152] *See* 28 U.S.C. § 1391(c) (2006).

[153] 28 U.S.C. § 1409(e) (2006).

[154] 28 U.S.C. § 1412 (2006).

[155] *See* Jeffrey T. Ferriell, *The Perils of Nationwide Service of Process in a Bankruptcy Context*, 48 Wash & Lee L. Rev. 1199 (1991); Maryellen Fullerton, *Constitutional Limits on Nationwide Personal Jurisdiction in the Federal Courts*, 79 NW. U. L. Rev. 1 (1984-85); Jackie Gardina, *The Bankruptcy of Due Process: Nationwide Service of Process, Personal Jurisdiction and the Bankruptcy Code*, 16 Am. Bankr. Inst. L. Rev. 37 (2008).

[156] Fed. R. Bankr. P. 7004(d).

through the long-arm statute in the state where the district court is located.[157]

Nationwide service of process permits the bankruptcy court to consolidate disputes between the debtor and anyone else located in the United States in a single forum. This is particularly useful in cases where the estate might have to collect property owned by or owed to the estate (sometimes as a result of the bankruptcy trustee's avoiding powers) or in simple collection cases to recover funds owed to the estate as a result of pre-bankruptcy transactions.

The power of nationwide service is magnified by the liberal venue rules that permit affiliated debtors to file their bankruptcy cases in the same district and with the broad "home court" venue rule that permit bankruptcy litigation to be commenced in the same district in which the debtor's bankruptcy case is pending. For example, assume that Titanic Industries, Inc. is a Delaware corporation with a wholly-owned subsidiary, Ismay, Inc., which is incorporated and doing business in New Mexico. If Titanic Industries files a Chapter 11 petition in Delaware, where venue for its case is proper, Ismay, Inc. could file its own Chapter 11 case in Delaware, even though Ismay, Inc. is incorporated in New Mexico and neither conducts business nor owns assets outside that state. If Ismay, Inc. has a preference claim against one of its New Mexico creditors, it could bring that action in Delaware and serve process on the creditor in New Mexico, even though the creditor has no contact with the parent corporation or anyone else in Delaware.

Although it might seem that this application of nationwide service of process might raise procedural due process difficulties under *International Shoe Co. v. Washington*[158] and it progeny, courts have almost universally ruled that no such difficulties arise if the defendant has minimum contacts with the United States or any part of it.[159]

§ 5.05   SOVEREIGN IMMUNITY[160]

The Eleventh Amendment prohibits a citizen of one state from suing another state. Enacted as a response to the Supreme Court's 1793 decision in *Chisolm v. Georgia*,[161] its precise scope, as a narrow or broad grant of sovereign immunity, has been in flux for over a hundred years. Until 1996, Supreme Court decisions implied that a state's sovereign immunity could be abrogated by Congress, pursuant to the Commerce Clause, to allow a suit for money damages so long as that intention was

---

[157] *See* Fed. R. Civ. P. 4(d).

[158] 326 U.S. 310 (1945).

[159] *See* Jeffrey T. Ferriell, *The Perils of Nationwide Service of Process in a Bankruptcy Context*, 48 Wash. & Lee L. Rev. 1199 (1991).

[160] Ralph Brubaker, *Explaining Katz's New Bankruptcy Exception to State Sovereign Immunity: The Bankruptcy Power as a Federal Forum Power*, 15 Am. Bankr. Inst. L. Rev. 95 (2007); Richard Lieb, *State Sovereign Immunity: Bankruptcy is Special*, 14 Am. Bankr. Inst. L. Rev. 201 (2006); Martin H. Redish & Daniel M. Greenfield, *Bankruptcy, Sovereign Immunity and the Dilemma of Principled Decision Making: The Curious Case of* Central Virginia Community College v. Katz, 15 Am. Bankr. Inst. L. Rev. 13 (2007).

[161] Chisholm v. Georgia, 2 U.S. (2 Dall.) 419 (1793).

"clearly stated."[162] However, in *Seminole Tribe v. Florida*,[163] the Court held that Congress's legislative powers under the Indian Commerce Clause do not empower Congress to abrogate the states' Eleventh Amendment sovereign immunity.[164] This holding has been read to extend to the Commerce Clause as well.

Nevertheless, in *Tennessee Student Assistance Corporation v. Hood*,[165] the Court subsequently held that a state student loan authority was subject to the bankruptcy discharge injunction of § 524, despite the Eleventh Amendment.[166] The Supreme Court reasoned that the power to grant a discharge emanated not from the power to sue or bind the state, but from the bankruptcy court's *in rem* jurisdiction over the bankruptcy estate.

Later still, in *Central Virginia Community College v. Katz*,[167] the Supreme Court further limited the effect of *Seminole Tribe*[168] in bankruptcy cases, and held that in ratifying the Bankruptcy Clause in Article I,[169] states ceded their sovereign immunity to the extent necessary to effectuate the purposes of that clause. Specifically, the *Katz* Court found that state sovereign immunity is not a defense to a trustee's action under Bankruptcy Code § 547, to recover a money judgment for a preferential transfer made to a state agency.[170]

The precise issue before the Court in *Katz* was whether Congress effectively abrogated state sovereign immunity by enacting § 106(a), which provides that "sovereign immunity is abrogated as to a governmental unit . . . with respect to" specific sections of the Bankruptcy Code authorizing actions against creditors and others.[171] However, the Court did not decide whether Congress' enactment of § 106(a) — which made states susceptible to suits seeking a money judgment — was actually within the scope of its power to enact "Laws on the subject of Bankruptcies."[172] Instead, the Court reasoned that the Framers would have understood the Bankruptcy Clause to give Congress the power to authorize courts to avoid preferential transfers to state agencies and to recover the transferred property. If

---

[162] United States v. Nordic Village, Inc., 503 U.S. 30 (1992); Hoffman v. Connecticut Dept. of Income Maintenance, 492 U.S. 96 (1989).

[163] 517 U.S. 44 (1996).

[164] 517 U.S. at 72-73. Because the Eleventh Amendment was passed after Article I was ratified, that Amendment creates a limitation on Congress' Article I powers. After *Seminole Tribe*, the Court reaffirmed its holding that Congress may not abrogate the states' Eleventh Amendment sovereign immunity based on powers enumerated in Article I. *See* Bd. of Trs. of Univ. of Ala. v. Garrett, 531 U.S. 356, 362 (2001).

[165] Tenn. Student Assist. Corp. v. Hood, 541 U. S. 440 (2004).

[166] Tenn. Student Assist. Corp. v. Hood, 541 U. S. 440 (2004).

[167] 546 U.S. 356 (2006).

[168] 517 U.S. at 72 n.16. However, in confronting the issue of sovereign immunity as it pertains to bankruptcy cases, the Court recently retreated from dicta in *Seminole Tribe* indicating that "[i]t has not been widely thought that_._._ bankruptcy . . . statutes abrogated the States' sovereign immunity." *Id.*

[169] The Bankruptcy Clause authorizes Congress to enact "uniform Laws on the subject of Bankruptcies throughout the United States." U.S. Const. Art. 1, § 8, cl. 4.

[170] *See infra* Chapter 15 Avoidable Preferences.

[171] Bankruptcy Code § 106(a)(1).

[172] *Katz*, 546 U.S. at 378-379 (2006).

this was the understanding, then the states surrendered their sovereign immunity from preference avoidance when they ratified the Bankruptcy Clause of the Constitution.

Moreover, because the critical element of a bankruptcy proceeding is the court's exercise of jurisdiction over the debtor's property (i.e., in rem jurisdiction), the Court theorized that a proceeding to recover a money judgment for a preferential transfer is "ancillary" to the bankruptcy courts' in rem jurisdiction. Thus, the Court declared that state sovereign immunity was relinquished under the Bankruptcy Clause with respect to bankruptcy courts' issuing "ancillary orders enforcing their in rem adjudications."[173]

Since the Court's ruling in *Katz*, the Eighth Circuit has stressed that the *Katz* exception for bankruptcy cases is narrow and, quoting language from *Katz*, indicated that the exception is based on the "unique history" of the Bankruptcy Clause and the "singular nature of bankruptcy courts' jurisdiction."[174] At the same time, however, the Court's ruling in *Katz* has been criticized as having the potential to be read too broadly. "[A]lthough its holding saved bankruptcy from the reach of the Eleventh Amendment, the Court neither specified what other bankruptcy proceedings will similarly overcome a sovereign immunity defense" — for example, if a state government seized property in violation of the automatic stay[175] — "nor sufficiently explored the implications of its original intent analysis."[176] In addition, it has been argued that the *Katz* decision "cannot be reconciled with precedent."[177]

Where *Katz* will lead regarding the defense of state sovereign immunity in various bankruptcy proceedings remains to be seen. Some scholars have regarded *Katz* as slowing down if not stopping the development of the jurisprudence of sovereign immunity,[178] while others have pointed out that "Katz will likely face close scrutiny and resistance in the future."[179] Thus far, at least, this scrutiny has not, at least in the bankruptcy context, materialized.

---

[173] 546 U.S. at 370.

[174] St. Charles County, Miss. v. Wisc., 447 F.3d 1055 (8th Cir. 2006).

[175] *See, e.g.*, In re Omine, 485 F.3d 1305 (11th Cir. 2007).

[176] *State Sovereign Immunity — Bankruptcy*, 120 Harv. L. Rev. 125, 126 (2006). *See also* Richard Lieb, *State Sovereign Immunity: Bankruptcy is Special*, 14 Am. Bankr. Inst. L. Rev. 201, 203 (2006) ("[*Katz's*] 'ancillary order' theory is broad enough to preclude the states from asserting immunity as a defense to *any* proceeding grounded on a provision of the Bankruptcy Code or which affects property of the debtor's estate.") (emphasis added).

[177] Suzanna Sherry, *Logic Without Experience: The Problem of Federal Appellate Courts*, 82 Notre Dame L. Rev. 97, 114 (2006).

[178] Patrick McKinley Brennan, *Against Sovereignty: A Cautionary Note on the Normative Power of the Actual*, 82 Notre Dame L. Rev. 181, 188-89 (2006).

[179] *State Sovereign Immunity — Bankruptcy*, 120 Harv. L. Rev. 125, 134 (2006). *See* Richard Lieb, *State Sovereign Immunity: Bankruptcy is Special*, 14 Am. Bankr. Inst. L. Rev. 201, 233 (2006) ("It is unclear just how far the Supreme Court intended to go in *Katz* . . . . It remains to be seen whether the lower courts will apply *Katz*, as logically required, to all ancillary bankruptcy proceedings, or will restrict it to avoidance proceedings brought pursuant to the Bankruptcy Code. It can be expected that they will reach conflicting results.").

§ 5.06   ARBITRATION CLAUSES IN BANKRUPTCY[180]

Although arbitration is popular, it is controversial in bankruptcy cases. The Federal Arbitration Act (FAA), encourages the enforcement of arbitration agreements.[181] The Bankruptcy Code, on the other hand, directs that all actions against the debtor are stayed and must be resolved in one centralized proceeding in bankruptcy court. The generally applicable policies of reducing delay and minimizing expense are particularly important in bankruptcy cases where the debtor's precarious financial condition and the goal of preserving value for all creditors weigh strongly in favor of resolving disputes quickly, through the normal bankruptcy process.[182]

Moreover, bankruptcy is, at its most fundamental level, a collective proceeding to resolve the competing interests of all interested parties, not a process for resolving discreet disputes between parties to a specific transaction.[183] Thus, the FAA's policy in favor of enforcing arbitration agreements is in direct conflict with a key feature of the bankruptcy system: centralized collective dispute resolution before judges with expertise in bankruptcy cases. This conflict has led courts to disagree widely about the enforceability of arbitration clauses in disputes that would otherwise be resolved in bankruptcy court.[184]

The conventional rule has been that normal bankruptcy claims process is the appropriate method for resolving disputes that arise during the bankruptcy process, and that arbitration agreements should not supplant this process. After all, once a debtor is in bankruptcy, other creditors also have a stake in how the debtor's property is handled, and they were not parties to any agreement the debtor may have signed, submitting its rights to resolution in an arbitration proceeding.

Although it was not a bankruptcy case, the Supreme Court's 1986 decision in *Shearson/American Express, Inc. v. McMahon*[185] has had a significant influence on how later courts have resolved the conflicting policies in the Bankruptcy Code and the Federal Arbitration Act. Before *McMahon*, bankruptcy courts had taken a flexible approach to whether arbitration agreements should supplant the normal bankruptcy dispute resolution process,[186] but generally erred on the side of

---

[180] Patrick M. Birney, *Reawakening Section 1334: Resolving the Conflict Between Bankruptcy and Arbitration Through an Abstention Analysis*, 16 Am. Bankr. Inst. L. Rev. 619 (2008); Michael D. Fielding, *Elevating Business above the Constitution: Arbitration and Bankruptcy Proofs of Claim*, 16 Am. Bankr. Inst. L. Rev. 563 (2008); Alan N. Resnick, *The Enforceability of Arbitration Clauses in Bankruptcy*, 15 Am. Bankr. Inst. L. Rev. 183 (2007). *See also* Erwin Chemerinsky, *Decision-Makers: In Defense of Courts*, 71 Am. Bankr. L.J. 109 (1997); Glenn A. Guarino, Annotation, *Disposition by Bankruptcy Court of Request for Arbitration Pursuant to Arbitration Agreement to Which Debtor in Bankruptcy Is a Party*, 72 A.L.R. Fed. 890 (1985).

[181] 9 U.S.C. §§ 1-14 (2006).

[182] Zimmerman v. Cont'l Airlines, 712 F.2d 55, 58 (3d Cir. 1983).

[183] Marianne B. Culhane, *Limiting Litigation over Arbitration in Bankruptcy*, 17 Am. Bankr. Inst. L. Rev. 493, 496 (2009).

[184] Alan N. Resnick, *The Enforceability of Arbitration Clauses in Bankruptcy*, 15 Am. Bankr. Inst. L. Rev. 183, 183-84 (2007).

[185] 482 U.S. 220 (1987).

[186] *See* Zimmerman v. Continental Airlines, Inc., 712 F.2d 55 (3d Cir. 1983).

refusing to enforce arbitration agreements in disputes over claims against the estate, motions for relief from the automatic stay, and dischargeability proceedings. *McMahon* ruled that the FAA's mandate to enforce valid arbitration decisions was overidden by legislation that demonstrated an intent to preclude arbitration,[187] but that the burden of showing that Congress had intended to displace an otherwise valid arbitration agreement lay on the shoulders of the party opposing arbitration.[188] The Court explained further that "Congressional intent [with respect to the issue could be] deduced from the statute's text or legislative history, or from 'an inherent conflict between arbitration and the statute's underlying purposes.' "

In ensuing years, the Circuit Courts seem to have come full circle on this issue, severely limiting the power of bankruptcy courts to disregard arbitration clauses. There currently is a circuit split. The Second and Fourth Circuits hold that an arbitration clause may only be disregarded if arbitration would inherently conflict with the purpose of the Bankruptcy Code.[189] The Third and Fifth Circuits take an even harsher view, saying that enforcing the arbitration clause would not only have to contravene the purpose of the Bankruptcy Code, but would have to conflict with a particular statutory provision.[190] bankruptcy courts have demonstrated a greater willingness to enforce arbitration agreements in disputes that are merely related to a bankruptcy cases are not "core proceedings" as defined by the post-Marathon Pipe Line jurisdictional scheme enacted by the Bankruptcy Amendments and Federal Judgeship Act of 1984.[191] Some decisions have gone further and permitted enforcement of arbitration agreements even in core proceedings, when the underlying dispute did not require consideration of the Bankruptcy Code,[192] or where resolution of the dispute would have no impact on the debtor's bankruptcy estate.[193] In these proceedings the key question is whether enforcement of the arbitration agreement would have an adverse impact, usually in the form of a delay, on the administration of the debtor's estate.[194]

---

[187] *Id.* at 227.

[188] *Id.* at 226.

[189] *See* MBNA America Bank N.A. v. Hill, 436 F.3d 104, 110 (2d Cir. 2006); Philips v. Congelton L.L.C. (In re White Mountain Mining Co.), 403 F.3d 164, 170 (4th Cir. 2005).

[190] Mintze v. American Gen. Fin. Serv. Inc. (In re Mintze), 434 F.3d 222, 231 (3d Cir. 2006); Gandy v. Gandy (In re Gandy), 299 F.3d 489, 495 (5th Cir. 2002).

[191] *See, e.g.*, Hays & Co. v. Merrill Lynch, Pierce, Fenner, & Smith, Inc., 885 F.2d 1149, 1159-60 (3d Cir. 1989); Gandy v. Gandy (In re Gandy), 299 F.3d 489, 495 (5th Cir. 2002); U.S. Lines, Inc. v. Am. S.S. Owners Mut. Prot. & Indem. Ass'n, Inc. (In re U.S. Lines, Inc.), 197 F.3d 631, 640 (2d Cir. 1999).

[192] Mintze v. Am. Gen. Fin. Servs., Inc. (In re Mintze), 434 F.3d 222 (3d. Cir. 2006) (arbitration clause enforceable in debtor's counterclaim for violation of Truth in Lending Act).

[193] MBNA America Bank, N.A. v. Hill, 436 F.3d 104, 108 (2d Cir. 2006) (arbitration agreement enforced in debtor's post-discharge action against creditor for violations of the automatic stay); Ins. Co. of N. Am. v. NGC Settlement Trust and Asbestos Claims Management Corp. (In re Nat'l Gypsum Co.), 118 F.3d 1056 (5th Cir.1997).

[194] *See* In re Rarities Group, Inc., 434 B.R. 1 (D Mass. 2010).

Chapter 6

COMMENCEMENT

§ 6.01 COMMENCEMENT OF BANKRUPTCY CASES[1]

[A] Voluntary Cases

Although the Code permits creditors to file involuntary petitions against a debtor, nearly all bankruptcy cases are filed voluntarily.[2] Voluntary bankruptcy cases begin when the debtor files a petition, together with the necessary fee, with the bankruptcy court, accompanied by an array of schedules of assets, debts, and other information about the debtor's financial affairs.[3] Since 2005, debtors have also been required to file a "means test" form measuring the debtor's ability to repay his or her debts, as well as a certificate showing that the debtor has had a pre-filing credit counseling briefing. In voluntary cases, the filing of a petition operates as an "order for relief," without the necessity of further action.[4] Somewhat surprisingly, except for municipal entities seeking relief under Chapter 9 of the Bankruptcy Code, a person does not have to be insolvent to seek bankruptcy relief.[5]

Debtors without the cash to pay the filing fee may be permitted to pay it in installments.[6] Further, the court may waive the filing fee entirely for individual Chapter 7 debtors whose income is "less than 150 percent" of the federal poverty line.[7] However, Chapter 13 debtors, who will be submitting payments from their future income in any event, cannot escape the filing fee.

---

[1] Frank R. Kennedy, *The Commencement of a Case under the New Bankruptcy Code*, 36 Wash. & Lee L. Rev. 977 (1979).

[2] *See* Susan Block-Lieb, *Why So Few Involuntary Petitions and Why the Number is Not Too Small*, 57 Brook. L. Rev. 803, 804 & Appendix A at 863 (1991); David S. Kennedy et al., *The Involuntary Bankruptcy Process: A Study of the Relevant Statutory and Procedural Provisions and Related Matters*, 31 U. Mem. L. Rev. 1, 3 (2000); Lynn LoPucki, *A General Theory of the Dynamics of the State Remedies/Bankruptcy System*, 1972 Wis. L. Rev. 311.

[3] Bankruptcy Code § 301. *See* Fed. R. Bankr. P. 1002(a).

[4] Bankruptcy Code § 301(b).

[5] *See* Connell v. Coastal Cable T.V., Inc. (In re Coastal Cable T.V., Inc.), 709 F.2d 762 (1st Cir. 1983) (debtor must "owe debts").

[6] 28 U.S.C. § 1930(a) (2006); Fed. R. Bankr. P. 1006.

[7] 28 U.S.C. § 1930(f) (2006).

[B] Involuntary Cases

Creditors may also initiate a bankruptcy proceeding by commencing an involuntary proceeding. Involuntary petitions may be brought only under Chapter 7 or Chapter 11, and require the petitioning creditors to prove that the debtor is not paying its debts as they become due or has had a custodian appointed outside of bankruptcy. An order for relief is entered against the debtor only if the creditor makes this showing, or if the debtor fails to defend the creditor's petition and thus acquiesces to the proceeding.[8] As explained below, some debtors, such as farmers and charities, are insulated from involuntary petitions, even though they are otherwise eligible for voluntarily bankruptcy.

§ 6.02 COMMENCEMENT OF A VOLUNTARY CASE[9]

[A] Filing a Voluntary Petition

A voluntary bankruptcy case is "commenced," when the debtor files a petition in bankruptcy court.[10] The form for the voluntary petition itself is quite simple,[11] though some of the other paperwork required to be filed along with the petition is more complex.[12] A petitioning debtor is not required supply a justification for his petition, which operates as an immediate "order for relief" in the case.[13] Debtors who file skeleton petitions, without submitting the necessary additional schedules of assets and debts, or the required "statement of [financial] affairs," in accordance with the court's schedule,[14] will find their cases dismissed in due course.

Filing a petition has several consequences. Most importantly, it creates the debtor's estate and simultaneously transfers all of the property owned by the debtor when the petition was filed, to that estate.[15] It also triggers an automatic stay enjoining nearly every type of action a creditor might take to try to collect, including lawsuits, repossessions, and telephone calls.[16] Further, it establishes the base point for various time periods, such as the preference period,[17] the fraudulent transfer period,[18] and the period of time in which both creditors and debtors may

---

[8] Bankruptcy Code § 303(h). *See infra* § 6.03 Commencement of Involuntary Cases.

[9] John C. McCoid, II, *The Origins of Voluntary Bankruptcy*, 5 Bankr. Dev. J. 361 (1988); Randal C. Picker, *Voluntary Petitions and the Creditors' Bargain*, 61 U. Cin. L. Rev. 519 (1992).

[10] Bankruptcy Code § 301.

[11] *See* Official Bankruptcy Form 1.

[12] Bankruptcy Code § 521.

[13] Bankruptcy Code § 301(b). Those familiar with practice under the Bankruptcy Act will recall that before 1979, the clerk's office would stamp a filed petition with "ADJUDICATED" instead of "FILED" as is the custom today. This reflected that the debtor had been voluntarily "adjudicated" to be a "bankrupt."

[14] Fed. R. Bankr. P. 1007(a).

[15] Bankruptcy Code § 541(a)(1). *See infra* § 7.01 Creation of the Debtor's Estate.

[16] Bankruptcy Code § 362. *See infra* Chapter 8 — The Automatic Stay.

[17] *See infra* § 15.02[E] Preference Period.

[18] *See infra* Chapter 16 Fraudulent Transfers

file various documents with the court.[19] For these and other reasons, the phrase "commencement of the case," referring to the filing of a petition, is one of the most important and frequently used phrases in the Bankruptcy Code.[20]

[B] Debtors' Eligibility for Voluntary Bankruptcy

[1] General Restrictions on Eligibility for Bankruptcy Relief

Bankruptcy petitions under chapters 7, 11, 12, and 13 may be filed voluntarily by debtors with few restrictions other than the debtor's willingness to file. With limited exceptions, some kind of bankruptcy relief is available under the Bankruptcy Code to nearly every "person that resides or has a domicile, a place of business, or property in the United States, or [is] a municipality."[21] "Person" is defined broadly to include individuals, partnerships, corporations, and other entities.[22] Even incompetent persons, prisoners, and minors are eligible for relief.[23]

[a] Connection to the United States

There is a general requirement, rarely litigated but applicable to all debtors, that the debtor must have some nexus with the United States. Individual and business entities must either reside in or have a domicile, a place of business, or property in the U.S.[24] However, there is no requirement that the debtor be a citizen. In addition, political subdivisions, public agencies or instrumentalities[25] of one of the fifty states may be a debtor under Chapter 9.[26] States themselves, however, are not eligible.

---

[19] *E.g.*, Fed. R. Bankr. P. 1007(c) (fifteen days to file debtor's schedules and statement); Fed. R. Bank. P. 3002(c)(1) (proof of claim by governmental unit to be filed not later than 180 days after the date of the order for relief).

[20] In cases initiated via an involuntary petition, an "order for relief" will not be entered simultaneously with the commencement of the case. It will either be delayed until the debtor fails to contest the petition, until a trial is held on merits of the petition, or never entered if the petitioning creditors fail to prevail on those merits. Bankruptcy Code § 303(h). See *infra* § 6.03 Commencement of Involuntary Cases.

[21] Bankruptcy Code § 109(a).

[22] Bankruptcy Code § 101(41).

[23] In re Murray, 199 B.R. 165 (Bankr. M.D. Tenn. 1996). *See* Elizabeth Warren, Essay, *Bankrupt Children*, 86 Minn. L. Rev. 1003 (2002).

[24] Bankruptcy Code § 109(a).

[25] Bankruptcy Code § 101(40).

[26] Bankruptcy Code § 109(c). Municipal bankruptcies are highly specialized and generally beyond the scope of this book. Students interested in one of the largest municipal bankruptcies in the Nation's history may wish to consult Mark Baldassare, When Government Fails: The Orange County Bankruptcy (Univ. of Cal. Press 1998). The case was large enough to warrant its own directory on the Lexis database: BKRTCY/ORANGE.

[b] Abusive Repetitive Filings[27]

Debtors sometimes file repetitive petitions, usually in an effort to take advantage of the Bankruptcy Code's automatic stay,[28] even though their petitions are destined to be dismissed. Section 109(g) restricts the ability of individuals and "family farmers"[29] from deploying this tactic. The court may dismiss a case if the debtor was involved in an earlier case that was filed within the 180 days immediately before his most recent petition, if the earlier case was dismissed for any one of several reasons: 1) the debtor's willful failure to abide by the bankruptcy court's orders, 2) the debtor's failure to appear before the court to prosecute the earlier case,[30] or 3) in response to the debtor's request for dismissal after a creditor's request for relief from the automatic stay.[31]

For example, if Jack Dawkins is facing a real estate foreclosure sale, he might file a Chapter 13 petition, even though he has no realistic hope of having a Chapter 13 plan confirmed. His petition invokes the automatic stay and stops the sale. If Jack voluntarily dismisses his Chapter 13 case after the mortgage holder files a motion for relief from the automatic stay, Jack is ineligible to file another bankruptcy petition for 180 days after the date of his first petition. In many states, this will be long enough for the creditor to complete its foreclosure sale.[32]

Several courts have regarded § 109(g) as discretionary.[33] However, its plain language leaves little room for this conclusion. It provides: "no individual or family farmer may be a debtor" if the circumstances described in the remainder of the section exist.[34] Most courts have agreed that this is the only permissible result.[35]

Sections 362(c)(3) & (4) also attempt to frustrate the efforts of repeat filers by terminating the automatic stay quickly if the debtor has filed multiple petitions within a one year period. As explained in more detail elsewhere, § 362(c)(3) terminates the stay thirty days after the debtor's second petition within a year, unless the debtor demonstrates that the second petition was filed in good faith.[36] Section 362(c)(4) prevents the stay from going into effect *at all* in a third or

---

[27] John Golmant & Tom Ulrich, *Bankruptcy Repeat Filings*, 14 Am. Bankr. Inst. L. Rev. 169 (2006); Lawrence Ponoroff & F. Stephen Knippenberg, *The Implied Good Faith Filing Requirement: Sentinel of an Evolving Bankruptcy Policy*, 85 Nw. U. L. Rev. 919 (1991); Ned W. Waxman, *Judicial Follies: Ignoring the Plain Meaning of Bankruptcy Code § 109(g)(2)*, 48 Ariz. L. Rev. 149 (2006).

[28] *See infra* Chapter 8 — The Automatic Stay.

[29] Bankruptcy Code § 101(18). *See infra* Chapter 20 Family Farmer and Family Fisherman Reorganization.

[30] Bankruptcy Code § 109(g)(1).

[31] Bankruptcy Code § 109(g)(2).

[32] *See supra* § 2.07[A] Real Estate Foreclosure.

[33] *E.g.*, In re Luna, 122 B.R. 575 (B.A.P. 9th Cir. 1991); In re Beal, 347 B.R. 87 (E.D. Wis. 2006).

[34] Ned W. Waxman, *Judicial Follies: Ignoring the Plain Meaning of Bankruptcy Code § 109(g)(2)*, 48 Ariz. L. Rev. 149 (2006).

[35] *E.g.*, In re Steele, 319 B.R. 518 (E.D. Mich. 2005).

[36] Bankruptcy Code § 362(c)(3). *See infra* § 8.06[A][3]Automatic Termination — Prior Petition Within One Year.

subsequent case filed by a debtor within a one-year period.[37]

[c] Mandatory Credit Counseling Briefing[38]

Despite serious doubts about its efficacy, individual debtors must participate in a credit counseling briefing to be eligible for any type bankruptcy relief.[39] The briefing must outline "the opportunities for available credit counseling" and provide assistance in "performing a related budget analysis."[40] It may be conducted in person, over the telephone, or via the internet, and must be provided by an "approved nonprofit budget and credit counseling agency."[41] Debtors' lawyers, who have a financial stake in their clients' decisions to file a bankruptcy petition, are not trusted to provide sufficient information in an objective manner. This briefing may now be obtained any time "during the 180-day period *ending on* the date of filing of the petition . . . ."[42] This language, added in 2010,[43] legislatively overrules decisions based on language that required the briefing to be conducted during the 180 days "preceding" the petition, that prevented debtors from receiving their briefing on the same day as their petition.[44]

This briefing is rarely excused on the limited grounds available: the difficulty of obtaining a briefing, or the presence of exigent circumstances.[45] Otherwise, the court has no authority to excuse the debtor from obtaining the briefing, even, according to some courts, if the debtor wishes to file a petition on an emergency basis, such as to prevent an imminent foreclosure sale.[46]

Given their limited scope, these briefings seem unlikely to reduce the number of bankruptcy petitions or provide debtors with useful information about how to

---

[37] Bankruptcy Code § 362(c)(4). *See infra* § 8.06[A][4] Automatic Termination — Multiple Prior Petitions Within One Year.

[38] Jeffery A. Deller & Nicholas E. Meriwether, *Putting Order to The Madness: BAPCPA and the Contours of the New Prebankruptcy Credit Counseling Requirements*, 16 J. Bankr. L. & Prac. 1 (2007); Gary Neustadter, *A Consumer Bankruptcy Odyssey*, 39 Creighton L. Rev. 225, 234-58 (2006); Andrew P. MacArthur, *Pay to Play: the Poor's Problems in the BAPCPA*, 25 Emory Bankr. Dev. J. 407 (2009). *See generally* Laurin Willis, *Against Financial Literacy Education*, 94 Iowa L. Rev. 197 (2008).

[39] Bankruptcy Code § 109(h). *See* In re Piontek, 346 B.R. 126 (Bankr. W.D. Pa. 2006) (case of debtor's spouse dismissed due to failure of spouse to obtain briefing); In re Salazar, 339 B.R. 622 (Bankr. S.D. Tex. 2006) ("striking" petition of debtor who failed to obtain briefing); Alan Eisler, *The BAPCPA's Chilling Effect on Debtor's Counsel*, 55 Am. U.L. Rev. 1333, 1339-41 (2006); U.S. Gov't Accountability Office, GAO-07-203, Value of Credit Counseling Requirement Is Not Clear 19 (2007).

[40] Bankruptcy Code § 109(h).

[41] Bankruptcy Code § 109(h).

[42] Bankruptcy Code § 109(h)(1) (as amended in 2010).

[43] Bankruptcy Technical Corrections Act of 2010, Pub. L. 111–327, 124 Stat. 3557 (Dec. 22, 2010).

[44] In re Francisco, 390 B.R. 700, 702 (B.A.P. 10th Cir. 2008) (collecting cases). Robin Miller, Annotation, *Validity, Construction, and Application of Credit Counseling Requirement Under Bankruptcy Abuse Prevention and Consumer Protection Act (BAPCPA)*, 11 A.L.R. Fed. 2d 43 (2006).

[45] Bankruptcy Code § 109(h)(4).

[46] *Compare* Dixon v. LaBarge (In re Dixon), 338 B.R. 383 (B.A.P. 8th Cir. 2006) (foreclosure sale not exigent circumstances), *with* In re Henderson, 364 B.R. 906 (Bankr. N.D. Tex. 2007) (imminent foreclosure an exigent circumstance that excused the pre-petition briefing).

improve their financial circumstances.[47] Apart from the additional cost, the briefing requirement imposes an additional burden on pro se debtors, who may file a petition without learning of the requirement. Most courts rule that the court must dismiss the debtor's case if the petition is not accompanied by the necessary briefing certificate.[48] Allowing debtor to obtain the briefing and amend her petition to include the required certificate[49] would save debtors the filing fee for a second petition, and prevent them from running afoul of other rules that impose penalties on debtors who file multiple petitions in a short period of time.[50] But, the statute requires the briefing to occur before the petition, so this alternative is not permitted.

[d]   Abstention

In rare circumstances, the court may abstain from a case even though the debtor meets § 109's requirements. Section 305 gives the court broad authority to abstain from entertaining a petition in "the interests of creditors and the debtor."[51]

The legislative history of § 305 outlines the circumstances where abstention is appropriate. It suggests that abstention should be limited to involuntary cases filed by a small number of creditors when most creditors oppose the bankruptcy, where a state insolvency proceeding or other out-of-court arrangement was already pending, and where dismissal of the case was otherwise in the best interests of the debtor and all creditors.[52] Some courts take a restrictive approach, and limit abstention to the specific circumstances mentioned in the legislative history.[53] However, most courts take a more liberal stand and, based on the express language of § 305, permit abstention in a broader range of circumstances.[54] These cases have considered a wide variety of factors, but boil down to the effect of abstention on the efficiency of the administration of the debtor's financial affairs,[55] the availability of an alternative mechanism or forum which will protect the interests of all of the

---

[47] *See* Jean Braucher, *A Guide to Interpretation of the 2005 Bankruptcy Law*, 16 Am. Bankr. Inst. L. Rev. 349, 365-66 (2008) ("By [the time they consult a bankruptcy lawyer and learn of the briefing requirement] most debtors already are in deep debt trouble and have terrible credit ratings . . . ."). Susan Block-Lieb & Edward J. Janger, *The Myth of the Rational Borrower: Rationality, Behavioralism, and the Misguided "Reform" of Bankruptcy Law*, 84 Tex. L. Rev. 1481, 1561 (2006).

[48] *E.g.*, In re Hedquist, 342 B.R. 295, 297 (B.A.P. 8th Cir. 2006); In re Cleaver, 333 B.R. 430 (Bankr. S.D. Ohio 2005). *But see* In re Hess, 347 B.R. 489 (Bankr. D. Vt. 2006) (finding room for discretion in § 707(a)).

[49] In re Anderson, 391 B.R. 758 (Bankr. S.D. Tex. 2008).

[50] *See* Jean Braucher, *The Challenge to the Bench and Bar Presented by the 2005 Bankruptcy Act: Resistance Need Not Be Futile*, 2007 U. Ill. L. Rev. 93, 106-107, 109 (2007).

[51] Bankruptcy Code § 305(a)(1).

[52] *See* S. Rep. No. 95-989, at 35-36 (1978), *reprinted in* 1978 U.S.C.C.A.N. 5787, 5821-22; H.R. Rep. No. 95-595, at 325 (1977) *reprinted in* 1978 U.S.C.C.A.N. 5787, 6281.

[53] In re RAI Marketing Serv., Inc., 20 B.R. 943 (Bankr. D. Kan. 1982). *See supra* § 2.10 Compositions and Workouts.

[54] *E.g.*, In re Spade, 258 B.R. 221, 231-33 (Bankr. D. Colo. 2001); In re Tarletz, 27 B.R. 787 (Bankr. D. Colo. 1983).

[55] *See* In re Fortran Printing, Inc., 297 B.R. 89 (Bankr. D. Ohio 2003) (considering, *inter alia*, the economy and efficiency of administration; the likelihood that the debtor and the creditors would be able

parties,[56] and the purposes for which bankruptcy jurisdiction has been sought.[57] Under this multi-faceted approach, abstention is warranted in two-party "collection cases" where there is no need for collective creditor relief,[58] or in cases where a foreign debtor is technically eligible for relief because of the existence of some small amount of property in the United States, but where a relief in a foreign country would be more appropriate because of the debtor's more prominent presence there.

[2] Eligibility for Relief Under Chapter 7 — Liquidation

Virtually any individual, charitable, or business entity qualifies for voluntary liquidation under Chapter 7. The only exceptions are for railroads, domestic insurance companies, banks and similar financial institutions,[59] and municipalities.[60] These exclusions reflect the availability of other avenues of relief for these types of debtors, such as FDIC proceedings to restructure insolvent banks. Likewise, there is a special subchapter in Chapter 11 for railroad reorganizations,[61] and Chapter 9 of the Code deals with insolvent municipalities.[62]

This broad eligibility must nevertheless be read in conjunction with the de facto limitation placed on the eligibility of consumer debtors for Chapter 7 relief by § 707(b), which requires the court to dismiss petitions that are "abusive."[63] Whether a debtor's petition is abusive depends initially on whether the debtor's household income is above or below the state median income for similar sized households in the debtor's home state. If the debtor's household income is below this threshold, Chapter 7 relief is not presumed to be abusive. If the debtor's household income exceeds the state median, relief is denied if the debtor has sufficient disposable income to make meaningful payments to creditors under a Chapter 13 plan, based on a complicated statutory formula.[64]

---

to work out a less expensive out-of-court arrangement, which would better serve all interests in the case; the effect on the debtor's business).

[56] *Id.*; In re Int'l Zinc Coatings & Chem. Corp., 355 B.R. 76 (Bankr. N.D. Ill. 2006).

[57] *E.g.*, In re Fortran Printing, Inc., 297 B.R. 89 (Bankr. D. Ohio, 2003); In re Trina Associates, 128 B.R. 858, 867 (Bankr. E.D. N.Y. 1991).

[58] *E.g.*, In re Spade, 258 B.R. 221 (Bankr. D. Colo. 2001).

[59] Bankruptcy Code § 109(b)(1)-(3). *See* Richard M. Hynes & Steven D. Walt, *Why Banks are Not Allowed in Bankruptcy*, 7 Wash. & Lee L. Rev. 985 (2010).

[60] This last exception arises from the fact that only a "person" may under file Chapter 7 (Bankruptcy Code § 109(b)) and, with one exception that is not relevant here, the term "person" does not include a governmental unit. Bankruptcy Code § 101(41).

[61] Bankruptcy Code §§ 1161-1174.

[62] Bankruptcy Code §§ 901-946. All of these specialized proceedings are beyond the scope of this book.

[63] Bankruptcy Code § 707(b).

[64] *See infra* § 17.03[B] Dismissal of Consumer Cases Due to Abuse.

[3] Eligibility for Relief under Chapter 9 — Municipalities

Chapter 9 is available only for the reorganization of a municipality,[65] such as a city, county, or other subdivision of state government.[66] States themselves are not eligible. Further explanation of cases under Chapter 9 is beyond the scope of this book.

[4] Eligibility for Relief Under Chapter 11 — Reorganization

Chapter 11's eligibility requirements are virtually the same as those for Chapter 7, with two significant differences. First, stockbrokers and commodity brokers are ineligible for Chapter 11, though they may liquidate under Chapter 7.[67] Second, railroads, which are not eligible for Chapter 7, may utilize Chapter 11.[68] However, railroad reorganizations are governed by a special set of rules that do not apply to other debtors.[69]

For many years, it was uncertain whether Chapter 11 included an implicit "going concern" requirement that prevented debtors with no current business operations, like most individuals, from "reorganizing." The dispute was resolved by the Supreme Court's 1991 decision in *Toibb v. Radloff*, which held that nothing in the Bankruptcy Code imposed such a requirement.[70] Accordingly, even individual consumer debtors are eligible for Chapter 11. However, given its expense and complexity, consumers rarely find Chapter 11 desirable if they have the option to file under either Chapter 7 or 13. However, as discussed below, debtors who are now rendered ineligible for Chapter 7 relief by the means test, because their income is too high, and whose debts exceed the limits for Chapter 13, may be required to file under Chapter 11.

[5] Eligibility for Relief Under Chapter 12 — Family Farmers and Family Fishermen[71]

Chapter 12 provides for the rehabilitation of family farmers and family fishermen through a court-approved repayment plan.[72] It is crafted to deal with the uncertainties of income from farming and fishing. Eligibility depends on

---

[65] Bankruptcy Code § 109(c).

[66] Bankruptcy Code § 101(40).

[67] Bankruptcy Code § 109(d).

[68] Bankruptcy Code § 109(d).

[69] Bankruptcy Code §§ 1161-1174. *See generally infra* § 19.15 Railroad Reorganizations.

[70] Toibb v. Radloff, 501 U.S. 157 (1991). *See* Michael J. Herbert, *Consumer Chapter 11 Proceedings: Abuse or Alternative?*, 91 Com. L.J. 234 (1986).

[71] Linda King, *Chapter 12: Adjustment of Debts of a Family Farmer with Regular Income*, 29 S. Tex. L. Rev. 615 (1988); Katherine M. Porter, *Phantom Farmers: Chapter 12 of the Bankruptcy Code*, 79 Am. Bankr. L.J. 729 (2005); Susan A. Schneider, *Bankruptcy Reform and Family Farmers: Correcting the Disposable Income Problem*, 38 Tex. Tech L. Rev. 309 (2006); Ralph V. Seep, Annotation, *What Constitutes "Family Farmer" Entitled to Relief under Chapter 12 of Bankruptcy Code*, 101 A.L.R. Fed. 502 (1991).

[72] *See infra* Chapter 20 — Family Farmer and Family Fisherman Reorganization.

whether the debtor fits the definition of "family farmer" or "family fisherman." Debtors falling outside the scope of these definitions may still reorganize under Chapter 13, if they are eligible, or under the far more expensive provisions of Chapter 11.

Relief under Chapter 12 is available only to a "family farmer or family fisherman with regular income."[73] A family farmer with regular income is a "family farmer whose annual income is sufficiently stable and regular to enable such family farmer to make payments under a [Chapter 12 plan.]"[74] A family fisherman with regular income is similarly a "family fisherman whose annual income is sufficiently stable and regular to enable such family fisherman to make payments under a [Chapter 12 plan.]"[75] Not surprisingly, the debtor qualifies even if the family farm or fishing operation has operated at a loss.[76]

[a]   Stable and Regular Income

The requirement that the family farmer or family fisherman have income sufficiently stable and regular to make payments under a Chapter 12 plan possible adds little meaning to these definitions. If the debtor's income is inadequate to fund a Chapter 12 plan, the plan probably will not be confirmed due to Chapter 12's requirement that the plan is feasible.[77] So long as the debtor qualifies as either a family farmer or a family fisherman, the plan need not be funded with revenue derived from the family farming or fishing business.[78] However, as will be seen, a significant portion of the debtor's income must be derived from farming or fishing for the debtor to qualify for relief.

To determine whether a debtor is eligible for relief under Chapter 12, the definitions of "family farmer," "farming operation," "family fisherman," and "commercial fishing operation" must be examined.

[b]   Family Farmer

Unlike Chapter 13, certain corporations and partnerships are eligible for relief under Chapter 12. Thus, the definition of "family farmer" contains several elements that vary depending on whether the debtor is on the one hand, an "individual or individual and spouse"[79] or instead, a "corporation or partnership."[80]

---

[73] Bankruptcy Code § 109(f).

[74] Bankruptcy Code § 101(19).

[75] Bankruptcy Code § 101(19B).

[76] In re Sandifer, 448 B.R. 382 (Bankr. D.S.D. 2011).

[77] Bankruptcy Code § 1225(a)(6). *See infra* § 20.08 Confirmation of Chapter 12 Plans.

[78] *E.g.*, In re Mikkelsen Farms, Inc., 74 B.R. 280 (Bankr. D. Or. 1987).

[79] Bankruptcy Code § 101(18)(A).

[80] Bankruptcy Code § 101(18)(B).

[i]   Farming Operation

The debtor must be "engaged in a farming operation" at the time the case begins.[81] A "farming operation" includes, but is not strictly limited to[82] "farming, tillage of the soil, dairy farming, ranching, production or rasing of crops, poultry, or livestock, and production of poultry or livestock products in an unmanufactured state."[83] This excludes merely renting farmland to others,[84] crop dusting, or harvesting manure from a third party's farm,[85] but encompasses breeding dogs,[86] raising timber,[87] or running a feed lot.[88] The most important factor in determining whether a particular activity qualifies as a farming operation is whether the debtor's operation is exposed to the inherent risks of farming.[89]

[ii]   Debt Limit for Family Farmers

In addition, the debtor's aggregate debts must not exceed the statutory limit, which in 2012 is $3,792,650.[90] Debtors engaged in farming operations with debts exceeding this amount may reorganize under Chapter 11's more elaborate procedures or may simply liquidate under Chapter 7.

[iii]   Source of Family Farmers Debts

In addition, at least half of the debtor's "aggregate noncontingent liquidated debts," measured as of the debtor's petition, must have arisen out of the debtor's farming operation.[91] To determine whether this 50% threshold is satisfied, "a debt for the [debtor's] principal residence" is not included unless that debt "arises out of

---

[81]   Bankruptcy Code § 101(18)(A).

[82]   In re Watford, 898 F.2d 1525 (11th Cir. 1990).

[83]   Bankruptcy Code § 101(21).

[84]   In re Tim Wargo & Sons, Inc., 869 F.2d 1128 (8th Cir. 1989). *But see* In re Blanton Smith Corp., 7 B.R. 410 (Bankr. M.D. Tenn. 1980) (debtor who owned chickens that were tended by another was eligible for Chapter 12 relief).

[85]   Federal Land Bank of Columbia v. McNeal (In re McNeal), 848 F.2d 170 (11th Cir. 1988). *See also* In re Blackwelder Harvesting Co., 106 B.R. 301 (Bankr. M.D. Fla. 1989) (fruit picking service conducted for citrus growers).

[86]   In re Maike, 77 B.R. 832 (Bankr. D. Kan. 1987).

[87]   In re Sugar Pine Ranch, 100 B.R. 28 (Bankr. D. Or. 1989) (harvesting timber and replanting on a sustained yield basis).

[88]   In re Cattle Complex Corp., 54 B.R. 50 (Bankr. D.N.M. 1985) (for purposes of determining whether chapter 11 debtor could be compelled to convert case to chapter 7).

[89]   In re Osborne, 323 B.R. 489 (Bankr. D. Or. 2005).

[90]   Bankruptcy Code § 101(18)(A). Before the 2005 amendments, this amount was lower: only $1,500,000. As with most dollar amounts in the Bankruptcy Code, the figure in § 101(18)(A) is adjusted every three years by a factor reflecting the change in the United State's Department of Labor's Consumer Price Index, and rounded to the nearest $25 amount that represents the change. Bankruptcy Code § 104(b). The amounts were last adjusted on April 1, 2010 and are set to be adjusted again in 2013, 2016, and 2019.

[91]   Bankruptcy Code § 101(18)(A). Before the 2005 amendments, 80% of the debtor's aggregate debts must have arisen from the farming operation. *See* In re Sandifer, 448 B.R. 382 (Bankr. D.S.C. 2011) (income of LLC included in debtor's income for eligibility purposes).

a farming operation."[92]

[iv]   Source of Family Farmers' Income

Moreover, if the debtor is an individual or an individual and spouse, 50% of the debtor's *gross income* must have been derived from the debtor's farm operations.[93] Debtors who have been too successful in finding other sources of income to support their failing farm finances must seek relief either under Chaptrs 7, 11, or 13.[94]

[v]   Corporate Family Farmers

There are additional requirements if the debtor is a corporation or a partnership. First, a corporation or a partnership only qualifies as a "family farmer" if more than 50% of the stock or equity of the debtor is held by "one family, or by one family and the relatives of the members of such family," and if those family members and their relatives conduct the farming operations.[95] In addition, the debtor's stock must not be publicly traded.[96]

Second, more than 80% of the debtor's assets must relate to the farming operation.[97] As with individual family farmers, the debtor's aggregate debts must be within the $3,792,650 threshold, and at least half its total debt must arise from the farm.[98]

[c]   Family Fisherman

The expansion of the scope of eligibility for relief under Chapter 12 to include "family fisherman" resolves most uncertainties regarding whether commercial fishing and aquacultural operations qualify debtors for Chapter 12. The definition of a "family fisherman with regular annual income" is similar to the definition of a family farmer with regular income. So long as the debtor is a "family fisherman" and has income sufficient to feasibly fund a Chapter 12 plan, relief is available. As with family farmers, the devil is in the details of who qualifies as a family fisherman.

---

[92] Bankruptcy Code § 101(18)(A). In the case of a corporation or partnership, this exclusion is for a dwelling owned by the debtor and used as a principal residence by one of the debtor's shareholders or partners; however, consistent with the rule for individual debtors, the exclusion does not apply if the debt arises out of the farming operation. *Id.* § 101(18)(B)(ii).

[93] Bankruptcy Code § 101(18)(A). The debtor's income is based either on the taxable year immediately preceding the taxable year in which the petition was filed, or on "each of the 2d and 3d taxable years" preceding the year of the petition. *Id.* § 101(18)(A)(i)-(ii).

[94] *See also* In re Easton, 883 F.2d 630 (8th Cir. 1989) (rental income from farm land is not income from debtor's farming operation). *But see* In re Bircher, 241 B.R. 11 (Bankr. S.D. Iowa 1999) (capital gain from real estate that was previously used in farming operation included in farming operation's income).

[95] Bankruptcy Code § 101(18)(B). "Family" is not defined, but "relative" means an "individual related by affinity or consanguinity within the third degree as determined by the common law, or individual in a step or adoptive relationship within such third degree." Bankruptcy Code § 101(45).

[96] Bankruptcy Code § 101(18)(B)(iii).

[97] Bankruptcy Code § 101(18)(B)(i).

[98] Bankruptcy Code § 101(18)(B)(ii).

[i]   Commercial Fishing Operation

As with the definition of a family farmer, individuals, individuals and their spouses, corporations, and partnerships may all qualify for Chapter 12 relief as a family fisherman. Under this sub-category, the debtor must conduct a "commercial fishing operation."[99] A commercial fishing operation means either "the catching or harvesting of fish, shrimp, lobsters, urchins, seaweed, shellfish, or other aquatic species or products of such species" or "aquaculture activities consisting of raising for market any species or product [listed above]."[100]

[ii]   Debt Limit for Family Fishermen

The debt limit for family fishermen is lower than that for family farmers. As of 2012, it is pegged at $1,757,475, less than half of the limit imposed on family farmers. Thus, for otherwise-eligible debtors with debts between $1,757,475 and $3,792,650, the distinction between farming and fishing persists.[101]

[iii]   Source of Family Fishermens' Debts

For prospective Chapter 12 debtors who are individuals, 80% or more of the debtor's "aggregate noncontingent, liquidated debts" must arise from the commercial fishing operation, excluding debt for a family residence that did not arise out of the fishing operation. Thus, if the debtor lives on his fishing boat, the debt on the boat is included to determine whether the 80% threshold has been met. For family farmers, only 50% of an individual's debt must have arisen from the debtor's farming operation, again making the distinction between agriculture and aquaculture important to a debtor's eligibility under Chapter 12.[102]

[iv]   Source of Family Fishermens' Income

As with family farmers, a majority of the family fishermen's income must be derived from the family's fishing operation.[103] Income is measured based on the taxable year preceding the taxable year in which the case was filed.[104] Thus, family fishermen who wish to take advantage of Chapter 12 must be careful not to earn too much money from other activities.

---

[99] Bankruptcy Code § 101(19A).

[100] Bankruptcy Code § 101(7A). *Cf.* In re Watford, 898 F.2d 1525, 1529 (11th Cir. 1990) ("stone crabbing" not a farming operation).

[101] As with most dollar amounts in the Bankruptcy Code, the amount in § 101(19A)(A)(i) will be adjusted every three years by a factor reflecting the change in the Department of Labor's Consumer Price Index, and rounded to the nearest $25 amount that represents the change. Bankruptcy Code § 104(b)(1). The amounts were last raised on April 1, 2010 and are set to be adjusted again in April, 2013, and 2016, and 2019.

[102] Before 2005, the debt threshold for family farmers was 80%. The 2005 legislation reduced the required percentage to 50%, and at the same time, it established an 80% threshold for family fishermen.

[103] Bankruptcy Code § 101(19A)(A)(ii).

[104] *Id.*

[v]   Corporate Family Fishermen

Also like family farmers, the Code provides for commercial fishing operations operated as a proprietorship, a partnership, or a corporation. If the debtor is an individual or an individual and spouse, the income received from the fishing operation must be more than 50% of the couple's total income.[105] If the debtor is a corporation or a partnership, more than 50% of the stock or equity of the debtor must be held by "the family that conducts the commercial fishing operation, or by the family and the relatives of the members of such family [who] conduct . . . the . . . operation."[106] As with family farms, if the debtor is a corporation, its stock must not be publicly traded.[107] Further, more than 80% of the debtor's assets must relate to the fishing operation.[108] Likewise, as with individual family fishermen, the debtor's aggregate debts must be within the $1,757,475 threshold, and at least 80% of its total debt must arise from the fishing operation.[109]

[6]   Eligibility for Relief Under Chapter 13 — Individuals with Regular Income

"Individuals with regular income" can obtain relief under Chapter 13 by submitting a plan to restructure their debts.[110] Eligibility for relief is also somewhat restricted, but in ways that are less complicated than for Chapter 12.

[a]   Individual or Individual and Spouse

A Chapter 13 debtor must be either an individual, or an individual and his or her spouse. Corporations, partnerships, and other artificial entities need not apply. Further, stockbrokers and commodity brokers are ineligible and may seek relief only under Chapter 7, which provides special provisions for these debtors.[111]

[b]   Regular Income

The debtor must have income that "is sufficiently stable and regular to enable such individual to make payments under a [Chapter 13 plan]."[112] The source of the income does not matter.[113] Unlike old Chapter XIII, which required the debtor's income to be from wages or salaries, Chapter 13 permits the debtor to use income from such things as pensions, public assistance payments, self-employment, or investments. And, although income derived from the "kindness of strangers" may

---

[105] Bankruptcy Code § 101(19A)(A)(ii). Here, however, the debtor's income is based only on the taxable year immediately preceding the taxable year in which the petition was filed.

[106] Bankruptcy Code § 101(19A)(B)(i)(I)-(II).

[107] Bankruptcy Code § 101(19A)(B)(i)(III).

[108] Bankruptcy Code § 101(18)(B)(i).

[109] Bankruptcy Code § 101(18)(B)(ii).

[110] *See infra* Chapter 18 — Rehabilitation of Individuals with Regular Income under Chapter 13.

[111] Bankruptcy Code § 101(30).

[112] Bankruptcy Code § 101(30).

[113] Under the Bankruptcy Act of 1898, in effect until 1979, former chapter XIII was available only to "wage earners."

not be adequate, support payments and stable and predictable income from friends and family sometimes qualifies.[114] Likewise, reasonably predictable fluctuations in a debtor's income, such as those associated with seasonal employment, or from a sole proprietorship in a seasonal business, do not necessarily preclude the debtor from Chapter 13 relief. However, seasonal fluctuations might make it difficult for debtor to satisfy § 1325(a)(5)(B)(iii)(I)'s requirement that installment payments to secured creditors be in "equal monthly amounts."

It is important to distinguish the regular income requirement, which is a threshold for eligibility, from the feasibility standard for confirmation of a plan. The difference is that a party seeking to dismiss a debtor's case must show that the debtor does not have regular income. By contrast, to confirm a plan under 1325(a), the debtor must demonstrate that the debtor has sufficient income to make the payments provided for under the proposed plan.[115] Thus the problem of fluctuating income may be solved (at least with regard to unsecured creditors) by a plan that accommodates the fluctuations.

[c]　　Chapter 13 Debt Limits[116]

As of 2012, the debtor must have noncontingent, liquidated, unsecured debts less than $360,475, and noncontingent, liquidated, secured debts less than $1,081,400.[117] In a joint case involving a married couple, debts are aggregated to determine whether they exceed these thresholds.[118] However, there is no requirement that both spouses file, nor any requirement that if they both file, that they file jointly.

These limits, which were once much lower,[119] were originally designed to restrict Chapter 13 to debtors with relatively modest debts. These now larger limits allow some small sole proprietorships to reorganize without using the more

---

[114] *See* James Lockhart, *Who Is "Individual with Regular Income" Eligible to Be Chapter 13 Debtor under Secs. 101(30) and 109(e) of Bankruptcy Code*, 161 A.L.R. Fed. 127 (2000). *Compare* In re Baird, 228 B.R. 324 (Bankr. M.D. Fla. 1999) (voluntary support from debtor's son), *and* In re Murphy, 226 B.R. 601 (Bankr. M.D. Tenn. 1998) (income supplied by live-in companion of unmarried debtor), *with* In re Brock 365 B.R. 201 (Bankr. D. Kan. 2007) (plan could not be confirmed absent testimony or affidavit from debtor's mother to continue support payments to her son) *and* In re Duval, 226 B.R. 116 (Bankr. D. Mont. 1998) (debtor's monthly allowance from live-in boyfriend not regular and stable income).

[115] Bankruptcy Code § 1325(a)(6). *See infra* § 18.08[B] Feasibility.

[116] Tim A. Thomas, Annotation, *Classification of Debt as Liquidated, Unsecured, or Contingent, for Purposes of Determining Debtor's Eligibility, under § 109(e) of 1978 Bankruptcy Code, for Chapter 13 Proceeding*, 95 A.L.R. Fed. 793 (1991).

[117] Bankruptcy Code § 109(e). As with most dollar amounts in the Bankruptcy Code, the figures in § 109(e) will be adjusted every three years by a factor reflecting the increase in the Department of Labor's Consumer Price Index and rounded to the nearest $25 amount that represents the change. Bankruptcy Code § 104(b)(1). The amounts were last raised on April 1, 2010 and are set to be adjusted again in April, 2013, and 2016, and 2019.

[118] *But see* In re Werts, 410 B.R. 67 (Bankr. D. Kan. 2009) (each debtor must fall within the limits).

[119] In the 1978 Bankruptcy Reform Act, they were $100,000 for unsecured debts and $350,000 in secured debts. Bankruptcy Reform Act of 1978, Pub. L. No. 95-958, 92 Stat. 2549, 2557. They were increased in 1994, the same time that the periodic escalation provision was added, to $250,000 and $750,000 respectively. Pub. L. No. 103-394 § 108, 108 Stat. 4106, 4112. The amounts were last raised on April 1, 2010 and are set to be adjusted again in 2013, 2016, and 2019.

cumbersome processes of Chapter 11. Corporations are not eligible, regardless of the small size of their debts.

[i]　Non-Contingent Debts

Debts are included in these calculations only if they are both "noncontingent" and "liquidated."[120] Debts that are either contingent or unliquidated are excluded from the calculation. A debt is contingent if, on the petition date, it is still uncertain whether the debtor will be liable at all. In other words, the debt is contingent if the debtor's liability depends on the occurrence on non-occurrence of an event that is uncertain at the time of the debtor's petition.[121]

The most common circumstance that makes a debt continent is where the debtor is liable only as a guarantor, and the principal debtor was not yet in default at the time in question. For example, if Harland Wolff has guaranteed a $400,000 unsecured note owed by Titanic Industries, Inc. to North Atlantic Finance Co., but Titanic Industries has not yet defaulted, Wolff's contingent liability on the note does not render him ineligible for Chapter 13 relief. However, if Titanic has already fallen into default at the time of Wolff's Chapter 13 petition, removing all contingencies on his liability, the amount of this unsecured debt alone place's Wolff beyond the limit on unsecured debts for Chapter 13 debtors.[122]

The mere fact that the creditor has not yet sued or obtained a judgment against the debtor whose *legal responsibility* for the debt is not contingent, does not make the debt contingent.[123] Instead, if all events giving rise to liability occurred prior to the filing of the bankruptcy petition, the claim is not contingent.[124] Thus, a person injured in an auto accident holds a noncontingent claim, because the events that gave rise to the liability — the accident — occurred before the bankruptcy case was filed. However, as explained below, such a claim is likely to be regarded as "unliquidated" unless the fact and amount of the debtor's liability has been determined.

[ii]　Liquidated Debts

To be counted toward the maximum, a debt must be "liquidated." Whether a debt is liquidated or unliquidated depends on whether it is "subject to 'ready determination and precision in computation of the amount due.' "[125] The mere fact

---

[120]　Bankruptcy Code § 109(e).

[121]　The fact that there was still a condition to be fulfilled after the petition date confirms that the debt in question was not noncontingent when the debtor entered Chapter 13, and, thus, the debt should not be considered in the § 109(e) eligibility analysis. *E.g.*, Mazzeo v. United States (In re Mazzeo), 131 F.3d 295 (2d Cir. 1997); In re Knight, 55 F.3d 231, 234 (7th Cir. 1995) (quoting S. Rep. No. 95-989 at 22 (1978), *reprinted in* 1978 U.S.C.C.A.N. 5787, 5809). *See also* H.R. Rep. No. 95-595 at 310 (1978), *reprinted in* 1978 U.S.C.C.A.N. 5963, 6267.

[122]　*E.g.*, In re Winston, 309 B.R. 61 (Bankr. M.D. Fla. 2004).

[123]　*E.g.*, In re Flaherty, 10 B.R. 118 (Bankr. N.D. Ill. 1981).

[124]　In re Nicholes, 184 B.R. 82, 88 (B.A.P. 9th Cir. 1995).

[125]　*E.g.*, In re Slack, 187 F.3d 1070, 1073 (9th Cir. 1999); In re Huelbig, 299 B.R. 721, 723 (Bankr. D.R.I. 2004).

that a debt remains disputed does not necessarily make it unliquidated, if the amount of the debt, if it is owed at all, is readily ascertainable.[126] The most common example of an unliquidated debt is liability on a personal injury claim where the amount of the victim's medical bills, pain and suffering, lost income, and other damages are uncertain.[127] This should be distinguished from liability on a promissory note, where the amount of the debtor's liability is ascertainable, even though the amount might change from day to day, as interest accumulates.

Some courts treat disputed debts as liquidated if nothing more than a simple hearing is necessary to determine the amount owed, but as unliquidated if the determination requires a more elaborate proceeding.[128] Other courts regard disputed debts as liquidated if the process to establish the amount is "fixed, certain, or otherwise determined by a specific standard" regardless of how simple or complicated the process for applying the standard may be.[129]

Still other courts recognize that the nature of the dispute over liability might make the amount of the debt difficult to determine, and refuse to exclude questions of liability from the test.[130] Under this method, disputed tort claims are far more likely to be unliquidated than disputed tax and contract claims. Debtors facing unresolved tort claims will find it best to file their Chapter 13 petition before such claims are adjudicated, rather than wait until after judgment, only to find that the size of the judgment makes them ineligible.[131]

The debtor's eligibility depends on circumstances as they existed when the debtor's petition was filed. Debts that first become noncontingent or liquidated while the debtor's case is pending do not impair the debtor's ability to continue his case, even if this places him beyond § 109(e)'s debt limits.[132]

Of course, the debtor may not become eligible simply by contesting liability for a debt that would otherwise place him above the limit. Merely scheduling a debt as disputed will not lead a court to treat the debt as unliquidated, if its amount can readily be determined.[133]

---

[126] *See, e.g.*, In re De Jounghe, 334 B.R. 760 (B.A.P. 1st Cir. 2005). *But see* Ho v. Dowell (In re Ho), 274 B.R. 867, 872-75 (B.A.P. 9th Cir. 2002). *See* Tim A. Thomas, *Classification of Debt as Liquidated, Unsecured, or Contingent, for Purposes of Determining Debtor's Eligibility, under § 109(e) of 1978 Bankruptcy Code for Chapter 13 Proceeding*, 95 A.L.R. Fed. 793 (1989).

[127] In re Solomon, 166 B.R. 832 (Bankr. D. Md. 1993) (creditor's personal injury claim for $160,000,000 remained unliquidated even though debtor did not dispute liability, where amount had not yet been determined).

[128] Slack v. Wilshire Ins. Co. (In re Slack), 187 F.3d 1070, 1073-74 (9th Cir. 1999).

[129] In re Barcal, 213 B.R. 1008, 1014 (B.A.P. 8th Cir. 1997); In re Adams 373 B.R. 116 (B.A.P. 10th Cir. 2007).

[130] Ho v. Dowell (In re Ho), 274 B.R. 867, 872-75 (B.A.P. 9th Cir. 2002).

[131] These debtors can still obtain relief in Chapter 11, which contains no debt limits. *See* Bankruptcy Code § 109(d).

[132] In re Slack, 187 F.3d 1070, 1073 (9th Cir. 1999).

[133] In re Pearson, 773 F.2d 751, 756 (6th Cir. 1985) (holding that the court will look only to the schedules to see if made in good faith and to determine if the debt meets the statutory limitations).

[iii]   Secured Debts

The valuation test of § 506(a) is used to determine the extent to which a debt is secured or unsecured.[134] Under that test, a "claim" is secured only to the extent of the value of the collateral.[135] Thus, if a debtor had a liquidated, noncontingent debt of $40,000, secured by collateral worth $25,000, only the $25,000 secured portion of the claim would count toward the secured credit limit.[136] The remaining $15,000 unsecured portion of the claim would be added to the limit on the amount of unsecured claims.[137]

Courts are divided over whether debts partially secured by the debtor's home should be treated differently. Because these claims cannot be modified in Chapter 13, some courts treat the entire amount of the claim as secured.[138] Other courts permit bifurcation of these partially secured debts for the purpose of determining the debtor's eligibility for relief, even though the debts may not be bifurcated in the debtor's plan.[139]

Courts are similarly divided over how to treat debts secured by property that is owned by someone other than the debtor. Some treat the debt as secured, to the extent of the value of the collateral,[140] and others treat the debt as unsecured.[141]

[C]   Petition, Lists, Schedules, Statements, Certificates and Disclosures[142]

A debtor's petition must usually be accompanied by a number of other documents, as specified by the Bankruptcy Rules and their accompanying Official Forms. The main purpose of these other documents is to provide the court, the trustee, and creditors with information about the debtor's financial situation. These forms are designed to be easily completed and for the most part they are. Greater simplicity arises from the fact that there is excellent software available from several sources to assist in translating raw information to completed forms.

---

[134] Scovis v. Henrichsen (In re Scovis), 249 F.3d 975 (9th Cir. 2001).

[135] The modest difference between the language of § 506(a), which refers to secured "claims," and that in § 109(e), which refers to secured "debts," has not yielded a different result.

[136] This result might also be true for debts secured by liens that are subject to avoidance under § 522(f). *See* Scovis v. Henrichsen (In re Scovis), 249 F.3d 975 (9th Cir. 2001).

[137] *E.g.*, In re Groh, 405 B.R. 674 (Bankr. S.D. Cal. 2009) (unsecured debt eligibility threshold surpassed when unsecured portion of secured claims were added to other unsecured debts).

[138] *E.g.*, In re Munoz, 428 B.R. 516 (Bankr. S.D. Cal. 2010).

[139] *E.g.*, In re Brammer, 431 B.R. 522 (Bankr. D.D.C. 2009).

[140] *E.g.*, In re Belknap, 174 B.R. 182 (Bankr. W.D.N.Y. 1994).

[141] In re Fuson, 404 B.R. 872, 876 (Bankr. S. D. Ohio 2008); In re Lower, 311 B.R. 888 (Bankr. D. Colo. 2004).

[142] Henry E. Hildebrand, III & Keith M. Lundin, *Selected Changes Affecting Consumer Bankruptcy Practice in the Bankruptcy Abuse Prevention and Consumer Protection Act of 2005*, 59 Consumer Fin. L.Q. Rep. 370 (2005); Henry J. Sommer, *Trying to Make Sense Out of Nonsense: Representing Consumers Under the "Bankruptcy Abuse Prevention and Consumer Protection Act of 2005,"* 79 Am. Bankr. L.J. 191, 211 (2005).

Corporate debtors must submit a declaration by an officer or other authorized agent that the schedules are true and correct.[143] Individual debtors must sign a similar declaration.[144] Other documents may be required, depending on the type of bankruptcy case involved. These initial documents usually must be filed within fifteen days after the petition is filed.[145] Unless the court grants an extension, the case is likely to be dismissed if the items are not promptly filed.

[1] Petition

The debtor's petition contains, among other information, the debtor's name and address; whether the debtor is an individual, partnership, corporation or other entity; the chapter under which the debtor seeks relief; the estimated number and amount of debts; the basis for proper venue in the district in which the petition is filed; and several other matters required by the Code or the Rules.[146]

[2] Schedules of Debts and Assets; Statement of Affairs

Along with their petition, debtors must file a list of their creditors[147] and Schedules A through J, providing detailed information concerning their property, debts, executory contracts, co-debtors, income, and expenses.[148] The required schedules consist of:

- Schedule A — All real property interests of the debtor, other than leasehold interests, and any encumbrances.

- Schedule B — All personal property, other than leases or executory contracts. Encum-brances on the property are not included on Schedule B.

- Schedule C — All property that the debtor claims as exempt.

- Schedule D through F — All secured, priority, and general unsecured claims.

- Schedule G — Executory contracts and unexpired leases.

- Schedule H — Co-debtors.

- Schedule I — Individual debtor's current income.

- Schedule J — Individual debtor's current living expenses.[149]

---

[143] *See* Official Bankruptcy Form 2.

[144] *See* Official Bankruptcy Form 1.

[145] Fed. R. Bankr. P. 1007.

[146] *See* Official Bankruptcy Form 1.

[147] Fed. R. Bankr. P. 1007(a). In a voluntary case, the list of creditors is not required if the schedule of liabilities is filed with the petition. Also note that in Chapter 11 and Chapter 9 proceedings, the debtor must supply a separate list of the twenty largest unsecured claims. Fed. R. Bankr. P. 1007(d).

[148] Bankruptcy Code § 521(a)(1).

[149] Fed R. Bankr. P. 1007(b)(1). *See also* Official Bankruptcy Form 6, which sets out the standardized form of the various schedules.

- A Statement of Financial Affairs, which provides information about the debtor's recent financial history.[150]

Cases of individuals who fail to file the required documents within 45 days of their petition are to be automatically dismissed.[151] However, the apparent conflict between the hanging paragraph at the end of § 521(a)(6) and § 521(i), leads some courts to say that dismissal is discretionary.[152]

[3] Additional Documents for Individual Consumer Debtors[153]

Individual Chapter 7 debtors must provide a variety of other documents, designed to assist the trustee and creditors in evaluating the debtor's compliance with the Code's requirements, and in detecting abuse. Some items must be filed with the court; others must be submitted to the trustee.[154] This lengthy list of additional documents, some of which may be waived by the court,[155] includes:

- a statement of the debtor's intention regarding his secured debts, indicating whether he expects to reaffirm the debts, redeem the collateral, avoid the lien, or surrender the collateral to the creditor;[156]

- a certification that the debtor has received an appropriate pre-bankruptcy credit briefing from an approved nonprofit budget-and-credit-counseling agency within 180 days prior to the debtor's petition;[157]

- a copy of any debt repayment plan developed through the debtor's credit counseling briefing;[158]

- a certificate from the debtor's attorney or petition-preparer indicating that the debtor has been given the notice required by § 342(b), briefly explaining Chapters 7, 11, 12, and 13 and the general purpose, benefits, and costs of

---

[150] *See* Official Bankruptcy Form 7.

[151] Hanging paragraph at the end of Bankruptcy Code § 541(a)(6) & § 521(i).

[152] In re Bliek, 456 B.R. 241 (Bankr. D.S.C. 2011). *See also* In re Riddle, 344 B.R. 702, 702-03 (Bankr. S.D. Fla. 2006) (poem on automatic dismissal).

[153] Henry J. Sommer, *Trying to Make Sense Out of Nonsense: Representing Consumers Under the "Bankruptcy Abuse Prevention and Consumer Protection Act of 2005,"* 79 Am. Bankr. L.J. 191, 211 (2005).

[154] *E.g.*, Bankruptcy Code § 521(e)(2)(A)(i).

[155] *See* Bankruptcy Code § 521(a)(1)(B). *See* Wirum v. Warren (In re Warren), 568 F.3d 1113 (9th Cir. 2009); Segarra-Miranda v. Acosta-Rivera (In re Acosta-Rivera), 557 F.3d 8 (1st Cir. 2009). *Contra* In re Spencer, 388 B.R. 418 (Bankr. D.D.C. 2008). In some jurisdictions, courts have exercised their authority to require some specified items, such as the debtor's pay stubs, to be submitted to the trustee rather than filed with the court. One might speculate that this was done at the request of the bankruptcy court clerk, who bears the burden of storing items that are filed with the court.

[156] Bankruptcy Code § 521(2)(A); Fed. R. Bankr. P. 1007(b)(2).

[157] Bankruptcy Code §§ 109(h), 521(b). Individual consumer debtors are also required to complete a "personal financial management course from an appropriate credit counseling agency," prior to receiving a discharge. Bankruptcy Code §§ 111, 727(a)(11), 1328(g). Current Official Bankruptcy Form 1 includes a certification that this briefing has occurred as part of the debtor's petition.

[158] Bankruptcy Code § 521(b)(2).

proceeding under each of those chapters; describing "the types of services available from credit counseling agencies;"[159] alerting the debtor about the criminal penalties associated with concealing assets or making a false oath or statement in the case; and advising the debtor that the information supplied in connection with his petition is subject to review by the United States Attorney General;[160]

- if the debtor has an attorney, the written contract with the debtor and his attorney;[161]

- a copy of the debtor's most recent year's federal tax return;[162]

- upon request by the court, the trustee, or a creditor, a copy of any post-petition tax returns filed by the debtor while the case is pending;[163]

- copies of the debtor's pay stubs ("payment advices"), or other evidence of payment, received by the debtor during the sixty 60 days prior to his petition;[164]

- a statement of the debtor's "monthly net income, itemized to show how the amount is calculated";[165]

- in a Chapter 13 case, a statement disclosing any reasonably anticipated increase in the debtor's income or expenditures over the twelve months after the date of the debtor's petition;[166] and

- the record of any interest the debtor has in an education IRA or under a qualified state tuition program;[167]

---

[159] Bankruptcy Code §§ 521(a)(1)(B)(iii) & 342(b)(1). *See* Official Bankruptcy Form 1; Paul M. Black & Michael J. Herbert, *Bankcard's Revenge: A Critique of the 1984 Consumer Credit Amendments to the Bankruptcy Code*, 19 U. Rich. L. Rev. 845, 852-55 (1985).

[160] Bankruptcy Code §§ 521(a)(1)(B)(iii) & 342(b)(2). This latter section refers primarily to the Office of the United States Trustee, a branch of the United States Department of Justice, and also potentially to the Office of the United States Attorney for the district in which the petition was filed.

If the debtor is not represented by an attorney, and his petition is not signed by a "petition preparer," the debtor must supply a certificate that the necessary notice was "received and read by the debtor." Bankruptcy Code § 521(a)(1)(B)(iii)(II).

[161] Bankruptcy Code § 528(a)(1).

[162] Bankruptcy Code § 521(e)(2)(A)(i). In addition, the debtor must supply a copy of the return to any creditor who requests one. *See* In re Collins, 93 B.R. 835 (Bankr. E.D. Wis. 2008). In addition, Chapter 13 debtors must file copies of their federal, state, and local tax returns with the appropriate tax authorities, when they are due, or face dismissal. Bankruptcy Code § 1308. *See* In re Cushing, 401 B.R. 528 (B.A.P. 1st Cir. 2009) (Chapter 13 case dismissed due to debtor's failure to file returns on time).

[163] Bankruptcy Code § 521(f).

[164] Bankruptcy Code § 521(a)(1)(B)(iv). *See* Community Bank, N.A. v. Ruffle, 617 F.3d 171 (2d Cir. 2010) (adopting a "payment focused" rather than a "document-focused" reading of the requirement).

[165] Bankruptcy Code § 521(a)(1)(B)(v). *See* Official Forms B22A (Chapter 7) and B22C (Chapter 13). These are the forms used in Chapter 7 cases to determine whether the debtor's Chapter 7 case is abusive. *See* Bankruptcy Code § 707(b)(2)(C) and 18 U.S.C.S. § 2075 (2006) (that's right, it's part of the United States Criminal Code).

[166] Bankruptcy Code § 521(a)(1)(B)(vi).

[167] Bankruptcy Code § 521(c).

Section 707(b)(4)(D) provides that "[t]he signature of an attorney on the petition shall constitute a certification that the attorney has no knowledge *after an inquiry* that the information in the schedules filed with such petition is incorrect."[168] This language should be read in the context of a variety of other "attorney liability" provisions, which seek to impose additional duties on attorneys who represent consumer debtors.[169] The principal question in interpreting § 707(b)(4)(D) is the extent of the "inquiry" necessary to avoid running afoul of any consequences of signing and thus certifying a set of inaccurate schedules.[170]

[D] Joint Petitions

As a practical matter, many individual bankruptcies are rooted in the mutual financial difficulties of a married couple. Accordingly, the Code explicitly permits joint filing by spouses.[171] The key advantage to joint filing is lowered costs for both the court and the debtors. A joint case may make administration of the estate more efficient. At minimum, it at least limits the filing fee. In a joint case, only a single filing fee is required.

However, joint filing does not necessarily mean that the debtors' cases will be "consolidated" — handled as if they were a single case. Unless they are consolidated, each spouse's estate is separate.[172] Depending on the extent of the married couple's joint ownership of property and joint liability for their debts, the court may either leave both estates independent of each other, consolidate the estates in part, or consolidate them entirely.[173] For example, if the spouses held little property in joint ownership and had few obligations for which both were liable, the court would probably administer the case as two separate estates. However, most married debtors' assets and debts are considerably intermingled, making joint administration more sensible.

---

[168] Bankruptcy Code § 707(b)(4)(D) (emphasis added).

[169] *See infra* § 6.02[F] Attorney's Obligations Regarding Debtor's Schedules. *See generally* Gary Neustadter, *A Consumer Bankruptcy Odyssey*, 39 Creighton L. Rev. 225, 311-54 (2006); Henry J. Sommer, *Trying to Make Sense Out of Nonsense: Representing Consumers Under the "Bankruptcy Abuse Prevention and Consumer Protection Act of 2005*," 79 Am. Bankr. L.J. 191, 204-211 (2005); Catherine E. Vance & Corinne Cooper, *Nine Traps and One Slap: Attorney Liability Under the New Bankruptcy Law*, 79 Am. Bankr. L.J. 283 (2005); Ad Hoc Committee on Bankruptcy Court Structure, ABA section of Business Law, *Attorney Liability Under Section 707(b)(4) of the Bankruptcy Abuse Prevention and Consumer Protection Act of 2005*, 61 Bus. Law. 697 (2006).

[170] Henry J. Sommer, *Trying to Make Sense Out of Nonsense: Representing Consumers Under the "Bankruptcy Abuse Prevention and Consumer Protection Act of 2005*," 79 Am. Bankr. L.J. 191, 206 (2005).

[171] Bankruptcy Code § 302(a). *See In re Somers*, 448 B.R. 677 (Bankr. S.D.N.Y. 2011) (same-sex married couple's case not required to be dismissed by Federal Defense of Marriage Act); In re Balas, 449 B.R. 567 (Bankr. C.D. Cal. 2011) (Defense of Marriage Act unconstitutional).

[172] In re Jorczak, 314 B.R. 474 (Bankr. D. Conn. 2004); Carpenter v. Fanaras (In re Fanaras), 263 B.R. 655 (Bankr. D. Mass. 2001).

[173] Bankruptcy Code § 302(b). *See generally* Reider v. FDIC (In re Reider), 31 F.3d 1102 (11th Cir. 1994).

[E] Filing Fees

As of mid-2012, filing fees in bankruptcy cases range from $281 for Chapter 13 case, $306 for Chapter 7, and $1,047 for Chapter 11.[174] In addition, a $46 administrative fee is imposed for all cases and an additional $15 trustee's fee is charged in Chapter 7 cases.[175]

For many years, there was no such thing as a free bankruptcy case; the Bankruptcy Code made no provision for an *in forma pauperis* bankruptcy petition.[176] This changed in 2005 when Congress authorized bankruptcy courts to waive the filing fee for Chapter 7 debtors whose income is less than 150 percent of the federal poverty line.[177] Where the filing fee is not waived, it may be paid in installments with permission from the court.[178]

[F] Attorneys' Obligations Regarding Debtor's Schedules[179]

The Bankruptcy Code imposes several due diligence obligations on debtors' attorneys. It also subjects debtors' attorneys to sanctions if they fail to meet these obligations. These obligations arise primarily in connection with the new means testing rules that are used to assess whether a debtor's Chapter 7 petition is abusive.

Section 707 permits the court to use existing procedures under Bankruptcy Rule 9011 to order the debtor's attorney to "reimburse the trustee for all reasonable costs in prosecuting a [successful] motion" under § 707(b), seeking to have the debtor's case converted or dismissed due to abuse.[180] It similarly permits the court to assess an appropriate civil penalty and provide for payment of that penalty to the trustee if the attorney for the debtor violates Rule 9011 in some other manner.[181] Rule 9011 emulates Federal Rule of Civil Procedure 11 by permitting the court to impose a civil penalty on attorneys who violate its provisions by advancing unwarranted arguments.[182] Thus, § 707 does not, by itself, impose

---

[174] 28 U.S.C. § 1930(a) (2006).

[175] 28 U.S.C. § 1930(b) (2006).

[176] *See* United States v. Kras, 409 U.S. 434 (1973) (denial of right to *in forma pauperis* bankruptcy petition not a deprivation of due process); Philip Tedesco, *In Forma Pauperis in Bankruptcy*, 84 Am. Bankr. L.J. 79 (2010).

[177] 28 U.S.C. § 1930(f) (2006); In re Bradshaw, 349 B.R. 511, 515 (Bankr. E.D. Tenn. 2006) (court has discretion to grant or deny waiver to qualifying debtors); In re Nuttall, 334 B.R. 921 (Bankr. W.D. Mo. 2005) (granting waiver).

[178] Fed. R. Bankr. P. 1006(b).

[179] Alan Eisler, *The BAPCPA's Chilling Effect on Debtor's Counsel*, 55 Am. U.L. Rev. 1333, 1335-39 (2006); Gary Neustadter, *A Consumer Bankruptcy Odyssey*, 39 Creighton L. Rev. 225, 342-344; Henry J. Sommer, *Trying to Make Sense Out of Nonsense: Representing Consumers Under the "Bankruptcy Abuse Prevention and Consumer Protection Act of 2005*," 79 Am. Bankr. L.J. 191, 204 (2005); Catherine E. Vance & Corinne Cooper, *Nine Traps and One Slap: Attorney Liability under the New Bankruptcy Law*, Am. Bankr. L.J. 283, 286-88 (2005).

[180] Bankruptcy Code § 707(b)(4)(A).

[181] Bankruptcy Code § 707(b)(4)(B).

[182] Fed. R. Bankr. P. 9011(b).

significant additional risks on debtors' attorneys than they already face as a result of their own misconduct.[183]

However, § 707(b)(4)(C) goes further and imposes additional and more burdensome obligations on debtors' attorneys. It provides:

> The signature of an attorney on a petition, pleading, or written motion shall constitute a certification that the attorney has —
>
> (i) performed a reasonable investigation into the circumstances that gave rise to the petition, pleading, or written motion; and
>
> (ii) determined that the petition, pleading, or written motion —
>
> (I) is *well grounded in fact*; and
>
> (II) is warranted by existing law or a good faith argument for the extension, modification, or reversal of existing law and does not constitute an abuse under [§ 707(b)(1)].[184]

This requires attorneys to conduct a "reasonable investigation" into the accuracy of the information that is relayed to the attorney by his or her client and to make a "determination" that his or her client's positions are "well grounded in fact." This goes well beyond the traditional obligations imposed by Bankruptcy Rule 9011, which only require an attorney to certify that the factual assertions in the debtor's petition and schedules have "evidentiary support."[185] This lower standard would likely be satisfied based on the debtor's statements to the debtor's attorney. The additional requirement of a reasonable investigation and a determination that the information filed with the court is "well grounded in fact" requires the debtor's attorney to go further and conduct an independent investigation of the accuracy of the information provided by the debtor.[186] The attorney is likely required to seek independent verification of the nature and extent of the debtor's assets, their value, the number and amount of the debtor's obligations, the sources and amount of the debtor's income, and other aspects of the debtor's financial circumstances that are reflected in the debtor's petition and accompanying schedules. It also requires the debtor's attorney to verify that the debtor has not filed a bankruptcy petition during the past eight years. This does not quite make the debtor's attorney a guarantor of the accuracy of the information contained in these documents, but it comes dangerously close.[187] Courts addressing the issue so far have indicated that the attorney is not a guarantor of the information's accuracy, but, instead, that the information in the schedules must be "based upon the attorney's best knowledge, information and belief, 'formed after an inquiry reasonable under the circum-

---

[183] Gary Neustadter, *A Consumer Bankruptcy Odyssey*, 39 Creighton L. Rev. 225, 311-54 (2006). *See* In re Kayne, 453 B.R. 372 (B.A.P. 9th Cir. 2011) ($21,000 in sanctions for deliberate failure to include promissory note owned by debtor on schedule of debtor's assets).

[184] Bankruptcy Code § 707(b)(4)(C) (emphasis added).

[185] Fed. R. Bankr. P. 9011(b)(3).

[186] Task Force on Attorney Discipline Best Practices Working Group, Ad Hoc Committee on Bankruptcy Court Structure and Insolvency Processes, ABA Section of Business Law, *Working Paper: Best Practices for Debtors' Attorneys*, 64 Bus. Law. 79 (2008).

[187] *See* In re Withrow, 405 B.R. 505 (B.A.P. 1st Cir. 2009).

stances.' "[188] Attorneys who simply take their client's word for information do so at considerable risk.[189]

There are, of course, horror stories about the misconduct of disreputable lawyers who create facts out of thin air in an effort to assist their clients,[190] or who wilfully fail to report their client's known assets to the court. But, other provisions of the Bankruptcy Code and widely applicable standards of professional conduct already prohibit this sort of dishonest behavior. Making bankruptcy lawyers responsible for investigating the accuracy of information provided by their clients is likely to drive up the costs of providing bankruptcy services to consumer debtors.[191] And, at least until the scope of the duty becomes better understood, the provision may drive away risk-averse bankruptcy practitioners,[192] and those who only handle bankruptcy cases occasionally. These, and other requirements of the 2005 amendments appear to have increased the price charged by those who continue to provide these services.[193] This may have been part of Congress's intent in enacting these and other elements of the 2005 bankruptcy "consumer protection" legislation.

§ 6.03 COMMENCEMENT OF INVOLUNTARY CASES[194]

[A] Purpose of Involuntary Petitions

"Involuntary Bankruptcy" refers to a bankruptcy case commenced by a debtor's creditors without the debtor's consent. Involuntary bankruptcy permits creditors to force the debtor to deal with its creditors as a group, at a time when the debtor

---

[188] In re Withrow, 405 B.R. 505, 512 (B.A.P. 1st Cir. 2009); Nosek v. Ameriquest Mortg. Co. (In re Nosek), 386 B.R. 374, 381 (Bankr. D. Mass. 2008).

[189] In re Dean, 401 B.R. 917 (Bankr. D. Idaho 2008) (attorney failed to verify perfection of security interest in debtor's mobile home, granted to debtor's mother, compelled to disgorge half his fee).

[190] E.g., In re Diaz, 348 B.R. 752 (Bankr. S.D. Tex. 2006) (attorney or members of his staff fabricated $800 monthly charitable contribution in completing client's schedules).

[191] The Congressional Budget Office estimated that attorney costs would increase between $150 and $500 per Chapter 7 cases as a result of the requirement that debtor's attorneys conduct a reasonable investigation of a debtor's financial affairs and that they compute the debtor's eligibility for Chapter 7 under the new means testing rules in § 707(b). Congressional Budget Office Cost Estimate, S. 256 Bankruptcy Abuse Prevention and Consumer Protection Act of 2005, 14 (2005), available at http://www.cbo.gov/ftpdocs/62xx/doc6266/s256hjud.pdf (last viewed on July 7, 2006). See also Robert J. Landry, III & Amy K. Yarbrough, *An Empirical Examination of the Direct Access Costs to Chapter 7 Consumer Bankruptcy: A Pilot Study in the Northern District of Alabama*, 82 Am. Bankr. L.J. 331 (2008).

[192] One of your authors is aware of law school clinic programs that quit handling bankruptcy cases as a result of these new requirements.

[193] Gary Neustadter, *A Consumer Bankruptcy Odyssey*, 39 Creighton L. Rev. 225, 347-53 (2006). In Columbus, Ohio, where one of your co-author's resides, local attorneys report that the price of a no frills Chapter 7 case rose $250-500 after the 2005 amendments went into effect. *Compare* In re Murray, 348 B.R. 917 (Bankr. M.D. Ga. 2006) (administrative order raising amount that Chapter 13 debtor's attorney could charge without a separate detailed fee application, from $1,500 to $2,500), *with* In re Grunau, No. 9:06-bk-20573-ALP, 2006 Bankr. LEXIS 2503 (Bankr. M.D. Fla. Oct. 4, 2006) (Paskay, J.) (ordering attorney to disgorge fees charged to Chapter 13 debtors above $2,000).

[194] Susan Block-Lieb, *Why Creditors File So Few Involuntary Petitions and Why the Number is Not Too Small*, 57 Brook. L. Rev. 803 (1991); David S. Kennedy, James E. Bailey, III, & R. Spencer Clift, III, *the Involuntary Bankruptcy Process: a Study of the Relevant Statutory and Procedural Provisions and*

still has sufficient assets to make meaningful payment to its creditors. It also permits creditors to take advantage of the Bankruptcy Code's preference and other avoiding powers to recover assets that the debtor may have transferred to favored creditors and others, before the final fall into total insolvency. As will be seen, these are tools that are not available in collective procedures under state law, such as receiverships and assignments for the benefit of creditors.[195]

An involuntary petition is an extreme remedy with serious consequences for the unwilling debtor.[196] Accordingly, the Code imposes several restrictions which make it a difficult, risky, and unattractive alternative for creditors, when other avenues of relief are available.

The Code's approach has been successful. As some scholars have noted, the number of involuntary bankruptcies is much lower than one might expect.[197] Indeed, there are so few that the Administrative Office of the United States Courts no longer keeps separate records of them. Some scholars have suggested that the large percentage of unsuccessful Chapter 11 reorganizations indicates that a loosening of the standards to force debtors into bankruptcy might induce debtors to file voluntary petitions sooner, before their financial condition becomes so desperate that their prospects for reorganization are slim.[198] Despite these suggestions, it is impossible to determine the number of voluntary bankruptcy cases that are filed as a result of a threat of an involuntary bankruptcy petition.

[B]　Chapters Under Which Involuntary Petition are Permitted

The Bankruptcy Code permits involuntary proceedings only under Chapters 7 and 11. The Code prohibits involuntary Chapter 9, 12 or 13 cases. Nearly all involuntary proceedings are filed under Chapter 7, with creditors seeking to liquidate the debtor, not reorganize it.

[C]　Persons Against Whom an Involuntary Petition May Be Filed

As a threshold requirement, the debtor must be eligible for relief in the type of proceeding involved. Railroads may not file voluntarily under Chapter 7[199] and thus may not be forced into Chapter 7.[200] Financial institutions and insurance

---

Related Matters 31 U. Mem. L. Rev. 1 (2000); Lynn M. LoPucki, *A General Theory of the Dynamics of the State Remedies/Bankruptcy System*, 1982 Wis. L. Rev. 311, 352-62; John C. McCoid II, *The Occasion for Involuntary Bankruptcy*, 61 Am. Bankr. L.J. 195 (1987).

[195] *See supra* § 2.09 State Insolvency Proceedings.

[196] Huszti v. Huszti, 451 B.R. 717 (E.D. Mich. 2011).

[197] Susan Block-Lieb, *Why Creditors File So Few Involuntary Petitions and Why the Number is Not Too Small*, 57 Brook. L. Rev. 803 (1991).

[198] *See* Lynn M. LoPucki, *A General Theory of the Dynamics of the State Remedies/Bankruptcy System*, 1982 Wis. L. Rev. 311.

[199] Bankruptcy Code § 109(b)(1).

[200] Bankruptcy Code § 303(a).

companies are excluded from bankruptcy proceedings entirely, because their insolvency is governed by state law or by other federal law. Consequently, they cannot be debtors in an involuntary bankruptcy case.[201]

Farmers, family farmers, and non-profit corporations can never be put into involuntary bankruptcy.[202] The first two categories reflect the fact that although this has been a predominantly urban nation since 1920 (and although suggestions that there are now more lawyers in this country than farmers is a gross exaggeration),[203] the great bankruptcy compromise of 1898 that protected farmers from being forced into bankruptcy remains intact. Indeed, the compromise was broadened by the current Bankruptcy Code. Under the 1898 Act, farmer really meant farmer: an individual who worked the land.[204] Under the current law, the term includes any person that receives more than 80 percent of its gross income from farming operations,[205] and "person" includes individuals, partnerships and corporations.[206] Thus, the "farmer" sheltered by a kindly Congress from being crushed by creditors may well be a multi-million dollar limited partnership, run by accountants from air-conditioned offices in the city. Family fishermen, engaged in commercial fishing operations on the other hand, are not exempt, except to the extent they might fit also the broader definition of a "farmer."[207]

Section 303(a) further provides that an involuntary petition may not be filed against "a corporation that is not a moneyed, business, or commercial corporation."[208] This somewhat obscure phrase means that non-profit or charitable corporations cannot be the target of an involuntary petition.[209] Thus, most churches, colleges, foundations, and political campaigns cannot be forced into bankruptcy. These charities remain eligible to file voluntarily.

An involuntary petition must be against one debtor; there are no joint involuntary cases.[210] If there is a group of related debtors or a married couple who owe money to the same creditors, those creditors might file separate petitions against each of the debtors and seek to have the cases consolidated.[211] However, each petition must comply with all of the Code's requirements.

---

[201] Bankruptcy Code §§ 109(b), (d); 303(a).

[202] Bankruptcy Code § 303(a).

[203] Some say that there are more employees of the Department of Agriculture than farms. As of 2007 there were approximately 2.2 million farms in the United States, 96% of which were operated by individuals or families.

   http://www.csrees.usda.gov/nea/ag_systems/in_focus/familyfarm_if_overview.html

(last visited on August 24, 2011). At the same time there were about 1 million lawyers.

[204] Bankruptcy Act of 1898 § 1(17), 30 Stat. 544, 545 ("Farmer shall mean an individual personally engaged in farming or tillage of the soil") (repealed 1979).

[205] Bankruptcy Code § 101(20).

[206] Bankruptcy Code § 101(41).

[207] Bankruptcy Code § 101(21).

[208] Bankruptcy Code § 303(a).

[209] *E.g.*, In re Memorial Medical Center, Inc., 337 B.R. 388 (Bankr. D.N.M. 2005).

[210] *E.g.*, In re Bowshier, 313 B.R. 232, 234 (Bankr. S.D. Ohio 2004).

[211] *See infra* § 23.05 Consolidated Cases Involving Related Debtors.

[D] Petitioning Creditors[212]

The Code contains barriers that seek to prevent a single disgruntled creditor from forcing the debtor into an involuntary case. For most debtors, three unsecured creditors must join in the petition, though this rule is relaxed for debtors with fewer than twelve creditors. Further, these creditors' aggregate claims must meet a statutory minimum, and, as explained below, some claims are excluded from the amount necessary to satisfy the statutory threshold.

[1] Three Creditors

In most cases, an involuntary petition must be joined by a minimum of three creditors.[213] Each of these creditors must have a claim that is both non-contingent and not the subject of a bona fide dispute.[214] The three petitioning creditors must each either hold a claim or be an "indenture trustee representing" the holder of a claim. Those who do not hold a claim do not qualify to be one of the three petitioning creditors. "Claim" includes a broad array of rights to legal and equitable remedies.[215]

The petitioning creditor's claims also must not be "the subject of a bona fide dispute as to liability or amount."[216] The Code makes it clear that a bona fide dispute disqualifies the creditor regardless of whether the dispute is over liability itself, or only over the size of the creditor's claim.[217]

The requirement of multiple petitioners is a fundamental part of the compromise that opened the door to involuntary bankruptcy in 1898 and continues in the current Code. Judge Friendly explained the compromise in a famous case:

> [T]he entire process that resulted in the enactment of the Act of 1898 was a pitched battle between those who wanted to give the creditor an effective remedy to assure equal distribution of a bankrupt's assets and those who were determined to protect the debtor from the harassment of ill-considered or oppressive involuntary petitions, including those by a single

---

[212] David S. Kennedy, James E. Bailey III & R. Spencer Clift III, *The Involuntary Bankruptcy Process: A Study of the Relevant Statutory and Procedural Provisions and Related Matters*, 31 U. Mem. L. Rev. 1 (2000); Eric J. Taube, *Involuntary Bankruptcy: Who May be a Petitioning Creditor*, 21 Hous. L. Rev. 339 (1984).

[213] The "three creditor" standard was a compromise, added to the Bankruptcy Code in the Bankruptcy Act of 1898, as a compromise between the liberal standard in the short-lived Bankruptcy Act of 1841 and the stricter requirement of the 1867 Act. *See* In re Gibralter Amusements, 291 F.2d 22 (2d Cir. 1961).

[214] Lawrence Ponoroff, *The Limits of Good Faith Analyses: Unraveling and Redefining Bad Faith in Involuntary Bankruptcy Proceedings*, 71 Neb. L. Rev. 209 (1992).

[215] Bankruptcy Code § 101(5). *See infra* § 10.02[A] Definition of Claim.

[216] Bankruptcy Code § 303(b)(1). *See* Lawrence Ponoroff, *Involuntary Bankruptcy and the Bona Fides of a Bona Fide Dispute*, 65 Ind. L.J. 315 (1989-1990).

[217] Bankruptcy Abuse Prevention and Consumer Protection Act of 2005, Pub. L. No. 109-8, § 1234(a)(1)(A), 119 Stat. 23, 204.

creditor interest. The requirement of three creditors was one of many provisions reflecting a compromise between the two opposing positions.[218]

Some debtors have only a few creditors. For these debtors, involuntary petitions may sometimes be brought by one of them. If the debtor has fewer than twelve creditors who hold non-contingent, undisputed claims,[219] then the petition may be filed by a single creditor who is owed the statutory minimum amount.[220]

[2] Determining Whether the Debtor Has Twelve Creditors

In calculating the number of creditors, employees, insiders, and creditors who have received various types of avoidable transfers are not counted.[221] Thus, the actual number of creditors may be twelve, twenty, or a hundred, and a single creditor may still be able to initiate an involuntary petition on its own.

An aggressive creditor might try to circumvent the minimum required amount by purchasing a claim from another creditor. Likewise, a creditor might seek to sidestep the three-creditor requirement by splitting its claims and transferring some of them to another friendly entity, such as a subsidiary, or a relative, who is willing to join in the petition.[222] However, a claim will not be counted toward the minimum amount necessary if it was transferred or split for the purpose of filing an involuntary petition.[223] For example, suppose Industrial Supply Co. wished to file an involuntary petition against Franklin Manufacturing, but was unable to persuade two other creditors to join in the petition. If Industrial Supply split its claim into three parts, and assigned two parts to two of its subsidiaries and then joined with those subsidiary corporations in an involuntary petition, relief would be denied because the three petitioners will count as one creditor rather than three.

The rule against multiplying creditors by splitting claims is designed to protect the policy underlying the three-creditor requirement. The rule protects most debtors from being put into bankruptcy by a single creditor whose motivations may include personal animus or simple refusal to deal reasonably with an unpaid debt.

This policy, however, is not always rigorously deployed. Closely affiliated creditors that have separate claims against the debtor have been counted as separate petitioners, as long as each claim arose separately and the parties were not

---

[218] In re Gibraltor Amusements, 291 F.2d 22, 28 (2d Cir.) (Friendly, J., dissenting), *cert. denied*, 368 U.S. 925 (1961).

[219] Following the 2005 amendments, § 303(b)(1) is clear that petitioning creditors are required to hold claims that were not the subject of dispute regardless of whether the dispute was over the debtor's liability or the amount of the creditor's claim.

[220] Bankruptcy Code § 303(b)(2).

[221] Bankruptcy Code § 303(b)(2). *See* In re DemirCo Group (North America), L.L.C., 343 B.R. 898 (Bankr. C.D. Ill. 2006) (former employees are not "employees" within meaning of § 303(b)(2) and are thus not excluded from calculation of the number of creditors).

[222] Fed. R. Bankr. P. 1003(a). A transferee of a claim must attach to the petition the documents that evidence the transfer.

[223] Fed. R. Bankr. P. 1003(a); In re McMeekin & Shoreman, 16 B.R. 805, 808-09 (Bankr. D. Mass. 1982).

simply alter-egos of one another.[224]

The claims of petitioning creditors must be both "not contingent" and "undisputed."[225] As explained in a different context earlier in this chapter,[226] a claim is contingent "when the debtor's duty to pay arises only upon the occurrence of a future event that was contemplated by the parties at the time of the contract's execution."[227] Thus, if one of three petitioning creditors' claims is based on the debtor's liability as a guarantor of the creditor's claim against another principal debtor and the principal debtor is not yet in default, the petitioning creditor's claim remains contingent. The creditor may not be one of the three petitioning creditors who are needed to join in the petition.

[3] Aggregate Minimum of Unsecured Claims

The petitioning creditors claims must, in the aggregate total at least $14,425 in unsecured claims.[228] Thus, if the three petitioning creditors claims are $4,750 each, the $14,250 aggregate total is not enough to satisfy the threshold. But, if one of the petitioning creditors holds a claim for $14,423 and each of the others is owed $1, the minimum is met and the involuntary case may proceed.

Creditors with collateral for their claims may join the petition, but only the unsecured portion of their claims may count toward the $14,425 minimum. Thus, a creditor with a $10,000 claim, secured by collateral worth $7,000, counts only as $3,000 of the required amount.

Note that fully secured creditors rarely have a reason to force a debtor into bankruptcy. Their rights can be protected far more easily through a traditional mortgage foreclosure action; or, in the case of creditors with security interests on personal property under Article 9 of the U.C.C., through self-help repossession and sale of the collateral.

---

[224] Subway Equip. Leasing Corp. v. Sims (In re Sims), 994 F.2d 210 (5th Cir. 1993); In re Gibraltor Amusements, 291 F.2d 22 (2d Cir.), *cert. denied*, 368 U.S. 925 (1961).

[225] Bankruptcy Code § 303(b).

[226] *See supra* § 6.02[B][6] Eligibility for Relief Under Chapter 13 — Individuals with Regular Income.

[227] Chicago Title Ins. Co. v. Seko Invs., Inc. (In re Seko Invs., Inc.), 156 F.3d 1005, 1008 (9th Cir. 1998); In re All Media Properties, Inc, 5 B.R. 126, 133 (Bankr. S.D. Tex. 1980), *aff'd* 646 F.2d 193 (5th Cir. 1981).

[228] Bankruptcy Code § 303(b)(1). Prior to the 1994 Amendments, this amount was only $5,000. In 1994, the amount was raised to $10,000. As with most dollar amounts in the Bankruptcy Code, the amount in § 303(b) has been adjusted every three years, since 1994, by a factor reflecting the increase in the Department of Labor's Consumer Price Index and rounded to the nearest $25 amount that represents the change. Bankruptcy Code § 104(b)(1)(2006). The amount will continue to be increased, at three-year intervals, in accordance with any rise in the consumer price index. The amounts were last raised on April 1, 2010 and are set to be adjusted again in April, 2013, and 2016, and 2019.

[4]   Special Involuntary Petition Rules for Certain Debtors

There are some special additional rules for debtors who are partnerships. First, an involuntary petition against a partnership may also be filed by "fewer than all of the general partners."[229] Petitions filed by all of the general partners are perfectly valid, but they are regarded as voluntary. Second, if all of the general partners are debtors in their own separate bankruptcy cases, an involuntary petition against the partnership itself may be filed either by a single general partner, by the trustee of any general partner, or by any creditor of the partnership.[230] There is no requirement that any set number of creditors file the petition, or that there be any particular amount of debt owed to the filing creditor.

There is also a special rule that deals with debtors who are already the subject of a foreign bankruptcy. An involuntary petition may be filed by a foreign representative of the estate in a foreign proceeding concerning the debtor.[231] For example, suppose that InterGalactic Trading Corp., a multinational firm, is in receivership in Great Britain. If InterGalactic owns an office building, equipment, and inventory in New Jersey, the British receiver may file an involuntary bankruptcy petition against InterGalactic in the proper New Jersey district. The American bankruptcy case deals with the property in the U.S., while the British receivership administers the property located in Great Britain. Although the U.S. proceeding is technically separate from the British case and operates under American rules, the British receiver has the opportunity to initiate the American proceeding to handle the New Jersey assets. Recognition of the foreign receiver is handled under Chapter 15 of the Code, which was adopted in 2005.[232]

[E]   Grounds for Entering an "Order for Relief"[233]

A small group of unpaid creditors are not entitled to force a debtor into bankruptcy simply because the debtor has defaulted on its obligations to them. An order for relief will be entered only if 1) the debtor fails to resist the petition, 2) the debtor is generally not paying its debts as they come due, or 3) a custodian has already been appointed under state law to take control of substantially all of the debtor's assets.[234]

---

[229] Bankruptcy Code § 303(b)(3)(A). *See* Karen Blaney, Note, *What Do You Mean My Partnership Has Been Petitioned into Bankruptcy?*, 19 Fordham Urb. L.J. 833 (1992).

[230] Bankruptcy Code § 303(b)(3)(B).

[231] Bankruptcy Code § 303(b)(4).

[232] *See generally infra* Chapter 22 — International Bankruptcy.

[233] John C. McCoid II, *The Occasion for Involuntary Bankruptcy*, 61 Am. Bankr. L.J. 195 (1987); Israel Trieman, *Acts of Bankruptcy: A Medieval Concept in Modern Bankruptcy Law*, 52 Harv. L Rev. 189 (1938).

[234] Bankruptcy Code § 303(h).

[1] Petition Not Controverted

As with any lawsuit in which the defendant does not answer, a debtor who fails to answer an involuntary petition will suffer a default judgment and an order for relief will be granted, forcing it into bankruptcy. Section 303(h) provides: "If the petition is not timely controverted, the court shall order relief against the debtor in an involuntary case under the chapter under which the petition was filed."[235]

After an involuntary petition is filed, the bankruptcy court clerk's office issues a summons to be served on the debtor.[236] The debtor has twenty days to respond.[237]

If the debtor contests the petition, the creditors must prove that the grounds warranting relief asserted in their petition are true. This may require a trial to determine whether the statutory grounds to enter an order for relief exist. Or, where there is no dispute of material facts, an order for relief may be entered by summary judgment.[238]

[2] Debtor Generally Not Paying Debts as They Become Due

The main ground for granting involuntary relief is that the debtor is insolvent in the "equitable" sense of not paying its debts as they come due.[239] Section 303(h)(1) provides: the court shall order relief against the debtor in an involuntary case under the chapter under which the petition was filed, only if (1) the debtor is not generally paying such debtor's debts as such debts become due unless such debts are the subject of a bona fide dispute as to liability or amount.[240]

The fact that the debtor is insolvent in the "legal" sense, because its liabilities exceed its assets, is not enough to justify granting an involuntary petition. Many businesses (and many law students) are insolvent in this legal sense but are able to pay their monthly bills when they are due. If a debtor's cash flow is sufficient to remain current on its debts, there is no need for the debtor to be in bankruptcy.

Apart from this, the precise meaning of § 303(h)(1) is unclear. It does not specify whether a debtor who has fallen behind on numerous small debts, but remains current with all of its larger obligations is not generally paying. Nor is the statutory language clear about whether a debtor who is current on all of its smaller obligations, constituting a majority of its debts, but is in default on a few large debts that constitute a large proportion of its debt, is insolvent in this sense.[241]

In determining whether the standard has been met, most courts focus on the size and number of debts that the debtor is not paying, the extent of the debtor's default

---

[235] Bankruptcy Code § 303(h).

[236] Fed. R. Bankr. P. 1010.

[237] Fed. R. Bankr. P. 1013(b).

[238] In re Bishop, Baldwin, Rewald, Dillingham & Wong, Inc., 779 F.2d 471 (9th Cir. 1985).

[239] See Adams v. Richardson, 337 S.W.2d 911, 916 (Mo. 1960).

[240] See Adams v. Richardson, 337 S.W.2d 911, 916 (Mo. 1960).

[241] E.g., Perez v. Feinberg (In re Feinberg), 238 B.R. 781 (B.A.P. 8th Cir. 1999) (involuntary petition dismissed where debtor was in default on a single massive debt, but current on all other obligations).

on debts that have not been paid, and the state of the debtor's business and financial affairs generally.[242] Many other factors are frequently considered in this "totality of the circumstances" approach.[243]

Ordinarily, failing to pay a single creditor does not warrant relief, even though the size of the claim may be large in relation to the debtor's other obligations.[244] This general reluctance to approve a one-creditor involuntary bankruptcy reflects a broader concern about whether it is appropriate to use bankruptcy proceedings to resolve disputes that involve only two parties.[245] State collection law usually provides an ample solution to the problem of a debtor who is not paying a single creditor. Bankruptcy is designed to resolve the problems that arise due to the competing claims of multiple creditors where a debtor is in general default, not to handle disputes between a debtor and a single creditor.[246]

There is also a concern about the possibility of creditors improperly using the threat of involuntary bankruptcy as a tool in settlement negotiations.[247] This explains why disputed debts are not counted when the court determines whether the debtor is equitably insolvent.[248]

Whether a particular debt is the subject of a bona fide dispute depends on the same test that applies under § 303(b) to determine which creditors are eligible to join the petition.[249] The debt is excluded regardless of whether it is either the "liability or amount" that is in dispute.[250] This statutory language, added in 2005, overrules cases that held that it was only disputes about the fact of liability, not the amount, that would prevent a creditor from being included among the qualifying petitioning creditors.[251]

[3] Appointment of a "Custodian" of the Debtor's Property

Section 303(h)(2) provides a second, far less frequently used basis for granting an involuntary petition. Regardless of the debtor's equitable solvency, the court must grant the petition if a "custodian," such as a receiver, trustee, or assignee for benefit of creditors, was appointed or took possession of the substantially all of the debtor's

---

[242] E.g., In re Green Hills Dev. Co., 445 B.R. 647, 657 (Bankr. S.D. Miss. 2011).

[243] E.g., In re ELRS Loss Mitigation, LLC, 325 B.R. 604, 633 (Bankr. N.D. Okla. 2005).

[244] E.g., Soc'y of Lloyd's v. Harmsen (In re Harmsen), 320 B.R. 188 (B.A.P. 10th Cir. 2005); Perez v. Feinberg (In re Feinberg), 238 B.R. 781 (B.A.P. 8th Cir. 1999).

[245] See also § 23.04 Single-Asset Real Estate Reorganizations.

[246] Brad R. Godshall & Peter M. Gilhuly, The Involuntary Bankruptcy Petition: The World's Worst Debt Collection Device?, 53 Bus. Law. 1315 (1998).

[247] See Lawrence Ponoroff, Involuntary Bankruptcy and the Bona Fides of a Bona Fide Dispute, 65 Ind. L.J. 315 (1990).

[248] Bankruptcy Code § 303(h)(1).

[249] In re Busick, 65 B.R. 630 (N.D. Ind. 1986), aff'd, 831 F.2d 745 (7th Cir. 1987).

[250] Bankruptcy Abuse Prevention and Consumer Protection Act of 2005, Pub. L. No. 109-8, §§ 1234(a)(1), 1234(b), 119 Stat. 23, 203; H.R. Rep. No. 109-31 (Part I), at 148 (2005), as reprinted in 2005 U.S.C.C.A.N. 88, 206.

[251] See Riverview Trenton R.R. Co. v. DSC, Ltd. (In re DSC, Ltd.), 486 F.3d 940, 947 (6th Cir. 2007).

property within the 120 days before the petition was filed.[252] Thus, if a state insolvency proceeding is pending in state court, creditors have the right bring the proceeding into Bankruptcy Court. This makes an involuntarily proceeding similar to removal of an insolvency proceeding from state court to bankruptcy court, where provisions of federal bankruptcy law that have no analog in state receiverships, will apply. Consistent with the Bankruptcy Clause of the Constitution,[253] the fundamental rationale for this is that the federal bankruptcy courts are the better forum, with the better "uniform" law, and either the debtor or its creditors have the right to have a debtor's financial affairs administered under the Bankruptcy Code.

On the other hand, if the state court proceeding involves less than substantially all of the debtor's assets,[254] which might occur in a conventional mortgage foreclosure proceeding, involuntary relief is not automatically warranted without an independent showing that the debtor is generally not paying its debts as they mature under § 303(h)(1).

[F]   Dismissal of an Involuntary Petition

Involuntary petitions may be dismissed, without a determination of their merits, on the motion of any petitioning creditor, with the consent of all of the petitioners and the debtor, or for lack of prosecution by the petitioning creditors.[255] Dismissal requires notice to "all creditors" and an opportunity for a hearing.[256] This notice gives other creditors, who may want the bankruptcy to go forward, an opportunity to join in the petition, or to otherwise intervene.

Otherwise, an involuntary petition is dismissed if the petitioning creditors fail to show that the debtor is not generally paying its debts as they become due or that a custodian has assumed control of the debtor's assets, as required for an order for relief under § 303(h).

[G]   Penalties for Unsubstantiated Petitions[257]

Creditors dare not cavalierly file an involuntary petition in an effort to use it as leverage in their settlement negotiations with the debtor. If the court dismisses an involuntary petition on its merits, the court may grant judgment against all of the petitioning creditors for the costs and attorney's fees the debtor incurs in contesting the petition.[258] Moreover, if the court find that a petitioner acted in bad

---

[252] Bankruptcy Code § 303(h)(2).

[253] U.S. Const. art. I, § 8, cl. 4.

[254] Bankruptcy Code § 303(h)(2).

[255] Bankruptcy Code § 303(j).

[256] Bankruptcy Code § 303(j).

[257] Kurtis A. Kemper, *Award of Attorney's Fees Under § 303(i)(1)(B) of Bankruptcy Code on Dismissal of Involuntary Petition in Bankruptcy*, 179 A.L.R. Fed. 549 (2002); Isabella C. Lacayo, Note, *After the Dismissal of an Involuntary Bankruptcy Petition: Attorney's Fees Awards to Alleged Debtors*, 27 Cardozo L. Rev. 1949 (2006).

[258] Bankruptcy Code § 303(i)(1). The wording of § 303(i) is somewhat ambiguous. It states that the court may grant judgment for costs "or" attorney's fees, suggesting that the court may be compelled to choose between awarding either the debtor's costs or the debtor's reasonable attorney fees. Nevertheless,

faith, the court may award additional damages against that petitioner, including any damages proximately caused by the bad faith filing, plus punitive damages.[259]

Courts have established a variety of tests for bad faith based on the petitioning creditor's subjective honesty in filing the petition, their motivations for filing the petition, whether a reasonable person would have filed the petition, and whether the petition was an proper use of the bankruptcy code.[260] Bad faith is most likely to be inferred in circumstances where an involuntary petition was filed in disregard of facts that did not warrant relief,[261] where a petitioning creditor is motivated by a desire to harm the debtor,[262] or where the creditor used the involuntary petition to obtain leverage in what otherwise was merely a two-party dispute.[263]

The consequences for the debtor of an unfounded or bad faith petition can be substantial.[264] A teetering but not yet equitably insolvent debtor may fail as a result of bad publicity or expense caused by the involuntary petition. Ambiguity about the proper application of the "generally not paying" standard and the difficulty creditors might encounter before filing a petition in obtaining information relevant to the merits of their petition should lead creditors to be cautious about joining an involuntary petition precipitously.

[H]　Transactions During the "Gap Period"

Unlike the circumstances when a debtor voluntarily files a bankruptcy petition, an involuntary petition does not immediately or even necessarily result in the entry of an order for relief. As explained earlier, the debtor has the opportunity to contest the petition; if it does, a hearing must be conducted to determine whether the debtor is not generally paying its debts as they come due. As in any adversary litigation, there is likely to be a time period for discovery of relevant evidence. Consequently, the status of the debtor may remain in doubt for weeks or longer, while the involuntary petition is pending. This period of time between the petition and the entry of an order for relief is known as the "gap period" or the "involuntary gap."

---

it is reasonably clear that this means that the court may award one or the other, or neither, or both. It does not mean that the court may award only one or the other. *See* Kenneth N. Klee, *Legislative History of the New Bankruptcy Code*, 54 Am. Bankr. L.J. 275, 297 (1980). *See also* Bankruptcy Code § 102(5) (" 'or' is not exclusive").

[259]　Bankruptcy Code § 303(i)(2). *See, e.g.*, In re John Richards Homes Bldg. Co., 291 B.R. 727 (Bankr. E.D. Mich. 2003) (compensatory damages, punitive damages, and attorney's fees totaling $6.4 million).

[260]　*E.g.*, In re Cannon Express Corp., 280 B.R. 450 (Bankr. D. Ark. 2002); In re Landmark Distribs., Inc., 189 B.R. 290, 309 (Bankr. D.N.J. 1995).

[261]　In re Cadillac by DeLorean & DeLorean Cadillac, Inc., 265 B.R. 574, 581-82 (Bankr. N.D. Ohio 2001).

[262]　In re John Richards Homes Bldg. Co., 291 B.R. 727 (Bankr. E.D. Mich. 2003) (petitioning creditors went so far as to hire a public relations firm to publicize the bankruptcy case).

[263]　*E.g.*, In re Cannon Express Corp., 280 B.R. 450 (Bankr. D. Ark. 2002); In re John Richards Homes Bldg. Co., 291 B.R. 727 (Bankr. E.D. Mich. 2003).

[264]　*E.g.*, In re John Richards Homes Bldg. Co., 439 F.3d 248 (6th Cir. 2006) ($2 million punitive damages); In re Salmon, 128 B.R. 313 (M.D. Fla. 1991) ($250,000 punitive damages).

During the involuntary gap, the debtor is likely to continue operating its business, buying and selling property, paying employees, suppliers, and creditors, and incurring additional debts. Creditors who have not joined the petition may wish to continue efforts to collect claims owed by the debtor outside of bankruptcy court. Moreover, the petitioning creditors may become concerned that the debtor's continued operations will result in little more than a continued depletion of assets that will ultimately be available to pay their claims. A variety of provisions of the Bankruptcy Code deal with these problems that the gap period creates.

[1]   Control of the Debtor During the Involuntary Gap

As with voluntary petitions, the filing of an involuntary petition results in the creation of a bankruptcy estate and the transfer of all of the debtor's property to that estate. According to Bankruptcy Code § 541(a), creation of this estate is triggered by the "commencement of a case,"[265] not the entry of an "order for relief." However, unless the court orders otherwise, the debtor continues to manage its business and financial affairs and may continue to use, acquire, or dispose of property as if no case had been filed.[266]

Consistent with this rule, there is no automatic appointment of a trustee, even in an involuntary Chapter 7 case. Instead, the debtor remains in possession and control of the estate's assets. Where there is a risk that the debtor will dissipate its assets while the involuntary petition is pending, the court may appoint an interim trustee.[267] However, an interim trustee will be appointed only if necessary to preserve the property of the estate or to prevent loss to the estate.[268]

[2]   Effect of the Automatic Stay

As in voluntary cases, the filing of an involuntary petition invokes the automatic stay of § 362(a).[269] The stay restrains virtually every type of activity in which creditors might engage to collect. Thus, even creditors who do not join in the involuntary petition are stayed from further efforts to collect their claims while the court determines whether to act on the involuntary petition and enter an order for relief.

[3]   Transfers of Estate Property During the Involuntary Gap

A debtor's transfer of its property during the involuntary gap depletes the debtor's estate and may harm creditors. As a consequence, Bankruptcy Code § 549 permits a bankruptcy trustee to avoid a wide range of post-petition transfers of a debtor's property. It permits avoidance of post-petition transfers that are not

---

[265] Bankruptcy Code § 541(a).

[266] Bankruptcy Code § 303(f).

[267] Bankruptcy Code § 303(g).

[268] Bankruptcy Code § 303(g).

[269] Bankruptcy Code § 362(a). *See infra* Chapter 8 — The Automatic Stay.

authorized by either the court or a specific provision of the Bankruptcy Code.[270]

Despite this avoiding power, certain post-petition transfers are protected.[271] Transfers made in the ordinary course of business are protected, as are those made with the express approval of the court.[272] For purposes of this discussion, the most important exception to the trustee's avoiding power is for transfers of the estate's property during the involuntary gap to a transferee who gave value to the debtor in exchange for the property it received, so long as the transfer was something more than a payment for a pre-petition debt.[273] The transferee is protected, even if it knew that the involuntary petition was pending.

For example, if during the involuntary gap period, Titanic Industries manufactures and sells 500 deck chairs for the usual market price of $200 each, receiving a total price of $100,000, the buyer is permitted to keep the deck chairs, even if the buyer knew at the time that he received the goods that the bankruptcy case was pending.[274] Without this protection, Titanic's customers would be reluctant to deal with Titanic for fear that an order for relief would be granted and that the bankruptcy trustee would subsequently be able to recover the deck chairs or their value. Titanic's suppliers would be equally nervous that even cash transactions they entered into with the involuntary debtor would be overturned, leaving the supplier with nothing more than an unsecured claim against a financially troubled debtor. The reluctance of customers and suppliers to deal with the debtor would likely aggravate whatever financial difficulties the debtor was already facing, and drive otherwise financially viable debtors into liquidation.

Transfers that are nothing more than a payment of or security for a pre-petition debt are not protected. If an involuntary petition was filed against Titanic Industries on June 10, and on June 20 Titanic received a truckload of raw materials from one of its suppliers and gave the supplier a check in payment for those the materials, the transfer is protected. But, if the raw materials were delivered on May 20, and Titanic did not pay for them until June 15, five days after the petition had been filed against it, the payment would be subject to avoidance unless authorized by a specific provision of the Bankruptcy Code or by the court. Not surprisingly, employees who are paid for work done during the gap period are allowed to keep their wages.

Section 549 also provides limited protection for certain real estate transactions that are completed during the gap period. Protection is provided only to a "good faith purchaser without knowledge of the commencement of the case" who pays a "present fair equivalent value,"[275] but only if the transfer was recorded before notice of the bankruptcy case was recorded. Thus, a cautious purchaser, concerned about the possibility of the transferor's bankruptcy, will not part with value until it confirms that its deed or mortgage was recorded in the appropriate county recorder's office before notice of the debtor's bankruptcy case was recorded.

---

[270] Bankruptcy Code § 549(a).

[271] *See generally infra* § 14.05 Post-Petition Transfers of Estate Property.

[272] Bankruptcy Code § 363.

[273] Bankruptcy Code § 549(a), (b).

[274] Bankruptcy Code § 549(b).

[275] Bankruptcy Code § 549(c).

A purchaser who pays less than the fair equivalent value of the property may still have some protection. Suppose, for example, that a gap-period buyer paid only $100,000 for property that was worth $250,000.[276] The buyer may not keep the property, because she did not pay a fair equivalent value for it. However, she will enjoy a lien on the property for the $100,000 she paid, and be treated as a secured creditor in the debtor's bankruptcy case.

Finally, § 549(c) provides no protection for those who purchase estate property at a post-petition foreclosure sale. Language protecting these buyers was removed from the Code in 1984,[277] and the definition of "purchaser" in § 101(43) is limited to a transferee in a "voluntary transfer"[278] to make it clear that these buyers are not protected.

[4] Priority for Involuntary Gap Creditors

The final protection given to gap creditors is found in § 507. It gives certain post-petition gap creditors special priority, not only over other general unsecured creditors, but also over most other priority unsecured claims. Section 507(a) generally establishes priorities for a wide variety of unsecured claims, including those for the administrative expenses of the bankruptcy case, support claims, wages, and many taxes.[279] Section 507(a)(3) accords unsecured claims held by involuntary-gap creditors the third highest priority, behind support claims and claims for the administrative expenses of the bankruptcy case itself.[280] The priority is limited to claims arising in the ordinary course of the debtor's business or financial affairs after the commencement of an involuntary case but before the appointment of a trustee or the entry of an order for relief, whichever occurs first.[281]

Nevertheless, as a practical matter, priority may be of little help to these creditors. In many cases, more senior priority claims for the trustee's expenses in administering the bankruptcy case are left unpaid.[282] Thus, once creditors learn of an involuntary petition against a debtor, they are unlikely to be willing to deal with the debtor on anything but a cash basis. The risk of nonpayment, even with a third-priority claim, is simply too high.

---

[276] Financially troubled debtors sometimes sell assets at a bargain basement price in order to obtain a quick infusion of cash.

[277] Pub. L. No. 98-353, § 464, 98 Stat. 333, 379 (1984).

[278] Bankruptcy Code § 101(43); 40235 Washington Street Corp. v. Lusardi, 329 F.3d 1076, 1081 (9th Cir. 2003).

[279] Bankruptcy Code § 507(a). *See infra* § 10.04[B] Priority Claims.

[280] Bankruptcy Code § 507(a)(3). The relative priority between support claims and those for the administrative expenses associated with the bankruptcy case itself is complicated. *See infra* § 10.05[A][1] Support Claims.

[281] Bankruptcy Code § 502(f).

[282] In a typical Chapter 7 case, there are no assets available to distribute to creditors. Such cases are colloquially referred to as "no asset" cases. *See* Michael J. Herbert & Dominic E. Pacitti, *Down and Out in Richmond, Virginia: The Distribution of Assets in Chapter 7 Bankruptcy Proceedings Closed During 1984-87*, 22 U. Rich L. Rev. 303 (1988). Note, however, that most involuntary cases involve businesses, and the chance for a distribution on priority claims is higher than in most consumer-debtor cases.

This helps to explain why there are so many restrictions on involuntary petitions. The mere filing of an involuntary petition can have a devastating effect on a debtor's ability to obtain credit, even from suppliers who have extended credit in the ordinary course in the past. Thus, the mere fact that a petition has been filed may drive a basically sound company into insolvency.

§ 6.04 CLOSING BANKRUPTCY CASES[283]

[A] Closing a Case

When a bankruptcy case is over, the case is "closed." Section 350 specifies that a case shall close "[a]fter the estate is fully administered and the court has discharged the trustee."[284] This usually happens after all of the estate's assets are either distributed or abandoned, and other matters relating to administration are complete.

Bankruptcy Rule 5009 governs closing cases under chapters 7, 12 and 13, which commonly involve consumers or sometimes, particularly in the case of Family Farmer and Fishermen cases under Chapter 12, small businesses. Rule 5009 provides that the case is regarded as fully administered and can be closed 30 days after the trustee's final account and report have been filed.[285] In Chapter 11 cases, Rule 3022 permits the case to be closed after the plan has been confirmed and "fully administered." But, as the Rules Advisory Committee Notes reflect, the case need not remain open simply because payments to be made under the plan, remain to be made.[286]

[B] Reopening a Case

If necessary, a case can be reopened, sometimes even decades after it has been closed.[287] Reasons for reopening a case are numerous, including: adding a creditor to the debtor's schedules, avoiding a lien, administering a previously undisclosed asset, determining the dischargeability of a debt, obtaining relief from the discharge injunction or the automatic stay, recovering improper distributions, interpreting terms of a plan or otherwise enforcing orders of the court.[288]

---

[283] Michael P. Saber, *Section 350(b): the Law of Reopening*, 5 Bankr. Dev. J. 63, 83 (1987).

[284] Bankruptcy Code § 350(a).

[285] Fed. R. Bankr. P. 5009.

[286] *See* Fed. R. Bankr. P. 3022, advisory committee's note.

[287] In re Dunning Bros. Co., 410 B.R. 877 (Bankr. E.D. Cal. 2009).

[288] In re OORC Leasing, LLC, 359 B.R. 227, 231 (Bankr. N.D. Ind. 2007).

Chapter 7

PROPERTY OF THE ESTATE

§ 7.01 CREATION OF THE DEBTOR'S ESTATE

Filing a bankruptcy petition results in the automatic creation of an "estate,"[1] in much the same way a person's death results in the creation a decedent's estate. Indeed, the bankruptcy estate is treated, in many respects, as if it were a new legal entity, separate and distinct from the debtor.

With a few exceptions, the bankruptcy estate acquires title to all of debtor's "legal or equitable interest in . . . property" at the moment she filed her petition.[2] As will be seen, the estate may acquire additional assets by succeeding to certain property acquired by the debtor after the case commenced,[3] by avoiding transfers made by the debtor before the petition was filed,[4] or more simply, by engaging in revenue generating activities after the petition is filed. In cases under Chapters 12 and 13, the estate also becomes the owner of revenue earned by the debtor while the case is pending.[5]

In voluntary Chapter 7 liquidation cases, an interim trustee is appointed to act as the representative of the estate, to take control of the estate's property, and to conduct any of the estate's other financial affairs. Between the time the petition is filed and the time the interim trustee is appointed, the debtor usually remains in possession of the estate's property, but the debtor holds it in trust for the estate. Bankruptcy Code § 549, which generally deals with post-petition transfers, protects those who deal with the debtor in good faith without knowledge that the property involved in any such deal belongs to the estate. Once a trustee is in place, she has the right to take possession of property of the estate and may bring an action to compel the debtor or others to "turn over" any property of the estate that is under their control.[6]

In reorganization cases, the debtor generally remains in possession of the estate's property. In Chapter 12 and 13 cases, the debtor remains in possession of most of the estate's property and remits a portion of her income to a standing trustee who is responsible for distributing the debtor's payments to creditors, as

---

[1] Bankruptcy Code § 541(a).

[2] Bankruptcy Code § 541(a).

[3] Bankruptcy Code § 541(a)(5).

[4] Bankruptcy Code § 541(a)(3).

[5] *See infra* § 7.06 Expanded Estate in Reorganization

[6] Bankruptcy Code § 542(a).

specified in the debtor's plan. If a trustee is appointed in a Chapter 11 case,[7] the trustee assumes control over the estate's property in the same way as a Chapter 7 trustee. But, in most Chapter 11 cases, no trustee is appointed, and the debtor retains control of the estate's property, as "debtor-in-possession."

§ 7.02   PROPERTY INCLUDED IN THE ESTATE[8]

Determining the scope of the estate is critical to the bankruptcy process. This determines what property is subject to both the court's jurisdiction and the trustee's control, and what property is protected by the automatic stay.[9]

Under the old Bankruptcy Act, the rules regarding property of the estate were complicated by the fact that exempt property never became part of the estate. The Code's approach is different: virtually everything the debtor owns goes into the estate. It is then divided between the debtor and creditors. Thus, exempt property begins as property of the estate, even though ownership is later turned back over to the debtor. Likewise, the debtor's encumbered property is property of estate, even if it will be abandoned into the hands of a secured creditor. This approach avoids preliminary squabbles over what is or is not part of the estate, leaving for later an orderly determination of who takes what from the pot.

The debtor's estate is comprised of the following property, regardless of where it is located or who possesses it, unless it is expressly excluded from the estate:[10]

- any interest in property held by the debtor when the case commenced;[11]

- community property interests of the debtor or the debtor's spouse, if those interests are under the management and control of the debtor, or if the property is liable under relevant state community property law for claims against the debtor;[12]

- property recovered by the trustee or a debtor-in-possession from third parties under various avoiding powers, such as the power to avoid preferences, to reverse setoffs, or to avoid security interests that were unperfected when the case commenced;[13]

- property interests preserved for the benefit of the estate under Bankruptcy Code §§ 510(c) or 551;[14]

- certain property acquired by the debtor within 180 days after commencement of the case, such as property obtained by inheritance, as a result of a

---

[7] *See infra* § 19.03[D] Appointment of Trustee or Examiner.

[8] Thomas E. Plank, *The Outer Boundaries of the Bankruptcy Estate*, 47 Emory L.J. 1193 (1998).

[9] Bankruptcy Code § 362(a)(2)-(4). *See generally infra* § 8.02 Scope of the Automatic Stay.

[10] Bankruptcy Code § 547(b). *See infra* § 7.04 Property Excluded from the Debtor's Estate.

[11] Bankruptcy Code § 541(a)(1).

[12] Bankruptcy Code § 541(a)(2). *See infra* § 7.02[B] Community Property.

[13] Bankruptcy Code § 541(a)(3). *See infra* § 7.02[C] Property Recovered Under Avoiding Powers.

[14] Bankruptcy Code § 541(a)(4). *See infra* § 7.02[D] Property Preserved for the Benefit of the Estate.

divorce decree, or as proceeds of a life insurance policy;[15]

- proceeds, products, offspring, rents and profits generated by property of the estate;[16] and

- property acquired by the estate itself after commencement.[17]

The remainder of this section reviews the details each of these basic categories.

[A] Debtor's Interests in Property at Commencement of the Case

[1] Debtor's Property Included in the Estate

With limited exceptions, a debtor's estate acquires ownership of "all legal or equitable interests of the debtor in property as of the commencement of the case."[18] Thus, anything the debtor owned when the case began belongs to the estate.[19] This ordinarily includes any type of property interest, regardless of whether it is in real estate, goods, receivables, intellectual property, or other intangible personal rights. It includes rights the debtor may have to sue someone.[20]

Normally, the nature of the debtor's interest has no effect on whether the estate aquires the interest.[21] Thus, if the debtor holds title to real estate in fee simple absolute, the estate acquires the property in fee simple absolute. If the debtor owns a mere life estate, the life estate becomes property of her bankruptcy estate. For example, if, as part of her estate plan, Agnes has conveyed title to her ancestral home to her daughter, and taken back a life estate, but files a bankruptcy petition when she is 99 years old, Agnes's life estate belongs to her bankruptcy estate. The same is true if the debtor's interest is a contingent remainder, a springing executory interest, an easement, or a mortgage — the debtor's estate acquires whatever rights the debtor owned. The property might not be worth much to the creditors, but this does not prevent it from entering the estate.

Inchoate expectancies, on the other hand, such as a beneficiary's rights under an unmatured life insurance policy, are not estate property.[22] In most cases, the owner

---

[15] Bankruptcy Code § 541(a)(5). *See infra* § 7.02[E] Post-Petition Property Acquired by the Estate.

[16] Bankruptcy Code § 541(a)(6). *See infra* § 7.02[F] Post-Petition Earnings.

[17] Bankruptcy Code § 541(a)(7). *See infra* § 7.02[G] Post-Petition Property Acquired by the Estate.

[18] Bankruptcy Code § 541(a)(1).

[19] *E.g.*, In re Paige, 443 B.R. 878 (D. Utah 2011) (internet domain name part of Chapter 11 debtor's estate).

[20] *See* In re Upshur, 317 B.R. 446 (Bankr. D. Ga. 2004) (bankruptcy case re-opened to permit trustee to pursue previously undisclosed employment discrimination claim held by debtor when case was commenced); Anderson v. Acme Mkts., 287 B.R. 624 (D. Pa. 2002) (debtor lacked standing to bring discrimination claim that had accrued before bankruptcy petition was filed because it was property of the estate under the control of the case trustee).

[21] *See generally* George R. Pitts, *Rights to Future Payment as Property of the Estate Under Section 541 of the Bankruptcy Code*, 64 Am. Bankr. L.J. 61, 73-80 (1990) (regarding contingent future interests).

[22] Wornick v. Gaffney, 544 F.3d 486 (2d Cir. 2008).

of the policy has an unfettered right to change the beneficiary,[23] and this prevents the current beneficiary from having any rights in the policy benefits, until the policy matures (until the insured dies).

A debtor's rights in jointly held property are included in her estate. Undivided interests held in joint tenancy or tenancy in common are part of a debtor's estate.[24] The extent of the estate's interest is identical to whatever interest the debtor held under state law. Thus, a bankrupt spouse's undivided joint interest in stock or other property held in joint tenancy with the debtor's spouse is property of the bankruptcy estate of the spouse who filed the bankruptcy case.[25] The interest of the other spouse (the "non-debtor spouse"), on the other hand, is not part of the estate and is protected.[26] Thus, if Merl and Agnes own real estate as joint tenants and Merl alone files a bankruptcy petition, only Merl's undivided interest belongs to the estate. Depending on state law regarding the effect of a transfer of one joint tenant's interest in property, this may result in a severance of the joint property. In the common situation in which a husband and wife file a joint petition, their respective joint tenancy interests become part of their respective estates and are "jointly administered" by the bankruptcy trustee.

Interests held in a tenancy by the entirety present problems in bankruptcy cases filed by only one spouse.[27] A tenancy by the entirety is an ancient form of ownership that rests upon the legal fiction that "husband and wife are but one person."[28] Many states have eliminated entireties property, but the form of ownership persists in about twenty states.[29] Entireties property generally cannot be transferred by one spouse alone, and the property cannot be taken to pay debts owed by only one spouse.[30] This means that entireties property is not a part of the estate of a bankruptcy case filed by only one spouse.[31] Whether this is true may turn on how a particular state defines entireties property. While at least one court has held that entireties property, at least in Indiana, comes into the estate,[32] most courts treat entireties property as beyond the scope of an individual spouse's bankruptcy

---

[23] *See* In re Greenberg, 271 F. 258, 259 (2d Cir. 1921).

[24] One of your co-authors holds a 1/64 interest in several oil wells. They produce income of $200-400 per year. If he were to file a bankruptcy petition, these undivided interests would be part of his bankruptcy estate. His sister's 1/64th interest and his aunt's 1/32 interest would be unaffected.

[25] In re Becker, 136 B.R. 113 (D.N.J. 1992) (stock certificates); In re Fey, 91 B.R. 524 (E.D. Mo. 1988) (real estate).

[26] *E.g.*, In re Nicholson, 90 B.R. 64 (Bankr. W.D.N.Y. 1988).

[27] Benjamin C. Ackerly, *Tenants by the Entirety Property and the Bankruptcy Reform* Act, 21 Wm. & Mary L. Rev. 701 (1980); William G. Craig, Jr., *An Analysis of Estates by the Entirety in Bankruptcy*, 48 Am Bankr. L.J. 255 (1974); Lawrence Kalevitch, *Some Thoughts on Entireties in Bankruptcy*, 60 Am. Bankr. L.J. 141 (1986).

[28] Tyler v. United States, 281 U.S. 497, 503 (1930). *See* In re Bellingroehr, 403 B.R. 818, 820 (Bankr. W.D. Mo. 2009).

[29] 7 Richard R. Powell & Michael Allan Wolf, Powell on Real Property § 52.03[3] (2006).

[30] Thompson on Real Property § 33.07(e) (David A. Thompson ed. 1994).

[31] *E.g.*, In re Paeplow, 972 F.2d 730 (7th Cir. 1992).

[32] Chippenham Hosp. Inc. v. Bondurant, 716 F.2d 1057, 1058 (4th Cir. 1983) (dicta). *See* H.R. Rep. No. 95-595, at 368 (1977), *reprinted in* 1978 U.S.C.C.A.N. 5963, 6324; S. Rep. No. 95-989, at 82 (1978), *reprinted in* 1978 U.S.C.C.A.N. 5787, 5868.

estate.[33] As discussed in the next section, it is not one hundred percent clear whether a state might be able to define its entireties estate in such a way that it would be excluded from a debtor's bankruptcy estate. While determining whether something is "estate property" is undoubtedly a question of federal law, the extent to which courts will disturb state definitions of property rights in this area remains unclear.

Bankruptcy Code § 363(h) provides a mechanism for a bankruptcy trustee to administer jointly owned property by selling the estate's interest, together with the interest of the non-debtor spouse, after giving the non-debtor what amounts to a right of first refusal to buy the property at the proposed price.[34] Following a sale of the property, the non-debtor spouse is entitled to her share of the proceeds.

[2] Relationship Between Bankruptcy Law and State Property Law

Because property law is a creature of state law, there both is an inherent connection and an inherent tension between state property law and bankruptcy law. State law determines the nature and extent of the debtor's rights,[35] but bankruptcy law determines whether those rights are "property" that become part of a bankrupt debtor's estate.[36]

This is true even though state law might not treat a debtor's interest as "property," in the strictest sense. This fundamental principal was established in *Chicago Board of Trade v. Johnson*,[37] decided under the Bankruptcy Act. The debtor held a seat on the Chicago Board of Trade. Under Illinois law, the membership was not regarded as "property," even though it was transferable, and even though it had substantial economic value.[38] Nevertheless, the membership was treated as "property" of the estate within the meaning of federal bankruptcy law, and consequently the debtor's estate acquired the interests the debtor held in connection with his membership. Otherwise enforceable limitations on the debtor's membership, which could not be transferred under applicable state law because of the debtor's unpaid obligations to other members, remained effective, making its characterization as property of limited benefit to the debtor's estate.[39]

---

[33] *E.g.*, In re Bellingroehr, 403 B.R. 818 (Bankr. W.D. Mo. 2009).

[34] Bankruptcy Code § 363(h). *E.g.*, In re Hunter, 970 F.2d 299 (7th Cir. 1992).

[35] Butner v. United States, 440 U.S. 48 (1979).

[36] Chicago Bd. of Trade v. Johnson, 264 U.S. 1 (1924). The Supreme Court recently made a similar point in a tax case, holding that even though Michigan's entireties law stated that one spouse had no property interest in property held by the entireties, a taxpayer had sufficient interest in entireties property for a tax lien to attach. United States v. Craft, 535 U.S. 274 (U.S. 2002).

[37] Chicago Bd. of Trade v. Johnson, 264 U.S. 1 (1924).

[38] The market value in 1924 when the case was decided was $10,500. This would be approximately $139,000 in 2012 dollars, adjusted for inflation based on changes in the consumer price index. *See* http://146.142.4.24/cgi-bin/cpicalc.pl (last visited Feb. 21, 2012).

[39] Chicago Bd. of Trade v. Johnson, 264 U.S. at 15.

This rule was solidified by *Butner v. United States.*[40] There, a mortgagee claimed the right to receive rent generated by the debtor's property after the petition was filed. The Supreme Court ruled that whether the creditor was entitled to receive the rents depended in the first instance on applicable state law. If state law creates an interest in the creditor's favor, those rights are to be respected in bankruptcy, unless "some federal interest requires a different treatment."[41] Thus, bankruptcy first identifies the nature and extent of the creditor's right, whatever it may be, under state law. Whatever interest the debtor held at the time of its petition becomes estate property under § 541(a)(1). Bankruptcy law might invalidate limitations on the rights established under state law, but only if some specific provision of the Bankruptcy Code requires a reallocation of those rights. To do otherwise, the *Butner* Court indicated, would increase uncertainty, encourage forum shopping, and create the possibility of a windfall, merely because the parties' rights were being resolved in a bankruptcy proceeding instead of in state court.[42] Although *Chicago Board of Trade* and *Butner* were decided under the now-repealed Bankruptcy Act, the basic principles of the cases remains intact under the Bankruptcy Code.

[B] Community Property

Some states have a community property system for marital property. Under community property laws, most property acquired by a married person is treated as "community property" and is both subject to the management and control of either spouse and available to satisfy the debts of either spouse. Thus, if Dave and Kathy are married to one another, wages earned by Dave are subject to Kathy's control and are available to satisfy Kathy's debts, even though Dave might not be personally responsible for her debts.

Section 541(a)(2) of the Bankruptcy Code includes any interest of the debtor and the debtor's spouse in community property when the debtor's case commenced, if either:

- the property is under the sole, equal, or joint management and control of the debtor, or

- the property is "liable" for an allowable claim against the debtor or the debtor and the debtor's spouse.

Property that is under the exclusive control of only the non-debtor spouse or that is liable under applicable state law only for debts of the non-debtor spouse does not become property of the debtor's estate, even if state law otherwise labels it as "community property."

Although the Bankruptcy Code has extensive rules to deal with property owned by married couples, it does nothing to consolidate the property rights of unmarried couples who have not structured their affairs in compliance with more traditional

---

[40] 440 U.S. 48 (1979).

[41] 440 U.S. at 55.

[42] 440 U.S. at 55.

forms of joint ownership, such as a tenancy in common or joint tenancy.[43]

[C] Property Recovered under Avoiding Powers

Section 541(a)(3) brings any property recovered by the trustee pursuant to the trustee's array of avoiding powers, into the debtor's estate.[44] Thus, the debtor's estate includes property recovered from a third party as a fraudulent conveyance[45] an avoidable preference,[46] or otherwise. Further, because a Chapter 11 debtor-in-possession enjoys all of the same rights, powers, and duties of a trustee,[47] § 541(a)(3) also operates to bring property recovered by a debtor-in-possession into the debtor's estate.

However, property that is subject to avoidance, but not yet avoided, is not yet property of the estate. Therefore, this recoverable but not yet recovered property is not "estate property" that is subject to the automatic stay or otherwise under the immediate control of the debtor or the trustee.

[D] Property Preserved for the Benefit of the Estate

Section 541(a)(4) facilitates the operation of several other provisions of the Bankruptcy Code by including in the estate any property right that is preserved for the benefit of the estate or ordered to be transferred to the estate.[48] The most common application of § 541(a)(4) occurs in connection with the bankruptcy trustee's avoidance of a senior lien. Preservation of the avoided lien for the benefit of the estate permits the trustee to enjoy the benefit of whatever priority the avoided senior lien may have had over other secured creditors, whose liens may not themselves be avoidable.

For example, the trustee may be able to avoid a creditor's preferential security interest because it was conveyed, within ninety days of the debtor's bankruptcy petition, to secure a previously unsecured debt.[49] If not avoided, the creditor's security interest might have been senior to a competing but junior security interest that is not avoidable. Preserving the avoided senior creditor's lien for the benefit of

---

[43] *See* Elizabeth Fella, Comment, *Playing Catch Up: Changing the Bankruptcy Code to Accommodate America's Growing Number of Non-Traditional Couples*, 37 Ariz. St. L.J. 681 (2005).

[44] The scope of § 541(a)(3) is somewhat deceptive. The Code's language refers to property recovered under §§ 329(b), 363(n), 543, 550, 553, and 723. Bankruptcy Code § 550 is a broad provision, permitting the trustee to avoid transfers made by the debtor under an expanded number of other provisions, including § 544(a) (the strong-arm clause), § 544(b) (transfers avoidable by unsecured creditors under state law), § 545 (statutory liens), § 547 (preferences), § 548 (fraudulent conveyances), § 549 (post-petition transfers), § 553 (setoffs), and § 724(a) (securing a fine or penalty). *See* Bankruptcy Code § 550. *See generally infra* Chapter 14 — Trustee's General Avoiding Powers; Limits on Avoiding Powers, Chapter 15 — Avoidable Preferences, and Chapter 16 — Fraudulent Transfers.

[45] *See infra* Chapter 16 — Fraudulent Transfers.

[46] *See infra* Chapter 15 — Avoidable Preferences.

[47] Bankruptcy Code § 1107. *See supra* § 4.02[B] Debtor in Possession.

[48] Bankruptcy Code § 541(a)(4).

[49] *See* Bankruptcy Code § 547(b)(4); *infra* Chapter 15 — Avoidable Preferences.

the estate, and transferring the preserved lien to the estate preserves value for the estate.

Assume, for example that North Atlantic Finance Co. has a preferential senior mortgage on Titanic Industries' land, securing a $5 million dollar debt, and that White Star Bank has an unavoidable second mortgage on the land securing a $4 million debt. If the land is only worth $7 million, avoidance of North Atlantic's mortgage results in White Star Bank's junior lien being promoted to senior status. This would leave the estate to enjoy only $3 million of value in the land as a result of avoiding North Atlantic's lien. However, § 541(a)(4) preserves North Atlantic's lien for the benefit of the estate. With this lien preserved, the estate recovers the first $5 million of the property's value and thus permits White Star Bank to recover only the $2 million it would have received from its collateral had North Atlantic's lien not been avoidable. In effect, § 541(a)(4), working in conjunction with § 551, transfers North Atlantic's senior lien to the trustee for the benefit of the debtor's estate, and prevents junior lienholders from jumping ahead in priority as a result of the trustee's avoidance action.

[E]   Certain Post-Petition Property Acquired Within 180 Days of the Petition[50]

Property acquired by an individual Chapter 7 debtor after her petition is filed does not generally become part of her bankruptcy estate. Instead, a liquidating debtor gives up the property she has when she files her petition, but is entitled to keep any property she receives afterwards. This is a key part of the Bankruptcy Code's "fresh start" policy.[51]

However, § 541(a)(5) brings some property interests into the estate, even though the debtor first acquires them after filing her petition. This "post-petition property" is brought into the estate in three distinct situations where the property would have been part of the estate if the debtor had already owned it when the case began, and if the debtor "acquires or becomes entitled to acquire [the property] within 180 days after" the date of her petition. These three situations are:

- the debtor acquired the property by "bequest, devise, or inheritance";[52]

- the debtor acquired the property received as a result of a spousal property settlement or divorce decree;[53] or

---

[50] Adam J. Hirsch, *Inheritance and Bankruptcy: The Meaning of the "Fresh Start,"* 45 Hastings L.J. 175 (1994); C.T. Foster, Annotation, *Construction and Application of Provision of Bankruptcy Act (§ 70, subd. (a)(8)) with Respect to Property Vesting in Bankrupt After Bankruptcy By Bequest, Devise, or Inheritance,* 11 A.L.R.2d 738 (1950).

[51] *See supra* § 1.01[B] Bankruptcy as a Debtors' Remedy: Fresh Start for Honest Debtors.

[52] Bankruptcy Code § 541(a)(5)(A). *But see* Holter v. Resop (In re Holter), 401 B.R. 372 (Bankr. W.D. Wisc. 2009) (amount received post-petition as the beneficiary of a "payable on death" account was not received by "bequest, devise, or inheritance" and was not property of the estate).

[53] Bankruptcy Code § 541(a)(5)(B).

- the debtor acquired the property as a "beneficiary of a life insurance policy or a death benefit plan."[54]

All three situations involve windfalls to the debtor that might otherwise permit the debtor to time the filing of her bankruptcy petition in an attempt to prevent creditors from reaching valuable assets that she expected to receive.

For example, suppose that Dora files a bankruptcy petition on July 1, 2013 and a week later, on July 8, inherits $1,000,000 from her rich aunt. Although the property was received post-petition, it becomes part of Dora's bankruptcy estate and is available to pay Dora's creditors in her bankruptcy case. If Dora is able to anticipate her aunt's death by more than six months, she may be able to inherit the million dollars after discharging her debts. However, few deaths can be planned with such precision.[55]

Similarly, if Dora had been the beneficiary of her aunt's $250,000 life insurance policy, the $250,000 Dora obtained the right to on July 8, when her aunt died, would likewise be part of Dora's bankruptcy estate.

In both cases, the date Dora actually receives the payment from her aunt's estate or the life insurance company does not matter. The date of her aunt's death is the critical date — this is the date Dora acquired the right to receive the property. Otherwise, it would be far too easy for debtors to avoid the effect of § 541(a)(5) by simply delaying receipt of the payments to which they are entitled.

Property the debtor receives as a result of a property settlement with her spouse is treated the same way.[56] If the debtor acquires her interest within 180 days of her petition, the property is included in her estate.

The usual reason given for these rules is that otherwise a debtor, foreseeing these events, might rush into bankruptcy to prevent the assets from becoming available to her creditors.[57] Section 541 prevents debtors from capitalizing on this moral hazard, to the detriment of their creditors.

[F] Post-Petition Earnings

After the debtor's petition is filed, both the debtor and the estate may continue to generate income. Depending on the source of these funds, they may or may not be included as property of the bankruptcy estate. The estate may generate income as a result of estate property being sold, invested, or otherwise producing a return. These funds are part of the estate. The simplest example is the interest earned on a bank account that the debtor owned when her petition was filed. The estate owns

---

[54] Bankruptcy Code § 541(a)(5)(C).

[55] Having said this, however, as morally repugnant it is, it is not difficult to imagine an unscrupulous debtor filing a bankruptcy petition and then refusing to implement his mother's living will until the 180 period days has elapsed. Legal advice about the potential financial benefits of prolonging the life of a loved one in this situation would be difficult to provide.

[56] Bankruptcy Code § 541(a)(5)(B).

[57] See In re Woodson, 839 F.2d 610 (9th Cir. 1988) (debtor filed petition a few days after the death of his wife, whose life was insured for $1,000,000) (one of your co-authors represented Mr. Woodson in this matter).

the account, so naturally, the estate has the right to any interest earned on the account. Likewise, if the estate owns real estate that had been owned by the debtor when her petition was filed, rent received from tenants in the building belongs to the estate. The estate owns the building, and it gets the rent.

In cases involving a individual — a living breathing human being — the debtor might generate income by earning wages or income from other services after her petition is filed. As explained in more detail below, inclusion of these post-petition earnings as property of the estate depends on whether the earnings are derived from the debtor's pre-petition or post-petition services.

[1] Proceeds, Products, Offspring, Rents and Profits from Property of the Estate Included

Section 541(a)(6) brings into the estate any "[p]roceeds, product, offspring, rents, or profits of or from property of the estate." However, it sets a boundary between income that is attributable to property of the estate and income that is attributable to an individual debtor's post-petition labor.[58] Including earnings from post-petition labor would make the debtor a virtual indentured servant and impede the Code's purpose of providing her with a "fresh start."

Money received when property of the estate is sold is "proceeds" from estate property and is naturally included in the debtor's estate. Otherwise, the estate could not benefit from the trustee's sale of its assets. Similarly, funds obtained by the debtor through any wrongful conversion of estate property also rightfully belongs to the estate.

If the debtor owns an office building, an apartment building, or a fleet of rental cars, any rent received from lessees of this property is "rents" that are owned by the estate. Similarly, if the estate includes livestock, offspring of the livestock are property of the estate, and milk produced by the estate's dairy cows, or eggs or manure produced by the estate's chickens are also estate property as "products . . . of property of the estate."

Any post-petition "proceeds" from a secured creditor's collateral, though unquestionably included among the estate's property, remain subject to a creditor's security interest, under U.C.C. § 9-315(2). However, under § 552(a), other collateral acquired by the estate after commencement that is covered by the terms of an after-acquired collateral clause in a creditor's security agreement (or "floating lien"), is not subject to a creditor's security interest, unless it is "proceeds, products, offspring, or profits" of the pre-petition collateral to which the security interest otherwise extends.[59] This distinction between proceeds and other post-petition property makes the meaning of "proceeds, products, offspring, or profits" particularly important.

---

[58] Bankruptcy Code § 541(a)(6).

[59] Bankruptcy Code § 546(b).

[2] Earnings from Individual Debtor's Post-Petition Services Excluded[60]

The Bankruptcy Code's "fresh start" policy warrants a special rule for a debtor's personal earnings attributable to services that the debtor performs after her petition is filed. Section 541(a)(6) expressly excludes from the estate "earnings from services performed by an individual debtor after the commencement of the case."[61]

In simple cases, this rule is easy to apply. If Ray files Chapter a 7 bankruptcy petition at the end of the day on Friday, June 28, 2015, the earnings he receives for work he does the following week are not part of his bankruptcy estate. Paychecks Ray receives for work he performed after his petition do not belong to the estate and are not available for distribution to creditors in his bankruptcy case.

But, a paycheck Ray receives on July 13, 2015, compensating him for services he rendered in the last two weeks of June, before he filed his petition, belongs to the estate. Although the compensation is received post-petition, he earned the right to receive it before the case was filed.

The key is to determine when he performed the services for which the payment was made. If the work was done before his petition, the paycheck belongs to the estate, even though a good portion of it may be "exempt" under § 522(b). If the work was done after his petition, Ray owns it free and clear, without regard to any limits on what amount may be protected by the applicable exemption statute.

Applying the rule is more difficult when a debtor receives payment for work that he performed partially before and partially after his bankruptcy petition. In these cases, the court must allocate the payment between the pre-petition and the post-petition work. The former is property of the estate; the latter belongs to the debtor.[62]

Jess v. Carey (In re Jess),[63] illustrates how this rule operates. The debtor was a lawyer who, before filing his bankruptcy petition, had done work for one of his clients pursuant to a "contingent fee" contract. He finished work on the case after filing his petition. He then sought to exclude the entire fee from his estate, claiming that it was due only as a result of personal services he provided to his client after the date of his petition. The court held that "the estate is entitled to recover the portion of post-petition payments attributable to [his] pre-petition services."[64] The fact that the debtor's eventual receipt of the fee was contingent upon services

---

[60] Louis M. Phillips & Tanya Martinez Shively, *Ruminations on Property of the Estate — Does Anyone Know Why a Debtor's Postpetition Earnings, Generated by Her Own Earning Capacity, Are Not Property of the Bankruptcy Estate?*, 58 La. L. Rev. 623 (1998); George R. Pitts, *Rights to Future Payment as Property of the Estate Under Section 541 of the Bankruptcy Code*, 64 Am. Bankr. L.J. 61 (1990); James L. Rigelhaupt, Jr., Annotation, *Exception from Bankruptcy Estate, under 11 U.S.C.A. Sec. 541(a)(6), of Earnings from Services Performed by an Individual Debtor after Commencement of Case*, 76 A.L.R. Fed. 853 (1986).

[61] Bankruptcy Code § 541(a)(6).

[62] *See* Rav v. Ryerson (In re Ryerson), 739 F.2d 1423 (9th Cir. 1984).

[63] 169 F.3d 1204 (1999).

[64] 169 F.3d at 1207 (1999).

provided after the petition did not mean that all of the fee was earned from services provided after the petition was filed.[65]

In other situations, the debtor's entire earnings may be property of the estate, even though the debtor performed some additional services after his petition was filed. In *Smith v. Hanrahan (In re Smith)*,[66] the trustee successfully recovered real estate commissions that the debtor earned from two real estate sales contracts that were entered into before the debtor's petition, but which closed afterwards. Although the debtor worked after his petition to ensure that the real estate deals closed, and was involved in negotiations that extended the time for the closing, none of these services altered the debtor's right to the commission, which had already been earned before his petition was filed.[67]

This result should make it clear that a debtor's rights to tax refunds[68] and accrued vacation pay[69] that are derived from services the debtor provided before her petition, are part of her bankruptcy estate.[70] These rights, in the words of the Supreme Court's decision in *Segal v. Rochelle*,[71] are "sufficiently rooted in the pre-bankruptcy past and so little entangled with the bankrupts' ability to make an unencumbered fresh start that it should be regarded as 'property' . . . [of the estate]."[72]

The problem of determining which of debtor's past earnings are included in his estate can be complicated if the earnings involve bonuses or similar compensation related to or calculated on the basis of the debtor's performance over an extended period of time.[73] Assume, for example, that Jerrod is an assistant sales manager for Global Manufacturing and that he receives a base salary of $54,000 per year, plus a year-end performance bonus tied to his personal full-year sales results, combined with a year-end bonus representing a share of the firm's overall profits that is entirely within the discretion of his employer to award. If on September 1, 2015, Jerrod files a Chapter 7 bankruptcy petition and on December 31, 2015 he is awarded both a $10,000 personal results bonus based on his individual sales and a

---

[65] *See also* Turner v. Avery, 947 F.2d 772 (5th Cir. 1991); In re Ballard, 238 B.R. 610 (Bankr. M.D. La. 1999).

[66] 402 B.R. 687 (B.A.P. 8th Cir. 2009).

[67] *See also* Parsons v. Union Planters Bank (In re Parsons), 280 F.3d 1185, 1187 (8th Cir. 2002) (real estate commissions part of the debtor's estate despite his post-petition efforts to ensure that contingencies in underlying real estate contract were performed).

[68] *E.g.*, Weinman v. Graves (In re Graves), 609 F.3d 1153 (10th Cir. 2010) (action to recover portion of tax refund that debtor had irrevocably applied to prepayment of their taxes for the next tax year); In re Rash, 22 B.R. 323 (Bankr. D. Kan. 1982). *See* Kokoszka v. Belford, 417 U.S. 642 (1974) (Bankruptcy Act decision).

[69] Matter of Nichols, 4 B.R. 711 (Bankr. D. Mich. 1980) (noting that the Supreme Court's Bankruptcy Act decision in *Lines v. Frederick*, 400 U.S. 18 (1970), which held that the estate did not include accrued, but unpaid, vacation pay of the bankrupt, was overruled by the enactment of § 541(a)(6)). H.R. Rep. No. 95-595, 95 Cong., 1st Sess. 368 (1988), *reprinted in* 1978 U.S.C.C.A.N. 5787, 6324.

[70] *See* In re Edwards, 400 B.R. 345 (Bankr. D. Conn. 2008) (debtor and non-debtor spouse's tax refund must be apportioned based on their respective tax witholdings).

[71] Segal v. Rochelle, 382 U.S. 375 (1966) (interpreting § 70a(5) of the former Bankruptcy Act).

[72] 382 U.S. at 380.

[73] *E.g.*, In re Palmer, 57 B.R. 332 (Bankr. W.D. Va. 1986).

$5,000 discretionary bonus based on the firm's profits, there might be a dispute about how much of these bonuses should be swept into his estate. Jerrod may contend that all of the bonuses are attributable to the post-petition period, because his right to earn the bonus did not accrue until after the petition was filed. He might conclude that one-third of the bonuses are attributable to his post-petition work during the last four months of the year. He might even argue that the percentage should be higher, if most of his results or most of the company's profits were earned during those last four months. The trustee might claim all of the $5,000 profit-share bonus, arguing that since Jerrod's sales took a real nose dive after he filed for bankruptcy, that his bonus was attributable to his pre-petition efforts.

Similar issues arise in connection with the compensation of corporate executives and other highly-compensated employees,[74] whose access to Chapter 7 was severely limited by the means testing provisions in Code's 2005 Amendments. They likewise arise in cases involving debtors who earn commissions earned from post-petition renewals of sales, like those of insurance policies, that the debtor initially generated before her petition was filed.[75]

However, for many debtors the issue will most likely arise in connection with her right to receive an income tax refund. The simplest way to allocate the estate's portion of a debtor's right to a tax refund is to prorate the amount of the refund between the pre-petition and post-petition portions of the year during which the income from which the tax was withheld, was earned.[76] However, this method may not work where the debtor's stream of income was disrupted or enhanced during the year. If the debtor filed her petition after six months of unemployment, and then began a new job from which income was withheld, any resulting refund should not be attributed to the pre-bankruptcy period during which the debtor earned no income and during which no withholdings were made.

A similar issue was presented in the wake of the $600 payment that many Americans received in 2008, as part of the 2008 Economic Stimulus Act. Debtors who filed their bankruptcy petitions before receipt of their $600, but after the February 13, 2008 effective date of the Stimulus Act,[77] were surprised when their bankruptcy trustees sought to recover the amount of their stimulus payment. Many courts held that because the stimulus payments were crafted as a tax credit against Americans' 2007 income taxes, that they were sufficiently rooted in the pre-bankruptcy past to be included in the debtors' estates, even though they were

---

[74] *See infra* § 17.03[B] Dismissal of Consumer Cases Due to Abuse. *Compare* Vogel v. Palmer (In re Palmer), 57 B.R. 332 (Bankr. W.D. Va. 1986) (post-petition bonus not property of the estate because employer had discretion not to award any bonus until after debtor's petition had been filed), *with* Towers v. Wu (In re Wu), 173 B.R. 411 (B.A.P. 9th Cir. 1994) (estate's right to post-petition insurance policy renewal commissions depended upon whether debtor's postpetition services were a prerequisite for right to renewal commissions, and if so, the extent to which commissions were attributable to postpetition as opposed to prepetition services).

[75] In re Wu, 173 B.R. 411 (B.A.P. 9th Cir. 1994).

[76] In re Meyers, 616 F.3d 626 (7th Cir. 2010).

[77] Economic Stimulus Act of 2008, Pub. L. No. 110-185 § 101 amending 26 U.S.C. § 6428 (Supp. 2010).

received post-petition.[78] These payments therefore ended up as a stimulus, not for the debtors, but for unsecured creditors and bankruptcy trustees of debtors whose financial circumstances drove them to bankruptcy court before their stimulus payments arrived. Debtors who were able to fend off bankruptcy until after they had received (and spent) their stimulus money, enjoyed the benefits of the government's generosity.[79]

[G]   Post-Petition Property Acquired by the Estate

In most respects, the Bankruptcy Code sharply distinguishes between the estate and the debtor as if they were distinct legal entities. A consequence of this is that property acquired post-petition by the estate, rather than by the debtor, belongs to the estate. Section 547(a)(7) provides that "[a]ny interest in property that *the estate acquires* after commencement of the case" is property of the estate.[80]

This provision is an extension of § 541(a)(6), discussed above. Section 547(a)(7) makes it clear that even if the property acquired by the estate is not "proceeds, product, offspring, rents, or profits" arising from property of the estate, if the property was acquired by the estate and not by the debtor, the property belongs to the estate, not to the debtor. For example, if Titanic Development Corp. designs computer software and continues to operate this business during its bankruptcy case, programs developed by the company might not qualify as "proceeds, product, offspring, rents, or profits," but they are unquestionably property acquired by the estate and thus part of the estate's property under § 547(a)(7).

Likewise, funds the debtor borrows while the case is pending, pursuant to § 364, or contracts made by the trustee or debtor in possession, are post-petition estate property under § 541(a)(7).

§ 7.03   EFFECT OF RESTRICTIONS ON TRANSFER OF DEBTOR'S PROPERTY[81]

The debtor's property interests are sometimes saddled with limitations and restrictions. If enforced, these limits would prevent the debtor's assets from becoming property of her bankruptcy estate. This would operate to the detriment of creditors and in possible violation of the Bankruptcy Code's "equal treatment" policy.[82] As will be seen, many of these types of restrictions are invalid in

---

[78] E.g., In re Alguire, 391 B.R. 252 (Bankr. W.D.N.Y. 2008); In re Smith, 393 B.R. 205 (Bankr. S.D. Ind. 2008).

[79] Presumably, the effects on the national economy were the same regardless of whether debtors, their bankruptcy trustees, or their creditors ultimately received these funds.

[80] Bankruptcy Code § 541(a)(7) (emphasis added).

[81] Marie Rolling-Tarbox, Note, *Powers of Appointment under the Bankruptcy Code: A Focus on General Testamentary Powers*, 72 Iowa L. Rev. 1041 (1987).

[82] *See* Whitaker v. Power Brake Supply (In re Olympia Holding Corp.) 188 B.R. 287 (M.D. Fla. 1994), aff'd 68 F.3d 1304 (11th Cir. 1995); S. Rep. No. 95-989, at 83 (1977), *reprinted in* 1978 U.S.C.C.A.N. 5787, 5869.

bankruptcy. Some, however, such as those that might appear in an ERISA-qualified pension plan, or another spendthrift trust, are effective to keep these assets out of the debtor's estate and insulated from creditors' claims.

The common law rule *nemo dat qui non habet* (he who hath not, cannot give),[83] generally applies in bankruptcy as it does in other settings. The debtor's estate cannot usually acquire greater rights than the debtor owned when his petition was filed. Thus, most limits inherent in a debtor's property rights remain intact in bankruptcy. If the debtor held only a life estate, the bankruptcy estate acquires a only life estate. Likewise, if the debtor held only a one-half undivided interest as a tenant in common, the estate acquires the same undivided interest and nothing more. However, the Bankruptcy Code contains various provisions that invalidate debtors' attempts to gerrymander their ownership or contractual rights to avoid the effects of bankruptcy.

[A] Ipso-Facto Clauses Ineffective

Sometimes a debtor's property interest purportedly terminates upon the filing of a bankruptcy petition or upon the occurrence of some other event related to the debtor's financial condition. Restrictions of this type, commonly referred to as "ipso-facto clauses," do not prevent the estate from acquiring whatever interest the debtor held. Section 541(c)(1)(B) provides:

> [A]n interest of the debtor in property becomes property of the estate under [§ 541(a)(1), (2), or (5)] notwithstanding any provision in an agree-ment, transfer instrument, or applicable nonbankruptcy law . . . (B) that is conditioned on the insolvency or financial condition of the debtor, on the commencement of a case under [the Bankruptcy Code], or on the appoint-ment of or taking possession by a [bankruptcy] trustee . . . or a custodian before such commencement, and that effects or gives an option to effect a forfeiture, modification, or termination of the debtor's interest in prop-erty.[84]

Thus, these ipso-facto provisions that might be found in the debtor's deeds or contracts, that automatically terminate a debtor's property interest if the debtor files a bankruptcy petition, are ineffective.[85] For example, in *In re Robert L. Helms Construction & Development Co., Inc.*, the debtor entered into an option contract that contained a provision purporting to terminate the debtor's option if it filed a bankruptcy petition. Section 541(c) prevented the clause from operating as intended to prevent the debtor's bankruptcy estate from exercising the option.[86] Likewise, in *In re Mitchell* a security agreement contained language purporting to terminate the debtor's residual ownership rights in a creditor's collateral upon the filing of a bankruptcy petition. This too, was ineffective. The collateral remained property of

---

[83] Black's Law Dictionary 1735 (8th ed. 2004).

[84] Bankruptcy Code § 541(c)(1)(B).

[85] Bankruptcy Code § 541(c)(1)(B).

[86] In re Robert L. Helms Constr. & Dev. Co., 139 F.3d 702 (9th Cir. 1998).

the estate and the automatic stay of § 362(a) prevented the creditor from repossessing the collateral.[87]

Permitting these types of provisions to operate would allow the debtor to prefer particular creditors and would impair the effectiveness of bankruptcy as a means to resolve creditors' claims to the debtor's assets collectively. It would also impair debtors' ability to obtain a fresh start by reorganizing with their property rights intact. For example, without § 541(c), the estate would not succeed to the debtor's valuable option in *Robert L. Helms Construction*, described above. Likewise, if filing a bankruptcy petition deprived *Mitchell* of title to his property, the automatic stay would lose its bite. It would, in effect, slam the barn door closed after the horses had escaped. Section 541(c) prevents this from happening.

[B]   Transfer Restrictions Ineffective

Creditors sometimes attempt to restrict a borrower's ability to transfer her property to another person. Such restraints are rarely effective under state law.[88] But, when they are, they prevent a debtor's bankruptcy estate from succeeding to the debtor's property.[89] Giving effect to them might impair a financially troubled debtor's chances of reorganizing, by preventing the debtor's estate from acquiring the debtor's assets. Accordingly, Bankruptcy Code § 541(c)(1)(A) makes "any provision in an agreement, transfer instrument, or applicable nonbankruptcy law . . . that restricts or conditions transfer of such interest by the debtor . . ." ineffective to prevent *the estate* from acquiring the debtor's property.[90] Thus, restraints on alienation that might be effective outside of bankruptcy do not prevent the debtor's bankruptcy estate from succeeding to the debtor's property.[91]

For example, suppose that Doug owns property subject to a security interest held by Consumer Finance Co., and that the security agreement prohibits Doug from selling or otherwise transferring title to the collateral without the prior written permission of the finance company. Such restraints are usually not enforceable under state law. But, even if they were, Bankruptcy Code § 541(c)(1)(A) makes them unenforceable in bankruptcy. The collateral is part of Doug's bankruptcy estate, despite the restriction in the security agreement and regardless of whether it is otherwise enforceable under state law.

This does not mean Consumer Finance Co. will lose its lien. In general, properly created liens survive bankruptcy. However, by ensuring that the encumbered property remains in the debtor's estate, the Bankruptcy Code preserves the trustee's ability to administer the property and to preserve any equity for the benefit of the debtor's other creditors. It also ensures that the lien holder is

---

[87] *E.g.*, In re Mitchell, 85 B.R. 564 (Bankr. D. Nev. 1988).

[88] *See, e.g.*, U.C.C. § 9-406(d) (2010).

[89] Whitaker v. Power Brake Supply (In re Olympia Holding Corp.), 188 B.R. 287 (M.D. Fla. 1994), *aff'd* 68 F.3d 1304 (11th Cir. 1995).

[90] Bankruptcy Code § 541(c)(1)(A).

[91] In re Chambers, 451 B.R. 621 (Bankr. N.D. Ga. 2011) (funds contributed to debtor's state legislative campaign were part of his bankruptcy estate despite statutory restrictions on use of funds for campaign purposes).

restrained from attempting to enforce its security interest while the bankruptcy case is pending, without first obtaining relief from the automatic stay, under § 362(d).

Franchise agreements frequently contain language prohibiting the franchisee from transferring the franchise to another person without the franchisor's consent. If enforced, this type of a restriction prevents a debtor's fast food restaurant, auto dealership, or other franchise from becoming property of the debtor's bankruptcy estate and impairs the franchisee's ability to reorganize. Section 541(c)(1)(A) makes these types of transfer restrictions ineffective and ensures that the debtor's estate owns and can operate the debtor's franchise.

Section 541(c)(1)(A) addresses only a very narrow issue: whether the transfer restriction prevents the *debtor's estate* from acquiring the property. In many cases, it may also be important to determine whether the restriction prevents the estate from transferring the property to a third person. This is a separate issue, dealt with by other provisions of the Bankruptcy Code.[92] But § 541(c)(1)(A) makes it clear that these restrictions generally do not, in the first instance, prevent the estate from acquiring whatever rights the debtor owned when it filed its petition.

[C]   Restrictions on Transferability of Governmental Licenses Ineffective

Restrictions on the transferability of governmental licenses, such as liquor licenses, drivers licenses, broadcast licenses, and professional licenses have sometimes led to the suggestion that the license was not estate property, either because, under state law, the license was not regarded as "property," or because the government's interest in regulating the activity for which the license was required effectively restrained the estate's ability to succeed to the debtor's rights.[93] True to the text of § 541(c)(1)(A), courts now generally regard liquor licenses[94] and FCC broadcast licenses[95] as property of the bankruptcy estate, regardless of any restriction imposed on the transferability of the license by the regulating authority.

For example, in *In re Barnes*, the court ruled that an Indiana liquor license was property of the estate even though it was not regarded as "property" under state law, and even though it was both nontransferable without the state's consent and was revocable by the state due to the licensee's misconduct.[96] In *In re Burgess*,

---

[92] *See infra* § 10.06 Assignment of Executory Contracts and Unexpired Leases. *See also infra* § 9.03[E] Continuation of Liens and Other Interests; Sales Free and Clear.

[93] *E.g.*, In re D.H. Overmyer Telecasting Co., 35 B.R. 400 (Bankr. N.D. Ohio 1983), *but see* Ramsay v. Dowden (In re Cent. Ark. Broad. Co.), 68 F.3d 213, 215 (8th Cir. 1995) (expressing disagreement).

[94] *E.g.*, In re Barnes, 276 F.3d 927, 928-29 (7th Cir. 2002) (Posner, J.); In re Nejberger, 934 F.2d 1300 (3d Cir. 1991).

[95] *E.g.*, Ramsay v. Dowden (In re Cent. Ark. Broad. Co.), 68 F.3d 213, 214-15 (8th Cir. 1995); In re LAN Tamers, Inc., 329 F.3d 204 (1st Cir. 2003); In re Schmitz, 270 F.3d 1254, 1257 (9th Cir. 2001). *See* FCC v. NextWave Personal Communications, Inc., 537 U.S. 293 (2003).

[96] *E.g.*, In re Barnes, 276 F.3d 927, 928-29 (7th Cir. 2002) (Posner, J.). *See also* Ramsay v. Dowden (In re Cent. Ark. Broad. Co.), 68 F.3d 213 (8th Cir. 1995) (FCC broadcast license).

even a license to operate a Nevada brothel was treated as estate property.[97]

Significantly, the Supreme Court's decision in *FCC v. NextWave Personal Communications, Inc.* assumed that an FCC spectrum license was an asset of the bankrupt debtor's estate while holding that § 525, which generally prohibits the government from discriminating against bankrupt debtors,[98] prevented the FCC from terminating the debtor's license solely because the debtor had filed a bankruptcy petition.[99]

As with other restrictions on transfers of a debtor's property that do not prevent the property from becoming property of the debtor's estate, license restrictions may nevertheless prevent the debtor or the estate from transferring the license to a third party. Consider, for example, the absurdity of a rule that would permit an airline pilot to transfer her pilot's license to someone with no flight experience, or that would permit an attorney to transfer her license to practice law to someone who had not graduated from law school. The effectiveness of transfer restrictions to prevent the estate from transferring property to a third person requires a complex analysis that is considered elsewhere in connection with rules governing the debtor's "use, sale, and lease" of estate property[100] and the debtor's ability to assign executory contracts that are part of the debtor's estate.[101]

§ 7.04 PROPERTY EXCLUDED FROM THE DEBTOR'S ESTATE

Although the Bankruptcy Code's general approach is to include everything in the estate, and then to remove certain property from the estate when it is distributed, abandoned, or exempted, there are a few exceptions. These exceptions are narrowly drawn and exclude only very limited types of property. Most of these exclusions deal with interests arising from trusts or similar divisions of property into legal and equitable interests. Others deal with various types of employment benefits, including pensions, as well as with certain educational savings plans that are promoted by federal law.

[A] Property Held by Debtor for the Benefit of a Third Person

The first category of property that does not become part of a debtor's estate deals with powers of the debtor that may be exercised by the debtor solely for the benefit of someone else.[102] The most obvious example of this is a power of

---

[97] 234 B.R. 793 (Bankr. D. Nev. 1999). One of your authors once represented a debtor who owned un-rated video tapes, copyrights to such movies, and the phone number to a phone-sex service. Persuading the trustee to sell these items proved difficult, even though there was a buyer waiting in the wings to take over the debtor's business.

[98] *See infra* § 13.06[D][1] Governmental Discrimination.

[99] 537 U.S. 293 (2003).

[100] *See infra* Chapter 9 — Operation the Debtor's Business and Financial Affairs.

[101] *See infra* Chapter 11 — Executory Contracts and Unexpired Leases.

[102] Bankruptcy Code § 541(b)(1).

appointment under a trust that can only be exercised for the benefit of someone other than the debtor. For example, a trust might be created that empowers Terrel to assign the principal to one of his two nephews, Abdur or Basil, but not to himself. If Terrel goes into bankruptcy, his power to designate Abdur or Basil as recipients of the assets of the trust does not become part of Terrel's bankruptcy estate, and cannot be exercised by the trustee. The reason for this rule is to preserve the ability of the settlor of the trust — the person who created it — to determine both who would benefit and who would decide who would benefit from the trust. Since Terrel's creditors cannot directly gain anything from Terrel's exercise of the power, there is no sound reason to subvert the settlor's intention by handing the power of appointment over to the trustee of Terrel's bankruptcy estate.

On the other hand, if the debtor is among those for whose benefit the power might be exercised, the power of appointment does become part of the estate, with the trustee empowered to exercise the debtor's power for the benefit of the debtor's estate. Thus, if Terrel has the power to designate himself as the beneficiary of a life insurance policy and withdraw the cash value of the policy, the power is property of his estate, and the trustee will exercise Terrel's authority to designate Terrel, and thus the estate, as the beneficiary.

[B] Expired Leases of Non-Residential Real Estate

The second exclusion from the debtor's estate is of broader significance. Section 541(b)(2) specifies that the estate does not acquire any interest of the debtor as lessee of nonresidential real property once the stated term of the lease expires.[103] If the lease expires before bankruptcy, the leasehold interest is never part of the estate; if it expires during the bankruptcy case, the leasehold interest ceases to be part of the estate at that time.[104] Thus, holdover tenants cannot claim any right to the leasehold premises.

For example, suppose that Dottie Lane, Inc. is the lessee of a warehouse, but that the lease expires on July 1, 2015, with no right of renewal. If the company files a bankruptcy petition on August 1, 2015, her previously expired lease would not be property of the estate. If it files its petition on June 1, 2015, with only one month remaining on the lease, the leasehold interest initially becomes part of the estate, but ceases to be a part of the estate when the lease expires on July 1. This result is consistent with the general rule of § 541(a)(1) that the estate acquires whatever the debtor owned when its petition was filed. If only one month remains on the lease when the petition is filed, the estate succeeds only to what the debtor had at that time — one month.

The negative implication of § 541(b)(2) is that other types of leases might become property of the estate, despite having expired before the petition was filed. Thus, the language of § 541(b)(2) could easily be interpreted to imply that an expired lease of residential real estate or of an automobile or other personal property becomes property of the estate, notwithstanding its expiration before the lessee's bankruptcy petition. "Nonresidential lease" is not defined.

---

[103] Bankruptcy Code § 541(b)(2).

[104] Erickson v. Polk, 921 F.2d 200 (8th Cir. 1990).

A holdover tenant's right to possession under a residential property lease is part of the debtor's estate.[105] For example, in *In re Butler*, the debtor defaulted on the rent obligations on her month-to-month tenancy.[106] Her landlord obtained a judgment for unlawful detainer, and on the same day her Chapter 7 petition was filed, served the debtor with a notice to vacate the premises. The court ruled that the debtor's possessory interest in the premises was part of her estate. Accordingly, the automatic stay of § 362(a)(1)-(3), which prevents creditors from taking action against property of the estate, restrained the landlord from proceeding with the debtor's eviction, at least while the case was pending. At least conceptually, the tenant's month to month tenancy may not arise from the lease, but the tenant still has an interest that is part of the estate and subject to the automatic stay.

In reaching this conclusion, the court explained that "[t]he doctrine of expressio unius est exclusio alterius" was applicable and that Congress's creation of § 541(b)(2)'s express exception to § 541(a)(1) for "an expired lease of nonresidential property suggest[ed] that Congress intended possessory interests in residential property to be included in property of the estate."[107] The court went further and pointed out that Congress had considered and rejected proposed amendments to the Bankruptcy Code to treat expired leases of residential real estate in the same manner as expired non-residential leases under § 541(b)(2).[108]

The opinion in *In re Butler* emphasizes an important point: the landlord's right to evict the debtor is still governed by the automatic stay. Efforts to remove a holdover tenant from the premises by eviction will violate the automatic stay, absent express approval of the bankruptcy court.[109] And, even though the Bankruptcy Code has been amended to provide an express exception to the stay to permit landlords to continue with evictions of residential tenants pursuant to a pre-petition judgment ordering their eviction,[110] prudent landlords seek the bankruptcy court's permission before permitting an eviction to continue after the case has commenced.

Further, § 541(b)(2) applies only to leases that expire as scheduled according to the terms of the lease. It does not apply to leases that are "terminated" by the landlord due to the tenant's breach.[111] If the landlord terminates the lease due to the tenant's default, § 541(b)(2) does not apply and the lease remains part of the tenant's bankruptcy estate when the tenant files a petition. The estate's authority to assume, reject, or assign the lease are governed by Bankruptcy Code § 365,

---

[105] *See, e.g.*, Convenient Food Mart No. 144, Inc. v. Convenient Indus. of Am., Inc. (In re Convenient Food Mart No. 144, Inc.), 968 F.2d 592, 594 (6th Cir. 1992)

[106] In re Butler, 271 B.R. 867 (Bankr. C.D. Cal. 2002).

[107] In re Butler, 271 B.R. 867, 872 (Bankr. C.D. Cal. 2002).

[108] In re Butler, 271 B.R. 867, 872 (Bankr. C.D. Cal. 2002).

[109] *E.g.*, In re Sims, 213 B.R. 641 (Bankr. W.D. Pa. 1997).

[110] Bankruptcy Code § 362(b)(22). *See infra* § 8.03[A] Private Right Exceptions to the Stay.

[111] *See, e.g.*, In re Turner, 326 B.R. 563, 575 (Bankr. W.D. Pa. 2005); In re Morgan, 181 B.R. 579 (Bankr. N.D. Ala. 1994).

dealing with "executory contracts and unexpired leases."[112]

[C] Debtor's Right to Participate in Educational Program; Accreditation

The third exclusion is of limited significance. The right of a debtor to participate in certain specified educational programs is not estate property. Nor is the the the debtor's accreditation or licensing as an educational institution.[113] While § 541(b)(3) might provoke jokes about prominent colleges, such as Harvard, Yale, or Stanford being unable to use bankruptcy to sell their accreditation, it is far more important in the context of private elementary and secondary schools, where questions might be raised about the estate's ability to continue to operate the school. Not surprisingly, though, § 541(b)(3) has generated virtually no reported litigation.[114]

[D] Specific Oil Industry Rights

The fourth exclusion is also narrow and reflects the impact that lobbying groups for specific industries sometimes have on bankruptcy policy. Property of the estate does not include certain interests in liquid or gaseous hydrocarbons that had been transferred or are subject to an agreement to transfer.[115] This exemption was designed to deal with specific problems created for the energy industry by the Bankruptcy Code's rules regarding the scope of a debtor's estate.

[E] Proceeds of Money Orders

The 1994 Amendments added a fifth exclusion from the estate for a debtor's interest in certain proceeds of a sale by the debtor of a money order.[116] These proceeds are excluded if the debtor sold the money order within fourteen days prior to the filing of the petition under an agreement that prohibited the commingling of the proceeds with other property of the debtor.[117]

[F] Spendthrift Trusts[118]

Section 541(c)(2) prevents many spendthrift trusts from becoming part of the debtor's estate. Its greatest significance is with respect to assets in debtors' pension funds, but it also applies to family trusts and other spendthrift trusts that

---

[112] Bankruptcy Code § 365(b). *See infra* § 11.05[C] Restrictions on Assumption.

[113] Bankruptcy Code § 541(b)(3).

[114] *See* In re Betty Owen Sch., Inc., 195 B.R. 23 (Bankr. S.D.N.Y. 1996).

[115] Bankruptcy Code § 541(b)(4).

[116] Pub. L. No. 103-394, § 223, 108 Stat. 4106, 4128 (1994).

[117] Bankruptcy Code § 541(b)(9)(2006) (previously codified at § 541(b)(5)). Note that it does not matter whether the proceeds were segregated from other funds or commingled. The key question is whether the agreement prohibited commingling.

[118] Robert B. Chapman, *A Matter of Trust, or Why "ERISA-Qualified" Is "Nonsense Upon Stilts": The Tax and Bankruptcy Treatment of Section 457 Deferred Compensation Plans as Exemplar*, 40 Willamette L. Rev. 1, 8 n.21 (2004); Patricia E. Dilley, *Hidden in Plain View: The Pension Shield Against Creditors*, 74 Ind. L.J. 355, 366 n.34 (1999); Anthony Michael Sabino, *A Final Battle at the Last Line of*

are valid under state law.[119] The statutory language provides: "A restriction on the transfer of a beneficial interest of the debtor in a trust that is enforceable under applicable nonbankruptcy law is enforceable in a case under [the Bankruptcy Code]."[120] This language effectively makes spendthrift trusts just as enforceable in bankruptcy as they are outside of bankruptcy.

[1] Meaning of "Spendthrift Trust"

The exclusion from the debtor's estate for certain spendthrift trusts is particularly important to consumer debtors. It deals with non-assignable beneficial interests held in trust. The non-assignability provision of the trust, if enforceable, prevents its beneficiary from spending the principal assets of the trust, and more importantly in this context, prevents the beneficiary's creditors from seizing those assets to satisfy the beneficiary's debts. It also prevents creditors or the beneficiary's bankruptcy trustee from reaching the beneficiary's remainder interest in the trust.[121]

There are at least three roles, usually involving three persons, in every "trust." The "settlor" is the person who creates and funds the trust by transferring money or other property to the trust; the "trustee," who administers the trust; and the "beneficiary," who is entitled to receive distributions from the trust, and may enjoy a remainder interest in the trust.[122] There may be multiple beneficiaries. The trustee holds legal title to the property placed in trust, with the beneficiary enjoying the equitable or "beneficial" interest in the property.[123] If a trust permits the beneficiary to assign the beneficial interest in the trust to a third party, the beneficiary's interest in the trust is property of the estate and will be distributed to its creditors.[124] However, spendthrift trusts prohibit the beneficiary from assigning the beneficial interest either as a gift, or to her creditors. In many circumstances, these restrictions are enforceable under non-bankruptcy law.

Where spendthrift restrictions on transfer of the beneficial interest are enforceable, creditors of the beneficiary cannot seize the corpus of the trust. No matter how much the beneficiary of such a trust owes, no matter how delinquent he is on his debts, and no matter how flush with cash the trust has become, creditors may latch onto the property only when and if the funds in the trust are received by the beneficiary. Creditors may not reach the property while it is still held in trust.[125]

Defense — The Struggle to Keep ERISA-Qualified Pension Plans Outside the Reach of Creditors in Bankruptcy Cases, 12 Am. Bankr. Inst. L. Rev. 501 (2004).

[119] *E.g.*, Wachovia Bank, N.A. v. Levin, 419 B.R. 297 (E.D.N.C. 2009).

[120] Bankruptcy Code § 541(c)(2).

[121] Levin v. Wachovia Bank, 436 Fed. Appx. 175 (4th Cir. 2011).

[122] Restatement (Third) of Trusts § 3 (2003).

[123] The trust corpus or "res" is the property that is administered. Restatement (Third) of Trusts § 40 (2003). It usually consists of various investment property, such as stocks, bonds, or other securities, but may be real estate, tangible personal property or anything else.

[124] Restatement (Third) of Trusts § 56 (2003).

[125] Restatement (Third) of Trusts § 58 (2003). *See generally* George G. Bogert & George T. Bogert, The Law of Trusts and Trustees §§ 221, 223, 225-227 (Rev. 2d ed. 1992).

Trusts subject to these type of transfer restrictions are usually called "spend-thrift trusts." This is because restrictions on transfer of beneficial interests in trusts have sometimes been used to ensure a continued income for the feckless offspring of the very rich. A wealthy parent or grandparent, dismayed by the uncanny ability of their potential heirs to squander money on snipe ranches and pearl mines, may set up a trust that pays out $5,000 per month for bare maintenance expenses and prohibits the transfer of the beneficiary's interest to anybody else.[126]

[2] Enforceability of Spendthrift Trusts in Bankruptcy

There is nothing in the Constitution that compels Congress to recognize spendthrift trusts in bankruptcy, and it is arguable that such recognition is unfair to those debtors whose ancestors had neither the wealth nor the wit to provide for their prodigal offspring.[127] However, § 541(c)(2) continues a long tradition of giving effect to this type of restriction on the transfer of an asset. Thus, if Bertie Wooster's rich aunt has had the good sense to restrict his ability to transfer his beneficial interest in the Wooster family trust, Bertie's future prosperity is secure from his creditors outside of bankruptcy, and from the bankruptcy trustee, should he file a bankruptcy case.[128]

Because of the effect on creditors, courts usually examine the terms of these trusts to determine whether they are a true spendthrift trust or merely a sham. Self-settled trusts are particularly vulnerable. For example, in *In re Nichols*, assets that the debtor placed in a spendthrift trust established for her own benefit, and over which she retained complete control, were not excluded from the estate. The trust was invalid under state law and its assets could be taken by the trustee to administer for the benefit of the debtor's creditors.[129] Similarly, in *Shurley v. Texas Commerce Bank-Austin, N.A. (In re Shurley)*, the Fifth Circuit ruled that a spendthrift trust that was partially self-settled, and thus invalid to the extent of the settlor's contribution to the trust and was part of the settlor's bankruptcy estate to the same extent it would have been invalid under governing state law.[130] If the trust's restrictions are unenforceable under state law, they will be equally unenforceable in bankruptcy. However, a growing number of state legislatures have protected these trusts, perhaps as method to permit doctors to protect their assets, and thus to attract them to practice medicine their states.[131] The validity in bankruptcy of these self-settled "spendthrift" trusts has yet to be determined. And,

---

[126] Restatement (Third) of Trusts § 58 cmt. a (2003).

[127] Note, however, that recognition of spendthrift trusts is in line with one theory of bankruptcy, that bankruptcy law should be transparent to state property and creditor's rights law, neither broadening nor narrowing the substantive rights of creditors but only enforcing them more efficiently.

[128] *E.g.*, Ehrenberg v. S. Cal. Permanente Med. Group (In re Moses), 167 F.3d 470, 473 (9th Cir. 1999). *See generally* Pelham G. Wodehouse, The World of Jeeves (1967).

[129] In re Nichols, 434 B.R. 906 (Bankr. M.D. Fla. 2010). *See also* In re Herzig, 167 B.R. 707 (Bankr. D. Mass. 1994); In re Gallagher, 101 B.R. 594, 601 (Bankr. W.D. Mo. 1989). *See generally* David B. Young, *The Pro Tanto Invalidity of Protective Trusts: Partial Self-Settlement and Beneficiary Control*, 78 Marq. L. Rev. 807 (1995).

[130] 115 F.3d 333 (5th Cir. 1997); In re Phillips, 411 B.R. 467 (Bankr. S.D. Ga. 2009).

[131] *See* David G. Shaftel, *Comparison of the Twelve Domestic Asset Protection Statutes*, 34 Am. Coll. Tr. & Est. C. J. 293 (2009).

as discussed in the next section, even if the spendthrift nature of these trusts is respected for estate purposes, the transfer of assets into the trust may be subject to attack as a fraudulent conveyance.[132]

[3] Offshore Asset Protection Trusts[133]

Wily debtors, seeking to retain their assets and avoid financial responsibility for their debts (as well as tax on their income), have recently added a new quiver to their bows in the form of offshore "asset protection" trusts. These trusts, which operate under the laws of foreign countries, are intended to do little other than frustrate the efforts of American courts to recover assets placed in the trust by an uncooperative debtor.

Debtors wishing to use these asset protection trusts to shield their wealth from the claims of creditors must transfer their assets to a trust in a foreign jurisdiction that does not recognize or comply with judgments or other legal processes originating in the United States.[134] Courts where such trusts are established will not enforce an order from a state or federal court in the United States that compels turnover of the trust assets to a creditor who was defrauded under United States law or to a bankruptcy trustee representing the beneficiary's creditors.[135] The asset protection trust documents specify that upon the occurrence of an "event of duress," such as the issuance of a court order that would impair the trustee's ability to control the direction of the trust's assets, the debtor will be terminated as the trustee and control of the trust's assets is transferred to a foreign trustee who is beyond the jurisdiction of the United States.

American courts have reacted in predictable ways to these dishonest schemes. The debtor in *United States v. Brennan* was convicted of the federal crime of bankruptcy fraud for misrepresenting the extent of his assets and repatriating funds held in an offshore asset protection trust after his bankruptcy case was closed.[136] Other debtors who have used these devices have been held in contempt[137] and denied any discharge from their debts pursuant to Bankruptcy Code § 727.[138] Whether these debtors eventually recover their assets, after paying the price for their misconduct, is uncertain.

A number of states have sought to join the asset protection party by validating so-called "self settled" trusts under state law, and treating them as spendthrift

---

[132] Bankruptcy Code §§ 544, 547.

[133] Richard C. Ausness, *The Offshore Asset Protection Trust: A Prudent Financial Planning Device or the Last Refuge of a Scoundrel?*, 45 Duq. L. Rev. 147, 193 (2007); Stewart E. Sterk, *Asset Protection Trusts: Trust Law's Race to the Bottom?*, 85 Cornell L. Rev. 1035 (2000).

[134] One may wonder how these debtors expect to recover their assets if they are converted by the unscrupulous trustees in violation of their fiduciary duties.

[135] FTC v. Affordable Media, LLC, 179 F.3d 1228, 1240 (9th Cir. 1999). *See* James T. Lorenzetti, *The Offshore Trust: A Contemporary Asset Protection Scheme*, 102 Com. L.J. 138, 143-44 (1997).

[136] 395 F.3d 59 (2d Cir. 2005).

[137] *E.g.*, In re Lawrence, 279 F.3d 1294 (11th Cir. 2002); FTC v. Affordable Media, 179 F.3d 1228 (9th Cir. 1999).

[138] *See infra* § 13.02 Denial of Discharge.

(unreachable by creditors).[139] Even if state law validates a self-settled spendthrift trust, however, the 2005 Amendments explicitly permit the bankruptcy trustee to recover transfers to a self-settled trust made within the last ten years prior to the debtor's bankruptcy petition if the transfer was made with the intent to defraud an existing creditor.[140]

The Bankruptcy Code contains language specifically directed at these and other self-settled trusts. Section 548(e)(1) permits the trustee to avoid any:

> transfer of an interest of the debtor in property that was made on or within 10 years before the date of the filing of the petition if —
>
> (A) such transfer was made to a self-settled trust or similar device;
>
> (B) such transfer was by the debtor;
>
> (C) the debtor is a beneficiary of such trust or similar device; and
>
> (D) the debtor made such transfer with actual intent to hinder, delay, or defraud any entity to which the debtor was or became, on or after the date that such transfer was made, indebted.[141]

Section 548 has always provided that transfers made with the intent to hinder, defraud, or delay creditors are avoidable. The most important aspect of this new language is the portion that looks back ten years before the debtor's petition was filed, thus effectively expanding the scope of § 548 beyond the two-year period that applies to fraudulent transfers generally.[142]

[4] Employee Pension Plans[143]

The spendthrift trust provision has its most dramatic effect in connection with the type of pension funds that many middle-class Americans hold. It has long been clear that restrictions on the transfer of pension funds held in trust, if recognized or required by state law, fit within the exclusion. In its 1992 decision in *Patterson v. Shumate*,[144] the Supreme Court held that spendthrift trust restrictions imposed under ERISA[145] are equally effective. In doing so, the Court effectively further

---

[139] *See* Stewart E. Sterk, *Asset Protection Trusts: Trust Law's Race to the Bottom?*, 85 Cornell L. Rev. 1035, 1044 (2000).

[140] Bankruptcy Code § 548(e).

[141] Bankruptcy Code § 548(e)(1)(A).

[142] Bankruptcy Code § 548(a)(1). The trustee might also be able to avoid a fraudulent transfer under state fraudulent transfer law, through Bankruptcy Code § 544(b). *See infra* § 16.01[D] Sources of Fraudulent Conveyance Law.

[143] Patricia E. Dilley, *Hidden in Plain View: The Pension Shield Against Creditors*, 74 Ind. L.J. 355, 387 (1999); Donna Litman, *Bankruptcy Status of "ERISA Qualified Pension Plans" An Epilogue to* Patterson v. Shumate, 9 Am. Bankr. Inst. L. Rev. 637, 655 (2001); C. Scott Pryor, *Rock, Scissors, Paper: ERISA, the Bankruptcy Code and State Exemption Laws for Individual Retirement Accounts*, 77 Am. Bankr. L.J. 65 (2003); Ann K. Wooster, Annotation, *Retirement Funds Benefits or Refunds of Retirement Fund Contributions as "Property" of Bankruptcy Estate Under § 541 of Bankruptcy Code of 1978*, 174 A.L.R. Fed. 587 (2001).

[144] 504 U.S. 753 (1992).

[145] "ERISA" is the Employee Retirement Income Security Act of 1974. Most of ERISA was codified

broadened the scope of § 541(c)(2) beyond what had traditionally been assumed. As a result of *Patterson*, funds in employee's ERISA-qualified pension plans are completely excluded from their bankruptcy estates and protected from their creditors' claims, regardless of the size of their pension fund, and regardless of whether or not the debtor needs those funds for retirement.

Patterson resolved a long-standing dispute over whether the phrase "applicable nonbankruptcy law' " in § 541(c)(2) referred to any law outside of the confines of the bankruptcy code or only to state law. The Court's analysis was uncomplicated. The debtor's pension plan contained an ERISA-mandated spendthrift clause, preventing alienation of the plan's funds.[146] It seemed evident to the Court that ERISA, appearing as it does outside of the Bankruptcy Code, was the type of "applicable nonbankruptcy law" to which § 541(c)(2) refers.[147] The Court held: "[a] debtor's interest in an ERISA-qualified pension plan may be excluded from the property of the bankruptcy estate pursuant to § 541(c)(2)."[148]

Unfortunately, the Court's cryptic phrase "ERISA-qualified" has left bankruptcy courts baffled about the scope of the exclusion.[149] The *Patterson* decision left open the possibility that the pension plan could still be invaded by the trustee if, due to some oversight, the pension plan failed to qualify for favorable tax treatment under ERISA. It also left open questions about the extent to which other pension plans, not governed by ERISA, qualified for the exclusion.

Most courts have applied one of several two- or three-pronged tests to determine if a debtor's pension is excluded by § 541(c)(2). One of these two-pronged tests asks whether the plan (1) is subject to title I of ERISA and (2) contains the necessary anti-alienation term prohibiting plan benefits from being assigned or alienated.[150] Another test modifies the second prong by requiring that the anti-alienation provision be enforceable under ERISA.[151] Other courts have deployed a third requirement, insisting that the plan also be qualified under § 401 of the Internal Revenue Code.[152]

---

in Title 29 of the United States Code, but a significant part of it is contained in Title 26 (the Internal Revenue Code). A basic explanation of ERISA's provisions in relation to the exclusion of ERISA pension funds from the debtor's estate can be found in C. Scott Pryor, *Rock, Scissors, Paper: ERISA, the Bankruptcy Code and State Exemption Laws for Individual Retirement Accounts*, 77 Am. Bankr. L.J. 65, 71-74 (2003).

[146] ERISA specifies that "[e]ach pension plan shall provide that benefits provided under the plan may not be assigned or alienated." ERISA § 206(d)(1), 29 U.S.C. § 1056(d)(1) (2000).

[147] 504 U.S. at 760. *See generally* Donna Litman, *Bankruptcy Status of "ERISA Qualified Pension Plans" — An Epilogue to* Patterson v. Shumate, 9 Am. Bankr. Inst. L. Rev. 637, 655 (2001).

[148] 504 U.S. at 765.

[149] *E.g.*, In re Goldschein, 244 B.R. 595 (Bankr. M.D. Md. 2000). *See generally* Donna Litman, *Bankruptcy Status of "ERISA Qualified Pension Plans" — An Epilogue to* Patterson v. Shumate, 9 Am. Bankr. Inst. L. Rev. 637, 648-656 (2001).

[150] *E.g.*, Traina v. Sewell (In re Sewell), 180 F.3d 707, 712 (5th Cir. 1999); In re Baker, 114 F.3d 636, 638-39 (7th Cir. 1997).

[151] *E.g.*, In re Hanes, 162 B.R. 733 (Bankr. E.D. Va. 1994).

[152] *E.g.*, In re Hall, 151 B.R. 412, 419-20 (Bankr. W.D. Mich. 1993). *See generally* J. Gordon Christy & Sabrina Skeldon, Shumate *and Pension Benefits in Bankruptcy*, 2 J. Bankr. L. & Prac. 719, 722-23 (1992).

Benefits under a retirement plan that is not valid under ERISA should not be excluded from the debtor's estate under § 541(c)(2) even if the plan includes an anti-alienation or spendthrift provision and is thus otherwise "tax qualified" under the Internal Revenue Code.[153] But, in *Raymond B. Yates, M.D., P.C. Profit Sharing Plan v. Hendon,* the Supreme Court ruled that the owner of a business who also works as an employee of his business may qualify as a "participant" in an ERISA plan if the plan covers employees other than the business owner and his spouse. Thus, an employee who also serves as the employer is not disqualified from enjoying the benefits of participating in the firm's ERISA pension plan, including the right to have the employee's pension assets excluded from his or her bankruptcy estate.[154]

Language in the *Yates* decision, limiting its holding to situations were there are employees in addition to the debtor and his spouse, lends support to the holdings of some courts that the exclusion would not apply to funds in a profit-sharing plan whose sole beneficiary is the same person who is the owner of the business and its only employee.[155]

Further consensus is hard to find. Courts using the two-pronged approach have taken the decidedly pro-debtor view that the debtor's pension funds are excluded under § 541(c)(2) and *Patterson* if the plan is generally regulated under ERISA and contains the necessary spendthrift trust language, even if the plan's administrators have not handled the plan or its funds in strict compliance with ERISA's requirements.[156] However, other courts have denied owner-employees the benefit of the exclusion where they have misused their control over the plan's assets in complete disregard of ERISA's restrictions, effectively using the plan as if it were a personal bank account.[157]

Debtors might have pension funds invested in a wide variety of pension plans and savings accounts, which, depending on their characteristics, may be included in their bankruptcy estate. Funds in a "Simplified Employee Pension Plans" (SEP), a type of Individual Retirement Account (IRA),[158] which are neither required to be held in trust, nor required to be protected by an anti-alienation provision,[159] are usually not excluded from a debtor's estate by this provision.[160] In addition, funds in either a conventional IRA or a "Roth" IRA are not excluded.[161] However, particularly since the 2005 Amendments, these funds are at least partially exempt

---

[153] 26 U.S.C. § 401(a)(13) (2006).

[154] Raymond B. Yates, M.D., P.C. Profit Sharing Plan v. Hendon, 541 U.S. 1, 6 (2004).

[155] *E.g.*, In re Sutton, 272 B.R. 802 (Bankr. D. Fla. 2002) (pension not excluded from estate because it did not comply with ERISA as a result of the debtor's status as sole employee and sole participant under the fund).

[156] In re Baker, 114 F.3d 636 (7th Cir. 1997); In re Handel, 301 B.R. 421 (Bankr. D.N.Y. 2003).

[157] In re Goldschein, 244 B.R. 595 (Bankr. D. Md. 2000); In re Harris, 188 B.R. 444, 449 (Bankr. M.D. Fla. 1995), *aff'd* Harris v. Jensen, 116 F.3d 1492 (11th Cir. 1997), *cert. denied*, 522 U.S. 950 (1997).

[158] C. Scott Pryor, *Rock, Scissors, Paper: ERISA, the Bankruptcy Code and State Exemption Laws for Individual Retirement Accounts*, 77 Am. Bankr. L.J. 65 (2003).

[159] 26 U.S.C. § 408(k) (2006).

[160] *E.g.*, In re Kellogg, 179 B.R. 379 (Bankr. D. Mass. 1995).

[161] *E.g.*, Velis v. Kardanis, 949 F.2d 78 (3d Cir. 1991). Individual retirement accounts fail to satisfy two

from administration by the trustee under § 522.[162]

In 2005, Congress added language to § 541(b) excluding both amounts withheld by an employer from an employee's wages or received as contributions by the employee to one of several types of retirement funds or to health insurance plans.[163] Some pension funds provide for funding from both sources: the employer and the employee. This language supplements § 541(c)(2) and the *Patterson v. Shumate* decision by excluding amounts withheld by an employer or contributed by an employee, even if the withheld or contributed funds have not yet been remitted by the employer to the employee's pension plan.

This language resolves several issues that had been frequently litigated under *Patterson* and resolves most of the issues against inclusion of these types of assets in the debtor's estate. However, the amendment fails to address several related issues, including inclusion of amounts that may have been contributed by an employer without being withheld from the employee's wages, earnings acquired before the withheld or contributed amounts are remitted to the pension plan, and a debtor's right to receive payments under one of the enumerated plans.[164] Depending on the amounts involved, aggressive trustees might be expected to pursue employers to recover such funds that are not expressly excluded from the estate either under *Patterson* or under this new provision.

[G] Debtor's Right as Trustee

The final blanket exception excludes property in which the debtor holds only legal title and not an equitable interest.[165] This is property that the debtor holds in trust, of the benefit of someone else. All that the estate would acquire under § 541(a) is bare legal title; the real value of the property — the equitable interest — is not part of the estate in any event. Assume, for example, that the debtor, Uncle Ernie, is the trustee of his niece Bertie's spendthrift trust. As trustee, he holds bare legal title. He is not entitled to take money out of the trust; to do so would violate his fiduciary duty and give rise to a non-dischargeable debt.[166] Thus, the property in the trust does not belong to the debtor, is not normally subject to the claims of his creditors, and is not a part of his bankruptcy estate.[167] However,

---

criteria for ERISA qualification. IRAs are explicitly excluded from ERISA's scope. ERISA § 201(6), 29 U.S.C. § 1051(6) (2006). Likewise, IRAs are not qualified under Internal Revenue Code § 401. Moreover, even though an IRA might include an anti-alienation provision, nothing in ERISA, or any other provision of federal law, requires them to do so.

[162] Margaret Howard, *Exemptions Under the 2005 Bankruptcy Amendments: A Tale of Opportunity Lost*, 79 Am. Bankr. L.J. 397 (2005).

[163] Bankruptcy Abuse Prevention and Consumer Protection Act of 2005, Pub. L. No. 109-8 § 323, 119 Stat 23, 97 (2005).

[164] Bankruptcy Code § 541(b)(7). This new language refers to both employer and employee payments to (1) employee benefit plans subject to Title 1 of ERISA; (2) government employee plans under I.R.C. § 414(d); (3) deferred compensation plans under I.R.C. § 457; (4) tax deferred annuities under I.R.C. § 403(b); and (5) health insurance plans regulated by state law.

[165] Bankruptcy Code § 541(d).

[166] Bankruptcy Code § 523(a)(4).

[167] *See* Tort Claimants Committee v. Roman Catholic Archbishop of Portland in Oregon, Inc. (In Re

if the transfer of the property into the trust is avoidable as a fraudulent transfer or under one of the bankrupcy trustee's other avoiding powers, the limitation imposed by § 541(d) does not impair the trustee in bankruptcy's ability to avoid the transfer and recover the property for the debtor's estate.[168]

[H]   Education IRAs and Tuition Credits

In 2005, Congress added exclusions from a debtor's estate for certain federally protected education benefits.[169] Subject to specified limits, a debtor's contributions to "Coverdell" educational IRAs and for the purchase of state "tuition credits" are excluded from the debtor's estate.[170] The Code also excludes similar amounts that the debtor "used to purchase a tuition credit or certificate or contributed to an account . . . under a qualified State tuition program."[171] Income earned by these funds, established pursuant to § 529 of the Internal Revenue Code, are exempted from taxation.[172]

[I]   Pawned Goods

New § 541(b)(8) excludes from the estate tangible personal property that the debtor has pawned, as long as the debtor is not obligated to repay the loan made by the pawnshop or redeem the property from the shop to which it has been delivered.[173] The exclusion operates primarily for the benefit of licensed pawnshops who do not have to surrender pawned property, even though the debtor may still retain the right to redeem it under applicable state law. The property is part of the estate if the debtor has already exercised any right to redeem it[174] or if the transaction with the pawnshop is otherwise subject to avoidance under any of the trustee's avoiding powers.[175]

[J]   Social Security Benefits

Social Security Administration benefits, although not governed by § 541(c)(2)'s spendthrift trust provisions, may also be excluded from the debtor's estate. These benefits are exempt under § 522(d)(10)(A) for debtors who elect the federal exemption scheme, and may be exempt under state exemption statutes for debtors whose bankruptcy exemptions are governed by state law. However, until recently,

---

Roman Catholic Archbishop of Portland in Or., Inc.), 345 B.R. 686 (D. Or. 2006).

[168] Bakst v. Corzo (In re Corzo), 406 B.R. 154 (Bankr. S.D. Fl. 2008).

[169] Bankruptcy Abuse Prevention and Consumer Protection Act of 2005, Pub. L. No. 109-8, § 225(a)(1)(C), 119 Stat 23, 65 (2005).

[170] Bankruptcy Code § 541(b)(5).

[171] Bankruptcy Code § 541(b)(6). *See* In re Werth, 468 B.R. 412 (Bankr. D. Kan. 2012) (contributions within 1 year of petition are excluded).

[172] 26 U.S.C. § 529 (2006).

[173] Bankruptcy Code § 541(b)(8).

[174] Bankruptcy Code § 541(b)(8)(C).

[175] This latter result is made plain by language subjecting the exclusion to "subchapter III of chapter 5" of the Bankruptcy Code, where the trustee's various avoiding powers are located. Bankruptcy Code § 541(b)(8).

they have generally been regarded as falling within the ambit of the estate's property. Recent Court of Appeals decisions, based on the anti-assignment provision of the Social Security Act,[176] have drawn this conclusion into question.

The conflict between § 541(a)(1) of the Bankruptcy Code, which makes "all legal or equitable interests of the debtor in property"[177] part of the debtor's estate, is in direct conflict with 42 U.S.C. § 407. Section 407 expressly provides: "none of the moneys paid or payable or rights existing under [the Social Security Act] shall be subject to . . . the operation of any bankruptcy or insolvency law."[178] This conflict is even more evident in Chapter 13 bankruptcy cases, which were designed, in part, to permit Social Security benefit recipients to use the benefits to fund a Chapter rehabilitation plan.[179]

Faced with this apparent conflict, some courts regard the Bankruptcy Code as having implicitly repealed § 407[180] while others treat § 407 as nothing more than an exemption provision.[181] If § 407 creates an exemption, in addition to those provided in § 522(b), the debtor must claim her Social Security benefits as exempt, or lose them. Still other courts take § 407 at face value, and regard a debtor's Social Security benefits as completely outside the debtor's estate, not subject to administration by the bankruptcy trustee regardless of whether the debtor claims them as exempt in her bankruptcy case.[182] This conflict is particularly acute for debtors whose exemptions are governed by state law in a state that does not exempt Social Security benefits from the estate.

§ 7.05 SECURITIZATION

Asset securitization transactions, which involve trillions of dollars, raise difficult issues about property of a debtor's estate. Securitization deals are an alternative way for a business to use its accounts, chattel paper, rental payments and other receivables to generate immediate cash. The traditional way for a business to transform its receivables into cash is to sell them to a commercial factor, who is engaged in the business of buying receivables, or to use them as collateral for a loan. A securitization transaction combines the aspects of factoring (which involves the sale of receivables) with secured financing. These transactions have become immensely popular for a pair of reasons — liquidity enhancement and perceived advantageous treatment in bankruptcy. The first of these is efficiency enhancing, while the second is potentially more troubling.[183]

---

[176] 42 U.S.C. § 407 (2006).

[177] Bankruptcy Code § 541(a)(1).

[178] 42 U.S.C. § 407(a)(2006).

[179] *See* United States v. Devall, 704 F.2d 1513, 1516 (11th Cir.1983); Toson v. United States, 18 B.R. 371, 373-75 (Bankr. N.D. Ga.1982).

[180] *Id.*

[181] Walker v. Treadwell (In re Treadwell), 699 F.2d 1050, 1052 (11th Cir.1983).

[182] Carpenter v. Ries (In re Carpenter), 614 F.3d 930 (8th Cir. 2010); Hildebrand v. Social Security Administration (In re Buren), 725 F.2d 1080 (6th Cir. 1984).

[183] Edward J. Janger, *The Death of Secured Lending*, 25 Cardozo L. Rev. 1759 (2004); Edward J. Janger, *Muddy Rules for Securitization Transactions*, 7 Fordham J. Corp. & Fin. L. 301 (2002).

In a securitization transaction, the debtor (in this case known as an "originator") incorporates a company for the sole purpose of purchasing the debtor's accounts — a "Special Purpose Vehicle" or "SPV"[184] — and then sells its receivables to the SPV. The SPV then issues securities ("Asset Backed Securities" or "ABS"), backed by the stream of accounts purchased from the debtor, to outside investors. Assume, for example, that Titanic Industries regularly generates accounts receivables owed by its customers. This makes Titanic the "originator" of the accounts. Titanic would then sell the receivables to an SPV, "Ocean Receivables." Ocean Receivables would, in turn, obtain the cash necessary to pay for the receivables by selling bonds to investors. Collections from the receivables would then pay off the SPV's obligations to the bondholders. This form of financing often allows debtors to receive a more favorable interest rate than a conventional loan secured by the same assets.

The first reason for this price advantage is liquidity enhancement — the principle efficiency created by securitization transactions. Asset Backed Securities issued by the SPV can be classified in denominations with risk attributes that are attractive to capital market participants such as mutual funds and pension plans. This increases the number of investors who are available to purchase Titanic's debt beyond banks and factors, and renders debt markets more competitive. A second key component of ABS transactions, and another reason that the interest rate may be better, is the perception by the market that the receivables sold to the SPV will not, or indeed cannot be brought back into the originator's bankruptcy estate in the event that the originator goes bankrupt. In other words, the SPV is "bankruptcy remote." Unless the transaction is supported by an opinion of counsel that the transaction is structured in a way that protects the SPV's purchase of the receivables from the originator's bankruptcy, the bonds issued by the SPV will not receive an investment grade rating and will be difficult to sell. As such, the success of the entire transaction depends on whether the sale of the accounts can be insulated from recovery by the originator's bankruptcy in the event that the originator must seek bankruptcy protection from its creditors.

This, of course, is where the difficulty lies. In the originator's bankruptcy proceeding, the transaction is vulnerable to attack on three potential grounds: that it is a fraudulent transfer; that the transaction is "intended for security" and thus is not a "true sale"; or that the relationship between the originator and the SPV warrants piercing the SPV's corporate veil and therefore the originator and the debtor should be "substantively consolidated," thereby bringing the SPV's assets into the originator's bankruptcy estate.

The sale of receivables from the originator to the SPV might be a fraudulent transfer.[185] Depending on the originator's financial condition, if the price paid by the SPV to the originator was not a reasonably equivalent value for the transferred accounts (as may occur where the sale is "overcollateralized"), the entire transaction might be avoidable as a constructively fraudulent transfer.[186] Though less

---

[184] *See* Steven L. Schwarcz, *The Alchemy of Asset Securitization*, 1 Stan. J.L. Bus. & Fin. 133, 134 (1994).

[185] Edward J. Janger, *Muddy Rules for Securitizations*, 7 Fordham J. Corp. & Fin. L. 301, 308-10 (2002). *See infra* § 16.03[B] Specific Transactions Involving Constructive Fraud.

[186] Bankruptcy Code § 548(a)(1)(B). *See* Peter V. Pantaleo et al., *Rethinking the Role of Recourse in*

likely, the transaction might also be a fraudulent transfer if the circumstances surrounding the transaction indicate that it was merely a means to insulate the originator's assets from its creditors and thus "intended to hinder, delay, or defraud" the originator's creditors.[187]

A second avenue of attack, to bring the "sale" of the receivables back into the originator's bankruptcy estate is to characterize the transaction as one that was "intended for security" and thus not a "true sale."[188] This is a particular risk if the terms of the sale obligate the originator to repurchase accounts that fall into default, or if the originator guaranties or warrants to the SPV that it will receive a particular rate of return on the purchased assets. Giving the buyer of accounts a "right of recourse" exposes the seller to the risk that the accounts may not be collectible. Placing this attribute of ownership back on the originator makes the transaction appear more a like loan from the SPV, secured by a floating lien in the originator's accounts.[189] This gives the SPV nothing more than a secured claim in the originator's bankruptcy and give the originator's bankruptcy estate the right to any surplus value in the accounts. More importantly, if the assets of the SPV are considered property of the estate, then they would be considered "cash collateral" and could be used (with appropriate protections) to fund the debtor/originator's reorganization.[190] In the wake of a decision in the *LTV* bankruptcy that allowed securitized assets to be used as cash collateral, proponents of securitization transactions sought to avoid this risk by amending the Bankruptcy Code to prevent recharacterization of the transaction if the parties labeled it as a true sale.[191] This tactic was rejected as a matter of federal law, leaving the substance of the transaction to control its characterization, rather than the label at the top of the page. Nonetheless similar provisions have been enacted by a number of states. Whether these state statutes are effective to eliminate the doctrine of "true sale" as a matter of federal law has not yet been tested.[192]

Finally, depending on the intercorporate relationship between the originator and the SPV, the transaction might be collapsed and the accounts brought back into the originator's estate by piercing the corporate veil — or by its bankruptcy equivalent, "substantive consolidation" of the estates of the originator and the SPV.[193]

---

the Sale of Financial Assets, 52 Bus. Law. 159, 185 (1996).

[187] Bankruptcy Code § 548(a)(1)(A).

[188] Stephen J. Lubben, *Beyond True Sales: Securitization and Chapter 11*, 1 N.Y.U. J. L. & Bus. 89 (2004). *See* In re LTV Steel, Inc., 274 B.R. 278 (Bankr. N.D. Ohio 2001).

[189] Thomas E. Plank, *The True Sale of Loans and the Role of Recourse*, 14 Geo. Mason U. L. Rev. 287 (1991).

[190] For an example of a case where this issue was litigated, see In re LTV Steel Co., Inc., No. 00-43866, 2001 Bankr. LEXIS 131 (Bankr. N.D. Ohio 2001).

[191] The proposed amendment is described in detail in Edward J. Janger, *Muddy Rules for Securitization Transactions*, 7 Fordham J. Corp. & Fin. L. 301 (2002).

[192] For a discussion of these state statutes, see Edward J. Janger, *The Death of Secured Lending*, 25 Cardozo L. Rev. 1759 (2004).

[193] Steven L. Schwarcz, Securitization Post-Enron, 25 Cardozo L. Rev. 1539 (2004); Edward J. Janger, *Muddy Rules for Securitizations*, 7 Fordham J. Corp. & Fin. L. 301, 308-10 (2002).

§ 7.06 EXPANDED ESTATE IN REORGANIZATION CASES UNDER CHAPTERS 11, 12, AND 13

[A] Expanded Estate in Chapter 11 Cases

The basic provisions of § 541 apply in Chapter 11 reorganization cases the same as they do in Chapter 7 liquidation cases.[194] There are no special rules in Chapter 11 regarding the inclusion of post-petition property of the estate being included in the debtor's estate. However, in the typical Chapter 11 proceeding, the debtor's post-petition property is property of the estate under §§ 541(a)(6) and (7). Under those provisions, the estate includes "proceeds, product, offspring, rents, or profits of or from property of the estate," and "property acquired by the estate." This language encompasses most of what a Chapter 11 debtor normally receives after its case is commenced.

Significantly, however, and unlike Chapters 12 and 13, nothing in Chapter 11 brings earnings from an individual Chapter 11 debtor's post-petition services into his estate. Although Chapter 11 petitions by individuals who are not engaged in any business are rare, they are permitted, as the United States Supreme Court held in *Toibb v. Radloff*.[195] Thus, § 541(a)(6)'s exclusion of such earnings from the debtor's estate applies in Chapter 11 cases involving individual debtors.

Because a Chapter 11 debtor is likely to need these post-petition earnings to fund his plan, the primary significance of the exclusion of these assets from an individual debtor's Chapter 11 estate is in connection with the scope of the automatic stay. For example, § 362(b)(2)(B) permits creditors to bring or maintain actions to collect amounts owed for a "domestic support obligation from property that is not property of the estate,"[196] without violating the automatic stay. A Chapter 11 debtor's spouse might be permitted to bring a wage garnishment action to collect a pre-petition support obligation from the debtor's post-petition earnings without running afoul of the automatic stay.[197]

[B] Expanded Estate in Chapter 12 Cases

Chapter 12 proceedings provide for the reorganization of family farmers and family fishermen.[198] These reorganization proceedings necessarily involve the debtor's post-petition earnings. Accordingly, the scope of property included in a Chapter 12 estate is broader than in a Chapter 7 liquidation case. Section 1207 brings into the estate not only the property included by § 541, but also any "property . . . that the debtor acquires after the commencement of the case"[199]

---

[194] Bankruptcy Code § 103(a).

[195] 501 U.S. 157 (1991).

[196] Bankruptcy Code § 362(b)(2)(B).

[197] The Bankruptcy Abuse Prevention and Consumer Protection Act of 2005 added several related exceptions to the automatic stay, all dealing with various domestic relations and support obligations. Pub. L. No. 109-8, § 214, 119 Stat. 23, 54 (2005).

[198] *See* Chapter 20 — Family Farmer and Family Fisherman Reorganization under Chapter 12.

[199] Bankruptcy Code § 1207(a)(1).

and "earnings from services performed by the debtor after the commencement of the case."[200] This includes virtually every type of property that the debtor might acquire. Property acquired after the case is closed, dismissed, or converted to a Chapter 7 case is excluded from the Chapter 12 estate.[201] For example, income that the debtor earns from the operation of his farm or fishing operation while the case is pending belongs to the estate. Generally speaking, this would not be true in a Chapter 7 proceeding; under Chapter 7, only the income that is attributable to the property of the estate or received by the estate is included.

[C] Expanded Estate in Chapter 13 Cases

Chapter 13 of the Bankruptcy Code provides for the reorganization of individuals with regular income.[202] Like Chapters 11 and 12, Chapter 13 involves a reorganization; thus, it necessarily deals with property acquired by the debtor after his petition was filed. Indeed, the debtor's post-petition income is nearly always necessary to effectuate the plan of reorganization. Under Chapter 13, property of the estate includes everything included in a Chapter 7 estate;[203] any property that the debtor acquires after the commencement of the case but before the case is either closed, dismissed, or converted to Chapter 7, 11 or 12;[204] and all earnings from labor performed by the debtor after the commencement of the case but before the case is closed, dismissed, or converted to Chapter 7, 11, or 12.[205] This, of course, includes property acquired after the plan is confirmed.[206] Most importantly, the debtor's wages earned post-petition are property of the Chapter 13 estate, even though they would not be included in his estate in a liquidation case under Chapter 7, where they are explicitly excluded by § 541(a)(6).

---

[200] Bankruptcy Code § 1207(a)(2).

[201] Bankruptcy Code § 1207(a).

[202] *See* Chapter 18 — Rehabilitation of Individuals with Regular Income under Chapter 13.

[203] Bankruptcy Code § 1306(a).

[204] Bankruptcy Code § 1306(a)(1).

[205] Bankruptcy Code § 1306(a)(2).

[206] In re Waldron, 536 F.3d 1239 (11th Cir. 2008).

Chapter 8

THE AUTOMATIC STAY

§ 8.01 PURPOSE OF THE AUTOMATIC STAY

The automatic stay cements the bankruptcy court's jurisdiction over the estate and gives the debtor breathing room to arrange his or her affairs. The stay is an automatic injunction that stops virtually all creditors' collection activities, including lawsuits, repossessions, foreclosure sales, as well as the barrage of dunning phone calls and letters that debtors receive. Creditors who continue these efforts violate the stay and run the risk of being cited for contempt. The stay, together with the discharge injunction at the end of the case, implement the debtor's "fresh start," the main incentive for individual debtors to file a bankruptcy petition.

The first issue that must be addressed in connection with the automatic stay is its scope: who or what does it protect, and what creditor activity does it prohibit? Related to this issue is the nature and extent of an ever growing number of exceptions to the stay. The Code also provides for several ancillary stays, which apply in Chapters 12 and 13 to protect those who are jointly liable for the debtor's obligations, and courts sometimes grant supplemental stays in Chapter 11 when they are necessary to assist the debtor in focusing on its efforts to reorganize.

The second key issue pertaining to the stay deals with the circumstances under which creditors will be granted relief from the stay, usually to permit them to enforce their rights as secured creditors. In consumer cases, relief from the stay can result in the debtor losing her home or her car. In business cases, relief from the stay heralds the end of the debtor's efforts to reorganize and results in the termination of the debtor's business and the beginning of the liquidation process.

Finally, the third key issue discussed in this chapter are the consequences for those who violate the automatic stay. As will be seen, actions taken in violation of the stay are void, and creditors who violate the stay are liable for the harm they cause, and are sometimes subject to punitive damages as well.

§ 8.02 SCOPE OF THE AUTOMATIC STAY

Section 362(a) imposes an automatic stay prohibiting most judicial and administrative proceedings as well as most informal actions a creditor might take in an effort to collect.[1] Section 362(a) indicates that the stay protects the debtor, property of the estate,[2] and property that an individual debtor continues to own post-

---

[1] Bankruptcy Code § 362(a).

[2] Bankruptcy Code § 362(a)(2), (3), (4), (5).

petition.[3]

The stay's scope is broad. It extends to a wide array of efforts creditors might take, including lawsuits, repossessions, foreclosure sales, assessments, and setoffs. Still, there are a few narrow gaps between its various provisions that permit some creditors a small amount of leeway to continue their collection efforts. Morever, § 362(b) contains a number of explicit, narrow exceptions that permit action that otherwise would be prohibited.[4]

[A] Judicial and Administrative Proceedings

The automatic stay blocks the commencement or continuation of any judicial or administrative action against the debtor that was or could have been commenced before the commencement of the case. It also bars judicial and administrative actions against the debtor to recover a pre-petition claim.[5]

For example, suppose that Daniel negligently injured Alice in an auto accident on July 7, and that on August 1, he entered into a contract with Belinda, but breached on October 30. If Daniel files a petition on November 27, and neither Alice nor Belinda have yet filed suit, they are prohibited from doing so. Their claims arose pre-petition. Their only recourse is to file proofs of claim in Daniel's bankruptcy case.

Even if Alice and Belinda had previously filed suit against Daniel, the stay applies. Their actions must not continue. Even status conferences violate the stay.[6] Pending state proceedings must simply stop, even if the jury has already begun its deliberations.[7] Without getting relief from the court to permit these suits to continue, any action taken in the pending litigation violates the stay and is void.[8]

Significantly, for many debtors who file for bankruptcy in order to try to hold on to their homes and other property, § 362(a)(1) prevents creditors from continuing real estate foreclosure and replevin actions against the debtor's real and personal property. Once the petition has been filed, a pending foreclosure proceeding must cease.[9] Sales conducted after the bankruptcy case starts are void.

The stay only prohibits actions based on claims that arose "before the commencement of the [bankruptcy case]."[10] Thus, it does not prevent post-petition creditors, those who extended credit after the bankruptcy case was filed, from pursuing suits against the debtor, even though the bankruptcy case may still be pending. This gap in the scope of § 362(a)(1) is particularly important in

---

[3] Bankruptcy Code § 362(a)(5).

[4] Bankruptcy Code § 362(b). *See infra* § 8.03 Exceptions to the Automatic Stay.

[5] Bankruptcy Code § 362(a)(1).

[6] In re Hall-Walker, 445 B.R. 873 (Bankr. N.D. Ill. 2011).

[7] Though in such a case, the court might grant relief from the stay to conclude the action. *See infra* § 8.06[B][2] For Cause — Other than for Lack of Adequate Protection.

[8] *See infra* § 8.07[A] Actions in Violation of the Stay Are Void.

[9] *E.g.*, In re Ebadi, 448 B.R. 308 (Bankr. E.D.N.Y. 2011).

[10] Bankruptcy Code § 362(a)(1).

reorganization cases under Chapters 11, 12, and 13, which might continue for several years.[11] However, other portions of the stay prevent a post-petition creditor from taking steps to enforce its judgment against assets that belong to the debtor's bankruptcy estate.[12] On the other hand, the bankruptcy estate is not a static entity. Assets that once belonged to the estate might be transferred back to the debtor, as commonly occurs when a Chapter 11 or 13 plan is confirmed. Once these assets have been revested in the estate, post-petition creditors are free to pursue them to collect their post-petition judgments.[13]

[B] Enforcement of Judgments

The automatic stay also prohibits actions to enforce judgments that were obtained before the bankruptcy case commenced. These judgments cannot be enforced against either the debtor or against property of the estate.[14] Thus, if on March 14, Chelsea obtains a products liability judgment against Franklin Manufacturing Inc., and Franklin files a bankruptcy petition on April 1, Chelsea is stayed from taking any action to enforce her judgment against either the debtor or against property of the bankruptcy estate.[15] Her judgment is still valid, but she may not enforce it outside the bankruptcy proceeding.[16]

Although § 362(a)(2) is not directed at creditors' efforts to enforce their pre-petition judgments against property that belongs solely to the debtor, and not to the estate, § 541 is likely to make virtually all of the debtor's property, even exempt and encumbered property, part of the estate and thus protects it against these enforcement efforts.[17] Property that the debtor exempts will be abandoned by the trustee and exit the estate, but it is protected by the debtor's exemptions under state law, or under § 522.[18] Property that is subject to a pre-petition lien is protected from foreclosure by § 362(a)(5), discussed below. Thus, it is rare that there is much property of the debtor that can be seized while the bankruptcy case is pending, without express permission from the bankruptcy court.

Many debtors file their bankruptcy cases in direct response to creditors' enforcement actions. The automatic stay stops foreclosure, garnishment, and other similar actions, cold. Thus, the opportunity to take advantage of the automatic stay is among the strongest motivations for a debtor to file a bankruptcy case.

If the enforcement process is underway, but still incomplete, the stay prevents it from continuing. For example, if the sheriff is in the midst of selling the debtor's home in a mortgage foreclosure sale, but the sale has not been completed, the stay

---

[11] *See, e.g.*, Fritz Fire Protection Co. v. Chang (In re Chang), 438 B.R. 77 (Bankr. M.D. Pa. 2010).

[12] Bankruptcy Code § 362(a)(3), (4).

[13] *See* Fritz Fire Protection Co. v. Chang (In re Chang), 438 B.R. 77 (Bankr. M.D. Pa. 2010).

[14] Bankruptcy Code § 362(a)(2).

[15] Bankruptcy Code § 362(a)(2).

[16] *E.g.*, Lunde v. Am. Family Mut. Ins. Co., 297 S.W.3d 88 (Mo. Ct. App. 2009).

[17] *See supra* Chapter 7 — Property of the Estate.

[18] *See infra* Chapter 12 — Preserving Property: Exemptions and Redemption.

prevents the sale from going forward.[19] If the sale is completed after the case is filed, the sale is void and will be vacated, even though no-one associated with the sale knew that the case had been commenced and the stay imposed.

[C] Acts to Obtain Possession or Control of Estate Property

Section 362(a)(3) prohibits "any act to obtain possession of property of the estate, to obtain possession of property from the estate, or to exercise control over property of the estate."[20] This language extends the stay beyond formal judicial or administrative proceedings and restricts even informal actions to interfere with estate property. Most significantly, it prohibits self-help repossession, even though self-help is otherwise permitted by the U.C.C.[21]

Because creditors are prohibited from exercising control over estate property, creditors who have successfully repossessed collateral before the debtor's petition was filed, but have not yet sold it, must return the property to the debtor upon learning of the debtor's bankruptcy petition.[22] Although this rule is well-established, creditors sometimes persist in violating the stay by refusing to turn over estate property in their possession.[23]

Although § 523(a)(3) applies only to property of the estate, and not to property of the debtor, both exemption laws and the discharge injunction of § 524(a)[24] prevent most efforts that creditors might take to seize the debtor's property, such as a Chapter 7 debtor's post-petition earnings, that do not belong to the bankruptcy estate.

[D] Acts to Create, Perfect, or Enforce Liens

Section 362(a)(4) restrains acts a creditor might take to "create, perfect, or enforce" liens against estate property. Section 362(a)(5) does the same thing, but with respect to the debtor's property in connection with any pre-petition claim. Thus, creditors who have not recorded their mortgages, filed their financing statements, or filed other public documents necessary to perfect their liens are restrained from doing so after the debtor's petition is filed.

Although these provisions encompass purchase money security interests that might not yet have been perfected when the debtor's petition is filed, §§ 362(b)(3) and 546(b) permit creditors to take advantage of state statutory relation-back rules to perfect their interests, even after the debtor's bankruptcy petition is filed. Thus a creditor who obtained a purchase money security interest on April 1 is permitted

---

[19] *E.g.*, In re Ebadi, 448 B.R. 308 (Bankr. E.D.N.Y. 2011).

[20] Bankruptcy Code § 362(a)(3).

[21] In re Holman, 92 B.R. 764 (Bankr. S.D. Ohio 1988).

[22] *E.g.*, In re Knaus, 889 F.2d 773 (8th Cir. 1989); Unified People's Fed. Credit Union v. Yates (In re Yates), 332 B.R. 1 (B.A.P. 10th Cir. 2005); In re Castillo, 456 B.R. 719 (Bankr. N.D. Ga. 2011).

[23] Rutherford v. Auto Cash, Inc. (In re Rutherford), 329 B.R. 886 (Bankr. N.D. Ga. 2005); Metromedia Fiber Network Servs. v. Lexent, Inc. (In re Metromedia Fiber Network, Inc.), 290 B.R. 487 (Bankr. S.D.N.Y. 2003); Nissan Motor Acceptance Corp. v. Baker, 239 B.R. 484 (N.D. Tex. 1999).

[24] *See infra* § 13.06 Effect of Discharge.

to file a financing statement perfecting its interest within twenty days of the time the debtor receives possession of the goods,[25] even if the debtor files a bankruptcy petition on April 7, before the twenty days has run out.[26] Similarly, creditors who must file continuation statements, or refile in another jurisdiction, to maintain the perfection of their security interests and thus preserve the pre-petition status quo, may do so.

[E]   Acts to Collect[27]

Section 362(a)(6) is the broadest prong of the automatic stay. It prohibits "*any act* to collect, assess, or recover a claim against the debtor that arose before the commencement of the case."[28] This restricts virtually every type of collection action a creditor might take. It even stops creditors from continuing the barrage of dunning letters and phone calls designed to persuade the debtor to pay.[29] Creditors who persist, after learning of the debtor's bankruptcy petition, run the risk of liability for actual and punitive damage awards.[30] Colleges that refuse to provide students with a transcript, until they pay their discharged tuition debt, violate the automatic stay.[31]

However, a commercial trash hauler who dumped a container of fresh trash on the home driveway of the debtor's vice president did not violate the automatic stay. The court said that the creditor's retaliatory actions were offensive and improper, tortious and possibly criminal, but were not an "act to collect."[32]

Although creditors are permitted to discriminate against those who discharge their debts in bankruptcy, they are not allowed to condition their willingness to deal on the debtor's willingness to pay. For example, in *In re Sechuan City, Inc.*,[33] the creditor (a hotel) violated the stay when it tried to coerce payment from the debtor (the restaurant in the hotel) by refusing to allow restaurant patrons to order from the hotel bar and by posting signs that encouraged hotel guests not to use the restaurant. In *In re WVF Acquisition, LLC*, the court assessed $50,000 in punitive damages against an internet service provider who terminated the debtor's internet service in wilful violation of the stay.[34] And, in *In re Sportfame of Ohio,*

---

[25] *See* U.C.C. § 9-317(e) (2010).

[26] Bankruptcy Code § 362(b)(3). *See infra* § 8.03[A][2] Perfection of Certain Pre-Petition Security Interests.

[27] Daniel Keating, *Offensive Uses of the Bankruptcy Stay*, 45 Vand. L. Rev. 71 (1992).

[28] Bankruptcy Code § 362(a)(6) (emphasis added).

[29] In re Waldo, 417 B.R. 854, 889-890 (Bankr. E.D. Tenn. 2009).

[30] *E.g.*, In re White, 410 B.R. 322 (Bankr. M.D. Fla. 2009) (creditor's post-petition phone calls to debtor's "emergency contacts" and dozens of communications with the debtor warranted award of $5000 actual and $10,000 punitive damages for wilful violation of the stay); In re Perviz, 302 B.R. 357 (Bankr. N.D. Ohio 2003) (debtor awarded $8,000 punitive damages).

[31] In re Kuehn, 563 F.3d 289 (7th Cir. 2009) (Easterbrook, J.) (violation of automatic stay and discharge injunction).

[32] In re The Original Barefoot Floors of Am., Inc., 412 B.R. 769 (Bankr. E.D. Va. 2009).

[33] In re Sechuan City, Inc., 96 B.R. 37, 40-42 (Bankr. E.D. Pa. 1989).

[34] *E.g.*, In re WVF Acquisition, LLC, 420 B.R. 902 (Bankr. S.D. Fla. 2009).

Inc.,[35] one of the debtor's suppliers was held in contempt for refusing to deal with the debtor, even for cash, with the sole purpose of trying to collect on its pre-petition debt. If it had simply refused to do business with the debtor, it would not have violated the stay. But indicating its willingness to continue to deal with the debtor if the debtor repaid the pre-petition debt made its refusal a violation of the stay.[36]

Public utilities are subject to additional restrictions.[37] Section 366 prohibits a utility, such as a telephone, electric, water, or natural gas supplier, from refusing to provide service to a debtor or from altering the terms of continued service to a debtor, solely because of the debtor's use of bankruptcy to discharge its debt for past service.[38] However, these utility providers may discontinue service if the debtor fails to supply adequate assurance of payment for future services, within twenty days after the debtor's "order for relief."[39]

With other creditors, courts draw a line between efforts to collect and those that merely inform the debtor of the obligation or of the creditor's refusal to do business.[40] For example, secured creditors are permitted to engage in a limited amount of contact with the debtor in connection with negotiations leading to a reaffirmation agreement that would permit the debtor to retain the collateral.[41] Thus, they may continue to send billing statements to the debtor, "as long as [they] are not coercive."[42] Unless creditors are permitted to communicate their willingness to allow the debtor to reaffirm these debts, reaffirmation agreements would be virtually impossible.[43] The debtor might also need to receive information from secured lenders, particularly mortgage lenders, to learn about increases in property taxes or insurance premiums.[44] However, where the creditor goes further, by sending a payment coupon that requests voluntary payment,[45] or demands immediate payment of an overdue debt,[46] the creditor violates the automatic stay.

---

[35] Sportframe of Ohio, Inc. v. Wilson Sporting Goods Co. (In re Sportfame of Ohio, Inc.), 40 B.R. 47 (Bankr. N.D. Ohio 1987).

[36] *See* Donald Wayne, Note, *Postbankruptcy Refusals to Deal with the Debtor and the Automatic Stay: A Fresh Approach*, 72 Wash. U. L.Q. 507 (1994).

[37] *See infra* § 9.04 Utility Service.

[38] Bankruptcy Code § 366(a).

[39] Bankruptcy Code § 366(b). *See* Weisel v. Dominion Peoples Gas Co. (In re Weisel), 400 B.R. 457 (Bankr. W.D. Pa. 2009).

[40] Morgan Guaranty Trust Co. v. Am. Sav. and Loan Assoc., 804 F.2d 1487, 1491 n.4 (9th Cir. 1986).

[41] *See* Jamo v. Katahdin Fed. Credit Union (In re Jamo), 283 F.3d 392 (1st Cir. 2002); Pertuso v. Ford Motor Credit Co., 233 F.3d 417 (6th Cir. 2000).

[42] Morgan Guar. Trust Co. v. Am. Sav. & Loan Ass'n (In re Morgan Guar. Trust Co.), 804 F.2d 1487, 1491 (9th Cir.1986); Knowles v. Bayview Loan Serv. (In re Knowles), 442 B.R. 150 (B.A.P. 1st Cir. 2011); Cousins v. CitiFinancial Mortgage Co. (In re Cousins), 404 B.R. 281, 287 (Bankr. S.D. Ohio 2009).

[43] *See* Pertuso v. Ford Motor Credit Co., 233 F.3d 417, 423 (6th Cir. 2000).

[44] In re Zotow, 432 B.R. 252 (B.A.P. 9th Cir. 2010) (informational notice concerning escrow payment); Connor v. Countrywide Bank, N.A. (In re Connor), 366 B.R. 133, 137-38 (Bankr. D. Hawaii 2007).

[45] In re Draper, 237 B.R. 502, 506 (Bankr. M.D. Fla. 1999).

[46] In re Butz, 444 B.R. 301 (Bankr. M.D. Pa. 2011).

Along the same lines, creditors' bookkeeping entries, such as recording fees charged to the debtor in their own internal records regarding the debtor's account, are not violations of the automatic stay. They are not acts to collect under § 362(a)(6), and do not violate § 362(a)(3) or (a)(5)'s prohibitions of actions to obtain possession of the estate's property or those to create, perfect, or enforce a lien.[47]

[F] Setoff

While § 553 preserves any rights that a creditor may have to set off their claims against the debtor against mutual debts owed by the parties to one another, § 362(a)(7) prohibits any exercise of those setoff rights without court authorization.

Rights of setoff frequently arise between debtors and the banks where they hold their accounts. For example, if Franklin Manufacturing borrows $750,000 from Peninsula Bank while it has $600,000 on deposit with the bank, the bank may, before bankruptcy, exercise its right of setoff against the account to satisfy $600,000 of the $750,000 debt. However, § 362(a)(7) restricts the bank's ability to exercise its setoff rights after Franklin's case commences. Instead, the bank must obtain an order to lift the stay in order to set off the debts.

On the other hand, banks are permitted to impose a "freeze" on the debtor's account to protect their interest in the debtor's funds. Although some courts held that such freezes were violations of the automatic stay, the Supreme Court, in *Citizens Bank of Maryland v. Strumpf*, held that these administrative freezes did not violate the automatic stay but merely preserved the status quo between the parties. The Court ruled that §§ 542(b) and 553(b), which also deal with setoff, manifested Congress's intent to preserve the status quo in this manner.[48] The *Strumpf* Court's language, focusing on the temporary nature of the freeze, suggested that creditors who impose a freeze on a debtor's account should probably seek prompt relief from the automatic stay or request adequate protection of their setoff rights to avoid committing a violation.[49] This language has led subsequent courts to rule that extended freezes, imposed without an effort to seek relief from the stay, are impermissible.[50]

Section 362(b)(26) supplies a limited exception that permits a taxing authority, like the IRS or a state or local tax department, to set off any prepetition tax debt against a debtor's income tax refund.

The stay does not affect the creditor's rights in any other way. The creditor's right of setoff is included within the definition of a secured claim under § 506, and entitles the creditor to adequate protection for the value of its interest in the debtor's account. Moreover, the debtor is not permitted to withdraw the funds in its

---

[47] In re Jacks, 642 F.3d 1323 (11th Cir. 2011).

[48] 516 U.S. 16 (1995). The Court also held that an administrative freeze did not violate § 362(a)(3)'s proscription against acts to obtain possession of estate property, because the debtor's bank account was nothing more than an obligation to pay the deposited funds to the debtor.

[49] *See* Gregory P. Johnson, *Following* Strumpf — *Will Allowance of an Administrative Freeze Begin the Erosion of the Automatic Stay?*, 5 J.Bankr.L. & Prac. 193 (1995).

[50] *E.g.*, In re Radcliffe, 563 F.3d 627 (7th Cir. 2009).

account without court permission, because this would be an unauthorized use of cash collateral in violation of § 363(c)(2).[51] Thus, while the stay prevents the creditor from exercising its setoff rights, the value of that right is protected.

[G] Tax Court Proceedings

Section 362(a)(8) restricts "the commencement or continuation of a proceeding before the United States Tax Court" concerning a corporate debtor's tax liability for any tax period determined by the bankruptcy court or concerning the tax liability of an individual debtor for a tax period that ended before the date of the order for relief.[52] Because § 362(a)(1) already enjoins the commencement or continuation of any judicial, administrative, or other action or proceeding against the debtor, this final portion of the automatic stay adds little additional protection for the debtor or the estate. Nevertheless, by staying all Tax Court proceedings against anyone regarding the debtor's tax liability, § 362(a)(8) protects the debtor against pressure from corporate officers who might be responsible for the corporation's taxes or for penalties associated with its failure to remit the corporation's withholding taxes to the government.

§ 8.03 EXCEPTIONS TO THE AUTOMATIC STAY

There are many limitations on the automatic stay. More are added it seems, every time Congress goes into session. Some of the exceptions deal with the private rights of creditors; others deal with enforcement of the government's police and other regulatory powers. Some permit governmental entities to protect their financial interests. An important set of exceptions was added in 2005 insulating derivative and other capital markets transactions, in the interest of maintaining the stability of the banking system and financial markets.[53] Most of the exceptions attempt to balance the interests of creditors in preserving the value of the debtor's estate and permitting an orderly administration of the debtor's assets with the interests of enforcing the government's police power.

[A] Private Rights Exceptions to the Stay

A few exceptions to the automatic stay protect the private rights of the debtor's creditors. Most of these exceptions facilitate the purposes of the automatic stay to preserve creditors' rights as if the bankruptcy case had never been filed, without depriving the estate of valuable property. Others exceptions protect specific creditors, such as the debtor's spouse and children, who depend on the debtor for support.

---

[51] *See infra* § 9.03[B] Use of Cash Collateral.

[52] Bankruptcy Code § 362(a)(8).

[53] Bankruptcy Code §§ 555, 556, 559 & 560.

[1] Family and Domestic Obligations

The first of the major private rights exceptions to the automatic stay deals with a variety of family and domestic obligations. Significantly, the automatic stay does not apply to the commencement or continuation of actions to collect a "domestic support obligation."[54] The 2005 Amendments expanded this exception to permit "the withholding of income that *is property of the estate* or *property of the debtor* for payment of a domestic support obligation under a judicial or administrative order or a statute."[55] This permits wage garnishments to continue, if the garnishment is for spousal or child support. In a Chapter 7 case, where the debtor's post-petition earnings are not property of the estate,[56] the garnishment can continue against these post-petition earnings.[57] In a Chapter 13 case, where the debtor's earnings are part of the estate,[58] the garnishment can nevertheless continue, uninterrupted by the debtor's bankruptcy case.

The Code also permits the commencement or continuation a variety of actions involving family relationships, including those:

- to establish paternity;

- to establish or modify a domestic support obligation;

- concerning child custody or visitation rights;

- for dissolution of a marriage (but not including the division of estate property); and

- regarding domestic violence.[59]

These actions might distract the debtor from his bankruptcy case, but they do not otherwise affect the administration of the bankruptcy case or impinge upon the bankruptcy court's authority over estate property. Moreover, the Code permits actions that are designed to facilitate recovery of support, such as suspending the debtor's driver's or other licenses, reporting the overdue support to a credit reporting agency, intercepting tax refunds, and enforcing medical obligations as specified by the Social Security Act.[60]

These provisions are largely consistent with other Code provisions regarding domestic support obligations, which make support debts non-dischargeable,[61] give support obligations priority over other creditors,[62] and even authorize dismissal of

---

[54] *See* Bankruptcy Code § 101(14A).

[55] Bankruptcy Code § 362(a)(2)(C) (emphasis added).

[56] Bankruptcy Code § 362(b)(2)(B).

[57] Bankruptcy Code § 541(a)(6). *See supra* § 7.02[F][2] Earnings from Individual Debtor's Post-Petition Services Excluded.

[58] Bankruptcy Code § 1306. *See infra* § 18.04 Property of the Chapter 13 Estate.

[59] Bankruptcy Code § 362(b)(2)(A)(i)-(v).

[60] Bankruptcy Code § 362(b)(2)(D)-(G).

[61] Bankruptcy Code §§ 523(a)(5), 1141(d)(2), 1328(a)(2). *See generally infra* § 13.03[B][5][a] Domestic Support Obligations.

[62] Bankruptcy Code § 507(a)(1). See *infra* § 10.04[A][1] Support Claims.

the debtor's Chapter 11, 12, or 13 case if they are not paid.[63]

[2] Perfection of Certain Pre-Petition Property Interests

The second major private rights exception gives limited relief to persons who acquire interests in the debtor's property just before bankruptcy subject to a relation back rule. The biggest impact of this exception is its protection of purchase money security interests acquired shortly before a bankruptcy case commences. If a purchase money security interest is created during the preference period (which is usually ninety days before the filing of the bankruptcy petition),[64] it must be perfected within twenty days after the debtor receives possession of the collateral to be effective against subsequent lien creditors and the trustee.[65] Section 362(b)(3) permits purchase money lenders to file a financing statement to perfect their security interests, despite the automatic stay.[66]

For example, suppose that on June 1, Peninsula Bank loans Franklin Manufacturing $100,000 to enable Franklin to purchase a new piece of equipment. On the same day, the parties sign a security agreement giving Peninsula a security interest in the item, which is delivered to Franklin a week later, on June 7. On June 20, before Peninsula files a financing statement to perfect its purchase money security interest, Franklin files a bankruptcy petition. Section 362(b)(3) permits Peninsula to take advantage of the U.C.C.'s twenty-day grace period and file its financing statement after Franklin's bankruptcy petition is filed. This, together with other limits on the trustee's avoiding powers, protects Peninsula's purchase money security interest from avoidance by the trustee.

Section 362(b)(3) also permits creditors with already perfected interests to take action, such as filing a continuation statement, to ensure that perfection of their interest does not lapse.[67] Thus, if the five-year effective period of a U.C.C. financing statement is scheduled to lapse after the debtor's petition is filed, the secured creditor may file a continuation statement without violating the automatic stay.[68] Likewise, a creditor may file a new financing statement in a second state, in order to maintain the perfected status of a security interest already perfected under the law of one state.[69]

[3] Commercial Real Estate Leases

Section 362(a)(10) permits lessors of commercial real estate to retake possession of the leased premises when the term of the lease expires either before the case commenced or while it is pending. For example, if the debtor occupies space in a

---

[63] Bankruptcy Code §§ 1112(b)(4)(P), 1208(c)(10), 1307(c)(11).

[64] Bankruptcy Code § 547(b)(4)(A). *See infra* § 15.02[E] Preference Period.

[65] U.C.C. § 9-317(e) (2010).

[66] Bankruptcy Code § 362(b)(3).

[67] *See* U.C.C. § 9-515 (2010).

[68] H.R. Rep. 103-835, 21 (1994), *reprinted in* 1994 U.S.C.C.A.N. 3340, 3354. *See* In re Stetson & Assocs., Inc., 330 B.R. 613, 623 (Bankr. E.D. Tenn. 2005).

[69] *E.g.*, In re Halmar Distribs., Inc., 968 F.2d 121 (1st Cir. 1992) (refiling to continue perfection after debtor moved to a new state not in violation of the stay).

shopping mall under a lease that expired on June 1, 2013, two months after it filed its bankruptcy petition, the lessor may retake possession of the premises, despite the automatic stay. This permits landlords to evict holdover tenants, without the risk of running afoul of the bankruptcy court.[70]

[4] Presentment of Negotiable Instruments

The last important private rights exception is rooted in the requirements of U.C.C. Article 3 for enforcement of negotiable instruments. The exception permits a creditor to satisfy the U.C.C.'s procedural requirements of presentment, notice of dishonor, and in the rare circumstances where it is still necessary, protest, without violating the stay.[71] The creditor may not receive payment, but § 362(b)(11) prevents the creditor's rights from being prejudiced by its failure to take these key procedural steps.

[5] Other Private Rights Exceptions to the Automatic Stay

There are a wide variety of additional exceptions to the automatic stay that apply only in narrow circumstances. Although they are important to the participants in the affected transactions, their scope is too narrow for discussion here. They deal with:

- various setoffs in certain securities and commodities contracts, repurchase agreements, swap agreements, and master netting agreements;[72]

- withholding of wages to repay loans from employer sponsored pension plans;[73]

- acts to enforce liens or security interests in real estate after relief from the stay was granted in an earlier case filed by the same debtor;[74]

- acts to enforce liens and security interests in real estate in a case filed by an ineligible debtor;[75]

- enforcement of pre-petition eviction judgments;[76]

---

[70] John M. Tyson, *Automatic Stays and Administrative Expenses: Rights and Remedies of Landlords and Tenants in Bankruptcy Proceedings*, 31 Campbell L. Rev. 413, 417 (2009).

[71] Bankruptcy Code § 362(b)(11).

[72] Bankruptcy Code § 362(b)(6), (7), (17), (27); Jeanne L. Schroeder, *Repo Madness: The Characterization of Repurchase Agreements Under the Bankruptcy Code and the UCC*, 46 Syracuse L. Rev. 99 (1996); Shmuel Vasser, *Derivatives in Bankruptcy*, 60 Bus. Law. 1507, 1530 (2005).

[73] Bankruptcy Code § 362(b)(19); Lisa A. Napoli, *The Not-So-Automatic Stay: Legislative Changes to the Automatic Stay in a Case Filed by or Against an Individual Debtor*, 79 Am. Bankr. L.J. 749, 752 (2005). This is consistent with § 1322(f), which prevents a Chapter 13 plan from modifying the terms of this type of pension fund loan and excludes amounts paid to the pension fund from the debtor's disposable income.

[74] Bankruptcy Code § 362(b)(20).

[75] Bankruptcy Code § 362(b)(21).

[76] Bankruptcy Code § 362(b)(22); Alan M. Ahart, *The Inefficacy of the New Eviction Exceptions to the Automatic Stay*, 80 Am. Bankr. L.J. 125 (2006). Sections 362(l) & (m) provide a limited "safe harbor"

- actions to evict tenants due to illegal drug use on the premises;[77]

- certain post-petition mortgages recorded in connection with pre-petition real estate transfers;[78] and

- self-regulatory proceedings by private securities organizations, such as stock and commodities exchanges.[79]

[B] Public Rights Exceptions to the Stay — Governmental Action Permitted

The vast majority of exceptions to the automatic stay permit various types of governmental action, usually related to the government's police or other regulatory powers.

[1] Criminal Prosecutions

Bankruptcy is not a haven for criminals. The automatic stay does not provide even temporary protection for those accused of crimes. Section 362(b)(1) provides that "[t]he filing of a [bankruptcy] petition . . . does not operate as a stay . . . of the commencement or continuation of a criminal action against the debtor."[80]

Despite this exception, some criminal prosecutions border on "debt collection" either by governmental claimants or private parties, and bankruptcy courts are not insensitive to this point. For example, most states make issuing a check on insufficient funds a crime.[81] Zealous prosecutors sometimes use these statutes to operate as little more than a very powerful collection agency for disgruntled local merchants, by bringing criminal actions against debtors who have violated these statutes and subsequently dropping the charges if the debtor makes restitution to the merchant involved. Most courts hold that these criminal prosecutions do not violate the automatic stay.[82]

However, debtors sometimes seek a supplemental injunction under § 105, which permits the bankruptcy court to issue injunctions and to provide other relief as

---

from termination of the automatic stay in these circumstances, when the eviction judgment is due to a curable monetary default and the debtor or one of her dependents deposits rent with the court in an amount sufficient to cure the default. Bankruptcy Code § 362(l). *See, e.g.,* In re Griggsby, 404 B.R. 83 (Bankr. S.D.N.Y. 2009); In re Alberts 381 B.R. 171 (Bankr. W.D. Pa. 2008). *See* Eugene R. Wedoff, *Major Consumer Bankruptcy Effects of BAPCPA,* 2007 U. Ill. L. Rev. 31, 39.

[77] Bankruptcy Code § 362(b)(23).

[78] Bankruptcy Code § 362(b)(24). Section 362(b)(24) puts to rest questions raised by the Nithth Circuit's subsequently withdrawn decision in *Thompson v. Margen (In re McConville)* regarding whether recording certain mortgages violated the automatic stay. *See* H.R. Rep. No. 109-31, 75-76 (2005), *reprinted in* 2005 U.S.C.C.A.N. 88, 142-44 (*addressing* Thompson v. Margen (In re McConville), 84 F.3d 340 (9th Cir. 1996), *withdrawn,* 110 F.3d 47 (9th Cir.), *cert. denied,* 522 U.S. 966 (1997)).

[79] Bankruptcy Code § 362(b)(25).

[80] Bankruptcy Code § 362(b)(1).

[81] *E.g.,* Ohio Rev. Code § 2913.11 (Page Supp. 2012); N.Y. Penal Penal Law § 190.05 (McKinney 2010).

[82] Gruntz v. County of Los Angeles (In re Gruntz), 202 F.3d 1074, 1081 (9th Cir. 2000); Bartel v. Walsh (In re Bartel), 404 B.R. 584 (B.A.P. 1st Cir. 2009) (exception is absolute, regardless of whether the prosecution is being pursued in an effort to recover a debt).

necessary in furtherance of the provisions of the Bankruptcy Code.[83] Furthermore, creditors who bring the debtor's conduct to the attention of prosecutors, as part of an effort to have the debt collected, sometimes run afoul of the stay, even though the prosecution itself is not a violation.[84]

The issue is complicated by the interplay of federalism and the general reluctance of federal courts to interfere in state criminal matters. Because of these concerns, courts refuse to enjoin state criminal prosecutions unless they are brought in bad faith.[85] Courts sometimes deploy the more elaborate *Younger* abstention doctrine[86] to determine whether the court should abstain from interfering with state prosecutions. The *Younger* test examines whether the debtor lacks an adequate remedy at law, whether the debtor will suffer great and immediate irreparable injury if the proceeding is not restrained, and whether continuation of the prosecution would impair any of the debtor's federally created rights, such as his right to a bankruptcy discharge.[87]

The critical issue in actions to impose a supplemental stay under § 105 is whether the prosecutor's "principal motivation" in pursuing the prosecution is to collect a debt or to vindicate the public good.[88] Prosecutors who use their offices primarily to collect debts owed to local merchants are likely to be enjoined. Not surprisingly, this test rarely results in an injunction against continuation of the prosecution, but some courts take a more inventive approach and enjoin the creditor from participating in the efforts to prosecute the debtor.[89]

[2] Regulatory Enforcement

Similarly, the stay is mostly inapplicable to prevent the commencement or continuation of proceedings that "enforce [a] governmental unit's . . . police and regulatory power."[90] Whether an action is to enforce a police and regulatory power is determined by two tests: the "pecuniary purpose test and the public policy test."[91] Under the pecuniary purposes test, the focus is on "whether the governmental proceeding relates primarily to the protection of the government's pecuniary interest in the debtor's property, and not to matters of public safety."[92] Actions that

---

[83] Bankruptcy Code § 105(a). *See infra* § 8.05 Discretionary Stays.

[84] Pearce v. E.L.W. Corp. (In re Pearce), 400 B.R. 126 (Bankr. N.D. Iowa 2009).

[85] *E.g.*, Barnette v. Evans, 673 F.2d 1250 (11th Cir. 1982).

[86] Younger v. Harris, 401 U.S. 37 (1971).

[87] Barnette v. Evans, 673 F.2d 1250, 1252 (11th Cir. 1982); Winkler v. Rickert (In re Winkler), 151 B.R. 807 (Bankr. N.D. Ohio 1992).

[88] Evans v. Bank of Eureka Springs (In re Evans), 245 B.R. 852, 856-57 (Bankr. W.D. Ark. 2000). *But see* Gruntz v. County of Los Angeles (In re Gruntz), 202 F.3d 1074 (9th Cir. 2000).

[89] *See* In re Caldwell, 5 B.R. 740 (Bankr. W.D. Va. 1980).

[90] Bankruptcy Code § 362(b)(4). In 2005, exceptions for several specific governmental police and regulatory powers, and a broader generic exception for other police and regulatory powers, that had been split between former §§ 362(b)(4) and 362(b)(5) were merged into § 362(b)(4). Former § 362(b)(5) does not exist.

[91] Chao v. Hosp. Staffing Servs., Inc. 270 F.3d 374, 385 (6th Cir. 2001).

[92] *Id.*

are pursued to protect the government's pecuniary interest in the debtor's property are beyond the scope of the exception and are thus prohibited by the automatic stay. Under the public policy test, the court focuses on whether the action is brought primarily to resolve "private rights" or to "effectuate public policy."[93] Actions that primarily adjudicate the private rights of creditors remain subject to the stay.

For example, an action to force a polluter to desist from contaminating air, water, or land is not stayed when the polluter files a bankruptcy petition.[94] Environmental enforcement actions of this type are designed to protect the public from future harm.[95] Similarly, the stay does not apply to proceedings to compel a debtor to comply with local zoning ordinances,[96] or to impose sanctions against a disciplined attorney for participating in frivolous litigation.[97] These actions are all well within the state's police power.

On the other hand, many governments engage in a variety of commercial activities. Many cities operate water and electric departments and, like other public utilities, have customers who have not paid their utility bills. Actions to collect those bills are stayed; a utility's financial interest in being paid is not transformed into a police or regulatory power just because the utility happens to belong to the government.

Similarly, state colleges charge tuition and collect dormitory rent from their students. Actions to recover unpaid charges are pecuniary in nature and do not fall within the police power exception to the stay. Exercise of a government power for the purpose of vindicating a private pecuniary right, rather than a general public interest, is subject to the stay. Accordingly, actions to enforce money judgments are normally stayed.[98]

[3] Specific Governmental Pecuniary Interests

There are many narrow exceptions to the stay that protect certain governmental pecuniary interests. Beyond their listing here, they are not discussed further. They include:

- certain foreclosure proceedings brought by the Department of Housing and Urban Development;[99]

- certain Department of Transportation ship mortgage foreclosure proceedings;[100]

---

[93] *Id.*

[94] *See* Penn Terra Ltd. v. Dept. of Envtl. Res., 733 F.2d 267 (3d Cir. 1984).

[95] *See* Berg v. Good Samaritan Hosp., Inc. (In re Berg), 230 F.3d 1165 (9th Cir. 2000); Enron Corp. v. California (In re Enron Corp.), 314 B.R. 524 (Bankr. S.D.N.Y. 2004).

[96] Cournoyer v. Town of Lincoln, 790 F.2d 971 (1st Cir. 1986).

[97] In re Berg, 230 F.3d 1165 (9th Cir. 2000).

[98] *See* Penn Terra Ltd. v. Dept. of Envtl. Res., 733 F.2d 267 (3d Cir. 1984).

[99] Bankruptcy Code § 362(b)(8).

[100] Bankruptcy Code § 362(b)(12), (13).

- tax audit and assessment proceedings to administratively determine the debtor's tax liability;[101]

- proceedings regarding the accreditation, licensing, and eligibility of educational institutions to participate in guaranteed student loan programs;[102]

- creation and perfection of statutory liens securing certain ad valorem property taxes or special real estate taxes;[103]

- certain income tax refund setoffs;[104] and

- administrative exclusion of debtors from participating in certain federal health care programs, such as medicare.[105]

§ 8.04   CO-DEBTOR STAYS IN CHAPTERS 12 AND 13

In most bankruptcy proceedings, the automatic stay applies only to actions involving the debtor or the estate. Section 362 does not prevent a creditor from pursuing remedies against other persons or their property. Most significantly for a creditor, the stay does not affect its rights to collect from co-obligors, such as co-signers or guarantors.

A different rule applies in cases under Chapters 12 and 13. Both chapters impose a limited automatic stay that protects certain co-debtors. For the co-debtor stay to apply, two conditions must be met: the debt involved must be a consumer debt; and the co-debtor must be an individual, not an organization such as a corporation or partnership.[106] In addition, if the co-debtor is a professional surety — someone who is in the business of providing financial guarantees — the stay does not apply, even if the co-debtor is an individual.[107]

The legislative history confirms what is obvious from the Code's text; the co-debtor stay is designed to protect those who guaranteed obligations of friends or family members.[108] By doing so, the Code protects the debtor from the demands, both formal and informal, of the co-debtor. At least, that is the hope.

Although it is possible to imagine other situations in which the stay could apply, as a practical matter it is usually limited to circumstances such as a parent, spouse, or friend who has co-signed a note. Congress was concerned that because of the underlying relationship between these parties, the debtor would feel inordinate pressure to pay the obligation unless the co-debtor was protected, at least temporarily, by an automatic stay. Otherwise, the debtor's desire to pay his relatives and friends would disrupt the normal reorganization process. Congress may have

---

[101]   Bankruptcy Code § 362(b)(9). But proceedings before the United States Tax Court are restrained.

[102]   Bankruptcy Code § 362(b)(14), (15), (16).

[103]   Bankruptcy Code § 362(b)(18).

[104]   Bankruptcy Code § 362(b)(26).

[105]   Bankruptcy Code § 362(b)(28).

[106]   Bankruptcy Code §§ 1201(a), 1301(a).

[107]   Bankruptcy Code §§ 1201(a), 1301(a).

[108]   H.R. Rep. No. 95-595, 121-22 (1978), *reprinted in* 1978 U.S.C.C.A.N. 5963, 6081-82.

been naive about the degree to which the stay actually relieves pressure on the debtor; after all, the stay does not discharge the co-debtor's obligation but merely delays the enforcement of that obligation. Thus, the stay may not in fact be sufficient to shield the debtor from pressure from the guarantor.

These provisions are often colloquially referred to among bankruptcy professionals as the co-signer provisions. The term "co-signer" is somewhat misleading. It does not refer only to co-makers of an obligation; it encompasses all sureties. Indeed, although the word "co-signer" is used informally, the actual statutory text of §§ 1201 and 1301 provisions refer to any person who is liable on the debt with the debtor. Thus, it also applies when someone other than the debtor is jointly and severally liable with the debtor, such as someone who shared in the proceeds of the loan.

There is only one statutory exception to the co-debtor stay. Rooted in the requirements of U.C.C. Article 3 for enforcement of a negotiable instrument,[109] the exception permits the creditor to present a negotiable instrument and to give notice of its dishonor.[110] This exception is exactly the same as the exception to the automatic stay regarding actions to collect from the debtor in § 362(b)(11).[111]

Because the co-debtor stay is designed to protect the rehabilitative process, it does not apply in other situations. If the case is closed, dismissed, or converted to Chapter 7 or Chapter 11, the co-debtor stay terminates.[112] The stay may also be terminated by the court, as discussed in detail later in this chapter.[113]

§ 8.05 DISCRETIONARY STAYS[114]

Apart from these limited provisions in Chapter 12 and 13, the automatic stay does not prevent lawsuits or collection efforts against third parties who may be jointly liable for the debtor's obligations. Thus, shareholders, insurers, other tort-feasors, and others who may also be liable for these debts, are not protected from creditors' continuing efforts to collect.

Fortunately, the automatic stay is not the only source of the bankruptcy court's power to limit creditors' collection activities. Section 105 broadly empowers the

[109] See supra § 8.03[A][4] Presentment of Negotiable Instruments.

[110] Presentment, dishonor, and notice are required only for suretyship agreements manifested in a negotiable instrument, usually a promissory note. See generally U.C.C. §§ 3-419, 3-412 to 3-415 (2003).

[111] See supra § 8.03[A][4] Presentment of Negotiable Instruments.

[112] Bankruptcy Code §§ 1201(a)(2), 1301(a)(2).

[113] See infra § 8.06 Relief from the Automatic Stay; Duration and Termination.

[114] Alan M. Ahart, The Limited Scope of Implied Powers of a Bankruptcy Judge: A Statutory Court of Bankruptcy, Not a Court of Equity, 79 Am. Bankr. L.J. 1 (2005); Daniel B. Bogart, Resisting the Expansion of Bankruptcy Court Power Under Section 105 of the Bankruptcy Code: The All Writs Act and an Admonition from Chief Justice Marshall, 35 Ariz. St. L.J. 793 (2003); Ralph Brubaker, Nondebtor Releases and Injunctions in Chapter 11: Revisiting Jurisdictional Precepts and the Forgotten Callaway v. Benton Case, 72 Am. Bankr. L.J. 1 (1998); Steve H. Nickles & David G. Epstien, Another Way of Thinking About Section 105(a) and Other Sources of Supplemental Law Under the Bankruptcy Code, 3 Chap. L. Rev. 7 (2000); Barry L. Zaretsky, Co-Debtor Stays in Chapter 11 Bankruptcy, 73 Cornell L. Rev. 213 (1988).

court to "issue any order, process, or judgment that is necessary or appropriate to carry out the provisions of the [Bankruptcy Code]."[115] Courts sometimes use this language, which emulates the language of the Federal All Writs Act,[116] to impose temporary stays on actions taken by creditors against persons other than the debtor.

The normal rules governing the availability of equitable relief apply with equal force to injunctions issued under § 105. Before issuing an injunction, the court must find:

- the plaintiff is likely to succeed on the merits;

- irreparable injury will result unless the injunction is issued;

- issuing the injunction will not cause substantial harm to other interested parties; and

- the public interest is served by preserving the status quo until the merits of the controversy can fully be considered.[117]

Generally, discretionary injunctions are imposed only under circumstances where the progress of the bankruptcy case would be disrupted if relief is not granted. Indeed, many courts recast the first two parts of the four part test slightly to focus on whether (1) a reorganization is reasonably in prospect, and (2) failing to grant the injunction will cause irreparable harm to the debtor's chance of reorganizing.[118]

The most common situations in which co-debtor stays are sought are to protect insider guarantors such as a corporate debtor's controlling shareholders, officers, and directors, who, because of their relationship with the debtor, are frequently involved in the day-to-day management of the debtor's business. Courts sometimes enjoin actions against these individuals to enable them to devote all of their attention to the corporation's reorganization efforts.[119] Actions against insider guarantors who are not so heavily involved in the debtor's management, however, may be permitted to be continued.[120]

Injunctions are similarly sometimes granted because these individuals may contribute other personal assets to the reorganization process. Permitting some of the debtor's creditors from seeking recovery from those assets might end up impairing the debtor's overall efforts to reorganize by depriving it of access to those assets.[121]

---

[115] Bankruptcy Code § 105(a).

[116] 28 U.S.C. 1651(a) (2006).

[117] *See* A.H. Robins Co. v. Piccinin (In re A.H. Robbins Co.), 788 F.2d 994 (4th Cir. 1986).

[118] In re Otero Mills, Inc., 25 B.R. 1018 (D.N.M. 1982); In re FTL, Inc., 152 B.R. 61 (Bankr. E.D. Va. 1993).

[119] *See* United States v. Seitles, 106 B.R. 36 (S.D.N.Y. 1989); In re Otero Mills, Inc., 25 B.R. 1018 (D.N.M. 1982).

[120] *E.g.*, In re Third Eighty-Ninth Assocs., 138 B.R. 144, 145 (S.D.N.Y. 1992).

[121] FTL, Inc. v. Crestar Bank (In re F.T.L., Inc.), 152 B.R. 61 (Bankr. E.D. Va. 1993).

This same problem sometimes occurs when guarantees have been provided by the debtor's corporate affiliates, such as parent and subsidiary corporations, who have not filed their own Chapter 11 reorganization case. To the extent that corporate affiliates may contribute resources to the reorganization process, permitting actions against those affiliates to continue may well disrupt the Chapter 11 debtor's reorganization.

On the other hand, actions against insurers and sureties, who received payment for their guaranties, will not unduly distract the co-debtor from participating in the debtor's efforts to reorganize. However, if the action would deplete a fund that the debtor might use as part of its reorganization efforts, these types of suits might be prevented.[122] Of course, if these funds are part of the debtor's estate, actions to recover them violate the automatic stay of § 362(a),[123] and a supplemental stay is not necessary.

In other situations, a judgment against a third-party might either be the equivalent of a judgment against the debtor, or somehow interfere with assets of the debtor's estate. In *A.H. Robins Co. v. Piccinin*,[124] for example, the court issued an injunction preventing tort claimants from continuing their state court actions against Robins' co-defendants, including Robins' insurer. The court admitted that discretionary injunctions should be issued under § 105 only in "unusual circumstances" but determined that the situation in *Robins* met this standard. First, the court explained that, because of the "identity between the debtor and the third-party defendant, that the debtor [was] the real party defendant and that a judgment against the third-party defendant [would] in effect be a judgment or finding against the debtor."[125] In other words, if the third-party would be entitled to indemnification from the debtor, permitting a judgment to be entered against the third-party would have the same effect as a judgment against the debtor. In these circumstances, the debtor would find it necessary to assist in the defense of the action to protect its own interest and the interests of its other creditors.

Despite these and other cases in which a supplemental stay may be warranted, bankruptcy courts are extremely sparing in their exercise of power over non-bankruptcy proceedings concerning non-debtors. Only in the absence of any alternative is a court likely to enter such a discretionary stay. Moreover, the court is not likely to make the stay broader or longer than is absolutely necessary.

A closely related issue is whether § 105 justifies entry of a permanent injunction, restraining creditors from pursuing a co-debtor. A permanent injunction effectively discharges the co-debtor from his liability. Here, the court's authority is more questionable, but courts still sometimes find that extraordinary circumstances justify a post-confirmation injunction.[126]

---

[122] *E.g.*, Feld v. Zale Corp. (In re Zale Corp.), 62 F.3d 746 (5th Cir. 1995); Homsy v. Floyd (In re Vitek, Inc.), 51 F.3d 530 (5th Cir. 1995).

[123] *E.g.*, A.H. Robins Co., Inc. v. Piccinin (In re A.H. Robins Co., Inc.), 788 F.2d 994, 1001-1002 (4th Cir. 1986).

[124] 788 F.2d 994 (4th Cir. 1986).

[125] *Id.* at 999.

[126] *E.g.*, In re Master Mortgage Inv. Fund, Inc., 168 B.R. 930, 936 (Bankr. W.D. Mo. 1994).

In determining whether to grant a permanent injunction, courts frequently consider the following factors:

- whether there is identity of interest between the debtor and the non-debtor party;

- whether the non-debtor has contributed substantial assets to the debtor's reorganization;

- whether an injunction is essential to the debtor's reorganization;

- whether a substantial majority of creditors agree on the issuance of the injunction; and

- whether the debtor's Chapter 11 plan provides a mechanism for payment of all, or substantially all, of the claims or classes affected by the injunction.[127]

Similar injunctions are sometimes included in Chapter 11 plans of reorganization. When a plan containing such an injunction is confirmed, it is res judicata and prevents collateral attack in a subsequent suit to recover against the party, such as the debtor's insurer.[128] These so-called third-party releases are quite controversial.

§ 8.06 RELIEF FROM THE AUTOMATIC STAY; DURATION AND TERMINATION

The automatic stay does not last forever. It ends when the bankruptcy case ends. However, if the debtor receives a discharge, many features of the stay are continued through the discharge injunction of § 524, at least with respect to discharged debts.[129] It might also end, at least with respect to specific estate assets, when the trustee abandons specific assets, or when a secured creditor seeks and obtains relief from the stay, granting permission to continue with state court foreclosure proceedings against the specific property involved. These latter types of disputes, over whether creditors should be granted relief from the stay, are a critical part of any reorganization proceeding.

[A] Automatic Termination of the Stay

The automatic stay serves the limited purpose of giving the debtor in possession or trustee the opportunity to deal effectively with the property of the estate and the demands of creditors, while the bankruptcy case is pending. It terminates automatically when events in the bankruptcy case make it no longer necessary. In some circumstances, the stay automatically terminates to prevent debtors from using it in an abusive manner.

---

[127] *See* In re Swallen's, Inc., 210 B.R. 123 (Bankr. S.D. Ohio 1997); In re Master Mortgage Inv. Fund, Inc., 168 B.R. 930 (Bankr. W.D. Mo. 1994).

[128] Travelers Indem. Co. v. Bailey, 129 S. Ct. 2195 (2009).

[129] Bankruptcy Code § 524(c). *See infra* § 13.06[A] Discharge Injunction.

[1] Property No Longer in the Estate

The stay of any act against estate property terminates when the property is no longer part of the estate.[130] Property ceases to be part of the estate if it is abandoned, returned to the debtor because it is exempt, or revested in the debtor through a reorganization plan.[131] However, as other portions of the automatic stay remain in place until the case is closed or otherwise terminated, and the discharge stay of § 524 takes its place in many respects when the debtor is granted a discharge.

[2] Conclusion of the Bankruptcy Case

The stay of all other actions, including actions against the debtor, terminates when the case is closed or dismissed or when a discharge is granted or denied.[132] For example, if a case is dismissed under § 707(b) due to abuse, the debtor and the debtor's property are no longer protected by the automatic stay.[133] Likewise, if the debtor's Chapter 11 reorganization case is dismissed due to the absence of a reasonable likelihood of rehabilitation or the debtor's inability to consummate its confirmed plan,[134] the stay ends and creditors are free to pursue the debtor through the customary mechanisms in state court.

The fact that the stay terminates upon closure of the case or the grant of a discharge does not necessarily mean that the debtor is once again vulnerable to its creditors. If a discharge is granted, the discharge injunction of § 524 takes over where the automatic stay leaves off with respect to discharged debts.[135] However, although discharge relieves the debtor of his personal liability, it does not remove creditors' liens on the debtor's assets. Thus, termination of the automatic stay upon completion of the case leaves secured creditors free to pursue their collateral. To retain their property, debtors must come to some accommodation with the lien holder.

[3] Automatic Termination — Prior Petition Within One Year

The 2005 Amendments added provisions aimed at debtors who file repeated petitions in bad faith solely to take advantage of the stay, usually to stop a mortgage foreclosure. Section 362(c)(3) limits the duration of the automatic stay when the debtor has filed a previous petition within a year.[136] The automatic stay in the second case automatically terminates thirty days after the petition,[137] unless the court extends it. The automatic termination only applies in the case of an individual

---

[130] Bankruptcy Code § 362(c)(1).

[131] Bankruptcy Code § 1141(b).

[132] Bankruptcy Code § 362(c)(2).

[133] *See infra* § 17.03[B] Dismissal of Consumer Cases Due to Abuse.

[134] *See* Bankruptcy Code § 1112(b); *infra* § 19.05[B] Involuntary Conversion or Dismissal.

[135] Bankruptcy Code § 524(c). *See infra* § 13.06[A] Discharge Injunction.

[136] *See* In re Pope, 351 B.R. 14 (Bankr. D.R.I. 2006).

[137] Bankruptcy Code § 362(c)(3)(A).

or joint debtor and does not apply if the second case is under Chapters 11, 12, or 13 and was filed after dismissal of the earlier Chapter 7 case due to abuse under § 707(b).[138]

Courts have construed § 362(c)(3) in two ways.[139] Most courts conclude that the phrase "with respect to the debtor" unambiguously means that the stay terminates on the 30th day only with respect to the debtor and the debtor's property, but not with respect to property of the estate.[140] Other courts interpret the phrase in the broader context of § 362(c)(3) as a whole, and draw the conclusion that the automatic stay terminates in its entirety with respect to actions against the debtor, the debtor's property, or property of the estate.[141] According to these courts, the majority approach would be contrary to Congress' purpose of discouraging opportunistic and abusive petitions.[142]

The stay can be extended if the later case was filed in good faith with respect to all creditors whose actions are stayed.[143] The burden of proof on the question of good faith is on the party seeking to have the stay continued — usually the debtor.[144] A change in the debtor's financial circumstances, such as the debtor in *In re McMinn*, who suffered a postpetition injury that resulted in $40,000 in medical bills that were not covered by the plan, satisfies this burden.[145]

However, several specified circumstances create a presumption of bad faith that may be rebutted only by clear and convincing evidence.[146] This presumption arises with respect to all creditors if:

- the debtor was a debtor in more than one previous case within the preceding year;[147]

- the debtor's previous case was dismissed within the past year after the debtor failed to file documents required by the court, provide adequate protection required by the court, or perform the terms of a confirmed plan;[148] or

---

[138] Bankruptcy Code § 362(c)(3).

[139] Laura B. Bartell, *Staying the Serial Filer-Interpreting the New Exploding Stay Provisions of § 362(c)(3) of the Bankruptcy Code*, 82 Am. Bankr. L.J. 201 (2008).

[140] *See, e.g.*, Holcomb v. Hardeman (In re Holcomb), 380 B.R. 813 (B.A.P. 10th Cir. 2008); Jumpp v. Chase Home Fin., LLC (In re Jumpp), 356 B.R. 789 (B.A.P. 1st Cir. 2006).

[141] *E.g.*, Reswick v. Reswick (In re Reswick), 446 B.R. 362 (B.A.P. 9th Cir. 2011) (collecting cases).

[142] *See* In re Jupiter, 344 B.R. 754, 761 (Bankr. D.S.C. 2006).

[143] *See* In re Havner, 336 B.R. 98 (Bankr. M.D.N.C. 2006).

[144] *See* In re Kurtzahn, 337 B.R. 356 (Bankr. D. Minn. 2006); In re Baldassaro, 338 B.R. 178 (Bankr. D.N.H. 2006).

[145] In re McMinn, 452 B.R. 247 (Bankr. D. Kan. 2011).

[146] Bankruptcy Code § 362(c)(3)(C)(i); In re Collins, 335 B.R. 646, 651 (Bankr. S.D. Tex. 2005); In re Baldassaro, 338 B.R. 178 (Bankr. D.N.H. 2006).

[147] Bankruptcy Code § 362(c)(3)(C)(i)(I).

[148] Bankruptcy Code § 362(c)(3)(C)(i)(II).

- the debtor's financial circumstances or personal affairs have not substantially changed since the debtor's most recent case was dismissed.[149]

The presumption also arises with respect to a single creditor if the debtor's previous case was dismissed while that creditor's motion for relief from the stay was still pending or had not yet been resolved.[150] This takes direct aim at debtors who file a petition to stop a creditor's foreclosure action, dismiss the case when the creditor's motion for relief from the stay seems likely to be granted, and then file a subsequent case when the creditor's subsequent foreclosure proceeding is close to fruition.

An exception to these presumptions is hidden in § 362(i). The presumption of bad faith does not arise if the debtor's earlier case is dismissed "due to the creation of a debt repayment plan."[151]

[4] Automatic Termination — Multiple Prior Petitions Within One Year

Section 362(c)(4) applies in similar fashion, but more aggressively, to debtors who are repeat offenders — those who have had two or more bankruptcy cases dismissed within the prior year. With respect to these debtors, the automatic stay does not go into effect at all.[152] The limiting language that appears in § 362(c)(3), discussed above, limiting the effect of the stay's automatic termination does not appear in § 362(c)(4).

Assume, for example, that Gail and Charlie file a Chapter 13 petition in June, 2013, but subsequently dismiss it. In September, 2013, they file a Chapter 7 petition which is dismissed because of their failure to file the required schedules. If in January 2014 they file a third petition, the automatic stay does not take effect, ongoing lawsuits are not restrained, and "upon request of a party in interest, the court *shall* promptly enter an order confirming that no stay is in effect."[153] Thus, the stay is never imposed and creditors have the right to obtain an order from the bankruptcy court, that they can show to state court judges, that validates their assertions that the stay does not impair continuation of their collection efforts.

The debtor has the opportunity to invoke the stay, as to all or some creditors, by demonstrating to the court, after notice and a hearing, that the current case "is in good faith as to the creditors to be stayed."[154] But any stay obtained only goes into effect when the court enters its order — in other words, for debtors with multiple repeat petitions, the stay is not automatic at all. Moreover, in the hearing regarding the debtor's good faith, the debtor is burdened with the same presumption that the case was filed "not in good faith" in the circumstances where a similar assumption exists under § 362(c)(3), discussed above.[155]

---

[149] Bankruptcy Code § 362(c)(3)(C)(i)(III).

[150] Bankruptcy Code § 362(c)(3)(C)(ii).

[151] Bankruptcy Code § 365(i).

[152] Bankruptcy Code § 362(c)(4)(A)(i). *E.g.* In re Bates, 446 B.R. 301 (B.A.P. 8th Cir. 2011).

[153] Bankruptcy Code § 362(c)(4)(A)(ii).

[154] Bankruptcy Code § 362(c)(4)(B).

[155] *See supra* § 8.06[A][3] Automatic Termination — Prior Petition Within One Year.

[5]   Individual Debtor's Failure to File Statement of Intention

Section 362(h) terminates the stay in cases involving individual debtors who fail to comply with § 521(a)(2).[156] It requires individual debtors to file a "statement of intention with respect to the retention or surrender" of property subject to a security interest within thirty days of filing their petition.[157] Section 521(a)(6) further requires the debtor to enter into a reaffirmation agreement with the creditor holding the security interest, redeem the property pursuant to § 722, or turn the property over to the creditor within forty-five days of the "first meeting of creditors" under § 341.[158] Section 362(h) puts teeth into these requirements by terminating the stay with respect to the creditor's collateral if the debtor fails to take these actions.[159] There is an exception to the automatic termination of the stay if the trustee demonstrates that the property involved is of "consequential value or benefit to the estate."[160]

[B]   Relief from Stay Upon Request of a Party[161]

Creditors may also obtain relief from the automatic stay upon application to the court. Secured creditors are those most likely to obtain this relief, which is most commonly granted to protect them from losses they may suffer if their foreclosure is delayed.

Consider, for example, a security interest held by Peninsula Bank in $100,000 worth of equipment owned by Franklin Manufacturing. When Franklin files its Chapter 11 bankruptcy petition and becomes a debtor-in-possession, Peninsula Bank is stayed from repossessing the equipment, even if Franklin is in default. Assume further that Franklin defaulted by permitting the insurance policy it carried on the equipment to lapse due to nonpayment of premiums. Without the automatic stay, Peninsula could have repossessed and sold the equipment. If a fire at Franklin Manufacturing's factory destroys the collateral, Peninsula will lose its collateral and become unsecured. In effect, the automatic stay has impaired Peninsula's secured status.[162]

There are many less dramatic examples. Even properly maintained equipment depreciates in value over time. If the debtor fails to make regular payments, which undoubtedly include an interest component, the amount of the debt increases; this may result in unpaid debts that would never had been incurred if the creditor had been permitted to foreclose and sell the collateral. Moreover, as time passes and the debtor continues to use the collateral, it probably depreciates in value due to

---

[156] Bankruptcy Code § 362(h).

[157] Bankruptcy Code § 521(a)(2). *See infra* § 12.08[D] Debtor's Statement of Intent.

[158] Bankruptcy Code § 521(a)(6).

[159] *See* Samson v. W. Capital Partners, LLC (In re Blixseth), 684 F.3d 865 (9th Cir. 2012).

[160] Bankruptcy Code § 362(h)(2). *See* In re Record, 347 B.R. 450 (Bankr. M.D. Fla. 2006).

[161] David Gray Carlson, *Junior Secured Creditors and the Automatic Stay*, 6 Am. Bankr. Inst. L. Rev. 249 (1998).

[162] *E.g.*, In re Delaney-Morin, 304 B.R. 365 (B.A.P. 9th Cir. 2003).

normal wear and tear. Shifts in market interest rates may mean that the lender is involuntarily locked into a transaction that is less profitable than a new one might be. Thus, the automatic stay may worsen the creditor's position each day that the stay remains in effect. The Bankruptcy Code's rules regarding "adequate protection" and "relief from the automatic stay" are designed to mitigate these harms.

Section 362(d) sets out the rules for relief from the stay. Its key language provides:

> On request of a party in interest and after notice and a hearing, the court shall grant relief from the stay . . . such as by terminating, annulling, modifying, or conditioning such stay —
>
> (1) for cause, including the lack of adequate protection of an interest in property of such party in interest; or
>
> (2) with respect to a stay of an act against property . . . if —
>
> (A) the debtor does not have an equity in such property; and
>
> (B) such property is not necessary to an effective reorganization.

Section 365 provides two additional grounds for relief from the stay that apply to single-asset real estate cases[163] and to creditors with mortgages or other enforceable liens on the debtor's real estate.[164]

[1] For Cause: Lack of Adequate Protection

Most automatic stay litigation involves § 362(d)(1). It requires the court to grant relief from the stay "for cause, including the lack of adequate protection of an interest in property." Although the phrase "for cause" encompasses a number of other matters, nearly all of the disputes under § 362(d)(1) deal with "adequate protection" of a secured creditor's interest in its collateral.

Secured creditors frequently respond to a debtor's reorganization case by asking the court for relief from the automatic stay to permit them to foreclose, insisting that their interest in the collateral is not adequately protected. Debtors respond that they have provided adequate protection to the creditor and that the court should keep the stay in place.[165] If a secured creditor is granted relief from the stay and permitted to foreclose, the debtor has little chance of reorganizing. Without its land, equipment, or inventory, the debtor is likely to cease operations. Accordingly, debtors regard motions for relief from the stay as vital threats to the reorganization process and the ongoing business that it seeks to protect. The adequate protection standard attempts to balance secured creditors' interests in preventing the deterioration of their secured position with debtors' and unsecured creditors' interests in preserving the chance for a successful reorganization.

---

[163] Bankruptcy Code § 362(d)(3). *See infra* § 8.06[B][4] Single-Asset Real Estate Collateral.

[164] Bankruptcy Code § 362(c)(4). *See infra* § 8.06[5] Foreclosure in Cases Filed to Delay, Hinder, or Defraud Creditors.

[165] They sometimes also respond by seeking to avoid the creditor's security interest via one of the trustee's avoiding powers.

The concept of adequate protection is deeply rooted in the traditional respect given to property rights in bankruptcy. Although such respect may not be constitutionally required, it derives from the same concern for property rights that underlies the Fifth and Fourteenth Amendments to the Constitution.[166] The legislative history of the adequate protection standard reflects its quasi-constitutional roots:

> The concept is derived from the 5th Amendment protection of property interests. It is not intended to be confined strictly to the Constitutional protection required, however. This section, and the concept of adequate protection, is based as much on policy grounds as on Constitutional grounds. Secured creditors should not be deprived of the benefit of their bargain. There may be situations in bankruptcy where giving a secured creditor an absolute right to his bargain may be impossible, or seriously detrimental to the bankruptcy laws. Thus, this section recognizes the availability of alternate means of protecting a secured creditor's interest. Though the creditor might not receive his bargain in kind, the purpose of the section is to insure that the secured creditor receives in value essentially what he bargained for.[167]

The earliest formulations of the doctrine long predate the Code.[168] Indeed, § 361, which deals with adequate protection, is largely a codification of prior case law. It refers to two specific methods of giving adequate protection, and sets a standard by which other methods are to be measured.

First, adequate protection may be given by making cash payments to the creditor.[169] Cash payments are one of the most common forms of adequate protection. For example, if the collateral is depreciating at a rate of $300 per month, the debtor might provide the secured creditor with adequate protection payments of $300 per month to compensate it for this loss in value. If the debtor lacks the cash to make the required payments and is otherwise unable to provide the creditor with adequate protection, the creditor is entitled to relief from the automatic stay and will likely foreclose. If continued use of the collateral is essential to the debtor's ability to remain in business, its inability to make the $300 monthly payments will end its effort to reorganize.

Section 361(2) permits the debtor to provide adequate protection by providing the claimant with an additional or replacement lien. Thus, instead of making cash payments to make up for the $300 monthly depreciation, Franklin might adequately protect Peninsula by giving it a post-petition security interest on other property in which the debtor has some equity. This alternative is valuable to debtors that have limited cash flow but significant unencumbered assets.

---

[166] Adequate protection is largely irrelevant where unsecured creditors are concerned. *See* In re Tellier, 125 B.R. 348 (Bankr. D.R. I. 1991).

[167] H.R. Rep. No. 95-595, at 339 (1977), *reprinted in* 1978 U.S.C.C.A.N. 5962, 6295.

[168] *See* In re Murel Holding Corp., 75 F.2d 941 (2d Cir. 1935).

[169] Bankruptcy Code § 361(1).

Alternatively, depending on the value of the collateral, the presence of an "equity cushion" in the collateral might provide adequate protection. Alternative forms of adequate protection are sufficient if, in words borrowed from Judge Learned Hand in *In re Murel Holding Co.*,[170] they "result in the realization [by the creditor] of the indubitable equivalent" of the creditor's interest in the collateral.[171]

Judge Hand's opinion in *Murel Holding* provided more than a catchphrase. It supplied an attitude of skepticism toward anything but cash or other tangible property as a suitable equivalent for a creditor's property interest. The plan in *In re Murel Holding* substituted only a doubtfully secured and speculative promise of future payment for what otherwise would have been an immediate realization on a property interest. Hand found this inadequate and even suggested that permitting such a substitution might be unconstitutional. He explained:

> [W]e are to remember not only the underlying purposes of the section, but the constitutional limitations to which it must conform. It is plain that "adequate protection" must be completely compensatory; and that payment ten years hence is not generally the equivalent of payment now. Interest is indeed the common measure of the difference, but a creditor who fears the safety of his principal will scarcely be content with that; he wishes to get his money or at least the property. We see no reason to suppose that the statute was intended to deprive him of that in the interest of junior holders, unless by a substitute of the most indubitable equivalence.[172]

The Code supplies little guidance about what constitutes an indubitable equivalent; the one thing we are told is that it is not sufficient to give the creditor an administrative priority claim.[173] The protection must be something more tangible and certain than that.

The legislative history provides some suggestions but emphasizes flexibility:

> The [indubitable equivalent] method gives the parties and the courts flexibility by allowing such other relief as will result in the realization by the protected entity of the value of its interest in the property involved . . . . For example, another form of adequate protection might be the guarantee by a third party outside the judicial process of compensation for any loss incurred in the case. . . . The paragraph also defines, more clearly than the others, the general concept of adequate protection, by requiring such relief as will result in the realization of value. It is the general category, and as such, is defined by the concept involved rather than any particular method of adequate protection.[174]

---

[170] 75 F.2d 941 (2d Cir. 1935).

[171] Bankruptcy Code § 361(3).

[172] 75 F.2d at 942.

[173] Bankruptcy Code § 361(3).

[174] H.R. Rep. No. 95-595, at 340 (1977), *reprinted in* 1978 U.S.C.C.A.N. 5962, 6296.

An equity cushion frequently satisfies the indubitable equivalent standard of § 361(3).[175] If the collateral is worth sufficiently more than the amount of the secured creditor's claim, the cushioning effect of this additional value supplies the creditor with adequate protection against a wide variety of risks, such as depreciation and the accumulation of interest on the creditor's fully secured claim.[176] For example, if the collateral for Peninsula Bank's $20,000 claim is worth $100,000, the $80,000 of equity protects the debtor against quite a bit of depreciation. Courts have routinely ruled that much smaller equity cushions are more than sufficient to protect a secured creditor from harm due to normal wear and tear, or as a result of the accumulation of interest on the creditor's claim.

Moreover, fully secured creditors are not usually entitled to post-petition interest payments that ensure the maintenance of the size of their equity cushion.[177] Thus, fully secured creditors must usually wait to receive interest that accumulates on their claims until the plan is confirmed and consummated. In the meantime, of course, their equity cushion subsides. However, if an equity cushion is in danger of being completely eliminated due to the accrual of interest on the creditor's claim, post-petition interest payments must commence. A cushion of 20% is usually enough to guard against this. Thus, if the collateral is worth $24,000, the $4,000 cushion over Peninsula's $20,000 claim is adequate. If the equity cushion drops to only 10%, or only $2,000 above the claim, additional protection is probably necessary.[178] However, these are not hard and fast rules; much depends on the nature of the collateral involved, the rate of dissipation of the cushion, and the degree of certainty about the value the court places on the collateral in the first place, because all these factors might expose the creditor to a greater or lesser degree of risk of losing its secured status.

When adequate protection is based on an equity cushion, the creditor may seek relief later in the case. As time passes, the cushion shrinks, both from the accumulation of unpaid interest and from any decline in the value of collateral. As the amount of the debt creeps close to the value of the collateral, the depth of the cushion diminishes; the amount of the cushion might no longer be adequate to protect the creditor, even though it once was sufficient. This is an issue of particular significance in a protracted reorganization case.

On occasion, courts err. They sometimes overestimate the value of the collateral or underestimate the rate by which its value will decline. When they do, there is no realistic way to provide the claimant with the true full equivalent of its claim. There is almost certainly little or nothing left in the estate. The Code does the best it can. It provides the claimant with a "super-priority" unsecured claim, prior to all other

---

[175] *E.g.*, Prudential Ins. Co. v. Monnier (In re Monnier Bros.), 755 F.2d 1336 (8th Cir.1985); Pistole v. Mellor (In re Mellor), 734 F.2d 1396 (9th Cir. 1984).

[176] *E.g.*, Bankers Life Ins. Co. v. Alyucan Interstate Corp. (In re Alyucan Interstate Corp.), 12 B.R. 803 (Bankr. D. Utah 1981).

[177] *See* Orix Credit Alliance, Inc. v. Delta Res., Inc. (In re Delta Res., Inc.), 54 F.3d 722 (11th Cir. 1995).

[178] Matter of Mendoza, 111 F.3d 1264 (5th Cir. 1997); In re Kost, 102 B.R. 829, 831-32 (D. Wyo. 1989) (collecting cases).

unsecured claims, including administrative claims.[179]

For example, assume North Atlantic Bank has a $5 million claim, secured by a mortgage on Titanic's land and building, and the court decides that the claim is adequately protected based on its valuation of the collateral at $6 million. As things turn out, when the collateral is finally sold, it yields only $4.8 million. North Atlantic will have a super-priority unsecured claim for the $200,000 deficiency. Even with priority, however, it may not receive payment for its deficiency claim. Whether it does depends on whether there is enough other value in the estate to satisfy super-priority claims. Moreover, the administrative expenses of any liquidating trustee are entitled to an even higher priority,[180] and these expenses may consume whatever minimal assets remain available for distribution to creditors.

Just as fundamental to adequate protection analysis as the form the protection must take are rules on standing to insist on that protection. Not every claim must be protected. Unsecured claims are entitled to no protection, because they do not represent an interest in specific property.[181] Even secured claims may be entitled to only limited protection. This is particularly significant in reorganization proceedings. During the period between the petition and consummation of a confirmed plan, interest is added to fully secured claims. If the amount of the claim is less than the value of the property securing it, interest will accrue on the claim, but only to the extent of the surplus value.[182]

For example, if Peninsula Bank has a $45,000 claim, secured by collateral worth $50,000, up to $5,000 in interest may be added to the claim while the case is pending. By contrast, if the collateral were worth only $40,000, Peninsula Bank would hold a $40,000 secured claim and a $5,000 unsecured claim and would not be entitled to "pendency" interest on either claim.[183] If the collateral were worth exactly $45,000, the bank would hold a $45,000 secured claim but would have no right to add interest to its claim while the debtor attempted to forge a reorganization plan.[184]

These rules carry over to adequate protection. Only the nominal value of the secured claim is entitled to adequate protection. An oversecured creditor is entitled to protection of the principal plus allowed interest. In the example above, in which the collateral is worth $50,000, the bank is entitled to adequate protection of up to $50,000, depending on how much interest actually accrues on the $45,000 debt. The undersecured or exactly secured creditor is not so lucky. If the bank's secured claim is not entitled to interest, it is not entitled to obtain adequate protection for more than the original dollar value of its claim — in the last two examples above, $40,000 or $45,000, respectively. In short, for exactly secured or undersecured creditors, adequate protection only protects against a decline in the value of the collateral during the pendency of the automatic stay.

---

[179] Bankruptcy Code § 507(b). *See infra* § 10.04[B][1] Claims for Inadequate "Adequate Protection."

[180] *See infra* § 10.04[B][3] Post-Conversion Liquidation Expenses.

[181] In re Tellier, 125 B.R. 348, 349 (Bankr. D. R.I. 1991).

[182] Bankruptcy Code § 506(b). *See infra* § 10.03[B][3] Post-Petition Interest.

[183] Bankruptcy Code § 502(b)(2).

[184] Bankruptcy Code § 506(b).

This is true even though the real value of Peninsula's claim is declining. Because the stay prevents the bank from foreclosing, it incurs the opportunity cost of being unable to reinvest its funds. If Peninsula were permitted to foreclose, it could sell the collateral and invest the proceeds from the sale at whatever current rate of interest is then available. If the collateral and thus its secured claim is worth only $40,000, and the period between petition and confirmation lasts for one year, the stay causes Peninsula to lose the interest it could have otherwise earned during this time. In the 1980s, many commentators argued that this loss should be paid for — that Peninsula should be paid this interest as a price for keeping the stay in place.[185] Whatever the merits of this argument, the Supreme Court, relying on what it saw as the plain meaning of the Code, unequivocally rejected it in *Timbers of Inwood Forest*.[186] The undersecured creditor is entitled to nothing for its lost opportunity.[187] The Court clearly held that "adequate protection" does not include compensation for the time value of money. Therefore the "exactly secured" creditor — whose collateral equals but does not exceed the amount of the debt, and likewise the creditor who becomes exactly secured because of interest accrued during the pendency of the case, is not entitled to pendency interest as adequate protection.[188]

Thus, adequate protection entitles the creditor to the property that it had at the outset of the case, and to receive only as much protection from delay in bankruptcy as that collateral provides. To the extent that their collateral is insufficient to cover the delay occasioned by bankruptcy, then the remaining part of its claim is simply an unsecured claim for unmatured interest, and is disallowed under § 502(b). The policy justification for this is that bankruptcy is a common disaster, causing losses that ought to be shared in some reasonable way among those affected. Given the relatively good treatment afforded secured claimants, occasional opportunity costs represent little enough contribution from them for the greater good.

Most adequate protection issues are resolved through negotiation rather than through litigation. The most common reason for a secured creditor to seek relief from the stay is to force the debtor to negotiate reasonably. Because of the powerful position secured creditors have in most bankruptcies, the debtor is usually willing to come up with a reasonable method of providing protection, thereby avoiding both the cost and the risk of stay litigation. Given the relatively clear rules regarding what is normally required to pass judicial muster, the negotiated protection usually is identical to the protection a judge would order. The debtor commits to the maintenance of insurance and periodic payments equal to the depreciation of the property (plus, in some cases, the interest accruing on the debt). This does not mean that secured creditors are satisfied with what they can obtain, because most of the time they are not. But courts have developed fairly good guidelines as to what the debtor must give and what the creditor can get.

---

[185] *E.g.*, Douglas G. Baird & Thomas H. Jackson, *Corporate Reorganizations and the Treatment of Diverse Ownership Interests: A Comment on Adequate Protection of Secured Creditors in Bankruptcy*, 51 U. Chi. L. Rev. 97 (1984).

[186] United Sav. Ass'n of Tex.v. Timbers of Inwood Forest Assocs., Ltd., 484 U.S. 365 (1988).

[187] 484 U.S. at 382.

[188] David Gray Carlson, *Postpetition Interest under the Bankruptcy Code*, 43 U. Miami L. Rev. 577 (1987).

Finally, § 361's rules regarding adequate protection do not apply in cases involving a family farmer or a family fisherman brought under Chapter 12 of the Bankruptcy Code.[189] As explained elsewhere, Chapter 12 has a separate set of rules for what constitutes adequate protection.[190]

[2]   For Cause: Other Than for Lack of Adequate Protection

Although most of the litigation concerning relief from the stay deals with lack of adequate protection for secured creditors, courts sometimes find other reasons to grant relief from the automatic stay.

Courts are sometimes willing to grant relief from the stay when there is a more appropriate forum than the bankruptcy court to hear a matter that has some relationship to the debtor's bankruptcy case. This is especially true if the dispute is only tangentially connected with the bankruptcy case. For example, domestic and probate cases are frequently permitted to continue.[191] Divorce cases may even be permitted to continue to allow the domestic relations court to distribute the couple's assets between them.[192] As one court explained: "[a] determination of Debtor's property interests necessarily requires a division of marital property. The state court is best situated to complete this task."[193]

Similarly, ordinary civil suits might be permitted to continue to judgment where considerable work toward a judgment has already been completed, and where it is inefficient to require the action to be concluded in bankruptcy court.[194] The effect of a judgment against the debtor in such a suit, however, is simply to fix the amount of the creditor's claim. The resulting judgment will not be entitled to priority or other special treatment in the bankruptcy case.

Proceedings against the debtor are also sometimes permitted to continue when an action must be maintained against the debtor in order to recover from the debtor's insurance carrier.[195] As one court said, "[d]ebtors-defendants suffer little prejudice when they are sued by plaintiffs who seek nothing more than declarations of liability that can serve as a predicate for a recovery against insurers, sureties, or guarantors."[196]

---

[189] Bankruptcy Code § 361.

[190] Bankruptcy Code § 361(b). *See infra* § 20.05[A] Adequate Protection in Chapter 12.

[191] *E.g.,* In re Taub, 413 B.R. 55 (Bankr. E.D.N.Y. 2009). *See generally* Carver v. Carver, 954 F.2d 1573, 1578 (11th Cir. 1992).

[192] In re Dryja, 425 B.R. 608 (Bankr. D. Colo. 2010); In re Taub, 438 B.R. 39 (Bankr. E.D.N.Y. 2010) (relief from stay to permit state domestic relations court to resolve "equitable distribution" issues between debtor and his estranged spouse).

[193] *Id.* at 612.

[194] *E.g.,* In re Robbins, 964 F.2d 342 (4th Cir. 1992); In re Haines, 309 B.R. 668 (Bankr. D. Mass. 2004); In re Chacon, 438 B.R. 725 (Bankr. D.N.M. 2010).

[195] In re R.J. Groover Constr., L.L.C., 411 B.R. 460 (Bankr. S.D. Ga. 2009).

[196] *E.g.,* In re Fernstrom Storage and Van Co., 938 F.2d 731, 735 (7th Cir. 1991).

The stay also might be terminated or even annulled if the debtor's petition was filed in bad faith.[197] In *In re Ironsides, Inc.*, the court explained: "[I]f there is not a potentially viable business in place worthy of protection and rehabilitation, the Chapter 11 effort has lost its raison d'etre."[198] Among the factors that lead to a finding that a petition was filed in bad faith are that:

- the debtor has one asset;

- the debtor engaged in improper conduct prior to the petition;

- the debtor has few unsecured creditors;

- the debtor's property has been scheduled for foreclosure;

- the debtor and one creditor have proceeded to a standstill in state court litigation, and the debtor has either lost or has been required to post a supersedeas bond that it cannot afford;

- the filing of the petition permits the debtor to evade court orders in another dispute;

- the debtor has no ongoing business; and

- the debtor has no possibility of successful reorganization.[199]

These same reasons might lead the court to dismiss or convert the case.[200] If the case is dismissed, the automatic stay terminates under § 362(c)(2)(B). If it is converted to Chapter 7, the stay remains in place, but a trustee is appointed and will likely sell or abandon the property involved.

[3] No Equity and Property Not Necessary for Reorganization

Relief from the stay is also granted if the debtor has no stake in the property and no use for it. Section 362(d)(2) authorizes relief from the stay "of an act against property . . . if — (a) the debtor does not have an equity in such property; *and* (b) such property is not necessary to an effective reorganization."[201] Both requirements must be met.

This basis for relief from the stay is significant primarily in reorganization proceedings under Chapters 11, 12, and 13. In Chapter 7 proceedings, where no reorganization is contemplated, the trustee ordinarily abandons property in which the debtor has no equity, making relief from the stay superfluous.

---

[197] Laguna Assocs., Ltd. v. Aetna Cas. & Sur. Co. (In re Laguna Assocs., Ltd.), 30 F.3d 734 (6th Cir. 1994).

[198] In re Ironsides, Inc., 34 B.R. 337, 339 (Bankr. W.D. Ky. 1983).

[199] *See* In re Charfoos, 979 F.2d 390, 393 (6th Cir. 1992).

[200] *See* Trident Assocs. Ltd. v. Metro. Life Ins. Co. (In re Trident Assocs., Ltd.), 52 F.3d 127 (6th Cir. 1995).

[201] Bankruptcy Code § 362(d)(2) (emphasis added).

[a]   No Equity in the Property

If the debtor has equity in the property, relief is unavailable under this provision, even if the property is to be liquidated by the trustee. The debtor-in-possession may be in the best position to obtain a good price for it. An over-secured creditor with a lien on the property has little incentive to obtain the best price for the property; it is satisfied if the property is sold for enough to satisfy its senior lien.

Whether the debtor has equity in the property requires a comparison between the total of all liens against the property and the property's value.[202] Determining whether the debtor has any equity in the property thus requires a determination of the property's value. Whenever value must be determined, questions inevitably arise about the appropriate method of valuation to use. Consider, for example, equipment subject to a $100,000 security interest. If the liquidation value of the property of $95,000 is used, then the debtor has no equity. If the going concern value of the property (if it is left in place and sold as part of a sale of the entire premises in which it is installed) is $125,000, then the debtor has $25,000 of equity in the item. Similarly, if the property would cost $130,000 for the debtor to replace, it's replacement value is $130,000 and again the debtor has equity in the property. Thus, whether the first prong of § 362(d)(2) is satisfied depends on whether the property is appraised at its liquidation, going concern or replacement value. In individual cases under Chapter 7 and 13, § 506(a)(2) requires the use of "replacement value" for calculating the value of the collateral.

[b]   Property Not Necessary for Effective Reorganization

In addition, for relief to be granted, the debtor must have no important use for the property. Even property in which the debtor has no equity can be vital to the operation of the debtor's business, or, if not vital, nevertheless useful. If the property is needed for the debtor's reorganization, the automatic stay should remain in place unless a creditor with a lien on the property can establish other grounds, such as lack of adequate protection, to be permitted to foreclose. For example, if Road Runner Transport, Co., is engaged in the trucking business, it needs its tractor-trailers to continue in business and have any chance of reorganization. Even if the debt to Navigator's Bank exceeds the value of the collateral, the stay should not be lifted. Of course, if Road Runner cannot protect the Bank against a decline in the collateral's value, relief should be granted under § 362(d)(1) for lack of adequate protection, as explained above.[203]

In effect, § 362(d)(2) protects two values that property has to a debtor and its creditors. It protects the value of the property as a financial asset that might be sold to generate cash. It also protects the debtor's use value of the property in its reorganization. Thus, both the liquidation value and the going concern value of the debtor's property are protected. Relief from the stay is granted under this test

---

[202] In re Indian Palm Assoc., 61 F.3d 197, 206-07 (3d Cir. 1995); In re 3H River Turf Farm, LLC, 414 B.R. 751 (Bankr. D. Utah 2009).

[203] See supra § 8.06[B][1] For Cause — Lack of Adequate Protection.

only if the property lacks value to the debtor in either sense.

Courts usually take a pro-debtor stance in interpreting § 362(d)(2), particularly with respect to whether the property is "necessary for reorganization." While it is clear that retention of the property must be more than merely convenient to the estate, there is no requirement that the property be indispensable.[204] Thus, an individual debtor's car is usually regarded as necessary for a debtor's Chapter 13 rehabilitation plan, even though the debtor might be able to take the bus to her job.[205] Likewise, the debtor's home is necessary for the debtor's reorganization "because it provides necessary stability for the debtor's family" while the debtor is being rehabilitated.[206] Of course, in a Chapter 7 case, where no reorganization is contemplated, this branch of the test is satisfied.[207]

At the same time, implicit in the "necessary for effective reorganization" requirement is that there be some realistic possibility of successful reorganization. As the Supreme Court explained in *United Savings Association of Texas v. Timbers of Innwood Forest Associates*:

> Once the movant under Section 362(d)(2) establishes that he is an under-secured creditor, it is the burden of the *debtor* to establish that collateral at issue is "necessary to an effective reorganization." What this requires is not merely a showing that if there is conceivably to be an effective reorganization, this property will be needed for it; but that the property is essential for an effective reorganization *that is in prospect.* This means, as many lower courts, including the en banc court in this case, have properly said, that there must be a "reasonable possibility of a successful reorganization within a reasonable time."[208]

The usual textual justification for this reading of the rule is rooted in the fact that the statute refers to an "effective" reorganization.[209]

This is similar to the feasibility test for confirmation of a plan.[210] One of the points at which creditors may attack the entire reorganization is when they attempt to lift the stay. If the debtor has no equity in the property and there is no reasonable prospect for reorganization, the stay is lifted.[211] Most of the time, lifting the stay precipitates liquidation. The same issue arises when the debtor proposes the plan; one of the requirements for confirmation is that the plan be feasible.[212]

However, at the early stage of the case in which relief from the automatic stay is

---

[204]   *E.g.*, In re Fields, 127 B.R. 150 (Bankr. W.D. Tex. 1991).

[205]   In re George, 315 B.R. 624 (Bankr. S.D. Ga. 2004); In re Wyatt, 173 B.R. 698 (Bankr. D. Idaho 1994). *But see* In re Haines, 10 B.R. 856 (Bankr. D. Pa. 1981) (relief granted to repossess debtor's sports car where it was "not impossible for an individual to survive in an urban area without an automobile").

[206]   In re Timmer, 423 B.R. 870, 874 (Bankr. N.D. Iowa 2010).

[207]   *E.g.*, In re Sanabria, 317 B.R. 59 (B.A.P. 8th Cir. 2004).

[208]   United Sav. Ass'n of Tex. v. Timbers of Innwood Forest Assocs., Ltd., 484 U.S. 365, 375-76 (1988).

[209]   *See* In re 8th Street Village Ltd., 94 B.R. 993, 996 (N.D. Ill. 1988).

[210]   *See infra* § 19.10[J] Feasibility of Plan.

[211]   *E.g.*, In re Mullock, 404 B.R. 800 (Bankr. E.D. Pa. 2009).

[212]   Bankruptcy Code § 1129(a)(11); *see infra* § 19.10[J] Feasibility of Plan.

likely to be sought, the feasibility test is applied far less rigorously than late in the case when the court is considering the details of the debtor's plan. Early in the case, the debtor might not yet have had the opportunity to determine why it is losing money, much less to evaluate its prospects for stemming its losses.

For example, assume that a creditor seeks to lift the stay under § 362(d)(2) only thirty days after the petition is filed, and that the court holds a hearing on the creditor's motion another thirty days later. This is only sixty days beyond the debtor's petition, and only half-way through the 120-day "exclusivity'" period during which the debtor has the sole right to file a plan of reorganization.[213] In many cases, the debtor will simply not have had enough time to prepare and present a confirmable plan. The fact that it has not yet done so should not translate into an automatic lifting of the stay on the basis that there is no reasonable prospect for effective reorganization. While the debtor certainly must be able to present the court with more than "unsubstantiated hopes for a successful reorganization," it should not ordinarily be necessary to have an actual, finished plan in hand.[214]

In some circumstances, the debtor's situation is so obviously hopeless that lifting the stay is appropriate, even at the very beginning of the proceeding. Debtors with irreversibly negative cash flow, no reasonable prospects for additional income or refinancing, and deteriorating property should be forced into liquidation at the earliest possible opportunity. Stay litigation provides the courts with a vehicle for doing this. Alternatively, a creditor might move to convert or dismiss the case.[215]

As time goes by and the proceeding drags on, the court's attitude toward feasibility is likely to change. If a debtor cannot show a strong prospect for reorganization six months or a year after the petition is filed, the court should move the case toward its almost inevitable close.

[4] Single-Asset Real Estate Cases

The Code supplies a special rule for relief from the stay in a single-asset real estate cases. Single-asset real estate cases are those in which substantially all of the debtor's income is generated from leasing commercial real estate — usually an office building or an apartment complex.[216] If the debtor operates a business out of the real estate, such as a hotel or a golf course, from which substantial other revenues are generated, the Code's single-asset real estate rules do not apply.[217]

The rule requires the court to grant relief from the stay, unless within the later of (1) ninety days after the entry of an order for relief or a later date established by

---

[213] Bankruptcy Code § 1121(b). *See infra* § 19.08[B] Who May File a Plan; The Exclusivity Period.

[214] In re Canal Place Ltd., 921 F.2d 569, 577 (5th. Cir. 1991).

[215] Bankruptcy Code § 1112(b)(4). *See infra* § 19.05[B] Involuntary Conversion or Dismissal.

[216] Bankruptcy Code § 101(51B). *See* In re Khemko, 181 B.R. 47 (Bankr. S.D. Ohio 1995) (boat marina). *See generally* Kenneth N. Klee, *One Size Fits Some: Single Asset Real Estate Bankruptcy*, 87 Cornell L. Rev. 1285 (2002).

[217] *See* Centofante v. CBJ Dev., Inc. (In re CBJ Dev., Inc.), 202 B.R. 467 (B.A.P. 9th Cir. 1996) (hotel); In re Larry Goodwin Golf, Inc., 219 B.R. 391 (Bankr. M.D.N.C. 1997) (golf course).

the court,[218] or (2) thirty days after the court determines that the case is a single-asset real estate case, the debtor either: (i) files a reorganization plan that has a reasonable possibility of being confirmed within a reasonable time, or (ii) begins making regular monthly interest payments to the creditor.[219] The amount of payments that must be made to stave off relief from the stay is "an amount equal to interest at the then applicable non-default contract rate of interest on the value of the creditor's interest in the real estate."[220]

Thus, if the debt is $12 million but the collateral is only worth $10 million, and the regular interest rate in the mortgage documents is 12% per year, interest must be paid at 12% on the $10 million value of the creditor's interest in the land, or $100,000 per month (12% per year on $10 million). This prevents the case from languishing with no payments to the lender, while the debtor does nothing more than wait and hope that the local real estate market will improve. The source of the monthly payments may either be rents or other income generated from the property at any time before, on, or after commencement of the case.[221]

[5]   Foreclosure in Cases Filed to Delay, Hinder or Defraud Creditors

The 2005 Amendments added language that permits foreclosure of a real estate mortgage or other interest in real estate if the court finds that the debtor's petition was part of a "scheme to delay, hinder, and defraud creditors"[222] that involved either a transfer of ownership of the property to a third person without the creditor's consent or multiple bankruptcy filings affecting the same property.[223]

Section 362(d)(4) prevents efforts of debtors, like the one in *In re Wilke*,[224] to delay and perhaps frustrate a creditor's efforts to foreclose, by filing successive bankruptcy cases for different debtors to whom key assets have been transferred. In *Wilke*, the owner of residential real estate filed several successive Chapter 13 petitions despite her continued inability to make condominium assessment payments under a plan. Even though her Chapter 13 cases were dismissed, she enjoyed the benefit of the automatic stay while the cases were pending. The bankruptcy judge, fed up with her fifth Chapter 13 case, found that all of her petitions had been filed in bad faith and barred her from filing another petition for 180 days. Unable to file a sixth Chapter 13 petition, the debtor transferred her property to another individual who promptly filed his own Chapter 13 petition, as part of the same effort to avoid eviction from the condominium unit in question. Under these circumstances, the court had little difficulty finding that the debtor had participated in a scheme of the type that § 362(d)(4) was designed to frustrate, and granted the

---

[218] *See* In re Hope Plantation Group, LLC, 393 B.R. 98 (Bankr. D.S.C. 2007) (motion filed during 90 days is premature, even if hearing is held more than 90 days after debtor's petition).

[219] *See, e.g.*, In re Rim Dev. LLC, 448 B.R. 280 (Bankr. D. Kan. 2010).

[220] Bankruptcy Code § 362(d)(3)(B)(ii).

[221] Bankruptcy Code § 362(d)(3)(B)(i).

[222] Bankruptcy Code § 362(d)(4).

[223] Bankruptcy Code § 362(d)(4). *See* In re Muhaimin, 343 B.R. 159 (Bankr. D. Md. 2006).

[224] 429 B.R. 916 (Bankr. N.D. Ill. 2010).

condominium association relief from the stay to evict her from the unit.

[6]   Enforceability of Pre-Petition Waivers

Relief from the stay might also be granted if the debtor entered into a pre-petition agreement waiving the stay. For many years, the possibility that a contractual waiver of the automatic stay would be enforced was unthinkable.[225] However, courts have begun enforcing these pre-petition agreements, particularly where the waiver was negotiated between the parties in the course of a settlement of a foreclosure action.

The enforceability of a pre-petition waiver is controversial, because the automatic stay is designed to protect not just the debtor, but its creditors, as well. By preventing a single creditor from enforcing its lien, the stay helps preserve the value of estate assets that otherwise might either be distributed to creditors generally or to produce income that will help the debtor reorganize.[226] As a result, some courts view such waivers as tantamount to a waiver of the right to file a bankruptcy petition, and unenforceable.[227] On the other hand, courts that have enforced them have explained that they further "the legitimate public policy of encouraging out-of-court restructuring and settlements."[228]

When they are enforceable, waivers are not self-executing but are frequently considered, together with other factors, in determining whether relief should be granted.[229] Courts that are willing to consider enforcing the waiver usually conduct an inquiry to evaluate "(1) the sophistication of the party making the waiver; (2) the consideration for the waiver, including the creditor's risk and the length of time the waiver covers; (3) whether other parties, such as unsecured creditors and junior lienholders are affected by the waiver; and (4) the feasibility of the debtor's plan."[230]

[7]   Creditor Standing

The home mortgage foreclosure crisis that began in 2007, and continued well into 2012, and perhaps beyond, combined with the now common practice of securitizing home mortgages,[231] has led to questions concerning the requirements necessary for creditors to have standing to obtain relief from the automatic stay.[232] Disputes over

---

[225] Daniel B. Bogart, *Games Lawyers Play: Waivers of the Automatic Stay in Bankruptcy and the Single Asset Loan Workout*, 43 UCLA L. Rev. 1117 (1996); Michael Baxter, *Prepetition Waivers of the Automatic Stay: A Secure Lenders Guide*, 52 Bus. Law. 577 (1997); Marshall E. Tracht, *Contractual Bankruptcy Waivers: Reconciling Theory, Practice, and Law*, 82 Cornell L. Rev. 301 (1997).

[226] Matter of Pease, 195 B.R. 431 (Bankr. D. Neb. 1996).

[227] In re DB Capital Holdings, LLC, 454 B.R. 804 (Bankr. D. Colo. 2011).

[228] In re Cheeks, 167 B.R. 817, 818 (Bankr. D.S.C. 1994).

[229] *E.g.*, In re Desai, 282 B.R. 527 (Bankr. M.D. Ga. 2002); In re Bryan Road, LLC, 382 B.R. 844 (Bankr. S.D. Fla. 2008).

[230] 282 B.R. at 532.

[231] *See* Derrick M. Land, *Residential Mortgage Securitization and Consumer Welfare*, 61 Consumer Fin. L.Q. Rep. 208, 209-10 (2007).

[232] *See, e.g.*, In re Mentag, 430 B.R. 439 (E.D. Mich. 2010).

standing for relief from the stay mirror similar disputes over standing to bring foreclosure actions in state court.

The modern secondary mortgage market system, in which mortgages are bundled together and transferred as part of securitization transactions, with payments collected and processed by mortgage loan servicing companies, has resulted in uncertainty over who is legally entitled to enforce the mortgage. If the promissory note that the mortgage secures is a negotiable instrument governed by U.C.C. Article 3, then only a person "entitled to enforce" the instrument, has standing to enforce the instrument[233] in either a foreclosure proceeding or in a contested matter in bankruptcy court to obtain relief from the stay.[234] This is usually the "holder," or another person in possession of the instrument.[235] A person seeking relief from the stay who lacks possession of the original mortgage note might not be a proper person to enforce the instrument, under either U.C.C. Article 3 or common law rules governing non-negotiable instruments. Even if they have possession, unless the note is a "bearer" note, they may need to prove that they are the owner of the instrument by proving chain of title. If this person lacks standing to bring a foreclosure action, it should not have standing to obtain relief from the automatic stay simply because it claims to have received an assignment of the note and mortgage from the original lender. If the plaintiff does have possession of the note, it should have standing obtain to relief from the automatic stay and to bring a foreclosure action against the mortgagor.

[C]   Form of Relief from the Stay

Although most lawyers think of stay litigation as an effort to lift the stay completely, and most cases deal with that issue, the court has flexibility to craft more limited remedies. The court may provide relief by "terminating, annulling, modifying, or conditioning" the stay.[236]

At one extreme, the court may annul the stay *ab initio* and thereby validate prior actions that violated it. If the stay is annulled, it is as if it was never imposed. Annulment is rare. It is usually limited to situations in which the debtor's petition was filed in bad faith or where a creditor took action that the court would have permitted in any event, without knowledge that the debtor's petition had been filed.[237]

Alternatively, the court might modify the stay to permit a creditor to take very specific but limited actions against the debtor or its property. Thus, a secured creditor might be permitted to commence or continue a state court foreclosure proceeding because the debtor is unable to supply it with adequate protection. Other creditors are still restrained.

---

[233] U.C.C. § 3-301 (2010).

[234] *See* Veal v. Am. Home Mortgage Serv., Inc. (In re Veal), 450 B.R. 897 (B.A.P. 9th Cir. 2011).

[235] U.C.C. § 3-301 (2010).

[236] Bankruptcy Code § 362(d).

[237] *E.g.*, Mut. Benefit Life Ins. Co. v. Pinetree, Ltd. (In re Pinetree, Ltd.), 876 F.2d 34 (5th Cir. 1989).

The court also might deny relief but impose a condition on the continuation of the stay. For example, if the debtor fails to pay for casualty insurance on a creditor's collateral, the court may require the debtor to obtain and maintain adequate insurance in the future, and continue the stay subject to the condition that the debtor provide the necessary coverage. An order of this type can be self-executing; in other words, the court may order that the stay automatically and immediately terminate if there is another lapse in the insurance coverage. This type of order avoids the need for further stay litigation. The court may also lift the stay for some purposes, but not for others. For example, the stay may be lifted to permit a state court to determine liability and assess damages but kept in place with regard to collection efforts.[238]

Relief may be given to one claimant, but not to another. For example, if two creditors have liens on the same property and only one requests insurance as a condition of maintaining the stay, the court could order the debtor to maintain only enough insurance to protect the interest of the requesting creditor. This issue rarely arises, because in most cases, there is only one creditor with a lien, or a least a significant lien, on any given piece of property.

[D] Procedure for Obtaining Relief from the Stay

Congress hoped to provide not only direct substantive protection for claimants' rights, but also procedural protection. Accordingly, it set out rules designed to expedite stay litigation. In the view of many, this effort has not been successful, and further tightening of the rules is a consistent legislative demand of creditor groups.

Under § 362(e)(1), the court must take action upon a request for relief from the stay within thirty days after the request is made. If it does not do so, the stay terminates automatically.[239]

Alas, what one section of the Code gives, another section takes away. The court does not have to take any final action within that thirty-day period. Upon notice and an opportunity for a hearing, the court may — and often does — continue the stay, pending a final determination of the claimant's request.[240] Nevertheless, § 362(e) requires the final hearing to be *concluded* within thirty days after the conclusion of the preliminary hearing. But, the court is permitted to extend the stay with the consent of the parties or if the court finds that compelling circumstances warrant continuation of the stay for a specific additional time.[241]

In 2005, Congress added an exception to this thirty-day rule. It applies only in Chapter 7, 11, and 13 cases "in which the debtor is an individual."[242] Section 362(e)(2) terminates the stay sixty days after a creditor moves for relief, unless the court enters a final decision before the end of the sixty days, the parties agree to an extension of the sixty days, or the court finds that there is "*good cause*" to extend

---

[238] *See* In re Revco D.S., Inc., 99 B.R. 768, 777 (N.D. Ohio 1989).

[239] Bankruptcy Code § 362(e)(1).

[240] Bankruptcy Code § 362(e)(1).

[241] Bankruptcy Code § 362(e)(1).

[242] Bankruptcy Code § 362(e)(2).

the stay beyond the sixty days.[243] Thus, if the debtor is an individual, the court need not find compelling circumstances to continue the stay for more than sixty days beyond the time of the request for relief from the stay.

The Code also includes rarely used procedures for emergency ex parte relief from the stay. Ex parte relief is available only if two conditions are met. First, the action must be necessary to prevent irreparable damage to the claimant's property interest. Second, the damage must be imminent — if there is time for notice and a hearing, the court may not act without them.[244]

Finally, the Code establishes basic rules regarding the burden of proof. The party requesting the relief carries the burden of proof as to the debtor's equity in the property.[245] Thus, if Peninsula seeks relief from the stay because Franklin Manufacturing has no equity in Peninsula's collateral and the property is not necessary for Franklin's effective reorganization, then Peninsula bears the burden of proof on the question of Franklin's lack of equity.

As to all other issues, the trustee or debtor-in-possession carries the burden of proof.[246] Thus, if Peninsula Bank proves that Franklin has no equity in the property, the debtor must prove that the property is necessary for reorganization; if it fails to do so, the stay is lifted.

Although not explicitly stated in the Code, "burden of proof" means the burden of persuasion. The party that carries the burden of proof must not only put on evidence supporting its position, but also must convince the judge that its position is correct. The standard for carrying the burden of proof is the ordinary one in civil litigation — preponderance of the evidence.

§ 8.07   ENFORCEMENT OF THE STAY

[A]   Actions in Violation of the Stay are Void[247]

Actions in violation of the automatic stay are regarded by most courts as entirely void, even if the person taking the action had no notice of the stay.[248] Even actions taken or conducted by the government, such as a foreclosure sale,[249] are without legal effect. The fact that the action taken may have been entirely innocent and in good faith is a defense against sanctions, but this does not protect the action taken from being treated as void.

---

[243] Bankruptcy Code § 362(e)(2).

[244] Bankruptcy Code § 362(f); Fed. R. Bankr. P. 4001(a)(2).

[245] Bankruptcy Code § 362(g)(1).

[246] Bankruptcy Code § 362(g)(2).

[247] Donna Renee Tobar, *The Need for a Uniform Void Ab Initio Standard for Violations of the Automatic Stay*, 24 Whittier L. Rev. 3 (2002); Timothy Arnold Barnes, Note, *Plain Meaning of the Automatic Stay in Bankruptcy: The Void Voidable Distinction Revisited*, 57 Ohio St. L.J. 291 (1996).

[248] *E.g.*, Maritime Elec. Co., Inc. v. United Jersey Bank, 959 F.2d 1194 (3d Cir. 1991); Franklin Sav. Ass'n v. Office of Thrift Supervision, 31 F.3d 1020, 1022 (10th Cir. 1994). *But see* Jones v. Garcia (In re Jones), 63 F.3d 411, 412 (5th Cir. 1995) (not void, merely voidable).

[249] Anglemyer v. United States, 115 B.R. 510 (D. Md. 1990).

[B] Damages for Violating the Stay[250]

Willful violations of the stay are punishable under § 362(k) or as contempt under § 105.[251] Section 362(k)(1) provides: "[A]n individual injured by any wilful violation of a stay provided by this section, shall recover actual damages, including costs and attorneys' fees, and in appropriate circumstances, may recover punitive damages."[252] In many instances, the principal damage done by a violation of the automatic stay is the expense of resorting to the legal system to undo the effects of the improper action.

Assume, for example, that Auto Finance Co. repossessed Ray's car, despite having received formal notice of his bankruptcy petition from the court and that it refused to voluntarily return the car to Ray. Ray rented a car for $200 per week for six weeks so that he could commute to work and run family errands. Ray also had to pay his lawyer $800 to make a (successful) motion in the bankruptcy court to force Auto Finance to return the car and to establish the amount he had to pay to obtain the rental vehicle. Ray is entitled to recover not only the car, but also the rental cost ($1200), plus his attorney's fees ($800); his monetary recovery is $2000.[253]

The court might also award him damages for any mental distress he suffered after the car was repossessed as an element of actual damages caused by the creditor's violation.[254] However, "[f]leeting or trivial anxiety or distress does not suffice to support an award; instead, an individual must suffer significant emotional harm."[255] Thus, the debtor's mere embarrassment is not sufficient to justify an award of actual damages.[256]

Ray may also be able to recover punitive damages from the finance company for its wilful violation of the stay.[257] Courts are generally reluctant to grant punitive damages, because compensatory damages are usually sufficient both to recompense the debtor (or the estate) and to deter the creditor from future violations. Some courts have said that punitive damages are appropriate only if the

---

[250] Ann K. Wooster, Annotation, *What Constitutes "Willful Violation" of Automatic Stay Provisions of Bankruptcy Code (11 U.S.C.A. § 362(h)) Sufficient to Award Damages — Chapter 13 Cases*, 8 A.L.R. Fed. 2d 433 (2006); Ann K. Wooster, Annotation, *What Constitutes "Willful Violation" of Automatic Stay Provisions of Bankruptcy Code Sufficient To Award Damages — Chapter 11 and 12 Cases*, 2 A.L.R. Fed. 2d 459 (2005).

[251] Jove Eng'g, Inc. v. IRS, 92 F.3d 1539 (11th Cir. 1996).

[252] Bankruptcy Code § 362(k)(1).

[253] *See* Nissan Motor Acceptance Corp. v. Baker, 239 B.R. 484 (N.D. Tex. 1999) (after repossession without notice of bankruptcy, secured party failed to return car).

[254] *E.g.*, Dawson v. Wash. Mut. Bank (In re Dawson), 390 F.3d 1139, 1148 (9th Cir. 2004).

[255] *Dawson*, 390 F.3d at 1149. *See also* In re Repine, 536 F.3d 512 (5th Cir. 2008) (requiring specific information demonstrating existence and extent of emotional distress).

[256] In re Kinsey, 349 B.R. 48, 53 (Bankr. D. Idaho 2006).

[257] *E.g.*, In re WVF Acquisition, LLC, 420 B.R. 902 (Bankr. S.D. Fla. 2009) ($50,000 punitive damages imposed on internet service provider who terminated debtor's internet access).

creditor's conduct was not only willful, but also malicious or in bad faith.[258] However, if the creditor's action is sufficiently egregious, punitive damages may be awarded. For example, if Ray's employer continued to dock his paycheck after learning of the petition, punitive damages would be appropriate.[259]

Courts disagree over whether the reference to "an individual" prevents corporations, partnerships and other organizations from recovering under § 362(k).[260] Courts that give "individual" its normal meaning, impose damages under § 105(a).[261] It broadly permits the court to "issue any order, process, or judgment that is necessary or appropriate to carry out the provisions of this title."[262] Before the 1984 Amendments added specific language that authorizes damages for violations of the stay, courts routinely used § 105(a) to punish such violations by awarding damages.[263] In appropriate cases, punitive damages can be awarded. However, sanctions are inappropriate for an inadvertent violation[264] or one taken without notice of the stay.

A related issue is whether creditors of a bankrupt company have standing to recover damages for another creditor's violation of the automatic stay. To the extent that the automatic stay helps preserves value of the estate for ultimate distribution to all creditors, the wilful and improper actions of one creditor may easily cause the sort of harm that confers constitutional standing on a creditor under Article III's case or controversy standard.[265] Moreover, both § 1109(b) which makes it clear that any "party in interest" may be heard on any issue that arises in a Chapter 11 case, and the general legislative purposes of the automatic stay, indicate that creditors have standing to bring claims under § 362(k). The principal difficulty is whether such claims are property of the estate under § 541, that should be brought, if at all, by the debtor-in-possession or the trustee. However, to the extent that a creditor may suffer harm from another creditor's violation of the stay that is independent of whatever harm the debtor may suffer, courts permit creditors to pursue damages for wilful violations of § 362(a).[266]

---

[258] *See* In re Crysen/Montenay Energy Co., 902 F.2d 1098, 1105 (2d Cir. 1990); In re Hooker Inv. Co., 116 B.R. 375 (Bankr. S.D.N.Y. 1990).

[259] *E.g.*, In re Panek, 402 B.R. 71 (Bankr. D. Mass. 2009); In re Everett, 127 B.R. 781, 784 (Bankr. E.D.N.C. 1991).

[260] *See* Spookyworld, Inc. v. Town of Berlin (In re Spookyworld, Inc.), 346 F.3d 1, 7 & 7n.3 (2003).

[261] 346 F.3d at 8.

[262] Bankruptcy Code § 105(a).

[263] *See* In re Crysen/Montenay Energy Co., 902 F.2d 1098, 1104 (2d Cir. 1990);

[264] *E.g.*, Miller v. United States, 422 B.R. 168 (W.D. Wis. 2010) (post-petition seizure of income tax refund caused by computer "glitch").

[265] St. Paul Fire & Marine Ins. Co. v. Labuzan, 579 F.3d 533 (5th Cir. 2009); Homer Nat'l Bank v. Namie, 96 B.R. 652, 654 (W.D. La. 1989).

[266] St. Paul Fire & Marine Ins. Co. v. Labuzan, 579 F.3d 533 (5th Cir. 2009).

[C] Sovereign Immunity

Section 106 contains a broad abrogation of sovereign immunity with respect to actions brought against state governments under many provisions of the Bankruptcy Code. It provides in part: "Notwithstanding an assertion of sovereign immunity, sovereign immunity is abrogated as to a governmental unit to the extent set forth in this section, with respect to [many enumerated sections of the Bankruptcy Code including §§ 105 and 362]."[267] It expressly abrogates sovereign immunity with respect to "an order or judgment awarding a money recovery, but not including an award of punitive damages."[268] Moreover, § 106(b) provides:

> A governmental unit that has filed a proof of claim in the case is deemed to have waived sovereign immunity with respect to a claim against such governmental unit that is property of the estate and that arose out of the same transaction or occurrence out of which the claim of such governmental unit arose.[269]

Until 2006, Congress's power to abrogate sovereign immunity with respect to actions for damages against a state government was in serious question. In the years since the Supreme Court's 1996 decision in *Seminole Tribe v. Florida*,[270] § 106 was widely regarded as unconstitutional, at least with respect to actions to recover damages from state governments. In *Seminole Tribe*, the Court held that Congress lacked authority to abrogate state sovereign immunity to authorize suits by Indian tribes against states to enforce legislation that was enacted pursuant to the Indian Commerce Clause of the U.S. Constitution. *Seminole Tribe* did not involve § 362, § 105, or any other provision of the Bankruptcy Code, but its rationale, which was based on the limits imposed by the Eleventh Amendment on Congress's powers under Article I of the Constitution, seemed easily adaptable to Article I's Bankruptcy power. In the wake of *Seminole Tribe*, most courts held that § 106(a) was unconstitutional.[271]

There remained a question of whether the automatic stay and discharge injunction implicated sovereign immunity at all. Since the Supreme Court's decision in *Ex Parte Young*,[272] actions for an injunction brought against a state official acting in his or her official capacity were held not to be an "action" against the state itself. As such, enforcing the automatic stay against a state might not require an abrogation of sovereign immunity. The Supreme Court addressed this question in *Tennessee Student Assistance Corporation v. Hood*,[273] holding that sovereign immunity did not prevent a bankruptcy court from discharging a student loan made by a state. The Court held that the bankruptcy court's *in rem* jurisdiction over the estate gave it the power to adjudicate the dischargeability of the state's claim.

---

[267] Bankruptcy Code § 106(a).

[268] Bankruptcy Code § 106(a)(3).

[269] Bankruptcy Code § 106(b).

[270] 517 U.S. 44 (1996).

[271] *E.g.*, Ga. Higher Educ. Assistance Corp. v. Crow (In re Crow), 394 F.3d 918, 921 (11th Cir. 2004).

[272] Ex Parte Young, 209 U.S. 123 (1908).

[273] 541 U.S. 440 (2004).

Finally, in 2006, in response to a split in the circuits regarding the issue, the Court overruled these earlier decisions, and in *Central Virginia Community College v. Katz*, held that the Bankruptcy Clause authorized Congress to abrogate sovereign immunity in bankruptcy matters, and that states therefore are not immune from suit by a trustee to recover avoidable preferences.[274]

The court explained:

> States agreed in the plan of the Convention not to assert any sovereign immunity defense they might have had in proceedings brought pursuant to "Laws on the subject of Bankruptcies." . . . The scope of this consent was limited; the jurisdiction exercised in bankruptcy proceedings was chiefly in rem — a narrow jurisdiction that does not implicate state sovereignty to nearly the same degree as other kinds of jurisdiction. But while the principal focus of the bankruptcy proceedings is and was always the res, some exercises of bankruptcy courts' powers — issuance of writs of habeas corpus included — unquestionably involved more than mere adjudication of rights in a res. In ratifying the Bankruptcy Clause, the States acquiesced in a subordination of whatever sovereign immunity they might otherwise have asserted in proceedings necessary to effectuate the in rem jurisdiction of the bankruptcy courts.[275]

Thus, to the extent enforcement of the stay is "necessary to effectuate" the court's in rem jurisdiction over estate property, there seems little doubt that under *Katz*, actions against states for violations of the stay are permitted.

---

[274] 546 U.S. 356 (2006). *See* Bankruptcy Code § 547; *infra* Chapter 15 — Avoidable Preferences.

[275] 546 U.S. at 377-78.

Chapter 9

OPERATING THE DEBTOR

§ 9.01 RESPONSIBILITY FOR OPERATION OF THE DEBTOR

Debtors are not static entities. Many debtors are businesses, which must obtain supplies, sell goods or services, pay their employees, use equipment, and obtain credit. This may appear, principally, to be an issue for debtors that are reorganizing under Chapter 11, but even a liquidating debtor might need to continue some of its operations to protect its assets from harm, or to avoid selling assets in a hurry at fire sale prices. As a result, many debtors choose to conduct their liquidations in Chapter 11. But, even in Chapter 7, some debtors may seek to continue at least some of their operations while their bankruptcy case is pending.[1] However, for debtors who hope to reorganize, it is crucial to maintain continuous operations while developing a strategy to resuscitate the business.

It might not be clear who should make these important decisions about whether to reorganize or liquidate, sell an asset or keep it, develop a new business strategy or focus on a core business. Stakeholders may disagree about the best course. A fully secured creditor may believe that an immediate surrender of its collateral or a prompt liquidation would serve their interests better than a risky attempt to reorganize. Unsecured creditors, by contrast, might prefer to take a risk to improve the return on their claim, while vendors might wish to keep a customer and employees preserve their jobs. Owners (and managers) may see reorganization as the only opportunity to save some of their investment (or their careers).

The Bankruptcy Code balances the interests of those who support the debtor's continued operation and those who oppose it. The fulcrum of this balance is "adequate protection," a concept that is explored more deeply in conjunction with the automatic stay of § 362, discussed in the previous chapter.[2] The issue is the extent to which the Code should subject unwilling creditors to continued risks in an effort to reduce the harm to others.

Rules regarding a debtor's continued operation apply to all types of bankruptcy cases.[3] Even a Chapter 7 trustee may continue to operate the debtor for a time, if that is the most reasonable means to conduct its liquidation.[4] However, these rules are important primarily in reorganization cases, particularly those involving

---

[1] Bankruptcy Code § 721.

[2] *See supra* § 8.06[B] Relief from Stay Upon Request of a Party.

[3] Bankruptcy Code § 103(a).

[4] Bankruptcy Code § 721. *See infra* § 17.04[B] Duties of the Trustee.

business debtors. Chapter 11 cases nearly always involve a prolonged period of several months to several years between the time a case is filed, and the consummation of a confirmed reorganization plan.

§ 9.02 SUPERVISION OF THE DEBTOR'S BUSINESS

When Franklin Manufacturing, Inc. files a bankruptcy petition, it is in many respects treated as a new legal entity: Franklin Manufacturing, Inc., Debtor-in-Possession.[5] This new role is accompanied by new responsibilities and new restrictions. While the debtor-in-possession owns the same building and produces the same products that are shipped by the same employees, and it has the same angry bankers trying to extract their collateral, the estate is not the same person or entity as the prepetition debtor.[6] Instead of operating the business for the benefit of its shareholder owners, the debtor-in-possession must seek to maximize the value of the estate for the benefit of all stakeholders.

This has many implications, both major and minor. Members of the debtor's management team have new fiduciary duties to the debtor's creditors and are managing the debtor's business under court supervision. Failure to accept these limitations on their power can create dangerous situations for the debtor as well as civil and even criminal liability for the managers themselves. For example, in one large, well-publicized bankruptcy, the managers of the debtor-in-possession thought nothing of paying themselves huge bonuses without court approval. Those bonuses had to be returned and a trustee was nearly appointed.[7] Had the court decided that the managers had acted fraudulently, rather than just foolishly, far more severe sanctions probably would have resulted.

The debtor-in-possession or trustee's authority to operate the business is not unrestrained. Most importantly, the trustee or a debtor-in-possession is required to adhere to applicable state and federal law. Section 959(b) of the Judicial Code imposes the obligation to "manage and operate the [estate] according to the requirements of the valid laws of the State in which [the estate's] property is situated, in the same manner that the owner or possessor thereof would be bound to do if in possession thereof."[8] This does not mean, of course that state regulatory

---

[5] For many years, the debtor-in-possession was regarded by most as a distinct legal entity. However, strict treatment of the debtor-in-possession as a new legal entity is inconsistent with several provisions of the Bankruptcy Code. *See* NLRB v. Bildisco & Bildisco, 465 U.S. 513, 528 (1984). As a result, many commentators have ceased treating the debtor-in-possession as an entirely new legal person. *E.g.*, Michael T. Andrew, *Executory Contracts in Bankruptcy: Understanding "Rejection,"* 59 U. Colo. L. Rev. 845, 855 n.51 (1988). Nevertheless, referring to the debtor-in-possession as a new entity is a useful device to remember that its discretion is limited in ways that did not apply before its petition was filed.

[6] *See generally* David Gray Carlson, *Voidable Preferences and Proceeds: A Reconceptualization*, 71 Am. Bankr. L.J. 517, 519-20 (1997) ("new entity" theory explains powers and new duties of debtor-in-possession better than other theories); Brett W. King, *Assuming and Assigning Executory Contracts: A History of Indeterminate "Applicable Law,"* 70 Am. Bankr. L.J. 95, 125 (1996) (regarding utility of "new entity" theory); Thomas E. Plank, *The Bankruptcy Trust as a Legal Person*, 35 Wake Forest L. Rev. 251 (2000).

[7] Ronald J. Bacigal, The Limits of Litigation: The Dalkon Sheild Controversy 64-71 (1990).

[8] 28 U.S.C. § 959(b) (2006).

agencies may ignore the automatic stay.[9] But the trustee or the estate may be held liable for violating state law in their operation or management of the estate. And, they may be enjoined from taking action that would not comply with state and local law.

In addition, a Chapter 11 debtor's operations are likely to be subject to review and supervision by interested parties, including creditors' committees, the United States Trustee, the Securities and Exchange Commission, or a court appointed examiner or trustee. The roles of these parties in a Chapter 11 case is explained in more detail in a later chapter.[10]

§ 9.03 USE, SALE, OR LEASE OF ESTATE PROPERTY

Section 363 authorizes the trustee or debtor-in-possession to use, sell, or lease property of the estate, subject to a complicated array of controls, depending on the nature of the property, the proposed use, and whether the property is subject to a creditor's lien. As will be seen, the debtor has considerable leeway to deal with property in the ordinary course of business. On the other hand, the debtor is subject to greater restrictions in dealing with extraordinary uses or dispositions of estate property. The debtor must seek court approval in advance of any sale or use of property outside the ordinary course of business and must seek court approval for any use of cash-like property that is subject to a creditor's security interest whether or not the use is in the ordinary course.

[A] Use, Sale, or Lease In the Ordinary Course

Debtors[11] generally have authority to use estate property in the ordinary course of business *without* prior court approval.[12] This permits the debtor to continue its operations without consulting with the court about everything. The debtor may use its real estate and equipment as part of its ongoing operations and continue to sell inventory to its customers, as it had done before the bankruptcy case was filed. There is no requirement that there be any notice to the court or creditors, or any hearing.[13] There are special rules for co-owners[14] and for those claiming an interest arising from marital rights,[15] but even these rules do not give an absolute right to block the debtor's action.

---

[9] Hillis Motors, Inc. v. Hawaii Auto. Dealers' Ass'n, 997 F.2d 581 (9th Cir. 1993).

[10] *See infra* § 19.03 Roles of the Participants.

[11] At this point, this chapter ceases to refer to the "trustee or debtor-in-possession" on every occasion. Instead, it will usually just refer to the "debtor" and trust the reader to understand that, unless the context otherwise requires, this refers either to the trustee or to the debtor-in-possession, depending on whether a trustee has been appointed. In most cases, a trustee will administer the estate in a Chapter 7 liquidation case. In other cases, the debtor-in-possession is usually responsible for the administration of the estate. Referring to both the trustee and the debtor-in-possession in these situations is cumbersome and detracts from the readability of the text.

[12] Bankruptcy Code § 363(c)(1).

[13] Bankruptcy Code § 363(c)(1).

[14] Bankruptcy Code § 363(h), (j).

[15] Bankruptcy Code § 363(i), (j).

The reason for this is simple. The Bankruptcy Code recognizes that the value of a business debtor is not just the sum of its assets. The debtor's business operations themselves produce value, and all stakeholders benefit if this value can be preserved. To continue the operation of the business, the person responsible for the operation of a business needs flexibility. It is assumed that achievement of this goal produces benefits to creditors as a group. Also, continuing the debtor's ordinary course business operations preserves any value that might exist until an orderly decision can be made whether to dispose of the assets piecemeal, to sell off particular business units, or to reorganize the entire company. Thus, except with respect to "cash collateral"[16] and unless the court orders otherwise, the debtor "may enter into transactions, including the sale or lease of property of the estate, in the ordinary course of business . . . and may use property of the estate in the ordinary course of business."[17]

For example, if Franklin Manufacturing, debtor-in-possession, wishes to sell items it has manufactured to its customers, the company may continue to enter into the usual contracts to buy raw materials, employ factory workers, and sell completed items of its inventory, without any prior notice to creditors or approval from the court. Any other rule would seriously impair the ability of the business to operate, and the business would have no hope of successfully reorganizing.

On the other hand, the court has the authority to intervene to restrict the debtor's actions.[18] For example, if the court decides that Franklin's managers are engaged in self dealing, or entering into foolish or improper supply contracts, it might require Franklin to obtain prior court approval before entering into any future deals. However, when this happens, the more typical remedy is to appoint a trustee.

Whether a particular transaction is in the ordinary course is also of concern to the non-debtor who wants the transaction to be enforced. Whether a transaction is "ordinary" depends on two tests: the horizontal dimension test and the vertical dimension test.[19] The horizontal dimension test considers "whether from an industry-wide perspective, the transaction is of the sort commonly undertaken by companies in that industry."[20] The vertical dimension test considers creditors' expectations and whether the economic risk of the transaction is different from those accepted by creditors that extended credit to the debtor pre-petition.[21]

---

[16] Bankruptcy Code § 363(a). *See infra* § 9.03[B] Use of Cash Collateral.

[17] Bankruptcy Code § 363(c)(1).

[18] Bankruptcy Code § 363(c)(1).

[19] *E.g.*, In re Roth Am., Inc., 975 F.2d 949, 952-54 (3d Cir. 1992); Vision Metals, Inc. v. SMS DEMAG, Inc. (In re Vision Metals, Inc.), 325 B.R. 138, 143-45 (Bankr. D. Del. 2005). *See* Benjamin Weintraub & Alan N. Resnick, *The Meaning of "Ordinary Course of Business" Under the Bankruptcy Code — Vertical and Horizontal Analysis*, 19 UCC L.J. 364 (1987).

[20] In re Roth Am., Inc., 975 F.2d 949, 953 (3d Cir. 1992); Vision Metals, Inc. v. SMS DEMAG, Inc. (In re Vision Metals, Inc.), 325 B.R. 138, 143-44 (Bankr. D. Del. 2005).

[21] In re Roth Am., Inc., 975 F.2d 949, 953 (3d Cir. 1992); Vision Metals, Inc. v. SMS DEMAG, Inc. (In re Vision Metals, Inc.), 325 B.R. 138, 144-45 (Bankr. D. Del. 2005); In re James A. Phillips, Inc., 29 B.R. 391, 394 (S.D.N.Y. 1983).

A debtor's continued sale of inventory is likely to be in the ordinary course under both tests. However, if the debtor's inventory is subject to a creditor's security interest, its sale might leave the creditor without adequate protection. This is particularly true because § 552(a) prevents a creditor's pre-petition security interest in after acquired property from attaching to property acquired by the debtor after its case commenced — though it does attach to the proceeds of pre-petition collateral.[22] Section 363(d) protects secured creditors from dissipation of their collateral by preventing its sale, use, or lease in a way that would be inconsistent with any relief from the automatic stay provided to the creditor under § 362(d).[23] Moreover, since the proceeds of any disposition of the collateral will be covered by a replacement lien, and the debtor is not allowed to use cash that is collateral without court approval, creditors with security interests in the debtor's inventory who are fearful that the debtor will sell the collateral out from under them[24] and dissipate the proceeds, have recourse to the court.[25] If inventory lenders are granted relief from the stay and permitted to foreclose, the debtor's reorganization comes to an abrupt halt. To avoid this problem, many Chapter 11 debtors seek a court order, frequently on the first day of their case, that either sets the conditions for the use of cash collateral or approves a post-petition financing agreement. That order grants the inventory lender a security interest in after-acquired inventory that is purchased to replace items that are to be sold in the ordinary course of business to the debtor's customers.[26] Except in rare cases, failure to obtain such post-petition financing is likely to lead to dismissal or conversion of the debtor's case.

[B]　Use of Cash Collateral[27]

The most important restriction on a debtor's ability to use property in the ordinary course is with respect to "cash collateral." Cash collateral is cash and any cash equivalents in which someone other than the estate (such as a secured creditor) has an interest.[28] Section 363(c)(2) prohibits the debtor from using cash collateral without first obtaining either the consent of the creditor or authorization from the court. Neither the creditor nor the court are likely to approve unless the

---

[22] Bankruptcy Code § 522(a).

[23] Bankruptcy Code § 363(d)(2).

[24] *See* U.C.C. § 9-320(a) (2010) (buyer in the ordinary course takes free from perfected security interest).

[25] Bankruptcy Code § 362(d)(1). *See supra* § 8.06[B][1] For Cause: Lack of Adequate Protection for Secured Creditors.

[26] *E.g.*, In re CB Holding Corp., 447 B.R. 222 (Bankr. D. Del. 2010). Under state law, buyers in the ordinary course usually take free from the creditor's security interest. *See* U.C.C. § 9-320(a) (2003). *See generally* Bruce A. Henoch, Comment, *Postpetition Financing: Is There Life After Debt?*, 8 Bankr. Dev. J. 575 (1991).

[27] Stephen A. Stripp, *Balancing of Interests in Orders Authorizing the Use of Cash Collateral in Chapter 11*, 21 Seton Hall L. Rev. 562 (1991); Benjamin Weintraub & Alan Resnick, *The Use of Cash Collateral in Reorganization Cases*, 15 UCC L.J. 168 (1982); Donald T. Polednak, Note, *Is the Secured Creditor Really "Secure"?: A Survey of Remedies and Sanctions for a Debtor's Unauthorized Use of Cash Collateral in Chapter 11 Bankruptcy*, 31 Washburn L.J. 344 (1992).

[28] Bankruptcy Code § 363(a).

debtor provides the creditor with adequate protection against loss or dissipation of the collateral.[29]

This protection makes the definition of "cash collateral" particularly important. It means "cash, negotiable instruments, documents of title, securities, deposit accounts, or other cash equivalents . . . and . . . proceeds, products, offspring, rents or profits of property" that are subject to a creditor's security interest.[30] This includes cash generated from the sale of encumbered inventory, and sometimes rents received from tenants in an apartment or office building that is collateral for a debt.[31] It specifically includes "fees, charges, accounts or other payments for the use or occupancy of rooms and other public facilities in hotels, motels, or other lodging properties subject to a security interest [under § 552(b)]."[32]

Not only is the debtor prohibited from using cash collateral without court , but also the debtor must segregate and separately account for cash collateral, unless either the creditor consents to other treatment or the court relieves the debtor of this duty in an order permitting the use of cash collateral.[33] These provisions effectively place the burden on the debtor to raise the issue of adequate protection if it wishes to use cash to pay its employees, pay its utility bills, or purchase additional supplies or equipment. In many cases, the court simultaneously hears the debtor's request to use cash collateral with a creditor's demand for adequate protection of its interest in the property.[34]

There are practical problems of timing. A reorganizing debtor frequently needs immediate access to cash collateral to continue the operation of its business. Thus, the court is required to make a decision "promptly."[35] The court may hold a preliminary hearing upon the debtor's request to use cash collateral and may give temporary permission — but only if there is a "reasonable likelihood" that the debtor will prevail at the final hearing.[36] Rule 4001(b) gives more detailed guidance for the conduct of hearings on use of cash collateral. The final hearing must be at least fifteen days after service of the debtor's motion for authorization. If the movant requests, the court may conduct an earlier preliminary hearing. However, at the preliminary hearing, the court may only authorize the use of "that amount of cash collateral as is necessary to avoid immediate and irreparable harm to the estate pending a final hearing."[37] Obvious examples include an immediately due payroll or a vital shipment that is arriving C.O.D.

---

[29] *See* In re Las Torres Dev., LLC, 413 B.R. 687 (Bankr. S.D. Tex. 2009); In re Carbone Co., 395 B.R. 631 (Bankr. N.D. Ohio 2008).

[30] Bankruptcy Code § 363(a).

[31] *E.g.*, In re 400 Walnut Assoc., LP, 454 B.R. 601 (Bankr. E.D. Pa. 2011).

[32] Bankruptcy Code § 363(a). *But see* In re HT Pueblo Props., LLC., 462 B.R. 812 (Bankr. D. Colo. 2011).

[33] Bankruptcy Code § 363(d)(4).

[34] Bankruptcy Code § 363(c)(3)

[35] Bankruptcy Code § 363(c)(3).

[36] Bankruptcy Code § 363(c)(3).

[37] Fed. R. Bankr. P. 4001(b)(2).

Even Rule 4001, however, does not fully deal with the most difficult situation — one in which the need for cash collateral is so great and immediate that the ordinary forms of notice and hearing are not available. It is generally assumed that, if the emergency is sufficiently grave, the notice may be nothing more than a telephone call to those creditors who can be reached; the hearing may be nothing more than a conference call. This hearing is likely to be conducted in connection with a variety of other "first-day motions" that are frequently necessary if the debtor is to survive.[38]

[C]   Use, Sale, or Lease Outside the Ordinary Course[39]

In contrast to ordinary course of business transactions, non-ordinary course transactions are subject to prior court scrutiny. Section 363(b) requires any non-ordinary course use, sale, or lease of property to be preceded by notice and an opportunity for a hearing.[40]

This provision is likely to be invoked in two distinct situations. The first is a liquidation case in which the trustee is not authorized to conduct the business of the debtor — the typical Chapter 7 case. The second is one in which the debtor-in-possession, or perhaps even a trustee, is authorized to conduct the debtor's business but wishes to enter into a transaction that is outside the ordinary scope of that business's operations. In both circumstances, the standard for court approval of the sale is usually a routine "business judgment" test.[41] However, if the transaction is with an insider, a higher standard, whether the transaction "will serve the interests of creditors and of the debtor's estate," may apply.[42]

The former circumstance most commonly occurs in a Chapter 7 case in which the trustee has not been authorized to conduct the debtor's business, but instead, is liquidating the debtor's assets. The trustee is likely, in these circumstances to sell most or all of the debtor's assets outside the ordinary course.

In other circumstances, it may be more fruitful for the trustee to continue to operate the debtor's business perhaps in anticipation of selling it as a going concern. In these cases, the trustee needs court authorization to continue the debtor's business operations.[43] In the course of operating the debtor's business, the trustee may determine that some of the debtor's assets need to be jettisoned. If so, the trustee needs further court authorization to sell these assets outside the ordinary course.

The more common situation in which court authority is necessary involves a Chapter 11 debtor-in-possession that decides either that some of its real estate or equipment is unnecessary, or that an entire portion of the debtor's business cannot

---

[38] *See infra* § 19.06[C] First-Day Orders.

[39] Lee R. Bogdanoff, *Purchase and Sale of Assets in Reorganization*, 47 Bus. Law. 1367 (1992).

[40] Bankruptcy Code § 363(b)(1).

[41] *E.g.*, In re Psychrometric Systems, Inc., 367 B.R. 670, 674 (Bankr. D. Colo.2007).

[42] *See* In re Pilgrim's Pride Corp., 401 B.R. 229, 237 (Bankr. N.D. Tex. 2009).

[43] Bankruptcy Code § 721.

be operated at a profit. In either case, the debtor can seek court approval to sell the unproductive assets.

Section 363(b)(1) has been used to accomplish a sale of all or a substantial part of the debtor's assets in a single transaction.[44] This was done in *In re Adelphia Communications, Inc.*, involving the well-known cable-TV and Internet provider of the same name. The debtor sold substantially all of its assets to two of its competitors, Time-Warner Cable Co. and Comcast Corp., for $17 billion.[45] Such sales can effectively reorganize the debtor without complying with the normal process of preparing a disclosure statement and giving creditors the opportunity to vote on the plan. The recent going-concern sales of Chrysler and GM are controversial examples of such sales. This aspect of the Chrysler and GM sales is nothing particularly new.[46] Courts currently permit such sales upon a showing that there is a sound business purpose for the transaction,[47] unless aspects of the sale restructure the priority and other rights of creditors.[48] Often, they will implement special procedures to safeguard, as much as possible, the interests that are protected through the plan process.

The sale in *In re Lionel Corp.* is frequently cited as an example.[49] Even though the company is known primarily for the toy train sets that many of us of a certain age played with in our childhood, Lionel's most valuable asset was 82% of the common stock of Dale Electronics, Inc., a manufacturer of electronic components. Lionel sought to sell its holdings in Dale to a suitor who was interested in acquiring the subsidiary. The success of Lionel's reorganization plan depended on its sale of the Dale Electronics stock. Lionel could have submitted a reorganization plan calling for the Dale Electronics stock to be sold and waited for creditors to vote to approve the plan. However, this would have taken considerable time and the buyer of the stock might not have been willing to wait to see whether Lionel's creditors would vote their approval. Accordingly, Lionel sought court approval of the sale under § 363.

A committee of equity security holders was opposed. It believed that conducting the sale in this fashion deprived shareholders of the "safeguards of disclosure, solicitation and acceptance"[50] that proposing the sale as part of an overall

---

[44] Brad B. Erens & David A. Hall, *Secured Lender Rights in 363 Sales and Related Issues of Lender Consent*, 18 Am. Bankr. Inst. L. Rev. 535 (2010); John J. Hurley, *Chapter 11 Alternative: Section 363 Sale of all of the Debtor's Assets Outside a Plan of Reorganization*, 58 Am. Bankr. L.J. 233 (1984); George W. Kuney, *Misinterpreting Bankruptcy Code Section 363(f) and Undermining the Chapter 11 Process*, 76 Am. Bankr. L.J. 235 (2002).

[45] *See Bankruptcy Court Backs Adelphia Sale*, N.Y. Times, June 28, 2006, at C7.

[46] Stephen Lubben, *No Big Deal: The Chrysler and GM Sales in Context*, 83 Am. Bankr. L.J. 101 (2009).

[47] *E.g.*, Comm. of Equity Sec. Holders v. Lionel Corp. (In re Lionel Corp.), 722 F.2d 1063 (2d Cir. 1983).

[48] *See* Pension Benefit Guar. Corp. v. Braniff Airways, Inc. (In re Braniff Airways, Inc.), 700 F.2d 935 (5th Cir. 1983). *See also* Official Comm. of Unsecured Creditors v. Cajun Elec. Power, Coop., Inc. (In re Cajun Elec. Power Coop., Inc.), 119 F.3d 349 (5th Cir. 1997).

[49] Comm. of Equity Sec. Holders v. Lionel Corp. (In re Lionel Corp.), 722 F.2d 1063 (2d Cir. 1983).

[50] 722 F.2d at 1066.

reorganization plan would have provided. The court disapproved the sale, but also rejected the view advanced by the committee that this type of sale could be conducted only in an emergency. At the same time, however, the court also rejected any assertion that the bankruptcy court had *"carte blanche"* to approve sales of a substantial portion of a Chapter 11 debtor's assets.[51] The court indicated that the bankruptcy judge could approved a sale of a substantial portion of a debtor's assets if "from the evidence before him at the hearing [there was] a good business reason to grant [the] application [for the sale]."[52] In determining whether there was a good business reason for the proposed sale, the court should:

> consider all salient factors . . . [such as] the proportionate value of the asset to the estate as a whole, the amount of elapsed time since the filing, the likelihood that a plan of reorganization will be proposed and confirmed in the near future, the effect of the proposed disposition on future plans of reorganization, the proceeds to be obtained from the disposition vis-a-vis any appraisals of the property, which of the alternatives of use, sale or lease the proposal envisions and most importantly perhaps, whether the asset is increasing or decreasing in value.[53]

Even though, in the *Lionel* case itself, the standard was not met, and the sale was not approved, the "Lionel standard" has been widely followed,[54] and was relied on to permit a similar sale in the 2009 Chapter 11 proceeding of the auto manufacturer, Chrysler, where the court noted that the sale of most of Chrysler's assets as part of alliance with the Italian auto manufacturer, Fiat, was Chrysler's only viable option to an immediate liquidation.[55] The 2009 bankruptcy sale of a substantial portion of General Motors, Inc's. assets, accompanied by the assistance of the United States government, was handled in much the same way. The Chrysler sale was upheld by the Second Circuit under the *Lionel* standard, but that opinion was summarily vacated and the appeal was dismissed as moot without an opinion by the Supreme Court. As such, the law in this area is unsettled.[56]

[D]   Adequate Protection

Section 363(e) makes adequate protection an integral part of the rules regarding the debtor's use, sale, or lease of estate property. Upon request of a person who has an interest in estate property, the court must prohibit or condition its use, sale,

---

[51] 722 F.2d at 1069 (emphasis in original).

[52] 722 F.2d at 1071.

[53] 722 F.2d at 1071.

[54] *E.g.*, Contrarian Funds, LLC v. Westpoint Stevens, Inc. (In re Westpoint Stevens, Inc.), 333 B.R. 30 (S.D.N.Y. 2005); Official Comm. of Subordinated Bondholders v. Integrated Res., Inc. (In re Integrated Res., Inc.), 147 B.R. 650 (S.D.N.Y. 1992).

[55] In re Chrysler, LLC, 405 B.R. 84 (S.D.N.Y. 2009). *See* Fred N. David, *Interpreting the Supreme Court's Treatment of the Chrysler Bankruptcy and its Impact on Future Business Reorganizations*, 27 Emory Bankr. Dev. J. 25, 33-34 (2010).

[56] Fred N. David, *Interpreting the Supreme Court's Treatment of the Chrysler Bankruptcy and its Impact on Future Business Reorganizations*, 27 Emory Bankr. Dev. J. 25 (2010). *See* Ind. State Police Pension Trust v. Chrysler LLC, 130 S. Ct. 1015, 1015 (2009), remanded sub nom. In re Chrysler LLC, 592 F.3d 370 (2d Cir. 2010).

or lease to the extent necessary to provide adequate protection.[57] This protects lienholders, lessors, lessees, and co-owners. Thus, if the debtor wished to sell a parcel of the estate's real estate, it would need to conduct the sale in a way that provided adequate protection for the mortgagee, any lessees, and any joint tenant who had an interest in the land.

The nature of the interest protected and the means of providing protection are largely the same as they are under § 362 with respect to the automatic stay.[58] In most cases, where the interest involved is a security interest, mortgage, or other lien, the creditor usually seeks either some sort of protective relief as a condition to the debtor's proposed use of the property or to foreclose. The secured creditor has the right to protection against the loss in value of its interest. This can be accomplished in a variety of ways, such as by giving the creditor an interest in the proceeds obtained from the sale of the property or an interest in substitute property of equal value, such as after-acquired inventory.

When the debtor wants to sell the creditor's collateral, the necessity of providing adequate protection is more urgent. This is particularly true in the case of sales of inventory, where buyers are likely to acquire their interest in the property free of the creditor's lien.[59] But even the debtor's continued use of a creditor's collateral leads to its loss of value through accelerated depreciation or possible casualty loss.

Section 363(d) coordinates with § 362's rules regarding terminating, limiting, or conditioning the automatic stay with rules on the use, sale, or lease of estate property. It prevents the debtor from using property in any manner that is inconsistent with relief granted from the stay.[60] For example, suppose that Perpetual Motors Acceptance Corporation has a security interest in some light trucks owned by Franklin Manufacturing Co. Shortly after Franklin filed its bankruptcy petition, Perpetual Motors Acceptance obtained a court order that imposed certain conditions on continuation of the automatic stay. One of those conditions might prohibit Franklin from using the trucks to haul more than the maximum load recommended by the manufacturer. Another condition might prevent Franklin from selling or leasing the trucks to anyone else without the creditor's consent or court approval. These conditions on the continuation of the automatic stay also act as restrictions on the debtor's use of the trucks. If Franklin fails to comply with these conditions, the court will likely permit foreclosure. A serious misuse of the debtor's property may lead the court to appoint a trustee,[61] dismiss the case,[62] or refuse to confirm the debtor's plan.[63]

---

[57] Bankruptcy Code § 363(e).

[58] *See supra* § 8.06[B] Relief from Stay Upon Request of a Party.

[59] U.C.C. § 9-320(a) (2010).

[60] Bankruptcy Code § 363(d).

[61] Bankruptcy Code § 1104. *See infra* § 19.03[D] Appointment of Trustee or Examiner.

[62] Bankruptcy Code § 1112. *See infra* § 19.05[B][2] Failure to Comply with Code Requirements.

[63] Bankruptcy Code § 1129(a)(2). *See infra* § 19.10[A] Compliance with the Bankruptcy Code.

[E]   Continuation of Liens and Other Interests; Sales Free and Clear[64]

If property that is subject to a lien or other third-party interest is sold by the trustee or debtor-in-possession, one obvious question that arises is whether the buyer acquires ownership of the property free and clear of the other person's interest. Thus, if Franklin Manufacturing obtains court approval to sell some of the light trucks mentioned in the example immediately above, the issue is whether the buyer acquires them free and clear of Perpetual Motors' security interest or whether it must it satisfy the secured creditor's lien to acquire clear title to the trucks. Sale of the property by a judgment creditor outside of bankruptcy is usually subject to the secured creditor's rights. Section 363(f) changes this rule. If the secured creditor is adequately protected (usually by a replacement lien on the proceeds), the debtor can sell collateral free and clear of liens. However, the debtor must meet the requirements of § 363(f) regarding a sale "free and clear" of the other creditor's interest.

[1]   "Interests" that May be Removed by a Sale Free and Clear

Section 363(f) applies when the debtor wishes to sell estate property in which some person other than the estate also holds an interest. Most of the time, the "interest" § 363(f) refers to is some sort of a lien: a consensual lien, such as a mortgage or an Article 9 security interest;[65] a judicial lien, such as a judgment or execution lien;[66] or a statutory, common law, or equitable lien, such as a mechanic's lien, a construction lien, or a tax lien.[67] In other circumstances, the other person's interest may be that of a co-owner, such as a joint tenant or a tenant in common.

The more difficult question is what rights might a third-party assert against the estate's property that is not the type of "interest" to which § 363(f) applies. One subject of debate is whether the trustee may sell the property free and clear of the interest of a lessee. Although it should be clear that a lessee's right to remain in possession of estate property is an interest, § 365(h)(1) expressly gives tenants the right to remain in possession after the debtor has rejected the unexpired lease.[68] Courts have disagreed about how to resolve the apparent conflict between § 363(f), which permits such a sale free and clear of a tenant's rights, and § 365(h)(1), which permits the tenant to remain in possession.[69]

---

[64] Rosemary E. Williams, Special Commentary, *Sales of Property, Other than in Ordinary Course of Business, of Bankruptcy Estate Free and Clear of Consensual and Nonconsensual Liens, Claims, and Encumbrances Under sec. 363(f) of Bankruptcy Code of 1978*, 22 A.L.R. Fed. 2d 579 (2007)

[65] *See supra* § 2.02 Consensual Liens; Leases.

[66] *See supra* § 2.04 Judicial Liens.

[67] *See supra* § 2.05 Statutory, Common Law, and Equitable Liens.

[68] Bankruptcy Code § 365(h)(1). *See infra* § 11.04[A][2][b] Real Estate Leases.

[69] *Compare* Precision Indus., Inc. v. Qualitech Steel SBQ, LLC (In re Qualitech Steel Corp.), 327 F.3d 537, 543-48 (7th Cir. 2003), *and* Hill v. MKBS Holdings, LLC (In re Hill), 307 B.R. 821 (Bankr. W.D. Pa. 2004) (permitting sale free and clear of lessee's interest), *with* In re Taylor, 198 B.R. 142 (Bankr. D.S.C. 1996), *and* In re Haskell L.P., 321 B.R. 1 (Bankr. D. Mass. 2005) (tenant may remain in possession). *See*

Sometimes it is not clear whether the third party's right qualifies as an "interest." In *Futuresource LLC v. Reuters Ltd.*, the court held that a business could be sold free and clear of a contractual obligation to provide intellectual property to a third party.[70] And in *EEOC v. Knox-Schillinger (In re Trans World Airlines, Inc.)*, the court permitted a sale of a debtor's assets free and clear of employment discrimination claims against the debtor, thus ensuring that the purchaser could not subsequently be held liable on a successor liability theory.[71] Cases such as these might more easily be reasoned on a theory that the third party held no "interest" that made a sale free and clear necessary. Invoking § 363(f) might lead later courts to conclude, like in other situations where § 363(f) applies, that the sale cannot be completed without providing the third party with adequate protection for its "interest," as § 363(e) usually requires.

[2] Circumstances Permitting Sale Free and Clear

The primary rules under which property may be sold free and clear are set out in § 373(f). It permits the sale free and clear if one of five alternative circumstances exist:

- nonbankruptcy law permits the property to be sold free and clear of the other party's interest;[72]

- the holder of the conflicting interest consents to the sale free and clear of its interest;[73]

- the conflicting interest is a lien, and the property will be sold for more than the aggregate value of all liens on the property;[74]

- the conflicting interest is the subject of a bona fide dispute;[75] or

- the holder of the interest could be compelled to accept a money satisfaction of the interest.[76]

These alternative grounds are discussed in order, below.

Robert M. Zinman Fall, *Precision in Statutory Drafting: The* Qualitech *Quagmire and the Sad History of 365(h) of the Bankruptcy Code*, 38 J. Marshall L. Rev. 97 (2004); Michael St. Patrick Baxter, *Section 363 Sales Free and Clear of Interests: Why the Seventh Circuit Erred in Precision Industries v. Qualitech Steel*, 59 Bus. Law. 475 (2004).

[70] 312 F.3d 281 (7th Cir. 2002).

[71] 322 F.3d 283 (3d Cir. 2003).

[72] Bankruptcy Code § 363(f)(1).

[73] Bankruptcy Code § 363(f)(2).

[74] Bankruptcy Code § 363(f)(3).

[75] Bankruptcy Code § 363(f)(4).

[76] Bankruptcy Code § 363(f)(5).

[a] Nonbankruptcy Law Permits Property to be Sold Free and Clear

Section 363(f)(1) permits the sale if nonbankruptcy law permits the property to be sold free and clear. This recognizes that there is no reason to prohibit the sale free and clear in bankruptcy, if the property could have been sold free and clear outside of bankruptcy.

The most common circumstance in which applicable nonbankruptcy law permits property to be sold free and clear of a creditor's security interest is when the property is goods that are to be sold to a buyer in the ordinary course of business. In this situation, U.C.C. § 9-320(a) permits a buyer to obtain good title. Buyers usually qualify as buyers in the ordinary course of business if the seller, in this case the debtor, is in the business of selling goods of the kind and the buyer has no knowledge that the sale to him violates the secured party's rights.[77]

[b] Creditor Consents to Sale Free and Clear

The sale may also be made free and clear if the secured creditor or other person with an interest the property consents.[78] Of course, the other person may impose conditions on its consent. For example, a secured creditor may withhold consent unless the proceeds of the sale are remitted to the secured creditor, or unless its security interest attaches to those proceeds (probably making them cash collateral). In other words, the other party is likely to provide consent to a sale free and clear of its interest if the debtor voluntarily supplies adequate protection for the affected interest. Not surprisingly, however, consent need not be formal or express; it can be implied from notice of the proposed sale and failure to object.[79]

[c] Price Exceeds Aggregate Value of All Liens

Alternatively, the court may approve a sale of estate property free and clear of all interests if the interests in question are liens and the price received for the property "is greater than the aggregate value of all liens" on the property.[80] This does not mean that the lienholders must be paid in full. It simply means that they must receive as much as their liens were worth. Assume, for example, that Titanic Corporation owns a parcel of real estate that it does not need for its reorganization, which is subject to two mortgages: a senior mortgage that secures a $1.5 million debt and a junior mortgage that secures a $300,000 debt. If the proposed price of the property is $2 million and thus exceeds the $1.8 million aggregate of both liens, the property may be sold free and clear of the liens.

But § 363 goes further. If instead, the value of the property was only worth $1.5 million, the property could be sold free and clear of both liens, so long as the sale price exceeded $1.5 million.

---

[77] U.C.C. § 1-201(37) (2010).

[78] Bankruptcy Code § 363(f)(2).

[79] *E.g.*, In re Tabone, Inc., 175 B.R. 855, 858 (Bankr. D.N.J. 1994). *But see* In re Roberts, 249 B.R. 152, 154-57 (Bankr. W.D. Mich. 2000).

[80] Bankruptcy Code § 363(f)(3).

Even though the language of § 363(f)(3) seems quite explicit, it says only that the sale price must exceed the aggregate *value* of all liens on the property. It does not say "aggregate *amount.*"[81] Courts frequently permit a sale free and clear when the sale will generate less than enough to satisfy all liens,[82] applying the literal language of § 363(f), which refers to the "aggregate *value* of all liens."[83] Other courts, recognizing that the statutory language should have some meaning, take a contrary view, and regard § 363(f)(3) as permitting a sale free and clear only if the value of the collateral is more than the amount of the debts secured by these liens.[84]

[d]   Lien Subject to a Bona Fide Dispute

Section 363(f)(4) permits a sale free and clear of a conflicting interest if the creditor's interest is the subject of a bona fide dispute. This facilitates the sale of estate property without the necessity of delaying the sale until after the dispute can be resolved.[85] For example, suppose Peninsula Bank has an undersecured lien on Franklin Manufacturing's equipment, but there is some dispute over whether the security agreement adequately describes the collateral. Because the lien is potentially avoidable under § 544(a), the collateral can be sold free and clear of what might turn out to be an invalid lien. The same would be true if the lien was subject to potential avoidance under any of the trustee's avoiding powers.

[e]   Legal or Equitable Right to Compel Acceptance of Money Substitute

Section 363(f)(5) permits estate property to be sold free and clear of another party's interest in the property if the other party "could be compelled, in a legal or equitable proceeding, to accept a money satisfaction" of its interest.[86] Because of the breadth of circumstances in which a third party might be compelled to accept cash in lieu of its interest, this language has the potential to permit a sale free and clear in nearly every circumstance. In some states, secured creditors can be compelled to accept a money satisfaction of their interests.[87] However, it is significant in this regard that § 363(f)(5) is not limited to situations where

---

[81] *E.g.,* In re Riverside Inv. P'ship, 674 F.2d 634 (7th Cir. 1982).

[82] *See* In re Beker Indus. Corp., 63 B.R. 474, 477 (Bankr. S.D.N.Y. 1986) (interpreting "aggregate value of all liens" to refer to the economic value of the lien, rather than the face amount of the debt owed to the secured creditor). *See* George W. Kuney, *Misinterpreting Bankruptcy Code Section 363(f) and Undermining the Chapter 11 Process,* 76 Am. Bankr. L.J. 235, 244-45 (2002).

[83] *E.g.,* In re Collins, 180 B.R. 447, 450 (Bankr. E. D. Va. 1995); *see* Matsuda Capital, Inc. v. Netfax Dev., LLC (In re Netfax, Inc.), 335 B.R. 85 (D. Md. 2005).

[84] Clear Channel Outdoor, Inc. v. Knupfer (In re PW, LLC), 391 B.R. 25 (B.A.P. 9th Cir. 2008); In re Nance Props., Inc., No. 11-06197-8-JRL, 2011 Bankr. LEXIS 4418 (Bankr. E.D.N.C. Nov. 8, 2011). *See* Brad B. Erens & David A. Hall, *Secured Lender Rights in 363 Sales and Related Issues of Lender Consent,* 18 Am. Bankr. Inst. L. Rev. 535 (2010).

[85] *See* In re Clark, 266 B.R. 163, 171 (B.A.P. 9th Cir. 2001).

[86] Bankruptcy Code § 363(f)(5).

[87] *See* In re Boston Generating, LLC, 440 B.R. 302 (Bankr. S.D.N.Y. 2010) (referring to U.C.C. §§ 9-608 & 9-615 as adopted in New York, Massachusetts, and elsewhere).

"nonbankruptcy law" would permit the other party to be compelled to accept a money substitute. Thus, the fact that a Chapter 11 plan that provides for a cash payment might be confirmed over the objection of the other party[88] makes § 363(f)(5) potentially broad enough to swallow up whatever other limits might be imposed by the remainder of § 363(f).[89] Several courts have taken the position that § 363(f)(5) is inapplicable to liens and only applies to other interests, such as those held by co-owners of the estate's property and other similar interests.[90] They reason that if § 363(f)(5) is construed to permit the sale in all circumstances, simply because a confirmed Chapter 11 plan would permit the creditor's interest to be satisfied by a cash payment, then § 363(f)(5) effectively eliminates any restrictions on the ability of a debtor to sell property free and clear of a creditor's lien and makes the other restrictions in § 363(f) superfluous.

[3]　Right to Adequate Protection

The fact that estate property can be sold free and clear of another party's interest does not mean that the other party can be completely deprived of its rights. The other party is entitled to adequate protection for the value of its interest in the property.[91] Buttressing this right is the prohibition against any sale, use, or lease of estate property that is inconsistent with any conditions imposed under § 363(d)(2), that a court placed on continuation of the automatic stay.[92]

[4]　Additional Special Protections for Joint Owners

[a]　Protection of Dower and Curtesy Interests

There are a number of additional rules that deal with special situations. Section 363(g) makes it clear that regardless of any limitations imposed by § 363(f), estate property may be sold free and clear of any vested or contingent marital rights of dower or curtesy.[93] However, the affected spouse must be given a right of first refusal to purchase the property for whatever price the proposed buyer has agreed to pay.[94] Moreover, if the property is sold to someone else, the non-debtor spouse must be paid the portion of the net proceeds of the sale that corresponds to his or her dower or curtesy interest.[95]

---

[88] *See* Hunt Energy Co. v. United States (In re Hunt Energy Co.), 48 B.R. 472 (Bankr. N.D. Ohio 1985).

[89] *See also* EEOC v. Knox-Schillinger (In re Trans World Airlines, Inc.), 322 F.3d 283, 290-91 (3d Cir. 2003) (permitting sale free and clear where Chapter 7 trustee could sell property free and clear in liquidation case).

[90] In re Beker Indus. Corp., 63 B.R. 474 (Bankr. S.D.N.Y. 1986); In re Canonigo, 276 B.R. 257 (Bankr. N.D. Cal. 2002).

[91] Bankruptcy Code § 363(e).

[92] Bankruptcy Code § 362(d)(2).

[93] Bankruptcy Code § 363(g).

[94] Bankruptcy Code § 363(i).

[95] Bankruptcy Code § 363(j).

[b]   Protection of Joint Tenants, Tenants in Common and Tenants by the Entirety

Section 363(h) provides additional protection for those who own interests with the debtor as tenants in common, joint tenants, or tenants by the entirety. It protects not only the joint owner's interest in the value of the property, but also the joint owner's interest in the property itself. To the extent feasible, the bankruptcy court is supposed to distribute the property in kind or to sell the debtor's interest in the whole rather than sell the entire property (including the co-owner's interest) and distribute to the co-owner its portion of the proceeds of sale.[96]

If it is feasible to split the property between the debtor and the co-owner(s), the court must do so. For example, suppose Nick is in bankruptcy, and he and his wife Nora are equal joint tenants of 100 virtually indistinguishable acres of farmland. Suppose further that these acres could readily be divided into two equal halves, each half with adequate access, drainage, and water, and each half composed of equally tillable soil. Because partition in kind is practicable, the court may not sell the entire parcel in a single unit. If the parcel is partitioned, Nick's fifty acres will be sold and Nora's fifty acres will be left untouched.

An alternative to partition is the sale of the debtor's undivided interest in the whole. Thus, the court might sell Nick's undivided interest and leave Nora's joint interest alone, so that the buyer becomes joint owner with Nora. If this form of sale would result in substantially the same amount for the estate as would a sale of the whole, then neither the trustee nor the debtor-in-possession may sell the property as a whole.

However, distribution in kind or sale of the debtor's interest alone is appropriate only where that would not impair the success of the bankruptcy proceeding. The court must sell the property as a whole, including the interest of the co-owner(s), if all four[97] of the following conditions are met:

- partition in kind between the estate and the co-owners is impracticable;[98]

- sale of the estate's undivided interest in the property would realize significantly less for the estate than sale of the property free of the co-owner(s) interest;[99]

- the benefit to the estate outweighs the detriment to the co-owners;[100] and

- the property is not used in the production, transmission, or distribution for sale of electric energy or of natural or synthetic gas for heat, light, or power.[101]

The constitutionality of selling the entire property, including the interest of a co-

---

[96] Bankruptcy Code § 363(h).

[97] *See* In re Haley, 100 B.R. 13 (Bankr. N.D. Cal. 1989).

[98] Bankruptcy Code § 363(h)(1).

[99] Bankruptcy Code § 363(h)(2).

[100] Bankruptcy Code § 363(h)(3).

[101] Bankruptcy Code § 363(h)(4).

owner, has been challenged but upheld.[102]

[5]　Effect of Sale Free and Clear

The principal effect of a sale free and clear of liens is to release the property from any encumbrances. This vests clear title in the buyer. It also transfers the property from the debtor's estate and places it beyond the bankruptcy court's jurisdiction.[103]

[F]　Ipso Facto Clauses Ineffective

The Code generally limits the effect of "ipso facto" clauses. These are provisions that place a borrower or lessee in default whenever it is in financial trouble or files a bankruptcy petition. Enforcement of these provisions would seriously impair the ability of the debtor to be liquidated or reorganize because they deprive the debtor of needed property. Moreover, if they were enforceable, nearly every commercial transaction in the country would be subject to a provision that permits the non-bankrupt party to escape the deal upon the filing of a bankruptcy petition.

Section 363(l) impairs the effect of ipso facto clauses that would otherwise prevent the debtor from using, selling, or leasing estate property. It supercedes any conflicting state common law or statutory legal rule that would similarly impair the debtor's ability to use, sell, or lease estate property.[104]

[G]　Rigged Sales[105]

A sale of estate assets may be set aside by the trustee or the debtor-in-possession if the price was rigged — that is, controlled by an agreement among potential bidders at the sale.[106] Alternatively, the trustee or debtor-in-possession may enforce the sale but insist on an increase in the price. Section 363(n) specifies that the trustee may "recover . . . any amount by which the value of the property sold exceeds the price at which [the] sale was consummated."[107] A careful reading of § 363(n) reveals that it only applies to an agreement "among potential bidders."[108] Thus, it does not govern situations where the debtor enters into a conspiracy with a single buyer to control the price.[109]

---

[102] In re Tsunis, 39 B.R. 977 (E.D.N.Y. 1983), aff'd, 733 F.2d 27 (2d Cir. 1984). See Thomas E. Plank, *The Constitutional Limits of Bankruptcy*, 63 Tenn. L. Rev. 487, 571-74 (1996).

[103] Borrego Springs Bank v. Skuna River Lumber, L.L.C. (In re Skuna River Lumber, LLC), 564 F.3d 353 (5th Cir. 2009) (bankruptcy court lacked jurisdiction to impose surcharge on property pursuant to § 506(c) after its free and clear transfer from the estate).

[104] Bankruptcy Code § 363(l).

[105] C.R. Bowles & John Egan, *The Sale of the Century or a Fraud on Creditors?: The Fiduciary Duty of Trustees and Debtors in Possession Relating to the "Sale" of a Debtor's Assets in Bankruptcy*, 28 U. Mem. L. Rev. 781 (1998).

[106] Bankruptcy Code § 363(n). See Lone Star Indus., Inc. v. Compania Naviera Perez Compac (In re New York Trap Rock Corp.), 42 F.3d 747 (2d Cir. 1994).

[107] Bankruptcy Code § 363(n).

[108] Bankruptcy Code § 363(n).

[109] *E.g.*, Lone Star Indus., Inc. v. Compania Naviera Perez Companc (In re New York Trap Rock Corp.), 42 F.3d 747, 752-53 (2d Cir. 1994); C.R. Bowles & John Egan, *The Sale of the Century or a Fraud*

Whichever alternative (avoidance or increased price) is chosen, the trustee can also recover any costs, attorneys' fees, and expenses involved in the action to correct the rigged sale. Although the Code is not explicit on the point, it appears that these expenses may also be recovered from anyone who was involved in the bid rigging, not just the ultimate buyer. In addition, the court has the discretion to award punitive damages against any of the co-conspirators who acted "in willful disregard" of the Code's prohibition of this improper activity.[110] It appears from the wording of § 363(n) that the requirement of "willful disregard" requires some knowledge or at least notice of the Code's prohibition on bid-rigging.

[H] Burdens of Proof Regarding Sales

Whenever there is a dispute over the right to use, sell, or lease property, § 363(p) regulates the burden of proof.[111] The debtor bears the burden of proof on the issue of adequate protection.[112] The party asserting an interest in the property — usually a secured creditor — bears the burden of proof on the validity, priority, and extent of its interest.[113]

[I] Appeals from Orders Approving Sales of Estate Property

The Code imposes limits on the ability to effectively appeal decisions to permit a sale or lease of estate property. To preserve rights against bona fide purchasers, the appellant must obtain a stay of the sale or lease pending the appeal.[114] Otherwise, reversal or modification of the decision does not affect the validity of the sale or lease if the buyer or lessee acquired the property in good faith.[115] For example, if the court has approved the non-ordinary course sale of Franklin Manufacturing's property to a bona fide purchaser free and clear of Peninsula Bank's security interest and the court's decision authorizing the sale is later reversed, the sale to the buyer is still valid and the bank can only seek redress, if any, against Franklin.

Redress against the buyer is available only where it acted in bad faith. This can occur where, among other things, bidders have acted in illegal collusion with one another,[116] or where the buyer has entered into a sweetheart deal with the debtor's

---

on Creditors?: The Fiduciary Duty of Trustees and Debtors in Possession Relating to the "Sale" of a Debtor's Assets in Bankruptcy, 28 U. Mem. L. Rev. 781 (1998).

[110] Bankruptcy Code § 363(n).

[111] Bankruptcy Code § 363(p) (formerly at 11 U.S.C. § 363(o) (2000)).

[112] Bankruptcy Code § 363(p)(1).

[113] Bankruptcy Code § 363(p)(2).

[114] See Fed. R. Bankr. P. 6004(g) (routinely staying orders approving the sale, use, or lease of estate property, other than those for cash collateral, for ten days).

[115] Bankruptcy Code § 363(m). See, e.g., Hower v. Molding Sys. Eng'g Corp., 445 F.3d 935 (7th Cir. 2006) (effect of failure to obtain injunction); In re Abbots Dairies, Inc., 788 F.2d 14 (3d Cir. 1986) (regarding good faith).

[116] Bankruptcy Code § 363(n). See In re Rock Indus. Mach. Corp., 572 F.2d at 1198; Mark Bell Furniture Warehouse, Inc. v. D.M. Reid Assoc. (In re Mark Bell), 992 F.2d 7, 8 (1st Cir.1992); In re Abbotts Dairies, Inc., 788 F.2d 143, 147-48 (3d Cir. 1986).

executives, which may give them an incentive to favor the buyer's proposed purchase of estate assets.[117]

[J]   Transfer of Customers' Personal Identifiable Information[118]

The Bankruptcy Code protects members of the public from inappropriate transfers of private information about the debtor's customers when the debtor's assets are sold. It restricts the transfer of "personally identifiable information about individuals to persons that are not affiliated with the debtor."[119] This information includes customer names, addresses, e-mail addresses, telephone numbers, and social security numbers.[120] The protection applies if the debtor, in connection with the sale of a product or provision of a service has previously disclosed to its customer an internal "privacy policy" that prohibits the transfer of these pieces of information about the debtor's customers. The information may not be transferred unless its sale or lease is consistent with the advertised policy or a "consumer privacy ombudsman" is appointed, and the court gives due consideration to the circumstances and conditions surrounding the sale and finds that the sale was not shown to violate any "applicable nonbankruptcy law" regarding the dissemination of such information.[121] The consumer privacy ombudsman must be appointed pursuant to new § 332.[122] This is similar to the mechanism used in §§ 333 and 352 to protect medical records of patients of bankrupt heath care providers.[123]

---

[117] *See* In re Abbotts Dairies, Inc., 788 F.2d 143 (3d Cir. 1986).

[118] *See* Daniel J. Solove, *Privacy and Power: Computer Databases and Metaphors for Information Privacy*, 53 Stan. L. Rev. 1393 (2001); Xuan-Thao N. Nguyen, *Collateralizing Privacy*, 78 Tul. L. Rev. 553 (2004).

[119] Bankruptcy Code § 363(b)(1).

[120] Bankruptcy Code § 101(41A).

[121] Bankruptcy Code § 363(b)(1)(B).

[122] Bankruptcy Code § 363(b)(1). *See* Bankruptcy Code § 332.

[123] *See infra* § 9.07 Health Care Providers.

§ 9.04   UTILITY SERVICE[124]

Section 366 provides a series of special rules addressing the debtor's utility services, such as electricity, water, natural gas, and telephone,[125] but not cable television[126] or internet services, which are not usually regarded as utilities. In most cases, these utility providers are government-run or government-regulated monopolies. It is sometimes impossible for a debtor to obtain service from an alternate provider.[127] Consequently, utilities are in an extraordinarily powerful position over a business debtor. A utility's refusal to deal with a debtor virtually forces a business debtor to liquidate. For this reason, there are restrictions on a utility's ability to refuse or terminate service. In exchange, the utility is usually entitled to a special form of adequate protection — a deposit.[128]

Section 366(a) prevents utilities from altering, refusing, or discontinuing service to the trustee, a debtor-in-possession, or the debtor merely because the debtor filed a bankruptcy case or because the debtor's pre-petition utility bills remain unpaid.[129] It also prohibits the utility from discriminating against debtors in other ways, such as charging higher rates. These limitations are considerably more expansive than the automatic stay, which does not prevent creditors from refusing to deal, provided that refusal is not used to coerce payment of a pre-petition debt.[130] Under § 366(a), the utility's motives for refusing to deal with the debtor are irrelevant.

On the other hand, utilities are entitled to adequate assurances that they will be paid for future goods or services that they provides to the debtor.[131] They must be given "adequate assurance of payment [for post-petition services], in the form of a deposit or other security" within twenty days after the date of the order for relief.[132] The 2005 Amendments specify that assurance of payment may take the form of a cash deposit, a letter of credit, a certificate of deposit, a surety bond, a

---

[124] Richard Levin & Alesia Ranney-Marinelli, *The Creeping Repeal of Chapter 11: The Significant Business Provisions of the Bankruptcy Abuse Prevention and Consumer Protection Act of 2005*, 79 Am. Bankr. L.J. 603, 608-10 (2005); Veryl Victoria Miles, *Adequate Assurance of Payment under § 366 of the Bankruptcy Code: A Term for Interpretive Flexibility or Judicial Confusion*, 20 Akron L. Rev. 715 (1987); Bertrand Pan & Jennifer Taylor, *Sustaining Power: Applying 11 U.S.C. 366 in Chapter 11 Post-BAPCPA*, 22 Emory Bankr. Dev. J. 371 (2006); John F. Wagner, Jr, Annotation, *Debtor's Protection Under 11 U.S.C.A. § 366 Against Utility Service Cutoff*, 83 A.L.R. Fed. 207 (1987).

[125] One Stop Realtour Place, Inc. v. Allegiance Telecom, Inc. (In re One Stop Realtour Place, Inc.), 268 B.R. 430 (Bankr. D. Pa. 2001).

[126] *See* Darby v. Time Warner Cable, Inc. (In re Darby), 470 F.3d 573 (5th Cir. 2006) (cable television is not a utility governed by § 366).

[127] One Stop Realtour Place, Inc. v. Allegiance Telecom, Inc. (In re One Stop Realtour Place, Inc.), 268 B.R. 430 (Bankr. D. Pa. 2001).

[128] In re Steinebach, 303 B.R. 634 (Bankr. D. Ariz. 2004).

[129] Bankruptcy Code § 366(a).

[130] *See supra* § 8.02 Scope of the Automatic Stay.

[131] Daniel Keating, *Offensive Uses of the Bankruptcy Stay*, 45 Vand. L. Rev. 71, 98 (1992); Stephanie A. Reday, Note, *Adequate Assurance Under Section 366: In re Caldor, a Step in the Right Direction*, 6 Am. Bankr. Inst. L. Rev. 235 (1998).

[132] Bankruptcy Code § 366(b). *See* Cheryl F. Anderson, Comment, *Providing Adequate Assurance for Utilities Under Section 366*, 9 Bankr. Dev. J. 199 (1992).

prepayment, or another form of security agreed upon between the parties.[133] The Code now makes it clear that in Chapter 11 cases, giving the utility company an administrative expense priority for these future services is not enough.[134] Moreover, the utility does not need to ask for this protection; the debtor must offer it voluntarily. If protection is not proffered by the debtor, the utility may alter, refuse, or discontinue service.[135]

Despite this, some courts prevent utilities from demanding a deposit or other form of protection even if applicable state law regulations permit the utility to do so.[136] Furthermore, the debtor's failure to provide adequate assurance of performance does not permit the utility to discriminate — it may cut off or reduce the debtor's service, but it may not charge extra. If the parties cannot come to an agreement regarding the assurance of payment, the court may, upon notice and an opportunity for a hearing, determine what is required. The nature and extent of the protection that may be required is subject to the court's discretion.[137]

Language added in 2005 makes a Chapter 11 debtor's deadline for providing assurance of payment unclear.[138] Although § 366(b) suggests that the utility may refuse service to the debtor if the debtor does not provide assurance of payment within twenty days of the order for relief, new § 366(c)(2) permits a utility to "alter, refuse, or discontinue utility service, if during the thirty-day period beginning on the date of the filing of the petition, the utility does not receive . . . adequate assurance of payment."[139] The weight of authority is that the utility need not obtain relief from the automatic stay to terminate service, if the debtor fails to make the necessary deposit or take whatever other action the utility demands as "adequate assurance."[140] In voluntary Chapter 11 cases, where the filing of a petition results in an immediate order for relief, it is unclear whether a utility may "alter, refuse, or discontinue" twenty days after the petition or not until thirty days after the petition.[141] Moreover, § 363(c)(2) permits the utility to alter, refuse, or discontinue service unless the assurances supplied by the debtor are "satisfactory to the utility."[142] This appears to remove the court from the picture and place the

[133] Bankruptcy Code § 366(c)(1)(A). *But see* In re Astle, 338 B.R. 855 (Bankr. D. Idaho 2006) (§ 366(c) applies only in Chapter 11 cases).

[134] Bankruptcy Code § 366(c)(1)(B). In re Astle, 338 B.R. 855 (Bankr. D. Idaho 2006) (administrative expense may be sufficient in cases under Chapter 13).

[135] Bankruptcy Code § 366(b). *See* In re Hanratty, 907 F.2d 1418 (3d Cir. 1990).

[136] *See, e.g.*, In re Coury, 22 B.R. 766, 768 (Bankr. W.D. Pa.1982).

[137] Puget Sound Energy, Inc. v. Pac. Gas & Elec. Co. (In re Pac. Gas & Elec. Co.), 271 B.R. 626 (N.D. Cal. 2002).

[138] David G. Epstien, *BAPCPA and Commercial Credit: Who (Sic) Do You Trust*, 10 N.C. Banking Inst. 57, 77-78 (2006).

[139] Bankruptcy Code § 366(c)(2); Weisel v. Dominion Peoples Gas Co. (In re Weisel), 400 B.R. 457 (Bankr. W.D. Pa. 2009).

[140] *See* In re Jones, 369 B.R. 745 (B.A.P. 1st Cir. 2007); Weisel v. Dominion Peoples Gas Co. (In re Weisel), 400 B.R. 457 (Bankr. W.D. Pa. 2009).

[141] Richard Levin & Alesia Ranney-Marinelli, *The Creeping Repeal of Chapter 11: The Significant Business Provisions of the Bankruptcy Abuse Prevention and Consumer Protection Act of 2005*, 79 Am. Bankr. L.J 603, 608-09 (2005).

[142] Bankruptcy Code § 366(c)(2).

adequacy of the assurances supplied by a Chapter 11 debtor solely in the hands of the utility.[143]

§ 9.05 OBTAINING CREDIT[144]

Between the time a reorganization case is commenced and the debtor's plan is confirmed, most Chapter 11 debtors need additional credit. They are likely to require short-term credit, customarily supplied by utility providers and trade creditors, which is usually payable thirty days after it is extended. They are also likely to require continued financing to purchase inventory. Further, they may require long-term structural credit. A reorganizing debtor generally has to reorganize its entire financial structure, including its long-term institutional debt. For example, when Titanic Corporation reorganizes, it may need to pay existing mortgages by selling off some of its property to reduce and refinance the remainder of its debt with a lower monthly payment. It might wait to do this as part of its reorganization plan, or it might find it useful to restructure some of these debts while the case is pending.

[A] Unsecured Credit In the Ordinary Course

Section 364 governs a debtor's ability to obtain credit while the case is pending, before confirmation of a plan. Section 364 draws two key distinctions: (1) ordinary course debt vs. non-ordinary course debt; and (2) secured debt vs. unsecured debt. The degree of court control over the debtor's post-petition borrowing is at its nadir when the debt is ordinary course unsecured and at its zenith when the debt is secured. Note, however, that post-petition credit has an affect on prepetition creditors. Post-petition ordinary course debt is given administrative expense priority, and therefore is senior to prepetition unsecured debt. That said, so long as the debt does not encumber new assets, the new debt will be exchanged for value, so the creditors should be no worse off. The risk is greater if the proceeds of the new loan are going to be used for a new business venture, or other extraordinary purpose, and they are greater still if the debtor is encumbering its assets.

Under § 364(a), the debtor may usually obtain unsecured credit and incur unsecured debt in the ordinary course of business, without court approval.[145] No notice, hearing, or court order is required for any particular transaction. Thus, management is permitted to allow the debtor's employees to show up for work the morning after its petition is filed, and those employees are permitted to turn the lights on when they arrive. Both transactions cause the debtor to incur an unsecured debt: to pay the employees their wages and to pay the electricity bill. Likewise, if the debtor customarily receives a delivery from one of its vendors every morning, incurring an obligation to pay for them at the end of the month,

---

[143] David G. Epstein, *BAPCPA and Commercial Credit: Who (Sic) Do You Trust?*, 10 N.C. Banking Inst. 57, 78-79 (2006).

[144] Paul M. Baisier & David G. Epstein, *Postpetition Lending Under Section 364: Issues Regarding the Gap Period and Financing for Prepackaged Plans*, 27 Wake Forest L. Rev. 103 (1992); George G. Triantis, *A Theory of the Regulation of Debtor-in-Possession Financing*, 46 Vand. L. Rev. 901 (1993).

[145] Bankruptcy Code § 364(a).

these routine deliveries may continue. The resulting claims are allowed as administrative expenses and are accorded priority.[146]

The reason for this loose approach is obvious; it would be pointlessly time-consuming and expensive for the debtor to run to court for every little routine credit transaction it engages in. In a single day, even a modest business might enter into a dozen small contracts with suppliers, each of which involves a brief extension of credit. Requiring approval of each would effectively sink the debtor in a sea of attorneys' fees. If the debtor abuses its authority, an interested party can bring the matter to the court's attention and obtain an order restricting the debtor's leeway.

The test for whether a particular credit transaction is in the ordinary course has two components, that are the same as those applied under § 363 in determining whether a debtor's use, sale, or lease of estate property is in the ordinary course.[147] The transaction is evaluated on vertical and horizontal dimensions. The vertical test considers creditors' expectations and whether the economic risk of the transaction is different from those accepted by creditors that extended credit to the debtor pre-petition.[148] The horizontal dimension test, which some courts reject as unnecessary, considers "whether from an industry-wide perspective, the transaction is of the sort commonly undertaken by companies in that industry."[149] Some courts also apply a second test and require the loan transaction to be "actual, necessary costs and expenses of preserving the estate" as required by § 503(b)(1), to which § 363(a) explicitly refers.[150]

[B]   Unsecured Credit Outside the Ordinary Course

If the proposed transaction involves a loan or other extension of credit outside the ordinary course, the transaction requires court approval,[151] after notice and the opportunity for a hearing.[152] For example, if Franklin Manufacturing needs to obtain an unsecured $50,000 line of credit to help meet its payroll as it comes due, and Franklin has never had this type of credit facility in the past or such a line of credit is not customary in Franklin's industry, prior court approval is necessary. This is almost certainly a non-ordinary course transaction (at least, a cautious attorney for the lender will make that assumption) that requires prior court approval.

---

[146] Bankruptcy Code § 364(a). *See infra* § 10.04[A][2] Administrative Expenses.

[147] *E.g.*, In re Lodge America, 259 B.R. 728, 732 (D. Kan. 2001); In re Poff Constr., Inc., 141 B.R. 104 (W.D. Va. 1991).

[148] In re Roth Am., Inc., 975 F.2d 949, 953 (3d Cir. 1992); Vision Metals, Inc. v. SMS DEMAG, Inc. (In re Vision Metals, Inc.), 325 B.R. 138, 144-45 (Bankr. D. Del. 2005); In re James A. Phillips, Inc., 29 B.R. 391, 394 (S.D.N.Y. 1983).

[149] In re Roth Am., Inc., 975 F.2d 949, 953 (3d Cir. 1992); Vision Metals, Inc. v. SMS DEMAG, Inc. (In re Vision Metals, Inc.), 325 B.R. 138, 143-44 (Bankr. D. Del. 2005) (applying § 363(b)).

[150] *See, e.g.*, In re S. Soya Corp., 251 B.R. 302 (Bankr. D.S.C. 2001).

[151] Bankruptcy Code § 364(b). This rule also applies to situations in which a trustee who is not authorized to conduct the debtor's business seeks to obtain credit.

[152] Bankruptcy Code § 102(1).

[1] Administrative Expense Priority

With prior court approval, after whatever notice and hearing is appropriate, the lender's claim is entitled to administrative priority under § 503(b).[153] However, if the debtor fails to obtain court authorization, or if there is a flaw in the notice provided to interested parties, the court may subsequently relegate the claim to general unsecured priority status.[154] Indeed, it is by no means clear that the debt is enforceable at all, as it did not arise prepetition and was not properly authorized. On rare occasions, courts have retroactively validated the transaction and given the loan priority status.[155] However, creditors who provide credit outside the ordinary course, without obtaining prior court approval, do so at considerable risk.[156]

Priority status entitles the creditor to full payment, in cash, on the effective date of a Chapter 11 plan[157] and entitles it to first crack at any equity remaining in the estate in a Chapter 7 liquidation. Creditors without priority usually recover a portion of their claims, but sometimes they receive nothing.

[2] Super-Priority

Unfortunately, administrative expense priority is no guarantee of payment. If a Chapter 11 debtor is unable to confirm a plan and its case is converted Chapter 7, the debtor will be liquidated. After paying the expenses of liquidation, the estate may be inadequate to make payments even to those with administrative expense priority.

Accordingly, § 364(c)(1) permits the court to provide a post-petition creditor with a super-priority claim, entitled to seniority over both routine administrative expenses and the higher super-priority claims of secured creditors whose "adequate protection" was inadequate to protect the full value of their interests in the estate's property.[158] In effect, the creditor is given a "super-duper" priority claim. This higher priority is available only upon a showing that the normal administrative priority is an insufficient inducement to persuade the creditor to make the loan.[159]

---

[153] *See infra* § 10.04[A][2] Administrative Expenses.

[154] *E.g.*, Credit Alliance Corp. v. Dunning-Ray Ins. Agency, Inc. (In re Blumer), 66 B.R. 109 (B.A.P. 9th Cir. 1986), *aff'd* 826 F.2d 1069 (9th Cir. 1987).

[155] In re Am. Cooler Co., 125 F.2d 496, 497 (2d Cir. 1942); In re Photo Promotion Assoc's, Inc., 881 F.2d 6, 9 (2d Cir. 1989).

[156] *See, e.g.*, In re Lehigh Valley Prof. Sports Clubs, Inc., 260 B.R. 745, 751 (Bankr. E.D. Pa. 2001) (refusing to supply nunc pro tunc approval of earlier loan).

[157] Bankruptcy Code § 1129(a)(A). *See infra* § 19.10[H] Full Payment of Priority Claims.

[158] *See generally infra* § 10.04[B][1] Claims for Inadequate "Adequate Protection."

[159] Bankruptcy Code § 364(c)(1).

[C]   Secured Credit[160]

In many cases, the Code's provisions that authorize priority to unsecured credit extended outside the ordinary course are of little significance. Prospective creditors are simply reluctant to provide any unsecured credit to the debtor, even with an administrative or super-priority status, for the simple reason that a struggling debtor has great difficulty obtaining unsecured credit under any circumstances. Those who are willing to extend credit at all to a reorganizing debtor usually want every possible personal guarantee and scrap of collateral that is available.

In recognition of this difficulty, the Code permits debtors to incur additional debt and give the lender a security interest in its assets. Section 363(c)(2) permits the court to authorize credit that is secured by estate property that is not encumbered by other liens, and § 362(c)(3) permits the court to authorize credit that is secured by a junior lien on previously encumbered property.

If these steps are not sufficient to persuade a creditor to provide a loan, § 363(d) even permits the court to authorize credit that is secured by a lien that has senior priority over pre-existing liens. This final step is usually reserved for circumstances, such as a partially completed real estate project, where the new loan will be used to finish construction and thus significantly enhance the value of the collateral. However, existing liens cannot be "primed" unless they are adequately protected after their priority is demoted.[161]

[1]   Granting a Lien on Unencumbered Equity

Section 364(c) permits the court to authorize a post-petition creditor to receive either a security interest on unencumbered estate property or a junior security interest on previously encumbered property.[162] Thus, if Franklin Manufacturing owns equipment that is not subject to any security interest, the court can authorize Franklin to give a new creditor a security interest on this unencumbered asset.[163] Or, if Franklin has no completely unencumbered assets, a lender might be willing to make the loan in exchange for a junior lien on previously encumbered property. Thus, if Peninsula Bank holds a senior mortgage on Franklin's real estate, securing its $4.5 million claim, but the property is worth $7 million, another lender may be willing to loan up to another $2 million, and be reasonably confident that it is fully secured, and with a small half-million dollar equity cushion to spare. This causes no harm to Peninsula Bank, who is still protected by the $2.5 million cushion of value above the amount of it's $4.5 million claim.

However, the court should be cautious about permitting the debtor's assets to be further encumbered. If the new secured loan generates benefits above the cost of

---

[160] David Gray Carlson, *Postpetition Security Interest under the Bankruptcy Code*, 48 Bus. Law. 483 (1993); Ralph C. McCullough, II, *Analysis of Bankruptcy Code § 364(d): When Will a Court Allow a Trustee to Obtain Post-Petition Financing by Granting a Superpriority Lien?*, 93 Com. L.J. 186 (1988).

[161] In re Belk Props., LLC, 421 B.R. 221 (Bankr. N.D. Miss. 2009).

[162] Bankruptcy Code § 364(c)(2), (3).

[163] Bankruptcy Code § 363(c)(2).

encumbering property, it assists the estate in accomplishing its goal of successful reorganization. But, if the debtor's efforts are unsuccessful, despite the new loan, the accompanying lien reduces the amount available for pre-existing unsecured creditors in a later liquidation. As with grants of super-priority status, court approval for extensions of secured credit should not be granted unless the debtor is otherwise unable to obtain unsecured credit.[164]

[2] Granting an Equal or Priority Lien[165]

Sometimes it is impossible for debtors to obtain credit by giving the prospective creditor a lien on unencumbered equity. There may be no unencumbered assets and the creditor may refuse to accept a lien that is junior to a pre-existing creditor. The final and most drastic option is to permit the debtor to grant a lien that is equal to or possibly even senior to existing liens.[166] When an existing lien is subordinated to a lien provided to a new post-petition creditor, the existing lien is said to have been "primed." This step presents one of the clearest conflicts between the Code's general policy of protecting existing property interests and the desire to find a means to rehabilitate the debtor.

For example, suppose that Peninsula Bank has encumbered virtually all of Franklin Manufacturing's assets. Moreover, Peninsula refuses to extend more credit to Franklin and is seeking relief from the automatic stay to foreclose against all of its collateral and effectively terminate Franklin's efforts to reorganize. Sharque Investment Co., on the other hand, has offered to lend Franklin $2 million, but only if Sharque can obtain a senior lien on Franklin's real estate and equipment, with priority over Peninsula's preexisting lien. No other potential lender is even willing to discuss the possibility of making a loan to Franklin. The debtor is out of cash and is unable to make its payroll unless it receives Sharque's loan. Failure to pay its employees will, of course, mean the certain end of Franklin's reorganization case, and will result in Franklin's converting its case to Chapter 7 or dismissing the case entirely and permitting Peninsula to foreclose.

If Franklin obtains the loan, it will likely be able to survive for at least six more months. By then, Franklin anticipates that market conditions will have improved and it will be possible to submit a suitable plan of reorganization that fully pays both Sharque and Peninsula and distributes a substantial dividend to pre-petition unsecured creditors. If market conditions do not improve, Franklin may liquidate anyway. This may deprive Peninsula of the value of its lien. In short, if Sharque provides the loan, Franklin has a chance to succeed but no guarantee that it will; if Sharque does not make the loan, Franklin will be forced to liquidate almost immediately.

Section 364(d) attempts to balance the interests posed by this situation by permitting but restricting the grant of equal or priority liens. As with other post-petition extensions of credit outside the ordinary course, granting a post-

---

[164] Bankruptcy Code § 364(c)(1).

[165] James S. Rogers, *The Impairment of Secured Creditor's Rights in Reorganization: A Study of the Relationship Between the Fifth Amendment and the Bankruptcy Clause*, 96 Harv. L. Rev. 973 (1983).

[166] Bankruptcy Code § 364(d)(1).

petition creditor a security interest with equal or senior priority to that of a pre-petition creditor requires court approval, after notice and a hearing.[167] At the hearing, the debtor must show first that the debtor cannot obtain the necessary credit in any way other than providing the creditor with the equal or senior lien it demands[168] and second that the interest of any existing lien holder is adequately protected.[169] The burden of proof that the requested priority should be approved is on the debtor.[170]

Authorization of the requested priority presents grave risks for existing secured lenders. Suppose, for example, continuing with the above hypothetical, that the total value of Franklin Manufacturing's real estate and equipment is $7 million, and that the amount of Peninsula Bank's pre-petition secured claims is $4.5 million. Even after Sharque's $2 million loan and senior "priming" security interest, Peninsula is adequately protected by a $500,000 equity cushion. If the collateral is fully insured against casualty loss and Franklin has sufficient cash to make interest payments and cover any depreciation in the value of the collateral, both creditors will be paid in full, even if Franklin's reorganization subsequently fails for other reasons. In this situation, even though other creditors are placed at greater risk, Peninsula Bank is not harmed by granting Sharque Investment Co. a senior lien on Franklin's assets.

However, this result is based on the premise that the bankruptcy court correctly assessed the value of Franklin's property. If, despite the bankruptcy court's assessment of the value, Franklin's real estate and equipment are only worth $5 million, granting Sharque a senior lien for its post-petition loan results in Peninsula holding an undersecured claim in any subsequent liquidation. With its new senior lien, Sharque receives the first $2 million derived from a sale of the collateral, leaving Peninsula with only $3 million for its $4.5 million debt. Section 507(b) provides Peninsula with an unsecured super-priority claim for its $1.5 million deficiency,[171] but even this is subordinate to whatever senior super-priority has been granted to someone else pursuant to § 363(c)(1),[172] and also subordinate to the administrative expenses of any subsequent liquidating trustee.[173]

Moreover, the debtor's assets are so heavily encumbered, that there may be no equity remaining to pay any unsecured claims, regardless of any right to priority treatment. Sharque's secured loan may have completely captured all of the priority to which Peninsula Bank had previously been entitled. Indeed, Peninsula may prefer to extend the requested loan rather than allow Sharque to jump in front.

Because of these risks, priming liens are usually limited to situations where the proceeds of the new loan can be used to substantially enhance the value of the debtor's collateral. This is typically true only in circumstances involving partially completed construction or other projects where the funds obtained from the new

---

[167] Bankruptcy Code § 364(d)(1).

[168] Bankruptcy Code § 364(d)(1)(A).

[169] Bankruptcy Code § 364(d)(1)(B).

[170] Bankruptcy Code § 364(d)(2).

[171] Bankruptcy Code § 507(b). *See infra* § 10.04[B][1] Claims for Inadequate "Adequate Protection."

[172] Bankruptcy Code § 363(c)(1). *See infra* § 10.04[B][2] Post-Petition Credit Claims.

[173] Bankruptcy Code § 726(b). *See infra* § 10.04[B][3] Post-Conversion Liquidation Expenses.

creditor will be used to complete the project and enhance the value of the collateral for everyone. For example, in *In re Hubbard Power & Light Co.*, the court approved a priming lien that enabled the debtor to borrow funds to remove a hazard on its property that prevented the property from being used for any purpose. The existing hazard had made the debtor's property worthless. But, the proceeds of the new loan could be used to enhance the value of the property by several million dollars, far in excess of the amount of the new senior lien.[174] Where, on the other hand, the collateral is not likely to increase in value sufficiently to preserve the value of the collateral for the pre-existing creditor after the new senior creditor is paid in full, the existing lien is not adequately protected and the new lender cannot be given seniority.[175]

[3] Cross-Collateralization[176]

Among the more hotly contested debates with respect to post-petition credit is the enforceability of a security interest, authorized in connection with a post-petition loan, which secures both a post-petition and a pre-petition debt to the creditor who extended the loan. Suppose, for example, that at the time it files its bankruptcy petition, Franklin Manufacturing owes Peninsula Bank $35 million, secured by only $10 million of collateral, leaving Peninsula woefully undersecured. Assume further that Franklin needs an additional infusion of $3 million in cash to continue operating its business. Peninsula Bank is willing to loan Franklin the $3 million, but only if it receives a security interest in Franklin's other assets as collateral — not only for the $3 million post-petition loan, but also for the $25 million deficiency claim that was unsecured at the time of Franklin's petition.

Giving Peninsula a security interest for *both* its post-petition advance and its pre-petition unsecured claim is known as "cross-collateralization," or more specifically as "*Texlon* type cross-collateralization," after a famous Second Circuit case where the practice was first discussed.[177] The practice, though approved by some courts,[178] is controversial. Granting the lender a security interest for its pre-petition claim gives it a preference. If such a security interest were granted in the ninety days prior to the debtor's petition, it would undoubtedly be avoidable under § 547.[179] As with all preferences, it gives an advantage to a single creditor at the expense of others and thus frustrates bankruptcy's "equal treatment" policy.[180] On the other hand, the creditor's loan might make it possible for the debtor to reorganize successfully and to thus provide a substantially larger distribution to its unsecured

---

[174] 202 B.R. 680, 684 (Bankr. E.D.N.Y. 1996).

[175] In re Fontainbleau Las Vegas Holdings, Inc., 434 B.R. 716, 747-755 (S.D. Fla. 2010).

[176] Jeff Bohm, *The Legal Justification for the Proper Use of Cross-Collateralization Clauses in Chapter 11 Bankruptcy Cases*, 59 Am. Bankr. L.J. 289 (1985); Charles J. Tabb, *A Critical Reappraisal of Cross-Collateralization in Bankruptcy*, 60 S. Cal. L. Rev. 109 (1987); Benjamin Weintraub & Alan Resnick, *Cross-Collateralization of Prepetition Indebtedness as an Inducement for Postpetition Financing: A Euphemism Comes of Age*, 14 UCC L.J. 86 (1981).

[177] In re Texlon Corp., 596 F.2d 1092 (2d Cir. 1979).

[178] *E.g.*, In re Keystone Camera Prods. Corp., 126 B.R. 177 (Bankr. D.N.J. 1991).

[179] *See infra* Chapter 15 — Preferences.

[180] *See supra* § 1.01[D] Bankruptcy as a Creditor's Remedy.

creditors from the income it earns after its plan is confirmed.

The facts of the hypothetical described above outline the circumstances in *Shapiro v. Saybrook Manufacturing Co.*[181] There, the bankruptcy court approved a post-petition cross-collateralized loan, and several unsecured creditors appealed. The objecting creditors sought to stay the loan and security interest while their appeal was pending, but the bankruptcy court refused. The Court of Appeals refused to treat the dispute as moot and reversed the bankruptcy court's ruling that authorized the cross-collateralization aspects of the transaction. In reaching its decision, the court explained:

> [C]ross-collatereralization is inconsistent with bankruptcy law for two reasons. First, [it] is not authorized as a method of post-petition financing under section 364. Second, cross-collateralization is beyond the scope of the bankruptcy court's inherent equitable power because it is directly contrary to the fundamental priority scheme of the Bankruptcy Code.[182]

Thus, the creditor's lien was unenforceable, even though it made the loan in good faith, and even though the transaction had not been stayed by the court while the appeal was pending and the funds had already been distributed and spent. Not all courts take the same dim view of cross-collateralization. However, even those that approve such arrangements look closely to determine whether they are in the best interests of the creditors.[183] For example, in the Franklin Bank example described above, the debtor agreed to grant security to $25,000,000 in return for a $3,000,000 loan. If the cross-collateralization were recharacterized as a loan initiation fee, the charge for making the loan would be a remarkable 500% of the principal amount. It is hard to believe that this would be a good deal under any circumstances. Moreover, it is difficult to believe that some other creditor might not be available to make the loan on more favorable terms. Where, by contrast, the value of the cross-collateralized assets or the amount of cross-collateralized debt could be recharacterized as a reasonable fee for initiating a risky loan, then the practice seems less objectionable.

As a practical matter, however, debtors frequently negotiate their post-petition financing facilities on the eve of the bankruptcy filing, and the post-petition lender is likely to be an existing secured creditor with a strong interest in ensuring that its deficiency gets paid. The debtor has little leverage at this moment, and no other creditors are in the room. As a result, many courts and creditors committees look closely at financing orders presented early in the case for signs of overreaching provisions. These issues are discussed in the next section.

---

[181] 963 F.2d 1490 (11th Cir. 1992).

[182] 963 F.2d at 1494-95 (citing Charles J. Tabb, *A Critical Reappraisal of Cross-Collateralization in Bankruptcy*, 60 S. Cal. L. Rev. 109 (1987)). *See also* Bland v. Farmworker Creditors, 308 B.R. 109 (S.D. Ga. 2003).

[183] *E.g.*, In re Babcock & Wilcox Co., 250 F.3d 955 (5th Cir. 2001). *See also* In re Kmart Corp., 359 F.3d 866 (7th Cir. 2004).

[4] Emergency Loans[184]

The most difficult problems arise when the debtor is seeking emergency funding. In the early stages of a case, Chapter 11 debtors are frequently strapped for cash; yet they have immediate payroll obligations to meet, or need cash to pay for a shipment of vital supplies when they arrive on a C.O.D basis. If the debtor does not obtain the financing necessary to meet these obligations, it may find it necessary to shut down its operations.

In these emergency settings, providing interested parties with the necessary notice and the opportunity to be heard before the funds must be received may present an insurmountable pragmatic difficulty. Despite this, the exigence of the debtor's circumstances does not excuse the need for notice and a hearing. Further, even if the Code were amended to accommodate these emergency situations, constitutional due process requires some level of notice and the opportunity for a hearing, particularly where creditors' property interests are at stake.[185] Thus, some type of notice and some type of opportunity must be given, even if it is only a telephone conference with the most significant creditors.

Failure to provide notice or an opportunity to be heard is a more serious problem for the creditor than are errors of judgment by the court. An attack on the adequacy of the notice and hearing is not protected by the rule that immunizes good faith transactions. Even though the creditor may have acted in good faith, that is not necessarily sufficient to preserve its rights under the credit agreement if the court failed to provide due process when issuing the order.[186]

[5] Compliance with Securities Laws

Another potential barrier to the debtor's obtaining necessary cash is the securities laws. Both federal and state law regulates the issuance of certain kinds of credit instruments. For example, a company issuing a bond that is to be publicly traded must generally comply with complex and burdensome state and federal "registration" laws that are designed to give information about the bond to the investing public.[187] These laws are not just expensive to comply with; they are also to some degree redundant in bankruptcy because the information disclosed in the registration process is generally available through the bankruptcy court, the creditors' committee, or (in a Chapter 11 case) the disclosure statement that must be made when soliciting approval of a debtor's plan.[188] There is, in consequence, a limited exemption from these laws under section 364(f). Unless the debtor is a securities underwriter,[189] § 364(f) preempts all state and federal registration laws

---

[184] Charles Jordan Tabb, *Emergency Preferential Orders in Bankruptcy Reorganizations*, 65 Am. Bankr. L.J. 75 (1991).

[185] *See* Credit Alliance Corp. v. Dunning-Ray Ins. Agency, Inc. (In re Blumer), 66 B.R. 109, 113-14 (B.A.P. 9th Cir. 1986), *aff'd*, 826 F.2d 1069 (9th Cir. 1987).

[186] *See, e.g.*, In re Ellingsen MacLean Oil Co., 65 B.R. 358, 361-63 (W.D. Mich. 1986), *aff'd*, 834 F.2d 599 (6th Cir. 1987), *cert. denied*, 488 U.S. 817 (1988).

[187] 1 Louis Loss & Joel Seligman, Securities Regulation ch. 2 (3d ed. 1989).

[188] *See infra* § 19.09[B][1] Court Approval of Disclosure Statement — Adequate Information.

[189] An underwriter is a person who is distributing a security to others, rather than holding it for

with regard to the offer or sale under § 364 "of a security that is not an *equity security*."[190] Thus, a debtor who wishes to raise cash by issuing a debt security (such as a bond or commercial paper), whether for its operations or to fund its reorganization plan, may do so without registering the security. Note, however, that this exemption does not include equity securities, such as common or preferred stock. Moreover, the exemption only excuses the debtor from compliance with registration laws. The debtor is not excused from other features of state and federal securities statutes, particularly those that prohibit fraud.

[D]   Appeals of Orders Authorizing Post-Petition Credit[191]

Section 364(e), regarding appeals, provides only limited protection against improvident extensions of credit. Interested parties may appeal a court's decision that approves an extension of credit on a priority, secured, or senior secured basis, but they must act promptly to obtain a stay, preventing the transaction from proceeding pending the appeal.[192] Absent a stay, any reversal or modification of the authorization or a grant of a priority or lien does not affect the validity of the debt, the priority, or the lien if the creditor extended credit in good faith.[193]

Section 363(e) goes a long way to protect creditors who provide post-petition loans in good faith reliance on the court's authorization of the loan. However, if the creditor knew that it lacked statutory authority to make the loan, its reliance on the bankruptcy court's authorization may not suffice. As the court said in *In re EDC Holding Co.*:[194]

> We assume the statute was intended to protect not the lender who seeks to take advantage of a lapse in oversight by the bankruptcy judge but the lender who believes his priority is valid but cannot be certain that it is, because of objections that might be upheld on appeal. If the lender knows his priority is invalid but proceeds anyway in the hope that a stay will not be sought or if sought will not be granted, we cannot see how he can be thought to be acting in good faith.

For example, in *Shapiro v. Saybrook*, discussed above, the *Texlon* type cross-collateralization at issue was not protected by 364(e) because the extension was not "authorized" by the statute.[195]

---

investment. *See* 2 Louis Loss & Joel Seligman, Securities Regulation 1108-1110 (3d ed. 1989).

[190] Bankruptcy Code § 364(f) (emphasis supplied). If the debtor wants to issue equity securities, it also gets an exemption pursuant to Bankruptcy Code § 1145, but only for securities issued pursuant to a plan of reorganization.

[191] Charles Jordan Tabb, *Lender Preference Clauses and the Destruction of Appealability and Finality: Resolving a Chapter 11 Dilemma*, 50 Ohio St. L.J. 109 (1989).

[192] *See, e.g.,* In re Roberts Farms, Inc., 652 F.2d 793, 796-98 (9th Cir. 1981).

[193] Bankruptcy Code § 363(e).

[194] 676 F.2d 945, 948 (7th Cir. 1982).

[195] Shapiro v. Saybrook Mfg. Co., 963 F.2d 1490, 1496 (6th Cir. 1992).

§ 9.06   ABANDONMENT OF ESTATE PROPERTY

Section 554 authorizes the trustee or debtor-in-possession to abandon estate property. Abandonment means exactly what it sounds like: the property is simply dropped from the estate and taken by either the debtor or another interest holder, such as a secured creditor. While this provision is of primary importance in Chapter 7 liquidation cases, it applies across the board to all bankruptcy proceedings. The purpose of abandonment is to permit the trustee to shed property that is unduly difficult or expensive to retain or that is of such minimal value that it is not worth administering.

Section 554(a) permits the trustee or debtor-in-possession to abandon estate property "that is burdensome to the estate or that is of inconsequential value and benefit to the estate."[196] Similarly, § 554(b) permits any other party in interest to seek a court order to force the trustee to abandon burdensome or minimally valuable property.[197] In either case, there must be notice and an opportunity for a hearing.[198]

If, as is typically the case, no objection is made to the proposed abandonment after the notice is given, the court may dispense with a hearing; however, a hearing is required if someone objects.[199]

There are two substantive bases for abandonment. The first is that the property is burdensome; the second is that it is of inconsequential value and benefit. Although in many cases both bases are satisfied, the statute only requires one. The most common situation in which property is abandoned, arguably on both bases, is where property in a Chapter 7 liquidation case is subject to a lien that secures a debt that is greater than the value of the property. Thus, if Perpetual Motors Acceptance Corp. holds a perfected security interest in Ray's $7,000 car, securing an $8,000 debt, the trustee is likely to abandon the car. The same is true if the car is worth $9,000 and the debtor is entitled to a $1,000 exemption under the relevant state exemption statute. The debtor will take one of three actions: 1) redeem the car from the security interest under § 722, 2) enter into a reaffirmation agreement with the creditor pursuant to § 524(c) (probably for the full amount of the debt), or 3) surrender the vehicle to the creditor.[200]

In other settings, the property may be burdensome to the estate, even though there is some equity in the property. Equine enthusiasts of all types are familiar with the concept of being "horse poor." A horse-riding stable may own several horses, worth a total of $10,000 and subject to a security interest that secures a $9,500 debt. The debtor has some equity in the animals, but they cost $1,000 per month to feed and care for. If the stable is not earning more than $1,000 from the use of the horses, they are a source of a continued loss and are burdensome to the estate. Of course, if the horses are worth only $9,000 and cost more to maintain than

---

[196] Bankruptcy Code § 554(a).

[197] Bankruptcy Code § 554(b). *See* Fed. R. Bankr. P. 6007(b).

[198] Bankruptcy Code § 554(a), (b).

[199] Fed. R. Bankr. P. 6007(a).

[200] Bankruptcy Code § 521(a)(2)(A), (a)(6). *See infra* § 12.08 Retaining Collateral.

the income they can produce, they are both burdensome to the estate and of inconsequential value. If they are burdensome to the estate, holding on to them is affirmatively harmful to other creditors because their maintenance depletes the estate of funds that could otherwise be distributed to satisfy creditors' claims. They should be abandoned.[201]

The propriety of the abandonment may depend upon the nature of the proceeding or the point that the proceeding has reached when the issue arises. For example, while it is ordinarily appropriate in a liquidation to abandon property when there is no equity, this is not necessarily true in a reorganization setting. If the property is needed for an effective reorganization, then it has some value and benefit for the estate, even though the lien on it is in excess of the property's value and is, as they say, "under water." Similarly, it may be inappropriate to abandon property at the beginning of the case before the value of the property or its utility in producing income is determined. For this reason, it has long been established by the case law that the trustee may wait a reasonable time before deciding whether to abandon property.[202] In some cases, the trustee may have an affirmative duty to wait to abandon the property, especially if there is a reasonable possibility that the market price of the property will rise in the foreseeable future.

Under the Bankruptcy Act, it was often unclear whether abandonment had occurred, because it was not always necessary for the trustee to take any formal action to abandon. The Code appears to cure this problem (at least in a properly conducted proceeding) by requiring notice, and opportunity for a hearing to effectuate abandonment. Subsections 554(c) and (d) also help to clarify the issue.

Subsection 554(c) specifies that, unless the court orders otherwise, all property that is scheduled but not otherwise administered by the time the case is closed is abandoned to the debtor.[203] This does not add a substantive basis for abandonment. It is always improper for the trustee to abandon property that is valuable and not burdensome. Rather, § 554(c) addresses the circumstance where property that could properly have been abandoned by the trustee has not been administered or formally abandoned.[204] However, apart from this situation, formal abandonment is normally required. Section 554(d) makes this clear: "Unless the court orders otherwise, property of the estate that is not abandoned under this section and that is not administered in the case remains property of the estate."[205] This language applies primarily to property that was not scheduled, whether the failure to

---

[201] Here, we mean in the technical legal sense; not just let loose on the highway.

[202] Stanolind Oil & Gas Co. v. Logan, 92 F.2d 28 (5th Cir. 1937). Even astonishingly long periods of time may be permissible under rare circumstances. *See* In re Aldrich's Estate, 215 P.2d 724 (Cal. 1950) (twenty-five years). *Cf.* Sparhawk v. Yerkes, 142 U.S. 1 (1891) (majority held that twelve years was too long; two justices dissented, holding that the delay merely exhibited wise judgment).

[203] Bankruptcy Code § 554(c).

[204] Your authors are acquainted with a case in which the estate's principal assets were a collection of pornographic video tapes, copyrights on the works, and several telephone numbers used in the debtor's phone-sex business. The trustee was reluctant to sell the assets, despite the existence of a ready and willing buyer. The trustee was not interested in bringing a motion to abandon the assets, which had economic value to the estate. There is no end to the issues that bankruptcy lawyers sometimes must confront.

[205] Bankruptcy Code § 554(d).

schedule was fraudulent or merely an honest mistake.[206] It remains a part of the estate, and, where appropriate, the case can be reopened to permit distribution of that property to the creditors.[207]

§ 9.07 HEALTH CARE PROVIDERS

In 2005, special provisions that apply to all bankruptcy cases involving health care providers, were added.[208] They apply to any "health care business" as that term is defined in § 101(27A).[209] These provisions are designed to ensure the privacy of patient records, particularly in cases where the debtor may not have funds to ensure that patient's health care records are properly maintained. Section 351 requires the trustee to maintain these records for a year and to publish notice of their availability to patients and insurers in order to enable them to retrieve records to which they are entitled.[210] The trustee must then seek from any appropriate federal agency to take possession of these records and may destroy them if no agency is willing to assume this responsibility.[211] This assures, at least, that patients' medical records are not thrown into the nearest dumpster.

These provisions also require a bankruptcy trustee or debtor-in-possession to make a reasonable effort to transfer a closing health care provider's patients to "an appropriate health care business."[212] This puts bankruptcy trustees in the business of finding new doctors for a failed health care provider's patients.

Accompanying these obligations is language that gives the trustee or any appropriate federal agency an administrative expense claim for the costs of storing and disposing of patients' records and for the costs associated with the transfer of patients to a new health care provider.[213] The Code also provides for the appointment of a patient care ombudsman, to be appointed under the usual rules in § 330 for hiring professionals. The patient care ombudsman is responsible for making regular reports to the court regarding the quality of patient care provided by the debtor.[214]

---

[206] *See supra* § 6.02[C][2] Schedules of Debts and Assets; Statement of Affairs.

[207] In re Medley, 29 B.R. 84 (Bankr. M.D. Tenn. 1983).

[208] *See* In re 7-Hills Radiology, Inc., 350 B.R. 902 (Bankr. D. Nev. 2006); In re Anne C. Banes, D.D.S., Inc., 355 B.R. 532 (M.D.N.C. 2006).

[209] Bankruptcy Code § 101(27A). *See* In re Banes, No. 06-81341-7, 2006 Bankr. LEXIS 3194 (Bankr. M.D.N.C. Nov. 16, 2006); In re 7-Hills Radiology, Inc., 350 B.R. 902 (Bankr. D. Nev. 2006); In re Anne C. Banes, D.D.S., Inc., 355 B.R. 532 (M.D.N.C., 2006).

[210] Bankruptcy Code § 351(1)(A).

[211] Bankruptcy Code § 351(2).

[212] Bankruptcy Code § 704(a).

[213] Bankruptcy Code § 503(b).

[214] Bankruptcy Code § 333(b).

Chapter 10

CLAIMS AND INTERESTS

§ 10.01 MEANING OF CLAIMS AND INTERESTS; PRIORITY

Those who assert a right to a distribution from the estate are divided into two basic types: holders of "claims" and holders of equity "interests." "Claim" refers to the right to payment held by a creditor. It is a right based on either a debt owed by the debtor or a right to an equitable remedy against the debtor.[1]

In this context, "interest" refers to an ownership interest in the debtor itself.[2] Such an ownership interest includes the right to receive the residue of the debtor's estate after all creditors' claims have been paid. When used this sense, the term is synonymous with "equity," and is sometimes called an "equity interest." Common examples are the rights of stockholders of a bankrupt corporation, or the interest of a general or limited partner in a partnership.[3] The key attribute of an "equity interest" is that it does not represent an enforceable right to payment, but instead involves a right to a portion of the distribution of the debtor's property *after* all creditors' claims have been paid.

Claims are divided into several broad categories, based on the legal rights associated with the claim. Claims might be "secured claims," "unsecured 'general' claims" or "unsecured 'priority' claims."

A secured claim is one that is secured by collateral. In other words, it is a claim that is accompanied by an interest in specific property. The most common types of secured claims are debts secured by a real estate mortgage or security interest in personal property, but they also include debts secured by judicial and statutory liens.

---

[1] Bankruptcy Code § 101(6).

[2] Bankruptcy Code § 101(5).

In another context, "interest" might also refer to a legal or contractual right to be paid a finance charge imposed by creditors as compensation for the time value of money or for the risk of loaning the funds in the first place. Borrowers pay interest on funds they have borrowed. This interest is neither an interest in particular property nor a right to obtain the residue of the debtor's property when all debts are paid.

[3] When talking about "interests" or "equity interests," it is important to distinguish them from "security interests" which give rise to "secured claims" and represent an ownership interest in a particular asset of the debtor, or from "interest" when used to describe interest payable on a debt. *See* U.C.C. § 1-201(b)(35)(2010).

By contrast, an unsecured claim is simply a debt, such as a contract or a tort claim against the debtor; the creditor has no interest in any particular property of the debtor that it may foreclose upon if the debt is not paid. Unsecured claims are frequently also referred to simply as "general" claims.

Priority claims are unsecured claims that are entitled to priority under § 507. Priority claims are entitled to different levels of statutory priority, with some priority claims having seniority over others.[4]

Sometimes, unsecured claims are "subordinated." That is, their priority is lowered, so the claim is not paid until after other unsecured claims are satisfied. This might occur because the creditor has agreed to have its claim subordinated to the claims of other creditors, or because of some wrongdoing by the creditor that leads a court to subordinate its claim on statutory or equitable grounds.[5]

Ownership interests in the debtor are also sometimes divided into several levels of priority. A corporation might have issued several different classes of stock, with one or more senior classes entitled to some sort of "liquidation preference." If the debtor is liquidated, such a preference entitles these stockholders to be paid ahead of those who hold only common stock.

In general, each category of claims and interests is entitled to full satisfaction before any junior category is entitled to anything. This makes priority critically important to creditors and owners. A creditor whose claim is junior to another creditor might receive nothing if the value of the assets in the debtor's estate is insufficient to satisfy the claims of more senior creditors in full. For example, unless the administrative expense claims (priority 2 claims) are paid in full, wage claims (priority 4) are paid nothing. Unless all priority claims are paid in full, those with general unsecured claims receive nothing. Finally, unless the estate has enough to satisfy the claims of all creditors, shareholder's interests disappear. Payments to creditors leave nothing for distribution to shareholders or partners.

Thus, Titanic Industries might owe a total of $10 million to a variety of creditors, including those with priority claims for the administrative expenses of handling the bankruptcy case, former employees who are owed wages, tax authorities, and a variety of general non-priority trade creditors. If the debtor's estate is worth only $3 million, creditors with lower priority will likely receive nothing, while those higher on the priority ladder may be paid in full. If there are $1 million in priority administrative expenses and $2 million in priority wage and pension claims, nothing will be left to distribute to lower priority unsecured tax claims and non-priority general claims. In this situation, shareholders stand no chance of receiving anything.

In even a fairly simple business bankruptcy case, there might be claims and interests which are all entitled to different priority. Thus, it would not be unusual for claims and interests in such a case to consist of:

• Secured Claims

---

[4] *See infra* § 10.04[A] Priority Claims.

[5] *See infra* § 10.05 Subordinated Claims.

- Priority 2 — Administrative Expenses[6]

- Priority 4 — Priority Wage Claims

- Priority 5 — Pension Claims

- Priority 8 — Tax Claims

- General Unsecured Non-Priority Claims

- Subordinated Claims

- Interests based on Preferred Stock; and

- Interests based on Common Stock

Consumer cases are usually far less complicated, but can easily involve:

- Secured Claims

- Priority 1 – Domestic Support Obligations

- Priority 2 — Administrative Expenses

- Priority 8 — Tax Claims

- General Unsecured Non-Priority Claims

Of course, in consumer cases, there are rarely enough assets to even begin to satisfy the most senior priority unsecured claims, making wrangling for inclusion in a class of priority claims superfluous.

§ 10.02 CLAIMS[7]

[A] Definition of Claim

The Bankruptcy Code defines "debt" as "liability on a claim,"[8] and defines "claim" as any:

(A) right to payment, whether or not such right is reduced to judgment, liquidated, unliquidated, fixed, contingent, matured, unmatured, disputed, undisputed, legal, equitable, secured, or unsecured; or

(B) right to an equitable remedy for breach of performance if such breach gives rise to a right to payment, whether or not such right to an equitable remedy is reduced to judgment, fixed, contingent, matured, unmatured, disputed, undisputed, secured, or unsecured.[9]

---

[6] These might be further broken down, in order of priority, into super-super-priority claims under § 364(c)(1), super-priority claims under § 507(b), and priority administrative expense claims under § 503.

[7] Timothy B. Matthews, *The Scope of Claims Under the Bankruptcy Code*, 57 Am. Bankr. L.J. 221 (1983); Menachem O. Zelmanovitz & Elana C. Jacobson, *The Reconsideration of Contingent and Disputed Claims Under Bankruptcy Code Section 502(j)*, 23 Seton Hall L. Rev. 1612 (1993).

[8] Bankruptcy Code § 101(12).

[9] Bankruptcy Code § 101(5).

The definition of "claim" is important for two reasons. First, most claims are entitled to receive a distribution from the debtor's estate. Moreover, in the bankruptcy hierarchy of distribution, claims get paid before equity interests. This reflects a long-standing general rule that debt precedes equity. Indeed, this rule is virtually definitional, since equity is generally thought of as the residual right to assets after debts are satisfied in full.

Second, because of the relationship between the definition of "claim" and the definition of "debt," creditors' claims are subject to discharge. If the creditor has a claim, the debtor's liability is a debt, and other than with respect to several specific exceptions,[10] debts are dischargeable.[11]

The Code definition of "claim" is exceptionally broad. Virtually any kind of obligation owed or even potentially owed by the debtor is a claim. The term includes any "right to payment." The right to payment may be uncertain in amount (known as "unliquidated"). It may be conditional as to ultimate liability ("contingent"). It may be disputed or unmatured. It may be secured or unsecured.[12] "Claim" also encompasses most equitable remedies by including any "right to an equitable remedy for breach of performance if such breach gives rise to a right to payment."[13]

The breadth of this definition is reflected in several key Supreme Court decisions. In *United States v. Kovacs*, the Supreme Court held that a debtor's obligation to remove hazardous waste was a claim and thus could be discharged in a Chapter 7 case.[14] In *Pennsylvania Department of Public Welfare v. Davenport*,[15] the Court departed from earlier dictum[16] and ruled that the debtor's obligation to provide restitution to the victim of his crime was a claim, even though the victim had no legal right to privately enforce the restitution order, based on the criminal judgment alone. And in *Johnson v. Home State Bank*,[17] the Court ruled that a creditor's purely "in rem" right to enforce a mortgage against the debtor's real estate was a claim, even though the debtor's personal liability had previously been discharged in a Chapter 7 bankruptcy case. In all of these cases, the Court has emphasized that Congress's intent in framing the definition of a claim was to ensure that "all legal obligations of the debtor, no matter how remote or contingent, will be able to be dealt with in the bankruptcy. It permits the broadest possible relief in the bankruptcy court."[18]

---

[10] *See* Bankruptcy Code § 523(a); *infra* § 13.03 Non-Dischargeable Debts.

[11] *See* Ohio v. Kovacs, 469 U.S. 274 (1985) (debtor's environmental cleanup obligation was a claim and thus a debt included within the scope of the debtor's discharge); Penn. Dep't of Pub. Welfare v. Davenport, 495 U.S. 552 (1990) (criminal restitution obligation was a claim and thus a dischargeable debt under now repealed provisions of Chapter 13).

[12] Bankruptcy Code § 101(5)(A).

[13] Bankruptcy Code § 101(5)(B).

[14] United States v. Kovacs, 469 U.S. 274 (1985) (state court judgment requiring the removal of hazardous waste). *See generally* Kathryn R. Heidt, *Environmental Obligations in Bankruptcy: A Fundamental Framework*, 44 Fla. L. Rev. 153 (1992).

[15] 495 U.S. 552, 562 (1990).

[16] *See* Kelly v. Robinson, 479 U.S. 36 (1986).

[17] 501 U.S. 78 (1991).

[18] *See also* H.R. Rep. No. 95-595, at 309-10 (1977) *reprinted in* 1978 U.S.C.C.A.N. 5963, 6266-6267; S.

It is common among lawyers and judges to speak of the holders of claims as "creditors," "unsecured creditors," "priority creditors," "secured creditors," and the like. However, the Bankruptcy Code does not speak in these terms. Instead, it deals not with "debts" and "creditors," but with "claims" and "holders of claims."[19]

This seemingly nit-picking nomenclature clarifies that a creditor's status in the bankruptcy is based on its claim, rather than on the underlying obligation owed by the debtor. For example, if collateral for a debt is inadequate to satisfy the debt in full, the creditor is treated as having two claims in bankruptcy: a secured claim to the extent of the value of the collateral, and an unsecured claim for the balance of the debt.[20] The creditor's rights in connection with each claim are largely independent of one another, even though they may be governed by the terms of the same contract.

[B] Proof of Claim

Depending on the circumstances, creditors may have to file a "proof of claim." A proof of claim is a simple "written statement setting forth [the] creditor's claim,"[21] usually accompanied by documentation of the validity of the claim.[22] Filing a proof of claim is usually no more complicated than completing the blanks on a simple form, indicating the name and address of the creditor, the basis and amount of the claim, whether the claim is secured or unsecured, and whether the claim is entitled to priority.[23] In cases under Chapters 7, 12, or 13, creditors must file a timely proof of claim to receive a distribution from the estate. As explained below, the procedure in Chapter 11 cases is somewhat different and, depending on the circumstances, creditors may not be required to file a proof of claim.

A proof of claim may be filed by a creditor or by an indenture trustee acting on behalf of creditors.[24] An equity security holder is similarly entitled to file a proof of interest, reflecting its ownership interest in the debtor.[25] Moreover, the debtor, the trustee, or "an entity that is liable to [a] creditor with the debtor" may file a proof of claim on the creditor's behalf.[26]

However, in many Chapter 7 cases, there is no reason for creditors to file proof of their claims. Nearly all consumer liquidations are "no-asset" cases in which the debtor's assets, if any, are exempt. With no anticipated distribution to creditors, there is no reason for creditors to submit claims or to require the Bankruptcy Court clerk's office to collect them. In a no-asset case, court's notice advising

---

Rep. No. 95-989, at 22 (1978) *reprinted in* 1978 U.S.C.C.A.N. 5787, 5808.

[19] Indeed, the term "creditor" is defined in the Bankruptcy Code in terms of claims: a creditor is an "entity" that has a claim. Bankruptcy Code § 101(10).

[20] *See* infra § 10.03[C] Allowance of Secured Claims.

[21] Fed. R. Bankr. P. 3001(a).

[22] Fed. R. Bankr. P. 3001. *See* Caplan v. B-Line, LLC (In re Kirkland), 572 F.3d 838 (10th Cir. 2009) (claim disallowed due to creditor's failure to produce any supporting documentation).

[23] Official Bankruptcy Form 10.

[24] Bankruptcy Code § 501(a).

[25] Bankruptcy Code § 501(a).

[26] Bankruptcy Code § 501(a).

creditors of the case will notify them there is no reason to file a proof of claim. In the unusual event that the trustee discovers assets not reflected in the debtor's schedules, the trustee will provide a further notice to the creditors, alerting them of the need to file proofs of claim and establishing a deadline for them to be filed.[27]

In Chapter 11 reorganization cases, a proof of claim is deemed filed with respect to any claim listed in the debtor's schedules, unless the schedules indicate that the claim is "disputed, contingent, or unliquidated."[28] Of course, if the debtor fails to include a creditor's claim in its schedules, the creditor must file a proof of claim by the established deadline. A proof of claim must also be filed if the debtor's schedules indicate that the claim is disputed, contingent, or unliquidated.[29] A creditor will wish to file a proof of claim if it believes that its claim is incorrectly reflected in the debtor's schedules.

On the other hand, if a Chapter 11 case is subsequently converted to a liquidation case, creditors must file a proof of claim, just as they would in any other Chapter 7 case. The fact that the case started out as an effort to reorganize the debtor does not excuse creditors from filing a proof of claim after the case is converted to Chapter 7.[30]

The Bankruptcy Rules specify that a proof of claim must be filed no later than ninety days after the first date set for the § 341 "meeting of creditors."[31] Governmental units have additional time, until 180 days after the order for relief. Additionally, the court may extend the deadline for claims held by a governmental entity[32] and an "infant or an incompetent person" or his or her representative.[33] Moreover, in Chapter 13 cases, a special rule exists for a "claim of a governmental unit for a tax with respect to a return filed under [Bankruptcy Code] § 1308" as timely "if the claim is filed on or before . . . 60 days after the date on which [the] return was filed."

[C] Allowance of Claims

Section 502 narrows the otherwise broad definition of "claim" by distinguishing between claims that are "allowed" and those that are not. Allowed claims are entitled to receive payment from the debtor's estate. Disallowed claims receive no payment. Likewise, allowed claims may vote on a plan; disallowed claims may not participate.

---

[27] Official Bankruptcy Form 9 (for Chapter 7 Individual or Joint Debtor No Asset Case).

[28] Bankruptcy Code § 111(a); Fed. R. Bankr. P. 3003(b).

[29] Bankruptcy Code § 111(a); Fed. R. Bankr. P. 3003(b).

[30] Fed. R. Bank. P. 1019(3).

[31] Fed. R. Bankr. P. 3002(c).

[32] Bankruptcy Code § 502(b)(9); Fed. R. Bankr. P. 3002(c)(1).

[33] Fed. R. Bankr. P. 3002(c)(2).

Claims are "deemed allowed" if a proof of claim is filed,[34] unless a party in interest objects.[35] If someone objects, the court determines the allowable amount of the claim.[36] The proof of claim is prima facie evidence of the amount and validity of the creditor's claim.[37] Thus, unless credible evidence of the invalidity of the claim surfaces, the creditor's claim will be allowed.[38]

The person asserting the claim must, as in other settings, have standing to assert the claim.[39] This has been an issue of importance in bankruptcy court, as it has been in state litigation, with respect to residential mortgages. The way the secondary mortgage market has handled the original promissory notes signed by borrowers has raised questions about whether a person who does not currently have possession of the mortgage note is a "person entitled to enforce" the obligation and thus the real party in interest with the right to assert the claim in bankruptcy court.[40] The same issue arises with respect to mortgage loan servicers who seek relief from the automatic stay even though they are not "holders" of the mortgage note.[41]

The allowable amount of a claim is whatever was owed by the debtor "as of the date of the filing of the petition."[42] The effect of this rule is to accelerate any unmatured, contingent, or unliquidated claims.[43] Thus, even if the debtor is not in default at the time of the petition, the obligation is a claim for the full amount owed as if the claim had already matured. For example, if a debtor signed a promissory note, promising to pay $5,000 on June 1, 2018, but filed a bankruptcy petition before that date, on Oct. 15, 2015, the creditor's right to receive the $5,000 principal amount would be an allowed claim, even though it was not yet due. Any interest accumulated prior to the date of the petition would be included in the claim; however, as explained below, unmatured post-petition interest would not be allowed.

---

[34] A proof of claim must ordinarily be filed for a claim to be allowed. Fed. R. Bankr. P. 3002(a). However, in a Chapter 11 or Chapter 9 case, if the claim is scheduled by the debtor, the filing of a proof of claim is permitted, but not required. Fed. R. Bank. P. 3003(c).

[35] Bankruptcy Code § 502(a).

[36] Bankruptcy Code § 502(b).

[37] Fed. R. Bankr. P. 3001(f).

[38] *See* In re Lanza, 51 B.R. 125 (Bankr. E.D. Pa. 1985).

[39] Fed. R. Bankr. P. 7017, 9014(c). Fed. R. Civ. P. 17.

[40] *See* Veal v. Am. Home Mortgage Sev'g, Inc. (In re Veal), 450 B.R. 897 (B.A.P. 9th Cir. 2011); Dale A. Whitman, *How Negotiability Has Fouled Up the Secondary Mortgage Market, and What to Do About It*, 37 Pepp. L. Rev. 737 (2010).

[41] *E.g.*, In re Alcide, 450 B.R. 526 (Bankr. E.D. Pa. 2011); In re Smoak, 461 B.R. 510 (Bankr. S.D. Ohio 2011) (loan servicer, acting as agent of holder of note, had standing to file proof of claim). *See generally* Peter A. Holland, *The One Hundred Billion Dollar Problem in Small Claims Court: Robo-Signing and Lack of Proof in Debt Buyer Cases*, 6 J. Bus. & Tech. L. 259, 286 (2011); Katherine Porter, *Misbehavior and Mistake in Bankruptcy Mortgage Claims*, 87 Tex. L. Rev. 121 (2008).

[42] Bankruptcy Code § 502(b).

[43] *E.g.*, In re Manville Forest Prods. Corp., 43 B.R. 293, 298 (Bankr. S.D.N.Y. 1984) ("It is a basic tenet of the Bankruptcy Code that bankruptcy operates as the acceleration of the principal amount of all claims against the debtor.").

[1] Contingent and Unliquidated Claims[44]

A creditor's right to receive payment is an allowed claim, even if the creditor's right is contingent or unliquidated.[45] A claim is contingent if it does not become an obligation until the occurrence of a future event.[46] Sometimes the contingency is removed or the claim is liquidated before the bankruptcy proceeding is complete. For example, if Sam guaranteed a $1,000 debt owed by Dora but had not yet been called upon to pay the debt when Dora's petition was filed, Sam's claim for reimbursement from Dora is contingent.[47] If, during the course of Dora's bankruptcy case, however, Sam is forced to pay the entire amount of Dora's debt, the contingency is removed, rendering Sam's claim non-contingent.

Personal injury and other similar tort claims, on the other hand, are not contingent. Although the fact and amount of the debtor's liability may not have yet been determined in court, the facts upon which liability is predicated have already occurred.

Claims also might be unliquidated. A claim is unliquidated if the amount of liability depends on a future exercise of discretion. If the amount of the claim is easily ascertainable, it is liquidated. Thus, it is liquidated if it is determinable by reference to an agreement, such as a promissory note or other contract that specifies a fixed liability, or through simple computation.[48] If its amount depends instead on a future exercise of discretion, not restricted by some specific criteria, the claim is unliquidated. Tort claims, for example, are frequently regarded as unliquidated, at least until the plaintiff obtains a judgment fixing the amount of the debt.

In no-asset cases, such as most liquidations of consumer debtors, it is usually unnecessary determine the amount of these claims. In fact, unless the estate is large enough that some distribution to creditors is anticipated, the notice sent to creditors in consumer liquidations usually advises creditors not to bother filing a proof of claim.[49] Unless there are some assets available to distribute to creditors, even the simple task of filling out a proof of claim form[50] is a waste of time.

On the other hand, if the estate has some assets, or if the case involves a reorganization of the debtor, the value and amount of contingent and unliquidated claims must be determined. Otherwise it is impossible to calculate the amount to be

---

[44] Benjamin Weintraub & Alan N. Resnick, *Treatment of Contingent and Unliquidated Claims Under the Bankruptcy Code*, 15 UCC L.J. 373 (1983).

[45] Bankruptcy Code § 101(5).

[46] *E.g.*, Mazzeo v. United States (In re Mazzeo), 131 F.3d 295 (2d Cir. 1997); In re Knight, 55 F.3d 231, 234 (7th Cir. 1995) (*quoting* S. Rep. No. 95-989 at 22 (1978), *reprinted in* 1978 U.S.C.C.A.N. 5787, 5809; *and* H.R. Rep. No. 95-595, at 310 (1978), *reprinted in* 1978 U.S.C.C.A.N. 5963, 6267).

[47] *E.g.*, Mazzeo v. United States (In re Mazzeo), 131 F.3d 295, 303 (2d Cir. 1997); In re Knight, 55 F.3d 231, 236 (7th Cir. 1995). *See also* S. Rep. No. 95-989 at 22 (1978), *reprinted in* 1978 U.S.C.C.A.N. 5787, 5809; H.R. Rep. No. 95-595 at 310 (1977), *reprinted in* 1978 U.S.C.C.A.N. 5963, 6267.

[48] *E.g.*, Mazzeo v. United States (In re Mazzeo), 131 F.3d 295, 304 (2d Cir. 1997); In re Knight, 55 F.3d 231, 235 (7th Cir. 1995).

[49] *See* Official Bankruptcy Form 9.

[50] *See* Official Bankruptcy Form 10.

distributed to the holder of these claims from the debtor's estate. This is sometimes accomplished by lifting the automatic stay and permitting another court to conduct a trial to determine the extent of the debtor's liability. In other cases, this is not practical, either because of the time involved, or because there is no adequate way to measure the claim through normal litigation. In these circumstances, the bankruptcy court may estimate the amount of the claim at least for the purposes of creditors voting on a Chapter 11 plan of reorganization.[51]

[2] Future Claims[52]

Cases involving business debtors who are liable to a large number of potential claimants raise issues about the allowability of claims that might be asserted on behalf of future claimants. Such cases might include victims of the debtor's defective product who have been injured but who have not yet traced the source of their injuries back to the debtor's product. They might also include those who were exposed to the debtor's product, but who have not yet detected any injury. Thus, a construction worker exposed to asbestos fibers may not have yet developed symptoms of asbestosis when the manufacturer of the harmful fibers is undergoing reorganization. The problem might also arise with respect to claimants who do not use the defective product and suffer an injury until after the bankruptcy case has been closed, such as a person who is a passenger in a defectively manufactured automobile, years after the manufacturer's bankruptcy case is over.

To determine whether future claims are allowable against the debtor's estate — and discharged — courts have adopted several approaches. The first approach regards a claim as arising when the debtor's *conduct* that gave rise to the claim occurred, regardless of whether the creditor discovered his harm or had even been harmed when the bankruptcy case was pending. Thus, someone exposed to harmful asbestos fibers after the debtor's bankruptcy case is filed holds a claim if the debtor's manufacture and sale of the asbestos occurred before the bankruptcy case began.[53] This is the broadest of the three approaches.

A second approach depends on whether the claim is based on a relationship between the creditor and the debtor that arose before the debtor's bankruptcy case.[54] This test requires pre-bankruptcy conduct by the debtor, together with some sort of relationship between the creditor and the debtor that gave rise to the

---

[51] *See* infra § 10.02[E] Estimation of Claims.

[52] *See generally* Laura B. Bartell, *Due Process for the Unknown Future Claim in Bankruptcy — Is This Notice Really Necessary?*, 78 Am. Bankr. L.J. 339 (2004). *See also* Kathryn R. Heidt, *Products Liability, Mass Torts and Environmental Obligations in Bankruptcy: Suggestions for Reform*, 3 Am. Bankr. Inst. L. Rev. 117, 127 (1995); Ralph R. Mabey & Jamie Andra Gavrin, *Constitutional Limitations on the Discharge of Future Claims in Bankruptcy*, 44 S.C. L. Rev. 745, 752-53 (1993); Mark J. Roe, *Bankruptcy and Mass Tort*, 84 Colum. L. Rev. 846, 855-62 (1984); Frederick Tung, *Taking Future Claims Seriously: Future Claims and Successor Liability in Bankruptcy*, 49 Case W. Res. L. Rev. 435, 453, 457-58 (1999); J. Maxwell Tucker, *The Clash of Successor Liability Principles, Reorganization Law, and the Just Demand That Relief be Afforded Unknown and Unknowable Claimants*, 12 Bankr. Dev. J. 1, 55-56 (1995).

[53] *See, e.g.*, Grady v. A.H. Robins Co., 839 F.2d 198, 201 (4th Cir. 1988).

[54] *See, e.g.*, Epstein v. Official Comm. of Unsecured Creditors (In re Piper Aircraft Corp.), 58 F.3d 1573 (11th Cir. 1995).

debtor's injury. If the creditor had no contact with the debtor or its defective product before the bankruptcy case commenced, the rights asserted by the creditor do not constitute a claim.[55]

The third and narrowest approach depends on whether the creditor's cause of action *accrued* under applicable nonbankruptcy law, before the debtor's petition was filed.[56] This frequently-criticized approach had prevailed only in the Third Circuit,[57] which recently finally abandoned it.[58]

A few courts have developed a fourth approach which depends on whether the debtor could have fairly and reasonably contemplated the claim at the time of the debtor's petition, even if the claimant's cause of action had not yet accrued under the applicable nonbankruptcy law.[59] This fourth approach is very similar to the second "relationship" approach that most courts use.

[3] Debtor's Defenses

Claims are not allowable against the debtor's estate if they are unenforceable against the debtor or the debtor's property other than because they are contingent or unmatured.[60] Thus, the Bankruptcy Code does nothing to enhance the enforceability of creditors' claims.[61] This rule is reinforced by Bankruptcy Code § 558, which provides: "[t]he estate shall have the benefit of any defense available to the debtor as against any entity other than the estate, including statutes of limitation, statutes of frauds, usury, and other personal defenses."[62] The debtor's "waiver of any such defense" does not bind the estate if the waiver occurred after the case commenced.[63] Otherwise, the estate enjoys the benefits of whatever defenses the debtor has based on any agreement between the parties or that were available under applicable law when the case commenced.[64]

---

[55] For the creditor to have an allowable claim, one branch of this test also requires the creditor's harm to have been fairly contemplated by the creditor prior to the bankruptcy. *E.g.*, In re Jensen, 995 F.2d 925, 929-31 (9th Cir. 1993).

[56] Matter of M. Frenville Co., Inc., 744 F.2d 332 (3d Cir. 1984).

[57] Laura B. Bartell, *Due Process for the Unknown Future Claim in Bankruptcy — Is This Notice Really Necessary?*, 78 Am. Bank. L.J. 339 (2004); Ralph R. Mabey & Annette W. Jarvis, In re Frenville: *A Critique by the National Bankruptcy Conference's Committee on Claims and Distributions*, 42 Bus. Law. 697 (1987). *But see* Gregory A. Bibler, *The Status of Unaccrued Tort Claims in Chapter 11 Bankruptcy Proceedings*, 61 Am Bankr. L.J. 145, 157-61 (1987).

[58] In re Grossman's Inc., 607 F.3d 114 (3d Cir. 2010).

[59] E.g., In re Jensen, 995 F.2d 925, 930-31 (9th Cir. 1993).

[60] Bankruptcy Code § 502(b)(1). Vanston Bondholders Protective Comm. v. Green, 329 U.S. 156 (1946).

[61] *See* In re Cameron, 452 B.R. 754 (Bankr. E.D. Ark. 2011) (claim based on indefinite contract disallowed).

[62] Bankruptcy Code § 558.

[63] Bankruptcy Code § 558.

[64] *E.g.*, In re Rolling Thunder Gas Gathering, Inc., 348 B.R. 803 (Bankr. D. Del. 2006) (lack of consideration).

An obvious example is a defense based on the statute of limitations. Thus, in *In re Hess*,[65] the court disallowed three proofs of claims filed by creditors, because they were stale under the applicable New York statute of limitations. In reaching its decision, the court noted the broader nationwide problem caused by businesses that purchase claims in bulk, sometimes purchasing thousands of them in a single transaction, and filing claims against bankrupt debtors' estates without evaluating their enforceability. As the court explained: "it is incumbent on debtors, their counsel, and the Chapter 13 Trustee, carefully to scrutinize proofs of claims to identify and object, if appropriate, to stale claims."[66]

[4]　Interest on Claims[67]

If the debt was one on which interest accrued, either by contract or rule of law, the allowed claim includes any accrued *pre-petition* interest. This is limited to interest that accrued on the claim before the debtor's case commenced. Post-petition interest, unmatured at the time the debtor's petition was filed, is not allowable on unsecured claims.[68]

Most of the time it, is easy to distinguish between principal and interest on a claim and to determine the amount of allowable pre-petition interest that accrued on the claim before the debtor's petition. For example, if a promissory note provides for payment of a principal debt of $10,000 with 12% annual interest, it is a simple matter to calculate the amount of interest that had accumulated when the petition was filed. If the note was made on June 1, 2013, and the maker's bankruptcy petition was filed on December 1, 2013, six months of interest accumulated. At 12% per year (or 1% per month), simple interest of $600 ($100 per month) matured as of the date of the debtor's petition and is thus allowed as part of the creditor's claim.

However, if the stated principal amount of the note includes the interest that the parties anticipate will accumulate on the note before it is due, the amount of matured pre-petition interest needs to be calculated. Consider, for example, the claim of a creditor who makes a $10,000 loan, with the debtor agreeing to pay 12% annual interest for five years. Six thousand dollars of simple interest will accumulate over the life of the loan. The parties might prepare a promissory note calling for the debtor to pay $16,000 in equal monthly installments of $266.66, without any interest stated in the note, even though $6,000 of the $16,000 amount due is interest. If the maker of the note files a bankruptcy petition sometime during the five year

---

[65] 404 B.R. 747 (Bankr. S.D.N.Y. 2009).

[66] *Id.* at 752.

[67] Walter J. Blum, *Treatment of Interest on Debtor Obligations in Reorganizations Under the Bankruptcy Code*, 50 U. Chi. L. Rev. 430 (1983); David G. Carlson, *Postpetition Interest Under the Bankruptcy Code*, 43 U. Miami L. Rev. 577 (1989); John C. McCoid, II, *Pendency Interest In Bankruptcy*, 68 Am. Bankr. L.J. 1 (1994); Dean Pawlowic, *Entitlement to Interest under the Bankruptcy Code*, 12 Bankr. Dev. J. 149 (1995Scott K. Charles & Emil A. Kleinhaus, *Prepayment Clauses in Bankruptcy*, 15 Am. Bankr. Inst. L. Rev. 537 (2007); Alexander F. Porter, Note, *Postpetition Interest on Unsecured Claims in the Case of a Solvent Debtor: Toward a More Consistent Statutory Regime*, 81 S. Cal. L. Rev. 1341 (2008).

[68] Bankruptcy Code § 502(b)(2). *See, e.g.*, In re Tuttle, 291 F.3d 1238 (10th Cir. 2002). *See generally* Todd W. Ruskamp, Comment, *In the Interest of Fairness: Interest Payments in Bankruptcy*, 67 Neb. L. Rev. 646 (1988).

amortization period of the note, the court must determine what portion of the $16,000 was interest that matured before the petition was filed. Under § 502(b)(2) the unmatured interest is not allowable as a claim against the debtor's estate.[69] Thus, the parties may not "front load" interest into the principal debt and thus avoid the limitation on the allowability of unmatured interest.[70]

There are two exceptions to the rule disallowing claims for post-petition interest. The first is of little consequence. In the unusual event that a Chapter 7 debtor turns out to be solvent, then post-petition interest is allowed on all claims, but only at the "legal rate" rather than at the agreed contract rate.[71] Because solvent Chapter 7 debtors are so rare, this rule has little practical significance.

The second exception is important. Section 506(b) allows post-petition interest to holders of over-secured claims.[72] A claim is over-secured if the value of the collateral securing the claim is greater than the amount of the claim. Thus, a $90,000 claim secured by real estate worth $100,000 is fully secured and entitled to recover post-petition interest up to the surplus value of the collateral — $10,000.

Partially secured claims do not qualify for this treatment. If the collateral for this creditor's $90,000 claim were worth only $70,000, the creditor would not be entitled to interest, even on the $70,000 that was secured. Undersecured creditors may not add post-petition interest to their claims any more than creditors who are completely unsecured.[73] Furthermore, the Supreme Court made it clear in the *Timbers of Inwood Forest* case that adequate protection does not include compensation for the delay in foreclosure caused by the automatic stay.[74]

Note, however, that the rule disallowing post-petition interest on claims applies during only during the initial part of a reorganization proceeding, before a plan is implemented. Interest does not accrue during the "pendency period" of the case, from filing of the petition to implementation (or "consummation") of a plan. This may be anywhere from a few weeks to several years. The plan itself, however, must provide for paying interest on some claims. Secured creditors are entitled to interest on the secured portion of their claims, starting on the effective date of the plan of reorganization. Unsecured creditors will be entitled to interest on the portion of their claim that represents what they would have received if the debtor had liquidated on the effective date of the plan.[75]

---

[69] *E.g.*, In re Morris, 8 B.R. 924 (Bankr. N.D. Ohio 1981).

[70] *E.g.*, In re Auto Int'l Refrigeration, 275 B.R. 789 (Bankr. N.D. Tex. 2002). *See* In re Chateaugay Corp., 961 F.2d 378 (2d Cir. 1992) (regarding "original issue discount"); Craig Nemiroff, Note, *Original Issue Discount and the "LTV Risk" Reconsidered*, 105 Yale L.J. 2209 (1996).

[71] Bankruptcy Code § 726(a)(5). *E.g.*, In re Hoskins, 405 B.R. 576, 587-88 (2009).

[72] Bankruptcy Code § 506(b).

[73] United Sav. Ass'n v. Timbers of Inwood Forest, 484 U.S. 365, 372-73 (1988); Ford Motor Credit Co. v. Dobbins, 35 F.3d 860 (4th Cir. 1994).

[74] United Sav. Ass'n v. Timbers of Inwood Forest, 484 U.S. 365, 372-73 (1988).

[75] *E.g.* Bankruptcy Code § 1129(a)(7)(A)(ii); *infra* § 19.10[F] Plan in Best Interests of Creditors.

[5] Fees and Expenses[76]

Most loan agreements and many other contracts expressly provide for the creditor to recover attorneys' fees and other costs incurred in efforts to collect the creditor's claim. Attorneys' fees and expenses may also be available by statute. Otherwise, the "American Rule" usually bars their recovery.[77]

When they are authorized by agreement or statute, there is a further question of whether they are allowable as a claim against the debtor's estate. If they are allowed, the creditor receives a greater share of the debtor's estate, to the disadvantage of other creditors. In the case of secured creditors' claims, allowance of fees and expenses may impair the debtor's ability to obtain confirmation of its plan. In the case of unsecured creditors' claims, allowance primarily affects the debtor's other creditors, whose recovery will be diminished.[78] As explained below, allowance depends in part on whether the costs and fees arose before or after the debtor's petition, whether the claim is fully secured, and on the inferences to be drawn from the language of §§ 502(b)(2) and 506(b).

[a] Pre-Petition Costs and Attorneys Fees[79]

It would seem that the allowability of claims for pre-petition costs of collection and attorneys' fees should follow the general rule — that is, they should be disallowed if they would not have been recoverable under applicable non-bankruptcy law and allowed if they would have been recoverable against the debtor outside of bankruptcy. The general American rule is that attorneys' fees are not recoverable unless they are expressly provided for by agreement or expressly recoverable under an applicable statute.[80]

Thus, the allowability of pre-petition collection costs and attorneys' fees depends initially on whether the creditor would have been entitled to recover these expenses and fees under relevant non-bankruptcy law.[81] This is consistent with § 502(b)(1), which subrogates the debtor's estate to whatever defenses the debtor might have raised outside of bankruptcy court.[82] If state or other applicable non-bankruptcy law denies the creditor the right to recover these costs and fees, they should not suddenly be available because the debtor has filed a bankruptcy petition.

---

[76] David Gray Carlson, *Oversecured Creditors Under Bankruptcy Code Section 506(b): The Limits of Postpetition Interest, Attorneys' Fees, and Collection Expenses*, 7 Bankr. Dev. J. 381, 407-12 (1990).

[77] *See* Mark S. Scarberry, *Interpreting Bankruptcy Code Sections 502 and 506: Post-Petition Attorneys' Fees in a Post-Travellers World*, 15 Am. Bankr. Inst. L. Rev. 611 (2007).

[78] 674 F.2d 134 (2d Cir. 1982).ur*See* Mark S. Scarberry, *Interpreting Bankruptcy Code Sections 502 and 506: Post-Petition Attorneys' Fees in a Post-Travellers World*, 15 Am. Bankr. Inst. L. Rev. 611, 613 & 613 n. 16 (2007).

[79] George Singer, *Section 506(b) and the Oversecured Creditor's Right to Recover Fees: A Matter of Right under "Federal" Law?*, 16 Am. Bankr. Inst. L. Rev. 1 (1997).

[80] *See generally, Symposium on Fee Shifting*, 71 Chi.-Kent L. Rev. 415-697 (1995).

[81] *E.g.*, Thrifty Oil Co. v. Bank of Am. Nat'l Trust and Sav. Ass'n, 322 F.3d 1039 (9th Cir. 2003); Blair v. Bank One, N.A., 307 B.R. 906 (N.D. Ill. 2004).

[82] Bankruptcy Code § 502(b)(1). *See supra* § 10.02[C][3] Debtor's Defenses.

Language in § 506(b) that limits the allowability of fully secured creditor's claims for post-petition collection costs and attorneys' fees to those that are "reasonable" has led some courts to impose a federal bankruptcy standard of reasonableness on any pre-petition fees, regardless of whether the fees would have been recoverable under applicable state law.[83] However, most courts have drawn a different conclusion, noting that § 502 is silent about any such limit on pre-petition claims for attorneys' fees[84] other than those the debtor owes to its own attorney.[85]

[b] Post-Petition Costs and Attorneys' Fees for Fully Secured Claims

Section 506(b)(1) expressly gives fully secured creditors an allowed claim for both post-petition interest and "any reasonable fees, costs, or charges provided for under the agreement or State statute under which such claim arise."[86] Most courts hold that this language pre-empts state law rules dealing with the enforceability of agreements that provide for a creditor's recovery of these types of expenses, and that the "reasonableness" of the expenses under § 506(b) is the only standard by which the allowability of these expenses should be measured, at least to the extent of the value of the collateral.[87]

A creditor with an allowable $10,000 pre-petition claim, secured by property worth $12,000, is entitled to up to $2,000 in accumulated reasonable post-petition fees, costs, or charges — if those fees, costs and charges were either provided for in the parties' agreement or recoverable under an applicable *state* statute.[88] Thus, recovery of post-petition interest is unqualified, but recovery of fees, costs, and charges is allowed only if they are reasonable and if they were provided for either by agreement or in an applicable state statute.[89]

Before 2005, § 506(b) referred only to reasonable fees, costs, and charges that are provided for in the parties' agreement. Language referring to an applicable state statute was added in 2005. The revised language overrules decisions that denied fully secured creditors a claim for post-petition interest, costs, and fees where they were recoverable under a state statute, but not by an agreement between the parties.[90] This permits fully secured state tax authorities to recover post-petition interest and costs if permitted to do so by state statute.[91] Significantly, there is no explanation for the conspicuous absence of a reference to amounts that may be recoverable under a *federal* statute. The principal impact of this absence is to deny post-petition interest, costs, and attorneys' fees to fully

---

[83] Welzel v. Advocate Realty Inv., LLC (In re Welzel), 275 F.3d 1308 (11th Cir. 2001).

[84] *E.g.*, In re Nunez, 317 B.R. 666 (Bankr. E.D. Pa. 2004) (collecting cases).

[85] *See infra* § 10.02[D][4] Limits on Claims of Insiders.

[86] Bankruptcy Code § 506(b).

[87] *E.g.*, Welzel v. Advocate Realty Inv., LLC (In re Welzel), 275 F.3d 1308, 1313-16 (11th Cir. 2001).

[88] United States v. Ron Pair Enters., Inc., 489 U.S. 235, 241 (1989).

[89] Rushton v. State Bank (In re Gledhill), 164 F.3d 1338, 1342 (10th Cir. 1999).

[90] *E.g.*, In re Nunez, 317 B.R. 666, 669 (Bankr. E.D. Pa. 2004).

[91] *See* Jo Ann C. Stevenson & Charles E. Consalus, *Taxing Authorities, Section 506(b) and the "Curious Comma"*, 61 Am. Bankr. L.J. 275 (1987) (discussing § 506(b) prior to the 2005 Amendments).

secured federal tax claims and to fully secured private claims under federal statutes that permit the recovery of such costs and fees.

[c] Post-Petition Costs and Attorneys' Fees for Unsecured and Partially Secured Claims[92]

The Bankruptcy Code is silent about the allowability of post-petition attorneys' fees and collection costs for unsecured claims. This, together with its inclusion of language permitting recovery of such amounts by creditors with fully secured claims,[93] would seem to make it clear that creditors with partially secured or completely unsecured claims are not entitled to these items, even if such they are available under the terms of the parties' agreement or by statute. However, courts are not in agreement.

The Supreme Court's 2007 decision in *Travelers Casualty and Surety. Co. of America v. Pacific Gas and Electric Co.*[94] resolved the question of whether the allowance of post petition fees and expenses depended on whether the underlying dispute was based on state law or bankruptcy law,[95] but left open the more basic question of whether the bankruptcy code prohibits their allowance at all.[96] Since *Travelers*, courts have been divided, with some courts refusing to permit unsecured creditors' attorneys' fees for collection efforts after the debtor's petition was filed to be included as part of the creditor's claim,[97] and other courts allowing them.[98]

The disagreement is over the significance of language in § 506(b) that deals with secured claims.[99] It provides that "to the extent that an allowed secured claim is secured . . . there should be allowed to the holder . . . any reasonable fee . . . ."[100] Section 502, which deals with the allowance of unsecured claims, does not contain similar language about post-petition fees for unsecured creditors. The absence of any such parallel language in § 502 has led some courts to conclude that

---

[92] James Gadsden, *Recovery of Attorney Fees as an Unsecured Claim*, 114 Banking L.J. 594 (1997); Liore Z. Alroy & J. Michael Mayerfeld, Note, *Contracted-For Post-Petition Attorneys' Fees and Collection Costs:* United Merchants *Revisited*, 1992 Colum. Bus. L. Rev. 309.

[93] Bankruptcy Code § 506(b).

[94] 549 U.S. 443 (2007).

[95] Before *Travellers*, courts were split over whether claims for attorneys' fees incurred litigating bankruptcy law issues were allowable. *Compare In re Fobian*, 951 F.2d 1149 (9th Cir. 1991), *with* Official Comm. of Unsecured Creditors v. Dow Corning Corp., 456 F.3d 668, 686 (6th Cir. 2006).

[96] 549 U.S. at 456. *See* Michelle Arnopol Cecil, *A Reappraisal of Attorneys' Fees in Bankruptcy*, 98 Ky. L.J. 67, 101 (2010); Mark S. Scarberry, *Interpreting Bankruptcy Code Sections 502 and 506 in a Post-*Travelers *World*, 15 Am. Bankr. Inst. L. Rev. 611 (2007).

[97] *E.g.*, In re Cranston, 387 B.R. 480 (Bankr. D. Md. 2008).

[98] Ogle v. Fidelity & Deposit Co. of Md., 586 F.3d 143 (2d Cir. 2009); In re SNTL Corp., 571 F.3d 826 (9th Cir. 2009).

[99] *See* Ogle v. Fidelity & Deposit Co. of Md., 586 F.3d 143 (2d Cir. 2009).

[100] *See generally* Michelle Arnopol Cecil, *A Reappraisal of Attorneys' Fees in Bankruptcy*, 98 Ky. L.J. 67 (2010); Mark Scarberry, *Interpreting Bankruptcy Code Sections 502 and 506: Post-Petition Attorneys Fees in a Post-Travelers World*, 15 Am. Bankr. Inst. L. Rev. 611 (2007); Jennifer Taylor & Christopher Meretens, Travelers *and the Implication on the Allowability of Unsecured Creditors' Claims for Post-Petition Attorneys' Fees Against the Bankruptcy Estate*, 81 Am. Bankr. L.J. 123 (2007).

these post-petition fees and expenses are not allowable.[101] This conclusion has been buttressed by *United Savings Association of Texas v. Timbers of Inwood Forest Associates, Ltd.*,[102] in which the Supreme Court relied on language in § 506, which authorized post-petition *interest* to secured creditors, to deny post-petition *interest* to unsecured creditors. However, because the Court's decision in *Travelers* said that courts should presume that "claims enforceable under applicable state law will be allowed in bankruptcy unless they are expressly disallowed,"[103] it seems that the Court has taken a different turn since *Timbers of Inwood Forest*, on the relationship between §§ 502 and 506.[104]

[6] Disallowance of Claims of Recipients of Avoidable Transfers

Section 502(d) disallows claims of any creditor who has received an avoidable transfer, unless the creditor has paid the avoidable amount to the estate.[105] Thus, the claim a creditor who has received a partial payment is disallowed if the partial payment is recoverable by the trustee as an avoidable pre-petition preference under § 547(b), unless the creditor has paid the recoverable amount. Courts are divided over whether § 502(d) prevents allowance of an administrative expense.[106]

[D] Limits on Allowance of Claims

The Code contains several specific provisions disallowing or limiting the allowance of some specific claims.[107] These limitations address two potential problems. First, some claims are so large that their allowance might deprive other claimants of a meaningful share in the meager proceeds of the estate. Second, some claims may be unusually large because the claim may include damages that were expected to accrue over a long period of time, and may not take into account mitigation that might occur after the claim was allowed; the claimant is allowed to ask for damages without regard to whether those damages could have been avoided.

---

[101] *E.g.*, Adams v. Zimmerman, 73 F.3d 1164, 1177 (1st Cir. 1997).

[102] 484 U.S. 365 (1988).

[103] *Travelers*, 549 U.S. at 452.

[104] Ogle v. Fidelity & Deposit Co. of Md., 586 F.3d 143 (2d Cir. 2009); In re SNTL Corp., 571 F.3d 826 (9th Cir. 2009).

[105] Bankruptcy Code § 502(d).

[106] *Compare* In re Colonial Serv., Co. 480 F.2d 747 (8th Cir. 1973) (claim disallowed under § 502(d)'s predecessor in Bankruptcy Act), *and* In re Circuit City Stores, Inc., 426 B.R. 560 (Bankr. E.D. Va. 2010), *with* Ames Dept. Stores, Inc. v. ASM Capital, L.P., 582 F.3d 422 (2d Cir. 2009) (permitting allowance of administrative expense despite 502(d)).

[107] These limitations only apply if an objection is made. In the absence of an objection, a claim is equal to the amount stated in the proof of claim. Bankruptcy Code § 502(a).

[1]   Limits on Claims for Rent[108]

The Bankruptcy Code imposes a cap on the claim of a lessor of real property for unpaid future rent. Because of the duration of some real estate leases, such claims might be overwhelming, particularly if they are not limited by state law imposing a duty on the lessor to mitigate its damages. More importantly, it is not likely that the property will remain unrented for the entire remaining term on the lease. For example, imagine a lease that, at the time of rejection, had fifteen years to run, at a rate of $50,000 per year. The unpaid rent on the lease would be $750,000. However, if the space was actually relet two years after the debtor vacated, the actual damages would be only $100,000. It is not practical for the trustee to wait until all of the various landlords have relet their space. Instead, the Code takes a standardized approach. A landlord's claim for breach of a real estate lease cannot exceed the sum of any past due rent plus the greater of one year's rent or 15% of the remaining rent on the lease, but in no event can the claim exceed three years' post-petition rent.[109]

Suppose that at the time of the bankruptcy that the debtor was a lessee under a long-term real estate lease that had twenty-five years remaining. If the lessor were able to make a claim for all of the unpaid future rent, the amount of the claim might overshadow other claims. Thus, § 502(b)(6) limits the lessor's claim to whatever amounts the debtor already owed for past-due rent, and rent due for three years of the twenty-five years remaining on the term of the lease.[110] If the remaining term had been only fifteen years, the landlord would be entitled to the past-due rent, plus rent due for 15% of the remaining fifteen years (twenty-seven months). Courts are divided, however, over whether this is 15% of the remaining duration of the lease, or 15% of the total rent due for the balance of the lease,[111] with most courts applying the 15% limit to the amount of rent owed, rather than to the duration of the lease.[112]

The landlord cannot avoid the impact of these limits by accelerating the tenant's obligation to pay rent. Section 502(b)(7) provides that the amount of the allowable claim for "unpaid rent due under [the] lease [is to be calculated] without acceleration."[113]

If the lessor has mitigated damages, the claim may be limited further, based on any defenses the debtor has under state property law.[114] However, the traditional common law rule did not require the lessor to seek a new tenant. Although most states have abandoned this archaic rule, § 502(b)(6) further limits the effect of this

---

[108] Michael St. Patrick Baxter, *The Application of § 502(b)(6) to Nontermination Lease Damages: To Cap or Not to Cap?*, 83 Am. Bankr. L.J. 111 (2009).

[109] Bankruptcy Code § 502(b)(6).

[110] Fifteen percent of the remaining twenty-five years is three years and nine months, which is greater than one year, but there is a three-year cap on the duration of the remaining term for which a claim may be allowed.

[111] *See* In re Shane Co., 464 B.R. 32 (Bankr. D. Colo. 2012) (collecting cases).

[112] *Id.*

[113] Bankruptcy Code § 502(b)(6).

[114] Bankruptcy Code §§ 502(b)(11) & 558.

rule in jurisdictions where it has not been changed.[115]

[2] Limit on Claims for Salaries

Section 502(b)(7) limits the allowability of employee's claims for wrongful termination.[116] Such claims are allowable only for wages owed to the employee for up to one year after the employee's termination or the debtor's petition, whichever is earlier,[117] plus any past-due wages prior to that time.[118] Thus, an employee who is wrongfully terminated one month before the debtor's petition is filed, in the middle of a three-year employment contract, has a claim only for salary owed to her for work completed at the time of her termination, together with a claim for wages to which she was entitled for one year after she is let go, rather than wages for the entire contract.

Most employees are likely to be at-will employees with very limited claims for wages. Other employees, particularly highly-paid executives, may have long-term employment contracts that would result in sizeable claims without these limits. In addition, these employees, who may also have equity interests in the debtor, might otherwise be tempted to try to cause their employers to enter into long-term employment contracts immediately prior to bankruptcy in an effort to capture additional value from the business as a creditor. Thus, § 502(b)(8) prevents an executive from obtaining a sizeable claim against the estate and possibly considerable voting rights over the debtor's plan by causing her employer to enter into a twenty-year employment contract with her immediately before bankruptcy. It should also be noted that all or a part of an employee's allowable wage claim may be entitled to priority under § 507(a)(4), discussed below.[119]

[3] Limits on Property Tax Claims

Property tax claims are allowable only to the extent of the value of the estate's interest in the property.[120] If real property worth $40,000 has been assessed with real estate taxes of $50,000, only $40,000 of the claim is allowed. This limit treats property taxes as non-recourse claims, collectable only against the property subject to the tax. As explained below, allowable property tax claims may be entitled to priority under § 508(a)(8)(B). However, the claim must be allowable to qualify for priority treatment.

---

[115] *E.g.*, Stonehedge v. Square Ltd. P'ship v. Movie Merchants, Inc., 715 A.2d 1082 (Pa. 1998); Christopher Vaeth. Annotation, *Landlord's Duty, on Tenant's Failure to Occupy, or Abandonment of, Premises, to Mitigate Damages by Accepting or Procuring Another Tenant*, 75 A.L.R.5th 1 (2000).

[116] Bankruptcy Code § 502(b)(7).

[117] Bankruptcy Code § 502(b)(7)(A).

[118] Bankruptcy Code § 502(b)(7)(B).

[119] *See infra* § 10.04[A][4] Wage Claims.

[120] Bankruptcy Code § 502(b)(3).

[4] Limits on Claims of Insiders

Claims for services of insiders, such as close relatives and other affiliates of the debtor,[121] are allowable only to the extent the claim is for the reasonable value of the services supplied by the insider.[122] The same rule applies to claims held by the debtor's attorney.[123] Note that this limit is not related to the similar limit imposed by Bankruptcy Code § 329 with respect to services supplied by the debtor's attorney in connection with the case.

[5] Unmatured Support Claims

Past-due support is both allowable,[124] and, in most cases, entitled to priority.[125] However, support payments not yet due when the debtor's petition is filed are generally not allowed. Section 502(b)(2) prevents allowance of unmatured and non-dischargeable domestic support obligations.[126] Thus, unlike other claims, claims for post-petition support are not accelerated. Rather than receiving a distribution from the debtor's estate for the amount of future support, the child, former spouse, or other support claimant must rely on the fact that their claim is non-dischargeable.[127] They are relegated to whatever remedies they have in state court to recover post-petition support that the debtor fails to pay from his post-petition earnings. Moreover, because the automatic stay does not restrict a support claimant's ability to recover support from the debtor's earnings that are not included in the debtor's estate,[128] a support claimant might be able to pursue both her pre-petition and post-petition support claims in state court, while the debtor's bankruptcy case is pending. Finally, a debtor's failure to make post-petition support payments is grounds for dismissal or conversion of a Chapter 11, 12, or 13 case.[129]

Consider, for example, a Chapter 7 debtor who at the time of his petition owes $3,000 to his former spouse for a past-due domestic support obligation. After the case commences, the debtor further defaults on his duty to pay support at the rate of $1,000 per month. The $3,000 pre-petition support obligation is a fully allowable claim for which the receiving spouse is entitled to priority under § 507(a)(1).[130] Support beyond this amount, that did not mature until after the debtor's petition was filed, is neither allowable under § 502 nor entitled to priority under § 507. On the other hand, any portion of the past-due support that is not paid from the

---

[121] Bankruptcy Code § 101(31).

[122] Bankruptcy Code § 502(b)(4).

[123] Bankruptcy Code § 502(b)(4). Some lawyers may view this as a most regrettable provision.

[124] Bankruptcy Code § 502(a).

[125] Bankruptcy Code § 507(a)(1). The priority of past-due support obligations is somewhat complicated. *See generally infra* § 10.04[A][1] Support Claims.

[126] Bankruptcy Code § 502(b)(5).

[127] *See* Bankruptcy Code § 523(a)(5); *infra* § 13.03[B][5][a] Domestic Support Obligations.

[128] Bankruptcy Code § 362(b)(2)(B)-(C).

[129] Bankruptcy Code §§ 1112(b)(4)(P), 1208(c)(10) & 1307(c)(11).

[130] *See infra* § 10.04[A][1] Support Claims.

debtor's estate remains non-dischargeable.[131] Future support is similarly non-dischargeable. Thus, the receiving spouse will be able to recover unpaid support from the debtor in the future. Moreover, because of the limited scope of the automatic stay, the receiving spouse is permitted to garnish the debtor's post-petition earnings to the extent permitted by state law, even while the debtor's bankruptcy case is pending.

[6] Disallowance of Late Claims

Section 502(b)(9) specifies the effect of a tardily filed proof of claim.[132] The claim of a creditor who fails to file a timely proof of claim is completely disallowed, except to the extent expressly permitted by either § 726(a)(1)-(3)[133] or by the Bankruptcy Rules.[134] The Code's language overrules a series of earlier cases[135] that permitted tardily filed priority claims to share in the distribution of the debtor's estate, despite the creditor's failure to file a timely claim.[136] After the 1994 Amendments, late-filed claims are entitled to share in the distribution of a Chapter 7 estate, but these tardily filed claims are subordinated to claims of the same class that were timely filed.

[7] Unsecured Consumer Debts

In 2005, Congress added complicated language that permits the bankruptcy court to penalize recalcitrant creditors for failing to cooperate with the efforts of a credit counseling agency to restructure a consumer debtor's obligations. New § 502(k) permits the court to "reduce a claim . . . based in whole on an unsecured consumer debt"[137] by up to 20% of the claim if the creditor who asserts the claim "unreasonably refused to negotiate a reasonable alternative payment schedule proposed . . . by an approved nonprofit budget and credit counseling agency."[138] Congress's apparent belief that the threat of having their claims reduced by up to 20% if creditors unreasonably fail to renegotiate the terms of consumer debts overlooks the harsh reality that distributions to creditors in consumer liquidation cases are almost unheard of. Because distributions to unsecured creditors in Chapter 7 proceedings are so rare, § 502(k) is an empty threat to credit card companies and health care providers who refuse to cooperate with credit counseling agencies. This limits the practical impact of § 502(k) to Chapter 13 cases and creditors with secured claims.

---

[131] *See infra* § 13.03[B][5][a] Domestic Support Obligations.

[132] Bankruptcy Code § 502(b)(9).

[133] *See infra* § 17.08 Distribution of Estate Property.

[134] Bankruptcy Code § 502(b)(9).

[135] *E.g.*, United States v. Vecchio (In re Vecchio), 20 F.3d 555 (2d Cir. 1994); In re Hausladen, 146 B.R. 557 (Bankr. D. Minn. 1992).

[136] *See* Uwimana v. Gov't of Rwanda (In re Uwimana), 284 B.R. 218 (D. Md. 2002); Gregory G. Hesse, *Time Limitations for Objecting to Claims: Interplay Between Sections 502(d) and 546(a) of the Bankruptcy Code*, 26 St. Mary's L.J. 87 (1994).

[137] Bankruptcy Code § 101(8).

[138] Bankruptcy Code § 502(k)(1).

There are several important limitations in § 502(k) that further impair its utility. First, it only applies if the proposed repayment plan is "made at least 60 days before the date of the filing of the petition."[139] Thus, it can only be invoked by a debtor who is willing to wait at least two months after her proposal is submitted to a creditor for the creditor to manifest its unreasonable refusal to agree to the debtor's terms. Debtors who seek the assistance of a credit counseling agency in a last-ditch effort to avoid an impending bankruptcy will find § 502(k) unhelpful.

Second, the potential reduction in the amount of the claim only applies if the terms proposed on the debtor's behalf provide for payment of at least 60% of the debt "over a period not to exceed either the repayment period of the loan or a reasonable extension of that period." It is entirely unclear what a reasonable extension might be, particularly for the type of uninsured medical debts that many debtors owe, which are due immediately. How this rule might apply to credit card debts, which are payable over a period of seemingly unlimited years,[140] can only be surmised.

Third, the reduction can only be invoked by the debtor.[141] Other creditors who might have an incentive to pursue the motion lack standing. And debtors, the only ones with standing to bring the matter to the court's attention, have little incentive to do so. In a typical Chapter 7 case in which no assets are available to distribute to creditors, reducing the creditor's claim neither benefits the debtor nor harms the creditor. Even if there are assets to distribute in the Chapter 7 case, the reduction of the claim harms the creditor vis a vis other creditors, but does not free up assets for the debtor, or in any way change the nature of the debtor's fresh start. In a Chapter 13 case, where a debtor submits her disposable income to satisfy creditors' claims, the debtor's only incentive to move to reduce the creditor's claim is the personal satisfaction the debtor may enjoy at the prospect of punishing the creditor's intransigent conduct. Given the strident new standards for the amount of income debtors must contribute toward their Chapter 13 plans, it is unlikely that many debtors will be willing to contribute some of their limited remaining income to pay an attorney to pursue a motion under § 502(k).

Finally, the rare debtor who invokes § 502(k) in an effort to reduce the size of a creditor's claim is likely to find it difficult to prevail. The reduction only applies if the creditor "unreasonably refused to negotiate a reasonable alternative repayment schedule." Matters that must be litigated include whether the creditor's actions constituted a "refusal," whether any refusal was "unreasonable," and whether the

---

[139] Bankruptcy Code § 502(k)(1)(B)(i).

[140] The minimum payments required by many credit card companies are so low (typically around 4% of the principal balance, or $10, whichever is higher), it might take many years to fully amortize a credit card debt of several thousand dollars. A monthly 4% minimum payment on a $1000 credit card debt bearing interest at 18% per year, would require eighty-seven months (7.25 years) to fully amortize the debt. *See* http://www.bankrate.com/brm/calc/MinPayment.asp (last viewed on Sept. 1, 2006). If the debt were $3,000, payment of the debt would take 130 months. Until mid 2005, when the United States Office of Comptroller required banks to increase the minimum payments required to be made, a 2% minimum payment was the norm. At this level, the $1,000 debt would have taken 232 months (nearly twenty years) to pay in full. With interest accumulating at 1.5% per month ($15), the lion's share of the payment would be attributable to interest, with only .005% of the $1,000 balance ($5) being paid each month.

[141] Bankruptcy Code § 502(k)(1).

alternative repayment schedule proposed by the debtor was "reasonable." The debtor has the burden of proof on the issue of whether the creditor's refusal to negotiate was unreasonable.[142] In addition, the reduction does not apply at all if any "part of the debt under the alternative repayment schedule is nondischargeable."[143] This last limitation could turn the debtor's motion into a full-blown dispute over the dischargeability of the debt, which may be an issue the debtor will be reluctant to put on the table. Moreover, the statutory language is ambiguous concerning the meaning of "based in whole on an unsecured debt." These impediments are likely to result in few motions pursuant to § 502(k), making its inclusion in the Code an empty threat.

[E] Estimation of Claims[144]

Taking the time to determine the amount of unliquidated or contingent claims through the usual mechanism of a full-blown trial could delay the administration of a debtor's estate. Likewise, it may be difficult for a court to calculate the amount of payment that may be appropriate compensation for the loss of a "right to an equitable remedy for breach of performance."[145] Consequently, in these circumstances, the bankruptcy court must sometimes estimate the amount of the creditor's claim.[146] The claim might be estimated merely for the purpose of voting on a plan of reorganization, or to finally determine the allowed amount of the claims for the purpose of distribution of the estate.

The court has wide discretion to use a variety of mechanisms to estimate claims.[147] It may not deviate from the legal rules governing the claim, but it is otherwise permitted to estimate the claim by whatever procedures are best suited to the circumstances.[148] Methods used by courts have "run the gamut from summary trials to full-blown evidentiary hearings to a mere review of pleadings, briefs, and a one-day hearing involving oral argument of counsel,"[149] to arbitration.[150]

The process of estimating unliquidated claims may be particularly important in bankruptcy cases involving mass tort claims.[151] In cases like *In re A.H. Robins,*

---

[142] Bankruptcy Code § 502(k)(2)(A).

[143] Bankruptcy Code § 502(k)(1)(C).

[144] Francis E. Goodwyn, *Claims Estimation and the Use of the "Cleanup Trust"in Environmental Bankruptcy Cases*, 9 Am. Bankr. Inst. L. Rev. 769 (2001). *See* Barbara J. Houser, *Chapter 11 As A Mass Tort Solution*, 31 Loy. L.A. L. Rev. 451 (1998); David S. Salsburg & Jack F. Williams, *A Statistical Approach to Claims Estimation in Bankruptcy*, 32 Wake Forest L. Rev. 1119 (1997).

[145] Bankruptcy Code § 502(c)(2).

[146] Bankruptcy Code § 502(c)(1).

[147] *See* In re Windsor Plumbing Supply Co., 170 B.R. 503 (Bankr. E.D.N.Y. 1994).

[148] In re Brints Cotton Mktg., Inc., 737 F.2d 1338 (5th Cir. 1984).

[149] In re Windsor Plumbing Supply Co., 170 B.R. 503, 520 (Bankr. E.D.N.Y. 1994).

[150] In re Seaman Furniture Co. of Union Square, Inc., 160 B.R. 40 (S.D.N.Y. 1993).

[151] Georgene Vairo, *Mass Torts Bankruptcies: The Who, The Why and The How*, 78 Am. Bankr. L.J. 93 (2004). *See infra* § 23.02 Mass Torts.

Inc.,[152] which involved a defective and widely distributed intrauterine birth control device, and *In re Johns-Manville Corp.*,[153] which involved millions of asbestos claims, the court may be called upon to estimate not only the amount of pre-existing claims, but also to estimate the amount of claims held by victims who had no symptoms of their injuries at the time of the bankruptcy. These "future" claims present the court with two relatively unappetizing propositions. The court can treat the claims as arising prepetition (because the conduct which gives rise to the claim occured prepetition), and allow the claims to be discharged, even thought the claimants don't yet know that their interests are implicated, or the court can deem the claims "post-petition." If the debtor liquidates, there is little difference, because once the assets are distributed, there will be nothing left to pay the future claimants. However, if the debtor reorganizes, one result leaves the future claimants with nothing. The other leaves them with a windfall, at least as compared to other tort claimants, in that they will get paid in full out of the reorganized debtor. The first approach encourages reorganization. The second makes it impossible for a reorganizing debtor to deal with possibly crushing tort liability in Chapter 11.

Courts are divided over how to handle these problems. In the Dalkon Shield case, the court appointed a representative for the future claimants, but allowed their claims to be discharged.[154] In the *Piper Aircraft* case, the court held that the claims of creditors who had no relationship with the debtor at the time of the bankruptcy, and therefore no basis to know that they had a claim that was being discharged, could not be bound by the debtor's discharge.[155] How these future creditors are treated may depend, as it did in these two cases, on the underlying basis for their future claims, and the extent of their relationship with the debtor before its bankruptcy case was filed.

§ 10.03   SECURED CLAIMS[156]

The Bankruptcy Code distinguishes between secured claims and unsecured claims. Creditors with secured claims have senior priority over the estate's assets. Moreover, they are entitled to have their interests in the debtor's property

---

[152] *See* Grady v. A.H. Robins Co. (In re A.H. Robins Co.), 839 F.2d 198 (4th Cir.), *cert. dismissed*, 487 U.S. 1260 (1988); Georgene M. Vairo, *The Dalkon Shield Claimants Trust, and the Rhetoric of Mass Tort Claims Resolution*, 31 Loy. L.A. L. Rev. 79, 154 (1997).

[153] In re Johns-Manville Corp., 57 B.R. 680 (Bankr. S.D.N.Y. 1986). *See generally* Alan Resnick, *Mass Torts: Bankruptcy as a Vehicle for Resolving Enterprise-Threatening Mass Tort Liability*, 148 U. Pa. L. Rev. 2045 (2000). *See also* Nat'l Bankr. Rev. Comm'n, Bankruptcy: The Next Twenty Years: National Bankruptcy Review Commission Final Report 316 (1997); Thomas A. Smith, *A Capital Markets Approach to Mass Tort Bankruptcy*, 104 Yale L.J. 367, 369 (1994).

[154] Grady v. A.H. Robins Co. (In re A.H. Robins Co.), 839 F.2d 198 (4th Cir.), *cert. dismissed*, 487 U.S. 1260 (1988).

[155] Epstein v. Official Comm. of Unsecured Creditors (In re Piper Aircraft Corp.), 58 F.3d 1573 (11th Cir. 1995).

[156] Lucian Arye Bebchuk & Jesse M. Fried, *The Uneasy Case for the Priority of Secured Claims in Bankruptcy*, 105 Yale L.J. 857 (1996); Steven L. Harris & Charles Mooney, Jr., *A Property-Based Theory of Security Interests; Taking Debtors' Choices Seriously*, 80 Va. L. Rev. 2021 (1994); Alan Schwartz, *The Continuing Puzzle of Secured Debt*, 37 Vand. L. Rev. 1051 (1984).

adequately protected while the case is pending. Because of the primacy accorded to secured claims, drawing the distinction between secured claims, partially secured claims, and unsecured claims is a critical part of most bankruptcy cases.

[A]   Creditors with Secured Claims

A secured claim is a claim that is coupled with some interest in the debtor's property, usually a lien. The mere fact that a debtor owes money to a creditor does not mean that the creditor has an interest in the debtor's specific assets.[157] Creditors have no interest in a debtor's property unless the creditor has acquired a lien[158] or other interest in the debtor's property to secure the debtor's obligation.

A creditor might acquire a secured claim in several ways. They might obtain a mortgage or security interest in the debtor's property by agreement with the debtor (consensual liens).[159] Alternatively, they might have obtain a judgment or execution lien on the debtor's property through judicial process (judicial liens).[160] In addition, some creditors are favored with statutory or common law liens that arise by operation of law.[161]

The Bankruptcy Code does not generally distinguish between these types of liens. Nor does it generally distinguish between voluntary and involuntary liens: security interests and mortgages are treated in the same manner as judicial and statutory liens. With minor exceptions, all give rise to secured claims, and each of those claims has the priority given to it by the non-bankruptcy law that gave rise to the lien. What all of these lien claims have in common is that the holder does not have merely a claim for money; it also has a right to use specific property to satisfy the creditor's claim.

Regardless of the type of lien involved, a claim is secured only to the extent of the value of the debtor's interest in the property that secures the claim. Thus, a creditor whose $100,000 claim is secured by property worth only $60,000 has a secured claim only up to the $60,000 value of the collateral. The remaining $40,000 of the claim is unsecured. This simple rule has numerous important consequences.

---

[157] The mother of one of your co-author's learned this, to her dismay, when her son refused to repossess a car she had sold to a co-worker on credit. The generally dutiful son was reluctant to take the car in the absence of evidence of a security agreement giving his mother the right to do so. *See* Ohio Rev. Code §§ 2913.02, 2319.03 (LexisNexis 2006) (theft & unauthorized use of a vehicle).

[158] The term "lien' " should be used with caution. It is sometimes used broadly, to refer to any property interest that gives rights in property to enforce an obligation, whether voluntary or involuntary. For example, Bankruptcy Code § 101(37) says that " 'lien' means charge against or interest in property to secure payment of a debt or performance of an obligation." At other times, "lien" refers only to involuntarily created rights, such as a statutory lien or a judicial lien.

[159] *See supra* § 2.02 Consensual Liens; Leases.

[160] *See supra* § 2.04 Judicial Liens.

[161] *See supra* § 2.05 Statutory, Common Law, and Equitable Liens.

[B]   Effect of Bankruptcy on Secured Claims[162]

Although secured claims are protected in many ways in bankruptcy,[163] they are not completely unaffected by the filing of a bankruptcy petition. At the very least, they are subject to the automatic stay that restrains creditors from taking a variety of actions against the debtor and her property while the bankruptcy case is pending.[164] In Chapter 7 liquidation cases, this may result in delaying a secured creditor from foreclosing until the bankruptcy case is nearly over, though the court may grant permission to the creditor to proceed with foreclosure. In reorganization proceedings under Chapters 11, 12 and 13, the debtor has the power to use the collateral during the case. The debtor may be able to adjust the terms of repayment of a secured creditor's claim, such as by extending the time for payment, altering the amount of monthly installments, lowering the rate of interest, or, depending on the value of the collateral with respect to some claims, reducing the amount of the secured debt. And, unless the collateral is worth more than enough to satisfy the secured creditor's claim fully and is thus "oversecured," bankruptcy will stop the accumulation of interest on the amount of the claim while the case is pending. Finally, the filing of a bankruptcy petition prevents a security interest or other lien from attaching to after-acquired collateral that the debtor or the estate acquires after the petition has been filed. These topics are discussed in the remainder of this section, in varying degrees of detail, depending on their treatment in other sections of this book.

[1]   Foreclosure Delayed or Restrained

The automatic stay of Bankruptcy Code § 362(a) has a dramatic and immediate effect on secured creditors' ability to enforce their claims. As explained in more detail elsewhere, the filing of a bankruptcy petition operates as an automatic injunction against a variety of creditors' efforts to collect, including "any act to obtain possession of . . . or to exercise control over property of the estate [or] to create, perfect, or enforce any lien against property of the estate."[165] This prevents secured creditors from repossessing what they view as "their" collateral. It also prevents them from selling collateral they have already repossessed or from conducting foreclosure sales they have scheduled. It even requires them to return any property they have already repossessed to the trustee or to the debtor.[166]

---

[162] Lawrence Ponoroff, & F. Stephen Knippenberg, *The Immovable Object Versus the Irresistible Force: Rethinking the Relationship Between Secured Credit and Bankruptcy Policy*, 95 Mich. L. Rev. 2234, 2307 (1997); James S. Rogers, *The Impairment of Secured Creditors' Rights in Reorganization: A Study of the Relationship Between the Fifth Amendment and the Bankruptcy Clause*, 96 Harv. L. Rev. 973 (1983).

[163] The Bankruptcy Code, like other federal statutes, is limited by the Takings Clause of the Fifth Amendment to the United States Constitution. Dewsnup v. Timm, 502 U.S. 410, 419 (1992); Louisville Joint Stock Land Bank v. Radford, 295 U.S. 555, 589 (1935).

[164] Bankruptcy Code § 362. *See supra* Chapter 8 The Automatic Stay.

[165] Bankruptcy Code § 362(a)(3)-(4).

[166] In re Knaus, 889 F.2d 773 (8th Cir. 1989); Williams v. GMAC (In re Williams), 316 B.R. 534 (Bankr. E.D. Ark. 2004).

In liquidation cases, the automatic stay only delays foreclosure. In many cases, where there is no non-exempt equity in the collateral, the trustee is likely to be willing to abandon the collateral and to permit the secured creditor to foreclose.[167] Or the court may grant the creditor relief from the automatic stay to permit the foreclosure to proceed.[168] For example, if collateral worth only $5,000 secures an allowed $7,000 claim, there will be no surplus value available following the sale of the collateral to distribute to other creditors. In most liquidation cases, where no reorganization will occur, none of the debtor's property is necessary for reorganization. Accordingly, secured creditors are nearly always entitled to relief from the automatic stay and permitted to proceed with their foreclosure against the collateral.[169]

In other liquidation cases, where the collateral is worth more than enough to satisfy a secured creditor, the property is likely to be sold by the bankruptcy trustee. Upon a sale of the collateral, the trustee distributes the proceeds of the sale to the secured creditor in an amount necessary to satisfy the secured creditor's claim and uses any surplus to satisfy any priority and non-priority unsecured claims. This may result in delayed payment to secured creditors who must wait for the trustee to dispose of the collateral.[170]

In reorganization cases, secured creditors are unlikely to be permitted to foreclose, even if the debtor was in default when the debtor filed its bankruptcy petition. The debtor is allowed to use property of the estate during the course of the case, even if it is encumbered. As explained in detail elsewhere, the debtor's reorganization plan is likely to allow the debtor to retain its property and to restructure its debts. Payment may be extended over a longer period than called for in the debtor's contract with the secured creditor and both the interest rate and the amount of each installment payment might be reduced. Thus, a creditor with a $100,000 fully secured claim payable at 8% interest over a period of six years, might find its claim payable at only 6% interest with installments extended over ten years. In cases that involve partially secured claims, where the collateral is worth less than the amount of the outstanding debt, the reorganization plan may provide for a reduction of the amount of the secured portion of the creditor's claim.[171] Thus, if the creditor's $100,000 claim is secured by only $80,000 of collateral, the creditor will emerge from bankruptcy with collateral for only $80,000 if its claim, with payments extended over a longer period of time and at a reduced rate of interest. Its $20,000 unsecured claim will receive a distribution similar to that received by other unsecured creditors. In rarer cases, the debtor's reorganization plan may substitute alternative collateral or alter the seniority of a secured creditor's claim.[172] After the debtor's plan is confirmed by the court, the secured creditor's right to foreclose is

---

[167] *See* Bankruptcy Code § 554.

[168] Bankruptcy Code § 362(d)(2).

[169] *See supra* § 8.06[B] Relief From the Automatic Stay Upon Request of a Party.

[170] Fortunately, fully secured creditors have allowable claims for post-petition interest, up to the value of their collateral. *See supra* § 10.02[C][4] Interest on Claims.

[171] *See, e.g.,* Bankruptcy Code § 1123(b)(5) (generally permitting modifications of secured creditors' claims).

[172] *See* Bankruptcy Code § 364(d)(1); *supra* § 9.05[C] Secured Credit.

governed by the provisions of the plan, rather than by whatever rights the creditor had before the bankruptcy case began.[173]

[2] Acceleration

As with nearly all claims,[174] the filing of a bankruptcy petition accelerates the due date of a secured creditor's claim, making the entire amount of the claim immediately due, despite the agreement between the parties that does not call for payment until sometime in the future.[175] Most loan agreements permit a creditor to accelerate the due date of a debtor's obligations, upon the debtor's default. Regardless, bankruptcy accelerates the debtor's obligations, even if the parties' agreement does not provide for acceleration, and even though the creditor may not wish to accelerate the debt.[176]

[3] Post-Petition Interest

As explained in more detail below,[177] filing a bankruptcy petition generally stops the accumulation of interest on unsecured and partially secured claims. If the claim is fully secured, interest continues to accumulate up to the amount of the value of the collateral. If the debtor is in default, it may even accumulate at whatever enhanced "default rate" is specified in the parties' agreement.[178] However, the court may limit the rate of interest to the pre-default rate, based on equitable considerations.[179] If the claim is only partially secured, filing a bankruptcy petition stops interest from accruing on the claim while the case is pending.

[4] After-Acquired Collateral and Proceeds

Some secured creditors' rights extend to property acquired by the debtor after the security agreement or mortgage is executed.[180] This is particularly true with respect to claims secured by inventory, accounts, chattel paper, and other receivables, where the creditor necessarily relies on the value of these after-acquired

---

[173] *See, e.g.*, Bankruptcy Code § 1327(a).

[174] Claims for future support are not accelerated. Bankruptcy Code § 502(b)(5).

[175] *E.g.*, In re Manville Forest Prods. Corp., 43 B.R. 293, 297 (Bankr. S.D.N.Y. 1984). *See* Scott K. Charles & Emil A. Kleinhaus, *Prepayment Clauses in Bankruptcy*, 15 Am. Bankr. Inst. L. Rev. 537, 554 (2007).

[176] *See, e.g.*, In re Allegheny Int'l, Inc., 100 B.R. 247 (Bankr. W.D. Pa. 1989).

[177] *See infra* § 10.03[C][3] Post-Petition Interest on Secured Claims.

[178] General Elec. Capital Corp. v. Future Media Prods., Inc., 547 F.3d 956 (9th Cir. 2008) (citing Travelers Cas. & Sur. Co. of Am. v. Pac. Gas & Elec. Co., 549 U.S. (2007)).

[179] *See* Matter of Southland Corp., 160 F.3d 1054 (5th Cir. 1998); Matter of Terry Ltd. Partnership, 27 F.3d 241 (7th Cir. 1994); In re Wolverine, Proctor & Schwartz, LLC 449 B.R. 1 (Bankr. D. Mass. 2011). *But see* Casa Blanca Project Lenders v. City Commerce Bank (In re Casa Blanca Project Lenders), 196 B.R. 140 (B.A.P. 9th Cir. 1996).

[180] *See* U.C.C. § 9-204(a) (2010); *e.g.*, Stoumbos v. Kilimnik, 988 F.2d 949 (9th Cir. 1993) (absence of "after-acquired" collateral language did not prevent security interest from attaching to after-acquired inventory, but did preclude security interest from attaching to after-acquired equipment); United Okla. Bank v. Moss, 793 P.2d 1359 (Okla. 1990) (with appropriate language, mortgage could attach to after-acquired land).

assets as collateral for the debt owed to the creditor.[181] Some liens may extend much more broadly to after-acquired property. For example, an Article 9 security interest granted as part of a commercial transaction can encompass broad categories of collateral, both already owned and subsequently acquired by the debtor, if the parties so agree.[182] A business may grant a security interest in "all inventory, now owned or hereafter acquired." Under an after-acquired collateral clause of this type, the security interest immediately attaches to new inventory as soon as the debtor acquires it.

The attachment of a security interest, mortgage, or other lien to after-acquired collateral might have one of two possible effects. In most cases, it ensures that property subsequently acquired by the debtor serves as substitute collateral for the debtor's property that has been sold (in the case of inventory) or collected (in the case of accounts, chattel paper, and other types of receivables). For example, a creditor with a security interest in "existing and after-acquired inventory" may rely (sometimes desperately) on deliveries of new inventory the debtor receives to replace items that have been sold to customers.[183] Security interests in after-acquired collateral also might easily operate to expand the creditor's collateral, such as where the debtor expands its inventory or acquires new equipment, and thus provide the creditor with greater security than it previously enjoyed. In other situations, a creditor might depend on after-acquired collateral as a source of cash flow, such as where a mortgagor acquires a security interest in rents obtained from a mortgaged apartment building or office complex to secure the debtor's obligation to make monthly payments on the mortgage.[184]

Another type of after-acquired property is "proceeds." Proceeds consist primarily of money or other property obtained by the debtor when the encumbered property is sold or otherwise disposed of.[185] For example, suppose that Doug has given an Article 9 security interest in his car to Union Bank. If Doug sells his car to Boris for $2,000, that $2,000 is proceeds from the sale of the collateral and is automatically subject to the bank's security interest.[186]

Bankruptcy significantly curtails secured creditors' rights to after-acquired property. A pre-petition lien may encumber any property acquired up to the commencement of the case. However, unless the court orders otherwise, property acquired by the debtor after the commencement of the case is subject to the lien

---

[181] *See, e.g.*, In re Filtercorp, Inc., 163 F.3d 570 (9th Cir. 1998).

[182] There are many limitations on the ability to use after-acquired property clauses in consumer transactions. *See, e.g.*, U.C.C. § 9-204(2) (2010); Federal Trade Commission's Unfair Credit Practices Regulations, 16 C.F.R. § 444.2(a)(4) (2006).

[183] In most cases, these customers will acquire ownership of the items of inventory free and clear of the creditor's security interest, either because the secured party authorized the sale free of its interest, or because the buyers take free as buyers in the ordinary course of business. *See* U.C.C. §§ 9-315(a)(1) & 9-320(a) (2010).

[184] At least in states following the "lien theory" of mortgages, any right to rents prior to foreclosure must be based on the contract between mortgagor and mortgagee; it is not an automatic incident of the mortgage itself. *See* Grant S. Nelson & Dale A. Whitman, Real Estate Finance Law § 4.23 (4th ed. 2001).

[185] U.C.C. § 9-102(a)(64)(A) (2010).

[186] U.C.C. § 9-306 (2010).

only if: (1) the property qualifies as "proceeds, products, offspring, rents, or profits of property that was subject to a security agreement"[187] prior to the commencement of the case; (2) the security agreement provides that the lien extends to after-acquired property;[188] and (3) the provision in the security agreement that provides for inclusion of after-acquired property is otherwise enforceable under the non-bankruptcy law applicable to the security agreement.[189]

The court may alter the scope of after-acquired property subject to the lien, but only if it is appropriate "based on the equities of the case."[190] This occurs in reorganization when the debtor wishes to make a special court-approved deal with its secured creditors to permit the case to continue. The agreement may be necessary to obtain a loan of additional funds[191] or to provide a secured lender with adequate protection for its collateral.[192]

[C] Allowance of Secured Claims[193]

Claims are allowed as secured only to the extent of the value of the collateral securing the claim. Creditors with a right of setoff are treated as having secured claims to the extent of their right of setoff. Bankruptcy Code § 506(a)(1) provides: "An allowed claim of a creditor secured by a lien on property in which the estate has an interest . . . is a secured claim to the extent of the value of such creditor's interest in . . . such property."[194] The extent of the secured claim depends on the value of the collateral. If the collateral is worth more than the amount of the debt, the claim is "fully secured." Thus, if Franklin Manufacturing owes $100,000 to Peninsula Bank and the debt is secured by a senior unavoidable lien on Franklin's equipment, Peninsula's claim is secured to the extent of the value of the collateral. If the equipment is worth $100,000, or more, Peninsula has an allowed secured claim for the full $100,000.

---

[187] In bankruptcy, the term "security agreement" extends to all consensual liens, not just to Article 9 security interests. Bankruptcy Code § 101(50). Thus, when it appears in the Bankruptcy Code, the term "security agreement" refers not only to contractual liens arising under Article 9 but also to real estate mortgages and deeds of trust. However, it excludes judicial liens, statutory liens, and common law liens.

[188] Thus, even though U.C.C. Article 9 does not require a security agreement to refer specifically to "proceeds" for the security interest to attach, § 522(b)(1) makes such a reference necessary for the security interest to attach to proceeds acquired by the debtor after the case commences.

[189] Bankruptcy Code § 552(b)(1), (2). The 1994 Bankruptcy Code Amendments slightly revised this section to encompass "the fees, charges, accounts, or other payments for the use or occupancy of rooms and other public facilities in hotels, motels, or other lodging properties."

[190] Bankruptcy Code § 552(b)(1), (2).

[191] See supra § 9.05 Obtaining Credit.

[192] See supra § 8.06[B] Relief From the Automatic Stay Upon Request of a Party.

[193] Jean Braucher, Getting It for You Wholesale: Making Sense of Bankruptcy Valuation of Collateral After Rash, 102 Dick. L. Rev. 763 (1997); Lucian Arye Bebchuk & Jesse M. Fried, A New Approach to Valuing Secured Claims in Bankruptcy, 114 Harv. L. Rev. 2386 (2001); David Grey Carlson, Bifurcation of Undersecured Claims in Bankruptcy, 70 Am. Bankr. L.J. 1 (1996); Margaret Howard, Stripping Down Liens: Section 506(d) and the Theory of Bankruptcy, 51 U. Chi. L. Rev. 97 (1984).

[194] Bankruptcy Code § 506(a)(1).

Section 506(a)(1) further provides that a creditor's claim is an "unsecured claim to the extent that the value of [the] creditor's interest . . . is less than the amount of [the] allowed claim." A claim that is greater than the value of the collateral is a "partially secured claim" and is accompanied by an unsecured claim for any deficiency in the value of the collateral. Thus, if Franklin's equipment is worth only $80,000, Peninsula's allowed secured claim is only $80,0000. Peninsula also has an allowed unsecured claim for the remaining $20,000. When this bifurcation of an obligation occurs, the creditor has separate rights on each of its two claims.

A claim might also need to be bifurcated because of the existence of a senior secured claim, which might limit the secured status of a junior secured creditor's claim. For example, if Franklin's equipment is worth $200,000, Peninsula's $100,000 claim is only partially secured if there is $130,000 senior claim, secured by the same equipment in which Peninsula holds its lien. The senior secured creditor holds a $130,000 fully secured claim and Peninsula holds both a $70,000 secured claim and a $30,000 unsecured claim.

If a senior creditor's claim completely exhausts the value of the collateral, a junior secured creditor's claim might be completely "under water" and is merely an unsecured claim. If Franklin's equipment is worth only $130,000 and is subject to a senior security interest that secures a $150,000 debt, then Peninsula's claim is completely unsecured.

[1] Valuation of Collateral[195]

Because secured claims are limited by the value of the collateral, the method of determining that value is important. If, continuing with the above example, the court determines Franklin's equipment is worth $250,000, both creditors' claims are fully secured. If it were worth only $200,000, Peninsula's junior claim would be bifurcated. And if it is worth only $130,000, Peninsula's claim is be wholly unsecured.

Section 506(a)(1) specifies that the value of the debtor's property is to be determined "in light of the purpose of the valuation and of the proposed disposition or use" of the property.[196] This language seems to favor use of liquidation value in circumstances where the collateral is to be liquidated, and replacement value or going concern value where the collateral continues to be used by the debtor, as it might in a reorganization proceeding.[197] However, some courts use a liquidation or

---

[195] Jean Braucher, *Beneath the Surface of BAPCPA* Rash *and Ride-through Redux: The Terms for Holding on to Cars, Homes and Other Collateral under the 2005 Act*, 13 Am. Bankr. Inst. L. Rev. 457 (2005); Jean Braucher, *Getting It for You Wholesale: Making Sense of Bankruptcy Valuation of Collateral After* Rash, 102 Dick. L. Rev. 763 (1997); Lucian Arye Bebchuk & Jesse M. Fried, *A New Approach to Valuing Secured Claims in Bankruptcy*, 114 Harv. L. Rev. 2386 (2001); David Gray Carlson, *Secured Creditors and the Eely Character of Bankruptcy Valuations*, 41 Am U. L. Rev. 63 (1991); Lee Dembart & Bruce A. Markell, *Alive at 25? A Short Review of the Supreme Court's Bankruptcy Jurisprudence, 1979-2004*, 78 Am. Bankr. L.J. 373, 384 (2004); Robert M. Lawless & Stephen P. Ferris, *Economics and the Rhetoric of Valuation*, 5 J. Bankr. L. & Prac. 3 (1995); Chris Lenhart, *Toward a Midpoint Valuation Standard in Cram Down: Ointment for the* Rash *Decision*, 83 Cornell L. Rev. 1821 (1998).

[196] Bankruptcy Code § 506(a)(1).

[197] *E.g.*, In re Taffi, 96 F.3d 1190, 1191-92 (9th Cir. 1996).

foreclosure value standard to determine the amount of a secured creditor's allowed claim, even in cases where the debtor plans to continue using the collateral.[198] Other courts use the midpoint between the forced liquidation value and the replacement value.[199]

In *Associates Commercial Corp. v. Rash*,[200] the Supreme Court appeared to resolve this conflict by requiring use of the debtor's cost of replacing the collateral, at least in Chapter 13 cases where the debtor planned continued use of collateral. However, the opinion in *Rash* re-introduced considerable uncertainty regarding the proper valuation method by recognizing that "[w]hether replacement value is the equivalent of retail value, wholesale value, or some other value will depend on the type of debtor and the nature of the property."[201] The Court also acknowledged that the value should not include enhancements to the value that might be attributable to improvements made to the collateral, such as warranties or reconditioning, that might affect the retail value of many used automobiles.[202]

Some courts have ruled that the reasoning in *Rash* applies with equal force in Chapter 11 reorganizations.[203] Other courts resist *Rash*'s insistence on the use of replacement value by limiting the scope of the decision to its facts, which involved a determination of the amount of the allowed secured claim for purposes of confirming a Chapter 13 rehabilitation plan. For example, in *In re Weber*, a bankruptcy appellate panel approved using liquidation value to determine the size of a secured creditor's allowed secured claim to establish how much the debtor would be required to pay to accomplish a lump-sum redemption of the collateral under Bankruptcy Code § 722.[204] And, although some courts have applied *Rash* in Chapter 11 cases,[205] they have most frequently cited it for the proposition that valuation must be based in "light of the purpose of the valuation and of the proposed disposition or use of the property" rather than in direct support for use of the replacement cost of the collateral.[206] Thus, despite *Rash*'s explicit rejection of the use of the midpoint between retail and wholesale value,[207] courts continue to use

---

[198] In re Rash, 90 F.3d 1036 (5th Cir. 1996), *reversed*, Assoc. Commercial Corp. v. Rash, 520 U.S. 953 (1997).

[199] In re Hoskins, 102 F.3d 311, 316 (7th Cir. 1996).

[200] 520 U.S. 953 (1997).

[201] 520 U.S. at 965 n.6.

[202] 520 U.S. at 965 n.6. *See* Lucian Arye Bebchuk & Jesse M. Fried, *A New Approach to Valuing Secured Claims in Bankruptcy*, 114 Harv. L. Rev. 2386, 2397 n.41 (2001).

[203] See, e.g., In re Heritage Highgate, Inc., 679 F.3d 132, 141-42 (3d Cir. 2012); In re Mayslake Village — Plainfield Campus, Inc., 441 B.R. 309, 320 n. 2 (Bankr. N.D. Ill. 2010).

[204] *See supra* § 12.08[A] Lump-Sum Redemption by Debtor.

[205] In re T-H New Orleans Ltd. P'ship, 116 F.3d 790, 799 (5th Cir. 1997).

[206] In re LTV Steel Co., 285 B.R. 259 (Bankr. N.D. Ohio 2002). *See* Lucian Arye Bebchuk & Jesse M. Fried, *A New Approach to Valuing Secured Claims in Bankruptcy*, 114 Harv. L. Rev. 2386 (2001); Jean Braucher, *Getting It For You Wholesale: Making Sense of Bankruptcy Valuation of Collateral after Rash*, 102 Dick. L. Rev. 763, 764 (1998); Keith Sharfman, *Judicial Valuation Behavior: Some Evidence from Bankruptcy*, 32 Fla. St. U. L. Rev. 387 (2005).

[207] Chris Lenhart, *Toward a Midpoint Valuation Standard in Cram Down: Ointment for the Rash Decision*, 83 Cornell L. Rev. 1821 (1998).

this standard outside of the Chapter 13 context in which *Rash* was decided.[208]

A related issue is whether the anticipated costs associated with any sale of collateral should be deducted from the value in calculating the amount of the creditor's secured claim. In *Brown & Co. Securities Corp. v. Balbus (In re Balbus)*,[209] the issue was whether the debtor was ineligible for relief under Chapter 13 because his unsecured debt exceeded the ceiling imposed by Bankruptcy Code § 109(e).[210] The court refused to permit the anticipated costs of the sale of a secured creditor's collateral to be deducted from the amount of a secured claim, thus keeping the size of the debtor's unsecured claims just barely within Chapter 13's limits.

In 2005, Congress amended § 506(a) by adding new subsection (2), which governs valuation of personal property in cases involving individual debtors under Chapters 7 and 13. In those cases "such value . . . shall be determined based on the replacement value of such property as of the date of the filing of the petition without deduction for costs of sale or marketing."[211] This codifies the result in *Rash.*[212] The language further provides, "with respect to property acquired for personal, family, or household purposes, replacement value [means] the price a retail merchant would charge for property of that kind considering the age and condition of the property at the time value is determined."[213]

This new language overrules decisions that base the amount of a creditor's secured claim on the liquidation value of an individual Chapter 7 or 13 debtor's property and that indicate that any advertising, sales, or other marketing costs incurred in selling the property should be deducted from the value used to determine the amount of the creditor's secured claim.[214] Moreover, with respect to consumer goods, it directs the court to use the retail price of used goods, despite the nearly complete absence of information regarding the retail value of many used goods, except perhaps as it is determined by online auction services,[215] and the nearly complete absence of such a market, except, of course, with respect to motor vehicles for which an abundance of such information is readily available.[216] Broadly

---

[208] *E.g.*, Evabank v. Baxter, 278 B.R. 867, 876 (N.D. Ala. 2002); In re Younger, 216 B.R. 649, 656-657 (Bankr. W.D. Okla. 1998); In re Oglesby, 221 B.R. 515, 519 (Bankr. D. Colo. 1998). *See also* Lee Dembart & Bruce A. Markell, *Alive at 25? A Short Review of the Supreme Court's Bankruptcy Jurisprudence, 1979-2004*, 78 Am. Bankr. L.J. 373, 384 (2004).

[209] 933 F.2d 246 (4th Cir. 1991).

[210] *See infra* § 6.02[B][6][c] Chapter 13 Debt Limits.

[211] Bankruptcy Code § 506(a)(2).

[212] *See* Scott F. Norberg, *Consumer Bankruptcy's New Clothes: An Empirical Study of Discharge and Debt Collection in Chapter 13*, 7 Am. Bankr. Inst. L. Rev. 415, 426 (1999); Jean Braucher, *Rash and Ride-through Redux: The Terms for Holding on to Cars, Homes, and Other Collateral Under the 2005 Act*, 13 Am. Bankr. Inst. L. Rev. 457, 465 (2005).

[213] Bankruptcy Code § 506(a)(2).

[214] Jean Braucher, Rash *and* Ride-Through Redux: The Terms for Holding on to Cars, Homes, and Other Collateral Under the 2005 Act, 13 Am. Bankr. Inst. L. Rev. 457, 465 (2005).

[215] *See* Michael Korybut, *Online Auctions of Repossessed Collateral Under Article 9*, 31 Rutgers L.J. 29 (1999).

[216] *E.g.*, In re Pearsall, 441 B.R. 267 (Bankr. N.D. Ohio 2010). *See* Richardo I. Kilpatrick, *Selected*

speaking, the value of the collateral is likely to be set higher in a reorganization than in a liquidation. Moreover, in business cases, most litigation over the value of collateral occurs in the context of adequate protection and the automatic stay, not the allowance of the claim itself. These rules, however, do not explicitly apply to Chapter 11 or 12 cases or to claims secured by interests in real estate.

[2] Enforceability of Lien or Setoff

A claim's secured status depends on the enforceability of the creditor's lien or right of setoff under both applicable non-bankruptcy law and the Bankruptcy Code. Not surprisingly, a lien that is unenforceable outside of bankruptcy enjoys no greater rights in bankruptcy. Likewise, if the secured creditor's lien is avoidable via one of the bankruptcy trustee's numerous avoiding powers, the creditor's claim is relegated to unsecured status.

As long as the lien is otherwise enforceable, a secured claim can arise as a result of a consensual lien, a judicial lien, or a statutory lien.[217] A secured claim can also arise as the result of a creditor's right of setoff.[218] The nature or source of the lien does not matter.

[3] Post-Petition Interest on Secured Claims[219]

Most debt that is wholly or partially secured was originally incurred under an agreement that required the debtor to pay interest on the unpaid portion of the obligation. From the creditor's perspective, interest continues to accumulate on the debt after a bankruptcy petition is filed. However, whether the creditor is entitled to a claim for that post-petition interest depends on the value of the collateral in relation to the size of the claim.[220]

As explained above with respect to claims in general, unsecured creditors are not permitted to add post-petition interest to their claims. Although interest may accumulate on the debt, the creditor's claim for post-petition interest is not allowed as a claim against the debtor's estate, and an unsecured creditor receives no distribution for such interest in either a liquidation or a reorganization case. However, over-secured creditors are entitled to recover interest up to the value of the collateral securing their claims. Section 506(b) provides:

Creditor Issues Under the Bankruptcy Abuse Prevention and Consumer Protection Act of 2005, 79 Am. Bankr. L.J. 817, 826 (2005). *See generally* http://www.cars.com (last visited July 30, 2012, 2010) and http://www.kbb.com (last visited July 30, 2012).

[217] United States v. Ron Pair Enters., Inc., 489 U.S. 235, 240 (1989). *See generally supra* Chapter 2 — Creditors' Collection Rights.

[218] Boston Ins. Co. v. Nogg (In re Yale Express Sys., Inc.), 362 F.2d 111, 114 (2d Cir. 1966) (characterizing a right of setoff as the perfect kind of security); In re Bourne, 262 B.R. 745, 752 (Bankr. E.D. Tenn. 2001).

[219] Paul D. Bancroft, *Post Petition Interest on Tax Liens in Bankruptcy Proceedings*, 62 Am. Bankr. L.J. 327 (1988); John C. McCoid, II, *Pendency Interest in Bankruptcy*, 68 Am. Bankr. L.J. 1 (1994); Thomas H. Jackson & Robert E. Scott, *On the Nature of Bankruptcy: An Essay on Bankruptcy Sharing and the Creditors' Bargain*, 75 Va. L. Rev. 155 (1989); Dean Pawlowic, *Entitlement to Interest Under the Bankruptcy Code*, 12 Bankr. Dev. J. 149 (1995).

[220] United Sav. Ass'n of Texas v. Timbers of Inwood Forest Assocs., Ltd., 484 U.S. 365 (1988).

> To the extent that an allowed secured claim is secured by property the value of which . . . is greater than the amount of such claim, there shall be allowed to the holder of such claim, interest on such claim, and any reasonable fees, costs, or charges provided for under the agreement or State statute under which such claim arose.[221]

Thus, interest that continues to accumulate on the debt is added to the amount of the allowed secured claim, but only up to the value of the collateral for the debt. If a debt owed to Peninsula Bank is $100,000 and Franklin Manufacturing's equipment securing the debt is worth $120,000, Peninsula is allowed up to $20,000 in post-petition interest. Once the surplus has been exhausted, however, the creditor is not allowed either a secured or an unsecured claim for any further interest.

Correspondingly, if there were no surplus to begin with, the creditor would have no claim for post-petition interest. If Franklin Manufacturing's collateral were worth only $90,000, or even the full $100,000 amount of the debt, Peninsula would not have an allowed claim for interest that accumulates on the debt after Franklin's petition was filed.

A closely related issue is the rate of interest that must be paid. If the debtor is in default, the creditor will insist on payment at any "default" rate specified in the contract between the parties. Some courts have ruled that nothing in the Bankruptcy Code prevents such a default rate from continuing to accrue on the claim, at least prior to confirmation of the debtor's plan.[222] Here, the Supreme Court's decision in *Travelers Casualty & Surety Co. of America v. Pacific Gas & Electronic Co.*,[223] though not dispositive, has been influential. There, in analyzing whether unsecured creditors were entitled to have post-petition attorneys' fees as part of their claim, the court said: "[c]reditors' entitlements in bankruptcy arise in the first instance from the underlying substantive law creating the debtor's obligation, subject to any qualifying or contrary provisions of the Bankruptcy Code."[224] This language points to allowing creditors whatever they are entitled to under state law,[225] unless the Bankruptcy Code specifies otherwise. But, not all courts agree,[226] and the issue remains to be resolved.

After BAPCPA, secured tax claims are entitled to interest at whatever rate applies under relevant non-bankruptcy law.[227] Usually this is the rate established by the applicable state or federal statute that governs tax claims.[228]

Note that the secured claim may be increased not only by the interest that accrues on the loan, but also by "any reasonable fees, costs, or charges provided for

---

[221] Bankruptcy Code § 506(b).

[222] General Elec. Capital Corp. v. Future Media Prods., Inc., 547 F.3d 956 (9th Cir. 2008).

[223] 549 U.S. 443 (2007).

[224] *Id.* at 450.

[225] In re Sundale, Ltd., 410 B.R. 101 (Bankr. S.D. Fla. 2009).

[226] *See, e.g.*, In re Hollstrom, 133 B.R. 535, (Bankr. D. Colo. 1991) (36% default rate unreasonable).

[227] Bankruptcy Code § 511. *See* In re Bernbaum, 404 B.R. 39 (Bankr. D. Mass. 2009).

[228] *E.g.*, In re Bernbaum, 404 B.R. 39 (Bankr. D. Mass. 2009).

under the agreement or State statute under which such claim arose."[229] This means post-petition late fees, attorneys' fees, collection costs, and the like may be added to the allowed secured claim but, as with post-petition interest, only up the value of the collateral,[230] and only to the extent that these late fees, attorneys' fees, and collection costs are reasonable.[231]

In reorganization cases, a careful distinction must be drawn between post-petition "pendency" interest and interest required to be paid under the terms of a confirmed reorganization plan. Interest is likely to be required under the latter, even if the secured creditor is not entitled to a claim for the former. "Pendency" interest refers to interest accumulating on a secured debt between the time the debtor's petition is filed and the time its reorganization plan is implemented. As explained immediately above, creditors have no claim for pendency interest beyond the value of the their collateral. However, Chapters 11, 12 and 13 all require post-confirmation interest to be paid on the amount of the "allowed secured claim" to compensate the creditor for deferral of payment of his claim under the terms of the confirmed plan of reorganization.[232]

Consider Peninsula Bank's security interest in Franklin Manufacturing's equipment. If the equipment is worth only $90,000 and the debt owed to Peninsula is $100,000, Peninsula does not have an allowed claim for any interest that accumulates on the debt between the time Franklin files its Chapter 11 case and the time Franklin's plan is confirmed, even though this may be a period of at least several months, perhaps several years. However, if Franklin's reorganization plan provides for deferred payment of Peninsula's $90,000 secured claim, the plan must provide for interest payments to Peninsula on this amount, commencing at the time when Franklin's plan is implemented.

The unavailability of pendency interest under the *Timbers* rule[233] has been attacked for providing many secured claims with less than full payment during the pendency period. Since the secured creditor loses the use of its property during that period, and it is not compensated for that lost use, the secured creditor does not in fact receive the full value of the property.[234] If, for example, Peninsula Bank has exactly $100,000 of collateral available to secure its $100,000 claim, it is entitled to no pendency interest. This is in spite of the fact that, but for the automatic stay, Peninsula Bank could have seized and sold its collateral, and re-invested the proceeds. Although the bank eventually receives $100,000 through the bankruptcy proceeding, this is less than what it would have received outside of bankruptcy if it

---

[229] Bankruptcy Code § 506(b). The reference to fees, costs, and charges arising under a "State statute" was added in 2005.

[230] *See* Rushton v. State Bank (In re Gledhill), 164 F.3d 1338, 1342 (10th Cir. 1999).

[231] Eastman Nat'l Bank v. Sun 'N Fun Waterpark, LLC (In re Sun 'N Fun Waterpark, LLC), 408 B.R. 361, 366 (B.A.P. 10th Cir. 2009); In re Market Ctr. E. Retail Prop., Inc., 433 B.R. 335, 357-60 (Bankr. D.N.M. 2010).

[232] *See infra* § 19.11[B][1] Secured Claims.

[233] United Sav. Assoc. of Texas v. Timbers of Inwood Forest Assocs., Ltd., 484 U.S. 365 (1988).

[234] Douglas Baird & Thomas Jackson, *Corporate Reorganization and the Treatment of Diverse Ownership Interests: A Comment on Adequate Protection of Secured Creditors in Bankruptcy*, 51 U. Chi. L. Rev. 97 (1984).

had foreclosed and reinvested. It may be considerably less if the proceeding is protracted, with a long pendency period between the time the petition is filed and the time a plan is ultimately confirmed.

In the view of some, this improperly forces a secured creditor, who is unlikely to benefit from the reorganization, to subsidize the reorganization for the benefit of unsecured creditors, who may get a better payout if the reorganization succeeds.[235] On the other hand, the no-interest rule has been defended as recognizing that bankruptcy is a common disaster, like a shipwreck, in which the burden of loss should be shared among all stakeholders.[236] It is at least a crude means of helping to provide some payment on unsecured claims; virtually all or most debtors' non-exempt property already goes to pay secured claims,[237] allowing interest on claims that are not oversecured simply exacerbates this problem. In any event, any doubt about the proper interpretation of the Code has been resolved by the Supreme Court. It ruled in *Timbers of Inwood Forest* that the plain language of the Code mandates the denial of any pendency interest on debts that are not oversecured.[238] Thus, at least for now, the issue appears to be at rest.

[D] Surcharge of Secured Claims[239]

Generally, administering the debtor's estate cannot be charged to a particular secured creditor's collateral. Instead, these administrative expenses must be paid from other assets of the estate. However, in rare circumstances, § 506(c) subjects a secured creditor's claim to a "surcharge" to pay for the estate's expenses. A surcharge is permitted only when the expenses incurred have directly benefitted the secured creditor, such as where costs are incurred to keep the debtor's business open in a way that preserves the going concern value of the creditor's collateral, which is subsequently sold. A surcharge is permitted only when: (1) the expense was "necessary" to preserve or dispose of the creditor's collateral, (2) the expense was "reasonable," and (3) the expenses provided a "direct benefit" to the creditor with a lien on the property.[240]

---

[235] *E.g.*, Thomas H. Jackson, The Logic and Limits of Bankruptcy Law 189-90 (1986).

[236] *See* John C, McCoid II, *Pendency Interest in Bankruptcy*, 68 Am. Bankr. L.J. 1, 2 (1994). (Note that this is not Professor McCoid's own position.) The shipwreck model of bankruptcy dates back at least to the eighteenth century; Professor McCoid quotes a 1743 case, *Ex parte Bennet*: "[I]t is a dead fund, and in such a shipwreck, if there is salvage of part to each person, in this general loss, it is as much as can be expected." Ex parte Bennet, 26 Eng. Rep. 716, 717 (1743). *See also* Robert E. Scott, *A Relational Theory of Secured Financing*, 86 Colum. L. Rev. 901, 967-68 (1986); Robert E. Scott, *Through Bankruptcy with the Creditors' Bargain Heuristic*, 53 U. Chi. L. Rev. 690, 700-07 (1986).

[237] For a discussion regarding the percentage of a debtor's assets that are distributed on secured claims, see Michael J. Herbert & Dominic E. Pacitti, *Down and Out in Richmond, Virginia: The Distribution of Assets in Chapter 7 Bankruptcy Proceedings Closed During 1984-87*, 22 U. Rich. L. Rev. 303 (1988).

[238] United Sav. Assoc. of Texas v. Timbers of Inwood Forest Assocs., Ltd., 484 U.S. 365 (1988).

[239] David Gray Carlson, *Surcharge and Standing: Bankruptcy Code Section 506(c) after* Hartford Underwriters, 76 Am. Bankr. L.J. 43 (2002).

[240] *See* Bear v. Coben (In re Golden Plan of Cal., Inc.), 829 F.2d 705 (9th Cir. 1986).

After the Supreme Court's decision in *Hartford Underwriters Insurance Co. v. Union Planters Bank, N.A.,*[241] it is clear that § 506(c) may be invoked only by the trustee, or a Chapter 11 debtor-in-possession. The plain meaning of § 507(c) limits standing to obtain a surcharge to the trustee, and § 1107 extends all of the rights, powers and duties of a trustee to the debtor-in-possession. Thus, though it may not be the best policy, others who contribute value to a secured creditor's collateral are not entitled to a surcharge under § 507(c), and should obtain the agreement of the secured creditor for a surcharge, before incurring expenses that might result in conferring a benefit to the lender.

§ 10.04 UNSECURED CLAIMS[242]

Unsecured claims fall into two broad categories: priority claims and general claims. Among priority claims, there are a few super-priority claims that, when they exist, are entitled to be paid after secured claims, but before other priority claims. These super-priority claims are explained below after claims entitled to ordinary priority.

Priority claims are unsecured claims that are singled out by the Bankruptcy Code for favorable treatment, primarily in § 507. These claims are entitled to be paid in full after secured claims are satisfied, but before holders of general unsecured claims receive anything. In liquidation cases, priority claims are paid only to the extent the estate has enough assets to pay unsecured creditors. If all of the estate's assets are consumed by secured claims and nothing is left to provide payment to creditors with unsecured claims, priority status means nothing. In reorganization cases, holders of priority claims are entitled to insist on full payment,[243] though they will nearly always agree to less favorable treatment if liquidation of the debtor would result in receiving even less. In Chapter 11 cases, some priority claims are entitled to payment in full immediately upon implementation of the debtor's plan.[244]

General unsecured claims are those held by most creditors whose claims are neither secured nor entitled to any special bankruptcy priority. In liquidation proceedings, which usually involve consumer debtors with no non-exempt assets, these claims rarely receive payment. In reorganization proceedings, they may receive some payment, though nearly always less than 100% of the amount owed. Included among these claims are those of creditors whose security interests, mortgages, or other liens have been avoided by the bankruptcy trustee because they were unperfected, preferential, or otherwise,[245] and those of creditors whose collateral is inadequate to fully satisfy the entire claim.

---

[241] 530 U.S. 1 (2000).

[242] James W. Bowers, *Wither What Hits the Fan?: Murphy's Law, Bankruptcy Theory, and the Elementary Economics of Loss Distribution,* 26 Ga. L. Rev. 27 (1991); Donald R. Korobkin, *Rehabilitating Values: A Jurisprudence of Bankruptcy,* 91 Colum L. Rev 717 (1991); Lynn M. LoPucki, *The Death of Liability,* 106 Yale L.J. 1 (1996).

[243] Bankruptcy Code § 1129(a)(9). *See infra* § 19.10[H] Full Payment of Priority Claims.

[244] Bankruptcy Code § 1129(a)(9)(A).

[245] *See generally infra* Chapters 14-16.

[A] Priority Claims[246]

Section 507 establishes a group of claims entitled to priority status. Each claim in each priority class is entitled to payment in full before any payment is made on any claim in a lower priority class. When there is not enough to pay each claim in a particular class fully, all the claims in that class are paid pro rata, and no payment is made with regard to claims in a lower rung on the priority ladder. In business liquidation cases in particular, the difference between classification as a priority claim and a general claim can sometimes mean the difference between being paid in full or receiving nothing. Classification as a priority claim in a higher rung on the priority ladder (or a lower rung) can have the same importance.

[1] Support Claims

In 2005, after considerable political wrangling, a new first priority was added for "domestic support obligations . . . owed to or recoverable by a spouse, former spouse, or child of the debtor, or such child's parent, legal guardian, or responsible relative."[247] A related second priority is accorded to the same sort of domestic support obligations that have previously been assigned to a governmental unit or otherwise owed to a governmental unit.[248] These new provisions promote support claims from seventh priority to first.

Despite this assurance of highest priority, new § 507(a)(1)(C) subordinates these domestic support claims to the administrative expenses of a bankruptcy trustee.[249] This provision recognizes the harsh reality that unless payment to the trustee is assured, no one will be willing to serve as trustee, and no one will incur the expenses necessary to liquidate the debtor's assets to pay the claims of other creditors.[250] Thus, despite the appearance of support claims in § 507(a)(1), administrative expenses of a Chapter 7, 11, 12, or 13 trustee really occupy the first priority position.[251]

Bumping support claims up from seventh priority to almost first is even less meaningful when considered in the broader context of the funds generally available to distribute to creditors. Approximately 96% of all consumer liquidation cases are "no-asset" cases, in which no assets are available to distribute to creditors, regardless of their priority. Thus, the priority potentially comes into play in only 4% of liquidation cases. Corporate debtors, of course, do not owe support. In a large percentage of these remaining liquidation cases, the trustee's administrative expenses are likely to exhaust the estate's assets. With no funds to distribute to

---

[246] Hanoch Dagan, *Restitution in Bankruptcy: Why All Involuntary Creditors Should Be Preferred*, 78 Am. Bankr. L.J. 247 (2004).

[247] Bankruptcy Code § 507(a)(1)(A).

[248] Bankruptcy Code § 507(a)(1)(B). This priority does not apply if an assignment was voluntarily made to the governmental entity "for the purpose of collecting the debt."

[249] Bankruptcy Code § 507(a)(1)(C).

[250] Those who tried to insist on giving support claims priority over a trustee's administrative expenses ignored this practical reality.

[251] Samuel K. Crocker & Robert H. Waldschmidt, *Impact of the 2005 Bankruptcy Amendments on Chapter 7 Trustees*, 79 Am. Bankr. L.J. 333, 366 (2005).

spouses and children with support claims, their promotion from seventh priority is meaningful in only those rare consumer liquidation cases in which there are substantial assets available to distribute to creditors. In Chapter 12 and 13 cases, priority support claimants were already entitled to payment in full as a condition of confirming the debtor's rehabilitation plan, pursuant to their seventh position in former § 507(a)(7).

[2] Administrative Expenses

The expenses of administering the bankruptcy case itself are nearly always given the highest priority among unsecured claims and thus have the best chance of receiving payment. Section 507(a)(2) accords second priority to "administrative expenses allowed under section 503(b) of this title and any fees and charges assessed against the estate under chapter 123 of title 28." Administrative expenses are those that arise from the expenses involved in the bankruptcy proceeding itself. Section 503 sets out the various administrative expenses.

The most obvious administrative expense claims are those derived from the "actual, necessary costs and expenses of preserving the estate."[252] The most important categories of these expenses are:

- salaries paid to the debtor's employees for services rendered during the case;[253]

- taxes incurred by the estate;[254] and

- compensation to paid to the trustee, to any examiner appointed by the court, and to any other "professional person" engaged to render services to the estate, such as attorneys, accountants, investment bankers, appraisers, and real estate agents, pursuant to Bankruptcy Code § 330(a).[255]

While it might be thought that this latter category includes fees owed to the debtor's attorney for services rendered in connection with the "preservation of the estate," § 330 does not mention fees owed to an individual debtor's attorney in a Chapter 7 case. The exclusion of any provision for fees to a Chapter 7 debtor's attorney has been characterized as possibly a scrivener's error. Nevertheless, in *Lamie v. United States Trustee*, the Supreme Court felt constrained to take Congress at its word and denied the debtor's attorney a claim for fees in a Chapter 7 liquidation.[256] Section 330 specifically provides for recovery of attorneys' fees in

---

[252] Bankruptcy Code § 503(b)(1).

[253] Bankruptcy Code § 503(b)(1)(A). This includes any wages and benefits awarded as back pay attributable to the debtor's pre-petition violation of state or federal law, regardless of when the debtor's violations took place or when the employee's services were rendered. Bankruptcy Code § 503(b)(1)(A)(ii).

[254] Bankruptcy Code § 503(b)(1)(B)-(D) (this includes any fines, penalties, or reductions in credit relating to a post-petition tax). *See* Hall v. United States, 132 S. Ct. 1882 (2012) (capital gain tax on Chapter 12 debtor's post-petition sale of their farm, while case was pending, was not a tax liability "incurred by the estate" and thus not an administrative expense).

[255] Bankruptcy Code § 503(b)(2). The employment and compensation of such "professional persons" is subject to court approval in accordance with Bankruptcy Code § 330. *See infra* § 21.03 Professionals' Fees.

[256] 540 U.S. 526 (2004).

cases under Chapters 12 and 13, and explicitly provides for their recovery in Chapter 11 cases where the debtor's attorney is appointed to represent the "debtor in possession."[257] However, after *Lamie*, Chapter 7 debtors' attorneys must plan to recover their fees in advance or run the risk of not being paid at all. Section 330 does not prevent a debtor's attorney from obtaining a pre-petition retainer as compensation for post-petition services.[258]

In consumer liquidation cases, attorneys' fees are normally paid in cash by the debtor before the commencement of the case. This is usually also true in Chapter 13 cases, although the debtor's attorneys' fees are sometimes paid through distributions to creditors under the debtor's plan.[259] In Chapter 11 reorganization cases, the debtor's attorneys' fees can be considerable, running into the hundreds of thousands, and in large cases, millions of dollars.

Administrative expense claims are sometimes paid for the actual, necessary expenses of creditors or their attorneys, but only if their efforts have made a substantial contribution to the administration of the case itself, such as by filing an involuntary petition or recovering property for the estate.[260] The creditor's contribution must have resulted in some definite tangible benefit to the estate that will accrue to the benefit of all creditors. Apart from this exception, creditors generally bear the cost of their own expenses and attorneys' fees incurred in connection with their efforts to recover payment on their claims, even if they have generally been active participants in the case.[261]

The 2005 amendments added a pre-petition claim to this list, for unpaid sellers who delivered goods to the debtor in the twenty day period immediately before the debtor's petition.[262] This provides additional protection for unpaid sellers of goods,[263] that supplements the seller's right of reclamation under U.C.C. § 2-702 and Bankruptcy Code § 546(c)(1).[264] It provides no similar protection for those who provide services during the twenty days before the debtor's petition, even if the services were rendered in connection with the delivery of goods.[265]

---

[257] Bankruptcy Code § 330(a). *See* In re Busetta-Silvia, 314 B.R. 218 (B.A.P. 10th Cir. 2004).

[258] Lamie v. United States, 540 U.S. 526, 537-38 (2004).

[259] *See* In re San Miguel, 40 B.R. 481 (Bankr. D. Colo. 1984) (plan consisted primarily of payments to debtor's Chapter 13 attorney).

[260] Bankruptcy Code § 503(b)(3)-(4).

[261] *E.g.*, In re The Columbia Gas Sys., 224 B.R. 540 (Bankr. D. Del. 1998) (creditors' fee applications denied). *See* Edward A. Stone, Comment, *Encouraging Creditor Participation: Integrating the Allowance of Administrative Expenses with the Common Fund Theory*, 15 Bankr. Dev. J. 223 (1999).

[262] Bankruptcy Code § 503(b)(9). *See* In re Goody's Family Clothing, Inc., 401 B.R. 131 (Bankr. D. Del. 2009) (clothing retailer who supplied inspection, ticketing, and repackaging services for goods purchased from another vender not entitled to priority under § 503(b)(9)).

[263] *See* In re Erving Industries, Inc., 432 B.R. 354 (Bankr. D. Mass. 2010) ("electricity" is goods); In re Grede Foundries, Inc., 435 B.R. 593 (Bankr. W.D. Wis. 2010).

[264] *See supra* § 2.05[E][4] Bankruptcy Code Limits on Seller's Right of Reclamation.

[265] In re Pilgrim's Pride Corp., 421 B.R. 231 (Bankr. N.D. Tex. 2009) (distinguishing between services and goods and thus denying priority to pre-petition claims for transportation services and electricity but granting priority to claims for natural gas, and water).

[3] Involuntary Gap Creditors

Involuntary bankruptcy cases are initiated by creditors. Creditors seeking to force a debtor into bankruptcy usually must prove that the debtor is not generally paying its debts as they come due.[266] Unlike a voluntary case, in which an order for relief is entered at the same time the debtor's petition is filed, an order for relief is not entered in an involuntary case until the creditors prove facts that support this standard. As a result, there is usually a gap between the time the creditor's petition is filed and the time an order for relief is entered. Creditors whose claims arise in the ordinary course during this "involuntary gap period" are entitled to priority for their claims. Their claims are paid after other administrative expense claims but before other priority claims. This provides some measure of assurance to creditors who continue to provide credit to a debtor while an involuntary petition is pending.

[4] Wage Claims[267]

Fourth priority is given to certain employees' wage claims. To qualify for priority treatment, an employee's claim must have been earned within 180 days before either the date the debtor (the employer) filed its petition or the date when debtor ceased doing business, whichever occurred first.[268] The priority may not exceed $11,725 for each claimant.[269] In connection with an employee's severance pay, amounts are "earned" on the date that employment was terminated.[270]

Consider, for example, the claim of an employee who is owed a total of $12,000 in unpaid wages, earned during the last six months before the debtor's bankruptcy petition was filed at the rate of $2,000 per month.[271] Only $11,725 of the claim is entitled to priority. The remaining $250 is a general unsecured claim. Even though the entire $12,000 was earned during the 180 days preceding the employer's bankruptcy petition, the total claim exceeds the $11,725 maximum that may be accorded priority treatment.

This priority is intended to provide some protection for employees, because Congress assumes most employees have great need for, and little ability to obtain, protection against their employer's bankruptcy. If there are two employees, each owed $12,000, each employee is entitled to his own priority claim. Thus, the total amount entitled to priority depends on the number of unpaid employees and the size of their claims.

---

[266] Bankruptcy Code § 303(h). *See supra* § 6.03[E] Grounds for Entry of "An Order for Relief."

[267] C. Scott Pryor, *The Missing Piece of the Puzzle: Perspectives On the Wage Priority in Bankruptcy,* 16 Am. Bankr. Inst. L. Rev. 121 (2008).

[268] Bankruptcy Code § 507(a)(4). Before the 2005 amendments this time period was only 90 days.

[269] Bankruptcy Code § 507(a)(4). Before the 2005 Amendments, the amount was only $4925 for each claimant. As with most other dollar figures in the Bankruptcy Code, this amount is adjusted every three years, pursuant to Bankruptcy Code § 104, in accordance with increases in the Consumer Price Index. They were last adjusted on April 1, 2010, and are set to be adjusted again in April 2013 and 2016.

[270] Matson v. Alarcon, 651 F.3d 404 (4th Cir. 2011).

[271] Such claims, of course, are rare. Few employees remain on the job for six months without compensation.

Priority is accorded only to those who qualify as employees. Independent contractors are not eligible. However, independent contractors who earn sales commissions from selling goods or services — but not real estate — are entitled to priority if the claimant earned at least 75% of his earnings from the debtor during the 12 months prior to the filing of the debtor's petition.[272] Thus, a sales agent who earned commissions by making sales for several merchants would probably not qualify for the priority.

[5] Employee Benefit Plan Claims

Fifth priority is for contributions to employee benefit plans. Priority relates only to those contributions that arise from services rendered within the earlier of 180 days before the petition or 180 days before the debtor ceased doing business.[273] The amount of priority for each employee benefit plan is capped — it may not exceed the number of employees covered by the plan, multiplied by $11,725, but minus the aggregate amount that was distributed to employees for priority wage claims under the fourth priority, and minus the amount paid by the estate on behalf of such employees under any other employee benefit plan.[274]

For example, suppose that during the 180-day period, thirty employees had earned the right to a $200,000 benefit plan contribution to Benefit Plan A, and the debtor had failed to pay this contribution. Those thirty employees also established aggregate wage priority claims under § 507(a)(4) in the amount of $150,000, and the estate already paid $30,000 into Benefit Plan B on behalf of the same thirty employees. Benefit Plan A has priority for $191,750 of the $2000 pension benefit plan claim ($371,750 – $150,000 – $30,000 = $191,750).[275]

In 2006, the Supreme Court determined that an unsecured creditor's claim for unpaid workers' compensation liability insurance was not entitled to priority under this provision, because workers' compensation benefits were not intended as a substitute for wages.[276] Instead, the Court held that workers' compensation benefits (and thus the insurance premiums for those benefits) were substitutes for common law tort liability. As the court explained, tort claims, unlike claims for unpaid wages and other similar employee benefits, are not entitled to priority under § 507.

---

[272] Bankruptcy Code § 507(a)(4)(B).

[273] The priority does not extend to contributions owed to the plan for the benefit of retired former employees who did not provide services to the debtor during the 180 days before the petition. Consol. Freightways Corp. v. Aetna, Inc., 564 F.3d 1162 (2009).

[274] Bankruptcy Code § 507(a)(5). As with other dollar figures in the Bankruptcy Code, this amount is adjusted every three years, in accordance with increases in the Consumer Price Index. The last adjustments were made on April 1, 2010, and are set to be made again in April 2013 and 2016. *See* Bankruptcy Code § 104.

[275] *See* Consol. Freightways Corp. v. Aetna, Inc., 564 F.3d 1162 (2009).

[276] Howard Delivery Serv. Inc. v. Zurich Am. Ins. Co., 547 U.S. 651 (2006).

[6]   Certain Claims of Farmers and Fisherman

The sixth priority addresses the special problems of farmers and fishermen who have delivered grain or fish to bankrupt grain elevators or fish storage facilities. Each is given a priority claim for its products or proceeds. The priority is capped at $10,000.[277] No similar priority is provided to farmers who have claims for livestock that was delivered to a bankrupt meat packer or livestock dealer.[278]

[7]   Consumer Deposits

The seventh priority gives limited protection to consumer buyers who have made a down payment or layaway deposit to a now-bankrupt seller. The payment may be for the purchase, lease, or rental of property or for the purchase of services. The property or services must have been intended for personal, family, or household use. The priority is capped at $2,225 per individual claimant.[279] The suggestion that payment in full is not a "deposit"[280] and thus does not fit within the plain meaning of the statutory language, has been repeatedly rejected by nearly every court that has considered the issue.[281]

[8]   Tax Claims[282]

The eighth and most complex of the priority provisions deals with various taxes, customs duties, and penalties.[283] Instead of dollar limits, most tax priorities have various time limits. Claims for past-due income or gross receipts taxes are priority claims if they are for a tax "for a taxable year ending on or before the date of the filing of the petition for which a return, if required, is last due, including extensions, after three years before the date of the filing of the petition."[284] Thus, roughly speaking, unpaid income taxes for the debtor's previous three tax years enjoy

---

[277] Bankruptcy Code § 507(a)(6). As with other dollar figures in the Bankruptcy Code, this amount is adjusted every three years, in accordance with increases in the Consumer Price Index. It was last adjusted on April 1, 2010. The next adjustments are scheduled for 2013 and 2016. *See* Bankruptcy Code § 104.

[278] *See* Bankruptcy Code § 557(a)(1) (defining grain for this purpose as "wheat, corn, flaxseed, grain sorghum, barley, oats, rye, soybeans, other dry edible beans, or ride"). Thus, sunflower seed farmers and hops farmers do not qualify either.

[279] Bankruptcy Code § 507(a)(7). As with other dollar figures in the Bankruptcy Code, this amount is set to be adjusted every three years, in accordance with increases in the Consumer Price Index. It was last adjusted in 2010. The next adjustments are scheduled for April 1, 2013, and 2016. *See* Bankruptcy Code § 104.

[280] Bonner v. Allman (In re Heritage Village Church & Missionary Fellowship, Inc.), 137 B.R. 888 (Bankr. D.S.C. 1991).

[281] *See* Salazar v. McDonald (In re Salazar), 430 F.3d 992 (9th Cir. 2005).

[282] Patrick M. Castleberry, *Individual Tax Claims in Chapter 7 and 13 Bankruptcies: Administrative Priorities and Dischargeability*, 47 Consumer Fin. L.Q. Rep. 433 (1993); Barbara K. Morgan, *Should the Sovereign Be Paid First? A Comparative International Analysis of the Priority for Tax Claims in Bankruptcy*, 74 Am. Bankr. L.J. 461 (2000).

[283] Bankruptcy Code § 507(a)(8).

[284] Bankruptcy Code § 507(a)(8)(A)(i).

priority treatment.[285] By contrast, the property tax priority includes one year's worth of back taxes.[286] Priorities are available for three years of income taxes, one year of property taxes, all withholding taxes, three years of employment taxes, three years of excise taxes, and one year of custom's duties.[287]

Many tax claims are secured. An allowed secured claim arising from a valid tax lien has the same status as any other secured claim and has priority over all unsecured claims. Real estate property tax claims in particular are ordinarily secured by the debtor's interest in real estate subject to the tax. Federal tax claims may be secured as a result of the imposition and perfection of a federal tax lien under the Tax Lien Act.[288] If they are secured, tax claims are already senior to other claims. Consequently, § 507(a)(8) deals only with unsecured tax claims.

Claims for any tax penalties on a priority tax claim are also entitled to priority treatment, but only if the penalty is imposed as compensation for "actual pecuniary loss."[289] If other non-compensatory tax penalties were entitled to priority treatment, creditors with lower priority or general unsecured claims would be bearing the financial burden of the taxpayer's transgressions. If the purpose of the penalty is to compensate the taxing authority, the penalty is entitled to priority treatment; if its purpose is to punish the debtor, no priority is awarded.[290]

The priority includes income or gross receipts taxes "assessed within 240 days before the date of filing the petition," with the 240-day period expressly excluding "any time" that an offer in compromise with respect to the tax claim was pending.[291] This and other similar language effectively prevents taxpayers from using extended settlement negotiations with the IRS to demote the claim from priority to non-priority status.[292]

Another principal significance of the priority status of tax claims is that priority tax claims are non-dischargeable.[293] Thus, the debtor remains liable for any tax claim that is entitled to priority under § 507(a)(8) but remains unpaid due to the inadequacy of the estate. This makes § 507(a)(8) particularly important in many consumer bankruptcy cases involving unpaid and unsecured individual income taxes.

---

[285] The precise operation of this language is explained in connection with the non-dischargeability of income tax debts in Chapter 13. *See infra* § 13.03[B][1] Tax Debts.

[286] Bankruptcy Code § 507(a)(8)(B).

[287] Bankruptcy Code § 507(a)(8).

[288] I.R.C. §§ 6321-6323.

[289] Bankruptcy Code § 507(a)(8)(G).

[290] *See generally* United States v. Reorganized CF & I Fabricators of Utah, Inc., 518 U.S. 213 (1996) (distinguishing between a tax and a penalty).

[291] Bankruptcy Code § 507(a)(8)(A)(ii)(I).

[292] *See* Young v. United States, 535 U.S. 43 (2002).

[293] Bankruptcy Code § 523(a)(1). *See infra* § 13.03[B][1][a] Priority Taxes.

[9] Claims of Insured Depositary Institutions

The ninth priority, for claims of federally insured depositary institutions, had its genesis in the troubled financial world of the 1980s, when many federally insured financial institutions failed. It creates a priority claim for unkept commitments of the debtor to maintain the capital of an insured depository institution. This priority is uncapped.[294]

[10] Civil Liability for Driving While Intoxicated

In 2005, Congress added a tenth priority for claims "for death or personal injury resulting from the operation of a motor vehicle or vessel if such operation was unlawful because the debtor was intoxicated from using alcohol, a drug, or another substance."[295] This new priority is practically meaningless in most consumer liquidation cases, which are usually designated as "no asset" cases, with no property to distribute to unsecured creditors, with priority claims or otherwise.[296] Creditors in these cases will have to pursue the debtor after the bankruptcy case is closed, on this non-dischargeable debt.[297] On the other hand, it will have a significant effect in Chapter 13 cases, where debtors may find it difficult to propose a plan calling for full payment of these claims as required by § 1322(a)(2).[298]

[B] Super-Priority Claims

Other provisions grant several other types of claims "super-priority" status of one type or another. These are complex provisions that have their greatest impact in cases where most of the debtor's value is almost consumed by secured creditors' claims. Using this limited remaining value to pay claims entitled to super-priority might easily deprive other priority creditors of any distribution.

[1] Claims for Inadequate "Adequate Protection"[299]

Just ahead of other § 503(b) administrative priority claims are claims held by secured creditors who were granted "adequate protection" that turned out to be inadequate. Secured creditors are sometimes provided with "adequate protection" for their claims pursuant to §§ 362, 363, and 364 to protect them from the harm that they otherwise would suffer due to the automatic stay or some other potential impairment of their rights in the debtor's property. This protection is sometimes in the form of a lien on additional or substitute collateral. If the additional collateral

---

[294] Bankruptcy Code § 507(a)(9).

[295] Bankruptcy Code § 507(a)(10).

[296] *But see* In re Loader, 406 B.R. 72 (Bankr. D. Idaho 2009).

[297] Liability for these debts is non-dischargeable. Bankruptcy Code § 523(a)(9). In 2005, the non-dischargeability provision in § 523 was amended to make it apply to liability for death or personal injury while operating either a "vessel" or an "aircraft," but only the reference to operation of a "vessel" made it into the priority provision of new § 507(a)(10).

[298] *See* Bankruptcy Code § 1322(b)(2); *infra* § 18.06[B] Full Payment of Priority Claims.

[299] Julia A. Goatley, Note, *Adequate Protection and Administrative Expense: Toward a Uniform System for Awarding Superpriorities*, 88 Mich. L. Rev. 2168 (1990).

turns out not to compensate them as anticipated, the secured creditor is entitled to super-priority status above all other § 507 priority claims.[300]

Assume, for example, that a creditor with a security interest in the debtor's equipment demands and receives adequate protection against the continued depreciation of its collateral in the form of a security interest in the debtor's accounts. If the equipment depreciates and the accounts turn out to have no value, the "protection" provided by the accounts was inadequate and the creditor will be compensated with a priority claim under § 507(b) for the loss caused by the depreciation of the equipment. This is consistent with the property rights and senior status of secured creditors, who are senior to all priority claims.

However, a secured creditor is not entitled to a super-priority claim under § 507(b) simply because the court denies relief from the stay because of its belief that the creditor is already adequately protected by a sufficient equity cushion.[301] Thus, super-priority is awarded only if the trustee or debtor-in-possession has provided some sort of adequate protection in response to the creditor's insistence on it, to avoid a lack of adequate protection. Creditors are not entitled to a § 507(b) super-priority when they consent to the extent of protection provided by the debtor, such as when an inventory and accounts receivable lender consents to a cash collateral order it has negotiated with the debtor.[302]

[2] Post-Petition Credit Claims

In addition, § 364(c)(1) permits the court to grant an even more senior super-priority administrative expense claim to a creditor who is willing to provide the estate with unsecured credit while the case is pending. This assures such post-petition creditors that their claims will be paid ahead of other post-petition claims and thus provides them with an added inducement to extend credit to a debtor that is reorganizing or that needs financing in order to accomplish an orderly liquidation. Thus, if an unsecured creditor were granted this priority for post-petition credit it extended to the debtor, its administrative expense claim for the amount of the loan would be paid ahead of all other § 507 priority claims and ahead of the super-priority claim of the secured creditor whose adequate protection turned out to be inadequate.

[3] Post-Conversion Liquidation Expenses

There is one final super-priority claim that is even more senior to the two super-priority claims already described, but it applies only in liquidation cases that have been converted from a case under Chapter 11, 12 or 13. Section 727(b) provides for payment of any § 503(b) administrative expenses incurred in the liquidation of the debtor after the case was converted ahead of all other the administrative claims, including those permitted by §§ 507(b) and 364(c)(1).[303] This priority is necessary to

---

[300] Bankruptcy Code § 507(b).

[301] *See* LNC Investments, Inc. v. First Fidelity Bank, 247 B.R. 38 (S.D.N.Y. 2000).

[302] *E.g.*, In re Cheatham, 91 B.R. 382 (E.D.N.C. 1988).

[303] Bankruptcy Code § 726(b).

ensure the willingness of someone to wind up and liquidate the affairs of a debtor after its efforts to reorganize have failed.

[C] General Unsecured Claims

General unsecured claims are those in the great residual pot into which claims not otherwise classified fall. In consumer cases, these tend to consist of debts to retailers, health care providers, and credit card issuers.[304] In business cases, many general unsecured creditors are "trade creditors" who have delivered goods or services to the debtor in the ordinary course of their business, usually expecting payment in a month or two. In addition, it is not unusual for business debtors to owe unsecured debts to banks and other financial institutions. There may also be unsecured debt that is represented by investment securities. Long-term debt of this sort is generally represented by a bond; short-term debt is more often represented by commercial paper. Some or all of this type of unsecured debt may be publicly traded in the securities markets. Note, however, that bonds and commercial paper might be fully or partially secured.

Tort claimants, other than those secured by a non-avoidable judgment lien or an execution lien, are also nearly always general unsecured claims. Unlike those whose claims are based in contract, tort claimants have little or no opportunity to evaluate or to take precautions against the risk involved in dealing with the debtor.

In liquidation bankruptcy, general unsecured claims are likely to be paid little if anything.[305] By contrast, successful reorganizations may provide for substantial payment to claims of unsecured creditors. In rare cases, these claims might even be paid in full.

In liquidation, all general unsecured claims are treated equally; whatever assets remain after secured and priority claims are paid in full are divided among unsecured creditors pro rata. In reorganization, especially in Chapter 11 cases, general unsecured claims may be further subdivided by the plan into separate classes.[306] As long as the classifications are justified and the plan provides for payment of the liquidation value of each claim in each class, the plan may treat some classes more favorably than others.[307]

§ 10.05 SUBORDINATED CLAIMS

Claims are sometimes demoted in priority. This occurs as a result of a subordination agreement among creditors, due to equitable subordination or as the result of a specific statutory subordination rule. When a creditor's claim is subordinated, it falls further behind in the line for a right to receive a distribution

---

[304] *See* Teresa A. Sullivan, Elizabeth Warren & Jay Lawrence Westbrook, As We Forgive Our Debtors 275-76 (1989).

[305] *See* Dominic E. Pacitti & Michael J. Herbert, *Down and Out in Richmond, Virginia: The Distribution of Assets in Chapter 7 Bankruptcy Proceedings Closed During 1984-87*, 22 U. Rich. L. Rev. 303 (1988).

[306] *See infra* § 19.08[D] Classification of Claims.

[307] Bankruptcy Code § 1122. *See* § 19.08[D] Classification of Claims.

from the debtor's estate and thus runs the risk of receiving nothing, as if the claim had simply been disallowed.

Assume, for example, that Titanic Industries owes two trade creditors, DeckCo owes Titanic $100,000, but agrees to subordinate its claim to Atlantic Finance Co. in exchange for Atlantic making a $100,000 loan to Titanic. Later, FuelCo. delivers $100,000 of fuel to Titanic, for which it has not been paid. Later, when Titanic is insolvent, and only has $150,000 to distribute to its unsecured creditors, the subordination agreement will have a significant effect on how DeckCo.'s claim is treated.

But, because FuelCo. was not a party to the subordination agreement, it will have no affect on FuelCo.'s treatment. Without subordination, each of these three creditors would have received a pro-rata share of the $150,000 Titanic has left to pay its creditors, or $50,000 (1/3) each. However, by agreeing to subordinate its claim to Atlantic Finance Co., DeckCo. has agreed not to receive any payment until Atlantic is paid in full. Thus, Atlantic Finance Co. will receive payment in full, $100,000, and DeckCo. will receive nothing. FuelCo., is not affected by the subordination agreement, and will be paid exactly what it would have received if the subordination agreement had not been made, $50,000. FuelCo. is not adversely affected by the agreement, and will be indifferent to Atlantic Finance Co.'s preferred treatment. This is exactly the same as what happens at Thanksgiving dinner, when Uncle Dan agrees to give his piece of pie to Aunt Tina. Aunt Tina gets two pieces of pie; Cousin Fred should not care, because his slice of the pie is the same size that it would have been if Uncle Dan hadn't given his slice to Tina.

Section 510 partially codifies the rules regarding contractual and equitable subordination, but does not mention the concept of "recharacterization." Recharacterization or "reclassifications" of claims, is similar to equitable subordination, but is predicated on different facts and operates in a different way.

[A] Contractual Subordination[308]

Sometimes creditors agree to subordinate their claims to the claims of other creditors. A creditor may be willing to subordinate its claim if it is willing to accept additional risk for the opportunity for an additional reward, or in some cases, because the creditor wishes to make a quasi-equity investment. For example, the president of a closely held corporation may agree to subordinate any claim she has as a creditor of the corporation to another creditor as part of an effort to persuade the other creditor to loan money to her business. In addition, there is even a good deal of publicly traded subordinated debt, often referred to as debentures, which predictably offers a higher rate of interest than ordinary bonds to offset the higher risk of non-payment.[309]

---

[308] David Gray Carlson, *A Theory of Contractual Debt Subordination and Lien Priority*, 38 Vand. L. Rev. 975 (1985); Kevin C. Dooley & Thomas G. Rock, *Subordination Agreements: Suggested Approaches to Key Issues*, 113 Banking L.J. 708 (1996).

[309] *See* Taylor v. Standard Gas & Elec. Co., 306 U.S. 307 (1938); Pepper v. Litton, 308 U.S. 295 (1939).

Section 510(a) provides that "[a] subordination agreement is enforceable in a case under this title to the same extent that such agreement is enforceable under applicable nonbankruptcy law."[310] Thus, subordination agreements made between creditors are generally enforced in bankruptcy.[311]

The fact that post-petition interest is not allowable in bankruptcy might create difficulties in connection with the treatment of subordinated debt. The difficulty arises, for example, if there is a senior unsecured claim of $100 million, with $10 million of accumulated post-petition interest, and a subordinated junior claim of $15 million, but only $112 million of assets to distribute to these creditors. The $100 million senior claim will be paid first. Normally, the remaining $12 million in assets would be distributed to the holder of the junior $15 million claim. But, its contractual subordination to the holder of the $100 million claim arguably requires that the remaining $12 million in assets be paid first to satisfy the $10 million of post-petition interest on the senior claim, leaving only $2 million for the subordinated creditor.

Prior to adoption of the current Bankruptcy Code, courts applied the "Explicitness Rule," which permitted subordination of the junior debt to the senior creditor's post-petition interest only if the subordination agreement contained unequivocal language that "the general rule that interest stops on the date of the filing of the petition is to be suspended."[312] However, cases decided under § 510(a) have concluded that the Explicitness Rule was not carried forward into the Bankruptcy Code.[313] Of course, if the Explicitness Rule is part of the state law that generally governs the subordination agreement, the rule will still apply.

[B] Equitable Subordination[314] and Recharacterization

[1] Equitable Subordination and Recharacterization Compared

Courts sometimes forcibly subordinate a creditor's claim due to the creditor's bad behavior. This type of subordination originated as an equitable doctrine, imposed as part of the bankruptcy court's inherent equitable powers.[315] Although

---

[310] Bankruptcy Code § 510(a). *See* In re Sepco, 750 F.2d 51 (8th Cir. 1984). *But see* Bank of New England Corp. v. Branch (In re Bank of New England Corp.), 364 F.3d 355 (1st Cir. 2004).

[311] *E.g.*, In re Cliff's Ridge Skiing Corp., 123 B.R. 753 (Bankr. W.D. Mich. 1991).

[312] *See* In re Time Sales Fin. Corp., 841, 844 (3d Cir. 1974).

[313] In re Bank of New England Corp., 364 F.3d 355 (1st Cir. 2004). *See* Patrick Darby, *Southeast and New England Mean New York: The Rule of Explicitness and Post-Bankruptcy Interest on Senior Unsecured Debt*, 38 Cumb. L. Rev. 467 (2008).

[314] David Gray Carlson, *The Logical Structure of Fraudulent Transfers and Equitable Subordination*, 45 Wm. & Mary L. Rev. 157 (2003); Andrew DeNatale & Prudence B. Abram, *The Doctrine of Equitable Subordination as Applied to Nonmanagement Creditors*, 40 Bus. Law. 417 (1985); John J. Dvorske, Annotation, *Bankruptcy: Equitable Subordination, Under 11 U.S.C.A. § 510(c), of Insider Claims*, 2 A.L.R. Fed. 2d 119 (2005); Steven A. Karg, *A Bankruptcy Trap for the Unwary Creditor: Equitable Subordination Resulting from Excess Creditor Control*, 15 Seton Hall Legis. J. 434 (1991).

[315] *See* Taylor v. Std. Gas & Elec. Co., 306 U.S. 307 (1938); Pepper v. Litton, 308 U.S. 295 (1939).

now codified in § 510, it is still known as "equitable subordination."[316] When it applies, equitable subordination demotes the priority of a claim to the claims of those who were harmed by the subordinated creditor's misconduct.[317] Unless the debtor is solvent, this ordinarily results in the subordinated creditor receiving little or nothing. Accordingly, the possibility that a claim might be subordinated is a powerful tool in negotiations over the terms of a plan.

Recharacterization of a creditor's claim is similar to equitable subordination, except that it results in treating the creditor's claim as if it were not a claim at all, but as a contribution of equity. Thus, the claim does not share a distribution with creditors at all, but is treated as if it were an equity interest in the debtor. While subordination might only lower the priority of a claim with respect to the claims of other specific creditors who were harmed by the creditor's inequitable behavior, recharacterization subordinates the creditor's claim to the claims of all creditors and treats it on a par with the interests of shareholders.

The difference is illustrated by a simple example. Assume that Titanic Industries is worth $50 million and has secured claims of $35 million and unsecured claims of $17 million. Included in the $17 million of unsecured claims is a $5 million claim of an insider whose misconduct in connection with creation of the claim justifies its equitable subordination or recharacterization. Without subordination or recharacterization, the insider's claim will be entitled to 5/17th of the $15 million available for distribution to unsecured creditors, or approximately $4.4 million of the value of the reorganized company. If the $5 million claim is subordinated to the claims of other unsecured creditors, the plan will have to provide for full payment of the other $12 million in unsecured claims before the insider may receive anything. The other creditors will receive $12 million, the subordinated insider will receive only the remaining $3 million in value, and shareholders will receive nothing. If the creditor's claim is recharacterized as an equity interest, the remaining $3 million in value will be shared with other shareholders. Of course, in many cases, there will be insufficient assets to distribute anything to subordinated creditors or shareholders, and the consequences of subordination or recharacterization may be the same.[318]

[2] Equitable Subordination

Although it began as judicially created doctrine,[319] equitable subordination is now expressly authorized by the Bankruptcy Code. Section 510(c) provides: "[A]fter notice and a hearing, the court may (1) under principles of equitable subordination, subordinate for purposes of distribution all or part of an allowed claim to all or part

---

[316] Bankruptcy Code § 510(c). *See* Taylor v. Standard Gas & Elec. Co., 306 U.S. 307 (1939) ("Deep Rock doctrine" permitting subordination of debt below preferred stockholders interests).

[317] In re Winstar Commc'ns, Inc., 554 F.3d 382, 414 (3d Cir. 2009).

[318] This example does not explain the consequences of subordination of the insider's claim to the claims of only some creditors. This could occur if the insider's misconduct was harmful to some, but not all creditors.

[319] Taylor v. Standard Gas & Elec. Co., 306 U.S. 307 (1938); Pepper v. Litton, 308 U.S. 295 (1939); Sampsell v. Imperial Paper & Color Corp., 313 U.S. 215 (1941); Heiser v. Woodruff, 327 U.S. 726 (1946); Comstock v. Group of Institutional Investors, 335 U.S. 211 (1948).

of another allowed claim."[320]

As one might expect when the word "equitable" appears, there is no rigid test to apply the doctrine. The most widely used formulation from *In re Mobile Steel Co.* sets out a three-part test:

- the claimant must have engaged in some type of inequitable conduct;

- the misconduct must have resulted in injury to the creditors of the bankruptcy or conferred an unfair advantage on the claimant; and

- subordination must not be inconsistent with the provisions of the Bankruptcy Code.[321]

Although it is nearly impossible to catalog all of the actions that might be characterized as "inequitable conduct," the term unquestionably includes "(1) fraud, illegality, or breach of fiduciary duties; (2) undercapitalization;[322] and (3) the claimant's use of the debtor corporation as a mere instrumentality or alter ego."[323] *Pepper v. Litton*,[324] decided before equitable subordination was codified, provides a good example of subordination of a claim due to an insider creditor's fraudulent behavior. In *Pepper*, a controlling shareholder permitted the corporation to confess a judgment against itself on an old unpaid wage claim that was held by the shareholder in such a way that, if permitted to stand, would have resulted in other unsecured creditors receiving nothing.

Equitable subordination most commonly involves the misconduct of an insider, who owes a fiduciary duty to the debtor involved. However, the creditor's status as an insider is not enough — not nearly enough — to by itself warrant subordination of the insider's claim. Quite to the contrary, as indicated by the *Mobile Steel* test outlined above, the creditor must have engaged in some sort of inequitable conduct that harmed the debtor and its creditors.[325]

"Undercapitalization" is another type of inequitable conduct, that can result in subordination of a creditor's claim. Undercapitalization refers to a situation where the debtor's capital structure is heavily leveraged by debt. Assume, for example, that Close Corp. is a small company with only five shareholders and that is funded with a total of $100,000. On the books of the company, $1,000 of the initial capital is listed as common stock, and the remaining $99,000 is listed as loans made to the corporation by its five shareholders. This is a "highly leveraged" company in which nearly all of its capital comes from loans. It is leveraged at a ratio of 99:1 — that is, 99% debt and only 1% equity. Assume further that under the loan agreement between the company and its shareholders, interest on the loan accrues at an annual

---

[320] Bankruptcy Code § 510(c)(1).

[321] Benjamin v. Diamond (In re Mobile Steel Co.), 563 F.2d 692 (5th Cir. 1977).

[322] Jonathan A. Carson, *Pre-Petition Capital Contributions: The Road to Equitable Treatment in Bankruptcy*, 1999 Colum. Bus. L. Rev. 403 (1999).

[323] Matter of Herby's Foods, Inc., 2 F.3d 128, 131 (5th Cir. 1993); Fabricators, Inc. v. Technical Fabricators, Inc. (In re Fabricators, Inc.), 926 F.2d 1458, 1467 (5th Cir.1991); Wilson v. Huffman (In re Missionary Baptist Found. of Am., Inc.), 712 F.2d 206, 209, 212 (5th Cir. 1983).

[324] 308 U.S. 295 (1939).

[325] *See* In re Mobile Steel, 563 F.2d 692 (5th Cir. 1977).

"minimum" rate of 10%, but neither interest nor principal must be paid unless the company makes at least $20,000 in profits during a fiscal year. These terms make the loan seem as if it should be treated as a contribution of capital rather than as a loan. In other words, it represents an interest rather than a claim. If the company's liability to pay interest is forgiven in the event that the company earns less than $20,000 a year, this appearance is even more pronounced. And, if the "creditors" are entitled to a higher rate of "bonus" interest if the company turns a higher profit, the conclusion that this claim is really an ownership interest is hard to avoid. Such a loan, particularly when made by an insider, is highly vulnerable to being recast as equity and subordinated to the claims of outside creditors.[326]

Of greatest importance in this example is that the legal attributes of these types of debt are similar to those normally associated with stock. If the company does poorly, the investors recover little or nothing on their investment. If the company does extraordinarily well, the "lenders" receive a larger return. The usual mark of debt is that the debtor is obligated to pay regardless of financial condition, and conversely, that if the debtor earns more than expected, it need only pay a fixed amount of interest or interest at a rate pegged to an unmanipulable external standard, such as a prime interest rate. Equity, on the other hand, rises or falls with the success of the enterprise.[327]

Despite the frequent articulation of the statement that "undercapitalization" constitutes the type of inequitable conduct that justifies equitable subordination,[328] undercapitalization all by itself may not be enough.[329] However, subordination is usually sought with respect to an insider's claim for repayment of a loan made to the thinly capitalized business. It is the combination of the undercapitalization with the insider's loan that justifies subordination.[330] The fact that insiders have used their dominant power over the debtor to improve their position at the expense of outside creditors, such as by raising their own salaries while not paying creditors, can also be sufficient.[331] Creditors who are not insiders are even less frequently vulnerable to subordination.

Insiders might also be vulnerable to subordination of their claims when they have used their insider status to control the debtor as a "mere instrumentality" or as their "alter ego."

---

[326] *See* Fabricators, Inc. v. Technical Fabricators, Inc. (In re Fabricators, Inc.), 926 F.2d 1458, 1464 (5th Cir. 1991).

[327] *E.g.*, In re Carolee's Combine, Inc., 3 B.R. 324 (N.D. Ga. 1980).

[328] *E.g.*, Benjamin v. Diamond (In re Mobile Steel Corp.), 563 F.2d 692 (5th Cir. 1977). *See* Jonathan A. Carson, *Pre-Petition Capital Contributions: The Road to Equitable Treatment in Bankruptcy*, 1999 Colum. Bus. L. Rev. 403 (1999); Markus C. Stadler, *Treatment of Shareholder Loans to Undercapitalized Corporations in Bankruptcy Proceedings*, 17 J.L. & Com. 1 (1997).

[329] *See* In re Lifschultz Fast Freight, 132 F.3d 339 (7th Cir. 1997); Matter of Herby's Foods, Inc., 2 F.3d 128 (5th Cir. 1993); In re Fabricators, Inc., 926 F.2d 1458, 1469 (5th Cir. 1991); In re Phase I Molecular Toxicology, Inc., 287 B.R. 571 (Bankr. D.N.M. 2002).

[330] Matter of Herby's Foods, Inc., 2 F.3d 128, 132 (5th Cir. 1993).

[331] *See* In re Lemco Gypsum, Inc., 911 F.2d 1553 (11th Cir. 1990), *reh'g denied*, 930 F.2d 925 (11th Cir. 1991).

At one point it seemed as if creditors' claims might be vulnerable to subordination despite the absence of inequitable conduct by the creditor involved. However, in 1996, the Supreme Court unequivocally rejected subordination, based simply on the nature of the creditor's claim, where the creditor had engaged in no wrongdoing. In *United States v. Noland*,[332] the Court prohibited the subordination of a federal tax penalty, which was entitled to an administrative expense priority, as part of the bankruptcy court's effort to more "equitably" distribute the debtor's estate. The Supreme Court held that absent inequitable conduct on the creditor's behalf, subordination amounts to little more than a judicial realignment of the priority scheme established by Congress. Later the same year, the Court reinforced its holding in *Noland* by reversing a bankruptcy court's order that subordinated a similar tax penalty, despite the absence of any misconduct on the part of the government. The Court indicated that subordination based on nothing more than the nature of the creditor's claim was similarly "outside the scope of any leeway under § 510(c) for judicial development of the equitable subordination doctrine." As the Court held in *Noland*, bankruptcy courts are not permitted to engage in the type of "categorical reordering of priorities that takes place at the legislative level." To permit this type of subordination, the Court said, would be "beyond the scope of judicial authority."[333]

In re Windstar Communications, Inc. supplies a good example of the type of inequitable conduct that might result in a creditor's claim being equitably subordinated.[334] The creditor, Lucent Tecnhologies, Inc., combined its use of improper threats to induce the debtor to purchase unneeded equipment and delays in issuing a "refinancing notice" until after others disbursed funds to the debtor, to gain advantages over both the debtor and other creditors. Because the creditor's conduct caused other creditors to materially change their positions, with resulting harm to both the debtor and these third parties, the offending creditor's claim was subordinated to the claims of those creditors who had been harmed.

A creditor's claim should be subordinated only if the creditor's bad conduct caused some harm to other creditors.

[3] Recharacterization[335]

As explained above, recharacterization or "reclassification" of a creditor's claim as a contribution of equity, is somewhat different from equitable subordination, though, depending on the circumstances, it can have much the same effect.

---

[332] 517 U.S. 535 (1996).

[333] United States v. Reorganized CF & I Fabricators of Utah, Inc., 518 U.S. 213, 229 (1996).

[334] In re Winstar Commc'ns, Inc., 554 F.3d 382 (3d Cir. 2009).

[335] My Chi To & Matthew D. Siegel, *Debt Recharacterization Looks Back on a Good Year*, 26 Am. Bankr. Inst. J. 1, 58 (2007); Neil M. Peretz, *Recharacterization in the Ninth Circuit: Has the Supreme Court Finally Derailed the Pacific Express?*, 17 J. Bankr. L. & Prac. 297, 297-98 (2008); James M. Wilton & Stephen Moeller-Sally, *Debt Recharacterization Under State Law*, 62 Bus. Law. 1257 (2007); Michael R. Tucker, Note, *Debt Recharacterization During an Economic Trough: Trashing Historical Tests to Avoid Discouraging Insider Lending*, 71 Ohio St. L.J. 187 (2010).

The principle difference between the two doctrines is that a claim can be recharacterized, though not subordinated, in the absence of any inequitable conduct.[336] Recharacterization occurs when the court determines that, despite the initial characterization of the investment as a loan, the attributes of the transaction reveal that, in reality, it is more like a capital contribution of the type made by a shareholder.

In determining whether what might appear to be a loan should be recharacterized as a contribution of equity, courts consider a variety of factors, including:

> (1) the names given to the instruments, if any, evidencing the indebtedness; (2) the presence or absence of a fixed maturity date and schedule of payments; (3) the presence or absence of a fixed rate of interest and interest payments; (4) the source of repayments; (5) the adequacy or inadequacy of capitalization; (6) the identity of interest between the creditor and the stockholder; (7) the security, if any, for the advances; (8) the corporation's ability to obtain financing from outside lending institutions; (9) the extent to which the advances were subordinated to the claims of outside creditors; (10) the extent to which the advances were used to acquire capital assets; and (11) the presence or absence of a sinking fund to provide repayments.[337]

When these factors, taken together, demonstrate that the funds supplied were more in the nature of a contribution to the debtor's capital equity structure, the creditor's claim will be disallowed and recharacterized as an interest. The creditor will have a right to participate in the reorganization as if it were a shareholder, but will be on the losing end of the absolute priority rule of § 1129(b).

[C]   Statutory Subordination[338]

Subordination is also specifically required in several discreet situations. Section 510(b) requires subordination of claims "arising from rescission of a purchase or sale of a security of the debtor . . . or for reimbursement or contribution allowed . . . on account of such a claim."[339] This provision simply recognizes that the creditor's claim is based on an equitable ownership interest the creditor would have held, if not for the right to rescission, reimbursement, or contribution from the estate.

There are three other subordination provisions that apply only in liquidation cases. Section 724(b) provides for the subordination of certain tax liens. Section 726(a) subordinates claims that are filed late,[340] unless the delay occured through

---

[336] *E.g.,* Bayer Corp. v. MascoTech, Inc. (In re Autostyle Plastics, Inc.), 269 F.3d 726, 748 (6th Cir. 2001).

[337] Roth Steel Tube Co. v. Comm'r, 800 F.2d 625, 630 (6th Cir. 1986).

[338] Zach Christensen, Note, *The Fair Funds for Investors Provision of Sarbanes-Oxley: Is it Unfair to the Creditors of a Bankrupt Debtor?*, 2005 U. Ill. L. Rev. 339 (regarding potential conflict between Sarbanes-Oxley and Bankruptcy Code § 510(b)).

[339] Bankruptcy Code § 510(b).

[340] Bankruptcy Code § 726(a)(3).

no fault of the creditor.[341] Finally, claims for noncompensatory fines, penalties, and punitive damages are subordinated below both secured and general unsecured claims.[342] Creditors should not bear the burden of penalties that were designed to be imposed on the debtor.

§ 10.06 INTERESTS

[A] Meaning of Interests

The term "interest" has two primary meanings in the Code. When referring to specific property, the word refers to some form of co-ownership or lien. Thus, a secured creditor has an interest in property of the debtor or property of the estate. This type of interest is discussed throughout this book in the context of the treatment of liens and other divided property interests.

The other meaning refers to ownership interests in the debtor itself and thus obviously has meaning only if the debtor is a corporation, partnership, or entity other than an "individual." Interests of this type represent ownership not of particular property, but of the value of the entity above the amount of creditors' claims. This is the residual interest after all debt is paid. If the debtor is insolvent, there is no equity. The remainder of this section deals with this latter meaning of the term.

In liquidation proceedings, interests are nearly always ignored because there is hardly ever any residual value available to distribute to shareholders. Even in reorganization, interests in the debtor may be insignificant, because the debtor is still likely to be insolvent. However, in Chapter 11, it is possible for those who own interests to participate in the distribution under the plan, even if claims are not paid in full — so long as the claimants agree to this. Moreover, Chapter 11 proceedings are more likely to involve a debtor whose going concern value exceeds its liquidation value or who is in bankruptcy not because of an excess of debts over equity, but as a result of inadequate cash flow. In addition, to the extent shareholders' active involvement in the debtor's business contributes to its financial success, creditors may be anxious to ensure that these interest holders have a stake in the future profitability of the firm and thus may be willing to agree to yield some amount to which they otherwise might be entitled to facilitate implementation of the debtor's plan.

[B] Allowance of Owners' Interests

The procedure for allowing an interest is virtually identical to the procedure for allowing a claim. Ordinarily, a proof of interest must be filed. If no objection is made, the interest is allowed. Any party in interest may object, including a creditor of a general partner in a partnership that is a debtor. As is true with claims, however, a claim of interest need not be filed in Chapter 11 proceedings, so long as

---

[341] Bankruptcy Code § 726(a)(2)(C).

[342] Bankruptcy Code § 726(a)(4).

the interest is scheduled by the debtor.[343] Neither the Code nor the Bankruptcy Rules contain any detail concerning the adjudication of a contested interest. This is in contrast to the adjudication of contested claims. The reason for this lack of detail is undoubtedly that interests, which are almost always worthless, are rarely contested.

[C] Priority of Interests

Interests, like claims, might be entitled to different priority. These priorities, however, are not created by the Bankruptcy Code; rather, they are the result of the contract that created the interest. The most familiar example of a priority interest is stock with a liquidation preference. For example, assume Titanic Industries, Inc. issued a class of stock, Preferred Stock A, with $100 liquidation preference. This means that, upon liquidation of the company, whether in bankruptcy or out, a payment of up to $100 per share is paid to the holders of this stock before anything is paid on common stock. Thus, once all debt of every kind is paid, whatever is left is first applied to this liquidation preference. If there is not enough to pay the full $100 for each share, whatever remains is distributed pro rata among the outstanding preferred shares. Of course, as a practical matter it is highly unlikely that liquidation will produce anything for preferred stock. But, if the $100 liquidation preference is fully paid, holders of common stock will receive something for their junior interests.

[D] Subordinated Interests

At the very, very bottom of the Bankruptcy Code's priority pyramid are subordinated interests — interests that are even lower than typical common stock in a corporation. An interest may be subordinated in either of two ways. First, it may be subordinated by agreement. An agreement may have been entered into when the legal entity was created; it is certainly lawful to create a class of stock that is subordinated to common stock. A subordination agreement may also have been entered into after the stock was initially issued. The Bankruptcy Code makes subordination agreements enforceable to the extent they are enforceable under applicable non-bankruptcy law.[344]

Second, an interest may be equitably subordinated by the court. Although equitable subordination is usually thought of in the context of claims of creditors, the statutory provision that recognize equitable subordination applies to interests as well. Section 510(c) states, in part, "after notice and [an opportunity for] a hearing, the court may under principles of equitable subordination, subordinate for purposes of distribution . . . all or part of an allowed interest to all or part of another allowed interest."[345] The considerations discussed with equitable subordination of claims also control for equitable subordination of an interest. However, given the fact that virtually all interests are worthless, the chance that

---

[343] Bankruptcy Code § 1111(a); Fed. R. Bankr. P. 3003(b)(1), (c)(2).

[344] Bankruptcy Code § 510(a).

[345] Bankruptcy Code § 510(c)(1).

anyone would bother to seek equitable subordination of an interest is only slightly more than zero.

§ 10.07 CO-OWNERSHIP OF ESTATE PROPERTY

[A] Joint Property

In a number of cases, the property rights of the estate co-exist with the property rights of another. The most obvious example occurs when the debtor is a joint tenant or a tenant in common of real estate.[346] The co-owner in that type of situation has neither a claim against the estate[347] nor an interest in the debtor. Moreover, the co-ownership right is normally not an interest in property of the estate, because, with a limited exception for community property, the co-owner's interest does not become property of the estate.[348]

Ideally, co-owners would be unaffected by the debtor's bankruptcy. However, this is sometimes impossible. On occasion, it is necessary either to partition the property and sell the debtor's portion or to sell the property free and clear of all co-owners' interests.[349] If the latter is done, the co-owner who is not the debtor must be compensated for his interest in the jointly-owned asset.

[B] Leases

Leases, whether of real or personal property, have some of the features of liens. As students of Article 9 of the U.C.C. will recall, some personal property transactions that are called leases have the same economic effect as a credit sale of property subject to a security interest, and for that reason they are regarded as secured sales.[350] A true lease, however, is somewhat different, regardless of whether it is a lease of real or personal property. It is a form of divided ownership, but unlike a lien, the interest of the lessor exists for purposes other than ensuring payment. At the end of the lease, the property is returned to the lessor who, like any owner, may re-lease it, sell it, or use it. The assumption of both parties is that the lessor will get the property back, which is what differentiates it from a credit sale of the property. The lease also differs from other forms of joint ownership, such as joint tenancy, because in a lease, the interest of one of the "owners," the lessee, is limited in time and contingent upon the lessee making rent payments to the owner of the residual interest, the lessor.

---

[346] We do not discuss tenancies by the entirety at this point, because that form of ownership insulates both the rights of the debtor and the debtor's spouse if the debt incurred by the debtor was not a mutual debt.

[347] The term "claim" encompasses a right to payment and a right to an equitable remedy for breach of a duty. Bankruptcy Code § 101(5). *See supra* § 10.01 Meaning of Claims and Interests. In a typical co-ownership case, neither of these exist.

[348] Bankruptcy Code § 541. The limited exception for community property is contained in Bankruptcy Code § 541(a)(2). *See supra* § 7.02[B] Community Property.

[349] Bankruptcy Code § 363(f). *See supra* § 9.03 Use, Sale, or Lease of Estate Property.

[350] *See* U.C.C. § 1-201(37) (2010). *See* William H. Lawrence, William H. Henning & R. Wilson Freyermuth, Understanding Secured Transactions 14 (3d ed. 2004).

Insofar as bankruptcy is concerned, the interest of a lessor of real or personal property leased to the debtor is dealt with in a manner that recognizes its hybrid character. The lessor has a claim for rent. The lessor also has an interest in property of the estate; the debtor's leasehold is property of the estate, and the lessor has certain rights and obligations with regard to its ownership of the property. Finally, the lessor has a residual property interest that is not part of the estate. The lessor's right to possess the property at the end of the lease term is a right that never belonged to the debtor, and thus does not become part of the estate. The complexity of lease rights has generated difficult and complex rules, explained elsewhere.[351]

§ 10.08   ANOMALOUS RIGHTS

On occasion, it is extremely difficult to classify a particular right as a claim or an interest. As the discussion in the previous sections suggest, debt and equity are not two different species. They are simply shorthand ways of defining rights, and they exist on a continuum from the purest type of debt, a precisely defined right not in any way conditioned on the obligor's financial condition, to the purest form of equity, which is a variable right that wholly depends on the obligor's financial circumstances. A right to collect $10,000, whether or not the debtor can afford to pay, is unquestionably a claim. A right to participate in the obligor's profits, whatever they are, is unquestionably an interest. On the other hand, a right to collect $10,000, subject to a one-year postponement of the due date if the debtor is insolvent, a right to collect $10,000 which can at any time be converted into common stock, or common stock that can at any time be converted into debt at the rate of $100 per share tendered, falls somewhere in between these two guideposts.

As a general principle, the classification of anomalous rights is done functionally. If a particular right has the substance of equity, it is treated as equity.[352] However, this is sometimes entangled in the court's analysis of the propriety of the action that created the right. If it appears to the court that a particular right has odd features because it was used to cheat other claimants, the court will likely treat the right as one subordinate to those claimants.

§ 10.09   SETOFF[353]

"Setoff" refers to the right to offset one mutual debt against another.[354] The most obvious example is a bank's right to set off a debt owed to it by one of its customers against funds the customer has on deposit with the bank.[355] Thus, if Franklin

---

[351] *See infra* Chapter 11 Executory Contracts and Unexpired Leases.

[352] *See supra* § 10.05[B][2] Equitable Subordination.

[353] Lawrence Kalcvitch, *Sotoff and Bankruptcy*, 41 Clcv. St. L. Rcv. 599 (1993)

[354] *See supra* § 2.06 Setoff of Mutual Debts; John C. McCoid II, *Setoff: Why Bankruptcy Priority?*, 75 Va. L. Rev. 15 (1989); Michael Tigar, Comment, *Automatic Extinction of Cross Demands: Compensation From Rome to California*, 58 Cal. L. Rev. 224, 226-34 (1965); William H. Loyd, *The Development of Setoff*, 64 U. Pa. L. Rev. 541 (1916).

[355] *See, e.g.,* Citizens Bank of Md. v. Strumpf, 516 U.S. 16 (1995).

Manufacturing owes $50,000 to Peninsula Bank but also has $60,000 in an account at Peninsula Bank, the bank has a right to set off Franklin's $50,000 debt against the bank's obligation (represented by the deposit) to repay $60,000 to Franklin. The basic operation of the right of setoff and limitations on its use are explained in more detail elsewhere.[356]

The Bankruptcy Code treats a creditor's right of setoff as a secured claim. Section 506 provides:

> An allowed claim of a creditor . . . that is subject to setoff under section 553 of this title, is a secured claim . . . to the extent of the amount subject to setoff . . . and is an unsecured claim to the extent that . . . the amount so subject to setoff is less than the amount of such allowed claim.[357]

If Franklin only has $40,000 on deposit with Peninsula Bank, the bank has a secured claim as a result of its right of setoff for $40,000, and an unsecured claim for the $10,000 balance due from Franklin.

[A] Setoff Under Non-Bankruptcy Law

The bankruptcy code does not establish a right of setoff.[358] Whether a right of setoff exists depends entirely on non-bankruptcy law.[359] Where a right of setoff exists, Bankruptcy Code § 553 preserves it, subject to some limitations.[360] Section 553(a) specifies that the Bankruptcy Code "does not affect any right of a creditor to offset a mutual debt . . . that arose before the commencement of the case . . . except as otherwise provided" in §§ 553, 362, and 363.[361]

The most important limitation is one that usually emulates the operation of setoff under state law. Thus, the Bankruptcy Code does not create a right of setoff; it merely recognizes and (to some extent) limits any right of setoff that exists apart from bankruptcy law. As explained elsewhere, non-bankruptcy law usually only permits setoff of debts that are both "mutual" and "matured."[362]

Section 553 emulates the law of setoff in most states by permitting setoff only of "mutual debts."[363] However, if state law were to permit setoff of debts in the absence of mutuality, § 553 would nevertheless require that the debts be mutual, as an independent limitation on the exercise of the right of setoff in bankruptcy. This requirement is explicit in § 553, which only permits setoff by a creditor of "a mutual

---

[356] *See supra* § 2.06 Setoff of Mutual Debts.

[357] Bankruptcy Code § 506(a).

[358] *E.g.*, In re Lehman Bros. Holding, Inc., 433 B.R. 101, 107 (Bankr. S.D.N.Y. 2010).

[359] *See supra* § 2.06 Setoff of Mutual Debts.

[360] Official Comm. of Unsecured Creditors v. Mfrs. & Traders Trust Co. (In re Bennett Funding Group), 146 F.3d 136, 138-39 (2d Cir. 1998).

[361] Bankruptcy Code § 553(a).

[362] *See supra* § 2.06[A] Creditor's Right of Setoff. *E.g.*, In re Patterson, 967 F.2d 505 (11th Cir. 1992) (creditor's claim unmatured at time of debtor's bankruptcy).

[363] *See* In re Lehman Bros. Holdings, Inc., 433 B.R. 101 (Bankr. S.D.N.Y. 2010).

debt owing by such creditor to the debtor."[364]

[B]   Setoff Limited to Pre-Petition Claims

For a creditor to assert a right of setoff for its claim, the debt owed by the creditor to the debtor must be one "that arose before the commencement of the case."[365] Thus, a creditor's post-petition claim may not be set off against a prepetition debt owed by the creditor to the debtor. No provision is made for setoff of post-petition claims.

This limitation may require a determination of when the creditor's claim arose. Various tests have been used, in this and other contexts, to determine when a creditor's claim arose.[366] These include the "accrual" test, which depends on when liability accrued to the creditor under state law;[367] a "conduct" or "transactions" test, which depends on when the conduct that gave rise to the claim occurred;[368] the "relationship test," under which a claim cannot exist unless the parties had some pre-petition relationship that gave rise to the claim;[369] and a "foreseeability test," which depends on whether the debtor's liability arose from prepetition conduct that made the creditor's claim foreseeable or "fairly contemplated" by the parties.

[C]   No Setoff of Disallowed Claims

Not surprisingly, if the creditor's claim is disallowed, it may not provide the basis for a setoff.[370] This prevents a creditor who does not have a claim that is cognizable in bankruptcy from effectively reviving that claim in the form of a right of setoff.

The creation of a right of setoff on the eve of bankruptcy, like the transfer of a security interest or other lien to a creditor just before the debtor files a bankruptcy petition, can result in an inappropriate preference to a creditor at the expense of others. Section 553 imposes three limits on creditors' right of setoff that seek to avoid this result. It restricts a creditor's right of setoff if the right was acquired by the creditor during the last ninety days before bankruptcy and (1) results from transfer of a claim to the creditor, (2) results from a claim created for the purpose

---

[364] Bankruptcy Code § 553(a).

[365] Bankruptcy Code § 553(a).

[366] *See generally* In re Jensen, 127 B.R. 27 (B.A.P. 9th Cir. 1991).

[367] *E.g.*, Cooper-Jarrett, Inc. v. Cent. Transp. Inc., 726 F.2d 93 (3d Cir. 1984). *See also* Matter of M. Frenville Co., Inc., 744 F.2d 332, 337 (3d Cir. 1984), *cert. denied* 469 U.S. 1160 (1985) (overruled in In re Grossman's, Inc., 607 F.3d 114 (3d Cir. 2010)). *See* Lawrence Kalevitch, *Setoff and Bankruptcy*, 41 Clev. St. L. Rev. 599, 658 (1993) (noting criticism of the "accrual" test).

[368] *E.g.*, Braniff Airways, Inc. v. Exxon Co., 814 F.2d 1030 (5th Cir. 1987). *See generally* Grady v. A.H. Robins Co. (In re A.H. Robins Co.), 839 F.2d 198 (4th Cir.), *cert. dismissed sub nom.* Joynes v. A.H. Robins Co., 487 U.S. 1260 (1988).

[369] *E.g.*, In re Pettibone Corp., 90 B.R. 918 (Bankr. N.D. Ill. 1988).

[370] Bankruptcy Code § 553(a)(1). Note that the technical requirement is that the claim not be disallowed, rather than it be allowed. In re Davidovich, 901 F.2d 1533 (10th Cir. 1990).

of obtaining a right of setoff, or (3) improves the financial position of the creditor exercising the right of setoff.[371]

[1] Transfer of Claim

Section 553(a)(2) restricts the setoff of claims that the creditor has acquired through a transfer from another creditor.[372] Setoff is not permitted if the creditor's claim against the debtor was transferred to the creditor, by someone other than debtor, either after the debtor's petition was filed or during the ninety day period immediately before the petition was filed and while the debtor was insolvent.[373]

For example, suppose Franklin Manufacturing had $20,000 on deposit with Peninsula Bank while owing Industrial Supply Co. $15,000. State law would not ordinarily permit setoff in this situation, even if Industrial Supply Co. also owed a debt to the Bank. However, a right of setoff might be created if Industrial Supply were to assign its claim against Franklin to Peninsula Bank. After such an assignment, Peninsula would hold a $15,000 claim against Franklin and would be able to offset its claim against the $20,000 Franklin had on deposit with it. This might be an effective way for the Bank to collect the claim owed to it by Industrial Supply. If Franklin were insolvent at the time the Bank received the assignment that created the right of setoff, it would also effectively boost Industrial Supply's claim to a secured position, ensuring that it would be paid in full.

However, if the transfer of Industrial Supply's claim to Peninsula were within ninety days before Franklin's bankruptcy, and depending on the source of its claim, § 553(a)(2) would probably prevent Peninsula from exercising its right of setoff. Peninsula would still have a claim against Franklin, but could not assert a right of setoff or assert that its claim was secured as a result of its right of setoff.

This restriction discourages trafficking in setoff rights. Whether this trafficking is truly offensive is debatable. It is problematic where a creditor with no setoff rights sells its claim to somebody who owed the debtor money. The claim may be worth almost nothing in the hands of the assigning creditor, but worth 100% in the hands of the creditor with setoff rights. This creates an opportunity for abuse. Imagine that Franklin Bank owes the debtor $100. Imagine further that Sam Supplier is owed $100 by the debtor. Sam may anticipate a distribution of $10 on it's $100 claim from the estate. On the other hand, Franklin Bank might purchase the claim for $50 and then use the acquired setoff rights to settle its $100 obligation to the debtor. In some cases, however, the mere fact that a claim has been transferred from one creditor to another has no real impact on other creditors. Suppose, for example, if, that Industrial Supply had a right of setoff against Franklin Manufac-

---

[371] In 2005, these restrictions were removed with respect to setoff rights arising in a variety of narrow circumstances, most of which arise in connection with certain securities and commodities transactions, repurchase agreements, swap agreements, and master agreements that facilitate the operation of financial markets. Bankruptcy Abuse Prevention and Consumer Protection Act of 2005, Pub. L. No. 109-8, § 907, 119 Stat. 23 (2005).

[372] Bankruptcy Code § 553(a)(2).

[373] Bankruptcy Code § 553(a)(2). Note that for this purpose, the debtor is presumed to have been insolvent during the ninety days prior to bankruptcy. Bankruptcy Code § 553(c). This presumption may be rebutted by the creditor asserting the right of setoff.

turing as a result of other transactions between the parties, but that it transferred the claim for which it might have exercised its right of setoff to Peninsula Bank. Before the assignment to Peninsula, Industrial Supply had a right of setoff against Franklin. After the transfer, Peninsula enjoys the same right of setoff. The effect on other creditors is zero; both before and after the transfer, the offset reduces the assets available to other creditors by exactly the same amount.

[2] Intent to Create a Right of Setoff

Section 553(a)(3) operates similarly to § 553(a)(2), but deals with setoff of claims against debts owed by the debtor that are first created on the eve of the debtor's bankruptcy with the intent to create a right of setoff. The easiest illustration is where a debtor makes a deposit to its bank account, during the last ninety days before bankruptcy as part of an effort to supply the bank in which the deposit is made with collateral, in the form of a right of setoff, for what would otherwise be an unsecured claim against the debtor.

Assume, for example, that on June 1, Duarte owes $20,000 to Commerce Bank. If on July 1 Commerce Bank insists that Duarte makes a $20,000 deposit to his account at the bank and maintain a $20,000 balance in the account as a condition of preserving the status of the loan in good standing, § 553(a)(3) will likely restrict the resulting right of setoff. Otherwise, the effect of the deposit would be to convert the Bank's unsecured $20,000 claim to a secured claim, which would violate the Bankruptcy Code's anti-preference policy. This provision fits squarely into the concerns underlying § 547, regarding avoidable preferences. In these circumstances, the right of setoff created by Duarte's deposit is really no different from the transfer of a security interest in Duarte's property during the last ninety days before his bankruptcy petition. It has the same effect as a security interest in Duarte's $20,000 automobile being transferred to the bank.

[3] Setoff Resulting in Improvement in Position

Section 553(b) permits the court to set aside a setoff that was exercised during the last ninety days before the debtor's bankruptcy petition was filed if the exercise of the right of setoff resulted in an improvement in the creditor's position in a manner similar to an avoidable preference. This provision operates similarly to § 547(c)(5)'s rules regarding the improvements in position that a creditor with a security interest in after-acquired inventory and receivables can obtain, unless avoidance is allowed. Because this deals more with one of the trustee's avoiding powers than with a creditor's claim, and because of its similarity to issues involving preferences created by secured creditors' "floating liens," it is dealt with elswhere with in connection with the trustee's power to avoid preferences under Bankruptcy Code § 547.[374]

---

[374] *See infra* § 15.06 Setoff Preferences.

Chapter 11

EXECUTORY CONTRACTS AND UNEXPIRED LEASES

§ 11.01 RIGHT TO ASSUME OR REJECT; ASSIGNMENT[1]

The Bankruptcy Code respects property rights, but discharges contractual and other liability of the debtor. This raises a fundamental conundrum for the debtor. Most contractual relationships are a two-way street, involving both rights and duties. Parties to a contract act with the expectation that they will both be better off after their respective promises are performed. This is no less true when one of the parties suffers some financial difficulty and files a bankruptcy petition. Completing performance may remain advantageous for both parties.

However, in other situations, performance may be burdensome to the debtor. The contract is a loser, and requiring performance would be a drag on the estate and on the debtor's chances for rehabilitation. Section 365 recognizes this and allows the debtor to make a choice whether to breach or perform its contractual obligations. If the debtor chooses to perform, the contract is binding on the estate, and any breach claim is treated as arising after the petition was filed, and is entitled to adminsitrative expense priority. If the debtor chooses to breach, the breach is treated as having arisen prepetition, and is treated as a general unsecured claim. While this power to perform is quite straightforward, it has been the source of much confusion among judges. As a result, the statute, and the case law surrounding, it have grown increasingly complicated.

Section 365 preserves value for the debtor's estate by giving the debtor (through the trustee or current management acting as debtor-in-possession)[2] several options. A debtor may:

- reject the contract (breach it);

- assume the contract and perform it according to its terms;

- assume the contract and assign it to a third party to perform; or

---

[1] Michael T. Andrew, *Executory Contracts in Bankruptcy: Understanding "Rejection*," 59 U. Colo. L. Rev. 845, 889-94 (1988); Vern Countryman, *Executory Contracts in Bankruptcy*, 57 Minn. L. Rev. 439, 446 (1973) (the classic article); Jesse M. Fried, *Executory Contracts and Performance Decisions*, 46 Duke L.J. 517 (1996); Carl N. Pickerill, *Executory Contracts Re-Revisited*, 83 Am. Bankr. L.J. 63 (2009); Morris G. Shanker, *Bankruptcy Asset Theory and its Application to Executory Contracts*, 1992 Ann. Surv. Bankr. L. 97; Jay L. Westbrook, *A Functional Analysis of Executory Contracts*, 74 Minn. L. Rev. 227 (1989).

[2] Bankruptcy Code § 365.

- do nothing, and permit the contract to remain in effect, unaffected by the bankruptcy case.

The purpose of permitting the debtor to assume or reject these contracts is to give it the opportunity to realize the value of transactions that are favorable to the estate and to breach those that are burdensome. The Code is silent about the fourth alternative: neither assume nor reject the executory contract, but permit it to simply "right-through" the bankruptcy case, and remain in effect when the bankruptcy case is over.[3]

At a very basic level, each of these alternatives is easy to understand. Consider, for example, a contract for the sale of goods between Franklin Manufacturing Co. and Industrial Supply Co. Franklin has agreed to purchase and Industrial has agreed to sell 12,000 yards of insulated copper wire, which will be delivered at a rate of 1,000 yards each month for $10 per yard. Sometime during the year, Franklin files a Chapter 11 petition and must decide how to handle the contract.

If the contract price is relatively high due to fluctuations in the market for copper wire, Franklin might wish to reject the contract under § 365(a). To do so, Franklin must seek the court's approval.[4] Because rejection is a breach of the contract, its rejection gives Industrial Supply a claim for breach of contract. The conceptually difficult aspect of § 365 arises because, although the rejection (and breach) does not occur until after the debtor's petition was filed, the other party's claim is treated as if the breach occurred before the bankruptcy case began. If the breach is treated as occurring post-petition, the non-debtor might be deemed to have a post-petition claim with administrative expense priority. By contrast, if the breach is treated as occurring prepetition, the breach claim will be an unsecured claim, probably payable at a lower rate than administrative claims will be paid. The Code makes it clear that after rejection, Industrial Supply has a general unsecured claim, not an administrative expense claim.[5]

On the other hand, if Franklin still needs the copper wire and the contract price with Industrial Supply is favorable, it may wish to assume the contract, take delivery of the goods, and pay the contract price. Even if Franklin no longer needs the wire, if the contract price is low, Franklin may wish to go ahead with the sale and resell the wire to someone else. In either case, Franklin will seek to assume the contract and perform according to its terms.[6] Just as with the decision to reject, Franklin must obtain court approval to assume the contract. Upon assumption, the debtor's contractual duties are treated as post-petition obligations of the estate and, if unperformed, give rise to an administrative expense priority claim under §§ 503 and 507(a)(2).[7] Normally, the debtor will perform contracts it assumes. But, if it does not, it must pay the other party the damages caused by its breach, in full.[8]

---

[3] Mark R. Campbell & Robert C. Hastie, *Executory Contracts: Retention Without Assumption in Chapter 11 — "Ride-through" Revisited*, 19 Am. Bankr. Inst. J. 33, 34-35 (2000).

[4] Bankruptcy Code § 365(a).

[5] Bankruptcy Code § 365(g)(1).

[6] Bankruptcy Code § 365(a).

[7] Bankruptcy Code § 365(g)(2).

[8] Bankruptcy Code § 1129(a)(9)(A). *See infra* § 19.10[H] Full Payment of Priority Claims.

Alternatively, Franklin may anticipate the sale of one division as a going concern. If this were the division that expected to use the copper wire, Franklin may wish to assume the contract and assign the obligations and benefits to whomever buys this part of Franklin's business. To do so, Franklin must assume the contract and gain further court approval to assign it to the purchaser of the division in question. Even if Franklin does not plan to sell one of its divisions, it might determine that it will be profitable to assume the contract, and assign it to another business, perhaps even to one of its competitors.

The fourth alternative is to permit the contract to simply ride through the bankruptcy proceeding and emerge, at the conclusion of the case, unaffected.[9] Though this alternative is not expressly authorized by the Bankruptcy Code, and seems to conflict with § 524 on the effect of a discharge, Franklin may simply ignore the contract and emerge from bankruptcy with the contract neither assumed nor rejected, but nevertheless still intact.

Regardless of the debtor's choice, the Code imposes a variety of time limits and other constraints on the debtor's decision. The remainder of this chapter explains the meaning of "executory contract," examines the Code's restrictions on the debtor's various alternatives, and explores the consequences of each alternative the debtor might choose.

§ 11.02   MEANING OF "EXECUTORY CONTRACT" AND "UNEXPIRED LEASE"[10]

Section 365 permits the rejection of executory contracts and unexpired leases, not all contracts. Accordingly, the terms "executory contract" and "unexpired lease" must be defined.

[A]   "Executory Contract" Defined

For many years, courts have used a definition originally suggested by Professor Vern Countryman: "A contract under which the obligation of both the bankrupt and the other party to the contract are so far unperformed that the failure of either to complete performance would constitute a material breach excusing performance of the other."[11] Thus, a contract is executory if *both parties* have material duties remaining to be performed.

Consider a simple contract for the sale of goods, involving a single delivery. Crash Construction Co. enters into a contract with Builder's Supply Inc. to buy 100 sheets of plywood for $1,000. If Crash pays the price in advance and is awaiting

---

[9] *See generally* In re JZ, L.L.C., 371 B.R. 412 (B.A.P. 9th Cir. 2007).

[10] Michael T. Andrew, *Executory Contracts in Bankruptcy: Understanding "Rejection,"* 59 U. Colo. L. Rev. 845 (1988); Vern Countryman, *Executory Contracts in Bankruptcy*, 57 Minn. L. Rev. 439, 446 (1973); Carl N. Pickerill, *Executory Contracts Re-Revisited*, 83 Am. Bankr. L.J. 63 (2009); Jay L. Westbrook, *A Functional Analysis of Executory Contracts*, 74 Minn. L. Rev. 227 (1989).

[11] Vern Countryman, *Executory Contracts in Bankruptcy*, 57 Minn. L. Rev. 439, 446 (1973). *See* RCI Tech. Corp. v. Sunterra Corp. (In re Sunterra Corp.), 361 F.3d 257, 264 (4th Cir. 2004); Sharon Steel Corp. v. Nat'l Fuel Distrib. Corp., 872 F.2d 36, 39 (3d Cir. 1989).

delivery from Builder's Supply when Crash files its bankruptcy petition, the contract is not executory, because Crash has substantially performed. Crash's right to receive the drywall is simply an estate asset.[12] Likewise, if Builder's Supply has already delivered the drywall, but Crash has not yet paid for it, Builder's Supply is the one who has substantially performed. Builder's Supply is a creditor with a general unsecured claim. Thus, the contract is not executory within the Countryman definition. Courts agree that treating either one of these situations as invoking § 365 would expand the effect of the provision pointlessly, "since it is the rare agreement that does not involve unperformed obligations on either side."[13]

On the other hand, if neither party has substantially performed, with Crash still owing payment and Builder's Supply still in possession of the plywood, the contract is executory and is governed by § 365. Crash has the option to reject the contract, to assume and retain the contract, or to assume and assign the contract. Thus, if the contract involves *both* a set of rights (such as the right to receive the plywood) and a set of obligations (the duty to pay for the plywood), it is an executory contract.[14]

While the Countryman "material breach" test is useful in most situations, several commentators[15] and a few courts[16] have pointed out that it would make more sense to apply a more functional test, based on the effect of treating a contract as executory, rather than the traditional Countryman rubric. This functional test examines whether the debtor has remaining obligations to perform upon which the estate's right to receive the other party's performance is conditioned.[17] Unless there is some potential advantage to the estate from electing to assume or reject, the mechanisms of § 365 should play no role in connection with the contract. But, if the estate might gain a potential benefit from assumption, or avoid a significant detriment through rejection, § 365 applies and the estate may elect to assume or reject. This type of approach would make it unnecessary for courts to bend over backwards in an effort to find some remaining material obligation that would justify treating the contract as executory under the traditional Countryman test.[18] In other words, a court should consider "the goals that assumption or rejection were expected to accomplish: enhancement of the estate."[19]

---

[12] Bankruptcy Code § 541(a)(1).

[13] Mitchell v. Streets (In re Streets & Beard Farm P'ship), 882 F.2d 233, 235 (7th Cir. 1989).

[14] *See* Thomas H. Jackson, The Logic and Limits of Bankruptcy Law 106-07 (1986).

[15] *See* Michael T. Andrew, *Exectutory Contracts in Bankruptcy: Understanding "Rejection,"* 59 U. Colo. L. Rev. 845, 889-94 (1988); Michael T. Andrew, *Executory Contracts Revisited: A Reply to Professor Westbrook*, 62 U. Colo. L. Rev. 1 (1991); Morris G. Shanker, *Bankruptcy Asset Theory and its Application to Executory Contracts*, 1992 Ann. Surv. Bankr. L. 97; Jay L. Westbrook, *A Functional Analysis of Executory Contracts*, 74 Minn. L. Rev. 227 (1989).

[16] *E.g.*, In re Jolly, 574 F.2d 349 (6th Cir. 1978); In re Booth, 19 B.R. 53 (Bankr. D. Utah 1982).

[17] *See, e.g.*, In re Jolly, 574 F.2d 349 (6th Cir. 1978) (decided under the Bankruptcy Act).

[18] David G. Epstein & Steve H. Nickles, *The National Bankruptcy Review Commission's Section 365 Recommendations and the "Larger Conceptual Issues"* 102 Dick. L. Rev. 679 (1998).

[19] The National Bankruptcy Review Commission, General Issues in Chapter 11, Report p. http:// govinfo.library.unt.edu/nbrc/report/12chapt1.html#1151 (last viewed on March 17, 2012). *See In re*

Installment land sale contracts provide a good example of the difficulties in applying the Countryman test. In a land sale contract, the buyer promises to make regular installment payments over a period of time. The seller agrees to deliver good title when the payments are complete.[20] Under the Countryman definition, this is an executory contract: the buyer has a material obligation to make the balance of the promised payments and the seller has a duty to deliver a deed. Yet, treating it as an executory contract makes it necessary for the buyer to assume the contract and pay the full price, even if the value of the land is lower that what the buyer agreed to pay. If the buyer instead had acquired immediate title to the land and granted the seller a mortgage on it to secure payment of the price, no one would have difficulty treating the transaction as giving rise to a secured claim. Subject to some exceptions, the buyer would be able to retain the property by paying the creditor only the amount of its allowed secured claim, rather than the full amount of the mortgage debt, and giving the creditor an allowed unsecured deficiency claim for the unpaid balance.[21] Under a functional approach, this is not an executory contract. On the other hand, a debtor may have other contracts that do not meet the Countryman definition, but where the debtor's right to assume or reject may benefit the estate.

[B]   "Unexpired Lease" or Security Interest

Though it might seem easier to identify an unexpired lease, this is not always true. Here, the principal question is whether the transaction is a true lease or a disguised security agreement. The question is frequently considered in connection with leases of goods, but it has also presented itself in the context of a long-term lease of land.[22]

The economic realities of the transaction determine whether it is a true lease or a security interest.[23] If the lease leaves the lessor with no meaningful economic interest in the goods, it is a disguised security interest and should be handled by the Code's rules governing secured claims. On the other hand, if the lessor's residual interest is economically meaningful, it is a true lease which the debtor may assume or reject under § 365.

The most obvious example of a security interest disguised as a lease is one in which the "lessee" has a contractual obligation to make all of the payments provided for in the lease, without the right to early termination, and also has the

---

Government Sec. Corp., 101 B.R. 343, 349 (Bankr. S.D. Fla. 1989), aff'd, 111 B.R. 1007 (S.D. Fla.1990).

[20] See supra § 2.02[A][1][c] Installment Land Contracts.

[21] E.g., In re Booth, 19 B.R. 53 (Bankr. D. Utah 1982). See Jay L. Westbrook, A Functional Analysis of Executory Contracts, 74 Minn. L. Rev. 227, 317-22 (1989). See also Thomas C. Homburger & Karl L. Marsche, Recharacterization Revisited: A View of Recharacterization of Sale and Leaseback Transactions in Bankruptcy After Fifteen Years, 41 Real Prop. Prob. & Tr. J. 123 (2006).

[22] E.g., United Airlines, Inc. v. HSBC Bank USA, 416 F.3d 609 (7th Cir. 2005); In re PCH Associates, 804 F.2d 193, 198-200 (2d Cir. 1986).

[23] Margaret Howard, Equipment Lessors and Secured Parties in Bankruptcy: An Argument for Coherence, 48 Wash. & Lee L. Rev. 253 (1991); Shu-Yi Oei, Context Matters: The Recharacterization of Leases in Bankruptcy and Tax Law, 82 Am. Bankr. L.J. 635 (2008).

right to buy the goods, at the end of the lease for a nominal price.[24] Likewise, if the duration of the lease is for the entire anticipated useful life of the goods, the transaction is really a secured sale, not a lease.[25] If the economic reality of the transaction demonstrate that it is a sale, with the lessor retaining no meaningful interest in the goods at the end of the lease, the deal is a disguised financing transaction and is not governed by § 365.[26]

The consequences of the conclusion that a transaction is a security interest rather than a lease are significant. If it is a security interest, the creditor's secured claim may be modified and the lien "stripped down" to the value of the collateral. The rate of interest, and the duration of payments may be modified as well. If the transaction is really a lease, the debtor must assume the lease and make all payments provided for in the original lease agreement in order to retain the leased property.[27] The amounts involved may differ widely, and, if the transaction is a true lease, the debtor may not be able to afford to make the required payments.

§ 11.03　PROCEDURE FOR ASSUMPTION OR REJECTION

Section 365 imposes restrictions on the trustee or debtor-in-possession's option to assume or reject an executory contract. Time limits on this decision vary, depending on the nature of the transaction and the type of bankruptcy proceeding involved. Moreover, the debtors' desires do not control; the court must approve the choice. Finally, the Code imposes restrictions on the estate's treatment of executory contracts in any "limbo period" between commencement of the case and the decision to assume or reject. In Chapter 11 cases in particular, this may be an extended period of several months or even years.

[A]　Timing of Assumption or Rejection[28]

In liquidation cases, the trustee has sixty days from the order for relief to assume or reject. Afterwards, the agreement is "deemed rejected," unless the court has extended the sixty-day period.[29] However, the sixty-day limit does not apply to an unexpired lease of non-residential real estate.[30]

In reorganization cases under Chapters 11, 12, and 13, the determination may usually be deferred until confirmation of a plan. Thus, the debtor might ignore the contract while the case is pending, though the court has discretion to require a

---

[24] U.C.C. § 1-203(b)(2) (2010) (formerly U.C.C. § 1-201(37)).

[25] U.C.C. § 1-203(b)(1) (2010) (formerly U.C.C. § 1-201(37)).

[26] *See* Duke Energy Royal, LLC v. Pillowtex Corp. (In re Pillowtex, Inc.), 349 F.3d 711 (3d Cir. 2003).

[27] In re Smith, 449 B.R. 35, 40-41 (Bankr. E.D. Pa. 2011).

[28] Jennie D. Latta, *"What You Don't Know May Hurt You"* — *Time Limits Under the Bankruptcy Code and Rules*, 28 U. Mem. L. Rev. 911 (1998); Rosemary Williams, Annotation, *Time Limits on Assumption or Rejection of Executory Contract or Lease Under § 365 of Bankruptcy Code*, 137 A.L.R. Fed. 137 (1997).

[29] Bankruptcy Code § 365(d)(1).

[30] *Id.*

quicker decision.[31]

Leases of non-residential (commercial) real estate are treated differently. The Code requires assumption or rejection of a commercial real estate lease within 120 days of the order for relief, or the date an order confirming a plan is entered, whichever is earlier.[32] For cause, the court may extend the time period for an additional ninety days. But, any extension must be granted before the initial 120 day period expires.[33] Any further extension requires the lessor's consent.[34] If the debtor fails to assume by the deadline, the lease is "deemed rejected."

This short time frame places considerable pressure on debtors to determine which premises are needed for continued operations of their business. Debtors who are unsure whether to jettison certain locations may find it necessary to assume unexpired commercial real estate leases for property they may ultimately need. Because breach of an assumed lease gives the lessor an administrative priority expense claim, which must be paid in full in the debtor's Chapter 11 plan, the time limits operate to give some lessors a considerable advantage over other creditors.

[B]   Court Approval of Assumption or Rejection

Approval of the trustee or debtor-in-possession's motion to assume or reject an executory contract is not automatic. Most courts apply a "business judgment" standard to determine whether the debtor's motion to assume or reject should be granted.[35] Thus, the scope of the court's review is narrow, and the debtor's decision to seek assumption or rejection carries a presumption of reasonableness that is not normally disturbed absent a showing of bad faith or abuse of the debtor's discretion.[36]

[C]   Performance Before Assumption or Rejection[37]

In Chapter 11 cases, except with respect to commercial real estate leases, the time between the debtor's petition and its decision about assumption or rejection may be significant. Many months might lapse before the debtor promulgates a plan. And, even with respect to commercial real estate leases, the court may extend the time period for assumption or rejection for many months. This raises a question about how the contract will be handled before a decision is made.

---

[31]   Bankruptcy Code § 365(d)(2).

[32]   Bankruptcy Code § 365(d)(4)(A).

[33]   Bankruptcy Code § 365(d)(4)(B)(I); In re DCT, Inc., 283 B.R. 442 (Bankr. E.D. Mich. 2002); *but see* In re Sw. Aircraft Servs., Inc., 831 F.2d 848, 851 (9th Cir. 1987) (finding statute ambiguous and permitting extension of the motion that was made before expiration of the statutory period).

[34]   Bankruptcy Code § 365(d)(4)(B)(ii).

[35]   *E.g.*, Orion Pictures Corp. v. Showtime Networks, Inc. (In re Orion Pictures Corp.), 4 F.3d 1095, 1099 (2d Cir. 1993); Richmond Leasing Co. v. Capital Bank, N.A., 762 F.2d 1303, 1309 (5th Cir. 1985).

[36]   Phar-Mor, Inc. v. Strauss Bldg. Assocs., 204 B.R. 948, 951-52 (N.D. Ohio 1997); In re Lady Balt. Foods, Inc., No. 02-43428, 2004 Bankr. LEXIS 1413 (Bankr. D. Kan. Aug. 13, 2004).

[37]   Douglas W. Bordewieck, *The Postpetition, Pre-Rejection, Pre-Assumption Status of an Executory Contract*, 59 Am. Bankr. L.J. 197, 200 n.18 (1985); Thomas Plank, *Bankruptcy and Federalism*, 71 Fordham L. Rev. 1063, 1113-26 (2002).

Sections 365(d)(3) and (d)(5) specify the estate's duties during the period before assumption or rejection. However, the Bankruptcy Code is silent about the other party's duty to continue performing during this time, particularly if the debtor has committed a material breach that would ordinarily permit the other party to suspend or terminate its performance of the contract.[38] The parties' respective obligations during this interim period are discussed below.

[1] Debtor's Duties to Perform

[a] Commercial Real Estate Leases[39]

Section 365(d)(3) governs performance of nonresidential real estate leases. It requires the trustee or debtor-in-possession to "timely perform all the obligations of the debtor" until the lease is assumed or rejected.[40] During the first sixty days after the order for relief, the court may grant the estate a time extension for performance of the debtor's obligations, but the court is expressly forbidden from extending the debtor's obligations beyond this initial sixty-day period. This usually means that the debtor must make regular rental payments during the 210 days before it assumes or rejects the lease.[41] The debtor's failure to pay the rent during this time may impair its ability to subsequently assume the lease.[42]

[b] Equipment Leases

Section 365(d)(5) treats equipment leases differently. It applies only to personal property leased for business purposes. In Chapter 11 cases, the debtor must "timely perform all of the obligations of the debtor" that first arise "from or after 60 days after the order for relief . . . ."[43] The court has more flexibility with respect to permitting extensions or other deviations from timely full performance than it does with respect to commercial real estate leases. The court can use equitable considerations to adjust the debtor's obligations before the lease is assumed or rejected. However, this rule does not apply in Chapter 7, 12, or 13 cases; nor does it apply to leases of property used for personal, family, or household purposes.

---

[38] *See* In re Orla Enterprises, 399 B.R. 25 (Bankr. N.D. Ill 2009) (debtor's prepetition breach terminated contract, making it no longer executory).

[39] Jeffrey S. Battershall, *Commercial Leases and Section 365 of the Bankruptcy Code*, 64 Am. Bankr. L.J. 329 (1990); Joshua Fruchter, *To Bind or Not to Bind — Bankruptcy Code 365(d)(3): Statutory Minefield*, 68 Am. Bankr. L.J. 437 (1994).

[40] Bankruptcy Code § 365(d)(3).

[41] The debtor need not comply with "ipso facto" provisions that treat the debtor's financial condition as a default. Bankruptcy Code § 362(d)(3). *See* Bankruptcy Code § 362(b)(2).

[42] *See* South St. Seaport Ltd. P'ship v. Burger Boys, Inc. (In re Burger Boys, Inc.), 94 F.3d 755, 759 (2d Cir.1996); In re Sw. Aircraft Servs., Inc., 831 F.2d 848, 853-54 (9th Cir. 1987) (failure to pay is a factor, but is not dispositive of debtor's ability to assume); Matter of Condominium Admin. Servs., Inc., 55 B.R. 792 (Bankr. M.D. Fla. 1985) (payment is a condition of assumption).

[43] Bankruptcy Code § 365(d)(5) (formerly codified in 11 U.S.C. § 365(d)(10)).

[c]   Other Executory Contracts[44]

Sections 365(d)(3) and (d)(5) leave several conspicuous gaps regarding the estate's duties during this "limbo period" between commencement of the case and assumption or rejection. They are silent about the estate's duty to continue to make rental payments on leased equipment in Chapter 7, 12, or 13 cases or on leased consumer goods in type of case. Likewise, they say nothing about other executory contracts.

Cases decided under both the old Act and the current Code make it clear that these contracts are not enforceable against the estate until they have been assumed.[45] Nevertheless, the debtor must pay for the reasonable value of its use of the property involved.[46] A special rule is carved out for goods or services supplied to the estate in connection with an unexpired lease — the estate must pay at the contract rate.[47]

[2]   Non-Debtor's Duties Before Assumption or Rejection[48]

The Bankruptcy Code is conspicuously silent about the non-debtor's duties to continue performing while the case is pending, but before the debtor assumes or rejects. In Chapter 11 cases, where the debtor can delay its decision until confirmation of a plan, this may be quite a while.

The Supreme Court's most important executory contract decision, *NLRB v. Bildisco & Bildisco*,[49] provided some guidance, indicating that between the time of the debtor's petition, and the debtor's assumption, that the agreement "is not an enforceable contract."[50] This meant that, although it might be an enforceable pre-petition deal, that it was not enforceable as a contract against the debtor's estate. The debtor might have been bound, but the estate is not — at least not yet.

Cases decided under the Bankruptcy Act presumed that the debtor's rights under an executory contract were not even property of the debtor's estate. In *Hall v. Perry (In re Cochise College Park, Inc.)*,[51] the court indicated that where the debtor was in breach of an executory contract for the sale of real estate, the other party had no duty to continue making payments, thus suggesting that the contract was not property of the debtor's estate that the debtor could enforce prior to assumption.

---

[44] Douglas W. Bordewieck, *The Postpetiton Pre-Rejection, Pre-Assumption Status of an Executory Contract*, 59 Am. Bankr. L.J. 197 (1985); Howard Buschman, *Benefits and Burdens: Postpetition Performance of Unassumed Executory Contracts*, 5 Bankr. Dev. J. 241 (1988).

[45] NLRB v. Bildisco & Bildisco, 465 U.S. 513, 531 (1984); Philadelphia Co. v. Dipple, 312 U.S. 168 (1941), *aff'g* 111 F.2d 932 (3d Cir. 1940).

[46] Philadelphia Co. v. Dipple, 312 U.S. 168 (1941), *aff'g* 111 F.2d 932 (3d Cir. 1940).

[47] Bankruptcy Code § 365(b)(4).

[48] *See* Howard Buschman, *Benefits and Burdens: Post-Petition Performance of Unassumed Executory Contracts*, 5 Bankr. Dev. J. 341, 355-57 (1988).

[49] 465 U.S. 513 (1984).

[50] *Id.* at 532.

[51] 703 F.2d 1339 (9th Cir. 1983).

However, more in line with *Bildisco*, cases decided under § 541(a) reach a different result. *Data-Link Systems., Inc. v. Whitcomb & Keller Mortgage. Co. (In re Whitcomb & Keller Mortgage Co.)*,[52] provides a good example. There, the court held that the debtor did not assume a contract requiring Data-Link to provide computer services to the debtor even though it obtained a court order enjoining Data-Link from discontinuing its services in response to the debtor's pre-petition breach. The court said that "utilization of the [other party's] computer services during the administration of the estate did not support a finding that [the debtor] assumed the contract . . . ."[53] Thus, even though the other party may be compelled to continue performance, in return for the right to receive payment from the debtor, the debtor cannot otherwise be required to perform. As another court explained: "After a debtor commences a Chapter 11 proceeding, but before executory contracts are assumed or rejected under § 365(a), those contracts remain in existence, enforceable *by* the debtor *but not against* the debtor."[54]

Of course, if the debtor elects to receive benefits from the other party during this interregnum, the debtor must pay for the reasonable value of the goods or services it receives. The amount owed might be the same as the amount specified in the contract, which is strong evidence of the reasonable value of what the debtor receives. The other party enjoys an administrative expense claim for the value it contributed to the estate. However, amounts still owed for pre-petition goods or services remain general unsecured claims that are not entitled to any special treatment.[55]

§ 11.04 REJECTION OF EXECUTORY CONTRACTS[56]

[A] Effect of Rejection

[1] Pre-Petition Claim

Rejection of an executory contract or unexpired lease is treated as a *pre-petition* breach.[57] Thus, the non-debtor party has a general unsecured claim for the damages it has suffered. The claim is allowed or disallowed just as if the debtor had breached before the petition was filed.[58] Because *the estate* never became bound by the agreement, the creditor's claim is not entitled to administrative expense priority. Instead, it is a general unsecured claim, allowed, like other pre-petition

---

[52] 715 F.2d 375 (7th Cir. 1983).

[53] *Id.* at 379-80.

[54] United States ex rel. United States Postal Serv. v. Dewey Freight Sys., 31 F.3d 620, 624 (8th Cir. Mo. 1994) (emphasis added).

[55] NLRB v. Bildisco & Bildisco, 465 U.S. 513, 5301 (U.S. 1984). *See also* In re Jartran, Inc., 732 F.2d 584, 586-91 (7th Cir. 1984).

[56] See Michael T. Andrew, *Executory Contracts in Bankruptcy: Understanding "Rejection,"* 59 U. Colo. L.Rev. 845 (1988); Douglas Bordewieck & Vern Countryman, *The Rejection of Collective Bargaining Agreements by Chapter 11 Debtors*, 57 Am. Bankr. L.J. 293 (1983).

[57] Bankruptcy Code § 365(g)(1).

[58] Bankruptcy Code § 502(g).

claims, to the extent permitted by § 502.[59]

[2]   Effect of Rejection on Non-Debtor's Rights[60]

One key issue with respect to rejected executory contracts and leases is the effect of rejection on the rights of the other party. Rejection operates as a breach, which gives the other party a pre-petition claim against the estate. But, it is not a rescission or termination of the contract. Nor does it act as an avoidance power or undo conveyances of property that have already occurred pursuant to the rejected contract. As will be seen, when courts forget about this, they sometimes reach disastrous conclusions. Congress has reacted to several of these situations by enacting very specific provisions that correct these poorly reasoned decisions.

[a]   Land Sale Contracts and Timeshares

The Code directly addresses the buyer's rights when the seller rejects a land sale contract or a contract for the sale of a timeshare interest. These sales contracts are in part conveyances of property, and in part contractual obligations. Section 365(i) respects this distinction when the debtor is the seller who decides to reject. If the buyer is already in possession when the seller rejects, the buyer may elect to treat the contract as terminated and file a claim against the estate, or it may remain in possession and offset its damages against amounts remaining due to the seller.[61] In other words, rejection does not operate to undo the conveyance to the buyer. If the buyer chooses to remain in possession and offset its damages, it may do so, but has no further claim against the estate.[62] The debtor must deliver title to the buyer in accordance with the terms of the contract.[63]

If the buyer treats the rejection as a termination of the contract, it has a lien on the property involved in the sale as collateral for the buyer's right to recover the portion of the purchase price it paid before rejection.[64] Thus, its claim is secured, and the property interest it had is, at least to this extent, respected. But, this is the buyer's only recovery.

[b]   Real Estate Leases

Where a landlord rejects an unexpired real estate lease, the lessee's rights are similar to those of a buyer under a rejected land sale contract. Section 365(h) gives the lessee the same right it would have under applicable nonbankruptcy law to terminate the lease, vacate the premises, and file a claim against the estate to recover its damages.[65] Alternatively, assuming the term of the lease has already

---

[59] *See supra* § 10.02[C] Allowance of Claims.

[60] *See* Michael T. Andrew, *Executory Contracts in Bankruptcy: Understanding "Rejection,"* 59 U. Colo. L. Rev. 845 (1988).

[61] Bankruptcy Code § 365(i).

[62] Bankruptcy Code § 365(i)(2)(A).

[63] Bankruptcy Code § 365(i)(2)(B).

[64] Bankruptcy Code § 365(j).

[65] Bankruptcy Code § 365(h)(1)(A)(i).

commenced, the lessee may remain in possession, retain whatever other rights it has under the lease (such as the right to sublet or assign the lease), and offset whatever damages it suffers as a result of the landlord's rejection against the rent remaining due.[66] These damages may be significant, particularly in connection with an office building or an apartment complex in which the bankrupt landlord is responsible for maintenance of common areas such as parking lots, lobbies, hallways, and elevators. Similar rights are accorded to purchasers of timeshare interests who have made a deposit but have not yet taken possession.[67]

The Code expressly provides that the landlord's rejection does not affect the rights of a tenant in a shopping center with respect to "radius, location, use, exclusivity, or tenant mix or balance."[68] This specific language may imply that similar rights of tenants in other real estate projects may not be entitled to similar protection.

[c]   Intellectual Property Licenses[69]

Intellectual property licenses present issues similar to those involved in land sale contracts and unexpired real estate leases. When an intellectual property licensor files a bankruptcy petition, it may seek to reject contracts it has with licensees. Section 365(n) allows the licensor to walk away from its executory contractual obligations, but it does not allow it to rescind the conveyance of a property interest (the license) that has already occurred. Upon the licensor's rejection, the licensee may, however, treat the license as if it had been terminated.[70] Alternatively, it may retain its rights under the license.[71] However, unlike the rights of a lessee, an intellectual property licensee must make any future royalty payments as they come due and may neither set off any damages it suffers as a result of the rejection nor pursue any claim for damages as an administrative expense claim. Its only right to damages is as a general unsecured creditor.[72]

These provisions expressly preserve any exclusivity rights the licensee has under the license agreement.[73] Thus, if the debtor granted a licensee the exclusive right to use the debtor's patent, the licensee retains this exclusive right. The licensee can enforce this right through specific performance or an injunction, just as it could have if the licensor had not filed for bankruptcy. This overrules decisions

---

[66] Bankruptcy Code § 365(h)(1)(B).

[67] Bankruptcy Code § 365(h)(2).

[68] Bankruptcy Code § 365(h)(1)(C).

[69] Madlyn Gleich Primoff & Erica G. Weinberger, *E-Commerce and Dot-Com Bankruptcies: Assumption, Assignment and Rejection of Executory Contracts, Including Intellectual Property Agreements, and Related Issues Under Sections 365(c), 365(e) and 365(n) of the Bankruptcy Code*, 8 Am. Bankr. Inst. L. Rev. 307 (2000).

[70] Bankruptcy Code § 365(n)(1)(A).

[71] Bankruptcy Code § 365(n)(1)(B).

[72] Bankruptcy Code § 365(g)(1).

[73] Bankruptcy Code § 365(n)(1)(B).

such as *In re Lubrizol*[74] and *In re Logical Software, Inc.*,[75] which held that rejection terminated the license and stripped the licensee of its property rights.[76]

A careful reading of § 365 reveals that its rules apply only to trade secrets, patents, and copyrights. They do not apply to trademarks, which are not mentioned in the Code's definition of "intellectual property."[77]

[d]   Personal Property Leases

If a lessee of personal property rejects the lease, the lease is no longer property of the estate.[78] Moreover, the automatic stay is automatically terminated, giving the lessor the right to recover possession of its property under applicable state law.[79]

[e]   Covenants Not To Compete[80]

A related issue, which Congress has not directly addressed, is the effect of rejection on a covenant not to compete with the debtor. This issue commonly arises in employment contracts, franchise agreements, and agreements for the sale of a business. The principal question is whether the non-complete clause survives rejection, or whether the debtor, having rejected the agreement, is free to complete with the other party.

In *In re Rovine*, for example, the franchisee of a fast-food chain rejected its franchise contract with the franchisor. The franchisor sought to enforce the agreement's covenant not to compete, seeking to prevent the debtor from continuing its hamburger business. The court treated rejection as a complete termination of the contract that relieved the debtor of its responsibilities. This result deprived the franchisor of its ability to enjoin the debtor from violating the restrictive covenant in the rejected contract.[81]

When this issue arises outside of bankruptcy, the covenant not to compete would be enforceable through specific performance, and the aggrieved franchisor would also have a claim for damages. Specifically enforceable contract rights straddle the

---

[74] Lubrizol Enter., Inc. v. Richmond Metal Furnishers (In re Lubrizol Enter., Inc.), 756 F.2d 1043, 1048 (4th Cir. 1985).

[75] In re Logical Software, Inc., 66 B.R. 683, 686 (Bankr. D. Mass. 1986), *rev'd, and remanded on other grounds*, Infosystems Tech. v. Logical Software, No. 87-0042, 1987 U.S. Dist. LEXIS 6285 (D. Mass. June 25, 1987).

[76] *See generally* Robert L. Tamietti, *Technology Licenses Under The Bankruptcy Code: A Licensee's Mine Field*, 62 Am. Bankr. L.J. 295 (1988); Michael T. Andrew, *Executory Contracts in Bankruptcy: Understanding Rejection*, 59 U. Colo. L. Rev. 845 (1988).

[77] Bankruptcy Code § 101(35A). *See* Xuan-Thao N. Nguyen, *Bankrupting Trademarks*, 37 U.C. Davis L. Rev. 1267 (2004).

[78] Bankruptcy Code § 365(p)(1).

[79] Bankruptcy Code § 365(p)(1).

[80] See Michael T. Andrew, *Executory Contracts in Bankruptcy: Understanding "Rejection,"* 59 U. Colo. L.Rev. 845 (1988); Jeffrey C. Sharer, *Noncompetition Agreements in Bankruptcy: Covenants (Maybe) Not to Compete*, 62 U. Chi. L. Rev. 1549 (1995).

[81] In re Rovine, 6 B.R. 661 (Bankr. W.D. Tenn. 1980).

conceptual line between property rights that are respected in bankruptcy, and contract rights that are discharged. Rejection of the contract converts the damage claim to a pre-petition claim. However, this raises the question of whether covenant can be specifically enforced, even though the underlying claim has been discharged.

The issue also arose in *In re Ortiz*,[82] where a professional boxer's bankruptcy trustee rejected a pre-petition contract the boxer had entered into with a boxing promoter. The court reached a result different from that in *In re Rovine* and ruled that the trustee's rejection of the contract did not terminate it. Instead, the promoter's right to an equitable remedy to prevent the debtor from working with a different promoter, was preserved.[83]

Rovine and Ortiz characterize two competing approaches to the effect of rejection on a personal services contract. Because the definition of claim includes "equitable remedies for breach of performance" of a contractual obligation, so long as the equitable remedy gives rise to a right to payment, courts like *Rovine* have ruled that the creditor's claim supplants any right to an equitable remedy that might otherwise exist in state court. Courts like *Ortiz* recognize that even though rejection gives rise to a claim against the estate, it does not otherwise completely eliminate the creditor's equitable rights against the debtor, which might remain enforceable.[84] On the one hand, it preserves the non-debtor's property rights. On the other hand, it does not explore the question whether, under non-bankruptcy law, those rights would have been enforceable against third parties who were not parties to the contract.[85]

[3] Rejection (Breach) after Assumption

If a debtor-in-possession assumes a contract, it assumes the contract in its entirety, with all of its burdens and responsibilities attached. Damages for any subsequent rejection or breach by the debtor are treated as administrative expenses that are entitled to priority under §§ 503(b) and 507(a)(2).[86]

[B] Employees' Rights

In general, employment contracts are treated the same as other executory contracts. A bankrupt employer has the right to reject any long-term employment contract with its employees. Upon rejection, the employee has a pre-petition claim for damages. But, allowance of an employee's damages is limited by § 502(b)(7).[87] On the other hand, such claims are likely entitled to limited priority under

---

[82] In re Ortiz, 400 B.R. 755 (C.D. Cal. 2009).

[83] *Id.* at 769.

[84] *Compare* In re Rovine, 6 B.R. 661 (Bankr. W.D. Tenn. 1980), *with* Sir Speedy, Inc. v. Morse, 256 B.R. 657 (D. Mass. 2000), *and* Watman v. Groman (In re Watman), 331 B.R. 502 (D. Mass. 2005).

[85] *See* In re Exide Techs., 607 F.3d 957 (3d Cir. 2010).

[86] Bankruptcy Code § 365(g)(2); Mason v. Official Comm. of Unsecured Creditors (In re FBI Distrib. Corp.), 330 F.3d 36, 42 (1st Cir. 2003).

[87] *See supra* § 10.02[D][2] Limit on Claims for Salaries.

§ 507(a)(4).[88]

In addition to these general rules, the Code contains detailed provisions regarding the rejection of collective bargaining contracts[89] and termination of employees' retirement benefits.[90] These provisions are discussed elsewhere.[91]

§ 11.05 ASSUMPTION OF EXECUTORY CONTRACTS[92]

One of the estate's key alternatives is to assume executory contracts and leases entered into by the debtor. The principal effect of assumption is to bind the estate to the contract and give the other non-debtor party the right to an administrative expense claim for any subsequent breach, while the case is pending. Courts generally defer to the debtor's business judgment about whether to assume or reject. However, the Code imposes several restrictions which make certain contracts non-assumable.

[A] Effect of Assumption

It is well established that assumption is all or nothing. If the debtor assumes the contract or lease, the debtor assumes all the obligations it contains. "Cherry picking" is not allowed. The debtor may not assume the favorable terms and reject those it prefers to avoid. To escape burdens in this way, the debtor needs to negotiate consent to a modification of the agreement. The obligations created by the assumption bind the estate, and if they are not performed, give rise to a priority claim for administrative expenses.[93] As noted above, the breach claim created by rejection, on the other hand, is treated as a pre-petition claim.[94]

[B] Cure of Defaults Required for Assumption[95]

Financially troubled debtors are frequently in default on their pre-petition contracts. Sometimes these defaults are a material breach which, under contract law, justifies the other party in suspending or terminating its performance under the contract. This creates a barrier if the debtor-in-possession wants to assume the contract.

To assume, the debtor must cure its defaults. Section 365(b)(1) requires the debtor who wants to assume a broken contract to "cure, compensate, and assure."

---

[88] *See supra* § 10.04[A][4] Wage Claims.

[89] Bankruptcy Code § 1113.

[90] Bankruptcy Code § 1114.

[91] *See infra* Chapter 23 — Special Problems in Bankruptcy.

[92] Daniel J. Bussel, & Edward A. Friedler, *The Limits on Assuming and Assigning Executory Contracts*, 74 Am. Bankr. L.J. 321, 339+ (2000); David Hahn, *The Internal Logic of Assumption of Executory Contracts*, 13 U. Pa. J. Bus. L. 723 (2011).

[93] NLRB v. Bildisco & Bildisco, 465 U.S. 513, 531-32 (1984).

[94] Bankruptcy Code § 502(g).

[95] Jason B. Binford, *Beyond Chimerical Possibilities: The Meaning and Application of Adequate Assurance of Future Performance under the Bankruptcy Code*, 18 Am. Bankr. Inst. L. Rev. 191 (2010).

It must:

- "cure" any pre-petition defaults;

- "compensate" the other party for damages it suffered as a result of these defaults; and

- "assure" that it will continue to perform, with "adequate assurance of future performance."[96]

Suppose, for example, that Franklin Manufacturing was leasing its computer equipment from CompuWorld Corp. and that Franklin failed to make two $10,000 rental payments in the months before its Chapter 11 petition. In addition, the debtor let the insurance policy it was required to maintain on the equipment, lapse. If Franklin wants to assume the lease, it must pay the past-due rent and reinstate the insurance policy (cure), pay CompuWorld interest on the missed payments (compensate), and provide CompuWorld adequate assurances that these and other defaults will not recur (assure).

If the debtor does not have the cash necessary to cure the pre-petition defaults and pay for the damages that the other party suffered immediately, the debtor may nevertheless assume the contract or lease if it is able to provide adequate assurance that it will "promptly cure" its defaults[97] and "promptly compensate"[98] the other party for its harm.

Providing adequate assurance of future performance may be difficult and is likely to require more than a simple promise.[99] The debtor-in-possession might be required to place sufficient funds in escrow to cover future rent and insurance payments or to obtain a letter of credit or guarantee that will ensure payment of sums that come due. In addition, the Code contains special rules for adequate protection of future performance with respect to shopping center leases.[100]

[1] Nonmonetary Defaults[101]

Many debtors' pre-petition defaults are monetary — the debtor missed a rental or other payment due under the contract. Other defaults arise from failure to perform a "nonmonetary obligation." Due to their very nature, some nonmonetary obligations cannot, by their very nature, be cured. For example, a commercial real estate lease may require the debtor to maintain regular business hours from 9 a.m. to 6 p.m. six days per week. If, as a cost-savings effort, the debtor did not open until noon on Saturdays for several month before its petition was filed, its failure to have done this cannot be cured. The default is a historical fact that cannot be undone

---

[96] Bankruptcy Code § 365(b)(1).

[97] Bankruptcy Code § 365(b)(1)(A).

[98] Bankruptcy Code § 365(b)(1)(B).

[99] *See* In re DBSI, Inc., 405 B.R. 698 (Bankr. D. Del. 2009).

[100] Bankruptcy Code § 365(b)(3). *See infra* § 11.07 Shopping Center Leases.

[101] Andrea Coles-Bjerre, *Ipso Facto: the Pattern of Assumable Contracts in Bankruptcy*, 40 N.M. L. Rev. 77, 101-105 (2010).

without a time machine.[102] As the court explained in *In re Deppe*:[103] "[t]he lapse in operations . . . took place. The estate simply cannot overcome that historical fact."

The 2005 Amendments addressed non-curable non-monetary defaults in real estate leases. Such defaults can be cured by taking action to resume performance at the time of assumption and compensating the other party for any harm caused by the breach.[104] Thus, the debtor need not turn back the clock; it is sufficient if it resumes performance going forward.

The new language does not apply to nonmonetary defaults of franchise agreements.[105] Nor does it apply to service contracts[106] or personal property leases.[107] It is unclear whether the new language applies to commercial real estate leases where the debtor's pre-petition breach was in connection with mishandling of goods it was required to purchase from the lessor, such as in *In re Deppe*, where a gas station breached its lease and supply contract with an oil refinery by mixing gasoline delivered by the refinery with fuel from another supplier.[108] Thus, the conflict in the circuits that led to the adoption of the new language may still need to be resolved.[109]

[2] Ipso Facto Clauses[110]

Ipso facto clauses purport to make the debtor's financial condition or the filing of bankruptcy a default that automatically terminates the contract or lease. Section 365(b)(2) exempts these types of default from the necessity of being cured.[111]

The same rules effectively apply with regard to the assignment of the contract or lease. To be assigned, the contract or lease must first be assumed properly.[112] This means that defaults, other than those under ipso facto clauses, must be cured. Moreover, whether or not there are defaults, the debtor must provide adequate

---

[102] *E.g.*, In re Claremont Acquisition Corp., 113 F.3d 1029, 1033-35 (9th Cir. 1997) (auto dealership ceased operations in violation of its franchise agreement). *See* James I. Stang, *Assumption of Contracts and Leases: The Obstacle of the Historical Default*, 24 Cal. Bankr. J. 39 (1998).

[103] 110 B.R. 898, 904 (Bankr. D. Minn. 1990).

[104] Bankruptcy Code § 365(b)(1)(A).

[105] *E.g.*, In re Claremont Acquisitions, Inc., 113 F.3d 1029 (9th Cir. 1992).

[106] *E.g.*, Matter of GP Exp. Airlines, Inc., 200 B.R. 222 (Bankr. D. Neb. 1996).

[107] Richard Levin & Alesia Ranney-Marinelli, *The Creeping Repeal of Chapter 11: The Significant Business Provisions of the Bankruptcy Abuse Prevention and Consumer Protection Act of 2005*, 79 Am. Bankr. L.J. 603, 625-26 (2005).

[108] 110 B.R. 898 (Bankr. D. Minn. 1990).

[109] *Compare* In re Claremont Acquisitions, Inc., 113 F.3d 1029 (9th Cir. 1992) (duty to cure applies to nonmonetary default), *with* In re BankVest Capital Corp., 360 F.3d 291 (1st Cir. 2004) (cure of nonmonetary defaults unnecessary). *See* David G. Epstein & Lisa Normand, *"Real-world" and "Academic" Questions about "Nonmonetary Obligations" Under the 2005 Version of 365(b)*, 13 Am. Bankr. Inst. L. Rev. 617 (2005).

[110] Andrea Coles-Bjerre, *Ipso Facto: The Pattern of Assumable Contracts in Bankruptcy*, 40 N.M. L. Rev. 77 (2010).

[111] Bankruptcy Code § 365(b)(2).

[112] Bankruptcy Code § 365(f)(2)(A).

assurance of future performance by the assignee of the lease or contract.[113]

[3]   Penalty Rates & Penalty Provisions

Some executory contracts, and many leases, provide for an increase in the price if the debtor falls into default. Thus, a commercial lease might provide for a 15% increase in the debtor's rent, if the debtor fails to make a timely payment or is otherwise in breach of the lease. Section 365(b)(2)(D) eliminates the necessity of satisfying this type of provision in order to cure a default.[114]

[C]   Restrictions on Assumption

Some executory contracts and unexpired leases cannot be assumed. If assumption is impossible, a Chapter 11 debtor-in-possession is unable to take full advantage of the favorable terms of the contract as part of its reorganization effort. At a minimum, the debtor must renegotiate the terms of the contract; at worst, the debtor loses the deal entirely. Further, because assumption is necessary for any assignment of the contract to a third party, an unassumable contract cannot be sold by a Chapter 7 trustee to obtain valuable cash to make payments to the debtor's creditors. Likewise, a Chapter 11 debtor-in-possession is unable to assign the contract to obtain cash to fund its operations or make payments to creditors upon implementation of the plan.

[1]   Pre-Petition Termination

To be assumed, the contract must remain in effect when the debtor's petition is filed. If the contract or lease has expired or has been terminated due to a pre-petition breach, it cannot be assumed. Thus, a three-year lease that expired a month before the debtor's petition was filed cannot be assumed. It is not an "unexpired" lease. Further, the lease may not be assumed if the lease has terminated and the debtor has been evicted before commencement due the debtor's default.[115] As one court explained: "[s]imply put, if a lease of nonresidential real property has been terminated under state law before the filing of a bankruptcy petition, there is nothing left for the trustee to assume."[116]

Most of the difficulty with respect to pre-petition termination deals with the effect of a pre-petition breach under applicable state law. First, not every breach gives the other party the right to terminate the contract. Second, lessors and other parties sometimes waive a breach, even though it was material and could have served as justification for termination. Third, the contract itself or governing law many give the debtor the right to cure the breach, even if it was material. But, if the contract terminated before the debtor's case began, it cannot be assumed.[117]

---

[113] Bankruptcy Code § 365(f)(2)(B). *E.g.*, In re DBSI, Inc., 405 B.R. 698 (Bankr. D. Del. 2009).

[114] Bankruptcy Code § 365(b)(2)(D).

[115] Bankruptcy Code § 365(c)(3).

[116] In re Windmill Farms, Inc., 841 F.2d 1467, 1469 (9th Cir. 1988).

[117] Moody v. Amoco Oil Co., 734 F.2d 1200, 1212 (7th Cir. 1984).

[2] Termination Under an Ipso Facto Clause

An ipso facto clause that purports to terminate an executory contract or unexpired lease automatically, based on the debtor's financial condition, commencement of its bankruptcy case, or the appointment of a custodian of the debtor's property, is ineffective.[118] Thus, the parties may not impair the effect of § 365 through a contractual provision that purports to end the contract at the outset of the debtor's bankruptcy case. The same rule applies to a provision in applicable law that would automatically terminate a contract under these circumstances.[119] Thus, lobbying groups may not seek relief from § 365 by appealing to state courts or legislatures.

[3] Anti-Assignment Clauses Ineffective

Many contracts contain provisions purporting to prohibit their assignment or delegation. In most cases, these clauses are ineffective to prevent assumption of the contract.[120] Thus, parties who are adverse to the risk of their long term contracts being assumed in a bankruptcy filed by their contracting partner may not sidestep the risk by negotiating for an anti-assignment clause in their contract. Rather, as explained immediately below, the contract must be unassignable *under applicable law*, without regard to whether it contains an anti-assignment clause, to be non-assumable.

[4] Non-Delegable Duties[121]

The Code prevents both assumption and assignment of a contract if applicable non-bankruptcy law[122] (usually state law) excuses the other party from accepting performance from or rendering performance to any person who does not consent to the assumption or assignment.[123] This applies regardless of whether there is a contractual restriction on assignment.[124]

Thus, § 365(c)(1) implements the staple rule of basic contract law that some duties cannot be delegated. These duties are often misleadingly referred to as "personal services." This is not quite accurate. Many personal services can be delegated; and, some non-delegable duties are not for personal services.[125] The real

---

[118] Bankruptcy Code § 365(e)(1).

[119] Bankruptcy Code § 365(e)(1).

[120] Bankruptcy Code § 541(c)(1), § 365(c)(1)(A).

[121] Daniel J. Bussel & Edward A. Friedlander, *The Limits on Assuming and Assigning Executory Contracts*, 74 Am. Bankr. L.J. 321 (2000); Michelle Morgan Harner, et al., *Debtors Beware: The Expanding Universe of Non-assumable/Non-assignable Contracts in Bankruptcy*, 13 Am. Bankr. Inst. L. Rev. 187 (2005); Michael J. Kelly, *Recognizing the Breadth of Non-assignable Contracts in Bankruptcy: Enforcement of Nonbankruptcy Law as Bankruptcy Policy*, 16 Am. Bankr. Inst. L. Rev. 321 (2008).

[122] This encompasses all law applicable to the particular contract, whether state or federal.

[123] Bankruptcy Code § 365(e)(2)(A).

[124] *E.g.*, In re Pioneer Ford Sales, Inc., 729 F.2d 27 (1st Cir. 1984).

[125] *E.g.*, In re Pioneer Ford Sales, Inc., 729 F.2d 27, 29 (1st Cir. 1984) (Breyer, J.) (automobile franchise).

issue is whether performance by a particular person or organization is a fundamental part of the bargain.

The personal nature of the services may make it clear that performance by a particular person is a fundamental part of the bargain. For example, if Radio Shack hires Bradley Wiggins to ride as the leader on its professional bicycle racing team, Wiggins could not file a Chapter 11 petition and assign the contract to actor Dennis Christopher (who starred in the classic bicycle racing movie "Breaking Away"), or the co-authors of this casebook, both of whom are old and slow. The identity and appearance of the professional athlete and his racing skill are fundamental parts of the bargain.

Of course, not many bicycle racing legends file bankruptcy petitions.[126] The issue is more likely to arise in other business contexts, such as the assignment of a franchise contract, a partnership agreement, or a trademark license.[127]

Even rarer than non-delegable duties are non-assignable benefits. There are now very few circumstances under which a party to a contract is prohibited from assigning the benefit of its bargain to another. Although Bradley Wiggins may not be able to delegate his duty to race in the Tour de France to Dennis Christopher, he would probably be permitted to assign his right to receive payment for one of his product indorsements to Merchant's Finance Company. Many of the few restrictions that still exist are nothing more than indirect ways of restricting improper delegations.

There are three distinct situations in which this issue arises with respect to assumption of executory contracts in a bankruptcy case: (1) performance of the contract by the debtor-in-possession; (2) performance of the contract by the trustee; and (3) performance of the contract by a third party. Technically speaking, the first two situations involve performance of the contract by the estate, following assumption of the contract, under the supervision of either the debtor-in-possession or the trustee. The third situation involves a two step process: assumption of the executory contract by the estate and its subsequent assignment to a third party.

In dealing with these contracts, the meaning of the precise text of the Code has proven quite elusive, leading to a serious division of authority with respect to the first of these three issues: whether a debtor-in-possession can assume and perform an otherwise non-delegable duty in a personal services contract.

---

[126] Notable counterexamples of TV, movie, and sports celebrities as well as political figures who have sought bankruptcy protection are: P.T. Barnum, Samuel Clemens (aka Mark Twain), William (Buffalo Bill) Cody, Texas Governor John Connelly (who was wounded in the JFK Assassination), Walt Disney, Mick Fleetwood (of Fleetwood Mac), Alan Iverson, Larry King, Cindy Lauper, Jerry Lee Lewis, Randy Quaid, Mike Tyson, Tammy Wynette, and both Ulysses. S. Grant and Abraham Lincoln (whose grocery store went bust).

[127] *See* Michelle Morgan Harner, Carl E. Black & Eric R. Goodman, *Debtors Beware: The Expanding Universe of Non-Assumable/Non-Assignable Contracts in Bankruptcy*, 13 Am. Bankr. Inst. L. Rev. 197 (2005); Michael J. Kelly, *Recognizing the Breadth of Non-assignable Contracts in Bankruptcy: Enforcement of Nonbankruptcy Law as Bankruptcy Policy*, 16 Am. Bankr. Inst. L. Rev. 321 (2008); David R. Kuney, *Restructuring Dilemmas for the High Technology Licensee: Will "Plain Meaning" Bring Order to the Chaotic Bankruptcy Law for Assumption and Assignment of Technology Licenses?*, 44 Gonz. L. Rev. 123, 158 (2009).

The relevant language is found in § 365(c):

> The trustee may not assume or assign any executory contract or unexpired lease of the debtor, whether or not such contract or lease prohibits or restricts assignment of rights or delegation of duties if:
>
> (1)(A) applicable law excuses a party, other than the debtor, to such contract or lease from accepting performance from or rending performance to an entity other than the debtor or the debtor-in-possession, whether or not such contract or lease prohibits or restricts assignment of rights or delegation of duties; and
>
> (B) such party does not consent to such assumption.

In parsing this language, it is critical to remember that a debtor-in-possession has all of the same rights, powers, and duties of the trustee.[128] This justifies substituting the phrase "debtor-in-possession" for "trustee" in the first part of this language. With this adjustment, the statutory language seems to say:

> The [debtor-in-possession] may not assume . . . any executory contract . . . if applicable law excuses [the non-debtor] from accepting performance from or rendering performance to [anyone] other than the debtor or the debtor-in-possession.

In other words, it establishes a "hypothetical test"[129] that asks whether the debtor could assign the contract to a stranger. If the contract could be assigned to the stranger, it can be assumed by the estate. If it could not be assigned to a stranger, it cannot be assigned to a stranger, and, more importantly, *cannot be assumed* in order to be performed by the debtor or the trustee. The plain language of the statutory text, which surely must be a mistake,[130] leads to the conclusion reached in cases such as *In re Catapult Entertainment, Inc,*[131] where the court said:

> Policy arguments cannot displace the plain language of the statute; that the plain language of § 365(c)(1) may be bad policy does not justify a judicial rewrite. And a rewrite is precisely what the actual test requires. The statute expressly provides that a debtor in possession "may not assume *or* assign" an executory contract where applicable law bars assignment and the nondebtor objects. 11 U.S.C. § 365(c)(1) (emphasis added). The actual test effectively engrafts a narrow exception onto § 365(c)(1) for debtors in possession, providing that, as to them, the statute only prohibits assumption and assignment, as opposed to assumption or assignment.[132]

---

[128] Bankruptcy Code § 1107.

[129] *See* In re W. Elec. Inc., 852 F.2d 79, 83 (3d Cir. 1988).

[130] *See* In re Hartec Enter., Inc., 117 B.R. 865 (Bankr. W.D. Tex. 1990).

[131] 165 F.3d 747 (9th Cir. 1999). *Ssee also* Allentown Ambassadors, Inc. v. Northeast Am. Baseball, LLC (In re Allentown Ambassadors, Inc.), 361 B.R. 422 (Bankr. E.D. Pa. 2007); RCI Tech. Corp. v. Sunterra Corp. (In re Sunterra Corp.), 361 F.3d 257 (4th Cir. 2004); City of Jamestown v. James Cable Partners (In re James Cable Partners), 27 F.3d 534 (11th Cir. 1994); In re W. Elec., Inc. 852 F.2d 79 (3d Cir. 1988).

[132] In re Catapult Entmt. Inc., 165 F.3d 747, 754 (9th Cir. 1999).

However, a majority of other courts, such as in *Summit Investment and Development Corp. v. Leroux*[133] and *Institut Pasteur v. Cambridge Biotech Corp.*,[134] have deployed an "actual test" that permits a debtor-in-possession to assume an executory contract, as long as the assumption does not actually require the other party to accept performance of the contract from a stranger.[135] These courts have generally permitted the estate to assume the debtor's executory contracts.[136]

Cases taking the first approach would prevent Bradley Wiggins, as debtor-in-possession, from assuming his own contract to race in the Tour de France. Cases taking the second approach would prevent Wiggins' bankruptcy trustee from assuming the contract[137] and would prevent him from assigning it to an actor, but would permit Wiggins, as a Chapter 11 debtor-in-possession, to assume the contract and participate in the race himself. This result reflects the likely intent of § 365.

In re Footstar takes a creatively different approach to the issue that reaches the same result as cases applying the "actual" test, but adopts reasoning that is compatible with both the general policy thrust of § 365 and its plain language.[138] Under this approach, as the plain language of § 365(c)(1) provides, a trustee may not assume a non-assignable contract, but the debtor-in-possession may. In reaching this conclusion, the *Footstar* court focused on the text of § 365(c)(1) which prohibits "the trustee" from assuming or assigning an executory contract if the non-bankrupt party could not be compelled to accept performance from a stranger to the deal. The court explained that this prohibition says nothing about the ability of a debtor-in-possession from assuming the contract, and that even though a debtor-in-possession's rights, powers, and duties are generally equated with those of the trustee, the DIP should not be regarded as the equivalent of the trustee for all purposes. Where it is the debtor who seeks to assume the contract in its role as debtor-in-possession, the proscription of § 365(c)(1) does not apply. Instead, assumption by the debtor-in-possession makes the debtor — and the debtor's estate — responsible for performance of the contract just as it would have been if no bankruptcy case had been filed. Although it has limited precedential effect, the *Footstar* approach has met with approval from courts[139] and commentators who have considered its reasoning.[140]

---

[133] 69 F.3d 608 (1st Cir. 1995).

[134] 104 F.3d 489 (1st Cir. 1997).

[135] In re Catapult Entmt. Inc., 165 F.3d 747 (9th Cir. 1999). *See generally* Daniel J. Bussel & Edward A. Friedlander, *The Limits on Assuming and Assigning Executory Contracts*, 74 Am. Bankr. L.J. 321 (2000).

[136] Thomas M. Mackey, *Post-Footstar Balancing: Toward Better Constructions of § 365(c)(1) & Beyond*, 84 Am. Bankr. L.J. 405 (2010).

[137] Whether the trustee could assume the contract and then assign it to herself is fun to consider, but it is difficult to imagine such a circumstance even occurring.

[138] In re Footstar, Inc., 323 B.R. 566 (Bankr. S.D.N.Y. 2005).

[139] In re Aerobox Composite Structures, LLC, 373 B.R. 135 (Bankr. D.N.M. 2007); In re Adelphia Comm. Corp., 359 B.R. 65 (Bankr. S.D.N.Y. 2007).

[140] David R. Kuney, *Restructuring Dilemma for the High Technology Licensee: Will "Plain Meaning" Bring Order to the Chaotic Bankruptcy Law for Assumption and Assignment of Technology*

The *Footstar* court's analysis notwithstanding, determining the meaning of § 365(c)(1) is made even more difficult by the trouble reconciling it with the text of § 365(f)(1), which is discussed in more detail below. Section 365(c)(1), just discussed, impairs efforts by the trustee or debtor-in-possession to "assume or assign" an executory contract or unexpired lease. Section 365(f)(1) on the other hand applies only to attempts to "assign" such a contract. It specifies: "[N]othwithstanding a provision in an executory contract or unexpired lease of the debtor, *or in applicable law*, that prohibits, restricts, or conditions the assignment of such contract or lease, the trustee may assign such contract or lease . . . ."[141] This language permits the assignment of a contract despite its non-assignability under relevant state or federal law. Moreover, it fails to recognize that such contracts must be assumed before they can be assigned[142] and that under the language of § 365(c)(1), they cannot be assumed. The two provisions are irreconcilable. Or, as the court in *In re Antonelli* said: "What section 365(f) appears to give, section 365(c) seems to take away."[143]

[5] Contracts to Extend Credit or Issue Securities

In contracts to make a loan or otherwise extend credit, the identity (and credit record) of the borrower is a fundamental part of the bargain. Although one might question whether this logic entirely applies to modern mass-marketed credit cards, the Bankruptcy Code draws no distinction between them and other extensions of credit. It explicitly makes all contracts to "make a loan, or extend other debt financing or financial accommodations . . . or to issue a security of the debtor"[144] unassumable, regardless of how they are treated outside of bankruptcy.

This limitation applies regardless of the presence or absence of language in the agreement regarding its non-assumability.[145] Moreover, because there is no provision in this subsection regarding consent, the prohibition applies regardless of the consent of the other party.[146] Of course, this does not prevent the lender and the debtor from entering into a new, post-petition credit agreement; that agreement, however, would nearly always require court approval.[147]

The limitation has been narrowly construed. It applies only when the focus of the contract is an extension of credit. For example, many contracts for the sale of goods or services, and virtually all leases, involve an extension of credit, because the buyer or lessee is not obligated to pay for the property or services immediately. But, the

---

Licenses?, 44 Gonz. L. Rev. 123, 149-54 (2009); Thomas M. Mackey, *Post-Footstar Balancing: Toward Better Constructions of § 365(c)(1) & Beyond*, 84 Am. Bankr. L.J. 405 (2010); Jay R. Indyke, Richard S. Kanowitz, and Brent Weisenberg, *Ending the "Hypothetical" vs. "Actual" Test Debate: A New Way To Read Section 365(c)(1)*, 16 J. Bankr. L. & Prac. 2 Art. 3 (2007).

[141] Bankruptcy Code § 365(f)(1) (emphasis added).

[142] Bankruptcy Code § 365(f)(2)(A).

[143] In re Antonelli, 148 B.R. 443, 447 (D. Md. 1992). *See also* RCI Tech. Corp. v. Sunterra Corp. (In re Sunterra Corp.), 361 F.3d 257, 267 (4th Cir. 2004).

[144] Bankruptcy Code § 365(c)(2).

[145] Bankruptcy Code § 365(c).

[146] In re Sun Runner Marine, Inc., 945 F.2d 1089 (9th Cir. 1991).

[147] *See supra* § 9.05 Obtaining Credit.

mere fact that a contract for sale of goods provides for thirty days' unsecured open account credit does not mean that the contract is non-assumable or non-assignable.

[D]   Executory Contract Ride-Through[148]

In Chapter 11 cases, a possible alternative to assumption or rejection, that is not specified in the Bankruptcy Code, but is nevertheless recognized in numerous cases, is to permit the unexpired lease or executory contract to ride through the bankruptcy proceeding unaffected, or in other words, to do nothing. This option is not mentioned in the Bankruptcy Code and "is purely a creature of case law."[149] It has been applied in cases where debtors, possibly through oversight, have neglected to take affirmative action to assume or reject an executory contract before their plans were confirmed. When this happens, the contract passes through the bankruptcy case completely "unaffected" by the bankruptcy.[150]

When the contract rides through bankruptcy, the other party may then enforce the contract, after the case is concluded, outside of the bankruptcy proceedings. With respect to the contract in question, it is as if the bankruptcy had never occurred.

However, this alternative is not universally accepted. Moreover, it is at odds with § 524 regarding discharge and the procedures required by § 524(c) for reaffirming discharged debts. It also conflicts with language placed in most Chapter 11 plans, purporting to reject any unexpired lease or executory contract that has not been assumed.

§ 11.06   ASSIGNMENT OF EXECUTORY CONTRACTS AND UNEXPIRED LEASES

If the estate may assume an executory contract or unexpired lease, a separate question arises over whether the contract may be assigned to a third party. Some contracts that may be assumed by the trustee or a debtor-in-possession may not be assigned to a stranger to the contract. Assumption by the estate and assignment to a third party are distinct events, and any effort to assign the contract must be evaluated independently from the question of whether the contract may be assumed.

[A]   Effect of Assignment

Assignment of an executory contract or unexpired lease operates as a novation of the contract. Section 365(k) makes this clear: "Assignment . . . relieves the trustee and the estate from any liability for any breach of [the] contract or lease

---

[148] Mark R. Campbell and & Robert C. Hastie, *Executory Contracts: Retention Without Assumption in Chapter 11 - "Ride-through" Revisited*, 19 Am. Bankr. Inst. J. 33, 34-35 (2000).

[149] In re Hernandez, 287 B.R. 795, 799 (Bankr. D. Az. 2002).

[150] Gray v. W. Envtl. Servs. & Testing, Inc. (In re Dehon, Inc.), 352 B.R. 546, 5601 (Bankr. D. Mass. 2006); In re Pub. Serv. Co. of N.H., 884 F.2d 11, 15 (1989).

occurring after [its] assignment."[151] This, of course, is quite different from the usual treatment of delegated duties under the law of contracts, where a person who delegates a duty remains responsible for performance unless the other party to the original contract consents to her release.[152]

For example, if Franklin Manufacturing Inc. enters Chapter 11, assumes its long-term sales contract with Industrial Supply Co., and assigns the contract to Hocking Fabrications Corp., Franklin is off the hook with Industrial Supply. If Hocking Fabrications subsequently breaches, Industrial Supply's only recourse is to recover from Hocking Fabrications. It has no claim against Franklin. Under state law, assignment of the contract to Hocking would not, all by itself, relieve Franklin of its obligation to Industrial Supply.

This is also quite different from the consequence if Franklin breached the contract after assuming it, without an assignment to a third party. In that case, Industrial Supply would not only have a claim against Franklin, it would have a § 507(a)(2) priority administrative expense claim, entitled to payment in full in Franklin's reorganization plan.[153] The disparity of treatment between breach after assumption and breach after assignment suggests the wisdom of delaying assumption until it is clear whether the contract will be assigned to a third person.

[B]   Restrictions on Assignment

The Code's language restricting assignments of executory contracts and unexpired leases is nearly incoherent. Section 365(f), which addresses assignments directly, must be read in conjunction with § 365(c) on assumptions. As explained below, the two sections do not fit well together.

[1]   Assumption Required for Assignment

Not surprisingly, the estate can only assign contracts that it has assumed.[154] This means that the Code's restrictions on assumption of an executory contract operate as restrictions on assignment of the contract. This includes the requirement of curing any defaults and compensating the other party for any damages it has suffered as a result of the debtor's breach. Thus, a contract remaining in default can neither be assumed nor assigned.

---

[151]   Bankruptcy Code § 365(k).

[152]   *See* Restatement (Second) of Contracts § 318(3) (1981); Jeffrey Ferriell, Understanding Contracts § 19.08[B] (2009).

[153]   Bankruptcy Code § 365(g)(2).

[154]   Bankruptcy Code § 365(f)(2)(A).

[2]   Assurance of Future Performance by the Assignee[155]

In addition, assignment to a third party is possible only if the assignee provides "adequate assurance of future performance" of the contract.[156] Significantly, the assignee must provide adequate assurance of future performance even if there has been no previous default. Thus, the Bankruptcy Code treats proposals to assign an executory contract or unexpired lease as if the proposal to assign the contract constituted the type of "reasonable grounds for insecurity" which, under non-bankruptcy contract law, gives the other party the right to demand adequate assurances of performance.[157]

[3]   Legal and Contractual Restrictions on Assignment[158]

The law regarding the effect of legal and contractual restrictions on assignments is a mess. The principle difficulty is in attempting to reconcile the conflicting language of § 365(c) with that of § 365(f). Section 365(f)(1) permits the trustee or debtor-in-possession to assign an executory contract "notwithstanding a provision in [the contract], or in *applicable law* that prohibits . . . the assignment."[159] Read in isolation, this seems to take a very liberal approach to the assignability of executory contracts and unexpired leases. If applied without consulting other provisions of the Code, it completely abrogates state and non-bankruptcy federal law that restricts delegability of contractual duties.

However, § 365(f)(2)(A) makes it clear that a contract may not be assigned unless it is first assumed.[160] Some courts take the view that § 365(c)(1) prevents assumption if the contract could not be assigned to a third party under applicable law. Where this is the case, a contract that is unassignable under "applicable law" (without regard to any contractual non-assignment provision) would not be assumable. Therefore, by default, the effect of § 36f(f)(1) would be *only* to override *contractual* non-assignment provisions. This distinction makes a fair amount of sense, preserving the value of the contract for the debtor, where applicable law would allow assignment, and preventing the debtor from contracting that right away prior to bankruptcy. Indeed, even the courts that apply the "actual" test would

---

[155] Jason B. Binford, *Beyond Chimerical Possibilities: The Meaning and Application of Adequate Assurance of Future Performance Under the Bankruptcy Code*, 18 Am. Bankr. Inst. L. Rev. 191 (2010).

[156] Bankruptcy Code § 365(f)(2)(B).

[157] *See* U.C.C. § 2-609 (2010).

[158] Daniel J. Bussel & Edward A. Friedler, *The Limits on Assuming and Assigning Executory Contracts*, 74 Am. Bankr. L.J. 321 (2000); Thomas H. Jackson, *Translating Assets and Liabilities to the Bankruptcy Forum*, 14 J. Leg. Stud. 73, 108 (1985); Morris W. Macey & James R. Sacca, *Reconciling Sections 365(c)(1) and (f)(1) of the Bankruptcy Code: Should Anti-Assignment Laws Prohibit Assumption of Contracts by a Debtor in Possession?*, 100 Comm. L.J. 117 (1995); Thomas E. Plank, The *Bankruptcy Trust as a Legal Person*, 35 Wake Forest L. Rev. 251, 290 (2000); Thomas H. Jackson, Translating Assets and Liabilities to the Bankruptcy Forum, 14 J. Leg. Stud. 73, 108 (1985). Even commentators who advocate a literal application of the mangled statute acknowledge that doing so is at best dubious from a bankruptcy policy perspective. See, e.g., Thomas E. Plank, The Bankruptcy Trust as a Legal Person, 35 Wake Forest L. Rev. 251, 290 (2000); Daniel J. Bussel, Edward A. Friedler, 74 Am. Bankr. L.J. 321, 339+ (2000).

[159] Bankruptcy Code § 365(f)(1) (emphasis added).

[160] Bankruptcy Code § 365(f)(2)(A). *See supra* § 11.06[B][1] Assumption Required for Assignment.

appear to agree that a non-assignable contract cannot be assumed if the debtor does not intend to perform the contract him or herself.

However, where courts apply the "actual" test, the asymmetry between 365(c) and 365(f) creates a potential linguistic problem. The debtor might assume the contract, proclaiming his or her intent to perform, and then later seek to assign the contract to a third party. This would violate the spirit of the statute, but might be approved by a court using a plain language reading of the statute.

Several courts have attempted to reconcile the provisions in the manner suggested above. In *In re Pioneer Ford Sales, Inc.*, an auto dealership sought authority to assume and assign its Ford franchise to a Toyota dealer, over the Ford Motor Company's objection.[161] Under applicable Rhode Island law, auto dealers could not assign a franchise without the consent of the manufacturer.[162] The court reconciled the two provisions by indicating that § 365(c)(1)(A) applies to contracts where applicable nonbankruptcy law prohibits assignment, regardless of what the contract says, while § 365(f)(1) overrides contractual provisions prohibiting assignment.[163] As commentators and several courts have pointed out, this is not what the statute says.[164]

Similar problems arise in connection with the enforceability of ipso facto clauses under § 365(e)(2). That section contains language similar to§ 365(f)(2) overriding an ipso facto clause only if "applicable law excuses a party, other than the debtor . . . from accepting performance from or rendering performance to the trustee or to an assignee."[165] Courts applying this language, like those interpreting § 365(f)(2), usually take a liberal approach to the question and preclude enforcement of the ipso facto clause against the debtor-in-possession, even if the other party could resist performance of the contract by a trustee or a third party.[166]

[C] Appeals of Orders Permitting Assignment

Once the bankruptcy court has issued an order authorizing assignment of an executory contract or unexpired lease, the assignee may rely on the court's order and begin performance. This makes appeals of a court's order permitting assignment problematic. Accordingly, orders approving the assignment of an executory contract or unexpired lease are stayed for ten days after they are entered.[167] This facilitates parties who oppose the assignment in seeking a longer stay while an appeal of the bankruptcy court's decision is pending.

---

[161] In re Pioneer Ford Sales, Inc., 729 F.2d 27 (1st Cir. 1984).

[162] The manufacturer could not, however, unreasonably withhold its consent.

[163] 729 F.2d at 28-29.

[164] In re Magness, 972 F.2d 689, 695 (6th Cir. 1992); Everex Sys. v. Cadtrak Corp. (In re CFLC, Inc.), 89 F.3d 673 (9th Cir. 1996); Daniel J. Bussel & Edward A. Friedler, *The Limits on Assuming and Assigning Executory Contracts*, 74 Am. Bankr. L.J. 321, 336-37 (2000); Theresa J. Pulley Radwan, *Limitations on Assumption and Assignment of Executory Contracts by "Applicable Law*," 31 N.M. L. Rev. 299 (2001).

[165] Bankruptcy Code § 365(e)(2)(A)(i).

[166] *E.g.*, In re Footstar, Inc., 337 B.R. 785 (Bankr. S.D.N.Y. 2005).

[167] Fed. R. Bankr. P. 6006(d).

§ 11.07 SHOPPING CENTER LEASES

Shopping center leases are singled out for special treatment. The Code's special shopping center provisions are designed to protect the shopping center from particular hardships they may suffer if an important tenant goes bankrupt. Among the many goals of those who operate shopping centers is to have the right mix of stores. The classic shopping center has one or more "anchor" stores (usually large all-purpose retailers) and a variety of specialized shops. Certain kinds of stores may be prohibited entirely; for example, many shopping malls prohibit liquor stores and adult bookstores on the theory that these detract from the family atmosphere they are trying to create. Also, shopping center developers frequently promise particular stores that they will be the only store of their type in the center. For example, in order to induce Famous Pharmacy to locate in the shopping center, Colossal Developer may promise the pharmacy that it will be the only pharmacy in the shopping center. If Sam's Sporting Goods goes bankrupt, and seeks to assign its lease to Discount Drug Stores, it will disturb the tenant mix and may create a violation in the lease agreement between Developer and Famous Pharmacy. Other considerations include common opening and closing times and avoidance of empty space. Nothing horrifies a mall manager more than the possibility of closed and shuttered shops.[168] Section § 365(b)(3) requires the debtor to provide the lessor with adequate assurance of a variety of matters:

- that there will be a sufficient source of rent and other consideration due under the lease;

- if the lease is assigned, that the financial condition and the operating performance of the assignee is similar to the financial condition and the operating performance that the debtor had when the debtor and the lessor entered into the lease;[169]

- that the percentage rent will not decline "substantially;"[170]

- that the assumption or assignment of the lease is subject to all the provisions of the lease, particularly those that deal with "radius, location, use, or exclusivity";[171]

- that there will be no breach of any provision contained in any other lease relating to the shopping center, any financing agreement relating to the shopping center, or any master agreement relating to the shopping center;[172] and

- that assumption or assignment of the lease will not disrupt any tenant mix or balance in the shopping center.[173]

---

[168] This is why vacant space, when it does exist, is usually hidden behind a facade.

[169] Bankruptcy Code § 365(b)(3)(A).

[170] Bankruptcy Code § 365(b)(3)(B).

[171] Bankruptcy Code § 365(b)(3)(C).

[172] Bankruptcy Code § 365(b)(3)(C).

[173] Bankruptcy Code § 365(b)(3)(D).

Note that these requirements are in addition to all of the other requirements imposed on an assuming or assigning trustee or debtor-in-possession, including the other requirements that relate generally to leases of real property.

Chapter 12

PRESERVING ASSETS: EXEMPTIONS & REDEMPTION

§ 12.01 DEBTOR'S RETENTION OF ESTATE PROPERTY

In Chapter 7 liquidation cases, debtors are supposed to give up their assets in exchange for being released from liability for their debts. However, debtors have never been required to give up all of their assets. Through several avenues, including exemptions, redemption, and reaffirmation, many Chapter 7 debtors are able to keep a large share, if not all of their assets.

Chapter 12 or 13 reorganization usually permits debtors to keep their non-exempt assets.[1] But this privilege does not come for free. Reorganizing debtors are required to use their future income to pay creditors at least what they would have received if the debtor's non-exempt property had been liquidated.[2]

Debtors who value their current assets more than their anticipated future income may find reorganization an attractive alternative. Debtors who either value their future income more highly than their current property, or who determine that they will be able to use their exemption rights to protect much of their current property from liquidation, will seek bankruptcy protection in a Chapter 7 liquidation case.

§ 12.02 EXEMPTIONS IN BANKRUPTCY

Bankruptcy Code § 522 permits bankrupt debtors to retain some of their property as "exempt" from liquidation by the trustee. Although exempt property is part of the debtor's estate, it is not available for sale by the trustee or for distribution to unsecured creditors.

However, exemptions do not generally impair the rights of creditors who hold liens on the debtor's property.[3] Thus, creditors with a security interest or mortgage on otherwise exempt property are normally entitled to enforce their rights against their collateral, despite the debtor's exemption rights.[4] For example, if Charlie owns a car worth $8000, subject to a security interest in favor of Olympic Bank, securing a $10,000 debt, Olympic can enforce its security interest in Charlie's bankruptcy

---

[1] *See infra* Chapter 18 — Rehabilitation of Individuals with Regular Income under Chapter 13.

[2] *See infra* § 18.08[E][1] Best Interests of Creditors; § 19.10[F] Plan in Best Interests of Creditors.

[3] *See generally* Owen v. Owen, 500 U.S. 305, 308-09 (1991).

[4] *See infra* § 12.05[B] Liens on Exempt Property.

case and recover the full value of the car, even though the Bankruptcy Code supplies a $3450 exemption for motor vehicles. Because the car is worth less than Olympic's secured debt, Charlie has no "equity" in the vehicle to exempt.

Exemptions are available only for an "individual debtor."[5] Corporations and partnerships enjoy no such rights. Thus, while exemptions play a significant role in consumer liquidation cases under Chapter 7, nearly all of which are "no-asset" cases,[6] they are rarely important in business bankruptcies.

Exemptions are also important in Chapter 13 rehabilitation cases. Although Chapter 13 debtors are generally permitted to keep their property regardless of whether it is exempt, exemptions have an effect on the extent of payments necessary to meet the "best interests of creditors" test for confirmation of a Chapter 13 plan. The best interests test requires Chapter 13 debtors to pay creditors an amount that is equivalent to what the creditors would have received in a liquidation case.[7] More generous exemption rights reduce the amount necessary to satisfy this test. Less generous exemption rights require debtors, or at least those who have more assets, to pay a higher price for their Chapter 13 discharge.

[A] Exemption Policy

Exemptions have been an integral part of debtor-creditor and bankruptcy law for many years. The underlying policy for permitting debtors to keep some of their property is simple: debtors should not be utterly deprived of the basic necessities of life. For this reason, creditors have long been prohibited from seizing such things as clothing, cooking and eating utensils, beds, linens, and other basic furnishings. Without these items, debtors are likely to become a burden on society in other ways. Moreover, sale of such items is unlikely to generate much value for creditors, and the debtor's cost of replacing these necessities is likely to far exceed any marginal payment to creditors that might result from their seizure.

For many years, exemption laws remained static. They preserved, in legal amber, a picture of nineteenth century rural American life, exempting a cow, a couple of pigs, a spinning wheel, a family Bible, and the like.[8] However, most states have now updated their exemption laws to reflect what are commonly regarded as the necessities of life in modern urban society. The most obvious example of this is the nearly universal inclusion of at least a portion of a debtor's equity in an automobile among the property that is exempt. Many modern exemption statutes

---

[5] Bankruptcy Code § 522(b)(1).

[6] When a Chapter 7 case is filed, the clerk of the court initially determines, based on the schedules filed with the debtor's petition, whether a "dividend" will be available for creditors. If not, Bankruptcy Rule 2002(e) provides that the clerk informs creditors of this fact in the notice that is sent to them, formally advising them of the bankruptcy case and alerting them that they should not bother to file a proof of claim. If the trustee subsequently determines that assets are available for distribution, a revised notice is sent that advises creditors of the ninety day deadline to submit proofs of claim. Fed. R. Bankr. P. 3002(c)(5).

[7] Bankruptcy Code § 1325(a)(4). *See infra* § 18.08[E][1] Best Interests of Creditors.

[8] Mich. Comp. Laws Serv. § 600.6023(1)(d) (LexisNexis 2012).

protect radios and televisions, and sometimes even personal computers.[9] Curiously, however, no special exemption has yet been carved out for cell-phones, MP3 players, GPS receivers, or tablet computers.[10]

Even in bankruptcy, exemption laws have traditionally been the province of state governments. Although many state exemption statutes are quite similar to one another, a few state statutes stand out as notably pro-creditor or pro-debtor. Florida and Texas are often singled out by critics as debtor's havens, permitting some debtors to exempt literally millions of dollars' worth of real estate.[11] However, in most states exemptions are relatively modest, protecting only basic items, such as clothing, limited furniture, appliances, and limited equity in a car and a home.[12]

There has been much debate over whether exemption levels matter very much either as an incentive to borrow or to default and file bankruptcy. Theoretically, generous exemptions should encourage bankruptcy, because they permit a debtor to discharge debt "cheaply"; that is, without the surrender of much property. However, there is surprisingly little evidence to support that contention. To the contrary, the evidence indicates that exemption levels have little or no impact on the frequency of bankruptcy.[13] This does not mean that there are no bankruptcies in which the debtor exploits generous exemptions; it merely means that the number of such bankruptcies is so small as to be statistically invisible. Nevertheless, widely disseminated publicity about even a few examples of abuse carries with it the potential to detract from public confidence in the bankruptcy system. Despite these concerns, the most recent round of revisions to the Bankruptcy Code left the most generous state exemption schemes largely intact,[14] though they did limit the ability of debtors to increase the value of their homesteads during the period immediately before their bankruptcy petition.

---

[9] Iowa Code § 627.6(5) (2012).

[10] Though exemptions for "a radio" might, in the right circumstances, be applied to these ubiquitous electronic devices.

[11] In Texas, debtors are permitted to exempt an "urban home" of land comprised of up to ten acres of contiguous real estate, together with any improvements that have been made to the land. Texas Prop. Code Ann. § 41.002(a) (Vernon 2000). Up to 200 acres of land, including a "rural home," may be exempted, though an unmarried adult is limited to a meager 100 acre ranch. Texas Prop. Code Ann. § 41.002(b). With respect to an "urban home," the Texas statute permits the exempted ten acres of homestead property to include a place to "exercise a calling or business" and thus does not limit the number of square feet of apartment or office space that might be part of the improvements to the urban home.

There is historical evidence that the Republic of Texas adopted America's first exemption statute as an inducement to settlers (immigrants?) from the United States. *See* Richard M. Hynes et al., *The Political Economy of Property Exemption Laws*, 47 J.L. & Econ. 19, 23 (2004) (citing Paul Goodman, *The Emergence of Homestead Exemptions in the United States: Accommodation and Resistance to the Market Revolution, 1840-1880*, 80 J. Am. Hist. 470, 477 (1993)). Thus it is possible that early Texas sought freedom, not from General Antonio López de Santa Anna, but from Chase Manhattan.

[12] *E.g.*, Ohio Rev. Code Ann. § 2329.66 (LexisNexis 2012 Supp.).

[13] Teresa Sullivan, Elizabeth Warren & Jay Lawrence Westbrook, As We Forgive Our Debtors: Bankruptcy and Consumer Credit in America 241-42 (1989).

[14] Margaret Howard, *Exemptions under the 2005 Bankruptcy Amendments: A Tale of Opportunity Lost*, 79 Am. Bankr. L.J. 397 (2005); Susan Jensen, *A Legislative History of the Bankruptcy Abuse Prevention and Consumer Protection Act of 2005*, 79 Am. Bankr. L.J. 485, 511-12 (2005).

[B] State or Federal Exemptions; Opt-Out[15]

Since the 1898 Act, federal bankruptcy law has largely left the level and extent of exemptions up to the states. The Bankruptcy Act permitted debtors to use the applicable state exemption statute to determine what they could retain in a bankruptcy case. This had the advantage of transparency to state law and thus limited forum shopping between state and federal courts. It had the disadvantage of limiting national uniformity, since exemptions differed so much from state to state. This non-uniformity has not, despite occasional challenges, posed any serious constitutional difficulties.[16] Unfortunately, it also had the effect of preserving exemption rules that were increasingly obsolete. Until recently, few states had amended their rules to account for the vast twentieth century migration of Americans from farms with horses, pigs and goats, to suburban tract houses with cars and garages.

In 1978, the drafters of the Bankruptcy Code were concerned that state exemption laws were too varied, too out of date, and too limited. There was some support for completely federalizing exemption law, but this turned out to be politically impossible. A compromise was reached that left ultimate control of debtors' exemption rights with state legislatures. The Bankruptcy Code now contains a set of federal exemptions and permits debtors to choose between the federal exemptions provided in the Bankruptcy Code or the exemptions authorized under state law. However, it also permits individual states to prohibit their residents from using the federal exemptions by "opting out" of the federal exemption scheme. Within a few years of implementation of this compromise, most states had opted out. Not surprisingly, the states that have not opted out are primarily those with more generous exemptions than those contained in what some had hoped would be a uniform schedule of federal exemptions. Thus, despite the Bankruptcy Code's list of exempt property, exemption law remains largely a state preserve.

In the opt-out states,[17] debtors may only use the state exemptions, plus a few related federal exemptions.[18] However, some courts have held that states may not

---

[15] Judith Schenck Koffler, *The Bankruptcy Clause and Exemption Laws: A Reexamination of the Doctrine of Geographic Uniformity*, 58 N.Y.U. L. Rev. 22 (1983).

[16] In re Sullivan, 680 F.2d 1131 (7th Cir. 1982). *See* Erwin Chemerinsky, *Constitutional Issues Posed in the Bankruptcy Abuse Prevention and Consumer Protection Act of 2005*, 79 Am. Bankr. L.J. 571, 592-95 (2005).

[17] States that have opted out are: Alabama, Arizona, California, Colorado, Delaware, Florida, Georgia, Idaho, Illinois, Indiana, Iowa, Kansas, Kentucky, Louisiana, Maine, Maryland, Mississippi, Missouri, Montana, Nebraska, Nevada, North Carolina, North Dakota, Ohio, Oklahoma, Oregon, South Carolina, South Dakota, Tennessee, Utah, Virginia, West Virginia and Wyoming.

[18] The federal exemptions that always apply are: civil service retirement benefits, 5 U.S.C. § 8346 (2006); Central Intelligence Agency retirement and disability payments, 50 U.S.C. § 2094 (2006); Congressional Medal of Honor winners' special pensions, 38 U.S.C. § 3101 (2006); fishermen, seamen, and apprentices' wages, 46 U.S.C. § 11109 (2006); foreign service employees disability and retirement benefits, 22 U.S.C. § 4060 (2006); government employees' disability and death benefits, 5 U.S.C. § 8130 (2006); longshoremen's and harbor workers' death and disability benefits, 33 U.S.C. § 916 (2006); military survivors' benefits, 10 U.S.C. § 1450(i) (2006); military annuities, 10 U.S.C. § 1440 (2006); military pension benefits, 38 U.S.C. § 5301 (2006); railroad workers' pensions and annuities, 45 U.S.C. § 231m (2006);

adopt special exemption statutes for use in bankruptcy, that are not generally available to their residents. To attempt to do so, these courts hold, would violate the Supremacy Clause.[19] However, a few states have adopted bankruptcy specific exemption statutes,[20] and some of them have been approved.[21]

In states that have not opted out, each debtor may choose either the state or the federal exemptions. The choice is all or nothing; a debtor may not "mix and match" his exemptions, choosing the most favorable state and the most favorable federal rules.[22] Moreover, if the case is a joint husband-and-wife bankruptcy, both must choose the same set of exemptions; if they cannot agree, then both are "deemed" to have chosen the federal exemptions.[23]

Opt-out affects only the list of exempt property. It does not affect other provisions of § 522. For example, even in an opt-out state, the Bankruptcy Code's rules permitting avoidance of certain liens on exempt property still apply.[24] In addition, married debtors are usually permitted to double the effective amount of state exemptions.

The federal exemptions have had an impact even in many of the opt-out states. During the 1980s many states updated their exemption statutes, often using parts of the federal exemption scheme as a model.[25] Thus, although the goals of those who wanted to federalize the exemptions available to bankrupt debtors were not fully achieved, exemptions today are considerably more modern and at least somewhat more uniform than they were before enactment of the current Bankruptcy Code.[26]

A number of opt-out states have adopted bankruptcy-specific exemption statutes that apply only in bankruptcy cases, but not in routine collection proceedings. States with these types of exemption statues have two sets of exemptions: one for

---

railroad workers' unemployment insurance benefits, 45 U.S.C. § 352(e) (2006); servicemembers' and veterans group life insurance benefits, 38 U.S.C. § 1970 (2006); student loans, grants, and work assistance payments, 20 U.S.C. § 1095a(d) (2006); social security payments, 42 U.S.C. § 407 (2006); veterans' benefits, 38 U.S.C. § 5301 (2006); and war hazard injury or death compensation payments, 42 U.S.C. § 1717 (2006).

[19] In re Schafer, 455 B.R. 590 (B.A.P. 6th Cir. 2011) (Michigan's statute); In re Applebaum, 422 B.R. 684 (B.A.P. 9th Cir. 2009) Oregon's statute).

[20] These include Arkansas, California, Delaware, Georgia, Iowa, Maryland, Michigan, Montana, Ohio, New York, and West Virginia.

[21] E.g., Sheehan v. Peveich, 574 F.3d 248 (4th Cir. 2009) (approving West Virginia's bankruptcy specific exemption statute).

[22] Bankruptcy Code § 522(b).

[23] Bankruptcy Code § 522(d). This provision was added by in 1984 to curb the then-existing practice of "stacking" exemptions — that is, each spouse choosing a different set to get the largest overall number and value of exemptions. Stacking still might be possible for married debtors who do not file jointly and whose cases are not ordered to be jointly administered.

[24] See Bankruptcy Code § 522(f). See infra § 12.07[B] Avoiding Non-Purchase Money Security Interests.

[25] See, e.g., Ohio Rev. Code § 2329.66 (LexisNexis Supp. 2012).

[26] See James B. Haines, Jr., Section 522's Opt-Out Clause: Debtors" Bankruptcy Exemptions in a Sorry State, 1983 Ariz. St. L.J. 1, 11-15.

use in state court collection proceedings and another for use in bankruptcy cases.[27] Courts that have addressed the constitutional propriety of this practice, under the Supremacy Clause, have taken differing views. Some courts have approved the practice, saying that § 522(b) grants state legislatures broad authority to opt out of § 522(d)'s "uniform" exemptions.[28] Other courts have held these types of exemption schemes unconstitutional, usually on the grounds that they depart from the scope of the authority delegated to the states, and thus violate the Supremacy Clause.[29]

[C] Debtor's Domicile Controls Exemptions[30]

State exemption statutes vary, and debtors may be tempted to change their residence to take advantage of another state's more generous exemptions.[31] However, § 522(b)(3) makes this extremely difficult. It requires the debtor to use the exemption statute in the state where the debtor has been domiciled "for the 730 days immediately preceding [the debtor's petition.]"[32] Thus, debtors who want to employ this tactic need to plan their bankruptcies well in advance. If the debtor has not been domiciled in the same place for the entire two-year period immediately before his petition, the Code applies the exemption statute of the state where the debtor lived for more than half of the 180 day period *before* the 730-day period.[33] Thus, if the debtor filed his petition on December 31, 2012, but lived in both Texas and Ohio during 2011 and 2012, the exemption statute where he lived for the last half of 2010 would govern. This might be Texas, Ohio, or somewhere else, depending on the debtor's residence more than two years before his bankruptcy case began.[34] Few debtors will be able to plan their bankruptcies this far in advance.

Debtors who move around a lot, and who have not lived in any one state for the two years before their petition, may find themselves ineligible for any state's exemptions. The 2005 amendments addressed this difficulty by adding language after the end of § 522(b)(3)(C),[35] permitting debtors who are otherwise ineligible

---

[27] *E.g.*, Mich. Comp. Laws. Serv. § 600.5451 (LexisNexis 2012).

[28] Sheehan v. Peveich, 574 F.3d 248, 252 (4th Cir. 2009).

[29] *E.g.*, In re Kanter, 505 F.2d 228 (9th Cir.1974); In re Regevig, 389 B.R. 736 (Bankr. D. Ariz. 2008) (California's exemption statute with wild-card exemption for double the amount permitted outside of bankruptcy); In re Pontius, 421 B.R. 814 (Bankr. W.D. Mich. 2009).

[30] Laura B. Bartel, *The Peripatetic Debtor: Choice of Law and Choice of Exemptions*, 22 Emory Bankr. Dev. J. 401 (2006).

[31] *See generally* John M. Norwood & Marianne M. Jennings, *Before Declaring Bankruptcy, Move to Florida and Buy a House: The Ethics and Judicial Inconsistencies of Debtors' Conversions and Exemptions*, 28 Sw. U. L. Rev. 439 (1999).

[32] Bankruptcy Code § 522(d)(3)(A).

[33] Bankruptcy Code § 522(d)(3)(A).

[34] *See, e.g.*, In re Stanton, 457 B.R. 80 (Bankr. D. Nev. 2011) (Nevada, where debtor owned a home, was her domicile, even though she had lived in rental property near her mother in Colorado for several years, where she regularly returned to Nevada to play bridge, filed her tax returns from Nevada, paid utility bills in Nevada, and regarded Nevada as her home the entire time she was away); In re Porvaznik, 456 B.R. 738 (Bankr. M.D. Pa. 2011) (debtor's residence with her husband in Louisiana, where husband was stationed in the military, did not mean that debtor was no longer domiciled in Pennsylvania).

[35] Bankruptcy Abuse Prevention and Consumer Protection Act of 2005 (BAPCPA), Pub. L. No. 109-8,

for any state's exemption statute to take the uniform federal exemptions in § 522(d). This could occur if the otherwise applicable exemption statute requires debtors to reside in the state to assert the exemptions,[36] or if the exemption statute does not permit debtors to exempt property located outside the state.[37]

A debtor's "domicile" is generally regarded as the place where the debtor actually resides if the debtor has a present intent to remain there.[38] A person's "residence" is considered as a less permanent place of abode.[39] For example, a few years ago, one of your co-authors resided in Seattle, Washington, for the better part of a year while he was a Visiting Professor at Seattle University. Throughout that time, however, he planned to return to Ohio, where his wife, his house, and his cats were permanently located. Seattle was his temporary residence, but not his place of domicile.

Not every state's homestead exemption applies to property located outside the boundaries of the state. Thus, a debtor who files a bankruptcy petition eighteen months after moving from Florida, might not be able to claim the nearly unlimited Florida homestead exemption, even though he is directed by § 522(b)(3) to use the Florida exemption statute.[40] Other states, that do not have express statutory prohibitions on the extraterritorial use of their exemption for residential real estate, would not result in the same difficulties.[41] If the exemption statute of the specified jurisdiction may not be applied to property in territory outside the state, the debtor might simply lose his right to an exemption for residential real estate. Alternatively, a court might draw an analogy to the last paragraph of § 522(b)(3) and permit the debtor to take an exemption pursuant to § 522(d).[42] Other courts have ruled that such territorial restrictions are preempted by § 522(b)(3) as they apply to debtors in bankruptcy proceedings.[43]

The 730 day rule can lead to anomalies. For example, in *In re Camp*, a Texas resident, who had not lived in Texas for the 730 day period before his bankruptcy petition, was required to apply the law of Florida, the state where he had lived for the majority of the 180 days before the 730 days prior to his petition.[44] Florida has opted out of the federal exemptions, pursuant to statutory language that prevents

---

§ 307(2) (2005). This is the other "hanging paragraph" added by BAPCPA. *See* Henry E. Hildebrand, III, *Getting Noticed: The New Notice Requirements of Section 342*, 13 Am. Bankr. Inst. L. Rev. 533, 538 n. 27 (2005). It should probably should have been designated as § 522(b)(3)(D).

[36] *E.g.*, In re West, 352 B.R. 905 (Bankr. M.D. Fla. 2006).

[37] *E.g.*, In re Adams, 375 B.R. 532 (Bankr. W.D. Mo. 2007).

[38] *E.g.*, Morad v. Xifaras (In re Morad), 323 B.R. 818 (B.A.P. 1st Cir. 2005).

[39] One of your co-authors temporarily resides each summer on the bucolic island of Martha's Vineyard, off the coast of Massachusetts, where he and his wife own real estate. He is domiciled elsewhere.

[40] In re Camp, 396 B.R. 194 (Bankr. W.D. Tex. 2008).

[41] In re Stephens, 402 B.R. 1 (B.A.P. 10th Cir. 2009).

[42] In re Adams, 375 B.R. 532, 533 (Bankr. W.D. Mo. 2007) (Missouri residents were unable to use the applicable Florida exemption statute for their Missouri residence).

[43] In re Garrett, 435 B.R. 434 (Bankr. S.D. Texas 2010).

[44] Bankruptcy Code § 522(b)(3)(A).

"residents of this state" from utilizing the exemptions in § 522(d).[45] But, nothing in Florida law prevents non-residents from utilizing the federal exemption statute, if it otherwise applies. Accordingly, the debtor was permitted to use the uniform Federal exemptions in Bankruptcy Code § 522(d), which were more favorable to him than either the Florida or the Texas exemption statutes, even though Florida law applied and even though Florida had opted out. The same result would have applied even if both Florida and Texas had opted out.

[D]   Joint Debtors' Exemption Rights

Married couples who jointly own their exempt property and who are jointly liable for their debts frequently file joint bankruptcy petitions. Their cases are nearly always consolidated for the purposes of administration and are effectively treated as if they were only one bankruptcy case.[46]

This nearly always permits married debtors to double the amount of any limit on the amount of their available exemptions. Thus, if both spouses are liable for the same debts and jointly own their exempt property, each debtor is entitled to his or her own separate exemption. For example, under § 522(d)(2)'s motor vehicle exemption, each debtor is entitled to a separate exemption for $3,450 in equity in a motor vehicle, effectively making up to $6,900 of the couple's equity in a car, exempt.[47] Of course, if the property is not jointly owned, but belongs to only one debtor, only that debtor may assert an exemption.[48]

This result applies because most exemption statutes are phrased in terms that permit an exemption to be claimed in "the debtor's interest in" the exempt category of property.[49] Section 522(d)(2), dealing with a debtor's exemption rights in a motor vehicle, supplies a good example. It exempts "[t]he debtor's interest, not to exceed $3,450 in value, in one motor vehicle."[50] State exemption statutes nearly always contain equivalent language.[51] If the state exemption statute only permits a married couple to assert one exemption, this result might not apply.

[E]   Exemption Planning[52]

Debtors with extensive non-exempt assets sometimes employ a variety of strategies in an effort to protect some of their property. Some debtors simply liquidate property that is not exempt and use the cash to buy items that fit an

---

[45] Fla. Stat. Ann. § 222.20.

[46] Bankruptcy Code § 302. *See supra* § 6.02[D] Joint Petitions.

[47] This amount is set to change every three years. 11 U.S.C. § 104(a) (2006). The next changes are slated to occur on April 1, 2013, 2016, and 2019.

[48] In re Steiner, 459 B.R. 748 (Bankr. D. Idaho 2010); In re Miller, 427 B.R. 616 (Bankr. N.D. Ohio 2009).

[49] *E.g.*, Ohio Rev. Code Ann. § 2329.66 (LexisNexis Supp. 2012).

[50] Bankruptcy Code § 522(d)(2).

[51] *E.g.*, Ohio Rev. Code Ann. § 2329.66(A)(2) (LexisNexis Supp. 2012) ("*The person's interest*, not to exceed three thousand two hundred twenty-five dollars, in one motor vehicle.") (emphasis supplied).

[52] A. Jay Cristol, William J. Cassidy & Alexandra Sarmiento Walden, *Exemption Planning: How Far*

exempt category. Other debtors try change their state of domicile before filing their bankruptcy petition, in an effort to take advantage of another state's more generous exemption statute. A few debtors seek to move their assets offshore, where they believe that neither the creditors nor a bankruptcy trustee will be able to reach them. Such strategies are sometimes successful, but are fraught with difficulty, including the risk that the debtor will be denied a discharge for having fraudulently transferred his property in an effort to "hinder, delay, or defraud, his creditors."[53] Moreover, the Code contains several restrictions that directly prevent the most extreme examples of these strategies.

[1]   Conversion of Assets to Exempt Status

Debtors with a surplus of non-exempt property sometimes try to expand their exemptions by converting non-exempt assets into types of property covered by an exemption. For example, the debtor in *In re McCabe* bought a $10,000 Belgian Browning shotgun, not because of his interest in hunting or his dedication to the Second Amendment, but because he knew that Iowa's exemption for a "family gun" had no dollar limit.[54] While debtors might be tempted to load up (so to speak) on exempt household furnishings, wearing apparel, or even pets, the limited value of these items, combined with what is usually a ceiling on the exempt value of such assets, usually makes these exemptions less attractive havens for protecting non-exempt property.[55] The debtor in *McCabe* found a category of exempt property without this type of restriction.

Exemptions for residential real estate, various retirement accounts, annuities, and life insurance sometimes contain very high or unlimited ceilings, making them them more attractive targets for debtors seeking to protect non-exempt cash.[56] For example, in *In re Jennings*,[57] the debtor, who was exposed to a $50 million uninsured personal injury judgment, bought a $925,000 Florida house and spent over $84,000 refurbishing it before spending another quarter of a million dollars making renovations to its adjoining airplane hanger. All of these expenditures were part of a scheme to shield his property from one large debt. Other debtors

---

May You Go?, 48 S.C. L. Rev. 715 (1997); Theodore Eisenberg, *Bankruptcy Law in Perspective*, 28 U.C.L.A. L. Rev. 953, 995 (1981); Juliet M. Moringiello, *Distinguishing Hogs from Pigs: A Proposal for a Preference Approach to Pre-Bankruptcy Planning*, 6 Am. Bankr. Inst. L. Rev. 103 (1998); John M. Norwood & Marianne M. Jenning, *Before Declaring Bankruptcy, Move to Florida and Buy a House: The Ethics and Judicial Inconsistencies of Debtors' Conversions and Exemptions*, 28 Sw. U. L. Rev. 439 (1999); Lawrence Ponoroff & F. Stephen Knippenberg, *Debtors Who Convert Their Assets on the Eve of Bankruptcy: Villains or Victims of the Fresh Start*, 70 N.Y.U. L. Rev. 235 (1995); Alan N. Resnick, *Prudent Planning or Fraudulent Transfer? The Use of Nonexempt Assets to Purchase or Improve Exempt Property on the Eve of Bankruptcy*, 31 Rutgers L. Rev. 615 (1978).

[53] Bankruptcy Code § 727(a)(2). *See infra* § 13.02[B][2] Fraudulent Transfers; Destruction or Concealment of Property.

[54] In re McCabe, 280 B.R. 841 (Bankr. N. D. Iowa 2002).

[55] *See, e.g.*, Ohio Rev. Code Ann. § 2329.66 (LexisNexis Supp. 2012).

[56] *E.g.*, In re Orso, 214 F.3d 637 (5th Cir. 2000) (annuities held not exempt); Hanson v. First Nat'l Bank (In re Hanson), 848 F.2d 866 (8th Cir. 1988) (debtor converted about $34,000 of non-exempt property to $31,000 of exempt property, consisting of a $20,000 exempt life insurance policy and an $11,000 payment on the mortgage).

[57] Jennings v. Maxfield (In re Jennings), 533 F.2d 1333 (11th Cir. 2008).

sometimes liquidate their non-exempt investments to pay off as much of their mortgage as possible, in order to take full advantage of their state's liberal homestead exemption statute.

The legislative history of § 522 seems to expressly sanction these types of pre-bankruptcy conversions. The House and Senate Reports accompanying the 1978 Bankruptcy Code contained the same language:

> As under current law, the debtor will be permitted to convert non-exempt property into exempt property before filing a bankruptcy petition. The practice is not fraudulent as to creditors, and permits the debtor to make full use of the exemptions to which he is entitled under the law.[58]

Despite this apparent legislative approval, debtors who get carried away with these strategies sometimes find it necessary to meet creditors' objections. Creditors sometimes object directly to the debtor's claim of exemption. On other occasions, they use the far more devastating strategy of seeking denial of the debtor's discharge.

Successful objections to the debtor's claim of exemption lead only to the debtor's loss of the exemption and thus put the debtor and his creditors back into the position they would have been in if the debtor had not embarked on his plan to convert his assets to exempt status. Debtors who have converted assets into exempt forms have had some success in meeting creditors' objections to their claimed exemptions, as bankruptcy courts are usually constrained to adhere to the exemptions provided by state law in the debtor's domicile.[59] Absent a limitation in the state exemption statute, bankruptcy courts are unable to restrain these tactics. However, creditors' objections sometimes result in limitations being imposed on the debtor's claim of exemption, particularly if the court finds that the debtor's actions were part of a scheme to defraud creditors.[60]

Debtors whose conversion of assets from non-exempt to exempt status was part of an effort to defraud creditors face more serious consequences. Section 727(a)(2) permits the court to deny the debtor a discharge entirely if the debtor "with intent to hinder, delay, or defraud a creditor . . . has transferred, removed, destroyed, mutilated, or concealed" his property.[61] A debtor whose global discharge is denied gains no relief from his debts. The risk of denial of discharge makes exemption planning risky business for debtors whose creditors may feel cheated by the debtor's scheme.

For example, the debtor in *In re Tveten* was denied a discharge after socking away over $700,000 in various life insurance and annuity contracts, which were fully exempt under his state exemption statute.[62] The debtor had moved otherwise

---

[58] H.R. Rep. No. 95-595, 361 (1977), *reprinted in* 1978 U.S.C.C.A.N. 5963, 6317; S. Rep. No. 95-989, 76 (1978), *reprinted in* 1978 U.S.C.C.A.N. 5787, 5862.

[59] *E.g.*, First Tex. Sav. Assoc., Inc. v. Reed (In re Reed), 700 F.2d 986 (5th Cir. 1983).

[60] *E.g.*, In re Lacounte, 342 B.R. 809 (Bankr. D. Mont. 2005).

[61] Bankruptcy Code § 727(a)(2). *See infra* § 13.02[B][2] Fraudulent Transfers; Destruction or Concealment of Property.

[62] Norwest Bank Neb., N.A. v. Tveten (In re Tveten), 848 F.2d 871 (8th Cir. 1989). The debtor was

non-exempt funds into these exempt resources in the last several months before filing his petition. In the notorious example of *In re Reed*, the debtor was denied a discharge after he held off his creditors' efforts to collect with a settlement agreement that held out the prospect of future payment and then liquidated nearly all of his assets, using the proceeds to build equity in his exempt home.[63] And, in *In re Jennings*, a debtor who bought a million dollar Florida home, and then spent considerable additional funds to renovate the property, was denied a discharge, when the court found that he had taken these actions in an effort to avoid paying a $50 million debt arising from a gunshot injury involving a defective firearm he had designed.[64]

Despite similar facts, other debtors have not been denied a discharge. During the fifteen days before filing their bankruptcy petition, the debtors in *In re Bowyer* used $24,000 in savings to reduce their mortgage, building exempt equity in their home in the process.[65] The debtor in *In re McCabe*, mentioned above, purchased a $10,000 "family gun" solely to take advantage of his state's liberal exemption statute.[66] Both of these debtors held on to their discharge.

The difficulty is in drawing the distinction between a debtor's intent to defraud his creditors in cases like *Tveten* and *Reed* and an honest effort to take full advantage of the reasonable expectations supplied by a state's exemption statute.[67] Most courts draw the distinction by inquiring whether there is "extrinsic evidence of fraud" beyond the conversion of assets to exempt status.[68] The debtor's conduct in *Reed*, enticing his creditors into a settlement agreement that he did not intend to perform so that he could obtain the time he needed to convert his assets, provides an obvious example of an overt act involving fraudulent intent. The exempt family gun in *McCabe* notwithstanding, some courts deny the debtor's discharge if the assets the debtor acquired prior to filing for bankruptcy seemed "unwise, uneconomical or unusual" for the debtor, apart from his attempt to protect his assets from bankruptcy.[69] These decisions make pre-bankruptcy planning a risky strategy. On the other hand, decisions like *In re Vangen*, permitting the debtor's conversion of $136,000 of nonexempt equity in her home into an exempt retirement fund, was regarded as part of an appropriate effort to ensure that she had funds available for her future retirement.[70]

---

facing over $19 million in liabilities as a result of a failed but highly leveraged real estate development project.

[63]　First Tex. Sav. Assoc., Inc. v. Reed (In re Reed), 700 F.2d 986 (5th Cir. 1983).

[64]　Jennings v. Maxfield (In re Jennings), 533 F.3d. 1333 (11th Cir. 2008).

[65]　932 F.2d 1100 (5th Cir. 1991) (en banc).

[66]　280 B.R. 841 (Bankr. N.D. Iowa 2002).

[67]　Martin Marietta Materials Sw., Inc. v. Lee (In re Lee), 309 B.R. 468 (Bankr. W.D. Tex. 2004).

[68]　In re Crater, 286 B.R. 756 (Bankr. D. Ariz. 2002).

[69]　Jensen v. Dietz (In re Sholdan), 217 F.3d 1006, 1010 (8th Cir. 2000) (evidence of fraud where debtor's acquisition of assets represented a "radical departure from his previous lifestyle").

[70]　In re Vangen, 334 B.R. 241 (Bankr. W.D. Wis. 2005).

Another risky approach that is deployed by some debtors is to transfer property into an offshore "asset protection trust."[71] These trusts are usually maintained in island nations that have established themselves as debtor's havens.[72] The debtor transfers his assets to the trust naming himself as beneficiary of the trust. The duties of trustee are shared by the debtor and the offshore organization, frequently a bank or trust company. Under the terms of the trust, the debtor has complete control over the trust assets unless an "event of duress" occurs. An attempted garnishment by one of the debtor's creditors or a turnover order by a bankruptcy trustee qualifies as an event of duress. When such an event occurs, the debtor is automatically removed as trustee and loses his right to control disposition of the funds. The purpose, of course, is to frustrate the efforts of U.S. courts to seize the debtor's assets to satisfy the claims of creditors.

While these mechanisms have protected debtors' assets from the claims of creditors, they have occasionally led to contempt citations,[73] and seem likely to result in bankruptcy courts denying debtors Chapter 7 discharges,[74] or refusing to confirm their rehabilitation plans due to lack of good faith[75] or otherwise.[76] The further possibility of criminal prosecution for bankruptcy fraud cannot be ignored.[77]

Alaska, Delaware and Nevada attempted to take advantage of the demand for "asset protection," by passing statutes that recognized self settled asset protection trusts as valid spendthrift trusts. The hope was that this would have the effect of excluding the assets in the trust account from the debtor's bankruptcy estate under § 541(c)(1). However, § 548 has since been revised to explicitly permit avoidance of transfers to a self-settled trust that are made with the intent to defraud creditors, regardless of whether these trusts are valid under state law.[78] Section 548 has always permitted the trustee to recover transfers made with the intent to hinder,

---

[71] *See supra* § 7.04[F][3] Offshore Asset Protection Trusts.

[72] *See* Elena Marty-Nelson, *Offshore Asset Protection Trusts: Having Your Cake and Eating it Too*, 47 Rutgers L. Rev. 11, 62 (1994) (indicating that "the Bahamas, Belize, Cayman Islands, Cook Islands, Cyprus, Gibralter, and the Turks and Caicos Islands" are popular offshore jurisdictions); *e.g.*, Marine Midland Bank v. Portnoy (In re Portnoy), 201 B.R. 685, 699 (Bankr. S.D.N.Y. 1996) (providing a history of debtor protection in the Channel Islands).

[73] FTC v. Affordable Media, 179 F.3d 1228 (9th Cir. 1999). *See also* In re Lawrence, 279 F.3d 1294 (11th Cir. 2002).

[74] *See infra* § 13.02 Denial of Discharge.

[75] *See infra* § 18.08[C] Good Faith.

[76] *See infra* § 18.08[E][1] Best Interests of Creditors.

[77] Two federal criminal statutes govern bankruptcy fraud. Section 152 of the Federal Criminal Code prohibits knowing concealment of assets in connection with a bankruptcy case. If the law of the offshore jurisdiction, together with the terms of the trust instrument, deprives the settlor-debtor of power to control trust assets, and if the debtor discloses the trust's terms to the bankruptcy court, it might be difficult to find that the debtor had "knowingly and fraudulently conceal[ed] . . . property belonging to the estate of the debtor." 18 U.S.C. § 152 (2006). Section 157 criminalizes a debtor's filing of a bankruptcy petition "for the purpose of executing . . . a scheme" to defraud. 18 U.S.C. § 157 (2006). Under these provisions, debtors who disclose their asset protection trusts are unlikely to face prosecution by the United States.

[78] Bankruptcy Code § 548(e)(1).

defraud, or delay creditors.[79] The most important feature of § 548(e)(1) is the preamble, which looks back ten years before the debtor's petition was filed, effectively expanding the scope of § 548 beyond the two-year period that applies to such transfers generally.[80]

[2] Federal Limits on Certain Exemptions[81]

[a] Limit on IRA Exemptions[82]

The Bankruptcy Code imposes only a few restrictions on a debtor's ability to assert the most generous state exemptions. Section 522(n) prevents a debtor from asserting an exemption in more than $1 million in an Individual Retirement Account (IRA), but allows this ceiling to be raised by the court "if the interests of justice so require." Moreover, it only applies to IRAs funded by the debtor's contributions. Because of the $4,000 annual limit on IRA contributions, it seems unlikely that many bankrupt debtors will accumulate enough funds in their IRAs for the limit to have any practical impact. Debtors with over $1 million in an IRA are more likely to have accumulated such a large amount as a result of a rollover of their more traditional pension benefits into an IRA. IRA's funded by contributions from debtors' employers are not subject to the $1 million limit.[83]

[b] Limit on Homestead Exemptions[84]

The Code also sets limits on pre-bankruptcy transfers that might otherwise dramatically enhance a debtor's homestead exemption. These limits, added in 2005, apply primarily to exemptions that would otherwise protect a debtor's residence, but also apply to burial plots.[85]

Section 522(o) prevents debtors from claiming an exemption in an otherwise exempt residence or burial plot that the debtor acquired any time during the ten

---

[79] See generally infra § 16.01 Purposes and Sources of Fraudulent Conveyance Law.

[80] Bankruptcy Code § 548(a)(1). The trustee might also be able to avoid a fraudulent transfer under state fraudulent transfer law, through Bankruptcy Code § 544(b). See infra § 16.01 Purposes and Sources of Fraudulent Conveyance Law.

[81] Juliet M. Moringiello, Has Congress Slimmed Down the Hogs?: A Look at the BAPCPA Approach to Pre-bankruptcy Planning,15 Widener L.J. 615 (2006).

[82] John Hennigan, Rousey and the New Retirement Funds Exemption, 13 Am. Bankr. Inst. L. Rev. 777, 796 (2005); Margaret Howard, Exemptions Under the 2005 Bankruptcy Amendments: A Tale of Opportunity Lost, 79 Am Bankr. L.J. 397, 417 (2005).

[83] Margaret Howard, Exemptions Under the 2005 Bankruptcy Amendments: A Tale of Opportunity Lost, ,79 Am. Bankr. L.J. 397, 417-18 (2005).

[84] Samuel K. Crocker & Robert H. Waldschmidt, Impact of the 2005 Bankruptcy Amendments on Chapter 7 Trustees, 79 Am. Bankr. L. J. 333, 349-54 (2005); Margaret Howard, Exemptions Under the 2005 Bankruptcy Amendments: A Tale of Opportunity Lost, 79 Am. Bankr. L.J. 397, 399-408 (2005); David M. Holliday, Annotation, Construction and Application of Bankruptcy Abuse Prevention and Consumer Protection Act's (BAPCPA) Limitation of Homestead Exemption, 11 U.S.C.A. § 522(p), 52 A.L.R. Fed. 2d 541 (2011).

[85] New §§ 522(o)(3) and 522(p)(1)(C) impose the same limits on exemptions for debtors' interests in a "burial plot," a somewhat more or less permanent place of either domicile or residence, depending on your perspective on other issues unrelated to bankruptcy law. Bankruptcy Code § 522(o)-(p).

years before his petition through the conversion of non-exempt property "with the intent to hinder, delay, or defraud a creditor."[86] This overrules decisions such as *In re Reed*, where the court felt constrained to allow the exemption despite the debtor's apparent fraud, because nothing in the state exemption statute that applied to the debtor's case limited the exemption.[87] But, it is not inconsistent with cases that take a traditional "badges of fraud" approach to whether a pre-bankruptcy conversion warrants denial of the debtor's exemption.[88]

Four requirements must be met to limit the debtor's homestead exemption under § 522(o): (1) the debtor must have disposed of property within the 10 years before his bankruptcy filing; (2) the property that debtor disposed of must have been nonexempt; (3) some of the proceeds from the sale of nonexempt property must have been used to buy, improve or reduce debt on a homestead; and (4) the debtor must have disposed of the nonexempt property with intent to hinder, delay or defraud creditors.[89]

In addition, § 522(p) prohibits debtors from asserting an exemption in a residence or burial plot if the interest was acquired by the debtor during the 1215 days (three years and four months) before his bankruptcy petition and exceeds $146,450 in value.[90] The dollar limit is doubled for joint debtors who co-own the property.[91] Debtors who have changed residences during the 1215-day period are protected, at least to the extent that they simply reinvested equity from their original residence into a new home during that period.[92] Otherwise, this limit applies regardless of the debtor's intent.

This new language impairs debtors' efforts to take unfair advantage of several states' highly favorable homestead exemption laws.[93] Courts have divided over whether § 522(p) applies in states that have opted-out of the federal exemption

---

[86] Bankruptcy Code § 522(o). *See* In re Maronde, 332 B.R. 593 (Bankr. D. Minn. 2005); In re Agnew, 355 B.R. 276 (Bankr. D. Kan. 2006).

[87] In re Reed, 12 B.R. 41 (Bankr. N.D. Tex. 1981).

[88] In re Wilmoth, 397 B.R. 915 (B.A.P. 8th Cir. 2008); In re Booth, 417 B.R. 820 (Bankr. M.D. Fla 2009) (debtor's action not intended to hinder, delay, or defraud creditors).

[89] Danussi v. Kaska, 424 B.R. 616 (N.D.N.Y. 2010); In re Presto, 376 B.R. 554, 568 (Bankr. S.D. Tex. 2007).

[90] Bankruptcy Code § 522(p)(1). The limit applies to four types of property interests that are potentially exempt under applicable state law:

> (A) real or personal property that the debtor or a dependent of the debtor uses as a residence; (B) a cooperative that owns property that the debtor or a dependent of the debtor uses as a residence; (C) a burial plot for the debtor or a dependent of the debtor; or (D) real or personal property that the debtor or dependent of the debtor claims as a homestead.

As with many other dollar figures in the Bankruptcy Code, the amount in § 522(p) is adjusted on April 1, every 3 years to reflect changes in the consumer price index. The last adjustment was in 2010 and it is scheduled to be adjusted again on April 1, 2013, 2016, and 2019. Bankruptcy Code § 104.

[91] Dykstra Exterior, Inc. v. Nestlen (In re Nestlen), 441 B.R. 135 (B.A.P. 10th Cir. 2010).

[92] Bankruptcy Code § 522(p)(2)(B); In re Wayrynen, 332 B.R. 479 (Bankr. S.D. Fla. 2005).

[93] Florida, Iowa, Kansas, South Dakota, and Texas, have no cap on the value of a homestead that may be exempted by their residents. *E.g.*, Fla. Const. art. 10 § 4(a)(1) (West Supp. 2006) (½ acre in town; 160 acres in the country); Iowa Code Ann. § 561.2 (West 1992) (½ acre in town; 40 acres in the country); Kan. Stat. Ann. § 60-2301 (2005) (one acre in town; 160 acres in the country); S.D. Codified Laws Ann. § 43-31-4

scheme.[94] Courts that have concluded that it does not apply in opt-out states, based their decisions on language in § 522(p) that imposes the limit only when a debtor exempts a larger amount of property "as a result of *electing* under [Bankruptcy Code § 522(b)(3)(A)] to exempt property under State or local law."[95]

In most states, debtors do not "elect" their home state's exemption statute. As a result of their state legislature's decision to "opt out" of the federal exemptions, they have no choice but to exempt property protected by their home state's exemption statute. Despite this suggestion, most courts impose the limitation on debtors in states that have opted-out of the uniform federal exemptions.[96]

In addition, courts have now ruled that the limit only applies to equity accumulated by the debtor as a result of transfers made by the debtor during the 1215-day period.[97] It does not apply to passive appreciation of the property due to market forces that increases the debtor's equity beyond the dollar limit established by § 522(p). Moreover, debtors who obtained title to the property more than 1215 days before their petition, but began using it as their residence during the 1215 period, are not subject to the limitation.[98]

A similar limit is imposed with respect to debtors who have been convicted of certain bankruptcy crimes, securities fraud, fiduciary fraud, or criminal, intentional, wilful, or reckless misconduct resulting in personal injury or death.[99] This limit applies regardless of when the debtor acquired the exempt property.

[F]   Effect of Debtor's Misconduct on Exemptions

Section 522(q) imposes limitations on the amount of exemptions for debtors who have engaged in certain types of misconduct. It limits the effect of some particularly generous state exemption statutes that provide debtors, even those who have committed securities fraud, breached their fiduciary duties, or committed heinous criminal and tortious acts, with virtually unlimited exemptions.

Under § 522(q), debtors are limited to an aggregate of $146,450 in exempt real estate if they have been convicted of a felony which demonstrates that their bankruptcy petition was filed as an abuse of the Bankruptcy Code.[100] The debtor's

---

(one acre in town; 160 acres in the country); Texas Prop. Code Ann. § 42.001(a) (Vernon 2000) (10 acres in town; 200 acres in the country).

[94] *Compare* In re Summers, 344 B.R. 108 (Bankr. D. Ariz. 2006), *and* In re Kane, 336 B.R. 477 (Bankr. D. Nev. 2006) (applies in both opt-out and non opt-out states), *with* In re McNabb, 326 B.R. 785 (Bankr. D. Ariz. 2005) (does not apply in non opt-out states).

[95] In re McNabb, 326 B.R. 785, 788 (Bankr. D. Ariz. 2005).

[96] In re Summers, 344 B.R. 108 (Bankr. D. Ariz. 2006) (collecting cases); In re Kaplan, 331 B.R. 483 (Bankr. S.D. Fla. 2005); In re Virissimo, 332 B.R. 201 (Bankr. D. Nev. 2005).

[97] *E.g.*, In re Rasmussen, 349 B.R. 747 (Bankr. M.D. Fla. 2006); Wallace v. Rogers (In re Rogers), 354 B.R. 792 (N.D. Tex. 2006). *See also* Parks v. Anderson, 406 B.R. 79, 95 (D. Kan. 2009).

[98] Greene v. Savage (In re Greene), 583 B.R. 614 (9th Cir. 2009).

[99] Bankruptcy Code § 522(q).

[100] Bankruptcy Code § 522(q)(1)(A). This is adjusted on April 1, every 3 years to reflect changes in the consumer price index. The last adjustment was in 2010 and it is scheduled to be adjusted again on April 1, 2013, 2016, and 2019. Bankruptcy Code § 104.

state exemptions are similarly limited if the debtor "owes a debt arising from" state or federal securities fraud,[101] fiduciary fraud,[102] RICO violation,[103] or "any criminal act, intentional tort, or wilful and reckless misconduct that caused serious physical injury or death to another individual in the preceding 5 years."[104] The only exception for this limitation is where state exemptions are reasonably necessary for the support of the debtor and any dependent of the debtor.

§ 12.03 TYPES OF EXEMPTIONS

A wide variety of exemptions are available under both the Bankruptcy Code and under applicable state law. Any effort to catalog them all would be beyond the scope of this book. Instead, we provide a general description of the most important categories of exempt property available under both Bankruptcy Code § 522(d) and many modern state exemption statutes.

[A] Residential Property — Homestead Exemptions

An exemption for property used as the debtor's residence is available in all states. In most jurisdictions, the exemption applies to either real or personal property used as a residence, avoiding questions about whether motor homes or interests in a "cooperative" are real or personal property.[105] The exemption has been applied to a wide variety of types of personal property that a debtor uses as a residence, including boats,[106] trucks, and buses.[107] As the court in *In re McClain*, explained: "so long as a debtor actually lived on real property being claimed as exempt, a non-exempt tree-house or tent would establish the requisite degree of permanency."[108] The homestead exemption is extended to any "burial plot" owned by the debtor.[109]

Most states impose a dollar limit on the value of the debtor's interest that may be exempt, though the range of these limits is considerable, extending from only

---

[101] *Id.* § 522(q)(B)(i).

[102] *Id.* § 522(q)(B)(ii).

[103] *Id.* § 522(q)(B)(iii).

[104] *Id.* § 522(q)(B)(iv).

[105] The Bankruptcy Code's homestead exemption is illustrative. It exempts the debtor's interest in:

> real property or personal property that the debtor or a dependent of the debtor uses as a residence, in a cooperative that owns property that the debtor or a dependent of the debtor uses as a residence, or in a burial plot for the debtor or a dependent of the debtor.

Bankruptcy Code § 522(d)(1). *See also* Ohio Rev. Code Ann. § 2329.66(A)(1)(b) (LexisNexis Supp. 2012) ("the person's interest, not to exceed twenty thousand two hundred dollars, in one parcel or item of real or personal property that the person or a dependent of the person uses as a residence.").

[106] *Compare* In re Ross, 210 B.R. 320 (Bankr. N.D. Ill 1997) (fishing boat exempt as residence), *with* Norris v. Thomas, 215 S.W.3d 851 (Tex. 2007) (yacht not a homestead).

[107] In re Tullar, 434 B.R. 69 (Bankr. W.D.N.Y. 2010).

[108] In re McClain, 281 B.R. 769 (Bankr. M.D. Fla. 2002).

[109] *See* Bankruptcy Code § 522(d)(1). There is no requirement that the debtor *reside* in his burial plot. Many other states have separate exemptions for burial plots.

$5,000 in Alabama[110] and Tennesee,[111] to $75,000 in California,[112] $150,000 in Arizona,[113] and $500,000 in Massachusetts.[114] The Bankruptcy Code's residential property exemption stands at $21,625, but is slated, together with all other dollar limits on debtors' uniform federal exemption rights, to be increased on April 1, 2013 and every three years afterward to reflect inflation as measured by the U.S. Department of Labor's Consumer Price Index.[115] Dollar limits on most state exemptions are not subject to this periodic increase. In Texas and Florida, long regarded as debtor's havens, the limit is virtually nonexistent, with Texas domiciliaries enjoying protection for residential real estate and improvements in an urban area of up to ten contiguous acres, and in a rural area of up to either 100 or 200 acres, depending on whether the debtor is single or part of a "family." The Florida Constitution is less generous, only permitting Florida residents to exempt up to one-half acre of an urban residence or 160 acres of a rural homestead, without regard to the debtor's marital status.[116]

Like other exemptions, the homestead exemption does not give the debtor any guarantee of keeping his home. Indeed, in most cases, it will not. The debtor must still deal with the mortgage debt, if any, and must also purchase any excess equity above the amount of the available exemption. That excess equity belongs to his bankruptcy estate and will be distrbiuted, after sale of the debtor's home, to unsecured creditors.

For example, if a debtor's home is worth $100,000, but is subject to a $75,000 mortgage, the debtor has $25,000 equity in the house. If the applicable exemption statute protects only $15,000 of that equity, an additional $10,000 of "non-exempt equity" remains. Funds received from the sale are first distributed to satisfy the mortgage, second to fulfill the debtor's exemption rights, and third to distribute to other creditors.

In situations like this, the debtor must make some deal with both the mortgage holder and the trustee in order to keep his home. This could theoretically be accomplished through refinancing or via a combination of reaffirmation of the debt with the mortgagee and the sale of other exempt property to pay the trustee the amount of the non-exempt equity to which the estate is entitled. Anecdotal evidence indicates that trustees are generally willing to sell the excess equity to the debtor, as long as the debtor is willing to pay its full value. But if the excess is large, it may be impossible for the debtor to raise enough money to purchase it.

Debtors with excess equity in their homes are more likely to find it useful to file a Chapter 13 plan. However, the viability of this strategy depends on whether the debtor has enough income to make his house payments and other payments under

---

[110] Ala. Code § 6-10-2.

[111] Tenn. Code Ann. § 26-2-301 (LexisNexis Supp. 2005).

[112] Cal. Civ. Proc. Code § 704.730(a)(3) (West Supp. 2006).

[113] Ariz. Rev. Stat. Ann. § 33-1101(A) (2000).

[114] Mass Gen. Laws. Ann. ch. 188 § 1 (West Supp. 2006).

[115] Bankruptcy Code § 104.

[116] *See* Peter Currin, *Florida's Homestead Exemption: Does This Chameleon Ever Die?*, 50 U. Fla. L. Rev. 573 (1998).

the plan. Debtors with inadequate income will run afoul of the requirement that their plans be "feasible."[117]

Likewise, if the house in the above example is only worth $80,000, the debtor may not enjoy the full extent of his $15,000 exemption, as all but $5,000 of the value of the property is consumed by the mortgage.[118] Debtors in this situation may be able, as described in the following section, to apply some or all of the unused portion of their homestead exemption to protect other assets.[119]

[B] Wildcard Exemptions[120]

Some jurisdictions provide debtors with a so-called "wildcard" exemption, permitting the debtor to exempt a limited value of *any* property, without the necessity of limiting the exemption to a legislatively approved list of specific assets.[121] For example, § 522(d)(5) provides an exemption of $1,150 for the debtor's interest in "any property."[122] These types of exemption statutes provide a supplemental exemption in addition to the exemptions for specific but limited types of property.[123] Thus, an avid bicyclist might use this provision to protect one or several of his bicycles, even though the exemption statute otherwise does not protect sporting goods or does not protect them to this extent.[124]

Under some state exemption statutes and under the Bankruptcy Code's uniform federal residential exemption, debtors are not required to use their homestead exemption to protect equity in a residence but may instead apply all or some of their unused homestead exemption to other non-exempt property.[125] When available, this type of provision enhances whatever wildcard exemption might otherwise be provided.

Section 522(d)(5) permits this in states that have not opted out. In those states, debtors can to use up to $10,825 of the unused portion of his homestead exemption to protect the debtor's interest "in any property."[126] This provides debtors with less than the full amount of equity protected by the homestead exemption, with some flexibility in the use of their exemption. Under § 522(d)(5), a debtor with only

---

[117] Bankruptcy Code § 1325(a)(6). *See infra* § 18.08[B] Feasibility.

[118] *See infra* § 12.05[B] Liens on Exempt Property.

[119] *See infra* § 12.03[B] Wildcard Exemptions.

[120] Stephen F. Yunke, Comment, *The General Exemption of Section 522(d)(5) of the 1978 Bankruptcy Code*, 49 U. Chi. L. Rev. 564 (1982).

[121] *E.g.*, Tex. Prop. Code Ann. § 42.001(a) (Vernon 2000) ($60,000 for a family; $30,000 for a single adult).

[122] Bankruptcy Code § 522(d)(5). This amount is scheduled to be adjusted in 2013, 2016, and 2019, in accordance with Bankruptcy Code § 104, to reflect changes in the consumer price index.

[123] *See also, e.g.*, Ohio Rev. Code Ann. § 6323.66(A) (LexisNexis Supp. 2012); Cal. Civ. Proc. Code §§ 704.010-704.200 (West Supp. 2006).

[124] Both of your authors have invested in bicycles with values exceeding this amount. With twelve of them in his basement, one of your authors has invested in bicycles considerably beyond this amount.

[125] *See also, e.g.*, Ohio Rev. Code Ann. § 2329.66(A)(4) (LexisNexis Supp. 2012).

[126] Bankruptcy Code § 522(d)(5). This amount is scheduled to be adjusted in 2013, 2016, and 2019, in accordance with Bankruptcy Code § 104, to reflect changes in the consumer price index.

$10,000 equity in a home could use Bankruptcy Code § 522(d)(1) to exempt this equity and apply $11,525 of the remaining unused $11,625 homestead exemption, together with the $1150 general wildcard to exempt property not covered by other exemptions. This amount might also be used to protect other property in which the debtor has too much equity, such as a car worth more than the $3450 currently protected by Bankruptcy Code § 522(d)(2).[127]

These types of provisions also provide some measure of protection for renters. At the same time, however, it reflects the strong societal preference for home-ownership, by giving renters only half of the exemption that is available to homeowners. Similar provisions exist in some state exemption schemes.[128]

[C]　Exemptions for Personal Property

Not surprisingly, most exemption statutes permit debtors to exempt a wide array of items of personal property commonly found in nearly all of our homes. These usually include clothes, furniture, appliances, and similar household items. There is usually both a per-item and aggregate limit on the value of these items that can be claimed as exempt.[129]

[1]　Categories of Exempt Property

Bankruptcy Code § 522(d)(3) is a typical example of an exemption for personal, family, and household items. It protects

> [t]he debtor's interest, not to exceed $550 in value in any particular item or $11,525 in aggregate value, in household furnishings, household goods, wearing apparel, appliances, books, animals, crops, or musical instruments that are held primarily for the personal, family, or household use of the debtor or a dependent of the debtor.[130]

Given the low value of most household items, this and similar state exemptions permit most debtors to keep virtually all of their clothes, furniture, and appliances.

Exemption statutes typically protect a debtor's interest in limited value in a "motor vehicle."[131] Here, however, there is wide disparity, with some jurisdictions protecting as much as $20,000 equity in a car[132] and some others protecting

---

[127] This amount is scheduled to be adjusted in 2013, 2016, and 2019, in accordance with Bankruptcy Code § 104, to reflect changes in the consumer price index.

[128] *See, e.g.*, Ohio Rev. Code Ann. § 2329.66(A)(4) (LexisNexis Supp. 2012).

[129] Without an aggregate limit, debtors may be able to protect a treasure trove of smaller items. *E.g.*, In re Wahl, 14 B.R. 153 (Bankr. E.D. Wis. 1981) ($6,000 worth of silverware exempt under earlier version of § 522(d) limiting the debtor's exemption to $200 per item, without regard to the number of related items claimed).

[130] Bankruptcy Code § 522(d)(3). These amount are scheduled to be adjusted in 2013, 2016, and 2019, in accordance with Bankruptcy Code § 104, to reflect changes in the consumer price index.

[131] *E.g.*, Bankruptcy Code § 522(d)(2) (currently $3450).

[132] Kan. Stat. Ann. § 60-2304(c) (2005). Married debtors in Texas can exempt a whopping $60,000 in a car, providing they claim no other personal property as exempt. Tex. Prop. Code. Ann. §§ 42.001(a), 42.002 (Vernon 2000).

significantly less.[133] As with other exemptions, the protection does not extend to value that is subject to an outstanding consensual security interest. Thus, debtors who wish to keep their automobiles, trucks, buses, and motor scooters must frequently enter into some sort of arrangement with their secured creditors to be able to retain the asset after their bankruptcy.

Exemptions are typically also provided, usually subject to both per-item and possibly aggregate value restrictions, for jewelry[134] and tools of a debtor's trade, business, or profession.[135] Nearly all jurisdictions[136] provide an unlimited exemption for professionally prescribed heath aids,[137] though some statutes provide an exemption for such items if they are either "professionally prescribed" *or* "medically necessary."[138] The exemption is most commonly used to exempt wheelchairs, valuable medications, eyeglasses, and hearing aids (which are more expensive than you imagine), but is sometimes used to protect more valuable assets, including vans equipped with devices to facilitate those with physical disabilities,[139] and in one instance, a condominium apartment.[140]

Likewise, most exemption statutes protect the debtor's interest in a "burial plot,"[141] presumably to prevent creditors from frustrating debtors' efforts to be laid to rest in plots adjoining loved ones rather than to ensure that they are not relegated to a pauper's funeral. After 2005, these exempted interests are limited, together with interests in the debtor's homestead, to a ceiling of $146,450, to the extent the interest was acquired by the debtor within the 1215-day period before the filing of his bankruptcy petition.[142] Moreover, the entire exemption can be

---

[133] In most states, the amount seems to be between $2000-3,000, with a few up in the $5,000 range. *See* John H. Williamson, The Attorney's Handbook on Consumer Bankruptcy and Chapter 13, Appendix III — Exempt Property (2005 ed.).

[134] Bankruptcy Code § 522(d)(4) ($1,450 aggregate limit). *See also* Ohio Rev. Code Ann. § 6323(A)(4)(b) (LexisNexis Supp. 2012) ("one or more items of jewelry, not to exceed one thousand three hundred fifty dollars . . . .").

[135] *E.g.*, Bankruptcy Code § 522(d)(6) ($1,850 aggregate limit for "implements, professional books, or tools of the trade of the debtor or [his] dependent."); Ohio Rev. Code Ann. § 2329.66(A)(5) (LexisNexis Supp. 2012) ($2,025 "in all implements, professional books, or tools of the person's profession, trade, or business, including agriculture").

[136] Such an exemption is conspicuously missing from the exemption statutes in Delaware. One sometimes wonders what wheel-chair bound debtors do in states without such an exemption. Such items might be claimed as "furniture" or even "wearing apparel."

[137] Bankruptcy Code § 522(d)(9).

[138] Ohio Rev. Code Ann. § 2329.66(A)(7) (LexisNexis Supp. 2012) ("professionally prescribed *or* medically necessary health aids") (emphasis added).

[139] *See* In re Reardon, 403 B.R. 822, 830 (Bankr. D. Mont. 2009) (van); In re Allard, 342 B.R. 102 (Bankr. M.D. Fla.2005) (van); In re Johnson, 101 B.R. 280 (Bankr. W.D. Okla.1989) (water treatment system).

[140] *See* In re Man, 428 B.R. 644 (Bankr. M.D.N.C. 2010) (condominium, which debtor had extensively renovated as directed by her physician to ensure that she was living in a chemical-free "safe environment" to mitigate her extreme sensitivity to environmental irritants, was exempt as professionally prescribed and medically necessary under applicable state exemption statute).

[141] *E.g.*, Bankruptcy Code § 522(d)(1) (part of the homestead exemption); Ohio Rev. Code § 2329.66(A)(8) (LexisNexis Supp. 2012).

[142] *See* Bankruptcy Code § 522(p)(1)(C).

denied if the debtor acquired the interest in the burial plot within the ten-year period before his bankruptcy petition with the intent to "hinder, delay, or defraud a creditor."[143]

[2] Categorization Issues

The detail included in many exemption statutes inevitably leads to curious and sometimes amusing categorization issues.[144] For example, the absence of a value limitation on the exemption for wearing apparel or household goods, combined with a meaningful limit on the exemption for jewelry, might lead to questions over whether a Rolex watch is more properly characterized as wearing apparel or jewelry.[145] Numerous cases have addressed the question of whether cameras qualify as the type of household goods that are typically exempt either with or without a limit on their value.[146] Similarly, aggressive trustees have sometimes raised questions about whether ATVs[147] buses,[148] boats, motorcycles,[149] riding lawn mowers,[150] tractors,[151] and airplanes[152] qualify as either a "motor vehicle" or an "automobile," with varying results. For example, in *In re McMillin* the debtor successfully contended that his collection of unassembled parts for an antique Model A Ford, that the debtor hoped one day to assemble, qualified as a "motor vehicle" for the purposes of the debtor's state exemption statute.[153]

Due to the wide variety of terminology used in exemption statutes, it is difficult to draw broad conclusions about the proper characterization of specific items. Generally, however, courts are reluctant to permit items to be claimed as exempt under a general category when it also fits within a more specific class of exempt property. Thus, items regarded as jewelry do not ordinarily qualify as wearing

---

[143] Bankruptcy Code § 522(o).

[144] *See* In re Wilkinson, M.D., 402 B.R. 756 (Bankr. W.D. Texas 2009) (debtor's antique guns retained their status as "firearms" despite being mounted on plaques and hung on the walls of the debtor's home).

[145] *Compare* In re Lynch, 139 B.R. 868 (Bankr. N.D. Ohio 1992) (separate exemption for jewelry prevents its characterization as household goods), *with* In re Stanhope, 76 B.R. 165, (Bankr. D. Mont. 1987) ($5,000 Rolex watch exempt as "wearing apparel" absent evidence that it had been purchased for investment purposes). One of your co-authors wears a geeky Timex watch that also keeps track of his appointments and stores important phone numbers — no one would confuse it with jewelry.

[146] *E.g.*, In re Whitney, 70 B.R. 443 (Bankr. D. Colo. 1989).

[147] *Compare* In re Moore, 251 B.R. 380 (Bankr. W.D. Mo. 2000) (ATV qualified as a motor vehicle under state exemption statute even though it was used solely for recreational purposes), *with* In re Bosworth, 449 B.R. 104 (Bankr. D. Idaho 2011) (ATV characterized as motor vehicle under applicable state exemption statute).

[148] In re Johnson, 14 B.R. 14 (Bankr. W.D. Ky. 1981) (" 'bus' and 'automobile' [are] species of the genus 'motor vehicle'").

[149] *Compare* In re Drewes, 217 B.R. 978 (Bankr. D.N.H. 1998) (motorcycle not an "automobile"), *with* In re Clemons, 441 B.R. 519 (N.D Miss. 2010) (motorcycle was a "motor vehicle").

[150] Harris v. State, 686 S.E.2d 777 (Ga. 2009).

[151] In re Matthews, 449 B.R. 833 (Bankr. M.D. Ga. 2011).

[152] In re Wilbur, 25 B.R. 405 (Bankr. D. Me. 1982) (airplane not a motor vehicle).

[153] In re McMillin, 441 B.R. 348 (Bankr. D. Oregon 2010).

apparel or household goods.[154] And, in *In re Holzapfel*, the Montana Supreme Court determined that an all terrain vehicle (or "ATV") did not fit the state's exemption for "firearms and sporting goods" because it fit squarely within the exemption for motor vehicles.[155] Similarly, debtors frequently face difficulty in having their motor vehicles characterized as "tools of the trade," even if they are used in the debtor's trade or business.[156]

Characterization issues like this also arise under § 522(f), which permits debtors to avoid non-possessory, non-purchase money security interests in certain types of exempt property.[157]

[3] Regional Exemption Patterns

There are, in addition, a number of exemptions that seem to reflect a different lifestyle than the ones imagined by most law students. For many years, and well into the last quarter of the twentieth century, many states' exemption statutes seemed to reflect a far more agrarian society than the one most Americans now enjoy.[158] A few of these persist. Thus, it is not unusual to find exemptions for certain quantities of firewood, chickens, church pews, and "horses, mules, or donkeys."[159] Other exemptions are hard to understand from any point of view. One state has an exemption for a debtor's leasehold interest in a piano.[160] At least one protects liquor licenses.[161]

The adoption of the Bankruptcy Reform Act of 1978, with its effort to establish a set of uniform bankruptcy exemptions, and its provision authorizing states to opt-out of the uniform exemptions, led many states to revise their archaic exemption statutes in favor of new provisions that reflect life in the latter part of the twentieth century. One can only surmise how long it will be before these recently enacted statutes will become relics in need of further revision.[162] Indeed, without exemptions for laptop computers, cell phones, or tablets, this may already have occurred.

---

[154] In re Lynch, 139 B.R. 868 (Bankr. N.D. Ohio 1992) (separate exemption for jewelry prevents its characterization as household goods).

[155] In re Holzapfel, 262 P.3d 1114 (2011).

[156] *Compare* In re Patterson, 825 F.2d 1140 (7th Cir. 1987) (farmer's tractor was not a tool of the trade under § 522(d)(6)), *with* Nazarene Fed. Credit Union v. McNutt (In re McNutt), 87 B.R. 84 (B.A.P. 9th Cir. 1988) (pickup truck a tool of the debtor's drywall hanging trade even though it was not specially equipped), *and* In re Giles, 340 B.R. 543 (Bankr. E.D. Pa. 2006) (milliner's auto, used to transport hats to various festivals was a tool of the trade).

[157] *E.g.*, Parrotte v. Sensenich (In re Parrotte), 22 F.3d 472 (2d Cir. 1994) (dairy farmers' "bulls" were a tool of their trade). *See infra* § 12.07[B] Avoiding Non-Purchase Money Security Interests.

[158] *See* Vern Countryman, *For a New Exemption Policy in Bankruptcy*, 14 Rutgers L. Rev. 678, 681 (1960); William T. Vukowich, *The Bankruptcy Commission's Proposals Regarding Bankrupts' Exemption Rights*, 63 Cal. L. Rev. 1439, 1441-46 (1975).

[159] Tex. Prop. Code Ann. § 42.002(10)(A) (Vernon 2000).

[160] Del. Code Ann. tit. 10 § 4902 (LexisNexis 2004).

[161] Conn. Gen. Stat. § 30-14(a) (West Supp. 2006) (tools of the trade in other states?).

[162] No state provides a separate exemption for a personal computer. However, new Bankruptcy Code § 522(f)(4)(A) includes a personal computer among the items that are within the term "household goods" and thus potentially subject to lien avoidance by the debtor. *See infra* § 12.07 Avoiding Liens on Exempt Property.

[4] Dollar Limits

Most exemptions are subject to dollar limits. These limits raise valuation issues.[163] The trustee may question the debtor's valuation of the asset, either by objecting to the claimed exemption,[164] or simply by seeking permission to sell the exempt asset and distribute the proceeds of the sale to the debtor, up to the amount of her exemption, with the surplus deposited with the estate for distribution to creditors.[165]

[D] Earnings and Other Financial Assets

A wide variety of financial assets are exempt, either under § 522(d), or under the applicable state exemption statute. Principal among these are wages, which are protected by the federal Consumer Credit Protection Act, and sometimes more extensively by state law. Certain other substitutes for wages, such as payments under life insurance policies,[166] payments due on account of the wrongful death of a person on whom the debtor was dependent,[167] spousal support,[168] and disability payments[169] are also commonly exempt. Both federal and state law also provide broad exemptions for a variety of types of retirement assets, which, after all, are nothing more than deferred wages. A mish-mash of provisions protect other forms of financial assets.

[1] Wage Exemptions

Wages are exempted pursuant to the Consumer Credit Protection Act.[170] It was enacted to make sure wage earners are able to receive at least enough of their take-home pay to enable them to meet their basic needs, and it was hoped at least to permit them to avoid being forced into bankruptcy.[171] In most cases, the Act exposes a maximum of only 25% of a person's "disposable earnings" to the claims of creditors.[172] Individuals whose weekly earnings are less than forty times the federal minimum wage receive greater protection.[173] Not surprisingly, protection for

---

[163] David Gray Carlson, *The Role of Valuation in Federal Bankruptcy Exemption Process: The Supreme Court Reads Schedule C*, 18 Am. Bankr. Inist. L. Rev. 461 (2010).

[164] Bankruptcy Code § 522(l).

[165] Schwab v. Reilly, 560 ___ U.S. ___, 130 S. Ct. 2652, 177 L. Ed. 2d 234 (2010).

[166] *E.g.*, Bankruptcy Code § 522(d)(11)(B); Ohio Rev. Code Ann. § 2329.66(A)(6)(b) (LexisNexis Supp. 2012)

[167] *E.g.*, Bankruptcy Code § 522(d)(11)(B); Ohio Rev. Code Ann. § 2329.66(A)(12)(b) (LexisNexis Supp. 2012)

[168] *E.g.*, Bankruptcy Code § 522(d)(10)(D); Ohio Rev. Code Ann. § 2329.66(A)(11) (LexisNexis Supp. 2012).

[169] *E.g.*, Bankruptcy Code § 522(d)(10)(C); Ohio Rev. Code Ann. § 2329.66(A)(9)(f) (LexisNexis Supp. 2012)

[170] 15 U.S.C. § 1673(a)(1) (2006).

[171] *See* In re Kokoszka, 479 F.2d 990 (2d Cir. 1973), *aff'd sub. nom* Kokoszka v. Belford, 417 U.S. 642, *reh'g denied*, 419 U.S. 486 (1974).

[172] 15 U.S.C. § 1673(a)(1) (2006).

[173] Section 303 of the Consumer Credit Protection Act always protects "thirty times the Federal

earnings is less if the creditor seeking to recover those earnings is owed "support."[174]

This maximum percentage can only be garnished from a person's "disposable earnings." These are defined as "that part of earnings of any individual remaining after the deduction from those earnings of any amounts required by law to be withheld."[175] Amounts required to be withheld include deductions for social security, medicare, and income withholding taxes. Significantly, however, amounts required to be withheld do not include sums deducted from the debtor's earnings pursuant to an order of support for another creditor.[176]

Courts have generally been restrictive in determining what payments are earnings and thus entitled to protection. For example, neither lump sum severance payments owed to a former employee[177] nor a debtor's tax refund owed by the government[178] have qualified for protection. Further, although state exemption statutes may provide greater protection, the few decisions that exist have concluded that these federal restrictions do not apply to wages after they have been deposited into the debtor's bank account.[179]

Many states' wage exemption statutes adhere closely to the restrictions imposed by federal law and expose wages to garnishment to the full extent permitted by the Consumer Credit Protection Act.[180] Other states provide even greater protection than what the federal law requires. California, for example, exempts wages beyond the federal limits to the extent "necessary for the support of the judgment debtor or the judgment debtor's family"[181] and Pennsylvania does not permit wage

---

minimum hour wage." 15 U.S.C. § 1673(a)(2) (2006). As of October 2006, the federal minimum wage is $5.15 per hour. Thus, employees in sectors not governed by the minimum wage or who work less than forty hours may always protect $154.50 in wages per week from their creditors. Employees who earn more than the minimum wage and who work at least forty hours per week may protect more, with only 25% of their earnings subject to garnishment. For example, an employee who works forty hours, earning $8.00 per hour, may protect up to $240 from garnishment, without adjusting for the smaller portion of his total wages that constitute "disposable earnings."

In early 2007, each house of Congress had passed separate bills proposing several increases in the federal minimum wage over a twenty-six month period to $7.25 per hour. If enacted, the proposed legislation would raise the federal minimum wage in 3 increments: to $5.85 per hour 60 days after enactment; to $6.55 per hour for 12 months thereafter; and, finally to $7.25 per hour. This would affect the minimum amounts that debtors could protect from wage garnishment to $175.50 for wage garnishments occurring two months after its enactment, to $196.50 for the next twelve months, and then to $217.50.

[174] A support claimant may recover anywhere from 50% to as much as 65% of a debtor's disposable earnings, depending on whether the debtor has other dependents and on whether the support claim involved, as so many of them are, is for past-due support. 15 U.S.C. § 1673(b) (2006).

[175] 15 U.S.C. § 1672(b) (2006).

[176] Marshall v. Dist. Court for Forty-First-b Judicial Dist. of Mich., Mount Clemens Div., 444 F. Supp. 1110 (E.D. Mich. 1978).

[177] Aetna Cas. & Sur. Co. v. Rodco Autobody, 965 F. Supp. 104 (D. Mass. 1996).

[178] In re Trudeau, 237 B.R. 803 (B.A.P. 10th Cir. 1999).

[179] John O. Melby & Co. Bank v. Anderson, 276 N.W.2d 274 (Wis. 1979).

[180] See Ohio Rev. Code Ann. § 2329.66(A)(13) (LexisNexis Supp. 2012).

[181] Cal. Civ. Proc. Code § 706.051 (West 1987) (and those who have no dependents).

garnishment at all, except with respect to support and student loan claimants.[182]

Debtors in states that have opted out, as well as debtors in other, usually more generous states that have not opted out, who elect their home state's exemption statute receive the benefit of their own state's federally mandated restriction on wage garnishment. Debtors in states that have not opted out and who elect the uniform federal exemptions under § 522(d) appear to be out of luck, as that section contains no provision to exempt wages owed to the debtor from his bankruptcy estate.

[2] Wages Substitutes

Many exemption statutes contain provisions exempting a variety of wage substitutes. These commonly include payments under a life insurance policy due because of the death of a person on whom the debtor was dependent,[183] payments on account of the wrongful death of a person on whom the debtor was dependent,[184] spousal support,[185] disability payments,[186] awards for lost earnings,[187] unemployment, and social security benefits.[188]

Some of these exemptions are specifically limited to the amount reasonably necessary for the support of the debtor and the debtor's dependents.[189] For example, the uniform federal exemptions protect support, wrongful death, and life insurance payments only "to the extent reasonably necessary for the support of the debtor and any dependent of the debtor,"[190] but they fully exempt veterans' benefits, unemployment benefits, and social security benefits.[191] State exemption statutes contain similar differences, reflecting an array of policies and political compromises.[192]

---

[182] 42 Pa. Cons. Stat. Ann. § 8127 (West Supp. 2006) (it also permits wage garnishment for "board of four weeks or less," and student loans).

[183] E.g., Bankruptcy Code § 522(d)(11)(B); Ohio Rev. Code Ann. § 2329.66(A)(6)(b) (LexisNexis Supp. 2012).

[184] E.g., Bankruptcy Code § 522(d)(11)(B); Ohio Rev. Code. Ann. § 2329.66(A)(12)(b) (LexisNexis Supp. 2012).

[185] E.g., Bankruptcy Code § 522(d)(10)(D); Ohio Rev. Code Ann. § 2329.66(A)(11) (LexisNexis Supp. 2012).

[186] E.g., Bankruptcy Code § 522(d)(10)(C); Ohio Rev. Code Ann. § 2329.66(A)(9)(f) (LexisNexis Supp. 2012).

[187] E.g., Bankruptcy Code § 522(d)(11)(E); Ohio Rev. Code § 2329.66(A)(12)(d) (LexisNexis Supp. 2012). See In re Lewis, 406 B.R. 518 (E.D. Mich. 2009) (exemption covered buyout option payments from former employer, and was not limited to right to receive payments due to bodily injury).

[188] E.g., Bankruptcy Code § 522(d)(10)(A); Ohio Rev. Code Ann. § 2329.66(A)(9)(c) (LexisNexis Supp. 2012).

[189] E.g., Bankruptcy Code § 522(d)(10)(D).

[190] Bankruptcy Code § 522(d)(10)(D), (11)(B), (11)(C).

[191] Bankruptcy Code § 522(d)(10)(A).

[192] The Ohio statute, with which one of your author's is particularly familiar, fully exempts benefits from "life insurance," but protects payments for wrongful death claims only to the extent they are reasonably necessary for the support of the debtor and the debtor's dependents. Compare Ohio Rev. Code Ann. § 2329.66(A)(6)(b) with § 2329.66(A)(12)(b) (LexisNexis Supp. 2012).

[3] Retirement Funds[193]

Retirement assets are widely exempt. Many state exemption statutes protect a variety of traditional "defined benefit" pension plans,[194] more modern "defined contribution" plans,[195] and other modern tax-deferred retirement savings plans, such as the various types of IRAs, Keough Plans, SEPs, and so on, from the claims of creditors. Not surprisingly, state exemption statutes are not always drafted to cover what seems like an ever-expanding type of retirement savings accounts and trust funds.

Funds in an "ERISA qualified" pension plan are excluded entirely from a debtor's estate under the Supreme Court's ruling in *Patterson v. Shumate*,[196] interpreting § 541(c)(2). Section 541(b) extends this exclusion to a variety of tax deferred retirement, health, and educational savings accounts, including those under §§ 403(b), 414(d), 457, 529(b)(1), and 530(b)(1) of the Internal Revenue Code.[197]

Retirement assets that remain included in the debtor's estate are now protected by exemptions that apply regardless of whether the debtor's home state has opted out of other federal exemptions. At the same time, they impose limits on the size of some of these exemptions.

Section 522(b)(3)(C) exempts "retirement funds to the extent that those funds are in a fund or account that is exempt from taxation under section 401, 403, 408, 408A, 414, 457, or 501(a) of the Internal Revenue Code."[198] This exemption applies regardless of whether the debtor's state has opted out of the uniform federal exemptions and regardless of whether a debtor in a state that has not opted out has elected his own state's exemptions or those in § 522(d).[199] As a result, the following types of retirement funds are now completely exempt:

- Traditional employer-sponsored and defined-contribution pension, profit-sharing, and stock-bonus plans governed by I.R.C. § 401;

---

[193] John Hennigan, *Beneath the Surface of BAPCPA, Rousey, and the New Retirement Funds Exemption*, 13 Am. Bankr. Inst. L. Rev. 777 (2005); C. Scott Pryor, *Rock, Scissors, Papers: ERISA, the Bankruptcy Code and State Exemption Laws for Individual Retirement Accounts*, 77 Am. Bankr. L.J. 65 (2003).

[194] A defined benefit retirement plan specifies the amount of benefits the employee will receive upon his retirement. The amount is usually a percentage of the employee's highest salary, with the percentage dependent upon the total number of years of the employee's service to the employer. Defined benefit plans remain common for public employees but are now rare for those in the private sector.

[195] In a defined contribution plan, the employer contributes a specific amount (usually a percentage of the employee's salary) to the employee's pension fund. Employees also frequently contribute to the fund. The accumulated funds provide the basis for the employee's pension, which may be large or small depending on the sums contributed and their earnings performance while they accumulate.

[196] 504 U.S. 753 (1992).

[197] *See supra* § 7.04[F] Spendthrift Trusts.

[198] Bankruptcy Code § 522(b)(3)(C). *See* In re Patrick, 411 B.R. 659 (Bankr. C.D.Cal. 2008); Margaret Howard, *Exemptions under the 2005 Bankruptcy Amendments: A Tale of Opportunity Lost*, 79 Am. Bankr. L.J. 397, 413-18 (2005).

[199] This result is accomplished by the addition of identical language to the uniform federal exemptions in new § 522(d)(12).

- Qualified annuity plans for employees of non-profit employers under I.R.C. § 503;

- Traditional Individual Retirement Accounts under I.R.C. § 408;[200]

- "Roth" IRAs under I.R.C. § 408A;

- Retirement plans for certain controlled groups of employees under I.R.C. § 414;

- Deferred Compensation plans maintained by certain eligible employers under I.R.C. § 457; and

- Retirement plans established and maintained by certain defined tax-exempt organizations under I.R.C. § 501(a).

While many of these retirement assets were already excluded from the debtor's estate under § 541(c)(2), the new language brings those that were not excluded, such as Individual IRAs and Roth IRAs, under a broad umbrella of protection. No longer will debtors whose retirement assets have been rolled over from an ERISA pension plan into an IRA need to decide whether to trade their security in retirement for a fresh start in bankruptcy.

However, the exemption for both traditional and Roth IRAs is capped at $1 million, though the limit does not apply to funds that have been deposited into the IRA as a "rollover" contribution from other traditional retirement funds that contain contributions from the debtor's employer. Also, it is anticipated that few debtors will have successfully accumulated over $1 million in IRA assets from accumulated $5000 annual contributions. Even then, the $1 million limit may be increased by the court "if the interests of justice so require."[201]

[E] Tracing Exemptions into Non-Exempt Property

When property changes form, the question arises whether it remains exempt in the new form. A debtor might sell his home and deposit the proceeds in a bank account. Later, he might use the funds to buy a motorcycle. If the equity in his home was exempt, this might raise questions about whether he can apply the exemption to the bank account, or even the motorcycle.

Wages provide a key illustration. As explained above, seventy-five percent of a person's earnings are exempt from garnishment.[202] An initial question is whether the exemption applies when the debtor's wages are deposited into the debtor's bank account.[203] Although the federal wage garnishment limits do not require the exemption to be traced into other forms of property, many state exemption statutes extend their own wage garnishment protections to wages that have been deposited

---

[200] *See* In re Chilton, 674 F.3d 486 (5th Cir. 2012); In re Nessa, 426 B.R. 312 (B.A.P. 8th Cir. 2010) (both dealing with inherited IRAs).

[201] Bankruptcy Code § 522(n).

[202] 15 U.S.C. § 1673 (2006). *See supra* § 2.11[A][4][a] Federal Restrictions on Wage Garnishment.

[203] *See* In re Palidora, 310 B.R. 164 (Bankr. D. Ariz. 2004).

into a bank account or other liquid asset readily available to meet the debtor's living expenses.

Extending the exemption further might easily lead to the conclusion that all of a debtor's property attributable to the debtor's wages should enjoy a 75% exemption. However, this has not been done.

Whether wages are exempt after being deposited into a debtor's bank account depends on the exemption statute the debtor relies on. Some states' exemption statutes expressly provide for tracing wages into other forms.[204] In some other states, where the exemption statute is not explicit, courts have ruled that the exemption continues notwithstanding the transfer of the wages to the debtor's bank account.[205] Other states' wage exemption statutes provide no such protection,[206] and the federal wage exemption limits do not require states to do so.

The question of tracing might also be applied to income substitutes such as workers' compensation benefits or personal injury awards. Decisions run in both directions, with some courts permitting the exemption to continue as long as the funds are contained in a segregated account,[207] and others permitting it to continue even if the funds have been commingled, as long as the amount of the award can be traced into the account using standard tracing methods.[208]

A dramatic example of the importance of the issue occurred in *Woodson v. Fireman's Fund Ins. Co. (In re Woodson)*. The court refused to trace the debtor's exemption in an unmatured whole life insurance policy on the life of his wife, into the $1 million proceeds he received after his wife expired.[209] The court treated the proceeds of the policy as a separate asset, brought into the estate under § 541(a)(5) and exempt only to the extent they were reasonably necessary for the support of the debtor and his remaining dependents.[210]

[F] Exemption Protections for a Debtor's Dependents

The Bankruptcy Code contains several protections for debtors' dependents in connection with property that could be claimed as exempt. If the debtor does not submit a schedule of exempt property, the debtor's dependents are permitted to file

---

[204] *See* Fla. Stat. Ann. § 222.11(3) (West 1998). Before the Florida statute was specifically amended to address this issue, wages placed into an account were not exempt. In re Ryzner, 208 B.R. 568, 569 (Bankr. M.D. Fla. 1997).

[205] Daugherty v. Central Trust Co., 504 N.E.2d 1100, 1103 (Ohio 1986).

[206] *E.g.*, In re Sinclair, 417 F.3d 527 (5th Cir. 2005) (applying the Louisiana exemption statute); In re Adcock, 264 B.R. 708 (D. Kan. 2000) (Kansas wage exemption statute). Nor does the federal Consumer Credit Protection Act require states to exempt wages after their deposit into an account. Usery v. First Nat'l Bank, 586 F.2d 107 (9th Cir.1978); *cf.* Kokoszka v. Belford, 417 U.S. 642, 651 (1974) (right to tax refund not exempt).

[207] *E.g.*, In re Nolen, 65 B.R. 1014 (Bankr. D.N.M. 1986).

[208] Matthews v. Lewis, 617 S.W.2d 43 (Ky. 1981).

[209] 839 F.2d 610 (9th Cir. 1988). In a previous life, one of your co-authors assisted in representing Mr. Woodson in his pursuit of this exemption.

[210] *See* In re Tessendorf, 449 B.R. 793 (Bankr. D. Kan. 2011) (investment of exempt life insurance proceeds into a Certificate of Deposit).

the list or submit a claim of property as exempt from the estate on the debtor's behalf.[211] This provides a hedge against debtors who are either irresponsible in this regard, or who are perhaps estranged from their spouses or children and not interested in protecting property that may be in the dependents' possession.[212] However, if the debtor files a schedule of exemptions, a dependent may not file a different or conflicting schedule,[213] unless the debtor's schedule was supplied in bad faith.[214] In addition, § 522(e) makes a debtors' waiver of his exemptions or of his avoiding powers with respect to exempt property, unenforceable.[215]

[G] Valuation of Exempt Property

Most consumer debtors' attorneys advise their clients to state the value of their assets based on what the client believes he would be able to recover from a sale of the asset at a garage sale. This usually comports with the definition of value in § 522(a)(2), which indicates that "value" means "fair market value" as of the date of the debtor's petition.[216] Fair market value is generally regarded as "[t]he amount at which property would change hands between a willing buyer and a willing seller, neither being under any compulsion to buy or sell and both having reasonable knowledge of the relevant facts."[217] Most courts have used "liquidation" value as the market value for the purpose of the debtor's exemption rights,[218] though this might vary according to differences in state exemption schemes.[219]

Courts usually accept the debtor's valuation in the absence of persuasive evidence to the contrary. Where expert appraisal testimony is available regarding the market value of an asset, rebutting this presumption is not difficult.[220] Where there is no available market for the exempt property, the court is likely to accept the debtor's view, particularly with respect to unusual assets, such as a cause of action under the Truth in Lending Act or some other claim the debtor has against a third party.[221]

---

[211] Bankruptcy Code § 522(l).

[212] The debtor's spouse is specifically designated as one of the debtor's "dependents" even though he or she might not be financially dependent on the debtor in the ordinary sense. 11 U.S.C. § 522(a)(1). Bankruptcy Rule 4003(a) provides a mechanism permitting a dependent to claim the debtor's exemptions.

[213] *E.g.*, Kapila v. Morgan (In re Morgan), 286 B.R. 678 (Bankr. E.D. Wis. 2002).

[214] In re Crouch, 33 B.R. 271 (Bankr. E.D.N.C. 1983).

[215] *See generally* H.R. Rep. No. 95-595, 362 (1977), *reprinted in* 1978 U.S.C.C.A.N. 5963, 6318; S. Rep. No.95-989, 76 (1978) *reprinted in* 1978 U.S.C.C.A.N. 5787, 5862.

[216] Bankruptcy Code § 522(a)(2).

[217] Black's Law Dictionary 537 (5th ed. 1979) (cited in *In re Johnson*, 165 B.R. 524 (Bankr. S.D. Ga. 1994).

[218] *E.g.*, In re Walsh, 5 Bankr. 239 (Bankr. D.D.C. 1980).

[219] *E.g.*, In re Belsome, 434 F.3d 774 (5th Cir. 2005) (applying Louisiana exemption statute which specifies use of National Automobile Dealers Association (NADA) valuations).

[220] Matter of Salzer, 52 F.3d 708 (7th Cir. 1995).

[221] In re Polis, 217 F.3d 899 (7th Cir. 2000).

New requirements imposed on debtors' attorneys by § 707(b)(4)(C) undoubtedly influence how property values are determined. Section 707(b)(4)(C) provides that the debtor's attorney's signature on the debtor's petition certifies that the attorney has conducted a "reasonable investigation" into the underlying circumstances and that the documents submitted with the petition are "well grounded in fact."[222] Thus, debtors' attorneys are not permitted to rely solely on their client's representations about the value of the assets that are claimed as exempt.[223] They must conduct their own investigation.

§ 12.04 TENANCY BY THE ENTIRETY

States that still permit married couples to hold property as tenants by the entirety provide limited protection for property held in this manner. Further, although entirety property is usually associated with real estate, some states recognize the form of ownership for items of personal property.[224]

Tenancy by the entirety is a form of joint ownership available only to married couples, which prevents transfer or encumbrance by the unilateral action of only one spouse. It is based on the "ancient common law principle that, upon marriage, each spouse loses his or her individual identity, and the two people become one entity."[225] Its original purpose was chauvinistic: "to protect a wife from the husband who might irresponsibly lose the family home or other assets."[226]

As a result, a deed or mortgage executed solely by a husband or a wife has no effect. Similarly, if a judgment is rendered on a debt incurred solely by a wife, no judicial lien arising from that judgment can attach to the entirety property held by her and her husband. The property can be transferred or encumbered by both spouses acting jointly; it can also be subject to a judicial lien arising from a jointly incurred obligation. But, it cannot be used to satisfy a debt owed by only one of them.

For example, suppose Merl and Agnes own their home as tenants by the entirety. If Merl conveys a mortgage on the property to Red Rose Bank, the mortgage is unenforceable. If Agnes incurs an individual credit card debt to the bank, the bank is unable to obtain a judgment lien on their home to satisfy Agnes's individual debt. Only by acting jointly in incurring an obligation can Merl and Agnes subject their entirety property to any voluntary or involuntary lien.[227]

In the context of a bankruptcy case, this means only joint creditors have any rights to the debtors' home. If there are no joint creditors, the debtors may keep all

---

[222] Bankruptcy Code § 707(b)(4)(C).

[223] *See supra* § 6.02[F] Attorney's Obligations Regarding Debtor's Schedules; Gary Neustadter, *A Consumer Bankruptcy Odyssey*, 39 Creighton L. Rev. 225, 338-353 (2006); Henry J. Sommer, *Trying to Make Sense Out of Nonsense: Representing Consumers Under the "Bankruptcy Abuse Prevention and Consumer Protection Act of 2005*," 79 Am. Bankr. L.J. 191, 211 (2005).

[224] *E.g.*, In re Caliri, 347 B.R. 788 (Bankr. M.D. Fla. 2006) (catamaran sailboat).

[225] In re Hunter, 970 F.2d 299, 301 (7th Cir. 1992).

[226] *E.g.*, In re Bellingroehr, 403 B.R. 818, 820 (Bankr. W.D. Mo. 2009).

[227] *See* 7 Richard R. Powell & Michael Allan Wolf, Powell on Real Property § 52.03[3] (2006).

of their entirety property, not just the amount protected by a homestead exemption. Thus, their mode of ownership operates as if it were an exemption, at least insofar as individual debts are concerned. Section 522(b)(3)(B) recognizes this by explicitly exempting property held with a non-debtor spouse as tenants by the entirety under applicable state law.[228]

However, most married couples have numerous joint debts. If both are liable on the family credit card, they can protect their entirety property against the creditor's claim only to the extent of their ordinary homestead and wildcard exemptions.[229] Savvy creditors who provide credit to individual spouses in states that protect entirety property in this way frequently take care to obtain guarantees from their borrower's spouses to protect themselves from this limitation inherent in the tenancy by the entirety form of ownership.

§ 12.05 LOSS OF EXEMPTIONS

[A] Exemption Waivers Unenforceable

Under the old Bankruptcy Act and in many states today, the benefit of the exemption laws can be waived by agreement. However, under the Bankruptcy Code, such a waiver is ineffective. Section 522(e) makes any exemption waiver that is executed in favor of a creditor who holds an unsecured claim unenforceable.[230] Also unenforceable is any attempted waiver of the debtor's power to avoid certain liens on exempt property under § 522(f).[231]

The purpose for these provisions is consumer protection. Congress was concerned that many exemption waivers were made without full understanding of the consequences. This provision operates in parallel with other state and federal enactments that similarly restrict or prohibit exemption waivers.[232]

Of course, a debtor might effectively waive his exemptions by failing to assert them. In such a case, § 522(l) permits the debtor's dependents to file a schedule of exemptions on the debtor's behalf. Still, if no one files the list, the debtor's exemptions may be lost.[233]

[B] Liens on Exempt Property

Although waivers of exemptions are not enforceable, security interests are generally enforceable. Security interests impair a debtor's exemptions much in the same way that an exemption waiver would, if the waiver could be enforced.

---

[228] Bankruptcy Code § 522(b)(3)(B). *See, e.g.*, In re Bellingroehr, 403 B.R. 818, 820 (Bankr. W.D. Mo. 2009).

[229] *See* 7 Richard R. Powell & Michael Allan Wolf, Powell on Real Property § 52.03[3] (2006).

[230] Bankruptcy Code § 522(e).

[231] Bankruptcy Code § 522(e).

[232] *See, e.g.*, Federal Trade Commission Unfair Credit Practices Regulations, 16 C.F.R. § 444.2(a)(2).

[233] This appears to be rather a remote contingency, however, since even if the debtor misses the deadline to list exemptions, amendments are rather freely allowed.

Exemptions can only be claimed in "the debtor's interest" in his property.[234] The debtor's interest is only his equity in the asset. The value of this equity is the value of the property above the amount necessary to satisfy any valid liens against the property, such as mortgages and security interests.

Consider, for example, a debtor who owns a home worth $100,000, but subject to a $90,000 mortgage. This leaves the debtor with only $10,000 equity in his house. If the applicable exemption statute protects $15,000 of a debtor's interest in his residence, the debtor is unable to take advantage of more than $10,000 of the exemption, because his equity is only worth $10,000. If the debtor had encumbered his home with a second mortgage, such as by using it as collateral for an "equity line" credit card with a $12,000 balance due, the home would be subject to two contractual liens, one for a $90,000 debt and another for a $12,000 debt, with no equity left for the debtor. He would be unable to use any of the $15,000 exemption to protect the house.

The reason for making a debtor's exemption rights subordinate to the rights of a creditor with a contractual lien, such as a real estate mortgage or an Article 9 security interest, is to enhance people's ability to borrow funds. If a debtor could assert his exemption rights to protect a house from a mortgage, lenders might be more likely to insist that borrowers put up a down payment equal to the amount of the applicable exemption. At the margins, this would reduce the number of people who could qualify for a loan. Consider what would happen if debtors could assert their § 522(d)(2) $3,450 exemption rights in a car. For married couples, who jointly owned the car, this amounts to a $6,900 exemption. Car buyers would need at least a $6,900 down payment to purchase a car — and probably more, to protect the dealership from the immediate decline in the value of the car after it rolls off the showroom floor. Not only would car buyers be unhappy — car manufacturers would find it difficult to locate customers who could afford to make the necessary down payment. Fewer cars would be sold, and the auto industry would stall.

As will be discussed elsewhere in this chapter, debtors can sometimes avoid non-purchase money security interests that impair their exemptions. Some states have followed suit in their own exemption laws.[235] Because this right is limited to non-purchase money security interests, it does not impair people's ability to borrow money to buy things.

Because security interests survive bankruptcy, and are not affected by debtor's exemption rights, debtors usually find it necessary to either surrender the collateral to the secured party, enter into a reaffirmation agreement with the secured creditor, or more rarely, "redeem" the collateral from the lien by making a lump-sum payment to the creditor in the amount of the allowed secured claim.[236]

---

[234] *E.g.*, Ohio Rev. Code Ann. § 2329.66(A)(1)(b) (LexisNexis Supp. 2012) (exempting *"the person's interest*, not to exceed twenty thousand, two hundred dollars, in one parcel or item of real or personal property that the person or a dependent of the person uses as a residence.") (emphasis added).

[235] *See, e.g.*, Va. Code Ann. § 34-28 (LexisNexis 2005), which provides for the avoidance of non-purchase money liens on most types of exempt property.

[236] Bankruptcy Code § 521(a)(2). *See infra* § 12.08[D] Debtor's Statement of Intent.

If the debtor has any non-exempt equity in the property, any deal with the secured creditor must include the trustee. The trustee wants to sell the property and distribute the surplus equity to the debtor's other creditors. For example, if a mortgage secures a debt of only $80,000, the debtor's $15,000 exemption is not sufficient to protect all of the debtor's $20,000 equity in the home. The trustee will probably want to sell the house for $100,000, distribute $80,000 to the mortgagee, $15,000 to the debtor on account of his exemption, and the $5,000 balance to unsecured creditors. To save the house, the debtor needs to come up with an additional $5,000, possibly from the sale of other exempt assets or through an additional loan from the mortgage company or someone else. The debtor would thereby purchase the surplus equity from the trustee. As noted above, trustees are often willing to sell the excess to the debtor, so long as the debtor is willing, and able, to pay the full value of that excess. Alternatively, the trustee may simply wish to sell the property as the only way to determine the true amount of the surplus equity.

[C] Debtor Misconduct

A debtor may also be deprived of the benefit of his exemptions because of his fraud or other misconduct in the bankruptcy proceeding itself. The power of the court to strip the debtor of his exemptions may arise from any of several sources. First, and most obvious, exemptions created by state law are subject to state law restrictions (except where those restrictions are superseded by the Code). If the debtor's misconduct would deprive him of the exemption under state statutory or case law, the same result ordinarily applies in bankruptcy.[237]

Second, § 522(g) imposes a limit on exemptions claimed with respect to property recovered by the trustee from a third party.[238] The debtor may not exempt recovered property unless: (1) the transfer was involuntary and the debtor did not conceal the property; or (2) the debtor could have avoided the transfer himself under the rules in § 522(f) regarding avoidance of non-purchase-money security interests in household property, tools of the trade, and health aids.[239]

Thus, as a general rule, voluntarily transferred property recovered by the trustee under rules such as those for avoiding preferences or fraudulent transfers may not be exempted by the debtor. Section 522(g) does not require a showing of fraud or other specific misconduct; rather, it requires only a showing that the avoided transfer was made voluntarily. If the debtor voluntarily parted with possession of the property, the debtor effectively demonstrated that he did not need it to make his way in life.

Another potential problem arises if the debtor converted his non-exempt assets into an exempt category immediately prior to filing for bankruptcy. Although there is no general rule prohibiting debtors from converting their non-exempt assets into an exempt category, the Code now imposes some express limits on the practice, particularly with respect to residential property and burial plots. Section 522(o),

---

[237] *E.g.,* In re Clemmer, 184 B.R. 935 (Bankr. E.D. Tenn. 1995).

[238] Bankruptcy Code § 522(g).

[239] *See infra* § 12.07 Avoiding Liens on Exempt Property.

enacted as part of the 2005 amendments, prohibits debtors from asserting an exemption in residential real or personal property or a burial plot that was acquired with non-exempt property that the debtor disposed of during the ten-year period prior to his bankruptcy petition "with the intent to hinder, delay, or defraud a creditor."[240]

The enactment of § 522(o) opens an avenue of support for the contention that other pre-bankruptcy conversions, not specifically prohibited by this new language, are permitted. Section 522(o) may be regarded as an exception to the normal rule that conversions of assets into exempt status are not prohibited.[241] Thus, although a debtor who used non-exempt assets to build exempt equity in his home with the intent to hinder his creditors, would not be able to assert an otherwise available homestead exemption, a debtor who converted non-exempt assets to build up the value of an exempt life insurance policy or retirement plan might be able to assert the exemption, even though the conversion was accomplished with the same intent.[242]

§ 12.06 PROCEDURES FOR CLAIMING AND OBJECTING TO EXEMPTIONS

As with most matters in bankruptcy, specific procedures are available for asserting and objecting to exemptions. Failure to follow these procedures may result in the debtor's losing valuable exemption rights, with a resulting windfall to creditors (and the trustee), or in a windfall to the debtor who may be able to retain property that should not have been exempt.

[A] What to File; Who May File; When to File

Exemptions are not automatically given to the debtor; the debtor must claim them. This is accomplished by filing a list of exempt property with the bankruptcy court, on "Schedule C," one of the documents a debtor files in connection with his bankruptcy case.[243] The list of exemptions is ordinarily filed with the debtor's petition but may be filed up to fifteen days after the petition, unless the court grants an extension.[244]

Since exemptions are personal, they may generally be claimed only by the debtor. However, if the debtor fails to file the list (or "schedule" as it is usually called), a dependant of the debtor may submit the schedule.[245] If the debtor does

---

[240] Bankruptcy Code § 522(o).

[241] *But see* In re Crater, 286 B.R. 756 (Bankr. D. Ariz. 2002). *See also* In re Sholdan, 217 F.3d 1006 (8th Cir. 2000) (96-year-old living in assisted care facility converted all of his assets into a new home which far exceeded his housing needs).

[242] *See, e.g.,* First Tex. Sav. Ass'n, Inc. v. Reed (In re Reed), 700 F.2d 986 (5th Cir. 1983) (denial of discharge due to conversion of non-exempt property with intent to hinder, delay, and defraud creditors).

[243] Bankruptcy Code § 522(l). *See* Fed. Rule Bankr. P. 4003(a); Official Bankruptcy Form 6, Schedule C.

[244] Fed. R. Bankr. P. 1007(c) ("with the petition or within 14 days thereafter . . . .").

[245] Bankruptcy Code § 522(l); Fed. Rule Bankr. P. 4003(a).

not file, a dependant has thirty days from the time normally required for the debtor to file his schedules to file on the debtor's behalf.[246] This schedule may be examined by parties in interest who then may file objections.

Debtors enjoy a liberal right to amend their claim of exemptions.[247] However, debtors who act in bad faith, such as by concealing assets and dissipating them with the knowledge that they should have been included on their schedules, may be denied the right to amend their exemptions in a retrospective effort to avoid the adverse consequences of their actions.[248]

[B]   Objections to Exemptions[249]

Objections to the debtor's exemptions must be filed within thirty days of the creditors' meeting or the filing of any amendment to the list of exempt property.[250] They may be filed by the case trustee or any creditor.[251] The burden of proving that an item of property is not exempt is on the objecting party.[252]

Trustees who fail to submit timely objections are unlikely to find sympathy from the court. In *Taylor v. Freeland & Kronz*, the Supreme Court ruled that the thirty-day period in § 522(l) is absolute, even if the debtor's claim of exemption is entirely specious.[253] In *Taylor*, the debtor's schedules asserted an exemption in the proceeds of the employment discrimination suit that was pending against her former employer. The trustee, believing that the claim against the employer was meritless and thus that it lacked any value, failed to object. When the debtor subsequently settled the claim for $110,000, the trustee objected to the exemption, asserting that the debtor had "no statutory basis" to claim the cause of action as exempt. The Court flatly rejected the trustee's objection, explaining, "[d]eadlines may lead to unwelcome results, but they prompt parties to act and they produce finality." In reaching this conclusion, the Court applied the plain language of Bankruptcy Rule 4003(b) in a straightforward manner, denying the trustee's assertion that the bankruptcy court's equitable powers permitted it to circumvent the thirty day limit, even though the debtor's claimed exemption was both meritless and probably made in bad faith. Courts after *Taylor* have sometimes tried to mitigate its harsh outcome, either by distinguishing its facts,[254] or by construing

---

[246] Fed. R. Bankr. P. 4003(a).

[247] *E.G.*, Kaelin v. Bassett (In re Kaelin), 308 F.3d 885, 889 (8th Cir. 2002).

[248] Barrows v. Christians (In re Barrows), 408 B.R. 239 (B.A.P. 8th Cir. 2009).

[249] David Gray Carlson, *The Role of Valuation in Federal Bankruptcy Exemption Process: The Supreme Court Reads Schedule C*, 18 Am. Bankr. Inst. L. Rev. 461 (2010).

[250] Fed. R. Bankr. P. 4003(b). The court may extend this if a request for extension is made before the thirty-day period expires.

[251] Fed. R. Bankr. P. 4003(b).

[252] Fed. R. Bankr. P. 4003(c).

[253] Taylor v. Freeland & Kronz, 503 U.S. 638 (1992).

[254] Dean v. Telegadis (In re Dean), 317 B.R. 482 (Bankr. W.D. Pa. 2004) (exempt property acquired after deadline for objections); In re Ruggles, 210 B.R. 57 (Bankr. D. Vt. 1997) (objection to good faith of Chapter 13 plan, based on flaws in debtor's asserted exemptions).

debtors' exemption claims narrowly.[255]

Taylor's scope was tested in *Schwab v. Reilly.* There, the debtor scheduled her restaurant equipment as having a value of $10,718, and combined a $1850 tools of the trade exemption with a $10,225 "wild card" exemption to exempt the entire value. After the thirty-day period of Rule 4003(b) expired, the trustee obtained an appraisal of the equipment, which indicated that it was worth over $17,000. Accordingly, the trustee sought to sell the property to recoup its value in excess of the $10,718 that the debtor had claimed as exempt. The Court of Appeals, relying on *Taylor*, affirmed the bankruptcy court and district court in denying the trustee the opportunity to take late advantage of the debtor's mistaken valuation of the otherwise exempt property.[256]

The Supreme Court, in a decision that appears to cut directly against *Taylor*, reversed, and held that the thirty-day deadline did not impair the trustee's ability to object to the debtor's claimed valuation of the exemption, and permitted the trustee to sell the property, and keep any excess beyond the exempt amount.

The Court in *Schwab* claimed that its decision in *Taylor* was distinguishable, because, unlike Reilly, the debtor in *Taylor* had not specified the value of the claimed exemption and thus sought to exempt all of the property, regardless of its value.[257] In *Schwab*, the debtor only claimed an exemption for the amount permitted by the applicable exemption statute. Thus, the Court concluded, the trustee did not have a duty to make a timely objection until it became clear that the debtor was seeking to exempt portions of the property that exceeded the allowed exemption. According to the Court in *Schwab*, *Taylor* merely established that the trustee was required to "object to a claimed exemption if the amount the debtor lists as the 'value claimed exempt' is not within statutory limits, a test the value (unknown) in *Taylor* failed, and the values . . . in this case pass."[258]

Thus, the thirty-day limit applies when the debtor claims an exemption for property that does not fit an exempt category, when the amount claimed as exempt exceeds the applicable amount of the exemption, or where the debtor does not specify the amount that is claimed as exempt. If the debtor's claimed exemption fits within the applicable statutory limits, and it later surfaces that the debtor wishes to exempt more, the time limit in Rule 4003(b) does not apply.

§ 12.07 AVOIDING LIENS ON EXEMPT PROPERTY[259]

Although liens generally trump the debtor's exemption rights, the Bankruptcy Code carves out a few exceptions to this basic principle. Section 522(f) permits a debtor to avoid judgment liens and some consensual security interests to the extent

---

[255] *E.g.,* In re Clark, 266 B.R. 163 (B.A.P. 9th Cir. 2001) (initial claim regarded as ambiguous).

[256] In re Reilly, 534 F.3d 173 (3d Cir. 2008).

[257] Schwab v. Reilly, 130 S. Ct. 2652, 2666-67 (2010). The debtor in *Taylor* listed the value of the property as "unknown." *Id.* at 2665.

[258] *Id.* at 2666.

[259] Robert H. Bowmar, *Avoidance of Judicial Liens That Impair Exemptions in Bankruptcy: The Workings of 11 U.S.C. § 552(f)(1),* 63 Am. Bankr. L.J. 375, 400 (1989); David Gray Carlson, *Security*

that they impair the debtor's exemptions. This avoiding power is not subject to states' power to opt out of the uniform federal exemptions. But, it applies only to judicial and consensual liens, not to statutory liens, such as mechanics liens and artisans liens.[260]

The ability to avoid liens can help some debtors keep their property. For example, if state law creates a homestead exemption but prohibits a debtor from asserting it against a judgment lien-holder, the federal rule permitting avoidance of such liens when they impair exemptions prevails, and the exemption may be claimed.[261] Attempts by several states to restrict the effect of the bankruptcy rule avoiding some security interests on exempt property have been held unconstitutional as violations of the Supremacy Clause.[262] However, as explained below, a few state limits on avoidance have since been expressly sanctioned by § 522.

[A]　Avoiding Judicial Liens[263]

Section 522(f)(1) allows the debtor to avoid the "fixing" of most judicial liens to the extent the lien impairs an exemption to which the debtor otherwise would be entitled.[264] It applies to all exempt property, and is particularly useful with respect to property held in tenancy by the entirety, in the few states that still recognize this estate.[265]

Section 522(f) does not permit avoidance of statutory liens. Section 101(36) defines a "judicial lien" as a "lien obtained by judgment, levy, sequestration, or other legal or equitable process or proceeding." Conversely, section 101(52) defines "statutory lien" as a "lien arising solely by force of a statute on specified circumstances or conditions . . . ." As a result, section 522(f)(1) expressly provides relief only for judicial liens and does not allow a debtor to avoid statutory liens.[266]

When it applies, § 522(f) does not entirely destroy the judicial lien. Instead, it permits avoidance of the lien only to the extent the lien "impairs an exemption to which the debtor would have been entitled under [§ 522(b)]."[267] Therefore, the lien remains enforceable to the extent that the property was not exempt.

Consider, for example, a debtor with a $100,000 home, subject to both a $40,000 mortgage and a $60,000 judgment lien, located in a jurisdiction that provides a

Interests On Exempt Property After the 1994 Amendments to the Bankruptcy Code, 4 Am. Bankr. Inst. L. Rev. 57 (1996).

[260] In re Helms, 438 B.R. 95 (Bankr. W.D.N.C. 2010). *See generally supra* § 2.05 Statutory, Common Law, and Equitable Liens.

[261] Owen v. Owen, 500 U.S. 305 (1991).

[262] *E.g.*, In re Pelter, 64 B.R. 492 (Bankr. W.D. Okla. 1986); In re Vaughn, 67 B.R. 140 (Bankr. C.D. Ill. 1986); In re Strain, 16 B.R. 797 (Bankr. D. Idaho. 1982).

[263] Lawrence Ponoroff, *Exemption Impairing Liens under Bankruptcy Code Section 522(f): One Step Forward and One Step Back*, 70 U. Colo. L. Rev. 1 (1999).

[264] Bankruptcy Code § 522(f)(1)(A).

[265] *See* Allan v. Putnam County Nat'l Bank (In re Allan), 431 B.R 580 (Bankr. M.D. Pa. 2010).

[266] In re Helms, 438 B.R. 95 (Bankr. W.D.N.C. 2010); In re Chambers, 264 B.R. 818 (Bankr. N.D. W. Va. 2001).

[267] Bankruptcy Code § 522(f)(1).

$25,000 homestead exemption for residential real estate. Section 522(f)(1) permits avoidance of the judgment lien to the extent it impairs the debtor's $25,000 exemption. If the house is sold, the mortgagee receives $40,000, the debtor receives $25,000, and the judgment lien-holder receives the remaining $35,000. Thus, the lien is not completely avoided, but is only set aside to the extent that it impairs the debtor's $25,000 homestead exemption.

The Supreme Court found it significant that this provision refers not to the lien itself but rather to the "fixing" of the lien. In *Farrey v. Sanderfoot*,[268] the Court held that this means the debtor's property interest must exist before the lien attaches to it. In *Sanderfoot*, the debtor's divorce decree granted him sole title to a home previously held in joint tenancy with his wife. His wife was simultaneously given a judgment lien against the property to secure his obligation to pay her for half of the value of the house. Because the interest was created simultaneously with the creation of his right to the property, it was treated not as a lien that had "fixed' " to his property but as an encumbrance that the debtor took along with the real estate, "as if he had purchased an already encumbered [property]."[269]

Since *Sanderfoot*, most courts have ruled that judicial liens securing support obligations in divorce decrees are invulnerable to attack under § 522(f) where the debtor acquires a new interest in the property subject to the lien as a result of a realignment of marital property rights in the divorce decree. Using the analysis deployed by *Sanderfoot*, § 522(f)(1)(A) could not apply because the debtor's property interest arose simultaneously with the creation of the lien.[270]

In 2005, Congress amended § 522(f)(1) by proscribing its use to avoid judicial liens that secure non-dischargeable "domestic support obligations."[271] This expands decisions following *Sanderfoot*, but only to the extent the judicial lien secures a support obligation. Judicial liens securing property settlement obligations or other debts remain subject to avoidance, unless under the *Sanderfoot* analysis, the lien is created simultaneously with a realignment of the debtor's property rights.

The *Sanderfoot* "fixing" approach is particularly troublesome with respect to the attachment of liens to after-acquired property in which the debtor did not acquire an interest in the property subject to the lien until after the lien was in place. Some courts have applied the *Sanderfoot* analysis to prevent use of § 522(f)(1)(A) in these settings.[272] Others have distinguished *Sanderfoot* and permitted the lien to be avoided by limiting *Sanderfoot* to its precise facts, involving situations where the debtor's property interest and the lien were created simultaneously.[273]

---

[268] 500 U.S. 291 (1991).

[269] 500 U.S. at 300.

[270] *E.g.*, Estate of Catli, 999 F.2d 1405 (9th Cir. 1993). *See also* In re Parrish, 7 F.3d 76 (5th Cir. 1993), *cert. denied sub nom.*, McVay v. Parrish, 511 U.S. 1006 (1994) (lien imposed on that property previously owned by debtor alone remained subject to avoidance).

[271] Bankruptcy Code § 522(f)(1)(A).

[272] Marine Midland Bank v. Scarpino (In re Scarpino), 113 F.3d 338 (2d Cir. N.Y. 1997).

[273] General Motors Acceptance Corp. v. Bates (In re Bates), 161 B.R. 965 (N.D. Ill. 1993).

[B]   Avoiding Non-Possessory, Non-Purchase Money Security Interests

Section 522(f)(1)(B) also permits the avoidance of some consensual security interests in certain items of the debtor's tangible personal property. The debtor may avoid the fixing of a non-possessory, non-purchase money security interest to the extent it impairs one of the debtor's exemptions in:

- household furnishings, household goods, clothing, appliances, books, animals, crops, musical instruments, or jewelry held primarily for the personal, family, or household use of the debtor or a dependent;

- implements, professional books, or tools of the debtor's trade or a dependent's trade; or

- professionally prescribed health aids for the debtor or a dependent of the debtor.[274]

This rule is narrow. First, it does not apply to all exempt property, but only to those few types specified in § 522(f)(1)(B).[275] Second, it does not avoid all security interests, but only those that are both "non-possessory" and "non-purchase-money.' " Thus, it does not impair the possessory security interests of pawn shops. Third, it does not impair purchase money security interests — security interests of those who have sold the collateral to the debtor or provided credit to the debtor to enable him to acquire the goods.[276]

The primary impetus for the § 522(f) avoidance power was Congress's concern about the personal loan industry's practice of obtaining security interests in all of a family's household goods and furnishings. These security interests had little to do with the value of those items, which were for the most part scarcely worth selling. However, the creditor's right to repossess all of a debtor's household property gave the creditor considerable leverage over the debtor because of the "in terrorem" effect of the creditor's lien. A room full of used furniture, worn clothing, and an array of umatched and dented old pots and pans has little market value. But these items might be difficult for a bankrupt debtor to replace. Consumer creditors believed that debtors faced with repossession of these goods would make extraordinary efforts to pay the debt, despite the minimal amount creditors would recover upon their sale.[277]

It was thus not the value of the property lost but the pressure imposed by the possibility of repossession that concerned Congress. Significantly however, § 522(f) does not impair the ability of a secured purchase money lender to seize its

---

[274] Bankruptcy Code § 522(f)(1)(B)(i)-(iii). Language added in 2005 supplies a detailed definition of "household goods." Bankruptcy Code § 522(f)(4).

[275] See Cleaver v. Warford (In re Cleaver), 407 B.R. 354 (B.A.P. 8th Cir. 2009) (debtor was permitted to show that motor vehicle was a "tool of the trade" for the purpose of § 522(f) avoidance, even though it was exempt as motor vehicle and not as tool of the trade under state exemption statute).

[276] See U.C.C. § 9-103 (2003).

[277] See Michael J. Herbert, *Straining the Gnat: A Critique of the 1984 Federal Trade Commission Consumer Credit Regulations*, 38 S.C. L. Rev. 329, 352 (1987).

collateral, even if it is of the type described in section 522(f)(1)(B). Permitting debtors to avoid purchase money loans would restrict the supply of credit available for the purchase of these items and impair economic growth generally.

Section 522(f)(3) imposes an additional limit on the debtor's ability to avoid security interests on tools of the debtor's trade, farm animals, professional books, and crops. The statutory language is nearly incomprehensible, but seems to apply only if (1) the debtor is claiming exemptions under state law, (2) the state has "opted out" of the federal exemption scheme, and (3) state law either has an unlimited exemption or prohibits avoidance of consensual liens on otherwise exempt property.[278] If these three conditions are met, the debtor may not use § 522(f) to avoid the fixing of a non-possessory, non-purchase money security interest in these limited types of property "to the extent that the value of [the property] exceeds $5,850."[279] Because no state permits debtors "to claim exemptions without limitation in amount," the literal language of § 522(f)(3) seems not to apply to any real-world situations. The text of the statute may have been intended to apply if the state permits the debtor to claim an exemption in an unlimited amount of tools of the debtor's trade, but the language of the statute does not say this.

Since the enactment of § 522(f), the enforceability of non-purchase money security interests in most household items has largely been dealt with by other bodies of law. Some states restrict the use of non-purchase money security interests in consumer transactions.[280] More significantly, the Federal Trade Commission's (FTC) rule treating non-purchase money security interests in most types of household goods as an unfair trade practice,[281] has made these types of security interests virtually non-existent. The FTC rule thus diminishes the significance of § 522(f)(2).

But, the FTC rule does not completely deprive § 522(f) of its effect. It still applies to types of property that are not protected by the Federal Trade Commission's rule, such as tools of the debtor's trade. Likewise, § 522(f) encompasses a wider range of creditors. For example, the FTC's rule applies only to professional creditors, and not to other more casual lenders.[282]

The potential conflict between § 522(f) and the constitutional prohibition on taking property without just compensation was resolved by the Supreme Court in *United States v. Security Industrial Bank*.[283] The Court ruled that although the

---

[278] Bankruptcy Code § 522(f)(3).

[279] Bankruptcy Code § 522(f)(3). This amount is set to be adjusted every three years. Bankruptcy Code § 104. The next changes will be on April 1, 2013, 2016, and 2019.

[280] Unif. Cons. Credit Code § 3.301 (1974).

[281] 16 C.F.R. §§ 444.1-444.5 (2012). *See* Michael J. Herbert, *Straining the Gnat: A Critique of the 1984 Federal Trade Commission Consumer Credit Regulations*, 38 S.C. L. Rev. 329, 352 (1987) (once described to its author by a supporter of the rule as "unduly negative and unnecessarily sarcastic"); Jean Braucher, *Defining Unfairness: Empathy and Economic Analysis at the Federal Trade Commission*, 68 B.U. L. Rev. 349 (1988).

[282] 16 C.F.R. §§ 444.2(a), 444.1(a) (2012).

[283] 459 U.S. 70 (1982).

retroactive application of § 522(f) might have been unconstitutional, Congress intended for it to apply only prospectively. This determination sidestepped the constitutional issue that had been brewing over its retroactive application to security interests created before adoption of the 1978 Bankruptcy Code.

§ 12.08   RETAINING COLLATERAL[284]

Debtors have several options to permit them to retain collateral covered by a creditor's security interest. In liquidation cases, § 722 permits debtors to "redeem" collateral by paying the secured creditor, in a lump sum, the amount of the "allowed secured claim" — either the amount of the debt or the value of the collateral, whichever is lower. Second, the debtor may enter into a "reaffirmation agreement" with the secured creditor holding the lien. These agreements usually reinstate the debtor's personal liability to the creditor but permit the debtor to keep the collateral. Before 2005, debtors who were not in default on their obligations to their secured creditors had a third option of simply retaining the collateral and continuing to make payments according to the terms of their original agreement with the creditor. However, language added in 2005 seems to have eliminated this alternative, unless the creditor is willing to cooperate. Finally, debtors might keep their collateral pursuant to the terms of a confirmed plan under Chapters 11, 12, or 13. As will be seen, debtors who deploy these strategies, are likely to remain saddled with debt after their bankruptcy cases are over.[285]

Debtors who implement none of these alternatives are required to surrender the collateral to the secured creditor. In addition, if the property is valuable enough, there may be non-exempt equity in the property that the trustee will wish to capture for distribution to unsecured creditors. However, as explained below, if the collateral is worth too much, the debtor may be deprived of most, if not all of these choices.

[A]   Lump-Sum Redemption by Debtor[286]

Under some circumstances, the debtor has the right to "redeem" property from a lien holder. Redemption simply means that the debtor may buy out the lien and become the owner of the property. Most states provide debtors with various rights of redemption, before or after the collateral is sold, as described elsewhere.[287]

---

[284] David Gray Carlson, *Redemption and Reinstatement in Chapter 7 Cases*, 4 Am. Bankr. Inst. L. Rev. 289 (1996); Scott B. Ehrlich, *The Fourth Option of Section 521(2)(A) — Reaffirmation Agreements and the Chapter 7 Consumer Debtor*, 53 Mercer L. Rev. 613 (2002); Margaret Howard, *Stripping Down Liens: Section 506(d) and the Theory of Bankruptcy*, 65 Am. Bankr. L.J. 373, 388 (1991); Lawrence Ponoroff & F. Stephen Knippenberg, *The Immovable Object Versus the Irresistible Force: Rethinking the Relationship Between Secured Credit and Bankruptcy Policy*, 95 Mich. L. Rev. 2234, 2239 (1997).

[285] *See* Katherine Porter, *Bankrupt Profits: The Credit Industry's Business Model for Postbankruptcy Lending*, 93 Iowa L. Rev. 1369 (2008).

[286] Lucian Arye Bebchuk & Jesse M. Fried, *A New Approach to Valuing Secured Claims in Bankruptcy*, 114 Harv. L. Rev. 2386 (2001); David Gray Carlson, *Redemption and Reinstatement in Chapter 7 Cases*, 4 Am. Bankr. Inst. L. Rev. 289 (1996).

[287] *See supra* § 2.07 Foreclosure Procedures.

These rights are not disturbed by bankruptcy. However, the Code goes beyond the traditional recognition of state-created redemption rights. It includes an additional right of redemption, limited to individual Chapter 7 debtors who seek to retain property that is exempt or abandoned.

The main problem with the typical state law redemption right is that the debtor must pay the underlying debt in full. Often, this is impossible. Insofar as personal property is concerned, the key provision is U.C.C. § 9-623, which requires full payment for redemption.[288] By contrast, the Bankruptcy Code permits Chapter 7 debtors to redeem for the lesser of (i) the obligation owed or (ii) the value of the property redeemed.

Bankruptcy Code § 722 permits an individual debtor to redeem property from a lien if the property is "tangible personal property intended primarily for personal, family, or household use."[289] This right applies even if the debtor has previously waived his or her redemption rights. In addition, the property either must be exempt under § 522 or must have been abandoned by the trustee under § 554.[290] Other property, such as real estate, is not subject to redemption. A further limit prohibits redemption if the debt involved is non-dischargeable under § 523.[291]

The key benefit for the debtor is that full payment of the debt is unnecessary. The debtor only needs to pay the lien holder the amount of the allowed secured claim.[292] Because the secured claim cannot exceed the value of the collateral,[293] if the debt is more than the value of the collateral the debtor must pay only the latter, not the former in order to redeem.

Assume, for example, that Doug owes Island Bank $10,000, representing the purchase price of a car financed by the bank. Assume further that the car is collateral for the debt but is only worth $7,000. Because the bank's lien is "under water," the trustee has no incentive to sell the car and will most likely be amenable to abandoning the estate's interest in it.[294] Even if the property has not been formally abandoned, redemption would probably be permitted, because the motor vehicle is probably subject to an available exemption, even though the exemption does not cover the entire value of the property.[295]

---

[288] U.C.C. § 9-623 (2003). In this context, full payment includes not only the principal and interest but also other contractual obligations, such as late fees and lawyer's fees. It also includes "the expenses reasonable expenses and attorney's fees" incurred in enforcing the security interest and preparing the collateral for sale.

[289] Bankruptcy Code § 722.

[290] *See supra* § 9.06 Abandonment of Estate Property.

[291] *See generally infra* § 13.03 Non-Dischargeable Debts.

[292] Bankruptcy Code § 722.

[293] Bankruptcy Code § 506(b). *See supra* § 10.03[A] Creditors with Secured Claims.

[294] Section 554 permits such abandonment when property can be shown to be burdensome to the estate or of inconsequential value and benefit to the estate. Bankruptcy Code § 554. Property that is covered by a lien securing a debt for more than the value of the collateral is of "inconsequential value and benefit to the estate." *See supra* § 9.06 Abandonment of Estate Property.

[295] *See* In re Fitzgerald, 20 B.R. 27 (Bankr. N.D.N.Y. 1982).

Under the U.C.C., Doug would have to pay at least $10,000 to redeem the car from the bank's security interest. If the agreement provided for other costs, such as Island Bank's attorneys' fees and collection costs, Doug would also have to pay those expenses.[296] However, under § 722, Doug may redeem the car by paying only the amount of the allowed secured claim: $7,000. By cutting the potential cost of redemption, § 722 provides some help to those debtors who are trying to keep property — at least those who are trying to keep property that is worth less than the debt it secures. The secured party, who receives the full value of its collateral, but from the debtor rather than another buyer, is not harmed.

The 2005 Amendments require the court to base the amount of the allowed secured claim on the "replacement value" of the collateral, rather than its liquidation value.[297] In many cases, however, the "price a retail merchant would charge" for property of the kind will be difficult to determine, given the general absence of a market for such goods.

Historically, the help promised by § 722 was meaningless for most debtors. In the example given, it may be just as difficult for Doug to raise $7,000 as $10,000. In most cases, debtors are unable to find a source for either sum, unless well-heeled relatives or sub-prime lenders are willing to step in to provide the necessary cash. However, with the growth of subprime lending in recent years, a market has emerged for loans to allow Chapter 7 debtors to redeem their cars.[298]

Section 722 would be more meaningful if it permitted debtors to make an installment redemption by paying the amount of the allowed secured claim over an extended period of time. However, § 722 has consistently been interpreted to deny debtors the right to make installment payments to redeem the property[299] and the 2005 Amendments added language removing any lingering doubt about the issue.[300] Consequently, unless they qualify for a redemption loan from a willing lender, debtors who wish to retain more property than § 522's exemption provisions allow must enter into a reaffirmation agreement with their current lender or file for reorganization under Chapters 11, 12, or 13. A reorganization plan in one of these proceedings may be used to make payments over time, without the creditor's consent.[301]

---

[296] See U.C.C. § 9-623(b) (2003).

[297] Bankruptcy Code § 506(a)(2). See Jean Braucher, *Beneath the Surface of BAPCPA Rash and Ride-through Redux: The Terms for Holding on to Cars, Homes and Other Collateral under the 2005 Act*, 13 Am. Bankr. Inst. L. Rev. 457 (2005).

[298] See, e.g., http://www.freshstartloans.com/fslc/home.asp (last visited March 15, 2012); http://www.722redemption.com (last visited March 15, 2012). See generally Katherine Porter, *Life After Debt: Understanding the Credit Restraint of Bankruptcy Debtors*, 18 Am. Bankr. Inst. L. Rev. 1 (2010).

[299] See In re Edwards, 901 F.2d 1383 (7th Cir. 1990); In re Bell, 700 F.2d 1053 (6th Cir. 1983); In re Horne, 132 Bankr. 661 (Bankr. N.D. Ga. 1991).

[300] BAPCA added the words "in full at the time of redemption." See also Fed. R. Bankr. P. 6008.

[301] See infra § 18.07[B][2] Modifying Secured Claims.

[B]   Reaffirmation[302]

Debtors wishing to retain property subject to a security interest, but who are unable to obtain the cash necessary to redeem the collateral with a lump-sum payment under § 722, may be able to retain it by entering into a reaffirmation agreement with the creditor holding the security interest. A reaffirmation agreement would contain the debtor's renewed post-petition promise to repay the debt secured by the collateral, possibly with a revised payment schedule, in exchange for the creditor's agreement to refrain from exercising its right to immediately repossess the collateral.[303]

Bankruptcy Code §§ 524(c) & (m) impose limitations on the enforceability of these reaffirmation agreements. To be enforceable, a reaffirmation agreement must:

- be in writing;[304]

- have been made before the debtor's discharge is granted;[305]

- be preceded by the debtor's receipt of several disclosure statements regarding the debtor's right not to enter into a reaffirmation agreement and about the consequences of making the agreement;[306]

- be filed with the court;[307]

- in a case in which an attorney represents the debtor in connection with the reaffirmation agreement, be accompanied by the attorney's affidavit,[308] stating that the reaffirmation agreement was 1) fully informed and voluntary, 2) does not impose an undue hardship on the debtor or the debtor's dependents, and 3) was made only after the attorney fully advised

---

[302] Marianne B. Culhane & Michaela M. White, *Debt after Discharge: An Empirical Study of Reaffirmation*, 73 Am. Bankr. L.J. 709 (1999); Gregory M. Duhl, *Divided Loyalties: The Attorney's Role in Bankruptcy Reaffirmations*, 84 Am. Bankr. L.J. 101 (2010); Lisa A. Napoli, *Reaffirmation after the Bankruptcy Abuse Prevention and Consumer Protection Act of 2005: Many Questions, Some Answers*, 81 Am. Bankr. L.J. 259 (2007).

[303] A secured creditor's agreement not to repossess provides consideration for the debtor's renewed promise, but the debtor's promise does not need consideration to be enforceable under the common law of contracts. *See* Restatement (Second) of Contracts § 83 (1981) (making promises to repay debts discharged in bankruptcy enforceable without consideration).

[304] Bankruptcy Code § 524(c)(3). Though not explicitly stated, the requirement that the agreement be filed with the court necessitates that it be in writing.

[305] Bankruptcy Code § 524(c)(1); In re Giglio, 428 B.R. 397 (Bankr. N.D. Ohio 2009) (reaffirmation agreement unenforceable because it was executed after discharge); In re Golladay, 391 B.R. 417 (Bankr. C.D. Ill. 2008).

[306] Bankruptcy Code § 524(c)(2), (k). *See* David B. Wheeler & Douglas E. Wedge, *A Fully-Informed Decision: Reaffirmation, Disclosure, and the Bankruptcy Abuse Prevention and Consumer Protection Act of 2005*, 79 Am. Bankr. L.J. 789 (2005); Jean Braucher, *Counseling Consumer Debtors to Make Their Own Informed Choices — A Question of Professional Responsibility*, 5 Am. Bankr. Inst. L. Rev. 165 (1997).

[307] Bankruptcy Code § 524(c)(3). *See* Fed. R. Bankr. P. 4008.

[308] In re Minardi, 399 B.R. 841 (Bankr. N.D. Okla. 2009) (attorney's effort to limit the scope of his representation to exclude supplying affidavit regarding reaffirmation was ineffective).

the debtor about the effect and consequences of the agreement;[309]

- the debtor has signed the "reaffirmation statement" specified in § 524(k)(6), before or at the time he signed the agreement;

- in a case in which the debtor is not represented by an attorney in connection with the reaffirmation agreement, and the debt is not a consumer debt secured by real estate, must have been approved by the court as both 1) not imposing an undue hardship[310] and 2) "in the best interest of the debtor;[311] and

- not have been rescinded by the debtor either before a discharge was granted or during the sixty days thereafter.[312]

Further, in the rare circumstance in which the court conducts a "discharge hearing," the court must as part of the hearing repeat the disclosures about the debtor's reaffirmation agreement that were to have been supplied to the debtor.[313]

[1] Agreement with Creditor

Of course, the most important limitation on reaffirmation agreements is that there must be an agreement between the parties. The debtor cannot unilaterally retain the collateral, but must obtain the secured party's assent to the terms of the reaffirmation agreement permitting him to do so. The practical impact of this limitation, which is inherent in the concept of reaffirmation, is that debtors will usually have to repay the entire debt owed to the secured party under the terms of the original agreement, and perhaps more.[314]

For many years it was unclear whether creditors' efforts to persuade a debtor to enter into a reaffirmation agreement are violations of the automatic stay. Section 362(a)(6) prohibits "*any act* to collect, assess, or recover a claim against the debtor that arose before the commencement of the case."[315] This seems to prohibit creditors from soliciting reaffirmation agreements while still permitting debtors to approach their lenders about reaffirming.

Courts have disagreed about the extent to which creditors can attempt to persuade a debtor to enter into a reaffirmation agreement without violating the automatic stay. Although § 362(a)(6) prohibits creditors from engaging in any act to

---

[309] Bankruptcy Code § 524(c)(3). It is completely unclear how debtors' attorneys are supposed to assess whether the agreement will impose an "undue hardship" on the debtor or the debtor's dependents. If "undue hardship" means the same thing as it does in the context of dischargeability of student loans under § 523(a)(8), then undue hardship will be found only in extreme situations. *See infra* § 13.03[B][8] Student Loans.

[310] *E.g.*, In re Reed, 403 B.R. 102 (Bankr. N.D. Okla. 2009) (reaffirmation agreement with monthly installments of $285 with a final "balloon payment" of over $37,000 imposed an undue hardship).

[311] Bankruptcy Code § 524(c)(5); E.g., In re Stillwell, 348 B.R. 578 (Bankr. N.D. Okla. 2006) (debtors' schedules reflected that their income inadequate in to meet expenses).

[312] Bankruptcy Code § 524(c)(4).

[313] Bankruptcy Code § 524(c)(5), (d).

[314] 283 F.3d 392 (1st Cir. 2002); In re Paglia, 302 B.R. 162 (Bankr. W.D. Pa. 2002).

[315] Bankruptcy Code § 362(a)(6) (emphasis supplied). *See supra* § 8.02[D] Acts to Collect.

collect a pre-petition debt, the text of § 524(c) is rife with references to the necessity for an "agreement," which implies the right of the creditor to hold out for terms it prefers. As the court said in *In re Turner*: "Implicit in the statute's repeated reference to an 'agreement'. . . is the requirement that the creditor as well as the debtor consent to the reaffirmation."[316] Agreements, like the proverbial tango, require two participants. Prohibiting creditors from negotiating with debtors over the terms of a reaffirmation agreement would render much of § 524(c) meaningless.[317]

This does not permit the creditor to engage in "harassment or coercion."[318] However, secured creditors are permitted to invite the debtor to enter into a reaffirmation agreement and to inform the debtor about the consequences of either accepting or rejecting the creditor's proposed terms.[319] They are also permitted, during the course of these negotiations, to "make plain" their intent to foreclose on the collateral if the debtor does not agree to reaffirm the debt.[320]

Creditors also seem to be permitted to insist that the debtor agree to repay other debts owed to the them as a condition of being permitted to retain the collateral. This practice, though controversial, seems consistent with the principles of freedom of contract inherent in § 524(c) and has been permitted by a few courts.[321] It is in tension, however, with the automatic stay. Thus, if Robert owes $10,000 to Island Bank for the purchase price of his $7,000 pickup truck and also has an outstanding unpaid $6,000 balance on his Island Bank credit card, the bank might agree to permit him to keep the truck only if he agrees to repay the entire $16,000 owed on both debts combined.

[2] Undue Hardship

Where debtors are represented by an attorney in connection with the reaffirmation agreement, the debtor's attorney must submit an affidavit that the agreement will not result in an undue hardship on the debtor or her dependents.[322] Debtors' attorneys who sign these affidavits will want to act with due diligence to assure themselves that their clients' reaffirmation agreements will not result in an undue hardship on their clients or on any of the client's dependents. The requirement of providing an affidavit carries the risk of placing the attorney in a conflicted situation, with a duty to act at the behest of her client and a duty to

---

[316] 156 F.3d 713, 718 (7th Cir. 1998).

[317] *See, e.g.*, In re Duke, 79 F.3d 43, 45 (7th Cir. 1996); Pertuso v. Ford Motor Credit Co., 233 F.3d 417, 423 (6th Cir. 2000).

[318] Pertuso v. Ford Motor Credit Co., 233 F.3d 417, 423 (6th Cir. 2000); Cox v. Zale Del. Inc., 239 F.3d 910 (7th Cir. 2001).

[319] Pertuso v. Ford Motor Credit Co., 233 F.3d 417, 423 (6th Cir. 2000).

[320] Jacqueline B. Stuart, *All or Nothing Reaffirmation: Can Secured and Unsecured Debts Be Linked?*, 58 Bus. Law. 1309, 1317 (2003).

[321] Jamo v. Katahdin Fed. Credit Union (In re Jamo), 283 F.3d 392 (1st Cir. 2002); In re Jacobs, 321 B.R. 451 (Bankr. N.D. Ohio 2004).

[322] Bankruptcy Code § 524(c)(3)(B).

provide an honest personal assessment of the client's situation, to the court.[323]

Where debtors are not represented by an attorney, the court must assess whether the agreement would impose an undue hardship on the debtor or his dependents. If the reaffirmation statement submitted by the debtor pursuant to § 524(k)(6)[324] reflects that the debtor cannot afford to make the payments required by the agreement, the court will refuse to approve the agreement.

In some cases, debtors are presumed to face an undue hardship, regardless of whether they are represented by an attorney. Debtors whose reaffirmation agreements would result in their monthly expenses being in excess of their monthly income must rebut this presumption to obtain court approval of their reaffirmation agreements.[325] The presumption may be rebutted if the debtor supplies a written statement that identifies the additional sources of funds that will be used to fund the payments required by the reaffirmation agreement.[326] Curiously, however, this presumption does not apply if the creditor involved in the reaffirmation agreement is a credit union.[327] Apparently, Congress is not quite so concerned about imposing undue hardships on debtors when the beneficiary of the hardship is a credit union, rather than a bank or finance company.

The undue hardship test applies primarily to debtors' efforts to retain possession of their automobiles, and sometimes to items of household furniture. It does not apply in connection with reaffirmations of debts secured by the debtor's home.[328]

[3]   Best Interest of the Debtor

In cases involving debtors who are not represented by counsel in connection with the reaffirmation agreement, the court must also find that the agreement "is in the best interest of the debtor." Like the undue hardship test, the "best interests" test does not apply in connection with "a consumer debt secured by real property" — usually the debtor's home.[329] Some courts refuse to find that the agreement is in the debtor's bests interests if it will result in the debtor owing more than the collateral she is seeking to retain is worth.[330] However, most debtors need their cars to get to work and to perform other routine family errands. Even though reaffirming a debt to pay more for a car than it is worth does not seem wise, a reaffirmation agreement is the only source of credit available for many debtors. Without the ability to reaffirm their secured debt and retain possession of the family auto, bankrupt debtors would face additional burdens and inconveniences; some, without transportation, would lose their jobs.

---

[323] Gregory M. Duhl, *Divided Loyalties: The Attorney's Role in Bankruptcy Reaffirmations*, 84 Am. Bankr. L.J. 101 (2010).

[324] *See* Fed. R. Bankr. P. 4008(b).

[325] Bankruptcy Code § 524(m). *See* In re Grisham, 436 B.R. 896 (Bankr. N.D. Tex. 2010).

[326] Bankruptcy Code § 524(m)(1).

[327] Bankruptcy Code § 524(m)(2).

[328] Bankruptcy Code § 524(c)(6)(B). *E.g.,* In re Law, 421 B.R. 735, 737 (Bankr. W.D. Pa. 2010).

[329] Bankruptcy Code § 524(c)(6)(B).

[330] In re Delano, 7 B.R. 72 (Bankr. D. Me. 1980).

[4] Agreement Before Discharge

The agreement must also have been executed "before the granting of the [debtor's] discharge."[331] Thus, agreements made after the bankruptcy case has been concluded, or after the debtor's discharge has been entered, are unenforceable. This may trip the debtor up if the creditor has been neglectful in getting the paperwork necessary to form the reaffirmation agreement until a late stage in the debtor's bankruptcy case, or after it has been concluded.

[5] Required Disclosures

Sections 524(c)(2) and (k) also require certain disclosures to be made to the debtor, no later than the time the debtor signed the reaffirmation agreement. These disclosures, imposed in 2005, must be made "clearly and conspicuously, and in writing."[332] The details are specified in § 524(k)(3) and are designed to ensure that the debtor understands the total amount she is agreeing to reaffirm, the total of any fees and costs associated with the reaffirmation agreement, the "annual percentage rate" of interest that will accrue on the debt, and other details of the agreement, including the debtor's right to rescind.

[6] Right to Rescind

Section 524(c)(4) makes reaffirmation agreements enforceable only if the debtor does not rescind the agreement. The debtor may rescind before his discharge is granted, or within sixty days after the agreement is filed with the court.[333] All that is required is for the debtor to give notice of his exercise of the right to rescind to the creditor who holds the claim.

[7] Relationship to "Abuse"

Finally, debtors who seek to reaffirm debts to retain luxury items run the risk that the court will find that their Chapter 7 petition is abusive, and dismiss their case altogether. Section 707(b) permits the court to dismiss a case if "the granting of relief would be an abuse of [Chapter 7 of the Bankruptcy Code]." In determining whether a particular debtor's case is abusive, courts consider a variety of factors, including the debtor's ability to pay. A debtor who has sufficient income to reaffirm debts secured by luxury items, may have sufficient income to make substantial payments to his other creditors, if debts secured by luxury items are not reaffirmed.[334]

---

[331] Bankruptcy Code § 524(c)(1).

[332] Bankruptcy Code § 524(k)(2).

[333] Bankruptcy Code § 524(c)(4).

[334] *Compare* In re Brenneman, 397 B.R. 866, 874 (Bankr. N.D. Ohio 2008), *and* In re Boyle, 412 B.R. 108, 109 (Bankr. W.D.N.Y. 2009), *with* In re Honkomp, 416 B.R. 647 (Bankr. N.D. Iowa 2009).

[C] Retention without Redemption or Reaffirmation — "Ride-Through"[335]

Before 2005, debtors were able to deploy a fourth strategy to hold on to property that was covered by a security interest. A debtor who was not in default could simply continue making his regularly scheduled payments, without reaffirming the debt. Absent a default, the creditor had no right to repossess or foreclose.[336] The advantage of this, over entering into a reaffirmation agreement was that the debtor's personal liability to repay the debt was discharged. If the debtor subsequently fell into default, the creditor could foreclose on the collateral, but the debtor would not be liable for a deficiency.

The strategy was controversial. Courts were divided over whether § 521(2) permitted it at all.[337] Like current § 521(a)(2), former § 521(2)(A) required individual debtors to file a statement of intention regarding their plans for dealing with collateral securing a consumer debt. Debtors are required to file a statement that expresses whether they intend to surrender the collateral, redeem the collateral under § 722, or enter into a reaffirmation agreement with the secured creditor under § 524(c).[338] Former § 521(2)(C), which has since been renumbered and amended further, specified that "nothing in the remainder" of § 521(2) shall alter the debtor's . . . rights" with respect to the collateral.[339] This language gave debtors an avenue to claim that the statement of intent required to be filed by the debtor was purely procedural and that it did not create a substantive rule that required the debtor to surrender, redeem, or reaffirm. A majority of circuits addressing the issue agreed.[340]

In 2005, Congress amended § 521 to eliminate this option with respect to debts secured by personal property. The revised language now provides:

> [I]n a case under chapter 7 . . . [an individual debtor may] not retain possession of personal property as to which a creditor has an allowed claim

---

[335] Jean Braucher, *Beneath the Surface of BAPCPA*, Rash *and Ride-Through Redux: The Terms for Holding on to Cars, Homes and Other Collateral Under the 2005 Act*, 13 Am. Bankr. Inst. L. Rev. 457 (2005); Marianne Culhane & Michaela White, *But Can She Keep the Car? Some Thoughts on Collateral Retention in Consumer Chapter 7 Cases*, 7 Fordham. J. Corp. & Fin. L. 471, 477-78, 487-88 (2002); David Gray Carlson, *Redemption and Reinstatement in Chapter 7 Cases*, 4 Am. Bankr. Inst. L. Rev. 289 (1996); Scott B. Ehrlich, *The Fourth Option of Section 521(2)(A) — Reaffirmation Agreements and the Chapter 7 Consumer Debtor*, 53 Mercer L. Rev. 613 (2002); Henry J. Sommer, *Trying to Make Sense Out of Nonsense: Representing Consumers Under the "Bankruptcy Abuse Prevention and Consumer Protection Act of 2005*,*" 79 Am. Bankr. L.J. 191 (2005); Christopher M. Hogan, Note, *Will the Ride-through Ride Again?*, 108 Colum. L. Rev. 882 (2008).

[336] *See, e.g.*, U.C.C. § 9-601 (2003) (making the secured party's rights to foreclose contingent upon "default.").

[337] *See* Price v. Delaware State Police Fed. Credit Union (In re Price), 370 F.3d 362 (3d Cir. 2004).

[338] *See* Bankruptcy Code § 521(a)(2)(A) (containing language identical to that in former § 521(2)(A)).

[339] Bankruptcy Code § 521(2)(C).

[340] *Compare* In re Price, 370 F.3d 362, 379 (3d Cir. 2004) (joining the second, fourth, ninth, and tenth circuits in treating former § 521(2) as procedural, not substantive), *with* Bank of Boston v. Burr (In re Burr), 160 F.3d 843, 849 (1st Cir. 1998) (joining the fifth, seventh, and tenth circuits in regarding § 521(2) as substantive and prohibiting ride-through).

for the purchase price secured in whole or in part by an interest in such personal property unless the debtor, not later than 45 days after the first meeting of creditors under section 341(a) either —

(A) enters into an agreement with the creditor pursuant to section 524(c) with respect to the claim secured by such property; or

(B) redeems such property from the security interest pursuant to section 722.[341]

On its face, subject to some narrow exceptions, this language proscribes the debtor's ability to permit the security interest to ride-through the bankruptcy, at least with respect to some security interests.[342] Thus, debtors who do not either surrender the collateral, redeem under § 722, or reaffirm under § 524(c) will find the creditor released from the automatic stay and free to repossess the collateral, even though the bankruptcy case is still pending.

However, the 2005 amendments did not completely eliminate ride-through.[343] First, the proscription applies only to individual debtors in Chapter 7 cases. Second, it applies only to security interests in personal property, not to real estate mortgages.[344] Thus, in *In re Hart*,[345] the debtors were permitted to retain their nine-acre poultry farm, and to continue making the monthly $14,000 payments owed to the creditor, without entering into a reaffirmation agreement and renewing their personal liability or the debt. The discharge did not affect the creditor's lien, but the debtors could keep the collateral since they were not in default.

Finally, some courts have ruled that ride-through survives in cases in which the debtor negotiated a reaffirmation agreement, only to have the court disapprove it.[346] In these cases, the debtor substantially complied with the requirements of §§ 521(a)(2), 521(a)(6), and 362(h).[347] However, where the debtor is unwilling to enter into a reaffirmation agreement, ride-through is unavailable, for individual debtors seeking to retain items of personal property.[348]

---

[341] Bankruptcy Code § 521(a)(6).

[342] Bankruptcy Code § 362(h); Dumont v. Ford Motor Credit Co. (In re Dumont), 581 F.2d 1104 (9th Cir. 2009).

[343] *See* In re Price, 370 F.3d 362 (3d Cir. 2004), and its progeny. In re Baker, 400 B.R. 126 (Bankr. N.D. Iowa 2009); In re Hart, 402 B.R. 78 (Bankr. D. Del. 2009). Seems to depend on court disapproval of reaffirmation — this may be an anomaly based on a D. Del Bankruptcy judge's weird ruling about 521 after BAPCA and the impact of *In re Price*. *See* Christopher M. Hogan, Note, *Will the Ride-Through Ride Again?*, 108 Colum. L. Rev. 882 (2008).

[344] In re Lopez, 440 B.R. 447 (Bankr. S.D. Ohio 2010). *See* Jean Braucher, *Beneath the Surface of BAPCPA, Rash and Ride-Through Redux: The Terms for Holding on to Cars, Homes and Other Collateral under the 2005 Act*, 13 Am. Bankr. Inst. L. Rev. 457, 479-81 (2005).

[345] 402 B.R. 78 (Bankr. D. Del. 2009).

[346] *See* In re Dumont, 581 F.3d 1104 (9th Cir. 2009); In re Donald, 343 B.R. 524 (Bankr. E.D.N.C. 2006); Coastal F. Credit Union v. Hardiman, 398 B.R. 161 (E.D.N.C. 2008). *See* Christopher M. Hogan, Note, *Will the Ride-through Ride Again?*, 108 Colum. L. Rev. 882 (2008).

[347] In re Dumont, 581 F.3d 1104, 1112 n. 14 (9th Cir. 2009).

[348] In re Dumont, 581 F.3d 1104 (9th Cir. 2009).

Naturally, debtors still have the option to retain the collateral if the secured creditor acquiesces.[349] In addition, the reference to "personal property as to which a creditor has an allowed claim for the purchase price" leaves open the possibility that § 521(a)(6) will be limited to creditors either who were either the sellers of the collateral or whose claims arise from an assignment of the seller's rights. The plain language of the statute leaves it inapplicable to secured creditors who made loans to the debtor, enabling him to pay the price in cash.[350]

[D]   Debtor's Statement of Intent[351]

One of an individual debtor's duties is to file a notice, ordinarily within thirty days after filing his petition,[352] indicating his intent with respect to property that is subject to a security interest.[353] The statement of intent must indicate whether the debtor intends to surrender the collateral to the secured party, to redeem the property under § 722, or to enter into a reaffirmation agreement with the creditor holding the lien pursuant to § 524(c).[354]

Section 521(c) further specifies that the debtor "shall perform his intention with respect to such property" within thirty days after the "first date set for the meeting of creditors" under § 341, or "within such additional time as the court, for cause" may fix.[355]

As indicated above, the language of § 521(a)(2)(B) now seems to preclude a debtor who is not in default from simply maintaining his payments to the creditor and thus permitting the security interest to "ride-through" the bankruptcy case.

---

[349] Jean Braucher, *Beneath the Surface of BAPCPA, Rash and Ride-Through Redux: The Terms for Holding on to Cars, Homes and Other Collateral under the 2005 Act*, 13 Am. Bankr. Inst. L. Rev. 457, 475-77 (2005).

[350] The distinction between a secured seller and an enabling lender is reflected in U.C.C. § 9-103(b)(2) (2003) (defining "purchase money obligation). Further, Bankruptcy Code § 547(c)(3) uses broader language to refer to all purchase money security interests, not just those retained by the seller. Bankruptcy Code § 547(c)(3).

[351] Jean Braucher, *Beneath the Surface of BAPCPA, Rash and Ride-Through Redux: The Terms for Holding on to Cars, Homes and Other Collateral under the 2005 Act*, 13 Am. Bankr. Inst. L. Rev. 457 (2005).

[352] If the "meeting of creditors" conducted pursuant to § 341 is held earlier than thirty days after the petition, the debtor must file his § 521(a)(2) statement of intent prior to that meeting. Bankruptcy Code § 521(a)(2)(A).

[353] Bankruptcy Code § 521(a)(2). *See* Fed. R. Bankr. P. 1007(b)(2).

[354] Bankruptcy Code § 521(a)(2).

[355] Bankruptcy Code § 521(a)(2)(B). The language requires the court to make its decision whether to extend the time for performance during the initial thirty-day period after the date set for the § 341 meeting.

[E] Chapter 7 Lien-Stripping[356]

A fundamental axiom of bankruptcy law is that creditors' liens on a debtor's property pass through bankruptcy unaffected by the debtor's discharge.[357] This historic rule raises difficult questions with respect to the effect of bankruptcy on partially secured claims in which the value of the collateral at the time of bankruptcy is less than the debt the collateral secures.

In *Dewsnup v. Timm*, the Supreme Court held that § 506(d) could not be used to "strip down" a lien by avoiding the unsecured *portion* of a real estate mortgage.[358] Thus, if land securing a $120,000 debt is worth only $90,000, and the trustee abandons the property without selling it, the debtors may not rescue the land from the creditor's mortgage by paying only the $90,000 value of the collateral. The lien remains on the property to satisfy the full $120,000 debt even though the debtor's in-personum liability for the $120,000 debt is discharged.

To reach this result, the *Dewsnup* Court read § 506(d) in a highly unorthodox manner. The section provides: "To the extent that a lien secures a claim against the debtor that is not *an allowed secured claim*, such lien is void."[359] The conventional meaning of "allowed secured claim" is supplied by § 506(a)(1): "An allowed claim of a creditor secured by a lien on property in which the estate has an interest . . . is a secured claim to the extent of the value of such creditor's interest in the . . . property."[360] For other purposes, the creditor's allowed secured claim would be only $90,000 and § 506(d) would permit the lien to be avoided to the extent that it secured the $30,000 balance. In *Dewsnup*, the Court read the word "secured" out of § 506(d) and refused to permit the debtor to avoid the lien.[361]

Whether *Dewsnup* permits a Chapter 7 debtor to use § 506(d) to "strip off" a completely unsecured and thus valueless junior lien from real property has left courts divided.[362] Most courts apply *Dewsnup* with equal vigor to liens that are wholly unsecured, and refuse to permit a debtor to avoid or "strip off" the junior lien.[363] Nothing in the 2005 Amendments changed this trend.[364] Thus, if the

---

[356] *See* David Gray Carlson, *Bifurcation of Undersecured Claims in Bankruptcy*, 70 Am. Bankr. L.J. 1 (1996); Margaret Howard, *Dewsnupping the Bankruptcy Code*, 1 J. Bankr. L. & Prac. 513 (1992); Jane Kaufman Winn, *Lien Stripping After Nobelman*, 27 Loy. L.A. L. Rev. 541 (1994).

[357] Farrey v. Sanderfoot, 500 U.S. 291, 297 (1991) ("Ordinarily, liens and other secured interests survive bankruptcy"); Johnson v. Home State Bank, 501 U.S. 78 (1991); Dewsnup v. Timm, 502 U.S. 410, 417 (1992).

[358] Dewsnup v. Timm, 502 U.S. 410, 417 (1992).

[359] Bankruptcy Code § 506(d) (emphasis added).

[360] Bankruptcy Code § 506(a)(1). *See supra* § 10.03[C] Allowance of Secured Claims.

[361] Margaret Howard, *Dewsnupping the Bankruptcy Code*, 1 J. Bankr. L. & Prac. 513, 516 (1992).

[362] In re Talbert, 344 F.3d 555 (6th Cir. 2003).

[363] In re Talbert, 344 F.3d 555 (6th Cir. 2003); Ryan v. Homecomings Financial Network, 253 F.3d 778 (4th Cir. 2001); Concannon v. Imperial Capital Bank (In re Concannon), 338 B.R. 90 (B.A.P. 9th Cir. 2006); Grano v. Wells Fargo Bank (In re Grano), 422 B.R. 401 (Bankr. W.D. N.Y. 2010); In re Pomilio, 425 B.R. 11 (Bankr. E.D.N.Y. 2010).

[364] *E.g.*, In re Spears, 421 B.R. 47 (Bankr. W.D.N.Y. 2009); Cook v. IndyMac Bank, FSB (In re Cook), 449 B.R. 664 (D.N.J. 2011).

property were worth $80,000 and subject to both a senior $90,000 mortgage and a junior $30,000 mortgage, the junior mortgage could not be "stripped-off." Accordingly, if after bankruptcy, the property increased in value to $120,000, the creditor with the junior mortgage could still foreclose. To redeem her property from these creditors' claims, debtor would have to pay both the $90,000 debt and the $30,000 debt.

Other courts rule that *Dewsnup* applies only to partially secured claims.[365] Whether a reconstituted Court would heed the plain meaning of § 506(d) and overrule *Dewsnup* to permit lien stripping, or adhere to stare decisis and apply *Dewsnup* to completely worthless liens, depends on which of these two restraints on judicial power holds the strongest sway with the new Supreme Court.[366]

Dewsnup and its progeny apply only to Chapter 7 cases, and only to property that is not sold by the trustee as part of the case. Chapters 11, 12, and 13 all contain provisions expressly permitting the sort of strip-down and strip-off that *Dewsnup* precludes.[367]

[F] Buying Non-Exempt Equity

Another way for the debtor to retain his non-exempt property is to purchase it from the trustee. The debtor may use other exempt assets, or borrowed funds to complete the purchase.[368] This strategy can only be implemented with the cooperation of the trustee, but the trustee is likely to be far more interested in obtaining the best possible price for the property than in the identity of the buyer. Moreover, selling the estate's property to the debtor will avoid transaction costs, such as a real estate agent's commission, that otherwise might have to be paid from the proceeds of the sale and reduce the amount realized by the estate for distribution to creditors. For example, in *In re Weathers*,[369] the debtor's sought to pay the trustee $11,000 for the non-exempt 0.05 acre portion of their otherwise exempt 0.3 acre residence, which was worth a total of $66,000.[370] The court approved the sale over the objection of creditors, who preferred to have the property sold and the proceeds divided between the debtors and the estate. Conducting such a sale would have resulted in a delay, and would have reduced the amount available for distribution to creditors by the creditors' share of the cost of the sale. Selling the exempt portion to the debtors was justified because it would produce the largest amount for creditors, based on the available appraisal evidence.

---

[365] *E.g.*, In re Lavelle, No. 09-72389-478, 2009 Bankr. LEXIS 3795 (Bankr. E.D.N.Y. Nov. 19, 2009) (restricting *Dewsnupp* to situations involving "strip-down"); Howard v. Nat'l Westminister Bank, U.S.A. (In re Howard), 184 B.R. 644 (Bankr. E.D.N.Y. 1995).

[366] Dewsnup v. Timm, 502 U.S. 410, 421-31 (1992) (Scalia, J., dissenting).

[367] *See* Bankruptcy Code §§ 1129(b)(2)(A), 1225(a)(5) & 1325(a)(5); Grano v. Wells Fargo Bank (In re Grano), 422 B.R. 401 (Bankr. W.D.N.Y. 2010).

[368] *See generally* Katherine Porter, *Life After Debt: Understanding the Credit Restraint of Bankruptcy Debtors*, 18 Am. Bankr. Inst. L. Rev. 1 (2010).

[369] In re Weathers, 423 B.R. 530 (Bankr. W.D. Ark. 2009).

[370] The applicable homestead exemption statute protected a maximum of .25 acres of land. Their lot was .3 acres — ½ acre more than the exemption statute permitted.

In other cases, debtors may wish to purchase any non-exempt value of their automobile, or household goods and furnishings, which are usually far more valuable to the debtor than to any other prospective buyer. And, as in *Weathers*, sale of the non-exempt portion of these assets to the debtor is the most cost effective way to reduce the asset to cash. Most trustees also see that making deals like this with the debtor is the most cost effective use of the trustee's time.

Chapter 13

DISCHARGE

§ 13.01 THE NATURE OF DISCHARGE[1]

The main goal of nearly all debtors is to obtain relief from their debts, through a discharge.[2] Discharge is the feature that distinguishes bankruptcy from state insolvency proceedings. Discharge prohibits creditors from ever taking further action to collect most prepetition debts.[3] Discharge provides debtors with a valid legal defense in any action brought by creditors in an effort to collect. This is the essence of the debtor's "fresh start."[4] Some debtors may feel a moral responsibility to pay their discharged debts, but they have no legal obligation to do so.[5]

The Bankruptcy Code contains a number of discharge rules. Both the availability and the scope of a discharge depend on the type of bankruptcy proceeding involved, and in some cases, on whether the debtor is a live human being or some sort of organization, such as a corporation. Further, discharge may be denied entirely because of the debtor's misconduct.[6]

In addition, even if the debtor is generally entitled to a discharge, individual debts may be "nondischargeable" and thus excluded from the scope of the debtor's discharge. Moreover, some debts are dischargeable in one bankruptcy chapter but not in others. Still other debts may be dischargeable or not, depending on the debtor's financial circumstances.

---

[1] Barry Adler, Ben Polak & Alan Schwartz, *Regulating Consumer Bankruptcy: A Theoretical Inquiry*, 29 J. Legal Stud. 585 (2000); Vern Countryman, *Bankruptcy and the Individual Debtor — And a Modest Proposal to Return to the Seventeenth Century*, 32 Cath. U. L. Rev. 809 (1983); Margaret Howard, *A Theory of Discharge in Consumer Bankruptcy*, 48 Ohio St. L.J. 1047 (1987); Thomas Jackson, *The Fresh-Start Policy in Bankruptcy Law*, 98 Harv. L. Rev. 1393 (1985); Michael D. Sousa, *The Principle of Consumer Utility: A Contemporary Theory of the Bankruptcy Discharge*, 58 Kan. L. Rev. 553 (2010); Charles Jordan Tabb, *The Historical Evolution of the Bankruptcy Discharge*, 65 Am. Bankr. L.J. 325 (1991).

[2] It is not the only goal, however. Some debtors file in order to delay imminent foreclosure on their house. Others use bankruptcy to utilize the bankruptcy court's ability to sell assets free and clear of liens. Indeed, it should be noted that corporate debtors that liquidate do not receive a discharge at all.

[3] Bankruptcy Code § 524(a)(2). *See supra* § 13.09 Effect of Discharge.

[4] Katherine Porter, *Life After Debt: Understanding the Credit Restraint of Bankruptcy Debtors*, 18 Am. Bankr. Inst. L. Rev. 1 (2010).

[5] Conscientious students may remember from their course in contract law that this moral obligation supplies the consideration necessary to make any renewed promise to pay a discharged debt (in the form of a reaffirmation agreement) enforceable. However, the Bankruptcy Code provides further restrictions on these agreements, discussed elsewhere. *See supra* § 12.08[B] Reaffirmation.

[6] Bankruptcy Code § 727.

Discharge is an individual benefit given to the debtor who files the bankruptcy case. If other persons are liable for the debtor's obligations, they remain liable both during and after the debtor's bankruptcy case. For example, if Mark and Amy are jointly liable on a debt incurred while they were married, and Amy files a bankruptcy petition after their divorce, Amy's discharge has no effect on Mark's liability for the debt. If Mark wants relief, he will have to file his own bankruptcy petition. Similarly, if Betty, who owns of all of the stock of Metcalf, Inc., has signed a promissory note as an accommodation party,[7] guaranteeing repayment of a loan made to Metcalf, Inc., a bankruptcy discharge of the corporation does not relieve Betty from her personal responsibility for the debt, as a guarantor.

A final preliminary point bears emphasis. A bankruptcy discharge affects debts, not liens. Courts frequently reiterate the rule that liens survive discharge.[8] Although discharge prevents a creditor from obtaining payment from the debtor personally, it does not restrain a creditor from enforcing any property rights the creditor had, such as consensual, judicial, or statutory liens. In precise legal terms, discharge provides debtors with relief from their in personam liability but does not affect creditors' in rem rights against a debtor's property.[9]

For example, suppose that Carrie owes $12,000 to Friendly Finance Co. and that the debt is secured by a security interest in Carrie's carpenter's tools, which are worth $9,000. In Carrie's bankruptcy case, Friendly Finance has a $9,000 secured claim and a $3,000 unsecured claim.[10] Because Carrie had no equity in her tools that can be distributed to her other creditors, the bankruptcy trustee is unlikely to sell them. Instead, the trustee will likely abandon the estate's interest in the tools and permit Friendly Finance to enforce its lien against them.[11]

After Carrie's discharge, Friendly Finance retains its property interest in the tools and retains its right to sell them to satisfy its claim. But any amount of Carrie's debt that is not satisfied from the sale of the tools has been discharged and Friendly Finance is not entitled to recover the deficiency from Carrie personally.

As will be seen, the discharge provisions of the Bankruptcy Code have been the battleground for much of the debate over bankruptcy policy.[12] In many critics' view, discharge is too easy and too cheap. According to them, discharge is granted without sufficient inquiry into the debtor's ability to pay and thus provides debtors

---

[7] *See* U.C.C. § 3-419 (2003).

[8] H.R. Rep. No. 95-595, 361 (1977), *reprinted in* 1978 U.S.C.C.A.N. 5963, 6317; S. Rep. No. 95-989, 76 (1978), *reprinted* in 1978 U.S.C.C.A.N. 5787, 5862. *See* Dewsnup v. Timm, 502 U.S. 410, 420 (1992); Farrey v. Sanderfoot, 500 U.S. 291, 297 (1991); Long v. Bullard, 117 U.S. 617 (1886).

[9] Johnson v. Home State Bank, 501 U.S. 78, 83 (1991).

[10] Bankruptcy Code § 506.

[11] *See* Bankruptcy Code § 554. Under § 554, the trustee has the right to abandon property that is "burdensome" to the estate. *See supra* § 9.06 Abandonment of Estate Property.

[12] *See generally* Susan Block-Lieb & Edward J. Janger, *The Myth of the Rational Borrower: Behaviorism, Rationality and the Misguided "Reform" of Bankruptcy Law*, 84 Tex. L. Rev. 1481 (2006); Charles Jordan Tabb, *The Historical Evolution of the Bankruptcy Discharge*, 65 Am. Bankr. L.J. 325 (1991); John M. Czarnetzky, *The Individual and Failure: A Theory of the Bankruptcy Discharge*, 32 Ariz. St. L.J. 393 (2000).

with an incentive to resort to bankruptcy unnecessarily and wastefully.[13] They contend that these inefficiencies burden the entire economy, especially for those whose economic situations force them to seek high-risk credit. Discharge risk may make such credit unavailable or very expensive. Worse, it may contribute to a society of individuals who feel no responsibility for their actions and thus result in a relaxation of the ties that bind society together generally.

In the view of those who defend the Code, the discharge rules have engendered little abuse, especially by consumers.[14] These scholars contend that, except in rare cases, discharge merely confirms what is all too palpably the case — the debtor cannot pay, or at least cannot pay without enduring undue hardship or imposing unconscionable difficulties on her dependents. According to them, bankruptcy discharge merely imposes an official end to an already fruitless collection effort. Any serious attempt to impose a higher cost on discharge will be either futile or cruel.

In 2005, this debate led to the "Bankruptcy Abuse Prevention and Consumer Protection Act."[15] The 2005 amendments imposed new restrictions on the availability of a Chapter 7 bankruptcy discharge, based primarily on what was determined to be an ability of debtors to pay a substantial portion of their debts. It also led to a statutory formula for determining how much of their income some Chapter 13 debtors would have to devote to paying their unsecured creditors in a Chapter 13 rehabilitation plan.

§ 13.02　DENIAL OF DISCHARGE[16]

Discharge from their obligations is the principal remedy individual debtors seek in liquidation cases. But, if the debtor is ineligible for a discharge, she will not receive the "fresh start" that bankruptcy provides. As a result, after the bankruptcy case ends and the automatic stay expires, her creditors may continue to pursue her, as if the bankruptcy had never been filed.

---

[13] *See* Gordon Bermant & Ed Flynn, *Consumer Filings in a Complex Economy*, 18 J. Am. Bankr. Inst. J. 22 (Dec./Jan. 2000). The best elaboration of this argument is found in the Purdue Study, which argued that $1,100,000,000 of debt was unnecessarily discharged each year. Credit Research Center, Krannert School of Management, Purdue University Monograph No. 23, Consumer Bankruptcy Study, vol. 1 at 88-91 (1982).

The methodology used by the Purdue Study, which was funded by members of the consumer credit industry, has been criticized. *See, e.g.*, Teresa A. Sullivan, Elizabeth Warren & Jay Lawrence Westbrook, *Limiting Access to Bankruptcy Discharge: An Analysis of the Creditors' Data*, 1983 Wis. L. Rev. 1091 (1983) (indicating that the Purdue Study's methodology suffered from a selection bias); Elizabeth Warren, *Reducing Bankruptcy Protection for Consumers: A Response*, 72 Geo. L.J. 1333, 1338-39 (1984) (arguing that the Purdue Study lacked crucial expertise, was improperly designed, gathered data poorly, mis-analyzed the data, and drew erroneous and biased conclusions).

[14] Teresa A. Sullivan, Elizabeth Warren & Jay Lawrence Westbrook, As We Forgive Our Debtors: Bankruptcy and Consumer Credit in America 219-24 (1989).

[15] Bankruptcy Abuse Prevention and Consumer Protection Act of 2005, Pub. L. No. 109-8, 119 Stat 23 (2005). *See generally* Susan Jensen, *A Legislative History of the Bankruptcy Abuse Prevention and Consumer Protection Act of 2005*, 79 Am. Bankr. L.J. 485 (2005).

[16] William Houston Brown, *Taking Exception to a Debtor's Discharge: The 2005 Bankruptcy Amendments Make it Easier*, 79 Am. Bankr. L.J. 419 (2005).

When discharge is denied, it is usually because of the debtor's own wrongdoing, either in connection with the bankruptcy case itself or in dealing with creditors generally. Further, discharge is denied to debtors who seek the protection that bankruptcy offers, too frequently. Relief is also now denied, under the Code's "means testing" eligibility rules, to those who are deemed capable of making meaningful payments to their creditors.

[A] Consequences of Denial of Discharge

Denial of discharge means that the debtor is not relieved of responsibility for her debts. Instead, she remains saddled with whatever obligations she owed at the beginning of the case, reduced only by whatever amount was paid to her creditors through liquidation of her assets.

Without a discharge, a debtor does not enjoy the benefits of the discharge stay of § 524. Instead, creditors are permitted to engage in any of the collection activities they had been permitted to deploy in state court before the bankruptcy case began.[17] These include informal collection efforts to persuade the debtor to pay voluntarily, initiation or continuation of action to obtain a judgment against the debtor in court, and enforcement of any judgment that they have already obtained.

However, denial of discharge does not mean that the debtor's assets are unaffected by the bankruptcy case. The debtor's property is still assembled and sold by the trustee, with the proceeds distributed to creditors. The debtor thus loses her non-exempt assets. In precise statutory jargon, the trustee still fulfills its duties to "collect and reduce to money the property of the estate"[18] and to distribute the money collected according to the priorities established by the Code.[19] Thus, the debtor is deprived of any non-exempt equity she has in her property, but does not receive the "fresh start" that a bankruptcy discharge would otherwise provide.[20]

Denial of discharge is mostly commonly an issue in Chapter 7 liquidation cases. Discharge is most often denied because of some sort of misconduct by the debtor, usually in connection with the bankruptcy case itself.

It should also be remembered that dismissal of a Chapter 7 case at the outset due to "abuse" under § 707(b) has the same effect as a denial of discharge: the debtor obtains no relief from her debts and creditors remain free to pursue the debtor informally or in state court. However, denial of discharge is different from dismissal in that the debtor's assets are administered by the trustee even though discharge is denied; if a case is dismissed the trustee does not collect, sell, or distribute the debtor's assets.

In reorganization cases, the issue of discharge is dealt with primarily in the context of court confirmation of a reorganization plan; the debtor's misconduct in

---

[17] *See supra* Chapter 2 — Creditors' Collection Rights.

[18] Bankruptcy Code § 704(1).

[19] *See* Bankruptcy Code § 726.

[20] *See* Local Loan v. Hunt, 292 U.S. 234 (1934).

connection with the case is punished by the court's refusal to confirm a plan. Since discharge in these types of proceedings cannot occur unless a plan (providing for reorganization rather than liquidation) is confirmed,[21] denial of confirmation in a reorganization case has roughly the same effect as denial of discharge in a liquidation case. This section deals with the denial of discharge under these various types of proceedings but focuses primarily on denial of discharge in liquidation cases under Chapter 7.

[B]   Denial of Discharge in Chapter 7[22]

As indicated above, the reasons for denying discharge are nearly always rooted in the debtor's misconduct. The most common basis for denying the debtor a discharge is because of their fraudulent transfer or concealment of assets or their failure to provide the information necessary for the administration of their bankruptcy case. Debtors are also denied a discharge if they have obtained another discharge in a case commenced within eight years of the time of a subsequent petition.

The right to challenge the debtor's eligibility for a discharge is extended to all "parties in interest."[23] This includes the trustee, creditors, and the office of the United States Trustee. Further, on request of any party in interest, the court may order the trustee to examine the debtor's actions and conduct to determine whether there is a basis for denying discharge.[24]

[1]   Eligibility for Chapter 7 Discharge — Individual Debtors

Individuals are eligible for a Chapter 7 discharge,[25] even if they are deceased.[26] Other entities, such as corporations and partnerships, are not eligible for a Chapter 7 discharge and must seek relief, if at all, under Chapter 11.[27] While this may seem odd, when these other entities are deprived of all of their assets, they are likely to dissolve. Denying them the right to a discharge prevents trafficking in corporate shells and bankrupt partnerships.[28]

---

[21] In Chapter 11 cases, discharge occurs upon confirmation of a plan. Bankruptcy Code § 1141(d). In Chapter 12 and 13 cases, discharge occurs upon the debtor's completion of the terms of a previously confirmed plan. Bankruptcy Code §§ 1228(a), 1328(a).

[22] William Houston Brown, *Taking Exception to a Debtor's Discharge: The 2005 Bankruptcy Act Makes it Easier*, 79 Am. Bankr. L.J. 419 (2005).

[23] Bankruptcy Code § 727(c)(1).

[24] Bankruptcy Code § 727(c)(2). One of your authors once observed a bankruptcy judge angrily departing from the bench, in the belief that one of his clients had concealed assets from the court, in order to make an immediate call to the trustee to suggest that he make such a motion. Ouch!

[25] Bankruptcy Code § 727(a)(1).

[26] H.R. Rep. 95-595, 384 (1977), *reprinted in* 1978 U.S.C.C.A.N. 5963, 6340; S. Rep. No. 95-989, 98 (1978), *reprinted in* 1978 U.S.C.C.A.N. 5787, 5885.

[27] Bankruptcy Code § 727(a)(1).

[28] H.R. Rep. 95-595, 384 (1977), *reprinted in* 1978 U.S.C.C.A.N. 5963, 6340; S. Rep. No. 95-989, 98 (1978), *reprinted in* 1978 U.S.C.C.A.N. 5787, 5885.

The 2005 amendments imposed further restrictions on which debtors are eligible for discharge by restricting their ability to file a bankruptcy petition in the first place. As explained elsewhere, Chapter 7 liquidation cases of debtors whose income is high enough to enable them to make what Congress has determined are meaningful payments to their creditors are either dismissed or converted to Chapter 13.[29]

[2] Fraudulent Transfers; Destruction or Concealment of Property[30]

Debtors who hide their property from their creditors are not the type of "honest debtors" who deserve the fresh start that bankruptcy supplies. Consequently, § 727(a)(2) denies a discharge of debtors who "with intent to hinder, delay, or defraud a creditor [or the trustee, have] transferred, removed, destroyed, mutilated, or concealed" their property either within one year before the date of their bankruptcy petition or after it was filed.[31] Section 727(a)(2) is based on the premise that debtors who intentionally seek to deny creditors access to their assets should not be entitled to enjoy the benefits of Chapter 7.

[a]   Transfers with Intent to Defraud

The relationship between § 727(a)(2) and fraudulent conveyance law is clear. Both § 4 of the Uniform Fraudulent Transfer Act and § 548(a)(1)(A) of the Bankruptcy Code permit intentionally fraudulent transfers of the debtor's property to be avoided.[32] Section 727(a)(2) compounds the consequences of this bad behavior by denying the debtor a discharge. But, § 727(a)(2) goes further than fraudulent conveyance law. It denies a discharge to debtors who, with fraudulent intent: "transferred, removed, destroyed, mutilated, or concealed, or has permitted to be transferred, removed, destroyed, mutilated, or concealed" property of the debtor or property of the estate.[33] Thus, debtors who intentionally omit references to their property in the schedules of assets that they file with the court, and take other affirmative steps to conceal its existence from the trustee, receive no discharge.[34]

The fact that the property involved is ultimately recovered by the bankruptcy trustee and used to pay creditors' claims does not preserve the debtor's discharge. Thus, the fact that the debtor's effort to conceal his assets was unsuccessful is not a defense.[35] The debtor's intentional misconduct is enough. If this were not the

---

[29] *See infra* § 17.03[B][2] Presumptive Abuse — Means Testing.

[30] James L. Buchwalter, Annotation, *Application of Bankruptcy Code Provision Denying Chapter 7 Debtor Discharge for Fraudulently Transferring or Concealing Property, 11 U.S.C.A. § 727(a)(2)(A) — Real Property,* 50 A.L.R. Fed. 2d 307 (2010).

[31] Bankruptcy Code § 727(a)(2).

[32] *See infra* Chapter 16 — Fraudulent Transfers.

[33] Bankruptcy Code § 727(a)(2).

[34] Cotton v. Derer (In re Derer), 400 B.R. 97 (Bankr. E.D. Tex. 2008).

[35] *E.g.,* In re Smiley, 864 F.2d 562, 569 (7th Cir. 1989).

case, debtors might have too great an incentive to try to hide their assets.[36]

In many cases, there will be no direct evidence of the debtor's fraudulent intent. However, as under fraudulent conveyance law generally, circumstantial evidence, or "badges of fraud," are used to infer the requisite scienter. The commonly recurring circumstances that reflect the intent to defraud creditors have not changed much since *Twyne's Case* in 1601.[37] They still include the inadequacy of consideration, the existence of a family or other close relationship between the parties, the debtor's retention of the possession of the property, the financial circumstances of the debtor before and after the transfer, and the proximity in time between the transfer and the initiation of creditors' efforts to collect.[38]

However, transfers of property that are only constructively but not intentionally fraudulent, do not warrant denial of discharge,[39] even though the transfer might be recoverable by the trustee. Thus, a debtor who sells her property at a steep discount in an effort to raise cash to pay her creditors or meet her current living expenses will not be denied a discharge.[40] Because the debtor's intent was benign, she still qualifies for relief from her debts.

[b]   Concealment of Transfer

The text of § 727(a)(2) denies the debtor a discharge only on account of intentionally fraudulent transfers that occurred within one year before the debtor's petition. However, transfers made more than one year before the case was filed might still result in a denial of discharge if the debtor continued to conceal the transfer, pursuant to the "continued concealment" doctrine. It treats transfers of property as continuing up through the time of the petition if the debtor retains secret ownership of the property during the year before filing for bankruptcy.[41] Thus, a debtor who arranges to re-acquire the transferred property may be denied a discharge, even though she initially transferred her property more than a year before filing her bankruptcy petition.

---

[36] The debtor's misconduct might also constitute a federal crime punishable by up to five years in prison. 18 U.S.C. § 152(1) (2000). *See generally* Tamara Ogier & Jack F. Williams, *Bankruptcy Crimes and Bankruptcy Practice*, 6 Am. Bankr. Inst. L. Rev. 317 (1998).

[37] 76 Eng. Rep. 809 (Star Chamber 1601).

[38] *See* Unif. Fraudulent Transfer Act § 4(b) (1984). *See e.g.*, Village of San Jose v. McWilliams, 284 F.3d 785, 791 (7th Cir. 2002); Martin v. Bajgar (In re Bajgar), 104 F.3d 495 (1st Cir. 1995) (transfer to spouse in exchange for love and affection). *See also infra* § 16.02 Actual Fraud: Intent to Hinder, Delay or Defraud Creditors.

[39] *See* Unif. Fraudulent Trans. Act § 5(a) (1984).

[40] Commerce Bank & Trust Co. v. Burgess (In re Burgess), 955 F.2d 134 (1st Cir. 1992) (debtor used assets his meet its payroll).

[41] *E.g.*, Keeney v. Smith (In re Keeney), 227 F.3d 679 (6th Cir. 2000).

[c]   Conversion of Non-Exempt Property

A debtor's conversion of non-exempt property into an exempt form might also constitute grounds for denial of discharge.[42] For example, in *In re Reed*, the debtor sold many of his nonexempt assets and used the proceeds to make mortgage payments on his otherwise fully exempt residence. Because this was done with the actual intent to place his assets beyond the reach of his creditors, Reed's discharge was denied.[43] Despite this result, cases like *Reed* have usually been limited to situations where the debtor committed some act extrinsic to the conversion that hindered, delayed, or defrauded his creditors. Reed, for example, had entered into an agreement with his creditors that delayed their collection efforts in a way that facilitated his efforts to place his assets beyond his creditors' reach.[44]

The debtor in *In re Tveten* also ran afoul of § 727(a)(2).[45] Dr. Tveten sought bankruptcy protection, not, as one might imagine in the case of a physician, as a result of medical malpractice liability, but as a result of the collapse of a highly leveraged $19 million investment scheme. In an effort to protect his assets from his creditors, Dr. Tveten participated in seventeen separate transfers, which resulted in the conversion of nearly $700,000 worth of non-exempt assets into exempt life insurance policies and annuities. The court regarded this systematic conversion of non-exempt assets into exempt categories as an attempt to obtain not just a "fresh start" but a "head start." Although his assets were exempt under state law, denial of his discharge meant that he would not be able to reconvert them back into non-exempt status without running the risk that they would become exposed to the claims of his creditors in the years after his bankruptcy.

Other debtors whose conversions of non-exempt assets into exempt categories have been less dramatic usually receive more generous treatment. Courts generally require some extrinsic evidence of fraudulent intent other than the mere conversion of nonexempt assets into an exempt class.[46]

---

[42] *E.g.*, Ford v. Poston, 773 F.2d 52 (4th Cir. 1985) (transfer of property held in joint tenancy by husband and wife to themselves in "tenancy by the entireties" accompanied by extrinsic evidence of intent to defraud creditors warranted denial of discharge).

[43] First Tex. Sav. Ass'n, Inc. v. Reed (In re Reed), 700 F.2d 986 (5th Cir. 1983). *See also* Norwest Bank Neb. v. Tveten (In re Tveten), 848 F.2d 871, 874 (8th Cir. 1988). *See generally* Lawrence Ponoroff & F. Stephen Knippenberg, *Debtors Who Convert Their Assets on the Eve of Bankruptcy: Villains or Victims of the Fresh Start?*, 70 N.Y.U. L. Rev. 235 (1995); Theodore Eisenberg, *Bankruptcy Law in Perspective*, 28 UCLA L. Rev. 953, 992-96 (1981); Alan N. Resnick, *Prudent Planning or Fraudulent Transfer? The Use of Non-Exempt Assets to Purchase or Improve Exempt Property on the Eve of Bankruptcy*, 31 Rutgers L. Rev. 615 (1978).

[44] *See also* Grover v. Jackson, 472 F.2d 589 (9th Cir. 1973); In re Adlman, 541 F.2d 999 (2d Cir. 1976); Love v. Menick, 341 F.2d 680 (9th Cir. 1965); Forsberg v. Sec. State Bank of Canova, 15 F.2d 499 (8th Cir. 1926); In re Johnson, 80 B.R. 953 (Bankr. D. Minn. 1987).

[45] Norwest Bank Neb. v. Tveten (In re Tveten), 848 F.2d 871 (8th Cir. 1988).

[46] Gill v. Stern (In re Stern), 345 F.3d 1036 (9th Cir. 2003). On the question of whether the debtor will be denied the exemption, *see supra* § 12.02[E] Exemption Planning.

[d]   Destruction, Mutilation or Concealment

It is not only fraudulent transfers of property that lead to denial of discharge. The debtor's discharge might also be denied, under § 727(a)(2), on account of the debtor's "removal, destruction, mutilation or concealment of property" during the year before her petition.[47]

[e]   Delayed Recording

The authorities are divided over whether discharge should be denied if property is transferred more than a year before the debtor's petition, but the transfer is not recorded until later, within a year of bankruptcy.[48] This might easily occur with real estate, particularly where the transferee does not realize that the transfer is part of the debtor's fraudulent scheme, or that recording is necessary.

[3]   Failure to Maintain Records[49]

A debtor may also be denied a discharge for failure to keep or preserve her financial records, unless she supplies some justification for her failure to keep them. Section 727(a)(3) provides that the debtor's discharge can be denied if:

> the debtor has concealed, destroyed, mutilated, falsified, or failed to keep or preserve any recorded information, including books, documents, records, and papers, from which the debtor's financial condition or business transactions might be ascertained, unless such act or failure to act was justified under all of the circumstances of the case.[50]

Under this provision, the court must first determine whether the debtor's existing financial records are sufficient, and, if not, whether the debtor has a suitable justification for failing to maintain better records.[51]

Even though some debtors destroy their financial records or fail to create them in the first place as part of a dishonest scheme, most who lack adequate financial records are simply careless.[52] Nevertheless, the impact of inadequate records on the estate's creditors is likely to be the same regardless of the debtor's motivation. Without adequate financial records, the trustee may find it difficult or be unable to locate the debtor's assets, to determine whether the debtor transferred assets before her petition, or evaluate the allowability of creditors' claims. As one court explained, "[t]he purpose of this provision is to ensure that the trustee and creditors receive sufficient information to trace a debtor's financial history for a reasonable

---

[47] *See, e.g.*, Buckeye Retirement Co. v. Swegan (In re Swegan), 383 B.R. 646 (B.A.P. 6th Cir. 2008).

[48] *Compare* Dean Witter Reynolds, Inc. v. MacQuown (In re MacQuown), 717 F.2d 859 (3d Cir. 1983) (applying former § 14(c)(4)), *with* Finalco, Inc. v. Roosevelt (In re Roosevelt), 87 F.3d 311 (9th Cir. 1996).

[49] *See* David S. Kennedy & James E. Bailey, III, *Gambling and the Bankruptcy Discharge: An Historical Exegesis and Case Survey*, 11 Bankr. Dev. J. 49 (1994); Leslie R. Masterson, *Rolling the Dice: The Risks Awaiting Compulsive Gamblers in Bankruptcy Court*, 83 Am. Bankr. L.J. 749 (2009).

[50] Bankruptcy Code § 727(a)(3).

[51] Floret, L.L.C. v. Sendecky (In re Sendecky), 283 B.R. 760, 764 (B.A.P. 8th Cir. 2002).

[52] *E.g.*, Ledbetter v. Zaidan (In re Zaidan), 86 B.R. 296 (Bankr. S.D. Fla. 1988).

period past to present."[53] Accordingly, intent is not an element of this ground for denial of discharge; instead, the standard imposed is one of reasonableness.[54]

The court's decision in *In re Caneva*[55] provides a good example. There, the debtor claimed to have transferred $500,000 to a third party as a brokerage fee in connection with a $20 million loan. However, the debtor had no records of the transaction. In denying the debtor's discharge, the court said: "when a debtor transfers a substantial amount of money to a third party, the failure to keep any documentation evidencing the terms of the transfer or the fact that the payment actually took place establishes a prima facie violation of § 727(a)(3)."[56]

In determining the adequacy of the debtor's records, courts consider a wide variety of factors, including the complexity of the debtor's business, the customary business practices for record keeping in that type of business, the degree of accuracy of any existing books, the debtor's level of education, and the debtor's courtroom demeanor.[57] According to the leading case decided under similar language in the Bankruptcy Act, "[t]he law is not unqualified in imposing a requirement to keep books or records, and it does not require that if they are kept they shall be kept in any special form. . . . It is a question in each instance of reasonableness in the particular circumstances."[58] The obligation of some debtors to keep records may be satisfied by something pretty sketchy, especially if minimal records are normal in the debtor's line of work. Courts in general require very little of ordinary wage earners whose financial activities are not complex.[59]

Although debtors without records have the opportunity to provide a reason for the lack of sufficient records, debtors who present unsubstantiated or fanciful claims about the loss of their records receive the same treatment as elementary school students who claim that their homework was eaten by the family dog. Debtors who claim that their records were stolen, despite their obvious lack of market value,[60] or who assert, as one debtor claimed, that they were inadvertently removed from the garage by the garbage man,[61] have little success in justifying their failure to produce adequate records. On the other hand, debtors who get rid

---

[53] United States v. Trogdon (In re Trogdon), 111 B.R. 655, 658 (Bankr. N.D. Ohio 1990).

[54] Wolfe v. Wolfe (In re Wolfe), 232 B.R. 741, 745 (B.A.P. 8th Cir. 1999); Riley v. Riley (In re Riley), 305 B.R. 873 (Bankr. W.D. Mo. 2004).

[55] 550 F.3d 755 (9th Cir. 2008).

[56] *Id.* at 762.

[57] The Cadle Co. v. Duncan (In re Duncan), 562 F.3d 688, 796 (5th Cir. 2009); Floret, L.L.C. v. Sendecky (In re Sendecky), 283 B.R. 760, 764 (B.A.P. 8th Cir. 2002).

[58] In re Underhill, 82 F.2d 258, 259-60 (2d Cir. 1936).

[59] In re Weismann, 1 F. Supp. 723 (S.D.N.Y. 1932); Simcich v. Haugen (In re Haugen), 9 B.R. 4 (Bankr. S.D. Fla. 1980) (laborer who worked about eight days a month should not be denied a discharge for failing to retain the passbook from a closed savings account that contained nominal sums). *Compare* Buckeye Retirement Props. of Ind., Inc. v. Tauber (In re Tauber), 349 B.R. 540 (Bankr. N.D. Ind. 2006) (lack of records of $35,000 in gambling losses did not warrant denial of discharge), *with* Kaler v. Huynh (In re Huynh), 392 B.R. 802 (Bankr. D. N.D. 2008) (absence of corroboration of $100,000 in gambling losses warranted denial of discharge).

[60] Vetri v. Meadowbrook Mall Co., 174 B.R. 143 (M.D. Fla. 1994).

[61] In re Harron, 31 B.R. 466 (Bankr. D. Conn. 1983).

of their financial records with the knowledge that copies can easily be obtained from their bank, probably have a reasonable justification for shredding the originals.[62]

[4] Misconduct in the Debtor's Bankruptcy Proceeding

Sections 727(a)(4)-(6) deny the debtor a discharge due to the debtor's misconduct in her own bankruptcy proceeding. This misconduct might consist of perjury, bribery, withholding records, failure to account for missing assets, refusal to obey court orders, and the like.[63]

Debtors who knowingly and fraudulently misrepresent their financial affairs,[64] either on the schedules they file in connection with their petition,[65] when examined by the trustee at the § 341 meeting of creditors,[66] or in an examination of the debtor conducted pursuant to Bankruptcy Rule 2004,[67] are intentionally impeding the orderly administration of their estate and should not receive the benefit of a discharge.

The standard for denial a discharge for lying is high: to be denied a discharge under § 727(a)(4)(A), for making a "false oath," it must be proven that: "(1) Debtor made a statement under oath; (2) the statement was false; (3) Debtor knew the statement was false; (4) Debtor made the statement with fraudulent intent; and (5) the statement related materially to the Debtor's bankruptcy case."[68] Fraudulent intent might be shown through circumstantial evidence, which is sufficient if it shows that the debtor was recklessly indifferent to the truth or falsity of his statement.[69]

For example, the debtor in *In re Weiner* was denied a discharge because he had intentionally and seriously undervalued his assets on the schedules filed with his petition.[70] His discharge was denied because his misrepresentation was both material and was made with the intent to defraud his creditors.[71] Similarly, in *In re Freese*, the debtor was denied a discharge because he failed to disclose the existence of several valuable assets, $25,000 of income, and certain pre-petition transfers.[72] Debtors who lie about their assets are trying to evade the basic bargain that the bankruptcy code supplies: a discharge in exchange for the debtor's non-exempt assets. Having attempted to evade the Code's mechanisms for distributing their

---

[62] Lassman v. Hegarty (In re Hegarty), 400 B.R. 332 (Bankr. D. Mass. 2009).

[63] Bankruptcy Code § 727(a)(4)-(6).

[64] Bankruptcy Code § 727(a)(4)(A).

[65] *See* Fed. R. Bankr. P. 1007(a).

[66] *See* Bankruptcy Code § 341; Fed. R. Bankr. P. 2003. *E.g.*, Korte v. IRS (In re Korte), 262 B.R. 464 (B.A.P. 8th Cir. 2001).

[67] *See* Fed. R. Bankr. P. 2004.

[68] In re Freese. 460 B.R. 733, 738 (B.A.P. 8th Cir. 2011).

[69] *Id. See also* In re Taylor, 461 B.R. 420 (E.D. Mich. 2011).

[70] Weiner v. Perry, Settles & Lawson, Inc. (In re Weiner), 208 B.R. 69 (B.A.P. 9th Cir. 1997).

[71] *See also* Korte v. Internal Revenue Serv. (In re Korte), 262 B.R. 464, 474 (B.A.P. 8th Cir. 2001).

[72] 460 B.R. 733 (B.A.P. 8th Cir. 2011).

assets to the creditors, it is no surprise that they do not receive the benefit of this bargain.

Debtors' attorneys share responsibility to participate in this effort. Section 527(a)(2) requires them to provide written notice to their clients, advising them that they must supply "complete, accurate, and truthful" information in their petition and schedules, and that "all assets and liabilities are required to be completely and accurately disclosed in the documents filed to commence the case . . . ."[73] Moreover, debtor's attorneys who sign the debtor's petition certify that they have "performed a reasonable investigation into the circumstances that gave rise to the petition . . ." and that the petition is "well grounded in fact."[74] Attorneys who fail to meet these obligations risk the imposition of sanctions under Bankruptcy Rule 9011.[75]

Likewise, debtors who knowingly and fraudulently either present a false claim,[76] commit or attempt bribery,[77] or withhold otherwise available financial records in their own bankruptcy case[78] may be denied a discharge. In *In re Gioele*,[79] a debtor who, on the day before a scheduled hearing, went to a creditor's home and angrily threatened to kill the creditor's horses, was denied a discharge under § 727(a)(4)(C), which has been interpreted to penalize debtors who engage in extortion or bribery in an effort to undermine the bankruptcy process.[80]

Not surprisingly, debtors who fail to provide a satisfactory explanation for the loss of their assets are also denied a discharge.[81] Debtors have sometimes attempted to explain the loss of their assets by claiming that they "lost it all" at a casino or in a poker game.[82] In *In re McNamara* the debtor claimed to have lost over $130,000 in a poker game, but was suspiciously unable to describe the location of the game, the names of the participants, or any of the details of the session. Other evidence suggested that he had simply hidden his assets in an offshore account. The court explained, "[a] person who loses $130,000 in a poker game would be expected to have some recollection of the details of the event which could be corroborated, or at least a credible explanation for why he did not."[83] Likewise, the debtor in *In re Shahid* was denied a discharge when his explanation for the loss of $25,000 received

---

[73] Bankruptcy Code § 528(a)(2).

[74] Bankruptcy Code § 707(b)(4)(C). *See supra* § 6.02[F] Attorney's Obligations Regarding Debtors' Schedules.

[75] *See* Taylor v. Freeland & Kronz, 503 U.S. 638 (1992).

[76] Bankruptcy Code § 727(a)(4)(B).

[77] Bankruptcy Code § 727(a)(4)(C).

[78] Bankruptcy Code § 727(a)(4)(D).

[79] In re Gioele, 452 B.R. 581 (Bankr. M.D. La. 2011).

[80] It was significant to the court that 18 U.S.C. § 152 (2006) treats "giving, offering, receiving or attempting to obtain money or property, remuneration, compensation, reward advantage, or promising to do the aforementioned, for acting or forbearing to act in a bankruptcy case" as a felony.

[81] Bankruptcy Code § 727(a)(5); David S. Kennedy & James E. Bailey, *Gambling and the Bankruptcy Discharge: An Historical Exegesis and Case Survey*, 11 Bankr. Dev. J. 49 (1994).

[82] *E.g.*, In re Wilbur, 211 B.R. 98 (Bankr. M.D. Fla. 1997).

[83] In re McNamara, 310 B.R. 664 (Bankr. D. Conn. 2004).

as a loan from a bank was simply that he had "spent it" with no further elaboration on what expenditures he had incurred.[84] Finally, in *In re Vilhauer*,[85] the claim of a farmer who explained that he had lost 117 head of cattle over the winter and burned their carcases in a pit, did not stand up to evidence that the normal rate of loss would have accounted for only about 20 of the lost steers and that the pit contained only 56 carcases, some of which had predated the time of the claimed loss. Debtors who supply far-fetched stories to explain the loss of their assets run the risk of losing their entire discharge.

Debtors who fail to cooperate with the bankruptcy court's orders understandably receive the same treatment. Section 727(a)(6) provides that a Chapter 7 discharge may be denied if the debtor has refused, in her own case "to obey any lawful order of the court."[86] Usually the debtor's refusal consists of her failure to supply information about her assets, or to turn property over to the trustee.[87]

The debtor's duty to comply with the court's orders does not compel her to surrender her constitutional right against self-incrimination.[88] However, if she refuses to answer questions about her financial affairs after being granted immunity from prosecution, her discharge will be denied.[89]

[5] Misconduct in Prior or Concurrent Bankruptcy Proceedings

Discharge can be denied not only because of the debtor's misconduct in her current case but also because of her misconduct in an earlier case involving either the debtor herself or a closely related person.[90] Thus, the debtor cannot escape the consequences of her misconduct simply by filing another case. If, during the year before the debtor's petition, the debtor has made a fraudulent transfer, concealed or destroyed records, lied in conjunction with a case, committed perjury, or committed any of the acts specified in section 727(a)(2)-(6), discharge may be denied. Discharge may also be denied if, during the case, the debtor has done any of these things in another case that concerns an "insider" of the debtor.[91]

Cases where this has been an issue frequently involve cases of spouses or other family members, or those of corporations with which the debtor is affiliated. Debtors who fail to cooperate in cases filed by their relatives may be unable to obtain their own Chapter 7 discharge. Likewise, an officer, director or other insider of a corporation, who acts improperly in the corporation's bankruptcy may

---

[84] In re Shahid, 334 B.R. 698 (Bankr. N.D. Fla. 2005).

[85] 458 B.R. 511 (B.A.P. 8th Cir. 2011).

[86] Bankruptcy Code § 727(a)(6)(A). *See, e.g.*, United States Trustee v. Lebbos (In re Lebbos), 439 B.R. 154 (E.D. Cal. 2010) (debtor wilfully repeatedly failed to appear for examination and to produce required documents).

[87] In re Mora, 399 B.R. 330 (Bankr. E.D. Mo. 2008).

[88] Bankruptcy Code § 727(a)(6)(B).

[89] Bankruptcy Code § 727(a)(6)(B).

[90] Bankruptcy Code § 727(a)(7).

[91] "Insiders" are close affiliates of the debtor, such as relatives or related legal entities. *See* Bankruptcy Code § 101(31).

subsequently be denied a Chapter 7 discharge in her own individual bankruptcy case.

[6]   Repeat Filings — The 8-Year Bar[92]

There is a time limit on how frequently a debtor can obtain a Chapter 7 discharge. Otherwise, it would be too easy for debtors to run up their debts, enjoy the benefits of their profligate spending, and discharge their obligations whenever their creditors started to close in.[93] For many years, debtors were prohibited from obtaining a Chapter 7 discharge within six years of the filing of any earlier Chapter 7 or Chapter 11 case in which a discharge was supplied.[94] In 2005, the bar following a Chapter 7 or Chapter 11 discharge was extended to eight years.[95] The period remains at six years following a prior discharge in an earlier Chapter 12 or 13 case.

The rules discussed here only apply to the availability of a discharge in a Chapter 7 case. Rules regarding the availability of a discharge in Chapters 11, 12, or 13, after a discharge in an earlier proceeding are explained elsewhere.[96]

[a]   Prior Chapter 7 or 11 Discharge

A debtor who receives a Chapter 7 or Chapter 11 discharge is barred from a subsequent Chapter 7 discharge for eight years.[97] The eight year period is measured from the filing of the petition in the first case to the filing of the petition in the second case. Thus, if Debbie filed a Chapter 7 petition on June 30, 2013, and received a discharge, she cannot obtain another Chapter 7 discharge in any proceeding filed before July 1, 2021.

This "eight-year bar" partially explains why individuals who have discharged their debts sometimes find it surprisingly easy to obtain credit: lenders know that they will not be able to discharge their debts again for another eight years.[98] However, the bar does not prohibit a debtor from submitting a second petition; it only prohibits her from obtaining a second discharge more than twice in eight years.

---

[92] Saul Schwartz, *The Effect of Bankruptcy Counseling on Future Creditworthiness*, 77 Am. Bankr. L.J. 257, 267 (2003).

[93] Although one might imagine that debtors who have received a bankruptcy discharge would find it impossible to obtain credit, this has not proven to be true. *See* Saul Schwartz, *The Effect of Bankruptcy Counseling on Future Creditworthiness*, 77 Am Bankr. L.J. 257 (2003).

[94] Bankruptcy Code § 727(a)(8).

[95] Bankruptcy Abuse Prevention and Consumer Protection Act of 2005, Pub. L. No. 109-8, § 312, 119 Stat. 23, 87.

[96] *See infra* §§ 13.05 Chapter 13 Discharge & 13.06 Chapter 11 Discharge.

[97] Bankruptcy Code § 727(a)(8).

[98] Jay L. Zagorsky & Lois R. Lupica, *A Study of Consumers' Post-Discharge Finances: Struggle, Stasis, or Fresh-Start?* 16 Am. Bankr. Inst. L. Rev. 283 (2008).

[b]   Prior Chapter 12 or 13 Discharge

The time bar is more relaxed if the earlier discharge was in a Chapter 12 or a Chapter 13 case. In those cases,[99] the debtor must wait only only six years before obtaining a Chapter 7 discharge. Thus, if Debbie filed a Chapter 13 case on June 30, 2013 and completed her Chapter 13 plan three years later, she would be eligible for a Chapter 7 discharge in a case filed anytime after July 1, 2019. This is true even if her prior Chapter 13 plan provided only for negligible payments to her creditors. Thus, debtors gain a two-year advantage by filing under Chapter 13 rather than Chapter 7, even if the payments made to their creditors under the Chapter 13 plan are modest.

A few Chapter 12 and 13 debtors pay 100% of what they owe. The six-year bar does not apply *at all* if the debtor's earlier Chapter 12 or 13 discharge was granted after completing a plan that provided for payment of 100% of her allowed unsecured claims.[100] This makes sense: debtors who have paid their creditors in full should remain eligible for a subsequent discharge if their financial circumstances again turn sour.

Whether a debtor's prior Chapter 12 or 13 case resulted in 100% payment, there is some question about whether the plan payments must be equal to the *value* of the claims or simply to their *amount*. In other words, the question is whether 100% payment is required to include an interest component on the amount of the unsecured claims to compensate the creditor for the delay in receiving payment. The Code says that the payments must equal "the allowed unsecured claims," not "the value" of the amount of the allowed unsecured claims.[101] The plain meaning of this language, at least in "bankruptcy-speak," is that the plan need not provide for payment of interest on the amount of the creditors' claims in order to avoid the six-year bar.

For example, if a debtor's allowed unsecured claims in her earlier Chapter 13 cases were $7200, and the debtor made 36 $200 payments over three years, totaling $7200, the requirement appears to have been satisfied, even though the payment was made over a three-year period, without interest. The *value* of this stream of payments would have been something less than $7200, but because the *amount* was equal to the amount of the creditors' claims, the debtor remains eligible for a subsequent Chapter 7 discharge.

Even if the debtor's prior Chapter 12 or 13 plan did not provide for 100% payment, the six-year bar of § 727(a)(9) does not apply if the earlier plan provided for payment of at least 70% of her unsecured claims and "the plan was proposed by the debtor in good faith and was the debtor's best effort."[102] "Best effort" is a somewhat uncertain standard. The legislative history to § 727(a)(9) indicates that in

---

[99] Under Chapters 12 and 13, discharge is ordinarily granted only if the debtor has fully performed the terms of her plan. *See generally infra* § 13.05 Chapter 13 Discharge.

[100] Bankruptcy Code § 727(a)(9)(A).

[101] Bankruptcy Code § 727(a)(9)(A).

[102] Bankruptcy Code § 727(a)(9)(B).

determining whether the debtor's plan represented his or her best effort, the court should:

> balance the debtor's assets, including family income, health insurance, retirement benefits, and other wealth, a sum which is generally determinable, against the foreseeable necessary living expenses of the debtor and the debtor's dependents, which unfortunately is rarely quantifiable. In determining the expenses of the debtor and the debtor's dependents, the court should consider the stability of the debtor's employment, if any, the age of the debtor, the number of the debtor's dependents and their ages, the condition of equipment and tools necessary to the debtor's employment or to the operation of his business, and other foreseeable expenses that the debtor will be required to pay during the period of the plan, other than payments to be made to creditors under the plan.[103]

Significantly, it is not unusual for debtors to include language in their Chapter 12 and 13 plans specifying that the payments provided for in their plans constitute their "best effort." This is done in an effort to preclude creditors in any Chapter 7 discharge hearing in a subsequent case, from contending otherwise. Moreover, the means-testing standards of § 1325(b), which require debtors to submit all of their disposable income to their plan for a minimum of three years, makes it easier for debtors to claim that their plan represented their best effort.

[7] Waiver of Discharge

Debtors also are denied a discharge if they have made an effective waiver of their right to receive one.[104] To be effective, a waiver of the right to a discharge must be in writing, be executed by the debtor after the order for relief (in a voluntary case, after the filing of the petition), and be approved by the court.[105] Not surprisingly, discharge waivers are rare. They are to be expected generally only as a result of a settlement agreement in a denial of discharge proceeding.

Waiver of discharge is completely different from reaffirmation of individual debts. After a waiver of discharge, the debtor remains liable for all of her debts. A reaffirmation agreement affects only the single debt involved in the agreement. The enforceability of reaffirmation agreements is governed by § 524(c).[106]

[8] Failure to Complete Credit Counseling Course[107]

To receive a discharge, individual debtors must "complete an instruction course concerning personal financial management."[108] Debtors who fail to complete a "credit counseling" course with an approved "non-profit budget and credit counsel-

---

[103] 124 Cong. Rec. H11,908 (Sept. 28, 1978) (statement of Rep. Edward); 124 Cong. Rec. S17415 (Sept. 28, 1978) (statement of Senator DeConcini).

[104] Bankruptcy Code § 727(a)(10).

[105] In re Asbury, 423 B.R. 525 (B.A.P. 8th Cir. 2010).

[106] Bankruptcy Code § 524(c). *See supra* § 12.08[B] Reaffirmation.

[107] Susan Block-Lieb et al., *The Coalition for Consumer Bankruptcy Debtor Education: A Report on Its Pilot Program*, 21 Bankr. Dev. J. 233 (2005); Jean Braucher, *An Empirical Study of Debtor*

ing agenc[y]"[109] are ineligible for a Chapter 7 discharge.[110] This instructional course in personal financial management is different from the far less extensive credit-counseling briefing that debtors must obtain before filing their petition.[111]

Both § 727(a)(11) and § 1328(g) provide for a waiver of this requirement based on either the debtor's personal circumstances or on the unavailability of approved courses in the debtor's geographic region.[112] Among the circumstances that justify a waiver are "incapacity, disability, or active military duty in a combat zone."[113] Thus, in *In re Hall*, an 81-year old debtor who was hearing impaired, confined to a scooter for mobility, and suffering from other ailments including prostate cancer, was excused from completing an instructional course in personal financial management after he had made a reasonable effort to do so.[114] Likewise, in *In re Trembulak*,[115] a debtor who died before his discharge hearing, was excused from completing the required course of instruction. But, debtors who suffer from less serious impediments are unlikely to be excused.[116]

Such credit counseling programs are not free, and the debtor's dire financial circumstances do not provide a basis for a waiver. The necessity of completing a credit counseling program adds to the cost of obtaining a bankruptcy discharge.

Many are skeptical about the long-term benefits of these mandatory credit counseling programs, though there is some empirical evidence that voluntary financial education programs are beneficial.[117] Whether these reported benefits

---

Education in Bankruptcy: Impact of Chapter 13 Completion Not Shown, 9 Am. Bankr. Inst. L. Rev. 557 (2001); A. Michele Dickerson, *Can Shame, Guilt, or Stigma Be Taught? Why Credit-Focused Debtor Education May Not Work*, 32 Loy. L.A. L. Rev. 945 (1999); Gary Neustadter, *A Consumer Bankruptcy Odyssey*, 39 Creighton L. Rev. 225, 258-270 (2006); Saul Schwartz, *The Effect of Bankruptcy Counseling on Future Creditworthiness*, 77 Am. Bankr. L.J. 257 (2003); Robin Miller, Annotation, *Validity, Construction, and Application of Credit Counseling Requirement Under Bankruptcy Abuse Prevention and Consumer Protection Act (BAPCPA)*, 11 U.S.C.A. § 109(h), 11 A.L.R. Fed. 2d 43 (2006).

[108] Bankruptcy Code § 727(a)(11). Debtors must also participate in a credit counseling "briefing" prior to filing their petition. *See* Bankruptcy Code § 521(b)(1). *See generally supra* § 6.02[B][1][c] Mandatory Credit Counseling Briefing.

[109] Bankruptcy Code § 111(a)(1).

[110] Completion of a credit counseling program is also required in order to obtain relief under Chapter 13. Bankruptcy Code § 1328(g). *See infra* § 13.05[A] Debtors Eligible for Chapter 13 Discharge.

[111] Bankruptcy Code § 109(h). *See supra* § 6.02[B][1][c] Mandatory Credit Counseling Briefing.

[112] Bankruptcy Code §§ 727(a)(11) & 1328(g). *See* Fed. R. Bankr. P. 4004(c)(1)(H).

[113] Bankruptcy Code § 109(h)(4).

[114] In re Hall, 347 B.R. 532 (Bankr. N.D. W. Va. 2006). *See also* In re Tulper, 345 B.R. 322, 326 (Bankr. D. Colo. 2006).

[115] 362 B.R. 205 (Bankr. D.N.J. 2007).

[116] In re Ferrell, 391 B.R. 292 (Bankr. D.S.C. 2008) (medical inability to participate in person, not a sufficient excuse).

[117] *See* Susan Block-Lieb, Karen Gross & Richard L. Wiener, *Lessons from the Trenches: Debtor Education in Theory and Practice*, 7 Fordham J. Corp. & Fin. L. 503 (2002); Susan Block-Lieb, Corinne Baron-Donovan, Karen Gross & Richard Wiener, *The Coalition for Consumer Bankruptcy Debtor Education: A Report on its Pilot Program*, 21 Bankr. Dev. J. 233 (2004); Karen Gross & Susan Block-Lieb, *Beneath the Surface of BAPCPA Empty Mandate or Opportunity for Innovation? Pre-petition Credit Counseling and Post-petition Financial Management*, 13 Am. Bankr. Inst. L. Rev. 549 (2005); Richard L. Stehl, *The Failings of the Consumer Credit Counseling and Debtor Education*

exist where the debtors are compelled to take the course remains to be seen.

[9] Criminal Convictions

New § 727(a)(12) also permits the court to deny the debtor a discharge if "there is reasonable cause to believe that . . . the debtor may be found guilty of a felony" in a pending criminal proceeding in which the debtor is charged with a bankruptcy crime, securities fraud, RICO violations, or a crime involving wilful or reckless misconduct that resulted in personal injury or death,[118] if the debtor sought a homestead exemption otherwise available under a state exemption statute, in excess of $125,000. Thus, executives of large corporations who are found guilty of criminal activity in connection with the management of their financially troubled employers will find relief from their own personal financial difficulties unavailable. However, because of the working of §§ 727(a)(12) and 522(q)(1), denial of discharge under § 727(a)(12) applies only to debtors who elect to exempt property under the applicable state exemption statute.[119] Moreover, it may not apply to debtors in states that have opted out, as these debtors have not "elected" to exempt property under state or local law.[120]

[10] Failure to Supply Tax Returns

Although not formally listed as grounds for denial of a discharge, a debtor's failure to provide the trustee with her most recent year's federal tax return will result in dismissal of the debtor's case, effectively denying her a discharge.[121] An exception is made only for debtors who are able to demonstrate that their failure to comply is due to circumstances beyond their control.[122]

[C] Denial of Discharge in Chapter 11

Most Chapter 11 cases involve corporations or partnerships. The debtor nearly always receives a discharge upon confirmation of its Chapter 11 plan.[123] Without confirmation of a plan that will continue the operations of the business, there is no discharge. Some debtors choose to liquidate in Chapter 11. In such cases, even where a plan is confirmed, the debtor does not receive a discharge.

This does not mean that the debtor's misconduct is irrelevant. Rather, the issue will arise in the context of a confirmation hearing on the debtor's plan, rather than in a separate discharge proceeding. If the court refuses to confirm the debtor's plan, it will effectively deny the debtor a discharge. The Chapter 11 requirement

---

Requirements of the Proposed Consumer Bankruptcy Reform Legislation of 1998, 7 Am. Bankr. Inst. L. Rev. 133 (1999); Richard L. Wiener, Susan Block-Lieb, Karen Gross & Corinne Baron-Donovan, *Debtor Education, Financial Literacy, and Pending Bankruptcy Legislation*, 23 Behav. Sci. & L. 347 (2005).

[118] *See* Bankruptcy Code § 522(q).

[119] In re Jacobs, 342 B.R. 114 (Bankr. D.D.C. 2006).

[120] *See* Bankruptcy Code § 522(q)(1).

[121] Bankruptcy Code § 521(e)(2)(A)(i).

[122] Bankruptcy Code § 521(e)(2)(B).

[123] Bankruptcy Code § 1141(d).

that the debtor's plan be proposed in good faith[124] provides a sufficient standard to deny confirmation due to the debtor's misconduct. Further, in most cases, creditors can prevent confirmation of the debtor's plan, and its discharge, by voting in sufficient numbers against the plan.[125] Dismissal or conversion of the debtor's entire Chapter 11 bankruptcy case has the same effect.

However, there is no express limitation on frequency of Chapter 11 discharges. Unlike Chapter 7 discharges, which are available only once every eight years, Chapter 11 discharges are available anytime, provided that a plan can be confirmed. However, because it is difficult (though not impossible) to obtain confirmation of a Chapter 11 plan without the consent of a majority of the debtor's creditors,[126] their reluctance to vote in favor of a debtor's plan is the most imposing barrier to a Chapter 11 discharge. This, and the other requirements for confirmation under Chapter 11 are discussed elsewhere.[127]

The principle exception to the general availability of a Chapter 11 discharge is § 1141(d)(3). It precludes discharge in the same circumstances as those in which a Chapter 7 discharge would be denied if the plan provides for nothing more than the debtor's liquidation. A liquidating plan might result in the Chapter 11 case being virtually indistinguishable from a Chapter 7 case. Accordingly, Chapter 7's rules for denial of discharge apply to Chapter 11 cases in which "(1) the plan provides for the liquidation of all, or substantially all, the property of the estate, (2) the debtor does not engage in business after consummation of the plan, and (3) discharge would have been denied under section 727(a) if the case had been brought under chapter 7."[128] Corporations, of course, are never eligible for a Chapter 7 discharge. Thus, corporations that liquidate, may not receive a Chapter 11 discharge, even if their liquidating plans are confirmed.

Finally, as in Chapter 7, a Chapter 11 discharge can be waived. To be effective, the waiver must be in writing; it must be executed by the debtor after the order for relief (i.e., in a voluntary case, after the filing of the petition), and it must be approved by the court.[129]

Although individuals only rarely seek relief in Chapter 11, those who do will not receive their discharge until they complete all of the payments provided for in their plan.[130] For individuals, this is the same result as in Chapter 13. Other Chapter 11 debtors receive their discharge immediately upon confirmation of their plan.[131]

---

[124] Bankruptcy Code § 1129(a)(3).

[125] Bankruptcy Code §§ 1126 & 1129(a)(8).

[126] *See generally infra* § 19.09 Acceptance of Plan by Holders of Claims and Interests: Disclosure and Voting.

[127] *See infra* § 19.10 Confirmation of Chapter 11 Plans.

[128] Bankruptcy Code § 1141(d)(3).

[129] Bankruptcy Code § 1141(d)(4).

[130] Bankruptcy Code § 1141(d)(5)(A).

[131] Bankruptcy Code § 1141(d)(1)(A).

[D]   Denial of Discharge in Chapters 12 and 13[132]

Ordinarily, a discharge is granted under Chapters 12 and 13 only upon completion of the payments required by their plan. Confirmation of the plan can be denied, even if it complies with the financial requirements, if the plan has not been proposed in "good faith."[133] The court may refuse confirmation — and thus effectively preclude discharge — for many of the same reasons that it would directly rule on discharge in a Chapter 7 case.

A Chapter 13 debtor is ineligible for discharge if she received a discharge in an earlier Chapter 7, 11, or 12 case that was filed within four years before the date of the "order for relief" in the subsequent Chapter 13 case.[134] For example, if Gail obtains a Chapter 7 discharge in a case filed on October 1, 2013, she is not eligible for a Chapter 13 discharge in a case filed before October 2, 2018. And, because a Chapter 13 discharge is not usually granted until completion of the debtor's plan, the earliest Gail will be able to receive a Chapter 13 discharge is in the winter of 2016, and not until 2018 if it is a five year plan.

This rule prevents debtors from filing sequential Chapter 7 and 13 cases in a strategy that was unofficially known as "Chapter 20." Before this rule was adopted, it was possible for debtors to discharge their personal liability in Chapter 7 and immediately file a Chapter 13 case. The subsequent Chapter 13 case would be used to restructure the debtor's secured debts, or perhaps to cure and reinstate a home mortgage that was vulnerable to foreclosure due to the debtor's default. In 1991, the United States Supreme Court ruled that the debts discharged in the earlier Chapter 7 case were still "claims" (as that term is defined in Bankruptcy Code), in the subsequent Chapter 13 case, and could thus be dealt with in the debtor's Chapter 13 plan.[135] Section 1328(f)(2)'s restrictions on the debtor's ability to obtain a subsequent Chapter 13 discharge in a case filed on the immediate heels of an earlier Chapter 7 discharge now prevents this strategy.

The Code also restrict debtors' eligibility for successive Chapter 13 discharges. New § 1328(f)(2) prohibits a debtor from obtaining a discharge in a Chapter 13 case if the debtor received a Chapter 13 discharge in a case *filed*[136] within two years before the date of filing the later case.[137] The way this language is written, it will rarely, if ever, prevent a debtor from obtaining a discharge. Most Chapter 13 plans

---

[132] William Houston Brown, *Taking Exception to a Debtor's Discharge: The 2005 Bankruptcy Amendments Make It Easier*, 79 Am. Bankr. L.J. 419, 448-49 (2005).

[133] Bankruptcy Code §§ 1225(a)(3), 1325(a)(3). *See generally* Robert Bein, *Subjectivity, Good Faith and the Expanded Chapter 13 Discharge*, 70 Mo. L. Rev. 655 (2005); *infra* § 18.08[C] Good Faith.

[134] Ordinarily the date of the "order for relief" is the same as the date the debtor's Chapter 13 petition was filed. However, it might be later if the order for relief in the Chapter 13 case is entered following the conversion of a case filed by the same debtor under Chapter 7, 11, or 12. Bankruptcy Code § 1328(f)(1). *See, e.g.*, In re Lewis, 339 B.R. 814 (Bankr. S.D. Ga. 2006); In re Sours, 350 B.R. 261 (Bankr. E.D. Va. 2006) (earlier Chapter 13 cases converted to Chapter 7). *See generally infra* § 18.03[B] Conversion and Dismissal of Chapter 13 Cases.

[135] Johnson v. Home State Bank, 501 U.S. 78 (1991).

[136] Carroll v. Sanders (In re Sanders), 551 F.3d 397 (6th Cir. 2008).

[137] Bankruptcy Code § 1328(f)(2).

take a minimum of three years to complete. Although it is possible for a debtor to receive a discharge sooner, by completing a 100% payment plan in less than three years, or by obtaining a hardship discharge, these circumstances are rare. It is even rarer for a debtor to obtain a Chapter 13 discharge and file a second Chapter 13 case within two years of the time of the first petition. Nevertheless, the plain language of § 1328(f)(2) indicates that its two-year period runs from the dates the petitions are filed.[138]

There is no similar provision restricting the availability of a Chapter 12 discharge. Chapter 12 debtors are denied a discharge only if they have been involved in certain types of criminal conduct.[139]

A Chapter 12 or a Chapter 13 discharge can be waived. The waiver must be in writing, it must be executed by the debtor after the order for relief (i.e., after the filing of the petition), and it must be approved by the court.[140] Discharge waivers are rare.

§ 13.03 NONDISCHARGEABLE DEBTS[141]

[A] Meaning of Nondischargeability

A debtor who is granted a global discharge nevertheless may not be relieved from all of her debts. Section 523 lists the debts that are not included within the scope of a debtor's discharge. Debts excluded from a discharge are said to be "nondischargeable." Debts are nondischargeable usually because of the debtor's misconduct or because permitting their discharge would result in the debtor receiving an unfair benefit or a creditor bearing an unfair burden. Some grounds for nondischargeability reflect broader public policies about individual responsibility and preserving public perceptions about the integrity of the bankruptcy system.

Whether nondischargeable debts will ever actually be paid is, of course, speculative. What little data there are suggests that nondischargeable debts are seldom recovered, either because the debtor rarely acquires enough money to pay them or because the cost of monitoring the debtor to determine whether the debtor has the ability to pay is burdensome to creditors.

There is a long tradition of interpreting the exceptions to discharge narrowly. Many cases have held that, to be nondischargeable, the debt must fit clearly within one of the exceptions. On the other hand, Congress has gradually expanded the categories of nondischargeable debts, further limiting the scope of a debtor's fresh start.

---

[138] *See* In re West, No. 4:06-BK-11215E, 2006 Bankr. LEXIS 2562 (Bankr. E.D. Ark., Oct. 10, 2006).

[139] Bankruptcy Code § 1228(f).

[140] Bankruptcy Code §§ 1228(a), 1328(a).

[141] William Houston Brown, *Taking Exception to a Debtor's Discharge: The 2005 Bankruptcy Act Makes it Easier*, 79 Am. Bankr. L.J. 419 (2005); George H. Singer, *Section 523 of the Bankruptcy Code: The Fundamentals of Nondischargeability in Consumer Bankruptcy*, 71 Am. Bankr. L.J. 325 (1997).

Whether a particular debt is nondischargeable depends on the type of bankruptcy proceeding involved. As part of its effort to make Chapter 13 more attractive to consumer debtors than Chapter 7, Congress historically has provided a broader discharge in Chapter 13 cases than in Chapter 7 cases. Thus, some of the obligations discussed in this section may be discharged upon completion of a Chapter 13 plan. For some debtors, this broader discharge, though narrowed considerably in 2005, is one of the main attractions of Chapter 13.

Section 523(a) now contains nearly two dozen categories of nondischargeable debts.[142] The major ones that consumer debtors are likely to owe are family obligations, student loans, tax debts, and debts for various types of intentional torts, including fraud. Other less commonly occurring categories abound.

[B] Types of Nondischargeable Debts[143]

[1] Tax Debts

As Justice Holmes said "taxes are the price we pay for civilization." Not surprisingly, many tax debts to federal, state, and local governments, are nondischargeable.

[a] Priority Taxes[144]

As discussed elsewhere, some unsecured claims are entitled to priority. But priority provides no assurance of payment. Most debtors' estates are inadequate to pay even those debts that are entitled to priority. Any tax debt that would have been entitled to priority under § 507, but which was not paid by funds in the debtor's bankruptcy estate, is not discharged. Thus, if priority tax claims are not paid through the administration of the debtor's estate, the government is entitled to recover the unpaid taxes from the debtor after her bankruptcy case is closed.

[i] Income Taxes

Foremost among the nondischargeable tax debts that individual debtors are likely to be concerned about are those for income taxes. Income tax debts are nondischargeable if the tax was due "for a taxable year ending on or before the date of the filing of the [bankruptcy] petition for which a return . . . is last due, including extensions, after three years before the date of the filing of the

---

[142] Twenty-one to be precise. *See* Bankruptcy Code § 523(a)(1)-(19) (including §§ (14A) and (14B), lest it appear that your authors cannot count).

[143] William Houston Brown, *Taking Exception to a Debtor's Discharge: The 2005 Bankruptcy Amendments Make it Easier*, 79 Am. Bankr. L.J. 419 (2005); Margaret Howard, *Theory of Discharge in Consumer Bankruptcy*, 48 Ohio St. L.J. 1047 (1987); George H. Singer, *Section 523 of the Bankruptcy Code: The Fundamentals of Nondischargeability in Consumer Bankruptcy*, 71 Am. Bankr. L.J. 325 (1997).

[144] William H. Brown & Daniel A. Hawtof, *Tolling the Three-year Period for Discharge of Income Taxes: Is There Plain Meaning in 11 U.S.C. § 507(a)(8)(A)(i)?*, 18 Miss. C. L. Rev. 483 (1998); Stephen W. Sather, Patricia L. Barsalou & Richard Litwin, *Borrowing from the Taxpayer: State and Local Tax Claims in Bankruptcy*, 4 Am. Bankr. Inst. L. Rev. 201 (1996).

petition."[145] This is the dreaded "after three years before" language that sometimes confounds law students and lawyers. However, when considered in the context of several simple examples, the language is not so difficult to fathom.[146]

Consider a debtor who filed her bankruptcy petition on March 20, 2013, and who owes unpaid income tax obligations for the past several years, extending through the 2009 tax year. If she owes income tax for 2012, the debt is entitled to priority under § 507 and is thus nondischargeable under § 523. The first part of § 507(a)(8)(A)(i) asks whether the tax owed is for a taxable year that ended before the date of the filing of the debtor's bankruptcy petition. Our debtor's bankruptcy petition was filed on March 20, 2013. Absent unusual circumstances, her 2012 tax year ended at midnight on December 31, 2012, and thus her income tax liability for 2012 was for a taxable year that ended before her bankruptcy petition was filed.

Further, still following the text of § 507(A)(8)(A)(i), we must determine whether the deadline for any required return for the debtor's 2012 taxes was "after three years before" the date her petition was filed. The deadline for filing a federal tax return is usually April 15 of the year following the end of the tax year involved, so the normal deadline for the filing of this debtor's 2012 return would be April 15, 2013.[147] Thus, the question is whether April 15, 2013, is sometime after "three years before" the date she filed her bankruptcy petition. The point in time three years before her bankruptcy petition was March 20, 2010. Put another way: Is April 15, 2013, *after* March 20, 2010? On our calendars it is.

Because the debtor's 2012 tax year ended before her bankruptcy petition was filed, and because her 2012 return was due sometime after three years before her bankruptcy petition, any taxes she still owes for the 2012 tax year are nondischargeable. The debtor's only hope is that there will be enough funds in her bankruptcy estate to ensure that this debt will be paid from funds she was going to lose to her creditors in the bankruptcy case anyway.

If the debtor still owes taxes for 2011, the result is the same. Her 2011 tax year ended before she filed her bankruptcy petition, and her 2011 return was due on April 15, 2012, which is *after* March 20, 2010. Thus, any unpaid income taxes she still owes for 2011 are nondischargeable.

Any taxes she still owes for 2010 will suffer the same fate because her 2010 return was due on April 15, 2011, which is still sometime *after* March 20, 2010. Worse yet, any taxes she owes from back in 2009 are also nondischargeable. Her 2009 tax return was due after 3 years before the date of her bankruptcy petition. The bankruptcy petition was March 20, 2013. Three years before that date was March 20, 2010, and her 2003 tax return was *due* twenty-five days *after* that date, on April 15, 2010.

---

[145] Bankruptcy Code § 508(a)(8)(A).

[146] In understanding the detailed operation of this rule, it is helpful to remember that the general statute of limitations for unpaid federal income taxes is three years. In a broad sense, income tax debts that are beyond this statute of limitations are dischargeable, while those that are still within the statute of limitations are nondischargeable. The text of § 507 closely follows the rules in the Internal Revenue Code regarding this statute of limitations for unpaid income taxes.

[147] *See* In re Bisch, 437 B.R. 355 (Bankr. E.D. Mo. 2010).

Note that this debtor could have obtained a discharge of her 2009 taxes simply by waiting a month, until after April 15, 2010, to file her bankruptcy petition. Then, the April 15, 2010 due date for her 2009 return would have been *before* three years before her bankruptcy petition and her 2009 tax debt, at least, would not fit the language of § 507(a)(8)(A)(i). Taxes due for 2010, 2011, and 2012 would still be nondischargeable.

If this debtor had sought an automatic extension for the due date for her 2009 return, until July 15, 2010, then she would have to wait until July 16, 2013, to file her bankruptcy petition to ensure that any 2009 income taxes still owed would be dischargeable. The problem with waiting, of course, is that the IRS (and other creditors) might in the meantime succeed in garnishing her wages, seizing her property, or simply obtaining a tax lien to secure the debt.

Although these examples refer to federal income tax obligations, §§ 506 and 523 apply with equal force to state and local income taxes. Other language in § 507 prevents taxpayers from entering into settlement negotiations with tax collectors in an effort to obtain an delay that might result in another year's tax liabilities becoming dischargeable by falling outside the three year period.[148]

[ii]   Property Taxes

A debtor's real estate and personal property taxes are entitled to priority under § 507 and are thus nondischargeable under § 523(a)(1) if the tax was "assessed before the commencement of the case and last payable without penalty *after one year before the date of the filing of the petition.*"[149] This language provides for a similar reach-back period to that applicable to income taxes, for property taxes that were assessed less than one year before the date of the debtor's petition.

A debtor who filed her petition on March 20, 2013, would find that all of her property tax debts that were assessed before she filed her bankruptcy petition but that were payable without the imposition of a penalty sometime after March 20, 2012, are nondischargeable. The dischargeability of her debts depends on when any property taxes she owes were assessed and when, under applicable tax law, they were payable without the imposition of a penalty. If her 2011 real estate taxes were assessed on December 31, 2011, and could have been paid without the imposition of a penalty anytime after March 20, 2012, then they are nondischargeable. If the deadline for payment of her 2011 taxes, without the imposition of a penalty, was before March 20, 2012, the property tax is dischargeable.

Discharge of the debtor's tax liability does not affect the enforceability of any otherwise enforceable tax lien that has been imposed on her property. Thus, although the debtor might obtain a discharge of her personal liability for an earlier year's unpaid property tax, her property might remain subject to a lien for the unpaid tax.

---

[148] Bankruptcy Code § 507(a)(8)(A)(ii).

[149] Bankruptcy Code § 507(a)(8)(B).

[iii]   Other Nondischargeable Priority Taxes

Section 507 also accords priority to taxes "required to be collected or withheld"; thus trust fund taxes, such as income and social security taxes withheld from employees' paychecks[150] and sales taxes collected from customers[151] are nondischargeable. The employer's share of social security taxes, and federal unemployment taxes are entitled to a similar priority, also making them nondischargeable.[152] Significantly, this category includes the personal liability of a "responsible officer" for the employee's share of income and social security taxes that were withheld from an employee's pay but not remitted to the IRS.[153]

Finally, excise taxes and customs duties, entitled to priority under § 507(a)(8)(E) and (F) are also nondischargeable.

[iv]   Tax Penalties

Section 507(a)(8)(G) provides that tax penalties that are related to a priority tax claim are also entitled to priority and thus are similarly nondischargeable, so long as the penalty imposed is "in compensation for actual pecuniary loss."[154] But this language must be read in conjunction with § 523(a)(7), which generally makes debts for a non-compensatory "fine, penalty, of forfeiture payable to and for the benefit of a governmental unit" nondischargeable. Exceptions to this rule leave tax penalties dischargeable if the penalty relates to an otherwise dischargeable tax or if the penalty was "imposed with respect to a transaction or event that occurred [more than] three years before the date of the filing of the petition."[155]

[v]   Involuntary Gap Period Taxes

Taxes arising during the gap between the time an involuntary bankruptcy petition is filed and the time an order for relief is entered are entitled to priority under Bankruptcy Code § 507(a)(2) and are thus nondischargeable under § 523(a)(1)(A). In involuntary cases, an order for relief is entered, requiring the debtor's estate to be administered only if the petitioning creditors demonstrate that relief is warranted. Taxes accumulating between the filing of the creditors' petition and the entry of an order for relief are entitled to priority. If not paid as a result of the administration of the case, they are nondischargeable.

For example, if an involuntary petition is filed against a debtor on January 10, 2012, but the court does not enter an order for relief against the debtor until April 20 of that year, the debtor is likely to incur taxes during the interim. Any taxes that become due during this "involuntary gap" period are nondischargeable.[156]

---

[150]   *E.g.*, Billingsley v. United States (In re Billingsley), 146 B.R. 775 (Bankr. S.D. Ill. 1992).

[151]   *E.g.*, Western Sur. Co. v. Waite (In re Waite), 698 F.2d 1177 (11th Cir. 1983) (taxes on liquor sales).

[152]   Bankruptcy Code § 507(a)(8)(D). *E.g.*, In re Reichert, 138 B.R. 522 (Bankr. W.D. Mich. 1992) (federal unemployment tax).

[153]   I.R.C. § 6672 (2000). *See* United States v. Sotelo, 436 U.S. 268 (1978).

[154]   Bankruptcy Code § 507(a)(8)(G).

[155]   Bankruptcy Code § 523(a)(7)(B).

[156]   *See supra* § 10.04[A][3] Involuntary Gap Creditors.

[b]   Taxes Owed on Unfiled or Late Filed Return

Debtors who fail to file their tax returns, or who delay until the eve of bankruptcy to file them, should not be surprised to learn that unpaid taxes associated with these returns cannot be discharged.[157] If the debtor never filed a return, the tax owed is nondischargeable, regardless of how long ago the tax was incurred or when the return for the tax was due.[158] Thus, a debtor who failed to file her 1970 tax return will be unable to discharge her taxes for that year in a bankruptcy case commenced in 2020.

Debtors will find it difficult to evade the effect of § 523(a)(1)(B) by filing any overdue returns on the eve of bankruptcy. Section 523(a)(1)(B)(ii) makes taxes nondischargeable if the late return was filed "after two years before the date of the filing of the [bankruptcy] petition."[159] Thus, to avoid nondischargeability, a debtor must file her return more than two years before the filing of her bankruptcy petition. Further, the "after two years before" language makes it clear that delaying the return until after the date of the petition achieves nothing. A return filed after the date the bankruptcy petition is still filed sometime *after* the point in time two years before the petition. If the petition is filed on March 20, 2013, a tax return filed on March 30, 2013, is "after" two years earlier, March 20, 2011.

For the purposes of these and other rules that depend on the date a tax return was filed, "return" means "a return that satisfies the requirements of applicable nonbankruptcy law . . . ."[160] In the case of a federal return, this means a return prepared pursuant to § 6020(a) of the Internal Revenue Code.[161] However, because a state return does not fit the definition of a "return," because it is not filed pursuant to the federal tax code, late state tax returns are not "returns" and the taxes associated with them are simply non-dischargable.[162]

[c]   Fraudulent Tax Returns

Debtors who attempt to evade their taxes by filing fraudulent returns or by otherwise willfully attempting to evade tax liabilities receive similar treatment. A tax "with respect to which the debtor made a fraudulent return or willfully attempted in any manner to evade or defeat such tax . . ." is nondischargeable.[163] The date the tax or return was due or filed is irrelevant.

---

[157] Bankruptcy Code § 523(a)(1)(B).

[158] In re Bergstrom, 949 F.2d 341 (10th Cir. 1991); In re McAdam, 402 B.R. 473 (Bankr. D.N.H. 2009) (corporate president, personally liable for corporate unemployment tax, could not discharge liability for tax for which return was not filed).

[159] Bankruptcy Code § 523(a)(2)(B)(ii). Mueller v. State of Wisconsin (In re Mueller), 243 B.R. 346, 350 (Bankr. W.D. Wis. 1999).

[160] The "undesignated paragraph" after the end of Bankruptcy Code § 523(a)(19).

[161] The "undesignated paragraph" after the end of Bankruptcy Code § 523(a)(19). *See* Cannon v. United States (In re Cannon), 451 B.R. 204 (Bankr. N.D. Ga. 2011) (return filed by debtors after assessment was made did not qualify as "return" to make debt dischargeable under 523(a)(1)(B)).

[162] *See* In re McCoy, 666 F.3d 924 (5th Cir. 2012).

[163] Bankruptcy Code § 523(a)(1)(C). *See* United States v. Jacobs (In re Jacobs), 490 F.3d 913, 921 (11th Cir. 2007); United States v. Fretz (In re Fretz), 244 F.3d 1323, 1326 (11th Cir. 2001).

[d]　Debts Incurred to Pay Nondischargeable Taxes

Sections 523(a)(14) and 523(a)(14A) make debts incurred to pay a nondischargeable tax owed either to the United States or to any other governmental unit nondischargeable.[164] Thus, a debtor may not evade the effect of § 523(a)(1) by borrowing the funds necessary to repay her nondischargeable tax debts and then seeking a discharge of the loan. A debtor who charges her otherwise nondischargeable property tax bill to her credit card,[165] or takes advantage of overdraft protection on her checking account to pay her taxes,[166] will find that the debt to her bank is nondischargeable. The creditor who extended the funds to pay the tax need not prove that the debtor borrowed the funds as part of a fraudulent scheme to attempt to discharge an otherwise nondischargeable debt.[167] However, in order to support a finding of nondischargeability, the lender must trace the amount of the borrowed funds to the repayment of the nondischargeable tax debt. On the other hand, debts incurred to prevent what would be a nondischargeable tax debt from arising, do not fall within the ambit of these provisions.[168]

[2]　Debts Fraudulently Incurred[169]

Section 523(a)(2) makes debts incurred through various types of fraud nondischargeable.[170] Debtors who dishonestly obtain money, property, or services, or who obtain an extension, renewal, or refinancing of existing credit remain liable for these debts after their bankruptcy case is over. This rule implements the broad general policy of the Bankruptcy Code of providing a fresh start to "honest debtors," but not to others. Those who have behaved dishonorably in their dealings with their creditors are not entitled to be relieved from debts owed to the creditors they have defrauded.

Section 523(a)(2) divides this basis for nondischargeability into two main categories. The broadest of these makes debts incurred through "false pretenses, a

---

[164] Bankruptcy Code § 523(a)(14)-(14A).

[165] In re Redmond, 399 B.R. 628 (Bankr. N.D. Ind. 2009).

[166] Kaukauna v. VanDynHoven (In re VanDynHoven), 460 B.R. 214 (Bankr. E.D. Wisc. 2011).

[167] Id. at 633-34.

[168] In re White, 455 B.R. 141 (Bankr. N.D. Ind. 2011).

[169] Margaret Howard, *Shifting Risk and Fixing Blame: The Vexing Problem of Credit Card Obligations in Bankruptcy*, 75 Am. Bankr. L.J. 63, 143 (2001); Richard H. Gibson, *Credit Card Dischargeability: Two Cheers for the Common Law and Some Modest Proposals for Legislative Reform*, 74 Am. Bankr. L.J. 129 (2000); David F. Snow, *The Dischargeability of Credit Card Debt: New Developments and the Need for a New Direction*, 72 Am. Bankr. L.J. 63 (1998); Lawrence M. Ausubel, *Credit Card Defaults, Credit Card Profits, and Bankruptcy*, 71 Am. Bankr. L.J. 249 (1997); Barry Zaretsky, *The Fraud Exception to Discharge Under the New Bankruptcy Code*, 53 Am. Bankr. L.J. 253 (1979). *See also* Elizabeth Lea Black, Annotation, *Credit Card Debt as Nondischargeable under Bankruptcy Code Provision Concerning Nondischargeability of Individual Debt Obtained Through False Pretenses, False Representation, or Actual Fraud, Other than Statement Respecting Debtor's or Insider's Financial Condition*, 158 A.L.R. Fed. 189 (1999).

[170] Bankruptcy Code § 523(a)(2).

false representation, or actual fraud," nondischargeable.[171] Debts incurred through the use of a false financial statement are dealt with separately.[172]

[a]   Actual Fraud

To have a debt determined to be nondischargeable due to actual fraud, other than through the use of a false financial statement, a creditor must establish:

- the debtor made false representations to the creditor;[173]

- the debtor knew the representations were false;

- the debtor made the representations with the intent of deceiving the creditor;

- the creditor justifiably relied on the representations; and

- the creditor sustained a loss as a result of the debtor's misrepresentations.[174]

The most troublesome issues have been proof of the debtor's intent and the extent of the creditor's reliance on the debtor's representations.

The level of the creditor's reliance necessary to make the debt nondischargeable has been the subject of some debate. Although courts at one time required "reasonable" reliance on the a debtor's intentionally false representation, the United States Supreme Court ruled in *Field v. Mans* that this standard was too strident.[175] Instead, "justifiable" reliance is regarded as sufficient.[176] The precise point of demarcation between "reasonable" reliance and mere "justifiable" reliance remains unclear. Cases interpreting *Field* have indicated that an issuer of a credit card justifiably relies on a debtor's representation of intent to pay as long as the account is not in default and any initial investigations into the debtor's credit report "did not raise red flags that would make reliance unjustifiable."[177] Thus, although creditors have no affirmative duty to investigate the truth of the debtor's representations, the creditor cannot purport to rely on "preposterous representations or close his eyes to avoid discovery of the truth."[178]

One court has held that credit card charges are dischargeable despite the debtor's misrepresentation of their intent to repay if the creditor failed to conduct a sufficient inquiry into the debtor's financial circumstances.[179] And, in *In re*

---

[171] Bankruptcy Code § 523(a)(2)(A).

[172] Bankruptcy Code § 523(a)(2)(B).

[173] *But see* In re McClellan v. Cantrell, 217 F.3d 890 (7th Cir. 2000) (fraudulent conveyance constituted actual fraud, despite lack of misrepresentation).

[174] McCrory v. Spigel (In re Spigel), 260 F.3d 27, 32 (1st Cir. 2001); Am. Express Travel Related Serv. Co. v. Hahemi, 104 F.3d 1122 (9th Cir. 1996).

[175] Field v. Mans, 516 U.S. 59, 75 (1995).

[176] *See* Lentz v. Spadoni (In re Spadoni), 316 F.3d 56 (1st Cir. 2003).

[177] In re Anastas, 94 F.3d 1280, 1296 (9th Cir. 1996).

[178] In re Hashemi, 104 F.3d 1122, 1126 (9th Cir. 1996); In re Mercer, 246 F.3d 391, 421 (5th Cir. 2001).

[179] In re Ellingsworth, 212 B.R. 326 (Bankr. W.D. Mo. 1997). *But see* Bankruptcy Abuse Prevention

Curtis, a college-educated investor was held not to have justifiably relied on the debtor's promise of a 2,000% return on a risk-free investment of $100,000, making the debtor's obligation to return the funds dischargeable despite the debtor's obviously fraudulent intent.[180]

It may be thought that a debtor who has passed a bad check in payment for goods or services runs afoul of § 523(a)(2)(A). However, the mere fact that a check has been dishonored due to insufficient funds is not, standing alone, sufficient to constitute fraud. Issuance of the check is a "promise" as required by § 523(a)(2)(A).[181] But the fact that a check is dishonored due to insufficient funds does not necessarily reflect any fraudulent intent on the part of the debtor when she issued the check. And, as the Supreme Court ruled in *Williams v. United States*, it does not involve any representation of fact at all about funds on deposit in the account.[182] The check might have been written on insufficient funds because of a the drawer's mistake about the balance in her account.[183] Or the debtor might have intended to make a subsequent deposit of funds sufficient to cover the item. If so, the debtor lacks the necessary fraudulent intent necessary for the debt to be declared nondischargeable under § 523(a)(2)(A).

However, a debtor who issues a bad check with the intent not to pay its amount commits garden variety fraud by misrepresenting her intent to perform the obligation for which the check was issued.[184] Thus, obligations incurred in check-kiting or other similarly dishonest schemes are nondischargeable.[185] Likewise, obligations incurred on the eve of bankruptcy, after the debtor has already formed the intent to file a bankruptcy proceeding, are nondischargeable due to fraud. For example, in *In re Reibesell*, a licensed attorney borrowed funds from his clients until shortly before he filed his bankruptcy petition, while at the same time engaging in fraudulent transfers in an attempt to shield his assets from his creditors.[186] It goes without saying that debtors are ill-advised to borrow the cash necessary to pay their bankruptcy lawyer.

Many fraud cases involve credit card charges. A debtor's use of a credit card is treated as an implied representation to the credit card company that the cardholder intends to pay the charges incurred.[187] The debtor's representation of

---

and Consumer Protection Act of 2005, Pub. L. No. 109-8, § 1229, 119 Stat. 23, 200 (sense of Congress provision casting doubt on *Ellingsworth*).

[180] In re Curtis, 345 B.R. 870 (Bankr. N.D. Ill. 2006).

[181] Goldberg Sec., Inc. v. Scarlata (In re Scarlata), 979 F.2d 521 (7th Cir. 1992); Bednarsz v. Stanislaw Brzakala (In re Brzakala), 305 B.R. 705, 710 (Bankr. N.D. Ill. 2004). The drawer of a check issues an "order." U.C.C. § 3-104 (2003).

[182] Williams v. United States., 458 U.S. 279 (1982).

[183] As students of the law of commercial paper know, the account might even have been drawn down because of checks containing a forgery of the drawer's signature, which, because they were not properly payable from the drawer's account, should not have been paid. *See* U.C.C. § 4-401 (2003).

[184] *E.g.*, In re Mercer, 246 F.3d 391 (5th Cir. 2001) (listing factors used to determine absence of intent to perform).

[185] *See* In re Eashai, 87 F.3d 1082 (9th Cir. 1996).

[186] 586 F.3d 782 (10th Cir. 2009).

[187] AT & T Universal Card Servs. v. Mercer (In re Mercer), 246 F.3d 391, 404 (5th Cir. 2001).

her intent to pay occurs not at the time the credit card was initially obtained, but at the time she incurred the charges in question.

A debtor who intended to pay, but who was unable to pay at the time her debts were incurred, might also run afoul of § 523(a)(2)(A). However, drawing an analogy to the Supreme Court's decision in *Williams v. United States*,[188] courts have begun to reject the contention that use of a credit card implies the debtor's representation that she is in fact able to pay for the goods or services acquired with the use of the card.[189] The standard should be the debtor's intent to repay rather than her ability to repay, even though her knowledge of any inability to pay may be a relevant factor in the inquiry concerning into the debtor's intent. Thus, the debtor's inability to pay for transactions charged to her account is evidence of fraud, but it is not dispositive.

Courts consider a wide variety of factors to evaluate the debtor's intent to repay charges to her credit card. These factors frequently include the time between use of the card and the debtor's bankruptcy,[190] whether the debtor consulted an attorney about bankruptcy before incurring the charges, the number of charges, the amount of the charges, the debtor's financial condition when the card was used, whether any credit limit was exceeded, whether multiple charges were made on the same day, whether the debtor was employed, the debtor's employment prospects, the debtor's financial sophistication, whether the debtor's buying habits changed suddenly, and whether the card was used to purchase luxuries or necessities.[191]

The devastating losses suffered by stock market investors and the bankruptcy of investment firms and investment advisors of 2008 and 2009, has precipitated numerous nondischargeability complaints by defrauded investors. For example in *Thoroughman v. Savittieri*, a debtor who had intentionally misrepresented to investors the liquidity of their funds and how the money would be used, found his liability to investors who had justifiability relied on his representations, nondischargeable.[192]

Whether fraud committed by one person can be imputed to others, and make the debt non-dischargeable in the bankruptcy of a person, such as a spouse or business partner who did not participate in the fraud, remains unsettled. The central bankruptcy policy of providing a fresh start to "honest debtors" suggests that a partner's fraud should not be imputed to other partners who did not

---

[188] 458 U.S. 279 (1982).

[189] *See* In re Mercer, 246 F.3d 391 (5th Cir. 2001); Larry Bates, *Excepting Credit Card Debt from Discharge in Bankruptcy: Why Fraud Can't Mean What the Courts Want it to Mean*, 78 N.D. L. Rev. 23 (2002).

[190] *See* Chase Bank USA, N.A. v. Swanson (In re Swanson), 398 B.R. 328 (Bankr. N.D. Iowa) ($3200 charged for clothing and household items during a thirteen day period immediately before consulting bankruptcy counsel).

[191] *See* Citibank S.D., N.A. v. Dougherty (In re Dougherty), 84 B.R. 653, 657 (B.A.P. 9th Cir. 1988). Other courts have rejected their use as not reflective of the statutory subjective standard in § 523(a)(2)(A). *E.g.*, Am. Express Travel Related Servs. Co., Inc. v. Christensen (In re Christensen), 193 B.R. 863, 866 (N.D. Ill. 1996) (multi-factor "objective" test inconsistent with common-law "subjective" standard).

[192] Thoroughman v. Savittieri, 323 Fed. Appx. 548 (9th Cir. 2009).

participate in the dishonest conduct. On the other hand, these partners may well have obtained a financial benefit as a result of the other partner's misbehavior, and ought not benefit from conduct they benefitted from. Moreover, nondischargeability provides a measure of protection for victims of the partners' fraud that the innocent partner was in perhaps the best position to have prevented. As the Supreme Court said in *Grogan v. Garner*:

> The statutory provisions governing nondischargeability reflect a congressional decision to exclude from the general policy of discharge certain categories of debts — such as child support, alimony, and certain unpaid educational loans and taxes, as well as liabilities for fraud. Congress evidently concluded that the creditors' interest in recovering full payment of debts in these categories outweighed the debtors' interest in a complete fresh start.[193]

Accordingly, early decisions, interpreting former Bankruptcy Act § 17(a)(2), on which current § 523(a)(2) is based, refused to extend the discharge to these debts.[194] This result, of course, comports with the general rule regarding the civil liability of partners for obligations incurred by other members of the partnership in the course of conducting partnership business.[195]

In the past, courts were split over whether the debtor must personally receive money or other value from the fraudulent conduct, in order to have the debt excepted from his discharge. Some courts have required that the debtor personally receive the fruits of his partner's fraud.[196] A second group of courts takes a "receipt of benefits" approach which requires that the debtor gain a benefit from the money that was obtained by fraudulent means for the debt to be nondischargeable due to a partner's fraud.[197] A third group of courts takes the broadest view, that the plain language of § 523(a)(2) does not require the debtor to have received any gain or benefit at all from his partner's fraud for the debt to be excluded from his discharge.[198] This is the approach that courts have taken more recently.[199]

This result presupposes that the debtor is liable for the debt in the first place. In some jurisdictions, a partner who neither knows of the fraud nor should have known is not liable for his partner's fraud. Thus, in *In re Treadwell*,[200] a debtor was not responsible for his partner's fraudulent misrepresentation, because he neither knew nor should have known of his wife's fraudulent misrepresentation to one of their travel agency customers.

---

[193] 498 U.S. 279, 287 (1991).

[194] Strang v. Bradner, 114 U.S. 555, 556-61 (1885) ("his partners cannot escape pecuniary responsibility therefor upon the ground that such misrepresentations were made without their knowledge"); McIntyre v. Kavanaugh, 242 U.S. 138, 140-42 (1916).

[195] Revised Unif. Partnership Act § 9 (1994).

[196] *See* In re Wade, 43 B.R. 976 (Bankr. D. Colo. 1984).

[197] *Id. See* In re Winfree, 34 B.R. 879, 883 (Bankr. M.D. Tenn. 1983).

[198] In re Wade, 43 B.R. 976, 981 (Bankr. D. Colo. 1984).

[199] *E.g.*, Casablanca Lofts, LLC v. Abrham, 436 B.R. 530 (N.D. Ill. 2010).

[200] 423 B.R. 309 (B.A.P. 8th Cir. 2010).

[b] Luxury Goods or Services — Presumption of Fraud

Section 523(a)(2)(C)(i)(I) establishes a rebuttable presumption of fraud for consumer debts owed to a single creditor for "luxury goods or services" and aggregating more than $600 [201] "within 90 days before the order for relief."[202] The rule is based on the premise that debtors who incur such charges do so without the intent to repay their debts.

The most difficult question has been determining what types of purchases qualify as "luxury goods or services." Luxury goods or services do not include those which are "reasonably *necessary* for the support or maintenance of a debtor or a dependent of the debtor."[203] Note, however, that this does not exempt charges that were reasonably necessary for support or maintenance from a claim that they are nondischargeable. It merely exempts them from the presumption that they were incurred through fraud. Even if the goods or services were not luxurious, a defrauded creditor might still prove actual fraud, but it will have to do so without the benefit of a statutory presumption.

Cases interpreting § 523(a)(2)(C) have inquired into whether the items purchased served any significant family function and whether the transaction evidenced fiscal irresponsibility. Purchases that are "extravagant, indulgent, or nonessential under the circumstances are considered luxury goods."[204] In *Carroll & Sain v. Vernon*, legal services necessary to obtain a divorce were not regarded as a luxury and thus did not raise this evidentiary presumption in the creditor's favor.[205] In *In re Allen*, where most of the debtor's charges were made at gas stations, grocery stores, department stores such as Wal-Mart, Sears, and J.C. Penney, a pharmacy, and several restaurants, the court was unwilling, without further information about the nature of the transactions, to regard the transactions as involving purchases of luxury goods or services. Without more specific information about the items purchased (a hamburger and fries or fillet mignon?), a mere listing of the merchant's name and the amount of the charge was not sufficient to raise the presumption.[206] However, in *In re Simpson*,[207] the court had

---

[201] As with most other dollar amounts in the Bankruptcy Code, this figure is adjusted every three years by a factor reflecting the increase in the Department of Labor's Consumer Price Index, and rounded to the nearest $25. Bankruptcy Code & 104(b)(1). It was last adjusted on April 1, 2010 and is set to be adjusted again, in 2013, 2016, and 2019.

[202] Bankruptcy Code § 523(a)(2)(C)(i)(I). Before the 2005 amendments, this provision applied to consumer debts to a single creditor for luxury goods or services incurred during the last 60 days before the debtor's petition aggregating more than $1,000. Expansion of the time period in which the charges were incurred and reducing the dollar threshold, expanded this category of nondischargeability.

[203] Bankruptcy Code § 523(a)(2)(C)(ii)(II) (emphasis supplied). This language has recently changed. Before 2005, "luxury goods or services" were those not "reasonably *acquired*" for support or maintenance.

[204] In re McDonald, 129 B.R. 279 (Bankr. M.D. Fla. 1991).

[205] 192 B.R. 165 (Bankr. N. D. Ill. 1996).

[206] 296 B.R. 849 (Bankr. N.D. Ala. 2003). *See also* In re Zeman, 347 B.R. 28 (Bankr. W.D. Tex. 2006) (judge suggested that creditor's lack of proof that receipts from fast-food restaurants, discount retailers, grocery store, movie theater, and beauty salon were for luxury goods and services was nothing more than a "shake-down" tactic that might warrant Rule 9011 sanctions).

[207] 319 B.R. 256 (Bankr. M.D. Fla. 2003).

little difficulty in concluding that charges for over $200,000 in gambling losses in the period immediately before the debtor's bankruptcy petition were "luxury goods or services" and thus presumably nondischargeable even though it remains a question whether gambling losses constitute "consumer debts."[208]

Decisions like those in *In re Olwan*,[209] and *In re Woodman*,[210] regarding a debtor's pre-petition purchase of tobacco products, raises the question of how the 2005 change to § 523(a)(2)(C) regarding what is regarded as "luxury goods and services" will be applied. Before BAPCPA, luxury goods and services excluded purchases that were "reasonably acquired" for the maintenance or support of the debtor and the debtor's dependents. BAPCPA narrowed the exclusion to only those goods or services that are "reasonably necessary" for the maintenance or support of the debtor. This language matches that used for determining disposable income under Chapter 13 (and the means test), and may bring the standard for what does not qualify as luxury goods or services *in pari materia* with the standard for the kinds of expenses that are not to be deducted in determining a debtor's disposable income in determining amounts that must be devoted to payments under a Chapter 13 plan. In making this decision in a Chapter 13 case, the *Woodman* court remarked:

> If smoking is "bad" and therefore not "reasonably necessary," could not similar arguments be made in favor of ruling that any Chapter 13 debtor's expense, however minimal, for alcohol (even one can of beer), lottery tickets (a single one), cosmetics, sugared breakfast cereal, candy bars, or even, say, scented soap is never reasonably necessary, as well? Could not the same be said as to automobiles that seat more than (or fewer than), say, four adults, or achieve less than twenty-three-point-five miles-per-gallon?

Applying § 523(a)(2)(C)'s presumption regarding luxury goods and services inherently involves moral judgments that may not be well-suited to judicial determination.[211]

The presumption applies only to "consumer debts," which are defined as those incurred "by an individual primarily for a personal, family, or household purpose."[212] Debts incurred for a business purpose, however extravagant or frivolous they may be, do not fit within the presumption.

The presumption can be overcome by evidence that the debtor experienced a sudden change in circumstances or that the debtor did not contemplate filing a bankruptcy petition until after the transaction took place.[213] For example, in *In re*

---

[208] Richard I. Aaron, *Collection of Gambling Debts and the Bankruptcy Reform Act of 2005*, 9 Gaming L. Rev. 299 (2005); Leslie R. Masterson, *Rolling the Dice: The Risks Awaiting Compulsive Gamblers in Bankruptcy Court*, 83 Am. Bankr. L.J. 749 (2009).

[209] 312 B.R. 476 (Bankr. E.D.N.Y. 2004).

[210] 287 B.R. 589 (Bankr. D. Maine 2003).

[211] *See* Theresa J. Pulley Radwan, *Sword or Shield: Use of Tithing to Establish Nondischargeability of Debt Following Enactment of the Religious Liberties and Charitable Donation Protection Act*, 19 Am. Bankr. Inst. L. Rev. 471 (2011).

[212] Bankruptcy Code § 101(8).

[213] Sears, Roebuck & Co. v. Green (In re Green), 296 B.R. 173 (Bankr. C.D. Ill. 2003).

Davis, the debtor successfully rebutted the presumption by demonstrating that she had commenced payments on charges for luxury items according to the terms of her contract with the creditor before filing bankruptcy.[214] And, in *In re Leaird*, the debtor rebutted the presumption by explaining that he had purchased the luxury goods on an impulse and did not form the intent to file for bankruptcy until after the purchases had been made.[215]

[c]   Cash Advances

A similar presumption of nondischargeability applies to "cash advances aggregating more than $875[216] that are extensions of consumer credit under an open end credit plan obtained by an individual debtor on or within 70 days before the order for relief."[217] The presumption applies regardless of the debtor's use of the funds.

Debtors on the verge of bankruptcy are presumed to have made these withdrawals without the intent to repay, even if the charges are incurred for food, clothing, or shelter. Thus, debtors who use their credit cards to purchase "reasonably necessary" items are not faced with the presumption of § 523(a)(2)(C)(i)(I), but those who withdraw cash to make the same type of purchases need to rebut the presumption of § 523(a)(2)(C)(i)(II).

As with the presumption regarding credit purchases of luxury goods, the presumption regarding cash advances can be rebutted. However, courts have reached different conclusions about the effect of the presumption.[218] Some courts adhere to Federal Rule of Evidence 301 and treat the presumption as doing nothing more than shifting the burden of going forward with evidence regarding the debtor's fraud and leaving the ultimate burden of proof on the creditor.[219] Other courts have treated the presumption of placing the burden of proving that the debt is dischargeable "squarely on the shoulders of the debtor."[220]

In *In re Ritter*,[221] the debtor successfully rebutted the presumption by showing that charges made to her credit card in the seventy days immediately before her petition were to pay for increased expenses after her car broke down. And, in *In re Manning*,[222] the debtor successfully rebutted the presumption that his repeated transfers of balances from one credit card account to another account that offered

---

[214] 56 B.R. 120 (Bankr. D. Mont. 1985).

[215] 106 B.R. 177 (Bankr. D. Wis. 1989).

[216] As with most other dollar amounts in the Bankruptcy Code, the figures in § 523(a) are adjusted every three years by a factor reflecting the increase in the Department of Labor's Consumer Price Index and rounded to the nearest $25 amount. Bankruptcy Code § 104(b)(1). It was last adjusted on April 1, 2010 and is set to be adjusted again in 2013, 2016, and 2019.

[217] Bankruptcy Code § 523(a)(2)(C)(i)(II). Before 2005, the thresholds were $1,225 advanced within sixty days of the debtor's petition.

[218] In re Manning, 280 B.R. 171 (Bankr. S.D. Ohio 2002).

[219] *E.g.*, Sears, Roebuck & Co. v. Green (In re Green), 296 B.R. 173 (Bankr. C.D. Ill. 2003).

[220] *E.g.*, Novus Servs., Inc. v. Cron (In re Cron), 241 B.R. 1, 8 (Bankr. S.D. Iowa 1999).

[221] In re Ritter, 404 B.R. 811 (Bankr. E.D. Pa. 2009).

[222] Nat'l City Bank v. Manning (In re Manning), 280 B.R. 171 (Bankr. S.D. Ohio 2002).

a lower introductory rate was not a fraudulent credit card kite, but was part of his attempt to keep afloat financially until obligations imposed by his divorce court had ended. In both of these cases, facts demonstrating the circumstances of the charges that were consistent with the debtor's intent to repay were sufficient to rebut the presumption of fraud.

[d]   False Financial Statements

Section 523(a)(2)(B) carves out a separate rule for debtors who use a false financial statement to incur or restructure a debt. Loan application forms usually seek information concerning a debtor's obligations, assets, and income. A debtor's exaggeration of her assets or income or an omission of her debts could easily lead to a claim that the debt owed to the creditor who relied on the information from the debtor is nondischargeable.

On the other hand, loan and credit card application forms usually provide only a few lines for the debtor to list all of her debts. Moreover, loan applicants are sometimes advised by the creditor's loan officer to list only their most important debts on these applications.[223] In addition, creditors nearly always obtain credit reports to gain a fuller picture of their borrower's ability to pay. These factors make it difficult for a creditor to successfully pursue a complaint that debt is nondischargeable under § 523(a)(2)(B).

Courts are divided over whether less formal written misrepresentations are the type of statement about the debtor's financial condition to which § 523(a)(2)(B) applies. Most courts insist that the representation must be a more or less formal statement of financial condition, purporting to provide the creditor with an overall picture of the borrower's financial standing.[224] Other courts permit other less comprehensive statements, that might contain information about only some, or even one of the debtor's assets to be enough.[225]

In order to have a debt declared nondischargeable because of an inaccurate financial statement, a creditor must show that (1) the statement is in writing;[226] (2) it is materially false; (3) it is a statement regarding the financial condition of the debtor or an insider; (4) the creditor to whom the debt is owed reasonably relied on the statement; and (5) the debtor supplied the statement with the intent to deceive the creditor.[227]

Section 523(a)(2)(B) requires that the debtor's statement about her financial condition be "in writing." The debtor's oral representations about her financial condition may not be used to have a debt ruled nondischargeable.[228]

---

[223] H.R. Rep. No. 95-595, 130-131 (1977), *reprinted in* 1978 U.S.C.C.A.N. 5787, 6091.

[224] In re Belice, 461 B.R. 564 (B.A.P. 9th Cir. 2011).

[225] *See* Douglas v. Kosinski (In re Kosinski), 424 B.R. 599, 608–09 & n. 8 (B.A.P. 1st Cir. 2010).

[226] *See* In re Gulevsky, 362 F.3d 961 (7th Cir. 2004).

[227] Bankruptcy Code § 523(a)(2)(B). *See* Ins. Co. of N. Am. v. Cohn (In re Cohn), 54 F.3d 1108 (3d Cir. 1995); In re Bogstad, 779 F.2d 370 (7th Cir. 1985).

[228] In re Belice, 461 B.R. 564, 573 (B.A.P. 9th Cir. 2011); In re Sharpe, 351 B.R. 409 (Bankr. N. D. Tex. 2006).

Misinformation about a debtor's substantial debts, assets, or income is likely to be regarded as material, as these matters have a "natural tendency to influence" a creditor's decision about whether to advance a loan.[229] Likewise, inaccurate information on a financial statement is material if it "influences a influences a creditor's decision to extend credit [or] if it is so substantial that a reasonable person would have relied upon it, even if the creditor did not in fact rely upon it in the case at hand."[230]

Section 523(a)(2)(B) applies only to a debtor's more formal written financial statements regarding his financial condition or regarding the financial condition of an "insider" of the debtor. Such statements usually consist of a schedule of assets, liabilities, and income that reflects a debtor's net worth,[231] cash flow, or both.

The reference to the debtor's "insiders"[232] is most likely to be important with respect to representations about the financial condition of the debtor's spouse[233] or of a partnership or corporation for which the debtor is a general partner, officer, or director.

False representations regarding other matters are dealt with in § 523(a)(2)(A), nondischargeability due to fraud, discussed above.[234]

Whether a creditor has "reasonably relied" on the debtor's false financial statement depends on a variety of factors. Courts examine the extent to which the creditor acted in compliance with its normal business practices, as well as the extent to which it followed the standards or customs of others in the creditor's industry, in evaluating the debtor's credit worthiness.[235] Quite naturally, a creditor who has obtained a credit report with accurate information about the debtor's credit history or other financial condition is unable to claim that it "reasonably relied" on conflicting inaccurate information in a financial statement supplied by the debtor.[236]

A few courts have held that a creditor who fails to take simple steps to verify the accuracy of a debtor's financial statement assumes the risk that it contains inaccurate information; this preserves the dischargeability of the debt despite the debtor's factual misrepresentations.[237] However, this assumption of the risk

---

[229] United States v. Keefer, 799 F.2d 1115, 1127 (6th Cir. 1986); cf. Kungys v. United States, 485 U.S. 759, 771 (1988).

[230] Ins. Co. of N. Am. v. Cohn (In re Cohn), 54 F.3d 1108 (3d Cir. 1995).

[231] See, e.g., In re Batie, 995 F.2d 85, 90 (6th Cir. 1993).

[232] "Insider" is defined in Bankruptcy Code § 101(31).

[233] In re Batie, 995 F.2d 85, 90 (6th Cir. 1993).

[234] See supra § 13.03[B][2][a] Actual Fraud.

[235] Ins. Co. of Am. v. Cohn (In re Cohn), 54 F.3d 1108, 1114, 1117 (3d Cir. 1995).

[236] Under § 523(a)(2)(B) the statutory standard is "reasonable" reliance. In Field v. Mans, the Supreme Court interpreted § 523(a)(2)(A) to impose a lesser standard of "justifiable" reliance. 516 U.S. 59 (1995). Thus, the standard for the level of a creditor's reliance that is necessary to have a debt determined nondischargeable under § 523(a)(2) varies slightly depending on whether the debt is claimed to be nondischargeable due to the fraudulent use of a false financial statement or due to some other type of fraudulent misrepresentation.

[237] In re Ward, 857 F.2d 1082 (6th Cir. 1988).

approach has been discredited at least in cases involving credit cards, where each use of the card involves an independent promise to pay for the charges incurred.[238] And, where internal inconsistencies or other matters in the debtor's financial statement raise "red flags" about the debtor's financial condition, the creditor may not ignore the adverse information and claim to have reasonably relied only on the favorable contents of the debtor's credit application.[239] Finally, a creditor who disbelieves the information contained on the debtor's financial statement cannot claim to have relied on it at all.[240]

The reliance standard of § 523(a)(2)(B) is different from that under § 523(a)(2)(A) where the Supreme Court has ruled that only "justifiable reliance" need be shown.[241] The "reasonable reliance" standard of § 523(a)(2)(B) is harder to satisfy, though quantifying the difference between "justifiable" and "reasonable" reliance is difficult.

Finally, the debtor must have supplied the false financial statement with the intent to deceive the creditor. The debtor's intent to deceive can be established either through a showing of her subjective intent to trick the creditor or through evidence exhibiting the debtor's reckless disregard for the truth or falsity of information in her financial statement.[242]

[e] Securities Fraud

Section 523(a)(19) makes debts incurred through securities fraud nondischargeable, regardless of whether the liability was incurred as a result of a violation of federal securities laws or regulations, state securities laws or regulations, or "common law fraud, deceit, or manipulation in connection with purchase or sale of any security."[243] To fit within the scope of this category of nondischargeable debts, the liability must be based on a judgment, settlement agreement, court order, or administrative decree.[244] Thus, § 523(a)(19) merely gives preclusive effect to a prior judgment or settlement and makes the liability imposed on the debtor as a result of that judgment or settlement nondischargeable.[245]

---

[238] *E.g.*, In re Burdge, 198 B.R. 773 (B.A.P. 9th Cir. 1996).

[239] Branch Banking & Trust Co. v. Adam (In re Adam), 406 B.R. 717 (Bankr. E.D. Va. 2009); In re Hill, No. 07–4106 AT, 2008 Bankr. LEXIS 1668 (Bankr. N.D. Cal. May 23, 2008).

[240] Shaw Steel, Inc. v. Morris, 240 B.R. 553 (N.D. Ill. 1999), *aff'd*, 223 F.3d 548 (7th Cir. 2000).

[241] Field v. Mans, 516 U.S. 59 (1995).

[242] Ins. Co. of N. Am. v. Cohn (In re Cohn), 54 F.3d 1108, 1119 (3d Cir. 1995); In re Batie, 995 F.2d 85 (6th Cir. 1993).

[243] Bankruptcy Code § 523(a)(19)(A).

[244] Bankruptcy Code § 523(a)(19)(B).

[245] *E.g.*, Frost v. Civiello (In re Civiello), 348 B.R. 459 (Bankr. N.D. Ohio 2006). *See also* S.E.C. v. Sherman, 406 B.R. 883 (C.D. Cal. 2009) (liability for funds derived from securities violations by others nondischargeable, even though debtor did not violate securities laws).

[3]   Unscheduled Debts[246]

Debts not listed on the schedule of debts filed in conjunction with the debtor's bankruptcy petition may be excluded from the scope of the debtor's discharge. The purpose of § 523(a)(3) is to ensure that creditors will have time to file a proof of claim in the case.[247] Thus, a debt is nondischargeable if the debtor has not scheduled it in time for the creditor to file a "timely . . . proof of claim."[248]

In no-asset cases, where nothing is available to distribute to unsecured creditors, there is no reason to file a proof of claim. Creditors are notified that there is no need to file a proof of claim. Accordingly, the traditional rule is that a creditor omitted from the debtor's schedules is not harmed by the debtor's failure and the exception to discharge in § 523(a)(3) does not apply.[249] However, this rule has recently been challenged by the decision in *Colonial Surety Co. v. Weizman*,[250] where the First Circuit applied § 523(a)(3) to exclude a surety's claim from the debtor's discharge where the debtor failed to list the surety among its creditors. In departing from the traditional rule, the court explained:

> Nothing in the language or history of the 1978 revision of section 523(a)(3) indicates that Congress aimed to carve out no asset bankruptcies from what we perceive to be a general rule that listing the creditor is a condition of discharge. The qualifying phrase about timely filing recognizes that notice may be given late in the bankruptcy-proceeding day but still in time for the creditor to participate in the bankruptcy proceeding. Here, the bankruptcy proceeding was completed with no notice to Colonial.[251]

In the case of debts that are dischargeable under § 523(a)(2), (4), (6), or (15), the debt must be scheduled in time for the creditor to permit both a "timely filing of a proof of claim and [a] timely request for a determination of dischargeability."[252] Because the bankruptcy court has exclusive jurisdiction to determine the dischargeability of such debts, they must be scheduled by the debtor in time for creditors to bring their right to have the debt determined nondischargeable under these provisions. Some courts have read § 523(a)(3)(B) expansively including debts for which the creditor had only a colorable claim for nondischargeability under these provisions.[253]

---

[246] Lauren A. Helbling & Christopher M. Klein, *The Emerging Harmless Innocent Omission Defense to Nondischargeability under Bankruptcy Code § 523(a)(3)(A): Making Sense of the Confusion Over Reopening Cases and Amending Schedules to Add Omitted Debts*, 69 Am. Bankr. L. J. 33 (1995).

[247] Tidwell v. Smith (In re Smith), 582 F.3d 767, 779-80 (7th Cir. 2009).

[248] Bankruptcy Code § 523(a)(3).

[249] In re Beezley, 994 F.2d 1433, 1435-37 (9th Cir. 1993) (O'Scannlain, J., concurring); In re Nielsen, 383 F.3d 922, 925 (9th Cir. 2004); In re Madaj, 149 F.3d 467, 470 (6th Cir. 1998); Judd v. Wolfe, 78 F.3d 110, 111 (3d Cir. 1996); Stone v. Caplan, 10 F.3d 285, 291 n. 13 (5th Cir. 1994).

[250] 564 F.3d 526 (1st Cir. 2009).

[251] *Id.* at 532. *See also* Francis v. Nat'l Revenue Service, Inc. (In re Francis), 426 B.R. 398 (Bankr. S.D. Fla. 2010) (factual issues over debtor's intentional failure to schedule the creditor precluded summary judgment).

[252] Bankruptcy Code § 523(a)(3)(B).

[253] *See, e.g.*, Haga v. Nat'l Union Fire Ins. Co. (In re Haga), 131 B.R. 320, 327 (Bankr. W.D. Tex. 1991).

However, the debtor's failure to schedule the debt does not result in nondischargeability if the creditor had "notice or actual knowledge of the [bankruptcy] case in time" to meet the deadline in question. Thus, even if the debtor failed to schedule a debt, if the creditor learns of the bankruptcy through other means, the unscheduled debt remains dischargeable.

[4] Fraud or Defalcation in a Fiduciary Capacity; Embezzlement; Larceny[254]

Section 523(a)(4) specifies that a debt for "fraud or defalcation while acting in a fiduciary capacity, embezzlement, or larceny" is nondischargeable.[255] Debts incurred through most other types of fraud are nondischargeable under § 523(a)(2).[256]

Use of the word "defalcation" raises the question of whether § 524(a)(4) involves a different standard of misconduct than § 524(a)(2).[257] Courts have interpreted § 523(a)(4) in three different ways.[258] Some courts permit § 523(a)(4) to apply to any kind of loss by a fiduciary in breach of her fiduciary obligation, even if it was by mistake or otherwise innocent.[259] Some courts apply it only when the fiduciary's conduct was negligent or worse.[260] Other courts limit it to reckless or even more serious defalcations.[261]

FNFS, Ltd. v. Harwood (In re Harwood)[262] supplies a good example of how § 523(a)(4) may establish a lower standard for nondischargeability than § 523(a)(2). A corporate president and chief operating officer failed to take action to record mortgages that he had granted to the corporation on his own property to secure a loan that the corporation had made to him. The court determined that even if the making of the loans themselves was not a breach of his fiduciary duty, the debtor's willfully reckless conduct in failing to protect the corporation against the increasing financial risk created by those loans by failing to take steps to perfect the liens securing them was the type of defalcation by a fiduciary that made the debt nondischargeable under § 523(a)(4).

---

[254] Peter M. Reinhardt and William G. Horlbeck, *Defalcation While Acting in a Fiduciary Capacity: What Does it Mean?*, 24 Colo. Law. 1773 (1995); Jennifer Liotta, Comment, *ERISA Fiduciaries in Bankruptcy: Preserving Individual Liability for Defalcation and Fraud Debts under 11 U.S.C. § 523(a)(4)*, 22 Emory Bankr. Dev. J. 725 (2006).

[255] Bankruptcy Code § 523(a)(4).

[256] *See supra* § 13.03[B][2] Debts Fraudulently Incurred.

[257] *See* Cent. Hanover Bank & Trust Co. v. Herbst, 93 F.2d 510 (2d Cir. 1937) (Hand, J.).

[258] Rutanen v. Baylis (In re Baylis), 313 F.3d 9, 18 (1st Cir. 2002).

[259] *E.g.*, Republic of Rwanda v. Uwimana (In re Uwimana), 274 F.3d 806 (4th Cir. 2001); Commonwealth Land Title Co. v. Blaszak (In re Blaszak), 397 F.3d 386 (6th Cir. 2005); Mountbatten Sur. Co. v. McCormick (In re McCormick), 283 B.R. 680 (Bankr. W.D. Pa. 2002).

[260] Antlers Roof-Truss & Builders Supply v. Storie (In re Storie), 216 B.R. 283 (B.A.P. 10th Cir. 1997).

[261] *E.g.*, Schwager v. Fallas (In re Schwager), 121 F.3d 177 (5th Cir. 1997); Rutanen v. Baylis (In re Baylis), 313 F.3d 9, 20 (1st Cir. 2002).

[262] In re Harwood, 637 F.3d 615 (5th Cir. 2011).

Another example of this lower standard is supplied by *First National Bank v. Bingaman (In re Bingaman).*[263] There, a debtor who withdrew funds from a trust fund established for her daughter, to purchase a car for her own use, found her liability nondischargeable under § 523(a)(6) even though she did not realize that her actions were wrongful.[264] Moreover, her husband's liability was also non-dischargeable, even though he was not involved in making the withdrawals, because, as the court put it, he could not "escape liability . . . by putting his head in the sand and claiming that he did not know what was going on with his daughter's accounts."[265]

Some years ago, the Supreme Court ruled that the exception for fiduciary capacity under the former Bankruptcy Act applied only to express trusts and not to equitable trusts created by the debtor's conduct.[266] Thus, it does not apply to breaches of duties by mere agents whose responsibilities do not rise to the level of a fiduciary obligation,[267] such as those owed by a trustee to the beneficiaries of a trust[268] or by an attorney to her client.[269]

However, general contractors have sometimes had debts due to their suppliers and subcontractors declared nondischageable under § 523(a)(4) on the theory that they held payments received from the owner in trust, for the benefit of these creditors. In *Gamboa v. ASCI Readi-Mix and Asphalt Specialities, Co. (In re Gamboa),*[270] the court held that the general contractor's obligation to pay these suppliers from funds he had received from the owner was nondischargeable as a breach of a fiduciary duty under § 523(a)(4), where a state construction trust fund statute made it clear that the contractor held these funds in trust. In states with similar statutes, debts that otherwise might look like ones for garden variety breach of contract claims, could easily turn into nondischargeable debts, based on the state's characterization of the contractor's obligation as a fiduciary duty.[271]

Embezzlement is not defined in the Code. However, courts assume that Congress used the term with the common law in mind.[272] Under the common law, embezzlement is "the fraudulent conversion of the property of another by one who is already

---

[263] 397 B.R. 444 (Bankr. C.D. Ill. 2008).

[264] *See also* In re Harwood, 637 F.3d 615 (5th Cir. 2011).

[265] *Id.* at 449.

[266] Davis v. Aetna Acceptance Co., 293 U.S. 328, 333 (1934) (interpreting former Bankruptcy Act § 17(a)(4)); Peerless Ins. v. Swanson (In re Swanson), 231 B.R. 145, 148 (Bankr. D.N.H. 1999).

[267] Angelle v. Reed (In re Angelle), 610 F.2d 1335 (5th Cir. 1980); Quaif v. Johnson, 4 F.3d 950 (11th Cir. 1993) (insurance agent).

[268] *See generally* Fowler Bros. v. Young (In re Young), 91 F.3d 1367 (10th Cir. 1996).

[269] *E.g.,* Ball v. McDowell (In re McDowell), 162 B.R. 136 (N.D. Ohio 1993).

[270] 400 B.R. 794 (Bankr. D. Colo. 2008).

[271] *See also* Ficher Constr., LLC v. Ecker, 400 B.R. 669 (Bankr. D. Wis. 2009) (state "theft by contractor" statute); In re Cline, No. 08-8104, 431 B.R. 307 (B.A.P. 6th Cir. Jan. 6, 2010) (debtor embezzled property from unsecured creditors who had financed auto dealership's purchase of inventory by selling automobiles to friends & family members without remitting proceeds to lenders).

[272] Sherman v. Potapov (In re Sherman), 603 F.3d 11 (1st Cir. 2010).

in lawful possession of it."[273]

In addition to the rules concerning larceny, embezzlement, and breach of fiduciary duty in § 523(a)(4), §§ 523(a)(11) and (12) provide special rules for certain types of debts owed to federal depository institutions. Section 523(a)(11) makes such debts nondischargeable if they are for a judgment, order, or consent decree "arising from any act of fraud or defalcation while acting in a fiduciary capacity committed with respect to any depository institution or insured credit union."[274] Section 523(a)(12) applies more specifically to any "malicious or reckless failure to fulfill any commitment . . . to a Federal depository institutions [sic] regulatory agency to maintain the capital of an insured depository institution."[275]

[5] Family Obligations[276]

In the past, the Bankruptcy Code drew a sharp distinction between support obligations and property settlement debts.[277] Support obligations have never been dischargeable. For many years, other obligations could be discharged. For a time, between 1994 and 2005, property settlement debts, that did not qualify as "domestic support obligations" were dischargeable, or not, depending on two factors: 1) the debtor's ability to pay; and 2) the relative hardship on the parties if the debt were discharged.[278] In 2005, this balancing test was eliminated and all domestic obligations were made nondischargeable in Chapter 7 cases.[279] In Chapter 13 cases, on the other hand, the distinction between support obligations and property settlement debts remains in place. The latter are dischargeable; the former are not.

[a] Domestic Support Obligations[280]

Section 523(a)(5) contains the traditional rule that any debt "for a domestic support obligation" is nondischargeable.[281] Domestic support obligations are defined broadly to include nearly every imaginable type of support obligation[282]

---

[273] United States v. Young, 955 F.2d 99, 102 (1st Cir. 1992).

[274] Bankruptcy Code § 523(a)(11).

[275] Bankruptcy Code § 523(a)(12).

[276] Peter C. Alexander, *Another Perspective: The Bankruptcy Code Harms Women and Children* 15 Widener L.J. 599 (2006); Judith K. Fitzgerald, *We All Live in a Yellow Submarine: BAPCPA's Impact on Family Law Matters*, 31 S. Ill. U. L.J. 563 (2007); Janet Leach Richards, *A Guide to Spousal Support and Property Division Claims under the Bankruptcy Abuse Prevention and Consumer Protection Act of 2005*, 18. 41 Fam. L.Q. 227 (2007); Sheryl L. Scheible, *Bankruptcy and the Modification of Support: Fresh Start, Head Start, or False Start?*, 69 N.C. L. Rev. 577 (1991); Jana B. Singer, *Divorce Obligations and Bankruptcy Discharge: Rethinking the Support/Property Distinction*, 30 Harv. J. on Legis. 43 (1993); Catherine E. Vance, *Till Debt Do Us Part: Irreconcilable Differences in the Unhappy Union of Bankruptcy and Divorce*, 45 Buff. L. Rev. 369 (1997).

[277] *E.g.*, In re Farelli, 347 B.R. 501 (Bankr. W.D. Pa. 2006).

[278] *See* Pub. L. No. 103-394 § 304(e), 108 Stat 4106, 4133 (repealed) (formerly codified at 11 U.S.C. § 523(a)(15)(A), (B) (2000)).

[279] *See* In re Blackburn, 412 B.R. 710 (Bankr. W.D. Pa. 2009); In re Golio, 393 B.R. 56 (Bankr. E.D.N.Y. 2008).

[280] Daniel A. Austin, *For Debtor or Worse: Discharge of Marital Debt Obligations Under the*

owed to the debtor's spouse, a former spouse, the debtor's child, a parent or guardian of the debtor's child, or to even a governmental unit.[283] The support obligation qualifies for nondischargeability if it was established in any one of a wide variety of ways, including a separation agreement, a divorce decree, a property settlement agreement, a court order, or an order of any other governmental unit.[284] But the obligation is not a domestic support obligation if it has been "assigned to a non-governmental entity," unless the obligation was assigned voluntarily by the original obligee for the purpose of collecting the debt.[285]

A debtor's obligation to his or her former spouse's attorney, for services provided to the spouse in connection with these matters are usually regarded as support.[286] The debt is one that the bankrupt spouse owes to the non-debtor spouse.

The Code makes this clear in its definition of domestic support obligations, which includes those that are "owed to *or recoverable by*" the spouse.[287] This clearly applies to obligations owed to the debtor's spouse's attorney. The extent to which it might apply more broadly, to other third-parties remains unclear.

Thus, the Code's language now indicates that an obligation is dischargeable even if it is not payable directly to the debtor's spouse, former spouse, or child, and courts continue to treat these debts to third parties as nondischargeable if they are in the nature of support.[288] Whether a particular debt is support is not dictated by its characterization in the divorce settlement or decree.[289] Instead, the determination depends on a variety of factors,[290] including:

- the intent of the parties;[291]

Bankruptcy Abuse Prevention and Consumer Protection Act of 2005, 51 Wayne L. Rev. 1369, 1371-2 (2005); James L. Musselman, *Once Upon a Time in Bankruptcy Court: Sorting Out Liability of Marital Property for Marital Debt Is No Fairly Tale*, 41 Fam. L.Q. 249 (2007); Michaela M. White & James P. Caher, *The Dog That Didn't Bark: Domestic Support Obligations and Exempt Property After BAPCPA*, 41 Fam. L.Q. 299 (2007).

[281] Bankruptcy Code § 523(a)(5).

[282] Section 101(14A)(B) includes any debt that is "in the nature of alimony, maintenance, or support (including assistance provided by a governmental unit) . . . whether such debt is expressly so designated." Bankruptcy Code § 101(14A)(B).

[283] Bankruptcy Code § 101(14A)(A).

[284] Bankruptcy Code § 101(14A)(C).

[285] Bankruptcy Code § 101(14A)(D).

[286] *See* In re Andrews, 434 B.R. 541 (Bankr. W.D. Ark. 2010).

[287] Bankruptcy Code § 101(14A) (emphasis supplied).

[288] *See, e.g.*, In re Andrews, 434 B.R. 541 (Bankr. W.D. Ark. 2010); In re Sullivan, 423 B.R. 881 (Bankr. E.D. Mo. 2010); Simon, Schindler & Sandberg v. Gentilini (In re Gentilini), 365 B.R. 251 (Bankr. S.D. Fla. 2007).

[289] *E.g.*, Sylvester v. Sylvester, 865 F.2d 1164 (10th Cir. 1989).

[290] Peter C. Alexander, *"Herstory" Repeats: The Bankruptcy Code Harms Women and Children*, 13 Am. Bankr. Inst. L. Rev. 571 (2005).

[291] *E.g.*, Forsdick v. Turgeon, 812 F.2d 801 (2d Cir. 1987) (labels in settlement agreement may reflect the parties' intent).

- the parties' financial circumstances and their relative need;[292]

- the amount and division of their property;[293]

- whether the obligation terminates upon the recipient's death or remarriage, or on her children becoming adults;[294]

- the number and frequency of the debtor's payments;[295]

- whether alimony or support is waived in the divorce decree;[296]

- the availability of state court mechanisms to modify and enforce the obligation;[297]

- and the income tax treatment of the obligation.[298]

With this many factors, courts have a wide degree of leeway, with decisions in individual cases affected by facts and circumstances that vary considerably from one case to the next.

Characterization of a claim as one for domestic support obligations is also important because of their priority under § 507(a)(1)(A). In chapter 7 cases, domestic support obligations are entitled to priority payment, if there are funds sufficient to pay them. In cases under Chapters 12 and 13, they are entitled to full payment sometime during the plan.[299] In the rare Chapter 11 case involving an individual debtor, they must be paid, in cash, when the plan is consummated.

[b] Other Obligations to a Spouse, Former Spouse, or Child[300]

Section 523(a)(5), discussed immediately above, deals with support obligations. But divorcing spouses also frequently owe property settlement and other debts to one other. The most obvious example is where one spouse keeps the marital home. He or she will likely be obligated to pay the other spouse for his or her joint ownership in the property. In addition, divorce and separate agreements frequently provide for one spouse to pay specific marital debts and hold the other spouse "harmless" for the obligation. Creditors, of course, are not bound by these agreements and may seek recovery from either spouse, regardless of the agreement between the divorcing couple. These obligations are now completely

---

[292] *E.g.*, In re Evert, 342 F.3d 358, 366 (5th Cir. 2003); Dennis v. Dennis (In re Dennis), 25 F.3d 274 (5th Cir. 1994).

[293] *See* Goin v. Rives (In re Goin), 808 F.2d 1391 (10th Cir. 1987).

[294] Fitzgerald v. Fitzgerald (In re Fitzgerald), 9 F.3d 517, 521 (6th Cir. 1993).

[295] Forsdick v. Turgeon, 812 F.2d 801 (2d Cir. 1987).

[296] *See* Sylvester v. Sylvester, 865 F.2d 1164 (10th Cir. 1989).

[297] In re Albin, 591 F.2d 94 (9th Cir. 1979).

[298] Tilley v. Jessee, 789 F.2d 1074 (4th Cir. 1986).

[299] 11 U.S.C. §§ 1129(a)(9)(B), 1222(a)(5) & 1325(a)(4) (2006).

[300] Michael Satz & Elizabeth Barker Brandt, *Representing Victims of Domestic Violence in Property Distribution of Proceedings After the Bankruptcy Abuse and Consumer Protection Act of 2005*, 41 Fam. L.Q. 275 (2007).

nondischargeable in cases under Chapters 7, 11, and 12, without regard to the debtor's ability to pay or to the relative impact on the other spouse. Thus, for dischargeability purposes, the difficult distinction between support and property settlement, needs to be made only in Chapter 13 cases, where property settlement debts remain dischargeable.[301]

[6] Willful and Malicious Injury

Section 523(a)(6) makes any debt for a "willful and malicious injury" to a person or property nondischargeable under § 523(a)(6). This makes liability for traditional intentional torts, such as assault, battery,[302] intentional infliction of emotional distress,[303] invasion of privacy,[304] defamation,[305] and trespass[306] nondischargeable. It also embraces more modern causes of action, such as intentional sexual harassment,[307] copyright infringement,[308] and intentional illegal discrimination of all types.[309] However, it does not encompass knowing, intentional, or deliberate breaches of contract, unless, in rare circumstances, the debtor intended to cause harm as a result of his breach.[310]

[a]   Recklessness

Liability for conduct that is merely negligent or reckless does not fall within the ambit of § 523(a)(6). The Supreme Court's decision in *Kawaauhau v. Geiger* rejected language in a much older case that had suggested that liability for any voluntary act which resulted in an injury fell within its ambit.[311] The older case, *Tinker v. Colwell*, ruled that liability for the largely archaic tort of "criminal

---

[301]   *See, e.g.*, In re Clark, 441 B.R. 752 (Bankr. M.D. N.C. 2011); In re White, 408 B.R. 677 (Bankr. S.D. Tex. 2009); In re McCollum, 415 B.R. 625 (Bankr. M.D. Ga. 2009) (debts due on marital home and car awarded to debtor's spouse in divorce proceeding were not support).

[302]   *E.g.*, In re Owens, 449 B.R. 239 (Bankr. E.D. Va. 2011) (parking lot fight); Taylor v. Fechnay (In re Fechnay), 425 B.R. 212 (Bankr. E.D. Pa. 2010) (clinical psychologist's sexual misconduct); In re Levin, 434 B.R. 910 (Bankr. S.D. Fla. 2010) (fatal shooting); In re Brown, 263 B.R. 832 (Bankr. S.D. Ohio 2000) (homicide); In re Love, 47 B.R. 349 (Bankr. W.D. Mo. 2006) (child molestation).

[303]   In re Elder, 262 B.R. 799 (C.D. Cal. 2001) (stalking); In re Cunningham, 59 B.R. 743 (Bankr. N.D. Ill. 1986); *but see* In re Lopez, 292 B.R. 570 (E. D. Mich. 2003) (limiting collateral estoppel effect of state court judgment where state law permits liability based on reckless or negligent conduct).

[304]   Mazurczyk v. O'Neil (In re O'Neil), 268 B.R. 1 (Bankr. D. Mass. 2001).

[305]   Jefferson v. Holland (In re Holland), 428 B.R. 465 (Bankr. N.D. Ill. 2010); Muse v. Day (In re Day), 409 B.R. 337 (Bankr. D. Md. 2009).

[306]   In re Bundick, 303 B.R. 90 (Bankr. E.D. Va. 2003).

[307]   *See* Sells v. Porter (In re Porter), 539 F.2d 889 (8th Cir. 2008); Jones v. Svreck (In re Jones), 300 B.R. 133 (B.A.P. 1st Cir. 2003); In re Busch 311 B.R. 657 (Bankr. N.D.N.Y. 2004) (distinguishing hostile environment claims); Andy Gaunce, Note, *Rethinking In re Busch: Bankruptcy Discharge of Sexual Harassment Judgments under Section 523(a)(6)*, 56 S.C. L. Rev. 645 (2005).

[308]   In re Albarran, 347 B.R. 369 (B.A.P. 9th Cir. 2006); In re Barboza, 545 F.3d 702 (9th Cir. 2008) (reckless copyright violation not willful and malicious).

[309]   Speaking of all types, see Jeffries v. Sullivan (In re Sullivan), 337 B.R. 210 (Bankr. W.D. Mo. 2005) (to make a long story short, the debtor willfully rammed the creditor's vehicle with her own).

[310]   Humility of Mary Health v. Garritano (In re Garritano), 427 B.R. 602 (Bankr. N.D. Ohio 2009).

[311]   Kawaauhau v. Geiger, 523 U.S. 57 (1998).

conversation" (with the plaintiff's spouse) was nondischargeable because it was an inherently malicious act that had been done intentionally.[312] *Geiger* resolved the issue and made it clear that § 523(a)(6) applies only to "intentional torts" where "the actor intend[ed] the consequences of an act, not simply the act itself."[313]

Thus, neither negligent nor reckless conduct are enough to make the debt nondischargeable.[314] Liability for medical, legal,[315] or other professional malpractice, based on simple negligence, is not a willful and malicious injury and is thus fully dischargeable.[316] Likewise, liability for many traditional intentional torts, which might be based on a finding of recklessness, might not satisfy the scienter standard required by *Geiger.* Courts interpreting *Geiger* have sometimes required the bankruptcy court to inquire into the debtor's subjective motive to inflict injury while other courts have been satisfied that the necessary finding of willful and malicious intent can be found if harm from the debtor's intentional conduct was substantially certain to occur.[317]

[b]   Conversion of Secured Creditor's Collateral[318]

Secured creditors sometimes claim that the debtor's sale of their collateral is a conversion, making the debt nondischargeable under § 523(a)(6), at least to the extent of the value of the converted collateral.[319] Although earlier cases support this result,[320] decisions after *Kawaauhau v. Geiger* have been more resistant to these claims. The debtor's sale of the collateral renders the debt nondischargeable only when the debtor both knew of the creditor's security interest and knew that the sale would harm the lender.[321] For example, an auto dealership who sells items of inventory "out of trust" in violation of the terms of the security agreement and fails to remit the proceeds from the sale to the lender, as required by the terms of

---

[312] Tinker v. Colwell, 193 U.S. 473 (1904) (applying § 14(a)(6) of the Bankruptcy Act).

[313] 193 U.S. at 63 (quoting the Restatement (Second) of Torts § 8A, comment a, (1964)).

[314] 193 U.S. at 64.

[315] Greenwood v. Dickhaus (In re Dickhaus), 425 B.R. 827 (Bankr. E.D. Mo. 2010).

[316] Kawaauhau v. Geiger, 523 U.S. 57 (1998); James L. Rigelhaupt, Jr., Annotation, *When Does Medical Practitioner's Treatment of Patient Constitute "Willful and Malicious Injury" So as to Make Practitioner's Debt Arising from Such Treatment Nondischargeable Under Section 523(a)(6) of Bankruptcy Act*, 77 A.L.R. Fed. 918 (1986).

[317] *Compare* Carrillo v. Su (In re Su), 290 F.3d 1140, 1142 (9th Cir. 2002), *and* Markowitz v. Campbell (In re Markowitz), 190 F.3d 455, 464 (6th Cir. 1999) (subjective intent), *with* Raspanti v. Keaty (In re Keaty), 397 F.3d 264 (5th Cir. 2005), *and* Miller v. J.D. Abrams, Inc. (In re Miller), 156 F.3d 598 (5th Cir. 1998).

[318] Charles J. Tabb, *The Scope of the Fresh Start in Bankruptcy: Collateral Conversions and the Dischargeability Debate*, 59 Geo. Wash. L. Rev. 56 (1990); Annotation, *Conversion as Willful and Malicious Injury to Property Within Provision of Bankruptcy Act Preventing Discharge from Liability for Such Injury*, 98 A.L.R. 1454 (1935).

[319] *E.g.*, In re Burns, 276 B.R. 441 (Bankr. N.D. Miss. 2000).

[320] *See* McIntyre v. Kavanaugh, 242 U.S. 138 (1916); Davis v. Aetna Acceptance Co., 293 U.S. 328 (1934) (dealer's sale of inventory out of trust). *See also* C.I.T. Fin. Serv. v. Posta (In re Posta), 866 F.2d 364 (10th Cir. 1989).

[321] *See* Federal Nat'l Title Ins. Co. v. Garcia (In re Garcia), 442 B.R. 848 (Bankr. M.D. Fla. 2011).

the floor-planning agreement, is likely to run afoul of § 523(a)(6).[322]

Debtors who attempt to conceal their sales of a creditor's collateral are also likely have their debts determined to be nondischargeable under § 523(a)(6). But, after the Supreme Court's decision in *Kawaauhau v. Geiger*,[323] described above, creditors should be required to show that the debtor's sale or concealment of the collateral was malicious — that is, accomplished with the intent to cause the creditor harm.[324] When the debtor's action was intended to deprive the creditor of its property right, it might also make the debt nondischargeable under § 523(a)(4), as larcenous.[325]

[7] Governmental Fines, Penalties, or Forfeitures

[a]   Non-Compensatory Fines and Penalties

It will surprise no one to learn that criminal fines and other penalties owed to a governmental unit are nondischargeable. Section 523(a)(7) excludes debts that are "for a fine, penalty, or forfeiture payable to and for the benefit of a governmental unit" from the scope of a debtor's discharge so long as the obligation is "not compensation for actual pecuniary loss."[326] Obligations to pay restitution to a victim of the debtor's crimes, entered as a condition of the debtor's probation or parol, are similarly nondischargeable.[327] Even awards of attorneys' fees can be such a fine or penalty, such as where they are assessed in a consumer protection enforcement action.[328] Likewise, depending on state law, fees and costs assessed against a disciplined attorney, are nondischargeable as a fine or penalty assessed against the attorney in favor of the state bar.[329] On the other hand, tax penalties are dischargeable if they either relate to an otherwise dischargeable tax[330] and were imposed in connection with a "transaction or event that occurred [more than] three years before the date of [the debtor's bankruptcy] petition."[331]

---

[322] *E.g.*, Automotive Fin. Corp. v. Rigoroso (In re Rigoroso), 453 B.R. 612 (Bankr. D.S.C. 2011).

[323] Kawaauhau v. Geiger, 523 U.S. 57 (1998).

[324] *Compare* In re Crump, 247 B.R. 1 (Bankr. W.D. Ky. 2000) (debtor's sale of collateral and disposition of proceeds in effort to keep business afloat was not intended to harm creditor), *and* In re Tomlinson, 220 B.R. 134 (Bankr. M.D. Fla. 1998) (sale of inventory and use of proceeds with intent to save business was not done with intent to harm secured creditor), *with* The Magic Lamp, Inc. v. LeBanc (In re LeBlanc), 346 B.R. 706 (Bankr. M.D. La. 2006) (debtor disposed of collateral and converted proceeds with knowledge of harmful effect on secured creditor), *and* Ocean Equity Group, Inc. v. Wooten (In re Wooten), 423 B.R. 108 (Bankr. E.D. Va. 2010) (debtor sold creditor's collateral and used proceeds to pay his home mortgage with knowledge of security interest and no hope to maintain the business in which collateral was used).

[325] *See* In re Sohail, 438 B.R. 398 (E.D. Va. 2010).

[326] Bankruptcy Code § 523(a)(7).

[327] Kelly v. Robinson, 479 U.S. 36 (1986); Colton v. Verola (In re Verola), 446 F.3d 1206 (11th Cir. 2006).

[328] In re Jenson, 395 B.R. 472 (Bankr. D. Colo. 2008).

[329] State Bar of Calif. v. Findley (In re Findley), 593 F.3d 1048 (9th Cir. 2010).

[330] *E.g.*, In re Roberts, 906 F.2d 1440 (10th Cir. 1990).

[331] Bankruptcy Code § 523(a)(7).

[b]   Federal Election Law Fines

Section 523(a)(14B) now makes it clear that debts "incurred to pay fines or penalties imposed under federal election law" nondischargeable.[332] Thus, a debtor who borrows money in order to pay his or her federal election law penalties cannot escape the penalty by using bankruptcy to discharge the debt to the creditor who provided financing for the debtor to pay her fine.[333] The narrow language of § 523(a)(14B) implies that debts incurred to pay other fines or penalties, including election law penalties imposed under state law, remain dischargeable. Any unpaid fines or penalties themselves are nondischargeable under § 523(a)(7), but only if they are not compensatory.

[c]   Federal Criminal Restitution Orders

Federal criminal restitution obligations, imposed under the United States Criminal Code are also nondischargeable.[334] Unlike § 1328(a)(3), which only applies to Chapter 13 cases,[335] it does not make state-imposed criminal restitution orders nondischargeable.

[8]   Student Loans[336]

Section 523(a)(8) makes a wide variety of student loans nondischargeable "unless excepting the debt from discharge would impose an undue hardship on the debtor and the debtor's dependents."[337] The language of the statute presents two different issues: first, whether the debt is a student loan; and second, whether the debtor suffers from an undue hardship.

[a]   Types of Nondischargeable Student Loans

Section 523(a)(8) applies to virtually every imaginable type of student loan. Foremost among them are educational loans made directly or guaranteed by a federal, state, or local government unit,[338] or loans made under a program "funded in whole or in part by a governmental unit or nonprofit institution."[339] Thus, if the

---

[332] Bankruptcy Code § 523(a)(14B).

[333] This language is similar to that contained in § 523(a)(14) & (14A) regarding debts incurred to pay otherwise nondischargeable tax debts.

[334] Bankruptcy Code § 523(a)(13).

[335] *See infra* § 13.05[C] Scope of Chapter 13 Discharge.

[336] Thad Collins, *Forging Middle Ground: Revision of Student Loan Debts in Bankruptcy as an Impetus to Amend 11 U.S.C. § 523 (a)(8)*, 75 Iowa L. Rev. 733 (1990); Darell Dunham & Ronald A. Buch, *Educational Debts Under the Bankruptcy Code*, 22 Mem. St. U. L. Rev. 679 (1992); Rafael I. Pardo & Michelle R. Lacey, *The Real Student-loan Scandal: Undue Hardship Discharge Litigation*, 83 Am. Bankr. L.J. 179 (2009); Rafael I. Pardo & Michelle R. Lacey, *Undue Hardship in the Bankruptcy Courts: An Empirical Assessment of the Discharge of Educational Debt*, 74 U. Cin. L. Rev. 405 (2005); John A. E. Pottow, *The Nondischargeability of Student Loans in Personal Bankruptcy Proceedings: The Search for a Theory*, 44 Canadian Bus. L.J. 245 (2006).

[337] Bankruptcy Code § 523(a)(8).

[338] Bankruptcy Code § 523(a)(8)(A)(i).

[339] Bankruptcy Code § 523(a)(8)(A)(i).

source of even part of a loan provided to a student is either a governmental agency or a nonprofit organization, such as the college itself, a fraternal organization, or other charitable entity, the entire loan is nondischargeable. Most decisions also make it applicable to debts incurred in trade-sponsored apprenticeship programs.[340]

Section 523(a)(8) also applies to any "obligation to repay funds received as an educational benefit, scholarship, or stipend." If a student accepted a scholarship or fellowship that was subject to the condition that the student engage in some sort of public or community service job after graduation, she would find her obligation to repay the amount of the scholarship nondischargeable if she failed to fulfill the terms of the program.

Finally, § 523(a)(8) now makes any educational loan that qualifies for tax deductible interest payments nondischargeable.[341] Deductible interest represents a smaller but nevertheless discernable federal subsidy that gives the government a stake in ensuring that these loans are repaid. This category makes most privately funded student loans non-dischargeable.[342]

Curiously, unpaid tuition bills are fully dischargeable. Thus, a student who borrows money to pay her tuition is likely to find that the debt is nondischargeable, but a student who simply fails to pay her tuition bill is able to obtain relief from the debt.[343] Colleges that wish to preserve their ability to collect unpaid tuition bills usually refuse to permit students to register for classes without a formal loan agreement containing the student's express promise to repay the extension of credit provided by the college. Obtaining a promissory note or other acknowledgment of liability for the unpaid tuition bill, after it is overdue, is not enough to invoke the non-dischargeability provision.[344] However, in *McKay v. Ingleson*, the court held that a student account and deferment agreement that the college student had signed before attending classes, promising to pay charges for tuition, housing, meals, laundry, books, copies, prescriptions, and vending machine purchases was a student loan within the meaning of § 523(a)(10).[345]

Separate rules outside the Bankruptcy Code govern the dischargeability of certain health educational loan programs, such as those under the Health Education Assistance Loan Act[346] and the National Health Service Corp

---

[340] *See* In re Capron, 454 B.R. 738 (Bankr. N.D. Iowa 2011).

[341] Bankruptcy Code § 523(a)(8)(B).

[342] Rafael I. Pardo & Michelle R. Lacey, *The Real Student-Loan Scandal: Undue Hardship Discharge Litigation*, 83 Am. Bankr. L.J. 179, 181 (2008).

[343] *E.g.*, In re Chambers, 348 F.3d 650 (7th Cir. 2003); In re Moore, 407 B.R. 855 (Bankr. E.D. Va. 2009) (unaccredited "online" law school violated discharge by refusing to issue transcript to student with discharged tuition debt). *See* Matthew C. Welnicki, *Dischargeability of Students' Financial Obligations: Student Loans Versus Student Tuition Account Debts*, 31 J. C. & U. L. 665 (2005).

[344] In re Renshaw, 222 F.3d 82 (2d Cir. 2000) (student's formal acknowledgment of obligation to pay overdue tuition did not transform the unpaid tuition debt into an educational loan).

[345] 558 F.3d 888 (9th Cir. 2009).

[346] 42 U.S.C. § 292f(g) (2006).

Scholarship Program.[347] These benefits are nondischargeable under a stricter standard, depending on whether more than five years have expired since the first payment became due and whether requiring repayment would be "unconscionable."[348]

[b] Undue Hardship[349]

Obligations to repay educational loans and benefits are dischargeable if excluding the debt from discharge "will impose an undue hardship on the debtor and the debtor's dependents."[350] Whether a particular debtor's situation presents a case of undue hardship has been subject to several tests, but none of them are easy to satisfy.

Most courts employ the three-part test adopted by the court in *Brunner v. New York State Higher Education. Services Corp.*,[351] which permits discharge of a student loan due to undue hardship if: (1) the debtor cannot maintain, based on current income and expenses a "minimal" standard of living for himself and his dependents if she is forced to repay the debt; (2) additional circumstances exist indicating that the debtor's circumstances are likely to persist for a significant portion of the repayment period for the loan; and (3) the debtor has made a good faith effort to repay the loan.[352] Debtors have found it difficult to satisfy all three prongs.

For example, in *Educational Credit Management Corp. v. Mason (In re Mason)*,[353] a debtor who had successfully completed eight years of military service, obtained an undergraduate philosophy degree, and completed law school, was unable to pass the bar exam when he was deprived of the special testing accommodations that his law school had provided to compensate for the learning disability he had suffered from since the third grade. Though his $1200 monthly wages as a part-time laborer was insufficient to meet his monthly living expenses, his abandonment of any plans to retake the bar exam, unwillingness to look for a second part-time job, and failure to take advantage of the federal Income Contingent Repayment Plan (ICRP) to reduce his monthly student loan repayment obligation,[354] led the court to refuse to discharge his student loans

---

[347] 42 U.S.C. § 254o(c)(3) (2006).

[348] 42 U.S.C. § 292f(g) (2006).

[349] Andrew M. Campbell, Annotation, *Bankruptcy Discharge of Student Loan On Ground of Undue Hardship Under § 523(a)(8)(B) of Bankruptcy Code of 1978 — Discharge of Student Loans*, 144 A.L.R. Fed. 1 (1998); Richard Fossey, *The Certainty of Hopelessness: Are Courts Too Harsh Toward Bankrupt Student Loan Debtors?*, 26 J.L. & Educ. 29 (1997); Rafael I. Pardo & Michelle R. Lacey, *Undue Hardship in the Bankruptcy Courts: An Empirical Assessment of the Discharge of Educational Debt*, 74 U. Cin. L. Rev. 405 (2005); Robert F. Salvin, *Student Loans, Bankruptcy, and the Fresh Start Policy: Must Debtors Be Impoverished to Discharge Educational Loans?*, 71 Tul. L. Rev. 139 (1996).

[350] Bankruptcy Code § 523(a)(8).

[351] Brunner v. N. Y. State Higher Educ. Serv. Corp., 831 F.2d 395 (2d Cir. 1987).

[352] 831 F.2d at 396. *See* In re Tirch, 409 F.3d 677 (6th Cir. 2005); Educ. Credit Mgmt. Corp. v. Mason (In re Mason), 464 F.3d 878, 881-885 (9th Cir. 2006).

[353] 464 F.3d 878 (9th Cir. 2006).

[354] *See* 34 C.F.R. § 685.209(c)(4)(iv) (2005). *See also* In re Bender, 338 B.R. 62 (Bankr. W.D. Mo. 2006)

under second and third prongs of the *Brunner* test.[355] Cases like *Mason*, which deny relief to debtors who have failed to take advantage of the ICRP program, or otherwise exhaust any available administrative remedies,[356] are legion.[357]

The difficulty debtors have in satisfying the *Brunner* test is also illustrated by *In re Goodman*,[358] where the debtor's financial responsibility for seven dependent children and expenses to treat her husband's skin cancer, were still not sufficient to satisfy the second "additional circumstances" prong of the *Brunner* test. The court explained that "although the Debtors' children will always be their children, the children will not always be [the debtor's] dependents" and thus the debtor's financial circumstances did not reflect the "certainty of hopelessness" that the *Brunner* test requires.[359]

Against the background of examples like these, it should not be surprising that debtors who live too comfortably are unlikely to qualify for discharge of their student loans, despite other physical and emotional challenges they may be facing. In *In re Miller*,[360] the court ruled that the debtor had failed to satisfy the first part of the *Brunner* test, despite her malformed brain, bipolar disorder, diabetes, and possible multiple sclerosis, because she had not demonstrated that her family could not move to a smaller, less expensive home than the five-bedroom $280,000 residence they occupied. In doing so, however, the court agreed with the debtor that the "means testing" standards, used to determine whether the debtor's case was "abusive," are not the sole basis for evaluating whether a debtor has reduced her living standards sufficiently to qualify for discharge of her student loans.[361]

Likewise, debtors with too many discretionary expenses are unlikely to satisfy the *Brunner* good faith effort standard. Bankruptcy judges are not impressed with debtors who spend money on large-screen projection televisions, manicures,[362] cell phones, cable tv, and even cigarettes,[363] who claim that paying their student loans would result in an undue hardship.

Two circuits take a somewhat more flexible approach based on the "totality of the circumstances." The totality of the circumstances test:

(assistant public defender who failed to participate in ICRP program ineligible for discharge of student loans); In re Booth, 410 B.R. 672 (Bankr. E.D. Wash. 2009) (debtor's zero payment obligation in ICRP did not preclude discharge of student loans due to undue hardship). *See generally* Terrence L. Michael & Janie M. Phelps, *Judges?! — We Don't Need No Stinking Judges!!!: The Discharge of Student Loans In Bankruptcy Cases And The Income Contingent Repayment Plan*, 38 Tex. Tech L. Rev. 73 (2005).

[355] The court nevertheless provided the debtor with a "partial" hardship discharge. *See infra* § 13.03[B][8][c] Partial Discharge of Student Loans.

[356] *E.g.*, In re Willis, 457 B.R. 829, 831 & 831 n.4 (Bankr. D. Kan. 2011).

[357] In re Barrett, 487 F.3d 353 (6th Cir. 2007); Educ. Credit Mgmt. Corp. v. Jesperson, 571 F.3d 775, 789 (8th Cir. 2009).

[358] 449 B.R. 287 (Bankr. N.D. Ohio 2011).

[359] *See also* In re Bush, 450 B.R. 235 (Bankr. M.D. Ga. 2011).

[360] 409 B.R. 299 (Bankr. E.D. Pa. 2009).

[361] *Id.* at 317-19.

[362] In re Armstrong, 394 B.R. 43 (Bankr. M.D. Pa. 2008).

[363] In re Mosko, 515 F.3d 319 (4th Cir. 2008).

requires a debtor to prove by a preponderance of evidence that (1) his past, present, and reasonably reliable future financial resources; (2) his and his dependents' reasonably necessary living expenses; and (3) other relevant facts or circumstances unique to the case, prevent him from paying the student loans in question while still maintaining a minimal standard of living, even when aided by a discharge of other prepetition debts.[364]

Under this test, courts consider all relevant evidence: "the debtor's income and expenses, the debtor's health, age, education, number of dependents and other personal or family circumstances, the amount of the monthly payment required, the impact of the general discharge under chapter 7 and the debtor's ability to find a higher-paying job, move or cut living expenses."[365]

The two tests take largely converging tacks. The "totality of circumstances test" examines past, present, and future financial resources and necessary living expenses, and whether, taken together with other factors, the debtor has the ability to repay while maintaining a minimal standard of living. The *Brunner* test, used in nine circuits, asks the same question looking to current income and expenses, then considers whether circumstances inhibiting repayment are likely to persist. Under either test, debtors who could adjust their standard of living stand little chance of discharging their student loans.

[c] Partial Discharge of Student Loans[366]

The straightforward text of § 523(a)(8) seems to make student loans either completely nondischargeable or completely dischargeable, depending on whether excepting the debt from discharge would impose an undue hardship. Despite this "all or nothing" language, some courts have relied on Bankruptcy Code § 105 to grant a partial discharge of a student loan "to the extent" that excluding it from the debtor's discharge would impose an undue hardship.[367] Other courts have rejected this interpretation as unsupported by the plain language of § 523(a)(8).[368]

[d] Discharge Through Confirmation in Chapter 13

Debtors sometimes try to discharge student loans in Chapter 13 without demonstrating that they suffer from an undue hardship, through the simple expedient of including the debt in their Chapter 13 plans. Creditors are normally

---

[364] In re Lorenz, 337 B.R. 423, 431 (B.A.P. 1st Cir. 2006).

[365] Hicks v. Educ. Credit Mgmt. Corp. (In re Hicks), 331 B.R. 18, 31 (Bankr. D. Mass.2005).

[366] Frank T. Bayuk, *The Superiority of Partial Discharge for Student Loans Under 11 U.S.C. § 523(a)(8): Ensuring a Meaningful Existence for the Undue Hardship Exception*, 31 Fla. St. U. L. Rev. 1091, 1119 (2004); Brendan Hennessy, Comment, *The Partial Discharge of Student Loans: Breaking Apart the All or Nothing Interpretation of 11 U.S.C. § 523(a)(8)*, 77 Temp. L. Rev. 71 (2004). *See also* Kevin C. Driscoll Jr., Note, *Eradicating the "Discharge by Declaration" for Student Loan Debt in Chapter 13*, 2000 U. Ill. L. Rev. 1311 (2000).

[367] *See* Educ. Credit Mgmt. Corp v. Mason (In re Mason), 464 F.3d 878 (9th Cir. 2006); Alderete v. Educ. Credit Mgmt. Corp. (In re Alderete), 412 F.3d 1200 (10th Cir. 2005); Miller v. Penn. Higher Educ. Assist. Agency (In re Miller), 377 F.3d 616 (6th Cir. 2004).

[368] *E.g.*, Salinas v. United Student Aid Funds, Inc. (In re Salinas), 258 B.R. 913 (Bankr. W.D. Wis. 2001).

bound by the terms of a confirmed plan, unless they successfully object. Upon completion of the terms of the plan, the debt is discharged, even though debtor did not pay the entire amount of the otherwise non-dischargeable student loan. Courts were split over whether this strategy was viable until early 2010, when the United States Supreme Court, in *United Student Aid Funds, Inc. v. Espinosa*,[369] laid the issue to rest by determining that the plan's provisions were controlling even though the debtor failed to comply with the usual requirements of § 523(a)(8) by filing a complaint to determine the dischargeability of the debt.

[9] Liability for Personal Injuries while Driving Drunk

Debts owed for simple negligence are generally fully dischargeable. However, liability for personal injury and wrongful death "caused by the debtor's operation of a motor vehicle, vessel, or aircraft if such operation was unlawful because the debtor was intoxicated from using alcohol, a drug, or another substance" is nondischargeable.[370] Thus, it applies to impaired driving, boating, and flying, but not to drunk horseback riding or drunk bicycling.[371] Liability for property damage on the other hand is not nondischargeable under this provision. Section 523(a)(9) applies only to liability for "death or personal injury." Nondischargeability also depends on whether the debtor's operation of the vehicle was unlawful under applicable local law "because the debtor was intoxicated."[372] If the debtor's operation of the vehicle was unlawful for some other reason, the debt remains dischargeable.

[10] Debts Excluded from Discharge in Prior Bankruptcies

Not surprisingly, debts that were not discharged in an earlier bankruptcy involving the same debtor, either because they were unlisted in the debtor's earlier case or because the debtor waived her discharge or was denied a discharge under § 727(a)(2)-(7), may not be discharged through the simple expedient of filing a subsequent bankruptcy case.[373] For example, in *In re Buckely*,[374] the debtor owed $508,680.99 to a former client, whose funds he had misappropriated prior to his earlier bankruptcy case, in which a discharge was denied. Because the facts that gave rise to the debtor's liability occurred before his earlier bankruptcy case, in which a discharge was denied, the debt was non-dischargeable in the subsequent case, without regard to whether the debt was incurred through fraud, conversion, or some other basis for non-dischargeability. Thus, debtors who are denied a

---

[369] United Student Aid Funds, Inc. v. Espinosa, 130 S. Ct. 1367 (2010).

[370] Bankruptcy Code § 523(a)(9).

[371] *See* Young v. Schmucker (In re Schmucker), 409 B.R. 477 (Bankr. N.D. Ind. 2008) (horse and buggy are not a "vessel" under § 523(a)(9)).

[372] *See* In re Hart, 347 B.R. 635 (Bankr. W.D. Mich. 2006) (operation unlawful due to impairment even though the debtor was not criminally charged); Wood v. Loader (In re Loader) 424 B.R. 464 (Bankr. D. Idaho 2009) (eyewitness evidence that debtor was "loud, rowdy, obnoxious" or "cowboy drunk" insufficient to establish that debtor's ability to operate a motor vehicle was impaired under applicable state standard, in the absence of evidence of blood-alcohol concentration).

[373] Bankruptcy Code § 523(a)(10).

[374] 404 B.R. 877 (Bankr. S.D. Ohio 2009).

discharge cannot evade the consequences of their ineligibility for discharge in one case, by filing a later case and obtaining a discharge.

However, if denial of discharge in the earlier case was due either to the eight-year bar of § 727(a)(8) or to the six-year bar of § 727(a)(9), debts scheduled in that earlier case are not automatically nondischargeable in a later case filed after the time barrier to discharge has passed. Likewise, if discharge was denied only because the debtor failed to complete a financial education program, as now required by § 727(a)(11), debts scheduled in the earlier case can be discharged in a subsequent case if the debtor participates in the necessary course of study.

[11] Other Nondischargeable Debts

A variety of other obligations are nondischargeable under the ever-growing list of debts excluded from the scope of a Chapter 7 discharge. Among these are:

- condominium or cooperative fees that become due "after the order for relief";[375]

- certain court imposed fees on state and federal prisoners in connection with civil actions they might pursue while incarcerated;[376] and

- debts owed to pension funds for loans permitted under certain provisions of ERISA.[377]

[C] Procedure for Determining Nondischargeability; Exclusive Jurisdiction

[1] Jurisdiction over Dischargeability

In most cases, the dischargeability of a debt can be determined either in bankruptcy court or state court. However, bankruptcy courts have exclusive jurisdiction to determine the nondischargeability of debts under § 523(a)(2), (4), or (6). Thus, actions to determine the dischargeability of a debt incurred through fraud, fiduciary fraud, embezzlement, larceny, or for willful and malicious injuries must be brought in bankruptcy court while the bankruptcy case is pending.

[2] Adversary Proceeding to Determine Dischargeability

Bankruptcy court actions to determine the dischargeability of a debt are "adversary proceedings" governed by Part VII of the Rules of Bankruptcy Procedure.[378] These rules are similar in most every respect to the Federal Rules of Civil Procedure.

---

[375] Bankruptcy Code § 523(a)(16).

[376] Bankruptcy Code § 523(a)(17).

[377] Bankruptcy Code § 523(a)(17).

[378] See Fed. R. Bankr. P. 4007(e), 7001(6).

Under Bankruptcy Rule 4007, either the debtor or a creditor may initiate an action to determine the dischargeability by filing a complaint.[379] The debtor may seek to have any question about a debt's dischargeability resolved in bankruptcy court rather than in what might be viewed as a less friendly state forum.

Most dischargeability complaints can be filed any time while the bankruptcy case is pending.[380] However, complaints to determine the nondischargeability of a debt under § 523(a)(2), (4), or (6) must be filed "no later than 60 days after the first date set" for the § 341(a) meeting of creditors.[381] To prevent creditors from being unfairly surprised by this short time frame, Bankruptcy Rule 4007 requires the standard notice that is sent to all creditors regarding the debtors bankruptcy case to include information about the 60 day limit.[382] The court has authority to extend the limit "for cause" upon the motion of the debtor, a creditor, or any other party in interest.

[D]   Collateral Estoppel Effect of Earlier Judgments[383]

If a creditor has obtained a pre-bankruptcy judgment against the debtor regarding a debt that might be nondischargeable, the prior judgment may have some collateral estoppel effect on a subsequent bankruptcy court dispute of the dischargeability of the debt. If the creditor has previously established that the debt was incurred through fraud or that it involved some willful and malicious personal injury, the creditor may attempt to set up the earlier judgment to prevent the debtor from relitigating those issues in bankruptcy court.[384] Alternatively, if the creditor previously alleged, but failed to prove elements of some basis for determining the nondischargeability of the debt, the debtor may attempt to use the earlier judgment to preclude the creditor from renewing its assertion that the element can be satisfied.[385]

Because the earlier judgment is likely to have been in state court, the federal full faith and credit statute[386] requires bankruptcy courts to give the earlier state court judgment the same collateral estoppel effect that it would be given by the state that issued the judgment.[387] Thus, if the underlying judgment, such as a settlement decree, would not have been given preclusive effect by the state where

---

[379]   Fed. R. Bankr. P. 4007(a).

[380]   Fed. R. Bankr. P. 4007(b).

[381]   Fed. R. Bankr. P. 4007(c).

[382]   Fed. R. Bankr. P. 4007(c).

[383]   Jeffrey T. Ferriell, *The Preclusive Effect of State Court Judgments in Bankruptcy, Part I*, 58 Am. Bankr. L.J. 349 (1984), and *Part II*, 59 Am. Bankr. L.J. 55 (1985); Christopher Klein, Lawrence Ponoroff, & Sarah Borrey, *Principles of Preclusion and Estoppel in Bankruptcy Cases*, 79 Am. Bankr. L.J. 839 (2005).

[384]   *E.g.* Muse v. Day (In re Day), 409 B.R. 337 (Bankr. M.D. 2009) (state court judgment established non-dischargeability of defamation liability).

[385]   *See* In re Ryals, 424 B.R. 539 (Bankr. M.D. Fla. 2009) (conviction for tax evasion).

[386]   28 U.S.C. § 1738 (2006).

[387]   Grogan v. Garner, 498 U.S. 279 (1991). *See* Smith v. Cornelius (In re Cornelius), 405 B.R. 597, 601-02 (Bankr. N.D. Ohio 2009); Colemichael Invs., L.L.C. v. Burke (In re Burke), 405 B.R. 626 (Bankr. N.D. Ill. 2009).

the judgment was issued, the bankruptcy court is not bound by the earlier decision.[388]

§ 13.04   CHAPTER 7 DISCHARGE

Because most bankruptcies are filed, and still more are closed, under Chapter 7, eligibility for discharge and the scope of discharge are primarily issues that arise under Chapter 7. Moreover, because there are usually no assets to distribute to creditors in Chapter 7 cases, discharge is the only real function of most Chapter 7 cases.[389]

[A]   Debtors Eligible for Chapter 7 Discharge

In order to be eligible for a Chapter 7 discharge, debtors must be eligible to file a Chapter 7 petition in the first place. As explained elsewhere in more detail, Chapter 7 is generally available to individuals, corporations, partnerships, trusts, non-profit organizations, and unincorporated associations. However, railroads, insurance companies, and banks or other financial institutions are ineligible for Chapter 7 relief.[390]

Although a wide variety of other types of entities are eligible to file a petition under Chapter 7, natural persons — human beings — are the only ones eligible for a Chapter 7 discharge.[391] Organizations, such as corporations, partnerships, trusts, and other business entities may not receive a Chapter 7 discharge. This rule prevents "shell" corporations from obtaining tax advantages that might otherwise be available to a company that has discharged its debts in liquidation. State and federal tax laws sometimes permit a profitable company to acquire and use the net operating loss of a defunct firm, thus enabling the acquiring company to reduce its taxes. Drafters of the Bankruptcy Code disapproved of this practice and consequently imposed a price on companies who might seek to deploy this strategy. A profitable company may acquire a company that has been in Chapter 7 and, if the Internal Revenue Code permits, may use its net operating losses to defray its income. However, it may have to pay a steep price. If, to obtain the tax benefits, the acquiring entity must merge with the shell, the acquiring entity thereby becomes liable for the shell's remaining debts because those debts have not been discharged.

As a result of this rule, few business entities seek relief under Chapter 7. When these types of debtors find themselves in a Chapter 7 case, it is usually because they have failed in their attempt to successfully reorganize under Chapter 11. Indeed, while it is permissible to liquidate in Chapter 11, corporations that

---

[388] Archer v. Warner, 538 U.S. 314 (2003).

[389] *See* Michael J. Herbert & Domenic E. Pacitti, *Down and Out in Richmond, Virginia: The Distribution of Assets in Chapter 7 Bankruptcy Proceedings Closed During 1984-87*, 22 U. Rich. L. Rev. 303, 311 (1988) (92.3% of Chapter 7 cases are no-asset cases).

[390] Bankruptcy Code § 109(b). *See supra* § 6.02[B][2] Eligibility for Relief in Chapter 7 — Liquidation.

[391] Bankruptcy Code § 727(a)(1).

liquidate in Chapter 11 do not receive a discharge either.[392]

As is true throughout the Code, any particular debtor may be denied discharge because of various types of misconduct. Denial of discharge due to various types of misconduct is discussed earlier in this chapter.[393]

[B]   Timing of Discharge

A Chapter 7 discharge is supposed to be granted promptly. Under Bankruptcy Rule 4004, once the time is set for filing objections to discharge and motions to dismiss for substantial abuse, the court is to grant the discharge "forthwith" after expiration of whatever time has been fixed.[394] The discharge need not be granted if there is a pending objection to discharge[395] or to dismiss the case entirely due to abuse.[396] Moreover, the court may on its own motion delay entry of the order of discharge for thirty days, and if a party in interest makes a motion within that thirty day period, to a further date certain.[397]

[C]   Scope of Debtor's Chapter 7 Discharge

The full list of nondischargeable debts set out in Bankruptcy Code § 523 is discussed earlier in this chapter.[398] This means that under some circumstances, Chapter 7 will be a poor choice for the debtor. For example a debtor who owes a property settlement obligation to a former spouse, may find it more advantageous to file under Chapter 13 and obtain its somewhat more expansive discharge.

Otherwise, a Chapter 7 discharge extends to all debts that arose before the order for relief.[399] In voluntary cases, this means all dischargeable pre-petition debts. As a general rule, post-petition debts are not discharged.[400] This is part and parcel of the structure of Chapter 7, which is designed to deal with pre-petition debts and pre-petition assets. Some post-petition debts are encompassed in the discharge, but only if some specific provision of the Code treats them as if they were incurred pre-petition. These include claims of involuntary gap creditors, who extended credit after an involuntary petition but before the order for relief; the claims of those from whom property was recovered by the trustee; and claims arising from the rejection of executory contracts and unexpired leases.[401]

---

[392] *See infra* § 19.05 Conversion and Dismissal of Chapter 11 Cases.

[393] *See supra* § 13.02[B] Denial of Discharge in Chapter 7.

[394] Fed. R. Bankr. P. 4004(c).

[395] *See supra*, § 13.02[B] Denial of Discharge in Chapter 7.

[396] *See infra*, § 17.03[B] Dismissal of Consumer Cases Due to Abuse.

[397] Fed. R. Bankr. P. 4004(c)(2).

[398] *See supra* § 13.03 Nondischargeable Debts.

[399] Bankruptcy Code § 727(b).

[400] *E.g.*, In re Johnson, 460 B.R. 328 (Bankr. S.D. Fla. 2011) (landlord's claim for post-petition rent due under pre-petition lease outside the scope of debtor's discharge).

[401] Bankruptcy Code §§ 502, 727(b).

§ 13.05 CHAPTER 13 DISCHARGE

A Chapter 13 discharge is broader than the discharge available in a Chapter 7 liquidation case. But, a Chapter 13 discharge is normally granted only upon completion of the debtor's repayment plan, usually at least three years after her petition has been filed, and for debtors with too much disposable income, not until five years after the petition has been filed.

[A] Debtors Eligible for Chapter 13 Discharge

Chapter 13 is available only to individual debtors.[402] Corporations, partnerships, and other organizations who seek relief in a reorganization proceeding must file under either Chapter 11, or if they qualify as a "family farmer," under Chapter 12. Consequently, there is no need for any additional limitation on those eligible for discharge. Since corporations, partnerships, and other business organizations cannot use Chapter 13, there are no concerns about the sale of shell companies emerging from it.

Chapter 13 debtors who have engaged in misconduct in connection with their case may have difficulty obtaining confirmation of their plans.[403] Because Chapter 13 debtors are generally only eligible for a discharge upon completion of the terms of their confirmed Chapter 13 plan,[404] misconduct that results in denial of confirmation prevents the debtor from satisfying the requirements for a Chapter 13 discharge. Further, as explained earlier, a debtor's prior Chapter 7 or 13 discharge may prevent her from obtaining a discharge too closely on the heels of the earlier case.[405]

[B] Timing of Chapter 13 Discharge

Ordinarily, a Chapter 13 discharge is granted only upon completion of the debtor's repayment plan. The court is to grant the discharge "as soon as practicable" after the debtor makes the last plan payment.[406] In most cases, this means that the debtor will not receive a discharge until either 3 or 5 years after her case had been filed. An earlier, hardship discharge may be requested under some circumstances, involving "hardship" as explained later in this chapter.[407]

---

[402] Bankruptcy Code § 109(e).

[403] *See infra* § 18.08[C] Good Faith.

[404] *See supra* § 13.02[D] Denial of Discharge Under Chapters 12 and 13.

[405] Bankruptcy Code § 1325(a). *See supra* § 13.02[D] Denial of Discharge in Chapters 12 and 13.

[406] Bankruptcy Code § 1328(a).

[407] *See infra* § 13.05[C][2] Chapter 13 Hardship Discharge.

[C] Scope of Chapter 13 Discharge[408]

The scope of discharge under Chapter 13 depends on whether the debtor successfully completes her plan. Successful completion of a plan entitles the debtor to a broader discharge than is available under other chapters. Debtors who do not complete their plans may, under some circumstances, obtain a narrower hardship discharge.

In general, the discharge encompasses only those debts that were provided for under the plan and those that were disallowed under Bankruptcy Code § 502. It also permits discharge of a few post-petition debts that involve either taxes or consumer obligations arising from property or services necessary for the debtor's performance under the plan.[409]

[1] Full-Compliance Chapter 13 Discharge[410]

As discussed in depth in a subsequent chapter, the core feature of a Chapter 13 case is the debtor's repayment plan. Chapter 13 plans usually provide for repayment of a portion of the debtor's obligations over either a three or five year period.[411] As one of the incentives to convince debtors to choose Chapter 13 over Chapter 7, Congress provided a broader discharge for those who complete their Chapter 13 plans. Under § 1328, all plan obligations and all disallowed obligations are discharged, except for:

- "long term" debts — claims on which the last payment is due after the due date of the final payment under the plan;[412]

- tax debts entitled to priority under § 507(a)(8)(C) or nondischargeable under § 523(a)(1)(B) or (C);[413]

- debts fraudulently incurred under § 523(a)(2);[414]

- unscheduled debts under § 523(a)(3);[415]

- debts for fiduciary fraud, embezzlement, or larceny under § 523(a)(4);[416]

- domestic support obligations under § 523(a)(5), as defined in § 101(a)(14A);[417]

---

[408] Scott F. Norberg, *Consumer Bankruptcy's New Clothes: An Empirical Study of Discharge and Debt Collection in Chapter 13*, 7 Am. Bankr. Inst. L. Rev. 415 (1999).

[409] *See* Bankruptcy Code § 1305(a).

[410] Farris E. Ain, Comment, *Never Judge a Bankruptcy Plan by its Cover: The Discharge of Student Loans Through Provisions in a Chapter 13 Plan*, 32 Sw. U. L. Rev. 703 (2003).

[411] *See infra* Chapter 18 — Rehabilitation of Individuals with Regular Income.

[412] Bankruptcy Code §§ 1328(a)(1), 1322(a)(5).

[413] *See supra* § 13.03[B][1] Tax Debts.

[414] *See supra* § 13.03[B][2] Debts Fraudulently Incurred.

[415] *See supra* § 13.03[B][3] Unscheduled Debts.

[416] *See supra* § 13.03[B][4] Fraud or Defalcation in a Fiduciary Capacity; Embezzlement, Larceny.

[417] *See supra* § 13.03[B][5][a] Domestic Support Obligations.

- student loans under § 523(a)(8);[418]

- debts for wrongful death or personal injury while driving, boating, or flying drunk under § 523(a)(9);[419]

- criminal restitution orders or fines;[420] and

- damages awarded in civil judgments against the debtor for personal injuries or death suffered as a result of wilful or malicious injuries inflicted by the debtor.[421]

This means of course that some debtors may gain considerably from a Chapter 13 filing, instead of seeking relief under Chapter 7. The most important categories of debts that are nondischargeable in Chapter 7 but that can be discharged in Chapter 13 are those owed to a former spouse for something other than support,[422] liability for property damage due to intentional torts,[423] and debts incurred to repay otherwise nondischargeable non-priority tax debts.[424]

It might appear from § 1328(a)(2) as if tax debts are dischargeable in Chapter 13. Although § 1328 leaves most tax debts fully dischargeable, what § 1328 giveth, § 1322 taketh away. Section 1322(a)(2) requires Chapter 13 plans to "provide for full payment . . . of all claims entitled to priority under section 507." Most income, property, excise, and other tax debts are entitled to priority under § 507.[425] This, combined with delaying the debtor's discharge until she has completed the terms of her plan, effectively makes § 507(a)(8) tax obligations dischargeable only after they have been fully paid pursuant to the debtor's plan. To be confirmed, the debtor's plan has to provide for payment of these debts in full. To obtain a discharge, the debtor must fully perform her plan.

Congress has shown considerable ambivalence about the breadth of the Chapter 13 discharge. The scope of the Chapter 13 regular discharge has gradually narrowed since it was implemented in 1978. The 2005 amendments dramatically reduced the scope of the Chapter 13 discharge by, among other things, excepting debts fraudulently incurred, and, at the same time, expanding the presumption of fraud in § 523(a)(2)(C).

Nothing could better illustrate the difficulties presented by any effort to strike a reasonable balance between competing interests in bankruptcy. Congress at first sought to draw debtors into Chapter 13 by offering a generous discharge; then,

---

[418] *See supra* § 13.03[B][8] Student Loans.

[419] *See supra* § 13.03[B][9] Liability for Personal Injuries while Driving Drunk.

[420] Bankruptcy Code § 1328(a)(3).

[421] Bankruptcy Code § 1328(a)(4). *See* In re Waag, 418 B.R. 373 (B.A.P. 9th Cir. 2009) (judgment need not be prepetition). Lepore v. Kerner, 2010 U.S. Dist. LEXIS 112590 (D.N.J. 2010) (same).

[422] *See* Bankruptcy Code § 523(a)(15); *supra* § 13.03[B][5][b] Other Obligations to a Spouse, Former Spouse, or Child. *See, e.g.*, In re Clark, 441 B.R. 752 (Bankr. M.D.N.C. 2011).

[423] *See* Bankruptcy Code § 523(a)(6); *supra* § 13.03[B][6] Wilful & Malicious Injury.

[424] *See* Bankruptcy Code § 523(a)(14), (14A); *supra* § 13.03[B][1] Tax Debts. Note, however, that such debts may be nondischargeable due to fraud, under §§ 1328(a)(2) and 523(a)(2) if the debt was incurred in anticipation of discharging the debt in a subsequent Chapter 13 bankruptcy proceeding.

[425] Bankruptcy Code § 507(a)(8). *See supra* § 13.03[B][1][a] Priority Taxes.

seemingly appalled by the fact that people actually took advantage of that offer, it gradually made Chapter 13's discharge more and more restrictive.

Despite the restrictions imposed by § 1328, Chapter 13 debtors may be able to discharge debts that are otherwise nondischargeable in Chapter 13 through the simple expedient of including language in their plan providing for discharge of the debt. In *Espinosa v. United Student Aid Funds, Inc.*,[426] the Supreme Court ruled that such a provision was binding on the creditor if the creditor failed to object to the plan after receiving notice of its provisions, even though the debtor had failed to commence and serve an adversary proceeding to have the student loan involved in the case declared dischargeable under § 523(a)(8). The creditor received notice of the proposed discharge of the student debt when it received notice of the debtor's plan, and, although the bankruptcy court's confirmation of the plan was a mistake, it was not void. Thus, the creditor could not obtain relief from the confirmation order under Federal Rule of Civil Procedure 60(b)(4), which, the Court explained, did "not provide a license for litigants to sleep on their rights."[427]

[2] Chapter 13 Hardship Discharge

Many Chapter 13 debtors find that they are unable to complete the terms of their plans. Consider the difficulty of living within a strict budget for three to five years. Few of us manage more than a week or two on such a strict regimen, even without the intervention of unforseen adverse circumstances.

Debtors in this situation may modify their plan, and if the modified plan is confirmed and completed, the debtor is still eligible for a full Chapter 13 discharge.[428] However, depending on the circumstances that make completion of the original plan more difficult, modification may be impractical.[429] The debtor may fall ill, lose her job, or need to quit working to care for a sick child. If neither modification nor completion seems possible, a Chapter 13 debtor might choose to convert the case and obtain a Chapter 7 discharge. Alternatively, the debtor might ask the court to grant a Chapter 13 hardship discharge.[430] Either way, the debtor's discharge is the same.[431] The principal difference is that by seeking a hardship discharge, the debtor avoids the loss of any further property beyond what she had already contributed to the payment of her debts through her plan.

[a] Grounds for Hardship Discharge

A hardship discharge is not always available. Section 1328(b) permits the court to grant a hardship discharge only if:

- the debtor's failure to complete the plan payments is due to circumstances

---

[426] 130 S. Ct. 1367 (2010).

[427] *Id.* at 1380.

[428] *See* Bankruptcy Code § 1329; *infra* § 18.10 Modification of Chapter 13 Plan.

[429] *See* In re Bond, 36 B.R. 49 (Bankr. E.D.N.C. 1984) (Chapter 13 debtor's death made completion or modification impossible).

[430] Bankruptcy Code § 1328(b).

[431] Bankruptcy Code § 1328(c).

for which the debtor should not justly be held accountable;

- the creditors have received at least the Chapter 7 liquidation value of their unsecured claims; and

- modification of the plan is not practicable.[432]

In determining whether the debtor's failure to complete the plan is as a result of circumstances for which the debtor should not justly be held accountable, courts frequently decide that disruptions in the debtor's income stream due to previously unforeseeable circumstances that make performance of the plan impossible such as a permanent disruption of the debtor's income or an unanticipated increase in the debtor's expenses, qualifies.

Although courts have sometimes indicated that the debtor need not show that she was facing "catastrophic circumstances" to obtain a hardship discharge, courts have sometimes denied a hardship discharge in situations many of us would regard as catastrophic. For example, in *In re Easley*, married debtors were denied a hardship discharge where the husband's position with his employer was completely eliminated, because the husband remained healthy, they lived in an area where the rate of unemployment was generally low, and there was no evidence that the wife, who had not been looking for work, was unable to work outside the home.[433]

Among the factors courts frequently consider in making this determination are (1) whether the debtor has presented substantial evidence that she had the ability and intent to perform the plan when it was confirmed; (2) whether the debtor materially performed the plan up to the time of the event that impaired her ability to perform; (3) whether the disrupting event was foreseeable at the time the plan was confirmed; (4) whether the intervening circumstances that impair the debtor's ability to continue performing are reasonably expected to continue; (5) whether the debtor had direct or indirect control of the intervening circumstances; and (6) whether the intervening events were a sufficient and proximate cause of the debtor's inability to continue performance under the terms of the plan.[434]

Consistent with the basic bargain struck in Chapter 13 cases, a hardship discharge is available only if the payments made to unsecured creditors, at the time the hardship discharge is sought, is the equivalent of what they would have received if the debtor had liquidated in Chapter 7. Thus, the value of payments made to unsecured creditors under the plan must be discounted to their present value, and then compared with what unsecured creditors would have received if the debtor had simply liquidated. This makes sense, as unsecured creditors would be seriously prejudiced by a hardship discharge if they have not received payments compensating them for at least what they would have received if the debtor had liquidated.

For example, if the debtor owned $10,000 in non-exempt equity that would have been distributed to unsecured creditors if the debtor had liquidated, the *value* of

---

[432] Bankruptcy Code § 1328(b).

[433] 240 B.R. 563 (Bankr. W.D. Mo. 1999).

[434] Bandilli v. Boyajian (In re Bandi), 231 B.R. 836 (B.A.P. 1st Cir. 1999).

payments made under the plan must equal that same amount. If a total of exactly $10,000 has been distributed to unsecured creditors through 2 years of payments under the plan, a hardship discharge cannot be granted. Payments totaling $10,000, spread out over two years does not have the same value as the $10,000 the unsecured creditors would have received immediately if the debtor had previously liquidated. A hardship discharge can be granted if the payments distributed under the plan exceed $10,000 by a sufficient amount to compensate her creditors for the delay in receiving the liquidation value of her estate.

Finally, in order to grant the debtor a hardship discharge, the court must determine that modification of the debtor's plan is not feasible. In most cases, the same circumstances that make continued payments under the plan impossible makes modification impractical. If the debtor has lost her job or suffered some injury, making continued employment impossible, it is unlikely that she can fund any plan. Still, before a hardship discharge is granted, the debtor's circumstances should be evaluated to determine if a plan, which is feasible and meets the financial standards imposed by §§ 1325 and 1329 for confirmation, can be proposed.

[b]   Scope of a Hardship Discharge

Unfortunately, the scope of a Chapter 13 hardship discharge is no broader than a Chapter 7 discharge, and in some respects, it is narrower. Section 1328(c)(2) provides that a hardship discharge "discharges the debtor from all unsecured debts provided for by the plan or disallowed under section 502 . . . except any debt . . . of a kind specified in section 523(a)."[435] Thus, a Chapter 13 hardship discharge is subject to the same limits as those imposed by § 727 in a Chapter 7 discharge. Also excluded from the hardship discharge are any long-term debts, which would ordinarily extend beyond the terms of the debtor's plan within the meaning of § 1322(b)(5).[436]

The principal advantage of obtaining a hardship discharge is that it permits the debtor to retain her non-exempt assets. The alternative, converting the case to Chapter 7 would result in the appointment of a trustee who would administer any non-exempt assets that the debtor owns. Thus, although a hardship discharge does not provide the debtor with an expanded discharge, it at least permits the debtor to retain her property.

§ 13.06   CHAPTER 11 DISCHARGE

[A]   Persons Eligible for Chapter 11 Discharge

Chapter 11 is broadly available to nearly every type of person eligible for relief generally under the bankruptcy code.[437] Railroads, which are ineligible for relief under Chapter 7, may reorganize under Chapter 11. Stockbrokers and commodity

---

[435] Bankruptcy Code § 1328(c).

[436] Bankruptcy Code § 1328(c)(1).

[437] *See supra* 6.02[B] Debtor's Eligibility for Voluntary Relief.

brokers, however, are ineligible for reorganization and must seek relief, if at all, under Chapter 7.[438]

[1] Corporations, Partnerships and other Organizations

Most Chapter 11 cases involve corporations or partnerships. In these cases, the debtor receives a discharge upon confirmation of its Chapter 11 plan.[439] If no plan is confirmed, the debtor receives no discharge, and the case will most likely be dismissed or converted to Chapter 7. Thus, the ability to obtain confirmation is the principal barrier to obtaining a discharge in Chapter 11.

This does not mean that questions about the debtor's conduct are irrelevant in Chapter 11. They are likely to arise, if at all, in connection with whether to confirm the debtor's plan, rather than in a separate adversary proceeding to determine whether to grant or deny a discharge. Thus, by refusing to confirm the debtor's plan, the court can effectively deny discharge for one or more of the same reasons that it would directly rule on denial of discharge in Chapter 7.

Chapter 11 contains nothing like the eight-year bar of § 727 that prevents debtors from obtaining successive Chapter 7 discharges.[440] Debtors may receive a Chapter 11 discharge as frequently as they are able to obtain confirmation of a Chapter 11 plan.

However, it is difficult to obtain confirmation of a Chapter 11 plan without the consent of a majority of the debtor's creditors. In Chapter 11, creditors have the right to vote to approve or reject the debtor's plan.[441] A Chapter 11 debtor's past misconduct may lead creditors to refuse to vote in favor of the debtor's plan, making confirmation difficult or impossible. Likewise, creditors who have voted to "accept" a plan in a recent Chapter 11 case may be reluctant to give the debtor a second chance to reorganize and may effectively deny a corporate debtor a second successive Chapter 11 discharge simply by refusing to vote in favor of the second plan.[442]

As noted above, there is one circumstance in which a Chapter 11 debtor may be denied a discharge even though it has obtained confirmation of a plan. If the debtor's Chapter 11 plan provides for liquidation rather than reorganization, the debtor may not receive a discharge. Section 1141(d)(3) prevents discharge if: (1) the plan provides for the liquidation of all, or substantially all of the property of the estate; (2) the debtor does not engage in business after consummation of the plan; and (3) discharge would have been denied under § 727(a) if the case had been brought under Chapter 7.[443] Because corporations are not entitled to a Chapter 7 discharge, corporations whose plans call for an orderly liquidation in Chapter 11, may not receive a Chapter 11 discharge.

---

[438] Bankruptcy Code § 109(d).

[439] Bankruptcy Code § 1141(d).

[440] See supra § 13.02[B][6] Repeat Filings — The 8-Year Bar.

[441] See generally infra § 19.09 Acceptance of Plan by Holders of Claims & Interests: Voting.

[442] See infra § 19.10 Confirmation of Chapter 11 Plans.

[443] Bankruptcy Code § 1141(d)(3).

Finally, as in Chapter 7, a Chapter 11 discharge can be waived. There are procedural requirements that must be met. To be effective, the waiver must be in writing; it must be executed by the debtor after the order for relief (i.e., in a voluntary case, after the filing of the petition); and it must be approved by the court.[444]

[2] Discharge of Individual Debtors in Chapter 11

Although Chapter 11 is generally regarded as suitable primarily for corporations, partnerships, and other organizations, individual debtors are also eligible for Chapter 11 relief.[445] Indeed, individuals who are ineligible for Chapter 7 because they cannot satisfy the means test, and who do not satisfy the Chapter 13 debt limits, must file in Chapter 11 to obtain any bankruptcy relief at all. However, a Chapter 11 discharge relieves individuals debtors only from their dischargeable debts.[446] Debts excluded from the scope of discharge by § 523 are not within the scope of a Chapter 11 discharge.[447] However, for a Chapter 11 plan to provide the debtor with effective relief, the debtor's plan will normally provide for the payment of nondischargeable debts. Otherwise the plan may not be feasible, as required by § 1129(a)(11), and cannot be confirmed.[448]

[B] Timing of Chapter 11 Discharge

Unlike under Chapters 12 and 13, a Chapter 11 discharge is normally granted as soon as the plan becomes effective. Indeed, it is the fact of confirmation itself that ordinarily discharges the debtor. As noted earlier, the only exception to this is in cases involving individual debtors who are not normally eligible for discharge until their plans are fully performed.

However, mere confirmation of a Chapter 11 plan does not provide an individual debtor with a discharge. Unlike other entities, individual debtors must wait to receive their discharge until "the court grants a discharge on completion of all payments under the plan."[449]

A discharge may be granted earlier if the payments made to unsecured creditors under the plan are the equivalent of what the creditors would have received in a Chapter 7 liquidation case and modification of the plan is not practicable.[450] This emulates the rules applicable in cases under Chapters 12 and 13 where the debtor finds herself unable to complete a confirmed plan after making payments that would at least provide her unsecured creditors with the amount they would have received if the debtor had simply liquidated.

---

[444] Bankruptcy Code § 1141(d)(4).

[445] Toibb v. Radloff, 501 U.S. 157 (1991).

[446] Bankruptcy Code § 1141(d)(2).

[447] *See supra* § 13.03 Nondischargeable Debts.

[448] *See infra* § 19.10[J] Feasibility of Plan.

[449] Bankruptcy Code § 1141(d)(5)(A).

[450] Bankruptcy Code § 1141(d)(5)(B).

[C] Scope of Chapter 11 Discharge

The scope of a Chapter 11 discharge is simple. The obligations under the Chapter 11 plan substitute for the debtor's pre-confirmation obligations. Insofar as corporations and other artificial entities are concerned, virtually all existing debt is discharged, and the sole remaining obligations are those undertaken in the plan.[451]

The situation of an individual Chapter 11 debtor is more complicated. She remains obligated on all the debts listed in § 523 as nondischargeable, the same as she would have been if she had obtained relief under Chapter 7. Thus, individual Chapter 11 debtors remain liable for family obligations, debts incurred through fraud, willful and malicious injuries, student loans, and other debts specified in § 523, even though their plans have been confirmed, and even though they have received a Chapter 11 discharge.

§ 13.07 CHAPTER 12 DISCHARGE

[A] Persons Eligible for Chapter 12 Discharge

The Chapter 12 discharge is available to anyone who may be a Chapter 12 debtor. Eligibility for Chapter 12 is limited to family farmers and family fishermen and thus can include some closely held family corporations and partnerships.[452] Otherwise, discharge is available to any eligible debtor whose Chapter 12 plan is confirmed and completed.

[B] Timing of Chapter 12 Discharge

Ordinarily, a Chapter 12 discharge is granted only upon completion of the plan of reorganization. The court is to grant the discharge "as soon as practicable" after the debtor makes the last plan payment (other than certain payments permitted on long-term debt).[453] An earlier hardship discharge may be requested under circumstances similar to those in which a hardship discharge may be granted in cases under Chapter 13.[454] A hardship discharge may be granted if the debtor's failure to complete the plan is excusable, if creditors have received at least the liquidation value of their claims, and if modification of the plan is not practicable. In this respect, Chapter 12 is similar to Chapter 13.

---

[451] Bankruptcy Code § 1141(d)(1)(A).

[452] *See supra* § 6.02[B][5] Eligibility for Relief in Chapter 12 — Family Farmers & Family Fishermen.

[453] Bankruptcy Code § 1228(a).

[454] Bankruptcy Code § 1228(b). *See supra* § 13.05[C][2] Chapter 13 Hardship Discharge.

[C]   Scope of Chapter 12 Discharge

A Chapter 12 discharge encompasses debts provided for under the plan, administrative expenses, and claims that were disallowed under § 502.[455] Unlike a Chapter 13 discharge, a Chapter 12 discharge does not encompass otherwise nondischargeable debts. The Chapter 12 debtor thus remains obligated, even after the discharge is granted, on the full list of § 523 debts.[456] In addition, the Chapter 12 debtor remains obligated on long-term debts that extend beyond the completion of the plan.[457]

§ 13.08   REVOCATION OF DISCHARGE

Under very limited circumstances, a discharge previously granted may be revoked. Revocation always involves serious misconduct by the debtor. In addition, revocation may only be requested within a relatively short time after the discharge was granted. Even when the debtor has committed a seriously wrongful act, the need for finality and closure militates for an early statute of repose. Because this need for finality is greater in a reorganization case than in a liquidation proceeding, the requirements for revoking confirmation under Chapters 11, 12 and 13 are even more restrictive than the requirements under Chapter 7.

[A]   Revocation of Chapter 7 Discharge

A Chapter 7 discharge may be revoked in five situations:

- the discharge was obtained by fraud;[458]

- the debtor failed to report its acquisition of estate property or failed to surrender the newly acquired property to the trustee;[459]

- the debtor refused to obey a lawful order of the court;[460] or

- the debtor failed to satisfactorily explain any misstatement that is discovered;[461] or

- the debtor failed to provide records in connection with a Justice Department audit of her case.[462]

Despite the various items on this list, the most common situation in which a discharge is revoked is where the debtor has obtained a discharge by fraudulently

---

[455] Bankruptcy Code § 1228(a) (2006).

[456] See supra § 13.03 Nondischargeable Debts.

[457] Bankruptcy Code § 1228(a)(1).

[458] Bankruptcy Code § 727(d)(1).

[459] Bankruptcy Code § 727(d)(2).

[460] Bankruptcy Code § 727(d)(3), (a)(6). Gargula v. Mora (In re Mora), 399 B.R. 330 (Bankr. E.D. Mo. 2008) (debtor failed to comply with court order to deliver tax refunds to trustee).

[461] Bankruptcy Code § 727(d)(4).

[462] Bankruptcy Code § 727(d)(4).

failing to fully disclose her assets.[463]

The court may not revoke the discharge without notice and an opportunity for a hearing.[464] Actions to revoke a Chapter 7 discharge are adversary proceedings conducted under Part VII of the Federal Rules of Bankruptcy Procedure.[465]

There are tight time limitations placed on invoking any of these grounds. Fraud may be raised only within one year after the discharge is granted.[466] Failure to report or surrender property and misconduct may only be raised within one year after the discharge is granted or within one year after the case is closed, whichever is later.[467] However, there is no time limit on the court's ability to revoke the debtor's discharge due to the debtor's failure to cooperate with an audit of the debtor's case conducted by the United States Department of Justice.[468]

[B]　Revocation of Chapter 11 Discharge

Under Chapter 11, confirmation is nearly always the point at which the debtor obtains a discharge. Because of this, revocation of the discharge is dealt with in conjunction with revocation of confirmation. Confirmation may be revoked if it was procured by fraud, but only if revocation is sought within 180 days after the order confirming the plan was entered.[469] If the confirmation is revoked, the court must, among other things, revoke the debtor's discharge.[470]

[C]　Revocation of Chapter 12 and 13 Discharge

Chapters 12 and 13 have identical revocation provisions. Unlike Chapter 11, Chapters 12 and 13 separate confirmation from discharge. Thus, revocation of an order of confirmation is unrelated to an order revoking the debtor's discharge. It is virtually impossible for a discharge to be granted during the time in which the confirmation could still be revoked.

Following completion of a plan, any party in interest may move for revocation of the discharge. The motion must be made within one year after the discharge was granted. The discharge may be revoked — if and only if — the discharge was obtained by fraud, and the moving party did not know of the fraud until after the

---

[463] *E.g.*, In re DePriest, 414 B.R. 518 (Bankr. W.D. Wis. 2009) (failure to disclose ownership of a Limited Liability Company).

[464] Bankruptcy Code § 727(d).

[465] Fed. R. Bankr. P. 7001(4).

[466] Bankruptcy Code § 727(e)(1).

[467] Bankruptcy Code § 727(e)(2).

[468] This appears to have been an oversight. The 2005 amendments added a mechanism that permits the United States Trustee's office to conduct audits of bankruptcy cases. 28 U.S.C. § 586(f) (2006). At the same time, Congress added § 727(d)(4), permitting the court to revoke a debtor's discharge if the debtor fails to provide a satisfactory explanation of any misstatement discovered in the course of such an audit or to provide information requested during such an audit. However, no corresponding amendment was made to § 727(e), which imposes a time limit for discharge revocations prompted by such an audit.

[469] Bankruptcy Code § 1144.

[470] Bankruptcy Code § 1144(2).

discharge was granted.[471] Prior to any revocation of the discharge, the court must provide notice and an opportunity for a hearing.[472]

§ 13.09 EFFECT OF DISCHARGE[473]

Discharge has a number of direct and indirect effects on the debtor and the debtor's obligations. A discharge voids any judgment based on the debtor's personal liability for a discharged debt.[474] It operates as an injunction against any action to collect, recover, or offset any discharged debt as a personal liability of the debtor.[475] Taken together, these two rules provide the debtor with considerable relief from her pre-petition debts: judgments against her are void and thus cannot be enforced,[476] and creditors are enjoined from "any action" to collect a discharged debt from the debtor. In addition, the Bankruptcy Code prohibits certain types of discrimination against debtors by creditors, governmental agencies, and employers.

[A] Discharge Injunction[477]

Discharge prevents creditors from attempting to collect discharged debts. The prohibition against any action to collect a discharged debt is broad. Section 524(a)(2) enjoins "the commencement or continuation of an action, the employment of process, or *an act*, to collect, recover or offset any [discharged] debt as a personal liability of the debtor."[478] This not only prevents creditors from suing debtors on discharged debts, it also prevents them from resuming the barrage of phone calls, dunning letters, or other efforts aimed at persuading the debtor to pay.[479]

This imposes upon creditors an obligation to maintain adequate procedures to prevent violation of § 524(a). Creditors and collection agencies who sell discharged debts may run afoul of the discharge stay if they fail to take steps to guard against the buyer's efforts to collect. Creditors who sell a discharged debt, without registering the discharge in their own records, violate § 524(a).[480]

---

[471] Bankruptcy Code §§ 1228(d), 1328(e).

[472] Bankruptcy Code §§ 1228(d), 1328(e).

[473] Susan N.K. Gummow & John M. Wunderlich, *Suing the Debtor: Examining Post-Discharge Suits Against the Debtor*, 83 Am. Bankr. L.J. 495 (2009).

[474] Bankruptcy Code § 524(a)(1).

[475] Bankruptcy Code § 524(a)(2).

[476] *See* Hamilton v. Herr (In re Hamilton), 540 F.3d 367 (6th Cir. 2008) (*Rooker-Feldman* doctrine does not prevent bankruptcy court from determining that state court judgment, entered in violation of discharge stay, was void).

[477] Susan N.K. Gummow & John M. Wunderlich, *Suing the Debtor: Examining Post-Discharge Suits Against the Debtor*, 83 Am. Bankr. L.J. 495 (2009).

[478] Bankruptcy Code § 524(a)(2) (emphasis supplied).

[479] *E.g.*, In re Latanowich, 207 B.R. 326 (Bankr. D. Mass. 1997) (Sears, Roebuck & Co.'s deliberate efforts to persuade debtor to enter into a reaffirmation agreement without complying with the requirements of § 524(c)); In re A.G. Wassem, 456 B.R. 566 (Bankr. M.D. Fl. 2009) (50 post-discharge phone calls made in effort to collect discharged debts).

[480] *E.g.*, In re Nassoko, 405 B.R. 515 (Bankr. S.D.N.Y. 2009); In re Lafferty, 229 B.R. 707 (Bankr. N.D.

Creditors' efforts to shame the debtor into paying, such as by posting signs publicizing the debtor's default or parking a car outside the debtor's place of business containing a sign publishing a "public service announcement" about the debtor's failure to pay also likely violate the stay.[481] Colleges and universities have occasionally violated the discharge stay by refusing to issue transcripts to students who discharged unpaid tuition bills.[482] Creditors who do nothing more than refuse to do business with the debtor violate the stay if the creditor expresses a willingness to resume business with the debtor upon repayment of the discharged debt.[483] Creditors whose claims against the debtor have been discharged can refuse to provide future service to the debtor, but they may not condition future service on repayment of the discharged debt or actively seek repayment through other means.

Despite these rules, § 524(j) now permits home mortgage lenders to act in the ordinary course to obtain monthly payments due from the debtor, rather than pursuing their in rem rights to foreclose the mortgage and have the property sold.[484] There is no similar provision expressly permitting creditors with a security interest in personal property, such as an automobiles or furniture, to send even routine reminders to the debtor, seeking resumption of payments, as an alternative to foreclosure.

In addition, special rules deal with the effect of the discharge on a debtor's community property.[485]

Although § 524 enjoins creditors from efforts to collect, it does not provide a private right of action for debtors who are injured by a creditor's violation of the injunction.[486] Nevertheless, the bankruptcy court can use its civil contempt power under § 105 to award damages to the debtor for harm she suffers as a result of a creditor's wilful violation of § 524.[487] However, courts have split over whether this extends to damages for emotional distress the debtor may suffer as a result of the creditor's actions.[488]

The discharge injunction does not prevent creditors from pursing claims that arose after the debtor's Chapter 7 case was filed or which are not dealt with by a

---

Ohio 1998). *But see* Finnie v. First Union Nat'l Bank, 275 B.R. 743 (E.D. Va. 2002). *See generally* Guy B. Moss, *The Risks of Purchasing and Collecting Consumer Debt*, 10 Am. Bankr. Inst. L. Rev. 643 (2002).

[481] *E.g.*, In re Crudup, 287 B.R. 358 (Bankr. E.D. N.C. 2002) (creditor's First Amendment rights not impaired by prohibition against signs posted in effort to collect); In re Andrus, 189 B.R. 413 (N.D. Ill. 1995).

[482] *E.g.*, In re Kuehn, 563 F.3d 289 (7th Cir. 2009) (Easterbrook, J.) (violation of discharge stay and of the automatic stay).

[483] Olson v. McFarland Clinic, P.C. (In re Olson), 38 B.R. 515 (Bankr. N.D. Iowa 1984).

[484] Bankruptcy Code § 524(j). This is consistent with rule that provides that creditors' liens on the debtor's property survive discharge.

[485] Bankruptcy Code § 524(a)(3), (b), (e).

[486] *See* Walls v. Wells Fargo Bank, 276 F.3d 502, 509 (9th Cir. 2002).

[487] *See* Walls v. Wells Fargo Bank, 276 F.3d 502, 509 (9th Cir. 2002); Bessette v. Avco Fin. Servs., Inc., 230 F.3d 439, 444-445 (1st Cir. 2000).

[488] *See* In re Feldmeier, 335 B.R. 807 (Bankr. D. Or. 2005); In re Wassem, 456 B.R. 566 Bankr. M.D. Fla. 2009).

reorganization plan. Those claims are outside the scope of the discharge and beyond the purview of the discharge stay.[489] Nor does it prevent creditors, who believe they were victims of the debtor's criminal activity, such as securities fraud or larceny, from reporting the debtor's conduct to the police or prosecutors,[490] so long as the creditor's action is not part of a bad faith effort to coerce payment through a threatened criminal action.[491]

[B]   Enforcement of Liens Permitted

The discharge stay applies only to actions aimed at collecting from the debtor personally. Unavoided liens on the debtor's property survive and can be enforced in an *in rem* action, such as one to foreclose a real estate mortgage or to obtain possession of personal property in order to have it sold, despite discharge of the debtor's *in personum* responsibility for the debt.[492]

Thus, if Julie and Richard default on their mortgage payments and discharge their debt in bankruptcy, the mortgagee, Empire Bank, is nevertheless permitted to foreclose on their home. Likewise, if New Motors Acceptance Corporation holds a security interest in their car, it is allowed to repossess or replevy the car after the case is closed.[493]

Creditors with real estate mortgages are now expressly permitted to communicate with the debtor in the ordinary course of business to obtain monthly or other "periodic payments" associated with the creditor's mortgage.[494] Before 2005, creditors with security interests in personal property were given some modest leeway in advising the debtor of its right to repossess the collateral if payments were not resumed. In *Garske v. Arcadia Financial, Ltd. (In re Garske)*, the court permitted a secured creditor's phone calls to the debtor advising the debtor of its right to repossess and requesting the debtor to pay in order to avoid repossession.[495] As the court explained: "because [the] Debtor must pay . . . to retain the Vehicle, contact between them is unavoidable."[496] Whether this leeway for creditors with security interests in personal property will survive the enactment of § 524(j), which is limited to creditors who retain "a security interest in real property that is the principal residence of the debtor" remains to be seen.[497] Even if decisions like *Garske* continue to be followed, creditors who barrage the debtor with requests and demands for repayment, that go beyond the type of contact necessary to facilitate the debtor's intent to retain the collateral, still run

---

[489]   Paul v. Iglehart (In re Paul), 534 F.3d 1303 (10th Cir. 2008).

[490]   Williams v. Meyer (In re Williams), 438 B.R. 679 (B.A.P. 10th Cir. 2010).

[491]   *E.g.*, In re McMullen, 189 B.R. 402, 411 (Bankr. E.D. Mich. 1995).

[492]   *See* Long v. Bullard, 117 U.S. 617 (1886).

[493]   *See supra* § 2.07 Foreclosure Procedures.

[494]   Bankruptcy Code § 524(j).

[495]   287 B.R. 537 (B.A.P. 9th Cir. 2002).

[496]   287 B.R at 544.

[497]   *See* In re Sosa, 443 B.R. 263 (Bankr. D.R.I. 2011).

afoul of § 524(a)(2).[498]

[C] Recovery from Co-Debtors

The discharge stay of § 524(a)(2) does not prohibit creditors from pursuing others who may be liable, such as guarantors and insurers.[499] Section 524(g) imposes a limited exception to this rule by prohibiting actions against insurers who otherwise might be liable for claims against the debtor arising from asbestos injuries.[500]

The co-debtor stays that apply in Chapters 12 and 13 expire upon conclusion of the case and thus do not prevent creditors from pursuing these third parties in the event that the entire debt is not repaid through the debtor's completed plan. In Chapter 11 cases, debtors frequently seek co-debtor stays, to protect corporate insiders, who are likely to be distracted from their jobs with the debtor, if they must defend litigation against themselves while the case is pending. But, these discretionary stays usually expire upon confirmation of the debtor's plan.

Thus, it is not unusual for the debtor to propose plan language seeks to discharge any such insider guarantors and contributors.[501] Whether these provisions should be permitted remains open to dispute.[502] Some circuits broadly prohibit releases of third parties.[503] Other circuits permit narrowly tailored releases that are necessary to achieve reorganization of the debtor.[504]

[D] Discrimination Against Debtors

The Bankruptcy Code also contains several limited prohibitions against certain types of discrimination against bankrupt debtors. These apply primarily to discriminatory treatment by governmental bodies and employers. Creditors, on the other hand, are usually free to discriminate against debtors, so long as they do not

---

[498] *E.g.*, Mooney v. Green Tree Serv., LLC (In re Mooney), 340 B.R. 351 (Bankr. E.D. Tex. 2006).

[499] *E.g.*, Green v. Welsh, 956 F.2d 30 (2d Cir. 1992); In re Castle, 289 B.R. 882 (Bankr. E.D. Tenn. 2003).

[500] Bankruptcy Code § 524(g).

[501] *See* Ralph Brubaker, *Bankruptcy Injunctions and Complex Litigation: A Critical Reappraisal of Non-Debtor Releases in Chapter 11 Reorganizations*, 1997 U. Ill. L. Rev. 959 (1997); Joshua M. Silverstein, *Hiding in Plain View: A Neglected Supreme Court Decision Resolves the Debate Over Non-Debtor Releases in Chapter 11 Reorganizations*, 23 Emory Bankr. Dev. J. 13, 69 (2006); Judith R. Starr, *Bankruptcy Court Jurisdiction to Release Insiders from Creditor Claims in Corporate Reorganizations*, 9 Bankr. Dev. J. 485, 487 (1993); Elizabeth Gamble, Note, *Nondebtor Releases in Chapter 11 Reorganizations: A Limited Power*, 38 Fordham Urb. L.J. 821 (2011).

[502] *Compare* Republic Supply Co. v. Shoaf, 815 F.2d 1046 (5th Cir. 1987) (treating such a provision as res judicata with respect to the guarantor's liability) *with* Gillman v. Continental Airlines (In re Continental Airlines), 203 F.3d 203 (3d Cir. 2000) (sustaining objections to provisions of the debtor's plan providing for discharge of guarantors), *and* Class Five Nev. Claimants v. Dow Corning Corp. (In re Dow Corning Corp.), 280 F.3d 648 (6th Cir. 2002) (permitting such provisions in unusual circumstances based on several complex factors).

[503] In re Lowenschuss, 67 F.3d 1394, 1401 (9th Cir. 1995); In re W. Real Estate Fund, Inc., 922 F.2d 592, 600 (10th Cir. 1990).

[504] *See* In re Berwick Black Cattle Co., 394 B.R. 448, 455-463 (Bankr. C.D. Ill. 2008).

discriminate in an effort to recover payment of a discharged debt.

[1] Governmental Discrimination

With a few narrow exceptions, governmental units are prohibited from discriminating against debtors with regard to licenses, permits, charters, franchises, or employment.[505] Thus, a debtor's drivers' license may not be suspended or revoked due to the debtor's failure to pay a dishcarged debt arising from an auto accident.[506] Business debtors who discharge their debts in reorganization may not have their business or other licenses revoked due to their discharge.[507]

The express language of § 525(a) prohibits such discrimination "solely because" of the debtor's discharge.[508] Any suggestion that discrimination is permitted if the government has some underlying motive associated with its refusal to grant or renew the debtor's license, was dispelled by the Supreme Court's decision in *Federal Communications Commission v. NextWave Personal Communications, Inc.*[509] In *NextWave*, the court explained that interpreting the "solely because" language to permit discrimination in order to implement whatever underlying motive the government had to discriminate against the debtor "would deprive § 525 of all force."[510] It ruled that "section 525 means nothing more or less than that the failure to pay a dischargeable debt must alone be the proximate cause of the cancellation — the act or event that triggers the agency's decision to cancel, whatever the agency's ultimate motive in pulling the trigger may be."[511] Discrimination is permitted only if there is some other reason, apart from discharge of the debt, that is the "proximate cause" of the government's action.[512]

One potential impact of the *NextWave* decision is that it may prevent state supreme courts from denying licenses to practice law to those whose only moral defect is the irresponsibility reflected by the decision to discharge their debts in bankruptcy. Unless there is some other aspect of the aspiring lawyer's background that reflects dishonesty, moral turpitude, or irresponsible behavior, denying a license to practice law to those who have invoked the Bankruptcy Code violates § 525(a).

The key question is whether the government is applying a test that is facially neutral — a test that applies equally to all. For example, a reasonably based rule that every person who wishes to obtain a business license must either have a minimum level of unencumbered assets or obtain a minimum level of insurance is normally permissible, even though this would disqualify a disproportionate number

---

[505] Bankruptcy Code § 525(a).

[506] *See* Perez v. Campbell, 402 U.S. 637 (1971).

[507] Fed. Commc'n. Comm'n v. NextWave Personal Commc'ns, Inc., 537 U.S. 293 (2003).

[508] Bankruptcy Code § 525(a).

[509] 537 U.S. 293 (2003).

[510] 537 U.S. at 301-02.

[511] 537 U.S. at 301-02.

[512] 537 U.S. at 301-02.

of former bankrupts. To put it in language familiar to civil rights attorneys, § 525(a) does not include a disparate impact test.

Most courts have been more flexible in their interpretation of the matters encompassed by the anti-discrimination prohibition. The language "license, permit, charter, franchise, or other similar grant" has been read to encompass a wide variety of government benefits. Obvious things, such as business licenses and drivers' licenses are covered; also certain entitlements, such as the right to remain in public housing and thus receive an indirect subsidy from the government, have been held to be protected.[513] On the other hand, if the government benefit involves an extension of credit, courts are likely to find that the government is not prohibited from discriminating, because that form of discrimination is not prohibited by § 525.

[2]   Employment Discrimination

Section 525(b) imposes a more limited prohibition on discrimination by private parties. Private employers may not terminate or otherwise discriminate against *current* employees solely because they obtain a discharge in bankruptcy or because their discharged debts remain unpaid.[514] However, private employers are permitted to discriminate against job applicants who have received a bankruptcy discharge.[515] Thus, although private employers may not discriminate against current employees, based on discharge of their debts, they can discriminate against prospective employees. This of course, is different from the approach of § 525(a), discussed above, which only applies to governmental employers.

Because the prohibition of § 525(b) only prevents discrimination "solely because" the debtor has received a discharge or been insolvent, employers are permitted to consider a bankrupt employee's financial circumstances among other factors used to fire or otherwise discriminate against current employees. Bankrupt employees who have suffered from such discrimination are likely to find it difficult to prove that this was the sole reason for their treatment.[516]

[3]   Credit Discrimination

Creditors are, of course, generally permitted to discriminate against debtors who have discharged their debts. This discrimination takes many forms, including denials of credit, increased interest charges, smaller debt limits, and more onerous default provisions.

The only exception to this general rule, permitting credit discrimination, is with respect to student loans. Both governmental units and private lenders are prohibited from denying a student loan to a previously bankrupt debtor.[517] The prohibition

---

[513] *E.g.*, In re Sudler, 71 B.R. 780 (Bankr. E.D. Pa. 1987).

[514] Bankruptcy Code § 525(b).

[515] Rea v. Fed'd Inv's, 627 F.3d 937 (3d Cir. 2010); Myers v. TooJay's Mgmt Corp., 640 F.3d 1278 (11th Cir. 2011); Burnett v. Stewart Title, Inc. (In re Burnett), 635 F.3d (5th Cir. 2011).

[516] *E.g.*, Banner v. ABF Freight Sys., Inc. (In re Banner), 422 B.R. 608 (Bankr. N.D. Tex. 2009).

[517] Bankruptcy Code § 525(c).

applies to the grant of a loan, a loan guarantee, or loan insurance.[518] This provision was apparently added in the belief that refusal of student loans to former bankrupts would, by restricting their access to further education, unduly increase the possibility of future financial trouble. Although the precise language does not seem to prohibit governmental entities or private lenders from charging higher interest rates to those who have discharged their debts in bankruptcy, most student loan programs carry a set rate of interest that does not vary from one borrower to the next.

---

[518] Bankruptcy Code § 525(c).

Chapter 14

GENERAL AVOIDING POWERS; LIMITATIONS ON AVOIDING POWERS

§ 14.01 AVOIDANCE OF TRANSFERS

In this and the next three chapters, we explore bankruptcy trustee's avoiding powers. The bankruptcy trustee — and a Chapter 11 debtor-in-possession — has authority to set aside various transactions that deplete the debtor's estate in ways that advantage one person at the expense of creditors generally. In some cases, the unfairness to creditors is obvious, such as a transfer of assets by an insolvent debtor for no consideration — a fraudulent conveyance. Debtors who are unable to pay their creditors are not permitted to give away their few remaining assets. In other circumstances, the rationale for permitting the trustee to avoid the transfer is less obvious. Some avoiding powers are available only in bankruptcy. Others are borrowed directly from state law. Most depend on state law to some extent, but a few rely exclusively on federal bankruptcy law.

This chapter discusses a number of general avoiding powers that, while important, do not require extensive discussion. Other avoiding powers are discussed in detail in the chapters that immediately follow. These include preferences,[1] fraudulent transfers,[2] and certain non-possessory, non-purchase money security interests.[3]

There are also limitations on the trustee's avoidance powers. Some of these limitations are specific to the power; others of broader application are discussed in this chapter.

In Chapter 7 cases, avoidance powers are exercised primarily by the trustee. In Chapter 11[4] and Chapter 12[5] cases, they are exercised by the debtor-in-possession, unless a trustee is appointed to take over administration of the case. There is some confusion about who exercises the avoidance rights in a Chapter 13 case, because the Chapter 13 debtor-in-possession is not explicitly given the broad powers that are provided to the debtor-in-possession in Chapters 11 and 12. Courts are divided over whether the Chapter 13 debtor-in-possession may avoid pre-petition transactions, though most have held that only the Chapter 13 trustee may exercise the

---

[1] *See* Chapter 15 — Preferences, *infra.*

[2] *See* Chapter 16 — Fraudulent Transfers, *infra.*

[3] *See* § 12.07 Avoiding Liens on Exempt Property, *supra.*

[4] Bankruptcy Code § 1107(a).

[5] Bankruptcy Code § 1203; *e.g.*, Hoeger v. Teigen (In re Teigen), 123 B.R. 887, 888 (Bankr. D. Mont. 1991).

avoidance powers.[6] The remainder of this chapter refers to the avoiding powers of the trustee with the understanding that in most situations a debtor-in-possession has the same right to invoke the avoiding power as the trustee.[7]

§ 14.02 STRONG-ARM POWER

Section 544(a), long known as the "strong-arm clause," is the trustee's most important avoiding power. Section 544(a) primarily affects transfers that were incomplete on the date the debtor's bankruptcy case began — the date the debtor's petition was filed. It gives the trustee the status of a hypothetical person whose rights as a lien creditor or bona fide purchaser of real estate whose interest becomes effective against third parties at the moment the bankruptcy petition was filed. This means that any transfer of the debtor's property that is not yet effective against such third parties can be avoided by the trustee. As explained in more detail below, this gives the trustee the power to avoid unperfected security interests in personal property and unrecorded or improperly recorded sales and mortgages of real estate. Because a Chapter 11 debtor-in-possession enjoys all of the same rights, powers, and duties of a trustee, the debtor-in-possession can avoid transfers, as the representative of the estate, even though the transfer would have been effective against the debtor under applicable state law.

[A] Trustee as Hypothetical Judicial Lien Creditor[8]

Section 544(a)(1) gives the trustee the status of a hypothetical judicial lien holder. More specifically, if gives the trustee the rights of a person who obtained, as of the commencement of the case, "a judicial lien on all property on which a creditor on a simple contract could have obtained such a judicial lien . . . ."[9] The trustee acquires this status whether or not there actually is such a creditor. Thus, § 544(a)(1) treats the trustee is a "hypothetical lien creditor." The trustee is sometimes said to "stand in the shoes" of a lien creditor.[10]

The single most significant impact of this rule is the effect it has on unperfected Article 9 security interests (including sales of accounts and chattel paper). An Article 9 security interest usually must be perfected to achieve priority over a judicial lien creditor.[11] Thus, an unperfected security interest is subject to the rights of the trustee.[12] As one court explained:

---

[6] *See, e.g.*, Wood v. Mize (In re Wood), 301 B.R. 558, 561-63 (Bankr. W.D. Mo. 2003) (collecting cases).

[7] *E.g.*, Gandy v. Gandy (In re Gandy), 299 F.3d 489, 497 (5th Cir. 2002).

[8] David Gray Carlson, *The Trustee's Strong Arm Power Under the Bankruptcy Code*, 43 S.C. L. Rev. 841, (1992); C. Scott Pryor, *How Revised Article 9 Will Turn the Trustee's Strong-Arm into a Weak Finger: A Potpourri of Cases*, 9 Am. Bankr. Inst. L. Rev. 229 (2001).

[9] Bankruptcy Code § 544(a)(1).

[10] *E.g.*, In re Halabi, 184 F.3d 1335, 1337 (11th Cir. 1999).

[11] U.C.C. § 9-317(a)(2) (2003); *see supra* § 2.02[B][1][d] Priority Rules Under U.C.C. Article 9.

[12] Most cases regarding the perfection or lack of perfection of an Article 9 security interest arise in the context of bankruptcy.

The Trustee stands in the shoes of a hypothetical lien creditor whose lien arose on the day the bankruptcy petition was filed. With this "strong-arm" power, she may avoid and recapture for the debtor's estate any junior claim. Thus, the security interest of a creditor who has not perfected is defeated by the Trustee's section 544 power and relegated to the status of an unsecured debt.[13]

On the other hand, if the security interest is perfected at the moment the debtor's bankruptcy was filed, it is unassailable under § 544(a),[14] though it may be vulnerable under one of the trustee's other avoidance powers.

Section 544(a) achieves this result indirectly. It does not expressly provide that the trustee can avoid unperfected security interests. Instead, it operates through the interplay between § 544(a)(1) and state law.[15] Section 544(a)(1) gives the trustee whatever priority rights a lien creditor would enjoy under state law. It treats the trustee as if it were a creditor who had obtained a judicial lien on all of the debtor's property at the precise moment the debtor's bankruptcy petition was filed.[16] Under state law (primarily U.C.C. Article 9), a creditor who acquired a judicial lien on the debtor's property would take priority over an unperfected security interest. Because of § 544(a), the trustee enjoys the same power.[17] As one court explained: "[a]lthough the rights of the trustee as a lien creditor are governed by federal law, our determination of whether [the creditor] possesses a perfected security interest which has priority over the trustee as a lien creditor is controlled by . . . state law."[18]

Section 544(a)'s reliance on state law means that the trustee's rights depend on whatever limits state law imposes on the rights of judicial lien creditors. If under state law, a secured creditor would prevail against a lien creditor, the secured creditor similarly prevails against the trustee's rights under § 544(a).

The most basic example of this is the effect of the relationship between § 544(a) and U.C.C. § 9-317. Section 9-317(b)(2) specifies that a "security interest . . . is subordinate to the rights of . . . a person that becomes a lien creditor before . . . the security interest . . . is perfected."[19] Section 544(a) gives the trustee the rights of a hypothetical lien creditor who acquired its lien at the moment the bankruptcy petition was filed. Thus, the trustee's power to avoid a security interest under

---

[13] Wind Power Sys. Inc. v. Cannon Fin. Group, Inc. (In re Wind Power Sys., Inc.), 841 F.2d 288, 292 (9th Cir. 1988).

[14] Aerocon Eng'g, Inc. v. Silicon Valley Bank (In re World Auxiliary Power Co.), 303 F.3d 1120 (9th Cir. 2002).

[15] *E.g.*, LMS Holding Co. v. Core-Mark Mid-Continent, 50 F.3d 1520 (10th Cir. 1995); *see* C. Scott Pryor, *How Revised Article 9 Will Turn the Trustee's Strong-arm Into a Weak Finger: A Potpourri of Cases*, 9 Am. Bankr. Inst. L. Rev. 229 (2001).

[16] It is as if the Bankruptcy Code were the trustee's "fairy godmother" who tapped the trustee on the head with her magic wand and said: "Congratulations — you are now a lien creditor with a judicial lien on all of the debtor's property."

[17] To continue the fairy godmother analogy, she might also tell the trustee: "Go out and avoid unperfected security interests, wherever you can find them."

[18] Pearson v. Salina Coffee House, Inc., 831 F.2d 1531, 1532-33 (10th Cir. 1987).

[19] U.C.C. § 9-317(b)(2) (2003).

§ 544(a) depends on whether the security interest was perfected at the moment the debtor's bankruptcy petition was filed, when the trustee acquired its rights as a lien creditor.

Assume, for example, that on January 1, Merchant's Bank loaned Franklin Manufacturing $100,000 and obtained and immediately perfected a security interest in Franklin's equipment. Later, on August 1, Franklin filed a bankruptcy petition. Section 544(a) treats the trustee as a lien creditor who acquired its lien on August 1. Because the bank's security interest was perfected back in January, before Franklin's bankruptcy petition was filed, the trustee may not use § 544(a) to set aside the bank's security interest.

If, on the other hand, Merchant's Bank failed to perfect its security interest in January and it remained unperfected on August 1 when Franklin filed its petition, the trustee could use its status as a lien creditor to avoid the bank's security interest.[20] If, in July, the bank realized that it was still unperfected and rushed to the state Secretary of State's office to file a financing statement and become perfected, its interest would be protected from attack under § 544(a). Unfortunately, a security interest that is perfected late would still be vulnerable to attack by the trustee under different grounds, as a voidable preference.[21]

Section 544(a) also permits the trustee to avoid security interests whose perfection lapsed before the debtor's bankruptcy petition. Thus, if Merchant's Bank perfected by filing on January 30, 2008, but failed to file a continuation statement by January 30, 2013, its perfection would have lapsed. If Franklin initiates a bankruptcy proceeding after January 31, 2013, before the bank has re-perfected, the bank's security interest will fall to the trustee's power under § 544(a).

Article 9's twenty-day grace period for purchase money security interests provides a wrinkle in the application of § 544(a) that illustrates how it is completely dependent on state law. Under Article 9, a creditor with a purchase money security interest can achieve priority over a judicial lien creditor who acquires its lien between the time the security interest attaches and the time it is perfected, if the purchase money lender perfects within twenty days of the time the debtor receives possession of the collateral.[22]

Thus, if Industrial Supply Co. sells goods to Titanic, Inc. on credit, and retains a security interest in the goods sold, Industrial Supply achieves priority over any subsequent judicial lien creditor if Industrial perfects its security interest within twenty days of when Titanic first received possession of the goods. Thus, if Industrial Supply delivered the goods to Titanic on July 10, and North Atlantic Bank obtained a judicial lien on them on June 17, but Industrial Supply perfected on June 28, Industrial Supply has priority. Likewise, if Titanic, Inc. filed a bankruptcy petition on June 17, and Industrial Supply perfected on June 28, the trustee's rights under § 544(a)(1) as a hypothetical lien creditor do not permit the

---

[20] *E.g.*, LMS Holding Co. v. Core-Mark Mid-Continent, 50 F.3d 1520 (10th Cir. 1995).

[21] *See* Chapter 15, *infra.*

[22] U.C.C. § 9-317(e) (2003). *See* Sovereign Bank v. Hepner (In re Roser), 613 F.3d 1240 (10th Cir. 2010).

trustee to avoid Industrial Supply's security interest.[23]

[B] Trustee as Creditor Whose Attempted Execution is Returned Unsatisfied

Section 544(a)(2) endows the trustee with the rights of a hypothetical creditor that extends credit to the debtor when the case is commenced and simultaneously has an attempted writ of execution against the debtor's property that is returned unsatisfied.[24] This aspect of the trustee's strong-arm power is relatively insignificant. It gives the trustee whatever rights would be accorded by state law to a creditor who had exhausted its legal remedies.[25]

One of the most important rights § 544(a)(2) gives to the trustee is to compel what is known as "marshaling of assets" for the benefit of the estate.[26] The equitable doctrine of marshaling applies where a debtor has two creditors, with senior and junior security interests, but with the senior lender having a lien on two parcels of collateral and the junior lender having a lien on only one parcel. Assume, for example, that Peninsula Bank has a senior mortgage on two parcels of land: Redacre and Greenacre, securing a $3 million debt, and Gosnold Bank has a junior mortgage on Greenacre alone, securing a $2 million debt. Further assume that Redacre and Greenacre are worth $3 million each. Without marshaling, Peninsula Bank might foreclose first upon Greenacre, exhausting its value and leaving Gosnold Bank completely unsecured. Gosnold Bank could use marshaling to compel Peninsula Bank to foreclose upon Redacre first. This would result in full payment to Peninsula and leave Greenacre available to foreclosure by Gosnold.

Some state laws give judgment creditors whose efforts to execute against the debtor's property through the customary legal mechanism, a writ of execution, are unsuccessful, the right to compel other creditors to marshal assets in this fashion. By anointing the trustee as such a judgment creditor, § 544(a)(2) gives the trustee a right similar to that of Gosnold to force Peninsula to marshal the assets it holds as collateral.[27]

---

[23] Section 362(b)(3) provides an express exception to the automatic stay to cover this situation, and § 546(b) makes it clear that the trustee's rights are subject to the purchase money secured creditor's rights under U.C.C. § 9-317(e). Sovereign Bank v. Hepner (In re Roser), 613 F.3d 1240, 1248 (10th Cir. 2010). *See* § 8.03[A][2] Perfection of Certain Pre-Petition Security Interests, *supra*.

[24] Bankruptcy Code § 544(a)(2).

[25] Whenever a "writ" is involved, the remedy is "legal" rather than "equitable."

[26] *See, e.g.*, Comm. of Unsecured Creditors v. Lozinski (In re High Strength Steel, Inc.), 269 B.R. 560 (Bankr. D. Del. 2001).

[27] *E.g.*, Comm. of Unsecured Creditors v. Lozinski (In re High Strength Steel, Inc.), 269 B.R. 560 (Bankr. D. Del. 2001) (Pennsylvania marshaling rules); In re Wilmot Mining Co., 167 B.R. 806, 811 (Bankr. W.D. Pa. 1994) (Ohio marshaling rules).

[C]   Trustee as Bona Fide Purchaser of Real Estate

Section 544(a)(3) also gives the trustee the rights of a hypothetical bona fide purchaser of real estate (other than fixtures), who acquires its rights at the moment the debtor's bankruptcy petition is filed.[28] Its most significant impact is with respect to unrecorded mortgages, leases, and deeds. If under applicable state law, a bona fide purchaser would prevail over these interests, then the trustee similarly prevails. However, if a hypothetical bona fide purchaser, who acquired its interest at the time the debtor's bankruptcy petition, would take subject to the mortgage, lease, or deed, the trustee is subordinate to that interest[29] — or, at least does not achieve priority under § 544(a)(3). The trustee's rights, although derived from § 544 of the Bankruptcy Code, depend entirely on the rights of a bona fide purchaser under state law.[30]

As with the trustee's power as a hypothetical lien creditor, § 544(a)(3) does not depend on whether there actually is a bona fide purchaser of the debtor's real estate or whether anyone has been injured by the failure to record the mortgage, lease, or deed. For example, suppose Dora executed a deed transferring Blackacre to Betty, on April 1, 2013. The deed was never recorded, and under state law, bona fide purchasers without notice take free of rights created by unrecorded deeds. If Dora files a bankruptcy petition on April 10, 2013, the trustee, as a hypothetical bona fide purchaser, can avoid the transfer to Betty. This pulls Blackacre back into the estate, with its value available for distribution to all of Dora's Creditors. Betty would have an unsecured claim against the estate, but would lose Blackacre. But, if Betty recorded her deed on April 9, it would be enforceable against a bona fide purchaser who acquired an interest on April 10th, and thus Betty's rights would prevail. The same would be true if Betty's interest was a mortgage, or some other recorded interest, such as a claim to the property that was protected pursuant to a "lis pendens."[31]

Likewise, the trustee's power does not depend on any actual knowledge that the trustee may have of the other party's mortgage or ownership interest. As one court put it: "we are talking about a metaphysical and not a real person."[32] Thus, any knowledge obtained by the trustee in another capacity, or due to information accompanying the debtor's bankruptcy petition, is not enough to give the trustee, acting in her capacity as a hypothetical or "metaphysical" lien creditor, knowledge sufficient to prevent avoidance of an unrecorded mortgage or deed.

State law limits the ability of bona fide purchasers to avoid unrecorded deeds. If the bona fide purchaser has or should have notice of the buyer's rights, the bona fide purchaser usually takes subject to those rights. For example, it is generally true that if the buyer is in possession of the property, a bona fide purchaser cannot

---

[28]   Bankruptcy Code § 544(a)(3).

[29]   *E.g.*, Flener v. Monticello Banking Co. (In re Estes), 429 B.R. 872 (Bankr. W.D. Ky. 2010).

[30]   *E.g.*, Flener v. Monticello Banking Co. (In re Estes), 429 B.R. 872 (Bankr. W.D. Ky. 2010).

[31]   *E.g.*, In re Seymour, 442 B.R. 652 (Bankr. S.D. Ohio 2011).

[32]   Chase Manhattan Bank, USA, N.A. v. Taxel (In re Deuel), 594 F.3d 1073, 1077 (9th Cir. 2010).

avoid the purchase even though the buyer failed to record her deed.[33] In the example above, if Betty had been in possession of Blackacre, her rights would probably have been superior to those of an actual bona fide purchaser, even though her deed was unrecorded.[34]

However, this type of limitation does not necessarily affect the rights of the trustee under § 544(a)(3). The bankruptcy question is not whether all bona fide purchasers take free of the purchaser's interest, but whether *any* bona fide purchaser takes free.[35] Thus, if under governing state law there is any type of bona fide purchaser who takes free of an unrecorded interest, the unrecorded interest is avoidable by the trustee. This is clear from the statutory language of § 544(a)(3): "The trustee shall have, as of the commencement of the case, *and without regard to any knowledge of the trustee or of any creditor* the rights and powers of . . . (3) a bona fide purchaser of real property."

If Betty's possession protected her interest against all bona fide purchasers, regardless of whether they had knowledge or notice of her occupancy of the land, then her interest is not vulnerable to avoidance by the trustee under § 544(a)(3).[36] However, if Betty's possession protected her interest only against those bona fide purchasers who knew or should have known that she was in possession, then her interest is avoidable by the trustee. All depends on how state law treats possession.

The biggest impact of § 544(a)(3) is with respect to unrecorded or improperly executed mortgages. It can have a devastating effect. For example, many mortgages in Ohio have been avoided due to creditors' failure to have the mortgage documents properly "acknowledged" by two witnesses before a notary public, as required by state law. Under Ohio law, this defect made the recorded mortgages ineffective against a bona fide purchaser for value and thus avoidable by the bankruptcy trustee.[37] In one Ohio case, a mortgage was avoided under the same provision because the acknowledgment page contained only the debtor's initials and not, as the statute required, the debtor's full name in print, type, or signature form.[38] Similarly, a Kansas mortgage was avoided under § 544(a) because the lender failed to pay the mortgage registration fee, when it recorded its mortgage in the county real estate records.[39] The court explained: "While the result may seem draconian, perfection requires strict adherence to the statutes."[40] Likewise, a secured creditor's deed of trust was ineffective in Idaho because it merely provided a street address of the encumbered property and not the more elaborate "legal description" required by Idaho real estate law.[41]

---

[33] *E.g.*, HSBC Bank USA v. Perkins, 451 B.R. 555 (N.D. Ala. 2011).

[34] *See* Richard R. Powell & Michael Allan Wolf, Powell on Real Property § 82.01 (2007).

[35] *See* In re Hojnoski, 335 B.R. 282 (Bankr. W.D.N.Y. 2006).

[36] Thacker v. United Cos. Lending Corp., 256 B.R. 724, 729 (W.D. Ky. 2000); HSBC Bank USA v. Perkins, 451 B.R. 555, 561-62 (N.D. Ala. 2011).

[37] Rhiel v. The Huntington (In re Phalen), 445 B.R. 830 (Bankr. S.D. Ohio 2011).

[38] Daneman v. Nat'l City Mortgage Co. (In re Cornelius), 408 B.R. 704 (Bankr. S.D. Ohio 2009).

[39] In re Coffelt, 395 B.R. 133 (Bankr. D. Kan. 2008).

[40] *Id.* at 144.

[41] In re McMurdie, 448 B.R. 826 (Bankr. D. Idaho 2010) (deed of trust unenforceable by creditor

On the other hand, a more generous Kansas decision prevented the trustee from avoiding a Chapter 13 debtor's mortgage that misstated the debtor's lot number, because a reasonably prudent buyer, who would have found the debtor's name in the grantor-grantee index, would have conducted a further reasonably inquiry to determine whether the mortgage covered the property involved despite the discrepancy. Such a further inquiry would have revealed the error and alerted a subsequent bona fide purchaser to the creditor's mortgage.[42] Thus, the effect of a mistake depends on the impact it would have on a subsequent bona fide purchaser under the law of the state in question. Whether a particular mistake exposes the mortgage to avoidance might vary from one state to the next, depending on the type of recording statute the state has, and the standards under that statute for what would give notice to a reasonably prudent searcher.

Somewhat surprisingly, § 544(a)(3) permits a Chapter 11 debtor-in-possession to avoid mortgages on the debtor's own property, even though debtor granted the mortgage itself.[43] This is true even though the debtor-in-possession obviously has notice that the mortgage exists. This is because the debtor-in-possession's right to invoke § 544(a)(3) is the same as the right of a trustee, and because a trustee would be able to avoid an unrecorded mortgage if *any* bona fide purchaser could avoid it. Thus, if Titanic Corporation grants a mortgage on its land to Pacific Bank and Pacific Bank fails to record it by the time Titanic files its Chapter 11 petition, Titanic, acting as debtor-in-possession, can avoid Pacific Bank's mortgage.

This ability to set aside unrecorded mortgages, together with the ability to set aside unperfected security interests under § 544(a)(1) provides some debtors with a powerful inducement to file a Chapter 11 petition. These debtors can avoid unrecorded or defectively recorded liens and thereby acquire equity in their property that may not have been available outside of bankruptcy court.

§ 14.03 POWER TO USE RIGHTS OF ACTUAL UNSECURED CREDITORS

Section 544(b) gives the trustee the power to avoid transactions that are avoidable by actual general unsecured creditors under non-bankruptcy law.[44] Unlike § 544(a), § 544(b) does not create a set of hypothetical rights. Rather, it merely permits the trustee to enforce rights that the actual unsecured creditors of the debtor already have.[45] Thus, for the trustee to take advantage of § 544(b), she must find an actual unsecured creditor who has standing to avoid the transaction in question. In effect, § 544(b) subrogates the trustee to any actual creditors who might have avoided the transfer if the bankruptcy had not occurred. However, the

---

under § 558, for failure to satisfy the Idaho statute of frauds).

[42] Hamilton v. Wash. Mutual Bank (In re Colon), 563 F.3d 1171 (10th Cir. 2009).

[43] Cox v. Griffin (In re Griffin), 319 B.R. 609, 612 (B.A.P. 8th Cir. 2005), *affirmed* 178 Fed. App'x 595 (8th Cir. 2006).

[44] Bankruptcy Code § 544(b).

[45] Specifically, it gives the trustee the rights of those creditors who have claims that are allowed under § 502 or that are disallowed only because of § 502(e) (disallows claims for reimbursement or contribution). Bankruptcy Code § 544(b).

trustee's claim under 544(b) is not limited by the size of the debt owed to the creditor whose rights she asserts.[46] The transfer can be avoided entirely, with the proceeds distributed to all creditors — even those who would not have enjoyed the benefits of avoiding the transfer if no bankruptcy case had been filed.[47]

Thus, while the avoidance power is derivative of the power held by a real creditor, it is exercised for the benefit of all the creditors. The effect can be dramatic. Consider, for example, a $30,000 transfer that could have been avoided, under applicable state law, only by a single creditor who was owed $100. Outside bankruptcy, this one creditor could have recovered the $100 from the person who received the $30,000. The trustee's recovery is not so limited. Section 544(b) permits the trustee to recover the entire $30,000. This result, derived from the classic case *Moore v. Bay*,[48] is controversial,[49] but legislative efforts to supercede the decision have failed repeatedly.[50]

Section 544(b)'s biggest impact is with respect to fraudulent conveyances. Although § 548 gives the trustee her own fraudulent transfer avoiding power, § 544(b) gives the trustee whatever additional fraudulent transfer avoiding powers that creditors generally have under state law. Because the statute of limitations under most state fraudulent conveyance statutes is three years, § 544(b) effectively expands the reach-back period of the trustee in connection with pre-petition fraudulent conveyances.

Section 544(b) is not limited to fraudulent transfers. It can be used to exploit any state or federal statute or doctrine that permits an unsecured creditor to attack a pre-bankruptcy transfer of the debtor's property. It has been used to avoid unrecorded mortgages, intercorporate guarantees,[51] illegal commissions,[52] and before the widespread repeal of U.C.C. Article 6, bulk transfers.[53]

§ 14.04   AVOIDANCE OF STATUTORY LIENS[54]

Statutory liens are liens created by statute.[55] They are usually enforceable in bankruptcy and give the lien holder a secured claim. However, some exceptions exist. Depending on the circumstances, § 545 sometimes permits the trustee to

---

[46] *E.g.*, Stalnaker v. DLC, Ltd. (In re DLC, Ltd.), 295 B.R. 593, 606 (B.A.P. 8th Cir. 2003).

[47] *See* Coleman v. Comm'y Trust Bank (In re Coleman), 426 F.3d 719, 726-27 (4th Cir. 2005).

[48] *See* Moore v. Bay (In re Estate of Sassard & Kimball), 284 U.S. 4 (1931).

[49] Douglas J. Whaley, *The Dangerous Doctrine of* Moore v. Bay, 82 Tex. L. Rev. 73 (2003).

[50] Douglas J. Whaley, *The Dangerous Doctrine of* Moore v. Bay, 82 Tex. L. Rev. 73 (2003).

[51] Scott F. Norberg, Comment, *Avoidability of Intercorporate Guarantees under §§ 548(a)(2) and 544(b) of the Bankruptcy Code*, 64 N.C. L. Rev. 1099 (1986).

[52] *E.g.*, Terlecky v. Abels, 260 B.R 446 (S.D. Ohio 2001).

[53] *E.g.*, In re Villa Roel, Inc., 57 B.R. 835 (Bankr. D. Colo. 1985). Article 6 required notice to be given to the unsecured creditors whenever substantially all of assets of an "inventoried" business were sold. Creditors who were not notified could set aside the sale. *See* Steven L. Harris, *Article 6: The Process and the Product — An Introduction*, 41 Ala. L. Rev. 549 (1990); Fred H. Miller, *The Scope of Uniform Commercial Code Article 6: A Tale of Two Proposals*, 41 Ala. L. Rev. 587 (1990); Benjamin Weintraub & Harris Levin, *Bulk Sales Law and Adequate Protection of Creditors*, 65 Harv. L. Rev. 418 (1952).

[54] Thomas H. Jackson, *Statutory Liens and Constructive Trusts in Bankruptcy: Undoing the*

avoid "the fixing of a statutory lien" on the debtor's property.[56]

A statutory lien is a lien that arises "solely by force of a statute on specified circumstances or conditions."[57] It includes liens "of distress for rent," whether or not that lien arises from a statute. But consensual liens, like security interests and mortgages, and judicial liens, such as those obtained through legal or equitable proceedings, are excluded.[58]

Avoidable statutory liens fall into three groups:

- those that first become effective based on the debtor's financial condition;

- those that are not perfected or enforceable when the debtor's bankruptcy case commences; and

- those that are for rent.

The Code properly treats state created statutory liens that do not become effective unless the debtor faces adverse financial circumstances as nothing more than legislative efforts to circumvent the bankruptcy priority scheme. If these statutory liens were permitted to stand, state legislatures would be able to give secured status to favored creditors who otherwise would be limited to unsecured status.[59] Thus, the trustee can avoid a statutory lien that "first becomes effective against the debtor": (1) when a bankruptcy or other insolvency proceeding is commenced,[60] when a custodian is appointed to take possession of the debtor's property,[61] when the debtor becomes insolvent or fails to maintain some other financial condition,[62] or when the debtor's property is levied upon by some other creditor.[63] Thus, if a state medical association were to persuade its state legislature to give health care providers a statutory lien their patient's homes, in the event that the debtor fails to pay for medical treatment, the lien would be avoidable as a lien that "first becomes effective against the debtor . . . when the debtor's financial condition fails to meet a specific standard."[64]

The second group of avoided statutory liens are those that are not "perfected or enforceable" when the debtor's case is commenced against a hypothetical bona fide

---

Confusion, 61 Am. Bankr. L.J. 287 (1987); John McCoid II, *Statutory Liens in Bankruptcy*, 68 Am. Bankr. L.J. 269 (1994); Gene S. Schneyer, *Statutory Liens Under the New Bankruptcy Code — Some Problems Remain*, 55 Am. Bankr. L.J. 1 (1981).

[55] *See supra* § 2.05 Statutory, Common Law, and Equitable Liens.

[56] Bankruptcy Code § 545.

[57] Bankruptcy Code § 101(53).

[58] *Id. See* In re A & R Wholesale Distrib., Inc., 232 B.R. 616, 618 (Bankr. D.N.J. 1999).

[59] *Cf.*, John A. E. Pottow, *Greed and Pride in International Bankruptcy: The Problems of and Proposed Solutions to "Local Interests,"* 104 Mich. L. Rev. 1899 (2006).

[60] Bankruptcy Code § 545(1)(A), (B).

[61] Bankruptcy Code § 545(1)(C).

[62] Bankruptcy Code § 545(1)(D), (E).

[63] Bankruptcy Code § 545(1)(F).

[64] Bankruptcy Code § 545(1)(E).

purchaser that purchases the property subject to the lien at that time.[65] This overlaps to a large extent with § 544(a)'s strong-arm clause. As is true with § 544(a), there is no requirement that there be an actual bona fide purchaser of the encumbered property. Rather, the trustee is treated as if she were a bona fide purchaser with respect to any statutory liens on the debtor's property.

The third group of avoided liens is for rent and distress for rent.[66] Most states provide landlords with a lien on their tenants' property as security for rent. These liens need not be statutory to be vulnerable to avoidance. Because these liens would disrupt the priority rules of the Bankruptcy Code, they are avoidable by the trustee. However, consensual landlords liens, such as a security interest granted by the terms of the lease agreement between the parties, are not avoidable under § 545.

§ 14.05 POST-PETITION TRANSFERS OF ESTATE PROPERTY[67]

As explained elsewhere, when a debtor files a bankruptcy petition, all of her property is instantaneously transferred to her bankruptcy estate.[68] Nevertheless, the debtor still has possession of most if not all of her property and might transfer it without proper authority.

[A] Unauthorized Transactions[69]

The trustee may avoid transfers of property of the estate that occur after the commencement of the case, if the transfer is neither authorized by the Bankruptcy Code nor by the court.[70] For example, if after filing her petition the debtor uses funds in her bank account (estate property) to pay some of her creditors, the court can compel the creditors who received the payments to return the funds. Such payments are not authorized by the code and would be unlikely to be authorized by the court.

Limited protection against avoidance is provided for post-petition real estate transfers. A transferee of real estate may keep the property if: (1) she is a good faith purchaser; (2) she had no knowledge that the debtor's bankruptcy case had commenced; (3) she paid a fair equivalent value for the property;[71] and (4) her

---

[65] Bankruptcy Code § 545(2).

[66] Bankruptcy Code § 545(3), (4).

[67] David Gray Carlson, *Bankruptcy's Acephalous Moment: Postpetition Transfers under the Bankruptcy Code*, 21 Bankr. Dev. J. 113 (2004); Darrell W. Dunham, *Postpetition Transfers in Bankruptcy*, 39 U. Miami L. Rev. 1 (1984).

[68] Bankruptcy Code § 541(a)(1); *see* § 7.02 Property Included in the Estate, *supra.*

[69] William J. Rochelle, III & Gwen L. Feder, *Unauthorized Sales of a Debtor's Property: The Rights of a Purchaser Under § 549 of the Bankruptcy Code*, 57 Am. Bankr. L.J. 23 (1983).

[70] Bankruptcy Code § 549(a)(1), (2)(B).

[71] *Compare* T.F. Stone Co. v. Harper, 72 F.3d 466 (5th Cir. 1995) (value received in regularly conducted, non-collusive post-petition foreclosure sale deemed to have been for "present fair equivalent value") *with* Miller v. NLVK, LLC (In re Miller), 545 F.3d 899 (8th Cir. 2006) (regularly conducted foreclosure sale not dispositive regarding whether innocent buyer paid present fair equivalent value).

interest was recorded before any recorded notice of the bankruptcy case.[72] If the transferee meets all of the requirements except for paying a fair equivalent value for the property, she is given a lien on the property for whatever value she paid.[73] Thus, if Doug files a bankruptcy petition, but then sells his house to Vicky for $150,000, only 75% of its fair market value, Vicky will retain a lien for the $150,000 she paid. But, if she bought it in bad faith, or knew about the bankruptcy case, she will not enjoy this protection.

There is a limited period during which such post-petition transfers may be avoided. An action or proceeding must be commenced before the earlier of two years after the date of the transfer, or the time the case is closed or dismissed.[74]

[B] Involuntary Gap Transfers

In an involuntary case, there can be a gap between the filing of the petition and the court's determination as to whether an order for relief should be entered.[75] The debtor's property might be transferred during this period. The somewhat more favorable treatment of these transfers, is discussed elsewhere.[76]

§ 14.06 PRESERVATION OF AVOIDED TRANSFERS FOR THE BENEFIT OF THE ESTATE[77]

Section 551 provides that any transfer that is avoided under §§ 522 (Exempt Property), 544 (Strong-arm Clause), 545 (Statutory Liens), 547 (Preferences) 548 (Fraudulent Transfers), 549 (Post-Petition Transfers), or 724(a) (Liens Securing Noncompensatory Damages), and any lien that is void under § 506(d) (Underse-cured Creditors), can be preserved for the benefit of the estate.[78] This preservation permits the trustee to take advantage of whatever priority an avoided transfer might have against other transferees of the same property.

The most common circumstance in which preservation of an avoided transfer is beneficial to the estate is when the property involved is subject to a junior lien that would otherwise move up in priority to take the place of the avoided senior lien.[79] Assume, for example, that Franklin Manufacturing's land is encumbered by two

---

[72] Bankruptcy Code § 549(c).

[73] Bankruptcy Code § 549(c). For a somewhat more detailed discussion of this provision in context of the protection of those transferees during the "involuntary gap" period between the filing of an involuntary petition and the entry of an order for relief see § 6.03[H][2] Transfers of Estate Property During the Involuntary Gap, *supra.*

[74] Bankruptcy Code § 549(d).

[75] Bankruptcy Code § 303; *see* § 6.03[E] Grounds for Entering "An Order for Relief," *supra.*

[76] *See* § 6.03[H][3] Transfers of Estate Property During the Involuntary Gap, *supra.*

[77] John C. Chobot, *Preserving Liens Avoided in Bankruptcy — Limitations and Applications*, 62 Am. Bankr. L.J. 149 (1988); John C. McCoid, II, *Preservation of Avoided Transfers and Liens*, 77 Va. L. Rev. 1091 (1991).

[78] Bankruptcy Code § 551.

[79] According to the legislative history, the purpose of § 551 is to prevent "junior lienors from improving their position at the expense of the estate when a senior lien is avoided." H.R. Rep. 95-595, 376

liens: a senior mortgage for $4.5 million held by First National Bank and a junior judgment lien that secures a $6 million judgment in favor of Industrial Supply Co., one of Franklin's suppliers. Franklin's land and building are now worth only $5 million. Assume further that First National's senior mortgage was recorded only within the last ninety days before bankruptcy, but that First National's mortgage is senior to Security Bank's mortgage under the applicable state recording statute because Industrial Supply had prior notice of the earlier First National Bank mortgage.

Because of its delay in recording, First National's mortgage is avoidable, under § 547(b), as a preference. Without § 551, avoidance of First National's mortgage moves Industrial Supply's judgment lien into the senior position. Because the land is worth less than the amount of Industrial Supply's lien, avoiding First National's mortgage brings no additional value into the estate to be distributed to creditors. Section 551 prevents this from happening. It preserves First National's mortgage "for the benefit of the estate" and keeps Industrial Supply in the junior position it would have held had the bankruptcy not been filed. In effect, the bankruptcy trustee takes over First National's senior position. When the land and building are sold for $5 million, the trustee receives the first $4.5 million and Industrial Supply receives only $500,000.

Section § 551 effectively subrogates the trustee to the rights of the person whose rights she avoids. As is true with other subrogation rights, it puts the trustee in exactly the same position as the holder of the avoided transfer or the void lien, neither better nor worse. Section 551 represents a decision by Congress that the benefit of the avoidance should go to the unsecured creditors, and not to the holder of the junior interest in the property involved.

§ 14.07   RECOVERY OF AVOIDED TRANSFERS

The trustee's avoidance powers are not self-executing. If property has been transferred, and that transfer is avoidable, there has to be a mechanism for getting the property back. Even a court judgment ruling that a transfer is avoidable requires further action to recover the property involved, unless the transferee surrenders it. Section 550 contains rules that govern the actual recovery of avoidable transfers. If a transfer is avoided under §§ 544 (Strong-arm Clause), 545 (Statutory Liens), 547 (Preferences), 548 (Fraudulent Transfers), 549 (Post-Petition Transfers), 553(b) (Set-Off Preferences), or 724(a) (Liens Securing Noncompensatory Damages), the trustee may recover the property transferred, or if the court so orders, the value of the property.[80]

Section 550 comes into play only if there has been a transfer of ownership. Avoidance of a lien does not usually require any action beyond entry of a declaratory judgment. In most cases, the previously encumbered property is in the custody of the trustee or the debtor-in-possession and there is no way for the creditor to exercise any power over the property. However, if tangible property has been

---

(1977), *reprinted in* 1978 U.S.C.C.A.N. 5963, 6332; S. Rep. No. 95-989, 91 (1978), *reprinted in* 1978 U.S.C.C.A.N. 5787, 5877.

[80] Bankruptcy Code § 550(a).

physically transferred, or if money has been credited to the transferee's account, then the property must be physically recaptured or the transfer reversed on the books of the banks involved.

[A] Recovery of the Property or Its Value

The ability of the trustee to recover either the property transferred or its value is particularly significant when the avoidable transfer was something other than a cash payment. Although court approval is required to obtain the value of the property (money), rather than the property itself, courts routinely grant such permission. Particularly in a liquidation case, the trustee often prefers money rather than the property itself, which the trustee would then have to turn around and sell. Moreover, the property may have been damaged or destroyed after the transfer; or it may have simply depreciated in value over time. It is well established that the value the trustee can recover is the value it had when it was transferred, not the value at the time of recovery.[81] If the property has increased in value since its transfer, some courts permit recovery of the higher value and give the transferee a lien on the property for the amount of any expenses the transferee incurred in making the improvements.[82] This is consistent with the plain language § 550(a), which permits the trustee to recover the value of the property or the property itself.

[B] Recovery from Transferees

The trustee may recover the transferred property, or its value, from the "initial transferee," "the entity for whose benefit the transfer was made," or "any immediate or mediate transferee of the initial transferee."[83] However, the trustee may not obtain multiple recoveries from different persons; she is limited to a single recovery from one of these persons.

This means that the trustee can pursue a recovery not only from the person who received the transfer directly from the debtor, but also from anyone who was the beneficiary of the transfer and any subsequent transferee. For example, suppose that shortly before the bankruptcy Vicki fraudulently transferred her car to her husband, Doug. Doug then transferred the car to his cousin, Sam. In Vicki's bankruptcy case, the trustee can recover the value of the car from Doug (the trustee cannot recover the car itself *from Doug* because he no longer has it), or recover either the car or its value from Sam. Of course, the trustee is entitled to only one recovery; if the trustee recovers the value of the car from Doug, the trustee cannot also recover from Sam.[84] But, the trustee may recover part of the value from each of them, so long as she does not recover more than the value of the vehicle.

---

[81] *E.g.*, Drewes v. FM Da-Sota Elevator Co. (In re Da-Sota Elevator Co.), 939 F.2d 654 (8th Cir. 1991).

[82] *E.g.*, Feltman v. Warmus (In re Am. Way Serv. Corp.), 229 B.R. 496, 531 (Bankr. S.D. Fla. 1999).

[83] Bankruptcy Code § 550(a)(1), (2).

[84] Bankruptcy Code § 550(d) provides: "The trustee is entitled to only a single satisfaction under sub-section (a) of this section."

However, the trustee may not recover the amount of the transfer from someone who served as a mere conduit of the funds to someone else. Thus, if Sue makes a preferential payment of a debt to her brother, Scott, by depositing funds in Scott's account at Wells Fargo Bank, Wells Fargo is not the immediate transferee; it is a mere conduit of the funds for Scott. The transfer cannot be recovered from the bank.[85] On the other hand, when a preferential payment is made to a bank, which is serving as the trustee of a securitized investment pool, the bank, who is the owner of the investment pool's funds, is not a mere conduit of the funds — it is the legal owner of the pool's assets, and is a proper target of the trustee's preference recovery action.[86]

Although the transfer may be recovered from subsequent transferees, the code carefully distinguishes between the "initial transferee" and any "immediate or mediate transfer of [the] initial transferee."[87] These subsequent transferees receive greater protection than initial transferees, as more fully described below.[88]

§ 14.08   GENERAL LIMITATIONS ON AVOIDING POWERS

There are a number of limitations on the avoiding powers of the trustee. Some of these are discussed in the context of the specific avoiding power — for example, the exceptions to the preference avoidance rules under § 547. Others are of such narrow applicability that they are beyond the scope of this book.[89]

[A]   Statute of Limitations

There are a number of time-based limitations on the trustee's avoidance powers. Some of these relate to the filing of the petition; for example, most preferential transfers that occur more than ninety days before the petition are unavoidable.[90] Others relate to non-bankruptcy statutes of limitation. For example, when the trustee seeks to use § 544(b) to avoid a transfer that an unsecured creditor could have avoided outside of bankruptcy, the trustee is limited by whatever time limits the underlying state law avoidance power imposes.[91] In addition, § 546 sets time limits for the avoidance of transfers under §§ 544 (Strong Arm Clause), 545 (Statutory Liens), 547 (Preferences), 548 (Fraudulent Transfers) and 553 (Setoff). Section 550(f) imposes a further statute of limitations on actions to recover property or the value of property that have been the subject of an avoidable transfer. Thus § 546(a) imposes a limit on when an action to declare that the transfer is *avoidable* must be filed; § 550(f) imposes a limit on when an action to

---

[85] Bonded Fin. Serv., Inc. v. European Am. Bank, 838 F.2d 890 (7th Cir. 1988).

[86] Paloian v. Lasalle Bank, N.A., 619 F.3d 688 (7th Cir. 2010).

[87] Bankruptcy Code § 550(a)(2).

[88] *See* § 14.08[D], *infra.*

[89] *See* Bankruptcy Code § 546(e)-(g). These provisions limit avoidance of margin payments and transfers under swap agreements. *See, e.g.,* Enron Creditors Recovery Corp v. Alfa, S.A.B. de C.V., 651 F.3d 329 (2d Cir. 2011) (regarding avoidability of "settlement payments" under § 546(e)).

[90] *See* § 15.02[E] Preference Period, *infra.*

[91] *See* § 14.03 Power to Use Rights of Actual Unsecured Creditors, *supra.*

implement its avoidance by *recovering the property or its value* must be filed.

In most cases, an avoidance action must be commenced within two years after the entry of the order for relief or the closing or dismissal of the case, whichever is earlier. However, if a trustee is first appointed or elected in the case more than one year but less than two years after the entry of the order for relief, then the avoidance action must be commenced by the earlier of one year after appointment or election of the trustee or the closing or dismissal of the case.[92] This is designed to give a trustee who is appointed late in the game, a reasonable opportunity to investigate avoidable transfers. This might easily occur in Chapter 11 cases in which the debtor-in-possession manages the estate for a period of time before its gross mismanagement or fraud leads the court to appoint a trustee. Rather than force the trustee to hastily investigate transfers that might be avoided, the limitations period is extended beyond the normal two-year limit to give the trustee a minimum of one year to bring an appropriate action.

Section 549 (Postpetition Transfers) has its own limitations period. An action to avoid a postpetition transfer must be commenced by the earlier of two years after the transfer or the closing or dismissal of the case.[93]

Section 550, which deals with the recovery of property or its value after its transfer is avoided, imposes a different limit. An action to recover the property transferred, or its value, must be commenced by the earlier of one year after the transfer was avoided or the time the case is closed or dismissed.[94]

For example, suppose Titanic Industries filed its voluntary Chapter 11 petition on May 1, 2012, resulting in an immediate order for relief, and wants to bring an action to avoid a payment that it made to one of its suppliers as an avoidable preference. Under § 546(a), Titanic, as debtor-in-possession, must bring an action to avoid the transfer by May 2, 2014, "2 years after the entry of the order for relief."[95] If a trustee is appointed, the trustee has until one year after her appointment to bring the action, even if that delays its deadline until after May 2, 2014.[96] But in no event may the avoidance action be brought, by either Titanic as debtor-in-possession or a trustee, after the case is closed or dismissed.[97]

Further assume that Titanic files the avoidance action on April 30, 2014, and that on June 1, 2014, obtains a judgment avoiding the transfer. Section 550(f)(1) requires any action to recover the avoided transfer be brought within one year of the June 1, 2014, judgment.

---

[92] Bankruptcy Code § 546(a).

[93] Bankruptcy Code § 549(d).

[94] Bankruptcy Code § 550(e).

[95] Bankruptcy Code § 546(a)(1)(A).

[96] Bankruptcy Code § 546(a)(1)(B).

[97] Bankruptcy Code § 546(a)(2).

[B]   Effect of Non-Bankruptcy Law Grace Periods

The right of the trustee to avoid a transfer under §§ 544 (Strong-Arm Clause), 545 (Statutory Liens), and 549 (Postpetition Transfers) is subject to any "generally applicable law" that permits perfection of an interest in property to be effective against an entity that acquired rights in the property before perfection.[98] This protects two-step transactions that are incomplete at the time of bankruptcy, such as security interests and mortgages.[99]

A simple example of this is contained in Article 9 of the Uniform Commercial Code. Security interests in personal property are two-step transactions; the first step is attachment, which transfers the security interest from the debtor to the secured party; the second step is perfection, usually accomplished by the filing of a financing statement in the office of the secretary of state. Perfection protects the transfer against subsequent third parties, such as other secured parties and those who acquire a judicial lien on the property.[100] Generally, an interest in the property that arises between attachment and perfection has priority over the security interest. However, there are exceptions. The most important of these relates to "purchase money security interests" (PMSI), which are created in conjunction with the debtor's acquisition of the property used as collateral.[101] Article 9 supplies a twenty-day period during which the PMSI may be perfected and remain effective against interests that arose during the grace period.[102]

Section 546(b) protects these two-step transfers from avoidance by the trustee when the petition is filed during whatever grace period other law, such as the U.C.C., provides. Its purpose "is to protect, in spite of the surprise intervention of a bankruptcy petition, those whom State law protects by allowing them to perfect their liens or interests as of an effective date that is earlier than the date of the perfection."[103]

For example, if on March 10, Industrial Supply delivers equipment to Franklin Manufacturing, that is subject to Industrial Supply's purchase money security interest, and Franklin files a Chapter 11 petition on March 17, before Industrial Supply has filed a financing statement to perfect its security interest, the security interest might be avoidable under the strong-arm clause of § 544(a). Outside of bankruptcy, Industrial Supply enjoys a twenty-day grace period beginning on March 10, the day Franklin received possession of the collateral, to file its financing statement and perfect the security interest. Section 546(b) preserves Industrial Supply's right to file within the twenty-day period and prevents the trustee from avoiding Industrial's security interest. Section 362(b)(2) facilitates the operation of § 546(b) by creating an exception to the automatic stay for creditors whose conduct

---

[98]   Bankruptcy Code § 546(b). This limitation does not apply to other avoiding powers, such as those involving preferences or fraudulent transfers.

[99]   *See* § 2.02[A][2] Two Step Process: Agreement and Recordation, *supra.*

[100]   *See* § 2.02[B] Security Interests in Personal Property, *supra.*

[101]   U.C.C. § 9-103 (2003).

[102]   *See* U.C.C. § 9-317(d) (2003).

[103]   S. Rep. No. 95-989, at 86 (1978), *reprinted in* 1978 U.S.C.C.A.N. 5787, 5872.

merely takes advantage of the type of generally applicable law to which § 546(b) refers.[104]

[C]   Limits on Seller's Reclamation Rights

Another limitation on avoidance powers that protects a state-created creditor right relates to reclamation by an unpaid seller. One of the traditional rights given to credit sellers of goods is the ability to reclaim those goods after delivery if the seller discovers (after delivery) that the buyer is insolvent. This right is codified in the Uniform Commercial Code[105] and recognized, with limitations, by the Bankruptcy Code.

The U.C.C. gives sellers the right to reclaim goods sold on credit to an insolvent buyer if the seller demands return of the goods within ten days of the buyer's receipt. In some instances, the ten-day limit is expanded to three months.[106]

Instead of permitting the creditor to recover the goods themselves, § 546(c) permits the court to implement the seller's rights by ordering the debtor to return the goods, giving the seller a lien on the goods to secure the seller's claim for payment, or granting the seller an administrative priority claim for payment.[107] The last alternative is appropriate only if it is probable that all administrative claims will be paid in full.

More significantly, it gives the seller a maximum of either forty-five days after the buyer's receipt of the goods or twenty days after commencement of the case, whichever is earlier, regardless of what state law permits. Thus, to reclaim, the seller must satisfy both the requirements imposed by the U.C.C. and the limits imposed by the Bankruptcy Code.

[D]   Protection for Good Faith Transferees

Immediate transferees from the debtor generally enjoy little protection and must return the property or its value to the estate, though in some cases they have the right to a lien for the amount they paid in good faith for the transferred property or for improvements they have made since acquiring the property. Remote transferees, who acquired the property from the initial transferee, enjoy greater protection.

[1]   Remote Transferees

Some protection against avoidance is given to remote good faith transferees. The rule is similar to the rules regarding holders in due course of negotiable instruments and good faith purchasers of investment securities. The trustee may not

---

[104] Bankruptcy Code § 362(b)(2); *see* § 8.03 Exceptions to the Automatic Stay, *supra.*

[105] U.C.C. § 2-702(2) (2003); *see* § 2.05[E] Seller's Right of Reclamation, *supra.*

[106] U.C.C. § 2-702(2). Moreover, revisions to U.C.C. § 2-702 that have not been widely adopted, remove both ten-day and three-month limits in favor of a requirement that the seller demand reclamation within a "reasonable time." U.C.C. § 2-702 (2003).

[107] *See supra* § 10.04[B] Super-Priority Claims.

recover from a subsequent transferee if the transferee "takes for value, including satisfaction or securing of present or antecedent debt, in good faith, and without knowledge of the voidability of the transfer avoided."[108] Moreover, any transferee of the property after a protected remote transferee who takes the property in "good faith" is also protected from liability.[109]

Assume, for example, that shortly before he filed his bankruptcy case, Charlie fraudulently transferred his car to his sister, Gail. Gail sold the car for its fair market value to Reliable Motors, who had no knowledge of Charlie's fraudulent transfer of the car to Gail. Reliable Motors then sold the car to Bonita, who bought it in good faith.

In Charlie's bankruptcy case, the trustee can recover the value of the car from Gail, as the "initial transferee of the transfer."[110] However, the trustee cannot recover the value of the car from Reliable Motors, nor can it recover anything from Bonita. As a transferee for value, in good faith, and without knowledge of the voidability of the transaction, Reliable Motors meets all the requirements for protection under § 550(b)(1). Bonita is protected as an "immediate . . . good faith transferee of [the initial] transferee" under § 550(b)(2). These provisions apply only to transferees *after* the first transferee. Even if Gail had acted in good faith and without knowledge that the transfer was a fraudulent transfer, she would not be protected; the trustee could still recover from her.

[2] Amounts Paid by a Transferee

Several provisions of the Code protect good faith transferees for the amount they paid for property transferred to them by the debtor. The Code's protections are generally supplied by the portion of the Code that makes the transfer avoidable in the first place.

With respect to fraudulent transfers, § 548(c) protects good faith transferees by giving them a lien on the transferred property "to the extent that [the] transferee gave value to the debtor in exchange for the transfer."[111] Thus, if Gail (from the example above) acted in good faith in buying the car from Charlie, she has a lien on the recovered property to the extent of her payment. Section 549 provides similar protection for good faith purchasers of property transferred by the debtor after commencement of the case.[112]

No similar protection is supplied to transferees of property under §§ 544 (Strong-Arm Clause), 545 (Statutory Liens), or 547 (Preferences). However, these transferees have a claim against the estate for the amount of the transferred property; this restores them to the position they would have been in if the transfer had not been made.

---

[108] Bankruptcy Code § 550(b)(1).

[109] Bankruptcy Code § 550(b)(2).

[110] Bankruptcy Code § 550(a)(1).

[111] Bankruptcy Code § 548(c).

[112] Bankruptcy Code § 549(c).

[3] Improvements by a Transferee

Additional protection is given to transferees who make improvements to the transferred property. A good faith transferee from whom the trustee may recover has a lien on the property recovered to secure the lesser of (a) the cost to the transferee of any improvement made after the transfer, less the amount of any profit realized by or accruing to the transferee from the property, and (b) any increase in the value of the property as a result of the improvement.[113]

For example, assume that before his bankruptcy, Jerry transferred a parcel of real estate to Chu in satisfaction of a $150,000 debt he owed to Chu. Although the transfer was a preference, Chu acted in good faith with no knowledge that Jerry was preparing to file a bankruptcy petition. After taking possession of the property, Chu spent $50,000 renovating the kitchen. His efforts increased the value of the land by $40,000. When the trustee recovers the property, Chu is entitled to a lien on the property for the amount by which his improvements increased the value of the land — $40,000. If his work had increased the value to $60,000, Chu would be entitled to a lien for the full $50,000 he spent, but because he was willing to spend $50,000 to improve the value by only $40,000, the Code limits his lien to the expenses incurred or the enhancement in value achieved, whichever is lower.

The lien exists only if improvements are made on the property, and only if those improvements increase the value of the property. If the property increases in value on its own, and not because of any improvements made by the transferee, the transferee has no lien at all. The term "improvement" encompasses physical additions or changes to the property, repairs to the property, payment of tax on the property, payment of any debt secured by a lien that is superior to or equal to the rights of the trustee, and preservation of the property.[114]

No similar protection is provided to transferees who act in bad faith. Thus, if Chu, in the example above, had knowingly assisted in Jerry's fraudulent transfer of his land, and later paid to make improvements to the land, Chu would not be entitled to a lien for the money spent for his improvements.

---

[113] Bankruptcy Code § 550(d)(1).

[114] Bankruptcy Code § 550(d)(2).

Chapter 15

PREFERENCES

§ 15.01 PREFERENCE POLICIES

This chapter deals with the power of the trustee (or debtor-in-possession)[1] to avoid certain pre-petition transactions known as "preferences." The preference power, contained in Bankruptcy Code § 547, allows the bankruptcy trustee to recover payments and other property transfers made by the debtor to creditors on the eve of the bankruptcy filing. The purpose of the preference power is to discourage creditors from engaging in a race to dismember the debtor, and to reverse the consequences of such a race when it occurs.[2]

Broadly speaking, a preference occurs whenever a debtor favors one creditor over another in paying out its limited resources. For example, if Donna owes $1000 to Chuck and $500 to Carla, but has only $500 in available assets, Donna may decide to pay the entire $500 to Carla shortly before filing for bankruptcy. Such a payment "prefers" Carla over Chuck. Preferences are generally legal under state law, but the Bankruptcy Code takes the view that, when the debtor is insolvent, similarly situated creditors should be treated equally. In bankruptcy, therefore, many such preferences may be avoided (returned to the estate).[3]

In the above example, if the payment to Carla is an avoidable preference, Donna's bankruptcy trustee will recover the $500 payment from Carla and use the cash to make payments to all of Donna's creditors. In return, Carla will receive a $500 claim against the estate.[4] Unfortunately for Carla, her $500 claim will share with other claims against the estate, and she is likely therefore to receive far less than $500. The difference between the $500 returned by Carla to the estate, and the estate's payment to Carla on account of her claim is the gain to the estate.

---

[1] Section 547 speaks in terms of the ability of the trustee to avoid preferences. However, in a Chapter 11 case, the debtor usually remains in possession of the property of the estate and controls the reorganization process. Consequently, the debtor manages the estate as the "debtor-in-possession" and has all of the same rights, powers, and duties of a trustee, including the right to deploy the trustee's avoiding powers. Bankruptcy Code § 1107(a); *see* § 4.02[B] Debtor-in-Possession, *supra*.

[2] Vern Countryman, *The Concept of a Voidable Preference in Bankruptcy*, 38 Vand. L. Rev. 713 (1985); Thomas H. Jackson, *Avoiding Powers in Bankruptcy*, 36 Stan. L. Rev. 725 (1984); Charles J. Tabb, *Beneath the Surface of BAPCPA: The Brave New World of Bankruptcy Preferences*, 13 Am. Bankr. Inst. L. Rev. 425 (2005).

[3] Bankruptcy Code § 550.

[4] Bankruptcy Code § 502(h).

Many justifications for preference law have been advanced. The two most widely cited are "preservation of the estate" and "equality of distribution."[5] The former is based on the not-unreasonable assumption that creditors as a whole are likely to receive a greater payout if the debtor's assets remain intact until bankruptcy.[6] If they do, the trustee can conduct an orderly liquidation or the debtor-in-possession will have a greater chance of reorganizing. Orderly liquidation tends to produce more money than piecemeal dismemberment; reorganizations are likely to produce more money than any form of liquidation. In theory, preference law, by forcing the return of property transferred to creditors, preserves the estate. If creditors must return what they have obtained from the debtor by individual actions, they have no incentive to pick off the debtor's assets one by one; thus, the debtor's assets will remain intact to be administered as a whole through the bankruptcy proceeding.

The most sophisticated version of this theory is rooted in the Creditor's Bargain theory of bankruptcy law, advanced by several influential bankruptcy scholars. It assumes that creditors would generally prefer to receive equal treatment in a larger asset pool than unequal treatment in a smaller pool, even though they might sometimes benefit from taking a disproportionate share of the smaller pool.[7]

The second traditional rationale is that preference law protects the Bankruptcy Code's policy of equal distribution among creditors by forcing those who have received unequal distributions to return the excess they received.[8] A more subtle version of this rationale recognizes that distributions under the Bankruptcy Code do not treat all unsecured creditors equally. Instead, it is probably more accurate to say that the preference rules help effectuate the Bankruptcy Code's system of distribution. Bankruptcy is the last opportunity for most creditors to obtain any payment from the debtor, and it is virtually certain that there will not be enough in the estate to go around. Given these facts, Congress has established a set of priorities that identify those debts it thinks should be given the best chance of payment. Congress has ranked debts in order of perceived importance and has further mandated pro rata payment of claims within each rank, so that each creditor in the rank bears only a proportionate share of the loss. Preferences disturb this statutory distribution system by allowing the preferred creditor to obtain more than the Code would give it. Preferences are thus avoided to increase the number and amount of claims, and the value of the assets, dealt with under the Code's system. In short, a creditor who "ought to have" received $10,000, but who in fact received $20,000 because of a preference must pay back the preference and be given

---

[5] *E.g.*, In re Bullion Reserve of N. Am., 836 F.2d 1214, 1217 (9th Cir. 1988); Vern Countryman, *The Concept of a Voidable Preference in Bankruptcy*, 38 Vand. L. Rev. 713, 748, 778 (1985).

[6] *See* § 1.01[B] Bankruptcy as a Debtors' Remedy: Fresh Start for Honest Debtors, *supra.*

[7] *See generally* Bruce R. Krause, Note, *Preferential Transfers and the Value of The Insolvent Firm*, 87 Yale L. J. 1449, 1450 (1978); Thomas H. Jackson, The Logic and Limits of Bankruptcy Law 124 (1986); John McCoid, *Bankruptcy, Preferences, and Efficiency: An Expression of Doubt*, 67 Va. L. Rev. 249 (1981); Lawrence Ponoroff, *Evil Intentions and an Irresolute Endorsement for Scientific Rationalism: Bankruptcy Preferences One More Time*, 1993 Wis. L. Rev. 1439; Robert Weisberg, *Commercial Morality, The Merchant Character, and the History of the Voidable Preference*, 39 Stan. L. Rev. 3 (1986).

[8] *See* § 1.01[C] Bankruptcy as a Creditor's Remedy; Equal Treatment of Creditors of the Same Class, *supra.*

instead the $10,000 that Congress says it deserved.[9]

§ 15.02 PREFERENCES DEFINED

The basic elements of a "preference" are established in § 547(b). A preference is a transfer (i) of the debtor's property, (ii) to or for the benefit of a creditor, (iii) on account of an antecedent debt, (iv) made while the debtor was insolvent, (v) made during the preference period (usually the ninety days before the bankruptcy, but one full year for insiders of the debtor), (vi) that enables the creditor to receive more than it would get in a Chapter 7 liquidation of the debtor.[10] Each of these six elements requires careful analysis of the statute and the very extensive case law.

[A] Transfer of Property; Date of Transfer

[1] Type of Transfer

A preference involves "any transfer of an interest of the debtor in property."[11] It is important to recognize that the property need not be in the form of money. It may be in the form of tangible property, intangible property, or in the form of security interest in the debtor's property.[12] The property transferred is frequently cash, but it might be anything. In *Homann v. R.I.H Acquisitions, In, LLC (In re Lewinksi)*, for example, it was $50,000 of poker chips.[13]

The transfer may also be voluntary or involuntary.[14] For example, a voluntary payment of a debt may be a preference; but so may the involuntary imposition of a judicial lien[15] or a tax lien on the debtor's property.[16] The transfer may be of all rights in the property or only a partial interest in the property. For example, the grant of a security interest in the property, which gives the secured party only limited rights, is a transfer that may be a preference.[17]

---

[9] *See generally* Charles Jordan Tabb, *Rethinking Preferences*, 43 S.C. L. Rev. 981 (1992); Vern Countryman, *The Concept of a Voidable Preference in Bankruptcy*, 38 Vand. L. Rev. 713 (1985).

[10] Bankruptcy Code § 547(b).

[11] Homann v. R.I.H Acquisitions, In, LLC (In re Lewinksi), 410 B.R. 828 (Bankr. N.D. Ind. 2009) ($50,000 of poker chips transferred in satisfaction of pre-existing debt).

[12] Bankruptcy Code § 101(54)(B).

[13] 410 B.R. 828 (Bankr. N.D. Ind. 2009).

[14] Bankruptcy Code § 101(54)(D).

[15] *See* § 2.04 Judicial Liens, *supra.*

[16] *See* § 2.05 Statutory, Common Law, and Equitable Liens, *supra.*

[17] *See* Irving A. Breitowitz, *Article 9 Security Interests as Voidable Preferences*, 4 Cardozo L. Rev. 357 (1982); David Gray Carlson, *Security Interests in the Crucible of Voidable Preference Law*, 1995 U. Ill. L. Rev. 211; Vern Countryman, *The Concept of a Voidable Preference in Bankruptcy*, 38 Vand. L. Rev. 713 (1985); Thomas M. Ward & Jay A. Shulman, *In Defense of the Bankruptcy Code's Radical Integration of the Preference Rules Affecting Commercial Financing*, 61 Wash. U. L.Q. 1 (1983).

[2] Debtor's Interest

A transfer is vulernable to avoidance only if it is a transfer of the debtor's property. Transfers of property owned by others, however, they may benefit a creditor, do not dissipate the property that is otherwise available for the debtor's creditors.[18] If a transfer doesn't diminish the assets that can be paid to the debtor's creditors in the debtor's bankruptcy case, the transfer does not harm creditors, and is not avoidable as a preference.

Although the Code does not expressly define "an interest of the debtor in property" the Supreme Court has indicated that it means "that property that would have been part of the estate had it not been transferred before the commencement of bankruptcy proceedings."[19] Thus, the key question is whether the property would have been held by the debtor at the time of its petition, if the property had not been transferred. This depends largely on state property law. A bankruptcy court looks to state law to determine whether property is an asset of debtor.[20]

This limitation on the preference power makes several common types of transfers to creditors invulnerable to avoidance as a preference. For example, payments made to a creditor by the issuer of a letter of credit are not preferences, because they are not transfers of the debtor's property,[21] though this may be different if the letter of credit is collateralized.[22] And, as explained in more detail below, where funds supplied by a third party are "earmarked" for payment to one of the debtor's creditors, the fact that they temporarily belong to the debtor, might prevent payment of the earmarked funds from constituting a preference.[23] Likewise, transfer to a creditor of funds the debtor holds in trust, which is not estate property,[24] is not a preference. Creditors who are able to establish that the debtor held funds in constructive trust for payment to the creditor, may evade a trustee's action to recover the funds as an avoidable preference.[25] Establishing the existence of such a trust, however, has proven difficult.[26]

---

[18] *See, e.g.,* Ellenberg v. First Nat'l Bank (In re Hollvey), 15 B.R. 850, 851 (Bankr. N.D. Ga. 1981).

[19] Begier v. IRS, 496 U.S. 53, 58 (1990).

[20] Bailey v. Big Sky Motors, Ltd. (In re Ogden), 314 F.3d 1190, 1197 (10th Cir. 2002).

[21] *See, e.g.,* North Shore & Cent. Ill. Freight Co. v. American Nat'l Bank & Trust Co. of Chicago (In re North Shore & Cent. Ill. Freight Co.), 30 B.R. 377, 379 (Bankr. N.D. Ill. 1983).

[22] Kellogg v. Blue Quail Energy, Inc. (In re Compton Corp.), 831 F.2d 586, 595 (5th Cir. 1987). *See* David Gray Carlson, *The Earmarking Defense to Voidable Preference Liability: A Reconceptualization* 73 Am. Bankr. L.J. 591 (1999); Alan N. Resnick, *Letter of Credit as a Landlord's Protection Against a Tenant's Bankruptcy: Assurance of Payment or False Sense of Security?* 82 Am. Bankr. L.J. 497 (2008).

[23] *See infra* § 15.03[J] Substitution of Creditors — Earmarking.

[24] Bankruptcy Code § 541(d).

[25] *See* Begier v. I.R.S., 496 U.S. 53 (1990); Unicom Computer Corp., 13 F.3d 321 (9th Cir. 1994); In re Golden Triangle Capital, Inc., 171 B.R. 79 (B.A.P. 9th Cir. 1994).

[26] *E.g.,* In re Omegas Group, Inc., 16 F.3d 1443 (6th Cir. 1994); In Taylor & Assocs., L.P. v. Diamant (In re Advent Mgmt. Corp.), 104 F.3d 293 (9th Cir. 1997).

[3] Time of Transfer

It is often important to determine the date on which the transfer occurred. Determining the time of transfer is important for three reasons: (1) the date may determine whether the transfer was within the preference period,[27] (2) whether it was a payment of antecedent (preexisting) debt,[28] and (3) whether the debtor was insolvent at the time the transfer occurred.[29] In cases involving "insider" preferences, the creditor must have been an insider on the date the transfer was made.[30] In some cases, the date of transfer may also determine whether an exception to the avoidance rule applies.[31]

Most of the difficulty regarding the date of transfer involves two-step transfers.[32] The first step makes the transaction effective between the original parties to the transaction. A second step is required to establish the transferee's rights against third parties. For example, a conveyance of real property generally requires both the execution of a deed and the recording of the deed.[33] Step one — execution — makes the transaction effective between the seller and the buyer. Step two — recording — is required to establish the buyer's rights against certain third parties, such as subsequent bona fide purchasers of the realty.

Similarly, an Article 9 secured transaction often requires two steps.[34] Step one is attachment, which establishes the rights and obligations of the debtor and the secured party.[35] Step two is an additional act to perfect the security interest, which establishes the secured party's rights in the collateral as against other claimant to the same collateral, such as the holder of a subsequent judgment lien the property.[36] Similar rules apply to other personal property security transactions, such as preferred ship mortgages.[37] Analysis of a transaction as a preference requires determining whether the transfer was made in the first step or not until the second step.

This issue is addressed directly by § 547(e). Its rules deal with transfers of both real property and personal property, and with one-step and two-step transfers.

Section 547(e)(2) sets out the basic rules for determining when a transfer is made. It distinguishes between the time at which the transfer is effective between the immediate parties and the time at which it is "perfected." It addresses four basic sets of circumstances. The first two deal with situations in which the transfer was

---

[27] See § 15.02[E] Preference Period, *infra.*

[28] See § 15.02[C] Antecedent Debt, *infra.*

[29] See § 15.02[D] Insolvent at Time of Transfer, *infra.*

[30] Zucker v. Freeman (In re NetBank, Inc.), 424 B.R. 568 (Bankr. M.D. Fla. 2010).

[31] See § 15.03 Exceptions to Avoidance of Preferences, *infra.*

[32] See § 2.02[A][2] Two Step Process: Agreement and Recordation, *supra.*

[33] See, e.g., In re Lewis W. Shurtleff, Inc., 778 F.2d 1416 (9th Cir. 1985); In re Freedlander, Inc., 107 Bankr. 88 (Bankr. E.D. Va. 1989).

[34] See § 2.02[B][1] Uniform Commercial Code Article 9, *supra.*

[35] U.C.C. § 9-203 (2003).

[36] U.C.C. §§ 9-317 to -339 (2003).

[37] In re Gottschalk, 46 B.R. 49 (Bankr. M.D. Fla. 1985).

perfected before commencement of the bankruptcy case. The second two deal with situations in which perfection occurred after the commencement of the case.

First, if the transfer is perfected at the time it becomes effective between the parties (the debtor and the creditor) or within thirty days thereafter, the transfer is deemed to have occurred on the date it becomes effective between them. For example, suppose the debt was incurred on January 1, and that transfer became effective between debtor and creditor on the same day, January 1, but was not perfected until January 15. The transfer is deemed to have occurred on January 1. Further, since this is simultaneous with the incurring of the debt, the transfer cannot be a preference because it is not on account of antecedent debt.[38]

Second, if the transfer is perfected more than thirty days after the time it becomes effective, the transfer occurs on the date it was perfected. If the debt was incurred and the transfer became effective on January 1, but was not perfected until February 15, the transfer is deemed to have occurred on February 15. This is important because the transfer is now on account of an antecedent debt that was incurred on January 1.[39]

This is exactly what happened in *Lange v. Inoval Capital Funding, LLC (In re Qualia Clinical Service, Inc)*.[40] The lender tried to perfect by filing in the state where the debtor was doing business, but its filing was meaningless, because the debtor was incorporated in a different state. Later, the lender filed a financing statement in the state where the debtor was incorporated, and thus became perfected. But, this was more than 30 days after the security interest attached. Thus, the transfer was completed upon perfection. Because this was within 90 days of the debtor's bankruptcy petition, and for a previously created (antecedent) debt, the transfer was an avoidable preference.[41] Delayed perfection can thus easily result in the security interest being avoidable as a preference.

Third, if the transfer was not perfected by the later of the date of commencement of the case or thirty days after the transfer became effective, the transfer occurs immediately before the date of the filing of the petition.[42] For example, suppose that the transfer became effective on January 1, the bankruptcy was filed on January 7, and the transfer was perfected on February 15. The transfer is deemed to have occurred immediately before January 7 (which apparently means that it is deemed to have occurred on January 6).[43] January 6 is within the 90 day preference period, so unless the loan was made on January 6, the transfer is avoidable.

Fourth, if the transfer was not perfected on the date of commencement of the case, but was perfected within thirty days after it became effective, the transfer

---

[38] Bankruptcy Code § 547(e)(2)(A).

[39] Bankruptcy Code § 547(e)(2)(B). *See* Schatz v. Imperial Capital Bank (In re Schatz), 402 B.R. 482, 486 (Bankr. D.N.H. 2009) (mortgage perfected by recording twenty-two months after mortgage was created).

[40] 652 F.3d 933 (8th Cir. 2011).

[41] *Id.* at 331.

[42] In most cases, if the transfer was not perfected at the time the petition is filed, it is avoidable under § 544(a). *See* § 14.02 Strong-Arm Clause — § 544(a), *supra*.

[43] Bankruptcy Code § 547(e)(2)(C).

occurs on the date it became effective. If the transfer became effective on January 1, the bankruptcy was filed on January 5, and the transfer was perfected on January 7, the transfer is deemed to have occurred on January 1.[44]

Two key problems are determining what is necessary to make the transfer effective between the parties and what is necessary to perfect the transfer. The Code does not deal with the first issue, which is consequently left entirely to non-bankruptcy law. Nor does the Code specify what acts are necessary to perfect the transfer; this too is a question resolved outside the Code.[45] However, the Code does define what legal status constitutes perfection. In other words, the Code does not tell you how to perfect (this is determined by relevant non-Code law) but it does tell you what legal result your actions must have for the transfer to be perfected under § 547.

If the property transferred is realty (other than fixtures), the transfer is perfected only when a bona fide purchaser (BFP) of that property from the debtor cannot acquire an interest that is superior to the right of the transferee.[46] This does not mean that there is such a purchaser, nor does it make the trustee a bona fide purchaser.[47] Neither does it mean that every bona fide purchaser would have a superior interest. For example, it is generally true that a bona fide purchaser who has notice of an existing interest takes subject to it. This is irrelevant in determining the date of perfection under § 547(e); the question is not whether a BFP would have a superior right but rather whether a BFP *could* have a superior right. Broadly speaking, a BFP can obtain rights superior to those of the holder of an unrecorded interest in the realty.[48] Thus, as a general principle, an interest in realty is not perfected until it is properly recorded in the real estate records — usually in the county recorder's office in the county where the land is located.[49]

For example, suppose that on August 1 Alice executes and delivers to Betty a mortgage on her home. Under relevant state law, a BFP without notice does not take subject to an unrecorded mortgage. Betty records the mortgage a week later, on August 8. Thereafter, it is effective against a subsequent BFP. The transfer became effective between Alice and Betty on August 1 and was perfected on August 8. Because it was perfected within § 547(e)(2)(A)'s 30 day grace period, the transfer is deemed to have occurred on August 1. If Betty had not recorded until September 12, the transfer would be deemed not to have occurred until September 12.[50]

---

[44] Bankruptcy Code § 547(e)(2)(A), (C).

[45] Webb v. General Motors Acceptance Corp. (In re Hesser), 984 F.2d 345, 348 (10th Cir. 1993); Grover v. Gulino (In re Gulino), 779 F.2d 546, 550 (9th Cir. 1985).

[46] Bankruptcy Code § 547(e)(1)(A).

[47] *E.g.*, Grover v. Gulino (In re Gulino), 779 F.2d 546, 551 (9th Cir. 1985).

[48] *See, e.g.*, Midlantic Nat'l Bank v. Bridge (In re Bridge), 18 F.3d 195 (3d Cir. 1994); In re Lewis W. Shurtleff, Inc., 778 F.2d 1416 (9th Cir. 1985).

[49] This remains a matter of state law, however; if in the relevant state a BFP takes subject to an unrecorded deed, then the transfer is complete when the deed is executed and delivered. Webb v. General Motors Acceptance Corp. (In re Hesser), 984 F.2d 345, 348 (10th Cir. 1993).

[50] *E.g.*, Schatz v. Imperial Capital Bank (In re Schatz), 402 B.R. 482 (Bankr. D.N.H. 2009) (creditor delayed recording mortgage for twenty-two months).

With regard to personal property and fixtures, the rule is only slightly different. A transfer is "perfected" when a creditor on a simple contract cannot acquire a judicial lien that is superior to the interest of the transferee.[51] There does not have to be such a creditor; nor must all such creditors have rights superior to the transferee. All that is required is that a creditor of that type could obtain a lien that has priority over the rights of the transferee.

This rule is of primary importance with regard to security interests under Article 9 of the Uniform Commercial Code. Indeed the Bankruptcy Code rule was designed to mesh with the related U.C.C. rules governing security interests.[52] Most, but not all security interests in personalty and fixtures are governed by Article 9. Like the Bankruptcy Code, Article 9 uses the word "perfection" to describe the status and priority of security interests. Article 9 security interests may either be perfected or unperfected. Under Article 9, a judicial lien generally has priority over a security interest that is not perfected under Article 9's rules.[53] By contrast, a security interest that is perfected under Article 9 has priority over a subsequent judicial lien.[54]

This means that, for all practical purposes, perfection under Article 9 is also perfection under § 547(e). Except with regard to purchase money security interests in consumer goods and possessory security interests, Article 9 perfection generally requires that a public record of the security interest be made.[55] For most transactions, this record is a document called a financing statement, or, more colloquially a "UCC-1."[56] Except for real estate related collateral, the financing statement is filed "centrally" in the state capital, usually with the office of the state's secretary of state. For fixtures or other real estate related collateral, "local" filing may be required at the county courthouse or register of deeds, in the county where the real estate involved is located.[57] There are other forms of recording for other types of property. For example, if the property is a titled motor vehicle, the record is a notation on the certificate of title.[58]

Suppose that on June 1 Paul lends money to Dinesh, and Dinesh executes a security agreement giving Paul rights in Dinesh's business equipment as collateral. Paul files the necessary financing statement on June 5. The transaction became effective between the parties on June 1, and was perfected on June 5. Because perfection was accomplished within 30 days of attachment, the transfer is deemed to have occurred on June 1. But, if it was not perfected until July 17, outside

---

[51] Bankruptcy Code § 547(e)(1)(B).

[52] *See* § 2.02[B][1][d] Priority Rules under U.C.C. Article 9, *supra.*

[53] U.C.C. § 9-317 (2003).

[54] This is not directly stated in the U.C.C., but derives from U.C.C. § 9-201, which states that the security interest is effective against third parties except as otherwise stated in Article 9. Note that a perfected security interest can be subordinate to a judicial lien with regard to certain advances of credit made to the debtor after the lien attaches. U.C.C. § 9-323 (2003).

[55] U.C.C. § 9-310 (2003).

[56] U.C.C. § 9-310(a) (2003). The proper form for an Article 9 financing statement is set out in U.C.C. § 9-502 (2003).

[57] U.C.C. § 9-501 (2003).

[58] U.C.C. § 9-311(a)(3) (2003). *See supra* § 2.02[B][1][c] Perfection of Security Interests.

§ 547(e)(2)(A)'s 30 day grace period, the transfer will be deemed to have occurred on July 17. Depending on the time the debt was created, the debtor's solvency on July 17, and whether July 17 was within the 90 day preference period, the transfer may be an avoidable preference. As with real estate deals, delays in perfection easily lead to avoidance as a preference.

A final aspect of the date of transfer rules is of special significance to security interests in the debtor's "after-acquired" property — collateral that the debtor acquires weeks, months, and perhaps even years after the security agreement has been signed and the financing statement has been filed. For the purposes of the trustee's preference power, no transfer can occur until the debtor has rights in the property transferred.[59] Under Article 9, the debtor and secured party may agree that the security interest will attach to "after acquired property," that is, property that the debtor does not have at the time the security agreement is entered into.[60] When the debtor does acquire the property, the security interest will automatically attach without any further action by the parties.[61]

For example, in *Official Committee of Unsecured Creditors v. Citicorp North America. Inc.*, a creditor's security interest in the debtor's tax refund did not attach until the beginning of the tax year for which the refund would become due. Because this was after the debt was incurred, it was a transfer on account of an antecedent debt and vulnerable to avoidance as a preference.[62] The debtor did not have rights in the tax refund until the tax year for the refund began and thus the transfer could not occur, under § 547(e)(3), until that day.

If a proper financing statement has been filed, that security interest will also be perfected.[63] These rules are replicated in § 547: the transfer of the interest in the after acquired property does not occur until the debtor acquires rights in it. For example, if on January 1, Franklin Manufacturing and Peninsula Bank enter into a security agreement that covers all of Franklin's inventory, including after-acquired inventory, and Franklin acquires new inventory on June 1, the transfer of the security interest in the new inventory occurs on June 1, not January 1. This has considerable significance in connection with the extent to which floating liens, which attach to after-acquired property as the debtor acquires it, are treated as preferences.[64]

---

[59] Bankruptcy Code § 547(e)(3).

[60] U.C.C. § 9-204(a), (b) (2003).

[61] U.C.C. § 9-204 cmt. 2 (2003).

[62] Official Committee of Unsecured Creditors v. Citicorp. N. Am., Inc. (In re Tousa, Inc.), 406 B.R. 421 (Bankr. S.D. Fla. 2009).

[63] U.C.C. § 9-502 cmt 2 (2003).

[64] Bankruptcy Code § 547(c)(5); *see* § 15.03[E] Floating Liens, *infra.*

[B]   To or For the Benefit of a Creditor

The preference may either be direct or indirect; that is, the property may either be transferred *to* a creditor (a direct preference) or *for the benefit* of a creditor (an indirect preference).[65] Most cases involve direct preferences, where this element is self-evident. If the debtor gives his cash to one of his creditors, there is no difficulty in concluding that the debtor's property was transferred directly to a creditor. The same is true when the debtor signs a security agreement granting its creditor a security interest in her property.

However, it has created problems in one main situation: a transfer to one creditor that indirectly benefits another creditor, who is a close affiliate or "insider" of the debtor.[66] Payments to creditors pursuant to criminal restitution orders are treated similarly, even though it was the state rather than the creditor who sought payment, and even though the payment was designed not just to benefit the creditor but also to benefit society.[67]

[C]   Antecedent Debt

A preference is a transfer made regarding an antecedent, or preexisting, debt — a debt that arose before the transfer was made.[68] A contemporaneous exchange is not a preference (although if inadequate value is received by the debtor, it may be a fraudulent transfer).[69] For example, if Doug pays $18,000 in cash to buy a new car during the 90 days before bankruptcy, his transfer of cash to the seller is not usually a preference. The antecedent debt requirement derives from the notion that preference law deals with transfers that deplete the estate — more precisely, transfers that reduce the amount available for distribution to creditors. The exchange of one asset for another — of Doug's $18,000 cash for an $18,000 car — does not diminish the amount available to creditors.[70]

The antecedent debt requirement is met if there is any legally meaningful time lag between the creation of the debt and the transfer to the creditor. Even a gap of a day or less is sufficient.[71] Thus, if Doug buys the car on Monday, but does not pay for it until Tuesday, his payment is for an antecedent debt and thus may be an avoidable preference.

The strict reading of the antecedent debt element creates several practical problems, because it is almost impossible for an exchange to be absolutely contemporaneous. To take the example given above, Doug is much more likely to

---

[65]   Bankruptcy Code § 547(b)(1).

[66]   *See* § 15.04 Indirect Preferences, *infra.*

[67]   In re Silverman, 616 F.3d 1001 (9th Cir. 2010).

[68]   Bankruptcy Code § 547(b)(2).

[69]   Bankruptcy Code § 548(a)(1)(B); *see* Chapter 16 — Fraudulent Transfers, *infra.*

[70]   Bankruptcy Code § 547(b)(2). This is true even though the car may diminish in value very, very quickly, as soon as Doug drives it off the dealer's lot.

[71]   For an extreme example, see National City Bank of New York v. Hotchkiss, 231 U.S. 50 (1913) (holding that a lapse of several hours between making loan and obtaining collateral meant that transfer of collateral was on an antecedent debt).

pay for his new car by giving the dealer a check than $18,000 in cash; yet payment by check is not technically a contemporaneous transfer.[72] Even if he pays cash, he might hand over the cash a moment, or twenty minutes after he signs the contract to purchase the car, thus creating the debt. These problems have been ameliorated in part by the thirty-day grace period in § 547(e) for two-step transfers and in part by various exceptions to the avoidance rules that are contained in § 547(c).

For example, suppose that a debt was incurred on January 1, and was secured by a mortgage signed and delivered to the creditor on the same day. The mortgage was not filed until January 4. There is no antecedent debt problem because the mortgage transfer was perfected within thirty days of the date it became effective between the parties; thus, the transfer is deemed to have occurred on January 1, contemporaneously with the creation of the obligation.[73] Similarly, § 547(c)(1) ordinarily protects payments by check where completion of the payment may take several days.[74]

[D]　Insolvent at the Time of Transfer

Another basic element of an avoidable preference is that the debtor must have been insolvent at the time the transfer was made.[75] When a solvent debtor pays one creditor before another, or does anything else with his or her money, other creditors are not harmed. If the debtor is still solvent, there are still enough assets available for all creditors to be paid in full.

A debtor is "insolvent," for the purposes of the preference power, when a debtor's assets are worth less than the amount of its debts.[76] This is the so called "balance sheet" test. It reflects the fact that, once a debtor is insolvent, the creditors are competing for a limited fund of assets, and their claims will not be paid in full.[77] There may be difficulties in valuing assets and debts, so the issue of insolvency can present considerable evidentiary problems. In this respect, the trustee is aided by a statutory presumption that the debtor was insolvent during the ninety days immediately before her bankruptcy petition.[78] This presumption shifts only the burden of going forward with the evidence, not the burden of persuasion; if the transferee adduces any significant evidence that the debtor was solvent at the time of the transfer, the presumption is rebutted.[79] If there is no evidence either way, however, the trustee has carried its burden of proving

---

[72] See H.R. Rep. No. 95-595, 373 (1977) ("Strictly speaking [a payment by check] may be a credit transaction because the seller does not receive payment until the check is cleared through the debtor's bank.").

[73] Bankruptcy Code § 547(e)(2)(A).

[74] See § 15.03[A] Substantially Contemporaneous Exchange for New Value, infra.

[75] Bankruptcy Code § 547(b)(3).

[76] Bankruptcy Code § 101(32).

[77] Bankruptcy Code § 101(32).

[78] Bankruptcy Code § 547(f).

[79] In re Taxman Clothing Co., 905 F.2d 166, 168 (7th Cir. 1990); In re Koubourlis, 869 F.2d 1319, 1322 (9th Cir. 1989); WJM, Inc. v. Mass. Dept. of Pub. Welfare, 840 F.2d 996 (1st Cir. 1988); Clay v. Traders Bank, 708 F.2d 1347 (8th Cir. 1983).

insolvency by virtue of the presumption. For preferences to insiders, made between 90 days and 1 year before bankruptcy, the trustee does not enjoy the benefit of this presumption, and has both the burden of proof, and the burden of going forward on the factual issue of the debtor's solvency. In many cases, because of the difficulties of mustering this evidence, whomever bears the burden of coming up with the necessary evidence usually loses (or is dissuaded from vigorously litigating the issue).

[E] Preference Period

Section 547 does not avoid all transfers that prefer one creditor over another. Only those that occur "on the eve of bankruptcy" are avoided. Under the current Code, the preference period generally extends back only ninety days, unless the creditor is an insider.[80] If the creditor is an insider, the preference period extends one year prior to the filing.[81]

Thus, if Deng pays Clara the $10,000 he owes her on January 1, but does not file bankruptcy until May 1, Clara has not received a preference. But, if Clara is Deng's sister, a "relative" and thus an insider,[82] and Deng was insolvent on January 1, Clara will have to repay the $10,000 to Deng's bankruptcy trustee. This longer preference period is based on the plausible theory that insiders have special knowledge of the debtor's financial state, special ability to coerce payment from the debtor, and often some level of control over whether and when to file bankruptcy. They thus have a great advantage over other creditors based on their relationship to the debtor; some of this advantage is taken away by subjecting them to greater preference risk.

"Insider" is defined in § 101(31). If the debtor is an individual, "insider" includes certain of the debtor's relatives, the debtor's business partners, and business entities of which the debtor is a general partner, officer, director, or control person.[83] If the debtor is a business organization, "insider" includes persons who are partners, officers, directors, or control persons, as well as business affiliates (such as subsidiary or parent corporations).[84]

Finally, it is important to keep in mind the significance of the thirty day grace period for two-step transfers. If the second step occurred during the preference period, but within thirty days of the first step, the transfer is deemed to have occurred when the first step was taken. If that was outside the preference period, there is no preference. Thus, before concluding that a particular transfer is within

---

[80] Zucker v. Freeman (In re NetBank, Inc.), 424 B.R. 568, 572 (Bankr. M.D. Fla. 2010) (creditor must have been an insider on the date of the transfer).

[81] Bankruptcy Code § 547(b)(4)(A), (B).

[82] *See* Bankruptcy Code §§ 101(31)(A)(i) & 101(45).

[83] Bankruptcy Code § 101(31)(A). *See* Prunty v. Terry (In re Paschall), 408 B.R. 79 (E.D. Va. 2009) (debtor's estranged wife remained an insider, even after commencement of their divorce action).

[84] The relevant definition of "insider" appears at Bankruptcy Code § 101(31)(b)-(c), (e)-(f); the definition of "affiliate" is at Bankruptcy Code § 101(2). *See, e.g.*, Longview Aluminum, L.L.C. v. Brandt, 431 B.R. 193 (N.D. Ill. 2010) (managing member of LLC was insider because it was analogous to director of a conventional corporation even though managing member was not a "person in control").

the preference period, care must be taken to determine the time of the transfer in question under § 547(e)'s complex set of rules.

[F] Improvement in Position

The final requirement focuses on whether the transfer allows the transferee to obtain more than it would under the Code's basic distributional structure. That structure, which is rigidly enforced in Chapter 7 (liquidation) bankruptcy becomes the yardstick by which the transferee's position is measured.[85] The law compares the actual, post-transfer position of the creditor with the position it would have been in if there had been no transfer and the claim had been dealt with under Chapter 7. Note that treatment in a hypothetical Chapter 7 is always the base line for improvement in position, even if the actual bankruptcy is under one of the other chapters. If the creditor, as a result of the transfer, is in a better position than it would have been in under Chapter 7, the requirement is met.[86]

For example, suppose that Clara holds a general unsecured claim in the amount of $500. During the preference period, Clara received a $100 payment on that claim, reducing it to $400. Suppose further that Clara would have received 6% of her $500 claim ($30) if her debtor had gone into Chapter 7 and no transfer had been made. The transfer enabled her to receive more than the $30 she would have got in the debtor's hypothetical Chapter 7 case. She has already received $100 and still has a $400 claim against the debtor. If the debtor is in an actual Chapter 7 proceeding, Clara will still receive about 6% on her remaining claim ($24 on her $400 claim); thus, the transfer has enabled her to receive $124 instead of $30. Her position has thus been improved by the transfer. Even if Clara had received only a $30 transfer during the preference period, she still would have improved her position; she would have not only the $30 she would have received in Chapter 7, but also her remaining $470 claim, for which she would receive about $28.20 in the bankruptcy.

The requirement that the transfer enable the creditor to improve its position is nearly always met if the debt is unsecured and the debtor is insolvent. Almost by definition, any payment on an unsecured debt by an insolvent debtor improves the creditor's position, because the debtor doesn't have enough to pay all creditors in full.

The only significant exception to this general rule is payment on a priority unsecured debt. If there would have been enough money in a Chapter 7 proceeding to pay in full all debts with the same priority, then there is no preference. For example, suppose that during the preference period the debtor paid $500 in back wages to one of its employees. Suppose further that these wages would have been entitled to priority under the rules of § 507(a)(4)[87] and that in a hypothetical Chapter 7 liquidation of the debtor, there would have been enough money to pay all of the priority wage claims, even though general non-priority claims would not have

---

[85] *See* § 10.01 Meaning of Claims and Interests, *supra.*

[86] Bankruptcy Code § 547(b)(5); Rafael I. Pardo, *On Proof of Preferential Effect*, 55 Ala. L. Rev. 281 (2003).

[87] Bankruptcy Code § 507(a)(4); *see* § 10.04[A][4] Wage Claims, *supra.*

been paid in full. As a result, there is no preference, because the claim would have been paid in full in the bankruptcy case, even if it had not been paid in advance.

By contrast with payments on unsecured claims, payments on secured claims are frequently protected against preference avoidance precisely because of the improvement in position rule. Broadly speaking, secured claims have the highest priority in the bankruptcy distribution structure. In Chapter 7 (and indeed in every Chapter) secured claims must almost always be paid in full.[88] Thus, payments on *fully* secured claims during the preference period do not improve the creditor's position and are not preferences.[89]

Consider, for example a creditor with a $50,000 claim, secured by $60,000 of collateral. If the debtor makes no payments, the creditor will receive $50,000 in the debtor's Chapter 7 liquidation case, because of its right to foreclose on the debtor's collateral. If the debtor makes a $20,000 payment, reducing the debt to only $30,000, the creditor will receive an additional $30,000 in the debtor's liquidation, for a total recovery of $50,000 — the same amount it would have received if the payment had not been made. Thus, because the $20,000 payment does not result in the creditor receiving more than it would have received if the payment had not been made, it is not an avoidable preference.

On the other hand, if the debt is only partially secured, the Bankruptcy Code treats that obligation as generating two claims: a secured claim and an unsecured claim.[90] The secured claim is equal to the value of the collateral. The unsecured claim is equal to the excess of the obligation over the value of the collateral. If there is $80,000 of collateral securing a $100,000 debt, the creditor has an $80,000 secured claim and a $20,000 unsecured claim.

This creates a preference problem for payments on an undersecured debt. To the extent the payment is credited to the unsecured claim, the creditor's position improves. To the extent the payment is credited to the secured portion of the claim, there is no improvement in the creditor's position. Generally, courts treat payments on undersecured obligations as applying first to the unsecured claim. In the example given ($80,000 collateral and $100,000 debt), if $15,000 in payments were made during the preference period, all of the payments would be credited to the unsecured claim, reducing it to only $5,000. Thus, the creditor's position is improved and the $15,000 payment is an avoidable preference.[91] If $30,000 in payments were made, only the first $20,000 would be subject to avoidance; the remainder would be payments on the secured claim, and would not improve the creditor's position.

---

[88] *See* § 10.03 Secured Claims, *supra.*

[89] *E.g.*, In re Smith's Home Furnishings, Inc., 265 F.3d 959, 964 (9th Cir. 2001).

[90] Bankruptcy Code § 506(a). For a fuller discussion of the Bankruptcy Code's treatment of undersecured obligations, see § 10.03 Secured Claims, *supra.*

[91] In re El Paso Refinery, 171 F.3d 249 (5th Cir. 1999). If the creditor were to release an equivalent value of collateral, the payment on the unsecured portion of the debt would not be avoidable. Michael A. Bloom, Richard D. Gorelick & Heather A. MacKenzie, *Exceptions to Bankruptcy Preferences: Countryman Updated*, 47 Bus. Law. 529 (1992); Vern Countryman, *The Concept of a Voidable Preference in Bankruptcy*, 38 Vand. L. Rev. 713, 744 (1985). *See also* Bankruptcy Code § 547(c)(1).

§ 15.03 EXCEPTIONS TO AVOIDANCE

Not all transfers that satisfy the elements of § 547(b) are actually avoided. Sometimes the trustee or debtor-in-possession will not bother to attempt recovery of the preference, because the amount is too small to warrant the costs of recovery. Of greater significance for the lawyer, however, are the statutory exceptions set out in § 547(c). It immunizes certain transactions from avoidance even though those transaction meet all of the requirements for avoidance in § 547(b).

The overarching goal of most of the exceptions is to seek to distinguish "ordinary" repayment of debt, from payments that constitute part of the race of diligence — the race of creditors to dismember an insolvent debtor. As such, the so-called "contemporaneous exchange," "ordinary course," "purchase money," "subsequent advance" and "floating lien" exceptions all seek to distinguish transfers where the creditor is simply "doing business" with an insolvent debtor from those where the creditor (or the debtor) is engaging in "opt out" behavior — seeking to give a particular creditor a better distribution than the Code would otherwise allow. Finally, several of the exceptions overlap; some parts of a transaction may fit into one exception while other parts fit into another exception. Also note that the § 547(c) exceptions only affect the trustee's power to avoid a transfer under § 547. If the transfer runs afoul of another avoidance power, such as the power to avoid fraudulent transfers, § 547(c) will not preserve it.

[A] Substantially Contemporaneous Exchange for New Value

The first exception, in § 547(c)(1), protects transfers to the extent they were intended by the debtor and the creditor to be a contemporaneous exchange for new value and were in fact substantially contemporaneous.[92] Most of the litigation has concerned two issues: (1) the scope of the exception, and (2) whether a particular exchange is "substantially contemporaneous."

The legislative history of § 547(c)(1) indicates that Congress had in mind the technical preference problem created when the debtor pays a bill by check. Payment by check is not complete until the check is paid by the bank on which it is drawn. Thus, payment is not strictly contemporaneous with the creation of the debt.

Suppose, for example, that Equipment Manufacturing Co. purchases equipment from Industrial Supply Inc., on January 1, and gives Industrial a check to pay for the items at the same time. Industrial deposits the check on January 2, but it is not paid by Equipment Manufacturing's bank until January 4. Technically, the payment was made on January 4, and was consequently on account of a debt created earlier, on January 1 — an antecedent debt. But, this transaction was intended to be contemporaneous and, provided that the check clears in a routine way, it is almost or "substantially" contemporaneous. Accordingly, it fits within § 547(b), but it is not avoidable.[93]

---

[92] Bankruptcy Code § 547(c)(1).

[93] H.R. Rep. No. 95-595, 373 (1977); S. Rep. No. 95-989, 88 (1978).

If the check was post-dated to January 15, it would be clear that the parties had not intended a the transfer to be contemporaneous; rather, they have intended payment to be delayed, in a credit transaction, for 14 days. Thus, payment via a post-dated check would not fall within the statutory exception. Similarly, if the seller failed to deposit the check within a reasonable period of time, it would not be a substantially contemporaneous exchange.[94] Finally, if the check bounces, it is not a substantially contemporaneous exchange, even if the check clears when it is submitted a second time.[95] There is nothing in the language of § 547(c)(1) that limits the exception to payments by check, and it has certainly been used to protect things other than check payments.[96]

The other major interpretive difficulty is created by the phrase "substantially contemporaneous." The legislative history suggests that a time lapse of thirty days or more between the debt and the payment might still be substantially contemporaneous.[97] Although courts say that the standard is a flexible one,[98] they have not always been so generous.[99] Probably the best rule of thumb is that a transfer is substantially contemporaneous if the time lag is caused by the normal processing of documents necessary to complete the transfer.

Courts have taken different approaches to the meaning of "substantially contemporaneous." Some courts have concluded that security interests that are perfected beyond the 30-day time period specified in §§ 547(e)(2)(A) and (B)[100] cannot be substantially contemporaneous.[101] As explained in more detail elsewhere,[102] these sections provide that a security interest or other transfer that is perfected within 30 days of the time it becomes effective between the transferor and transferee ("attachment" in security interest lingo), are deemed to have been made at the time they were effective between those parties rather than at the time they were perfected. Courts that draw a sharp line for what qualifies as "substantially contemporaneous" explain that permitting the time period to last longer than the 30 days of § 547(e)(2) would render that provision superfluous.

---

[94] Michael J. Herbert, *The Trustee versus the Trade Creditor: A Critique of Section 547(c)(1), (2) & (4) of the Bankruptcy Code*, 17 U. Rich. L. Rev. 667, 673 n.23 (1983).

[95] Goger v. Cudahy Foods Co. (In re Standard Food Servs., Inc.), 723 F.2d 820 (11th Cir. 1984).

[96] *See, e.g.*, Drabkin v. A.I. Credit Corp., 800 F.2d 1153 (D.C. Cir. 1986) (holding that release of security interest can constitute substantially contemporaneous exchange for new value under § 547(c)(1) exception).

[97] Michael J. Herbert, *The Trustee versus the Trade Creditor: A Critique of Section 547(c)(1), (2) & (4) of the Bankruptcy Code*, 17 U. Rich. L. Rev. 667, 673 n.23 (1983).

[98] Rouse v. Univ. Nat'l Bank, 434 B.R. 875 (Bankr. W.D. Mo. 2010).

[99] *See* In re JWJ Contr., Co., 371 F.3d 1079 (9th Cir. 2004) (eighteen days too long); In re Maracle, 159 Fed. Appx. 692 (6th Cir. 2005) (fourty-two days too long); In re Coco, 67 B.R. 365 (S.D.N.Y. 1986) (seven days not too long; thirty-four days too long); In re Arctic Air Conditioning, Inc., 35 B.R. 107 (Bankr. E.D. Tenn. 1983) (thirty days too long); *Cf.* In re Quade, 108 B.R. 681 (Bankr. N.D. Iowa 1989) (six days not too long).

[100] Before 2005, § 547(e)(2)(B)'s time period was only 10 days. BAPCPA extended the period to 30 days.

[101] In re Arnett, 731 F.2d 358 (6th Cir. 1984).

[102] *See* § 15.02[A] Transfer of Property; Date of Transfer, *supra.*

Other courts reject this reasoning. They conclude that the modifier "substantial" suggests a more flexible approach that necessitates a case-by-case inquiry into all of the surrounding circumstances.[103] They point to § 547(c)(3)'s rigid thirty-day grace period for the perfection of purchase money security interests[104] as evidence that Congress knew how to implement a rigid time period when it wanted to impose one.[105] They also reject the contention that this flexible approach makes the time period in § 547(e)(2) mere surplusage. They explain that § 547(e)(2) determines whether a transfer has occurred within the 90-day or one-year preference period of § 547(b)(4), and thus serves an essential purpose regardless of whether it's 30-day period is read into the substantially contemporaneous exchange exception of § 547(c)(1).[106]

Creditors sometimes attempt to push the limits of § 547(c)(1). In *United States Rentals Inc. v. Angell*,[107] the trustee sought to recover three payments, totaling approximately $76,000, that the debtor — a subcontractor — made to one of its equipment suppliers for equipment it had rented for several projects. The supplier defended by claiming that the debtor had received "new value" as part of a contemporaneous exchange, because of funds that the debtor subsequently received from the general contractor, on account of the sums paid to the equipment lessor. These funds represented amounts that the debtor's surety eventually would have received from the general contractors on the projects if the surety had paid the creditor on a bond claim. The Fourth Circuit refused to regard this as "new value" within the meaning of § 547(a)(2).

However, the exception is sometimes applied in unexpected ways. In *In re McCaskill*,[108] the debtors borrowed $131,500 from University National Bank and granted the bank a security interest in some of their property, including their 2007 Chevy Suburban. Several months later, they modified their loan agreement and substituted their 2006 BMW X3 for the 2007 Chevy Suburban, as collateral for the loan. Approximately six weeks thereafter, they traded their BMW X3 for a BMW 330 Xi,[109] and four days later, on September 19, 2009, executed another loan modification agreement, this time substituting the 330 Xi for the X3, as collateral for the loan. A little over a month later, on October 23, 2009, they filed their release of the lien on the X3 and perfected their substitute security interest on the 330 Xi. Less than 90 days later they filed their Chapter 7 Bankruptcy petition.

Because the lien on the X3 was released from the lien on September 19, when the bank signed the release and modification agreement, and the lien on the 330 Xi was not perfected until more than 30 days later, the transfer of the security

---

[103] In re Durholt, 224 F.3d 871 (8th Cir. 2000); Pine Top Ins. Co. v. Bank of Am. Nat'l Trust & Sav. Ass'n, 969 F.2d 321, 329-29 (7th Cir. 1992).

[104] *See* § 15.03[C] Grace Period for Late Perfection of Purchase Money Security Interests, *supra*. Before 2005, § 547(c)(3)'s grace period was only 20 days. BAPCPA increased it to 30 days.

[105] In re Durholt, 224 F.3d 871, 874 (8th Cir. 2000).

[106] *Id.*

[107] 592 F.3d 525 (4th Cir. 2010).

[108] Rouse v. Univ. Nat'l Bank (In re McCaskill), 434 B.R. 875 (Bankr. W.D. Mo. 2010).

[109] Don't buy one of these cars unless you want to spend $400 every couple of years replacing the window regulators — even if you hardly ever use your power windows.

interest in the 330 Xi did not occur until it was perfected. Thus, the security interest in the replacement collateral enabled the bank to receive more than it otherwise would have received, and satisfied the other elements of § 547(b). However, the bankruptcy judge determined that the parties had intended the transaction to be a contemporaneous exchange, substituting one car for the other as collateral for the loan, and that, despite the delay, the transaction was "substantially contemporaneous" within the meaning of § 547(c)(1). Thus, the security interest in the substitute collateral was protected from avoidance by the trustee.

[B] Ordinary Course of Business Transfers

The second exception is for certain transactions that are in the ordinary course of business for the debtor and the transferee. Specifically, a transfer is not avoidable to the extent that it meets the following requirements:[110]

- The debt was incurred in the ordinary course of business or financial affairs of the debtor and the transferee;[111] and either

- The transfer was made in the ordinary course of business or financial affairs of the debtor and the transferee; or[112]

- The transfer was made according to ordinary business terms.[113]

The purpose of this exception is to encourage normal credit transactions, in the hope that their facilitation will help financially distressed debtors avoid the need to file a bankruptcy in the first place.[114] Since it was originally adopted, in 1978, its scope has gradually been expanded. Initially, the defense applied only to debts that were incurred within forty-five days of the date of the payment. The 1984 amendments eliminated the forty-five day limit, but courts were divided over whether the defense applied only to short term trade debt. Until 1991, it was unclear whether this exception could apply to scheduled payments on long term obligations. Courts were split between the plain language of the text on the one hand, and policy arguments, linked to the legislative history and the purpose of preference law, on the other.[115] In *Union Bank v. Wolas*,[116] the Supreme Court

---

[110] Before 2005 there were three requirements, (1) that the debt be incurred in the ordinary course, (2) that the debt be paid in the ordinary course, and (3) that the transfer be made according to ordinary business terms. Prior to the 1984 Amendments, there was a fourth requirement that the transfer be made within forty-five days after the debt was incurred. Howard N. Gorney, *The Ordinary Course Defense to a Preference Payment: A Trade Creditor's Impossible Dream*, 21 Emory Bankr. Dev. J. 183 (2004).

[111] *See* Carrier Corp. v. Buckley (In re Globe Mfg., Corp.), 567 F.3d 1291 (11th Cir. 2009) (absence of prior course of dealing with each other sufficient to establish the routine nature of the late payments not sufficient to establish ordinary course defense).

[112] Bankruptcy Code § 547(c)(2)(A). *See* Carrier Corp. v. Buckley (In re Global Mfg. Corp.), 567 F.3d 1291 (11th Cir. 2009).

[113] Bankruptcy Code § 547(c)(2)(B).

[114] Carrier Corp. v. Buckley (In re Global Mfg. Corp.), 567 F.3d 1291, 1297 (11th Cir. 2009).

[115] A. Ari Afilalo, *The Impact Of Union Bank v. Wolas On The Ordinary Course Of Business Defense To A Trustee's Avoiding Powers*, 72 B.U. L. Rev. 625 (1992). For an extended critique of the issue, see

ruled in favor of the plain language of the statutory text and held that payments of long term debt could be protected by the ordinary course exception. This rule has, to say the least, been controversial. In the view of some, it profoundly undercuts the whole purpose of preference law.[117] In the view of others, it enhances the willingness of creditors to continue to deal with their borrowers in the ordinary course, even though bankruptcy may be in the offing.

Section 547(c)(2) involves a two-stage analysis that focuses first on the making of the loan, and then on the payment. Both stages must have been in the ordinary course for the exception to apply.

In most cases, the focus of attention is on whether the payments were made in the ordinary course. The 2005 amendments made it clear that a payment was in the ordinary course if it was either in accordance with general practice in the industry or in accordance with the prior course of conduct between the parties.[118] Even for quite long time lags between the date payment was due and the time payment was received, the transfer is in the ordinary course if it was consistent with an established practice between the parties.[119] Sporadic and irregular payments may indeed be ordinary course if they are consistent with the parties' mode of dealing.[120] As one court explained:

> It may seem odd that paying a debt late would ever be regarded as a preference to the creditor thus paid belatedly. But it is all relative. A debtor who has entered the preference period — who is therefore only 90 days, or fewer, away from plunging into bankruptcy — is typically unable to pay all his outstanding debts in full as they come due. If he pays one and not the others . . . the payment though late is still a preference to that creditor . . . The purpose of the preference statute is to prevent the debtor during his slide toward bankruptcy from trying to stave off the evil day by giving preferential treatment to his most importunate creditors, who may sometimes be those who have been waiting longest to be paid.[121]

The creditor's actions are also potentially significant. If the creditor put pressure on the debtor to make payments, most courts say the payments are not in ordinary

---

Lissa L. Broome, *Payments on Long-Term Debt as Voidable Preferences: The Impact of the 1984 Bankruptcy Amendments*, 1987 Duke L.J. 78; *see also* Michael J. Herbert, *The Trustee versus the Trade Creditor II: The 1984 Amendment to Section 547(c)(2) of the Bankruptcy Code*, 2 Bankr. Dev. J. 201 (1985).

[116] 502 U.S. 151 (1991).

[117] *See* Charles Jordan Tabb, *Rethinking Preferences*, 43 S.C. L. Rev. 981 (1992).

[118] Carrier Corp. v. Buckley (In re Global Mfg. Corp.), 567 F.3d 1291, 1298 n.4 (11th Cir. 2009).

[119] In re Gardner Matthews Plantation Co., 118 B.R. 384 (Bankr. S.C. 1989) (payments protected under ordinary course of business exception even though time lag between delivery and payment ranged from 108 to 191 days).

[120] In re National Office Products, Inc., 119 B.R. 896 (D.R.I. 1990).

[121] In re Tolona Pizza Prods. Corp., 3 F.3d 1029, 1032 (7th Cir. 1993) (Posner, J.). *See also* In re Issac Leaseco, 389 F.3d at 1212 ("A creditor who tolerates unusual delays in payment from a debtor on the verge of bankruptcy may be dependent on the debtor and aiding the debtor in forestalling the inevitable to the detriment of less dependent creditors.").

course.[122]

Ordinary course payments only qualify for the exception if they were for a debt that was incurred in the "ordinary course of business or financial affairs *of the debtor and the transferee.*"[123] If the initiation of the debt was outside the ordinary course, the exception does not apply regardless of how routine the stream of payments had become. For example, in *In re Gawronski*,[124] the debtor made consistent monthly payments of $431.57 to her brother-in-law in repayment of loan he had made. However, because the brother-in-law's loan was far outside the ordinary course of the family transactions that had previously taken place between the parties, the regular loan payments did not qualify for protection from avoidance. Even though the payments were in the ordinary course, they were recoverable by the trustee because the inception of the loan was not in the ordinary course of the parties' business or financial affairs. Similarly, where the loan to the debtor was made in furtherance of a debtor's fraudulent scheme, payments made on the debt, however regular, are not protected by the ordinary course exception to the preference power.[125]

On the other hand, in *Stevenson v. Turowski & Son Funderal Homes, Inc. (In re Nowlen)*,[126] a widow's payments to a funeral home, after she had received proceeds from her deceased husband's life insurance policy, were compatible with ordinary business terms in the funeral home industry, and in the ordinary course of the debtor's financial affairs, and protected from avoidance.

[C] Grace Period for Late Perfection of Purchase Money Interests

Section 547(c)(3) protects from preference avoidance certain purchase money security interests that were not perfected in a timely fashion.[127] This exception is exceedingly narrow in scope and has been almost indistinguishable from the grace period for perfection provided by § 547(e). It applies only to certain security interests that are given to enable the debtor to acquire the property that is used to secure the debt, and that are in fact so used. A typical example is a security interest in a car given to secure a loan made to acquire the car. Further, to qualify for protection under this exception, the security interest must be perfected within thirty days after the debtor receives possession of the property.

---

[122] Xtra, Inc. v. Seawinds, Ltd. (In re Seawinds), 888 F.2d 640 (9th Cir. 1989); Marathon Oil Co. v. Flatau (In re Craig Oil), 785 F.2d 1563 (11th Cir. 1986) (whenever the debtor's "normal" payments are the result of unusual collection activity by the creditor, the exception does not apply); In re Accessair, Inc., 314 B.R. 386 (B.A.P. 8th Cir. 2004).

[123] Bankruptcy Code § 547(c)(2) (emphasis supplied).

[124] Schlant v. Bartolucci (In re Gawronski), 411 B.R. 139 (Bankr. W.D.N.Y. 2009).

[125] *E.g.*, Computer World Solution, Inc. v. Apple Fund, L.P. (In re Computer World Solution, Inc.), 427 B.R. 680 (Bankr. N.D. Ill. 2010).

[126] 452 B.R. 619 (Bankr. E.D. Mich. 2011).

[127] Bankruptcy Code § 547(c)(3). Note that this provision applies to interests in both real estate and personalty; the term "security interest" is defined as any "lien created by agreement." Bankruptcy Code § 101(51).

In most cases in which the § 547(c)(3) exception applies, the § 547(e)(2)(B) grace period also applies, and there is thus no preference in the first place.[128] However, the grace period given under the two provisions differs in three respects, two slight and one significant. The grace period under § 547(e)(2)(B) runs from the time the transfer is effective between the parties (attachment) to the time it is perfected; the § 547(c)(3) grace period runs from the time of debtor's possession until the time it is perfected. In addition, the § 547(e)(2)(B) grace period merely establishes the date of the transfer, while the § 547(c)(3) exception protects the transfer regardless of its date. This is occasionally important if the debt was incurred prior to the date that the debtor obtained possession.

Suppose that on January 1, the debtor enters into a contract to purchase a farm tractor and incurs an obligation to pay for it. The purchase is on credit; the seller retains a security interest in the tractor to secure payment of the price. The tractor is delivered on January 5, and the financing statement is filed on January 7. Under § 547(e)(2)(b), the transfer of the security interest in the tractor occurred on January 5, because under Article 9 the transfer became effective between the parties on January 5 when the debtor acquired rights in the collateral, and was perfected within thirty days thereafter. This, however, does not cure the creditor's preference problem; the obligation was incurred on January 1, so the transfer of the security interest on January 5 was a transfer on account of an antecedent debt. However, the transfer is protected from avoidance under § 547(c)(3). The extension of credit enabled to debtor to acquire the tractor and was perfected within thirty days after the debtor received possession of the tractor. The exception in effect excuses the delay between the creation of the debt and the transfer of the security interest.

Before the 2005 Amendments, the grace period under 547(e) was ten days, and the grace period under 547(c)(1) was twenty days. This difference periodically created complicated problems. The 2005 Amendments fixed this problem by extending both periods to thirty days. It should be noted that Article 9 of the U.C.C. has a twenty day grace period for the perfection of purchase money security interests.[129]

[D]　Advance of New Value Subsequent to Preference

Section 547(c)(4) provides what amounts to a setoff of post-preference advances of credit against previous preferences.[130] The theory underlying the subsequent advance exception is that the transferee has "replenished" the estate by adding new value to it, and indeed that the preferential payment may in fact have been the reason that the transferee was willing to extend new credit.[131] To qualify, the advance must:

- either be unsecured, or secured by an avoidable security interest; and

---

[128] *See* § 15.02[A] Transfer of Debtor's Property; Date of Transfer, *supra.*

[129] U.C.C. § 9-324 (2003).

[130] Bankruptcy Code § 547(c)(4).

[131] Richard B. Levin, *An Introduction to the Trustee's Avoiding Powers*, 53 Am. Bankr. L.J. 173, 187 (1979).

- either be not paid by the debtor, or paid by the debtor, but the payment itself is avoidable.[132]

For example, suppose that Pushkin received a $3000 preference on January 1 and made a subsequent $2000 advance of credit to DuBois on February 1. If the February 1 advance was unsecured, and was not subsequently repaid by the debtor, the amount of the preference is reduced to $1000. If the February 1 advance was fully secured by collateral, and that security interest is not itself avoidable, then the preference is not reduced at all. If the February 1 advance was repaid, but $500 of that repayment is avoided by the trustee, then the preference is reduced to $2500.

The key thing to keep in mind about this exception is that the preference and the advance of credit must occur in a particular order: the advance must follow the preference.[133] For example, suppose that during the preference period the following transactions occurred:

January 1 Advance of $5000 by Pushkin to DuBois

February 1 Preference of $3500 paid by DuBois to Pushkin

February 15 Advance of $4000 by Pushkin to DuBois

February 20 Preference of $5500 paid by DuBois to Pushkin

The January 1 advance of new value may not be set off against either of the preferences, because it occurred before both of them. The February 15 advance of new value may be set off only against the prior preference, the February 1 preference. Thus, Pushkin still has a preference liability of $5,500. This is true even though the total of the two advances equals the total of the two preferences. The "subsequent advance rule" is sometimes erroneously referred to as the "net result rule," but the preceding example demonstrates that this is a mischaracterization. Section 547(c)(4) does not net out all transactions during the preference period but merely permits later advances of new value to reduce earlier preferences.[134]

[E] Floating Liens

Section 547(c)(5) creates an exception for certain Article 9 floating liens.[135] A floating lien is created when a security agreement creates a security interest in "after acquired property." Under such a security agreement, property floats into

---

[132] Bankruptcy Code § 547(c)(4). According to at least some courts, if the debt is paid by someone other than the debtor, and the payment has no effect on the debtor's property, the fact that the debt was paid does not preclude the application of this exception. In re Formed Tubes, Inc., 46 B.R. 645 (Bankr. E.D. Mich. 1985).

[133] In re Wingspread Corp., 120 B.R. 8 (Bankr. S.D.N.Y. 1990); In re Excel Enterprises, Inc., 83 B.R. 427 (Bankr. W.D. La. 1988).

[134] It is generally assumed that the non-statutory, pre-Code net result rule does not survive the enactment of the Code. In re Fulghum Constr. Corp., 706 F.2d 171 (6th Cir. 1983). Indeed, according to one authority, the net result rule should not have been applied after 1903, when an amendment to the Bankruptcy Act made it obsolete. Michael J. Herbert, *The Trustee versus the Trade Creditor: A Critique of Section 547(c)(1), (2) & (4) of the Bankruptcy Code*, 17 U. Rich. L. Rev. 667, 674-675 & n.29 (1983).

[135] U.C.C. § 2-204 (2003).

the creditor's lien when the debtor acquires it, and floats out again, when the debtor sells it. As such, the creditor has a security interest in a pool of collateral rather than specific items of collateral. For example, Peninsula Bank might have a security interest in all of Franklin Manufacturing Co.'s existing and after-acquired inventory and accounts receivable. As Franklin Manufacturing sells its inventory, it generates accounts receivable; as it collects its receivables it obtains cash; it uses the cash to pay Peninsula Bank, which then advances it more money to buy more inventory. The collateral is an ever-changing pool of inventory and receivables on which the security interest floats.

Prior to the 1970s, floating liens were subject to substantial preference risk, because each time the debtor obtained new collateral for the pool, a new transfer of property to the secured creditor was made. A series of cases largely eliminated the risk, holding that the transfer occurred at the time the creditor filed its financing statement.[136] The 1978 Bankruptcy Code took a different approach, taking the view that the transfer occurred when property floated into the floating line, but adding a defense under § 547(c)(5) to provide limited protection to the most common forms of the floating liens.

The floating lien exception applies to perfected security interests in inventory, receivables, and their proceeds.[137] It does not apply to floating liens on other types of collateral; but floating liens on things other than inventory or receivables are rare. Section 547(c)(5) applies what is commonly referred to as a "two point net improvement" test. A preference occurs for 547(b) purposes when property floats into the lien of an undersecured creditor. However, that transfer is insulated from avoidance if it does not result in an improvement of the creditor's position during the ninety day preference period. To the extent that the obligation secured by the floating lien is less undersecured (the lienholder's deficiency is smaller) on the date of the petition than it was at the beginning of the preference period (or on the date the lender first gave new value, if that date was later than the beginning of the preference period) there is a preference to the extent of that reduction in deficiency.[138]

For example, on July 1 Merchant's Bank had a security interest in the Reliable Motors' inventory. The obligation secured was $100,000; the inventory was worth $80,000; since Merchant's Bank was an outsider, the preference period was ninety days. Ninety days later, on September 30, Reliable Motors filed its petition. At that time, the obligation secured was $60,000 and the inventory was worth $55,000. Merchant's Bank was $20,000 undersecured at the beginning of the preference

---

[136] *See* Dubay v. Williams, 417 F.2d 1277 (9th Cir. 1969); Grain Merchants of Ind., Inc. v. Union Bank & Sav. Co., 408 F.2d 209 (7th Cir. 1969); In re Gibson Products of Arizona, 543 F.2d 652 (9th Cir. 1976); Richard F. Duncan, *Preferential Transfers, The Floating Lien, and Section 547(c)(5) of the Bankruptcy Reform Act of 1978*, 36 Ark. L. Rev. 1 (1982); Jeffrey T. Ferriell, Note, *Bankruptcy — Voidable Preferences — Uniform Commercial Code Section 9-306(4)(d) Operates as a Voidable Preference*, In re Gibson Products of Arizona, 17 Santa Clara L. Rev. 967 (1977) (the beginning of a lifelong interest in bankruptcy law).

[137] Bankruptcy Code § 547(c)(5).

[138] Bankruptcy Code § 547(c)(5)(A).

period and $5,000 undersecured at the time of filing the petition. Merchant's Bank must repay $15,000 to the estate.

There are several things to note about this exception. First, it is a true net result rule; the court does not look at the individual transactions that occurred during the preference period, but only the net result.[139] In the example given, there may have been a dozen or more payments by Reliable Motors and advances of credit by Merchant's Bank; these are all ignored. The court merely snapshots the beginning and the end of the ninety day or (in the case of an insider) one year period.

Second, the key to the provision is the value of the collateral on the two snapshot dates. As elsewhere under the Code, valuation can be a tricky business. It might make sense to use wholesale value, retail value, liquidation value, or going concern value. The cases indicate that value should be pegged to the actual situation of the debtor.[140] Thus, if the debtor is a wholesaler in liquidation, a liquidation wholesale value is appropriate. If, by contrast, the debtor is a retailer with a reasonable chance of reorganization, a going concern retail value would normally be appropriate.

Third, it is reasonably clear that if the creditor was fully secured or over secured at the beginning of the preference period, it does not matter at all what the creditor's position was at the end.[141] The exception, by its terms, preserves the lien to the extent it does not reduce a deficiency. If there is no deficiency to start with, there is no avoidance. Thus, a fully secured creditor who becomes even more secured apparently retains all of its collateral.[142]

Fourth, the rule deals with increases of value that relate to transfers made during the preference period. An increase in value due solely to an increase in market price does not raise a preference issue, let alone the application of the floating lien exception because there has been no transfer.[143] For example, if Finance Bank has a floating lien on an inventory of 100 $20 U.S. "Double Eagle" gold coins, and the market value of those 100 coins rises from $675 each to $750 each during the preference period, that $7,500 increase in value is not a preference. No new property was acquired; no transfer occurred; thus neither § 547(b) nor § 547(c)(5) apply. It is clear, however, that if any measurable part of the increase in value was due to new property incorporated into the inventory, there has been a transfer and thus may be a preference. For example, suppose the inventory became more valuable because it was completed by the addition of parts that were not previously inventory. The necessary transfer would occur; if the other

---

[139] *See* Matter of Missionary Baptist Foundation of America, Inc., 796 F.2d 752, 760 & n.11 (5th Cir. 1987) (two-point test); In re Parker Steel Co., 149 B.R. 834, 848 (Bankr. N.D. Ohio 1992) (intervening fluctuations are ignored).

[140] In re Ebbler Furniture and Appliances, Inc., 804 F.2d 87 (7th Cir. 1986); In re Lackow Brothers, Inc., 752 F.2d 1529 (11th Cir. 1985).

[141] In re Southwest Equip. Rental, Inc., 137 B.R. 263 (Bankr. E.D. Tenn. 1992).

[142] This appears to be so even though there is a potential betterment in position; the more oversecured a creditor is, the more interest it can potentially obtain on the debt during the pendency period.

[143] *See, e.g.*, In re Nivens, 22 B.R. 287 (Bankr. N.D. Tex. 1982).

requirements of §§ 547(b) and (c)(5) were met, the transfer would be voidable.[144]

[F] Statutory Liens

The sixth exception protects statutory liens, such as mechanic's liens and repair liens, that are not avoidable under § 545.[145] As discussed elsewhere, there are a variety of liens created by state and federal laws that give the lienholder the right to claim property as security for an unpaid obligation.[146] If the lien is triggered by the obligor's insolvency or bankruptcy, is unprotected from bona fide purchasers of the property, or is related to a rental obligation, the lien is avoided.[147] The § 547(c)(6) exception applies to those liens that are *not* avoidable under § 545 and protects them from avoidance under § 547.

A simple illustration: On February 1, Darcy takes her car to Garibaldi for repairs. The repairs are performed that day, giving rise to Darcy's obligation to pay Garibaldi, and Garibaldi gives Darcy an itemized bill. Under local state law, Garibaldi is given a lien on the car if Darcy does not pay within three days of being given an itemized bill, and this lien is good against a bona fide purchaser.[148] Darcy fails to pay, so the lien "fixes" on February 4. A few days later, Darcy goes into bankruptcy. Since the lien attached to the car several days after the debt was incurred, there was a transfer on an antecedent debt and most likely a § 547(b) preference. However, since Garibaldi's lien is not avoidable under § 545, it is not avoidable under § 547 either.

[G] Alimony, Maintenance, Support

To the extent that a preference is a payment of a "domestic support" obligation, it is not avoidable. The term domestic support obligation is defined in § 101(14A) of the Bankruptcy Code.[149] The debt must be owed to a "spouse, former spouse, child of the debtor . . . or a governmental unit." The debt must be embodied in a separation agreement, divorce decree, property settlement agreement, court order, or other administrative order, and must be in the nature of alimony, maintenance or support, regardless of whether it was designated as such. This definition is similar to that contained in former § 547(c)(7) except for the addition of payments of child support to a governmental unit.

---

[144] It is less clear whether this is true if the increase in value was due to the debtor's labor rather than the addition of new property. The increase in value due to labor is not an increase that merely relates to market fluctuation; however, it is not a transfer of property, either.

[145] Bankruptcy Code § 547(c)(6); John C. McCoid, II, *Statutory Liens in Bankruptcy*, 68 Am. Bankr. L.J. 269 (1994); *see* § 14.04 Avoidance of Statutory Liens, *supra.*

[146] *See* § 2.05 Statutory, Common Law, and Equitable Liens, *supra.*

[147] Bankruptcy Code § 545.

[148] *See* § 2.06[B] Repair or "Artisan's" Liens, *supra*

[149] *See* § 13.03[B][5][a] Domestic Support Obligations, *supra.*

[H]   Small Preferences[150]

Section 547(c)(8) provides a limited exception for relatively small payments made by debtors. If the debtor is an individual whose debts are primarily consumer debts, then the § applies to transfers aggregating less than $600 to a particular creditor.[151] If the debtor's debts are not primarily consumer debts, then § 547(c)(9) applies to protect transfers aggregating less than $5850.[152] The usual reason given for this exception is that such small transfers have little effect on the actual distribution of the estate and are often unduly expensive to recover.

There is considerable ambiguity in the wording of the exception. Two difficulties stand out. First, if there is a transfer of $600 or more ($5850 or more for a non-consumer debtor), the exception is unclear as to whether the transferee may keep $599.99 or must return the entire amount. The case law suggests that the provisions are not a safe-harbor for the first $599.99 or $5849.99, but that rather the entire transfer is avoidable if the threshold is passed.[153] This is consistent with the policy behind the provision, which prevents pursuit of small-in-value preferences, where the litigation costs to pursue or defend against trustee avoidance actions does not justify the benefit to the prevailing party. If the amount were a safe-harbor, that protected the first 599.99 or $5849.99, the practical effect of the provision would be expanded, because trustees would be reluctant to pursue $600 preferences to recover only 1¢, though it might make sense to pursue such a transfer to recover the entire $600.[154]

Second, the statute oddly links the phrases "aggregate value" and "such transfer." The aggregate value language might require aggregation of all transfers made to the same creditor on the same debt to determine whether the transfers have exceeded $600 limit; or the phrase "such transfer" might mean that only the amounts of property transferred at the same time should be aggregated. For example, suppose that a consumer debtor paid $500 on the first of each month on the same unsecured debt during the preference period. If the three payments are aggregated, the $600 ceiling is breached and the entire $1500 must be repaid. If each is viewed separately, all three are within the ceiling and are protected. The very few cases that are squarely on point have supported the view that payments to the same creditor within the preference period are to be aggregated; if together they exceed the statutory threshold for the exception, all are avoidable.[155]

---

[150] Paul Giorgianni, Note, *The Small Preference Exception of Bankruptcy Code Section 547(c)(7)*, 55 Ohio St. L.J. 675 (1994).

[151] Nelson v. E.R. Group (In re Nelson), 419 B.R. 338 (Bankr. W.D. Ky. 2009).

[152] Bankruptcy Code § 547(c)(8). The amount in § 547(c)(9) is among those that are adjusted every three years to reflect changes in the Consumer Price Index. Bankruptcy Code § 104(b)(1). They were last adjusted on April 1, 2010 and are set to change again on April 1, 2013, 2016, and 2019. However, the $600 figure in § 547(c)(8) does not automatically fluctuate in this manner.

[153] *See* In re Bay Area Glass, Inc., 454 B.R. 86 (B.A.P. 9th Cir. 2011).

[154] *See also* Christians v. Am. Express Travel Related Servs. (In re Djerf), 188 B.R. 586, 588 (Bankr. D. Minn. 1995); Ray v. Cannon's, Inc. (In re Vickery), 63 B.R. 222, 223 (Bankr. E.D. Tenn. 1986).

[155] Young v. Dantone (In re Transcon. Refrig'd Lines, Inc.), 438 B.R. 520 (Bankr. M.D. Pa. 2010); Electric City Merchandise Co. v. Hailes (In re Hailes), 77 F.3d 873 (5th Cir. 1996).

While it might be better policy to aggregate all of the payments, the statutory language seems clear that only payments made at the same time as part of the same transfer should be aggregated. If this is the correct reading, then, in the example given, all three payments should be protected. By contrast, if the debtor had made two of the $500 payments at the same time (for example, by simultaneously giving the creditor $500 in cash and a security interest in $500 of collateral) they should be aggregated.

[I] Payments Sanctioned by Credit Counseling Agency

The 2005 Amendments added an exception to the trustee's preference power, but hid it apart from other exceptions, in new § 547(h). The trustee may not avoid a transfer if it was made "as part of an alternative repayment schedule between the debtor and any creditor of the debtor created by an approved nonprofit budget and credit counseling agency."[156] This new exception may lead savvy creditors to encourage debtors to seek credit counseling and to enter into an approved repayment schedule as a means of attempting to insulate payments they receive from recovery by the trustee.

[J] Substitution of Creditors — Earmarking[157]

A final exception to the preference rules is not explicitly mentioned in the Code. Rather, it has been carved out by case law, both before and after enactment of the current Bankruptcy Code. Although it finds support in the text and policies of § 547(b), it is unclear whether it would find favor in the Supreme Court, particularly given the Court's insistence on adherence to the plain language of the Code and the absence of any express reference to it in the "exceptions" in § 547(c).

The exception relates to what are often referred to as "earmarked" loans — that is, loans earmarked for the repayment of a pre-existing debt. Suppose, for example, that Doreen owes State Bank $100,000. During the last ninety days before filing her bankruptcy petition, she refinances this loan by borrowing $100,000 from Merchant's Finance Co., with the specific purpose, agreed to by all, of repaying the debt to State Bank. She is, of course, insolvent at the time, and the payment to State Bank results in it receiving more than it otherwise would have received in bankruptcy.

On the face of it, the bank has received a preference. However, a long line of cases has ruled otherwise. The rationale is that there has been no diminution of the estate — the financial situation of Doreen, the liquidation shares of its creditors, are exactly the same as they were before the transaction.[158] All that has changed is the identity of one of those creditors: Merchant's Finance is now a creditor, State Bank is not. Courts have generally tried to fit this rationale into the structure of the preference rule by saying that the proceeds of the second loan never really

---

[156] Bankruptcy Code § 547(h).

[157] David Gray Carlson & William H. Widen, *The Earmarking Defense to Voidable Preference Liability: A Reconceptualization*, 73 Am. Bankr. L.J. 591, 648 (1999).

[158] Chase Manhattan Mortgage Corp. v. Shapiro (In re Lee), 530 F.3d 458, 464 (6th Cir. 2008).

became part of the debtor's assets; thus, there was no transfer by the debtor. Since a transfer by the debtor is an element of a preference, there is no preference.[159]

The reasoning is somewhat disingenuous. The rule applies not only where the payment is made directly by the new creditor to the old but also where the payment is made through the borrower. In the former situation, it is at least plausible to argue that the borrower never "owned" the money newly lent; in the latter it is not. However, in the latter situation, there must be a specific agreement that the new loan be for repayment of the old; where the payment is made directly, no such specific agreement is required.[160]

The earmarking defense is most likely to be available when the transfer is from one unsecured creditor to another, or from one fully secured creditor to another. When the refinancing changes the status of the debt from unsecured status to secured, the earmarking defense is not available.[161]

The earmarking defense is sometimes asserted when a debtor transfers a balance on one credit card to another credit card. Although this merely substitutes one creditor for another, the transaction is subject to attack as a preference to the creditor who benefitted from the transaction. The earmarking doctrine only protects the creditor if the lender, rather than the debtor, decides which creditor will receive the proceeds of the loan.[162] It does not protect the creditor who received payment if the debtor had control over the funds that were used to make the payment.[163] The same result occurs when the debtor uses "convenience checks" to transfer a credit card balance from one lender to another.[164] Avoidance not only enhances the debtor's estate, it advances the preference policy of promoting creditor equality by discouraging creditors' efforts to dismember financially troubled debtors.[165]

[K] Certain Payments by Repo, Swap, or Financial Participants

Sections 546(e)-(g) provides additional protection for certain payments by Repo Participants, Swap Participants, or Financial Participants in complex financial transactions. These safe harbor provisions are designed to ensure the stability of the derivatives and financial contracts markets.[166] They are designed to balance the competing polices of the Bankruptcy Code and the nation's securities laws by minimizing any displacement that might be "caused in commodities and securities

---

[159] *See, e.g.,* Grubb v. General Contract Purchase Corp, 18 F. Supp. 680 (S.D.N.Y. 1937), *aff'd,* 94 F.2d 70 (2d Cir. 1938); In re Sun Railings, Inc., 5 B.R. 538 (Bankr. S.D. Fla. 1980).

[160] In re Bohlen Enterprises, Ltd., 859 F.2d 561 (8th Cir. 1988).

[161] Betty's Homes, Inc. v. Cooper Homes, Inc., 411 B.R. 626 (W.D. Ark. 2009).

[162] Yoppolo v. MBNA, N.A. (In re Dilworth), 560 F.3d 562, 564-65 (6th Cir. 2009).

[163] Bank of Am. v. Mukamai (In re Egidi), 571 F.3d 1156, 1161-62 (11th Cir. 2009); Yoppolo v. MBNA, N.A. (In re Dilworth), 560 F.3d 562 (6th Cir. 2009).

[164] Meoli v. MBNA American Bank, N.A. (In re Wells), 382 B.R. 355 (B.A.P. 6th Cir. 2008).

[165] *Id.*

[166] *See* Kaiser Steel Corp v. Charles Schwab & Co., 913 F.2d 846, 849 (10th Cir. 1990).

markets in the event of a major bankruptcy affecting those industries."[167] Recoverability of amounts received in transactions covered by the provisions has the potential to impair the capital structure or liquidity of those who participate in these transactions which might place these participants and the securities markets themselves at risk of failure.[168]

Whether they are necessary, and whether the parameters of the safe harbor provisions provide the necessary stability, are both open to debate.[169]

§ 15.04   INDIRECT PREFERENCES

Preferences can either be direct or indirect: either "to" a creditor (direct) or "for the benefit" of a creditor (indirect).[170] A series of cases utilized this rule to create a somewhat strange result when an insider received an indirect benefit during the preference period. The 1994 Amendments overturned the cases discussed, but did not entirely eliminate indirect preferences. To understand this issue, it is first necessary to examine a bit of suretyship law and how it interacts with bankruptcy law.

Suppose that Harland Wolff, the president of Titanic Industries guarantees an obligation of Titanic to North Atlantic Finance Co. The president, as a guarantor (a form of surety), owes a contingent obligation to North Atlantic (if Titanic fails to pay, the president must). In addition, as a surety, the president has a right of reimbursement against Titanic — if he has to pay any of the debt Titanic owes to North Atlantic, he is entitled to recover an equal amount from Titanic. Thus, the president has a contingent claim against Titanic for any money paid to North Atlantic under the guarantee. The contingent claim against Atlantic makes Wolff a creditor of Titanic.[171] And, since every payment made by Titanic reduces Wolff's possible obligation to North Atlantic, Wolff indirectly benefits from those payments. Thus, each payment by Titanic on the loan is a payment that is both directly to one of its creditors (North Atlantic) and is indirectly for the benefit of another (Harland Wolff). Finally, Wolff, as president of Titanic Corporation, is an insider of the company.[172]

This created a problem for lenders, because a number of cases have held that this dual benefit means that the payments to the lender (North Atlantic Finance Company) fall under the one year insider preference period rather than the normal

---

[167] Kaiser Steel Corp. v. Charles Schwab & Co., Inc., 913 F.2d 846, 849 (10th Cir. 1990) (quoting H.R. Rep. 97–420, at 2 (1982), reprinted in 1982 U.S.C.C.A.N. 583, 583).

[168] Enron Creditors Recovery Corp. v. Alfa, S.A.B. de C.V., 651 F.3d 329 (2d Cir. 2011).

[169] Eleanor Heard Gilbane, *Testing the Bankruptcy Code Safe Harbors in the Current Financial Crisis*, 18 Am. Bankr. Inst. L. Rev. 241 (2010); Stephen J. Lubben, *Chapter 11 at the Crossroads: Does Reorganization Need Reform? Repeal the Safe Harbors*, 18 Am. Bankr. Inst. L. Rev. 319 (2010).

[170] Bankruptcy Code § 547(b)(1).

[171] Bankruptcy Code §§ 101(5), (10); Levit v. Ingersoll Rand Financial Corp. (In re V.N. Deprezio Construction Co.), 874 F.2d 1186 (7th Cir. 1989); Osberg v. Halling (In re Halling), 449 B.R. 911 (Bankr. D. Wis. 2011) (debtor's son, who guaranteed debtor's obligation to bank, was a "creditor" who benefitted from debtor's payment to the bank).

[172] *See* Bankruptcy Code § 101(31)(B)(ii).

ninety day preference period. In syllogistic form:

- Titanic's president is an insider creditor of Titanic.

- Titanic's payments to North Atlantic are for the benefit of Titanic's president.

- Therefore, Titanic's payments to North Atlantic are for the benefit of an insider creditor.

- The preference period for a payment that is for the benefit of an insider creditor is one year.

- Therefore, the preference period for Titanic's payments to North Atlantic is one year.

- Therefore, *North Atlantic* has to disgorge the payments it received during the year prior to bankruptcy.[173]

This was true even though the payments were made to North Atlantic, an outsider, rather than to the president.

This approach was criticized for various reasons. Some viewed it as taking several complex statutory provisions far too literally in a way that Congress never had in mind. Others complained that it unduly increased the risk to creditors by reducing the value of suretyship rights.[174] A few commentators were supportive, although even these tended to suggest that a more sophisticated analysis was in order.[175]

In 1994, Congress addressed the issue directly in an amendment to § 550, which deals with the recovery of avoidable transfers. Under the revised language, if a transfer for the benefit of an insider is avoidable under § 547(b)(4)(B), the trustee may not recover from the direct transferee who was not an insider.[176] It may only be recovered from the insider who benefited from the transfer. Thus, in the example supplied above, the payment made by Titanic to North Atlantic Finance Co. can be recovered from Titanic's president (the insider creditor) but not from North Atlantic Finance Co. (the outsider creditor). In essence, the new provision puts the outside creditor who obtains an insider guarantee in exactly the same position as the outside creditor who does not obtain such a guarantee. Either is at risk for payments made during the ninety-day period of § 547(b)(4)(A); neither is at risk for payments made during the ninety-one day to one-year period of § 547(b)(4)(B). However, the basic principle, that an indirect beneficiary may be forced to disgorge a preference remains largely intact. The insider guarantor (in our example, Titanic's president, Harland Wolff) who indirectly benefitted from the debtor's preferential transfers (in our example, the payments made by Titanic Corporation) may still be

---

[173] This syllogism encapsulates the core of the leading case, *Levit v. Ingersoll Rand Financial Corp. (In re Deprizio)*, 874 F.2d 1186 (7th Cir. 1989).

[174] *See* Donald W. Baker, *Repayments of Loan Guaranteed by Insiders as Avoidable Preferences in Bankruptcy: Deprizio and Its Aftermath*, 23 U.C.C. L.J. 115 (1990); Robert F. Higgins & David E. Peterson, *Is There a One-Year Preference Period for Non-Insiders?*, 64 Am. Bankr. L.J. 383 (1990).

[175] Jay Lawrence Westbrook, *Two Thoughts About Insider Preferences*, 76 Minn. L. Rev. 73 (1991).

[176] Bankruptcy Code § 550(c).

forced to disgorge the benefit it received to the estate.

The 2005 Amendments added language to facilitate these earlier revisions. New § 547(i) specifies that if the trustee avoids a preference made between ninety days and one year before the debtor's petition, "to an entity that is not an insider" the transfer is considered to be avoided "only with respect to the creditor that is an insider."[177]

§ 15.05 PROCEDURAL ISSUES; THE EFFECT OF AVOIDANCE

Preference law is not self-executing; the trustee or debtor-in-possession must take action to recover the transfer. This is normally done by adversary proceeding (a trial) in the bankruptcy court.[178] If the creditor has submitted itself to the jurisdiction of the bankruptcy court (as, for example, by filing a proof of claim) there is no right to a jury trial.[179] The trustee carries the burden of persuasion as to all elements of the preference; however, there is a rebuttable presumption that the debtor was insolvent during the nintey days prior to the filing of the petition.[180] The creditor carries the burden of persuasion as to the applicability of any exception to the avoidance rules.[181]

Occasionally a trustee or debtor-in-possession has refused or neglected to pursue a preference. Sometimes this decision is legitimate — for example, it might be unduly expensive to the estate to attempt recovery of a small preference or a preference made to a person not subject to service of process in the United States. Other times, however, the failure to recover a preference is based on neglect or even bad faith — for example, a debtor-in-possession might be reluctant to recover insider preferences made to its managers. This is clearly a breach of the fiduciary duty owed to the creditors. Less clear is the appropriate remedy. Some cases have held that a Chapter 11 creditor's committee has the implicit right to pursue a preference if the trustee or debtor-in-possession improperly fails to do so,[182] and it is not unusual for creditors' committees to pursue preference actions on behalf of the estate, where the debtor has declined to do so, and the court approves. An individual creditor, however, has no such right. It may be possible to have the DIP replaced with a trustee, or have the trustee replaced; it might also be possible to obtain an order from the court under § 105 to force the trustee to take appropriate action.[183]

---

[177] Bankruptcy Code § 547(i).

[178] In re McCombs Properties, VI, Ltd., 88 B.R. 261 (Bankr. C.D. Cal. 1988); In re Magic Circle Energy Corp., 64 B.R. 269 (Bankr. W.D. Okl. 1986).

[179] Langenkamp v. Culp, 498 U.S. 42 (1990).

[180] Bankruptcy Code § 547(f), (g).

[181] Bankruptcy Code § 547(g).

[182] In re Cybergenics Corp, 330 F.3d 548 (3d Cir. 2003) (en banc); In re STN Enterprises, 779 F.2d 901 (2d Cir. 1985).

[183] Bankruptcy Code § 105(a) permits the court to enter any "necessary or appropriate" orders.

The effect of avoidance varies with the nature of the transfer. If the transfer was merely of a lien on property still in possession of the debtor, the lien simply ceases to exist and the creditor is left with a general unsecured claim. If the transfer was of money or other property physically transferred to the creditor, the trustee may recover the property or (if the court so orders) the value of the property.[184] The trustee ordinarily seeks recovery against the preferee. However, the trustee may often recover from a subsequent transferee.[185] Subsequent transferees are given some protection by bona fide purchaser rules, which are discussed elsewhere.[186] Similarly, creditors who have improved property that is subsequently recovered by the estate are provided with some protection for the value of their improvements. The creditor who is forced to return property is given a general unsecured claim equal to the value of the property.[187] This may create practical problems for a Chapter 11 debtor if the resulting claim is large, because the preferee is likely to be a particularly hostile creditor, unwilling to cooperate in the formulation or confirmation of the plan.

§ 15.06　SETOFF PREFERENCES

Not all preference rules are contained in § 547. Section 553(b) contains a preference provision that in key respects resembles the net result rule applied to floating liens in the § 547(c)(5) exception. The § 553 provision permits the trustee to recover certain pre-petition setoffs as preferences.[188]

With certain limited exceptions, a setoff exercised within ninety days prior to the filing of the petition can be avoided to the extent there was a reduction in the insufficiency. "Insufficiency" means the amount by which the debt owed by the offsetting creditor to the debtor was larger than the debt owed by the debtor to the offsetting creditor.[189] The amount of the insufficiency is measured at two points — (1) the date of the setoff and (2) the later of (a) ninety days before the filing of the petition and (b) the first date during that ninety days on which there was an insufficiency.[190]

Suppose that on June 1, which is nintey days before the filing of the petition, Debussy owes Chopin $10,000 and Chopin owes Debussy $12,000. On August 15, Debussy owes Chopin $11,000 and Chopin owes Debussy $11,500. On August 15, Chopin offsets the two obligations, leaving a net obligation of $500 owed by Chopin to Debussy. At the beginning of the 90 day period, the insufficiency was $2000 ($12,000 – $10,000). At the time the debts were offset, the insufficiency was $500 ($11,500 – $11,000). Thus, a setoff preference of $1,500 occurred and that amount may be recovered.

---

[184] Bankruptcy Code § 550(a).

[185] Bankruptcy Code § 550(a)(2).

[186] *See* § 14.08[D] Protection of Good Faith Transferees, *infra.*

[187] Bankruptcy Code § 502(h).

[188] For a general discussion of setoff, see § 2.06 Setoff, *supra.*

[189] Bankruptcy Code § 553(b)(2).

[190] Bankruptcy Code § 553(b)(1).

Note that the setoff preference rule is much simpler than the § 547 preference rules. There are no elaborate requirements; most notably, there is no requirements that the debtor be insolvent. Similarly, there are no exceptions to the rule. One troubling question, however, about § 553 is whether it applies when the insufficiency has been reduced during the 90 days prior to bankruptcy, but the creditor does not set off.

Two other quasi-preference rules appear in §§ 553(a)(2) and (3). These are structured as provisions dealing with the basic right of setoff, rather than as provisions avoiding setoffs already made. For this reason, they are discussed in the general material on setoffs.[191]

---

[191] *See* § 10.09 Right of Setoff, *supra.*

Chapter 16

FRAUDULENT TRANSFERS

§ 16.01 PURPOSES AND SOURCES OF FRAUDULENT CONVEYANCE LAW[1]

[A] Fraudulent Conveyances

Among the avoidance powers given to the bankruptcy trustee or a debtor-in-possession is the power to avoid fraudulent transfers. Pre-bankruptcy transfers of the debtor's property are avoidable as fraudulent if they are intentionally or constructively fraudulent. The classic example of an intentionally fraudulent transfer is a person who, on the eve of suffering a $10,000,000 judgment, transfers all her assets to a trusted relative for $1. There are, however, many more far less obvious examples that even savvy bankers sometimes fail to detect before it is too late.

There is a strong policy, both inside and outside bankruptcy, of preventing debtors from harming their creditors by dissipating their assets in this fashion. Debtors who dispose of their assets, either in an effort to hide them from creditors, or even without wrongful intent, for far less than they are worth, deprive their creditors of assets that could have been used to make payments to creditors.

Many reasons have been advanced for avoiding fraudulent transfers. Some of these are simple moral statements — one should not seek to avoid liability on a contract or for a wrong by secreting assets. Others focus on creditors' expectations. The most commonly stated reason is that the debtor is violating an implied term of the agreement, and even implicitly misrepresenting its intentions regarding its assets. Despite this, even non-consensual creditors, such as tort claimants, have claims under fraudulent conveyance law.

[B] Fraudulent Obligations

Parallel to the fraudulent transfer is the fraudulent obligation, which is also prohibited. By making themselves appear more indebted than they really are, debtors sometimes dissuade legitimate creditors from attempting to collect. This is particularly true if the debtor's obligations appear to be secured, making the debtor appear to have few unencumbered assets. For example, Charlie might

---

[1] Robert Charles Clark, *The Duties of the Corporate Debtor to Its Creditors*, 90 Harv. L. Rev. 505 (1977); Michael L. Cook, *Fraudulent Transfer Liability Under the Bankruptcy Code*, 17 Hous. L. Rev. 263 (1980); James McLaughlin, *Application of the Uniform Fraudulent Conveyance Act*, 46 Harv. L. Rev. 404 (1933).

execute a promissory note to pay his cousin Gail $100,000 and give Gail a mortgage on his $100,000 home, even though Charlie has borrowed no money from Gail and owes her no debt. When other creditors conduct a title search, they will find Gail's recorded mortgage. This might make Charlie appear judgment proof and induce his creditors to avoid pursuing collection as vigorously as they otherwise might. Thus, the motivation to create fraudulent obligations is much the same as the motivation to make a fraudulent transfer; the difference is that the former involves the creation of a claim while the latter involves the transfer of property.

[C]   Fraudulent Transfers Distinct from Preferences

Fraudulent transfers differ in significant ways from preferences, although some transactions might be avoidable under both powers. Both deplete the debtor's estate in ways that harm creditors. Preferences involve payments by the debtor that undercut the equality of distribution inherent in the bankruptcy priority scheme. As such, preference law is almost entirely indifferent to the motivation of transferor and transferee.[2] Fraudulent transfer doctrine, on the other hand, is frequently concerned with the actual or presumed motivation underlying the transaction. Many preferences are received by creditors who are not even aware of the fact that the payments are preferential, and who did nothing to cause the preference to be made. By contrast, in many cases, the beneficiary of a fraudulent transfer or obligation had at least some notice that the transaction was flawed.

[D]   Sources of Fraudulent Transfer Law[3]

Fraudulent conveyance law is traced historically to the Statute of Elizabeth, enacted by Parliament in 1570.[4] The Statute of Elizabeth is startlingly similar to modern fraudulent conveyance law. For example, the language regarding transactions made with the "intent to hinder, delay, or defraud creditors" appears in both the Statute of Elizabeth and the modern Uniform Fraudulent Transfer Act that was promulgated over 400 years later.

Today, fraudulent transfer law appears in both state law and in the Bankruptcy Code. The Uniform Fraudulent Transfer Act (UFTA),[5] promulgated in 1984, applies in forty-three states and the District of Columbia. Its predecessor, the Uniform Fraudulent Conveyance Act (UFCA), developed in 1918,[6] still applies in some of the remaining states. In bankruptcy cases, the trustee may invoke state fraudulent transfer law through § 544(b), which permits the trustee to avoid any transfer that an actual unsecured creditor could have avoided outside of

---

[2] *See generally* Lawrence Ponoroff, *Evil Intentions and an Irresolute Endorsement for Scientific Realism: Bankruptcy Preferences One More Time*, 1993 Wis. L. Rev. 1439.

[3] Frank R. Kennedy, *Reception of the Uniform Fraudulent Transfer Act*, 43 S.C. L. Rev. 655 (1992).

[4] An Act Against Fraudulent Deeds, Alienations, 13 Eliz., ch. 5 (1570) (Eng.), *repealed by* The Law of Property Act, 15 Geo. 5, ch. 20, § 172 (1925).

[5] *See* Michael L. Cook & Richard E. Mendales, *The Uniform Fraudulent Transfer Act: An Introductory Critique*, 62 Am. Bankr. L.J. 87 (1988).

[6] *See* James McLaughlin, *Application of the Uniform Fraudulent Conveyance Act*, 46 Harv. L. Rev. 404 (1933).

bankruptcy.[7] In addition, § 548 gives the trustee his own fraudulent transfer avoiding power that is not dependent on either state law or upon the standing of any individual creditor to avoid the transfer.

The UFTA and § 548 both authorize avoidance of two types of transfers: (1) transfers that the debtor made with the "actual intent" to defraud his creditors; and (2) transfers based on "constructive fraud" because of their effect on creditors, without regard to the debtor's intent. A key difference between § 548 and the UFTA is that the UFTA reaches further back in time than § 548, making it a more effective tool for the bankruptcy trustee than § 548 to recover property transferred long before the debtor filed his bankruptcy petition.

§ 16.02　ACTUAL FRAUD: INTENT TO HINDER, DELAY, OR DEFRAUD CREDITORS

A creditor's actual intent to "hinder, delay, or defraud" creditors has formed the basis of fraudulent conveyance law since 1570. It is codified today in Bankruptcy Code § 548(a)(1)(A) and UFTA § 4(a)(1). Section 548(a)(1)(A) permits the bankruptcy trustee to avoid

> any transfer of an interest of the debtor in property . . . that was made within 2 years before the date of the filing of the petition, if the debtor voluntarily or involuntarily (A) made such transfer . . . with actual intent to hinder, delay, or defraud any entity to which the debtor was or became . . . indebted.[8]

UFTA § 4(a)(1) similarly provides:

> [a] transfer made by a debtor is fraudulent as to a creditor, whether the creditor's claim arose before or after the transfer . . . if the debtor made the transfer . . . (1) with the actual intent to hinder, delay, or defraud any creditor of the debtor.[9]

Both provisions make a transfer avoidable because of the debtor's fraudulent intent, and both make them avoidable regardless of whether the transfer occurred before or after the debtor became indebted. Likewise, both apply equally to voluntary and involuntary transfers, although it is unusual for an involuntary transfer to be made with actual fraudulent intent.[10]

The predicate intent to establish actual fraud can be difficult to prove. Indeed, it is very rare for a debtor to be so foolish as to declare openly an intention to injure his creditors. For this reason, intent must ordinarily be inferred from the circumstances surrounding the transaction. Since *Twyne's Case* in 1602,[11] intent has usually been proven through circumstantial evidence that demonstrates the

---

[7] *See supra* § 14.03 Power to Exercise Rights of Actual Unsecured Creditors.

[8] Bankruptcy Code § 548(a)(1)(A).

[9] UFTA § 4(a)(1).

[10] *Compare* Bankruptcy Code § 548(a)(1), *with* UFTA § 1(12) (defining transfer).

[11] 76 Eng. Rep. 809 (Star Chamber 1601). *See* Michael L. Cook, *Fraudulent Transfer Liability Under the Bankruptcy Code*, 17 Hous. L. Rev. 263, 270-71 (1980).

strong likelihood of the debtor's deceitful intent. These traditional "badges of fraud" are now codified in UFTA § 4(b) to include whether:

- the transfer or obligation was to an insider;[12]

- the debtor retained possession or control of the property transferred after the transfer;[13]

- the transfer or obligation was disclosed or concealed.[14]

- before the transfer was made or obligation was incurred, the debtor had been sued or threatened with suit;[15]

- the transfer was of substantially all of the debtor's assets;[16]

- the debtor absconded after making the transfer;[17]

- the debtor removed or concealed assets;[18]

- the value of the consideration received by the debtor was not reasonably equivalent to the value of the asset transferred or the amount of the obligation incurred;[19]

- the debtor was insolvent or became insolvent shortly after the transfer was made or the obligation was incurred;[20]

- the transfer occurred shortly before or shortly after a substantial debt was incurred;[21] and

- the debtor transferred the essential assets of the business to a lienor who transferred the assets to an insider of the debtor.[22]

---

[12] UFTA § 4(b)(1). *See* McWilliams v. Edmonson, 162 F.2d 454 (5th Cir. 1947) (sister); Levy v. Bukes, 65 F. Supp. 494 (W.D. Pa. 1946) (spouse).

"Insider' " as used in the UFTA has much the same definition as it has under the Bankruptcy Code. It encompasses close relatives and close business affiliates. *See* UFTA § 1(7).

[13] UFTA § 4(b)(2). *E.g.*, In re Nemeroff, 74 B.R. 30 (E.D. La. 1987). Under modern secured transactions law, the fact that a debtor remains in physical possession of property that is subject to a security interest is not a fraudulent transfer (nor does it create a badge of fraud), provided that the security interest has properly been perfected by the filing of a financing statement or other notice-giving device. Prior to the late nineteenth century development of laws that provided for public notice, however, such security interests were often struck down as fraudulent transfers.

[14] UFTA § 4(b)(3).

[15] UFTA § 4(b)(4).

[16] UFTA § 4(b)(5).

[17] UFTA § 4(b)(6). The modern extension of long-arm jurisdiction, permitting the service of process across state lines, has reduced the significance of this badge of fraud.

[18] UFTA § 4(b)(7).

[19] UFTA § 4(b)(8).

[20] UFTA § 4(b)(9).

[21] UFTA § 4(a)(10).

[22] UFTA § 4(b)(11).

This is by no means an exhaustive list of the "badges of fraud" that courts have used to detect the debtor's fraudulent intent. Rather, they are those that were sufficiently common for specific inclusion in the UFTA.

Transfers to family members, whom the debtor might more confidently trust to return the transferred property at a later date, are particularly suspect.[23] Thus, when Corbin Lacina deposited his annuity checks in an account held by his mother-in-law, who later disbursed the funds as Corbin directed, the court had no trouble deciding that Corbin's transfer of the funds to his wife's mother was intentionally fraudulent.[24] Transfers to family members are not per se fraudulent,[25] but they are highly suspicious, particularly where there was no apparent consideration for the transfer.[26]

However, none of the badges of fraud alone is dispositive. They are only guidelines, creating inferences that the trier of fact may or may not draw in any particular case. As one court explained: "proof of intent under a badges-of-fraud analysis is not like a carnival dart game, where simply popping a given number of balloons entitles one to the big prize."[27]

The "actual intent" branch of fraudulent conveyance law has greatly diminished in significance over the years. This is primarily due to the development of the rules that treat transfers by a person who was insolvent at the time of the transfer as "constructively fraudulent" without regard to the person's intent. There are very few cases covered by the actual intent rules that are not also covered by the insolvent transferor rules, and constructive fraud is usually easier to prove.

§ 16.03 CONSTRUCTIVE FRAUD

The second type of fraudulent conveyance arises when the transfer is made for grossly inadequate consideration by a person who is unable to pay his debts. These transfers are treated as fraudulent even if the debtor's intent was benign, because of the effect that the transfer has on his creditors. These transfers deprive creditors of valuable assets that could have been used to satisfy their claims.

[A] Elements of Constructive Fraud

Constructive fraud involves two elements. The first is that the debtor received less than "a reasonably equivalent value" in exchange for the transferred property.[28] The second is that the debtor was either insolvent or otherwise facing an inappropriate risk of being unable to pay its debts. As explained more fully

---

[23] *E.g.*, ACLI Gov't Securites, Inc. v. Rhodes, 653 F. Supp. 1388 (S.D.N.Y. 1987).

[24] Sullivan v. Gergen (In re Lacina), 451 B.R. 485 (Bankr. D. Minn. 2011).

[25] *See, e.g.*, In re Knippen, 355 B.R. 710, 733 (Bankr. N.D. Ill. 2006).

[26] *See* Chichester v. Golden, 204 F. Supp. 634 (S.D. Cal. 1962); First Nat'l Bank v. Enzler, 537 P.2d 517 (Alaska 1975).

[27] In re Lumbar, 446 B.R. 316, 332 (Bankr. D. Minn.), *rev'd on other grounds*, 457 B.R. 748 (B.A.P. 8th Cir. 2011).

[28] Bankruptcy Code § 548(a)(1)(B)(i); UFTA §§ 4(a)(2), 5(a).

below, the second element may be satisfied in several ways.

[1] No Reasonably Equivalent Value

Both the UFTA and § 548 make the debtor's receipt of less than a "reasonably equivalent value"[29] a key element of constructive fraud. But neither statute supplies a definition of reasonably equivalent value.

If the transfer was for reasonably equivalent value, the debtor's financial circumstances do not matter. Creditors are not harmed when the debtor receives a reasonable equivalent in exchange for his property. But, if the debtor receives considerably less than the property is worth, creditors are deprived of value that otherwise could have been used to make payments to them.

The classic fraudulent cases, in which property is transferred to a relative for no consideration (love and affection) or for nominal consideration ($1, or a peppercorn), are easy.[30] The transfers are avoidable and the trustee can recover the amount of the property that was transferred for the benefit of the debtor's creditors.

Under both statutes "value" means "property, or satisfaction or securing of a present or antecedent debt . . . but does not include an unperformed promise to furnish support to the debtor or to a relative of the debtor."[31] The latter phrase prevents debtors from shielding transfers by claiming that the transferee has made an unperformed promise to care for the debtor. For example, if Charlie transfers all of his property to his daughter Gail, in exchange for Gail's promise to take care of him for the rest of his life, value has not been given.[32]

More difficult are those in which the transferee is getting a good deal but not an incredible one. For example, Charlie might sell his car to Gail for $5,000, even though it is worth $7,000, in order to raise cash quickly to meet his living expenses and pay some of his creditors. Gail is getting a good deal, but Charlie may have no fraudulent intent.

It is clear that reasonably equivalent value does not mean dollar for dollar equivalence.[33] Whether sufficient value was received depends on the "totality of the circumstances."[34] The problem of determining whether value given was a reasonable equivalent is particularly acute if the value given is intangible. It is fairly easy to determine the value of fungible goods that are regularly sold in an established market. It is far more difficult to determine the value of an investment in an uncertain business venture.

---

[29] Bankruptcy Code § 548(a)(2)(A); UFTA §§ 4(a)(2); 5(a).

[30] Williams v. Marlar (In re Marlar), 267 F.3d 749 (8th Cir. 2001) (700 acres exchanged for $10 and "love and affection"); In re Tarin, 454 B.R. 179, 182-83 (Bankr. D.N.M. 2011).

[31] Bankruptcy Code § 548(d)(2)(A). *See* UFTA § 3(a) (1984). Section 548 contains language that does not appear in the UFTA regarding value in securities transactions, repurchase transactions, swap agreements, and master netting agreements. Bankruptcy Code § 548(d)(2)(B)-(E).

[32] *See, e.g.*, Taunt v. Hurtado (In re Hurtado), 342 F.3d 528, 530-32 (6th Cir. 2003).

[33] *See* In re Fairchild Aircraft Corp., 6 F.3d 1119 (5th Cir. 1993).

[34] In re Besing, 981 F.2d 1488, 1495-96 (5th Cir. 1993).

For example, *In re Fairchild Aircraft Corp.*[35] involved payments made by Fairchild for aviation fuel sold to its affiliate, Air Kentucky. Air Kentucky was a struggling commuter airline that Fairchild hoped to prop up (so to speak), so that it could purchase Fairchild's planes. The court held that the indirect benefits that Fairchild reasonably hoped it would gain were value in determining whether its fuel payments were for reasonably equivalent value.[36]

One plausible justification for the acceptance of indeterminate values as reasonably equivalent value is the hands-off approach that courts have long taken toward business decisions. In the corporate law arena, this is called the business judgment rule — which broadly means that boards of directors are free to take actions that have a legitimate business justification, and are not obviously adverse to shareholder interests. If courts were too narrow in their review of intangible sources of value, then fraudulent transfer law would significantly inhibit business decision making. That is generally assumed to be undesirable, usually on the basis that courts lack the experience necessary to make business judgments.

If the debtor transfers its property in exchange for something given to a third person, the transfer is avoidable. Transfers for value given to someone else harm the debtor's creditors in the same way as transfers for inadequate value. For example, in *In re Leonard*,[37] a father's payment of his adult son's college tuition was fraudulent, because the son, not the father, received the educational services that the college provided in exchange for the payment. In *Leonard*, it did not even matter that the funds used to pay the son's tuition were traceable to a student loan the son had obtained and subsequently deposited into his father's bank account. The court justified this result because deposit of the funds in the father's account created a presumption that they belonged to him, and because they were reachable by his creditors while they were in the account. Payment of the son's tuition therefore diverted funds that otherwise would have been available to pay the father's creditors, to his son's college and the father received nothing that was a reasonable equivalent value, in exchange.

On the other hand, in *In re Tarin*, parents who paid for goods and services supplied at their daughter's wedding received a reasonably equivalent value for their payment:

> debtors received value in form of the flowers that they and their guests got to smell, the food that they and their guests got to eat, the music that they and their guests got to listen and dance to, with market value equal to what debtors had paid, and mere fact that daughter also benefited from debtors' payment did not permit trustee to pursue fraudulent transfer claim against her any more than it permitted trustee to recover from guests.

The court did note, however, that if the expenditures on the wedding had been $100,000 instead of $10,000, the result might have been different. As the court explained: "at some level of expenditure, benefit to the debtor becomes inconse-

---

[35] 6 F.3d 1119 (5th Cir. 1993).

[36] 6 F.3d at 1126.

[37] In re Leonard, 454 B.R. 444 (Bankr. E.D. Mich. 2011).

quential compared to benefit to the transferee."[38]

[2] Debtor Insolvent

The second element of constructive fraud is stated in several alternative ways, all of which point to the debtor's actual or potential inability to pay his creditors. Debtors who remain able to pay their debts are free to squander their assets. However, those who are already unable to pay their debts, or who are at substantial risk of being unable to pay, must not exchange their assets for less than they are reasonably worth.

Section 548 and the UFTA express these elements in slightly different ways. Thus, if the debtor did not receive reasonably equivalent value in exchange for its property, the transfer is fraudulent if:

- the debtor was insolvent when the transfer was made;[39]

- the debtor became insolvent as a result of the transfer;[40]

- the debtor was engaged in a business or transaction for which its remaining property was an unreasonably small capital;[41]

- the debtor was about to engage in a business or transaction for which its remaining property was an unreasonably small capital;[42]

- the debtor intended to incur debts that would be beyond its ability to pay as they came due;[43] or

- the debtor believed that it would incur debts that would be beyond its ability to pay as they came due.[44]

The transfer involved may be either voluntary or involuntary.

In the context of these provisions, "insolvent" refers to balance-sheet insolvency; that is, fewer assets than debts.[45] For example, if the fair value of the debtor's property is $500,000, and it owes its creditors a total of $750,000, the debtor is insolvent. In calculating the debtor's solvency, the Bankruptcy Code excludes exempt assets.[46]

---

[38] *Id.* at 446 n. 5.

[39] Bankruptcy Code § 548(a)(1)(B)(ii)(I); UFTA § 5(a) (1984). *See* In re Gallagher, 417 B.R. 677 (W.D.N.Y. 2009) (debtor was solvent at time she returned engagement ring to her fiancee).

[40] Bankruptcy Code § 548(a)(1)(B)(ii)(I); UFTA § 5(a) (1984).

[41] Bankruptcy Code § 548(a)(1)(B)(ii)(II); UFTA § 4(a)(2)(i). *See* Bruce A. Markell, *Toward True and Plain Dealing: A Theory of Fraudulent Transfers Involving Unreasonably Small Capital*, 21 Ind. L. Rev. 469 (1988).

[42] Bankruptcy Code § 548(a)(1)(B)(ii)(II); UFTA § 4(a)(2)(i).

[43] Bankruptcy Code § 548(a)(1)(B)(ii)(III); UFTA § 4(a)(2)(ii) (1984).

[44] Bankruptcy Code § 548(a)(1)(B)(ii)(III); UFTA § 4(a)(2)(ii) (1984).

[45] Bankruptcy Code § 101(32); UFTA § 2(a).

[46] Bankruptcy Code § 101(32)(A)(ii).

The debtor's fraudulent or benign intent is irrelevant. Thus, the person challenging the transfer on this basis does not have to prove, directly or by inference, that the transferor meant to cheat creditors.

The Code also makes it clear that transfers to insider employees, that are outside the ordinary course of business, are fraudulent if the debtor received less than a reasonably equivalent value in exchange.[47] This new language is designed to enhance the level of scrutiny of payments made or obligations incurred to insider employees under "golden parachute" employment contracts. It is significant because it makes these contracts avoidable regardless of whether the employer was insolvent when the transfer was made or the obligation was incurred.[48]

[B]   Specific Transactions Involving Constructive Fraud

Bankruptcy trustees rarely have any difficulty avoiding gifts made by an insolvent debtor on the eve of bankruptcy.[49] Even when fraudulent intent cannot be shown, the constructive fraud provisions in the UFTA and § 548 makes recovery of these transfers fairly easy. The most difficult factual issue is proving the necessary element of the debtor's insolvency at the time transfer was made. But, the schedules of assets and liabilities supplied with the debtor's petition, usually reveals that the debtor was insolvent at the time of its petition. With these details available, it is not difficult to establish the debtor's insolvency a few weeks or months before the time the bankruptcy case began.

Other transactions that may be recoverable as fraudulent transfers do not so obviously fit within the Code's fraudulent transfer rubric. Among these are pre-petition mortgage and security interest foreclosure sales, where inadequate value is received for the encumbered collateral; intercorporate guarantees; asset securitization transactions; transfers by a partnership to its general partners; and leveraged buy-outs. As explained below, fraudulent transfer law is frequently applied to all of these transactions, with often uncertain results.

[1]   Pre-Petition Foreclosure Sales[50]

Foreclosure sales are usually concluded at bargain-basement prices. The winning bid is frequently far less than the supposed value of the property. This is frequently because of the customary practice of foreclosing creditors buying the property

---

[47]   Bankruptcy Code § 548(a)(1)(B)(IV).

[48]   *See* Steve H. Nickles, *Behavioral Effect of New Bankruptcy Law on Management and Lawyers: Collage of Recent Statutes and Cases Discouraging Chapter 11 Bankruptcy*, 59 Ark. L. Rev. 329, 349-60 (2006).

[49]   Detecting the transfer is usually the hard part, particularly if the transfer was made many months before the debtor's petition was filed. One of your authors recalls attending a § 341 meeting, with one of his first clients, and observing a meeting involving different debtors (a physician and his spouse), who had given each of their three adult daughters sets of valuable silverware as Christmas presents several months before filing their joint petition. If they had not listed these assets on a loan application several years earlier, with a lender who carefully compared the assets listed on the loan application with those provided to the bankruptcy court in the schedules filed with the debtor's petition, the transactions would never have been discovered.

[50]   Marie T. Reilly, *A Search for Reason in "Reasonably Equivalent Value" After* BFP v. Resolution

involved in their own foreclosure sale with a "credit bid." This refers to bidding the amount of the debt involved in the foreclosure and exchanging the right to collect the mortgage debt for the mortgaged property, without coming up with any cash. This, together with other factors that make buying property at foreclosure a risky proposition for other prospective bidders, keep foreclosure sale prices low.[51]

It was traditionally assumed that fraudulent transfer law did not apply to a properly conducted foreclosure sale. This tradition is reflected in the UFTA, which provides that a buyer gives reasonably equivalent value for property if the buyer acquired the property in a "regularly conducted, non-collusive foreclosure sale."[52] Thus, under state law, the focus is on the propriety of the sale procedure, rather than on any disparity between the foreclosure sale price and the fair market value.

However, § 548 is silent on the topic. In 1980, in *Durett v. Washington National Insurance Co.*, the Fifth Circuit Court of Appeals held that a properly conducted foreclosure sale could be a fraudulent conveyance because of the inadequacy of the price obtained at the sale.[53] The analysis was simple: the debtor was insolvent and the property had been transferred for less that it was worth — less than a reasonably equivalent value. The decision sent shock-waves through the banking industry and resulted in a storm of law review articles, continuing legal education programs, and academic presentations.[54]

Fourteen years later, the Supreme Court resolved the issue in *BFP v. Resolution Trust Corp.*[55] The Court held that the consideration received from a non-collusive real estate mortgage foreclosure sale, conducted in conformance with applicable state law, conclusively satisfies the reasonably equivalent value standard of § 548.

Thus, if Peninsula Bank forecloses its mortgage on Franklin Manufacturing's land and buys the property by making a "credit bid" with the $1.5 million mortgage debt, the purchase is not a fraudulent transfer even though the appraised value of the property was $2.5 million. As long as the sale was conducted in compliance with governing state law and that there was no collusive bidding involved in the sale, the sale would not be subject to attack.

However, foreclosure sales that do not conform to the established procedures remain vulnerable as fraudulent conveyances. Also, since *BFP v. Resolution Trust* is an interpretation of § 548, it is important to check state laws that might apply under § 544(b) to see if they diverge from the UFTA in this regard.

Trust Corp., 13 Am. Bankr. Inst. L. Rev. 261 (2005). *See* William Henning, *An Analysis of* Durett, *and Its Impact on Real and Personal Property Foreclosures: Some Proposed Modifications,* 63 N.C. L. Rev. 257 (1985).

[51] *See supra* § 2.07 Foreclosure Proceedings. *See generally* Robert M. Washburn, *The Judicial and Legislative Response to Price Inadequacy in Mortgage Foreclosure Sales,* 53 S. Cal. L. Rev. 843 (1980); Debra Pogrund Stark, *Facing the Facts: An Empirical Study of the Fairness and Efficiency of Foreclosures and a Proposal for Reform,* 30 U. Mich. J.L. Ref. 639 (1997).

[52] UFTA § 3(b).

[53] 621 F.2d 201 (5th Cir. 1980).

[54] Durrett v. Wash. Nat'l Ins. Co., 621 F.2d 201 (5th Cir. 1980). *See* Helen J. Durham, *A Decade of Division Among the Circuits: Application of Section 548(a)(2) of the Bankruptcy Code to Foreclosure Sales,* 19 Mem. St. U. L. Rev. 381 (1989).

[55] BFP v. Resolution Trust Corp., 511 U.S. 531 (1994).

Despite the decision in *BFP v. Resolution Trust*, courts have not always agreed about other forced sales.[56] Where the opportunity for competitive bidding exists, the Court's rationale has held sway, and the sale is not subject to attack.[57] However, where there has been neither a public sale nor competitive bidding, the foreclosure sale remains vulnerable.[58]

[2]　Intercorporate Guarantees[59]

Most of the foregoing discussion has focused on fraudulent "transfers." However, both § 548 and the UFTA permit avoidance of a fraudulent "obligation."[60] The most obvious example of a fraudulent obligation occurs when a debtor creates documents making it appear as if he owes money to someone to whom he is not indebted. These obligations, incurred with the intent to hinder, delay, and defraud creditors, are avoidable due to actual fraud. Intercorporate guarantees, such as ones that might be made by a corporation in exchange for a loan to a different company that is under the control of the same shareholders,[61] or a guarantee by a company in exchange for a loan to the company's shareholders, are less obviously fraudulent.[62]

These obligations may be fraudulent because the surety receives no benefit for its promise. Whatever benefit was involved in the transaction is received by the principal debtor, not the surety. For example, if Harland Wolff, the president of Titanic Industries, guarantees a loan to Titanic from Manufacturer's Bank, Wolff receives no direct benefit from the transfer. If Wolff was insolvent when he made the guarantee, it might be fraudulent as to Wolff's other personal creditors. Likewise, if Wolff pays Manufacturer's Bank in fulfillment of his obligation as a guarantor, the payment might be a fraudulent transfer because it deprives Wolff's other creditors of funds that would otherwise be available to pay their claims, and, as with the guarantee itself, Wolff received no direct benefit from the Bank for making the guarantee.

Assume further that Wolff is also the sole stockholder of Olympic, Inc., and that the two companies are involved in related businesses.[63] When the economic vitality of the companies begins to falter and Olympic is in need of cash, Olympic borrows additional funds from Manufacturer's Bank, with Titanic guaranteeing the debt

---

[56] Marie T. Reilly, *A Search for Reason in "Reasonably Equivalent Value" After* BFP v. Resolution Trust Corp., 13 Am. Bankr. Inst. L. Rev. 261 (2005).

[57] *E.g.*, T.F. Stone Co. v. Harper (Matter of T.F. Stone Co.), 72 F.3d 466 (5th Cir. 1995) (tax sale). In re Denaro, 383 B.R. 879 (Bankr. D.N.J. 2008).

[58] *E.g.*, In re Murphy, 331 B.R. 107 (Bankr. S.D.N.Y. 2005); In re Sherman, 223 B.R. 555 (B.A.P. 10th Cir. 1998).

[59] Scott F. Norberg, Comment, *Avoidability of Intercorporate Guarantees Under Sections 548(a)(2) and 544(b) of the Bankruptcy Code*, 64 N.C. L. Rev. 1099 (1986); Jack F. Williams, *The Fallacies of Contemporary Fraudulent Transfer Models as Applied to Intercorporate Guaranties: Fraudulent Transfer Law as a Fuzzy System*, 15 Cardozo L. Rev. 1403 (1994).

[60] Bankruptcy Code § 548(a)(1); UFTA §§ 4(a), 5 (1984).

[61] *See* Rubin v. Mfrs. Hanover Trust, 661 F.2d 979 (2d Cir. 1981); Leibowitz v. Parkway Bank & Trust Co. (In re Image Worldwide, Ltd.), 139 F.3d 574 (7th Cir. 1978).

[62] *See* Rubin v. Mfrs. Hanover Trust, 661 F.2d 979 (2d Cir. 1981).

[63] Frontier Bank v. Brown (In re N. Merch., Inc.), 371 F.3d 1056 (9th Cir. 2004).

owed by Olympic and supplying the bank with a security interest in Titanic's assets. To the extent Olympic's economic survival is essential to keep Titanic afloat,[64] Titanic receives a real benefit in exchange for its guarantee.

Whether such guarantees are fraudulent depends on the circumstances. The issues are whether the guarantors received any benefit in exchange for their guarantees, and if they did, whether the benefit obtained was a reasonably equivalent value for their guarantees.[65] In many cases, the guarantor receives an indirect benefit that provides reasonably equivalent value for the obligation.[66]

In *In re Jeffrey Bigelow Design Group, Inc.*, the corporate debtor's shareholders obtained a $1 million line of credit from First American Bank, accompanied by a guarantee from the debtor.[67] The corporation simultaneously executed a promissory note for $1 million payable to the shareholders. Funds drawn on the line of credit were paid to the debtor, and when the debtor made payments to First American for amounts that had been drawn, the debtor's obligation to the shareholders was reduced. In holding that the payments the debtor made on the shareholder's debt to the bank was not a fraudulent conveyance, the Fourth Circuit explained:

> [T]he proper focus is on the net effect of the transfers on the debtor's estate, the funds available to the unsecured creditors. As long as the unsecured creditors are no worse off because the debtor, and consequently the estate, has received an amount reasonably equivalent to what it paid, no fraudulent transfer has occurred. . . . It seems apparent that the transfers have not resulted in the depletion of the bankruptcy estate, [but rather] served simply as repayment for money received.[68]

In *Bigelow Design Group*, the indirect benefit to the corporate guarantor was clear and tangible. In cases where the benefit to the debtor is more obscure, the transfer may be fraudulent. Lenders must be wary of such guarantees and take steps to ensure that they can establish both the fact and the amount of any indirect benefit supplied to the guarantor, lest they lose the advantage of obtaining the guarantee in the very circumstances for which it was sought.

---

[64] We're sorry, after this many examples involving this name, we couldn't resist. "Olympic" was one of Titanic's sister ships.

[65] *See* In re Xonics Photochemical, Inc., 841 F.2d 198 (7th Cir. 1988) (Posner, J.).

[66] *See* Frontier Bank v. Brown (In re N. Merch., Inc.), 371 F.3d 1056 (9th Cir. 2004) (corporation's secured guarantee given in exchange for loan to shareholders not a fraudulent conveyance because of indirect benefit to the corporation).

[67] Harman v. First Am. Bank (In re Jeffrey Bigelow Design Group, Inc.), 956 F.2d 479, 481 (4th Cir. 1992).

[68] 956 F.2d at 484-85.

[3]   Distributions to Shareholders[69]

Corporate dividends by an insolvent company are vulnerable to attack both as fraudulent transfers and possibly as violations of state corporate law. The same is true for redemptions of shareholders' stock.[70] If the company is insolvent and thus unable to pay its debts, it has no business making payments to its shareholders and thus depriving creditors of assets needed to pay the company's debts.[71] Payments to shareholders violate creditors' priority rights.

State corporations statutes frequently proscribe such distributions and make them recoverable. The Model Business Corporation Act, as well as state statutes patterned after it, prohibit a corporation from making a distribution to shareholders if after the distribution the corporation would be insolvent, either in the "legal" balance sheet sense or in the "equitable" sense of being unable to pay its debts as they mature.[72] The estate succeeds to the corporation's right to recover these transactions, and under § 544(b), the trustee can act aside any transfer that an unsecured creditor could have avoided under applicable state law. However, even though these distributions are improper, state corporate law does not appear to give unsecured creditors the right to invoke this rule to recover the transfer. If the debtor can recover the money, its cause of action belongs to the estate under § 541(a). Alternatively, the transfers are potentially vulnerable to avoidance under § 548 or state fraudulent conveyance law.

[4]   Charitable Contributions[73]

If made by a person who is unable to satisfy his debts, contributions to a church, college, or other charity, look very much like fraudulent transfers. The debtor is insolvent and whatever benefits the debtor receives from the contribution are highly intangible. And, whatever one may think of the social benefits associated with charitable contributions, they are rarely of any value to a debtor's creditors.

Despite this, § 548(a)(2) provides protection for charitable contributions made by individuals. It provides:

> A transfer of a charitable contribution to a qualified religious or charitable entity or organization shall not be considered to be a [constructively fraudulent transfer under § 548(b)(1)(B)] in any case in which —

---

[69] Norwood P. Beveridge, Jr., *Does a Corporation's Board of Directors Owe a Fiduciary Duty to Its Creditors?*, 25 St. Mary's L.J. 589 (1994); Jonathan P. Lipson, *Directors' Duties to Creditors: Power Imbalance and the Financially Distressed Corporation,* 50 UCLA L. Rev. 1189 (2003).

[70] Robinson v. Wangemann, 75 F.2d 756 (5th Cir. 1935).

[71] *See* Wood v. Nat'l City Bank, 24 F.2d 661 (2d Cir. 1928) (Hand, J.).

[72] Model Bus. Corp. Act. § 6.40 (1984).

[73] Daniel Keating, *Bankruptcy, Tithing, and the Pocket-Picking Paradigm of Free Exercise*, 1996 U. Ill. L. Rev. 1041; Kenneth N. Klee, *Tithing and Bankruptcy*, 75 Am. Bankr. L.J. 157 (2001); Nicholas C. Rigano, *Fraudulent Conveyance Law: Destroying Free Exercise Rights at a Church Near You*, 17 Am. Bankr. Inst. L. Rev. 165 (2009); Judd M. Treeman, Comment, *Blessed be the Name of the Code: How to Protect Churches From Tithe Avoidance Under the Bankruptcy Code's Fraudulent Transfer Law*, 25 Emory Bankr. Dev. J. 599 (2009).

(A) the amount of that contribution does not exceed 15% of the *gross* annual income of the debtor for the year in which the transfer of the contribution is made; or

(B) the contribution made by a debtor exceeded the percentage of the amount of gross annual income specified in subparagraph (A) if the transfer was consistent with the practices of the debtor in making charitable contributions.[74]

Thus, for a debtor with gross annual income of $100,000 per year, a charitable contribution up to $15,000 is not fraudulent under § 548(a)(2)(B), though it may still be recoverable if the contribution was made with the actual intent to hinder, delay, or defraud creditors under § 548(a)(1)(A).

In re Lewis provides a dramatic example of the potential impact of this provision.[75] Mr. Lewis, was a sole proprietor of a small business, who contributed 15% of his business's gross receipts, before even deducting amounts for the costs of goods sold or for his other operating expenses. Under § 548(a)(2)(B), a failing sole proprietorship might be grossing $10 million in income a year and incurring $11 million of operating expenses and yet retain the ability to make $1.5 million in charitable contributions free from any claim that the transfers were constructively fraudulent. Furthermore, a charitable contribution of even more than 15% might be protected from attack if the contribution was consistent with the debtor's history of making charitable contributions.

This might at first appear to be a limit on the total percentage of charitable contributions a debtor makes, but it is not. Despite the language of § 548(a)(2)(B), the 15% threshold applies to the aggregate of transfers made to the same charity throughout the taxable year, not to each separate transfer that the debtor made at various times throughout the year. Thus, if a debtor who earns $100,000 per year makes two $10,000 contributions to the same charity, $5,000 of the transfers are recoverable by the trustee. Any other result would permit the debtor to transfer all of his income to a single charity.[76]

The Religious Liberty and Charitable Donation Protection Act added this protection in response to the Supreme Court's 1997 decision in *City of Boerne v. Flores.*[77] *City of Boerne* struck down as unconstitutional the Religious Freedom Restoration Act of 1993, which, among many other things, sought to protect contributions to religious organizations from attack as fraudulent transfers.[78]

---

[74] Bankruptcy Code § 548(a)(2) (emphasis added).

[75] *See* Wolkowitz v. Breath of Life Seventh Day Adventist Church (In re Lewis), 401 B.R. 431 (Bankr. C.D. Cal. 2009).

[76] The Universal Church v. Geltzer, 463 F.2d 218 (2d Cir. 2006). *But see* In re Zohdi, 234 B.R. 371, 380 n. 20 (Bankr. M.D. La. 1999).

[77] 521 U.S. 507 (1997).

[78] The same day, the Court granted certiorari and remanded *Christians v. Crystal Evangelical Free Church* to the Eighth Circuit for reconsideration in light of its decision in *City of Boerne.* 521 U.S. 1114 (1997). On remand, the Eighth Circuit held that the fraudulent conveyance provisions of RFRA were severable from its other unconstitutional provisions, and that Congress had the power under Article I of the Constitution to revise portions of the Bankruptcy Code regarding the avoidability of fraudulent

The current language prevents the trustee from recovering charitable donations, within these limits, as fraudulent conveyances, unless the trustee can establish that the donation was made with fraudulent intent. Section 544(b) was also amended to prevent the trustee from mounting a similar attack through state fraudulent conveyance law.[79] On the other hand, nothing in these changes prevents the trustee from avoiding a fraudulent "obligation" — a charitable pledge to make a contribution to a charity.

Likewise, charitable contributions might still be recoverable by creditors under state law outside of bankruptcy, even though they are largely invulnerable, within the limits outlined above, to attack once the debtor has filed its petition. As explained elsewhere, Chapter 13 contains similar language that permits debtors to deduct charitable contributions, up to 15% of their gross income, from the income they must submit to the trustee for distribution to creditors under their plan.[80] Likewise, Chapter 7's new means testing rules, used to determine whether a debtor's petition should be dismissed due to abuse, permit deduction of up to 15% of the debtor's gross income in calculating the amount of the debtor's disposable income.[81]

[5] Leveraged Buy-Outs[82]

During the 1980s, the so-called "leveraged buy-out" (LBO) became a popular tool to change control of publicly held corporations. The typical LBO involves a group of investors, who buy out the interests of the stockholders using borrowed money ("leverage"). The company that is purchased is an obligor (sometimes the only obligor) on the loan. In effect, the buyers use the credit worthiness of the company they are acquiring to buy out the equity interests of the shareholders. LBOs can be used for many purposes, including the spin-off of an unwanted division or subsidiary. However, the most publicized LBOs have involved taking a public company private. This means that the end result of the LBO is the conversion of a corporation with many stockholders, an actively traded stock, and lots of shareholder equity, to a corporation with few stockholders and stock that is rarely if ever traded. In place of most of the shareholder equity is a massive debt.

For example, suppose Franklin Manufacturing is a widely-held company whose major stockholders and leading managers are Adams, Brown, and Clay. The three of them borrow money from Peninsula Bank and use the funds to purchase all of the other stock of Franklin. After obtaining control, they cause Franklin to guarantee

---

conveyances in bankruptcy. Christians v. Crystal Evangelical Free Church, 41 F.3d 854 (8th Cir. 1998).

[79] Bankruptcy Code § 544(b)(2) (expressly pre-empting state fraudulent conveyance law to this extent).

[80] Bankruptcy Code § 1325(b)(2)(A)(ii). *See infra* § 18.08[E][2] Debtor's Projected Disposable Income.

[81] Bankruptcy Code § 707(b)(1). *See infra* § 17.03[B][2][b][iv] Deduction of Charitable Contributions.

[82] Douglas G. Baird & Thomas H. Jackson, *Fraudulent Conveyance Law and Its Proper Domain*, 38 Vand. L. Rev. 829, 850-54 (1985); John H. Ginsberg, et al., *Befuddlement Betwixt Two Fulcrums: Calibrating the Scales of Justice to Ascertain Fraudulent Transfers in Leveraged Buyouts*, 19 Am. Bankr. Inst. L. Rev. 71 (2011); Emily L. Sherwin, *Creditors' Rights Against Participants in a Leveraged Buyout*, 72 Minn. L. Rev. 449 (1988).

payment of the debt they owe and grant the bank a security interest in all of Franklin's assets. Subsequently, Franklin, not Adams, Brown, or Clay, makes payments on the debt to Peninsula when they fall due. When Franklin ends up bankrupt, its other creditors (and any bankruptcy trustee who is appointed) complain that Franklin's guarantee, security interest, and payments are all fraudulent transfers or obligations. Their rationale is simple: the secured guarantee rendered Franklin insolvent and it received nothing in exchange for its transfers. If Franklin was insolvent when the transfer was made, became insolvent as a result of the transfer, had inadequate capital, or lacked ability to pay its debts, the basic requirements of § 548 appear to be met.

The leveraged buyout of Crown Unlimited Machine, Inc., provides a recent example of a leveraged buyout that was successfully attacked as a fraudulent conveyance. Crown (or "Old Crown") sold all of its assets, including its name, to a newly formed corporation (referred to here as "New Crown") which was owned by Kevin Smith.[83] New Crown's purchase of the assets was financed by a loan from a bank, with the loan secured by the assets that were being purchased.[84] The loan proceeds were paid to Old Crown, which subsequently distributed them to its shareholders and ceased doing business. When New Crown "was a flop,"[85] it filed a bankruptcy petition and its trustee brought an action against Old Crown alleging that the $6 million New Crown paid to Old Crown for the company's assets was for less than a "reasonably equivalent value" and left New Crown with remaining assets which were "unreasonably small in relation to [its] business" and thus a fraudulent transfer under § 4(a)(2)(i) of the old Uniform Fraudulent Transfer Act.[86] The court subsequently collapsed the two-stage transaction, and gave the trustee a judgment not only against Old Crown, but also against the shareholders who had subsequently received the borrowed cash as a distribution from Old Crown.[87] It supplies a good example of how an effort to use borrowed funds to replace old managers with new blood can be upset when the new managers are unsuccessful in their efforts to operate the business.

As *Crown* illustrates, various aspects of LBO transactions are vulnerable to attack. In *Crown* it was the payment of assets from Crown's new incarnation to its old incarnation, that caused the problem. In the hypothetical involving Franklin Manufacturing, several aspects of the transaction might be problematical: Franklin's guarantee might be a fraudulent obligation; the transfer of the security interest in Franklin's assets might be a fraudulent transfer; or the stream of Franklin's payments to Peninsula might be fraudulent transfers. Depending upon whether the company met the other requirements for avoidance, they may be able to attack all or any of these steps in the LBO.

It should be clear that Franklin did not receive any direct benefit from the transaction. All of the money the bank provided was paid to Franklin's former

---

[83] Boyer v. Crown Stock Distrib., Inc., 587 F.3d 787 (7th Cir. 2009) (Posner, J.).

[84] *Id.* at 790.

[85] *Id.* at 791.

[86] *Id.*

[87] *Id.* at 796-97.

stockholders. Franklin did, however, arguably receive indirect benefits: Adams, Brown, and Clay may be especially hard-working managers now that they own the entire company, and that ownership interest is only valuable if the company can meet its debt obligations. The problem, almost insurmountable, is to convince a skeptical bankruptcy court that the value of the managers' sweat equity is real, let alone a reasonable equivalent.

The transaction might take one of several other forms too numerous to fully describe here.[88] Those who structure LBOs work tirelessly to skirt the provisions of § 548 and the UFTA. To a large degree, these efforts, at least insofar as they apply to reasonably equivalent value, have been unsuccessful. It is very difficult to convince a court that new or rejuvenated management constitutes a measurable, reasonably equivalent value.[89] The exact structure of the transaction makes little difference.[90] In some cases, the structure of the transaction may affect who is liable, because of the protections given by § 548 and other fraudulent transfer laws to bona fide purchasers. More important as a defense to fraudulent conveyance attack is ensuring that when the transaction is complete, the leveraged entity is not left insolvent or with unreasonably small capital.[91]

Similarly, a good faith transferee may escape liability. Courts have protected transfers made to former shareholders who were not insiders and who had no reason to believe that the debtor was insolvent or that the transaction would create any financial difficulty for it.[92]

[6] Asset Securitization Transactions[93]

Securitization transactions have emerged over the last fifteen-twenty years as a big business, involving several trillion dollars in transactions outstanding at any one time. They serve as a substitute for traditional sales of accounts or accounts receivable financing, but they provide significant advantages for their sponsors, who use them to obtain capital more cheaply than they otherwise might.

In a securitization transaction, the debtor incorporates a company to purchase its accounts, and issues securities in the company backed by the stream of accounts

---

[88] David G. Carlson, *Leveraged Buyouts in Bankruptcy*, 20 Ga. L. Rev. 73, 80-83 (1985).

[89] *See, e.g.*, Moody v. Sec. Pac. Bus. Credit, Inc., 127 B.R. 958 (W.D. Pa. 1991); Credit Managers Ass'n v. Fed. Co., 629 F. Supp. 175 (C.D. Cal. 1985).

[90] Keven J. Liss, *Fraudulent Conveyance Law and Leveraged Buyouts*, 87 Colum. L. Rev. 1491, 1499 (1987).

[91] *E.g.*, Comm. of Unsecured Creditors v. ASEA Brown, 313 B.R. 219, 230 (N.D. Ohio 2004).

[92] *E.g.*, Kupetz v. Wolf, 845 F.2d 842 (9th Cir. 1988); Zahn v. Yucaipa Capital Fund, 218 B.R. 656 (D.R.I. 1998). *But see* Bay Plastics, Inc. v. BT Comm'l Corp. (In re Bay Plastics, Inc.), 187 B.R. 315 (Bankr. C.D. Cal. 1995) (no protection for shareholders who did not pay value "to the debtor"). *See* Michael L. Cook, Brad J. Axelrod & Geoffrey S. Frankel, *The Judicially Created "Innocent Shareholder Defense" to Constructive Fraudulent Transfer Liability in Failed Leveraged Buyouts*, 43 S.C. L. Rev. 777 (1992).

[93] Rhett G. Campbell, *Financial Markets Contracts and BAPCPA*, 79 Am. Bankr. L.J. 697 (2005); Edward J. Janger, *Muddy Rules for Securitizations*, 7 Fordham J. Corp. & Fin. L. 301 (2002); Peter J. Lahny, *Asset Securitization: A Discussion of the Traditional Bankruptcy Attacks and an Analysis of the Next Potential Attack, Substantive Consolidation*, 9 Am. Bankr. Inst. L. Rev. 815 (2001).

purchased from the debtor. For example, Franklin Manufacturing, as the "originator" of the accounts, might transfer them to a second corporation, known in the business as a "special purpose vehicle" (SPV),[94] which was formed for the express purpose of purchasing the accounts. After purchasing the accounts from the originator, the SPV sells securities backed by the accounts (ABS). The ABS produce the revenue used to pay dividends to investors. Securitization transactions are regarded as superior to traditional methods of lending secured by a debtor's accounts receivable and sales of such accounts because it is less expensive and less risky than these traditional mechanisms.[95]

However, the transaction is attractive to investors who might be expected to purchase the securities only if it can be insulated from any bankruptcy proceeding that the originator might file. Unless this can be accomplished, the securities will not be sufficiently attractive to investors to be successful. Thus, the success of the entire transaction depends on whether the sale of the accounts can be insulated from recovery by the originator's bankruptcy in the event that the originator must seek bankruptcy protection from its creditors.

Securitization transactions are vulnerable to attack on several fronts, including avoidance as a fraudulent transfer.[96] Depending on the originator's financial condition, if the price paid by the SPV to the originator was not a reasonably equivalent value for the transferred accounts, the entire transaction might be avoidable as a constructively fraudulent transfer.[97] Though less likely, the transaction might also be a fraudulent transfer if the circumstances surrounding the transaction indicate that it was merely a means to insulate the originator's assets from its creditors and thus "intended to hinder, delay, or defraud" the originator's creditors.[98]

One of the difficulties that makes the transaction susceptible to attack as a fraudulent transfer is that investors in the SPV are likely to want the value of the underlying receivables to be high enough to assure them a meaningful return. This is likely to push the sale price lower in relation to the value of the underlying receivables, and thus increase the likelihood that a court might later conclude that the amount paid by the SPV was not a reasonably equivalent exchange for the receivables.[99]

As explained elsewhere, the securitization transaction might also be attacked as "intended for security" and thus not a "true sale" of the originator's receivables, or,

---

[94] *See* Steven L. Schwarcz, *The Alchemy of Asset Securitization*, 1 Stan. J.L. Bus. & Fin. 133, 134 (1994).

[95] *See, e.g.*, Gregory R. Salathé, Note, *Reducing Health Care Costs Through Hospital Accounts Receivable Securitization*, 80 Va. L. Rev. 549 (1994).

[96] Edward J. Janger, *The Death of Secured Lending*, 25 Cardozo L. Rev. 1759 (2004); Edward J. Janger, *Muddy Rules for Securitizations*, 7 Fordham J. Corp. & Fin. L. 301, 308-10 (2002). *See supra* § 7.05 Securitization.

[97] Bankruptcy Code § 548(a)(1)(B).

[98] Bankruptcy Code § 548(a)(1)(A).

[99] *See generally* Steven L. Schwarcz & Adam Ford, Structured Finance, A Guide to the Principles of Asset Securitization § 4:7 (3d ed. 2002); Jeffrey E. Bjork, *Seeking Predictability in Bankruptcy: An Alternative to Judicial Recharacterization in Structured Financing*, 14 Bankr. Dev. J. 119 (1997).

if corporate formalities have not been fully observed, through an effort to pierce the corporate veil of the SPV and bring its assets into the originator's bankruptcy estate.[100]

[7] Ponzi Schemes[101]

Ponzi schemes, of the type made famous again by Bernie Madoff in 2008 and 2009,[102] carry with them the risk that when the scheme falls apart, that successful investors, who received payoffs from the scheme's perpetrator, will be forced to disgorge their "earnings" as fraudulent conveyances. Investors in Ponzi schemes who are fortunate enough to receive a return on their investment, are liable under the UFTA and § 548 because, except to the extent of their investment, they did not provide reasonable equivalent value for the amount of their earnings.[103]

[8] Financial Derivatives & Commodity Forward Agreements[104]

The Bankruptcy Code provides safe harbor protection for a variety of financial derivatives transactions and long-term commodity contracts, against avoidance as a constructive fraudulent conveyance, or otherwise under most of the trustee's other avoiding powers. This protection applies to parties to swap agreements,[105] forward contracts,[106] commodity contracts,[107] securities contracts,[108] and repurchase agreements.[109] These safe harbor provisions permit parties to these transactions to exercise their contractual rights to terminate, liquidate or accelerate ("close-out") their agreements with bankrupt debtors without fear of violating the automatic stay or avoidance under most of the trustee's avoiding powers.

§ 16.04 TRANSFERS TO GENERAL PARTNERS

Section 548(b) provides for special treatment of transfers by bankrupt partnerships. The trustee may avoid any transfer of property or any obligation incurred within two years before the debtor's petition if the partnership was insolvent or the

---

[100] *See supra* § 7.05 Securitization.

[101] Arthur J. Steinberg & John F. Isbell, *The Need to Revisit the "Value in Good Faith" Defense to Fraudulent Transfer Claims*, 18 J. Bankr. L. & Prac. 4 (2009).

[102] One NPR Commentator suggested that Mr. Madoff's Ponzi scheme was of such significant proportions that he should be awarded "naming rights" to the scheme that bears Mr. Ponzi's name.

[103] Donell v. Kowell, 533 F.3d 762 (9th Cir. 2008).

[104] Eleanor Heard Gilbane, *Testing the Bankruptcy Code Safe Harbors in the Current Financial Crisis*, 18 Am. Bankr. Inst. L. Rev. 241 (2010); Stephen J. Lubben, *The Bankruptcy Code Without Safe Harbors*, 84 Am. Bankr. L.J. 123 (2010). *See generally* In re Nat'l Gas Distrib's, LLC, 556 F.3d 247 (4th Cir. 2009).

[105] Bankruptcy Code § 101(53B).

[106] Bankruptcy Code § 101(25).

[107] Bankruptcy Code § 761(4).

[108] Bankruptcy Code § 741(7).

[109] Bankruptcy Code § 101(47).

partnership became insolvent as a result of the transfer or obligation.[110] This rule is far more absolute than any of the other grounds for avoidance: fraudulent intent is immaterial, and the transfer is avoidable even if it the exchange was for a reasonably equivalent value.

In understanding this rule, it is important to stress that it only applies when the partnership, together with its general partners, has fewer assets than liabilities. A partnership is only insolvent when its assets, together with the excess of each partner's own properties over the partner's own debts, is less than the total debts of the partnership.[111] This is because general partners are answerable for the debts of a partnership; thus, the excess of the partners' assets over the partners' personal debts are for all practical purposes assets of the partnership and are available to the partnership's creditors. Therefore, to determine whether the partnership is insolvent, the financial condition of the partnership and all of its general partners must be determined.

For example, assume Arsenio and Bernice are partners. Their partnership owns $50,000 in assets and has $70,000 in debts. Arsenio and Bernice each own $10,000 in nonpartnership property and each has $4,000 of nonpartnership debts. Arsenio's "excess" is $6,000; Bernice's excess is $6,000. The sum of Arsenio's excess plus Bernice's excess plus the partnership's property is $62,000 — $8,000 less than the partnership's debts. Thus, the partnership is insolvent. Any transfer of property by the partnership to Bernice is fraudulent. Even if Bernice were to pay the partnership $5,000 for $5,000 worth of the partnership's property, the situation would be the same. In either case, the creditors of the partnership would be able to reach only a total of $62,000, regardless of whether the assets are held by Arsenio, Bernice, or their partnership. Thus, Bernice's purchase, although for a reasonably equivalent value, would be avoidable.

§ 16.05 REACH-BACK PERIODS FOR FRAUDULENT TRANSFER

Both § 548 and state fraudulent transfer law limit the reach-back period for fraudulent transfers. Transfers made and obligations incurred many years before the bankruptcy petition are not recoverable even though the debtor may have been insolvent when they were made. However, the limit under § 548 is shorter than it is under most state's laws. As explained below, state law generally has a much longer reach-back period, that in some states goes back as far as ten years. This is tempered by restrictions on which creditors have standing to recover the fraudulent conveyance. These limits are important, because the trustee must find an actual unsecured creditor who could have avoided the transfer, in order to recover it under state fraudulent conveyance law through § 544(b).

---

[110] Bankruptcy Code § 548(b). *See also* UFTA § 8 (1984).

[111] Bankruptcy Code § 101(32)(B).

[A] Bankruptcy Code's Fraudulent Transfer Recovery Period

Section 548 permits recovery of fraudulent transfers that occurred within two years before the debtor's petition.[112] The two-year period must be considered in light of other portions of § 548 that specify the time a transfer is deemed to have been made. Section 548(d)(1) states that a transfer occurs when the transfer "is so perfected that a bona fide purchaser . . . against whom applicable law permits such transfer to be perfected cannot acquire an interest . . . that is superior to [that of] the transferee."[113] This provision deals with the same two-step transfer problem discussed in other contexts, such as avoidable preferences[114] and the strong-arm clause of § 544(a).[115]

Some transfers require more than one step to become effective against third parties. For example, execution of a deed or mortgage does not make the conveyance good against all third parties until it is recorded. Usually, a bona fide purchaser can take free of the interest represented by the unrecorded deed or mortgage. Until recorded, the transaction has not occurred for the purposes of § 548.

For example, suppose that on February 1, 2013, Vera executes a deed in favor of Park. But, Park does not record the deed until August 15, 2013. If Vera files a bankruptcy petition on July 1, 2015. The transfer from Vera to Park occurred on August 15, 2013 and is thus within two years before her bankruptcy petition. If Vera was insolvent back in August, 2013, and the price Park paid was inadequate, the trustee may avoid the transfer under § 548(a)(1)(B). If the deed had been recorded on March 1, 2013, the transfer would have occurred more than two years before her July 1, 2015 bankruptcy petition. It would not be avoidable under § 548, though it might still be vulnerable under state fraudulent conveyance law, which the trustee might also be able to use. If the deed was never recorded, the transfer would have occurred "immediately before the date of the filing of the petition,"[116] which presumably means on June 30, 2015, the day before her bankruptcy petition.

[B] State Law Fraudulent Transfer Recovery Period

The trustee's power to avoid a fraudulent transfer is not limited to § 548. Section 544(b), permits the trustee to avoid a fraudulent transfer obligation that could have been avoided by someone who is actually a creditor in the bankruptcy proceeding.[117] Most states have a longer fraudulent transfer reach-back period that the two years in § 548. This makes state fraudulent transfer law especially

---

[112] Bankruptcy Code § 548(a)(1), (b). Before 2005, the reach-back period was only one year.

[113] Bankruptcy Code § 548(d)(1).

[114] See supra § 15.02 [A] Transfer of Property; Time of Transfer.

[115] See supra § 14.02 Strong-Arm Power.

[116] Bankruptcy Code § 548(d)(1).

[117] Bankruptcy Code § 544(b) gives the trustee the power to "avoid any transfer of an interest of the debtor in property or any obligation incurred by the debtor that is voidable under applicable law by a creditor holding an unsecured claim that is allowable." See generally supra § 14.03 Power to Use Rights of Actual Unsecured Creditors.

important, despite other limitations imposed by § 544(b).

The UFTA generally uses a four-year statute of limitations.[118] Because the trustee's right to use state fraudulent conveyance law depends on the rights of actual unsecured creditors, this effectively imposes a four-year reach-back period that prevents the trustee from recovering transfers that were made more than four years before the debtor's bankruptcy petition. For cases involving actual fraud under UFTA § 4(a)(1), the period is extended until "one year after the transfer or obligation was or could reasonably have been discovered by the claimant" whose rights the trustee asserts.[119] Some states impose longer periods,[120] though a few are shorter.[121]

The UFTA contains rules similar to those in § 548(d), that determine when a transfer occurred. With respect to transfers of real estate, the transfer is deemed to have been made when it was "so far perfected that a good-faith purchaser of the asset from the debtor . . . cannot acquire an interest in the asset that is superior to the interest of the transferee."[122] In most cases, this means that the transfer is made when recorded. With respect to personal property and fixtures, the transfer is made when it is sufficiently perfected to prevent a subsequent judicial lien creditor from acquiring a superior interest.[123]

However, in other respects state fraudulent transfer law is narrower than § 548. The trustee may only use state fraudulent transfer law if it can find an actual unsecured creditor with standing to set the transfer aside. UFTA § 4(a) permits a person who was a creditor before or after the transfer to set it aside,[124] but § 5(a), regarding transfers by an insolvent debtor for less than a reasonably equivalent value, only gives standing to those who were creditors before the transfer was made.[125] In addition, the creditor whose rights the trustee asserts must have an allowable claim in the bankruptcy case.

Thus, if Franklin Manufacturing made a transfer two years before its petition, that could have been set aside by its existing creditors, but Franklin then paid those creditors, state fraudulent transfer law is of no avail to the trustee. The rights of the trustee under § 544(b) are entirely derivative of those of an actual creditor — if there is no actual creditor who has standing to avoid the transaction under state fraudulent conveyance law, the trustee has no standing either.

This standing problem does not arise under § 548, which draws no distinction between types of creditors and in any event does not require that there be any

---

[118] UFTA § 9(a), (b).

[119] UFTA § 9(a) (1984).

[120] *E.g.*, Ala. Code § 8-9A-9 (2001) (ten-year statute of limitations for transfers of real property and a six-year statute for transfers of personal property in Alabama); Maio v. Gardino, 700 N.Y.S.2d 509 (App. Div. 1999) (six years in New York).

[121] *See* Pa. Cons. Stat. § 12-5109 (2001) (two years).

[122] UFTA § 6(1)(i).

[123] UFTA § 6(1)(ii).

[124] UFTA § 4(a) (1984).

[125] UFTA § 5 (1984).

actual creditor who is affected by the transfer. Section 548 conveys standing to the trustee if the transaction is avoidable under its provisions.

§ 16.06   LIABILITIES OF AND PROTECTIONS FOR BONA FIDE PURCHASERS[126]

As discussed more fully elsewhere,[127] the trustee may usually recover an avoided transfer from either the immediate recipient of the transferred property or from subsequent transferees. However, if a remote transferee is a bona fide purchaser, the trustee may not recover the property. Moreover, as a general rule, those who make valuable improvements to the transferred property are given a lien on the property — in effect, a secured claim for the improvements made. Finally, the trustee has the option to recover the value of the property rather than the property itself.

Section 548(c) also provides some protection to the immediate transferee. The protection is given only if three conditions are met. First, the transfer must not also be avoidable under §§ 544, 545, or 547. Second, the transferee must have given value. Third, the value must have been given in good faith. If these conditions are met, the transferee is given a lien on the transferred property for the amount of the value given. In some cases, the transferee may even be permitted to retain the transferred property.[128]

Actions brought under state fraudulent conveyance law through § 544(b) are subject to whatever protections are accorded by the state law that authorizes the transaction to be avoided. The UFTA generally exposes the immediate transferee[129] and any subsequent transferee to liability but protects subsequent transferees who acted in good faith and and acquired the property from a subsequent transferee for value.[130] The UFTA extends full protection to good faith transferees who supplied a reasonably equivalent value from liability due to an intentionally fraudulent transfer.[131] However, immediate transferees are usually aware of the debtor's fraudulent intent.

In addition, the UFTA provides good faith transferees with a lien on the property that was the subject of the avoided transfer. However, unlike § 548, it gives them no protection for the value of improvements they might have made after the transfer.

---

[126] Michael L. Cook, *Fraudulent Transfer Liability Under the Bankruptcy Code*, 17 Hous. L. Rev. 263 (1980).

[127] *See supra* § 14.08[D] Protection for Good Faith Transferees.

[128] Bankruptcy Code § 548(c).

[129] UFTA § 8(b)(1).

[130] UFTA § 8(b)(2).

[131] UFTA § 8(a).

Chapter 17

LIQUIDATION UNDER CHAPTER 7

§ 17.01 DEBTOR LIQUIDATION[1]

Chapter 7 bankruptcy cases are usually referred to as "straight" bankruptcy,[2] "liquidation," or more simply, "Chapter 7." In theory, debtors in a Chapter 7 liquidation give up all of their property in exchange for relief, in the form of a discharge, from their debts.[3] In contrast, in reorganization or rehabilitation cases under Chapters 11, 12 and 13, debtors usually keep their property and make payments to creditors from their future income, pursuant to a court-approved plan. Liquidation makes sense when creditors will receive more from an immediate sale of the debtor's assets than they would from the receipt of installment payments made by the debtor over a period of time.

The practical reality is quite different, particularly in cases involving consumer debtors.[4] Nearly all consumer debtors have few, if any assets available to distribute to unsecured creditors. In these "no-asset" cases, the debtor's assets are either exempt or completely encumbered by security interests and mortgages. Debtors receive an immediate discharge, retain their exempt property, and usually end up either surrendering any property that is subject to a security interest or mortgage, or more likely, entering into reaffirmation agreements with their secured creditors permitting them to keep their property in return for renewing their obligations to repay their secured debts. In this respect, some Chapter 7 liquidation cases are similar to rehabilitation cases under Chapter 13, but with no recovery for unsecured creditors.

Business cases are different, at least where there are some unencumbered assets.[5] But few businesses that intend to continue their operations file Chapter 7 cases. The prospect of the immediate appointment of a trustee, responsible for taking over the day-to-day operation of the debtor's business, discourages most corporate managers from seeking this type of relief. Nevertheless, some businesses

---

[1] Scott Fay, Erik Hurst & Michelle J. White, *The Household Bankruptcy Decision*, 92 Amer. Econ. Rev. 706, 706 (2002); Michelle J. White, *Why It Pays to File for Bankruptcy: A Critical Look at the Incentives Under U.S. Personal Bankruptcy Law and a Proposal for Change*, 65 U. Chi. L. Rev. 685 (1998).

[2] *E.g.*, In re Puffer, 674 F.3d 78 (1st Cir. 2012).

[3] *See supra* Chapter 13 — Discharge.

[4] Dalié Jiménez, *The Distribution of Assets in Consumer Chapter 7 Bankruptcy Cases*, 83 Am. Bankr. L.J. 795 (2009).

[5] Lynn M. LoPucki, *The Death of Liability*, 106 Yale L.J. 1 (1996). *But see* Steven L. Schwarcz, *The Inherent Irrationality of Judgment Proofing*, 52 Stan. L. Rev. 1 (1999).

end up in Chapter 7 when their efforts to reorganize in Chapter 11 fail. Likewise, consumer debtors who thought they could maintain payments under a Chapter 13 rehabilitation plan, frequently convert their cases to Chapter 7, or, instead, simply exit bankruptcy court without having completed their plans or receiving a discharge of their debts.

Although liquidation of the debtor is primarily the function of Chapter 7, liquidation may also occur under other chapters as well. A Chapter 11 plan may provide for partial or even complete liquidation of the debtor.[6] Moreover, Chapter 7 does not necessarily result in an immediate "fire sale" of all of the debtor's assets. When appropriate, the Chapter 7 trustee may opt for an extended, orderly liquidation and may even continue to run the debtor's business for a time, anticipating selling the enterprise as a going concern.

Despite the reluctance of businesses to seek Chapter 7 relief, most bankruptcies are filed under Chapter 7, and an even greater number are closed in it.[7] In addition, the amount that would be distributed to creditors in a Chapter 7 liquidation case provides the baseline for the minimum amount that creditors must receive under Chapters 11, 12, and 13. Thus, Chapter 7 is the touchstone for all other types of bankruptcy proceedings.

However, there are many respects in which Chapter 7 is distinctive. Its distinctive features are discussed in the sections that follow.

§ 17.02 COMMENCEMENT OF A CHAPTER 7 LIQUIDATION CASE

Details about the filing or "commencement" of a Chapter 7 liquidation case are covered elsewhere.[8] Most entities: individuals, corporations, partnerships, trusts, and unincorporated associations are all eligible for relief under Chapter 7 if they reside in the United States, have a domicile in the United States, have a place of business in the United States, or own property in the United States.[9] Among these debtors, only railroads, insurance companies, and financial institutions are prohibited from seeking relief in Chapter 7.[10]

Like other bankruptcy cases, Chapter 7 proceedings are commenced with the filing of a simple petition.[11] The petition contains the debtor's representation that she is eligible for relief, and that she has resided in the district in which the petition is filed for the preceding 180 days or that venue is proper for some other reason,

---

[6] *See* Bankruptcy Code § 1123(b)(4).

[7] In 2010, almost 1.6 million bankruptcy cases were filed. Of these, nearly 1.14 million were Chapter 7 cases. Fewer than 14,000 of them were Chapter 11 cases. Of the nearly 1.14 million Chapter 7 cases, slightly less than 40,000 were business cases. The remainder involved primarily consumer debtors. http://www.uscourts.gov/bnkrpctystats/statistics.htm (last visited on April 17, 2012).

[8] *See infra* Chapter 6 — Commencement.

[9] Bankruptcy Code § 109(a). *See supra* § 6.02[B][1][a] Connection to the United States.

[10] Bankruptcy Code § 109(b). *See supra* § 6.02[B][2] Eligibility for Relief in Chapter 7 — Liquidation.

[11] Bankruptcy Code § 301(a).

such as that an affiliate has a case pending in the same district.[12]

Voluntary Chapter 7 petitions are usually accompanied by a list of creditors; schedules of assets, liabilities, income and expenditures; and other documents that enable creditors and the bankruptcy trustee to administer the debtor's estate and make payments to creditors.[13] Among these other documents are copies of a debtor's pay stubs, an itemized statement of monthly income, and a statement disclosing any reasonably anticipated income or expenditures for the twelve-month period following filing of the petition.[14] If the debtor is an individual debtor whose debts are primarily consumer debts, she must include a certificate verifying that she received a notification, either from her attorney, a bankruptcy petition preparer, or the court, briefly describing "chapters 7, 11, 12, and 13 and the general purpose, benefits, and costs of proceeding under each of those chapters [and] the types of services available from credit counseling agencies."[15] The debtor must also supply a certificate verifying that she has received a statement alerting her that "a person who knowingly and fraudulently conceals assets or makes a false oath or statement under penalty of perjury in connection with [the bankruptcy case is] subject to fine, imprisonment or both [and] that all information supplied by a debtor . . . is subject to examination by the Attorney General."[16]

All individual debtors (not just those with primarily consumer debts) must also submit a certificate from an approved nonprofit budget and credit counseling agency, verifying that the debtor has participated in a consumer credit counseling "briefing" sometime within the 180 days immediately preceding her petition,[17] and a copy of any "debt repayment plan" that was developed in the course of this briefing.[18] The briefing must be provided by a non-profit credit counseling provider approved by the United States Trustee.[19] The necessity of this credit counseling briefing may be waived by the court if the debtor is unable to complete the briefing due to "disability or active military duty in a military combat zone."[20]

Once filed, a voluntary petition operates as the entry of an order for relief for the debtor.[21] As explained elsewhere, it invokes the automatic stay of § 362,[22] prevent-

---

[12] 28 U.S.C. § 1408 (2006); Official Bankruptcy Form 1.

[13] Bankruptcy Code § 521(a). See Fed. R. Bankr. P. 1007(a).

[14] Bankruptcy Code § 521(a)(1)(B)(iv)-(vi).

[15] Bankruptcy Code §§ 521(a)(1)(B)(iii), 342(b)(1).

[16] Bankruptcy Code §§ 521(a)(1)(B)(iii), 342(b)(2).

[17] Bankruptcy Code § 521(b)(1).

[18] Bankruptcy Code § 521(b)(2). *See generally* Karen Gross & Susan Block-Lieb, *Empty Mandate or Opportunity for Innovation? Pre-petition Credit Counseling and Postpetition Financial Management Education*, 13 Am. Bankr. Inst. L. Rev. 549 (2005).

[19] Bankruptcy Code § 109(h)(1). A list of approved non-profit credit counseling agencies is maintained on the United States Trustee's website: http://www.usdoj.gov/ust/eo/bapcpa/ccde/cc_approved.htm (last visited April 17, 2012).

[20] Bankruptcy Code § 109(h)(4).

[21] Bankruptcy Code § 301(b). Indeed, the practice for many years was for the bankruptcy court's clerk's office to stamp "ADJUDICATED" on the filed petition, instead of the more innocuous "FILED."

[22] *See supra* Chapter 8 — The Automatic Stay.

ing creditors from continuing their efforts to collect outside the bankruptcy court process.

§ 17.03   DISMISSAL AND CONVERSION OF A CHAPTER 7 CASE

The successful filing of a petition and the entry of an order for relief does not guarantee that a debtor will ultimately obtain relief in Chapter 7. Liquidation cases can be dismissed by the court for a variety of reasons, including due to "abuse" under the new financial means test incorporated into the Bankruptcy Code in 2005 as a key component of the Bankruptcy Abuse Prevention and Consumer Protection Act (BAPCPA).[23] In rare cases the court might "abstain" from the case.

[A]   Dismissal For Cause

Section 707(a) permits a Chapter 7 case to be dismissed for cause[24] and specifies three straightforward and non-controversial bases for doing so. A case can be dismissed due to: (1) "unreasonable delay by the debtor that is prejudicial to creditors,"[25] (2) "nonpayment of any [required] fees or charges,"[26] or (3) "failure of the debtor in a voluntary case to file . . . the information required by [Bankruptcy § 521(a)(1)] within fifteen days" of the time of the debtor's petition.[27] Only the United States Trustee may move for dismissal due to the debtor's failure to file the necessary additional documents by within the fifteen-day deadline. The necessary paperwork is usually filed, and dismissal under these provisions is rare.

There are some procedural requirements for dismissal. There must be a strict twenty days' notice to the debtor, the trustee, and all creditors.[28] In addition, unlike many matters before a bankruptcy court,[29] there must be an actual hearing on the motion to dismiss.[30]

---

[23] Bankruptcy Code § 707(b). *See infra* § 17.03[B] Dismissal of Consumer Cases Due to Abuse.

[24] Bankruptcy Code § 707(a). *See* In re Simmons, 200 F.3d 738, 743 (11th Cir. 2000).

[25] Bankruptcy Code § 707(a)(1).

[26] Bankruptcy Code § 707(a)(2). In most cases, this will be the debtor's filing fee, which can be paid in installments and can sometimes now be waived. *See supra* § 6.02[E] Filing Fees.

[27] Bankruptcy Code § 707(a)(3). *See* In re Fawson, 338 B.R. 505 (Bankr. D. Utah 2006). This information consists primarily of the debtor's schedules of assets, liabilities, income, and expenditures, with the required accompanying documents to verify the accuracy of the debtor's income. *See* Bankruptcy Code § 521(a)(1). The statutory reference in § 707(a)(3) is to a non-existing provision, "paragraph (1) of section 521" but undoubtedly was meant to refer to § 521*(a)* (1).

[28] Fed. R. Bankr. P. 2002(a).

[29] *See* Bankruptcy Code § 102(1)(b).

[30] Bankruptcy Code § 707(a).

[B] Dismissal of Consumer Cases Due to Abuse[31]

Chapter 7 cases of debtors whose debts are "primarily consumer debts" can also be dismissed due to "abuse." The principal means of detecting abuse is the presumptive "means test" of § 707(b)(2).[32] It requires a complex and somewhat artificial calculation of the debtor's ability to make payments to her creditors from whatever sources of income she has, after deducting amounts necessary to meet her basic living expenses and make payments to secured creditors. Chapter 7 cases filed by debtors who have the financial ability or "means" to make what Congress has determined are meaningful payments to their unsecured creditors must be dismissed. However, as a practical matter, debtors whose cases are destined to be dismissed, rarely file Chapter 7 cases. Instead, they seek relief through a Chapter 13 rehabilitation plan.

[1] Consumer Debts

Dismissal due to abuse is possible only in cases involving an "individual debtor . . . whose debts are primarily consumer debts."[33] Consumer debts are those "incurred by an individual primarily for a personal, family, or household purpose."[34] Thus, Chapter 7 cases of individuals in financial difficulty due to their inability to pay business debts are not vulnerable to dismissal due to abuse, regardless of their anticipated future ability to pay the debts that their business has incurred.[35]

Cases decided under former § 707(b), permitting dismissal of Chapter 7 cases of the same types of debtors due to the former standard of "substantial abuse," indicate that debts incurred in pursuit of a profit are not consumer debts,[36] even though the profit might have been sought in order to support the debtor's family. Although student loans might at first blush seem like consumer debts, the portion that is to pay for tuition and books are regarded as part of the start-up expenses for a business or profession. The portion that is for living expenses and support of the debtor's dependents are consumer debts.[37] Debts incurred as part of a marital

---

[31] Jean Braucher, *Means Testing Consumer Bankruptcy: The Problem of Means*, 7 Fordham J. Corp. & Fin. L. 407 (2002); Marianne B. Culhane & Michaela M. White, *Taking the New Consumer Bankruptcy Model for a Test Drive: Means-Testing Real Chapter 7 Debtors*, 7 Am Bankr. Inst. L. Rev. 27 (1998); Angela Littwin, *The Affordability Paradox: How Consumer Bankruptcy's Greatest Weakness May Account for its Surprising Success*, 52 Wm. & Mary L. Rev. 1933 (2011); Gary Neustadter, *2005: A Consumer Bankruptcy Odyssey*, 39 Creighton L. Rev. 225 (2006); Henry Sommer, *Trying to Make Sense Out of Nonsense: Representing Consumers Under the Bankruptcy Abuse Prevention and Consumer Protection Act of 2005*, 79 Am Bankr. L.J. 191 (2005); Eugene W. Wedoff, *Means Testing in the New 707(b)*, 79 Am. Bankr. L.J. 231 (2005).

[32] Susan Jensen, *A Legislative History of the Bankruptcy Abuse Prevention and Consumer Protection Act of 2005*, 79 Am. Bankr. L.J. 485 (2005); Jack F. Williams, *Distrust: The Rhetoric and Reality of Means-Testing*, 7 Am. Bankr. Inst. L. Rev. 105 (1999).

[33] Bankruptcy Code § 707(b)(1).

[34] Bankruptcy Code § 101(8).

[35] *See* In re Mohr, 425 B.R. 457 (Bankr. S.D. Ohio 2010).

[36] *E.g.*, Citizens Nat'l Bank v. Burns (In re Burns), 894 F.2d 361, 363 (10th Cir. 1990).

[37] In re Stewart, 175 F.3d 796, 806 (10th Cir. 1999); In re Gentri, 185 B.R. 368 (Bankr. M.D. Fla. 1995).

settlement or in making improvements to the debtor's home are consumer debts.[38] Liability for negligence seems not to be a consumer debt, because "volition" is a necessary element of incurring a debt for personal, family, or household "purposes."[39]

Whether debts are "primarily" consumer debts depends on whether more than a majority of the *amount* of the debtor's obligations are consumer debts,[40] without regard to whether the debt is secured or unsecured.[41] The sheer number of debts should not matter. Thus, a debtor who owes ten $1000 consumer debts but owes $100,000 to a business creditor is not subject to dismissal for abuse. The amount of her $10,000 in consumer debts pales in comparison to the $100,000 business debt.

However, for most individuals, their home mortgage is their biggest debt. Because it does not matter whether the debt is secured or unsecured, the size of most individual's home mortgages means that most individual debtors debts are primarily consumer debts.[42]

[2] Presumptive Abuse — Means Testing[43]

The financial means test of § 707(b)(2) provides a rigid, and in some places, incoherent set of presumptive standards to determine whether the case must be dismissed due to "abuse." Debtors whose cases are dismissed will have to seek relief under Chapter 13 or go it alone with their creditors, perhaps with the assistance of a credit counseling agency. The test is complex and in places difficult to fathom. It is also highly controversial.[44]

The presumptive means test begins by comparing the debtor's income with the median income of debtors with the same size household in the debtor's home state. If the debtor's income is equal to or below the state median, the debtor's case cannot be dismissed due to presumptive abuse under § 707(b)(2), though it is still

---

[38] In re Gentri, 185 B.R. 368 (Bankr. M.D. Fla. 1995).

[39] *E.g.*, In re Marshalek, 158 B.R. 704 (Bankr. N.D. Ohio 1993).

[40] *E.g.* In re Hlavin, 394 B.R. 441 (Bankr. S.D. Ohio 2008) (discussing cases); In re Kelly, 841 F.2d 908, 913 (9th Cir. 1988) (relying on dictionary definition of "primarily").

[41] *See* In re Kelly, 841 F.2d 908, 912-913 (9th Cir. 1988) (legislative history of § 101(7) expresses intent that home mortgage debts not be treated as consumer debts); In re Price, 353 F.3d 1135, 1139 (9th Cir. 2004).

[42] *See, e.g.*, In re Hlavin, 394 B.R. 441, 445-46 (Bankr. S.D. Ohio 2008).

[43] *See* Jean Braucher, *Getting Realistic: In Defense of Formulaic Means Testing*, 83 Am. Bankr. L.J. 395 (2009); Marianne B. Culhane & Michaela M. White, *Catching Can-Pay Debtors: Is the Means Test the Only Way?*, 13 Am. Bankr. Inst. L. Rev. 665 (2005); Angela Littwin, *The Affordability Paradox: How Consumer Bankruptcy's Greatest Weakness May Account for its Surprising Success*, 52 Wm. & Mary L. Rev. 1933 (2011); Eugene W. Wedoff, *Means Testing in the New 707(b)*, 79 Am. Bankr. L.J. 231, 235 (2005).

[44] *Compare* Judge Edith H. Jones & Todd J. Zwicki, *It's Time for Means-Testing*, 1999 B.Y.U. L. Rev. 177 (1999), *and* Eric A. Posner, *Should Debtors Be Forced Into Chapter 13?* 32 Loy. L.A. L. Rev. 965 (1999), *with* Jean Braucher, *Increasing Uniformity in Consumer Bankruptcy: Means Testing as a Distraction and the National Bankruptcy Review Commission's Proposals as a Starting Point*, 6 Am. Bankr. Inst. L. Rev. 1 (1998), *and* Elizabeth Warren, *The Bankruptcy Crisis*, 73 Ind. L.J. 1079, 1101 (1998).

vulnerable to dismissal under the court's discretionary standard for abuse in § 707(b)(1).

Debtors whose income is above the state median must make a complicated calculation of a combination of presumed and actual living expenses to determine the amount of their surplus or "disposable" income. Many of the expenses that are to be deducted from income do not depend on the debtor's actual living expenses but on a set of expense guidelines used by the IRS when it establishes repayment schedules for delinquent taxpayers. Other expenses, such as payments to secured creditors, health insurance premiums, childcare costs, and others, are based on the debtor's actual expenses.

After making this calculation, many debtors find that they have no surplus income. Those who have some, must compare their surplus income with another set of complex standards which are designed to determine whether they have enough income to make what Congress has determined are meaningful payments to their unsecured creditors. Debtors who have too much surplus income, will have their cases dismissed.[45] Cases of debtors with insufficient surplus income are not subject to dismissal under the presumptive test but are still theoretically subject to dismissal under the discretionary abuse standard, but only on the motion of either the United States Trustee or the court itself.[46]

What a mess!![47]

[a]   Current Monthly Income.[48]

The first step in applying the means test involves determining the debtor's "current monthly income." The Code defines this precisely as "the average monthly income from all sources that the debtor receives . . . during the 6-month period ending [in most cases] on the last day of the calendar month immediately preceding the date of commencement of the [debtor's] case."[49] The time the debtor

---

[45] Official Bankruptcy Form 22A is designed to help debtors determine whether their cases are presumptively abusive. Most of those who have too much disposable income, and whose cases would raise the presumption of abuse, do not file Chapter 7 cases, though a few try to rebut the presumption.

[46] Bankruptcy Code § 707(b)(1).

[47] Some basic bankruptcy courses go no further than this in exploring the means test of § 707(b). Bankruptcy practitioners, students taking an intensive course in consumer bankruptcy practice, clinic students, and those taking a course in "General Practice" must delve further into the statute and the accompanying official forms.

[48] Gary Neustadter, *2005: A Consumer Bankruptcy Odyssey*, 39 Creighton L. Rev. 225, 285-300 (2006); Eugene W. Wedoff, *Means Testing in the New 707(b)*, 79 Am. Bankr. L.J. 231, 276-84 (2005).

[49] Bankruptcy Code § 101(10A)(A)(i). The language goes on to indicate that if the debtor does not file a schedule of current income as required by § 521(a)(1)(B)(ii), then current income is based on income received by the debtor during the six months immediately preceding whatever date that the court ends making its determination of the debtor's current income. Thus, if the debtor fails to file the necessary schedule, the court must conduct a hearing to determine the amount of the debtor's income and make a finding of fact. Basing the income determination on income received by the debtor during the six months immediately before the court's decision makes it necessary for the court to have information that is accurate right up to the day of its decision. Alternatively, the court may dismiss the case under § 707(a)(3).

receives the income controls, the time it was earned does not matter.[50]

The statutory language does not specify whether income is before or after applicable taxes, but the official forms indicate that it should be income before taxes. Income includes court-ordered payments received by the debtor as well as "any amount paid by [anyone] on a regular basis for the household expenses of the debtor or the debtor's dependents." This includes voluntary contributions to the debtor's household by a family member, a companion, a friend, or a stranger, if they are made on a "regular basis."[51] Current monthly income includes retirement income, unemployment compensation,[52] disability payments,[53] interest and dividends, and any royalties received as well as rental or business income that the debtor might receive.[54]

On the other hand, it specifically excludes social security benefits,[55] even apparently for those individuals whose social security benefits, combined with their retirement income, would place them well above the state median income among households in their state.[56] Consider an example involving two married couples who live next door to one another in a small Ohio town: Fred and Wilma and Barney and Betty. Fred and Wilma both work and earn a combined $60,000 per year, before taxes. Barney and Betty, on the other hand, are retired. They receive $35,000 in dividend and retirement income from their defined contribution retirement funds and IRAs, and an additional $40,000 in social security benefits. Exclusion of their social security benefits from their "current monthly income" places them below the roughly $50,000 state median for a two-person Ohio household even though they have considerably more income than their working neighbors, Fred and Wilma, who are above the median.

There might easily be another retired couple in the neighborhood, Nick and Nora, who worked their entire careers in state government, where they made no social security contributions and accordingly live on income from their § 403(b)

---

[50] In re Arnoux, 442 B.R. 769 (Bankr. E.D. Wash. 2010).

[51] See In re Quarterman, 342 B.R. 647 (Bankr. M.D. Fla. 2006).

[52] In re Washington, 438 B.R. 348 (M.D. Ala. 2010).

[53] Blausey v. U.S. Trustee, 552 F.3d 1124 (9th Cir. 2009).

[54] The official forms indicate that only net profits from a business, farm, or rental property need to be included. This makes good sense, but is not fully compatible with the statutory language of § 101(10A), which indicates that "income from all sources that the debtor *receives*" shall be included. The statutory language does not provide for deducting expenses associated with the production of this income. Curiously, although the forms indicates that all "dividend" income must be included, it does not mention deducting expenses associated with the production of this dividend income, such as investment advisor fees, accounting fees, or even tax preparation expenses. These and other expenses might be deducted later, in making the calculations necessary to determine whether the debtor has enough surplus income for his or her petition to constitute an "abuse."

[55] Bankruptcy Code § 101(10A)(B). *See also* Fink v. Thompson (In re Thompson), 439 B.R. 140 (B.A.P. 8th Cir. 2010) (Social Security income not included in income for purposes of determining debtor's good faith in Chapter 13).

[56] To prevent what might otherwise have been a political disaster, current monthly income also excludes payments to victims of war crimes, crimes against humanity, and international and domestic terrorism under several federal statutes. Payments received under state crime victim statutes, on account of more mundane crimes such as rape, robbery, and murder, appear to be included in income.

defined-contribution pension fund and their generous state defined-benefit pension plans from which they receive exactly the same $60,000 annual income amount as their neighbors, Fred and Wilma. Like Fred and Wilma, they are subject to means testing under § 707(b), even though their "current monthly income" is below that of Barney and Betty, merely because of the source of their funds.

Moreover, a few courts have refused to include unemployment benefits in current monthly income, because those benefits are paid pursuant to the Social Security Act.[57] Other courts disagree, and rule that this reading of § 101(10A) is inconsistent with Congressional intent, which was to exclude only social security retirement and disability benefits.[58]

"Current monthly income" is then based on the "average monthly income" received from the included sources, making it necessary to divide the total income for the applicable six-month period by six.[59] Section 707(b)(7) then specifies that the amount of the debtor's current monthly income should be multiplied by twelve and compared with the "median family income" of the debtor for the same sized "household"[60] as determined with reference to available United States Census data for households in the state in which the debtor resides.[61]

Courts take different approaches to the manner of determining the size of the debtor's household. Some courts make this determination with reference to the number of individuals who live in the household, regardless of whether they are related to one another.[62] The IRS approach, in dealing with delinquent taxpayers, determines the size of the debtor's household based on the number of the debtor's dependents.[63] Other courts reject both the "heads on beds" and the "dependents"

---

[57] In re Munger, 370 B.R. 21 (Bankr. D. Mass. 2007) (unemployment compensation is a benefit received under the Social Security Act and therefore not part of current monthly income); In re Sorrell, 359 B.R. 167 (Bankr. S.D. Ohio 2007).

[58] In re Washington, 438 B.R. 348 (M.D. Ala. 2010); In re Baden, 396 B.R. 617 (Bankr. M.D. Pa. 2008). *See* Eugene R. Wedoff, *Means Testing in the New § 707(b)*, 79 Am. Bankr.L.J. 231, 247 (2005).

[59] "Average" presumably is to be taken to refer to the "plain meaning" of "average," the "arithmetic mean" or "[t]he number obtained by dividing the sum of a set of quantities by the number of quantities in the set." The American Heritage Dictionary of the English Language (1969).

[60] Bankruptcy Code § 707(b)(7).

[61] "Median family income" is defined in Bankruptcy Code § 101(39A). Tables containing information necessary for this calculation are available on the websites of the United States Trustee and the Bureau of the Census. Compare the figures at the United States Trustee's website, http://www.justice.gov/ust/eo/bapcpa/20111101/meanstesting.htm (last viewed April 17, 2012) with those supplied by the Census Bureau, available at http://www.census.gov/hhes/www/income/data/statemedian/ (last viewed April 17, 2012).

With respect to the statutory formula, those who have been paying close attention will note that the same figure for annual income can be reached in a more direct fashion: by multiplying the six-month income figure on which current monthly income is based by 2. In algebraic format, the Bankruptcy Code's calculation is: $((mi1+mi2+mi3+mi4+mi5+mi6)/6) \times 12$, where mi1 is monthly income in the month immediately preceding the debtor's petition, mi2 is monthly income in the month before the month represented by mi1, and so forth. The same figure can be arrived by using the formula: $(mi1+mi2+mi3+mi4+mi5+mi6) \times 2$.

[62] In re Epperson, 409 B.R. 503, 507 (Bankr. D. Ariz. 2009); In re Smith, 396 B.R. 214 (Bankr. W.D. Mich. 2008) (adult children); In re Ellringer, 370 B.R. 905, 910-11 (Bankr. D. Minn. 2007).

[63] *See* In re Robinson, 449 B.R. 473, 479 (Bankr. E.D. Va. 2011).

approach and assess how many individuals are part of the debtor's "economic unit," regardless of whether they are the debtor's dependents in any legal sense.[64]

Use of the six-month period immediately before the debtor's petition leads to dramatically different results for otherwise similarly situated debtors, depending on the financial circumstances they were facing in the six months before the filing of their petition. Debtors who received a bonus in the preceding six months may find their cases vulnerable to dismissal under the means test, while debtors who anticipate receipt of a bonus in the near future may be protected.[65] Debtors who have been working extraordinary hours in an effort to deal with their financial situations may similarly find their cases vulnerable to dismissal, while those who have been working only part time may remain eligible for relief.[66] Likewise, debtors with seasonal or erratic income may have an easier time avoiding dismissal for abuse, even though their annual income is greater than other debtors with identical annual income. Debtors who are relying on support from spouses who have lost their jobs, whose support payments will rapidly decline in the short-term future, may be vulnerable to dismissal, while debtors with spouses who have only recently started making support payments are protected. Whether the discretionary abuse standard of § 707(b)(1) and the escape hatch for debtors facing "special circumstances" under § 707(b)(2)(B)[67] will prove elastic enough to deal with these and other permutations, remains unclear.[68]

If the debtor's annual income is below the applicable median income figure, there is no presumption of abuse.[69] If the debtor's annual income is above the applicable state median household income, further calculations are necessary. A combination of the debtor's presumed and actual expenses will be subtracted from the debtor's income, to determine her "disposable income." The amount of disposable income is then measured against a standard to determine if the debtor can make meaningful payments to her creditors. If so, her case will be dismissed due to abuse. Debtors whose income is below the state median remain vulnerable to dismissal under the discretionary abuse standard of revised Bankruptcy Code § 707(b)(1).[70]

---

[64] *E.g.*, In re Jewell, 365 B.R. 796 (Bankr. S.D. Ohio 2007); In re Morrison, 443 B.R. 378 (Bankr. M.D.N.C. 2011); In re Robinson, 449 B.R. 473 (Bankr. E.D. Va. 2011).

[65] Debtors whose circumstances seem likely to radically change in the months immediately after their bankruptcy petition seem to be those most vulnerable to having their Chapter 7 cases dismissed under the discretionary abuse standard of § 707(b)(1). Significantly, § 521(a)(1)(B)(vi) requires debtors to include "a statement disclosing any reasonably anticipated increase in income or expenditures during the 12-month period following the date of the filing of the petition" as a supplement to their petition. Bankruptcy Code § 521(a)(1)(B)(vi).

[66] *See* In re Barraza, 346 B.R. 724 (Bankr. N.D. Tex. 2006) (debtor's past income based on 80-hour work weeks). One of your co-author's parents worked 80 hours per week for many years, due not to financial necessity but to an overdeveloped work ethic. It is not a pretty sight.

[67] *See infra* § 17.03[B][2][d] Special Circumstances.

[68] *See, e.g.*, In re Stocker, 399 B.R. 522 (Bankr. M.D. Fla. 2008) (prenuptial agreement preventing use of spouse's funds for payment of debtor's debts not a special circumstance).

[69] Moreover, only the judge or the United States Trustee may seek dismissal under the discretionary abuse standard of § 707(b)(3).

[70] *See infra* § 17.03[B][3] Abuse under the Discretionary Standard.

Consider, for example, a debtor living in Ohio, who was receiving disability payments of $1,500 a month for three of the months immediately preceding her bankruptcy petition and earning pre-tax wages of $6,000 per month for the other three months. Her total income in the six months immediately before filing was $22,500, with an average "currently monthly income" of $3,750 ($22,500 ÷ 6). If $3,750, multiplied by 12 ($45,000) is below her state's median annual income for debtors in the same sized household, her case will not be dismissed under the standard for presumed abuse. According to figures released by the Census Bureau and the United States Trustee's office for cases filed between May 1 and October 31, 2012,[71] Ohioans in a single person household have a median annual income of $41,748. Ohioans living in larger households have median incomes starting at $51,839. Thus, if the debtor lives alone, her annual income is above the state median and further calculations would be necessary to determine whether she presents a case of presumed abuse. If she is a single mother of one, with custody of her child, her income is below the $51,839 median a for two person Ohio household, and her case would not be presumed to constitute abuse.

[b]   Expenses[72]

Debtors whose current monthly income is above the applicable state median[73] must calculate their presumed and actual living expenses to determine whether they have sufficient surplus income to make what Congress has determined are meaningful payments to creditors. Portions of the expense calculation are based on the debtor's actual living expenses. However, a large part of the calculation, for food, clothing, housing, and transportation, is based on presumptive expenses derived from Internal Revenue Service Guidelines for use by IRS agents in developing payment plans for delinquent taxpayers.[74]

As will be seen, these calculations are complicated.[75] Fortunately, Official Form B22A, and its accompanying instructions, provide considerable guidance. Students hoping to develop a good understanding of how the formula works will compare the form to the statutory language on which it is based and complete it for several hypothetical debtors facing a variety of circumstances.

---

[71] http://www.justice.gov/ust/eo/bapcpa/20111101/bci_data/median_income_table.htm (last viewed on April 17, 2012). Links to median household incomes for other time periods are available at http:// www.justice.gov/ust/eo/bapcpa/meanstesting.htm (last viewed on April 17, 2012).

[72] Gary Neustadter, *2005: A Consumer Bankruptcy Odyssey*, 39 Creighton L. Rev. 225, 285-300 (2006); Eugene W. Wedoff, *Means Testing in the New 707(b)*, 79 Am. Bankr. L.J. 231, 251-77 (2005).

[73] Debtors whose income is below the applicable household median are not required to complete the portion of the official forms that are designed to calculate the debtor's presumed and actual expenses. Official Bankruptcy Form B22A, Line 15. However, Bankruptcy Code § 707(b) seems to require that the calculation be completed, despite the form's dispensation from the requirement.

[74] Links to these standards are available at the web site of the Executive Office of the United States Trustee: http://www.justice.gov/ust/eo/bapcpa/meanstesting.htm (last visited April 15, 2012).

[75] Comparing the precise language of § 707(b) with Official Bankruptcy Form 22A is likely to be of great assistance for those seeking to plow the depths of the Chapter 7 means testing calculation. Those doing so should be on the lookout for discrepancies between the statutory language and the official forms. Examining the relevant portions of IRS' Revenue Manual is also helpful in this regard.

[i]   Expenses in IRS Financial Analysis Handbook

Rather than deduct the debtor's actual expenses for food, clothing, housing, utilities, transportation, and other basic living expenses, the Code specifies that amounts for these expenses are to be based on a set of presumed expenses. Section 707(b)(2)(A)(i) provides:

> the debtor's monthly expenses shall be the debtor's applicable monthly expense amounts specified under the National Standards and Local Standards, and the debtor's actual monthly expenses for the categories specified as Other Necessary Expenses issued by the Internal Revenue Service for the area in which the debtor resides . . . in effect on the date of the order for relief.[76]

As explained by the House Report accompanying the BAPCPA, this language refers to portions of the Financial Analysis Handbook which was prepared by the Internal Revenue Service for use by IRS agents in their dealings with delinquent taxpayers. The Handbook contains a schedule of living expenses for agents to use in preparing repayment plans for these taxpayers.[77] The standards in the IRS Handbook contain expense schedules for

- "allowable living expense" for food, clothing, housekeeping supplies, personal care and other miscellaneous items;[78]

- "housing and utilities," including utilities and either rent or mortgage payments;[79]

- the "cost of ownership" of up to two motor vehicles;[80] and

- motor vehicle operating expenses.[81]

Debtors are able to deduct the amounts specified in the IRS standards, regardless of whether their actual expenses are lower than the amounts specified. But, courts were initially divided over whether debtors who have no such expenses could nevertheless deduct the specified amounts. This issue has arisen most prominently in connection with debtors' ability to deduct ownership expenses of cars and trucks that they own outright, for which they have no regular monthly payments.[82] Not surprisingly, the Internal Revenue Service Manual from which these standards are drawn, does not permit taxpayers without car payments to

---

[76]   Bankruptcy Code § 707(b)(2)(A)(ii)(I).

[77]   H.R. Rep. No. 109-31, pt. 1, at 13-14 (2005), *reprinted in* 2005 U.S.C.C.A.N. 88, 99-100. This manual is available on the IRS website, at http://www.irs.gov/irm/ and through online search engines, such as Lexis (in source "Internal Revenue Manual or IRM") and Westlaw (in library "RIA-IRM"). Eugene W. Wedoff, *Means Testing in the New 707(b)*, 79 Am. Bankr. L.J. 231, 253 n.50 (2005).

[78]   *See* Official Bankruptcy Form 22, Line 19a.

[79]   *See* Official Bankruptcy Form 22, Lines 20A and 20B.

[80]   *See* Official Bankruptcy Form 22, Line 23-24.

[81]   *See* Official Bankruptcy Form 22, Line 22.

[82]   *See* Tate v. Bolen (In re Tate), 571 F.3d 423 (5th Cir. 2009); Ross-Tousey v. Neary (In re Ross-Tousey), 549 F.3d 1148 (7th Cir. 2008); Eugene W. Wedoff, *Means Testing in the New 707(b)*, 79 Am. Bankr. L.J. 231, 256-58 (2005).

deduct "ownership expenses" from their monthly income, in determining how much of their income is available to pay their back taxes.[83]

The question was resolved by the Supreme Court in *Ransom v. FIA Card Services, N.A.*,[84] which concluded that ownership expenses applied only to ownership or rental payments, and not to repair and maintenance costs. Thus, debtors who own their cars outright, with no regular monthly payments to a secured creditor or lessor, may not deduct amounts specified in the IRS guidelines for "ownership expenses" of their cars. The Court's rationale was based partially on the Court's perception of the broad purpose of the 2005 amendments, to ensure that debtors who were able to pay meaningful amounts to their creditors were required to do so,[85] and partially on its construction of the word "applicable" in § 707(b)(2)(A)(ii)(I).[86] Though the percentage of Chapter 7 debtors who own their homes outright is small, the rationale applies with equal force to ownership or rental payments associated with the debtor's home.

Debtors are expressly permitted to adjust the amounts slated for food and clothing upward by 5%, as specified in the IRS's guidelines, if "reasonable and necessary."[87] Moreover, § 707(b)(2)(A)(ii)(V) permits debtors to deduct as monthly expenses "an allowance for housing and utilities" in excess of the amount permitted by the IRS's guidelines "based on the actual expenses for home energy costs, but only if the debtor provides documentation of such actual expenses and demonstrates that [they] are reasonable and necessary."[88]

In addition, the IRS standards for "Other Necessary Expenses"[89] permit the debtor to deduct her *actual expenses* for a variety of other items:

- income, social security, and medicare taxes;[90]

- mandatory payroll deductions for items such as mandatory retirement contributions, union dues, and uniform expenses;[91]

- term life insurance on the life of the debtor (but not her dependents);[92]

---

[83] The Internal Revenue Manual specifies: "If the taxpayer has no car payment, or no car, question how the taxpayer travels to and from work, grocer, medical care, etc. The taxpayer is only allowed the operating cost or the cost of transportation." Internal Revenue Manual, Financial Analysis Handbook § 5.15.1.7. *See generally* James P. Terpening III, Comment, *All or Nothing: Properly Deducting Vehicle Ownership Expenses Under § 707(b)(2)(A)(ii)(I)*, 25 Emory Bankr. Dev. J. 565 (2009).

[84] 131 S. Ct. 716 (2011).

[85] *Id.* at 721.

[86] *Id.* at 724.

[87] Bankruptcy Code § 707(b)(2)(A)(ii)(I). *See* Official Bankruptcy Form 22, Line 39.

[88] *See* Official Bankruptcy Form 22, Line 37. One wonders the extent to which inquiries will be made about the thermostat settings in debtors' homes.

[89] Internal Revenue Service, Internal Revenue Manual, Collecting Process, § 5.15.1.10, http://www.irs.gov/irm/part5/irm_05-015-001.html (last visited April 17, 2012).

[90] *See* Official Bankruptcy Form 22, Line 25.

[91] *See* Official Bankruptcy Form 22, Line 26.

[92] *See* Official Bankruptcy Form 22, Line 27. The statute does not authorize deductions for whole life insurance premiums or for term insurance on the lives of the debtor's dependents.

- court ordered payments of any kind, such as future spousal or child support;[93]

- education expenses that are required for a physically or mentally challenged dependent child for whom no public education providing similar services is available;[94]

- actual childcare expenses;[95]

- actual health care expenses;[96] and

- cell phone, pager, call waiting, caller ID, special long distance, and internet connection expenses, but only if these are "necessary for the health and welfare" of the debtor or her dependents.[97]

Nothing in the IRS standards or the bankruptcy code provide for deduction of voluntary retirement plan contributions.[98] Contributions that are mandated by the debtor's employment contract can be deducted, but additional amounts that the debtor might choose to contribute are not mentioned. The United States Trustee, not surprisingly, has contended that voluntary retirement contributions should be disallowed, and most courts have agreed.[99] Nor have they been treated as the type of extraordinary expense for which an exception to the usual rules may be made. One court described such contributions as the "antithesis of an expense for which there is no reasonable alternative."[100] Courts have also balked at debtor's attempts to deduct retirement plan loan payments.[101] Notably, although the IRS Standards provide for deduction of payments to certain other unsecured creditors, § 707(b)(2)(A)(ii) expressly prohibits deductions for "any payments for debts."

[ii] Other Statutory Living Expenses

In addition to these expenses specifically provided for in the IRS Guidelines, debtors may deduct specific items expressly mentioned in § 707(b)(2)(A). These include:

- reasonably necessary health and disability insurance premiums and health savings account contributions;[102]

---

[93] *See* Official Bankruptcy Form 22, Line 28.

[94] *See* Official Bankruptcy Form 22, Line 29.

[95] *See* Official Bankruptcy Form 22, Line 30.

[96] *See* Official Bankruptcy Form 22, Line 31.

[97] *See* Official Bankruptcy Form 22, Line 32. The IRS Guidelines indicate that these expenses are to be deducted only if they are necessary for the health and welfare of the taxpayer or her family, or for the production of income. *See* In re Lara, 347 B.R. 198 (Bankr. N.D. Tex. 2006).

[98] James Winston Kim, Comment, *Saving Our Future: Why Voluntary Contributions to Retirement Accounts Are Reasonable Expenses*, 26 Emory Bankr. Dev. J. 341 (2010).

[99] In re Siler, 426 B.R. 167 (Bankr. W.D.N.C. 2010).

[100] In re Tauter, 402 B.R. 903, 906 (Bankr. M.D. Fla. 2009).

[101] In re Egebjerg, 574 F.3d 1045 (9th Cir. 2009).

[102] Bankruptcy Code § 707(b)(2)(A)(ii)(I). *See* Official Bankruptcy Form 22, Line 34. This might lead some debtors to opt for better insurance coverage if alternative plans are available through their

- various types of expenses for disabled children and the care of elderly or otherwise infirm dependents;[103]

- reasonably necessary expenses incurred to maintain the safety of the debtor and her family under the federal "Family Violence Prevention and Services Act";[104]

- actual public or private or school expenses for dependent children under eighteen, up to $1750 if they are "reasonable and necessary" and "not already accounted for" in the IRS Standards;[105]

- the actual administrative expenses of administering a Chapter 13 plan in the debtor's federal judicial district as determined by schedules published by the Executive Office of the United States Trustee.[106]

[iii]   Payments to Secured and Priority Creditors

The Code also expressly permits the debtor to deduct payments to secured and priority creditors.[107] The provision permitting the deduction of payments owed to secured creditors introduces several ambiguities into the calculation, primarily in connection with payments to secured creditors that might overlap with amounts separately slated in the IRS Standards for deduction of housing and transportation expenses, but also in relation to the types of secured debts that qualify for these deductions.

Section 707(b)(2)(A)(i) permits the debtor to deduct her "average monthly payments owed on account of secured debts."[108] The amount that can be deducted includes the sixty-month average of

> amounts scheduled as contractually due to secured creditors in each month of the 60 months following the date of the petition . . . [plus] any additional payments to secured creditors necessary for the debtor, in filing a plan under chapter 13 . . . to maintain possession of the debtor's primary residence, motor vehicle, or other property necessary for the support of the debtor and the debtor's dependents, that serves as collateral for secured debts.[109]

---

employer. One of your author's employers offers several layers of protection, designated as "bronze, silver, or gold," with smaller co-pays and deductibles for the higher-priced coverage plans.

[103] Bankruptcy Code § 707(b)(2)(A)(ii)(II). See Official Bankruptcy Form 22, Line 35. This does not include the college tuition of adult children. In re Linville, 446 B.R. 522 (Bankr. D.N.M. 2011).

[104] Bankruptcy Code § 707(b)(2)(A)(ii)(I). See Official Bankruptcy Form 22, Line 35.

[105] Bankruptcy Code § 707(b)(2)(A)(ii)(IV). See Official Bankruptcy Form 22, Line 38. This amount is subject to adjustment every three years pursuant to § 104. It was last adjusted on April 1, in 2010 and is scheduled to be adjusted again in 2013, 2016, and 2019.

[106] Bankruptcy Code § 707(b)(2)(A)(ii)(III). See Official Bankruptcy Form 22, Line 45. Deduction of this amount, which would not be distributed to creditors in a Chapter 13 case in any event, is compatible with the "best interests" test of creditors in Chapter 13. See infra § 18.08[E][1] Best Interests of Creditors.

[107] Bankruptcy Code § 707(b)(2)(A)(iii).

[108] Bankruptcy Code § 707(b)(2)(A)(iii). See Official Bankruptcy Form 22, Line 42.

[109] Bankruptcy Code § 707(b)(2)(A)(iii)(I)-(II). See Official Bankruptcy Form 22, Line 43.

This language contemplates totaling the amount due to secured creditors in the sixty months after the date of the debtor's petition together with all arrearages that would be required to be paid to a more limited class of secured creditors and dividing the total by sixty to arrive at a monthly amount that will be deducted from the debtor's income in determining the amount of any surplus the debtor has available to make payments to creditors in a Chapter 13 plan or otherwise.

Using the average of the amounts required to be paid over sixty months could lead to anomalies. Consider, for example, a debtor who is contractually obligated to make monthly auto payments of $500 per month for an additional thirty-six months. The total of these payments is $18,000. However, the sixty-month average is only $300.

A debtor who owes arrearages to a secured creditor can add the total of the arrearages to the amount used as the basis for the average. Thus, if the debtor described above is three months behind in her $500 monthly payments, she may add the $1500 in arrearages to bring the total to be averaged to $19,500, for a monthly average over a sixty-month period to $325.[110]

The language of § 707(b)(2)(A)(iii)(I), which pertains to the amount of future payments that can be deducted, makes no distinction between debts secured by collateral that is reasonably necessary for the support of the debtor and her dependents and debts secured by assets that it might seem frivolous, irresponsible, or dare we say, "abusive" for the debtor to attempt to retain. It appears that the amount includes payments owed to any secured creditor, regardless of the type of collateral involved or whether the collateral for the debt is property that is reasonably necessary for the debtor's support.[111] Thus, payments owed to a creditor with a security interest in the debtor's boat,[112] private airplane, recreational vehicle, racing bicycle,[113] or vacation home[114] seem to be slated for deduction simply because of the creditor's secured status.[115]

---

[110] The arrearages that can be included in the total include "payments to secured creditors, necessary for the debtor, in filing a plan under chapter 13 . . . to maintain possession of the [collateral]." Bankruptcy Code § 707(b)(2)(A)(iii)(II). Under Chapter 13, the amounts necessary for the debtor to pay to retain possession of the collateral would be an amount necessary to provide "adequate protection" to the creditor under the standard for relief from the automatic stay in § 362(d)(2). Bankruptcy Code § 1325(a)(5)(B)(iii)(II). In addition, the payments must at least have a value equal to the amount of the creditor's "allowed secured claim." Bankruptcy Code § 1325(a)(5)(B)(ii). Further, in some cases, particularly those involving motor vehicles, a Chapter 13 debtor may be required to pay the entire debt. Bankruptcy Code § 1325(a). *See generally infra* § 18.08[F] Treatment of Secured Claims — Chapter 13 Secured Creditor Cramdown.

[111] *Cf.* In re Thompson, 350 B.R. 770 (Bankr. N.D. Ohio 2006) (payments on loan secured by 401(k) account).

[112] In re Sandberg, 433 B.R. 837, 845–46 (Bankr. D. Kan. 2010); In re Robert, 384 B.R. 777 (Bankr. S.D. Ohio. 2008).

[113] Have you priced high-quality racing bikes, lately? One of your authors used to drive to bicycle rides with a bicycle on top of his car that was worth more than the car underneath. Then he bought a nicer car.

[114] In re Rahim, 449 B.R. 527 (E.D. Mich. 2011).

[115] This conclusion is reinforced by the limitation contained in language in the second category of secured creditor payments that can be deducted, for arrearages that would have to be paid in a Chapter

This is made clear by the somewhat different language of § 707(b)(2)(A)(iii)(II) regarding the deduction of amounts owed for arrearages. This language permits the debtor to deduct arrearages only if their payment is necessary "to maintain possession of the debtor's primary residence, motor vehicle, or other property necessary for the support of the debtor and the debtor's dependents, that serves as collateral for secured debts."[116] Debtors who deduct these payments from their income, for the purposes of the presumptive test for abuse, find that although courts might permit the deduction to be made, as part of the statutory formula, it may constitute abuse under the discretionary standard for "abuse" under § 707(b)(1).

It is also somewhat unclear whether the phrase "amounts scheduled as contractually due to secured creditors" refers only to principal and interest payments or if it includes any casualty insurance or tax payments that the debtor is contractually required, under the terms of the mortgage or security agreement, to pay either directly to the secured creditor or to the appropriate insurance carrier or governmental entity. Most mortgages require the debtor to make these payments; many require them to be paid directly to the creditor, who will disburse the payments, when they are due, to the insurance company or tax authority involved.[117]

A related anomaly is that the strict statutory language appears to permit the debtor to deduct the amount of payments due to secured creditors, regardless of whether the debtor intends to reaffirm these debts. Although the cases are split, most courts permit a debtor to deduct payments scheduled to be paid to a secured creditor, even though he debtor intends to surrender the collateral to the lender.[118] This is mandated, these courts reason, by the plain meaning of § 707(b)(2)(A)(iii). Other courts give the phrase "scheduled as contractually due" to have a bankruptcy specific meaning, that refers to payments included in the debtor's "bankruptcy schedules" included in the debtor's § 521(a)(2)(A) "statement of intent."[119] This can have a dramatic effect on the debtor's eligibility for relief. For example, in *In re Ralston*,[120] the debtors were able to deduct their $2,235.31 monthly mortgage payment from their income, despite their plan to surrender their home to their

---

13 case to permit the debtor to retain possession of "the debtor's primary residence, motor vehicle, or other property necessary for the support of the debtor and the debtor's dependents." Bankruptcy Code § 707(b)(2)(A)(iii)(II).

[116] Bankruptcy Code § 707(b)(2)(A)(iii)(II). Even here, the phrasing is unclear. It seems as if the phrase "debtor's primary" does not modify "motor vehicle," even though that might be a fair conclusion to draw. The language seems limited to only one "motor vehicle" and no provision is made for a motor vehicle owned by the debtor's dependents. Even more unclear is whether the payments are only to be deducted if the motor vehicle that serves as collateral for the loan must be "necessary for the support of the debtor and the debtor's dependents."

[117] Official Bankruptcy Form 22A, Line 42 indicates that the debtor should deduct amounts for taxes and insurance that are required "by the mortgage." This presumably was meant to include similar amounts owed under the terms of a security agreement covering personal property.

[118] *See* In re Rudler, 576 F.3d 37, 45 (1st Cir. 2009); In re Ralston, 400 B.R. 854 (Bankr. M.D. Fla. 2009).

[119] *E.g.*, In re Burden, 380 B.R. 194, 200-01 (Bankr. W.D. Mo. 2007).

[120] 400 B.R. 854 (Bankr. M.D. Fla. 2009).

lender.[121] Although they undoubtedly planned to have a rent payment for a place to live, it was probably considerably lower than the mortgage payment they would have been making if they had not surrendered their home to the bank. Despite the court's conclusion in *Ralston* on the effect of the debtor's intended surrender, the court all but invited the United States Trustee to seek dismissal of the debtor's case under the discretionary abuse test of § 707(b)(3).[122]

[iv] Deduction of Charitable Contributions

Although a debtor's charitable contributions are not listed as a permissible deduction, § 707(b)(1) specifies: "In making a determination whether to dismiss a case under this section, the court may not take into consideration whether a debtor has made, or continues to make, charitable contributions . . . to any qualified religious or charitable organization."[123] The statute specifies no limit to the amount that can be deducted. The only restriction specified by the statute is that the contributions must be ones that the debtor "continues to make," though the mechanism for policing this requirement is unclear.[124] Although this provision is extraordinarily generous, it seems unlikely that many debtors will seek to evade the consequences of the means test by making large contributions to their favorite charities.[125] Debtors who perceive the opportunity for receiving something in exchange for their contributions, on the other hand, may seek to use this provision in ways that neither creditors nor bankruptcy trustees would approve.

[v] Expenses Not Deducted From Income

Some debtors have other significant expenses that are not deducted from their income in determining whether their cases are presumptively abusive. Most significant among these are expenses for non-dischargeable, non-priority payments to unsecured creditors that the debtor is required to pay. The most significant of these are unsecured property settlement payments, student loan payments, payments for debts incurred through fraud, drunk-driving liabilites, or wilful and malicious injuries, and any non-priority, non-dischargeable tax obligations. In some circumstances, these and other expenses may be deducted from income under the "special circumstances" escape hatch of § 707(b)(2)(B).[126]

[c] Excess Surplus Income

After deducting these expenses from current monthly income, the debtor must compare the amount of her surplus or "monthly disposable income" with the standards in § 707(b)(2)(A)(i). Abuse is presumed and the petition will likely be dismissed if the debtor's current monthly income, when multiplied by sixty

---

[121] *Id.* at 857.

[122] *Id.* at 869.

[123] Bankruptcy Code § 707(b)(1).

[124] *See* Eugene W. Wedoff, *Means Testing in the New 707(b)*, 79 Am. Bankr. L.J. 231, 271-272 (2005).

[125] Line 40 of Official Form 22A permits debtors to deduct their charitable contributions that the debtor will continue to make.

[126] *Infra* § 17.03[B][2][d] Special Circumstances.

(months), is enough to repay what Congress has determined is a meaningful amount to unsecured creditors. If the surplus is more than $11,725 (or $195.42 per month), abuse is presumed. If the surplus is less than $7025 ($117.08 per month), abuse is not presumed. If the surplus is between $7,025 ($117.08 per month), and $11,725 ($195.42 per month), a further calculation must be made.[127]

For debtors with a five-year surplus of between $7,025 and $11,725, the surplus must be compared to the debtor's total non-priority unsecured claims. Abuse is presumed if the surplus is more than 25% of the debtor's non-priority allowed secured claims. If the surplus is less than 25% of these claims, abuse is not presumed. However, the court may still find abuse under the discretionary standard of § 707(b).

Thus, a debtor with $32,000 of unsecured claims and $8,000 ($133.34 per month) in total surplus income would be subject to dismissal for abuse, because $8,000 is 25% of her $32,000 in unsecured claims. If this debtor had slightly less surplus income, such as only $130 per month, or slightly more non-priority debt, such as $32,100, her case would not be dismissed due to presumed abuse. Debtors on the margin of these thresholds might be able to avoid dismissal due to abuse simply by delaying the filing of their petition while interest accumulates on their unsecured debts. Other debtors might be able to avoid dismissal by cutting back slightly on their overtime, by turning the thermostat back up to seventy-two degrees, making additional contributions to a health savings account, enrolling their child in an after-school "pay to play" sports or music program, or increasing their charitable contributions. These maneuvers, of course, may expose the debtor's case to being dismissed under the discretionary standard.

[d]   Special Circumstances[128]

Debtors whose cases are vulnerable to dismissal might still escape demonstrating "special circumstances" under § 707(b)(2)(B), to rebut the presumption of abuse. The purpose of the special circumstances exception is to protect debtors from rigid and arbitrary applications of the otherwise mechanical presumptive means test.[129] Nevertheless, it was intended to be "reserved for debtors whose special circumstances require adjustments to income or expenses that place them in *dire need* of chapter 7 relief."[130]

Section 707(b)(2)(B)(i) provides examples of the types of circumstances that might satisfy these purposes. It specifies that a "serious medical condition or a call to order to active duty in the Armed Forces" qualify as the type of special

---

[127] The $7025 and $11,725 figures are adjusted every three years pursuant to Bankruptcy Code § 104. They were last adjusted in 2010 and are set to be changed again on April 1, 2013, 2016, and 2019.

[128] Robert J. Landry, III, *The Means Test: Finding a Safe Harbor, Passing the Means Test, or Rebutting the Presumption of Abuse May Not Be Enough*, 29 N. Ill. U. L. Rev. 245, 260-61 (2009); Kathleen Murphy & Justin H. Dion, *"Means Test" or "Just a Mean Test": An Examination of the Requirement That Converted Chapter 7 Bankruptcy Debtors Comply with Amended Section 707(b)*, 16 Am. Bankr. Inst. L. Rev. 413, 438 (2008).

[129] S. Rep. No. 106-49, at 6-7 (1999); In re Stocker, 399 B.R. 522 (Bankr. M.D. Fla. 2008).

[130] S. Rep. No. 106-49, at 6-7 (1999).

circumstances that warrant rebuttal of the presumption. The statute makes it clear that the nature of the expense is one that leaves the debtor with no reasonable alternative but to the incur expense.[131]

Courts take two distinct approaches in determining what constitutes "special circumstances." The first approach views the range of circumstances that are "special" narrowly, and requires that the debtor's additional expense or decrease in income must be truly extraordinary in some way.[132] First, a debtor must show that some sort of special circumstances exist. Then, the debtor must show that these special circumstances leave him with "necessary and reasonable" expenses "for which there is no reasonable alternative."[133] This approach permits the deduction for special circumstances only if the expense must be one that is out of the ordinary for the average family.[134]

A second line of cases takes a more relaxed approach, that does not require the circumstances involved to be beyond the debtor's control.[135] These courts regard any legitimate expense that is out of the ordinary for an average family, but which leaves the debtor with no reasonable alternative but to incur the expense, as a "special circumstance" that permits the debtor to deduct the expense from his or her income.[136] Not surprisingly, courts also take diverging views on whether the debtor's liability for a nondischargeable student loan constitutes special circumstances that rebuts the presumption of abuse.[137]

A question that undoubtedly will continue to arise is whether the debtor's inability to make substantial payment to her unsecured creditors in a Chapter 13 plan is sufficient to rebut the presumption of abuse established by § 707(b). Cases raising the issue indicate that this, by itself, is not sufficient evidence of special circumstances to avoid dismissal due to abuse.[138]

The procedural requirements involved in applying the exception, discourage courts from using special circumstances to rebut the presumption of abuse. Debtors seeking to rebut the presumption must provide "documentation" for any adjustments to their expenses or income and supply a "detailed explanation" of the special circumstances that make the adjustment necessary.[139] Morever, debtors are required to "attest under oath" regarding the accuracy of the already documented information they supply.[140] Even with testimony under oath and

---

[131] Bankruptcy Code § 707(b)(2)(B)(i).

[132] In re Siler, 426 B.R. 167, 172 (Bankr. W.D.N.C. 2010).

[133] *Id. See also* Eisen v. Thompson, 370 B.R. 762, 773 (Bankr. N.D. Ohio 2007).

[134] *E.g.*, In re Siler, 426 B.R. 167 (Bankr. W.D.N.C. 2010); In re Patterson, 392 B.R. 497 (Bankr. S.D. Fla. 2008).

[135] *E.g.*, In re Graham, 363 B.R. 844, 850 (Bankr. S.D. Ohio 2007); In re Thompson, 350 B.R. 770, 777 (Bankr. N.D. Ohio 2006); In re Tamez, No. 07–60047-RCM, 2007 Bankr. LEXIS 2763 (Bankr. W.D. Tex. August 13, 2007); In re Robinette, 2007 Bankr. LEXIS 3523 (Bankr. D.N.M. 2007).

[136] *See* In re Batzkiel, 349 B.R. 581, 586 (Bankr. N.D. Iowa 2006)).

[137] *E.g.*, In re Johnson, 446 B.R. 921 (Bankr. E.D. Wis. 2011) (collecting cases).

[138] In re Johns, 342 B.R. 626 (Bankr. E.D. Okla. 2006).

[139] Bankruptcy Code § 707(b)(2)(B)(ii).

[140] Bankruptcy Code § 707(b)(2)(B)(ii). The debtor's attorney might be subject to sanction under

documentary evidence, the presumption can be rebutted only if the debtor's surplus income, after further deductions for additional expenses or reduced earnings fall under the established thresholds for detecting abuse.[141]

[e]   Safe Harbor

Section 707(b) provides several safe harbor provisions, establishing various levels of protection for debtors, depending on their status and income. These safe harbors provide protection from dismissal due to presumptive abuse for disabled veterans[142] and, of course, for those with income below the applicable state household median.[143] However, these debtors remain vulnerable to having their cases dismissed under the discretionary abuse standard of § 707(b)(3), discussed below.[144]

However, § 707(b)(6) provides at least a protected (if not entirely safe) harbor for these debtors by permitting a dismissal for abuse motion to be made only by "the judge or United States trustee."[145] This is similar to the situation that existed for all debtors before the 2005 Amendments, when debtors were protected from creditors' dismissal motions that might have been made to harass debtors who lacked the resources to defend them.[146]

[3]   Abuse under the Discretionary Standard[147]

Debtors whose cases are not subject to dismissal under the presumptive standard might still be vulnerable to dismissal under two alternative discretionary standards.[148] In determining whether the debtor's case is abusive, § 707(b)(3) directs the court to "consider (A) whether the debtor filed the petition in bad faith; *or* (B) [whether] the totality of the circumstances . . . of the debtor's financial situation demonstrates abuse."[149]

This discretionary standard is most likely to apply to debtors whose current or anticipated income is considerably higher than their presumed income under the "current monthly income" standard of § 101(10A).[150] Because this standard is based on debtors' actual income for the six months prior to filing their petitions,

---

§ 707(b)(4)(C) if her pleadings in support of rebuttal are not "well grounded in fact."

[141] Bankruptcy Code § 707(b)(2)(B)(iv).

[142] The debtor must satisfy the definition of a disabled veteran in 38 U.S.C. § 3741(1) (2006).

[143] Bankruptcy Code § 707(b)(7).

[144] In re Paret, 347 B.R. 12 (Bankr. D. Del. 2006); Eugene Wedoff, *Means Testing in the New 707(b)*, 79 Am. Bankr. L.J. 231 (2005).

[145] Bankruptcy Code § 707(b)(6).

[146] *See infra* § 17.03[B][3][ii] Totality of the Circumstances.

[147] Wayne R. Wells, Janell M. Kurtz & Robert J. Calhoun, *The Implementation of Bankruptcy Code Section 707(b): The Law and the Reality*, 39 Clev. St. L. Rev. 15 (1991); Teresa A.Sullivan, Elizabeth Warren, and Jay Lawrence Westbrook, *The Persistence of Local Legal Culture: Twenty Years of Evidence from the Federal Bankruptcy Courts*, 17 Harv. J.L. & Pub. Pol'y 801 (1994).

[148] Bankruptcy Code § 707(b)(1).

[149] Bankruptcy Code § 707(b)(3) (emphasis added).

[150] Bankruptcy Code § 101(10A). *See supra* § 17.03[B][2][a] Current Monthly Income.

debtors whose income rose around the time their petitions were filed may not be ensnared by the presumptive test, even though they are actually able to make meaningful payments to creditors from their current or anticipated income.

For example, a young doctor, earning $60,000 in the final year of her surgical residency might not have sufficient income (depending on the size of her family and other circumstances) to fall into the presumptive abuse standard of § 707(b)(2). Upon completion of her residency, however, she is likely to earn in excess of $225,000. If she files a Chapter 7 case shortly after she starts earning income at this level, her total financial circumstances might be closely examined to determine if her case should be dismissed under the discretionary standard for abuse.[151]

[a]   Bad Faith

The first discretionary standard permits the court to dismiss the debtor's petition due to the debtor's "bad faith."[152] A wide variety of circumstances might demonstrate that the debtor's petition was filed in bad faith. Among them are serial filings designed primarily to take advantage of the automatic stay and thus forestall foreclosure, the debtor's concealment of assets, and intentional credit card abuse. Debtors who attempt to unfairly manipulate their exemption rights are also vulnerable to having their cases dismissed due to bad faith, even though their exemption claims are technically valid under applicable state law.[153]

Likewise, debtors who have lived what might be viewed as an extravagant lifestyle, in the months prior to their bankruptcy filing, might have their cases dismissed due to "bad faith." For example, in *In re Crink*,[154] the court explained:

> The Debtors irresponsibly spent money on numerous non-essential goods and services during a two-year period in which they had no income. Mr. Crink made no attempt to obtain a job in another industry, and Mrs. Crink, who had no employment restrictions, made no attempt to obtain employment at all. They spent money that they did not have on a private school for their daughter, luxury vehicles for themselves, dining in expensive restaurants, pet care, and a host of other goods that they did not need and services that they could perform for themselves or do without.[155]

However, other courts have refused to treat mere irresponsibility as bad faith. In *In re Reese*,[156] a debtor who made average monthly credit card charges approaching $40,000, including monthly payments of nearly $5,000 for high-end vehicles over $5000 in monthly entertainment expenses was not acting in "bad faith." The court determined that even though her belief that she would be able to pay these debts

---

[151] *See, e.g.*, In re Stewart, 175 F.3d 796 (10th Cir. 1999).

[152] Bankruptcy Code § 707(b)(3)(A).

[153] Marianne B. Culhane & Michaela M. White, *Catching Can-Pay Debtors: Is the Means Test the Only Way?*, 13 Am. Bankr. Inst. L. Rev. 665, 696-98 (2005); *Final Report of the Bankruptcy Foreclosure Scam Task Force*, 32 Loy. L.A. L. Rev. 1063 (1999).

[154] 402 B.R. 159 (Bankr. M.D.N.C. 2009).

[155] *Id.* at 176.

[156] In re Reese, 402 B.R. 43 (Bankr. M.D. Fla. 2008).

through an expansion of her medical practice was wildly irresponsible, it was not dishonest.

Under the bad faith standard of § 707(b)(3)(A), the court may consider a wide variety of factors including those unrelated to their financial circumstances, such as the nature and extent of purchases they made before their petition, whether the schedules they filed with their petition were complete and accurate, and the extent to which they fully cooperated with the bankruptcy trustee.[157]

[b]   Totality of the Circumstances

The totality of the circumstances standard seems to codify the numerous pre-2005 decisions that adopted a totality of the circumstances approach to determine whether the debtor's Chapter 7 filing constituted a "substantial abuse." Under that test, the debtor's ability to pay was a key factor, but was not dispositive.

The totality of circumstances approach takes the debtor's anticipated income and her resulting ability to pay her creditors into account, but in a more flexible way than the more rigid presumptive means test of § 707(b)(2).[158]

As with the good faith standard, the totality of circumstances test has also been used to dismiss cases involving debtors whose high payments to secured creditors permitted them to avoid dismissal under the presumptive test. In these cases, payments to secured creditors are to maintain what might be regarded as a luxurious lifestyle, in an expensive house, furnished lavishly, while driving expensive cars. Recall that the presumptive means test permits debtors to deduct from their income any payments that are "scheduled as contractually due to secured creditors . . . ."[159] Thus, many debtors' income, that would be available to make payments to unsecured creditors in a Chapter 13 plan, is gobbled up by payments contractually due to secured creditors, without regard to whether the collateral is reasonably necessary for the debtor's support.

Courts have sometimes been dismayed that the retention of these assets enable debtors to obtain Chapter 7 relief, even though they could fund a Chapter 13 plan by jettisoning some of these assets and reallocating their income to satisfying their unsecured creditors' claims. For example, in *In re Felske*,[160] the court dismissed the debtor's Chapter 7 case after finding that their $3500 monthly housing expense, made to retain a $390,000 home was unreasonable, given the existence of numerous less expensive housing alternatives in their geographic area.

However, in *In re Seeburger*,[161] the court refused to dismiss the debtor's case, based on the totality of the circumstances of the debtor's financial condition, even though the debtors were retaining their recently acquired 2100 square-foot home that required a $2049 monthly payment. The United States Trustee sought dismissal of their case after calculating that if they moved to less expensive

---

[157] In re Parada, 391 B.R. 492, 499 (Bankr. S.D. Fla. 2008).

[158] *See* § 17.03[B][2][a] Current Monthly Income.

[159] Bankruptcy Code § 707(b)(2)(iii)(I).

[160] 385 B.R. 649 (Bankr. N.D. Ohio 2008).

[161] 392 B.R. 735 (Bankr. N.D. Ohio 2008).

quarters, they could afford to pay their unsecured creditors in full in Chapter 13. In drawing this conclusion, the court considered that the debtors had reduced their monthly food budget from $600 to $200, their monthly clothing expense from $100 to zero,[162] transportation expense from $500 to $200, and replaced a vehicle carrying a $584 monthly payment with a car costing them a total of $500.[163]

Early suggestions by some scholars that permitting a debtor's ability to pay to be considered under the discretionary standard renders the presumptive test of § 707(b)(2) superfluous,[164] have mostly been rejected.[165] The close similarity between language in pre-2005 "totality of the circumstances" cases and the express language of § 707(b)(3)(B) cuts in favor of this interpretation.[166] Thus, the discretionary "totality of the circumstances" test permits consideration of the debtor's "ability to pay," with respect to debtors whose petition was not abusive under the means test, regardless of whether their income is above the state median,[167] or below it.

The precise language of § 707(b)(3)(B) also directs the court to consider "whether the debtor seeks to reject a personal services contract and the financial need for such rejection as sought by the debtor."[168] This parenthetical was aimed at a relatively small (but highly visible) number of debtors in the sports and entertainment industries who have sometimes attempted to use Chapter 7 primarily to renegotiate their contracts, or make a better deal with another team or recording label.[169]

---

[162] One wonders how realistic this is. Clothes eventually wear out.

[163] 392 B.R. at 738-39.

[164] *See* Marianne B. Culhane & Michaela M. White, *Catching Can-Pay Debtors: Is the Means Test the Only Way?*, 13 Am. Bankr. Inst. L. Rev. 665, 677-82 (2005). *But see* Eugene R. Wedoff, *Judicial Discretion to Find Abuse under Section 707(b)(3)*, 71 Mo. L. Rev. 1035 (2006).

[165] In re Castellaw, 401 B.R. 223 (Bankr. N.D. Tex. 2009); In re Pak, 343 B.R. 239 (Bankr. N.D. Cal. 2006). *But see* In re Johnson, 399 B.R. 72 (Bankr. S.D. Cal. 2008) (J. Wedoff). *See generally* David Gray Carlson, *Means Testing: The Failed Bankruptcy Revolution of 2005*, 15 Am. Bankr. Inst. L. Rev. 223 (2007); Robert J. Landry, III, *The Means Test: Finding a Safe Harbor, Passing the Means Test, or Rebutting the Presumption of Abuse May Not Be Enough*, 29 N. Ill. U. L. Rev. 245, 280+ (2009); John A. E. Pottow, *The Totality of the Circumstances of the Debtor's Financial Situation in a Post-Means Test World: Trying To Bridge the Wedoff/Culhane & White Divide*, 71 Mo. L. Rev. 1053 (2006); Eugene R. Wedoff, *Judicial Discretion To Find Abuse Under Section 707(b)(3)*, 71 Mo. L. Rev. 1035 (2006); Ned W. Waxman & Justin H. Rucki, *Chapter 7 Bankruptcy Abuse: Means Testing Is Presumptive, but "Totality" Is Determinative*, 45 Hous. L. Rev. 901, 937 (2008).

[166] *See* Eugene Wedoff, *Judicial Discretion to Find Abuse under § 707(b)(3)*, 71 Mo. L. Rev. 1035 (2006).

[167] In re Mestemaker, 359 B.R. 849 (Bankr. N.D. Ohio 2007); In re McGillis 370 B.R. 720 (Bankr. W.D. Mich. 2008). *See* In re Johnson, 399 B.R. 72 (Bankr. S.D. Cal. 2008) (debtor's high mortgage payment not sufficient under totality of circumstances test to warrant discretionary dismissal).

[168] Bankruptcy Code § 707(b)(3)(B).

[169] *See* H.R. Rep. 105-794, 123 (1998) (accompanying a much earlier version of what became BAPCPA); *see, e.g.*, In re Carrere, 64 B.R. 156 (Bankr. C.D. Cal. 1986) (dismissing Chapter 7 case of an "A Team" actress who sought bankruptcy relief in an effort to switch TV networks).

[4]   Attorney Sanctions[170]

Section 707(b)(4) now permits bankruptcy trustees to seek reimbursement from debtor's attorneys for the trustee's reasonable costs in prosecuting a motion for dismissal under either the presumptive or the discretionary abuse standard of § 707(b), if the "action of the attorney for the debtor in filing a case under [chapter 7] violated Bankruptcy Rule 9011." In addition, if the attorney's actions have violated Rule 9011, the court may assess civil penalties against the debtor's attorney, possibly awarding them to either the case trustee or the United States Trustee.[171]

Debtors' attorneys must remain mindful, in determining whether to file Chapter 7 cases on behalf of their clients, that their signatures on a petition, a pleading, or a motion "constitute a certification that the attorney has (i) performed a reasonable investigation into the circumstances that gave rise to the [pleading]" and (ii) determined that the pleading is both "*well* grounded in fact"[172] and "warranted by existing law or a good faith argument for the extension, modification, or reversal of existing law and does not constitute an abuse."[173]

While attorneys already have a professional obligation to have "evidentiary support" for their factual contentions,[174] the more rigorous language of § 707(b)(4)(C) regarding a certification that the petition is "well grounded in fact," combined with congressional encouragement to the United States Trustee's office to vigorously enforce these new provisions, seems destined to both to weed out attorneys who lack a thorough familiarity with the law and to discourage attorneys from pursuing aggressive positions on behalf of their clients, particularly with respect to the standards for presumptive abuse.

[C]   Conversion of Chapter 7 Cases

Debtors are usually permitted to convert their Chapter 7 cases to Chapter 11, 12, or 13, at any time. This right is limited by the requirement that the debtor be eligible for the chapter selected and that the case was not previously converted from one of those chapters to Chapter 7.[175] Thus, if the debtor is ineligible for Chapter 12, because she is not a "family farmer" or a "family fisherman," she may

---

[170] Walter W. Miller, Jr., *The Proposed "Bankruptcy Abuse Prevention and Consumer Protection Act of 2002"*, 22 Ann. Rev. Banking & Fin. L. 301 329-30 (2003); Henry J. Sommer, *Trying to Make Sense Out of Nonsense: Representing Consumers Under the "Bankruptcy Abuse Prevention and Consumer Protection Act of 2005"*, 79 Am. Bankr. L.J. 191, 204 (2005).

[171] Bankruptcy Code § 707(b)(4)(B).

[172] Bankruptcy Code § 707(b)(4)(C) (emphasis added). This goes well beyond the language of Rule 9011, which only requires the attorney certify that "to the best of the [her] knowledge, information and belief, formed after an inquiry reasonable under the circumstances . . . the allegations and other factual contentions have *evidentiary support* or . . . are likely to have evidentiary support after a reasonable opportunity for further investigation or discovery." Fed. R. Bank. P. 9011(b)(3) (emphasis added).

[173] Bankruptcy Code § 707(b)(4)(C).

[174] Fed. R. Bankr. P. 9011(b)(3).

[175] Bankruptcy Code § 706(a).

not convert her Chapter 7 case to Chapter 12.[176] Likewise, if the debtor is not "an individual with regular income" or has debts beyond the limits imposed for those seeking relief under Chapter 13, she may not convert her case.[177] Moreover, if the debtor's case under another chapter is vulnerable to conversion back to Chapter 7, the case may not be converted from Chapter 7 to that other chapter in the first place.[178]

Any purported waiver of the right to convert is unenforceable.[179] However, despite the unqualified language of § 706, which appears to impose no further limits on the debtor's right to convert, the court may prevent a debtor from converting a case if the debtor has acted in bad faith.[180]

Other parties in interest may also seek to have the case converted,[181] though conversion to Chapters 12 or 13 is not permitted without the debtor's consent.[182] This is in line with the wholly voluntary nature of Chapters 12 and 13. In fact, motions to convert a case *from* Chapter 7 to another chapter are rare and most commonly occur in the context of involuntary corporate or partnership Chapter 7 cases that are converted, at the request of the debtor, to Chapter 11. Creditors almost never seek conversion from a liquidation case to a reorganization proceeding. If the debtor is unwilling to try to reorganize, its chances of success are slim.

[D] Conversion to Chapter 7[183]

Debtors who have initially filed a Chapter 13 case may encounter changed financial circumstances that make it impossible to complete their plan.[184] Even if their circumstances have not changed, they sometimes find that their expectations about being able to live within a strict budget, were unrealistic. These debtors may find it necessary to convert from Chapter 13 to Chapter 7. As explained in more detail elsewhere,[185] Chapter 13 debtors may convert their case to a case under

---

[176] *See supra* § 6.02[B][5] Eligibility for Relief Under Chapter 12 — Family Farmers and Family Fishermen.

[177] *See supra* § 6.02[B][6] Eligibility for Relief Under Chapter 13 — Individuals with Regular Income.

[178] Marrama v. Citizens Bank, 549 U.S. 365 (2007). *See* John Rao, *Impact of Marrama on Case Conversions: Addressing the Unanswered Questions*, 15 Am. Bankr. Inst. L. Rev. 585 (2007).

[179] Bankruptcy Code § 706(a).

[180] Marrama v. Citizens Bank (In re Marrama), 549 U.S. 365 (2007).

[181] Bankruptcy Code § 706(b).

[182] Bankruptcy Code § 707(c).

[183] Kathleen Murphy & Justin H. Dion, *"Means Test" Or "Just a Mean Test": An Examination of the Requirement That Converted Chapter 7 Bankruptcy Debtors Comply With Amended Section 707(b)*, 16 Am. Bankr. Inst. L. Rev. 413 (2008).

[184] Very few individuals file cases under Chapter 11, making conversion from Chapter 11 to Chapter 7 rare. Conversion from Chapter 12 to Chapter 7 presents the same issues as conversion to Chapter 7 from Chapter 13.

[185] *See infra* § 18.03[B] Conversion or Dismissal of Chapter 13 Cases.

Chapter 7 "for cause,"[186] which includes a "material default" in performance of the terms of the plan.

Chapter 13 debtors who seek to convert to Chapter 7 may confront the question of whether they must pass the means test of § 707(b). Section 707(b) applies to cases originally filed under Chapter 7, but whether it applies to cases converted from Chapter 13 is unclear.[187] As with many other issues under BAPCPA, courts have split, with some decisions finding the meaning of § 707(b) clear and unambiguously applying only to cases that are "filed" under Chapter 7,[188] and others concluding that interpreting § 707(b) in this way would lead to an absurd result.[189]

§ 17.04   ROLE OF A CHAPTER 7 TRUSTEE

In Chapter 7, a trustee is appointed or (more rarely) elected and given broad administrative responsibility over the case. The trustee is generally responsible for collecting the property of the estate, selling it, and distributing its proceeds to creditors according to whatever priority rights they have under state law and the Bankruptcy Code. Trustees are usually appointed from a panel of those who have qualified, in each federal judicial district, to serve as trustees in bankruptcy cases.

The trustee is sometimes referred to as the "case trustee" or "TIB" as a means of distinguishing the trustee from the United State Trustee or "UST." The United States Trustee is a federal administrative agency, operating as part of the United States Department of Justice, to establish rules and procedures governing bankruptcy cases and to supervise case trustees who serve in individual cases. The United States Trustee selects and supervises panel trustees, but does not ordinarily exercise authority over individual Chapter 7 cases.

[A]   Selection of a Trustee

The Chapter 7 trustee may be elected by creditors, though in practice this rarely happens. If creditors want to elect a trustee, virtually every creditor who holds an allowable, undisputed, fixed, liquidated, unsecured claim may vote.[190] However, the appointed interim trustee, initially appointed by the United States Trustee from a panel of available private trustees, nearly always remains in place and administers the debtor's estate.[191]

---

[186] Bankruptcy Code § 1307(c).

[187] Kathleen Murphy & Justin H. Dion, *"Means Test" Or "Just a Mean Test": An Examination of the Requirement That Converted Chapter 7 Bankruptcy Debtors Comply With Amended Section 707(b)*, 16 Am. Bankr. Inst. L. Rev. 413, 446 (2008).

[188] In re Chapman, 431 B.R. 216 (Bankr. D. Minn. 2010); In re Dudley, 405 B.R. 790 (Bankr. W.D. Va. 2009); In re Fox, 370 B.R. 639, 642 (Bankr. D.N.J. 2007).

[189] In re Willis, 408 B.R. 803 (Bankr. W.D. Mo. 2009); In re Perfetto, 361 B.R. 27, 29 (Bankr. D.R.I. 2007).

[190] Bankruptcy Code § 702(a).

[191] Bankruptcy Code § 702(d).

[B]   Duties of the Trustee

The duties of a Chapter 7 trustee are extensive. One of her primary duties is to collect the property of the estate, reduce it to cash, and make distributions to creditors, "as expeditiously as is compatible with the best interests of parties in interest."[192] In consumer cases, much of the debtor's property will be exempt. Other property will be fully encumbered by secured creditors' liens and will be surrendered to them. Liquidation of the estate should occur promptly, but if the case is complicated, or if an orderly liquidation will better the position of creditors,[193] the trustee may and should take the time necessary. However, there appear to be more problems of undue delay than of unseemly haste. In the 1980s, there were problems in some districts with getting even simple Chapter 7 cases closed promptly.[194] However, with the United States Trustee's office supervising case trustees, case administration is now more expeditious.

The trustee is also accountable for all property received.[195] This is a part of the trustee's fiduciary duty to the estate. The trustee is personally liable for property misappropriated or just mislaid. It is also part of the reason why the trustee must post a bond, securing proper performance of her duties.[196]

The trustee is also responsible for ensuring that the debtor performs her stated intentions with respect to property subject to a security interest. Section 521 requires individual consumer debtors to file a statement of intention with regard to retention, surrender, exemption, and redemption of property subject to a security interest.[197] Section 521(a)(6) gives the debtor forty-five days to act on her stated intention by either entering into a reaffirmation agreement with the secured creditor pursuant to § 524(c),[198] redeeming the property with a lump-sum payment to the secured creditor pursuant to § 722,[199] or surrendering the collateral to the creditor. The trustee is expected to monitor the debtor's conduct to ensure that her stated intentions are performed.

The trustee is also required broadly to "investigate the financial affairs of the debtor."[200] In most cases, this investigation is slight and may consist of little more than reviewing the schedules and statements accompanying the debtor's petition and questioning the debtor at the § 341 meeting. In complex cases, it may be quite extensive and may involve hiring accountants, or other professionals, to investigate the debtor's circumstances. Most trustees are lawyers, and have paralegals, law

---

[192] Bankruptcy Code § 704(a)(1).

[193] *See* Bankruptcy Code § 721.

[194] Michael J. Herbert & Domenic E. Pacitti, *Down and Out in Richmond, Virginia: The Distribution of Assets in Chapter 7 Bankruptcy Proceedings Closed During 1984-87*, 22 U. Rich. L. Rev. 303, 317-18 (1988).

[195] Bankruptcy Code § 704(a)(2).

[196] Bankruptcy Code § 322.

[197] *See supra* § 12.08 [D] Debtor's Statement of Intent.

[198] *See supra* § 12.08[B] Reaffirmation.

[199] *See supra* § 12.08[A] Lump-Sum Redemption by Debtor.

[200] Bankruptcy Code § 704(a)(4).

clerks, and a clerical staff, to assist in this process.

"If a purpose would be served," the trustee is required to examine the proofs of claim and object to the allowance of any improper claim.[201] The opening passage of this provision recognizes the fact that in most Chapter 7 cases, there is no reason to examine proofs of claim. In no-asset cases, where there will be no assets distributed to unsecured creditors, there is no reason to evaluate the validity of creditors' claims.[202] In most such cases, proof of claim forms are not even submitted. In complicated cases, with assets to distribute to unsecured creditors, examining the extent and validity claims may be a large part of the trustee's role.

The estate enjoys the benefit of any defenses that would have been available to the debtor, and creditors with valid claims have a substantial interest in the trustee not permitting the estate to be distributed to those whose claims are invalid. Thus, in complicated cases with numerous claims, the trustee may have to defend against claims based largely on non-bankruptcy principles that would have provided the debtor with a defense had the bankruptcy proceeding not been filed.

The case trustee is also required, "if advisable," to oppose the debtor's discharge.[203] The available grounds to deny the debtor a Chapter 7 discharge are specified in § 727(a).[204] The trustee does not, on the other hand, have responsibility for seeking to have individual debts determined to be non-dischargeable.[205] This task is left to individual creditors.

Unless the court orders otherwise, the trustee is also required to supply any party in interest with any information requested about the estate and the estate's administration.[206] Thus, the case trustee is one of the primary conduits of information concerning the case to creditors.

In rare cases, the trustee might also have responsibility for operating the business of a Chapter 7 debtor. If the debtor operated a business, the trustee may, depending on the situation, continue to operate the business for a time, generally for the purpose of winding up profitable contracts, or selling it, as a going concern.[207] This is governed by § 721, which states: "the court may authorize the trustee to operate the business of the debtor for a limited period, if such operation is in the best interest of the estate and consistent with the orderly liquidation of the estate."[208] Whether the trustee does so is largely a matter of business

---

[201] Bankruptcy Code § 704(a)(5).

[202] In no-asset cases, creditors are directed not to file proofs of claims. *See* Official Bankruptcy Form B9A, for use in "No Asset Case."

[203] Bankruptcy Code § 704(a)(6).

[204] Bankruptcy Code § 707(a). *See supra* § 13.02 Denial of Discharge.

[205] *See supra* § 13.03 Non-Dischargeable Debts.

[206] Bankruptcy Code § 704(a)(7).

[207] One of your authors is familiar with a trustee, in Columbus, Ohio, who took over the operation of a local restaurant, before selling it as a going concern to another bankruptcy lawyer in the area who was interested in changing careers.

[208] Bankruptcy Code § 721.

judgment. A typical Chapter 7 case involves nothing more than a speedy liquidation of the debtor's meager assets.

If the trustee has been authorized to operate the debtor's business, she is required to supply the court, the United States Trustee's office, and any relevant governmental tax authority, with periodic reports and summaries of the operation of the business. These reports and summaries must include a statement of receipts and disbursements, as well as any other information that the U.S. Trustee or the court requires.[209] At the end of the case, the trustee is also required to "[m]ake a final report and file a final account of the administration of the estate with both the court and the United States trustee."[210]

The 2005 Amendments to the Bankruptcy Code added several very specific duties related to very narrow and specific circumstances that may or may not be relevant to every case. These duties include:

- providing the notice required by § 704(c) to holders of claims for domestic support obligations;[211]

- performing the debtor's duties of any ERISA employee benefit plan previously administered by the debtor;[212] and

- "us[ing] all reasonable and best efforts" to transfer patients of debtor who operates a health care business to a new health care provider.[213]

§ 17.05 UNITED STATES TRUSTEE

United States Trustees are government officials, supervised by the United States Attorney General who are charged with responsibility for a variety of matters related to bankruptcy cases. There are twenty-one separate U.S. Trustees, covering the entire country. Most U.S. Trustees operate in more than one federal judicial district, with many of the twenty-one U.S. Trustee regions cutting across state lines.[214]

These government employees' responsibilities include establishing and supervising panels of private trustees who are eligible to serve as case trustees in individual cases.[215] The U.S. Trustee actually serves as case trustee only if it must do so because of the unavailability of an eligible private trustee willing to serve in a particular case.[216] They also exercise discretion to supervise the administration of

---

[209] Bankruptcy Code § 704(a)(8).

[210] Bankruptcy Code § 704(a)(9).

[211] Bankruptcy Code § 704(a)(1), (c).

[212] Bankruptcy Code § 704(a)(12).

[213] Bankruptcy Code § 704(a)(12).

[214] 28 U.S.C. § 581 (2006). *See* http://www.usdoj.gov/ust/eo/ust_org/judicial_districts.htm (last visited April 17, 2012).

[215] 28 U.S.C. § 586(a)(1) (2006).

[216] 28 U.S.C. § 586(a)(2) (2006).

cases "whenever the United States trustee considers it to be appropriate."[217] In Chapter 7 cases, the United States Trustee's office is responsible for reviewing materials filed by individual debtors and determining whether their cases would be "presumed to be an abuse under § 707(b)."[218] The trustee's office must file its report regarding abuse within ten days after the date of the § 341 meeting.

In cases where the debtor's case should be presumed to be an abuse under the presumptive test set out in § 707(b)(2), the United States Trustee has a further duty to either file a motion to dismiss the debtor's case or file a statement explaining why a motion to dismiss is not appropriate.[219]

The United States Trustee has additional responsibilities in connection with "small business cases" where there has been a historic concern about the lack of creditor involvement.[220] In these cases, the United States Trustee conducts interviews with the debtor, investigates its viability, and monitors the debtor's activities to evaluate the likelihood that it will be able to have a plan confirmed.[221]

The United States Trustee's office also conducts research and disseminates information about bankruptcy cases generally. Further, its website collects data necessary to apply § 707(b)'s means test for presumptive abuse of Chapter 7.[222] It also approves and monitors the activities of non-profit credit counseling agencies from whom consumer debtors must obtain credit counseling briefings and training programs.

§ 17.06   CREDITORS' COMMITTEES

Creditors' committees can be appointed in Chapter 7 and 11 cases. However, they are extraordinarily rare in Chapter 7 cases, and are usually only active in larger Chapter 11 reorganizations.

In Chapter 7 cases, creditors may elect a creditors' committee at a § 341 meeting; every creditor who has the right to vote on a trustee has the right to vote for a creditors' committee. The committee must be composed of not fewer than three and not more than eleven creditors; each of the creditors must hold an allowed unsecured claim entitled to distribution in the proceeding.[223]

The powers of the Chapter 7 creditors' committee are rather circumscribed. The committee may consult with the trustee and the United States Trustee regarding the administration of the estate. It may make recommendations about the trustee's

---

[217] 28 U.S.C. § 586(a)(3) (2006).

[218] Bankruptcy Code § 704(b)(1)(A).

[219] Bankruptcy Code § 704(b)(2).

[220] These cases involve debtors engaged in commercial or business operations with not more than $2,000,000 in secured and unsecured debts in which there is either no committee of unsecured creditors or in which the committee "is not sufficiently active and representative to provide effective oversight of the debtor." Bankruptcy Code § 101(51D).

[221] 28 U.S.C. § 586(a)(7) (2006).

[222] *See* http://www.usdoj.gov/ust/eo/bapcpa/meanstesting.htm (last visited April 17, 2012).

[223] Bankruptcy Code § 705(a).

performance (i.e., it may complain about the trustee's performance). It may also submit either to the court or to the U.S. Trustee any question "affecting the administration of the estate."[224] In sum, the committee acts in purely an advisory capacity; it is expected to do so in the interests of all creditors, and not merely in the interests of its members.[225]

The key function of a creditors' committee in a Chapter 7 case is to make noise. Its chief right is to be heard by the court. It is likely that it has an absolute right to be heard on any matter materially affecting the liquidation. This would certainly include the proposed sale of property, the trustee's method of dealing with claims, and the discharge. The committee may take positions contrary to those of the trustee, and in some circumstances the committee may even have the right to appeal decisions of the bankruptcy court.[226]

§ 17.07   PARTNERSHIP LIQUIDATION

Partnership liquidations are somewhat more complicated than other cases because of the hybrid nature of partnerships. Partnerships have most of the attributes of a legal entity. They can own property in their own name, enter into contracts, and sue or be sued. In these respects, partnerships are like corporations. However, unlike the shareholders of a corporation, general partners of a partnership are personally liable for all of the partnership's debts. But, their liability is only secondary; a creditor of the partnership cannot reach the assets of a general partner unless and until the assets of the partnership have been exhausted.

This same basic pattern is preserved in bankruptcy. One of the provisions that reflects this is § 723, which deals with the rights of the partnership's bankruptcy trustee against its general partners. The trustee of the partnership, as representative of the partnership's creditors, is given the right to do what the creditors themselves would do outside of bankruptcy — to recover unpaid claims from the individual partners.

There are two somewhat different situations dealt with in § 723. The first deals with an action by the trustee against a general partner who is not in bankruptcy. The second deals with a claim by the trustee against a general partner who is a debtor in her own separate bankruptcy proceeding.

If neither of the individual partners is involved in a bankruptcy proceeding, the partnership's bankruptcy trustee has a claim against each partner to the extent that, under applicable non-bankruptcy law, the general partner is personally liable for the partnership's debts. Assume, for example, that Sam Spade and Miles Archer are general partners in the firm of Spade & Archer, and that the Spade & Archer partnership has filed a Chapter 7 bankruptcy case.[227] However, neither Sam Spade

---

[224] Bankruptcy Code § 705(b).

[225] In re Kenney Co., 136 F. 451 (D. Ind. 1905).

[226] SEC v. U.S. Realty & Improvement Co., 310 U.S. 434 (1940).

[227] Partnerships are eligible to file a petition under Chapters 7 and 11. *See* Bankruptcy Code §§ 109, 101(41). In the right circumstances, they might be eligible to file under Chapter 12 as a "family farmer" or a "family fisherman." *See* Bankruptcy Code §§ 101(18)(B), 101(19A)(B).

nor Miles Archer has filed any form of bankruptcy. The total assets of their partnership are worth $150,000. Its total obligations are $500,000.

Because the property of the estate is insufficient to pay all of the allowed claims, and because under state law both Sam Spade and Miles Archer are personally liable for the unpaid claims, the bankruptcy trustee of the Spade & Archer partnership has a claim against each individual partner to the extent that, under applicable non-bankruptcy law, the general partner is personally liable for the partnerships debts. Normally, this personal liability would be for the entire amount of the deficiency ($350,000).[228] The trustee may recover from either Sam Spade or Miles Archer or both; of course, the total recovery from both of them cannot exceed $350,000. One implication of this, assuming that at least one of the partners has sufficient assets, is that creditors of the partnership will be paid in full.

Of course, in many cases, the financial failure of a partnership also means the financial failure of its individual partners. It is thus quite common for one or more of the general partners to be in bankruptcy as well. Assume that, in the hypothetical given, Sam Spade is not in bankruptcy, but Miles Archer is. To the extent practicable, the trustee is required to seek recovery of the deficiency from a general partner who is *not* in bankruptcy.[229]

Thus, the trustee is normally required to seek recovery of the $350,000 deficiency first from the non-bankrupt partner; in this case, Sam Spade. If the trustee is unable to recover the entire deficiency from the non-bankrupt partner, the trustee can pursue a claim in the bankrupt partner's case. In this example, if the partnership's bankruptcy trustee is unable to recover the full $350,000 deficiency from Sam Spade, the trustee has a claim in Miles Archer's bankruptcy case for the unpaid balance.

There is an obvious problem created when the trustee pursues the bankrupt partner. This partner is already in bankruptcy and probably has other creditors, who are not related to the failed partnership, who have not been paid. These other creditors would prefer not to share with the creditors of the partnership.

For example, Sam Spade might have fled to Patagonia where the partnership trustee cannot find either him or his assets. His partner, Miles Archer, did not escape to South America, but instead, filed his own Chapter 7 bankruptcy proceeding and turned his assets over for administration by his own Chapter 7 trustee. Assume that his individual assets are worth $100,000, and that there are $200,000 of allowed unsecured claims against him, all of them unrelated to the failed partnership.

Archer's personal creditors receive a fifty percent distribution if the claims of his partnerships creditors are not considered. However, if the $350,000 of unpaid claims from the Spade & Archer partnership bankruptcy are allowed in Miles Archer's estate, then there is a total of $550,000 in claims against Archer, with only $100,000 in assets to be used to satisfy them. Creditors receive only about 18%. With a very limited exception, all of the claims against the partnership are bundled together into

---

[228] Bankruptcy Code § 723(a).

[229] Bankruptcy Code § 723(b).

the trustee's claim against the partner.[230]

§ 17.08 DISTRIBUTION OF PROPERTY OF THE ESTATE

Although assets are rarely available to provide creditors in a Chapter 7 case with any distribution, there is a fairly elaborate set of rules for those cases where such a "dividend" is available.[231] Secured claims are dealt with only indirectly, because encumbered property is either abandoned by the trustee to the lien holder, or, if the property is worth more than the lien, the property is sold and the lien holder is paid from the proceeds of the sale.[232]

The primary rule for the distribution of property with regard to unsecured claims is § 726(a). That section sets out six categories that are to be paid in order.

First payment goes to allowed priority claims in order of their priority.[233] Thus, claims entitled to priority under § 507 are paid first, in strict compliance with the levels of priority set out in that section.[234] If the available assets of the estate are sufficient only to pay the administrative claims provided for in § 507(a)(2), claims entitled to priority in § 507(a)(3) receive nothing.

Priority claimants must file a timely proof of claim, or if tardy, file it before the earlier of ten days before the mailing of the trustee's summary report or the date of the trustee's final distribution.[235] This category includes claims entitled to super-priority treatment, which are ahead of other § 507(a) priority claims.[236]

Second in line for payment are the allowed general unsecured claims, other than certain claims that were filed late and certain claims for fines, penalties, and punitive damages. To be included in this group, the claimant must have filed a timely proof of claim, or, if the proof of claim was late, the delay was excusable.[237]

The third group consists of those claims that, although they were filed late and the late filing was not excused, have still been allowed.[238] Thus, a creditor who files late does not necessarily lose its right to receive a distribution from the estate, but the likelihood that funds will be available is considerably diminished.

---

[230] Bankruptcy Code § 723(c). If this produces a surplus in the partnership bankruptcy, the surplus would be returned to Archer's estate. *See* Bankruptcy Code § 723(d).

[231] The colloquial reference to payments made to unsecured creditors as a "dividend" informally recognizes that when a debtor is insolvent, creditors are the ones who, as a practical matter, are entitled to the benefits of ownership.

[232] *Cf.* Bankruptcy Code § 725 (requiring the trustee, before final distribution of the property of the estate, and after notice and an opportunity for a hearing, to dispose of any property in which an entity other than the estate has an interest, such as a lien).

[233] Bankruptcy Code § 726(a)(1).

[234] *See generally supra* § 10.04[A] Priority Claims.

[235] Bankruptcy Code § 726(a)(1).

[236] *See supra* § 10.04[B] Super-Priority Claims.

[237] Bankruptcy Code § 726(a)(2).

[238] Bankruptcy Code § 726(a)(3).

The fourth group consists of those allowed claims, whether secured or unsecured, that represent any fine, penalty, or forfeiture; or represent multiple, exemplary, or punitive damages arising before the earlier of the order for relief or the appointment of a trustee, to the extent the fine, penalty, forfeiture, or damages do not represent compensation for actual pecuniary loss suffered by the holder of such claim.[239] For example, if a claimant has obtained a judgment for both compensatory damages and punitive damages arising out of a battery committed by the debtor, the compensatory damages would be paid under § 726(a)(2) and the punitive damages would fall in this fourth category. These non-compensatory fines and penalties are paid fourth, even if they otherwise constitute the type of claim entitled to priority under § 507. Any other treatment would impose punishment intended for the debtor on its creditors.

Fifth in line to receive payment are claims for post-petition interest on claims in the first four categories, charged at the legal rate from the date of the filing of the petition to the date of payment.[240] As explained elsewhere, interest does not otherwise accrue on unsecured claims,[241] and accrues on secured claims only to the extent that the value of the collateral exceeds the amount of the debt.[242] However, in the very, very rare cases in which there is property left in the estate after other claims have been paid, a further payment of interest on those claims will also be provided. Note that this further payment is at the "legal rate," which means the rate set by statute, not the rate established by the parties' contract.

Finally, if after the payment of all the claims and interest on the claims, there is still money in the estate, this surplus is paid to the debtor.[243] The availability of funds to distribute to the debtor means that the debtor was not insolvent. This is virtually unheard of.[244]

§ 17.09 LIQUIDATION TREATMENT OF CERTAIN LIENS

Section 724 supplies a variety of rules that permit the avoidance and subordination of certain liens. Appearing, as they do in Chapter 7, these rules do not apply in reorganization cases.[245] However, they do affect the dynamics of plan negotiation, since they give these lien claimants a stronger interest in confirmation of a reorganization plan than those secured claimants who will receive the value of their collateral regardless of whether the debtor liquidates.

---

[239] Bankruptcy Code § 726(a)(4).

[240] Bankruptcy Code § 726(a)(5).

[241] *See supra* § 10.02[C][4] Interest on Claims.

[242] *See supra* § 10.03[C][3] Post-Petition Interest on Secured Claims.

[243] Bankruptcy Code § 726(a)(6).

[244] Boyer v. Crown Stock Distribution, Inc., 587 F.3d 787, 797 (7th Cir. 2009).

[245] *See* Bankruptcy Code § 103.

[A]   Subordination of Liens Securing Non-Compensatory Penalties

Section 724(a) permits the trustee to avoid a lien that secures a claim for a noncompensatory "fine, penalty, forfeiture" or for an award of "exemplary or punitive damages."[246] This avoidance effectively subordinates the claims secured by such liens and prevents them from reducing distributions to other competing creditors who had nothing to do with the debtor's wrongdoing that led to the punitive claim. These claims are further subordinated by § 726(a)(4) and not paid until after all other priority and unsecured claims.[247]

[B]   Subordination of Secured Tax Claims.

Section 724(b) provides a complicated mechanism that subordinates other unavoidable *secured* tax claims to unsecured priority non-tax claims.[248] Property subject to an unavoidable tax lien is distributed first to any creditor with a senior lien on the property.[249] Any excess value would then normally be distributed to the holder of the tax lien in question, but § 724(b)(2) instead calls for this value to next be distributed to holders of most non-tax § 507(a) priority claims.[250] If there is any excess value that would have been distributed to the tax lien, after these unsecured priority claims are satisfied, it is distributed to the holder of the subordinated tax lien.[251]

A simple example illustrates how this first part of the rule operates. Assume Empire Bank holds a senior mortgage on Titanic Corporation's land and buildings, securing a $10 million claim. Humboldt County holds an unavoidable but junior real estate tax lien, securing an unpaid $1 million tax debt on the same property. Subordinate to the tax lien is Atlantic Finance Co.'s second $3 million mortgage on the property. Assume further that there are $700,000 in unsecured priority claims. When the property is sold, Empire Bank's senior mortgage is paid first. The next $1 million of value received from the property is distributed to the $700,000 in unsecured § 507(a)(1)-(7) priority claims; then, up to the $300,000 balance of the $1 million tax lien is paid to the holder of the subordinated tax lien.[252] This treatment subordinates the tax lien to unsecured priority claims, but preserves the priority of Atlantic Finance Co.'s junior mortgage. Atlantic Finance Co.'s mortgage will be be paid next.[253] Atlantic Finance Co. is not harmed by promoting the unsecured priority claims because it is in any event subordinate to $11 million worth of claims

---

[246] Bankruptcy Code §§ 724(a), 726(a)(4).

[247] *See supra* § 17.08 Distribution of Property of the Estate.

[248] Bankruptcy Code § 724(b).

[249] Bankruptcy Code § 724(b)(1).

[250] Bankruptcy Code § 724(b)(2). Non-wage administrative expenses incurred while the case was in Chapter 11, before it was converted to Chapter 7, are excluded from this distribution.

[251] Bankruptcy Code § 724(b)(3).

[252] This amount is distributed according to whatever priority would otherwise apply under § 507. Bankruptcy Code § 724(c).

[253] Bankruptcy Code § 724(b)(4).

— those of Empire Bank and Humboldt County. Atlantic Finance will likely be indifferent as to who receives this $11 million and to whether the amount of Humboldt County's $1 million tax claim is paid to Humboldt County or to other claimants.

The distribution of $700,000 of Humboldt County's $1 million tax claim to holders of § 507(a) priority claims leaves $700,000 of Humboldt County's tax claim unpaid. If the property is worth more than the $14 million necessary to pay all three secured claims, the balance is distributed to the holder of the subordinated tax lien and then to the estate, which distributes it in accordance with § 726(a), described in the immediately preceding section.[254]

Section 724 also provides for treating *any* statutory lien as a tax lien if the priority of the tax lien is determined in the same manner as a Federal Income Tax Lien under the provisions of the Federal Tax Lien Act.[255] To simplify matters somewhat, § 724(e) now provides for the equitable marshaling of assets in a manner that avoids the necessity of subordinating the tax lien if unencumbered assets could be used to satisfy the § 507 priority claims that are promoted through the operation of § 724(b).[256]

§ 17.10   SPECIAL LIQUIDATIONS

Chapter 7 contains several sets of rules that apply only to liquidations of particular types of debtors: stockbrokers, commodity brokers, and clearing banks (banks whose only business is to facilitate transfers of funds between banks). Sections 741-753 govern stockholder liquidations. Sections 761-767 apply to liquidations of commodity brokers. Sections 781-784 apply to clearing bank liquidations. All of these provisions are highly specialized and unlikely to be encountered except in the most sophisticated bankruptcy practice. They are far beyond the scope of this book.

---

[254] *See supra* § 17.08 Distribution of Property of the Estate.

[255] Bankruptcy Code § 724(d).

[256] Bankruptcy Code § 724(e).

Chapter 18

REHABILITATION OF INDIVIDUALS WITH REGULAR INCOME

§ 18.01 GOALS OF REHABILITATION OF INDIVIDUALS WITH REGULAR INCOME[1]

Chapter 13 provides individual debtors with an alternative to liquidation. In Chapter 7 liquidation cases, debtors give up their non-exempt property in exchange for an immediate discharge. In Chapter 13 rehabilitation cases, debtors give up a portion of their future income for 3-5 years in exchange for being permitted to keep all of their property. Most debts remaining unpaid after completing their plan are discharged.

Chapter 13 is the descendent of Chapter XIII of the old Bankruptcy Act's "Wage Earner Plans," which began as little more than a local rule implemented by a single bankruptcy referee in Birmingham, Alabama.[2] These plans gave wage earning individuals an opportunity to obtain the advantages of reorganization bankruptcy.[3] When drafting the Bankruptcy Code in 1978, Congress decided to broaden the old chapter and make it more attractive, in hopes that more debtors would use it rather than Chapter 7.[4]

Relief under Chapter 13 is no longer limited to wage earners. Since 1978 it has been available to all individuals with regular income sufficient to fund an appropriate plan.[5] This requirement means only that the debtor must have a source of income that is sufficiently regular to make it possible to fund a plan.[6]

Chapter 13 debtors obtain advantages not available to those who liquidate. The most obvious advantage is intrinsic to the nature of reorganization: they get to keep their assets. In addition, Chapter 13 debtors receive a somewhat broader discharge

---

[1] Donald Boren, *An Analysis of Changes In the Use of Chapter 13 Since the Enactment of the Bankruptcy Reform Act of 1978*, 23 Am. Bus. L.J. 451 (1985); William C. Whitford, *Has the Time Come to Repeal Chapter 13?*, 65 Ind. L.J. 85 (1989).

[2] Timothy W. Dixon & David G. Epstein, *Where Did Chapter 13 Come From and Where Should it Go?*, 10 Am. Bankr. Inst. L. Rev. 741, 741 (2002).

[3] *See generally* Harry H. Haden, *Chapter XIII Wage Earner Plans — Forgotten Man Bankruptcy*, 55 Ky. L.J. 564 (1967).

[4] Timothy W. Dixon & David G. Epstein, *Where Did Chapter 13 Come from and Where Should it Go?*, 10 Am. Bankr. Inst. L. Rev. 741 (2002).

[5] Bankruptcy Code § 109(e).

[6] Bankruptcy Code § 101(30). *See supra* § 6.02[B][6] Eligibility for Relief in Chapter 13 — Individuals with Regular Income.

than debtors who choose Chapter 7.[7] Also significant is Chapter 13's expanded automatic stay, which prevents creditors from seeking recovery from individual co-debtors while the case is pending,[8] thus making the debtors the sole source of payment during the plan.

§ 18.02   ELIGIBILITY FOR RELIEF UNDER CHAPTER 13

Chapter 13 is available only to individual debtors.[9] Chapter 13 also permits joint cases to be filed by individuals who are married to one anther.[10] Corporations, partnerships, unincorporated associations and other such entities must reorganize, if at all, under Chapter 11, or, if they qualify, as "family farmers" or "family fishermen," under Chapter 12.[11]

In addition, Chapter 13 debtors must have income that "is sufficiently stable and regular to enable such individual to make payments under a [chapter 13 plan]."[12] The source of the income does not matter.[13] Income from odd jobs and even collecting junk qualifies. So does income from government benefits, and maybe even regular contributions from family members. Individuals who operate a business as a sole proprietor are eligible for Chapter 13 relief, so long as their obligations do not exceed Chapter 13's debt limits. Thus, Chapter 13 is sometimes used for small businesses but only if they are operated as sole proprietorships, or husband-wife partnerships.

As explained in greater detail elsewhere,[14] the debtor (and, where applicable, the debtor's spouse) must have non-contingent, liquidated, unsecured debts of less than $360,475, and non-contingent, liquidated, secured debts of less than $1,081,400.[15] In a joint case involving a married couple, the debts are aggregated to determine whether they exceed these thresholds. These limits restrict Chapter 13 to relatively small cases, involving less complicated finances.

---

[7] Since its inception in 1978, the scope of a Chapter 13 discharge has gradually narrowed. Congress has discovered other ways, in the form a financial means test, described elsewhere, for providing debtors with a suitable incentive to seek relief in Chapter 13 rather than in Chapter 7. *See* § 17.03[B][2] Presumptive Abuse — Means Testing, *supra*.

[8] Bankruptcy Code § 1301; *see supra* § 8.04 Co-Debtor Stay in Chapters 12 and 13.

[9] Bankruptcy Code § 109(e).

[10] Bankruptcy Code § 101(30).

[11] Bankruptcy Code § 109(f). In some circumstances, a corporation may qualify as either a family farmer or a family fisherman. Bankruptcy Code §§ 19 & 19(A); *see supra* § 6.02[B][5] Eligibility for Relief in Chapter 12 — Family Farmers & Family Fishermen.

[12] Bankruptcy Code § 101(30).

[13] Under the Bankruptcy Act, in effect until 1979, former chapter XIII was available only to "wage earners."

[14] *See supra* § 6.02[B][6][c] Chapter 13 Debt Limits.

[15] Bankruptcy Code § 109(e). As with most other dollar amounts in the Bankruptcy Code, the figures in § 109(e) are adjusted every three years by a factor based on the increase in the Department of Labor's Consumer Price Index and rounded to the nearest $25 amount that represents the change. Bankruptcy Code § 104(b)(1). The most recent increase was April 1, 2010. The amounts are scheduled to be adjusted again in 2013, 2016, and 2019.

§ 18.03 FILING, CONVERSION, AND DISMISSAL OF CHAPTER 13 CASES

[A] Filing Chapter 13 Cases

A Chapter 13 bankruptcy may be filed by either an individual or an individual and his or her spouse.[16] As of late 2012, the filing fee was $235,[17] plus a $46 "administrative fee,"[18] for a grand total of $281.[19] As with Chapter 7 petitions, the filing fee may be paid in installments,[20] but unlike Chapter 7,[21] no provision is made for an in forma pauperis Chapter 13 petition.[22]

In most cases, the debtor files his plan together with his petition. The plan, in any event, must be filed within fifteen days after the petition.[23] Moreover, payments must commence within thirty 30 days of the time of the "order for relief" or the "filing of the plan," whichever is earlier.[24] Thus, payments nearly always commence before the plan is confirmed.

Chapter 13 debtors must also file a variety of other documents, including schedules of their debts and assets, a statement of current income and current expenditures, a statement of financial affairs, a statement that the debtor has received certain notices about the differences between chapter 7, 11, 12, and 13 and about the consequences of falsified schedules, a detailed statement concerning monthly net income, and a statement disclosing any reasonably anticipated increase in income or expenditures.[25] Like all individual debtors, they are also required to certify that they have participated in a credit counseling briefing from an approved nonprofit budget and credit counseling agency, and a copy of any repayment plan developed during that briefing.[26]

---

[16] Bankruptcy Code §§ 109(e), 302.

[17] 28 U.S.C.S. § 1930(a)(1)(B) (2006).

[18] 28 U.S.C. § 1930(b) (2006).

[19] See 28 U.S.C. § 1930 (2006).

[20] Fed. R. Bankr. P. 1006(b).

[21] See 28 U.S.C. § 1390(f) (2006) (permitting waiver of the Chapter 7 filing fee for debtors whose income is less than 150 percent of the poverty line).

[22] Karen Gross, *In Forma Pauperis in Bankruptcy: Reflecting On and Beyond* United States v. Kras, 2 Am. Bankr. Inst. L. Rev. 57 (1994).

[23] Fed. R. Bankr. P. 3015(b).

[24] Bankruptcy Code § 1326(a)(1). Involuntary Chapter 13 petitions are not permitted. Bankruptcy Code § 303. Thus, the order for relief will nearly always coincide with the filing of the petition, except in cases involving conversion from another chapter.

[25] Bankruptcy Code § 521(a); *see supra* § 6.02[C] Petition, Lists, Schedules, Statements, Certificates, and Dsiclosures.

[26] Bankruptcy Code § 521(b)(1)-(2).

[B] Conversion or Dismissal of Chapter 13 Cases

Chapter 13 filings are completely voluntary. Although debtors with too much disposable income can be precluded from filing a case under Chapter 7, they cannot be forced to seek relief under Chapter 13. The Code makes no provision for involuntary Chapter 13 cases. Compelling debtors to submit a portion of their income is regarded as impractical; further, it would smack of involuntary servitude.[27] As a result, Chapter 13 cases may nearly always be voluntarily dismissed at the debtor's request.[28] Although the voluntary nature of Chapter 13 would seem to make this right absolute, several courts have held that the debtor's bad faith may negate her right to voluntarily dismiss.[29] This limitation is based on the Supreme Court's 2007 decision in *Marrama v. Citizens Bank*,[30] where the Court denied a Chapter 7 debtor, who had acted in bad faith, an unqualified right to convert from Chapter 7 to Chapter 13.[31] With this qualification, Chapter 13 cases may also be voluntarily converted to Chapter 7, regardless of any waiver of this right that the debtor may have supplied.[32]

Chapter 13 cases may also be converted or dismissed "on request of a party in interest or the United States Trustee . . . for cause."[33] Good cause covers a wide range of territory, including failure to comply with any of the requirements of Chapter 13, failing to file a timely plan,[34] denial of confirmation, and "material default" of a term of a confirmed plan.[35] As might be expected, the most common reason for dismissal is the debtor's continued failure to make payments required under the plan.[36]

Further, a debtor's case can be dismissed if he fails to meet any "domestic support obligations" — support to his spouse or children — even if they are not

---

[27] *See* H. R. Rep. No 595, 95th Cong., 1st Sess. 322 (1977) *as reprinted in* 1978 U.S.C.C.A.N, 5963, 6278. Note, however, that, subject to limits imposed by federal law, a debtor's wages can be garnished through state court collection proceedings.

[28] Bankruptcy Code § 1307(b). *E.g.*, Barbieri v. RAJ Acquisition Corp. (In re Barbieri), 199 F.3d 616 (2d Cir. 1999).

[29] In re Jacobsen, 609 F.3d 647 (5th Cir. 2010); In re Rosson, 545 F.3d 764 (9th Cir. 2008); In re Armstrong, 408 B.R. 559 (Bankr. E.D.N.Y. 2009).

[30] 549 U.S. 365 (2007).

[31] *See also* In re Glenn, 408 B.R. 800 (Bankr. E.D. Mo. 2009). *See generally* John Rao, *Impact of Marrama On Case Conversions: Addressing the Unanswered Questions*, 15 Am. Bankr. Inst. L. Rev. 585 (2007).

[32] Bankruptcy Code § 1307(a).

[33] Bankruptcy Code § 1307(c).

[34] *See, e.g.*, In re Jensen, 425 B.R. 105 (Bankr. S.D.N.Y. 2010) (debtor's delay in filing feasible plan).

[35] *Id.*

[36] *See* Till v. SCS Credit Corp., 541 U.S. 465, 493 (2004) (Scalia, J., dissenting) (failure rate between 37% and 60%); Scott F. Norberg, *Consumer Bankruptcy's New Clothes: An Empirical Study of Discharge and Debt Collection in Chapter 13*, 7 Am. Bankr. Inst. L. Rev. 415, 440 (1999) (one-third completion rate); William C. Whitford, *The Ideal of Individualized Justice: Consumer Bankruptcy as Consumer Protection, and Consumer Protection in Consumer Bankruptcy*, 68 Am. Bankr. L.J. 397, 411 (1994) (31% completion).

being paid through the Chapter 13 trustee, as part of his confirmed plan.[37] Debtors who do not pay their spouses and children are thus prevented from enjoying the benefits of Chapter 13. If the rule were otherwise, debtors would have an incentive to miss their support payments in order to keep their Chapter 13 plan payments on course. The case may also be converted or dismissed if the debtor fails to "file a [post-petition] tax return . . ." as required by § 1308.[38]

In extreme cases, the court might dismiss a case "with prejudice," effectively barring the debtor from refiling another case in the ensuing six months.[39] Dismissal with prejudice might also prevent the debtor from *ever* discharging the debts included in the dismissed case.[40]

The only source of real dispute in interpreting the grounds for conversion or dismissal deals with whether a debtor's default in performance of the provisions of his plan is "material." If the default was due to circumstances that were beyond the debtor's control or unexpected, and the debtor's performance can easily be resumed, a default may not be material.[41] Otherwise, cases of debtors who miss payments required by their plan are dismissed.[42] Failure to complete the payments required by the plan, and dismissal of the case, usually prevents the debtor from obtaining a discharge. The only exception is for debtors who qualify for a "hardship discharge."[43]

§ 18.04 PROPERTY OF THE CHAPTER 13 ESTATE[44]

In Chapter 13, the debtor's estate includes more than in Chapter 7. A Chapter 13 estate includes all property specified by § 541, plus the income that the debtor earns during the case.[45] Because the case might last for up to 5 years, this makes a Chapter 13 estate considerably larger than the same debtor's estate would have been, if the debtor had filed a Chapter 7 case.

This is consistent with the basic approach of Chapter 13, in which the debtor pays a portion of his earnings to his creditors for up to five years.[46] Chapter 13 plans must provide for "the submission of . . . future earnings or future income of the debtor to the supervision and control of the trustee as is necessary for the execution

---

[37] Bankruptcy Code § 1307(c)(11).

[38] Bankruptcy Code § 1307(e). This new language will presumably overrule cases such as *Howard v. Lexington Investments, Inc.*, 284 F.3d 320 (1st Cir. 2002) (failure to timely file tax returns was not necessarily a "material" default).

[39] Bankruptcy Code § 349(a). *See* Wiese v. Community Bank, 552 F.3d 584, 591 (7th Cir. 2009).

[40] Ellsworth v. Lifescape Medical Assoc. (In re Ellsworth), 455 B.R. 904, 921–22 (B.A.P. 9th Cir. 2011).

[41] In re Durben, 70 B.R. 14 (Bankr. S.D. Ohio 1986) (no material default where debtor's payments were temporarily disrupted by debtor diverting funds to repair secured creditor's collateral).

[42] *E.g.*, In re Mallory, 444 B.R. 553 (Bankr. S.D. Tex. 2011).

[43] *See supra* § 13.05[C][2] Chapter 13 Hardship Discharge.

[44] David Gray Carlson, *The Chapter 13 Estate and its Discontents*, 17 Am. Bankr. Inst. L.J. 233 (2009).

[45] Bankruptcy Code § 1306(a).

[46] *See infra* § 18.08[D] Duration of Plan.

of the plan."[47] Chapter 13 plans ordinarily provide for the debtor to submit a portion of his post-petition earnings to the control of the trustee, who uses the funds to make payments to creditors.

Unlike Chapter 7, where the trustee takes control of the debtor's non-exempt property, Chapter 13 permits the debtor to remain in possession of all of his property, except as specified in the debtor's plan.[48] Most Chapter 13 plans require the debtor to submit whatever portion of his earnings are necessary for the plan, to the trustee.[49] The plan might also require the debtor to surrender specific assets to secured creditors, or that certain property will be sold. But, most Chapter 13 plans do no such thing — they merely require the debtor to pay a portion of his income to the trustee, who will make payments to secured and unsecured creditors, in accordance with the plan.

Chapter 13 debtors who are engaged in a business[50] are permitted to operate their business in the ordinary course. Consistent with the debtor's status as a "debtor-in-possession," the business can incur debt and sell, use or lease property in the ordinary course,[51] subject to the usual limitations on the operation of a business imposed by sections 363 and 364.[52] Naturally, the court can impose any additional limitations and conditions that it deems appropriate,[53] to prevent the debtor from squandering assets that might otherwise be used to pay creditors.

§ 18.05 PARTIES IN CHAPTER 13 CASES

The parties in Chapter 13 cases are much the same as those in other bankruptcy cases, though the debtor and the trustee perform significantly different roles than they do in Chapter 7. Moeover, unlike Chapters 7 and 11, there are no "creditors' committees" in Chapter 13 cases.

[A] Role of a Chapter 13 Debtor

All Chapter 13 estates are operated by a debtor-in-possession, who is always the debtor. The debtor has the same rights and obligations as debtors in other types of cases. In addition, the Chapter 13 debtor has many of the rights that a trustee would have regarding the use, sale and lease of property.[54]

As a practical matter, the typical Chapter 13 debtor does virtually nothing except pay his lawyer and submit payments to the trustee to fund the plan. The

---

[47] Bankruptcy Code § 1322(a)(1). *See also* Fed. R. Bankr. P. 3013.

[48] Bankruptcy Code § 1306(b).

[49] Bankruptcy Code § 1322(a).

[50] Robert Lawless & Elizabeth Warren, *The Myth of the Disappearing Business Bankruptcy*, 93 Cal. L. Rev. 743, 773 tbl. 2 (estimating that 19.7 percent of Chapter 13 bankruptcies are filed by those starting or operating a small business).

[51] Bankruptcy Code § 1304(b).

[52] *See generally* Chapter 9 — Operation the Debtor, *supra.*

[53] Bankruptcy Code § 1304(b).

[54] Bankruptcy Code § 1303.

estate is usually small and only rarely involves a business to manage; the debtor simply continues to go to work and collect a paycheck. Few Chapter 13 cases involve any litigation, and what litigation does exist focuses mainly on whether the plan can be confirmed.

Because Chapter 13 cases continue for several years, the debtor is also required to update the trustee about changes in his financial circumstances. He must provide copies of his income tax returns,[55] pay future support,[56] and report any increases in his income.[57]

[B] Role of Standing Chapter 13 Trustee

A Chapter 13 trustee has a different role than a trustee in a Chapter 7 case. In most federal judicial districts, there is a standing trustee who supervises all the Chapter 13 cases in the district.[58] In particularly large districts, there are two or more such trustees, and the work is divided among them.

The Chapter 13 trustee's duties are midway between those of a Chapter 7 case trustee and the United States Trustee. The duties are primarily to supervise the debtor,[59] to appear and be heard on questions of valuation, confirmation, and modification,[60] to ensure that the debtor begins making payments in a timely fashion,[61] and to disburse payments to creditors under the plan.[62]

There is evidence that the standing trustee can and in some districts does exercise considerable influence over the number of Chapter 13 cases filed and the structure of debtors' plans. The right of the trustee to object to confirmation places the standing trustee in a particularly powerful position with respect to the structure and content of Chapter 13 plans. Debtors without the funds necessary to finance litigation over a trustee's challenge to confirmation are likely to go along with the requirements imposed by a standing trustee in order to avoid such a challenge. And, debtor's attorneys, seeking to avoid confrontations with a standing trustee they will be facing in every case they handle, are unlikely to even present their clients with alternatives that might involve such a potential challenge.

Differences in the degree of such influence creates considerable differences in the operation of Chapter 13 from district to district, and even within districts within the same state. Supporters of active standing trustees, however, insist that their work not only benefits creditors by increasing the amount collected but also

---

[55] Bankruptcy Code § 1307(c)(11).

[56] Bankruptcy Code § 1307(c)(11).

[57] *See* Bankruptcy Code § 521(f)(4).

[58] Bankruptcy Code § 1302(a); The Executive Office of the United States Trustee maintains a list of standing Chapter 13 trustees. *See* http://www.usdoj.gov/ust/eo/private_trustee/locator/13.htm (last viewed May 30, 2006).

[59] Bankruptcy Code § 1302(b)(1).

[60] Bankruptcy Code § 1302(b)(2).

[61] Bankruptcy Code § 1302(b)(5).

[62] Bankruptcy Code § 1326(c).

debtors by restoring their pride and self-esteem.[63]

[C]   The United States Trustee in Chapter 13

United States Trustees have no formal role in individual Chapter 13 cases. Their responsibility is limited, as it is in most other consumer cases, to appoint and supervise the standing trustees who administer Chapter 13 cases in their region, and, if necessary, because of the unwillingness of a private trustee to serve, to act as the trustee in an individual case. They might take action, where necessary, to prevent fraud and abuse by parties connected to bankruptcy cases, such as the occasional dishonest standing trustee. The United States Trustee also monitors awards of professional fees to Chapter 13 trustees, their attorneys, and other professionals hired pursuant to §§ 327 and 330.

[D]   Creditors in Chapter 13 Cases

[1]   Secured Creditors in Chapter 13

Some secured creditors play an active role in Chapter 13 cases; other secured creditors do little more than cash the monthly checks they receive from the debtor or the trustee. Because debtors cannot use Chapter 13 to modify residential real estate mortgages, mortgage holders have little reason to be involved in most cases, except perhaps with respect to efforts to dismiss the case or to obtain relief from the automatic stay. Other secured creditors are likely to play an active role with respect to the valuation of their collateral for the purposes of determining the amount of the allowed secured claim. However, rules that require full payment of many purchase money debts make this role less significant than it previously had been.[64]

[2]   Unsecured Creditors in Chapter 13

Unsecured creditors play a minimal role in most Chapter 13 cases. Most of the time, the standing Chapter 13 trustee can be counted on to make any necessary challenges to confirmation of the debtor's plan. The Procrustean features of the rules for determining the amount of income that Chapter 13 debtors must pay to their unsecured creditors provides creditors with little incentive to become active in individual cases, apart perhaps from getting involved in an occasional test case. They are more likely to have a wider impact on the trustee's behavior, by pressing their complaints with the local offices of the United States Trustee.

---

[63] Jean Braucher, *Lawyers and Consumer Bankruptcy: One Code, Many Cultures*, 67 Am. Bankr. L.J. 501, 557–58 (1993).

[64] *See infra* § 18.08[F][6] Certain Purchase Money Security Interests.

§ 18.06 THE CHAPTER 13 PLAN — REQUIRED PROVISIONS

At the core of Chapter 13 is the debtor's plan. Chapter 13 plans are usually formulated without creditor participation. The debtor is the only one with the right to submit a plan and creditors do not vote on whether to "accept" the plan.[65] As a result, unsecured creditors especially are given no direct or even indirect role in the formulation of a repayment plan. The contents of the plan are almost entirely set by the statutory requirements for confirmation.[66] The requirements for confirmation under Chapter 13 are so well established that it is routine for debtors to file their plan with their petition.[67] Plans are so standardized that their preparation often requires no more than filling in a computerized checklist and printing out the result.

There are only three mandatory provisions of a plan spelled out in § 1322(a). However, these mandatory provisions must be read together with § 1325's requirements for confirmation, which have a significant influence on how both mandatory and permissive provisions are drafted.

[A] Submission of Sufficient Income to Fund the Plan

A Chapter 13 plan must provide for the submission of a sufficient portion of the debtor's future income and earnings to the supervision and control of the trustee.[68] This is consistent with the basic structure of Chapter 13, which contemplates that the debtor will pay creditors whatever surplus income the debtor has available, after meeting his basic living expenses. Section 1322(a)(1) does not specify exactly what portion of the debtor's income is required to be submitted to the trustee, but only mandates that it be "sufficient . . . to fund the plan." The amount necessary to fund the plan will depend on the other terms of the plan. This will, in turn, be determined by the requirements for confirmation in § 1325.

[B] Full Payment of Priority Claims

[1] Priority Claims in Chapter 13

Section 1322(a)(2) requires all Chapter 13 plans to "provide for the *full payment* . . . of all claims entitled to priority under section 507 . . . unless the holder of a particular claim agrees to a different treatment . . . ."[69] This, together with § 1325(a)(1)'s requirement that the plan comply with all of the provisions of Chapter

---

[65] *See infra* § 19.09 Acceptance of Plan by Holders of Claims and Interests: Disclosure & Voting.

[66] The standing Chapter 13 trustee may have a great deal of influence over what goes into the plan. *See* Jean Braucher, *Lawyers and Consumer Bankruptcy: One Code, Many Cultures*, 67 Am. Bankr. L.J. 501, 556–61 (1993).

[67] If the plan is not filed with the petition, it must normally be filed within fifteen days after the petition, although the court can extend this time "for cause shown and on notice as the court may direct." Fed. R. Bankr. P. 3015(b).

[68] Bankruptcy Code § 1322(a)(1).

[69] Bankruptcy Code § 322(a)(2).

13[70] makes paying priority claims in full necessary.

Chapter 13 debtors who do not operate a business are unlikely to have creditors with priority claims other than those for any administrative expenses such as trustee's fees and bankruptcy attorney fees,[71] unpaid tax claims,[72] and unpaid support claims.[73]

Section 1322(b)(2) requires only that the "amount" of the claim be paid in full. It does not require the stream of future payments to have the same "value" as the amount of the claim. Thus, as long as the total dollars paid to the priority creditor satisfy the claim, the plan can be confirmed, even though it does not provide for interest to compensate the creditor for the delay in receiving payment. This is completely different from the way § 1325(a)(5) deals with secured creditors' claims. Thus, if a debtor owes a $3,000 unsecured debt to the IRS, the debtor's plan can be confirmed if it provides for making 30 payments of $100 each to the IRS, totaling $3,000. If the claim were secured, § 1325 would permit the creditor to insist on interest for its $3,000 secured claim.

[2] Domestic Support Obligations

Domestic support obligations are among the § 507 priority claims that must be paid in full. However, § 1322(a)(2) must be read together with § 1322(a)(4). The latter permits a Chapter 13 plan to provide for less than full payment of *some* domestic support obligations if the plan requires the debtor to continue making payments of all of his projected disposable income for a five-year period.[74] In a five-year plan, domestic support obligations that have previously been assigned to "a governmental agency or unit" need not be paid in full.[75] Thus, a plan may provide for less than payment in full of past-due domestic support claims that have already been assigned to a governmental unit, but only if the debtor submits a 5-year plan. But, the plan must provide for full payment of domestic support obligations that have not yet been assigned to a governmental agency.

These are not the only rules that seek to ensure that debtors pay support. The debtor's plan cannot be confirmed if the debtor has fallen further into default on payment of his domestic support obligations, since his petition was filed.[76] Further, the debtor's failure to make timely payment of any future domestic support obligation is grounds to have his case dismissed.[77] Finally, unpaid portions of domestic support obligations are non-dischargeable in Chapter 13, even under the

---

[70] Bankruptcy Code § 1325(a)(1).

[71] *See* In re San Miguel, 40 B.R. 481 (Bankr. D. Colo. 1984) (plan provided for payments of only $1.00 each to unsecured creditors, but provided for payment in full to debtor's attorney for § 507(a)(2) administrative priority claim).

[72] Bankruptcy Code § 507(a)(8).

[73] Bankruptcy Code § 507(a)(1).

[74] Bankruptcy Code § 1322(a)(4).

[75] Bankruptcy Code § 507(a)(1)(B); *see supra* § 10.04[A][1] Support Claims.

[76] Bankruptcy Code § 1325(a)(8).

[77] Bankruptcy Code § 1307(c)(11).

hardship discharge provisions.[78] Thus, the debtor will remain liable, after completion of his plan, for any past due support that is not fully paid.[79]

Property settlement obligations to a spouse, former spouse, or child are not entitled to priority and need not be paid in full. These debts remain fully dischargeable in Chapter 13, which preserves the historical distinction between support and property settlement.[80]

§ 18.07 CHAPTER 13 PLAN — PERMISSIVE PROVISIONS

Section 1322(b) specifies a variety of optional provisions, that may or may not be included in a Chapter 13 plan. Many of these optional provisions are routinely utilized, such as those providing for the modification of secured and unsecured claims. The most important passages in § 1322(b) are those which impose limitations on these otherwise permissive terms. In addition, the range of latitude permitted by § 1322(b) must be read in conjunction with the standards for plan confirmation imposed by § 1325 which, in many cases, further restrict what the plan may provide.

[A] Classification of Claims[81]

Chapter 13 debtors may separate unsecured claims into separate classes, but only in limited ways.[82] Separating claims into distinct groups is called "classification." Claims are classified so that they can be treated differently from one another. The most obvious example of this is a plan that provides for paying one class 100% of the amount of their allowed claims while paying members of a separate and distinctly second class less, perhaps only 60%.

Claims might also be segregated into separate classes for the purpose of paying members of one class earlier in the life span of the plan. This is sometimes done as a hedge against the risk that the plan will fail. If this happens, the debtor may find it useful to have fully paid secured claims or claims for nondischargeable debts. Or, the debtor may have other reasons to be more concerned that one group of creditors, such as family members, co-workers, or, in the case of a debtor engaged in business, key suppliers, receive more than others.[83]

Section 1322(b)(1) permits a plan to separate claims of unsecured creditors into separate classes provided that the classification comports with § 1122, governing

---

[78] Bankruptcy Code § 1328(a)(2).

[79] *See supra* § 13.05[C] Scope of Chapter 13 Discharge.

[80] In Chapter 7 cases, both support and property settlement obligations are non-dischargeable. *See* § 13.03[B][5] Family Obligations, *supra.*

[81] Stephen L. Sepinuk, *Rethinking Unfair Discrimination in Chapter 13*, 74 Am. Bankr. L.J. 341 (2000); Kevin D. Hart, Annotation, *Payments to Partially Secured Creditors Outside Chapter 13 Plan as Unfair Discriminatory Treatment of Class of Unsecured Claims under Bankruptcy Code § 1322(b)(1) of Bankruptcy Code of 1978*, 50 A.L.R. Fed. 694 (1980).

[82] Bankruptcy Code § 1122(b)(1).

[83] In re Wolff, 22 B.R. 510 (B.A.P. 9th Cir. 1982) (classification favoring existing insurance carrier and materials supplier not justified).

classification in Chapter 11 cases, and provided that the classification does not "discriminate unfairly" against any class.

"Unfair discrimination" is not the clearest standard imaginable. All classifications discriminate; the question is under what circumstances is the proposed discrimination "unfair."

The Code singles out one permissible type of discrimination. If someone other than the debtor is also liable for the debt — such as a guarantor — the debt can be classified separately from other debts, and be treated more favorably. This is only possible for "consumer debts,"[84] and only possible if the co-debtor is another "individual" — not a corporation or other artificial legal entity.[85]

This is little more than a bow to reality. In many cases, consumer's co-debtors are family members or friends, and many debtors, feeling a strong moral obligation to protect the co-debtor, make efforts to pay the debt outside of the plan. These payments endanger the viability of the plan, since those extra payments come out of whatever funds the debtor has left after making the required plan payments. This risk to the plan, and the fact that many debtors would try to find some way to pay the debt regardless, led Congress to legitimize a degree of disparate treatment under the plan itself.[86]

Despite this, the fact that the plan may treat co-signed consumer debts differently than other debts does not mean that any degree of discrimination is permitted. The code still prohibits "unfair discrimination" in favor of these claims.[87]

The test of unfair discrimination that has flourished, under a variety of names,[88] considers four and sometimes five factors:

1.   Is there a reasonable basis for the discrimination?

2.   Can the debtor fulfill the plan without the discrimination?

3.   Is the discrimination in good faith?

4.   Are other creditors receiving meaningful payment?

5.   Is there a direct relationship between the degree of the discrimination and the rationale for the discrimination?

---

[84] Bankruptcy Code § 101(8). *See generally* In re Westberry, 215 F.3d 589 (6th Cir. 2000).

[85] Bankruptcy Code § 101(8).

[86] The Senate Committee report, prepared at the time this amendment was made explained: "If, as a practical matter, the debtor is going to pay the codebtor claim, he should be permitted to separately classify it in Chapter 13." S. Rep. 65, 98th Cong. 1st Sess., 18 (1983).

[87] In re Whitelock, 122 B.R. 582 (Bankr. D. Utah 1990).

[88] William Houston Brown & Katherine L. Evans, *A Comparison of Classification and Treatment of Family Support Obligations and Student Loans: A Case Analysis*, 24 Mem. St. U. L. Rev. 623 (1994); James B. McLaughlin, Jr. & Robert W. Nelms, *Classification of Unsecured Claims in Chapter 13 of the Bankruptcy Reform Act of 1978: What Is Fair?*, 7 Campbell L. Rev. 329 (1985); Stephen L. Sepinuk, *Rethinking Unfair Discrimination in Chapter 13*, 74 Am. Bankr. L.J. 341, 354–55 (2000).

Some courts simply inquire as to whether the classification scheme is "reasonable,"[89] but as others have pointed out, there is little reason to believe that this different articulation results in a markedly different approach to the question.[90]

In applying these tests, courts have generally been skeptical of plans that provide different treatment to creditors based on the non-dischargeability of claims in the favored class,[91] though separate classifications of nondischargeable support claims have been treated with more favor.[92]

Courts are deeply divided over whether non-dischargeable long-term student loan debts may sometimes be singled-out for special treatment. Section 1322(b)(5) provides for curing defaults on long-term debts "on which the last payment is due after the date on which the final payment under the plan is due," and maintaining regular payments on the debts during the plan.[93] But, § 1322(b)(5) does not indicate that this may be done in contravention of § 1322(b)(1), which prohibits "unfair discrimination."[94] Most courts conclude that §§ 1322(b)(1) and 1322(b)(5) must be read in conjunction with one another, and that any interpretation of the two provisions which would treat § 1322(b)(5) as a "stand-alone provision immune from the prohibition of unfair discrimination would render § 1322(b)(1) superfluous . . . ."[95] As one court explained:

> If Congress had wanted courts not to consider whether putting unsecured creditors in a separate class and providing for full monthly payments on the unsecured creditors' claims during the course of the plan constituted unfair discrimination, Congress would have drafted section 1322(b)(5) to read "notwithstanding paragraphs (1) and (2) of this subsection, [a plan may] provide for the curing of any default . . . and maintenance of payments. . . ." Congress did not draft the statute in such a manner.[96]

Despite this argument, a few courts persist in the conclusion that § 1322(b)(5) permits long-term student loan obligations to be treated more favorably than other creditors' claims.[97]

---

[89] *E.g.*, In re Alicea, 199 B.R. 862, 866 (Bankr. D.N.J. 1996).

[90] *See* Stephen L. Sepinuk, *Rethinking Unfair Discrimination in Chapter 13*, 74 Am. Bankr. L.J. 341, 355 (2000).

[91] *E.g.*, In re Groves, 39 F.3d 212 (8th Cir. 1994) (denying confirmation of a plan that favored nondischargeable educational loans over other unsecured debts). *But see* In re Potgieter, 436 B.R. 739 (Bankr. M.D. Fla. 2010) (permitting disparate treatment of long-term, nondischargeable student loan).

[92] *See* In re Crawford, 324 F.3d 539 (7th Cir. 2003); In re Bentley, 250 B.R. 475, 478 (Bankr. D.R.I. 2000). Such claims are now, of course, entitled to priority under § 507(a)(1) and must therefore, be paid in full.

[93] Bankruptcy Code § 1322(b)(5).

[94] In re Boscaccy, 442 B.R. 501 (Bankr. N.D. Miss. 2010); In re Bentley, 266 B.R. 229 (B.A.P. 1st Cir. 2001). *But see* In re Harding, 423 B.R. 568 (Bankr. S.D. Fla. 2010).

[95] In re Edmonds, 444 B.R. 898 (Bankr. E.D. Wis. 2010). *See* In re Coonce, 213 B.R. 344 (Bankr. S.D. Ill. 1997).

[96] In re Chandler, 210 B.R. 898, 903–04, (Bankr. D.N.H. 1997).

[97] *E.g.*, In re Pracht, 464 B.R. 486 (Bankr. M.D. Ga. 2012); In re Boscacy, 442 B.R. 501 (Bankr. N.D.

But, courts have not favored classification schemes which merely favor the debtor's friends and relatives, at the expense of creditors with whom the debtor is less well acquainted. On the other hand, it makes sense to permit the debtor to favor one creditor over another where the favorable treatment is likely to enhance the debtor's income and result in better treatment for other creditors generally. Restitution payments to the victims of the debtor's crimes, necessary to keep the debtor out of jail, are an obvious example. Likewise, discriminatory treatment should be permitted when the debtor would otherwise lose some financial advantage than can be gained only by paying the creditor in full, such as where a debtor engaged in business would have to shift to an otherwise more expensive supplier or to move to a more expensive location.[98] As one Court of Appeals panel explained: "if without classification the debtor is unlikely to be able to fulfill the Chapter 13 plan and the result will be to make his creditors as a whole worse off than they would be with classification, then classification will be a win-win outcome."[99]

Finally, any discrimination between claims or types of claims must be done through separate classifications.[100] A debtor may not place differently treated claims in the same class; rather, each claim in any class must be treated the same.[101]

[B] Modification of Creditors' Rights

One of Chapter 13's most important provisions permits a plan to "modify the rights of holders of secured claims . . . or holders of unsecured claims."[102] The simplest modification is extending the time for paying the creditor.[103] For example, a creditor who is legally entitled to immediate payment might find that the plan provides for making payments to the creditor over a five-year period. For creditors depending on cash flow from their customers, this kind of extension is not only disappointing, it can have a devastating effect on the creditor's own financial position.

Chapter 13 plans frequently also reduce the amount that the creditor will receive, sometimes down to almost nothing. The debtor's ability to do this is subject to specific restrictions in the language of § 1322(b)(2) itself, and in § 1325 governing confirmation.

Miss. 2010); In re Pageau, 383 B.R. 221 (Bankr. D.N.H. 2008).

[98] *See* Stephen L. Sepinuk, *Rethinking Unfair Discrimination in Chapter 13*, 74 Am. Bankr. L.J. 341, 372–73 (2000).

[99] In re Crawford, 324 F.3d 539, 543 (7th Cir. 2003).

[100] An example of how this is accomplished in the text of a plan is illustrated by the sample plan online at: http://vls.law.vill.edu/prof/cohen/cletranscripts/Sample-1-ch13plan.htm (last visited November 4, 2006).

[101] Bankruptcy Code § 1322(a)(3).

[102] Bankruptcy Code § 1322(b)(2).

[103] *See supra* § 2.10 Compositions and Workouts.

[1] Modifying Unsecured Claims

Debtors are given wide leeway to modify the rights of unsecured creditors. As mentioned above, payments to these creditors may be extended or reduced. However, § 1325 imposes indirect restraints on this latitude by requiring that the payments made to unsecured creditors are worth at least what they would have received if the debtor had liquidated.[104] Further, in most cases, it requires the debtor to submit all of his "projected disposable income" to paying unsecured creditors for a minimum of three years.[105] Another indirect limit is imposed by § 1322(a)(2), discussed above, which requires full payment of all priority claims.[106]

Here, it should be remembered that unsecured claims include the unsecured portion of any partially secured claim. Thus, a creditor who is owed $3,000, secured by a lien on the debtor's $2,000 garden tractor, holds two claims: a secured claim of $2,000 and an unsecured claim of $1,000.[107]

The unsecured claim can be dealt with in a variety of ways. Depending on the circumstances, the plan may provide for paying very little or even nothing with respect to the unsecured claim. Or, if the debtor has ample income, the plan might provide for full payment of the claim.

The amount the debtor must pay to unsecured creditors, as explained in detail below, depends on two factors: first, the amount of non-exempt equity owned by the debtor's estate that would have been distributed to unsecured creditors in a Chapter 7 case;[108] and second, the amount of disposable income available to the debtor to pay his or her creditors.[109]

[2] Modifying Secured Claims[110]

Chapter 13 permits debtors to change the terms of payment of many, but not all secured creditors' claims.[111] If done over the creditor's objections, it is known as "cramdown."[112] Secured claims can be modified by changing the amount or duration of monthly payments or by extending or accelerating the amortization schedule of the secured debt. Thus, payments to a creditor with a security interest in the debtor's garden tractor might be spread out over the entire three to five years of the debtor's plan, even though the contract between the debtor and the

---

[104] Bankruptcy Code § 1325(a)(4); *see infra* § 18.08[E][1] Best Interests of Creditors.

[105] Bankruptcy Code § 1325(b).

[106] Bankruptcy Code § 1322(a)(2); *see supra* § 18.06[B] Full Payment of Priority Claims.

[107] If the creditor holds a purchase money security interest in the tractor, securing a debt incurred within one-year before the debtor's petition, the paragraph hanging at the end of § 1325(a)(9) will prevent the debtor from bifurcating the claim in this manner. *See infra* § 18.08[F][6] Certain Purchase Money Security Interests.

[108] *See infra* § 18.08[E][1] Best Interests of Creditors.

[109] *See infra* § 18.08[E][2] Debtor's Projected Disposable Income.

[110] *See generally* Adam J. Levitin, *Resolving the Foreclosure Crisis: Modification of Mortgages in Bankruptcy*, 2009 Wis. L. Rev. 565, 579–80 (2009).

[111] Bankruptcy Code § 1325(a)(4).

[112] In re Wright, 492 F.3d 829, 830 (7th Cir. 2007) ("the court crams down the creditor's throat").

secured creditor calls for full amortization of the debt within the next six months.

A secured claim might also be modified by changing the rate of interest to be paid to the creditor on the unpaid balance of its secured claim. The contract might require the debtor to pay 18% interest; the plan might reduce this to a much lower rate. The plan can be confirmed over the creditor's objection as long as the interest rate is sufficient to ensure that the value of the payments made to the creditor over the life of the plan are worth as much as the amount of the allowed secured claim. Thus, even though the contract calls for interest to accumulate at 18%, if the appropriate cramdown rate, to ensure that the creditor receive the full value of the amount of its secured claim is 8%, the lower rate is sufficient.[113]

Most importantly, however, the payments are only required to be worth the amount of the allowed secured claim. If the claim is only partially secured, because the collateral is worth less than the debt owed, the stream of payments need only be worth the amount of this lower amount. Thus, if debtor's garden tractor is worth $800, but the debt secured by the item is $1,000, the payments made under the plan need only be worth the lower amount, $800. The remaining $200 balance is an unsecured claim and will be paid, or not, together with other unsecured claims. This bifurcation of the creditor's total claim into a secured claim and an unsecured claim is commonly referred to as "stripping" the lien down to the value of the collateral or "lien stripping."[114]

Despite this general rule, the Code restricts the debtor's ability to modify some secured claims: those secured by a mortgage on the debtor's home, and purchase money security interests in motor vehicles and some other personal property, as explained below.

[a]   Residential Real Estate Mortgages[115]

The most important restriction on modifications of secured debts is in § 1322(b)(2). It prevents creditors from modifying the rights of residential real estate mortgagees.[116] Chapter 13 debtors may not reduce the amount, duration, or interest rate of home mortgages, even if their home is worth less than what they owe.

The precise statutory language is a bit complicated. Section 1322(b)(2) permits the plan to "modify the rights of holders of secure claims, *other than a claim secured only by a security interest in real property that is the debtor's principal residence . . . .*"[117] Thus the creditor's claim cannot be modified if:

---

[113] Till v. SCS Credit Corp. 541 U.S. 465 (2004). *See infra* § 18.08[F][4][b] Payments Equivalent to Amount of Secured Claim.

[114] Shaw v. Aurgroup Fin. Credit Union, 552 F.2d 447, 451 n. 5 (6th Cir. 2009).

[115] John Eggum, Katherine Porter & Tara Twomey, *Saving Homes in Bankruptcy: Housing Affordability and Loan Modification*, 2008 Utah L. Rev. 1123 (2008); Adam J. Levitin, *Resolving the Foreclosure Crisis: Modification of Mortgages in Bankruptcy*, 2009 Wis. L. Rev. 565 (2009); Mark S. Scarberry, *A Critique of Congressional Proposals to Permit Modification of Home Mortgages in Chapter 13*, 37 Pepperdine L. Rev. 635 (2009).

[116] Bankruptcy Code § 1322(b)(2).

[117] *Id.* (emphasis supplied).

1. The collateral for the debt is the debtor's principal residence;[118]

2. The collateral is real property;

3. There is no other collateral for the creditor's claim.[119]

If the collateral is the principal residence of one of the debtor's dependents, but not the principal residence of the debtor, the claim can be modified. Similarly, if the collateral is vacation property, or a "second home" that is not the debtor's principal residence, the claim can be modified. If the residence is personal property, such as a motor home, rather than real estate, the claim can be modified. Further, if the creditor obtained a security interest in additional collateral, such as the debtor's car, or his furniture, the claim can be modified. Somewhat surprisingly, the "no modification rule" does not apply to debtors who own and live in multi-unit structures, and rent out the other units, because the debt is not secured "solely" by the debtor's residence.[120]

If the secured creditor's claim cannot be modified, the plan must provide for payments to be made according to the terms of the parties' contract. For most home mortgages, this means that the debtor cannot use Chapter 13 to alter the amount or duration of payments owed to the mortgagee.

[i] Cure and Reinstatement Permitted

If the debtor is already in default on his mortgage, he is nevertheless able to "cure and reinststate" the mortgage pursuant to § 1322(c)(1). This is an explicit statutory exception to the no modification of home mortgages rules of § 1322(b)(2). It permits the debtor to cure and reinstate any time before the debtor's home is sold at a foreclosure sale. It effectively permits the debtor to decelerate the debt and restore the mortgage to the pre-default status quo.[121] The debtor must make up any missed payments and resume regular payments according to the schedule called for by the parties' contract. Thus, the plan might call for the debtor to resume making regular monthly installment payments at the contract rate and make additional payments to the creditor for any payments he missed before filing his Chapter 13 petition.

This right exists as long as a mortgage foreclosure sale had not been concluded at the time the debtor filed her bankruptcy petition.[122] If the property has already been sold, when the debtor's case began, the property is no longer part of the

---

[118] *See* In re Santiago, 404 B.R. 564 (Bankr. S.D. Fla. 2009) (secured creditor opposing confirmation bears burden of proof on whether realty is the debtor's principal residence); In re Benafel, 461 B.R. 581 (B.A.P. 9th Cir. 2011) (date of petition determines debtor's principal residence).

[119] Pigs get fat; hogs get slaughtered! *Cf.* Juliet M. Moringiello, *Has Congress Slimmed down the Hogs?: A Look at the BAPCPA Approach to Pre-bankruptcy Planning*, 15 Widener L.J. 615 (2006); Lynn M. LoPucki & Walter O. Weyrauch, *A Theory of Legal Strategy*, 49 Duke L.J. 1405, 1455 (2000).

[120] *E.g.*, In re Scarborough, 461 F.3d 406 (3d Cir. 2006); In re Zaldivar, 441 B.R. 389 (Bankr. S.D. Fla. 2011).

[121] *E.g.*, In re Taddeo, 685 F.2d 24 (2d Cir. 1982).

[122] *See* Bankruptcy Code § 1322(c)(1).

debtor's bankruptcy estate[123] and his right to cure evaporates.[124]

This ability to "cure and reinstate" a home mortgage is a key provision of Chapter 13 that induces many debtors to seek bankruptcy protection in the first place. Unburdened by the requirement of making payments to other creditors, debtors sometimes find that they are able to resume their monthly mortgage payments and keep their homes.

[ii]   Short Term Mortgages

A key exception to the rule prohibiting modification of residential real estate mortgages applies when the last payment on the mortgage is due before the end of the debtor's plan.[125] This might occur if the debtor filed his Chapter 13 case sometime in the last few years of his residential mortgage, but it is more likely to arise when there is a balloon payment due sometime within 3-5 years after the debtor's Chapter 13 petition. In this situation, the secured creditor's plan can be modified within the restraints otherwise imposed by § 1325(a)(5) regarding cramdown of secured claims and within the restraints imposed by the five-year limit on the duration of a Chapter 13 plan.[126]

[iii]   Other Procedural Adjustments

Other modest procedural adjustments to the creditor's claim are also permitted. For example, courts have recently held that a plan may require the mortgage lender to provide notice to the trustee, the debtor, and the debtor's counsel if there are changes in to the debtor's interest rate, escrow amounts, or other sums owed by the debtor while the debtor's case is pending. These changes are not regarded as impermissible modifications of the creditor's claim, but rather as procedural mechanisms to ensure that the debtor does not default.[127]

Likewise plan provisions specifying the manner in which payments will be allocated, such as a provision requiring the creditor to apply arrearage payments only to arrears and post-petition payments only to post-petition obligations, are regarded as procedural protections, and not substantive modifications of the creditor's claim.[128]

---

[123] Johnson v. County of Chautauqua (In re Johnson), 449 B.R. 7 (Bankr. W.D.N.Y. 2011).

[124] *E.g.*, In re Connors, 497 F.3d 314 (3d Cir. 2007); In re Cain, 423 F.3d 617 (6th Cir. 2005); In re Medaglia, 402 B.R. 530 (Bankr. D.R.I. 2009). *Contra* Colon v. Option One Mortgage Corp., 319 F.3d 912, 918 (7th Cir. 2003).

[125] Bankruptcy Code § 1322(c)(2).

[126] *See* Timothy B. McCaffrey, Jr., Comment, *Cramdown under the New 1332(c)(2) from Dewsnup to Nobelman to the Bankruptcy Reform Act of 1994: Did Congress Intend to Change "Pre-amendment" Law When it Enacted 1322(c)(2)?*, 30 Loy. L.A. L. Rev. 841 (1997).

[127] In re Herrerra, 422 B.R. 698 (B.A.P. 9th Cir. 2010); In re Ramsey, 421 B.R. 431 (Bankr. M.D. Tenn. 2009).

[128] *Id.* at 435.

[iv]   Due on Sale Clauses

Courts are divided over whether a debtor who is not the original mortgagor and who acquired property in violation of a due on sale clause may use a Chapter 13 plan to prevent a lender from accelerating the mortgage by invoking the due on sale clause.[129] Some courts regard this an impermissible modification of the lender's rights that directly violates § 1322(b)(2).[130] Other courts interpret the term "claim" very broadly to permit inclusion of the mortgage, even though the debtor is not "in privity" with the secured lender.[131] However, the reasoning of these latter decisions is strained. Section 1322(b)(2) prevents modification. Preventing enforcement of the express terms of an otherwise enforceable due on sale clause seems like just the sort of modification that § 1322(b)(2), wisely or foolishly, was meant to prevent.

[b]   Certain Purchase Money Loans

The right to modify the rights of secured claims is further restrained by language appended at the end of § 1325(a)(9).[132] This "hanging paragraph" prevents bifurcation of some purchase money security interests in motor vehicles and other consumer goods. As explained in more detail below in connection with the standards for plan confirmation, this new restriction applies only to certain purchase money security interests secured either by motor vehicles acquired within 910 days before the debtor's petition, or by other personal property acquired within one year before the debtor's petition.[133]

[C]   Cure & Waiver of Defaults; Reinstatement

When debtors default on an installment debt, the creditor nearly always accelerates the debt, making the entire outstanding balance payable immediately in full. The debtor's Chapter 13 plan can provide for the reversal of this acceleration. Section 1322(b)(3) permits the plan to provide for the cure and waiver of any default.[134] Likewise, § 1322(b)(5) permits the plan to cure defaults and reinstate the payment schedule on long-term debts for which the last payment is due after the plan is scheduled to be completed.[135] This is particularly important with respect to home mortgages.

Debtors are sometimes permitted to continue making their regular monthly mortgage payments directly to the mortgagee, rather than making them indirectly through the plan, through the Chapter 13 trustee. Any arrearages necessary to effectuate the cure, on the other hand, are usually be paid through the trustee.

---

[129] In re Tewell, 355 B.R. 674, 680 (Bankr. N.D. Ill. 2006).

[130] In re Mullin, 433 B.R. 1 (Bankr. S.D. Tex. 2010).

[131] In re Garcia, 276 B.R. 627, 642–43 (Bankr. D. Ariz. 2002).

[132] Referring to it this way always seems like "the artist previously known as Prince."

[133] The hanging paragraph appearing immediately after Bankruptcy Code § 1325(a)(9). *See infra* § 18.08[F][6] Certain Purchase Money Security Interests.

[134] Bankruptcy Code § 1322(b)(3).

[135] Bankruptcy Code § 1322(b)(5).

The debtor's cure of arrearages must be accomplished within a reasonable time.[136] What qualifies as a reasonable time varies, on a case-by-case basis, within the discretion of the court.[137]

The only hard and fast limit is the three-five year duration of the debtor's plan.[138] But, courts have approved cure periods ranging from 6 months to the maximum 60-month plan duration allowed by § 1322(d).[139]

The ability to cure and reinstate long-term debts should be read in conjunction with § 1328(a)(1), which exempts these long-term debts from the scope of a Chapter 13 discharge.[140] Thus, the debtor remains liable for the unpaid portion of the de-accelerated debt, after his Chapter 13 plan has been fully performed and he receives a Chapter 13 discharge. At this point, the debtor is obligated to simply continue making payments under the terms of his long-term debt as if the Chapter 13 case had never been filed.[141]

The most common long-term debts are real estate mortgages, which might easily extend well beyond the duration of the debtor's relatively short-term Chapter 13 plan. Most such mortgages cannot be modified in any way in Chapter 13, other than by curing any pre-petition defaults and de-accelerating the debt.[142] But, real estate mortgages that are secured by property that is not the debtor's residence, or that are secured by additional collateral, may be stripped down to the value of the property, in the normal manner permitted by §§ 1325(a)(5) and 506(a)(1).[143]

Despite the proscription against modifying the rights of claims secured by residential real estate, this also permits the debtor to cure and reinstate payments due on residential mortgages with maturity dates within the duration of the plan.[144] This provision is has its greatest significance in connection with secured claims that the debtor wishes to reinstate, such as mortgages on residential real estate.

The ability to cure defaults and reinstate also applies to student loans and other long-term unsecured debts with an amortization period that extends beyond the duration of the plan.[145] However, this ability to cure and reinstate these obligations

---

[136] *E.g.*, United Cal. Sav. Bank v. Martin (In re Martin), 156 B.R. 47 (B.A.P. 9th Cir. 1993); Steinacher v. Rojas (In re Steinacher), 283 B.R. 768 (B.A.P. 9th Cir. 2002).

[137] *See* Steinacher v. Rojas (In re Steinacher), 283 B.R. 768 (B.A.P. 9th Cir. 2002).

[138] United Cal. Sav. Bank v. Martin (In re Martin), 156 B.R. 47, 50 (B.A.P. 9th Cir. 1993).

[139] *See, e.g.*, In re Ford, 221 B.R. 749, 754 (Bankr. W.D. Tenn. 1988) (six months); In re Chavez, 117 B.R. 730, 733 (Bankr. S.D. Fla. 1990) (thirty-six months); In re Anderson, 73 B.R. 993, 996 (Bankr. W.D. Okla. 1987) (seventeen months); In re East, 172 B.R. 861, 867 (Bankr. S.D. Tex. 1994) (fifty-two months); In re Cole, 122 B.R. 943, 951–52 (Bankr. E.D. Pa. 1992) (sixty months).

[140] Bankruptcy Code § 1328(a)(1). *See supra* § 13.05 Chapter 13 Discharge.

[141] *See* In re McGregor, 172 B.R. 718 (Bankr. D. Mass. 1994).

[142] Bankruptcy Code § 1322(b)(2).

[143] *See* In re McGregor, 172 B.R. 718 (Bankr. D. Mass. 1994) (collateral consisted of four units, only one of which was the debtor's residence).

[144] Bankruptcy Code § 1322(c)(2).

[145] *See* Labib-Kiyarash v. McDonald (In re Labib-Kiyarash), 271 B.R. 189 (B.A.P. 9th Cir. 2001).

does not alter the mandate of § 1322(b)(1), which prevents debtors from unfairly discriminating in favor of, or against some unsecured creditors. Thus, a debtor may not propose a plan that pays most unsecured creditors 30% of what they are owed while at the same time reinstating long-term student loans and paying these creditors 100% of their unsecured claims.[146]

[D] Concurrent or Sequential Payment of Claims

Section 1322(b)(4) gives the debtor considerable leeway with respect to the sequence of payments made under the plan, permitting payments to be made to different creditors concurrently or sequentially.[147] Because cramdown requirements make it necessary to pay interest to holders of secured claims, debtors frequently find it useful to pay these claims in the early months of a plan and save payments to unsecured creditors for later.

Moreover, § 1325(a)(5)(B)(iii)(II) now explicitly requires payments under the plan to be sufficient to provide adequate protection to secured creditors. This seems to require payments to keep up with the anticipated depreciation of the collateral.[148] This may make it necessary for the plan to accelerate the rate of payments to holders of secured claims in the early months of the plan, and made unsecured creditors wait to begin receiving payments.[149]

Likewise, because of the risk of default on the terms of the plan and either conversion or dismissal of the debtor's case, it may be beneficial for the plan to provide for early payment to creditors holding non-dischargeable claims. If unanticipated circumstances prevent the debtor from fully performing the plan for its entire duration, this may lead to full payment of claims held by creditors whose claims cannot be discharged either in Chapter 7, or in a hardship discharge in Chapter 13. Of course, a plan filed with the intent of such a conversion would be in bad faith, and should not be confirmed.

Note that § 1326(b) limits some of this leeway by requiring certain administrative priority expenses to be paid simultaneously with "each payment" made to creditors under the plan. Some courts have ruled that this permits only partial payment of these claims, which consist primarily of the standing trustee's fees. Other courts have ruled that the plain meaning of § 1326(b) is that these administrative expense priority claims must be paid in full as the plan progresses, rather than leaving a portion of the claims to be paid later.[150]

---

[146] *See, e.g.*, Labib-Kiyarash v. McDonald (In re Labib-Kiyarash), 271 B.R. 189 (B.A.P. 9th Cir. 2001); In re Harding, 423 B.R. 568 (Bankr. S.D. Fla. 2010).

[147] Bankruptcy Code § 1322(b)(4).

[148] *E.g.*, In re Denton, 370 B.R. 441, 448–9 (Bankr. S.D. Ga. 2007).

[149] *See generally* Stacia M. Stokes, Comment, *Fighting Finality and Debtor Waste in Chapter 13 Postconfirmation Collateral Surrender*, 27 Emory Bankr. Dev. J. 169 (2010).

[150] *E.g.*, In re DeSardi, 340 B.R. 790, 808–09 (Bankr. S.D. Tex. 2006); *see* Richardo Kilpatrick, *Selected Creditor Issues Under the Bankruptcy Abuse Prevention and Consumer Protection Act of 2005*, 79 Amer. Bankr. L.J. 817, 836 (2005).

[E] Payment of Post-Petition Claims

Chapter 13 also permits a plan to provide for the payment of post-petition claims, allowed with the approval of the court pursuant to § 1305.[151] Under that section, creditors with certain post-petition claims, such as for taxes or consumer debts for property or services necessary for the debtor's performance under the plan, may file proofs of claim, and receive payments under the plan.[152] Section 1322(b)(6) facilitates plan provisions calling for the payment of such claims.

Courts conflict over whether § 1305 applies at all to tax debts that are payable, but not yet overdue at the time of the debtor's petition.[153] Thus, if a debtor files her Chapter 13 petition on March 23, 2013, it is unclear whether her 2012 taxes are already payable, or whether they do not become payable until April 15, 2013, when her return is due and, her Chapter 13 case is pending. Some courts regard these taxes as already payable at the time the petition was filed, and thus within the scope of the debtor's Chapter 13 discharge.[154] Under this view, the debtor's tax liability is a pre-petition claim, not governed by § 1305 and thus not even potentially protected from discharge under some interpretations of § 1305 post-petition claims. Other courts regard them as not yet payable and thus within the scope of § 1305.[155]

[F] Assumption, Rejection or Assignment of Executory Contracts

Few Chapter 13 consumer debtors will have executory contracts. But, debtors who rent their homes or who drive leased automobiles, are likely to want to assume their unexpired leases. Section 1325(b)(7) permits the plan to provide for the assumption, rejection, or even the assignment of any such executory contract or unexpired lease pursuant to the requirements of § 365, which governs these matters generally.[156] That section's restrictions on assumption of leases of *non-residential* real estate obviously will not apply to debtors who wish to assume the lease of their living quarters. But it will impair the ability of some Chapter 13 sole proprietorship business debtors from assuming leases on their business premises.

This provision might also apply to certain "rent-to-own" transactions, unless they are more properly characterized as secured sales and thus not subject to § 365.[157] However, if the transaction is not an unexpired lease, but a secured sale, it might be subject to the cramdown restrictions now imposed by the paragraph hanging after the end of § 1325(a)(9).[158]

---

[151] Bankruptcy Code § 1322(b)(6).

[152] Bankruptcy Code § 1305.

[153] *See* In re Joye, 578 F.3d 1070 (9th Cir. 2009).

[154] In re Joye, 578 F.3d 1070 (9th Cir. 2009); In re Dixon, 218 B.R. 150 (B.A.P. 10th Cir. 1998).

[155] In re Ripley, 926 F.2d 440 (5th Cir. 1991).

[156] Bankruptcy Code § 1322(b)(7). *See supra* Chapter 11 — Executory Contracts and Unexpired Leases.

[157] *See* In re Smith, 262 B.R. 365 (Bankr. E.D. Va. 2000).

[158] *See infra* § 18.08[F][6] Certain Purchase Money Security Interests.

[G] Payment of Claims from Estate Property or Property of the Debtor

Though it is largely implied from the overall structure of Chapter 13, § 1322(b)(8) expressly permits the plan to provide for "the payment or all or part of a claim . . . from property of the estate or property of the debtor."[159] This will usually be done through the debtor's post-petition income submitted to the trustee under § 1322(a)(1). However, payments to creditors might also be made through the liquidation of other property that belongs either to the estate or to the debtor.[160] Thus, although one of the chief advantages of Chapter 13 is that it permits debtors to keep their property, debtors might choose to sell property in order to provide the funding necessary to fulfill the terms of the plan. Less frequently, a plan might simply provide for delivering property to a creditor in kind, in lieu of a cash payment.[161]

[H] Vesting of Property of Estate in the Debtor or Another Entity

A Chapter 13 plan might also provide for vesting estate property either in the debtor or in another entity.[162] This works in conjunction with § 1327(b) which automatically vests property of the estate in the debtor upon confirmation, unless the plan or a court order specifies otherwise. Delaying vesting of the property back in the debtor until the plan is fully performed and a discharge is granted may be useful to preserve the effect of the automatic stay with respect to estate property while the case is pending.[163]

[I] Payment of Interest on Nondischargeable Debts

Although post-petition interest on unsecured claims is not generally allowable,[164] § 1322(b)(10) permits the plan to "provide for the payment of interest accruing after the date of the filing of the petition on unsecured claims that are nondischargeable under section 1328(a) . . . ."[165] However, this is permissible only if the debtor has "disposable income available to pay such interest after making provision for full payment of all allowed claims . . . ."[166] In other words, the plan

---

[159] Bankruptcy Code § 1322(b)(8).

[160] *E.g.*, In re Lapin, 302 B.R. 184 (Bankr. S.D. Tex. 2003) (IRA liquidated to make payments to creditors under the plan).

[161] The only restriction on this is in § 1322(b)(2) which requires priority claims to be paid in cash. Bankruptcy Code § 1322(b)(2).

[162] Bankruptcy Code § 1322(b)(9).

[163] *See* Telfair v. First Union Mortgage Corp., 216 F.3d 1333 (11th Cir. 2000), *cert. denied*, 531 U.S. 1073 (2001) (no automatic stay protection for property revested in the debtor).

[164] Bankruptcy Code § 502(b)(2).

[165] Bankruptcy Code § 1322(b)(10).

[166] *Id.* Note that § 1322(b)(10)'s reference to "disposable income," which is required to be based on the debtor's past income, rather than to the "projected disposable income" that is required to be paid to unsecured creditors under the plan, could well lead to a quirky interpretive problem. As of mid-2006,

can provide for the payment of post-petition interest on nondischargeable claims only if it is providing for the payment of other allowed claims in full.

This new provision facilitates debtors' efforts to complete their Chapter 13 plans free of any otherwise non-dischargeable debts. Without the ability to make plan payments to creditors whose right to recover post-petition would not be discharged, the debtor would end up liable for paying this interest upon conclusion of his plan. The rule preventing debtors from paying such post-petition interest, unless they are able to make full payment to all other creditors is consistent with decisions refusing to permit Chapter 13 plans from discriminating between dischargeable and non-dischargeable debts.[167]

[J] Other Consistent Provisions

Finally, § 1322(b)(11) permits the inclusion of any other provision, so long as it does not directly conflict some some other provision of the Bankruptcy Code.[168] When considered together with § 1325(a)(3), which permits confirmation only if the plan has not be proposed by any means forbidden by law,[169] § 1322(b)(11) permits any provision that is not incompatible with any other aspect of federal or non-preempted state law.

§ 18.08 CONFIRMATION OF CHAPTER 13 PLANS

A chapter 13 plan can be confirmed only if it meets the standards of Bankruptcy Code § 1325. The court is required to confirm a Chapter 13 plan only if:

- the plan complies with the rest of Chapter 13 and the Bankruptcy Code;

- the debtor has paid the necessary filing fee and any other fees imposed on Chapter 13 debtors;

- the debtor's petition and the plan itself has been proposed in good faith and not by any means otherwise forbidden by law;

- the plan is in the best interests of creditors in that it pays them at least what they would have received had the debtor liquidated under Chapter 7;

- it provides for secured creditors to receive the value of their collateral (and sometimes more);

- the plan is financially feasible;

- the debtor is current on his or her support obligations; and

- the debtor has filed any required Federal, State, and local income tax returns.

---

several bankruptcy courts had already ruled that "disposable income," defined in § 1325(b)(2), and "projected disposable income," required to be paid to unsecured creditors under a plan are not synonymous. *See, e.g.*, In re Kibbe, 342 B.R. 411 (Bankr. D.N.H. 2006).

[167] *See supra* Bankruptcy Code § 1322(b)(1); § 18.07[A] Classification of Claims.

[168] Bankruptcy Code § 1322(b)(11).

[169] Bankruptcy Code § 1325(a)(3).

The requirements that the debtor pay any fees associated with the bankruptcy case and that he file his tax returns are easily understood. Some of the other requirements are more complicated.

[A] General Requirements for Confirmation

[1] Compliance with the Bankruptcy Code

In order to be confirmed, the debtor's plan must comply "with the provisions of [Chapter 13] and with the other applicable provisions of [the Bankruptcy Code]" in general.[170] The requirement that the plan complies with the other provisions of Chapter 13, might lead to objections based on the plan's failure to comply with the mandatory provisions of § 1322(a), such as the requirement that priority claims be paid in full. Or, the plan might be objectionable because it contains a provision prohibited by § 1322(b), or is for an improper duration.[171]

The requirement that the plan comply with the requirements of other applicable provisions of the Bankruptcy Code generally, brings all of the provisions of Bankruptcy Code Chapters 1, 3 and 5 into play as the basis for potential objections to confirmation.[172]

[2] Filing Tax Returns[173]

The requirement that the debtor comply with both the requirements of Chapter 13 and of the Bankruptcy Code generally, together with the language of § 1308, prevents confirmation of the debtor's plan if the debtor has not filed any tax returns due to be filed for the four tax years prior to the petition.[174] Failure to file any subsequent returns is grounds for dismissal of the case.[175]

[3] Payment of Fees and Charges

Section 1325(a)(2) makes confirmation depend upon the debtor's payment of the fees imposed by the relevant provision of the Judicial Code, primarily the $235 filing fee of 28 U.S.C. § 1930(a)(1)(B) and the $39 "administrative fee" of 28 U.S.C. § 1930(b).[176] These fees can be paid by installment[177] and in some districts are permitted to be paid through the plan.

---

[170] Bankruptcy Code § 1325(a)(1).

[171] *See* Bankruptcy Code § 1322(d).

[172] *See* Bankruptcy Code § 103.

[173] Carl M. Jenks, *The Bankruptcy Abuse Prevention and Consumer Protection Act of 2005: Summary of Tax Provisions*, 79 Am. Bankr. L.J. 893, 907–09 (2005).

[174] *See* Bankruptcy Code § 1308.

[175] Bankruptcy Code § 1307(e).

[176] 28 U.S.C. § 1930 (2006).

[177] 28 U.S.C. § 1930 (2006).

[B] Feasibility

Section 1325(a)(6) requires that "the debtor will be able to make all payments under the plan and to comply with the plan."[178] Thus, it must be feasible for the debtor to perform the plan according to its terms. If the debtor lacks sufficient income to fund the plan and to meet both his living expenses and those of his dependents, the plan cannot be confirmed. Likewise, if the debtor's ability to fund the plan depends upon his receipt of a lump-sum payment from someone who may not provide it, feasibility of the plan is too speculative, and it should not be confirmed.[179] But, if the source of the lump-sum is credible, the mere fact that the plan calls for such a payment will not prevent confirmation.[180]

In most cases, determining the feasibility of a plan will be easy. If the total of the amount of payments required to be paid under the plan combined with the debtor's actual anticipated other expenses exceed the debtor's income, the plan is not feasible. If the debtor's projected income is sufficient, the plan is usually feasible.

Here, it must be remembered that the amount required to be paid under the plan, based on the debtor's projected disposable income, may well exceed the actual amount available to the debtor after paying his real living expenses. To the extent that the debtor's presumed expenses, based on the allowable figures in the IRS's standards, are unrealistically low, the debtor's plan may not be feasible unless the debtor makes significant changes in his living arrangements. On the other hand, because disposable income is calculated after deducting contractually required payments to secured creditors, the debtor might end up with more than enough income to fund the plan by surrendering some of his collateral to the secured party.[181]

In Chapter 13 cases involving debtors engaged in a business, the feasibility of the debtor's plan will be more difficult to evaluate. It will depend on the accuracy of the debtor's projected business income and expenses, both matters that might be more difficult to evaluate than a wage-earning debtor's projections about his future salary.[182] Even a wage-earning debtor, whose ability to fund the plan depends on the availability of overtime hours, might face the same sort of difficulty.

---

[178] Bankruptcy Code § 1325(a)(6).

[179] *E.g.*, First Nat'l Bank v. Fantasia (In re Fantasia), 211 B.R. 420 (B.A.P. 1st Cir. 1997).

[180] Chelsea State Bank v. Wagner (In re Wagner), 259 B.R. 694 (B.A.P. 8th Cir. 2001) (plan was feasible where debtor's father indicated willingness to provide assistance in making lump-sum payment).

[181] One might wonder whether a creditor's acceptance of such a surrender, if not provided for in the plan, would violate the automatic stay, and if anyone would have the incentive to assert the violation. If a tree falls in the forest . . . .

[182] *E.g.*, In re Torelli, 338 B.R. 390 (Bankr. E.D. Ark. 2006).

[C] Good Faith[183]

Section 1325(a)(3) requires that "the plan has been proposed in good faith and not by any means forbidden by law."[184] In addition, § 1325(a)(7) requires that "the action of the debtor in filing the petition was in good faith."[185] Thus, if either the debtor's plan or his petition was not in good faith, confirmation should be denied.

[1] Good Faith Plan

Whether a plan is submitted in good faith involves an consideration of a wide range of circumstances including the amount of payments under the proposed plan, the amount of surplus income available to the debtor, the debtor's ability to earn income, the anticipated duration of plan, the accuracy of the plan's statements, the extent of preferential treatment between classes of creditors, the extent to which secured claims are modified, the types of debt to be discharged under the plan, whether any discharged debt is nondischargeable in Chapter 7, the presence or absence of special circumstances such as medical expenses, the frequency with which the debtor has sought bankruptcy relief, the motivation and sincerity of debtor, and the burden that the plan's administration would place upon the trustee.[186]

Some courts have used the good faith standard to require Chapter 13 plans to provide something beyond a negligible payment to unsecured creditors.[187] The addition of § 1325(b), which establishes minimum financial standards for the amounts that must be paid to unsecured creditors, did not lay the issue of how much debtors should pay into the plan to rest. Instead, courts have used the good faith requirement of § 1325(a)(3) to examine the debtor's pre-petition conduct and continuing lifestyle.[188] For example, in *In re Sandberg*,[189] the plan satisfied the Bankruptcy Code's disposable income test, but the court held that it was not proposed in good faith because it contemplated retaining and paying for a 36-foot "cabin cruiser" and debtor-husband's aircraft mechanic tools while paying only 2.3% of the approximate $127,000.00 of unsecured debt.

Likewise, in *In re Shafer*,[190] the debtor's petition was determined to have been in bad faith where the debtor's actions demonstrated a greater concern for maintain-

---

[183] Diane M. Allen, Annotation, *Effect, on "Good Faith" Requirement of § 1325(a)(3) of Bankruptcy Code of 1978 for Confirmation of Chapter 13 Plan, of Debtor's Offer of Less than Full Repayment to Unsecured Creditors*, 73 A.L.R. Fed. 10 (1985).

[184] Bankruptcy Code § 1325(a)(3).

[185] Bankruptcy Code § 1325(a)(7).

[186] *E.g.*, In re Doersam, 849 F.2d 237 (6th Cir. 1988); *see* Bradley M. Elbein, *The Hole in the Code: Good Faith and Morality in Chapter 13*, 34 San Diego L. Rev. 439 (1997); Diane M. Allen, *Annotation, Effect, on "Good Faith" Requirement of Sec. 1325(a)(3) of Bankruptcy Code of 1978 (11 U.S.C.A. Sec. 1325(a)(3)) for Confirmation of Chapter 13 Plan, of Debtor's Offer of Less than Full Repayment to Unsecured Creditors*, 73 A.L.R. Fed. 10 (1985).

[187] *E.g.*, In re Iacovoni, 2 B.R. 256 (Bankr. D. Utah 1980).

[188] *E.g.*, In re Leone, 292 B.R. 243 (Bankr. W.D. Pa. 2003).

[189] 433 B.R. 837 (Bankr. D. Kan. 2010).

[190] In re Shafer, 393 B.R. 655 (Bankr. W.D. Wis. 2008).

ing a comfortable standard of living than for paying creditors. The debtors enjoyed an annual income of $144,000, and held over $1 million in retirement funds, had spent $400,000 in home improvements, spent $800 for food each month, and had previously dismissed an earlier Chapter 13 petition in an effort to protect over $40,000 in preferential transfers from avoidance. The court characterized the debtors as attempting to use Chapter 13 as a means of making a transition to an early and comfortable retirement rather than as a means to make meaningful payments to their unsecured creditors.

On the other hand, in *In re Wick*, the court found that the debtors' pre-petition purchase of a home with a $4857 monthly mortgage payment, which would consume 60% of their income, was not in bad faith, even though it would result in only a 15% distribution to their unsecured creditors. As the court explained, their decision to purchase the home was made "when the real estate market was extremely strong . . . [and] in the context of increasing the family size."[191]

Likewise, in *In re Thompson*, the debtors' failure to include their social security payments from the income they used to calculate amounts available to make payments to creditors under the plan did not constitute bad faith.[192] The court explained that requiring social security payments to be included in the debtor's income, as part of the calculus of the debtor's good faith, would make the express exclusion of these payments from the means test calculation superfluous.[193]

In evaluating the debtor's good faith, some courts apply the multi-faceted *Flygare* test, based on the Tenth Circuit's decision in *Flygare v. Boulden*.[194] This test, which some courts and commentators have suggested should not be used in the post-BAPCPA era,[195] considers: (1) the amount of the proposed payments and the amount of the debtor's surplus; (2) the debtor's employment history, ability to earn and likelihood of future increases in income; (3) the probable or expected duration of the plan; (4) the accuracy of the plan's statements of the debts, expenses and percentage repayment of unsecured debt and whether any inaccuracies are an attempt to mislead the court; (5) the extent of preferential treatment between classes of creditors; (6) the extent to which secured claims are modified; (7) the type of debt sought to be discharged and whether any such debt is non-dischargeable in Chapter 7; (8) the existence of special circumstances such as inordinate medical expenses; (9) the frequency with which the debtor has sought relief; (10) the motivation and sincerity of the debtor in seeking Chapter 13 relief; and (11) the burden which the plan's administration would place upon the trustee.[196]

The technical details involved in calculating the amount of a debtor's disposable income, mandated by the 2005 BAPCPA amendments, are likely to further limit the significance of many of these factors. However, they are likely to resurface in

---

[191] In re Wick, 421 B.R. 206, 215 (Bankr. D. Md. 2010).

[192] Fink v. Thompson, (In re Thompson), 439 B.R. 140 (B.A.P. 8th Cir. 2010).

[193] *See also* Cranmer v. Anderson, 463 B.R. 548 (D. Utah 2011).

[194] 709 F.2d 1344 (10th Cir. 1983).

[195] Keith M. Lundin & William H. Brown, Chapter 13 Bankruptcy, 4th Edition, § 177.1 at ¶ 4, Sec. Rev. July 23, 2004, and § 197.1 at ¶ 3; Sec. Rev. June 7, 2004, www.Ch13online.com.

[196] 709 F.2d at 1347–48.

connection with payments made to secured creditors, particularly if the collateral for these debts are regarded as luxury items or otherwise not reasonably necessary for the support of the debtor and his dependents.[197]

The requirement of good faith may also serve as an alternative grounds for denying confirmation due to the debtors' financial circumstances.[198] However, the debtors in *In re Sweet*,[199] were able to obtain confirmation of their Chapter plan, despite their retention of a fully encumbered $300,000 home, which consumed approximately 1/3 of their gross monthly income, and which prevented them from paying more than 8% to their unsecured creditors. In determining that the debtor's petition and plan were in good faith, the court emphasized that the debtors had not purchased the house in anticipation of bankruptcy, and that they had sought relief in Chapter 13 despite being eligible for Chapter 7 relief.

Courts have sometimes refused to confirm Chapter 13 plans, as having not been filed in good faith, where the plan is nothing more than a means to pay the attorney's fees of the debtor's attorney. Cases in which this strategy has been attempted have not worked out well for the debtor's attorneys who propose them, or for their clients. For example, in *In re Paley*,[200] the court said:

> A plan whose duration is tied only to payment of attorney's fees simply is an abuse of the provisions, purpose, and spirit of the Bankruptcy Code. These cases, basically Chapter 7 cases hidden within Chapter 13 petitions, blur the distinction between the chapters into a meaningless haze. To allow them to go forward would, in effect, judicially invalidate § 727(a)(8)'s requirement of an eight year hiatus between Chapter 7 discharges and replace it with either the four year break required by § 1328(f)(1), or the two year gap mandated by § 1328(f)(2).[201]

The court's references, of course, are to Chapter 7's eight year bar, that prevents debtors from obtaining Chapter 7 discharges more often than once every eight years, and the similar four and two year delays between Chapter 13 discharges, depending on the debtor's circumstances. As the court notes, these Chapter 13 cases are disguised Chapter 7 cases, which seek to evade Chapter 7's proscription against payment of the debtor's attorney's fees from the bankruptcy estate.

[2] No Legally Forbidden Means

The requirement that the plan not be proposed by any means forbidden by any other law adds little to the requirement that the plan be submitted in good faith. It makes it clear that the plan must comply with legal requirements outside the Bankruptcy Code, including any aspect of state law that is not superceded by the

---

[197] *See, e.g.*, In re Deutscher, 419 B.R. 42 (Bankr. N.D. Ill. 2009) (42–foot yacht). *But see* In re Spruch, 410 B.R. 839 (Bankr. S.D. Ind. 2008) (luxury goods no barrier to confirmation).

[198] *See, e.g.* In re Styles, 397 B.R. 771 (Bankr. W.D. Va. 2008) (single debtor with two cars).

[199] In re Sweet, 428 B.R. 917 (Bankr. N.D. Ga. 2010).

[200] 390 B.R. 53 (Bankr. N.D.N.Y. 2008).

[201] *Id.* at 59–60. *See also* In re Montry, 393 B.R. 695 (Bankr. W.D. Mo. 2008).

Bankruptcy Code. This limitation prevented the debtor in *In re McGinnis*[202] from obtaining confirmation of plan that was to have been funded with income generated from the illegal sale of marijuana.

[3] Petition Filed in Good Faith

The requirement that the debtor's action in filing the petition must have been in good faith was added in 2005. The inclusion of this element as grounds for denying confirmation suggests that a bad faith petition should be grounds for denying confirmation, not for dismissal of the debtor's case entirely.[203] On the other hand, if a bad faith petition is grounds for denying any plan the debtor might file, the case would seem to be destined for dismissal in any event under § 1325(c)(5) regarding dismissal due to "denial of confirmation . . . ."[204]

[D] Duration of the Plan — "Applicable Commitment Period"[205]

For many years the customary duration of a Chapter 13 plan was three years, though the court could permit it to be extended for as long as five years. These three and five year time limits were imposed because of a concern that some plans under old Chapter XIII, plans extended far longer and thus amounted to virtual peonage for the debtor.[206] To get a sense of how long a time period this is, develop a household budget, and see how many weeks you can manage to live on it, without deviation. Three years is a long time. For many people, five years must seem like an eternity.

The required duration of a plan now depends on the "applicable commitment period."[207] Debtors with past annual income equal to or higher than their home state's median family income for households of similar size, are required to submit a five-year plan.[208] Debtors with income below the applicable state median can propose a plan of only three years.[209]

In cases in which the debtor's currently monthly income after deducting permitted expenses is zero, § 1325(B)(4)(A) has given rise to a dispute over

---

[202] In re McGinnis, 453 B.R. 770 (Bankr. D. Or. 2011).

[203] *E.g.*, Alt v. United States (In re Alt), 305 F.3d 413 (6th Cir. 2002) (bad faith petition by debtor who had intentionally failed to schedule tax debt warranted dismissal).

[204] In re Hall, 346 B.R. 420 (Bankr. W.D. Ky. 2006). *See* § 18.03[B] Conversion and Dismissal of Chapter 13 Cases, *supra.*

[205] Evan J. Zucker, Note, *the Applicable Commitment Period: A Debtor's Commitment to a Fixed Plan Length*, 15 Am. Bankr. Inst. L. Rev. 687 (2007).

[206] Discussing the unlimited time period for Chapter XIII plans, the House Report on the Bankruptcy Code remarked: "Extensions on plans, new cases, and newly incurred debts put some debtors under court supervised repayment plans for seven to ten years. This has become the closest thing there is to indentured servitude . . . ." H.R. Rep. No. 595, 95th Cong., 1st Sess. 117 (1977) *reprinted in* 1978 U.S.C.C.A.N. 5963, 6078.

[207] Bankruptcy Code § 1425(b)(1)(B) & (b)(4).

[208] Bankruptcy Code § 1325(b)(4)(A)(ii).

[209] Bankruptcy Code § 1325(b)(4)(A)(i).

whether its language operates as a financial multiplier, or if, on the other hand, it operates as a temporal requirement. Most courts regard the phrase "applicable commitment period" as temporal and, thus, require above-median-income debtors to pay their creditors in full or commit to a plan for a full sixty month time period.[210] Other courts regard it as a multiplier that requires the plan to provide for payments that are equal to the amount of the debtor's currently monthly income times the applicable number of months (36 or 60).[211] Under this approach, debtors with a relatively low current monthly income, as calculated pursuant to § 101(10A), can propose a plan that lasts for a shorter period, as long as the total amount paid to their creditors under the plan is equal to their current monthly income times the prescribed number of months. This approach permits confirmation of a plan for any period, perhaps even only a month or less, if the dollar amount paid to unsecured creditors matches the total required by the applicable multiplier.[212] A third line of authority relies on § 1325(b)(1)(B) to require only that the debtor's projected disposable income during the "applicable commitment period" be applied to payments to unsecured creditors. Thus, if the debtor has no projected disposable income, the "applicable commitment period" requirement does not apply at all.[213]

In calculating the debtor's income, for the purposes of determining whether the applicable commitment period is three years or five, the "currently monthly income of the debtor and the debtor's spouse" is combined.[214] This, of course, is different from the way that median income is determined for the purposes of the Chapter 7 means test, which does not include the income of a non-debtor spouse, except to the extent that a spouse's income (or anyone else's) is contributed to the debtor's household expenses.[215]

Otherwise, the same "current monthly income" figure that is used in connection with the Chapter 7 means test of presumptive abuse is used to determine whether the debtor's income is above or below the state median.[216] As explained in detail elsewhere, currently monthly income is a defined term[217] which is based on the debtor's past income, earned during the last six months before filing his petition.[218] This might mean that the applicable commitment period will be only three years,

---

[210] *E.g.*, Baud v. Carroll, 634 F.3d 327 (6th Cir. 2011); Whaley v. Tennyson (In re Tennyson), 611 F.3d 873, 877–78 (11th Cir. 2010).

[211] *See, e.g.*, In re Henderson, 2011 Tex. App. LEXIS 1696 (Bankr. D. Idaho 2011); Maney v. Kagenveama (In re Kagenveama), 541 F.3d 868 (9th Cir. 2008).

[212] *E.g.*, In re Reed, 454 B.R 790 (Bankr. D. Or. 2011) (debtor with negative monthly income had no "applicable commitment period").

[213] *See* In re Kagenveama, 541 F.3d 868, 876 (9th Cir. 2008); Musselman v. eCast Settlement Corp. (In re Musselman), 394 B.R. 801, 814 (E.D.N.C. 2008).

[214] Bankruptcy Code § 1325(a)(4)(A)(iii). *See* In re Stansell, 395 B.R. 457 (Bankr. D. Idaho 2008) (income of deceased wife required to be included).

[215] Official Form B22C permits debtors to eliminate the income of a non-debtor spouse, if the spouse is not contributing to meeting the debtor's household expenses. Official Bankruptcy Form B22C, Line 13, "Marital Adjustment."

[216] Bankruptcy Code § 1322(d).

[217] Bankruptcy Code § 101(10A).

[218] *See supra* § 17.03[B][2][a] Current Monthly Income.

even though the debtor's income has increased since the time her petition was filed. For example, in *In re Beasley*, the debtor's current monthly income, calculated according to the formula specified by § 101(10A) was below the applicable state median.[219] His current income, which would have been available to fund his plan, was above the state median. The court determined that it was constrained by the plain meaning of § 1322(d) and confirmed the debtor's three-year plan over the trustee's objection that the applicable commitment period should have been five years.[220]

Debtors whose income is below their state's median, and who are thus permitted to submit only a three-year plan, might still find it useful to seek court approval of a longer plan, up to a maximum of five years.[221] Doing so will result in a higher payment to the creditors, and will keep the automatic stay in place for a longer period, both of which may be important to debtors with nondischargeable debts. Doing so is possible, with the approval of the court, which is rarely denied.[222]

Cases decided before the 2005 amendments indicated that an extension beyond the presumptive three year period is justified by the debtor's inability to fully pay priority or secured debts in such a short time.[223] Similarly, extending the duration of a plan beyond three years may, by reducing the amount of monthly payments, enhance the feasibility of the plan.[224] Moreover, some few debtors, who own substantial non-exempt assets, are unable to satisfy the "best interests" test in only three years, and will need the additional time to ensure that their unsecured creditors receive at least the equivalent of what they would have obtained in a liquidation case.[225] The debtor's simple desire to repay a larger portion of his debts might also justify extension to a maximum of five years, particularly if it will enable the debtor to repay creditors in full.[226]

[E] Payments to Creditors with Unsecured Claims

Chapter 13 contains two requirements with respect to payments that must be made to unsecured creditors holding general non-priority claims. First, the plan must be in the "best interests of creditors" in that it must ensure that unsecured creditors receive at least the same value they would have received if the debtor had liquidated under Chapter 7. Second, unless unsecured creditors are being paid in full, the plan must provide for the debtor to pay all of his "projected disposable

---

[219] 342 B.R. 280 (Bankr. C.D. Ill. 2006). *See also* In re Dew, 344 B.R. 655 (Bankr. N.D. Ala. 2006).

[220] In re Beasley, 342 B.R. at 284.

[221] Bankruptcy Code § 1322(d)(2).

[222] Bankruptcy Code § 1322(d)(2). To fully appreciate how long a time period this is, it will be useful to recall the last time you prepared a household budget and resolved to live within its limits.

[223] *E.g.*, In re Norris, 175 B.R. 515 (Bankr. M.D. Fla. 1994).

[224] In re Capodanno, 94 B.R. 62 (Bankr. E.D. Pa. 1988).

[225] Bankruptcy Code § 1325(a)(4). *See infra* § 18.08[E][1] Best Interests of Creditors.

[226] *See* In re Greer, 60 B.R. 547 (Bankr. C.D. Cal. 1986); In re Festa, 65 B.R. 85 (Bankr. S.D. Ohio 1986); *but see* In re Walsh, 224 B.R. 231 (Bankr. M.D. Ga. 1998) (three-year plan inadequate with respect to debtor seeking to use Chapter 13 to retain a non-essential automobile while making negligible payments to unsecured creditors).

income" to "unsecured creditors" for the duration of his three or five year plan. As will be seen, this second requirement, which has been modified somewhat in connection with the new "means testing" standards of the 2005 BAPCPA amendments, is both complex and the subject of interpretive disputes.

[1] Best Interests of Creditors

The "best interests of creditors" test[227] ensures that creditors will receive no less from the debtor in a Chapter 13 case than they would have if the debtor had liquidated in Chapter 7. This makes perfect sense. Chapter 13 would be of little benefit to creditors if they could be compelled to both wait for payment *and* receive less than they would have received if the debtor had simply liquidated.

Thus, § 1324(a)(4) requires that:

> the value, as of the effective date of the plan, of property to be distributed under the plan on account of each allowed unsecured claim it not less than the amount that would be paid on such claim if the estate of the debtor were liquidated under chapter 7 . . . on such date . . . .[228]

The key word in this passage is *value*. The value of whatever payments the creditor receives must be worth at least the amount the creditor would have received if the debtor had liquidated. Because payments under a plan are made over several years, the payments made must be more than the nominal amount that the creditor would have received if the debtor had liquidated.[229]

Consider the simple example of an unsecured creditor, owed $1,000, who would have received the proverbial 10¢ on the dollar, or a total of $100, if the debtor had liquidated. A plan that provided for payment of a total of $100, in monthly cash payments of approximately $1.66 per month over a 5-year period would result in the creditor receiving something that was *worth* less than the $100 the creditor would have received in Chapter 7. To compensate the creditor for the delay in receiving payment in Chapter 13, the plan must provide for interest on the $100 that the creditor otherwise would have received.[230]

This creates a difficulty in determining the appropriate rate of interest that must be paid to ensure that the creditor receives the "present value" of what it would have received in liquidation as compensation for the delay in receiving payment. In

---

[227] The phrase "best interests of creditors" is derived from the same test employed under the Bankruptcy Act. Bankruptcy Act §§ 651, 652(a) (repealed 1978). The traditional phrase appears nowhere in the Bankruptcy Code but remains in wide use to refer to § 1325(a)(4). *E.g.*, In re Van Der Heide, 164 F.3d 1183 (8th Cir. 1999).

[228] Bankruptcy Code § 1325(a)(4).

[229] In re Hockenberry, 457 B.R. 646 (Bankr. S.D. Ohio 2011).

[230] As one court put it: "[The] Debtor would gladly pay his creditors Tuesday for a hamburger today. However, the Code recognizes that a hamburger eaten today is worth more than payment for it on Tuesday due to the time value of money and, in the view of some courts, the risk of nonpayment." In re Cook, 322 B.R. 336, 339 (Bankr. N.D. Ohio 2005). Students unfamiliar with the combined effects of inflation and risk sometimes fail to comprehend this logic. To drive the point home, one of your authors sometimes suggests that the student loan him $1000 and that it be repaid in 100 equal monthly payments of $10 each until the $1000 is fully repaid. At this stage of the discussion, everyone gets the point.

many Chapter 13 cases, the requirement of § 1325(b), that the debtor submit all of its disposable income for payments under the plan, will eclipse the significance of the best interests tests. In many Chapter 7 cases, it should be remembered, unsecured creditors would have received nothing. Even where they would have received a distribution, the debtor's payment of all of his disposable income for three to five years will frequently result in payments that will be more than sufficient to give unsecured creditors the same value as what they would have received in liquidation.

In the rare Chapter 13 case where this is not true, the interest rate necessary to satisfy the best interests test will be based on the prime interest rate together with whatever upward adjustment is necessary to reflect the creditor's risk of non-payment. This standard is based on the Supreme Court's 2004 decision in *Till v. SCS Credit Corp.*,[231] regarding a similar issue on the appropriate rate of interest required to be paid to holder of secured claims under § 1325(a)(5).[232] However, a few courts have rejected the use of the *Till* standard with respect to the best interests test of § 1325(a)(4), based partially on *Till's* status as a plurality decision, and continue to require the use of whatever method for picking the appropriate rate of interest that they deployed before *Till.*[233]

As indicated above, in most cases, the best interest test will have little practical effect on the debtor's case. If the debtor's non-exempt equity that would have been distributed to his creditors in Chapter 7 is zero, the best interests test is easily satisfied. If there are disputes about the inclusion of certain property in the debtor's estate, this might well result in a dispute over whether the best interests of creditors test has been satisfied. Thus, in *In re Boyd*,[234] there was a fight over whether certain property that had been acquired by the debtor's husband was properly regarded as "community property" that was part of the debtor's estate. Inclusion of the asset in the debtor's estate expanded the amount that would have been available to creditors in a liquidation, and thus prevented the plan from satisfying the best interests test.

Cases like *In re Boyd* notwithstanding, the second requirement that the debtor contribute all of his "projected disposable income" usually requires more to be paid for distribution to unsecured creditors than the best interests test mandates. As a result, in most Chapter 13 cases, attention is focused not on the best interests test, but on the manner in which the debtor's projected disposable income is to be determined.

---

[231] *Cf.* Till v. SCS Credit Corp., 541 U.S. 465 (2004) (present value for secured claims under § 1325(a)(5)).

[232] *See, e.g.*, In re Bivens, 317 B.R. 755 (Bankr. N.D. Ill. 2004); Carmen H. Lonstein & Steven A. Domanowski, *Payment of Post-petition Interest to Unsecured Creditors: Federal Judgment Rate Versus Contract Rate*, 12 Am. Bankr. Inst. L. Rev. 421 (2004).

[233] In re Cook, 322 B.R. 336, 345 (Bankr. N.D. Ohio 2005) (coerced loan approach based on current market interest rates for loans in similar situations). *Cf.* In re American HomePatient, Inc. 420 F.3d 559 (6th Cir. 2005) (applying § 1129(a)(5)). *See generally infra* §1 8.08[F][4][b] Payments Equivalent to Amount of Secured Claim.

[234] 410 B.R. 95 (Bankr. N.D. Fla. 2009).

[2]   Debtor's Projected Disposable Income[235]

Nearly all Chapter 13 debtors must submit all of their "projected disposable income [for either three or five years]" to their unsecured creditors.[236] The rare exception is when the plan provides for paying unsecured creditors in full during the plan.[237] Debtors who can make such payments, usually don't need to file a Chapter 13 case.

Most debtors are unable to fund 100% payment plans and thus must make payments according to their ability to pay, regardless of how little their creditors would receive in liquidation. Thus, for most debtors, the best interest test of § 1325(a)(4) has little meaning. The key to determining how much this second standard requires is to understand the meaning of "projected disposable income."

Despite its importance, the Code supplies no definition of "*projected* disposable income." The debtor's ability to pay is calculated in two alternative ways, depending on whether the debtor's household income is above or below the applicable state median income.

[a]   Debtors with Income Above the State Median

For debtors whose household income is above the state median, projected disposable income depends on a forward looking approach, which takes into account anticipated changes in the debtor's financial circumstances.

The basic approach used to determine the amount of income that the debtor is required to contribute to her unsecured creditors begins with the debtor's anticipated income during the life of the plan. In most cases, this will be based on the average income earned by the debtor during the six months immediately preceding her bankruptcy petition. But, some debtors' financial circumstances involve a recent or anticipated change in income. These changes are taken into account. The debtor's living expenses, including payments to secured creditors, are then deducted from her income. The sum is the amount that must be paid, over the life of the plan, in partial payment of unsecured claims.[238]

---

[235] Jean Braucher, *Getting Realistic: In Defense of Formulaic Means Testing*, 83 Am. Bankr. L.J. 395 (2009); Chelsey W. Tulis, *Get Real: Reframing the Debate Over How to Calculate Projected Disposable Income in § 1325(b)*, 83 Am. Bankr. L.J. 345 (2009).

[236] Bankruptcy Code § 1325(b)(1)(B).

[237] Bankruptcy Code § 1325(b)(1)(A). Courts are split over whether this 100% payment must be with or without interest, as compensation for the delay. *See* In re Adolph, 441 B.R. 909 (Bankr. N.D. Ill. 2011).

[238] The apparent simplicity of this approach is belied by the multi-step form used to make the calculation.

[i]   Income[239]

Before the Supreme Court's 2010 decision in *In re Lanning*,[240] it was unclear whether § 1325(b) called for a forward looking approach to "projected" income, or whether it contemplated a mechanical approach, similar to that used for the Chapter 7 means test,[241] based solely on the income earned by the debtor during the six months immediately before the debtor's petition.[242] This uncertainty was caused by the text of the Code, which defines "disposable income," but which fails to define "projected disposable income."

Before 2005, the Code defined disposable income in a general way as "income which is received by the debtor and which is not reasonably necessary to be expended" for the debtor's "maintenance or support." "Disposable income" is now defined very precisely as "current monthly income received by the debtor" less "amounts reasonably necessary to be expended" for the debtor's maintenance and support, qualifying charitable contributions, and business expenses.[243] "Current monthly income" is also carefully defined, as an average of income received by the debtor during the six-month period immediately preceding the debtor's bankruptcy petition. Amounts included in this calculation are specified in § 101(10A), which is described in more detail elsewhere.[244]

These definitions led many courts to calculate the debtor's "projected disposable income" using a "projection" from the income the debtor earned in the six months before her bankruptcy petition, without considering anticipated increases or decreases in the debtor's financial circumstances.[245] Other courts were disturbed by the anomalous results that this interpretation of § 1325(b) caused, and insisted on taking anticipated fluctuations in the debtor's income into account in making the "projection" required by § 1325(b).

In 2010, the Supreme Court's *Hamilton v. Lanning*[246] decision resolved the split in a forward-looking approach that takes anticipated fluctuations in the debtor's income into account. The Court's 8-1 decision, with only Justice Scalia dissenting, relied on the ordinary meaning of the word "projected," and the ways in which a historic, mechanical approach clashed with other portions of § 1325, to interpret "projected disposable income" to take into account any "changes in the debtor's income or expenses that are known or virtually certain at the time of confirmation."[247] However, absent these predictable changes in the debtor's income

---

[239] Annotation, *What Constitutes "Disposable Income" under Sec. 1325(b) of Bankruptcy Code of 1978 (11 U.S.C.A. Sec. 1325(b)), Providing That All Disposable Income for Specified Period must Be Applied to Plan for Payment of Creditors*, 138 A.L.R. Fed. 547 (1997).

[240] 130 S. Ct. 2464 (2010).

[241] *See supra* § 17.03[B][2].

[242] Bankruptcy Code § 101(10A).

[243] Bankruptcy Code § 1325(b)(2)(A)(i) & (ii).

[244] *Infra* § 17.03[B][2][a] Current Monthly Income.

[245] *E.g.*, In re Kavenveama, 541 F.3d 868 (9th Cir. 2008). These calculations are based on the debtor's entries on Official Bankruptcy Form B22C.

[246] 130 S. Ct. 2464, 2469 (2010).

[247] *Id.*

or expenses, the debtor's projected disposable income will be limited to his disposable income, as calculated based on §§ 1325(b)(2) and 101(10A)(B).

Since *Lanning*, courts have continued to disagree about whether a debtor's Social Security benefits should be included in this projection. Section 101(10A) expressly excludes social security benefits from the debtor's "current monthly income."[248] But, under *Lanning*, the projection made necessary by the phrase "projected disposable income" may depart from the statutory connection between "disposable income" as defined in § 1325(b)(2) and "currently monthly income" as defined in § 101(10A).[249] This has resulted in varying conclusions about whether a debtor's Social Security income may be included in the projection that is made under § 1325(b)(1)(B), for the purposes of determining how much income must be paid to unsecured creditors.[250]

[ii]　Living Expenses

With respect to the debtor's living expenses, § 1325(b)(2) indicates that the calculation of the debtor's "disposable income" should take into account "amounts reasonably necessary to be expended" in four categories: (1) maintenance and support of the debtor or her dependents,[251] (2) future domestic support payments,[252] (3) certain charitable contributions,[253] and (4) for debtors engaged in a business, the expenditures necessary for the operation of the business.[254]

With respect to the most of these categories (other than charitable contributions), § 1325(b)(3) directs that amounts reasonably necessary to be expended by debtors with income above the relevant household median are to be determined in accordance with the Chapter 7 means test in § 707(b)(2)(A) and (B),[255] and based on the size of the debtor's household.[256] This means deducting amounts specified by the IRS's National and Local Standards for items such as those for food, clothing, shelter, and transportation, as reflected in Official Form B22C. Also permitted to be deducted, in the same manner as they are under the Chapter 7 means test, are the debtor's actual expenses for taxes, mandatory retirement contributions, life insurance, child care, and other items permitted by

---

[248]　Bankruptcy Code § 101(10A). *Supra* § 17.03[B][2][a] Current Monthly Income, *infra*.

[249]　*E.g.*, In re Scholz, 447 B.R. 887 (B.A.P. 9th Cir. 2011) (Railroad Retirement Act benefits included in "current monthly income" but outside the meaning of "projected disposable income").

[250]　*Compare, e.g.*, In re Welsh, 440 B.R. 836 (Bankr. D. Mont. 2010) (SSI benefits excluded from projected disposable income), *with* In re Nichols, 458 B.R. 516 (Bankr. E.D. Ark. 2011) (SSI benefits included in projected disposable income despite their exclusion from "current monthly income").

[251]　Bankruptcy Code § 1325(b)(2)(A)(I). *See* In re Lofty, 437 B.R. 578 (Bankr. S.D. Ohio 2010) (adult son and adult grandson were not "dependents").

[252]　Bankruptcy Code § 1325(b)(2)(A)(i).

[253]　Bankruptcy Code § 1325(b)(2)(A)(ii).

[254]　Bankruptcy Code § 1325(b)(2)(B).

[255]　Bankruptcy Code § 1325(b)(3). *See* In re Fuller, 346 B.R. 472 (Bankr. S.D. Ill. 2006).

[256]　*See* In re Robinson, 449 B.R. 473 (Bankr. E.D. Va. 2011).

§ 707(b).[257]

Several issues have arisen in Chapter 13 in connection with the deduction of these expenses. Among them are whether a debtor is entitled to deduct the full amount specified in the IRS's Standards, even though the debtor's actual expenses are less than those permitted by those standards. For example, in *In re Phillips*, a debtor who found an extraordinarily good deal on rent was able to deduct the entire amount specified in the IRS standards, even though her low rent made it possible for her to pay more to her unsecured creditors.[258] *Lanning's* dicta, which specifies that "the court may account for changes in the debtor's income *or expenses* that are known or virtually certain at the time of confirmation," casts doubt on these decisions.[259]

Much of the post-2005 litigation over living expenses dealt with whether debtors who owned their cars free and clear were nevertheless permitted to deduct the amounts specified in the IRS Standards as "ownership expenses."[260] In Chapter 7 liquidation cases, the prevailing view had been debtors could deduct the amount for "ownership expenses" regardless of whether they make debt or lease payments on the vehicle.[261] In Chapter 13 cases, however, many courts prevented Chapter 13 debtors from deducting ownership costs for vehicles that they own free and clear of any debt.[262] The Supreme Court resolved the conflict[263] in early 2011 in *Ransom v. FIA Card Services, N.A.*, in what was the first opinion written by Justice Kagan.[264] The Court ruled that the "car ownership" category encompassed only the costs of a car loan or lease and not other expenses, such as repairs, maintenance, registration, and insurance, that might be thought of being included in the costs of owning a vehicle. A debtor who does not have these ownership expenses could not deduct the amount specified in the standards for this category. Although the statutory language suggests that a debtor may deduct the specified amount in the IRS standards, regardless of whether she incurs those expenses, the Court read the phrase "applicable monthly expense amounts" in § 707(b)(2)(A)(ii)(I) to refer only to expenses that were "applicable" to the debtor's circumstances.[265] Cases decided since *Ransom* have permitted debtors whose house and car payments are

---

[257] *See, e.g.*, In re Bermann, 399 B.R. 213 (Bankr. E.D. Wis. 2009) (projected amounts for homeowner's insurance and real estate taxes).

[258] In re Phillips, 382 B.R. 153 (Bankr. D. Mass. 2008) (debtor entitled to deduct entire housing deduction, despite paying only $250 per month in rent).

[259] 130 S. Ct. at 2478 (emphasis supplied).

[260] *See* Official Form B22C, Line 28. *See* http://www.uscourts.gov/bkforms/bankruptcy_forms.html (last viewed Sept. 8, 2009).

[261] Tate v. Bolen (In re Tate), 571 F.3d 423 (5th Cir. 2009); In re Ross-Tousey, 549 F.3d 1148 (7th Cir. 2008); In re Kimbro, 389 B.R. 518 (B.A.P. 6th Cir. 2008).

[262] In re Ransom, 577 F.3d 1026 (9th Cir. 2009).

[263] *See* In re Coffin, 396 B.R. 804 (Bankr. D. Me. 2008) (collecting cases); James P. Terpening III, Comment, *All or Nothing: Properly Deducting Vehicle Ownership Expenses under 707(b)(2)(A)(Ii)(i)*, 25 Emory Bankr. Dev. J. 565 (2009).

[264] Ransom v. FIA Card Services, N.A., 131 S. Ct. 116 (2011).

[265] *Id.* at 724.

lower than the amount specified in the IRS's manual, may deduct the entire amount permitted by the IRS.[266]

Another persistent issue is the extent to which the debtor's voluntary contributions to her retirement plan, or repayments to loans from her retirement plan, can be deducted from her income in calculating the amount of disposable income that is available for payment to unsecured creditors. Even though expenses for retirement contributions and loan repayment are not included in the categories set out in § 707(b)(2), Official Bankruptcy Form B22C specifically permits these amounts to be deducted from the debtor's income.[267] Statutory support for this deduction is found in an unlikely place. Section 541(b)(7)(A) and (B) provide that contributions for employee benefit plans, deferred compensation plan and tax-deferred annuities "shall not constitute disposable income, as defined in section 1325(b)(2)."[268] However, deductions of these amounts conflicts with the means testing provisions of Chapter 7, which do not expressly permit voluntary retirement contributions to be deducted in determining whether the debtor's Chapter 7 case should be dismissed due to presumed abuse.

Other recurring issues deal with discretionary expenses, such as amounts for cigarettes, clothing, cable-TV, cell phones, internet, tuition, and other items. Not surprisingly, these all lead to mixed results, frequently depending on individual circumstances confronting the debtor and her family and the extent to which the debtor has deducted the full amount for items specifically permitted by other portions of the formula.[269] In the right situation, some of these expenses might fit into the "special circumstances" provision of § 707(b)(2)(B) which permits the debtor to deduct additional expenses, as part of the Chapter 7 means test calculation, if there are "special circumstances such as a serious medical condition or a call to active duty in the Armed Forces, to the extent that special circumstances justify additional expenses or adjustments of current monthly income for which there is no reasonable alternative."[270]

[iii] Payments on Secured Debts

Among the expenses that are to be deducted from an above state median debtor's income as "reasonably necessary to be expended" under the means test are payments "scheduled as contractually due to secured creditors."[271] Deducting

---

[266] In re Scott, 457 B.R. 740 (Bankr. S.D. Ill. 2011).

[267] Line 55 on Form B22C states: "Enter the monthly average of (a) all contributions or wage deductions made to qualified retirement plans, as specified in § 541(b)(7) and (b) all repayment of loans from retirement plans, as specified in § 362(b)(19)."

[268] Bankruptcy Code § 541(b)(7)(A), (B).

[269] *See generally* Jean M. Radler, Annotation, *What Constitutes "Disposable Income" Under § 1325(b) of Bankruptcy Code of 1978 (11 U.S.C.A. § 1325(b)), Providing That All Disposable Income for Specified Period Must be Applied to Plan for Payment of Creditors,* 138 A.L.R. Fed. 547 (1997).

[270] Bankruptcy Code § 707(b)(2)(B). *See* § 17.03[B][2][d] Special Circumstances, *supra.* In re Barbutes, 436 B.R. 519 (Bankr. M.D. Tenn. 2010) (additional home maintenance expense for older, dilapidated house that were required to make it suitable for basic housing).

[271] Bankruptcy Code § 707(b)(2)(A)(iii). Section 707(b)(2)(A)(i) indicates that the calculation is based on the amount of "current monthly income reduced by the amounts determined under clauses (ii), (iii),

amounts scheduled to be paid for collateral that is not reasonably necessary for the debtor's support effectively overrules pre-BAPCPA decisions like *In re Hedges*,[272] and *In re Brooks*,[273] in which debtors were not permitted to deduct payments secured by luxury items in determining the amount of their disposable income that would have to be paid to their unsecured creditors. The question becomes far more difficult in dealing with items such as children's musical instruments or sports equipment that might not be considered luxury goods, but which are not necessary for their support.[274]

Sections 1325(b)(3) and 707(b)(2)(A)(iii)(I) require deducting amounts "scheduled as contractually due" even though the debtor's plan might provide for modification of the amounts due to be paid on account of the creditor's claim.[275] However, scheduled payments to junior secured creditors whose security interests are completely "under water," because of the value of the collateral in relation to a senior secured claim, may not be deducted.[276] Thus, if the debtor's $25,000 mobile home is subject to two security interests, with the senior lien securing a $26,000 debt and the junior lien securing a $4,000 debt, payments scheduled to be made to the junior lien holder may not be deducted.

On the other hand, if a secured creditor's claim is partially secured, the debtor may deduct the full amount specified in his contract with the creditor, even though the debtor's plan calls for lower payments following a cramdown. If the debtor's $25,000 mobile home is secured by a $30,000 debt, the debtor can deduct the regular monthly payments on the $30,000 debt, even though the plan provides for smaller payments in a cramdown of what is only a $25,000 secured claim under §§ 506(a) and 1325(a)(5).

Some courts have even held that debtors who plan to surrender the collateral to the secured creditor can nevertheless deduct the scheduled monthly payment.[277] This comports with similar decisions regarding application of the means test for "presumptive abuse" in Chapter 7 cases,[278] and with the Supreme Court's decision in *Hamilton v. Lanning.*[279] Other courts disagree, on the grounds that payments on property that the debtor does not intend to keep are not payments which are "reasonably necessary to be expended for the maintenance or support of the debtor" while the plan is pending.[280] These competing positions are consistent with

---

and (iv) . . . ." Section 707(b)(2)(A)(iii) then refers to payments scheduled to be paid to secured creditors. Sometimes, finding the thread between related provisions is a challenge.

[272] 68 B.R. 18 (Bankr. E.D. Va. 1986) (boat).

[273] 241 B.R. 184 (Bankr. S.D. Ohio 1999) (recreational vehicle).

[274] *See* In re King, 308 B.R. 522 (Bankr. D. Kan. 2004) (adult college student child's auto payments not to be deducted from income in calculating disposable earnings).

[275] Bankruptcy Code § 1325(a)(5)(B). *See infra* § 18.08[F] Treatment of Secured Claims — Chapter 13 Secured Creditor Cramdown.

[276] In re Pruitt, 401 B.R. 546 (Bankr. D. Conn. 2009).

[277] *E.g.,* In re Burbank, 401 B.R. 67, 73 (Bankr. D.R.I. 2009); In re Thomas, 395 B.R. 914, 920 (B.A.P. 6th Cir. 2008).

[278] In re Rudler, 388 B.R. 433, 438–439 (B.A.P. 1st Cir. 2008).

[279] 130 S. Ct. 2464 (2010). *See* In re Quigley, 673 F.3d 269 (4th Cir. 2012).

[280] Zeman v. Liehr (In re Liehr) 439 B.R. 179 (B.A.P. 10th Cir. 2010) (surrender of mortgaged house);

the competing views over whether the Code mandates a more mechanical approach to determining the amount of the debtor's projected disposable income, and those that take a more flexible, forward-looking view of these aspects of the Code's confirmation standards.[281]

On the other hand, debtors who purchase luxury items, in anticipation of filing a chapter 13 petition and diverting income to paying for these unnecessary items, may be found to have acted in bad faith, in violation of § 1325(a)(3).[282] This may be the result even if the purchase was made with the best of intentions before the debtor's financial condition soured.[283] Apart from the issue of good faith, decisions on whether payments to secured creditors for luxury items can be deducted are split, with some cases permitting the deduction, in accord with the text of §§ 1325(b)(3) and 707(b)(2)(A)(iii),[284] and others permitting the court to engage in a discretionary analysis of whether the payments are "reasonably necessary."[285]

The decisions are also split over whether the debtor can deduct payments that are to be made to secured creditors even though the debtor's plan contemplates "surrender" of the collateral,[286] with most courts concluding that the scheduled payments may not be deducted if the debtor does not plan to retain the collateral.[287] Likewise, decisions are split over whether payments may be deducted when the creditor's claim is "completely under water" with insufficient value to satisfy even a portion of the secured creditor's claim.[288] Permitting debtors to deduct payments that they will not make is at odds with Congress's intent to require those with the ability to pay their unsecured creditors to make payments commensurate with their ability. It is also incompatible with Chapter 13's

---

In re Rahman, 400 B.R. 362 (Bankr. E.D.N.Y. 2009) (mortgage and car payment on property to be surrendered); In re Suess, 387 B.R. 243 (Bankr. W.D. Mo. 2008) (mortgage payment).

[281] *See* Zeman v. Liehr (In re Liehr), 439 B.R. 179, 183 n.22 (B.A.P. 10th Cir. 2010) ("the epic battle between use of the 'mechanical approach' versus the 'forward-looking approach' for determining projected disposable income has been waged in what seems like an infinite number of bankruptcy and appellate courts for at least four years now, no doubt generating much weeping, and wailing, and gnashing of teeth").

[282] *See* In re Young, 237 F.3d 1168 (10th Cir. 2001) (affirming finding that purchase of luxury auto was in bad faith).

[283] In re Walsh, 224 B.R. 231 (Bankr. M.D. Ga. 1998) (additional car used to transport debtor's grandchildren). *But see* In re Wick, 421 B.R. 206 (Bankr. D. Md. 2010) (debtor's pre-petition decision to "trade-up" to a bigger house, with a $4857 monthly mortgage payment was not made in anticipation of bankruptcy and was not lacking in good faith).

[284] *E.g.*, In re Van Bodegom Smith, 383 B.R. 441, 445–49 (Bankr. E.D. Wis. 2008); In re Guzman, 345 B.R. 640, 645–46 (Bankr. E.D. Wis. 2006).

[285] *See, e.g.*, In re McGillis, 370 B.R. at 729–30 (1325(b)(2)'s "reasonably necessary" expense requirements control the determination of allowable expenses); In re Owsley, 384 B.R. 739, 748 (Bankr. N.D. Tex. 2008) (secured debts must be for items that are "reasonably necessary").

[286] *Compare* In re Hoss, 392 B.R. 463, 469 n. 24 (Bankr. D. Kan. 2008), *and* In re Spurgeon, 378 B.R. 197, 200–01 (Bankr. E.D. Tenn. 2007), *with* In re Rudler, 388 B.R. 433 (B.A.P. 1st Cir. 2008), *and* In re Thomas, 395 B.R. 914 (B.A.P. 6th Cir. 2008).

[287] *See* In re Hoss, 392 B.R. 463, 469 n. 24 (Bankr. D. Kan. 2008); In re Spurgeon, 378 B.R. 197, 200–01 (Bankr. E.D. Tenn. 2007); In re McGillis, 370 B.R. 720, 728 n. 12 (Bankr. W.D. Mich. 2007); In re Edmunds, 350 B.R. 636, 641 (Bankr. D.S.C. 2006).

[288] *See* In re Reyes, 401 B.R. 910 (Bankr. C.D. Cal. 2009).

provisions regarding the debtor's obligation to report changes in their financial circumstances,[289] and liberal provisions regarding modifications of confirmed plans.[290] As more and more Courts of Appeal reject a strictly mechanical backward-looking approach to "projected disposable income," bankruptcy courts may abandon these positions.

Courts seem to be in agreement, on the other hand, that the debtor may deduct regularly scheduled lease payments on leased property — usually a motor vehicle — but not beyond the amount permitted by the IRS standards for "vehicle ownership expenses."[291] If their lease payments are less than the ownership expenses contained in the IRS's standard, courts disagree about the amount that may be deducted.[292]

The text of § 1325(b)(3) is bound to create difficulties, particularly for courts who heed the Supreme Court's nearly constant drum-beat about using the "plain meaning" of statutory language. For example, it remains unclear how the administrative expenses of administering a Chapter 13 case should be handled. The reference to § 707(b)(2)(A), in § 1325(b)(3), would seemingly require deduction of the hypothetical administrative expenses of a Chapter 13 case from the debtor's income, in determining the amount of income available for payment into the plan, even though those payments will again be deducted, pursuant to § 1322(a)(2) as amounts required to be paid to the trustee under the plan, as part of the 100% payment of administrative expense claims.

Moreover, deducting from income actual payments contractually required to be made to secured creditors, regardless of whether retention of the collateral securing such debt is appropriate for a debtor in financial difficulty, might easily result in dramatically lowering the debtor's "disposable income" while the debtor maintains an otherwise extravagant lifestyle, rich with encumbered but frivolous assets.

What a mess![293]

[iv]   Charitable Contributions

In calculating his disposable income, debtors are also permitted to deduct up to 15% of their "gross income" for amounts contributed to qualified charities.[294] This could amount to a hefty sum, and is well beyond the level of charitable contributions made by most Americans.

---

[289] Bankruptcy Code § 521(f)(4).

[290] Bankruptcy Code § 1329.

[291] *See* In re Reyes, 401 B.R. 910 (Bankr. C.D. Cal. 2009).

[292] *Compare, e.g.*, In re Barrett, 371 B.R. 855, 859 (Bankr. S.D. Ill. 2007) (permitting deduction of the $471 under the IRS Standard, even though the debtor's car payment was only $75), *with* In re Rezentes, 368 B.R. 55, 56, 62 (Bankr. D. Hawaii 2007) (debtors can only deduct their actual monthly housing expense of $300, even though the full housing expense deduction under the IRS Standard was $2,000).

[293] Jean Braucher, *Getting Realistic: In Defense of Formulaic Means Testing*, 83 Am. Bankr. L.J. 395 (2009); Robert M. Lawless et al., *Did Bankruptcy Reform Fail? An Empirical Study of Consumer Debtors*, 82 Am. Bankr. L. J. 349 (2008).

[294] Bankruptcy Code § 1325(b)(2)(A)(ii).

[v] Business Expenses of Debtors Engaged in Business

Sole proprietors are eligible for Chapter 13 relief so long as their debts do not exceed Chapter 13's limits.[295] Individual Chapter 13 debtors engaged in business will naturally need to spend a good portion of their income to keep the business running. Accordingly, § 1325(b)(2)(B) permits these debtors to deduct "expenditures necessary for the continuation, preservation, and operation . . ." of their business in calculating their disposable income.[296] This could include expenses for the purchase and maintenance of office equipment, inventory expenses, employees' salaries, and other continuing expenses necessary to keep the doors of the debtor's business open.

[b] Disposable Income for Debtors with Income Below the State Median

The income of debtors with household income below the applicable state median is calculated in the same manner as it is for those with household income above the median, but without resort to Chapter 7's means testing rules to determine the "amounts reasonably necessary to be expended" for the debtor's maintenance and support. Instead, the amount of expenses that should be deducted from the debtor' income, to determine "disposable income" is largely discretionary, as it was before the 2005 amendments.

Such amounts might be higher or lower than amounts specified in § 707(b) and the IRS Guidelines stipulated to be used by those with household income above the state median. This also might mean that the court will have greater discretion in determining whether payments to secured creditors are not reasonably necessary for the debtor's maintenance or support. The means testing rules in Chapter 7 provide for deducting all payments to secured creditors, without regard to whether the collateral security their claims is reasonably necessary for the debtor's support. For debtors below the state median, a further inquiry into whether retaining the debtor's retention of the collateral may be appropriate.

[c] Payment to "Unsecured Creditors"

The text of § 1325(b)(1)(B) requires that the plan call for distribution of all of the debtor's projected disposable income, during the three or five year mandatory term of the plan, to "unsecured creditors."[297] The precise meaning of this poorly articulated rule remains obscure. First, the remainder of the Bankruptcy Code refers not to "creditors" or to "unsecured creditors" but to "holders of allowed claims" and "holders of allowed unsecured claims." If Congress intended for the debtor's projected disposable income to be distributed to holders of "allowed unsecured claims" it should have used this term, which has a well-understood meaning. It does not seem likely that the Code intended for payments to holders of

---

[295] *See supra* § 6.02[B][6][c] Chapter 13 Debt Limits.

[296] Bankruptcy Code § 1325(b)(2)(B).

[297] Bankruptcy Code § 1325(b)(1)(b).

disallowed claims to be included, such as those for post-petition interest, but its imprudent choice of the term "unsecured creditors" leaves the door open for that possible interpretation.

The phrase "unsecured creditors" also creates some uncertainty as to whether payments to holders of unsecured priority claims should be considered as part of this calculation. The deduction of amounts to be paid to holders of "all priority claims"[298] from the debtor's "disposable income"[299] suggests that amounts paid under the plan to these unsecured creditors should not be included when calculating whether § 1325(b)(1)(B)'s standard has been satisfied, but the plain meaning of the phrase "unsecured creditors" indicates otherwise.

Consider, for example, a debtor with "projected disposable income," after deduction of the amounts specified in § 707(b)(2)(A) & (B), of $30,000 over the five-year period of his plan. Assume further that this $30,000 figure was reached after deducting amounts necessary to pay the debtor's ex-spouse's unsecured § 507(a)(1) priority claim for past due support, as specified by the means test formula of § 707(b)(2)(A)(iv). Amounts to be paid under the plan to the debtor's ex-spouse on account of this priority claims would reduce the amount that would have to be distributed to other unsecured creditors. This would, in effect, result in deducting the amount to be paid for the priority support claim twice, in undoubted contravention of Congress's intent, but consistent with what otherwise might easily be viewed as the "plain meaning" of the Code's language. Perhaps significantly, the forms promulgated by United States Trustee's office call for deducting payments to be made to holders of priority claims in calculating the amount of a debtor's "disposable income."[300]

[F]   Treatment of Secured Claims — Chapter 13 Secured Creditor Cramdown

Chapter 13 permits debtors to handle secured claims in a wide variety of ways, depending on debtor's desire and ability, and on certain aspects of the creditor's claim. Debtors may sometimes wish to simply surrender the collateral to the creditor. A few debtors may be successful in persuading a secured creditor to "accept" less than what the creditor is entitled to insist on. Chapter 13 facilitates both of these alternatives, but also provides for the cramdown of most secured claims, permitting the debtor to retain the collateral and make payments to the secured creditor on terms the creditor might not prefer. For debtors who seek Chapter 13 relief in order to maintain possession of property subject to secured creditors' claims, cramdown will be the most common treatment of secured claims. As will be seen, it's precise form varies, depending on the nature of the collateral and the of the creditor's claim.

---

[298]   Bankruptcy Code § 707(b)(2)(A)(iv).

[299]   Bankruptcy Code § 1325(b)(2)(A)(i) & (b)(3).

[300]   *See* Official Bankruptcy Form B22C, Line 49.

[1]   Surrender of the Collateral to the Creditor

Section 1325(a)(5)(C) permits a plan to be confirmed over the objection of a secured creditor if "the debtor surrenders the property securing such claim to [the creditor] . . . ."[301] Surrender will be preferred by debtors who lack enough income satisfy the claim, or by debtors who do not desire to retain possession of the collateral.

Before the 2005 BAPCPA amendments, debtors who attempted to retain luxury items sometimes found that surrender of the collateral was the only way to obtain confirmation of their plans. The 2005 amendments, which *require* amounts owed to secured creditors to be deducted from income that otherwise would be available for distribution to unsecured creditors, may change this result. However, the newly promulgated Official Bankruptcy Forms,[302] inertia,[303] and debtors' attorneys' reluctance to risk the imposition of sanctions, all may lead to continuation of past practice.

[2]   Secured Creditor Acceptance of Plan

Alternatively, § 1325(a)(5)(A) permits a debtor's plan to be confirmed, regardless of what payments it requires to be submitted to a secured creditor, so long as the creditor "has accepted the plan."[304] Although a few of the debtor's family members might agree to accept less than they are otherwise legally entitled to demand, acceptance of a Chapter 13 plan by a secured creditor is so rare that there is no routine procedural mechanism for seeking acceptances from secured creditors.[305]

[3]   Cure & Reinstatement[306]

As explained earlier, plans sometimes provide for the debtor to cure any pre-petition defaults on obligations to holders of secured claims, and reinstate the stream of scheduled payments as if there had been no default. In cases involving mortgages on residential real estate, this "de-acceleration" may be the only adjustment of the secured creditor's rights that is permitted.[307]

---

[301]   Bankruptcy Code § 1325(a)(5)(C).

[302]   Official Bankruptcy Form B22C, Line 47, specifies that debtors should deduct amounts for the average monthly payment "for each of your debtors that is secured by an interest in property that you own . . . ."

[303]   Lex 1: Corpus omne perseverare in statu suo quiescendi vel movendi uniformiter in directum, nisi quatenus a viribus impressis cogitur statum illum mutare." Sir Isaac Newton, Philosophiae Naturalis Principia Mathematica (1687) (Every object in a state of uniform motion tends to remain in that state of motion unless an external force is applied to it.).

[304]   Bankruptcy Code § 1325(a)(5)(A).

[305]   This is in sharp distinction to what occurs in Chapter 11, where acceptances are solicited from all creditors pursuant to Bankruptcy Code § 1125. *See infra* § 19.09 Acceptance of Plan by Holders of Claims & Interests: Disclosure and Voting.

[306]   *See* David Gray Carlson, *Car Wars: Valuation Standards in Chapter 13 Bankruptcy Cases*, 13 Bankr. Dev. J. 1, 2 (1996).

[307]   Bankruptcy Code § 1322(b)(2). *See supra* § 18.07[C] Cure & Waiver of Defaults; Reinstatement.

In *In re Taddeo*, one of the early decisions in which this step was approved, the debtors had fallen into default on their home mortgage.[308] When the creditor brought an action to foreclose on the mortgage, the Taddeos tendered full payment of all of their arrearages, but the creditor refused to accept the debtor's proposed cure. The Taddeos responded by filing a Chapter 13 petition and filed a plan proposing to pay the arrearages in several equal monthly installments and to simultaneously resume making regular monthly principal and interest payments according to the amortization schedule required by the mortgage agreement. The court held that § 1322(b)(2)'s proscription against modifying home mortgages did not prevent the debtors from utilizing §§ 1322(b)(3) or (b)(5) to cure their default and thus negate the effect of the creditor's acceleration of the mortgage debt. In effect, such a cure and reinstatement was not a modification of the secured creditor's rights, or if it was a modification, it was one expressly permitted by § 1322(b)(5).

Payments made to cure the debtor's arrearages must be made over a reasonable time, and are customarily made through the trustee. Regular monthly mortgage payments, on the other hand, are usually made directly to the creditor, without the involvement of the trustee. This has the advantage of saving the administrative expenses that would normally accompany the trustee's distribution of plan funds.

Despite § 1322(b)(3), cure and reinstatement of a mortgage that enables the debtor to retain a home in which he has no or little equity, may be inconsistent with the other goals of Chapter 13. The court in *In re Naime* seized on this to refuse to confirm a Chapter 13 plan, on the basis of lack of good faith.[309] Consistent with cases involving continued payments to creditors with claims secured by luxury goods, under § 1325(b), the court said:

> Though [the] Debtor may have acquired the home during more prosperous times, it is apparent that the expense associated with the home led to [the] Debtor's current need to seek relief [from his debts]. . . . [The] Debtor's retention of a home that consumes all of his personal net disposable income, to the detriment of his significant number of unsecured creditors, is not in good faith.[310]

The right to cure defaults and reinstate a mortgage does not last forever. Permitting debtors to restore the status quo after their home has been sold at foreclosure would discourage prospective buyers and further deflate foreclosure sale prices. Accordingly, the right to de-accelerate a residential mortgage does not apply if the property has already been sold at a foreclosure sale which has been conducted in compliance with whatever non-bankruptcy law applies to the sale.[311] However, if any aspect of the state foreclosure sale process is not complete, the debtor's right to cure and reinstate survives.[312]

---

[308] 685 F.2d 24 (2d Cir. 1982).

[309] In re Namie, 395 B.R. 594 (Bankr. D.S.C. 2008).

[310] *Id.* at 597. *See also* In re Loper, 367 B.R. 660, 669–70 (Bankr. D. Colo. 2007).

[311] Bankruptcy Code § 1322(c)(1).

[312] *E.g.*, In re Jenkins, 422 B.R. 175 (Bankr. E.D. Ark. 2010) (consideration not yet paid and deed not yet delivered).

[4] Cramdown of Chapter 13 Plan over Secured Creditor's Objection[313]

In many cases, Chapter 13 permits debtors to change the terms of payments to secured creditors, over their objection. The amount, duration, and interest rate on payments made to the creditor can be altered, subject to limitations, described below. The plan can be confirmed so long as it: 1) permits the creditor to retain its lien on the collateral; 2) provides for making payments to the creditor that are the equivalent of the amount of the allowed secured claim, and 3) ensures that the stream of payments on claims secured by personal property are sufficient to adequately protect the creditor for the duration of the plan.[314]

[a]   Retention of the Creditor's Lien

The requirement that the secured claim holder retain its lien ensures that the creditor will not be left with only an unsecured claim against the debtor if the plan fails. Section 1325(a)(5)(B)(i) requires that the creditor retains its lien at least until the underlying debt is fully paid or is discharged in Chapter 13.[315] A Chapter 13 discharge is normally only obtained when the debtor fully performs the terms of his plan.[316] Permitting the creditor to retain its lien for the full underlying debt ensures that the creditor will keep its lien for any unpaid portion of the debt in the event that the case is dismissed or converted to Chapter 7 if the debtor defaults under the plan and does not receive a Chapter 13 discharge.

Consider, a creditor with a security interest in the debtor's $2,000 garden tractor, securing a $3,000 debt. A creditor in this situation has a $2,000 secured claim and a $1,000 unsecured claim. The plan will probably provide for making regular monthly installment payments to the creditor sufficient to amortize the $2,000 secured portion of the claim. It might also provide for additional payments to be made, together with those distributed to other unsecured creditors, in partial satisfaction of the $1,000 unsecured deficiency claim. If, after one year of payments, the secured claim is whittled down to around $1,700 with nothing yet paid to with respect to the unsecured portion of the claim, and the debtor defaults, the creditor will still have its lien securing the entire outstanding $2,700 balance due. This provides the creditor with some measure of protection from the risk that the court had undervalued the collateral at $2,000, and with the ability to repossess the collateral, after dismissal of the case, until the debtor pays the full $2,700 balance of the underlying debt. Lest there be any doubt about this result, § 1325(a)(5)(B)(i)(II) specifies that "if the [Chapter 13] case . . . is dismissed or converted without completion of the plan, such lien shall also be retained by such holder to the extent recognized by applicable nonbankruptcy law."[317]

---

[313] Michael Elson, Note, *Say "Ahhh!": A New Approach for Determining the Cram Down Interest Rate After* Till v. SCS Credit, 27 Cardozo L. Rev. 1921 (2006).

[314] Bankruptcy Code § 1325(a)(5)(B)(i)-(iii).

[315] In re Olde Prarie Block Owner, LLC, 464 B.R. 337 (Bankr. N.D. Ill. 2011) (applying § 1129(b)).

[316] Bankruptcy Code § 1328(a); *see* § 13.05 [C][1] Full-Compliance Chapter 13 Discharge, *supra.*

[317] Bankruptcy Code § 1325(a)(5)(B)(i)(II).

This will have a huge effect on partially secured claims dealt with by plans that fail after a substantial portion or even all of the secured portion of the claim is paid. Consider the result in the same situation if the plan fails after four and a half years of payments, with the secured portion of the claim having been paid after 4 years, but with a $500 balance due on the unsecured portion of the underlying debt. Even though the secured claim has been fully paid under the plan, § 1325(a)(5)(B)(i)(II) means that the creditor's lien will survive as security for the unpaid $500 balance of the underlying debt as recognized by applicable non-bankruptcy law. This overrules cases decided before the 2005 amendments went into effect, that eliminated the creditor's lien once the amount of the secured portion of the claim was paid.[318]

[b]   Payments Equivalent to Amount of Secured Claim

The most important aspect of secured creditor cramdown, not only in Chapter 13, but also under Chapters 11 and 12, is the requirement that the "value, as of the effective date of the plan, of property to be distributed under the plan on account of such claim is not less than the allowed amount of such claim."[319] The key component of this passage, as it is in connection with the best interests test of § 1325(a)(4), is "value." For a stream of payments to have the same value as the amount of the creditor's claim, the payments must include an interest component to compensate the creditor for the delay in receiving payment.

In 2004, after over 25 years of debate in the lower courts, the Supreme Court ruled that the appropriate method for determining the rate of interest that must be paid to satisfy § 1325(a)(5)(B)(ii) should be based on the national prime rate, applied by banks when making low-risk loans, augmented by whatever additional increase is necessary to account for the risk of the debtor's nonpayment.[320] However, the plurality nature of Supreme Court's opinion in *Till v. SCS Credit Corp*, leaves some doubt as to the lasting effect of the Court's decision.[321]

In addition, the *Till* Court provided guidance about the factors that should affect the amount over the prime rate that should be required. It indicated that bankruptcy courts should consider: (1) the probability that the plan would fail, (2) the rate at which the collateral would depreciate, (3) the general liquidity of market for the collateral, and (4) the administrative expenses of enforcement.[322] The Court further cautioned that the "requirement obligates the court to select a rate high enough to compensate the creditor for its risk but not so high as to doom the plan. If the court determines that the likelihood of default is so high as to necessitate an "'eye-popping'" interest rate, . . . the plan probably should not be confirmed,"

---

[318] *E.g.*, In re Rheaume, 296 B.R. 313 (Bankr. D. Vt. 2003).

[319] Bankruptcy Code § 1325(a)(5)(B)(ii).

[320] Till v. SCS Credit Corp., 541 U.S. 456 (2004).

[321] James D. Walker Jr. & Amber Nickell, *Bankruptcy*, 55 Mercer L. Rev. 1101, 1127–28 (2004); Carmen H. Lonstein & Steven A. Domanowski, *Payment of Post-petition Interest to Unsecured Creditors: Federal Judgment Rate Versus Contract Rate*, 12 Am. Bankr. Inst. L. Rev. 421 (2004).

[322] *See also* Michael Elson, Note, *Say "Ahhh!": A New Approach for Determining the Cram Down Interest Rate after Till v. SCS Credit*, 27 Cardozo L. Rev. 1921 (2006).

presumably on the grounds that performance is not feasible within the meaning of § 1325(a)(6).[323]

Cases decided since *Till v. SCS Credit Corp.* indicate that lower courts will follow the suggestion contained in the Court's opinion and set the rate necessary to supply the creditor with the present value of its secured claim at between 1% to 3% above the prime rate.[324] The extent to which *Till* applies to secured creditor cramdown in Chapters 11 and 12 remains up in the air.[325]

[c] Valuation of the Collateral

Another key component of determining whether the payments to be made to the secured creditor are the equivalent of the amount of the secured claim is determining the actual amount of the secured claim. This is determined pursuant to Bankruptcy Code § 506.[326] If the collateral is worth more than the debt, the secured claim will be the full allowed amount owed. This is rarely the case in Chapter 13, except with regard to claims secured by the debtor's home, which are not usually subject to cramdown in any event.[327] In cases involving security interests in the debtor's personal property, the collateral is often worth less than the amount of the secured debt, making the value of the collateral the amount of the allowed secured claim.[328]

In determining the value of the personal property, courts are now directed to use its "replacement value . . . as of the date of the filing of the petition without deduction for costs of sale or marketing."[329] This language, added to § 506 as part of the 2005 BAPCPA amendments, codifies most of the Supreme Court's 1997 decision in *Associates Commercial Corp. v. Rash.*[330] However, like *Rash*, it leaves the precise method for determining the property's replacement value up in the air, particularly in cases where it may be difficult to identify an appropriate secondary market for the property.[331]

In cases involving automobiles, replacement value is frequently based on the National Automobile Dealers Association (NADA) Guide, less whatever reconditioning and repair costs may exist.[332] Because the "retail" value of a car is determined after a dealer has "reconditioned" the vehicle and made any necessary repairs, bankruptcy courts routinely find that "replacement value" is lower than

---

[323] 541 U.S. at 480–81.

[324] In re Cantwell, 336 B.R. 688 (Bankr. D.N.J. 2006) (1%).

[325] *E.g.*, In re Deep River Warehouse, Inc., 2005 Bankr. LEXIS 1793 (Bankr. M.D.N.C. Sept. 22, 2005).

[326] Bankruptcy Code § 506. *See supra* § 10.03 Secured Claims.

[327] *See supra* § 18.08[F][5] Residential Real Estate Mortgages.

[328] *See supra* § 10.03 Secured Claims.

[329] Bankruptcy Code § 506(a)(2).

[330] 520 U.S. 953 (1997).

[331] E-bay?

[332] In re Scott, 437 B.R. 168 (Bankr. D.N.J. 2010); In re Morales, 387 B.R. 36 (Bankr. C.D. Cal. 2008).

the "retail value," in the auto dealer's bluebook.[333] As one court explained:

> There are numerous other sources for debtors to obtain automobiles at lower costs, avoiding the overhead costs inherent in purchases from automobile dealerships. Debtors are able to purchase automobiles at auctions, from private individuals, from used car lots, from family members, or from rental car companies, just to name a few options. That market is clearly broader than a purely retail market. . . . While it would be easier for this Court to accept the analyses of the courts that equate "retail value" with "replacement value," the Court does not believe this to be mandated by *Rash*. The Court finds that "retail value" and "replacement value" are not synonymous.[334]

[d]   Equal Monthly Installment Payments[335]

In most cases, secured creditors' claims will have to be satisfied with regular monthly installment payments. Language added in 2005 specifies that if "periodic payments" are to be distributed to the holder of a secured claim, the payments must be made in equal monthly amounts.[336] Thus unless the creditor agrees otherwise and thus "accepts" the plan, the plan may not provide for only annual or quarterly payments. Nor may it provide for a "balloon payment" after a series of monthly payments.[337] The "equal amounts" requirement could well prove to be a problem for debtors whose income is sporadic or seasonal.

The purpose § 1325(a)(5)(B)(iii)(I) was to restrict the practice that had developed prior to BAPCPA with respect to payments to secured creditors with depreciating collateral. Some debtors tried to "backload" their plans either with large balloon payments at the end of the plan or with gradually increasing payments during the life of the plan.[338] Other debtors' plans provided for reduced payments to secured creditors at various times of the year or for quarterly or semi-annual payments. The requirement of equal payments, made monthly, whenever periodic payments are provided for, was intended to prevent these practices.

It also conflicts with the customary practice in some districts of permitting debtors to cure any existing arrearages on their home mortgages before commencing payments to other secured lenders. This may make it necessary for debtors to extend the period during which these arrearages will be cured.[339]

It also might be difficult to reconcile the equal monthly payments requirement

---

[333] *See* In re Henry, 457 B.R. 402 (Bankr. E.D. Pa. 2011).

[334] In re Glueck, 223 B.R. 514, 519 (Bankr. S.D. Ohio 1998).

[335] David Gray Carlson, *Cars and Homes in Chapter 13 after the 2005 Amendments to the Bankruptcy Code*, 14 Am. Bankr. Inst. L. Rev. 301, 336 (2006).

[336] Bankruptcy Code § 1325(a)(5)(B)(iii)(I).

[337] *E.g.*, Hamilton v. Wells Fargo Bank, N.A. (In re Hamilton), 401 B.R. 539 (B.A.P. 1st Cir. 2009).

[338] *See* In re Erwin, 376 B.R. 897, 901 (Bankr. C.D. Ill. 2007).

[339] *Compare* In re McDonald, 397 B.R. 175 (Bankr. D. Me. 2007), *and* In re Hamilton, 401 B.R. 539 (B.A.P. 1st Cir. 2009) (equal monthly periodic payments required even in plan contemplating cure), *with* In re Davis, 343 B.R. 326 (Bankr. M.D. Fla. 2006) (Section 1325(e) regarding cure overrides § 1325(b)(5)(B)(iii)).

with the requirement of § 1325(a)(5)(b)(iii)(II) that the payments ensure that the creditor is adequately protected.[340] If the collateral depreciates at an uneven rate over the life of the plan, this may require the debtor to make unequal payments, as the rate of depreciation changes. Considering both requirements together will probably make it necessary for equal payments to be made at a rate which keeps up with the steepest portion of the anticipated depreciation rate for the collateral.[341] Alternatively, the court might permit adequate protection payments pursuant to §§ 362(d) & 1325(a)(5)(B)(iii)(II) as separate and distinct from the equal monthly installment payments made under § 1325(a)(5)(B)(iii)(I).[342] Likewise, the court might permit initial payments at a higher rate, to cure a default on a long term debt pursuant to § 1322(b)(5).[343]

Since this requirement was added to the code, a split of authority has developed over whether the stream of equal payments must begin immediately, with the debtor's first payment following confirmation. Some courts require the stream of equal payments to commence immediately.[344] Others permit a debtor to devote a portion of his payments to satisfying his attorneys' fees in connection with the case, in the early months of a case, and then step-up the amounts paid secured creditors, when these administrative expenses are fully paid.[345]

On the other hand, courts have consistently ruled against confirmation of plans that provide for pro-rata payments to secured creditors, where the amount paid into the plan by the debtor varied from month to month, or where payments to other creditors for less than the entire duration of the plan resulted in varying amounts to each secured creditor.[346]

[e]   Adequate Protection

As suggested above, the 2005 amendments also added language requiring that payments made on claims secured by personal property must be sufficient to ensure that the creditor remains "adequately protected" during the entire period of the plan.[347] In most cases, this will prevent debtors from delaying payments to secured creditors until sometime later in the time-span of the plan.[348] Further, payments might have to be made to secured creditors at an accelerated rate,

---

[340] *E.g.*, In re Denton, 370 B.R. 441, 445–46 (Bankr. S.D. Ga. 2007). *See* § 18.08[F][4][e] Adequate Protection, *infra*.

[341] *See* In re Denton, 370 B.R. 441, 448–49 (Bankr. S.D. Ga. 2007); In re Hill, 2007 Bankr. LEXIS 502 (Bankr. M.D.N.C. Feb. 12, 2007).

[342] In re DeSardi, 340 B.R. 790, 805–10 (Bankr. S.D. Tex. 2006). *But see* In re Hill, 397 B.R. 259 (Bankr. M.D.N.C. 2007). *See also* Bankruptcy Code § 1326(a)(1)(C) (requiring "adequate protection" payments to be made directly to the creditor, rather than through the Chapter 13 trustee).

[343] In re Davis, 343 B.R. 326 (Bankr. M.D. Fla. 2006) (relying on Bankruptcy Code § 1322(e)).

[344] In re Williams, 385 B.R. 468 (Bankr. S.D. Ga. 2008).

[345] In re Brennan, 455 B.R. 237 (Bankr. M.D. Fla. 2009).

[346] *E.g.*, In re Willis, 460 B.R. 784 (Bankr. D. Kan 2011).

[347] Bankruptcy Code § 1325(a)(5)(B)(iii)(II).

[348] Richardo Kilpatrick, *Selected Creditor Issues Under the Bankruptcy Abuse Prevention and Consumer Protection Act of 2005*, 79 Am. Bankr. L.J. 817, 836 (2005).

particularly if the collateral threatens to decline speedily in value.[349] In some cases, where the debtor lacks sufficient income to pay the claim at a fast enough rate, it may prevent confirmation of the plan.

In addition, § 1326(a)(4) now requires the debtor retaining possession of personal property that is subject to a purchase money security interest or a lease, to provide "reasonable evidence of the maintenance of any required insurance coverage" on the property and to "continue to do so for as long as the debtor retains possession of such property." The requirement of adequate protection probably requires no less.

[5]   Residential Real Estate Mortgages[350]

Claims secured solely by residential real estate cannot be modified in Chapter 13.[351] As explained above, the debtor can cure any pre-petition default and thus de-accelerate the debt and resume regular monthly payments, but otherwise the debtor is required to perform the terms of his residential mortgage in accordance with the terms of the contract.

Until the residential foreclosure crisis of 2008 and 2009,[352] most residential purchase money mortgages were fully secured. However, the same rules apply regardless of whether the mortgage secures a purchase money debt, a construction loan, a home equity line, or otherwise. And, they apply regardless of whether the debt is fully or only partially secured. Thus, if the debtor owns a $100,000 home subject to a $70,000 senior mortgage and a $40,000 junior mortgage, both debts must be paid in full according to the terms of the respective agreements between the creditors.[353]

On the other hand, if the value of the collateral is completely consumed by senior secured claims, leaving no value whatsoever for the junior lien holder, the lender's claim is regarded as not being secured.[354] Thus, if in the above example the home were worth only $68,000, the $40,000 junior mortgage could be stripped-off as completely unsecured.[355]

---

[349] *See* In re Denton, 370 B.R. 441, 448–49 (Bankr. S.D. Ga. 2007); In re White 352 B.R. 633, 649 (Bankr. E.D. La. 2006).

[350] Adam J. Levitin, *Resolving the Foreclosure Crisis: Modification of Mortgages in Bankruptcy*, 2009 Wis. L. Rev. 565 (2009); Robert M. Zinman & Novica Petrovski, *The Home Mortgage and Chapter 13: An Essay on Unintended Consequences*, 17 Am. Bankr. Inst. L. Rev. 133 (2009).

[351] Bankruptcy Code § 1322(b)(2).

[352] *See* Adam J. Levitin, *Resolving the Foreclosure Crisis: Modification of Mortgages in Bankruptcy*, 2009 Wis. L. Rev. 565, 565–67 (2009).

[353] Nobleman v. Am. Sav. Bank, 508 U.S. 324 (1993).

[354] *E.g.*, Lane v. W. Interstate Bancorp (In re Lane), 280 F.3d 663 (6th Cir. 2002); Zimmer v. PSB Lending Corp. (In re Zimmer), 313 F.3d 1220, 1227 (9th Cir. 2002); In re Bartee, 212 F.3d 277, 295 (5th Cir. 2000); McDonald v. Master Financial, Inc. (In re McDonald), 205 F.3d 606, 611 (3d Cir. 2000); Tanner v. FirstPlus Fin., Inc. (In re Tanner), 217 F.3d 1357 (11th Cir. 2000). *Contra* In re Hughes, 402 B.R. 325 (Bankr. D. Minn. 2009).

[355] *E.g.*, Zimmer v. PSB Lending Corp (In re Zimmer), 313 F.3d 1220 (9th Cir. 2002); Lane v. W. Interstate Bancorp (In re Lane), 280 F.3d 663 (6th Cir. 2002); Fisette v. Keller (In re Fisette), 455 B.R. 177 (B.A.P. 8th Cir. 2011).

This different treatment could lead to dramatic results, depending on the value of the collateral. Consider what would happen in the above example, if the property were worth $70,100. The $40,000 junior mortgage would be only marginally secured, to the extent of $100. The debtor's plan would have to pay the entire amount of the $40,000 debt, and, apart from any effort to cure past defaults, would have to pay it according to the terms of the parties' agreement. As courts have explained: "where even the slightest bit of equity remains in the subject property such that the lien in question is partially secured, the lien may not be avoided."[356] Thus, in the above example, the creditor's lien could not be stripped off.[357] On the other hand, if the property were worth $101 less, $69,999, the second mortgage could be stripped away and the lender treated as a purely unsecured creditor. This places a great deal of importance on the court's determination of the value of the property involved,[358] and might give the debtor, or perhaps unsecured creditors, an incentive to make the house look as bad as possible on the day it is scheduled to be appraised.

Section 1322(b)(2) only prevents modification if the only collateral for the debt is "real property that is the debtor's principal residence."[359] If the terms of the agreement add other collateral, not inextricably associated with the land,[360] the creditor's secured claim may be modified.[361] Likewise, if the collateral is a mobile home which does not qualify as real estate, or if the premises are not the debtor's principal residence,[362] the claim is subject to the same rules as other secured claims and may be modified consistent with § 1325(a)(5)'s usual secured creditor cramdown rules.[363]

---

[356] Mitchem v. Branch Banking and Trust Co. (In re Mitchem), 455 B.R. 108 (Bankr. W.D. Va. 2011).

[357] *E.g.*, In re Wright, 460 B.R. 581 (Bankr. E.D.N.Y. 2011).

[358] *Id. See also* In re Mitchem, 462 B.R. 608 (W.D. Va. 2011).

[359] Bankruptcy Code § 1322(b)(2).

[360] In re Davis, 989 F.2d 208 (6th Cir. 1992); *see* David Gray Carlson, *Rake's Progress: Cure and Reinstatement of Secured Claims in Bankruptcy Reorganization*, 13 Bankr. Dev. J. 273 (1997); David J. Jesulaitis, Comment, *Lien Stripping After Nobelman v. American Savings Bank: What Is "Additional Collateral"?*, 32 Hous. L. Rev. 201 (1995); James H. Longino, Note, *Nobelman v. American Savings Bank: Bankruptcy, Bifurcation, and Residential Mortgages — Lender Beware*, 47 Ark. L. Rev. 907, 936 (1994).

[361] *See* Daniel C. Fleming & Marianne McConnell, *The Treatment of Residential Mortgages in Chapter 13 After Nobleman*, 2 Am. Bankr. Inst. L. Rev. 147 (1994).

[362] *E.g.*, Scarborough v. Chase Manhattan Mortgage Corp. (In re Scarborough), 461 F.3d 406, 408, 412–13 (3d Cir. 2006) (three-unit building, with only one unit serving as the debtor's residence).

[363] *See* Williamson v. Wash. Mutual Home Loans, Inc., 400 B.R. 917 (M.D. Ga. 2009).

[6]   Certain Purchase Money Security Interests[364]

In 2005, Congress imposed additional limits on a debtor's ability to modify secured creditors' claims. This was accomplished through a "hanging paragraph"[365] appearing at the end of § 1325(a), between § 1325(a)(9) and the beginning of § 1325(b).[366] The language of the hanging paragraph provides:

> For purposes of paragraph (5) section 506 shall not apply to a claim described in that paragraph if the creditor has a purchase money security interest securing the debt that is the subject of the claim, the debt was incurred within the 910-day [sic] preceding the date of the filing of the petition, and the collateral for that debt consists of a motor vehicle . . . acquired for the personal use of the debtor, or if the collateral for that debt consists of any other thing of value, if the debt was incurred during the 1-year period preceding that filing.

[a]   Preventing Strip-Down

The hanging paragraph was intended to prevent debtors from using § 506(a)(1) to "strip-down" or bifurcate a partially secured claim into two separate claims. Normally, of course, § 506 would result in the bifurcation of a partially secured claim. A $20,000 auto loan secured by a vehicle only worth $16,000 otherwise would be bifurcated into a $16,000 secured claim and a $4,000 unsecured claim. In Chapter 13, the debtor's plan could modify the secured creditor's claim and satisfy the cram-down standards of § 1325(a)(5)(B) by calling for payments to satisfy the $16,000 secured claim, at an appropriate rate of interest to ensure that the creditor received the full "value" of the amount of its secured claim. The $4,000 unsecured claim would be thrown in with other unsecured claim and share in whatever distribution the plan provided to holders of those general unsecured claims.

The effect of the hanging paragraph is to require the debtor to treat the claim as if it were fully rather than only partially secured. As a fully secured claim, § 1325(a)(5)(B)(ii) could only be satisfied by a plan that provided for payment of the full $20,000 of the claim, with interest to be paid on the entire $20,000 debt.[367] Most

---

[364] Robin Miller, Annotation, *Effect of "Hanging" or "Anti-Cramdown" Paragraph Added to 11 U.S.C.A. § 1325(a) by Bankruptcy Abuse Prevention and Consumer Protection Act (BAPCPA)*, 19 A.L.R. Fed. 2d 157 (2007); William C. Whitford, *A History of the Automobile Lender Provisions of BAPCPA*, 2007 U. Ill. L. Rev. 143 (2007).

[365] *See* In re Carver 338 B.R. 521, 523 (Bankr. S.D. Ga. 2006). As a testament to the lack of care involved in enacting the 2005 Amendments, "hanging paragraphs" also appear in §§ 342(c) and 522(b)(3).

[366] The new language is sometimes hard to locate. *See* In re Carver 338 B.R. 521, 523 (Bankr. S.D. Ga. 2006); In re Payne, 347 B.R. 278 (Bankr. S.D. Ohio 2006); In re Phillips, No. 06–71604-SCS,2007 Bankr. LEXIS 791, *28 n. 7 (Bankr. E.D. Va. 2006). In some publications, it appears as if it were an additional lengthy sentence made a part of § 1329(a)(9). In other publications it is set apart as an unnumbered additional paragraph between §§ 1329(a) and 1329(b). Congress' failure to provide it with its own designated home in the Bankruptcy Code is a testament to the poor drafting that typifies the legislation that many bankruptcy professionals now refer to as "BAPCRAP." *Cf.* David C. Farmer, *Bankruptcy Reform: Like a BAPCPA Out of Hell?*, 10 Haw. B.J. 6 (2006).

[367] Though this is not yet entirely clear, new § 1325(a)(5)(B)(iii)(II), which requires that the stream of payments be sufficient to ensure that the creditor is adequately protected, would seem to be satisfied

courts applying the hanging paragraph have applied it in this fashion.[368]

Initially, a few commentators and at least one court suggested that the "plain meaning" of hanging paragraph of § 1325(a) turned a secured creditor's claim into an *unsecured* claim.[369] Despite this apparent plain meaning,[370] permitting the hanging paragraph to treat secured creditors as unsecured would have turned the legislative intent of the provision on its head.[371] As one court put it, it is "unlikely that Congress would create a new, undefined type of claim, and then furnish no guidance as to how such a claim should be handled. Rather, this Court turns to basic principles of Code interpretation and finds that a 910-paragraph claim is an allowed secured claim and may be treated under § 1325(a)(5)."[372]

A few other courts have made the similar suggestion that the hanging paragraph eliminates a partially secured creditor's deficiency claim after the debtor has surrendered the collateral to the creditor or after the creditor has repossessed and sold the collateral, after obtaining relief from the automatic stay. For example, in *In re Pinti*,[373] the bankruptcy court ruled that the hanging paragraph language precludes any bifurcation of claims secured by 910-day motor vehicles.[374] However, most courts have rejected this reasoning. The hanging paragraph operates in favor of secured creditors by restricting Chapter 13 cramdown.[375]

Before 2005, debtors enjoyed two benefits in Chapter 13 with respect to secured creditors. The debtor could strip down the lien and reduce the amount of its payments to reflect current interest rates. The 2005 amendments removed the debtor's ability to strip down purchase money liens on 910-day automobiles, but did not eliminate the debtor's ability to otherwise alter the terms of the secured debt, such as by reducing the interest rate, or extending the amortization period of the loan.[376] Although the hanging paragraph prohibits the debtor from stripping off the creditor's lien, it does not prohibit other modifications of the secured creditor's claim.

---

if the amortization rate of the debtor's payments keeps up with the depreciation rate of the $16,000 value of the collateral.

[368] In re Brown, 339 B.R. 818 (Bankr. S.D. Ga. 2006); In re Johnson, 337 B.R. 269 (Bankr. M.D.N.C. 2006); In re Robinson, 338 B.R. 70 (Bankr. W.D. Mo. 2006); In re Wright, 338 B.R. 917 (Bankr. M.D. Ala. 2006).

[369] Timothy D. Moratzka, *The "Hanging Paragraph" and Cramdown: Bankruptcy Code §§ 1325(a) and 506 after BAPCPA*, (Am. Bankr. Inst. J.) May 25, 2006, at 18, 57.

[370] *See* In re Dean, 537 F.3d 1315, 1319 n.4 (11th Cir. 2008).

[371] *Id.* at 1320.

[372] In re Lowder, 2006 Bankr. LEXIS 1191 (Bankr. D. Kan., June 28, 2006); In re DeSardi, 340 B.R. 790, 812 (Bankr. S.D. Tex. 2006); *see also* In re Montoya, 341 B.R. 41 (Bankr. D. Utah 2006); In re Brown, 339 B.R. 818 (Bankr. S.D. Ga. 2006).

[373] 363 B.R. 369 (Bankr. S.D.N.Y. 2007).

[374] *See also* In re Lanier, 372 B.R. 727, 730 (Bankr. M.D. Pa. 2007).

[375] AmeriCredit Fin. Serv's, Inc. v. Tompkins (In re Tompkins), 604 F.3d 753 (2d Cir. 2010); In re Miller, 570 F.3d 633, 637 (5th Cir. 2009).

[376] In re Velez, 431 B.R. 567 (Bankr. S.D.N.Y. 2010); In re Johnson, 337 B.R. 269, 271 (Bankr. M.D.N.C. 2006) (Chapter 13 plan may still modify the term of the loan and interest rate, even if bifurcation is not allowed).

[b]   910-Day Automobiles

The hanging paragraph only applies to certain purchase money security interests. Its biggest impact is with respect to purchase money security interests in recently purchased motor vehicles.[377] In these cases it applies only if the debt was "incurred within the 910-day [period] preceding the date of the filing of the petition . . . ." Nine-hundred and ten days is approximately two and a half years. With many auto finance deals now lasting for five and sometimes six years, the hanging paragraph will affect auto purchase loans only for the first half of so of their duration. The 910 day limit will have a dramatic effect when the debtor is unable to delay filing his Chapter 13 petition until after expiration of the time period. If debtor bought the car within the 910 days immediately before his petition, his plan will have to pay the outstanding amount of the debt in full. If the debtor bought the car more than 910 days before his petition, he will only have to pay what it would cost the debtor to purchase a similar car on the used car market.[378]

[c]   Personal Use

The provision is also limited to situations where the motor vehicle was "acquired for the personal use of the debtor." Thus, autos acquired for a business purpose are not subject to the rule.[379] The normal ways of expressing this would have been to refer to the collateral as "consumer goods,"[380] to refer to the debt secured by the collateral as a "consumer debt,"[381] or to make the language applicable only to motor vehicles purchased for "personal, family, or household purposes." The absence of these customary terms means that the section might not apply to goods purchased for use by someone else in the debtor's family, such as the debtor's spouse or child. On the other hand, it might mean that it will apply to motor vehicles purchased for a business purpose, so long as the debtor is the one who will ordinarily be expected to personally drive the car. Assuming these questions are resolved, in determining whether the debtor's use was personal, courts may examine loan application documents, whether business use was required by the debtor's employer, and whether the debtor's mileage logs sufficiently support the debtor's contention that his use was other than personal.[382]

---

[377] For the purpose of the hanging paragraph, "motor vehicle" is defined in accordance with 49 U.S.C. § 30102 (2000). This definition applies broadly to any "vehicle driven or drawn by mechanical power and manufactured primarily for use on public streets, roads, and highways, but does not include a vehicle operated only on a rail line." Non-motorized bicycles don't count.

[378] Section 506(a)(1) specifies that the amount of the allowed secured claim will be based on the replacement value of the collateral. *See* § 10.03[C] Allowance of Secured Claims, *supra.*

[379] *E.g.*, In re Ozenkoski, 417 B.R. 794 (Bankr. E.D. Mo. 2009) (traveling book salesman's auto).

[380] *Cf.* U.C.C. § 9-102 (2010).

[381] Bankruptcy Code § 101(8).

[382] *See* In re Powell, 2010 U.S. Dist. LEXIS 40718 (C.D. Ill. April 26, 2010).

[d]   Other Collateral

With respect to a purchase money security interest in other collateral, referred to in the hanging paragraph as "any other thing of value," the language only applies if the "debt was incurred during the 1-year period preceding [the debtor's petition]." Thus, with respect to collateral other than a motor vehicle,[383] it does not matter whether the collateral was acquired for the personal use of the debtor and thus applies to consumer goods, business equipment, and presumably even inventory owned by a Chapter 13 debtor. Of course, the rising use of unsecured credit cards for consumer purchases makes this provision somewhat less important than it otherwise might be, except with respect to big-ticket consumer items such as furniture and appliances, and even then only if the goods are purchased pursuant to a retail installment purchase contract or other purchase money loan.

[e]   Purchase Money Security Interest[384]

The term "purchase money security interest" has its usual meaning.[385] The provision applies when the security interest was granted to the seller to secure the debtor's obligation to pay the price of the goods, or where it secures a loan that was made and used to enable the debtor to acquire the collateral.[386]

Initially, courts were badly split about the effect of negative equity financing on the purchase money status of the creditor's claim.[387] Negative equity financing refers to the practice of including the amount necessary to pay the debt still owed on the debtor's trade-in vehicle, in the amount loaned to the debtor to purchase a new car. Assume, for example, that Walt owns a gas-guzzling 2007 SUV, worth $6,000, on which he still owes $7000, and that he trades-in the SUV as part of the purchase price of a new environmentally-friendly hybrid sedan. Because he owes $1000 more that the SUV is worth, the financing for the new hybrid will most likely include the $1000 necessary to satisfy debt on the SUV. Assume that the price of the new hybrid is $24,000. Walt will trade in his $6000 SUV for part of the purchase price and borrow an additional $18,000 to pay the balance due on the new car and $1000 more to pay off the balance due on the SUV. His total debt, secured by the new hybrid, will be $19,000.

If two years later, Walt files a chapter 13 case, and seeks to cram-down the debt he still owes on the hybrid, he may claim that the hanging paragraph does not restrict his treatment of the debt on the hybrid, because the debt secured by the hybrid is not solely a purchase money loan — part of the loan was used to pay off

---

[383] *Compare* In re Horton, 398 B.R. 73 (Bankr. S.D. Fla. 2008) ("any other thing" does not refer to motor vehicles used for business purpose), *with* In re Tanguay, 427 B.R. 663 (Bankr. E.D. Tenn. 2010) (plain meaning of "any other thing" includes motor vehicles other than those held for personal use).

[384] Dienna Ching, *Does Negative Equity Negate the Hanging Paragraph?*, 16 Am. Bankr. Inst. L. Rev. 463, 510+ (2008).

[385] Reinhardt v. Vanderbilt Mortgage and Finance Inc. (In re Reinhardt), 563 F.3d 558 (6th Cir. 2009) (mortgage on land and unattached motor home could be stripped-down to the value of the collateral).

[386] U.C.C. § 9-103(b) (2002).

[387] Dienna Ching, *Does Negative Equity Negate the Hanging Paragraph?*, 16 Am. Bankr. Inst. L. Rev. 463 (2008).

the debt on the SUV, not to acquire the hybrid.

While some courts still take a contrary view,[388] there is now a nearly overwhelming consensus that the negative equity portion of the debt is properly regarded as part of the "package deal" that enabled the debtor to acquire the new vehicle.[389] Accordingly, these courts treat the entire lien as a purchase money security interest that is subject to the hanging paragraph's limitations.[390] Moreover, given the absence from the Bankruptcy Code of a definition of "purchase money security interest," most courts look to state law to determine whether the negative equity portion of the debt should be regarded as within the definition.[391]

[f]   Effect of Surrender

Another issue in connection with the hanging paragraph deals with the effect of the debtor's surrender of the collateral on the creditor's unsecured deficiency claim. Debtors have contended that because the hanging paragraph provides that § 506 shall not apply to property covered by the hanging paragraph, that partially secured claims affected by the hanging paragraph are not bifurcated into a secured claim and an unsecured claim. This reasoning leads to the conclusion that surrender of the collateral to the creditor satisfies the claim in full and eliminates the creditor's unsecured claim for any deficiency for amounts owed beyond the value of the collateral. Although some courts adopted this reasoning, most jurisdictions now reject it, and hold that surrender does not eliminate the creditor's state-created right to recover for a deficiency.[392]

[7]   Direct Payments "Outside the Plan"[393]

Payments to secured creditors might also be made outside the plan. The cramdown provisions of § 1325(a)(5) apply only "with respect to each allowed secured claim *provided for by the plan . . . .*"[394] It has long been recognized that a debtor who is not seeking to use Chapter 13 to adjust the rights of a secured creditor through its cramdown provisions or to discharge a portion of the debt is permitted to pay a secured creditor directly on his own, independent of the services

---

[388] *E.g.*, AmeriCredit Fin. Serv. v. Penrod (In re Penrod), 611 F.3d 1158 (9th Cir. 2010); In re Hall, 400 B.R. 516 (Bankr. S.D. W. Va. 2008) (collecting cases).

[389] *See* Nuvell Credit Corp. v. Westfall (In re Westfall), 599 F.3d 498, 503 (6th Cir. 2010); In re Padgett, 408 B.R. 374 (B.A.P. 10th Cir. 2009); Robin Miller, Annotation, *Effect of "Hanging Paragraph" or "Anti-Cramdown" Paragraph Added to 11 U.S.C.A. § 1325(a) by BAPCPA*, 19 A.L.R. Fed. 2d 157 (2007).

[390] *E.g.*, In re Howard, 597 F.3d 852 (7th Cir. 2010) (Posner, J.); In re Ford, 574 F.3d 1279 (10th Cir. 2009); In re Price, 562 F.3d 618 (4th Cir. 2009); In re Dale, 582 F.3d 568 (5th Cir. 2009); In re Shaw, 552 F.3d 447 (6th Cir. 2009); In re Graupner, 537 F.3d 1295, 1301–02 (11th Cir. 2008).

[391] *E.g.*, In re Peaslee, 547 B.R. 177 (2d Cir. 2008); In re Ford, 574 F.3d 1279 (10th Cir. 2009).

[392] *E.g.*, In re Wright, 492 F.3d 829 (7th Cir. 2007); Capital One Auto Finance v. Osborn, 515 F.3d 817 (8th Cir. 2008).

[393] Michaela M. White, *Direct Payment Plans*, 29 Creighton L. Rev. 583 (1996).

[394] Bankruptcy Code § 1325(a)(5) (emphasis added).

of the Chapter 13 Trustee.[395]

[G] Hearing on Confirmation of Plan

The court is required to hold a hearing on confirmation of the debtor's proposed plan. This hearing is normally required to be held in a window between the 20th and the 45th day after the § 341 meeting of creditors, but the court may order the hearing held earlier if no-one objects and the court determines that an earlier hearing is in the best interest of creditors.[396] Twenty-five days advance notice of the hearing is required to be given to these parties.[397] Any party in interest may object to the confirmation.[398]

§ 18.09   EFFECT OF CONFIRMATION OF CHAPTER 13 PLAN

[A] General Effect of Chapter 13 Plan Confirmation

Confirmation of the Chapter 13 plan binds the debtor and every creditor, whether or not the creditor has been provided for by the plan and whether or not the creditor has accepted, objected to, or rejected the plan.[399] Confirmation also vests all property of the estate in the debtor, unless the order of confirmation provides otherwise.[400] Creditors with security interests in estate property will want to make sure that the debtor's plan provides for the creditor to retain its lien, as they are permitted to insist on.

Confirmation does not discharge a Chapter 13 debtor. Unlike most Chapter 11 debtors, Chapter 13 debtors are discharged only on completion of their plan, or upon the granting of a hardship discharge. But, because the case remains pending until the terms of the plan are completed or until the case is dismissed or converted, the automatic stay of § 362 remains in effect.

Confirmation is res judicata with respect to all matters that were or could have been litigated in connection with the confirmation process.[401] The addition of § 1325(a)(5)(B)(iii)(II), which prevents confirmation unless payments to secured creditors provide adequate protection for the creditor's interest in the collateral, removes any doubt that might have existed about whether confirmation precludes secured creditors from subsequently seeking relief from the automatic stay, due to

---

[395] In re Case, 11 B.R. 843, 846 (Bankr. D. Utah 1981) (R. Maybe, J.); *see, e.g.*, In re Aberegg, 961 F.2d 1307 (7th Cir. 1992).

[396] Bankruptcy Code § 1324(b).

[397] Fed. R. Bankr. P. 2002(b).

[398] Bankruptcy Code § 1324(a).

[399] Bankruptcy Code § 1327(a). As a general rule, of course, creditors neither accept nor reject a Chapter 13 plan, because they have no vote on it.

[400] Bankruptcy Code § 1327(b). Property vests free and clear in the debtor unless otherwise provided in the plan or the confirmation order. Bankruptcy Code § 1327(c).

[401] *E.g.*, In re Harvey, 213 F.3d 318 (7th Cir. 2000).

a lack of adequate protection, provided of course that the debtor complies with the terms of the plan.

[B]   Payments Before Confirmation

The commencement of payment is ordinarily pegged to the filing of the plan, not its confirmation. Unless the court orders otherwise, payments must begin within 30 days after the plan is filed.[402] And, plans are usually filed with the debtor's petition.

These pre-confirmation payments are held by the trustee until the plan is either confirmed or not confirmed. If the plan is confirmed, the trustee distributes those payments in accordance with the plan. If the plan is not confirmed, the trustee returns the payments, minus any allowed administrative expenses, to the debtor.[403] After 2005, however, the trustee is permitted to disburse payments to creditors that have "become due" even though the plan has not yet been confirmed.[404] Payments on any unpaid administrative priority debt and of any unpaid portion of the standing trustee's fee must occur prior to or at the same time as each payment to creditors under the plan.[405] Although nothing in the Code requires this, it is generally contemplated that the debtor's payments and the trustee's disbursements occur on a monthly basis.[406]

In addition to any payments provided for in the plan, the debtor must now make both "adequate protection" payments to creditors who hold claims secured by purchase money security interests secured by personal property, before the plan is confirmed.[407] The debtor is also required to make lease payments on leases of personal property that become due after the order for relief.[408] These payments to secured creditors and lessors are to be made directly to the creditor rather than to the trustee. Payments made directly to these creditors will reduce the amount that must be paid under the plan.

§ 18.10   MODIFICATION OF CHAPTER 13 PLANS

Once submitted, Chapter 13 plans are not written in stone. Because Chapter 13 is voluntary, debtors may propose to modify their plans, before or after confirmation. However, the modified plan must meet the same requirements for confirmation as the original plan.[409]

---

[402] Bankruptcy Code § 1326(a)(1).

[403] Bankruptcy Code § 1326(a)(2).

[404] *Id.*

[405] Bankruptcy Code § 1326(b).

[406] Further, § 1325(a)(5)(B)(iii)(I) requires that payments on account of secured claims will be "distributed" in equal monthly amounts. This language does not require the debtor to make payments to the trustee in equal monthly amounts. It refers, instead, to the amounts to be distributed to the secured creditor.

[407] Bankruptcy Code § 1326(a)(1)(C).

[408] Bankruptcy Code § 1326(a)(1)(B).

[409] Bankruptcy Code § 1323(a). *See supra* § 18.06 The Chapter 13 Plan — Required Provisions.

[A] Pre-Confirmation Modification of Chapter 13 Plans

The debtor has the right to modify the plan at any time prior to confirmation. The modified plan must comply with all of the mandatory requirements of section 1322.[410] After the debtor submits a modified plan it becomes "the plan" for the purposes of other provisions of the Code.[411] Any secured creditor who accepted or rejected the original plan is deemed to have accepted or rejected the modified plan unless (i) the modification changes the creditor's rights and (ii) the creditor changes its previous acceptance or rejection.[412] Since unsecured creditors do not vote on a Chapter 13 plan, their view of the modified plan is irrelevant.

[B] Post-Confirmation Modification of Chapter 13 Plans

The rules regarding modification of a plan after it has been confirmed depart somewhat from the notion that Chapter 13 cases must be entirely voluntary. A Chapter 13 case cannot be commenced by a creditor,[413] nor may a creditor file an initial plan.[414] Nevertheless, unsecured creditors or the standing trustee may propose modifications of the debtor's plan after it has been confirmed.[415] To this rather limited extent, a Chapter 13 debtor may be forced into a plan he or she does not want, or, more precisely, may be forced to chose between accepting an unwanted plan or converting to Chapter 7 or dismissing the case altogether.[416]

A modification may be proposed by the debtor, an unsecured creditor, or the trustee at any time after confirmation but before completion of payments. The modification may (i) increase or decrease payments, (ii) extend or reduce the time for payments, (iii) alter the distribution to a creditor to the extent necessary to take account of payments made outside the plan, or (iv) reduce the amounts to be paid under the plan by the amount of "the actual amount expended by the debtor to purchase health insurance for the debtor and any of the debtor's dependents who do not otherwise enjoy health insurance coverage."[417] For example, plans are commonly modified to require the debtor to turn over any tax refunds or inheritances to the trustee for distribution to creditors.[418]

---

[410] Bankruptcy Code § 1323(a). *See supra* § 18.06 The Chapter 13 Plan — Required Provisions.

[411] Bankruptcy Code § 1323(b).

[412] Bankruptcy Code § 1323(c).

[413] Bankruptcy Code § 303(a).

[414] Bankruptcy Code § 1321.

[415] Bankruptcy Code § 1329(a). *See* In re Midgley, 413 B.R. 820 (Bankr. D. Or. 2009).

[416] The debtor always has the right to convert to Chapter 7 and nearly always has the right to dismiss the case voluntarily. Bankruptcy Code § 1307(a), (b).

[417] Bankruptcy Code § 1329(a)(4). The expenses for the coverage must be "reasonable and necessary" and must not be "materially larger" than any expenses previously paid by the debtor or than the amount that would be incurred by an otherwise similarly situated debtor. *Id.* It is entirely unclear what the debtor is supposed to do if he cannot otherwise obtain health insurance.

[418] In re Rodger, 423 B.R. 591 (Bankr. D.N.H. 2010).

The plan must comply with the usual requirements for confirmation in "[s]ections 1322(a), 1322(b), 1323(c) . . . and 1325(a) . . . ."[419] However, in applying the best interests test and cram-down requirements, the court will not re-evaluate the debtor's financial position. Instead, these tests depend on the amount and value of the debtor's assets at the time the case was initially filed.[420] However, the rate of interest necessary to satisfy these tests can be re-evaluated, even though the rate of interest required to be paid to satisfy the best interests test and secured creditor cram-down requirements necessarily took into account the possibility that the rate of inflation or the debtor's risk of non-payment might change. Likewise, parties may not use the modification hearing to raise issues that could have been raised at the original confirmation hearing.[421]

Strangely, § 1329(b) does not expressly require a modified plan to comply with the "projected disposable income" requirement of § 1325(b). This seems odd, given that increases in the debtor's income seem to be the most likely circumstance that would give rise to an effort by a creditor or the trustee to seek a modification to the debtor's plan. Most courts that have addressed § 1329(b)'s lack of any reference to the disposable income test, have generally held that § 1325(b) does not apply and thus that the duration of a modified plan may be reduced, irrespective of the requirements of § 1325(b).[422] Other courts have noted that these decisions conveniently ignore the qualifying language of § 1325(a), which makes the confirmation requirements of § 1325(a) expressly subject to the limitations imposed by § 1325(b).[423] Thus, the plain language of § 1325(a), incorporates § 1325(b)'s requirements into the conditions for confirmation of the debtor's original plan, or a modified plan.

The omission of § 1325(b) from § 1329(b) should not be taken to mean that § 1325(b) is inapplicable to modified plans. Section 1329(b) requires that a modified plan comply with § 1325(a). Section 1325(a), in turn, provides that "except as provided in subsection (b), the court shall confirm a plan if" the six requirements of sections 1325(a)(1)-(a)(6) are satisfied.

However, even courts that do not take the qualifying language of § 1325(a) into effect are suspicious of planned efforts to sidestep the projected disposable income requirement. Debtors who submit an initial plan with the intent to subsequently modify it, in an effort to circumvent the time requirement of § 1325(b), are likely to be met with "bad faith" objections under § 1325(a)(3) which requires that the plan be proposed in "good faith."

---

[419] Bankruptcy Code § 1329(b)(1).

[420] Forbes v. Forbes (In re Forbes), 215 B.R. 183 (B.A.P. 8th Cir. 1997).

[421] In re Stage, 79 B.R. 487 (Bankr. S.D. Cal. 1987). However, in *Rowley v. Yarnall*, 22 F.3d 190 (8th Cir. 1994), creditors of a Chapter 12 debtor successfully contended that the plan failed to meet the disposable income test through an objection to the debtors' motion for discharge.

[422] In re Davis, 439 B.R. 863 (Bankr. N.D. Ill. 2010) (collecting cases). *See also* In re Sunahara, 326 B.R. 768 (B.A.P. 9th Cir. 2005) ("Section 1329(b) expressly applies certain specific Code sections to plan modifications but does not apply § 1325(b). Period."). *But see* Forbes v. Forbes (In re Forbes), 215 B.R. 183 (B.A.P. 8th Cir. 1997).

[423] In re King, 439 B.R. 129 (Bankr. S.D. Ill. 2010); In re Keller, 329 B.R. 697 (Bankr. E.D. Cal. 2005).

As with pre-confirmation modifications, any secured creditor who accepted or rejected the original plan is deemed to have accepted or rejected the modified plan unless (i) the modification changes the creditor's rights and (ii) the creditor changes its previous acceptance or rejection.[424] Since unsecured creditors do not vote on the plan, their view of the modified plan is irrelevant. The modified plan becomes "the plan" unless it is disapproved after notice and an opportunity for a hearing.[425]

§ 18.11   REVOCATION OF CONFIRMATION OF CHAPTER 13 PLANS

The rules regarding revocation of an order of confirmation must inevitably balance the interest in fairness to creditors with the interest of others in finality. Thus, the timing and the substantive basis for revocation are both limited. On request of a party in interest, and after notice and an opportunity for a hearing, the court may revoke confirmation if it was procured by fraud. The request must be made within 180 days after the date the order of confirmation was entered.[426] If the order of confirmation is revoked, the court may either convert or dismiss the case under § 1307, or, if the debtor submits a modified plan, that modified plan may be confirmed.[427] If so, the case continues under the new plan.

§ 18.12   "CHAPTER 20"[428]

Before 2005, debtors sometimes sought to gain greater leverage over their home mortgage holders by filing, in succession, a Chapter 7 case and a Chapter 13 case. Before 2005, Chapter 13 did not require a six-year wait between discharges. Thus, it was possible to obtain, in quick succession, a Chapter 7 discharge and a Chapter 13 discharge. These serial cases have been nicknamed "Chapter 20" (7 plus 13).[429]

Chapter 20 has several advantages for consumer debtors. First, it permits them to extend the duration of the automatic stay. Second, it allows them to discharge some debts that were not discharged in their Chapter 7 cases. Third, it delays or prevents foreclosure of their secured debts through "cure and reinstatement" or "cramdown," depending on the nature of the debt and type of collateral. Fourth, it may reduce the amount of the debtor's obligations, and thus make the debtor eligible for relief under Chapter 13's debt limits.[430]

---

[424] Bankruptcy Code § 1323(c).

[425] Bankruptcy Code § 1329(b)(2).

[426] Bankruptcy Code § 1330(a); *but see* In re Thomas, 337 B.R. 879 (Bankr. S.D. Tex. 2006) (invoking § 105(a) to permit revocation of confirmation more than 180 days after confirmation due to debtor's fraud).

[427] Bankruptcy Code § 1330(b).

[428] Peenesh Shah, *Post-BAPCPA Availability of Lien-Stripping to a Chapter 20 Debtor*, 85 Am. Bankr. L.J. 161 (Spring, 2011).

[429] *E.g.*, In re Frazier, 448 B.R. 803, 807 (Bankr. E.D. Cal. 2011).

[430] *See* Johnson v. Home State Bank, 501 U.S. 78, 80 (1991). The Chapter 13 debt limits were raised to caps were raised in 2010 to $336,900 in unsecured debt and $1,010,650 in secured debt. They are slated

Although Chapter 20 had been attacked, the Supreme Court's decision in *Johnson v. Home State Bank* broadly validated its use while at the same time noting that in particular cases confirmation of the debtor's Chapter 13 plan might be refused on the grounds of lack of good faith.[431]

The 2005 amendments eliminated most but not all of the incentives to file sequential Chapter 7 and 13 cases. Debtors are no longer able to obtain a Chapter 13 discharge "if the debtor has received a discharge in a case filed under chapter 7, 11, or 12 . . . during the 4-year period preceding the date of the order for relief under this chapter."[432] However, section 1328(f) does not prevent debtors from filing a Chapter 13 petition on the heels of a Chapter 7 discharge, it merely prevents the debtor from obtaining a subsequent Chapter 13 *discharge.*

Even without a discharge, debtors may still invoke Chapter 13 to reimpose the automatic stay and pay debts not discharged in the Chapter 7 case in an orderly fashion, pursuant to a plan, or to cure and reinstate secured debts. Some courts have suggested that Chapter 20 can still be used to invoke Chapter 13's lien-stripping provisions,[433] or to reduce monthly interest payments on secured debts, at least while the case is pending.[434] Despite these potential advantages, some courts have been skeptical of this strategy and have ruled that Chapter 13 debtors who are not eligible for a Chapter 13 discharge, because of their recent Chapter 7 discharge, cannot "strip off" even wholly unsecured junior mortgage liens from their homes, even after successfully completing payments required by their Chapter 13 plans.[435]

---

for periodic adjustment every three years. As with most other dollar amounts in the Bankruptcy Code, these amounts are adjusted every three years by a factor reflecting the increase in the Department of Labor's Consumer Price Index and rounded to the nearest $25 amount that represents the change. Bankruptcy Code § 104(b)(1)(2006). The next adjustments are scheduled for was on April 1, 2013 and 2016.

[431] 501 U.S. 78 (1991); *see* Lex A. Coleman, *Individual Consumer "Chapter 20" Cases After Johnson: An Introduction to Non-Business Serial Filings Under Chapter 7 and Chapter 13 of the Bankruptcy Code,* 9 Bankr. Dev. J. 357 (1992).

[432] Bankruptcy Code § 1329(f)(1).

[433] In re Waterman, 447 B.R. 324 (Bankr. D. Colo. 2011); In re Tran, 431 B.R. 230 (Bankr. N.D. Cal. 2010). *See* Peenesh Shah, *Post-BAPCPA Availability of Lien-Stripping to a Chapter 20 Debtor,* 85 Am. Bankr. L.J. 161 (2011).

[434] *See* In re Lilly, 378 B.R. 232, 236 (Bankr. C.D. Ill. 2007).

[435] *Compare* In re Gerardin, 2011 Bankr. LEXIS 970 (Bankr. S.D. Fla. Mar. 28, 2011), *and* In re Fenn, 428 B.R. 494, 500 (Bankr. N. D. Ill. 2010), *with* In re Okosisi, 451 B.R. 90 (Bankr. D. Nev. 2011), *and* In re Fair, 450 B.R. 853 (E.D. Wis. 2011) (debtor's ability to strip off a wholly unsecured junior mortgage did not depend on his eligibility for a Chapter 13 discharge).

Chapter 19

REORGANIZATION UNDER CHAPTER 11

§ 19.01 DEVELOPMENT OF CHAPTER 11[1]

The goal of bankruptcy reorganization under Chapter 11 is to enable viable but financially troubled businesses to remain in business to preserve their "going concern value." The alternative is usually thought to be piecemeal liquidation, in which the businesses's going concern value is lost. When going concern value is higher than liquidation value, reorganization benefits everyone involved. Creditors receive more, employees keep their jobs, suppliers keep their customers, and the owners may even preserve some of their original investment.[2] Today, the line between liquidation and reorganization is not always as stark, though the logic remains the same. Many "reorganizations" involve significant asset sales, and many "liquidations" seek to preserve the value of particular business units. In short, modern Chapter 11 seeks to preserve going concern value where it exists, and maximize the value of assets when they are sold.

The earliest attempts to reorganize businesses through insolvency law involved nineteenth century railroads that were reorganized through the use of equity receiverships.[3] Bankruptcy law moved into the railroad reorganization arena with old § 77 and into corporate reorganization with former § 77B.[4] Reorganization was embraced more broadly in 1938 by the Chandler Act, which provided four chapters (X, XI, XII, and XIII) that provided reorganization procedures for nearly every type of debtor. Chapters X and XI were the principle mechanisms for reorganizing troubled businesses.

Chapter 11 of the Bankruptcy Code is the successor to Chapters X and XI of the Bankruptcy Act.[5] Those were the business reorganization chapters, each theoreti-

---

[1] Daniel J. Bussel, *Coalition-Building Through Bankruptcy Creditors' Committees*, 43 UCLA L. Rev. 1547, 1552-58 (1996); Douglas G. Baird & Robert K. Rasmussen, *Control Rights, Priority Rights and The Conceptual Foundations of Corporate Reorganizations*, 87 Va. L. Rev. 92, 925-36 (2001); Elizabeth Warren & Jay Lawrence Westbrook, *The Success of Chapter 11: A Challenge to the Critics*, 107 Mich. L. Rev. 603 (2009).

[2] *See* United States v. Whiting Pools, Inc., 462 U.S. 198, 203 (1983).

[3] David A. Skeel, Jr., Debt's Dominion: A History of Bankruptcy Law in America 48-70 (2001); Stephen J. Lubben, *Railroad Receiverships and Modern Bankruptcy Theory*, 89 Cornell L. Rev. 1420 (2004); Edward S. Adams, *Governance in Chapter 11 Reorganizations: Reducing Costs, Improving Results*, 73 B.U. L. Rev. 581, 584-86 (1993); Douglas G. Baird & Thomas H. Jackson, *Bargaining After the Fall and the Contours of the Absolute Priority Rule*, 55 U. Chi. L. Rev. 738, 739-40 (1988).

[4] *See* William L. Cary, *Liquidation of Corporations in Bankruptcy Reorganization*, 60 Harv. L. Rev. 173, 174 (1946).

[5] Chapter 13 is the successor to old Chapter XIII.

cally designed for a different type of reorganization. Chapter X was designed for large public companies, while Chapter XI was designed for smaller, "mom and pop" businesses. This multiplicity of reorganization procedures, each with its own requirements, led to protracted struggles over whether the reorganization should proceed under Chapter X or Chapter XI.[6]

In 1978, Congress eliminated the distinctions between these proceedings, and merged Chapters X and XI into current Chapter 11, as a "one size fits all" reorganization proceeding. Chapter 11 draws on old Chapter XI in the dominant role it gives to the existing management of the debtor, or "debtor-in-possession," and, like old Chapter X, permits the debtor's plan to restructure debts owed to secured creditors. The SEC, which had a prominent a role under old Chapter X, is reduced to the level of a "party in interest" in Chapter 11, but without the right to appeal.[7]

Even individual debtors — living, breathing human beings — can seek protection in Chapter 11, regardless of whether they operate a business.[8] Indeed, now that the 2005 amendments deny high income debtors access to Chapter 7, Chapter 11 may be the only option for debtors who do not satisfy the Chapter 13 debt limits.

Chapter 11 is not without its detractors. In the view of some, Congress went too far in giving control of the Chapter 11 debtor to the debtor-in-possession, which puts members of the debtor's pre-bankruptcy management team in control of the case.[9] In the view of others, more value might be preserved through a swift and cheap auction of the debtor or its assets.[10]

---

[6] *See generally* SEC v. Am. Trailer Rentals Co., 379 U.S. 594 (1965). Note that Chapter XII, which was hardly ever used, was not implicated in this struggle between the two primary reorganization chapters.

[7] *See infra* § 19.03[E] Role of the Securities and Exchange Commission.

[8] Toibb v. Radloff, 501 U.S. 157 (1991). The Court relied primarily on the plain meaning of Bankruptcy Code § 109(e), not to mention the careful explication of the statute and the underlying policy set out in Michael J. Herbert, *Consumer Chapter 11 Proceedings: Abuse or Alternative?*, 91 Com. L.J. 234 (1986).

[9] Douglas G. Baird & Robert K. Rasmussen, *The End of Bankruptcy*, 55 Stan. L. Rev. 751 (2002); Michael Bradley & Michael Rosenzweig, *The Untenable Case for Chapter 11*, 101 Yale L.J. 1043 (1992); Robert M. Lawless & Elizabeth Warren, *The Myth of the Disappearing Business Bankruptcy*, 93 Cal. L. Rev. 743 (2005); Lynn M. LoPucki, *The Debtor in Full Control — Systems Failure Under Chapter 11 of the Bankruptcy Code*, pts. 1 & 2, 57 Am. Bankr. L.J. 99, 247 (1983); Elizabeth Warren & Jay Lawrence Westbrook, *The Success of Chapter 11: A Challenge to the Critics*, 107 Mich. L. Rev. 603, 641 (2009).

[10] Michael Bradley & Michael Rosenzweig, *The Untenable Case for Chapter 11*, 101 Yale L.J. 1043, & 1045 n.11 (1992). *But see* Elizabeth Warren, *The Untenable Case for Repeal of Chapter 11*, 102 Yale L.J. 437 (1992); Donald R. Korobkin, *The Unwarranted Case Against Corporate Reorganization: A Reply to Bradley and Rosenzweig*, 78 Iowa L. Rev. 669 (1993).

§ 19.02   GOALS OF REORGANIZATION[11]

Under Chapter 7, assets are sold piecemeal to provide payment to creditors.[12] Chapter 11, by contrast, allows the debtor to continue to operate its business, and use the income from its operations to repay creditors. Chapter 11 can also be used to liquidate, however, and most reorganizations involve a sale of at least some of the debtor's assets, and may even involve a sale of all of the debtor's operations as a going concern. The recent Chrysler and GM cases are examples of "all asset" sales conducted in Chapter 11.

To understand the goals of Chapter 11, it is necessary to understand the concept of "going concern" value. Consider a business debtor that owns a building, manufacturing equipment, and raw materials. The business employs fifty skilled production workers and seven competent managers. If sold piecemeal, the hard assets might yield $4 million for distribution to the creditors. On the other hand, if the business continues to operate, it might produce $1 million a year in income after the costs of running the business have been paid. If this annual stream of future income is worth more than the $4 million that could be obtained immediately, the debtor's business should be preserved. The key question is whether the income from operations is worth more than the proceeds of liquidation. Methods for valuing an income stream are discussed below, but for the present purposes the question is whether a rational creditor would prefer an income stream of $1 million for the foreseeable future to $4 million now. If the answer is yes, then it makes sense to preserve the business.

In many cases, a manufacturing company, with its equipment, supplies, and personnel already functioning as a combined unit, will be more valuable than the separate items that go into it. The workers have experience working with the machines and with each other. The company has name recognition, customers, and suppliers willing to do business with it. The stream of income that these resources produce is the going concern value that Chapter 11 seeks to preserve.

By contrast, if the firm produces low quality items that nobody wants, keeping it in business will simply burn through cash. The firm's assets would be more valuable if sold off. Needless to say, the devil is in the details, and there are many businesses where some parts of the business have going concern value, while others would be best sold off.

Modern uses of Chapter 11 sometimes seem far removed from its principal purposes. Many modern Chapter 11 cases, including the 2009 reorganizations of General Motors and Chrysler, do not follow the model that Chapter 11's procedures contemplate.[13] Instead of the debtor negotiating the terms of a plan, circulating a disclosure statement, and providing creditors the opportunity to vote on the plan's

---

[11] John D. Ayer, *The Role of Finance Theory in Shaping Bankruptcy Policy*, 3 Am. Bankr. Inst. L. Rev. 53 (1995); Alan Schwartz, *A Normative Theory of Business Bankruptcy*, 91 Va. L. Rev. 1199 (2005); Elizabeth Warren & Jay Lawrence Westbrook, *The Success of Chapter 11: A Challenge to the Critics*, 107 Mich. L. Rev. 603, 641 (2009).

[12] Stephen J. Lubben, *Business Liquidation*, 81 Am. Bankr. L.J. 65 (2007). *See supra* Chapter 17 Liquidation Under Chapter 7.

[13] Barry E. Adler, *Chapter 11 at the Crossroads: Does Reorganization Need Reform? A Reassess-*

provisions, many modern Chapter 11 cases involve a sale of the debtor's most productive assets early in the case, prior to confirmation of a plan of reorganization. As a result, the sale is completed without a full-scale disclosure statement and vote on the terms of the proposed sale. Deviating from the protections embodied in Chapter 11 carries the risk that its system for distributing assets to creditors will be circumvented.[14]

§ 19.03 ROLES OF THE PARTICIPANTS

There are several participants in Chapter 11 reorganizations. They include:

* the debtor and its existing management;

* creditors, who may participate on their own behalf, but who may also be represented by a creditors' committee;

* owners of the debtor, such as shareholders and partners, who, if the court permits, may also be represented by an equity security holders' committee;

* the U.S. Trustee;

* in some cases, a case Trustee, to replace existing management; and

* in cases involving public investors, the Securities and Exchange Commission (SEC).

[A] Role of Existing Management[15]

A unique innovation of Chapter 11 in the U.S. is that the debtor's business remains under the operation and control of incumbent management, as the "debtor-in-possession" of the estate.[16] Thus, the same people who operated the business before bankruptcy remain in control throughout the reorganization process.[17]

Section 1107 authorizes existing management to remain in control of the debtor's affairs. It gives the "debtor-in-possession" the same rights, powers, and duties of a trustee,[18] including the power to "operate the debtor's business."[19]

---

ment of Bankruptcy Reorganization After Chrysler and General Motors, 18 Am. Bankr. L. Inst. Rev. 305 (2010).

[14] *See* Ralph Brubaker & Charles Jordan Tabb, *Bankruptcy Reorganizations and the Troubling Legacy of* Chrysler *and* GM, 2010 Ill. L. Rev. 1375.

[15] *See* Edward S. Adams, *Governance in Chapter 11 Reorganizations: Reducing Costs, Improving Results,* 73 B.U. L. Rev. 581, 584-86 (1993); Thomas G. Kelch, *The Phantom Fiduciary: The Debtor in Possession in Chapter 11,* 38 Wayne L. Rev. 1323 (1992); Lynn M. LoPucki, *The Debtor in Full Control — Systems Failure Under Chapter 11 of the Bankruptcy Code,* pts.1 & 2, 57 Am. Bankr. L.J. 99, 247 (1983).

[16] Bankruptcy Code § 1101(1). *See also supra* § 4.02 Debtors and Debtors-in-Possession.

[17] Bankruptcy Code § 1107(a). *See supra* § 4.02[B] Debtor-in-Possession.

[18] Bankruptcy Code § 1107(a).

[19] Bankruptcy Code § 1108.

This raises some obvious concerns: if the debtor is in financial difficulty because of mistakes made by its managers, their retention seems foolish. On the other hand, replacing existing managers is risky and expensive. Members of any new management team hired to take over the failing debtor must learn about the business and its operations. They must do so at a time when the demands of both operation and reorganization allow little time for on-the-job training. In addition, the appointment of new managers sacrifices existing relations with suppliers, customers, and employees.

Indeed, in many cases, key creditor constituencies lose faith in existing management before the debtor files its bankruptcy petition. New managers may be installed before the case is filed. These new managers are often "turnaround specialists" who have particular skills with managing financially troubled businesses. If this transition does not happen before bankruptcy, it frequently happens shortly afterwards.

Even though no trustee is usually appointed, the officers and managers of the debtor cannot function the same way that they did before bankruptcy. The managers are now responsible principally to the creditors not the owners.[20] Their ability to run the business is constrained by rules requiring the debtor to seek court permission to enter into transactions that are outside the ordinary course of business. Creditors, who have additional access to information about the debtor's operations, must be given the opportunity to object to the debtor's proposed actions.

[B]   Role of Creditors and Creditors' Committees[21]

[1]   Individual Creditors

Individual creditors may play a large or small role in a Chapter 11 reorganization, depending primarily on the relative size of their claims and whether their claims are fully secured, partially secured, or unsecured. If the debtor wants to use a creditor's collateral to operate its reorganized business, the creditor's role will be significant. On the other hand, if the debtor plans to surrender or sell the creditor's collateral, the creditor's role is likely to be minimal.

---

[20] Susan M. Freeman, *Are DIP and Committee Counsel Fiduciaries for Their Clients' Constituents or the Bankruptcy Estate? What Is a Fiduciary, Anyway?*, 17 Am. Bankr. Inst. L. Rev. 291 (2009); Steven H. Nickles, *Behavioral Effect of New Bankruptcy Law on Management and Lawyers: Collage of Recent Statutes and Cases Discouraging Chapter 11 Bankruptcy*, 59 Ark. L. Rev. 329, 400-01 (2006).

[21] Daniel J. Bussel, *Coalition-Building Through Bankruptcy Creditors' Committees*, 43 UCLA L. Rev. 1547 (1996); Andrew DeNatale, *The Creditors' Committee Under the Bankruptcy Code — A Primer*, 55 Am. Bankr. L.J. 43 (1981); Kenneth N. Klee & K. John Shaffer, *Creditors' Committees Under Chapter 11 of the Bankruptcy Code*, 44 S.C. L. Rev. 995 (1993); Lynn M. LoPucki, *The Debtor in Full Control — Systems Failure Under Chapter 11 of the Bankruptcy Code?*, pts. 1 & 2, 57 Am. Bankr. L.J. 99, 247 (1983); Churchill Rodgers, *Rights and Duties of the Committee in Bondholders' Reorganizations*, 42 Harv. L. Rev. 899 (1929); Greg M. Zipes & Lisa L. Lambert, *Creditors' Committee Formation Dynamics: Issues in the Real World*, 77 Am. Bank. L.J. 229 (2003).

Chapter 11 plans cannot be confirmed consensually without the approval of creditors holding two-thirds of the amount of unsecured claims.[22] Thus, creditors with larger unsecured claims may have considerable influence in negotiations that lead to the debtor's plan. Creditors with more than a third of the debt in a class of claims can block confirmation of a debtor's plan, unless it meets the requirements of "cramdown." Large creditors whose claims are not quite large enough to block the plan entirely are still likely to have a big impact on the votes of smaller creditors who will follow the leadership of those with more at stake in the case. Small creditors, whose claims can be paid in cash at the outset of the plan's implementation, will have limited influence, and, in most cases, lack a sufficient incentive to try to take a larger role.

[2] Creditors' Committees[23]

Except for "small business" cases,[24] the U.S. Trustee appoints an official creditors' committee to assist the debtor in its effort to reorganize. In some cases, there may be more than one such committee.[25] The basic function of a creditors' committee is to act as advisor to and watchdog over the debtor, and to negotiate and appear on behalf of the creditors generally.

Ideally, the creditors' committee scrutinizes the debtor's actions, makes recommendations concerning such matters as appointment of a trustee or examiner, and serves as the creditors' representative in negotiating the plan. Unfortunately, committees do not function equally well in all cases. In cases where there is not likely to be a large distribution to creditors, the committee may not be active, and in small Chapter 11 proceedings, it is sometimes impossible to assemble a creditors' committee.[26] When this happens, the U.S. Trustee is left to fill the void and perform many of the committee's responsibilities.

Creditors' committees are required to provide other creditors with access to information about the debtor and the reorganization process.[27] Wide circulation of information about the debtor carries with it the risk of the inappropriate dissemination of trade secrets and other private information about the debtor's customers and employees. These concerns can be dealt with via an appropriate protective order.[28]

---

[22] *See infra* § 19.09[C] Voting by Classes of Claims and Interests.

[23] Kurt F. Gwynne, *Intra-Committee Conflicts, Multiple Creditors'Committees, Altering Committee Membership and Other Alternatives for Ensuring Adequate Representation Under Section 1102 of the Bankruptcy Code*, 14 Am. Bankr. Inst. L. Rev. 109 (2006).

[24] *See infra* § 19.14 Small Business Debtors.

[25] *See also supra* § 4.04[B] Creditors and Creditors' Committees.

[26] In an effort to encourage participation on creditors' committees, the court is permitted to reimburse committee members' out-of-pocket expenses from the estate. Bankruptcy Code § 503(b)(3)(F).

[27] Bankruptcy Code § 1102(b)(3). *See* In re S & B Surgery Center, Inc., 421 B.R. 546 (Bankr. C.D. Cal. 2009) (committee required to establish web-site to provide information to other creditors).

[28] *E.g.*, In re Refco, Inc., 336 B.R. 187 (Bankr. S.D.N.Y. 2006). *See* Jonathan C. Lipson & Christopher M. DiVirgilio, Controlling the Market for Information in Reorganization, 18 Am. Bankr. Inst. L. Rev. 647 (2010).

Significantly, expenses incurred by creditors' committees, including the expense of hiring attorneys, accountants, appraisers, and other professionals, are allowable administrative expenses.[29] In the right circumstances, members of the committee may even receive compensation from the estate for expenses that were incurred before the committee was officially established.[30]

Members of a creditors' committee are selected by the United States Trustee[31] from among eligible unsecured creditors.[32] The committee should be representative of the various types of unsecured creditors,[33] and is ordinarily comprised of holders of the seven largest unsecured claims who are willing to serve.[34]

This in itself can create problems. In some Chapter 11 cases, there are fewer than seven unsecured creditors. There are many in which only one or two unsecured claims are large enough to make it worth the creditors' while to serve on the committee. The U.S. Trustee has no power of conscription; only those who are "willing to serve" are appointed.[35]

There are also frequent conflicts of interest that prevent creditors from participating on a creditors' committee.[36] Large unsecured creditors may also hold a large secured claim. For example, a creditor owed $650,000 that is secured by $500,000 worth of collateral may be one of the largest unsecured creditors because of its $150,000 unsecured deficiency claim. Because of its secured status, this creditor may prefer that the debtor be liquidated, even where liquidation is not in the best interests of the unsecured creditors. The secured creditor might prefer quick repayment of the secured portion of the claim over the delay and risk associated with seeking a larger dividend on the unsecured claim through reorganization. It is generally accepted that the members of the creditors' committee owe a fiduciary duty to unsecured creditors[37] A partially secured creditor's conflict of interest in this regard may prevent it from fulfilling that duty. At the same time, if such a creditor is excluded, the likelihood that the committee will even exist, let alone do anything, is greatly reduced. For this and other reasons, partially secured creditors are not automatically disqualified from serving on the creditors' commit-

---

[29] Bankruptcy Code § 1103.

[30] *E.g.*, In re Motors Liquidation Co., 438 B.R. 365 (Bankr. S.D.N.Y. 2010).

[31] Bankruptcy Code § 1102.

[32] Bankruptcy Code § 1102(a)(1).

[33] Bankruptcy Code § 1102(a)(1).

[34] Bankruptcy Code § 1102(b)(1).

[35] Bankruptcy Code § 1102(b)(1).

[36] Carl A. Eklund & Lynn W. Roberts, *Bankruptcy Ethics: Article: The Problem with Creditors' Committees in Chapter 11: How to Manage the Inherent Conflicts Without Loss of Function*, 5 Am. Bankr. Inst. L. Rev. 129 (1997); Greg M. Zipes & Lisa L. Lambert, *Creditors' Committee Formation Dynamics: Issues in the Real World*, 77 Am. Bankr. L.J. 229 (2003).

[37] In the words of one case, a member of a creditors' committee must be "honest, loyal, trustworthy and without conflicting interests, and with undivided loyalty and allegiance to their constituents . . . . Conflicts of interest on the part of representative persons or committees are thus not [to] be tolerated." Johns-Manville Sales Corp. v. Doan (In re Johns-Manville Corp.), 26 B.R. 919, 925 (Bankr. S.D.N.Y. 1983).

tee.[38]

Creditors have also sometimes been disqualified because of their status as shareholders, officers, directors, competitors, customers, employees, or other insiders.[39] However, these creditors are not automatically disqualified either; whether they are permitted to serve depends not only on the creditor's status, but also on any conduct that demonstrates that it will not act in the best interests of its constituents.[40]

Creditors' committees are sometimes comprised of those who belonged to a pre-petition creditors' committee.[41] In cases where the debtor has engaged in extensive pre-bankruptcy negotiations with an informal creditors' committee in an attempt to frame a work-out agreement, permitting the existing committee to continue to function is more efficient than establishing a new committee. However, the United States Trustee may not appoint any such pre-petition committee as the creditors' committee unless it was "fairly chosen and is representative of the different kinds of claims to be represented."[42]

Occasionally, additional creditors' committees are appointed. This is done, upon the request of a party in interest, if necessary to assure adequate protection of some discreet group of creditors.[43] For example, in some of the mass tort bankruptcies, the tort victims have been given a separate creditors' committee to represent their distinct interests.[44]

[C] Role of Owners[45]

Owners of the debtor's business — in the Code's parlance, "interest holders" — have little formal function *as such* in the Chapter 11 reorganization process. Interest holders include stockholders, partners, and in the case of an individual sole proprietorship, the debtor. They have the right to be heard in matters that affect them,[46] and also have the right to vote on a plan of reorganization.[47]

---

[38] *Compare* In re Walat Farms, Inc., 64 B.R. 65 (Bankr. E.D. Mich. 1986) (partially secured creditor not per se disqualified), *with* In re Glendale Woods Apartments., Ltd., 25 B.R. 414 (Bankr. D. Md. 1982) (partially secured creditor should not serve because of its potential conflict of interest).

[39] Kenneth N. Klee & K. John Shaffer, *Creditors' Committees Under Chapter 11 of the Bankruptcy Code*, 44 S.C. L. Rev. 995, 1012-21 (1993).

[40] *Id.* at 1013.

[41] Bankruptcy Code § 1102(b)(1).

[42] Bankruptcy Code § 1103(b)(1).

[43] Bankruptcy Code § 1102(a)(2).

[44] *See* Ronald J. Bacigal, The Limits of Litigation: The Dalkon Shield Controversy 59-61 (1990). In the *A.H. Robbins* case, which involved a defective intrauterine birth control device, the first tort claimants' committee disintegrated and was replaced by a second committee.

[45] Douglas G. Baird, Robert K. Rasmussenm & Christopher W. Frost, Essay, *Control Rights, Priority Rights, and the Conceptual Foundations of Corporate Reorganizations*, 87 Va. L. Rev. 921 (2001); Christopher W. Frost, *The Theory, Reality and Pragmatism of Corporate Governance in Bankruptcy Reorganizations*, 72 Am. Bank. L.J. 103 (1998); Lynn LoPucki & William Whitford, *Corporate Governance in the Bankruptcy Reorganization of Large, Publicly Held Companies*, 141 U. Pa. L. Rev. 669 (1993).

[46] Bankruptcy Code § 1109(b).

However, some reorganization plans oust these owners and give them nothing on account of their ownership interests. If so, they are deemed to have rejected the plan and there is no need for them to vote.[48]

However, except in cases involving larger publicly-held corporations, the owners of the business are also likely to be its managers. As managers, they have an important role to play in the day-to-day affairs of the debtor-in-possession. But as owners, they are largely irrelevant unless they are able to convince the creditors to permit them to retain a stake in the debtor after it is reorganized.

In a case where creditors are not being paid in full, it is difficult to see why old equity should receive any distribution at all on account of its ownership interest. Nonetheless, creditors are often willing to consent to a small distribution to the old equity to obtain their cooperation. For example, a plan might provide that the reorganized company would be owned 98% by pre-petition creditors (who would in effect be trading their debt for equity in the new company) and 2% by pre-petition stockholders. Such a distribution to old shareholders is permitted only if the creditors agree. Otherwise it would violate the so-called "absolute priority rule."

In rare cases, there is a committee, similar in structure and purpose to a creditors' committee, to represent the interest holders. Upon the request of a party in interest, the court may order the U.S. Trustee to appoint a committee of equity security holders.[49] This is done only if necessary to assure adequate representation of the numerous equity holders when there is some chance that they might receive a distribution.[50] Normally, this committee again consists of the seven largest shareholders.[51]

There is some uncertainty about the degree to which equity holders can continue to assert control over the debtor's management. Outside of bankruptcy, the function of corporate management is to create the maximum return for shareholders on their investment. All of this changes in bankruptcy.[52]

The function of the debtor-in-possession (or, more precisely, those persons who are actually managing the debtor-in-possession) is to act on behalf of the entire bankruptcy estate.[53] This creates a diffuse and sometimes contradictory set of fiduciary duties to all stakeholders in the debtor.[54] As a practical matter, the

---

[47] Bankruptcy Code § 1126(a).

[48] Bankruptcy Code § 1126(g).

[49] Bankruptcy Code § 1102(a)(2).

[50] Bankruptcy Code § 1102(a)(2).

[51] Bankruptcy Code § 1102(b)(2).

[52] Rutherford B. Campbell, Jr. & Christopher W. Frost, *Managers' Fiduciary Duties in Financially Distressed Corporations: Chaos in Delaware (and Elsewhere)*, 32 J. Corp. L. 491 (2007); A. Mechele Dickerson, *Privatizing Ethics in Corporate Reorganizations*, 93 Minn. L. Rev. 875, 932 (2009); Henry T. C. Hu & Jay Lawrence Westbrook, *Abolition of the Corporate Duty to Creditors*, 107 Colum. L. Rev. 1321 (2007); Laura Lin, *Shift of Fiduciary Duty upon Corporate Insolvency: Proper Scope of Directors' Duty to Creditors*, 46 Vand. L. Rev. 1485 (1993).

[53] *See* Official Committee of Unsecured Creditors v. Chinery (In re Cybergenics Corp.), 226 F.3d 237, 243 (3d Cir. 2000); In re Pac. Forest Indus., Inc., 95 B.R. 740 (Bankr. C.D. Cal. 1989).

[54] Raymond T. Nimmer & Richard B. Feinberg, *Chapter 11 Business Governance: Fiduciary Duties,*

debtor-in-possession's efforts normally are aimed at producing a maximum return for creditors, because in nearly all Chapter 11 cases, the debtor is insolvent and the equity interests are completely under water.

One specific question that sometimes arises is whether the shareholders of a Chapter 11 debtor retain their state law right to replace the board of directors. Generally speaking, the courts have allowed shareholders to elect a board, provided this will not interfere with the reorganization process.[55] However, this may be a hollow right. The board cannot unilaterally exercise its most important power — replacing the debtor's management — before confirmation of the debtor's reorganization plan.[56]

[D] Appointment of Trustee or Examiner[57]

In most Chapter 11 reorganization cases, no trustee is appointed to take over the management of the debtor's affairs. Appointment of a trustee is an unusual remedy. Bankruptcy judges understand that replacing existing management with a trustee " 'may impose a substantial financial burden on a hard pressed debtor seeking relief under the Bankruptcy Code,' by incurring the expenditure of 'substantial administrative expenses' caused by further delay in the bankruptcy proceedings."[58]

These expenses are warranted only when both the creditors and the court have lost faith in the ability of incumbent management to turn the business around and no practical alternative exists other than to appoint a trustee to operate the debtor's business. Management may be so incompetent or corrupt that the impact of replacing them, however bad, is preferable to keeping them in place.[59]

Any time after commencement of the case and before confirmation of the plan, the United States Trustee or any party in interest may seek appointment of a trustee to displace management.[60] The Code specifies that after notice and an opportunity for a hearing, the court "shall order the appointment of a trustee" if either of two alternative statutory grounds is established: "for cause, including fraud, dishonesty, incompetence or gross mismanagement of the affairs of the debtor by current management," or "if such appointment is in the interests of

---

Business Judgment, Trustees and Exclusivity, 6 Bankr. Dev. J. 1 (1989).

[55] In re Johns' Manville Corp., 801 F.2d 60 (2d Cir. 1986); Saxon Indus. Inc. v. NKFW Partners (In re Saxon Indus., Inc.), 39 B.R. 49 (Bankr. S.D.N.Y. 1984).

[56] In re Lifeguard Indus. 37 B.R. 3 (Bankr. S.D. Ohio 1983).

[57] Richard Levin & Alesia Ranney-Marinelli, *The Creeping Repeal of Chapter 11: The Significant Business Provisions of the Bankruptcy Abuse Prevention and Consumer Protection Act of 2005,* 79 Am. Bankr. L.J. 603, 618-20 (2005); Clifford J. White III & Walter W. Theus, Jr., *Chapter 11 Trustees and Examiners After BAPCPA,* 80 Am. Bankr. L.J. 289 (2006).

[58] Adams v. Marwil (In re Bayou Group, LLC), 564 F.3d 541, 546-47 (2d Cir. 2009).

[59] *See* In re Bonneville Pac. Corp., 196 B.R. 868 (Bankr. D. Utah 1996) (requiring disgorgement of fees paid to attorneys who represented the debtor-in-possession, due to mismanagement of the debtor's affairs).

[60] Bankruptcy Code § 1104(a).

creditors, any equity security holders, and other interests of the estate."[61]

The mere fact that the debtor's business has been losing money and has found it necessary to file a bankruptcy petition is not, by itself, a sufficient justification for appointing a trustee. Likewise, the mere fact that current management has made bad decisions or has been guilty of some mismanagement is not enough to warrant the appointment of a trustee.[62] Quite to the contrary, Chapter 11 contemplates a strong presumption that the debtor should remain in control of the estate. It imposes the burden on the moving party to demonstrate, by clear and convincing evidence, that appointment of a trustee is necessary.[63]

The duties of a Chapter 11 trustee are nominally the same as those of a Chapter 7 trustee.[64] In practice, though, there are major differences.[65] Chief among these are that the Chapter 11 trustee has a somewhat broader duty to investigate the debtor and report on the results of his investigation to creditors and the court.[66] Moreover, if it is still possible to go forward in Chapter 11, the trustee will prepare a reorganization plan. If reorganization is not feasible, the trustee will recommend either a conversion of the case to Chapter 7, or dismissal.[67]

The court has a less drastic alternative to appointment of a trustee that is more commonly exercised: appointment of an examiner.[68] Upon request, the court will appoint an examiner to investigate the debtor if doing so is in the interests of creditors, equity security holders, and others with an interest in the estate,[69] or if the debtor's fixed, unliquidated, unsecured debts (excluding those for goods, services, or taxes, and those owed to an insider) exceeds $5 million.[70] Thus, if the debtor exceeds the $5 million threshold and a motion is made, the court must make the appointment.[71] But, appointment of an examiner is not mandatory unless someone asks to have one appointed.

In cases where appointment is not mandatory, the courts exercise considerable discretion, just as they do with appointment of trustees. Appointment of an

---

[61] Bankruptcy Code § 1104(a)(1)-(2).

[62] *See* In re Adelphia Commc'n Corp., 342 B.R. 122 (S.D.N.Y. 2006).

[63] Official Comm. of Asbestos Claimants v. G-I Holdings, Inc. (In re G-I Holdings, Inc.), 385 F.3d 313, 317-18 (4th Cir. 2004); In re Sharon Steel Corp., 871 F.2d 1217, 1225 (3d Cir. 1989). *See also* In re Adelphia Commc'n Corp., 336 B.R. 610 (Bankr. S.D.N.Y. 2006).

[64] Bankruptcy Code § 704. *See supra* § 4.05[A] Case Trustees.

[65] Bankruptcy Code § 1106(a).

[66] Bankruptcy Code § 1106(a)(3), (4).

[67] Bankruptcy Code § 1106(a)(5).

[68] Bankruptcy Code § 1104(c). *See* Paula Hunt, Note, *Bankruptcy Examiners Under Section 1104(b): Appointment and Role in Complex Chapter 11 Reorganizations of Failed LBOs*, 70 Wash. U. L.Q. 821 (1992).

[69] Bankruptcy Code § 1104(c)(1).

[70] Bankruptcy Code § 1104(c)(2).

[71] Morgenstern v. Revco. D.S., Inc. (In re Revco D.S., Inc.), 898 F.2d 498 (6th Cir. 1990) (plain language of the Code requires appointment of examiner if unsecured debt exceeds $5,000,000 and U.S. Trustee so moves). *But see* In re Rutenberg, 158 B.R. 230, 233 (Bankr. N.D. Fla. 1993) (examiner not mandatory where appointment would delay administration of the case).

examiner is far less disruptive to the debtor than the appointment of a trustee; thus, the considerations that underlie the reluctance to appoint the latter do not apply in full force when someone seeks appointment of an examiner. However, appointment of an examiner should not be routine. Examiners are expensive and can slow the progress of the case toward a successful plan. Moreover, much of what an examiner does can be done by the creditors' committee — assuming the debtor is cooperative.

An examiner's job is implicit in his title: to investigate "fraud, dishonesty, incompetence, misconduct, mismanagement or irregularity . . . by current or former management of the debtor."[72] The examiner is then to report the results of its investigation to the court and the creditors' committee.[73] The report may include recommendations for further action, such as the appointment of a trustee, or, in the case of misconduct by the debtor's counsel, disallowance of its fees.[74] Recently, examiners are sometimes appointed and given "enhanced powers," normally reserved to the debtor-in-possession or a trustee, such as to pursue lawsuits against third parties[75] (whom members of the debtor's management team may not want to offend) or to otherwise more closely supervise the debtor's affairs.[76]

[E]   Role of the Securities and Exchange Commission

Under the Bankruptcy Act, the Securities and Exchange Commission (SEC) played a crucial role in Chapter X cases, involving publicly traded securities.[77] Moreover, because of the uncertain line between Chapter X and Chapter XI, the SEC also had considerable influence in large Chapter XI cases, even though it had no formal role.[78]

The SEC's role is now considerably diminished. Under § 1109(a), it may raise, appear, and be heard on any issue in a Chapter 11 case.[79] However, it may not appeal from the court's decision on the matter.[80] For many years after enactment of the current Bankruptcy Code, the SEC virtually disappeared from the bankruptcy courts.[81] Whether its role will be expanded in the wake of the financial crisis of the late 2000s, remains to be seen.

---

[72] Bankruptcy Code §§ 1104(c), 1106(a)(3).

[73] Bankruptcy Code § 1106(a)(4).

[74] *See* In re The Leslie Fay Co., 175 B.R. 525 (Bankr. S.D.N.Y. 1994).

[75] *See, e.g.*, In re Apex Oil Co., 111 B.R. 235 (Bankr. D. Mo. 1990).

[76] *E.g.*, In re Boileau, 736 F.2d 503 (9th Cir. 1984); Schuster v. Dragone, 266 B.R. 268 (D. Conn. 2001).

[77] David A. Skeel, Jr., Debt's Dominion: A History of Bankruptcy Law in America 160-66 (2001).

[78] The SEC often engaged in negotiations with borderline Chapter X or Chapter XI debtors to determine the conditions under which the debtor would be, in effect, allowed by the SEC to use the latter chapter.

[79] Bankruptcy Code § 1109(a).

[80] Bankruptcy Code § 1109(a).

[81] Alistaire Bambach, *The SEC in Bankruptcy: Past and Present*, 18 Am. Bankr. Inst. L. Rev. 607 (2010).

[F] Role of the United States Trustee

Some of the vacuum left by the SEC has been filled by the United States Trustee. The U.S. Trustee is an agency of the United States government, operating as part of the United States Department of Justice, with responsibility for supervising some aspects of the country's bankruptcy system. The U.S. Trustee should not be confused with a case trustee, who is appointed to administer specific bankruptcy cases. Case trustees administer bankruptcy cases; the U.S. Trustee supervises case trustees and debtors-in-possession.

In Chapter 11 cases, the U.S. Trustee plays a role in convening meetings of creditors and equity security holders,[82] appointing official creditors' committees and equity interest holders' committees,[83] monitoring and commenting on applications for attorneys' fees and other professionals' compensation,[84] and monitoring cases that involve small business debtors.[85] The U.S. Trustee has standing to seek appointment of a trustee or an examiner,[86] but is unlikely to take this action if there is an active creditors' committee in the case. Likewise, the U.S. Trustee may seek to have a Chapter 11 case converted or dismissed if there are no active creditors and if the case does not seem to be making sufficient progress toward promulgation of a plan.[87]

[G] Role of Others; Insurers

Others may also have a stake in the debtor's reorganization. In cases involving mass tort claims, where the debtor's plan may be funded with proceeds from the debtor's liability insurer, the debtor's insurance carrier will play a significant role. For example, in *In re Global Industrial Technologies, Inc.*,[88] the debtor's plan proposed creation of a trust from which creditors' claims would be paid. The trust was to be funded with money received from various insurers, whose policies were to be assigned to the trust. Even though the insurers' liability to the debtor was contingent, the court held that the insurers were "parties in interest" with standing to challenge the debtor's plan. The court explained that the harm to the insurers was not too speculative to establish standing, because the insurers were the only ones with an adequate incentive to pursue allegations of collusion between the debtor and those who would assert claims against the trust during the process of negotiating terms of the plan. Thus, even though the plan was otherwise neutral with respect to the insurers' liability, and preserved the insurers' rights to contest the validity of individual claims, the insurers had standing to object to the plan's confirmation.

---

[82] *See* Bankruptcy Code § 341(a), (b).

[83] Bankruptcy Code § 1102.

[84] For a discussion of professional compensation under the Bankruptcy Code, see *infra* § 21.03 Professionals' Fees.

[85] 28 U.S.C.S. § 586(a)(7) (2006).

[86] Bankruptcy Code § 1104(a).

[87] Bankruptcy Code § 1112(e).

[88] 645 F.3d 201 (3d Cir. 2011) (en banc).

§ 19.04 PROPERTY OF A CHAPTER 11 ESTATE[89]

The property of a Chapter 11 estate is determined primarily by § 541.[90] Thus, it includes all property interests of the debtor when the petition was filed,[91] together with whatever proceeds, products, offspring, rents, or profits are earned from property of the estate.[92] Unlike a typical Chapter 7 liquidation case where the debtor's business has already ceased operations or is quickly wound up by the trustee, Chapter 11 debtors usually continue their business operations in much the same fashion as they had before the case began. Accordingly, these revenues will likely be considerable. Section 541 also contemplates that the estate will acquire new property rights after commencement of the estate, and that these new assets will belong to the estate.

The post-petition earnings of an individual Chapter 11 debtor are included in the estate, much in the same way that they are for an individual in Chapter 12 or 13.[93] This is consistent with Code language requiring debtors to submit all of their projected disposable income to payments under their plan.[94] However, because § 1129(a)(15) only incorporates § 1325(b)(2), and not § 1325(b)(3), the mechanical means testing rules in Chapters 7 and 13 for calculating the debtor's expenses, do not apply in Chapter 11 cases involving individuals.[95]

Transfer of the debtor's property to the estate is significant primarily because of the restrictions imposed by § 363 on a debtor's ability to use "estate property."[96] As explained in detail elsewhere, the debtor cannot use any estate property outside the ordinary course of business, without court approval.[97] Likewise, property that is "cash collateral" cannot be used even in the ordinary course, without the court's permission.[98] In addition, estate property is protected by the automatic stay.[99]

---

[89] Robert J. Keach, *Dead Man Filing Redux: Is the New Individual Chapter Eleven Unconstitutional?*, 13 Am. Bankr. Inst. L. Rev. 483 (2005).

[90] *See supra* Chapter 7 Property of the Estate.

[91] Bankruptcy Code § 541(a)(1).

[92] Bankruptcy Code § 541(a)(6).

[93] Bankruptcy Code § 1115. *See* Robert J. Keach, *Dead Man Filing Redux: Is the New Individual Chapter Eleven Unconstitutional?*, 13 Am. Bankr. Inst. L. Rev. 483 (2005).

[94] Bankruptcy Code § 1129(a)(15)(B). *See* James Nash, *18th Congressional District Race, Bankruptcy May Haunt Padget*, Columbus Dispatch, Sept. 29, 2006, at D1 (if elected, congressional candidate's salary as member of Congress would be submitted to bankruptcy court to fund candidate's Chapter 11 plan, filed in wake of small town hardware store collapse).

[95] *See* In re Roedemeier, 374 B.R. 264 (Bankr. D. Kan. 2007).

[96] Bankruptcy Code § 363.

[97] *Id.* § 363(c). *See supra* § 9.03[C] Use, Sale, or Lease Outside the Ordinary Course.

[98] Bankruptcy Code § 363(b). *See supra* § 9.03[B] Use of Cash Collateral.

[99] Bankruptcy Code § 362(a).

§ 19.05 CONVERSION AND DISMISSAL OF CHAPTER 11 CASES

Section 1112 provides for both voluntary and involuntary conversion or dismissal when the debtor's attempt to reorganize fails. "Voluntary" conversion or dismissal occurs when the debtor or trustee seeks to end the reorganization effort. They are "involuntary" when creditors or others push the debtor out of its attempt to reorganize.

"Conversion" refers to transferring the case from one chapter of the Bankruptcy Code to another. In the context of a Chapter 11 reorganization case, it involves converting the case from Chapter 11 to Chapter 7. If a case is converted to Chapter 7, a trustee is appointed to take over administration of the debtor's estate, and liquidation is the most likely outcome.

Not surprisingly, the case may be converted to Chapter 7 only if the debtor is otherwise eligible for Chapter 7 relief. Because railroads and some financial institutions are eligible for relief under Chapter 11 alone,[100] their cases cannot be converted. Likewise, because neither farmers nor non-profit organizations may be forced into liquidation through an involuntary bankruptcy petition,[101] their Chapter 11 cases cannot be converted to Chapter 7, over their objection.[102]

Alternatively, the case might be dismissed. This ends the case. Dismissal dissolves the automatic stay, terminates the bankruptcy estate, and permits creditors to renew their efforts to collect from the debtor in state court. Unless the debtor has recovered from its financial difficulties or is able to enter into an out-of-court settlement with its creditors, dismissal leads to piecemeal liquidation of the debtor's assets.

When the debtor has been managed poorly, but the prospects for reorganization are not remote, the court might alternatively appoint a trustee to manage the debtor's estate.[103]

[A] Voluntary Conversion or Dismissal

The language of § 1112(a), which says that "[t]he debtor may convert a case under this chapter," appears to give a Chapter 11 debtor a nearly absolute right to give up on its efforts to reorganize and convert the case to Chapter 7. However, courts usually read this language together with § 1112(b) regarding involuntary conversion and dismissal and dismiss the case, rather than convert it, where involuntary dismissal is otherwise warranted.[104]

---

[100] *See* Bankruptcy Code § 109.

[101] Bankruptcy Code § 303.

[102] Bankruptcy Code § 1112(c). *See* In re Berwick Black Cattle Co., 405 B.R. 907 (Bankr. C.D. Ill. 2009).

[103] *E.g.*, In re Prods. Int'l Co., 395 B.R. 101 (Bankr. D. Ariz. 2008).

[104] Monroe Bank & Trust v. Pinnock, 349 B.R. 493 (E.D. Mich. 2006); In re Adler, 329 B.R. 406 (Bankr. S.D.N.Y. 2005).

As specified in § 1112(a), the debtor also lacks the right to convert the case if (i) the debtor is not a debtor-in-possession (that is, if a trustee has been appointed to administer the estate and the business); (ii) the case began as an involuntary Chapter 11 case; or (iii) the case was previously converted *to* Chapter 11 on the motion of someone other than the debtor.[105]

[B] Involuntary Conversion or Dismissal

A debtor's case can be converted or dismissed involuntarily at the request of any party in interest.[106] Section 1112(b)(4) supplies a long but non-exclusive list of circumstances that require the court to convert or dismiss a case. However, the court always has the discretion to refuse to convert or dismiss if there are "unusual circumstances specifically identified by the court that establish that [conversion or dismissal] is not in the best interests of creditors and the estate."[107] Although the items contained in the laundry list of circumstances warranting conversion or dismissal are conjoined by the word "and,"[108] no-one would plausibly contend that all sixteen specified circumstances must exist to warrant conversion or dismissal.[109] The debtor or other party who resists conversion or dismissal must also demonstrate "that there is a reasonable likelihood that a plan will be confirmed within the time frames established [elsewhere in the Code],"[110] and if the grounds for granting the motion are not among the items specifically listed in § 1112(b)(4), that the act or omission involved both was reasonably justified and will be cured within a reasonable time.[111]

Like motions to lift the stay, hearings on motions for conversion or dismissal are supposed to be begun no less than 30 days after the motion was filed.[112] The court is expected to "decide the motion not later than 15 days after the commencement of [the] hearing, unless the movant expressly consents to a continuance for a specific period of time or compelling circumstances prevent the court from meeting the [specified] time limits."[113] Thus, courts are to decide motions to convert or dismiss a case quickly, before the debtor's assets are further depleted in a fruitless attempt to reorganize.

The specific statutory grounds for conversion or dismissal fall into several broad categories.[114] The most important grounds are those based on the despair that the

---

[105] Bankruptcy Code § 1112(a)(1)-(3).

[106] Bankruptcy Code § 1112(b)(1). Language in former § 1112(b), that explicitly permitted the U.S. Trustee or a bankruptcy administrator to bring the motion, has been removed. However, because § 307 explicitly permits the U.S. Trustee to "appear and be heard on any issue," the language in former § 1112(b) that refers to these parties may have been considered superfluous.

[107] Bankruptcy Code § 1112(b)(1).

[108] Bankruptcy Code § 1112(b)(4)(O).

[109] In re TCR of Denver, Inc., 338 B.R. 494 (Bankr. D. Colo. 2006) ("and" means "or").

[110] Bankruptcy Code § 1112(b)(2)(A).

[111] Bankruptcy Code § 1112(b)(2)(B).

[112] Bankruptcy Code § 1112(b)(3).

[113] Bankruptcy Code § 1112(b)(3).

[114] Bankruptcy Code § 1112(b)(4).

debtor will ever be able to reorganize, usually due to devastating financial circumstances that make the debtor's hopes for successful reorganization unrealistic. Other grounds for conversion or dismissal are based on the debtor's inability or unwillingness to comply with technical requirements imposed on Chapter 11 debtors. The debtor's bad faith in filing the petition, not surprisingly, also provides grounds for conversion or dismissal.

Since a discharge is normally granted when a Chapter 11 plan is confirmed,[115] conversion or dismissal prevents the debtor discharge. However, many of the grounds for conversion or dismissal might also justify appointment of a trustee.[116] In determining whether to convert or dismiss the case, the court is first required to determine whether appointment of a trustee or examiner would be in the best interests of creditors and the estate.[117]

[1] Inability to Reorganize

Cases involving debtors who are financially incapable of reorganizing should be converted or dismissed. The Bankruptcy Code identifies several specific circumstances that indicate a debtor's inability to reorganize successfully. These circumstances nearly always reflect terminal flaws in the debtor's business plan or the debtor's practical inability to effectuate its financial strategies.

Thus, conversion or dismissal is usually warranted if there has been a "substantial or continuing loss to or diminution of the estate," combined with "the absence of a reasonable likelihood of rehabilitation."[118] In other words, if the debtor's income cannot even sustain its operations during the case, there is no reason to believe that it will be able to earn enough money to begin making payments to its creditors.

Consider, for example, an auto repair shop, with rent, utilities, and salaries of $6,000 per month that is earning only $5,500 in monthly revenue. The debtor is losing $500 each month it remains in business, without taking into account its obligations to creditors. It has no hope of reorganizing, and because liquidation is inevitable, the court is likely to convert it to Chapter 7. In the blunt words of an old § 77B case, "however honest in its efforts the debtor may be, and however sincere its motives, the District Court is not bound to clog its docket with visionary or impracticable schemes for resuscitation."[119]

However, a creditor's motion to convert a case during the early stages of the case, when the debtor has not had sufficient time to resolve its underlying business problems, is unlikely to be successful. Chapter 11 debtors are likely to have been losing money in the months leading up to their decision to reorganize, and, other than relieving the debtor of the obligation to pay prepetition debt, there is nothing in Chapter 11 that automatically alters the debtor's ongoing business operations. Debtors should be given time to resolve the problems that led to their financial

---

[115] Bankruptcy Code § 1141(d).

[116] Bankruptcy Code § 1104(a)(1). *See supra* § 19.03[D] Appointment of Trustee or Examiner.

[117] Bankruptcy Code § 1104(a)(3).

[118] Bankruptcy Code § 1112(b)(4)(A).

[119] Tenn. Publ'g Co. v. Am. Nat'l Bank, 299 U.S. 18, 22 (1936).

difficulties. But, if the debtor delays taking action, with nothing more than hope that the estate will increase in value due to improved economic circumstances, conversion is warranted.[120]

Likewise, a debtor's failure to propose a plan or obtain confirmation of a plan within the time limits imposed by the Code is a powerful indicator that the debtor is unlikely to reorganize, and should be liquidated. Accordingly, the Bankruptcy Code specifies that the case should either be converted or be dismissed if, within the time limits imposed by the court, the debtor 1) fails to file a plan, 2) fails to file a disclosure statement regarding a plan that has already been submitted, or 3) fails to obtain confirmation of a plan.[121]

The debtor has an exclusive right to file a plan for 120 days and a minimum of 180 days to have it confirmed.[122] These deadlines can be extended by the court for an outside maximum of eighteen and twenty months, respectively.[123] The court's refusal to extend the deadlines indicates the court's belief that the debtor's prospects for reorganization are slim, and it is likely to prompt a creditor to seek conversion or dismissal. But during the exclusive period, courts generally give the debtor the benefit of the doubt.

"Gross mismanagement of the estate" is a key basis for conversion or dismissal.[124] Mismanagement of the debtor, however severe, before initiation of the case, is not sufficient; the mismanagement complained of must have been that of *the estate*. Moreover, mere negligence in the management of the estate does not constitute grounds for conversion or dismissal. The mismanagement must have been gross. Alternatively, gross mismanagement of the estate might warrant appointment of a trustee or an examiner, particularly if the debtor's prospects for reorganization would improve significantly with the substitution of new management.[125]

The Code also provides for dismissal or conversion due to circumstances that develop after a plan is confirmed. These circumstances include revocation of confirmation under § 1144,[126] the debtor's inability to effectuate "substantial consummation" of a confirmed plan,[127] the debtor's material default with respect to the terms of a confirmed plan,[128] or termination of a confirmed plan due to the failure of a condition specified in the plan.[129]

"Substantial consummation" is a defined term. It means (i) transfer of all or substantially all the property that the plan proposes be transferred; and (ii) the

---

[120] *See* In re Milford Conn. Assoc's, L.P., 404 B.R. 699 (D. Conn. 2009).

[121] Bankruptcy Code § 1112(b)(4)(J). *See* In re Woodbrook Assocs., 19 F.3d 312 (7th Cir. 1994).

[122] Bankruptcy Code § 1121(c).

[123] Bankruptcy Code § 1121(d).

[124] Bankruptcy Code § 1112(b)(4)(B).

[125] Bankruptcy Code § 1104(a)(1). *See supra* § 19.03[D] Appointment of Trustee or Examiner.

[126] Bankruptcy Code § 1112(b)(4)(L). *See infra* § 19.13[B] Revocation of Confirmation.

[127] Bankruptcy Code § 1112(b)(4)(M). *See infra* § 19.13[C] Implementation of the Plan.

[128] Bankruptcy Code § 1112(b)(4)(N).

[129] Bankruptcy Code § 1112(b)(4)(O).

debtor or its successor's assumption of the business or of the management of all or substantially all the property dealt with by the plan; and (iii) commencement of distributions under the plan.[130] It is important to distinguish "substantial consummation" from confirmation. A plan may be approved by the court — confirmed — but the debtor may nonetheless be unable to implement the plan, which usually involves making payments, transferring assets, or taking other practical steps to satisfy the claims of creditors. If the debtor is unable to accomplish these essential tasks, the plan has not been substantially consummated. In plain terms, the debtor's inability to do the things the plan requires justifies conversion or dismissal.[131]

[2] Failure to Comply with Code Requirements

The Bankruptcy Code imposes an array of duties on Chapter 11 debtors. Failure to perform these duties constitutes grounds for dismissal or conversion. Section 1112(b)(4) identifies several such failures that provide grounds for dismissal or conversion unless the debtor demonstrates that the failure was due to unusual circumstances, not customarily encountered in a Chapter 11 reorganization, and that conversion or dismissal is not in the best interests of creditors and the estate. Most of these specific grounds reflect the debtor's inability to maintain viable ongoing business operations. Others are designed to ensure the integrity of the reorganization process.

Thus, a debtor's case can be dismissed for any of the following:

- "failure to maintain appropriate [property or liability] insurance that poses a risk to the estate or to the public";[132]

- "unauthorized use of cash collateral [that is] substantially harmful to [one] or more creditors";[133]

- the debtor's "failure to comply with an order of the court," which can have a devastating effect on the viability of a case;[134]

- the debtor's "failure to satisfy timely any filing or reporting requirement established by this title or by any [applicable] rule";[135]

- the debtor's failure to attend the § 341 meeting of creditors convened after the filing of a Chapter 11 petition, or to attend an examination of the debtor ordered pursuant to Bankruptcy Rule 2004;[136]

---

[130] Bankruptcy Code § 1101(2).

[131] The plan can be modified either before or after its confirmation. If the modified plan is confirmed, it becomes the plan that must be substantially consummated. *See infra* § 19.12 Modification of Chapter 11 Plans.

[132] Bankruptcy Code § 1112(b)(4)(C). *See* In re Daniels, 362 B.R. 428, 435-36 (Bankr. S.D. Iowa 2007) (practicing attorney required to maintain professional malpractice insurance); In re KC's Pub, LLC, 428 B.R. 612 (Bankr. M.D. Pa. 2010) (dram shop liability coverage).

[133] Bankruptcy Code § 1112(b)(4)(D).

[134] Bankruptcy Code § 1112(b)(4)(E).

[135] Bankruptcy Code § 1112(b)(4)(F). *E.g.*, In re Robino, 243 B.R. 472, 485-86 (Bankr. N.D. Ala. 1999).

[136] Bankruptcy Code § 1124(b)(4)(G).

- the debtor's "failure timely to provide information or attend meetings reasonably requested by the U.S. Trustee";[137]

- the debtor's failure to pay any taxes "owed after the date of the order for relief or to file tax returns due after the date of the order for relief" warrants conversion or dismissal of the debtor's case;[138] and

- the debtor's failure to pay any "domestic support obligation that first becomes payable after the date of the filing of the petition" is grounds for conversion or dismissal.[139]

This final language only applies to the few Chapter 11 cases filed by individual debtors, as corporations and partnerships do not have domestic support obligations.[140]

[3] Bad Faith Filing[141]

In addition to these specific statutory grounds, a Chapter 11 case may be also dismissed if it was filed in bad faith.[142] The precise parameters of this judicially created rule are both uncertain and controversial. Courts do not agree whether good faith should be measured by a subjective test that focuses on the debtor's intent[143] or an objective test that focuses on the debtor's practical ability to reorganize.[144]

The issue of dismissal due to bad faith often arises in cases that deviate from the traditional pattern of Chapter 11. For example, good faith challenges have been made to the use of Chapter 11 as a means of dealing with products liability litigation.[145] The most important and common use of "bad faith" filing has been in single asset real estate cases.[146] These cases involve debtors with only one substantial asset, usually an apartment or office building. They usually also have

---

[137] Bankruptcy Code § 1112(b)(4)(H).

[138] Bankruptcy Code § 1112(b)(4)(I).

[139] Bankruptcy Code § 1112(b)(4)(P).

[140] Bankruptcy Code § 101(14A).

[141] Ali M.M. Mojdehi & Janet Dean Gertz, *The Implicit "Good Faith" Requirement in Chapter 11 Liquidations: A Rule in Search of a Rationale?*, 14 Am. Bankr. Inst. L. Rev. 143 (2006); Janet Flaccus, *Have Eight Circuits Shorted? Good Faith and Chapter 11 Bankruptcy Petitions*, 67 Am. Bankr. L.J. 401 (1993); Lawrence Ponoroff & F. Stephen Knippenberg, *The Implied Good Faith Filing Requirement: Sentinel of an Evolving Policy*, 85 Nw. U. L. Rev. 919 (1991).

[142] Little Creek Dev. Co. v. Commonwealth Mortgage Corp. (In re Little Creek Dev. Co.), 779 F.2d 1068, 1071 (5th Cir. 1986); In re Victory Constr. Co., Inc., 9 B.R. 549, 551-58 (Bankr. C.D. Cal. 1981).

[143] *See* In re Phoenix Piccadilly, Ltd., 849 F.2d 1393 (11th Cir. 1988).

[144] *See* Carolin Corp. v. Miller, 886 F.2d 693 (4th Cir. 1989).

[145] *See* In re Johns-Manville, 36 B.R. 727 (Bankr. S.D.N.Y. 1984), *appeal denied*, 39 B.R. 234 (S.D.N.Y. 1984); Sandrea Friedman, Note, Manville: *Good Faith Reorganizations or "Insulated Bankruptcy,"* 12 Hofstra L. Rev. 21 (1983); Jonathan C. Lipson, *Fighting Fiction with Fiction — The New Federalism in (A Tobacco Company) Bankruptcy*, 78 Wash. U. L.Q. 1271 (2000).

[146] Brian S. Katz, *Single Asset Real Estate Cases and the Good Faith Requirement: Why Reluctance to Ask Whether a Case Belongs in Bankruptcy May Lead to the Incorrect Result*, 9 Bankr. Dev. J. 77 (1992).

only one substantial creditor — the bank that loaned the money to purchase or build the building.[147] Chapter 11 is a "collective" proceeding designed to solve the coordination problems that arise when a debtor has multiple creditors competing for assets. In these cases, the concern is that it is the debtor using bankruptcy as a tactic to delay resolution of a simple two-party dispute (usually to stall a foreclosure) that could be just as easily handled in state court.[148] An apartment or office building has no real going concern value apart from the rent that it generates from its tenants. This cash flow is either sufficient to pay the mortgage (in which case the debtor has equity in the property, and bankruptcy is not necessary), or it is not, in which case the mortgage lender should be able to foreclose. There are no particular obstacles to negotiation that Chapter 11 can overcome, and courts are concerned that they are merely being used as a tool to add cost and delay while the debtor waits out the local economy.

§ 19.06 POST-PETITION OPERATION OF THE DEBTOR'S BUSINESS

Chapter 11 debtors-in-possession are automatically authorized to operate the debtor's business.[149] This authority may only be revoked upon the request of a party in interest after notice and an opportunity for a hearing.[150] However, this constitutes authority to operate in the ordinary course of business only; court permission must be obtained for non-ordinary course transactions (and for incurring secured debt).[151]

Because of the ongoing nature of a Chapter 11 case and the continued operation of the debtor's business, a number of the familiar provisions of the Code operate differently in that Chapter. For example, the automatic stay is of much longer duration in a Chapter 11 (and Chapter 13) case. As a result, the creditor's loss of its repossession rights are more significant. Moreover, during the pendency of the stay, the debtor may continue to use the creditor's collateral, which may decline in value. There are also a few rules that apply to very narrow issues that arise only in some Chapter 11 cases and an entire subchapter that deals with railroad reorganizations. In addition, Chapter 11 contains specific provisions for rejecting collective bargaining agreements[152] and employees' retirement benefit plans. Finally, there are a few special rules regarding security interests and leaseholds in ships and airplanes.[153]

---

[147] *See infra* § 23.04 "Single-Asset Real Estate" Cases.

[148] *E.g.,* In re WGMJR, Inc., 435 B.R. 423 (Bankr. S.D. Tex. 2010).

[149] Bankruptcy Code § 1108. A debtor-in-possession enjoys all the same rights, powers, and duties of a trustee. *Id.* § 1107.

[150] Bankruptcy Code § 1108.

[151] *See supra* Chapter 9 Operating the Debtor.

[152] *See infra* § 23.03 Employees' Rights: Collective Bargaining Agreements and Retirement Benefits.

[153] Bankruptcy Code § 1110.

[A] Sale and Use of Estate Property

[1] Sale and Use of Property in the Ordinary Course

The debtor's power to use and sell estate property in the ordinary course of business permits the debtor to continue to use its real estate and equipment as part of its ongoing operations and to continue to sell inventory to its customers. However, despite this general authority, continued use of any creditor's collateral, particularly sales of inventory, is likely to raise adequate protection issues under § 362(d)(1). Unless the debtor is able to maintain casualty insurance on the collateral, compensate the creditor for the depreciating value of the collateral, and provide the creditor with a security interest in new items of inventory purchased to replace what the debtor sells, secured creditors will seek relief from the automatic stay due to a lack of adequate protection.[154]

[2] Use of Cash Collateral

The principal exception to the debtor's ability to use estate property in the ordinary course without prior court approval is with respect to cash collateral. "Cash collateral" is "cash, negotiable instruments, documents of title, securities, deposit accounts or other cash equivalents . . . in which the estate and an entity other than the estate have an interest."[155] Cash collateral most commonly arises as proceeds of other property, such as inventory or accounts, in which a creditor holds a security interest. Section 363(c)(2) prohibits a debtor from using cash collateral without first obtaining the consent of the creditor with an interest in the cash collateral or permission from the court.[156] Thus, if the debtor's cash and bank accounts are subject to a creditor's security interest, the debtor usually needs court permission to use the cash in any way. The court must not grant the debtor permission to use cash collateral unless the creditor's security interest is adequately protected.[157] These restrictions impair the ability of most Chapter 11 debtors to continue their business operations for more than a few weeks without seeking court approval to use funds in their bank accounts and other cash equivalents. In many cases, debtors seek court approval to use their cash collateral immediately after filing their petition.[158]

[3] Sale or Use Outside the Ordinary Course

A Chapter 11 debtor needs prior court approval to use, sell, or lease estate property outside the ordinary course of business,[159] regardless of whether a creditor holds a security interest in the affected property. Thus, Chapter 11 debtors

---

[154] Bankruptcy Code § 362(d)(1). *See supra* § 8.06[B][1] For Cause — Lack of Adequate Protection for Secured Creditors.

[155] Bankruptcy Code § 363(a).

[156] Bankruptcy Code § 363(c)(2). *See supra* § 9.03[B] Use of Cash Collateral.

[157] *See* Bankruptcy Code § 363(d)(2); *supra* § 9.03[D] Adequate Protection.

[158] *See infra* § 19.06[C] First-Day Orders.

[159] Bankruptcy Code § 363(b)(1). *See supra* § 9.03[C] Use, Sale, or Lease Outside the Ordinary Course.

whose strategies for resolving their business difficulties include reducing the size of their business and selling or leasing surplus land or equipment must obtain prior court approval. Court approval is usually granted if the proposed sale or use satisfies the business judgment test and is otherwise in the best interests of the estate.

In some cases, the debtor may seek to sell substantially all of the assets of the estate in one or a series of transactions, leaving the estate with nothing but a large bank account. This has been done in many well-known Chapter 11 cases, including those of General Motors and Chrysler. In *In re Adelphia Communications, Inc.*, involving a once well-known cable-TV and internet provider, the debtor sold substantially all of its assets to two of its competitors, Time-Warner Cable Co. and Comcast Corp., for $17 billion.[160] Such sales can effectively reorganize the debtor without complying with the normal process of preparing a disclosure statement and giving creditors the opportunity to vote on the plan. Courts permit such sales if there is a sound business purpose for the transaction,[161] unless aspects of the sale restructure the priority and other rights of creditors.[162] Courts are generally sensitive to the "sub rosa" plan concerns (that the terms of the sale may constitute a de facto plan of reorganization), and will take steps to make sure that interested creditors receive notice and have an opportunity to object. A number of courts have adopted local rules to govern such asset sales.

When the debtor's assets are encumbered by liens of secured creditors, any sale outside the ordinary course will likely leave the buyer "subject to" the secured creditors' rights, unless the debtor obtains approval for the sale of the assets free and clear of existing liens. The Bankruptcy Code authorizes such a sale, provided the secured creditor consents to the sale.[163] Secured creditors are likely to supply their consent if the terms of the sale ensure that the creditor will receive at least as much as it would have obtained if it had been permitted to foreclose. If the sale price exceeds the aggregate value of all liens encumbering the property, creditors have no reason to object and their consent is not required.[164]

Establishing the value of the liens, however, may be an issue. A traditional solution to this problem is to allow the secured party to credit bid (bid the amount of its debt) at the sale. If the creditor thinks the price is too low, they can simply claim the property itself.

This right to credit bid may present a problem for all asset sales. The Supreme Court's 2012 ruling in *RadLAX Gateway Hotel, LLC v. Amalgamated Bank*[165] held that a Chapter 11 plan, which proposed selling a creditor's collateral free and clear

---

[160] *See Bankruptcy Court Backs Adelphia Sale*, N.Y. Times, June 28, 2006, at C7.

[161] *E.g.*, Comm. of Equity Sec. Holders v. Lionel Corp. (In re Lionel Corp.), 722 F.2d 1063 (2d Cir. 1983).

[162] *See* Pension Benefit Guar. Corp. v. Braniff Airways, Inc. (In re Braniff Airways, Inc.), 700 F.2d 935 (5th Cir. 1983). *See also* Comm. of Unsecured Creditors v. Cajun Elec. Power, Coop., Inc. (In re Cajun Elec. Power Coop., Inc.), 119 F.3d 349 (5th Cir. 1997).

[163] Bankruptcy Code § 363(f)(2).

[164] Bankruptcy Code § 363(f)(3).

[165] RadLAX Gateway Hotel, LLC v. Amalgamated Bank, 132 S. Ct. 2065 (2012).

of the creditor's lien, could not be confirmed over the objection of the creditor without giving the creditor the right to submit a "credit bid" for the collateral, pursuant to § 1129(b)(2)(ii).

In single asset cases, this does not present a problem. However, in cases where there are multiple secured creditors with claims against a variety of assets, it may be procedurally very difficult to permit credit bidding. Section 363(k) allows the court to deny the right to credit bid "for cause," but there is very little certainty as to what might constitute "cause."

[B] Post-Petition Financing

Few Chapter 11 debtors are capable of continuing in business without obtaining additional financing. Even turning the lights on every morning and permitting employees who expect to be paid to show up for work involves an extension of credit by the local electricity provider and by the debtor's employees. Further, most debtors require additional infusions of cash to finance adjustments that they must make to restore their profitability.

To facilitate this, the Bankruptcy Code permits the debtor to "obtain unsecured credit and incur unsecured debt in the ordinary course of business" without prior court approval.[166] Creditors' claims for such advances enjoy an administrative expense priority under § 503(b)(1).[167]

Chapter 11 debtors may also be permitted to incur unsecured debts outside the ordinary course if they obtain prior court approval, after notice and a hearing.[168] Creditors who provide such extensions of credit are also entitled to payment as an administrative expense priority under § 503(b)(1). This priority, combined with Chapter 11's requirement that the debtor's plan provide for full payment of all priority claims, provides post-petition creditors with a substantial assurance of eventual payment.

However, many prospective lenders will not be confident of the debtor's ability to propose, confirm, and consummate a successful reorganization plan. Thus, the debtor may not be able to find lenders who are willing to extend unsecured credit. Section 363(c) recognizes this and allows the debtor, with court approval, to grant a post-petition creditor either a super-priority claim or a security interest in the debtor's assets.[169] Moreover, if existing secured creditors can be adequately protected, the court may authorize the debtor to provide a new lender with a senior lien on already encumbered assets.[170] Post-petition lending is explained in more detail elsewhere.[171]

---

[166] Bankruptcy Code § 364(a). *See supra* § 9.05[B] Unsecured Credit Outside the Ordinary Course.

[167] Bankruptcy Code § 364(a).

[168] Bankruptcy Code § 364(b).

[169] Bankruptcy Code § 363(c). *See supra* § 9.05[C] Secured Credit.

[170] Bankruptcy Code § 363(d).

[171] *See supra* § 9.05 Obtaining Credit.

[C] First-Day Orders[172]

Chapter 11 debtors usually find it necessary to obtain immediate court approval of a variety of matters necessary to continue to operate debtor's business and to get the debtor's reorganization process off the ground.[173] As a result, debtors frequently file a long list of motions along with their petition. These "first-day" motions frequently regard:

- employment and compensation of bankruptcy professionals, such as attorneys, accountants, and investment bankers;[174]

- joint administration of cases involving related debtors;

- extension of deadlines for filing the debtor's schedules and its statement of financial affairs;

- extension of deadlines for giving utilities adequate assurance of future performance;[175]

- continuation of the debtor's cash-management operations and permission for the use of cash collateral;

- continued payment of employees and continued contributions to employee benefit programs;

- permission to pay pre-petition debts to "critical vendors," without whose cooperation the debtor's business would fail;[176]

- authority to pay pre-petition taxes;

- post-petition financing;[177]

- assumption or rejection of executory contracts and unexpired leases;[178]

- adjustment of investment and deposit guidelines;[179] and

- where necessary, authority to operate in a foreign country.[180]

Among the most controversial of these first-day motions are those that permit payment of pre-petition claims, such as the "critical vendor" motions and first day

---

[172] Debra Grassgreen, First-Day Motions Manual: A Practical Guide to the Critical First Days of a Bankruptcy Case (2003).

[173] See Official Comm. of Unsecured Creditors Metalsource Corp. v. U.S. Metalsource Corp. (In re U.S. Metalsource Corp.), 163 B.R. 260, 266-68 (Bankr. W.D. Pa. 1993).

[174] See infra Chapter 21 — Role of Professionals in Bankruptcy Proceedings.

[175] See Bankruptcy Code § 366.

[176] See generally In re Kmart Corp., 359 F.3d 866 (7th Cir. 2004); Mark A. McDermott, Critical Vendor and Related Orders: Kmart and the Bankruptcy Abuse Prevention and Consumer Protection Act of 2005, 14 Am. Bankr. Inst. L. Rev. 409 (2006).

[177] E.g., In re The Colad Group, Inc., 324 B.R. 208 (Bankr. W.D.N.Y. 2005); In re Ames Dep't Stores, Inc., 115 B.R. 34, 36 (Bankr. S.D.N.Y. 1990).

[178] Bankruptcy Code § 365. See supra Chapter 11 Executory Contracts and Unexpired Leases.

[179] Bankruptcy Code § 345.

[180] See Bankruptcy Code § 1505.

wage orders. The court's authority to authorize payment of pre-petition creditors is not specified in the Code. Some courts, however, have derived such a power from § 105 and the judicially developed "doctrine of necessity." Section 105 permits the court to "issue any order, process, or judgment that is necessary or appropriate to carry out the provisions of [the Bankruptcy Code]."[181] The doctrine of necessity developed in the context of railroad reorganizations of the nineteenth century,[182] which was based partially on the necessity of permitting payments to preserve the debtor's prospects for reorganization and partially on the public's interest in maintaining the Nation's transportation system.[183] The doctrine has gradually expanded to cover a wide range of payments to vendors whose refusal to deal with the debtor would impede the debtor's continued operations.[184] It is controversial, because these critical vendors are receiving, in effect, a "post-petition" preference. They will be paid in full, while other creditors may receive cents on the dollar. Where the prepetition arearage is small, this may not be a big problem, but where it is large, it might be better for the debtor to seek to do business with another supplier. For example, if, in return for a shipment of $1,000 in goods, the debtor must make good on prepetition debts of $20,000 or $30,000, the cost is disproportionate to the benefit. Since the Seventh Circuit's decision in *K-mart*,[185] these critical vendor motions have been scrutinized more closely.[186]

§ 19.07 TREATMENT OF CLAIMS AND INTERESTS IN CHAPTER 11

The status of the various claims and interests in Chapter 11 is generally the same as it is in other chapters of the Bankruptcy Code. Allowed claims and interests are divided into secured claims, priority unsecured claims, general unsecured claims, subordinated unsecured claims, and equity interests.[187] Disallowed claims are entitled to nothing and have no opportunity to vote on the debtor's plan.

---

[181] Bankruptcy Code § 105.

[182] Stephen J. Lubben, *Railroad Receiverships and Modern Bankruptcy Theory*, 89 Cornell L. Rev. 1420 (2004).

[183] *See* Miltenberger v. Logansport Ry., 106 U.S. 286 (1882) (authorizing payment of pre-receivership claims to prevent creditor from terminating delivery of supplies); In re Boston & Maine Corp., 634 F. 2d 1359, 1370 (1st Cir. 1980).

[184] *E.g.*, In re Ionosphere Clubs, Inc., 98 B.R. 174 (Bankr. S.D.N.Y. 1989); In re Eagle-Picher Industries, Inc., 124 B.R. 1021, 1023 (Bankr. S.D. Ohio 1991); Russell A. Eisenberg & Frances F. Gecker, *The Doctrine of Necessity and Its Parameters*, 73 Marquette L. Rev. 1 (1989); Charles J. Tabb, *Emergency Preferential Orders in Bankruptcy Reorganizations*, 65 Am. Bankr. L.J. 75 (1991). The propriety of such payments and the legal reasoning supporting such payments has recently been criticized as lacking statutory support. *See, e.g.*, In re Kmart Corp., 359 F.3d 866, 871-74 (7th Cir. 2004); In re Coserv, LLC, 273 B.R. 487, 493-95 (Bankr. N.D. Tex. 2002).

[185] In re Kmart Corp., 359 F.3d 866 (7th Cir. 2004).

[186] *See* In re Corner Home Care, Inc., 548 B.R. 122 (Bankr. D. Ky. 2010); Douglas G. Baird, Essay, *Bankruptcy from Olympus*, 77 U. Chi. L. Rev. 977 (2010); Mark A. McDermott, *Critical Vendor and Related Orders: Kmart and the Bankruptcy Abuse Prevention and Consumer Protection Act of 2005*, 14 Am. Bankr. Inst. L. Rev. 409 (2006).

[187] *See generally supra* § 10.01 Meaning of Claims and Interests.

[A] Priority of Claims and Interests

The priority scheme applicable in Chapter 7 liquidation cases applies with equal force in Chapter 11.[188] Secured claims are entitled to be paid the value of the collateral before other claims receive anything. Priority claims are entitled to payment in full, with administrative expenses, and some other priority claims are entitled to be paid in cash as soon as the plan is implemented.[189] General unsecured claims, such as those held by trade creditors, holders of commercial paper issued by the debtor, bond-holders, and partially secured creditors with deficiency unsecured claims, are paid next. As explained elsewhere, these claims are sometimes separated into classes for purposes of voting on the plan, and different classes receive different forms of payment under the plan. Subordinated claims are paid next, if the debtor has sufficient value to provide them anything. Finally, if the debtor was not insolvent, equity interest holders are entitled to receive something, usually shares of stock in the reorganized company.

Many Chapter 11 plans alter this strict hierarchy. Chapter 11 debtors frequently propose paying differing percentages to separate classes. If all classes of creditors accept the plan by the required majorities, the plan need not be "fair and equitable" with senior creditors paid in full before junior creditors receive anything and with all creditors of the same priority treated equally. In other words, as long as creditors consent, some creditors may be treated "more equally" than others. This is based on the assumption that the plan produces a going-concern surplus, which need not be divided as rigidly as the basic liquidation value. In other words, so long as the claimants are paid as much as they would have received in a liquidation case, the allocation of the surplus can be negotiated. In particular, if creditors believe that the going concern value of the debtor's business will be enhanced through the continued participation of existing managers who also hold stock in the debtor, these creditors may be willing to permit stockholders to retain some or all of their shares in the debtor as an inducement for them to participate. If unsecured creditors are unwilling to consent, shareholders may not receive a distribution on account of their pre-petition ownership interest.

[B] Proof of Claims and Interests

Although it is probably better practice to file a proof of claim or interest in Chapter 11, it is not always necessary. If the claim (or interest) is scheduled by the debtor, a proof of claim is "deemed" to have been filed, unless the debtor's schedules indicate that the claim or interest is disputed, contingent or unliquidated.[190] As is true throughout the Code, the filing of the proof of claim or interest establishes the claim or interest (the claim or interest is "allowed), unless the proof is disputed.[191]

---

[188] *See generally supra* § 10.01 Meaning of Claims and Interests.

[189] Bankruptcy Code § 1129(a)(9). *See infra* § 19.10[H] Full Payment of Priority Claims.

[190] Bankruptcy Code § 1111(a).

[191] *See supra* § 10.02[B] Proof of Claim.

[C] Chapter 11 Treatment of Partially Secured Claims

Under § 506(a), undersecured obligations are bifurcated into two claims: a secured claim for the value of the collateral and an unsecured claim for the balance.[192] This is true in Chapter 11, even where the secured creditors' claim is "non-recourse." Or to put it another way, the unsecured portion of the claim is allowed in bankruptcy even though the undersecured creditor would not have a claim for a deficiency under applicable non-bankruptcy law. For example, some secured creditors whose collateral consists of real estate, may not have the right to recover any deficiency because their loan agreement expressly waives the right to a deficiency. Others may have lost their right to a deficiency because of some state law "anti-deficiency" rule. Section 1111(b) grants recourse to these partially secured creditors unless they elect to waive it. Gaining an understanding of how this election works and the circumstances in which creditors might find it useful to make the election is a difficult hurdle for those seeking to understand the law of business bankruptcies under Chapter 11.

Section 1111(b) actually contains two related sets of rules. The first involves the treatment of non-recourse debt. The second involves the treatment of partially secured debtors, regardless of whether they involve recourse or non-recourse debts.

[1] Treatment of Non-Recourse Claims

Non-recourse debt is debt that is enforceable only against the property securing the debt. For example, suppose Triangle Development Co. borrows $10 million from Canal Bank, secured by Triangle's new office building. Under the loan agreement, the secured debt is "non-recourse." In other words, Triangle has no personal liability for the debt. Under their agreement, if Triangle defaults, Canal Bank may foreclose on the building and sell it. However, whether or not the foreclosure sale yields enough to cover the debt, Canal Bank cannot recover the balance from Triangle or any of its other assets.

Under section 1111(b), non-recourse creditors are treated as if they had recourse. In other words, they have a claim against the debtor for the unsecured portion of the debt, even though their loan agreement gives it no such rights. The practical significance of this is that an undersecured, non-recourse creditor has an unsecured claim for the amount of any deficiency. In the above example, if Triangle's office building was worth only $8 million, Canal Bank will have an $8 million secured claim and a $2 million unsecured claim, even though Canal Bank does not have any right outside of Chapter 11 to seize Triangle's other assets to satisfy the $2 million deficiency.[193]

There are two exceptions to this rule. The first applies if the creditor elects somewhat different treatment under § 1111(b)(2). The creditor may elect, under 1111(b), to give up its unsecured claim in exchange for a lien that secures the entire amount of its debt. If Canal Bank makes this election, it has a secured claim for the

---

[192] *See supra* § 10.03[C] Allowance of Secured Claims.

[193] Bankruptcy Code § 1111(b)(1)(A).

full $10 million and retains a lien on the office building for the entire $10 million debt. In doing so, it gives up its right to share in whatever distribution is made to unsecured creditors,[194] and it must receive a distribution on its secured claim of at least the nominal amount of its secured debt. This may seem like a no brainer to an undersecured creditor, but, as discussed below, making the 1111(b) election does not guaranty payment in full. It is only the nominal amount of the payments that must match the amount of the debt. The present value is only required to match the value of the collateral. As such, the debtor can comply with 1111(b) by adjusting the length of payments or the interest rate, leaving the creditor more or less where they started.

The second exception applies if the debtor sells the collateral under § 363[195] or pursuant to the debtor's reorganization plan. If the debtor disposes of the collateral, the creditor is entitled only to what it receives from the sale, and does not have a claim for any deficiency that may result.[196] Thus, if the debtor sells the building for only $8.3 million (net of sale costs), that is all Canal Bank recovers. The theory behind this latter exception is that the creditor is receiving exactly what it bargained for when it made a non-recourse loan — the proceeds from the sale of the encumbered property.

[2] The 1111(b) Election

The remainder of § 1111(b) deals with all undersecured claims, whether or not the claimant has recourse against the debtor. The underlying purpose of the § 1111(b) election is to protect secured creditors from the risk that debtors will use a temporary decline in the value of their collateral to obtain a bargain price. Although the election is available to all secured creditors, it has its greatest significance in cases involving debtors whose principal asset and primary source of income is a building — a "single-asset real estate" case.[197]

Under § 1111(b), as explained above, a secured claim is treated as a recourse claim, even though no recourse would be available under state law. Suppose, for example, that Ridge Bank has a claim for $15 million, secured by property worth only $12 million. Regardless of whether Ridge Bank's claim is a recourse claim or a non-recourse claim, it is treated as a recourse claim. As a result, Ridge will have a $12 million allowed secured claim and a $3 million unsecured deficiency claim. Ridge is entitled to $12 million on account of its secured claim and will share in whatever is distributed to unsecured creditors, for its $3 million unsecured claim.

But Ridge may make the "1111(b)" election. By doing so, Ridge waives its deficiency claim, and in return, its secured claim will be treated as if it were fully secured. To put it another way, it prevents the lien from being "stripped down" to

---

[194] *See infra* § 19.07[C][2] The 1111(b) Election.

[195] *See supra* § 9.03[C] Use, Sale, or Lease Outside the Ordinary Course.

[196] Bankruptcy Code § 1111(b)(1)(A)(ii).

[197] Technically, the provision states that the election must be made by the class of which the claim is a part, and that the election must be by at least two-thirds in amount and more than half in number of the allowed claims in the same class. Bankruptcy Code § 1111(b)(1)(A)(i). However, as a general rule, each secured claim is in its own class, and thus this election is ordinarily made by individual creditors.

the value of the collateral. In other words, if Ridge Bank has a $15 million claim secured by $12 million in assets, and if Ridge Bank makes the § 1111(b) election, it has a $15 million secured claim.[198] It retains its lien on the collateral to secure the entire $15 million debt. This means that if the debtor decides to sell the property during the life of the plan, then Ridge will receive the full sale proceeds up to $15 million. However, unlike most secured claims, which must receive payments of at least the "allowed amount" of their secured claim with a value of "allowed amount," Ridge Bank's claim must receive payments totalling the "allowed amount" (here $15 million), but they need only receive payments with a *present value* that equals the *value of the collateral* (here $12 million). Or, to put it another way, if the payments under the plan have a value equal to the value of the collateral — $12 million — and total, with interest, the allowed amount of the secured claim ($15 million), the plan can be approved over the creditor's objection.[199]

There are two circumstances where a creditor is not permitted to make the 1111(b) election. First, a creditor may not make this election if its interest in the property is of inconsequential value.[200] For example, if Ridge Bank's interest in the collateral were only worth $10, because it was junior to an $11,999,990 secure claim, it could not make the § 1111(b) election. Second, the election cannot be made if if the property will either be sold under § 363, or is to be sold under the plan.[201]

The goal of § 1111(b) was to prevent debtors from taking advantage of a temporary dip in the market to deprive the secured creditor of its bargain. It does this by preventing lien stripping.[202] Suppose, for example, that the property involved in the example above is worth $12 million only because of a temporary slump in the local real estate market. There is reason to believe that it will soon be worth more than $12 million.[203] In the normal circumstance, where Ridge Bank's claim is bifurcated between a secured and an unsecured claim, the debtor can keep the property by paying the $12 million secured claim in full and paying only a portion of the $3 million unsecured claim. Later, when the market recovers, the debtor captures the increase in value. Allowing Ridge Bank to elect to have a $15 million secured claim prevents the debtor from obtaining this advantage (at least if the debtor sells the property before payments under the plan are complete).

§ 19.08 CONTENTS OF A CHAPTER 11 PLAN

As is true with any reorganization proceeding, the goal of Chapter 11 is the confirmation and successful completion of a plan of reorganization. The Chapter 11 plan is fruit of a process of negotiation among the debtor, creditors, and (in some cases) equity interest holders. Nearly all creditors whose interests are affected vote

---

[198] *See supra* § 10.03[C] Allowance of Secured Claims.

[199] *See infra* § 19.08[H][4] Treatment of the § 1111(b) Election.

[200] Bankruptcy Code § 1111(b)(1)(B)(i).

[201] Bankruptcy Code § 1111(b)(1)(B)(ii).

[202] *See infra* § 19.08[H][3] Chapter 11 Lien Stripping.

[203] As the depression-era comedian and social commentator Will Rogers famously said: "Buy land, Buy land. They ain't making any more of the stuff." (Rogers was similar in many respects to Jon Stewart of Comedy Central's "Daily Show").

on the plan — it is difficult to obtain court approval of a plan unless the required majorities of creditors approve.

In Chapter 11, creditors vote under a modified form of majority rule. If the requisite majority is obtained, then all creditors in the accepting class are bound. Only in limited circumstances may the plan be "crammed down" — confirmed over the creditors' objection.

Chapter 11 plans are likely to involve considerably more property and debt than even a large Chapter 12 or 13 proceeding, therefore, their financial structure is likely to be more complicated, with multiple layers of claims and interests, each entitled to different priority. This, in and of itself, makes the Chapter 11 plan process more complex than in other chapters. Additional complexity is added by (1) the debtor's greater flexibility in formulating a plan; and (2) the plan confirmation process which gives creditors a vote, and hence, more voice in the plan negotiation process. The usual justification for this greater flexibility is precisely the fact that the Chapter 11 creditors have a much greater degree of input.

As noted elsewhere, Chapter 13 debtors usually file their plans simultaneously with their petition. By contrast, a Chapter 11 debtor files a plan only after the debtor has an opportunity to adjust its business operations to correct whatever circumstances led it into financial difficulty in the first place and has had an opportunity to negotiate with its creditors about how to reorganize its financial structure.[204]

[A] Process of Negotiating the Plan's Terms

In some cases, a plan is partially or fully negotiated even before the Chapter 11 petition is filed. Often a bankruptcy is filed after prepetitition attempts to negotiate a workout have failed. The principal advantages offered by bankruptcy are (1) the control that Chapter 11 gives to the debtor over the process; (2) the automatic stay, which gives the debtor some breathing room; and (3) the power to bind holdouts to the plan who are in a minority.

[B] Who May File a Plan; The Exclusivity Period[205]

The debtor may file a plan either with the petition or at any other time during the case.[206] However, except in so called "prepackaged" plan cases (or "prepaks"), Chapter 11 plans are rarely filed until well after the case begins. This is because

---

[204] Despite this, some debtors are able to file a so-called pre-packaged plan with their petition. These are usually plans that have been worked out in advance but that require Chapter 11's voting procedures to enforce the plan on a minority of dissenting creditors. For a fuller discussion of pre-packaged plans, and the various considerations that have made them especially popular, see Marc S. Kirschner, et al., *Prepackaged Bankruptcy Plans: The Deleveraging Tool of the '90s in the Wake of OID and Tax Concerns*, 21 Seton Hall L. Rev. 643 (1991).

[205] Neill D. Fuquay, Note, *Be Careful What You Wish For, You Just Might Get It: The Effect on Chapter 11 Case Length of the New Cap on a Debtor's Exclusive Period to File a Plan*, 85 Tex. L. Rev. 431 (2006); Novica Petrovski, *The Bankruptcy Code, Section 1121: Exclusivity Reloaded*, 11 Am. Bankr. Inst. L. Rev. 451 (2003).

[206] Bankruptcy Code § 1121(a).

Chapter 11, unlike Chapter 13, envisions negotiations with creditors over the plan, and the negotiation process takes time.

In most cases, the debtor has 120 days from the time of its voluntary petition during which it enjoys the exclusive right to file a plan.[207] If the debtor files a plan during this initial 120-day period, others are prohibited from filing a competing plan until 180 days after the petition date.[208] This gives the debtor two months to complete the confirmation process by disseminating a disclosure statement and obtaining a sufficient number of acceptances to have the plan confirmed. This "exclusive period" is designed to give the debtor time to negotiate and draft a plan.

The 120/180 day time limits may be extended, in the court's discretion. For many years, the Code provided for unlimited extensions of the 120- and 180-day periods, as long as the court thought the case was moving forward.[209] Lengthy extensions beyond the 120- and 180-day periods were commonly granted.[210]

In response to creditors' complaints, Congress added language prohibiting the 120-day period from being extended beyond "18 months after the date of [the voluntary petition]"[211] and prohibiting the 180-day period from being extended beyond "20 months after the date of the [voluntary petition]."[212] Creditors hope this new limitation will prevent debtors from using Chapter 11 to delay the inevitable liquidation of debtors who have no realistic hope of reorganizing. On the other hand, it may force debtors to propose plans prematurely, before their managers have had sufficient time to adjust their operations to return to profitability. Worse yet, because there is a known and firm end date to the debtor's period of control over the case, creditors may have an incentive to be obstructionist, or the debtor may be tempted to present a plan that is overly optimistic in order to get it approved. This may in turn lead to a round of refilings, or requests for modification or dismissal as the debtors are unable to comply with the plan's requirements.

After expiration of either of these two periods, or after the appointment of a trustee, "any party in interest . . . may file a plan."[213] Plans submitted by creditors frequently call for the debtor's liquidation and for eliminating the interests of existing stockholders.

---

[207] Bankruptcy Code § 1121(b).

[208] These time periods run from the date of the "order for relief." In a voluntary case, this is the same as the date of the petition. Few involuntary Chapter 11 cases are filed.

[209] Bankruptcy Code § 1121(d)(1).

[210] *See* Eric W. Lam, *Of Exclusivity and For Cause: 11 U.S.C. § 1121(d) Re-examined*, 36 Drake L. Rev. 533 (1986-1987).

[211] Bankruptcy Code § 1121(d)(2)(A).

[212] Bankruptcy Code § 1121(d)(2)(B). Somewhat different rules apply in cases involving "small business debtors," with less than $2,000,000 in debts. *See* Bankruptcy Code § 1121(e).

[213] Bankruptcy Code § 1121(c).

[C]   Mandatory and Optional Chapter 11 Plan Provisions

[1]   Mandatory Plan Provisions

Section 1123(a) contains a number of mandatory provisions — topics that must be addressed in the plan. However, as a practical matter, the Code's standards for confirmation have a further significant impact on what must be included in most plans.

[a]   Designation of Classes of Claims and Interests

All Chapter 11 plans are required to "designate . . . classes of claims . . . and classes of interests."[214] Thus, Chapter 11 plans divide creditors' claims into separate classes. Chapter 11 plans always divide claims based on their priority, and frequently divide them on other characteristics, such as the underlying transaction that gave rise to the claim, the maturity of the claim, and the size of the claim.

The plan's classification scheme must comply with § 1122.[215] Section 1122 permits a plan to "place a claim or an interest in a particular class only if such claim or interest is substantially similar to the other claims or interests of such class."[216] In other words, the plan may not lump together claims of creditors whose legal rights are substantially different from one another.[217] A separate question, and one on which the Code gives no direct guidance, is the question of when similar creditors may be segregated into separate classes.

[b]   Specification of Unimpaired Classes

The plan must also specify whether a class is "impaired" or "unimpaired" by the plan.[218] Whether a particular class is impaired is governed by § 1124.[219] A creditor is unimpaired if its legal and equitable rights are not altered by the plan. Creditors in classes that are not impaired by the terms of the plan are deemed to have accepted the plan and thus do not have the right to vote on the terms of the plan.[220]

[c]   Specification of Treatment of Impaired Claims and Interests

Most Chapter 11 plans impair one or all classes of claims and interests. The plan is required to specify how any impaired class of claims or interests is treated by the plan.[221] As explained in more detail later in this chapter, the range of treatment of impaired classes of claims is considerable and may extend from cash payment in

---

[214] Bankruptcy Code § 1123(a)(1).

[215] Bankruptcy Code § 1123(a)(1).

[216] Bankruptcy Code § 1122(a).

[217] *See infra* § 19.08[D] Classification of Claims.

[218] Bankruptcy Code § 1123(a)(2).

[219] *See infra* § 19.08[E] Impairment of Claims.

[220] Bankruptcy Code § 1126(f).

[221] Bankruptcy Code § 1123(a)(3).

full on the day the plan is first implemented, to nothing. Classes of equity interest holders in particular — shareholders — may be ousted and receive nothing.

[d]   Equal Treatment of Claims and Interests Within a Class

A Chapter 11 plan must provide "the same treatment for each claim or interest of a particular class."[222] In other words, every creditor included in a class must be treated the same as every other creditor in the same class. And, every equity interest holder in a class must be treated the same as every other interest holder in that class. If the debtor wishes to treat one group of creditors differently from others, they must be classified separately. Because creditors vote to approve or reject the plan in classes, this prevents creditors from receiving more favorable treatment by ganging up on creditors who are receiving less during the voting process.[223] However, separate classification can have tactical consequences for the plan proponent. Creating separate classes may be a way to create the necessary majorities for consensual confirmation of a plan, or where all classes are not accepting, for ensuring that there is at least one consenting class (a prerequisite if the plan is going to be approved over the objectin of a class, through cram-down). These tactics will be discused below, along with the limits on when it is permissible to group claimants together, and when it is appropriate to classify them separately.

[e]   Adequate Means for Implementing the Plan

The plan must provide adequate means for its implementation.[224] In a simple plan, the means may include nothing more than necessary adjustments to debt, such as curing defaults and de-accelerating debt,[225] reducing the amount of unsecured claims, and extending the maturity of secured claims.[226] In other cases, the reorganization is more profound, and might include the partial liquidation of the debtor and the merger of the remainder of its business with another, healthy company.[227] A corporate debtor may also have to rewrite its charter as part of its restructuring; and many larger debtors have to issue securities as part of the plan, or to raise additional capital. New stock or bonds may be issued as part of the plan distribution, or to new investors.[228] Section 1123 gives a partial list of the types of things that may be needed to make the plan work; it includes all of the matters just mentioned.

---

[222] Bankruptcy Code § 1123(a)(4). In re New Century TRS Holdings, Inc., 407 B.R. 576, 592 (D. Del. 2009).

[223] *See infra* § 19.08[D][3] Identical Treatment of Claims in the Same Class.

[224] Bankruptcy Code § 1123(a)(5).

[225] Bankruptcy Code § 1123(a)(5)(G). Defaults on obligations owed to creditors with secured claims can sometimes be cured, leaving the creditor unimpaired under § 1124. Creditors in classes that are unimpaired are deemed to have accepted the plan and do not vote. *See infra* § 19.08[E] Impairment of Claims.

[226] Bankruptcy Code § 1123(a)(5)(F).

[227] Bankruptcy Code § 1123(a)(5)(C).

[228] Bankruptcy Code § 1123(a)(5)(J). That's right! Existing stockholders may be eliminated. If so, new stock is to others — buyers, or sometimes to its creditors.

[f]   Protecting Shareholders' Voting Rights

If the debtor is a corporation, the plan must provide for the debtor's corporate charter to include certain provisions relating to the appropriate distribution of voting power among classes of voting securities.[229] In addition, the plan must "contain only provisions that are consistent with the interests of creditors and equity security holders and with public policy with respect to the manner of selection of any officer, director, or trustee."[230] These requirements ensure that the plan allocates voting power among various stakeholders according to their relative priority.[231] It is particularly important when creditors receive stock in the reorganized debtor that they obtain a voice in the management of the debtor that is commensurate with their stake in the success of the company.[232]

[g]   Provide for Payment of an Individual Debtor's Personal Earnings

The 2005 Amendments added language requiring the plan of any individual debtor to "provide for the payment to creditors . . . of all or such portion of earnings from personal services performed by the debtor after the commencement of the case or other future income of the debtor as is necessary for the execution of the plan."[233] This language makes it clear that an individual debtor who must file under Chapter 11, because he is ineligible for relief under either Chapter 7 (because of the "abuse" test), or under Chapter 13 (because of its debt limits), must submit a portion of his future income to creditors in his Chapter 11 plan. Indeed, § 1129(a)(15) requires most individual debtors to submit all of their projected disposable income for five years.[234] This is consistent with the projected disposable income test of § 1325(b)(1)(B) for debtors who seek relief under Chapter 13.[235]

[2]   Optional Plan Provisions

Many plans go far beyond the requirements of the statute to include other provisions that may facilitate reorganization. Section 1123(b) gives blanket authorization for a variety of these provisions. The plan may:

- impair, or leave unimpaired, any class of secured claims, unsecured claims, or interests;[236]

- provide for the assumption, rejection, or assignment of any executory

---

[229] Bankruptcy Code § 1123(a)(5)(J).

[230] Bankruptcy Code § 1323(a)(7).

[231] *See* Acequia, Inc. v. Clinton (In re Acequia), 787 F.2d 1352, 1361-62 (9th Cir. 1986). *See also* In re Machne Menachem, Inc., 304 B.R. 140 (Bankr. M.D. Pa. 2003).

[232] Myron N. Krotinger, *Management and Allocation of Voting Power in Corporate Reorganizations*, 41 Colum. L. Rev. 646, 649, 664 (1941); Alfred N. Heuston, *Corporate Reorganization under the Chandler Act*, 38 Colum. L. Rev. 1199, 1213-14 (1938).

[233] Bankruptcy Code § 1123(a)(8).

[234] Bankruptcy Code § 1129(a)(15)(B).

[235] *See supra* § 18.08[E][2] Debtor's Projected Disposable Income.

[236] Bankruptcy Code § 1123(b)(1). *See infra* § 19.08[E] Impairment of Claims.

contract or unexpired lease of the debtor, unless it has previously been rejected;[237]

- provide for the settlement or adjustment of any claim or interest that belongs to the debtor or the estate; or in the alternative, provide for the retention and enforcement by the debtor, the trustee (if any), or a representative of the estate of any claim or interest that belongs to the debtor or the estate;[238]

- provide for the sale of all or substantially all of the property of the estate and distribution of the proceeds of the sale among holders of claims or interests;[239]

- modify the rights of holders of secured and unsecured claims;[240]

- include any other "appropriate provision not inconsistent with the applicable provision of this title."[241]

The last of these provisions permits the plan to include almost anything that does not contradict the Code or frustrate its purposes.

[D] Classification of Claims[242]

As indicated above, § 1123(a)(2) requires a Chapter 11 plan to designate classes of claims and classes of interests.[243] "Classification" of claims and interests means that the debtor subdivides creditors and interest holders into narrower categories,

---

[237] Bankruptcy Code § 1123(b)(2). *See supra* Chapter 11 Executory Contracts and Unexpired Leases.

[238] Bankruptcy Code § 1123(b)(3). For example, if the estate has a claim for damages against a third party, this may be compromised or otherwise dealt with in the plan.

[239] Bankruptcy Code § 1123(b)(4). This is the provision that permits a "liquidation plan," under which Chapter 11 becomes a substitute for Chapter 7. *See* In re Cypresswood Land Partners, I, 409 B.R. 396 (Bankr. S.D. Tex. 2009) (confirmation of liquidating plan).

[240] Bankruptcy Code § 1123(b)(5). There is an important exception to this provision. As in Chapter 13, the plan may not modify the rights of a holder of a claim secured only by a security interest in real property that is the debtor's principal residence. *See supra* § 18.07[b][2][a] Residential Real Estate Mortgages. This exception is likely to apply only in the rare Chapter 11 case that involves an individual debtor. It was included to dissuade such debtors from seeking Chapter 11 relief as a means of evading the similar limitation in § 1322(b)(2).

[241] Bankruptcy Code § 1123(b)(6).

[242] William Blair, *Classification of Unsecured Claims in Chapter 11 Reorganization*, 58 Am. Bankr. L.J. 197 (1984); David Gray Carlson, *The Classification Veto in Single-Asset Cases Bankruptcy Code Section 1129(a)(10)*, 44 S.C. L. Rev. 565 (1993); Henry J. Friendly, *Some Comments on the Corporate Reorganizations Act*, 48 Harv. L. Rev. 39, 70-74 (1934); Bruce A. Markell, *Clueless on Classification: Toward Removing Artificial Limits on Chapter 11 Claim Classification*, 11 Bankr. Dev. J. 1 (1995); Peter E. Meltzer, *Disenfranchising the Dissenting Creditor Through Artificial Classification or Artificial Impairment*, 66 Am. Bankr. L.J. 281 (1992); Scott F. Norberg, *Classification of Claims Under Chapter 11 of the Bankruptcy Code: The Fallacy of Interest Based Classification*, 69 Am. Bankr. L.J. 119, 120 (1995); Stefan A. Riesenfeld, *Classification of Claims and Interests in Chapter 11 and 13 Cases*, 75 Cal. L. Rev. 391 (1987); Linda J. Rusch, *Gerrymandering the Classification Issue in Chapter Eleven Reorganizations*, 63 U. Colo. L. Rev. 163 (1992); Charles F. Vihon, *Classification of Unsecured Claims: Squaring a Circle?*, 55 Am. Bankr. L.J. 143 (1981).

[243] Bankruptcy Code § 1123(a)(1).

usually based on differences in their legal rights, but frequently also based on their business relationships to the debtor. For example, the Code treats all general unsecured debts alike. Under Chapter 7, all are paid pro-rata if anything is left over from the secured and priority claims.

Chapter 11 debtors have a broad right to classify claims, provided the creditors approve the plan and that each claim is paid at least its liquidation value. The Code itself says remarkably little about classification.

Since all claims or interests within a class are required to be substantially similar to each other,[244] secured claims cannot be placed in the same class as unsecured claims, priority claims cannot be placed in the same class as general unsecured claims,[245] and interests of shareholders who own preferred stock cannot be placed in the same class of as interests of shareholders who own common stock.

[1] Substantial Similarity of Claims in the Same Class

The rule prohibiting the grouping together of claims that are materially different from one another usually means that there is only one creditor in each class of secured claims. The rights of a creditor with a senior mortgage on the debtor's land is not substantially similar to the rights of a creditor with a senior security interest in the debtor's equipment.[246] Quite to the contrary — their rights are markedly different from one another because they have property interests in different collateral. Likewise, the rights of a creditor with a senior mortgage on the debtor's land are materially different from the rights of a creditor with a junior mortgage on the same land — they have different priority.[247] This means that this one creditor must vote in favor of the plan for that class to "accept" the plan by the requisite majority.[248]

The principal exception to this common pattern occurs when multiple creditors join together to contribute to a "participation" loan and share the same seniority in the same collateral.[249] Thus, if Ridge Bank, Peninsula Bank, and Valley Bank each loaned Franklin Manufacturing $1 million as part of a $3 million participation loan for which they share a senior mortgage in Franklin's land and building, it is appropriate to place all three creditors in the same class.

In determining whether claims are substantially similar, the focus is on the nature of the claim rather than on the identity of the claim holder.[250] This depends

---

[244] Bankruptcy Code § 1122(a).

[245] John C. Anderson, *Classification of Claims and Interests in Reorganization Cases Under the New Bankruptcy Code*, 58 Am. Bankr. L.J. 99, 117 (1984).

[246] Brady v. Andrew (In re Comm. W. Fin. Corp.), 761 F.2d 1329, 1338 (9th Cir. 1985).

[247] Mokava Corp. v. Dolan, 147 F.2d 340 (2d Cir. 1945); In re Commercial W. Fin. Corp., 761 F.2d 1329 (9th Cir. 1985).

[248] *See* Bankruptcy Code § 1126(c); *infra* § 19.09[C] Voting by Classes of Claims and Interests.

[249] *E.g.*, In re Keck, Mahin & Cate, 241 B.R. 583, 589-90 (Bankr. N.D. Ill. 1999). *See generally* W. Crews Lott, Larry A. Makel, and Walter E. Evans, *Structuring Multiple Lender Transactions*, 112 Banking L.J. 734 (1995).

[250] In re Martin's Point, Ltd., 12 B.R. 721 (Bankr. N.D. Ga. 1981). *See* J.P. Morgan & Co. v. Mo. Pac.

primarily on the relative rights and priority of the claims outside of bankruptcy.[251] This does not mean that all claims in the same class must be identical. For example, it is possible to lump together claims arising from accounts payable with claims arising from unsecured operating loans. These claims might have different due dates, but they are both unsecured and entitled to no special priority. Moreover, they all probably have the same stake in the proceeding and have similar goals in connection with the debtor's reorganization.

On the other hand, tort claimants and contract claimants may have very different interests at stake in the debtor's reorganization. Suppose, for example, that Titanic Corporation has both personal injury claimants and contract claimants, all of whom have general unsecured claims. The contract claimants have ongoing commercial relations with Titanic, and may be willing to accept a relatively protracted payout because they expect to recoup some of their losses by entering into new, profitable contracts with Titanic after it reorganizes. By contrast, the personal injury claimants are likely to want to receive as much as possible immediately. The contract claimants' primary benefit from reorganization is the new business it will generate in the future; the tort claimants' only benefit from reorganization is a quick maximum payout of the prior debt. Moreover, the suppliers may have more leverage with the debtor who may need their cooperation in order to continue to operate the business. Therefore, it could be argued that these groups are not sufficiently similar to be included in the same class. If the tort claims can easily be outvoted by the contract claims, the tort claimants' interests may not be adequately taken into account in formulating the plan.

[2] Separate Classification of Similar Claims

The Bankruptcy Code is conspicuously silent about the separate classification of substantially similar claims. Claims that are materially different cannot be lumped together, but the Code does not expressly prohibit the *separation* of substantially similar claims into different classes. Indeed, the debtor often seeks to separate apparently similar claims, for reasons that are sometimes clearly bona fide and at other times dubious.

[a] Small Claims Classified for Administrative Convenience

One basis for separate classification of similar claims is explicitly recognized in the Code. Section 1122(b) provides: "A plan may designate a separate class of claims consisting of every unsecured claim that is less than or reduced to an amount that the court approves as reasonable and necessary for administrative convenience."[252] Thus, it is common for plans to include a class of small claims that will be paid in full as soon as the plan is consummated. This has the advantage of avoiding making small payments to these creditors over a longer period of time.

R.R., 85 F.2d 351 (8th Cir.), *cert. denied*, 299 U.S. 604 (1936).

[251] Bruce A. Markell, *Clueless on Classification: Toward Removing Artificial Limits on Chapter 11 Claim Classification*, 11 Bankr. Dev. J. 1, 27 (1995).

[252] Bankruptcy Code § 1122(b).

The plan in *Troy Savings Bank v. Travelers Motor Inn, Inc.*[253] provides a good example. It established a separate class for all claims under $250 and provided for members of the class to receive a lump sum payment immediately upon confirmation of the plan. Without this separate designation, these creditors would have been included in the class of general unsecured creditors and payments to them would have been spread out over five years as with other members of the class.[254] With quarterly payments of no more than $5 to each creditor with a claim of less than $250, the administrative cost of making payments to these creditors would probably be greater than the total of what they would receive.[255]

One of the potential advantages of creating a class of small claims is that favorable treatment of the class is likely to lead the class to accept the plan, thus satisfying the requirement in § 1129(a)(10) that at least one class of impaired claims must accept the plan.[256] Without acceptance by at least one class of impaired claims, cramdown is not possible. While a class of claims may not be articificially impaired, the elimination of former § 1124(a)(3) makes it clear that paying the claim in cash on the effective date of the plan, without paying post-petition interest,[257] leaves the claim "impaired." The very existence of § 1122(b) indicates that treating members of the administrative convenience class better than other classes of unsecured claims is not "unfair discrimination" that would violate § 1129(b)(1).

[b]   Segregation of Substantially Similar Claims

Some classification of substantially similar claims is permitted, but the limits of such classifications are ill-defined. While classification frequently makes sense to accommodate the different interests that various creditors have in the debtor's reorganization, some classification schemes are the bankruptcy equivalent of political gerrymandering — defining the classes in order to assure confirmation of the plan or to provide favorable treatment to preferred constituencies.

The leading decision regarding separate classification of general unsecured claims, other than for administrative convenience, is *Teamsters National Freight Industry Negotiating Committee v. U.S. Truck Co. (In re U.S. Truck Co).*[260] The plan in *U.S. Truck Co.* segregated claims of several unsecured creditors based on the circumstances that gave rise to their claims. In particular, it segregated the unsecured claims of employees based on the debtor's rejection of its collective bargaining agreement with the Teamsters' union from most other general

---

[253] 215 B.R. 485, 489-90 (N.D.N.Y. 1997).

[254] *See* Bankruptcy Code § 1123(a)(4) (all members of a class must be treated the same).

[255] *See also* In re Jartran, Inc., 44 B.R. 331, 397 (Bankr. N.D. Ill. 1984). Plans usually also provide for creditors with larger claims to elect to reduce their claims to whatever dollar threshold is imposed on this class. Thus, a creditor with a $300 claim could elect to reduce its claim to $250 and receive $250 in immediate cash, rather than receive only a few dollars a year for several years.

[256] Bankruptcy Code § 1129(a)(10).

[257] Such interest is not part of the allowed claim. Bankruptcy Code § 502(b)(2).

[260] 800 F.2d 581 (1986).

unsecured claims above $200.[261] The class of Teamsters' union claims rejected the plan, and the debtor sought to have it confirmed over the class's objection. The class of general unsecured claims had accepted the plan. A special creditors' committee representing the Teamsters objected to confirmation, contending that these two classes had been improperly segregated from one another, and that if they had been combined, the plan could not have been confirmed. By segregating the Teamsters' claim from the claim of other general unsecured creditors and obtaining the class of general unsecured creditors' acceptance of the plan, the debtor was able to satisfy the cramdown requirement that at least one class of impaired claims accept the plan.[262] If the class was improperly constituted, this confirmation requirement would not have been met.

In reviewing the legislative history of § 1122 and pre-Code cases that Congress intended to incorporate into the Code's language, the court found "one common theme." "[L]ower courts were given broad discretion to determine proper classification according to the factual circumstances of each individual case."[263] The court also found that these earlier decisions had permitted and indeed required separate classification of claims where the interests of the creditors holding these claims "differ[ed] substantially from those of other impaired creditors."[264] Because creditors who represented employees had both a different stake in the future viability of the reorganized debtor and alternative means to protect their interests, segregating their claims into a separate class was justified.[265]

This same rationale has been used to justify the separate classification of trade claims held by the debtor's suppliers, because their continued cooperation with the debtor is essential to the success of the debtor's continued business and thus to the success of its reorganization. Other courts have been less persuaded, particularly when the segregated class of trade creditors is receiving no better treatment than another class that has rejected the plan.[266] Such identical treatment belies the assertion that the classification scheme was proposed as a means to ensure the cooperation of members of the segregated class and indicates that it was designed instead to artificially separate creditors into separate classes simply to obtain an affirmative vote on the plan of reorganization. Courts are in agreement that gerrymandering is inappropriate. As the court in *Greystone* put it, " 'one clear rule' has emerged from the otherwise muddled § 1122 caselaw: 'thou shalt not classify similar claims differently in order to gerrymander an affirmative vote on a

---

[261] There were two other classes of unsecured claims. A class of unsecured claims of less than $200, separately classified for administrative convenience pursuant to § 1122(b), and the unsecured deficiency claim of the bank that also held a secured claim on the debtor's land. *U.S. Truck*, 800 F.2d at 584.

[262] Bankruptcy Code § 1129(a)(10). *See infra* § 19.10[G] Acceptance by Impaired Classes. Note that if all impaired classes accept the plan, the plan is consensual and there is no "cramdown."

[263] 800 F.2d at 586.

[264] 800 F.2d at 588.

[265] To the extent that separate classification is being used to satisfy the requirement for cramdown that one impaired class accept the plan, the *U.S. Truck* court stated that the question was whether there was a substantially impaired creditor constituency that favored the plan.

[266] In re Coram Healthcare, Corp., 315 B.R. 321, 349 (Bankr. D. Del. 2004) (collecting cases).

reorganization plan.' "[267] But beyond that, there is little clarity. Some courts follow the *U.S. Truck* approach and are fairly permissive, while other courts say that if claims are similar enough to be classified together, then they must be so classified.[268]

[c] Classification in Single-Asset Real Estate Cases[269]

The gerrymandering issue frequently arises in cramdown cases that involve debtors whose principle asset is a single parcel of real estate, usually an office building or an apartment complex. These "single-asset real estate" cases commonly involve the same problem that existed in *U.S. Truck Co.* — the necessity of having at least one impaired class of claims accept the debtor's plan in order to "cram down" a dissenting class.

Single-asset real estate cases frequently involve a large secured claim and a large unsecured deficiency claim held by a lender who holds a partially secured mortgage on the debtor's land. Since such real estate loans are often made on a non-recourse basis, the deficiency claim may exist solely as a result of § 1111(b)'s creation of "artificial recourse." These creditors are usually opposed to reorganization and prefer the immediate sale of the real estate and immediate payment of the secured portion of the debt that would result from the debtor's liquidation, or allowing the secured creditor to take control of the property by credit bidding the amount of its loan. Including this creditor's claim in a single general class of claims of unsecured creditors would probably lead to the class's rejection of the debtor's plan.

Many single-asset real estate cases preclude debtors from segregating unsecured deficiency claims of mortgagees into a class separate from the claims of other unsecured creditors.[270] Some courts take the same view when the claim would have been a non-recourse claim, but for the effect of § 1111(b), which gives holders of non-recourse claims the right to a deficiency that they would not have had outside of bankruptcy.[271] However, a few courts take the complete opposite view and require segregation of recourse claims created by § 1111(b)(1)(A) into a separate class.[272] These courts take the view that claims that would not be entitled

---

[267] In re Greystone III Joint Venture, 948 F.2d F.2d 134, 139 (5th Cir. 1991), *cert denied*, 113 S. Ct. 72 (1992); In re Bryson Properties, XVIII, 961 F.2d 496 (4th Cir.), *cert. denied*, 506 U.S. 866 (1992).

[268] In re Bloomingdale Partners, 170 B.R. 984 (Bankr. N.D. Ill. 1994).

[269] David Gray Carlson, *Artificial Impairment and the Single Asset Chapter 11 Case*, 23 Cap. U. L. Rev. 339 (1994).

[270] *E.g.*, In re Greystone III Joint Venture, 948 F.2d F.2d 134, 139 (5th Cir. 1991), *cert denied*, 506 U.S. 821 (1992) (separate classification prohibited due to debtor's improper gerrymandering motive). *See also* In re Bloomingdale Partners, 170 B.R. 984 (N.D. Ill. 1994) (separate classification prohibited due to similarity of claims, irrespective of debtor's motive). *See generally* In re JRV Indus., Inc., 342 B.R. 635 (Bankr. M.D. Fla. 2006) (collecting cases).

[271] *E.g.*, Boston Post Rd. Ltd. v. FDIC (In re Boston Post Rd. Ltd.), 21 F.3d 477, 483 (2d Cir. 1994), *cert. denied*, 513 U.S. 1109 (1995). *See supra* § 19.07[C][1] Treatment of Non-recourse Claims.

[272] In re D & W Realty Corp., 156 B.R. 140, 144 (Bankr. S.D.N.Y. 1993); Beal Bank SSB v. Waters Edge Ltd., 248 B.R. 668, 691 (D. Mass. 2000). *See generally* In re SM 104, Ltd., 160 B.R. 202, 218-19 (Bankr. S.D. Fla. 1993).

to a deficiency outside of bankruptcy are significantly different from the claims of other unsecured creditors and thus are not permitted to be included in the same class with other general unsecured claims.[273]

[3] Identical Treatment of Claims in the Same Class

Although a plan can provide unequal treatment between classes, it must provide equal treatment within a class. Every claim or interest in a particular class must receive the same treatment, unless the holder of a particular claim or interest agrees to receive less.[274] This prevents a plan from lumping together creditors who get favorable treatment with those who get unfavorable treatment in the hope that the former will vote "yes" in a sufficient majority to override the "no" votes of the latter.

[E] Impairment of Claims[275]

Every class of claims and interests is either impaired or unimpaired by the debtor's reorganization plan. This distinction plays a crucial role, because impaired classes vote; if a creditors' rights are not altered in any way by the debtor's plan, there is no reason to give them a say. The Code's definition of impairment provides that a class of claims or interests is impaired *unless* the plan either:

- leaves the legal, equitable, and contractual rights of the holder of a claim or interest unaltered,[276] or

- cures the debtor's defaults, de-accelerates the obligation, compensates the holder of the claim or interest for damages, and does not otherwise alter the legal, equitable, or contractual rights of the holder.[277]

Although § 1124 speaks in terms of the impairment of classes of both claims and interests, its biggest practical impact is with respect to claims. Few Chapter 11 plans leave equity interest holders unimpaired.

[1] Rights Unaltered by the Plan

A class of claims is unimpaired if the plan preserves its legal, equitable, and contractual rights. Thus, to be unimpaired, the plan must provide for satisfaction of the claims in the class according to whatever rights they held outside of bankruptcy,

---

[273] *E.g.*, Matter of Woodbrook Assoc., 19 F.3d 312 (7th Cir. 1994); In re SM 104, Ltd., 160 Bankr. 202, 218-19 (Bankr. S.D. Fla. 1993).

[274] Bankruptcy Code § 1123(a)(4).

[275] David Gray Carlson, *Artificial Impairment and the Single Asset Chapter 11 Case*, 23 Cap. U. L. Rev. 339 (1994).

[276] Bankruptcy Code § 1124(1).

[277] Bankruptcy Code § 1124(2).

Prior to 1994, § 1124(3) provided a third method for leaving a class of claims unimpaired: paying members of the class in full, in cash, immediately upon consummation of the plan. It was eliminated to ensure that unsecured creditors of solvent debtors could obtain post-petition interest for claims treated in this fashion. *See* Linda Rusch, *Unintended Consequences of Unthinking Tinkering: The 1994 Amendments and the Chapter 11 Process*, 69 Am. Bankr. L.J. 349, 373-77 (1995).

unaffected by the provisions of the plan. This rarely occurs. When it does, it is usually with respect to a fully secured claim, such as a real estate mortgage.

Assume, for example, that Titanic Corp. is legally obligated to make regular monthly payments on a fully secured mortgage debt, and that the debtor has never missed a single payment or otherwise defaulted on any of the mortgage's terms. The claim is unimpaired if the plan provides for all payments to be made to the creditor in full when they are due and for the debtor to otherwise fulfill all the terms of the mortgage agreement.[278] However, the claim is impaired, even if it is to be fully paid, if the plan changes the duration of payments, the amount of monthly payments, or the rate of interest.

Claims remain unimpaired, even though they may be affected by statutory provisions of the Bankruptcy Code, rather than by the plan. For example, § 502(b)(6) imposes a statutory limit on claims of landlords that exist due to termination of a lease.[281] Enforcement of this mandatory Code provision does not alter the landlord's "legal, equitable, and contractual rights *to which such claim . . . entitles the holder of [the] claim*"[282] and thus does not impair the creditor's claim within the meaning of § 1124.[283] The distinction is between provisions of the plan that alter the creditor's rights and provisions of the Bankruptcy Code that alter the creditor's rights. Changes in the creditor's rights derived from the plan impair the creditor's claim; changes derived from the Code may define the creditor's claim, but do not alter the creditor's claim.[284]

[2] Defaults Cured and Rights Reinstated; De-Acceleration

A plan also leaves a class of claims unimpaired if it alters the claim of the creditor *only* by curing any of the debtor's defaults and reinstating the creditor's legal, equitable, and contractual rights to their status prior to the debtor's default.[285] The plan must not only cure any of the debtor's defaults,[286] but also must reinstate the maturity of the claim,[287] "compensate the holder of such claim . . . for any damages incurred as a result of any reasonable reliance by such holder on such contractual provision or applicable law,"[288] and otherwise leave the creditor's rights unchanged.

For example, assume Titanic Corp. owes a fully secured $1 million debt to North Atlantic Finance Co., which calls for regularly monthly payments of $10,000 per month, and permits North Atlantic to accelerate the debt, making the $1 million

---

[278] *E.g.*, In re Atlanta-Stewart Partners, 193 B.R. 79, 82 (Bankr. N.D. Ga. 1996) (regarding the deletion of former § 1124(3)).

[281] *See supra* § 10.02[D][1] Limits on Claims for Rent.

[282] Bankruptcy Code § 1124(1) (emphasis added).

[283] *E.g.*, Solow v. PPI Enters., Inc. (In re PPI Enters., Inc.), 324 F.3d 197 (3d Cir. 2003).

[284] *E.g.*, In re Monclova Care Ctr., Inc., 254 B.R. 167, 176-177 (Bankr. N.D. Ohio 2000).

[285] Bankruptcy Code § 1124(2).

[286] Bankruptcy Code § 1124(2)(A).

[287] Bankruptcy Code § 1124(2)(B).

[288] Bankruptcy Code § 1124(2)(C).

balance immediately due upon the debtor's default. Before bankruptcy, Titanic missed a payment and North Atlantic accelerated the debt, making it due in full, immediately. The plan calls for the Titanic to make the missed payment, pay North Atlantic any penalties and interest due on the missed payment, and resume regular monthly installment payments according to the schedule specified in the parties' agreement. This cures the debtor's default, reinstates the maturity of the debtor's obligations, and, by requiring interest and penalty payments, compensates the creditor for the debtor's default. Thus, North Atlantic's claim has been de-accelerated; it is unimpaired and the creditor is not entitled to vote on the debtor's plan.

If the agreement provides for a default rate of interest, there is an issue of whether cure and reinstatement requires the debtor to pay interest at the default rate to avoid impairment of the creditor's claim. Section 1123(d), added in 2005, indicates that the terms of the agreement should be enforced, at least to the extent that they would be enforceable under state contract law. It provides:

> Notwithstanding subsection (a) of this section and sections 506(b), 1129(a)(7), and 1129(b) of this title, if it is proposed in a plan to cure a default the amount necessary to cure the default shall be determined in accordance with the underlying agreement and applicable nonbankruptcy law.[289]

Some earlier decisions held that cure and reinstatement erased the effects of the debtor's previous default and that therefore any default rate of interest provided for in the agreement should not be required.[290] Courts dealing with the issue after the enactment of § 1123(d) disagree with these decisions and require the debtor to pay any default rate, provided that it is not a "penalty" or otherwise unenforceable under relevant state or federal law that otherwise applies.[291]

Certain technical defaults need not be cured. For example, § 365(b)(2) specifies that "ipso-facto clauses" in the debtor's contracts that make the commencement of a bankruptcy case or other circumstances related to the debtor's financial condition a default, need not be cured.[292] Section 1124(2) leaves creditors' claims unimpaired even though the plan does not provide for cure of these types of defaults.

[3] Artificial Impairment

"Artificial impairment" refers to the practice of impairing a class of claims in a negligible way, such as providing for paying 99.99% of the amount of the claim, or providing for payment one day later than the terms of the contract with the creditor require. This is done in the anticipation that the creditor who holds the claim will vote to "accept" the plan and thus permit the plan to satisfy § 1129(a)(10)'s

---

[289] Bankruptcy Code § 1123(d).

[290] *E.g.*, Great W. Bank & Trust v. Entz-White Lumber and Supply, Inc., 850 F.2d 1338 (9th Cir. 1988).

[291] In re General Growth Properties, Inc., 451 B.R. 323 (Bankr. S.D.N.Y. 2011). *But see* In re Phoenix Bus. Park Ltd. P'Ship, 257 B.R. 517, 522 (Bankr. D. Ariz. 2001).

[292] Bankruptcy Code § 365(b)(2). *See supra* § 11.05[B] Cure of Defaults Required for Assumption.

requirement that at least one class of impaired claims accept the plan.[293] Though lower level decisions are split over whether this is appropriate,[294] Court of Appeals decisions that have confronted this issue directly have rejected the practice.[295] Section 1129(a)(10)'s purpose is to ensure that there is some indicia of support for the plan, and permitting a favorable vote by an artificially impaired class to satisfy its requirement, completely frustrates this purpose.[296]

[F] Treatment of General Unsecured Claims

The Bankruptcy Code allows broad flexibility with respect to the treatment of classes of unsecured claims. Unless the plan leaves their claims unaffected and thus unimpaired, unsecured creditors have the right to reject the plan. Therefore the key protections accorded to unsecured creditors are those that prevent unfair discrimination, ensure that creditors receive at least what they would have received in liquidation, and protect the voting process by insuring adequate disclosure and fair voting procedures.

Although § 1123 purports to specify all of the required provisions of a reorganization plan, a plan's provisions must also contain whatever terms are necessary for it to be confirmed pursuant to § 1129.

As discussed earlier, § 1123 requires the plan to set out all classes of unsecured debt, specify whether the class is impaired or unimpaired, state the treatment of each class under the plan, and provide for equal treatment of all claims within a class.[297]

Section 1129 requires the plan to be in the best interests of creditors.[298] More precisely, any creditor who does not accept the plan must "receive or retain . . . property of a value, as of the effective date of the plan, that is not less than the amount [it] would . . . receive or retain if the debtor were liquidated under Chapter 7 . . . on such date."[299] This implements creditors' most basic entitlement in bankruptcy: their right to the liquidation value of their claims. Because Chapter 11 plans normally provide for payments over a period of time, the payments proposed must exceed the present value of the amount that would be paid if the

---

[293] Bankruptcy Code § 1129(a)(1). *See infra* § 19.11[A] Acceptance by One Impaired Class.

[294] Peter E. Meltzer, *Disenfranchising the Dissenting Creditor Through Artificial Classification or Artificial Impairment*, 66 Am. Bankr. L.J. 281 (1992).

[295] In re Combustion Eng'g, Inc., 391 F.3d 190, 243 (3d Cir. 2004); Windsor on the River Assocs. Ltd. v. Balcor Real Estate Fin. (In re Windsor on the River Assocs. Ltd.), 7 F.3d 127, 131 (8th Cir. 1993).

[296] Windsor on the River Assocs. Ltd. v. Balcor Real Estate Fin. (In re Windsor on the River Assocs. Ltd.), 7 F.3d 127, 131 (8th Cir. 1993). *See* David Gray Carlson, *Artificial Impairment and the Single Asset Chapter 11 Case*, 23 Cap. U. L. Rev. 339 (1994).

[297] Bankruptcy Code § 1123(a)(1)-(4). *See generally infra* § 19.08[D] Classification of Claims.

[298] Bankruptcy Code § 1129(a)(7)(A)(ii). Despite its familiar name, this test applies to both claims and interests — interests are also entitled to liquidation value. However, in virtually every case, the Chapter 7 value of an owner's equity interest is zero, so the "best interest of interest holders" test is virtually insignificant. *See infra* § 19.10[F] Plan in Best Interests of Creditors.

[299] Bankruptcy Code § 1129(a)(7)(A). This rule is subject to an exception if the creditor has made the § 1111(b) election. Bankruptcy Code § 1129(a)(7)(B). *See infra* § 19.08[H][4] Treatment of the § 1111(b) Election.

debtor was liquidated as of the time the plan is implemented. The present value of what the creditor receives under the plan must be worth at least what the creditor would get if the debtor were liquidated in Chapter 7.[300]

[G]   Treatment of Priority Unsecured Claims

Chapter 11 treats priority claims favorably. Section 1129(a)(9) divides these claims into three groups. The first group[301] consists of priority 2 (administrative)[302] and priority 3 (involuntary gap) claims.[303] The second group[304] consists of priority 1 (alimony, maintenance, support),[305] priority 4 (wages),[306] priority 5 (employee benefits),[307] priority 6 (grain elevators and fish processing facilities),[308] and priority 7 (consumer deposits)[309] claims. The third group contains priority 8 (tax) claims.[310] There is no special treatment required for priority 9 (bank bailout) claims[311] or priority 10 (drunk driving liability) claims.[312]

The first group (priorities 2 and 3) are given the most favored status in the plan. These claims, including super-priority administrative claims, are entitled to immediate full payment, in cash, on the effective date of the plan — the day it is implemented.[313] The only exception is if the holder of a claim agrees to less favorable treatment.[314] The class itself, however, cannot bind any particular claimant; the right to full, immediate cash payment is specific to each claim. Thus, even if only the statutory majority of claims entitled to priority 2 or 3 accepts a plan that calls for less favorable treatment, the plan cannot be confirmed. This requirement may cripple a cash-poor debtor's effort to gain court confirmation of its plan — the debtor must have a considerable amount of cash to make performance of this provision feasible.[315]

The second group (priorities 1, and 4 through 7) are given slightly less favorable treatment. Each claim in the class is entitled to payment in full, but the class can

---

[300] *See infra* § 19.10[F] Plan in Best Interests of Creditors.

[301] Bankruptcy Code § 1129(a)(9)(A).

[302] *See supra* § 10.04[A][2] Administrative Expense Claims.

[303] *See supra* § 10.04[A][3] Involuntary Gap Creditors.

[304] Bankruptcy Code § 1129(a)(9)(B).

[305] *See supra* § 10.04[A][1] Support Claims.

[306] *See supra* § 10.04[A][4] Wage Claims.

[307] *See supra* § 10.04[A][5] Employee Benefit Plan Claims.

[308] *See supra* § 10.04[A][6] Certain Claims of Farmers and Fisherman.

[309] *See supra* § 10.04[A][7] Consumer Deposits.

[310] *See supra* § 10.04[A][8] Tax Claims.

[311] *See supra* § 10.04[A][9] Claims of Insured Depositary Institutions.

[312] *See supra* § 10.04[A][10] Civil Liability for Driving While Intoxicated.

[313] Bankruptcy Code § 1129(a)(9)(A).

[314] Bankruptcy Code § 1129(a)(9)(A).

[315] The plan must also be feasible. *See infra* § 19.10[J] Feasibility of Plan. Unless the debtor has the means to implement the plan, it cannot be confirmed.

vote to accept deferred payments, spread out over time.[316] If the class rejects the plan, each member of the class must be treated in the same manner as claims in the first group: full payment, in cash, on the effective date of the plan.[317] Thus, each class of these claims can vote to permit the debtor to defer payments to members of the class. However, each member of the class remains entitled to receive payment in full.

Note that this is different from claims in the first group, where each claimant has the right to demand payment immediately, regardless of how the class votes. In the second group, the class may vote to accept deferred payment in full, and this vote binds dissenters. Any individual holder of a claim may agree to accept less than full payment, but this binds no one else.

The third group (priority 8 tax claims) is given somewhat less favorable treatment. Each claim remains entitled to payment in full, but neither specific claims nor the class is entitled to insist on immediate cash payment. Nonetheless, the payments, when reduced to their present value, must equal the allowed amount of each claim on the effective date of the plan.[318] Any deferred payments must be made over no more than five years after the date of the order for relief.[319]

Holders of secured tax claims that would have been entitled to priority treatment if they had been unsecured may not be treated less favorably than unsecured priority tax claims.[320] Without this rule, payments to secured tax claims that would have been entitled to priority if they were not secured, could have been paid over a longer period than if they had been unsecured. The Code also requires priority tax claims to be treated at least as well as non-priority unsecured claims paid under the plan.[321] Thus, if non-priority unsecured claims are paid in full over three years, priority unsecured tax claims may not be paid over five years as would otherwise be permitted.

[H] Treatment of Secured Claims[322]

As is true throughout bankruptcy, Chapter 11 treats secured claims very favorably. Although the Code permits considerable changes in the rights of secured creditors, the value of most secured claims remains intact throughout the proceeding and after the plan is confirmed. The holder of a secured claim is thus generally in a relatively powerful position, and many plans founder on the requirement that the secured claims receive full value.

---

[316] Bankruptcy Code § 1129(a)(9)(B)(i).

[317] Bankruptcy Code § 1129(a)(9)(B)(ii).

[318] Bankruptcy Code § 1129(a)(9)(C)(i).

[319] Bankruptcy Code § 1129(a)(9)(C)(ii). Note that this may be considerably less than five years from the effective date of the plan. Any individual claimant may accept a different treatment, but this does not bind other creditors.

[320] Bankruptcy Code § 1129(a)(9)(D).

[321] Bankruptcy Code § 1129(a)(9)(C)(iii).

[322] Darrell G. Waas, *Letting the Lender Have It: Satisfaction of Secured Claims by Abandoning a Portion of the Collateral*, 62 Am. Bankr. L.J. 97 (1988).

In considering the Code's treatment of secured claims, it is useful to remember that most of the time each secured claim is in its own class. This is partly for the sake of convenience, partly because secured claimants generally want to negotiate individual deals with the debtor, and partly because it is unusual for a secured claim to have rights that are similar to any other secured claim.

[1] Mandatory Treatment of Secured Claims

The key mandatory provision regarding impaired secured claims is contained in § 1129's requirements for confirmation. Specifically, the best interests of creditors test requires that each claimant receive over the course of the plan the present value of the liquidation value of its claim.[323] In other words, the value of the payment stream under the plan must have a present value equal to the lesser of the amount of the debt or the value of the collateral securing the debt.

Moreover, a secured creditor cannot be bound, without its consent, to a plan that does not provide it the minimum to which it would be entitled in a non-consensual plan — a "cramdown." As explained in more detail in connection with secured creditor cramdown, secured creditors are entitled to deferred cash payments that are worth as much as their allowed secured claim.[324] This nearly always requires the payment of interest on the amount of its secured claim to compensate the creditor for any delay in receiving payment.

For example, if the debt is undersecured and the property securing the debt is worth $100,000, the payments under the plan must have a present value of at least $100,000. Just as with the best interests of creditors test, this means that the payments must total more than $100,000. How much more depends on the length of the payout period and the estimated interest rates for that period. In effect, this means that even if the debt is undersecured, the debtor must pay interest on it.

In addition, the holder of a secured claim must retain the lien on its collateral for the full amount of its secured claim.[325] Otherwise, holders of secured claims would be vulnerable to becoming unsecured creditors in any subsequent bankruptcy case filed by the debtor after failing to fully perform the terms of its confirmed plan.

Alternatively, secured creditors are entitled to a lien on any proceeds derived from the sale of their collateral free and clear of their lien,[326] or anything else that permits the secured creditor to realize the "indubitable equivalent" of its claim.[327]

---

[323] Bankruptcy Code § 1129(a)(7)(A). Any individual creditor may agree to accept less, but this virtually never happens.

[324] Bankruptcy Code § 1129(b)(2)(A)(i)(II).

[325] Bankruptcy Code § 1129(b)(2)(A)(i)(I).

[326] Bankruptcy Code § 1129(b)(2)(A)(ii).

[327] Bankruptcy Code § 1129(b)(2)(A)(iii).

[2]   Optional Treatment of Secured Claims

As is true with unsecured debt, so long as the debtor does not resort to cramdown, the Code expressly permits the inclusion of "any other appropriate provision not inconsistent with the applicable provisions of this title."[328] Because there is usually only one creditor in each class of secured claims, acceptance of the proposed provisions depends on the consent of that one creditor. This makes negotiations over the terms of the plan with respect to a secured creditor more akin to the negotiations between any two parties to a business deal.

Except with respect to residential mortgages, claims of secured creditors can be modified by extending the due date, reducing the monthly payments, or adjusting the interest rate, and, unless the creditor makes the § 1111(b) election, stripping the lien down to the value of the collateral.[329] The plan might call for a sale of the debtor's assets[330] free and clear of any lien, with creditors' liens transferred to the proceeds obtained from the sale.[331] What the debtor may offer to its secured creditors is limited almost solely by the imagination, provided they agree to the proposed treatment,[332] or even without their consent, if they receive the "indubitable equivalent" of their secured claims.[333]

[3]   Chapter 11 Lien Stripping

Lien stripping refers to reducing the lien of a partially secured claim to the value of the collateral. Thus, a $10 million debt, secured by a mortgage on land worth only $8 million, is bifurcated into two claims: an $8 million secured claim and a $2 million unsecured claim. In other words, if the debtor were to try to keep the collateral outside of bankruptcy, it would have to repay the full $10 million, regardless of the value of the collateral. Once the lien has been stripped, the lien can be satisfied with a payment of $8 million. The creditor's lien is "stripped" of the amount beyond the value of the collateral.

Lien stripping is not permitted with respect to a residential real state mortgage, nor is any other modification of the contract.[334] This restriction parallels a similar rule in Chapter 13.[335] Because only individuals have a principal residence, it has no effect in business reorganizations that involve corporations. A corporation might have a "domicile," but only an living, breathing human being can have a "residence." However, there is nothing in Chapter 11 similar to the hanging paragraph at the end of § 1325(a)(9) which prevents lien stripping with respect to purchase money security interests in motor vehicles or other personal property.[336] Chapter 11

---

[328]   Bankruptcy Code § 1123(b)(6).

[329]   Bankruptcy Code § 1123(a)(5).

[330]   Bankruptcy Code § 1123(b)(4).

[331]   Bankruptcy Code § 1129(b)(2)(A)(ii).

[332]   Bankruptcy Code § 1129(a)(8)(A).

[333]   Bankruptcy Code § 1129(b)(2)(A)(iii).

[334]   Bankruptcy Code § 1123(b)(5).

[335]   Bankruptcy Code § 1322(b)(2). See *supra* § 18.07[B][2][a] Residential Real Estate Mortgages.

[336]   *See* Bankruptcy Code § 1325(a)(9); *supra* § 18.07[B][b] Certain Purchase Money Loans.

debtors are free to strip purchase money security interests away from personal property, without limitation.

[4] Treatment of the § 1111(b) Election[337]

As noted earlier, partially secured creditors may elect to have their claims treated as non-recourse secured claims for the entire nominal amount of the debt, rather than as recourse claims that are bifurcated into secured claims and unsecured claims.[338] If a creditor is owed $5 million, secured by property worth only $3 million, the creditor has the option to be treated in the "normal" way — to have a secured claim for $3 million and an unsecured claim for $2 million or to make the § 1111(b)(2) election and have a secured claim for the entire $5 million.

On the face of it, the election is very attractive and provides strong protection against lien stripping. However, most of the time, this apparent appeal is illusory. Section 1129(a)(7)(B) eliminates much of the benefit of § 1111(b)(2). This provision sets out the mandatory treatment of an 1111(b)(2) claim. It provides that the holder of a § 1111(b)(2) claim must receive or retain under the plan "property of a value, as of the effective date of the plan, that is not less than the value of such holder's interest in the estate's interest in the property that secures such claim."[339] This means that the best interests of creditors test[340] does not require payment of the present value of the entire claim, but only payment of the present value of the collateral. Thus, in the example given, the best interest of creditors test is met if the sum of all payments made equals at least $5 million and has a present value of at least $3 million. Thus, if any meaningful payment is provided to creditors with unsecured claims, a secured creditor who makes the § 1111(b) election may be worse off than it would have been if it had elected to have its claim treated in the usual fashion. If the creditor does *not* make the election, it would still be entitled to payments with a present value of $3 million and would also receive payments worth at least the liquidation value of the $2 million unsecured deficiency claim.

This does not always mean that making the § 1111(b) election is a bad idea. For example, it may not be possible for the debtor to extend the plan for such a long period of time that it will meet both the requirement of paying the nominal amount of the claim and the actual value of the collateral. The property also might be sold during the life of the plan for more than it is presently worth; and, under at least some circumstances, the § 1111(b) creditor will then be able to collect the full amount of its claim from the sale proceeds. Such a sale might occur in a subsequent liquidation, if, for example, the debtor's reorganization fails within several years after the plan has been implemented.

However, given the plan confirmation standards, the protection provided by § 1111(b) is so uncertain that the election is only rarely made. The most common setting in which it might be utilized is in a single-asset real estate case where unsecured claims are to receive very little or where the affected creditor has little

---

[337] Steven R. Haydon et al., *The 1111(b)(2) Election: A Primer*, 13 Bank. Dev. J. 99 (1996).

[338] Bankruptcy Code § 1111(b)(1). *See infra* § 19.07[C][1] Treatment of Non-Recourse Claims.

[339] Bankruptcy Code § 1129(a)(7)(B).

[340] *See infra* § 19.10[F] Plan in Best Interests of Creditors.

confidence in the debtor's ability to succeed following reorganization.

[I] Executory Contracts and Unexpired Leases in Chapter 11

As explained in more detail elsewhere, a Chapter 11 trustee or debtor-in-possession has the authority to assume, reject, or assign any executory contract or unexpired lease of the debtor.[341] The estate's treatment of these unperformed contracts plays a key role in many Chapter 11 reorganization cases. Section 365 might apply to permit the debtor to reject, assume, or assign a wide variety of executory contracts and unexpired leases, including:

- real estate leases of its retail outlets, factories, or storage facilities;

- equipment leases;

- intellectual property licenses;

- franchise agreements; and

- employment contracts, including collective bargaining agreements.[342]

The Code expressly permits the debtor's plan to provide for the assumption, rejection, or assignment of any executory contract or unexpired lease that has not previously been rejected under § 365.[343] Section 365 specifies that, although the court may require a Chapter 11 debtor to make an earlier decision, the debtor otherwise has until confirmation of its plan to determine how to handle these contracts.[344] Normally, debtors desire to defer their decision until after they have had sufficient time to evaluate their business operations to determine which contracts they want to retain and which make more sense to either reject or assume and assign.

§ 19.09 ACCEPTANCE OF PLAN BY HOLDERS OF CLAIMS AND INTERESTS: DISCLOSURE AND VOTING[345]

Chapter 11's core is the agreement between the debtor and its creditors on a plan of reorganization. Creditors express their agreement by participating in negotiations leading to the promulgation of the debtor's plan and by voting to accept it. Creditors vote in classes. But, rather than the traditional "one person, one vote" approach that prevails in politics, Chapter 11 plan voting proceeds on a combination of a "one creditor, one vote," and a "one dollar, one vote" regime. More than half of a debtor's creditors must vote for the plan, and at least two-thirds of the dollar value

---

[341] *See supra* Chapter 11 Executory Contracts and Unexpired Leases.

[342] Rejection of collective bargaining agreements is conducted pursuant to § 1113. *See infra* § 23.03[A] Rejection of Collective Bargaining Agreements.

[343] Bankruptcy Code § 1129(b)(2).

[344] Bankruptcy Code § 365(d)(2).

[345] *See* Daniel J. Bussel & Kenneth N. Klee, *Recalibrating Consent in Bankruptcy*, 83 Am. Bankr. L.J. 663 (2009).

of claims against the debtor must approve the plan.[346]

A claimant's decision to accept or reject the plan is meant to be an informed one. The debtor, who is in control of most of the information about its financial position and its prospects for future success, must provide that information to creditors and equity interest holders who are to vote on its plan. Moreover, this information must be presented in a way that enables the voter to make a reasoned decision, and it must be provided in a timely manner. This scheme, although simpler in structure, is a substitute for the disclosure laws which govern issuers of publicly traded stocks and bonds.

[A] Consensual Chapter 11 Plans

As suggested above, most Chapter 11 plans are confirmed with the acceptance of creditors. For confirmation to be consensual, every impaired class of creditors and interest holders must vote to "accept" the plan.

There still might be dissenters. Classes of creditors whose claims are not impaired are deemed to accept the plan. They do not have the right to vote, even though they are dissatisfied with the debtor's prospects for success.[347] Other dissenting creditors may belong to a class that has accepted the plan. Even though there are dissenters, confirmation is regarded as consensual if each class entitled to vote has accepted it by the requisite number and amount. This feature of Chapter 11 is its principle advantage over an out-of-court workout agreement, where dissenters can effectively block a plan's success.[348]

[B] Disclosure and Solicitation of Ballots

[1] Court Approval of Disclosure Statement; Adequate Information[349]

Section 1125 deals with the process of providing information to the creditors and owners of the debtor about a proposed reorganization plan. It prohibits anyone from soliciting the acceptance or rejection of a plan unless it has simultaneously or previously given the person solicited both a copy of the plan or a summary of the plan and a written disclosure statement approved by the court.[350] The disclosure statement provides creditors and owners with the information they need to make an informed judgment about accepting or rejecting a plan.

---

[346] Bankruptcy Code § 1126(c).

[347] Bankruptcy Code § 1126(f).

[348] *See supra* § 2.10 Compositions and Workouts.

[349] Glenn W. Merrick, *The Chapter 11 Disclosure Statement in a Strategic Environment*, 44 Bus. Law. 103 (1988); Nicholas S. Gatto, Note, *Disclosure in Chapter 11 Reorganizations: The Pursuit of Consistency and Clarity*, 70 Cornell L. Rev. 733 (1985); Note, *Disclosure of Adequate Information in a Chapter 11 Reorganization*, 94 Harv. L. Rev. 1808 (1981).

[350] Bankruptcy Code § 1125(b). This may not be necessary in a case involving a "small business." Bankruptcy Code § 1125(f). *See infra* § 19.14 Small Business Debtors.

The disclosure statement may be approved by the court only after there has been both notice and an opportunity for a hearing.[351] The court may approve the disclosure statement only if the court determines that it contains "adequate information."[352]

"Adequate information" means information that is sufficient to enable a hypothetical "reasonable investor typical of holders of claims or interests of the relevant class" to make an informed judgment about the proposed plan.[353] It should be as detailed as practicable given the "nature and history of the debtor and the condition of the debtor's books and records . . . [but it does not have to] include information about other proposed or possible plan[s]."[354] Thus, a small proprietorship with sketchy books may have a lesser burden in preparing its disclosure statement than a large, publicly-traded corporation, both because the issues are less complex and because its records are less complete.

[2] Contents of Disclosure Statement

The adequacy of the information is not measured against some absolute standard. Rather, it is measured from the perspective of the "typical investor," who is defined as an investor who has (1) a claim or interest of the relevant class; (2) the same type of relationship with the debtor as holders of claims or interests of that class generally have; and (3) the same ability to gather information about the debtor as holders of claims or interests of that class generally have.[355] The latter two requirements make it clear that information that would be adequate for, say, an insider, would not necessarily be adequate information if most persons who held claims or interests of the same class were not insiders. The debtor does not have to send the same disclosure statement to everybody. Different classes may receive different disclosure statements; however, everyone within a particular class must receive the same disclosure statement.[356]

One frequently cited decision provides a detailed list of the items courts frequently require to be included in a disclosure statement:

1. the circumstances that gave rise to the filing of the bankruptcy petition;

2. a complete description of the available assets and their value;

3. the anticipated future of the debtor;

4. the source of the information provided in the disclosure statement;

5. a disclaimer, which typically indicates that no statements or information concerning the debtor or its assets or securities are authorized, other than those set forth in the disclosure statement;

---

[351] Bankruptcy Code § 1125(b). *See* Fed. R. Bankr. P. 3017(a).

[352] Bankruptcy Code § 1125(b).

[353] Bankruptcy Code § 1125(a)(1).

[354] Bankruptcy Code § 1125(a)(1).

[355] Bankruptcy Code § 1125(a)(2).

[356] Bankruptcy Code § 1125(c).

6. the condition and performance of the debtor while in Chapter 11;

7. information regarding claims against the estate;

8. a liquidation analysis setting forth the estimated return that creditors would receive under Chapter 7;

9. the accounting and valuation methods used to produce the financial information in the disclosure statement;

10. information regarding the future management of the debtor, including the amount of compensation to be paid to any insiders, directors, or officers of the debtor;

11. a summary of the plan of reorganization;

12. an estimate of all administrative expenses, including attorneys' fees and accountants' fees;

13. the collectibility of any accounts receivable;

14. any financial information, valuations, or pro forma projections that would be relevant to creditors' determinations of whether to accept or reject the plan;

15. information relevant to the risks being taken by the creditors and interest holders;

16. the actual or projected value that can be obtained from avoidable transfers;

17. the existence, likelihood, and possible success of non-bankruptcy litigation;

18. the tax consequences of the plan; and

19. the relationship of the debtor with affiliates.[357]

The disclosure statement must also contain "a discussion of the potential material Federal tax consequences of the plan to the debtor, any successor to the debtor, and a hypothetical investor typical of holders of claims or interests in the case."[358] Section 1125(a)(1) tempers the requirements for disclosure statements, by specifying that in determining whether to approve a disclosure statement the court should consider the complexity of the case, the benefit to creditors and others of requiring additional information, and the costs of providing additional information.[359]

---

[357] In re Scioto Valley Mortg. Co., 88 B.R. 168 (Bankr. S.D. Ohio 1988). *See also* In re Malek, 35 B.R. 443 (Bankr. E.D. Mich. 1983).

[358] Bankruptcy Code § 1125(a)(1).

[359] Bankruptcy Code § 1125(a)(1).

[3] Soliciting Rejection of a Plan[360]

In some cases, dissenting creditors take a proactive approach to resisting confirmation and actively solicit other creditors to reject a proposed plan. The rules for soliciting votes in favor of a plan also apply to efforts to solicit rejections.[361] Thus, those opposed to a plan may not solicit rejections until after the disclosure statement has been approved by the court and transmitted to interested parties.[362]

Despite this, creditors who try to persuade others to reject a plan do not need to distribute their own disclosure statement. Moreover, they do not need to obtain prior court approval of all of the information they supply to creditors as part of their effort to persuade them to vote against a plan.

In *Century Glove, Inc. v. First American Bank*, a group of dissenting creditors solicited rejections of the debtor's plan and circulated a draft of an alternative plan. The bankruptcy court sanctioned them for doing so by "designating" their ballots under § 1121(e) and thus disqualifying them.[363] None of the circulated materials had been approved by the court, and they were not accompanied by a separate disclosure statement.

In reversing the bankruptcy court's disqualification of rejections received pursuant to these solicitations, the court of appeals read § 1125 narrowly to permit plan opponents to solicit rejections, provided that a disclosure statement containing "adequate information" about the debtor's plan had previously been made.[364] Subsequent decisions have taken a similar approach.[365]

However, the efforts of dissenting creditors to persuade others to reject the debtor's plan should be distinguished from attempts to obtain acceptances of an alternative plan. If the opponents of a plan go too far, and solicit acceptances of a different plan, their votes may be disqualified.[366]

---

[360] Douglas E. Deutsch, *Ensuring Proper Bankruptcy Solicitation: Evaluating Bankruptcy Law, the First Amendment, the Code of Ethics, and Securities Law in Bankruptcy Solicitation Cases*, 11 Am. Bankr. Inst. L. Rev. 213 (2003); Paul R. Glassman, *Solicitation of Plan Rejections under the Bankruptcy Code*, 62 Am. Bankr. L.J. 261 (1988); Claude D. Montgomery, et al., *Solicitation Under Section 1125 of the Bankruptcy Code:* Century Glove *and the First Amendment*, 23 Seton Hall L. Rev. 1570 (1993).

[361] Bankruptcy Code § 1125(b).

[362] Bankruptcy Code § 1126(e) (providing for disqualification of votes solicited before a disclosure statement is disseminated).

[363] 860 F.2d 94 (3d Cir. 1988).

[364] 860 F.2d at 100. *But see* In re Apex Oil Co., 111 B.R. 245 (Bankr. E.D. Mo. 1990).

[365] *E.g.*, In re Trans Max Technologies, Inc., 349 B.R. 80 (Bankr. D. Nev. 2006). *But see* In re Clamp-All Corp., 233 B.R. 198 (Bankr. D. Mass. 1999) (prohibiting distribution of materials that solicit rejections before approval and dissemination of proponent's disclosure statement). *See generally* John F. Wagner Jr., Annotation, *What Constitutes Improper Solicitation of Acceptance or Rejection of Reorganization Plan Under 11 U.S.C.A. Sec. 1125(b)*, 100 A.L.R. Fed. 226 (1990).

[366] *See* In re Kellogg Square P'ship, 160 B.R. 336, 341 n.6 (Bankr. D. Minn. 1993).

[4] Exemption from Registration with the SEC

In some Chapter 11 plans, the debtor issues "securities" as a means of satisfying creditors' claims. For example, the debtor might propose issuing voting stock to its unsecured creditors; say, one share for every $100 of claim. Or the debtor might issue a bond or other type of publicly traded debt security. This creates some potential problems with the securities laws. The issuance of stocks, bonds, and other securities is regulated by a number of state and federal laws; among the requirements is "registration" of the security with state and federal authorities. Compliance with the registration requirement is frequently time-consuming and expensive; imposing this requirement on a Chapter 11 debtor would create yet another barrier to effective reorganization,[367] even though the function of registration overlaps with that of the disclosure statement.

Because of this, the Bankruptcy Code provides a broad exemption from securities laws for most debtors who are issuing plan-related securities. Assuming the debtor is not an "underwriter,"[368] any securities it issues that are entirely or primarily in exchange for a claim or an interest are *entirely exempt* from federal, state, and local laws that require securities to be registered.[369] This exemption only applies to securities exchanged for existing debt or equity; it does not apply to securities issued to raise funds to finance the plan, although the narrower registration exemption in § 364(f) can be used for that purpose.[370] Likewise, the exemption only relates to the registration requirements. Other securities laws — most notably, those that prohibit fraud in securities transactions — still apply.[371] Chapter 11 provides no safe harbor against claims of securities fraud. Indeed, fraud committed in connection with promulgation of a disclosure statement would raise problems beyond violations of the securities laws.

[5] Disclosure in Small Business Cases

Disclosure may be considerably simplified in cases involving "small business debtors." These are business debtors with less than $2 million in claims held by creditors other than insiders.[372] These debtors' financial circumstances are usually fairly simple. Accordingly, the court may determine that the plan itself provides adequate information and that a separate and expensive disclosure statement is not necessary.[373] Alternatively, the court may approve a disclosure statement that is submitted on standardized disclosure statement forms that have previously been

---

[367] *See generally* Louis Loss & Joel Seligman, Securities Regulation (Rev'd 3d ed. 2004).

[368] Broadly speaking, an underwriter is a person who is distributing a security to others, rather than holding it for investment. *See* 2 Louis Loss & Joel Seligman, Securities Regulation 1138.44-1138.70 (Rev'd 3d ed. 2004).

[369] Bankruptcy Code § 1145(a)(1).

[370] *See supra* § 9.05 Obtaining Credit.

[371] *See generally* Thomas Lee Hazen, The Law of Securities Regulation 560-698 (2002).

[372] Bankruptcy Code § 101(51D). The definition excludes single-asset real estate debtors regardless of the small amount of their debt.

[373] Bankruptcy Code § 1125(f)(1).

approved by the court.[374] Further, the court may conditionally approve a disclosure statement and defer final approval of its adequacy until the hearing on plan confirmation.[375]

[6] Pre-Petition Solicitation

Debtors who have attempted to deploy an out-of-court workout or composition in an unsuccessful effort to avoid bankruptcy may have solicited acceptances before filing their bankruptcy petition. Such a debtor may seek to use Chapter 11 to obtain confirmation of the proposed out-of-court settlement. However, solicitations of acceptances or rejections of the debtor's plan prior to the filing of the petition are subject to state and federal securities laws.[376]

[C] Voting by Classes of Claims and Interests[377]

Consensual confirmation requires the approval of each impaired class of creditors and equity security holders.[378] Voting is primarily by claim, not by claimant, and is conducted by each class of claim and interest holders. Normally, every allowed claim has a vote. However, if a claim is held by an entity whose vote was in bad faith, or whose vote was solicited or procured in bad faith, the ballot may be disqualified and will not count.[379]

Some classes of claims or interests do not vote. A class and all of the members of a class whose claims are unimpaired are deemed to have accepted the plan and have no right to vote.[380] These stakeholders effectively voted when they entered into the contract with the debtor on the terms that are replicated by the plan. Likewise, claims on which nothing will be paid do not vote; these classes are deemed to have rejected the plan, without the necessity of conducting a vote.[381]

[1] Voting by Classes of Claims

Approval does not require a unanimous vote. Instead, it requires a two-pronged majority. The first prong requires a simple majority of more than half of the number of claims.[382] The second prong requires a super-majority of at least two-thirds in the amount of the claims of those voting.[383]

---

[374] Bankruptcy Code § 1125(f)(2). *See* 28 U.S.C. § 2075 (2006).

[375] Bankruptcy Code § 1125(f)(3).

[376] Bankruptcy Code § 1126(b)(1).

[377] David Arthur Skeel, Jr., *The Nature and Effect of Corporate Voting in Chapter 11 Reorganization Cases*, 78 Va. L. Rev. 461 (1992).

[378] *See supra* § 10.01 Meaning of Claims and Interests; Priority.

[379] Bankruptcy Code § 1126(c), (e).

[380] Bankruptcy Code § 1126(f). They can still object to the plan on the grounds that it is not feasible.

[381] Bankruptcy Code § 1126(g).

[382] Bankruptcy Code § 1126(c).

[383] Bankruptcy Code § 1126(c).

In each case, whether the requisite majority is reached depends on the number and amount of claims in the class who vote. Those who do not either accept or reject, do not count.

Both requisite majorities must be reached. For example, suppose a class consists of thirty claims, totaling $180,000. If sixteen claims totaling $120,000 vote to approve the plan, the class has approved the plan. More than half (16 of 30) of the claim holders have voted for the plan and two-thirds ($120,000 of $180,000) of the amount of the claims have voted in its favor. If fewer than sixteen claim holders accept the plan, the class has rejected it. Even if fifteen claim holders (exactly 50% in number) totaling $179,999.85 (not quite 100%) accept the plan, the class has rejected it, because both majorities must be achieved. Similarly, if twenty-nine claims totaling $119,999.99 vote in favor, the class rejects the plan.[384] This is due to the size of the one remaining claim, which was more than one-third of the total amount of claims in the class.

This dual majority requirement prevents a plan from being accepted by a few large creditors over the objections of many small creditors or accepted by many small creditors over the objections of a few large creditors. The latter probably has more practical significance; in many Chapter 11 cases, a single creditor can block consensual confirmation if it holds more than one-third of the debt in a class.[385]

[2] Voting by Classes of Interests

Equity interest holders are subject to a somewhat different rule. A class of interests accepts a plan if two-thirds in the amount of the allowed interests in the class accept the plan.[386] The number of interest holders voting to accept, does not matter.

[D] Disqualification ("Designation") of Votes[387]

Acceptances or rejections that are submitted in bad faith can be disqualified.[388] Section 1126(e) provides: "the court may designate any entity whose acceptance or rejection of [a] plan was not in good faith, or was not solicited or procured in good faith or in accordance with the provisions [of the bankruptcy code]."[389] Votes of creditors who are designated, are not counted. Disqualification by "designation" should not be misinterpreted as a requirement that creditors must vote in accordance with the debtor's best interests, or that they have a fiduciary duty to other creditors.[390] Rather, creditors are entitled to vote in accordance with their

---

[384] *See* In re Eitemiller, 149 B.R. 626, 628 (Bankr. D. Idaho 1993).

[385] *E.g.*, In re Eitemiller, 149 B.R. 626 (Bankr. D. Idaho 1993).

[386] Bankruptcy Code § 1126(d).

[387] Chaim J. Fortgang & Thomas Moers Mayer, *Developments in Trading Claims: Participations and Disputed Claims*, 15 Cardozo L.Rev. 733 (1993).

[388] Bankruptcy Code § 1126(e). *See generally* 255 Park Plaza Assocs. Ltd. v. Conn. Gen. Life Ins. Co. (In re 255 Park Plaza Assocs. Ltd.), 100 F.3d 1214, 1219 (6th Cir. 1996).

[389] Bankruptcy Code § 1126(e).

[390] *E.g.*, In re Fed. Support Co., 859 F.2d 17, 19-20 (4th Cir. 1988).

own self-interest.[391]

[1]   Bad Faith Motive

The questionable good faith of votes in favor of or against the plan (usually against it), usually arises in one of several contexts, all of which involve some ulterior motive on the part of the claimant casting the vote. A creditor's efforts to destroy the debtor's business out of malice or ill will toward the debtor, though rarely the source of a vote in contravention of the claimant's financial interests, is in bad faith.[392] Votes against the debtor's plan as part of an effort to assume control of the debtor,[393] or to put the debtor out of business in order to gain a competitive advantage are also regarded as cast in bad faith.[394]

[2]   Trading in Claims[395]

The most common circumstance in which good faith is called into question involves creditors who have purchased claims held by other creditors, as part of an effort to acquire enough votes to block the debtor's plan.[396] If a creditor assembles more than one-third of the amount of the claims in a class, it will be able to prevent the plan from achieving the necessary two-thirds majority to satisfy § 1126(c).

When this occurred in *In re Allegheny International, Inc.*,[397] the court disqualified the votes of an undersecured creditor who paid a premium to several unsecured creditors in order to acquire a sufficient amount in claims to prevent confirmation. With this huge block of claims disqualified, the class accepted the plan, and it was confirmed. Where the creditor's actions are not designed to obtain a better distribution in the bankruptcy case, but were undertaken as part of an effort to take over control of the debtor's business, after a successful effort to block its plan, the creditor's votes against the plan may be disqualified.[398]

Other courts have been more tolerant of this tactic. In *Figter Ltd. v. Teachers Ins. & Annuity Association (In re Figter Ltd.)*,[399] a fully secured creditor was dissatisfied with the debtor's plan to convert its collateral, an apartment complex,

---

[391]   *See, e.g.*, In re Figter, Ltd., 118 F.3d 635 (9th Cir. 1997).

[392]   *E.g.*, In re MacLeod Co., 63 B.R. 654, 655-56 (Bankr. S.D. Ohio 1986).

[393]   *E.g.*, In re Allegheny Int'l, Inc., 118 B.R. 282, 290 (Bankr. W.D. Pa. 1990).

[394]   In re DBSD North Am., Inc., 634 F.3d 79 (2d Cir. 2011) (creditor who acquired claim with the intention not to maximize its return on the debt, but to enter a strategic transaction to acquire debtors' telecommunications spectrum rights); In re Landing Assocs. Ltd., 157 B.R. 791, 807-08 (Bankr. W.D. Tex. 1993).

[395]   Michelle M. Harner, *Trends in Distressed Debt Investing: An Empirical Study of Investors' Objectives*, 16 Am Bankr. Inst. L. Rev. 69 (2008).

[396]   Andrew Africk, Comment, *Trading Claims in Chapter 11: How Much Influence Can Be Purchased in Good Faith under Section 1126?*, 139 U. Pa. L. Rev. 1393 (1991); Frederick Tung, *Confirmation and Claims Trading*, 90 Nw. U. L. Rev. 1684 (1996); David Arthur Skeel, Jr., *The Nature and Effect of Corporate Voting in Chapter 11 Reorganization Cases.*, 78 Va. L. Rev. 461 (1992).

[397]   118 B.R. 282 (Bankr. W.D. Pa. 1990).

[398]   *Id.* at 289. In re DBSD N. Am., Inc., 421 B.R. 133 (Bankr. S.D.N.Y 2009).

[399]   118 F.3d 635 (9th Cir. 1997).

into condominium units. The creditor purchased twenty-one of the thirty-four unsecured claims in the class of general unsecured creditors, paying the creditors the face value of their claims in full.[400] It then submitted rejections for all twenty-one claims. This prevented consensual confirmation of the plan.

The debtor, which had proposed the plan, contended that the creditor's acquisition of the twenty-one claims and its subsequent rejection of the plan was in bad faith. The court found otherwise. The court ruled that a creditor whose purchase of additional claims was implemented for the purpose of "protecting his own existing claim does not demonstrate bad faith or an ulterior motive."[401] Instead, the creditor was quite naturally concerned that if the plan were implemented, it would be left with a complex bundle of mortgages on nearly 200 different condominium units, instead of a single mortgage on a single apartment building. Thus, the purchase of other creditors' claims was part of its "enlightened self interest," even though it frustrated the debtor's hopes.[402]

Votes in favor of a plan are also sometimes disqualified. In *In re Quigley Co., Inc.*,[403] the debtor's parent company purchased claims from creditors for cash as part of an effort to confirm a plan that would squeeze out certain other claimants by stripping them of derivative claims against the parent company and limiting them to an anticipated 7.5% distribution from the debtor's estate.

[E]   Pre-Packaged Plans[404]

Sometimes Chapter 11 proceedings are presented to the court as "prepackaged" — that is, the plan has been negotiated and acceptances have been obtained before the case is filed.[405] Section 1126 facilitates these pre-packaged plans by obviating the need for a second round of disclosures or a second vote. When its requirements are met, holders of claims or interests who either accepted or rejected the plan prior to the commencement of the case are "deemed" to have accepted or rejected the plan. Such pre-packaged plans are used to facilitate quick confirmation where resort to bankruptcy court is necessary to deal with a small group of recalcitrant dissenters, or to obtain other legal benefits available only in bankruptcy.

For a pre-packaged plan (or "pre-pack") to pass muster, one of two requirements must have been satisfied. First, the pre-petition solicitation of creditors' acceptances or rejections must have complied with any applicable

---

[400] The transferee is required to file evidence of the transfer, and the clerk sends notice to the alleged transferor that evidence of a transfer has been filed. Fed. R. Bankr. P. 3001(e)(2).

[401] 118 F.3d at 639.

[402] 118 F.3d at 639.

[403] In re Quigley Co., Inc., 437 B.R. 102 (Bankr. S.D.N.Y. 2010).

[404] Lynn M. LoPucki & Joseph W. Doherty, *Why are Delaware and New York Bankruptcy Reorganizations Failing*, 55 Vand. L. Rev. 1933 (2002); Elizabeth Warren & Jay Lawrence Westbrook, *The Success of Chapter 11: A Challenge to the Critics*, 107 Mich. L. Rev. 603 (2009).

[405] *See* Douglas G. Baird & Robert K. Rasmussen, *Beyond Recidivism*, 54 Buff. L. Rev. 343, 347-48 (2006); Melissa B. Jacoby, *Fast, Cheap, and Creditor-Controlled: Is Corporate Reorganization Failing?*, 54 Buff. L. Rev. 401 (2006).

nonbankruptcy law, rule, or regulation.[406] In other words, if the debtor adhered to any state law requirements that govern efforts to obtain approval from creditors of a plan of reorganization, the bankruptcy court regards those procedures as sufficient. Second, if no applicable state law, rule, or regulation applies, the plan can be confirmed if pre-petition disclosures made to creditors and interest holders provided the type of adequate information that is necessary in a Chapter 11 disclosure statement.[407]

In addition, § 1125(g) now authorizes the debtor to continue soliciting those whose acceptances were solicited before the case was commenced, provided that the creditor or equity security holder "was solicited before commencement of the case in a manner complying with applicable nonbankruptcy law."[408]

Further, of course, all of the other requirements for confirmation must be satisfied. The debtor cannot use pre-petition acceptances to deprive dissenters of their right to insist that the plan was filed in good faith, and the debtor must still show that the distribution to creditors satisfies the best interests of creditors test, and that the plan meets the other Code's other requirements. But, the proponent of the plan need not obtain court approval of a new disclosure statement, disseminate new copies of the plan and disclosure statement, or require creditors to resubmit their ballots.

§ 19.10   CONFIRMATION OF CHAPTER 11 PLANS[409]

Confirmation of the plan is the court action that approves the plan and permits it to be implemented. Confirmation may occur only after notice and an actual hearing. It is not enough to provide the mere opportunity for a hearing.[410] The plan may be confirmed only if § 1129's long list of statutory requirements are met.

[A]   Compliance with the Bankruptcy Code[411]

Section 1129(a)(1) permits confirmation only if "the plan complies with the applicable provisions of [the Bankruptcy Code]." This brings the remainder of the Bankruptcy Code into play in determining whether the plan can be confirmed. For example, this means that the plan must classify and treat claims consistently with

---

[406] Bankruptcy Code § 1126(b)(1).

[407] Bankruptcy Code § 1126(b)(2).

[408] Bankruptcy Code § 1125(g). *See* Richard Levin & Alesia Ranney-Marinelli, *The Creeping Repeal of Chapter 11: The Significant Business Provisions of the Bankruptcy Abuse Prevention and Consumer Protection Act of 2005*, 79 Am. Bankr. L.J. 603, 630-31 (2005).

[409] *See* Richard M. Cieri, Barbara J. Oyer, & Dorothy J. Birnbryer, *"The Long and Winding Road": The Standards to Confirm a Plan of Reorganization Under Chapter 11 of the Bankruptcy Code (Part II)*, 3 J. Bankr. L. & Prac. 115 (1994); Richard M. Cieri, Barbara J. Oyer & Dorothy J. Birnbryer, *"The Long and Winding Road": The Standards To Confirm a Reorganization Plan Under Chapter 11 of the Bankruptcy Code (Part I)*, 3 J. Bankr. L. Prac. 3 (1993).

[410] Bankruptcy Code § 1128(a).

[411] Harley J. Goldstein & Craig A. Sloan, *Spending Other People's Money: Creditors' Remedies for the Misuse of Cash Collateral in Bankruptcy*, 7 U. Miami Bus. L. Rev. 243, 264-66 (1999).

§ 1123(a)(1)-(4) and § 1122.[412] Likewise, the plan may not call for modification of claims secured by an individual debtor's residence, in violation of § 1123(b)(5). Nor may it violate provisions of the Code outside of Chapter 11, such as those that deal with compensation of professionals.[413]

In addition, the "proponent of the plan" must comply with the provisions of the Bankruptcy Code.[414] This creates a potential minefield for Chapter 11 debtors who are in jeopardy of being unable to obtain confirmation as a result of every possible violation of the Code's provisions.[415] Courts have mitigated this potential in two ways. First, despite the clear language of § 1129(a)(2) that requires the proponent of the plan to comply "with the applicable provisions of this *title*,"[416] courts have sometimes held that it only mandates compliance with the reorganization provisions of the Code.[417] Other courts have permitted it to be used only for serious deviations from the Code's requirements, thus effectively creating a de minimis exception to the requirement that the proponent comply with all of the Code's provisions. Thus, if the proponent's misbehavior had no material effect on creditors or on the plan, confirmation is still permitted.[418] Debtors who violate the Code in some serious fashion may still find it impossible to obtain confirmation because of their defalcation.[419]

[B] Plan Proposed in Good Faith[420]

Section 1129(a)(3) specifies that the plan must have been "proposed in good faith and not by any means prohibited by law."[421] Lack of good faith might also lead to dismissal of the case under § 1112.[422] Good faith has a wide array of potential meanings. In this context, it most commonly deals with whether the plan's goals are consistent with Chapter 11's purposes.[423] Good faith has been a particular stumbling block in single-asset real estate cases, where the debtor's purposes may simply be to delay the inevitable foreclosure, rather than to restructure its

---

[412] *See supra* § 19.08[D] Classification of Claims.

[413] *E.g.*, In re Beyond.com Corp., 289 B.R. 138, 143 (Bankr. N.D. Cal. 2003).

[414] Bankruptcy Code § 1129(a)(2).

[415] *See, e.g.*, Matter of Cothran, 45 B.R. 836, 838 (S.D. Ga. 1984) (misuse of cash collateral); In re Wermelskirchen, 163 B.R. 793 (Bankr. N.D. Ohio 1994) (failure to schedule all creditors).

[416] Bankruptcy Code § 1129(a)(2) (emphasis supplied).

[417] *E.g.*, In re Landing Assocs., Ltd., 157 B.R. 791, 811 (Bankr. W.D. Tex. 1993). *But see* In re Briscoe Enters., Ltd. II, 138 B.R. 795, 809 (N.D. Tex. 1992) (taking the draconian view that § 1129(a)(2) might prevent confirmation even if code violations were cured or were approved by the court nunc pro tunc).

[418] *E.g.*, In re Greate Bay Hotel & Casino, Inc., 251 B.R. 213 (Bankr. D.N.J. 2000).

[419] *E.g.*, Cothran v. United States (In re Cothran), 45 B.R. 836, 838 (S.D. Ga. 1984).

[420] Ali M. Mojdehi & Janet Dean Gertz, *The Implicit "Good Faith" Requirement in Chapter 11 Liquidations: A Rule in Search of a Rationale?*, 14 Am. Bankr. Inst. L. Rev. 143 (2006).

[421] Bankruptcy Code § 1129(a)(3).

[422] *See supra* § 19.05[B][3] Bad Faith Filing. *E.g.*, In re SGL Carbon Corp., 200 F.3d 154 (3d Cir. 1999).

[423] In re Madison Hotel Assocs., 749 F.2d 410, 424-25 (7th Cir. 1984).

business's finances consistently with the purposes of Chapter 11.[424] Plans that contemplate obtaining confirmation through tainted votes designed to squeeze out certain claimants might also be rejected based on a lack of good faith.[425]

The requirement that the plan be proposed by any means not forbidden by law casts a wide net. It encompasses violations not only of bankruptcy law, but also of other applicable federal, state, and local law.[426] Thus, if the plan calls for a legally prohibited source of funding, a legally proscribed organizational structure, or illegal business activities, it cannot be confirmed.

[C] Court Approval of Previous Payments

For the plan to be confirmed, the court must have approved payments made by the proponent, the debtor, and certain other parties, if those payments are for services, costs, or expenses incident to the plan or to the case.[427] This is a part of the broader issue of court control of the costs of administration, which is more fully discussed elsewhere,[428] and overlaps to some extent with the requirement discussed above, that the plan comply with other applicable provisions of the Code.

[D] Disclosure of Identity of Insiders and Affiliates of Debtor

The proponent of the plan must disclose the identity and affiliations of: 1) individuals who will be directors, officers or voting trustees of the reorganized debtor; 2) any affiliate of the debtor who is participating with the debtor in a joint plan of reorganization; or 3) of any successor to the debtor under the plan.[429] Moreover, the appointment or retention of directors, officers, or any voting trustee must be consistent with the interests of creditors, equity security holders, and any applicable public policy.[430] In addition, the proponent of the plan must disclose the identity of any insider who will be retained or employed by the reorganized debtor and the nature of that insider's compensation.[431] These requirements ensure that the identity and affiliations of those who manage the debtor are fully disclosed to those who vote on the plan. These matters can be expected to be dealt with in disclosure statements that are distributed in connection with the plan.

---

[424] Brian S. Katz, *Single-asset Real Estate Cases and the Good Faith Requirement: Why Reluctance to Ask Whether a Case Belongs in Bankruptcy May Lead to the Incorrect Result*, 9 Bankr. Dev. J. 77 (1992).

[425] In re Quigley Co., Inc., 437 B.R. 102 (Bankr. S.D.N.Y. 2010).

[426] In re Koelbl, 751 F.2d 137, 139 (2d Cir. 1984).

[427] Bankruptcy Code § 1129(a)(4).

[428] *See generally supra* Chapter 9 Operation of the Debtor's Business and Financial Affairs; *infra* Chapter 21 Role of Professionals in Bankruptcy Proceedings.

[429] Bankruptcy Code § 1129(a)(5)(A)(i).

[430] Bankruptcy Code § 1129(a)(5)(A)(ii).

[431] Bankruptcy Code § 1129(a)(5)(B).

[E]   Regulatory Approval

Debtors engaged in an industry that is subject to rate regulation and whose plan provides for a change in rates must have their proposed new rates approved by the appropriate regulatory agency.[432] An electric utility company is a good example of the type of debtor who must comply with this provision. This helps to ensure that aspects of the debtor's plan that depend on changes in the debtor's revenue are realistic.

[F]   Plan in the Best Interests of Creditors

Section 1129(a)(7) requires that *each* holder of an impaired claim or interest has either "accepted the plan"[433] or:

> will receive or retain under the plan on account of such claim or interest property of a value, as of the effective date of the plan, that is not less than the amount that such holder would so receive or retain if the debtor were liquidated under chapter 7 of this title on such date.[434]

This statutory language has long been referred to as "the best interests of creditors" test.[435] The "property" that creditors receive usually consists of cash payments, though it may be any type of property, such as stock in the reorganized company, or even tangible property such as items of the debtor's inventory or some of its equipment.[436]

The best interests of creditors test only applies to claims and interests that belong to an impaired class. Each affected creditor is entitled to receive payments that, when reduced to their present value, equal at least the Chapter 7 liquidation value of the affected claim or interest. It is easy to understand a requirement that creditors receive at least as much in reorganization as they would in liquidation, but the requirement is more complex than it first appears. The key component of the statutory language is its requirement that creditors receive payments that are equivalent to the *value* of what they would receive in liquidation. Because Chapter 11 plans nearly always call for payments to creditors to be distributed over a period of time, the amount of these payments must be discounted to reflect their "present value" on the effective date of the plan. In simple terms, $10 paid out one dollar at a time over a ten-year period is worth less than $10 received today.

For example, if in a liquidation of Titanic Corp., $100,000 would be distributed to general unsecured creditors who have claims aggregating $1,000,000, each creditor would be paid 10% of its claim. In Titanic's liquidation, a creditor with a $300,000 claim would receive $30,000. A plan that provides for payments to unsecured creditors generally at the rate of $20,000 per year for five years for a total of

---

[432]   Bankruptcy Code § 1129(a)(6).

[433]   Bankruptcy Code § 1129(a)(7)(A)(i).

[434]   Bankruptcy Code § 1129(a)(7)(A)(ii).

[435]   Bankruptcy Code § 1129(a)(7).

[436]   One of your authors is acquainted with a San Francisco Bay Area bankruptcy lawyer who received several very nice tennis racquets as compensation for his pre-petition services to a sporting goods store.

$100,000 would result in this one creditor receiving $6,000 a year for a five-year total of $30,000. But, this does not satisfy the best interests of creditors test. Five annual $6,000 payments spread out over five years is worth less than the $30,000 immediate payment that the creditor would receive if Titanic were liquidated. For the plan to be confirmed, the stream of future payments must include an interest component to compensate this creditor for the delay.

Each and every creditor has the right to receive the liquidation value of its claim. This is clear from the language of § 1129(a)(7) that refers to "each holder of a claim." Thus, each creditor has the right to insist that the plan provides it with the liquidation value of its claim, even if the creditor's class has accepted the plan. This protects dissenters who voted against the plan.

Of course, a class of creditors rarely accepts a plan that gives its members less than this statutory minimum. Thus, it is unusual for a plan to be accepted by the requisite majority and still fail the best interests of creditors test. As a practical matter, the best interests test is more commonly invoked with respect to a plan that is being "crammed down" without the approval of a class of creditors.

Nevertheless, because it protects dissenting members of a class that has accepted the plan, it may still play a role in cases where dissenting members of the class have a more accurate assessment of the debtor's liquidation value than those who voted to accept the plan. Moreover, the fact that dissenters might object, and thus force the court to determine the debtor's liquidation value, gives these creditors bargaining leverage that they might use to induce the debtor to pay more to the members of the class than it otherwise might.

The best interests test requires the court to make two factual determinations.[437] First, it must determine how much the creditor would have received if the debtor had liquidated. This requires a calculation of the debtor's total liquidation value and a determination of how that value would be distributed in a Chapter 7 liquidation. The process of making this determination is difficult, expensive, and like any other valuation proceeding, inexact. And, because the debtor's business might be sold as a going concern in a Chapter 7 case, the court may find it necessary to calculate the value of the debtor's business as a going concern. However, most of the time, the liquidation value is based on appraisals of what the debtor would be worth if liquidated in piecemeal fashion.[438] This value depends on the future earnings of the debtor, and not the book value or the appraised value of the debtor's individual assets.[439]

Second, the court must determine what discount or interest rate to use in determining whether the stream of future payments are equivalent to the liquidation value creditors would have received in a Chapter 7 case. The appropriate interest rate was a subject of much debate. In 2004, the United States Supreme

---

[437] For a discussion of the best interest test as it applies to Chapter 13 plans, see *supra* § 18.08[E][1] Best Interests of Creditors.

[438] *E.g.*, In re Lason, Inc., 300 B.R. 227, 233 (Bankr. D. Del. 2003).

[439] *See* Consol. Rock Prods. Co. v. DuBois, 312 U.S. 510 (1941).

Court decided *Till v. SCS Credit Corp.*,[440] and perhaps confused the matter further.

Till was a Chapter 13 case regarding the appropriate discount rate to use in determining whether amounts paid to a creditor were the equivalent to the present value of its secured claim, as required by § 1325(a)(5). The Court's plurality decision required use of a formula based on the prime rate of interest, as adjusted upward to reflect risks facing the creditor in the circumstances of the case. It remains somewhat unclear whether this formula approach applies to the best interests test of § 1129(a)(7). A few courts have rejected its use under Chapter 13's best interests test, reasoning that *Till* was merely a plurality decision, and applies only to the facts of the case before it, which involved secured creditor cramdown under Chapter 13.[441] As a result, in Chapter 11, a number of different approaches are still used.[442]

Most courts now use a market or "coerced loan" rate, at least where there is sufficient evidence of an efficient market for the type of loan that would ordinarily be used for the obligation the plan created.[443] Where no such efficient market can be found, courts use the "prime-plus" formula approach announced in *Till*.[444]

Section 1129(a)(7) also imposes requirements for treatment of those secured creditors who have made the § 1111(b) election to have their claims treated as non-recourse claims. As explained in more detail elsewhere, it requires payments under the plan to have a present value equivalent to the value of collateral. Thus, if the creditor held a $500,000 claim, secured by $300,000 of collateral, the plan would have to provide for payments totaling $500,000, with a discounted present value of at least $300,000. This would seem to be implicit in 1129(a)(7), but, since a creditor who has made the election has an allowed secured claim equal to the amount of the debt, 1129(a)(7)(B) specifies that the payments made on account of that claim need only have a present value equal to the value of the collateral (not the amount of the debt), and § 1129(b)(2)(A) makes the same distinction.

[G] Acceptance by Impaired Classes

Section 1129(a)(8) seems to require each class of claims or interests to accept the plan by the required statutory majority or be unimpaired by the plan.[445] The language of § 1129(a)(8) appears to make this requirement mandatory, but it is not. Section 1129(b), dealing with Chapter 11 cramdown (when read in conjunction with § 1129(a)(10)), permits confirmation even though a class of impaired claims has

---

[440] *Cf.* Till v. SCS Credit Corp., 541 U.S. 465 (2004) (present value for secured claims under § 1325(a)(5)).

[441] In re Cook, 322 B.R. 336, 345 (Bankr. N.D. Ohio 2005) (coerced loan approach based on current market interest rates for loans in similar situations). *Cf.* In re Am. HomePatient, Inc., 420 F.3d 559 (6th Cir. 2005) (applying § 1129(a)(5)); Mercury Capital Corp. v. Milford Connect. Assoc, L.P., 354 B.R. 1, 4-5 (D. Conn. 2006). *See generally supra* § 18.08[F][4][b] Payments Equivalent to Amount of Secured Claim.

[442] *See* Gary W. Marsh & Matthew M. Weiss, *Chapter 11 Interest Rates after* Till, 84 Am. Bankr. L.J. 209 (2010).

[443] E.g., In re Brice Rd. Devs., LLC, 392 B.R. 274, 280 (B.A.P. 6th Cir. 2006).

[444] *E.g.*, Mercury Capital Corp. v. Milford Connect. Assoc., L.P., 354 B.R. 1, 4-5 (D. Conn. 2006).

[445] Bankruptcy Code § 1129(a)(8). *See infra* § 19.09[C] Voting by Classes of Claims and Interests, regarding the necessary voting majorities.

rejected the plan so long as at least one impaired class votes to accept the plan and certain other requirements are met.

Note that § 1129(a)(8) does not require every impaired claim or interest to accept the plan; it requires only that each *class* of impaired claims or interests accept. Thus, the plan may be confirmed over the objection of a dissenting group of creditors who are outvoted by creditors in the same class. This ability to bind a dissenting minority is one of the significant advantages of Chapter 11 over out-of-court workouts.

[H]   Full Payment of Priority Claims

As explained elsewhere, to be confirmed, a Chapter 11 plan must provide for full payment of most priority claims.[446] Administrative expenses associated with the bankruptcy case itself and § 502(f) involuntary gap period claims must be paid in full, in cash, on the effective date of the plan.[447] Most other priority claims must be paid in full, and in cash, but they may be paid over time if the class of affected claims has accepted the plan.[448] Otherwise, they must be paid in full immediately, with administrative claims, on the plan's effective date.[449] Priority tax claims must be paid in full, but may be paid over a maximum of five years after the order for relief[450] and not more slowly than any non-priority claim.[451] Other priority claims, such as those owed to the FDIC or for personal injury or death in a drunk driving incident, are not entitled to any special treatment other than that required by the absolute priority rule. A class of these claims can prevent confirmation if any class of general unsecured claims receives anything under the terms of the plan.[452]

[I]   Acceptance by One Impaired Class

Most Chapter 11 plans are confirmed with acceptances from all classes. However, a consensual plan may not be possible. If so, the proponent of the plan may seek to have it confirmed over the objection of a class of claims or interests. If no class of impaired claims has accepted the plan, it cannot be confirmed.[453] This is a key aspect of Chapter 11 cramdown. Unlike other aspects of the requirements for confirmation, this rule applies only with respect to classes of claims; it does not apply to classes of interests — acceptance by a class of interests does not satisfy the requirement.

---

[446] Bankruptcy Code § 1129(a)(9). *See supra* § 19.08[G] Treatment of Priority Unsecured Claims.

[447] Bankruptcy Code § 1129(a)(9)(A).

[448] Bankruptcy Code § 1129(a)(9)(B)(i).

[449] Bankruptcy Code § 1129(a)(9)(B)(ii).

[450] Bankruptcy Code § 1129(a)(9)(C). This may be considerably less than five years from the time of confirmation.

[451] Bankruptcy Code § 1129(a)(9)(C)(iii). The one exception is for small claims that are segregated into a separate class for administrative convenience under § 1122(b). These are usually paid in cash on the effective date of the plan.

[452] *See infra* § 19.11 Confirmation over Objection of Impaired Class; Cramdown.

[453] Bankruptcy Code § 1129(a)(10).

In determining that at least one impaired class of claims has accepted, the votes of insiders are not counted.[454] Thus, if the only class that accepts the plan contains five claims, with two of them held by insiders,[455] two of the three non-insiders must have accepted the plan. Otherwise, the requirement that more than half of the claims in the class has accepted the plan is not met.

[J] Feasibility of Plan

The plan must be feasible — there must be a realistic chance for it to be successfully implemented. Like "best interests," the term "feasibility" appears nowhere in the code. Instead, § 1129(a)(11) requires that: "[c]onfirmation of the plan is not likely to be followed by the liquidation, or the need for further financial reorganization, of the debtor, or any successor to the debtor under the plan, unless such liquidation or reorganization is proposed in the plan." This has long been known as the feasibility test.[456]

The goal of this requirement is to protect creditors from visionary schemes and prevent the need for repeated efforts at reorganization. Despite this, courts sometimes characterize the feasibility standard as "not rigorous."[457] Confirmed plans do not always succeed, and cases sometimes find themselves back in bankruptcy after their plan has been confirmed.[458] Moreover, if the statutory majority of creditors have voted for the plan, it is perhaps only rarely appropriate for the judge to second-guess them on its prospects for success.

Despite this drawback, the feasibility requirement gives dissenting creditors who doubt the viability of the debtor's business plan an avenue for attack. The feasibility requirement requires the court to determine whether the plan "offers a reasonable probability of success."[459] As one court explained: "Guaranteed success in the stiff winds of commerce without the protections of the Code is not the standard under [§ 1129(a)(11)] . . . . All that is required is that there be a reasonable assurance of commercial viability."[460]

The complexities and uncertainties of modern business make it far more difficult to evaluate the feasibility of a Chapter 11 plan than to make the same determination with respect to a Chapter 13 plan, where feasibility is also required. In evaluating whether the debtor has a reasonable probability of success, courts frequently examine a variety of factors, including:

---

[454] Bankruptcy Code § 1129(a)(10).

[455] Bankruptcy Code § 101(31).

[456] In re Hockenberry, 457 B.R. 646, 659 (Bankr. S.D. Ohio 2011).

[457] In re Greate Bay Hotel & Casino, Inc., 251 B.R. 213, 226 (Bankr. D.N.J. 2000); In re Orfa Corp., 129 B.R. 404, 410 (Bankr. E.D. Pa. 1991).

[458] *Compare* Lynn Lopucki, Courting Failure (2005) *with* Kennety Ayotte & David Skeel, *An Efficiency-Based Explanation for Current Corporate Reorganization Practice*, 73 U. Chi. L. Rev. 425 (2006).

[459] In re Monnier Bros., 755 F.2d 1336, 1341 (8th Cir. 1985).

[460] In re Prudential Energy Co., 58 B.R. 857, 862 (Bankr. S.D.N.Y. 1986).

(1) the adequacy of the debtor's capital structure; (2) the earning power of its business; (3) economic conditions; (4) the ability of the debtor's management; (5) the probability of the continuation of the same management; and (6) any other related matters which determine the prospects of a sufficiently successful operation to enable performance of the provisions of the plan.[461]

Projecting a business debtor's income and estimating its operating expenses may require sophisticated calculations. This might make it difficult to obtain confirmation of a plan calling for a "balloon" payment sometime in the future.[462] Moreover, where the debtor's plan is based on completely conjectural plans, with no reasonable prospect of success, confirmation should be denied. Thus, confirmation of a plan that depended on the success of a child-care facility that did not yet exist and which had not yet applied for the appropriate license should be denied.[463] As the court explained, "[a]lthough it is not required for the plan to guarantee success, it must present a reasonable assurance of success [which must be based on] a reasonable and workable framework for reorganization."[464] Likewise, a plan that depends on the financial success of a proposed sublessee of the debtor's leased property, or upon some key customer's financial viability, is not feasible absent reasonable assurances about the financial success of these third parties upon whom the debtor depends.[465]

[K] Payment of Bankruptcy Fees

For a plan to be confirmed, all court-imposed bankruptcy fees, such as quarterly fees payable to the U.S. Trustee and those permitted to be imposed by the Judicial Conference of the United States must either have been paid or scheduled to be paid by the effective date of the plan.[466]

[L] Continuation of Retirement Benefits[467]

Section 1114 contains detailed provisions for determining the amount of benefits a Chapter 11 debtor must pay to retired employees and their spouses.[468] If a debtor reorganizes, it must continue to make medical benefit payments to retirees unless they follow the procedures set forth in § 1114 to modify them. The court

---

[461] In re Temple Zion, 125 B.R. 910, 915 (Bankr. E.D. Pa. 1991).

[462] *E.g.*, SPCP Group, LLC v. Cypress Creek Assisted Living Residence, Inc, 434 B.R. 650 (M.D. Fla. 2010); In re Trenton Ridge Investors, LLC, 461 B.R. 440 (Bankr. S.D. Ohio 2011).

[463] In re The Christian Faith Assembly, 402 B.R. 794 (Bankr. N.D. Ohio 2009).

[464] *Id.* at 799.

[465] In re Hurricane Memphis, LLC, 405 B.R. 616 (Bankr. W.D. Tenn. 2009).

[466] Bankruptcy Code § 1129(a)(12).

[467] Daniel Keating, *Bankruptcy Code § 1114: Congress' Empty Response to the Retiree Plight*, 67 Am. Bankr. L.J. 17 (1993).

[468] Bankruptcy Code § 1114. *See* Daniel Keating, *Bankruptcy Code § 1114: Congress' Empty Response to the Retiree Plight*, 67 Am. Bankr. L.J. 17 (1993); Susan J. Stabile, *Protecting Retiree Medical Benefits in Bankruptcy: The Scope of § 1114 of the Bankruptcy Code*, 14 Cardozo L. Rev. 1911 (1993).

must appoint a representative for the retirees, and the representative bargains on behalf of the retirees over the modifications necessary to effectuate a reorganization. If those negotiations fail, the court may impose such modifications as are necessary. Section 1129(a)(13) mandates that Chapter 11 plans must provide for the debtor to continue to pay whatever meager retirement benefits § 1114 requires.[469]

[M] Individual Chapter 11 Debtors

The Code includes two requirements aimed at individuals who attempt to use Chapter 11 to reorganize. Chapter 11's procedures and requirements are too expensive to be useful for all but a few individuals. But, the Supreme Court's decision in *Toibb v. Radloff* made it clear that individuals are entitled to Chapter 11 relief regardless of whether or not they are engaged in a business.[470] Several provisions in Chapter 11 attempt to prevent individuals from evading certain restrictions imposed on Chapter 13 debtors.

First, § 109(h) requires all individual debtors to obtain a financial counseling and planning briefing with 180 days prior to filing their petition.[471] This is necessary regardless of whether the debtor's obligations are primarily business debts or consumer debts. However, Chapter 11 debtors do not need to complete the subsequent financial management course required for individuals in Chapter 7 or Chapter 13.

Second, § 1129(a)(14) prevents confirmation unless the debtor has paid any post-petition domestic support obligations owed under a "judicial or administrative order, or by statute." Thus, individual debtors who expect to obtain Chapter 11 relief must maintain any child or spousal support payments that become due after the debtor's petition. This requirement should be read in conjunction with § 1129(a)(9)(B), which requires Chapter 11 debtors to pay any past-due priority support obligations in full, either on the effective date of the plan, or, with acceptance by the affected class of creditors, in deferred cash payments.

Third, § 1129(a)(15) requires most individual debtors to submit all of their projected disposable income for five years.[472] This is consistent with the projected disposable income test of § 1325(b)(1)(B) for debtors, with household income above their state's median, who seek relief under Chapter 13.[473]

On the other hand, § 1129(b)(2)(B)(ii) now provides that an individual debtor may retain "property included in the estate under section 1115," indicating that individual debtors may retain earnings from their own personal services, possibly free from the constraints that otherwise would be imposed by the absolute priority

---

[469] *See* Amy Lassiter, Note, *Mayday, Mayday!: How the Current Bankruptcy Code Fails to Protect the Pensions of Employees*, 93 Ky. L.J. 939 (2005).

[470] 501 U.S. 157 (1991). *See* Michael J. Herbert, *Consumer Chapter 11 Proceedings: Abuse or Alternative?*, 91 Com. L.J. 234 (1986).

[471] Bankruptcy Code § 109(h)(1).

[472] Bankruptcy Code § 1129(a)(15)(B).

[473] *See supra* § 18.08[E][2] Debtor's Projected Disposable Income.

rule.[474] Courts have differed over whether this operates as a repeal of the absolute priority rule in cases involving individual debtors.[475]

[N] Transfer of Property by Non-Profit Organization

New § 1129(a)(16) prevents non-profit trusts and corporations from using bankruptcy to sidestep restrictions that many states impose on property owned by these organizations. It specifies that "[a]ll transfers of property of the plan shall be made in accordance with any applicable provisions of nonbankruptcy law that govern the transfer of property by a corporation or trust that is not a moneyed, business, or commercial corporation or trust."[476] It is expected that this provision will be enforced by State Attorney General's offices, which are commonly responsible for enforcing state laws on the transfer of property by non-profit entities.[477]

§ 19.11 CONFIRMATION OVER OBJECTION OF AN IMPAIRED CLASS; CRAMDOWN[478]

Ideally, a Chapter 11 plan will be approved by the requisite majority of creditors in each class. However, even where one or more of the classes rejects the plan, the debtor may still seek confirmation. Confirmation over the objection of a class of creditors is graphically known as "cramdown" (as in crammed down their throats).[479]

There are three key requirements for cramdown. First, the plan must be accepted by at least one class of impaired claims.[480] Second, the plan must be "fair and equitable" with respect to each dissenting class.[481] The test for whether a plan is fair and equitable is somewhat different with respect to classes of secured claims, classes of unsecured claims, and classes of interests,[482] but it adheres to the "absolute priority rule" that prevents a debtor from distributing anything to a junior class over the objection of a senior class, unless whatever is received by the senior class is the equivalent of payment in full. Third, the plan must not "discriminate unfairly" against a class of creditors or interest holders.[483]

---

[474] *See See generally* Robert J. Landry, II, *Individual Chapter 11 Reorganizations: Big Problems with the New "Big" Chapter 13*, 29 U. Ark. Little Rock L. Rev. 251, 272 (2007).

[475] *Compare* In re Maharaj, 681 F.3d 558 (4th Cir. 2012) (no repeal) *with* In re Friedman, 466 B.R. 471 (B.A.P. 9th Cir. 2012) (absolute priority rule inapplicable to individuals).

[476] Bankruptcy Code § 1129(a)(16).

[477] Pub. L. No. 109-8, § 1221(d) (2005).

[478] Kenneth N. Klee, *All You Ever Wanted to Know About Cram Down Under the New Bankruptcy Code*, 53 Am. Bankr. L.J. 133 (1979).

[479] Dissenting creditors in a class that has accepted the plan also have the plan "crammed down" their throats. Section 1129(b) comes into play, however, only when a class as a whole rejects the plan.

[480] Bankruptcy Code § 1129(a)(10).

[481] Bankruptcy Code § 1129(b)(1).

[482] Bankruptcy Code § 1129(b)(2)(A)-(C).

[483] Bankruptcy Code § 1129(b)(1).

[A] Acceptance by One Impaired Class

One limitation on cramdown already discussed is the requirement that at least one impaired class of creditors accept the plan.[484] Thus, confirmation over the objection of all classes is not possible. This means that at least one impaired creditor constituency must support the plan. And, since the votes of insiders do not count,[485] the existing owners cannot confirm a plan over the dissent of all other claimants.

This requirement is frequently a barrier to confirmation in single-asset real estate cases. In those proceedings, there is usually only one significant creditor, a financial institution, who would prefer to foreclose upon its collateral and terminate the debtor's business. Debtors in this situation have tried to work around this requirement by cobbling together a class of small claims that are technically impaired, but to such a slight degree that they are virtually certain to vote to accept the plan. As explained elsewhere, courts have generally disfavored this type of gerrymandering.[486] However, where there is a legitimate justification for separate classification, such as a "non-creditor" interest, as in *U.S. Truck*, where the national union was thought to be particularly concerned about its position in other cases, rather than its interest as a creditor in the particular case, separate classification has been permitted.[487] Courts are divided over how strong such a justification must be.[488]

[B] Fair and Equitable — The Absolute Priority Rule[489]

A Chapter 11 plan may not be confirmed over the objection of a class of claims or interests that has rejected the plan unless the plan is "fair and equitable" with respect to that class.[490] For the plan to be fair and equitable, it must conform to the "absolute priority rule." Stated briefly, for unsecured creditors, no junior class may receive any distribution unless all senior classes are paid in full, and for secured creditors, the creditor must retain a lien stripped down to the value of the collateral, and receive payments with a present value equal to the value of the collateral as of the effective date of the plan.

---

[484] Bankruptcy Code § 1129(a)(10).

[485] Bankruptcy Code § 1129(a)(10). For the definition of insider see Bankruptcy Code § 101(31).

[486] *See supra* § 19.08[D][2][c] Classification in Single-Asset Real Estate Cases.

[487] In re U.S. Truck Co., Inc., 800 F.2d 581 (1986).

[488] In re Bloomingdale Partners, 170 B.R. 984 (Bankr. N.D. Ill. 1994).

[489] John D. Ayer, *Rethinking Absolute Priority After* Ahlers, 87 Mich. L. Rev. 963 (1989); Douglas G. Baird & Thomas H. Jackson, *Bargaining After the Fall and the Countours of the Absolute Priority Rule*, 55 U. Chi. L. Rev. 739 (1988); Lynn M. LoPucki & William C. Whitford, *Bargaining over Equity's Share in the Bankruptcy Reorganizaton of Large Publicly Held Companies*, 139 U. Pa. L. Rev. 125 (1990); Bruce Marckel, *Owners, Auctions, and Absolute Priority in Bankrukptcy Reorganization*, 44 Stan. L. Rev. 69 (1991); Raymond T. Nimmer, *Negotiated Bankruptcy Reorganization Plans: Absolute Priority and New Value Contributions*, 36 Emory L.J. 1009 (1987); Elizabeth Warren, *A Theory of Absolute Priority*, 1990 Ann. Surv. Am. L. 9.

[490] Bankruptcy Code § 1129(b)(1).

The absolute priority rule and the phrase "fair and equitable" long predate the current Code. They are derived from early twentieth century railroad equity receivership cases, in which the rule was developed,[491] and from § 77B of the Bankruptcy Act, which codified the phrase "fair and equitable" to refer to the absolute priority rule.[492] Broadly speaking, it means that the plan must follow absolute, rather than relative priorities. As explained elsewhere, priority rights under the Bankruptcy Code range downward from secured claims, through priority and general unsecured claims to equity interests, with the residual rights of owners at the bottom.[493]

In Chapter 7 liquidation cases, this list is followed strictly; each rank is paid in full before the next rank is paid anything. When the money runs out, the last rank for which there is any money is paid pro rata.[494] Chapter 11 usually permits the debtor to follow relative priority — each rank is entitled to its liquidation value,[495] but the surplus realized through the reorganization's capture of going concern value may be distributed in almost any manner to which the debtor and creditors agree. However, if they cannot agree, the Code reimposes strict rank ordering. To put it another way, Chapter 11 permits relative priority in the distribution of the plan payments only with the creditors' consent.

When creditors do not consent, the absolute priority rule may make it impossible for the owners to participate in the reorganized entity. Equity comes last. Only in the rarest Chapter 11 cases are all debts paid; and under the absolute priority rule, only if all debts are paid may equity receive anything. Thus, it is very hard for the existing owners to retain any portion of the residual value of the company on account of their prepetition ownership interest. The most difficult and interesting issues in Chapter 11 derive from owners' efforts to circumvent this problem and retain a stake in the reorganized company without obtaining creditors' consent.[496]

Despite (or perhaps because of) the rule's historic antecedents, the drafters of the Code provided a detailed definition of "fair and equitable," with distinct but nevertheless compatible formulations for secured claims, unsecured claims, and equity interests. The first two formulations are of greatest significance, because when the rule is applied, there is rarely any value remaining to distribute to equity after secured and unsecured claims have been paid.

---

[491] N. Pac. Ry. Co. v. Boyd, 228 U.S. 482 (1913); Kan. City Terminal Ry. Co. v. Cent. Union Trust Co., 271 U.S. 445 (1926).

[492] *See* Case v. Los Angeles Lumber Prods. Co., 308 U.S. 106 (1939). Stephen J. Lubben, *Railroad Receiverships and Modern Bankruptcy Theory*, 89 Cornell L. Rev. 1420 (2004).

[493] *See supra* § 10.01 Meaning of Claims and Interests.

[494] *See supra* § 17.08 Distribution of Estate Property.

[495] Bankruptcy Code § 1129(a)(7)(A)(ii). See *supra* § 19.10[F] Plan in Best Interests of Creditors.

[496] *See infra* § 19.11[D] New Value Exception to Absolute Priority Rule.

[1] Secured Claims

The absolute priority rule is particularly important with respect to secured claims, even in cases involving a consensual plan. This is because secured creditors are unlikely to accept a plan that provides them with less than they would be entitled to if the plan were confirmed over their objection in a cramdown.[497] Fully secured creditors usually have nothing to lose by forcing the debtor to liquidate; and in most cases, that is what they would prefer. Consequently, although they frequently agree to debtors' plans, they rarely accept a plan that provides them with less than they could obtain if they forced a cramdown of the plan. In considering the application of the absolute priority rule to classes of secured claims, it is helpful to remember that in most cases each class is comprised of a single creditor.

A plan must handle secured claims in one of three ways: (1) make deferred cash payments to the creditor in the amount of the secured claim while permitting the creditor to retain a lien for the amount of its claim;[498] (2) sell the collateral and attach the creditor's lien to the proceeds;[499] or (3) any other treatment that provides the secured creditor with the "indubitable equivalent" of its claim.[500]

[a] Lien Retention and Full Payment[501]

The most common method of satisfying the absolute priority rule with respect to a secured creditor's claim is to permit the creditor to retain lien in the amount of the creditor's allowed secured claim[502] and make payments to the creditor in satisfaction of the claim. In other respects, the creditor's claim may be modified, such as by changing the monthly payment, extending the payment period, or reducing the interest rate.

Permitting the creditor to retain its lien gives the creditor the right to foreclose if the debtor defaults on the payments called for by the plan.[503] Moreover, it ensures that it will have a secured claim in any subsequent liquidation case that results from the failure of the debtor's plan to succeed. However, unless the creditor elects otherwise under § 1111(b), its lien applies only to the secured portion of its claim as of the effective date of the plan; it does not protect the unsecured deficiency claim of a partially secured creditor. For example, if Titanic Corp. owes North Atlantic Finance Co. $100,000, secured by equipment worth only $70,000, then North Atlantic has a $70,000 secured claim and a $30,000 unsecured claim. Titanic's plan is fair and equitable if it permits North Atlantic to retain a lien that secures its $70,000 claim. The $30,000 unsecured claim is handled separately

---

[497] Charles D. Booth, *The Cramdown on Secured Creditors: An Impetus Toward Settlement*, 60 Am. Bankr. L.J. 69 (1986).

[498] Bankruptcy Code § 1129(b)(2)(A)(i).

[499] Bankruptcy Code § 1129(b)(2)(A)(ii).

[500] Bankruptcy Code § 1129(b)(2)(A)(iii).

[501] Patrick Halligan, *Cramdown Interest, Contract Damages, and Classical Economic Theory*, 11 Am. Bankr. Inst. L. Rev. 131 (2003).

[502] Bankruptcy Code § 1129(b)(2)(B)(i)(I).

[503] *See* In re Olde Prarie Block Owner, LLC, 464 B.R. 337 (Bankr. N.D. Ill. 2011) (applying § 1129(b)).

and has nothing to do with how § 1129(b)(2)(A) applies to the $70,000 secured claim. If the collateral were worth $100,000 or more, North Atlantic's claim would be fully secured, and the plan would have to provide for it to retain a lien on the equipment to satisfy the full $100,000 debt.

If the collateral for Titanic's debt to North Atlantic were real estate worth $4 million, securing a $5 million claim, it might make sense for North Atlantic to make the § 1111(b) election.[504] If it did so, North Atlantic's claim would be secured for the full $5 million and the lien it would retain would secure the entire $5 million debt. If Titanic subsequently defaulted or sought to sell the collateral, North Atlantic could enforce its lien for up to $5 million. Obviously, this is not worth much if the value of the collateral was still only $4 million, but if the value of the property increased, say to $6 million, the 1111(b) election would permit the creditor to capture any increase in value of the collateral that occurred before the plan failed.

As noted above, the plan may modify the secured creditor's claim in other ways. It may alter the duration and frequency of payments, the amount of each payment, and the interest rate applicable to the claims. However, the interest rate must ensure that the creditor receives the *value* of its secured claim. Section 1129 requires any "deferred cash payments . . . of a value, as of the effective date of the plan, of at least the value of [the creditor's] interest in the estate's interest in [the collateral]."[505] To compensate a secured creditor for the delay, any deferred cash payments must include interest on the amount of the allowed secured claim.[506] This is similar to the approach followed with regard to secured claims in Chapter 13. However, it is unclear whether courts are required to follow the same "formula" approach used in *Till* in Chapter 11 cases.[507]

Applying these rules requires the court to make two determinations: the value of the collateral; and the interest rate necessary to provide the creditor with the present value of its secured claim.

Courts have used a variety of approaches to calculate the appropriate rate of interest.[508] Some courts take a "coerced loan" approach and require the rate of return to correspond to the rate that would be charged or obtained by the creditor making a loan to a third party with similar terms, duration, collateral, and risk.[509]

---

[504] As explained in more detail elsewhere, whether making the election would be an advantage for a secured creditor in this position, would depend on several other factors, including the plan's treatment of unsecured claims, the likelihood that the real estate would increase in value, the amortization period of the payments to be made to the secured creditor, and the likelihood that the debtor would default on the terms of the plan. See supra § 19.08[H][4] Treatment of the § 1111(b) Election.

[505] Bankruptcy Code § 1129(b)(2)(A)(i)(II).

[506] Bankruptcy Code § 1129(b)(2)(A)(i)(II).

[507] *See supra* § 18.08[F][4] Cramdown of Chapter 13 Plan.

[508] *See, e.g.,* Till v. SCS Credit Corp., 541 U.S. 465, 472 (2004); In re Bryson Properties, 961 F.2d 496, 500 (4th Cir. 1992); In re Memphis Bank & Trust Co., 692 F.2d 427, 431 (6th Cir. 1982). *See* Patrick Halligan, *Cramdown Interest, Contract Damages, and Classical Economic Theory*, 11 Am. Bankr. Inst. L. Rev. 131, 134-137 (2003).

[509] Bank of Montreal v. Official Comm. of Unsecured Creditors (In re Am. Homepatient, Inc.), 420 F.3d 559 (6th Cir. 2005); Wade v. Bradford, 39 F.3d 1126 (10th Cir. 1994); In re Byrd Foods, Inc., 253 B.R. 196, 200 (Bankr. E.D. Va. 2000).

Other courts use a presumptive contract rate method, adjusting the negotiated contract rate between the parties upward or downward to reflect circumstances in the case that have changed since the original loan was made.[510] A third "costs of funds" method, depends on the cost that the creditor would incur to obtain the cash equivalent of the collateral; in other words, the interest rate the creditor would pay on a loan of an amount equal to the value of the collateral.[511] Fourth, some courts use a formula approach, based on a benchmark "risk free" interest rate, with adjustments based on factors affecting the circumstances faced by the parties.[512]

The "formula" approach was adopted by the Supreme Court in *Till v. SCS Credit Corp.*[513] for use in Chapter 13 cramdown cases. However, instead of using the treasury bill rate, it used the commercial "prime rate" as the putative risk free rate.[514] As a result of the Court's decision in *Till*, lower courts have insisted on interest rates of 1% to 3% above prime in Chapter 13 cases.[515] However, a number of courts have rejected the formula method as inappropriate for use in Chapter 11 cases, where a coerced loan rate, based on information about market rates of interest for the type of loan involved, is preferred.[516] As a consequence, the applicability of *Till's* formula method outside the context of Chapter 13 cramdown remains uncertain.[517]

The second key component in applying the fair and equitable standard in this manner is to determine the value of the creditor's interest in the debtor's property. The value of the creditor's interest depends initially on the value of the collateral. For example, if North Atlantic Finance Co. is owed $100,000, secured by a senior security interest in $120,000 of Titanic's equipment, the value of the creditor's interest in the collateral is $100,000. But, if the equipment is only worth $70,000, North Atlantic's interest is worth only $70,000.

The value of the creditor's interest is affected by the existence of a senior lien on the collateral. If, for example, North Atlantic's security interest is subordinate to the senior security interest held by Pacific Bank, which has a claim for $50,000, and the equipment is worth only $70,000, North Atlantic's interest in the collateral is worth only $20,000, even though it is owed $100,000. This $20,000 is the value available to North Atlantic after Pacific's senior claim is paid.

Moreover, as explained in more detail elsewhere, courts use different methods to

---

[510] In re Munnier Bros., 755 F.2d 1336, 1339 (8th Cir. 1985).

[511] In re Till, 301 F.3d 583, 592 (7th Cir. 2002), *reversed, sub. nom*, Till v. SCS Credit Corp., 541 U.S. 465 (2004); In re Valenti, 105 F.3d 55, 59-60 (2d Cir. 1997).

[512] In re Fowler, 903 F.2d 694 (9th Cir. 1990); United States v. Doud, 869 F.2d 1144 (8th Cir. 1989).

[513] Till v. SCS Credit Corp., 541 U.S. 465 (2004).

[514] *See supra* § 18.08[F][4][b] Payments Equivalent to Amount of Secured Claim. *See also* Michael Elson, Note, *Say "Ahhh!": A New Approach for Determining the Cram Down Interest Rate After* Till v. SCS Credit, 27 Cardozo L. Rev. 1921 (2006).

[515] In re Cantwell, 336 B.R. 688 (Bankr. D.N.J. 2006) (1%).

[516] Bank of Montreal v. Official Comm. of Unsecured Creditors (In re Am. Homepatient, Inc.), 420 F.3d 559 (6th Cir. 2005) (characterizing *Till's* approach as catastrophic in Chapter 11 cases).

[517] *E.g.*, In re Deep River Warehouse, Inc., 2005 Bankr. LEXIS 1793, (Bankr. M.D.N.C. Sept. 22, 2005) (refusing to apply *Till* in Chapter 11).

determine the value of the collateral.[518] Section 506(a)(1) specifies that the value of the debtor's property is to be determined "in light of the purpose of the valuation and of the proposed disposition or use" of the property.[519] This language suggests using the collateral's liquidation value in circumstances where the collateral is to be liquidated, and replacement value in situations like those where the creditor will retain its lien and receive deferred payments from the creditor.[520] However, some courts use a liquidation or foreclosure value standard to determine the amount of a secured creditor's allowed claim, even in cases where the debtor's reorganization plan contemplates the debtor's continued use of the collateral.[521] Other courts use the midpoint between the forced liquidation value and the replacement value.[522]

In Chapter 13 cases, the Supreme Court's decision in *Associates Commercial Corp. v. Rash*[523] requires use of the cost to the debtor of replacing the collateral as the method of determining the amount of the secured creditor's allowed secured claim. The 2005 Amendments codified some aspects of *Rash* and require using replacement cost in Chapter 7 or 13 cases involving individual debtors.[524] Many courts regard *Rash* as binding in Chapter 11 cases, but the replacement cost method has not yet been seriously challenged in the context of a Chapter 11 cramdown.[525] The addition of § 506(a)(2), specifying use of replacement cost in Chapter 7 and 13 cases of individual debtors, leads to a negative implication that courts are free to use other methods of valuing the collateral in other cases. Moreover, the context of *Rash*, which involved a truck tractor, made use of replacement cost a more pragmatic method, because of the wider availability of market prices for similar items.[526] Determining the replacement cost of manufacturing equipment might be more difficult.

[b]   Sale of Property and Attachment of Lien to Proceeds

Debtors who do not need to use the creditor's collateral as part of their ongoing business operations might propose a sale of the collateral, with the creditor's lien to attach to the proceeds derived from the sale. The sale of the collateral must be conducted pursuant to § 363(k) with the lien on the proceeds treated in conformity to § 1129(b)(2)(A)(i) or (iii). A plan proposing this treatment is fair and equitable.[527] This treatment amounts to little more than a foreclosure sale, albeit with the

---

[518] *See supra* § 10.03[C][1] Valuation of Collateral.

[519] Bankruptcy Code § 506(a)(1).

[520] *E.g.*, In re Taffi, 96 F.3d 1190, 1191-92 (9th Cir. 1996).

[521] In re Rash, 90 F.3d 1036 (5th Cir. 1996), *rev'd, sub nom.*, Assoc. Commercial Corp. v. Rash, 520 U.S. 953 (1997).

[522] In re Hoskins, 102 F.3d 311, 316 (7th Cir. 1996).

[523] 520 U.S. 953 (1997).

[524] Bankruptcy Code § 506(a)(2).

[525] *E.g.*, In re T-H New Orleans Ltd., 116 F.3d 790, 799 (5th Cir. 1997); In re Mulvania, 214 B.R. 1 (B.A.P. 9th Cir. 1997).

[526] *See, e.g.*, http://www.trucker.com (last viewed May 29, 2012).

[527] Bankruptcy Code § 1129(b)(2)(A)(ii).

debtor in control of the manner of the sale. In many cases, property the debtor does not need will have been sold in a similar manner, pursuant to § 363,[528] before the debtor's plan was proposed.[529]

By referring explicitly to § 363(k), cramdown pursuant to this provision expressly preserves the secured creditor's right to participate in the sale of the collateral by submitting a "credit bid."[530] A "credit bid" permits a secured creditor to exchange the amount of all or part of its secured claim for the collateral, rather than paying cash. Section 363(k) provides:

> At a sale under subsection (b) of this section of property that is subject to a lien that secured an allowed claim, unless the court for cause orders otherwise the holder of such claim may bid at such sale, and if the holder of such claim purchases such property, such holder may offset such claim against the purchase price of such property.

Offsetting the claim against the purchase price, as described in this language, is the key feature of a "credit bid." As explained below, § 1129(b)(2)(A)(ii)'s reference to § 363(k) has raised difficult questions concerning whether a plan which provides for a sale of encumbered collateral free and clear of the creditor's interest can be confirmed under the "indubitable equivalent" standard of § 1129(b)(2)(A)(iii), or whether it can only be confirmed under § 112(b)(2)(A)(ii), which preserves the secured creditor's right to make a credit bid for its collateral, pursuant to § 363(k).

[c]   Creditor Receives the "Indubitable Equivalent" of its Claims

The third alternative is open-ended. A plan is fair and equitable if it provides "for the realization by such [secured claim] holders of the indubitable equivalent of [their] claims."[531] The "indubitable equivalent" standard is derived from Judge Learned Hand's opinion in *In re Murel Holding Co.*[532] The indubitable equivalent standard is also widely used in connection with methods for providing secured creditors with adequate protection, as required by § 362(d)(1), to forestall them from obtaining relief from the automatic stay.[533]

Alternative treatments that might satisfy this standard might take many forms, but undoubtedly include surrender of all of the collateral to the creditor[534] or

---

[528] *See* Daniel J. Bussel & Kenneth N. Klee, *Recalibrating Consent in Bankruptcy*, 83 Am. Bankr. L.J. 663 (2009).

[529] Bankruptcy Code § 363(f). *See* Daniel J. Bussel & Kenneth N. Klee, *Recalibrating Consent in Bankruptcy*, 83 Am. Bankr. L.J. 663 (2009); *supra* § 9.03[C] Use, Sale, or Lease Outside the Ordinary Course.

[530] Vincent S. J. Buccola & Ashley C. Keller, *Credit Bidding and the Design of Bankruptcy Auctions*, 18 Geo. Mason L. Rev. 99 (2010); Alan N. Resnick, *Denying Secured Creditors the Right to Credit Bid in Chapter 11 Cases and the Risk of Undervaluation*, 63 Hastings L.J. 323 (2012).

[531] Bankruptcy Code § 1129(b)(2)(A)(iii).

[532] 75 F.2d 941 (2d Cir. 1935).

[533] *See supra* § 8.06[B][1] For Cause — Lack of Adequate Protection.

[534] 124 Cong. Rec. 32,407 (1978) (statement of Rep. Edwards); *cf.* Bankruptcy Code § 1325(a)(5)(C).

transfer of the creditor's lien to other property with the same or higher value.[535] However, surrender of only some of the collateral to the creditor, in what has sometimes been called a "dirt-for-debt" plan, which usually involves real estate, is questionable. Substitution of collateral is also questionable where the new collateral is property of a different type which is more difficult to value or which is subject to different types of market forces than the original collateral.

Plans calling for a sale free and clear of a creditor's lien have sometimes been confirmed, under the indubitable equivalent standard, even though the creditor has not been accorded the right to participate in the sale of the collateral by making a "credit bid" as § 1129(b)(2)(ii), discussed above, seems to require.[536] The Supreme Court's 2012 decision in *RadLAX Gateway Hotel, LLC v. Amalgamated Bank*[537] held that a plan proposing such a sale could not be justified under the "indubitable equivalent" standard of § 1129(b)(2)(A)(iii). Justice Scalia, writing for an unanimous court, explained that permitting the more general indubitable equivalent standard to be used in this way, without complying with the more specific requirements of § 1129(b)(2)(A)(ii), was inconsistent with the cannon of statutory construction that usually makes a more specific provision supersede a more general section of the same statute. As a result, § 1129(b)(2)(A)(iii) can no longer be used to cram down a plan that proposes the sale of a secured creditor's collateral, free and clear of the creditor's lien, without allowing the lender to submit a competing "credit bid" for the collateral.

This may make it difficult for debtors to sell a collection of assets to a single buyer when the assets are encumbered by liens held by different lenders. Whether such sales can continue to be made will depend on whether selling a collection of assets in a single transaction is sufficient "cause" to deny the lenders the right to submit a credit bid, as § 363(k) suggests it might.[538]

Debtor's plans also sometimes propose to convey *part* of the creditor's collateral to a secured creditor in *full* satisfaction of the creditor's claim, in what is generally known as a "dirt-for-debt" plan (sometimes called an "eat dirt" plan).[539] The problem in most such cases is with the value of the parcel the debtor seeks to transfer and whether it is the "indubitable equivalent" of the creditor's claim. To serve as the indubitable equivalent, the transferred property must both (1) provide the creditor with the present value of its claim and (2) ensure the safety of the creditor's principal.[540]

---

[535] 124 Cong. Rec. 32,407 (1978) (statement of Rep. Edwards).

[536] *Compare* In re River Road Hotel Partners, LLC, 651 F.3d 642 (7th Cir. 2011) (affirming secured creditor's right to make a credit bid), *with* In re Pacific Lumber Co., 584 F.3d 229 (5th Cir. 2009), *and* In re Philadelphia Newspapers, LLC, 599 F.3d 298 (3d Cir. 2010) (no right of secured creditor to bid if plan otherwise have secured creditors the "indubitable equivalent" of their secured claims).

[537] RadLAX Gateway Hotel, LLC v. Amalgamated Bank,132 S. Ct. 2065 (2012).

[538] Bankruptcy Code § 363(k).

[539] In re Richfield 81 Partners II, LLC, 447 B.R. 653 (Bankr. N.D. Ga. 2011).

[540] In re Arnold & Baker Farms, 85 F.3d 1415, 1422 (9th Cir.1996); In re Sparks, 171 B.R. 860, 866 (Bankr. N.D. Ill. 1994).

Courts have not embraced these plans warmly.[541] They transfer all of the risks associated with selling the collateral, including the risk that the collateral will decline in value, or that it was improperly valued in the first place, to the lender.[542] Still, they are sometimes approved.

[2] Unsecured Claims[543]

The fair and equitable standard has its biggest impact on unsecured creditors. Even when a plan is not "crammed down," negotiations over the terms of the plan are usually conducted against the backdrop of the absolute priority rule.

The standard can be satisfied in one of two ways. First, a plan that provides for "each holder of a claim [to receive] property of a value as of the effective date of the plan, equal to the allowed amount of [its] claim" is fair and equitable.[544] In other words, a plan is fair and equitable if it provides for payment to unsecured creditors that amount to 100% of the value they are owed. Alternatively, the plan can be confirmed over the objection of a class of unsecured claims if junior claims receive nothing.[545]

[a] Payment in Full

Satisfying the fair and equitable standard by paying creditors in full requires paying them not only the full amount of their claims, but the full value of the amount of their claims. As with other situations where full *value* must be paid, this means that if payment is deferred, the payments must include interest to compensate the creditor for any delay.[546]

Paying holders of unsecured claims the entire value of their claims might be accomplished in several ways. First, many plans designate a class of creditors with small claims, segregated from claims of larger creditors for administrative convenience pursuant to § 1122(b). These claims are usually paid in full, in cash, on the effective date of the plan. This undoubtedly satisfies § 1129(b), but cramdown is rarely necessary with respect to a class treated in this manner. Given the opportunity to receive cash, creditors usually vote to accept the plan.

Claims of unsecured creditors might also be fully satisfied by distributing stock in the reorganized company to creditors in the class. This gives creditors an equity position in the reorganized debtor. Creditors who prefer cash can sell their stock, if there is a market for it. Nevertheless, this method of providing unsecured claim

---

[541] Alfred S. Lurey & Brett J. Berlin, *When Can Less than All of a Creditor's Collateral Serve as the Indubitable Equivalent of the Creditor's Secured Claim?*, 28 Cumb. L. Rev. 333 (1997-98).

[542] *E.g.*, In re Arnold & Baker Farms, 85 F.3d 1415 (9th Cir. 1996) (plan conveying 566.5 acres of the 1320 acres that stood as collateral for the debt did not provide the indubitable equivalent).

[543] Andrew A. Wood, *The Decline of Unsecured Creditor and Shareholder Recoveries in Large Public Company Bankruptcies*, 85 Am. Bankr. L.J. 429 (2011).

[544] Bankruptcy Code § 1129(b)(2)(B).

[545] Bankruptcy Code § 1129(b)(2)(B)(ii).

[546] *E.g.*, Liberty Nat'l Enters. v. Ambanc La Mesa Ltd. (In re Ambanc La Mesa Ltd.), 115 F.3d 650, 653-64 (9th Cir. 1997) (plan failed to provide interest payments to unsecured claims of dissenting class of creditors).

holders with payment in full is fraught with difficulty, primarily because it may require a difficult and expensive valuation of the business as a going concern to determine if the stock they are receiving is really the equivalent of the full value of their claims.

The plan might also simply provide for deferred cash payments to holders of unsecured claims in full satisfaction of their claims. This satisfies the absolute priority rule only with respect to debtors who are solvent as a going concern. Otherwise, such a plan is not feasible.

[b] Eliminating Junior Claims and Interests

Although fully paying a class of unsecured creditors makes a plan fair and equitable, it is rarely feasible. Financially troubled debtors do not often have enough capital to pay unsecured creditors in full. If they do not consent to receive less, the only other way to make a plan fair and equitable is if the plan provides nothing for those who are junior to the dissenting class. The key statutory language is in § 1129(b)(2)(B)(ii): A plan is fair and equitable "[w]ith respect to a class of unsecured claims . . . [if] the holder of any claim or interest that is junior to the claims of such class will not receive or retain under the plan on account of such junior claim or interest any property."[547] Thus, if the plan is to be confirmed over the objection of a dissenting class of unsecured creditors who are not to be paid in full, those junior to the members of the class may not receive anything on account of their prepetition rights. In plain terms, shareholders may not keep their stock.

This is the absolute priority rule. It makes the negotiations leading to the development of a plan a game of financial "chicken."[548] The debtor's shareholders, who may also be its directors, officers, and employees, hope to give unsecured creditors as little as possible of the remaining value of the reorganized company. They hope that the company will return to profitability and that they will resume receiving dividends on their capital investment. They also hope to keep their jobs, but they might find it easier to find new jobs than to recover their capital. Creditors would like to receive payment for money they have loaned or for goods or services they have provided to the debtor. Those who are vendors also prefer the debtor to remain in business. In addition, more often than not, creditors and debtors alike realize that the going concern value of the debtor's business is greater than the value its assets would produce in a piecemeal liquidation sale. At liquidation, unsecured creditors receive little or nothing; shareholders inevitably lose all of their investments, and if they are employed as members of the debtor's management team, they lose their jobs. The debtor threatens to liquidate, hoping to persuade creditors to accept whatever payment the debtor is offering in the plan. Creditors threaten to reject the plan, and force the debtor to deprive its existing stockholders of any interest in the company as a means of encouraging the

---

[547] Bankruptcy Code § 1129(b)(2)(B)(ii).

[548] *See* John D. Ayer, *Bankruptcy as an Essentially Contested Concept: The Case of the One-Asset Case*, 44 S.C. L. Rev. 863, 896 n.129 (1993); Daniel B. Bogart, *Games Lawyers Play: Waivers of the Automatic Stay in Bankruptcy and the Single Asset Loan Workout*, 43 UCLA L. Rev. 1117, 1201 (1996); J. Bradley Johnston, *The Bankruptcy Bargain*, 65 Am. Bankr. L.J. 213, 302 (1991).

debtor to pay more. It is as if the debtor were standing on the ledge outside the window on the thirtieth floor, threatening to jump, with the creditors hovering all around, threatening to push.[549]

Plans calling for the elimination of existing shareholders are sometimes proposed by unsecured creditors. They might propose a redistribution of the shares of the company to creditors, or a sale of the debtor (or its assets) as a going concern and a distribution of the cash obtained from the sale to creditors according to their established priorities. Such a plan might easily satisfy the absolute priority rule.

The principal difficulty with applying the absolute priority rule is that it frequently requires a valuation of the business as a going concern. This is particularly true where members of a dissenting class of unsecured creditors receive stock in full satisfaction of their claims and shareholders are to retain an interest in the reorganized company without contributing any new value. Without determining the value of the reorganized debtor as a going concern, it is impossible to know whether this treatment of unsecured creditors amounts to full satisfaction of their claims and thus whether the full-payment branch of the fair and equitable standard has been satisfied.[550] Determining the going concern value of the debtor is expensive and may deprive the debtor of the going concern value upon which the plan depends.

There is one final uncodified but inherent feature of the absolute priority rule: no class senior to a dissenting class may receive *more* than its full present value under the plan.[551] This, of course, makes sense. If a senior class of creditors is receiving payment of more than full value of its claim, the junior class is being deprived of some residual value of the debtor on a dollar-for-dollar basis.[552]

Additional rules apply to Chapter 11 cases involving individual debtors.[553] Language at the end of § 1129(b)(2)(B)(ii) now provides: "in a case in which the debtor is an individual, the debtor may retain property included in the estate under section 1115, subject to the requirements of subsection (a)(14) of this section." Section 1115, added at the same time as the above text, includes an individual debtor's earnings from post-petition services in her estate.[554] Thus, for an individual Chapter 11 debtor, the estate includes all of the property usually included in a debtor's estate, together with earnings derived from the debtor's post-petition personal services.

Courts are split over whether these changes create an exception to the absolute

---

[549] Elizabeth Warren & Jay Lawrence Westbrook, The Law of Debtors and Creditors (6th ed. 2009).

[550] Bankruptcy Code § 1129(b)(2)(B)(i).

[551] *See* Omer Tene, *Revisiting the Creditors' Bargain: The Entitlement to the Going-concern Surplus in Corporate Bankruptcy Reorganizations*, 19 Bankr. Dev. J. 287, 397 (2003).

[552] Kenneth Klee, *Cram Down II*, 64 Am. Bankr. L.J. 229, 231-32 (1990); Kenneth Klee, *All You Ever Wanted to Know About Cram Down Under the New Bankruptcy Code*, 53 Am. Bankr. L.J. 133, 144-56 (1979).

[553] Robert J. Keach, *Dead Man Filing Redux: Is the New Individual Chapter Eleven Unconstitutional?*, 13 Am. Bankr. Inst. L. Rev. 483 (2005).

[554] Bankruptcy Code § 1115(a)(2).

priority rule with respect to earnings individual debtors receive from their post-petition personal services.[555] Courts that have held that the absolute priority rule is partially abrogated have found that § 1129(b)(2)(B)(ii)'s phrase "included in the estate under section 1115" refers to both "the property specified in section 541" and the two types of property described in Sections 1115(a)(1) and 1115(a)(2).[556] These courts effectively conclude that Chapter 11 does not turn individual debtors into indentured servants.[557] The reference to § 1129(a)(4) makes it clear that, despite the change, the plan must still provide for the debtor to continue to make payments for post-petition support obligations.

Other courts interpret the new language of § 1129(b)(2)(B)(ii) more restrictively. They conclude that the effect of the new language in § 1129(b)(2)(B)(ii) is not to abrogate the absolute priority rule. Instead, these courts rule that the phrase "included in the estate under section 1115" includes the specific property identified in §§ 1115(a)(1) & (a)(2), and that therefore the absolute priority rule applies in the same way to individuals as it does to other Chapter 11 debtors, as it did before BAPCPA.[558]

[3] Equity Interests

Cramming a plan down over the objection of a class of interest holders is more common. If the debtor is insolvent, stockholders' interests are worthless. A plan can be confirmed over their objection in one of two ways. First, it can be confirmed if the plan permits interest holders to receive or retain property equal to the "value of their interest."[559] Worthless interests are satisfied in full even if they receive nothing.

Here, the principal difficulty is in determining whether the debtor is insolvent. Making this determination requires a difficult and expensive valuation of the debtor's business. In many cases, it may be cheaper to give stockholders something as a way to avoid this expense. A class of preferred stock must be paid any "fixed liquidation preference" or "fixed redemption price,"[560] even if the debtor is insolvent. However, this difficulty can be avoided if no interest junior to the affected class receives anything. A plan that gives nothing to holders of common stock is fair and equitable with respect to preferred shareholders, even if they are not paid their liquidation preference.[561]

---

[555] Bankruptcy Code § 1129(b)(2)(B)(ii). *See* Bankruptcy Code § 1115(a)(2). *See generally* Bruce A. Markell, *The Sub Rosa Subchapter: Individual Debtors in Chapter 11 After BAPCPA*, 2007 U. Ill. L. Rev. 67, 88-90.

[556] *See* In re Tegeder, 369 B.R. 477 (Bankr. D. Neb. 2007); In re Roedemeier, 374 B.R. 264 (Bankr. D. Kan.2007); In re Shat, 424 B.R. 854 (Bankr. D. Nev. 2010).

[557] In re Stephens, 445 B.R. 816 (Bankr. S.D. Tex. 2011).

[558] *E.g.*, In re Maharaj, 681 F.3d 558 (4th Cir. 2012).

[559] Bankruptcy Code § 1129(b)(2)(C)(i).

[560] Bankruptcy Code § 1129(b)(2)(C)(i).

[561] *E.g.*, Nw. Village Ltd. v. Franke (In re Westpointe), 241 F.3d 1005, 1007 (8th Cir. 2001).

[C]   New Value Exception to Absolute Priority Rule[562]

One of the most contentious issues regarding Chapter 11 cramdown is whether there is a new value exception to the absolute priority rule. More precisely, the question is whether shareholders may retain an interest in the reorganized debtor over the objection of an impaired class of unsecured creditors by contributing "new value" to the debtor as part of the reorganization.[563]

Consider, for example, a situation in which City Bank has a senior mortgage on BroadHigh, Inc.'s office building, the only asset that the debtor owns.[564] The debt is $90 million, but the office building is worth only $50 million. This leaves the Bank with a $40 million unsecured deficiency claim. In addition, there are $100,000 in claims of unsecured trade creditors who supply cleaning, security, and maintenance services to the debtor. BroadHigh Inc.'s plan proposes to pay City Bank's $50 million secured claim in full by extending payments for ten years beyond the original term. It proposes to pay only 15% of the Bank's $40 million unsecured claim. Under the debtor's proposal, shareholders of BroadHigh, Inc. will make an additional $4 million capital contribution to the corporation, and retain their stock. Not surprisingly, the bank prefers to immediately foreclose. As a result, it rejects the plan and objects to its confirmation.[565]

At first glance, the absolute priority rule appears to support the Bank's objection. The class of unsecured creditors is impaired and has rejected the plan. Thus, the plan can only be confirmed if it can be crammed down. However, the Bank is receiving only 15% of the value of its unsecured claim and thus § 1129(b)(2)(B)(i), which permits cramdown if the plan pays members of the dissenting class the full value of their claim, is not satisfied. Further, in apparent violation of § 1129(b)(2)(B)(ii), shareholders, who are junior in priority to the Bank retain an interest in the reorganized company. Thus, the plan does not have the necessary consent of every class, and it is not fair and equitable.

On the other hand, the shareholders will pay $4 million for their stock. Nothing would have prohibited an outside investor from purchasing the reorganized debtor's stock for $4 million. The only question would have been whether the price

---

[562] John D. Ayer, *Rethinking Absolute Priority After* Ahlers, 87 Mich. L. Rev. 963 (1989); Elizabeth Warren, *A Theory of Absolute Priority*, 1991 Ann. Surv. Am. L. 9 (1992); Lynn M. LoPucki & William C. Whitford, *Bargaining over Equity's Share in the Bankruptcy Reorganization of Large, Publicly Held Companies*, 139 U. Pa. L. Rev. 125 (1990); Kenneth N. Klee, *Cram Down II*, 64 Am. Bankr. L.J. 229 (1990); Douglas G. Baird & Thomas H. Jackson, *Bargaining After the Fall and the Contours of the Absolute Priority Rule*, 55 U. Chi. L. Rev. 738 (1988); Raymond T. Nimmer, *Negotiated Bankruptcy Reorganization Plans: Absolute Priority and New Value Contributions*, 36 Emory L. J. 1009 (1987).

[563] *See* Bank of Am. Nat'l Trust & Sav. Ass'n v. 203 N. Lasalle St. P'ship, 526 U.S. 434, 437 (1999).

[564] This example illustrates the most common situation in which the new value exception is invoked, a single-asset real estate case. *See* David Gray Carlson & Jack F. Williams, *The Truth About the New Value Exception to Bankruptcy's Absolute Priority Rule*, 21 Cardozo L. Rev. 1303, 1305 n.10 (2000). *See also* David R. Perlmutter, *Navigating a Proposed "New Value" Plan Through the Cross-Currents of the Confirmation Process: An Arduous Journey for the Debtor of a Single-Asset Real Estate Case*, 17 Whittier L. Rev. 427 (1996).

[565] With a few adjustments to supply round numbers, these were the basic facts facing the Supreme Court in its *203 North Lasalle Parntership* decision. Bank of Am. Nat'l Trust & Sav. Ass'n. v. 203 N. Lasalle St. P'ship, 526 U.S. 434, 437-41 (1999).

was fair. The new value exception is based on this idea that the old shareholders might be permitted to buy the company back from the creditors for a fair price. Whether this is allowed has been an issue since the development of the absolute priority rule in the early twentieth century.[566]

The Supreme Court has not yet addressed the issue directly, though it has discussed it in dictum on numerous occasions.[567] Its most recent references to the new value exception were in *Norwest Bank Worthington v. Ahlers*[568] and *Bank of America v. 203 North LaSalle Street Partnership*.[569] In *Ahlers*, the Court ruled that, assuming a "new value exception" existed, "sweat equity" was not sufficient to satisfy the exception. Shareholders could not perform services as new value for the stock they retained. But, the Court did not directly determine whether other, more concrete value, in money or money's worth, would have been sufficient.[570] In *LaSalle*,[571] the Court again assumed for the sake of argument that the new value exception existed, but held that if it did exist, shareholders could not retain an interest in the reorganized firm without permitting others to compete for the opportunity to obtain a share in the reorganized firm. Again, however, the Court explicitly reserved judgment on whether the exception itself exists.[572] Thus, although the Court has suggested that under the right circumstances shareholders might avoid elimination of their interests by contributing new value to the enterprise,[573] the Court has never found a case where the right circumstances were present. Lower court decisions after *Ahlers* and *LaSalle* have not settled the issue,[574] but most courts and commentators regard *LaSalle* as implicitly recognizing the general validity of the new value exception to the absolute priority

---

[566] *See* Case v. Los Angeles Lumber Co., 308 U.S. 106 (1939) (shareholders' proposal to contribute their managerial skill and stature in the community was rejected as insufficient new value). *See, e.g.*, Bonner Mall P'ship v. U.S. Bancorp Mortgage. Co. (In re Bonner Mall P'ship), 2 F.3d 899, 910-16 (9th Cir. 1993) (approving the new value exception); In re Coltex Loop Cent. Three Partners, L.P., 138 F.3d 39, 44-45 (2d Cir. 1998) (doubting its validity); Unruh v. Rushville State Bank, 987 F.2d 1506, 1510 (10th Cir. 1993) (skirting the issue). *See also* Elizabeth Warren, *A Theory of Absolute Priority*, 1991 Ann. Surv. Am. L. 9 (1992); John D. Ayer, *Rethinking Absolute Priority After* Ahlers, 87 Mich. L. Rev. 963 (1989).

[567] The Court dismissed *U.S. Bancorp Mortgage Co. v. Bonner Mall P'ship*, 513 U.S. 18 (1994), after granting certiorari, ruling that the dispute was moot due to a settlement agreement among the parties over the proposed reorganization.

[568] 485 U.S. 197 (1988).

[569] 526 U.S. 434 (1999).

[570] 485 U.S. 197 (1988).

[571] 526 U.S. 434 (1999).

[572] 526 U.S. at 545. *See* Anthony L. Miscioscia, Jr., *The Bankruptcy Code and the New Value Doctrine: An Examination into History, Illusions, and the Need for Competitive Bidding*, 79 Va. L. Rev. 917 (1993).

[573] Lee Dembart & Bruce A. Markell, *Alive at 25? A Short Review of the Supreme Court's Bankruptcy Jurisprudence, 1979-2004*, 78 Am. Bank. L.J. 373, 381 (2004).

[574] Barry E. Adler & George G. Triantis, *The Aftermath of North Lasalle Street*, 70 U. Cin. L. Rev. 1225 (2002); Paul B. Lewis, *203 N. Lasalle Five Years Later: Answers to the Open Questions*, 38 J. Marshall L. Rev. 61 (2004); Nicholas L. Georgakopoulos, *New Value After LaSalle*, 20 Bankr. Dev. J. 1 (2003); Bruce A. Markell, *LaSalle and the Little Guy: Some Initial Musings on the Ultimate Impact of Bank of America, NT & SA v. 203 North LaSalle Street Partnership*, 16 Bankr. Dev. J. 345 (2000); Omer Tene, *Revisiting the Creditors' Bargain: The Entitlement to the Going-Concern Surplus in Corporate Bankruptcy Reorganizations*, 19 Bankr. Dev. J. 287 (2003).

rule, on the one hand, but requiring that the equity be exposed to the market to at least some degree, either by holding an auction, shopping the company, or at least lifting the exclusive period.[575]

It is not even clear that the "new value" exception is really an exception. It may be implicit in the absolute priority rule itself. The absolute priority rule prevents old equity — existing shareholders — from receiving anything "on account of" its old equity interest. But, if the debtor has residual value after distributions to creditors are made, it seems reasonable to permit shareholders to purchase it. Moreover, shareholders who participate in management might be in a better position to operate the business successfully. On the other hand, creditors may be concerned that shareholders might be taking unfair advantage of their better information about the debtor's prospects to purchase any residual value at a bargain-basement price. This risk is acute when the market for prospective buyers of the debtor's residual value is limited. The Court's decision in *LaSalle* prevents shareholders from contributing new value without providing other potential contributors with an opportunity to invest in the debtor, but it does not explain the mechanisms that might be used to encourage other bidders if the opportunity were made available.

[D] Unfair Discrimination[576]

Section 1129(b)(1)'s cramdown rules also prohibit "unfair discrimination" in a non-consensual plan.[577] Remember that § 1122(a) prohibits a plan from combining dissimilar claims in a single class, but is silent about segregating similar claims into separate classes.[578] The prohibition against unfair discrimination prevents unfair differences in the treatment of classes who are entitled to the same priority. These are almost always classes of unsecured creditors, whose basic legal rights and priorities are the same, but who might have different motivations for consenting or objecting to the debtor's plan. The prohibition against unfair discrimination implements one of the Bankruptcy Code's key policies: equal treatment of creditors of the same class.

One justification for discrimination among classes of similar claims is expressly sanctioned by the Code. Small claims may be treated favorably for administrative convenience.[579] Thus, Chapter 11 plans typically establish a class of small creditors, perhaps those with claims of less than $1000, and pay these creditors 100% of what they are owed, in cash, when the plan is implemented. This makes far

---

[575] *See, e.g.,* In re Davis, 262 B.R. 791, 799 n.9 (Bankr. D. Ariz. 2001). *See* Paul B. Lewis, 203 N. Lasalle *Five Years Later: Answers to the Open Questions,* 38 J. Marshall L. Rev. 61, 83 (2004).

[576] G. Eric Brunstad, Jr. & Mike Sigal, *Competitive Choice Theory and the Unresolved Doctrines of Classification and Unfair Discrimination in Business Reorganization Under the Bankruptcy Code,* 55 Bus. Law. 1 (1999); Bruce A. Markell, *A New Perspective on Unfair Discrimination in Chapter 11,* 72 Am. Bankr. L.J. 227 (1998); Stephen L. Sepinuck, *Rethinking Unfair Discrimination in Chapter 13,* 74 Am. Bankr. L.J. 341 (2000).

[577] Bankruptcy Code § 1129(b)(1).

[578] *See supra* § 19.08[D] Classification of Claims.

[579] Bankruptcy Code § 1122(b). *See supra* § 19.08[D][2][a] Small Claims Classified for Administrative Convenience.

more sense than sending and keeping track of small payments to these creditors, over several years. Other creditors, with more sizeable claims, usually do not object to this, because the amount necessary to fully pay these relatively minuscule claims is so small.

However, debtors also sometimes segregate similar claims into different classes to isolate dissenting creditors into a class with other creditors who are likely to vote in favor of the plan, as a means of gaining acceptance of the plan by the requisite majorities. As explained in more detail elsewhere, § 1122(a) does not permit this type of gerrymandering, even in an otherwise consensual plan.[580] It is also not permitted where the purpose of the gerrymander is to obtain the one accepting class required by 1129(a)(10).

Similar creditors are also segregated into different classes, and treated differently, because of differences in what will induce these creditors to vote in favor of a plan. Trade creditors, for example, are usually willing to accept less than other creditors, because they are more interested in keeping one of their customers in business than in insisting on receiving a high percentage of payment for their claims. Other creditors, who will not continue doing business with the debtor, will want to receive more. Some creditors may be interested in receiving a higher payment, even though they might have to wait, while others will be willing to accept less, if they receive it more quickly. Thus, a plan may provide for some creditors to receive 40% of what they are owed, over a one year period, while others are paid 60% over several years. Similarly, some creditors may wish to receive payment in cash, while others may be willing to receive stock in the debtor's reorganized company as a means of payment. If all classes consent to these differences in treatment, the plan can be confirmed under § 1129(a). But, if a class of creditors objects, and a cramdown is necessary, these differences must not discriminate "unfairly."

The test most commonly used to determine whether separate treatment of a class of dissenting creditors is unfair considers several factors: (1) whether the discrimination has a reasonable basis; (2) whether the debtor can carry out a plan without the discrimination; (3) whether the discrimination is proposed in good faith; and (4) whether the degree of discrimination is directly related to the basis or rationale for the discrimination.[581] If one class of unsecured creditors is paid 50% in cash and another class is paid the same percentage, over three years, with interest, the difference is probably warranted, if based on the different motivations and concerns of each group of creditors.[582]

For example, a plan that treats the deficiency claim of the main secured creditor vastly differently from other long-term unsecured claims usually fails this test. Treating key suppliers differently from other creditors, however, usually passes

---

[580] *See supra* § 19.08[D][2][b] Segregation of Substantially Similar Claims.

[581] Amfac Distrib. Corp. v. Wolff (In re Wolff), 22 B.R. 510, 512 (B.A.P. 9th Cir. 1982); Mickelson v. Leser (In re Leser), 939 F.2d 669, 672 (8th Cir. 1991).

[582] *See* In re Jim Beck, Inc., 207 B.R. 1010, 1016-17 (W.D. Va. 1996) (cash to one shareholder, stock to another).

the test, for reasons similar to courts' willingness to recognize the doctrine of necessity at the outset of the case.[583]

More recently, some courts have adopted a different test which establishes a rebuttable presumption against confirmation, on the grounds of unfair discrimination, where:

> there is: (1) a dissenting class; (2) another class of the same priority; and (3) a difference in the plan's treatment of the two classes that results in either (a) a materially lower percentage recovery for the dissenting class (measured in terms of the net present value of all payments), or (b) regardless of percentage recovery, an allocation under the plan of materially greater risk to the dissenting class in connection with its proposed distribution.[584]

Under this test, the presumption of unfair discrimination could be rebutted by showing that outside bankruptcy the dissenting class would receive less or that the preferred class had supplied new value to the reorganized debtor that offsets the gain it is receiving under the discriminatory plan. Differences in risks assumed by the parties under the plan could be justified by showing that differences in the plan reflected different risks that had been assumed by the parties before the bankruptcy case began.[585]

[E] Valuation of the Debtor[586]

Confirming a plan via cramdown nearly always makes it necessary to determine the debtor's value as a going concern.[587] Evaluations of the debtor's financial prospects are also a key component of the evaluation of a plan's feasibility. If the debtor cannot generate enough value to make the payments called for in the plan, the plan should not be confirmed. As the Supreme Court said in *Consolidated Rock Products Co. v. Du Bois*,[588] "whether or not the earnings may reasonably be expected to meet the interest and dividend requirements of new securities is a sine qua non to a determination of the integrity and practicability of the new capital structure. It is also essential for satisfaction of the absolute priority rule."[589] While creditors will usually make their own judgment about the debtor's value as a going concern in deciding whether to vote in favor of a plan, this is not nearly as

---

[583] *E.g.*, Creekstone Apartments Assocs., L.P. v. Resolution Trust Corp. (In re Creekstone Apartments Assocs., L.P.), 168 B.R. 639 (Bankr. M.D. Tenn. 1994).

[584] In re Dow Corning Corp., 244 B.R. 696 (Bankr. E.D. Mich. 1999) (quoting Bruce A. Markell, *A New Perspective on Unfair Discrimination in Chapter 11*, 72 Am. Bankr. L.J. 227, 254 (1998)).

[585] *Id. See also* In re BWP Transport, Inc., 462 B.R. 225 (Bankr. E.D. Mich. 2011); In re Greate Bay Hotel & Casino, Inc. 251 B.R. 213 (Bankr. D.N.J. 2000).

[586] Kerry O'Rourke, *Valuation Uncertainty in Chapter 11 Reorganizations*, 2005 Colum. Bus. L. Rev. 403.

[587] Kenneth N. Klee, *All You Ever Wanted to Know About Cram Down Under the New Bankruptcy Code*, 53 Am. Bankr. L.J. 133 (1979).

[588] Consol. Rock Prods. v. Du Bois, 312 U.S. 510 (1941).

[589] 312 U.S. at 525 (1941). *See* Douglas G. Baird & Donald S. Bernstein, *Absolute Priority, Valuation Uncertainty, and the Reorganization Bargain*, 115 Yale L.J. 1930 (2006).

complicated as bringing the matter to the bankruptcy court and asking it to make a decision.

Accountants use three basic methods to evaluate an enterprise's reorganization value: (1) the "discounted cash flow" method, (2) the "market comparison" method, and (3) the "comparable transaction" method.[590] The discounted cash flow approach is the one most commonly used in bankruptcy settings.[591] It involves several steps but primarily bases the value of the enterprise on the discounted present value of a debtor's projected cash flows. The market comparison approach determines the debtor's value by examining the market value of other similar firms and making an appropriate comparison to the debtor's situation. The comparable transaction approach is similar, but examines actual market transactions that involve the sale of enterprises similar to the debtor.[592] Although business bankruptcy lawyers need not become accountants, they must have sufficient familiarity with these methods to both understand their client's own accountants, and to question those hired by adverse parties.

§ 19.12 MODIFICATION OF CHAPTER 11 PLANS

Many Chapter 11 plans prove unacceptable to creditors. Other plans are confirmed, but turn out to have been too ambitious. In the former case, the debtor may seek to amend the plan before it is submitted to the court for confirmation. In the latter situation, the debtor must seek court approval of a post-confirmation modification. Not surprisingly, the rules regarding amendment before confirmation are considerably more liberal than they are for modification afterwards. Before confirmation, amendments are made routinely as the debtor adjusts its formal proposal to conform to the results of ongoing negotiations with creditors. Thus, it is not unusual for debtors to file a third, fourth, or fifth amended plan of reorganization. Matters become a bit more complicated after creditors have voted on a plan, and they become considerably more complicated if the debtor wishes to modify a plan after it has been confirmed. In either event, the modified plan must conform to the usual requirements for confirmation,[593] and appropriate disclosures nearly always need to be made before creditors vote to accept or reject the modified plan.[594]

---

[590] *See* In re Exide Technologies, 303 B.R. 48 (Bankr. D. Del. 2003); Bank of Montreal v. Official Comm. of Unsecured Creditors (In re Am. Homepatient, Inc.), 298 B.R. 152, 174 (Bankr. M.D. Tenn. 2003).

[591] *E.g.*, In re Am. Home Mortgage Holdings, Inc., 637 F.3d 246 (3d Cir. 2011).

[592] *See* Peter V. Pantaleo & Barry W. Ridings, *Reorganization Value*, 51 Bus. Law. 419, 421-36 (1996); Bradford Cornell, Corporate Valuation 243-46 (1993). *See, e.g.*, In re Exide Technologies, 303 B.R. 48, 62-63 (Bankr. D. Del. 2003).

[593] Bankruptcy Code § 1127(f)(1).

[594] Bankruptcy Code § 1127(f)(2).

[A]   Pre-Confirmation Modification of Chapter 11 Plan

Before confirmation, the proponent of a plan may modify it at any time.[595] Others who wish to propose a modification need to submit their own plan.[596] The modified plan must still conform to the requirements of §§ 1122 and 1123. Once the modification is filed with the court, the modified plan becomes "the plan."[597]

If the plan needs to be modified after a disclosure statement has been approved and disseminated, and after votes have been solicited, the proponent must take additional steps to modify the plan. The proponent of the modification must comply with the disclosure and solicitation requirements of § 1125, with respect to the modified plan.[598] This means that further disclosures will need to be made to any creditor or interest holder whose rights are affected by the modification. These disclosures need to be approved by the court before they can be used to solicit acceptances.[599]

Bankruptcy Rule 3019 addresses the treatment of modifications that are proposed after the original plan has been accepted but before it has been confirmed. It requires the court to give notice, to conduct a hearing,[600] and to determine whether the proposed modification adversely changes the treatment of any creditor or equity security holder who has not formally accepted the modification. If the court finds that the change was not materially adverse to creditors who accepted the plan, those creditors may not change their votes.[601] If the plan materially affects some creditors who have previously accepted the plan, a new round of disclosure and voting must take place. But, if the modification has no adverse affect on creditors who have already accepted the plan, there is no reason to require approval and dissemination of a new disclosure statement.[602]

[B]   Post-Confirmation Modification of Chapter 11 Plan

After confirmation, a proposal to modify the plan may be made by only by a reorganized debtor or the proponent of the confirmed plan.[603] In most cases, where the proponent of the original plan was the debtor, this will be the same person.

---

[595] Bankruptcy Code § 1127(a).

[596] *See supra* § 19.08[B] Who May File a Plan; The Exclusivity Period.

[597] Bankruptcy Code § 1127(a).

[598] Bankruptcy Code § 1127(c). *See supra* § 19.09[B] Disclosure and Solicitation of Ballots.

[599] Bankruptcy Code § 1127(c).

[600] Notice must be given to the trustee (if one has been appointed), to any official committees, and to anyone else designated by the court, such as creditors whose rights are affected by the modification. Fed. R. Bankr. P. 3019.

[601] Fed. R. Bankr. P. 3019. See Enron v. The New Power Co. (In re The New Power Co.), 438 F.3d 1113 (11th Cir. 2006) (modification that extended examiner's powers to post-modification period was not materially adverse to creditor).

[602] In re Mount Vernon Plaza Cmty. Urban Redevelopment Corp. I, 79 B.R. 305 (Bankr. S.D. Ohio 1987). *See also* In re Enron Corp. v. The New Power Co. (In re The New Power Co.), 438 F.3d 1113, 1117-18 (11th Cir. 2006).

[603] Bankruptcy Code § 1127(b).

Any proposal to modify a confirmed plan must be submitted before the plan has been substantially consummated.[604] If, once the plan has been implemented, the debtor determines that a further adjustment of its finances is necessary, it must either enter into an out-of-court workout with its creditors or file a new petition and go through the entire reorganization process, all over again. Substantial consummation means:

(a) transfer of all or substantially all of the property proposed by the plan to be transferred;

(b) assumption by the debtor, or by the successor to the debtor, of the management of all or substantially all of the property dealt with by the plan; and

(c) commencement of distribution under the plan.[605]

If the plan has not yet been substantially consummated, the modification can be confirmed only if the circumstances warrant modification.[606] But, because most modifications are proposed to surmount unanticipated difficulties in implementing a plan, this requirement is rarely difficult to satisfy. Because post-confirmation modifications usually reduce payments to creditors, those affected by the modification are more likely to change their votes than those whose rights were enhanced by a pre-confirmation modification.

The Code contains special rules, applicable only to Chapter 11 debtors who are individuals, for modification after a plan has been substantially consummated.[607] These special rules conform to rules for modifying Chapter 13 plans.[608] In these cases, the plan may be modified upon the request of the debtor, the trustee, the U.S. Trustee, or the holder of any unsecured claim. Modifications may increase or reduce the amount of payments made to any class, extend or reduce the duration of the plan, or alter the amount of the distribution to any individual creditor to account for payments that the creditor is receiving under the terms of any other plan involving a related debtor.[609]

§ 19.13   POST-CONFORMATION ISSUES[610]

Confirmation of the plan does not end the case. Issues sometimes arise over the effect of confirmation. Moreover, the plan still must be implemented by distributing any property or securities called for by the plan, and payments must be commenced. In rare circumstances, involving fraud in the confirmation process,

---

[604] Bankruptcy Code § 1127(b).

[605] Bankruptcy Code § 1101(2). *See* In re Dean Hardwoods, Inc., 431 B.R. 387 (Bankr. E.D.N.C. 2010).

[606] Bankruptcy Code § 1127(b).

[607] Bankruptcy Code § 1127(e).

[608] *See supra* § 18.10[B] Post-Confirmation Modification of Chapter 13 Plan.

[609] Bankruptcy Code § 1127(e)(1)-(3).

[610] Frank R. Kennedy & Gerald K. Smith, *Chapter 11 Issues: Postconfirmation Issues: The Effects of Confirmation and Postconfirmation Proceedings*, 44 S.C. L. Rev. 621 (1993).

confirmation may be revoked. And the plan may provide for the bankruptcy court to retain jurisdiction over the case to consider these or other issues that may arise.

[A]　Effect of Confirmation

Confirmation has several consequences. First and most important, the confirmed plan binds the debtor, its creditors, and its owners, regardless of whether they accepted the plan.[611] This is the single most significant difference between a confirmed Chapter 11 plan and an out-of-court workout, which does not bind those who have not agreed.

Second, unless the plan provides otherwise, confirmation vests the estate's property in the debtor.[612] In effect, confirmation re-establishes the original entity and extinguishes the estate. Of course, many plans are likely to provide otherwise, at least to the extent that the plan permits creditors to retain their liens, or provides for the transfer of the estate's property to a third-party, such as someone who buys key assets from the estate as part of the consummation of the plan.

Third, confirmation discharges the debtor from all pre-confirmation debts.[613] In this respect, Chapter 11 differs from Chapters 12 and 13, in which a discharge is normally granted only when the plan is fully performed. Thus, with limited exceptions, all of the claims and interests that existed prior to confirmation cease to exist[614] and are replaced by whatever rights and obligations are created by the plan. In this respect, confirmation is roughly the equivalent of a novation, in which the new obligation contained in the plan is a complete substitute for the discharged obligation that existed before. It is the debtor's fresh start: a new financial structure of both debt and equity.

There are a few limited exceptions to this fresh start. An individual Chapter 11 debtor, unlike the successful Chapter 13 debtor, is subject to the full list of debts made non-dischargeable by § 523.[615] Thus, confirmation does not discharge an individual from those debts.[616] Moreover, a liquidating debtor who would be denied a discharge in Chapter 7 is not entitled to any discharge.[617]

Another key consequence of confirmation is the imposition of the discharge stay of § 524 in place of the automatic stay. The automatic stay terminates when a discharge is granted.[618] As a result, creditors may not pursue the debtor for claims they held prior to confirmation. Chapter 11 replaces their pre-confirmation claims

---

[611]　Bankruptcy Code § 1141(a).

[612]　Bankruptcy Code § 1141(b).

[613]　Bankruptcy Code § 1141(d).

[614]　Bankruptcy Code § 1141(d)(1)(A), (B). Note that claims are extinguished whether or not a proof of claim was filed or deemed filed; whether or not it was allowed; and whether or not the claimant voted to accept the plan. Bankruptcy Code § 1141(d)(1)(A). By contrast, interests are terminated only if the rights of holders of those interests are provided for by the plan. Bankruptcy Code § 1141(d)(1)(B).

[615]　*See supra* § 13.03 Non-Dischargeable Debts.

[616]　Bankruptcy Code § 1141(d)(2).

[617]　Bankruptcy Code § 1141(d)(3). *See supra* § 13.02[C] Denial of Discharge in Chapter 11.

[618]　Bankruptcy Code § 362(c)(2)(C).

with whatever rights they receive under the terms of the plan, even though this may be less than full satisfaction of their earlier claims.

Debtors sometimes try to expand the scope of the stay by including language in the plan that purports to enjoin creditors from pursuing claims against guarantors. Section 524(e) provides that "discharge of a debt of the debtor does not affect the liability of any other entity on, or the property of any other entity for" the debtor's obligations.[619] Some courts have held that this language prevents confirmation of plan that provides otherwise.[620] Other courts have held that the Anti-Injunction Act of the Internal Revenue Code[621] prevents a plan from expanding the scope of the discharge stay, to protect a corporate debtor's officers from the IRS's post-confirmation collection efforts.[622]

[B] Revocation of Confirmation

As is true in the other reorganization chapters, an order confirming the plan may be revoked only in very limited circumstances. Upon the request of a party in interest, made within 180 days of the entry of the confirmation order, the court, after notice and an opportunity for a hearing, may revoke the order "if and *only if*" it was procured by fraud.[623] The order revoking confirmation must contain provisions to protect any entity that acquired rights in good faith reliance on the confirmation.[624] It must also revoke the debtor's discharge.[625] The very limited time period and fraud as the only basis for revocation are imposed because the need for finality in the proceeding is so great. The debtor must be able to resume its normal business and financial affairs; those with whom it is dealing must have assurance that their transactions are valid.

[C] Implementation of the Plan

Chapter 11 differs from Chapters 12 and 13 in that the implementation of the plan is largely in the hands of the debtor. There is no standing trustee assigned to collect payments from the debtor and transmit them to creditors. Although the court retains the power to issue any orders necessary to implement the plan,[626] it is the debtor and any entity organized for this purpose, who puts the plan's provisions into action.[627] Payments due under the plan are paid directly by the debtor, or in some cases they are paid from a separate trust or similar entity created by the plan for this purpose.

---

[619] Bankruptcy Code § 524(e).

[620] In re Lewenschuss, 67 F.3d 1394 (9th Cir. 1995); In re Linda Vista Cinemas, L.L.C., 442 B.R. 724 (Bankr. D. Ariz. 2010).

[621] 26 U.S.C. § 7421(a) (2006).

[622] J.J. Re-Bar Corp., Inc. v. United States (In re J.J. Re-Bar Corp., Inc.), 644 F.3d 952 (9th Cir. 2011).

[623] Bankruptcy Code § 1144 (emphasis added).

[624] Bankruptcy Code § 1144(1).

[625] Bankruptcy Code § 1144(2).

[626] Bankruptcy Code § 1142(b).

[627] Bankruptcy Code § 1142(a).

[D] Bankruptcy Court Jurisdiction After Confirmation[628]

Most plans contain some provision for the court to retain jurisdiction over the case while the plan is implemented. However, the propriety and extent of the court's continued jurisdiction remains a contentious issue.

There is no doubt about the court's authority to issue appropriate orders in the time immediately after confirmation until the "effective date" of the plan, when its provisions become effective and it begins to be implemented. Section 1142 expressly authorizes the court to:

> direct the debtor and any other necessary party to execute or deliver or to join in the execution or delivery of any instrument required to effect a transfer of property dealt with by a confirmed plan, and to perform any other act, including the satisfaction of any lien, that is necessary for the consummation of the plan.[629]

Thus, the court has the authority to compel parties to sign or deliver any deeds, bills of sale, contracts, negotiable instruments, or other documents that may be necessary to implement the plan's provisions.

However, the parameters of the court's jurisdiction are established by the relevant provisions of the United States Judicial Code, primarily 28 U.S.C. § 1334, not by § 1142, much less by language in a plan that purports to grant the court continuing jurisdiction over the case. Once the plan has been substantially consummated, issues sometimes arise over whether the court retains jurisdictional authority over its implementation. In some cases, particularly those involving trust funds established to pay claims to hundreds and perhaps thousands of injured claimants, courts have retained broad jurisdiction over the case for many years.[630]

Despite these cases, bankruptcy courts generally adhere to the oft-quoted passage in *North American Car Corp. v. Peerless Weighing & Vending Machine. Corp.*:

> We have had occasion before to deplore the tendency of District Courts to keep reorganized concerns in tutelage indefinitely by orders purporting to retain jurisdiction for a variety of purposes, extending from complete supervision of the new business to modifications of detail in the reorganization. Since the purpose of reorganization clearly is to rehabilitate the business and start it off on a new and to-be-hoped-for more successful career, it should be the objective of courts to cast off as quickly as possible all leading strings which may limit and hamper its activities and throw

---

[628] Daniel B. Bogart, *Unexpected Gifts of Chapter 11: The Breach of a Director's Duty of Loyalty Following Plan Confirmation and the Postconfirmation Jurisdiction of Bankruptcy Courts*, 72 Am. Bankr. L.J. 303 (1998); Darrell Dunham, *Bankruptcy Court Jurisdiction*, 67 UMKC L. Rev. 229, 267-71 (1998); Benjamin Weintraub & Michael J. Crames, *Defining Consummation, Effective Date of Plan of Reorganization and Retention of Postconfirmation Jurisdiction: Suggested Amendments to Bankruptcy Code and Bankruptcy Rules*, 64 Am. Bankr. L.J. 245 (1990).

[629] Bankruptcy Code § 1142(b).

[630] *See, e.g.*, Official Dalkon Shield Claimants' Comm. v. Mabey (In re A.H. Robins Co.), 880 F.2d 769 (4th Cir. 1989).

doubt upon its responsibility. It is not consonant with the purposes of the Act, or feasible as a judicial function, for the courts to assume to supervise a business somewhat indefinitely.[631]

Bankruptcy courts have generally avoided becoming enmeshed in matters that have nothing to do with the provisions of the Bankruptcy Code, such as missed payments, foreclosure suits, or other disputes that are routinely handled in state court.[632] Where issues of state law predominate and the dispute has nothing to do with the administration of the bankruptcy case, bankruptcy courts decline to assume jurisdiction.[633]

[E]   Individual Debtors

Confirmation has a different effect on individual debtors than it has on corporations, partnerships, and other organizations. In cases involving individuals, discharge is delayed, as it is in Chapters 12 and 13, until the debtor completes "all payments under the plan."[634]

Because confirmation revests the estate's property in the debtor,[635] the automatic stay terminates with respect to actions against estate property, as soon as the plan is confirmed.[636] Thus, it might appear that creditors can enforce their pre-petition liens against the collateral after the plan is confirmed. This, of course, would turn Chapter 11 on its head. Because confirmation binds the creditor, its res judicata effect would seem to prevent the creditor from pursuing its pre-petition rights, even though the automatic stay has ended and the discharge stay has not yet gone into effect.

As in Chapter 13, a discharge may be granted before completion of the debtor's payments if unsecured creditors have received at least what they would have received in a Chapter 7 liquidation and modification of the plan is not practicable.[637] However, unlike the requirements for a "hardship discharge" in Chapter 13, Chapter 11 does not require the debtor to show that its inability to complete the plan was due to circumstances for which the debtor should not justly be held accountable.[638]

---

[631] 143 F.2d 938, 940 (2d Cir. 1944).

[632] *E.g.*, Bank of La. v. Craig's Stores of Tex., Inc. (In re Craig's Stores of Tex., Inc.), 266 F.3d 388 (5th Cir. 2002) (post-consummation action over alleged breach of an executory contract assumed under the plan). *See* Zahn Assocs. v. Leeds Bldg. Prods., Inc. (In re Leeds Bldg. Prods., Inc.), 160 B.R. 689 (Bankr. N.D. Ga. 1993) (missed payment).

[633] Guccione v. Bell, No. 06 Civ. 492 (SHS), 2006 U.S. Dist. LEXIS 49526 (S.D.N.Y. July 20, 2006) (action by former officer of magazine publishing business — you know which one — alleging breach of contract, fraud, unjust enrichment, promissory estoppel, failure to pay severance, breach of fiduciary duty, and conspiracy to defraud).

[634] Bankruptcy Code § 1141(d)(5).

[635] Bankruptcy Code § 1141(b).

[636] Bankruptcy Code § 362(c)(1).

[637] Bankruptcy Code § 1141(d)(5)(B).

[638] *See* Bankruptcy Code § 1328(b).

§ 19.14   SMALL BUSINESS DEBTORS[639]

Because of its elaborate and expensive procedures, Chapter 11 has sometimes been of little benefit to small businesses. This was one of the reasons Congress permitted small sole proprietorships to seek relief under Chapter 13. It was also one of the factors that led to the 1986 adoption of Chapter 12 for family farmers and its 2005 expansion to apply to family fishermen.[640] Pressure is occasionally exerted to enact a separate new small business reorganization Chapter. While Congress has largely resisted this pressure, in 1994 it added a few provisions to Chapter 11 to deal with small business reorganizations. These provisions were revised and expanded in 2005.

[A]   Small Business Debtor Defined

The term "small business debtor" is defined narrowly. It means any person engaged in commercial or business activities whose aggregate, non-contingent liquidated debts (both secured and unsecured) do not exceed $2,343,300 on the date of the debtor's petition.[641] However, this definition excludes debtors whose primary business activity is owning or operating real estate. Thus, small single-asset real estate cases do not fall within the special procedures for small business debtors.

Before 2005, debtors could elect to have the Bankruptcy Code's small business provisions applied to their case. The 2005 Amendments removed this "election" and applies the small business debtor provisions to all debtors who fit the definition.[642] However, as will be seen, some of the small business provisions apply only upon court approval of an appropriate motion.

[B]   Expedited and Simplified Procedures for Small Business Debtors

The procedures for small business cases are simpler than for other cases. For example, a creditors' committee is not required, though the Code still presumes that there will be a creditors' committee, unless the court approves a motion

---

[639] Thomas E. Carlson & Jennifer Fraiser-Hayes, *The Small Business Provisions of the 2005 Bankruptcy Amendments*, 79 Am. Bankr. L.J. 645 (2005); Hon. James B. Haines, Jr. & Philip J. Hendel, *No Easy Answers: Small Business Bankruptcies After BAPCPA*, 47 B.C. L. Rev. 71 (2005); Richard Levin & Alesia Ranney-Marinelli, *The Creeping Repeal of Chapter 11: The Significant Business Provisions of the Bankruptcy Abuse Prevention and Consumer Protection Act of 2005*, 79 Am. Bankr. L.J. 603 (2005); Hon. A. Thomas Small, *If You Fix It, They Will Come — A New Playing Field for Small Business Bankruptcies*, 79 Am. Bankr. L.J. 981 (2005).

[640] *See infra* Chapter 20 Family Farmers and Family Fishermen.

[641] Bankruptcy Code § 101(51D)(A). Debts to insiders and affiliates are excluded in calculating whether the debtor is within the financial million threshold. As with many other dollar amounts in the bankruptcy code, the $2,343,300 threshold is adjusted on April 1, every three years, in accordance with changes in the consumer price index. The current threshold was last set in 2010 and is set to be adjusted again in 2013, 2016, and 2019. Bankruptcy Code § 104.

[642] Interim Fed. R. Bankr. P. 1020 provides a mechanism for debtors to declare their status in conjunction with their petition and establishes deadlines for objections to this designation.

otherwise.[643]

The exclusivity period, during which only the debtor may file a plan, is limited in cases involving small debtors, to a maximum of 180 days.[644] Further, no one may file a plan more than 300 days after the order for relief.[645] These time periods may be extended, but only if the debtor "demonstrates by a preponderance of the evidence that it is more likely than not that the court will confirm a plan within a reasonable period of time."[646]

In addition, the court is permitted to dispense with the necessity of a disclosure statement if it determines that "the plan itself provides adequate information."[647] Alternatively, the court may approve a simplified disclosure statement, submitted in accordance with a set of standardized forms. Moreover, the court may conditionally approve a disclosure statement on an ex parte basis, subject to final approval after notice and the opportunity for a hearing.[648] Acceptances or rejections of the plan may be solicited based on the conditionally approved disclosure statement, and the court may combine the disclosure statement hearing with a confirmation hearing after the requisite number of acceptances have been obtained.[649] This eliminates one of the major hearings that would otherwise ordinarily occur in a Chapter 11 case.

The debtor must obtain confirmation of its plan within forty-five days of the time it was filed.[650] This period, like the period for filing the plan and disclosure statement, can be extended only upon a showing that confirmation is likely within a reasonable period of time.[651]

[C] Expanded Reporting in Small Business Cases

Accompanying these streamlined procedures are a bevy of additional reporting and record keeping requirements. Most of these duties are found in new § 1116. They include:

- appending the debtor's most recent balance sheets, statement of operations, and federal income tax returns to the debtor's petition;[652]

- attending an initial debtor's interview and other meetings and conferences with the U.S. Trustee, as further specified in the Judicial Code;[653]

---

[643] Bankruptcy Code § 1102(a)(3).

[644] Bankruptcy Code § 1121(e)(1)(A).

[645] Bankruptcy Code § 1122(e)(2).

[646] Bankruptcy Code § 1122(e)(3)(A).

[647] Bankruptcy Code § 1126(f)(1).

[648] Bankruptcy Code § 1125(f)(3). *See* Fed. R. Bankr. P. 3017.1(a).

[649] Bankruptcy Code § 1125(f)(3)(C).

[650] Bankruptcy Code § 1129(e).

[651] Bankruptcy Code §§ 1129(e), 1121(e)(3)(A).

[652] Bankruptcy Code § 1116(1). Fed. R. Bankr. P. 2015(a)(6).

[653] Bankruptcy Code § 1116(2); 28 U.S.C. § 586(a)(7) (2006). Section 586(a)(7) codifies current practices of the U.S. Trustees office.

- expediting filing of all schedules and statements of affairs that are not filed with the debtor's petition;[654]

- filing post-petition financial and other reports as specified by the Federal Rules of Bankruptcy Procedure or local bankruptcy rules;[655]

- maintaining insurance according to industry custom;[656]

- timely filing all relevant tax returns and other government filings and timely paying all post-petition taxes;[657] and

- permitting the U.S. Trustee or its designate to inspect the debtor's premises, books, and records.[658]

§ 19.15 RAILROAD REORGANIZATIONS

Much of our law of bankruptcy reorganizations is derived from early procedures that were developed to restructure the finances of the first great American businesses: the railroads. The great railroad reorganizations of the late nineteenth and early twentieth centuries presented unique issues, involving assets spread out over vast geographical areas and key components of the public interest. Thus, it is not surprising that the Bankruptcy Code retains special provisions, in Subchapter IV of Chapter 11,[659] to deal with railroad reorganizations. For a variety of reasons, railroad reorganizations have many distinct features. This section only highlights a few of the most notable among them.

First, in railroad reorganizations, there is always a trustee. As soon as practical after the order for relief, the United States Secretary of Transportation submits a list of five qualified, disinterested persons who are willing to serve as the trustee. The U.S. Trustee appoints the case trustee from this list.[660] The fact that the trustee is selected from among nominees of the Secretary of Transportation reflects the strong public interest in railroad reorganization cases, but leaves one to wonder why similar provisions are not made for bankruptcies of domestic airlines, or large trucking companies, which are also a key link in the nation's transportation system.

Second, the regulatory structures that govern the operation of the railroad remain largely in place. The Interstate Commerce Commission, the United States Department of Transportation, and state railroad regulatory bodies play the role that the SEC plays in other Chapter 11 proceedings. Like the SEC, these bodies may appear and be heard on any issue, but they may not appeal.[661] Moreover,

---

[654] Bankruptcy Code § 1116(3).

[655] Bankruptcy Code § 1116(4). *See* Bankruptcy Code § 308.

[656] Bankruptcy Code § 1116(5).

[657] Bankruptcy Code § 1116(6).

[658] Bankruptcy Code § 1116(7). *See* 28 U.S.C. § 587(a)(7)(B) (2006) (requiring the U.S. Trustee to conduct such an inspection where "appropriate and advisable").

[659] Bankruptcy Code §§ 1161-1174.

[660] Bankruptcy Code § 1163.

[661] Bankruptcy Code § 1164.

regulations that apply to railroads continue in force during the bankruptcy; and, with limited exceptions, the trustee is subject to the orders of any regulatory body.[662]

Third, as noted earlier, there is a greater emphasis on the "public interest" in railroad reorganizations. Both the court and the trustee are explicitly required, when applying some of the key provisions of subchapter IV, to consider the public interest in addition to the interests of the debtor, creditors, and equity security holders.[663] At a minimum, this means that the ability of the public to have access to railroad transportation is to be weighed along with the more conventional interests of the stakeholders in the railroad.[664]

Finally, there is an absolute time limit on the pendency period. If a plan has not been confirmed within five years after the date of the order for relief, the court "shall" order the trustee to cease operations and liquidate the estate.[665] This puts considerable pressure on the debtor and creditors to come to terms over a plan. However, the case is not converted to Chapter 7. Instead, the Code applies Chapter 11's special railroad liquidation provisions which provide for the liquidation to proceed "in the same manner *as if* the case were a case under Chapter 7.[666]

The rights of unions are also treated differently and more favorably in railroad reorganizations. Collective bargaining agreements are protected by § 1167. It provides that neither the court nor the trustee may change the wages or working conditions of employees under a collective bargaining agreement that is subject to the Railway Labor Act, except as provided in that Act.[667] The procedures of provisions of § 1113, which apply to collective bargaining agreements in other Chapter 11 cases, do not apply in railroad reorganizations.[668] The Railway Labor Act requires much more elaborate procedures and considerable government involvement, including the power to order cooling off periods.[669]

---

[662] Bankruptcy Code § 1166.

[663] Bankruptcy Code § 1165.

[664] The court is not required to consider the public interest in all important matters. For example, it need not do so when making decisions under Bankruptcy Code § 363 (use, sale, and lease of property) or Bankruptcy Code § 364 (obtaining credit), even though these are among the most important decisions made.

[665] Bankruptcy Code § 1174.

[666] Bankruptcy Code § 1174 (emphasis added).

[667] Bankruptcy Code § 1167.

[668] Bankruptcy Code § 1113(a).

[669] *See generally* Railway Labor Act, 45 U.S.C. §§ 151 et seq. (2006).

Chapter 20

FAMILY FARMERS AND FAMILY FISHERMEN REORGANIZATION UNDER CHAPTER 12

§ 20.01 GOALS OF FAMILY FARMERS AND FAMILY FISHERMEN REORGANIZATION[1]

Since 1986, the Bankruptcy Code has included a separate reorganization proceeding tailored to assist financially troubled "family farmers." Chapter 12 was added because Chapter 11 proceedings were considered too complicated and expensive to facilitate the reorganization of family farm operations and because many family farms were ineligible for relief under Chapter 13, either as a legal matter, because their level of debt was too high or because they were organized in corporate or partnership form, or as a practical matter, because their income was too unpredictable.[2]

Chapter 13 was initially enacted in response to the mid-1980s "farm debt crisis" that was brought on by the United State's embargo on selling grain to the Soviet Union, in response to the late 1979 Soviet invasion of Afghanistan.[3] The traditional congressional interest in protecting family farms led to the enactment of a "temporary" chapter modeled largely on Chapter 13.[4] Chapter 12 was originally set to expire in 1993, but between 1993 and 2005 it expired and was re-enacted several times, usually retroactively.[5]

There have not been many cases filed under Chapter 12.[6] From its inception in 1986 through June 30, 1993, only about 15,000 Chapter 12 cases were filed. In 2010,

---

[1] Patrick Bauer, *Where You Stand Depends on Where You Sit: A Response to Professor White's Sortie Against Chapter 12*, 13 J. Corp. L. 33 (1987); Janet A. Flaccus, *A Comparison of Farm Bankruptcies in Chapter 11 and the New Chapter 12*, 11 U. Ark. Little Rock L. Rev. 49 (1988-89); David Ray Papke, *Rhetoric and Retrenchment: Agrarian Ideology and American Bankruptcy Law*, 54 Mo. L. Rev. 871, (1989); Katherine M. Porter, *Phantom Farmers: Chapter 12 of the Bankruptcy Code*, 79 Am. Bankr. L.J. 729 (2005); Katherine M. Porter, *Going Broke the Hard Way: The Economics of Rural Failure*, 2005 Wis. L. Rev. 969; James J. White, *Taking From Farm Lenders and Farm Debtors: Chapter 12 of the Bankruptcy Code*, 13 J. Corp. L. 1 (1987).

[2] *See supra* § 6.02[B][6] Eligibility for Relief in Chapter 13 — Individuals with Regular Income.

[3] Katherine M. Porter, *Phantom Farmers: Chapter 12 of the Bankruptcy Code*, 79 Am. Bankr. L.J. 729, 730-33 (2005).

[4] *See generally* David Ray Papke, *Rhetoric and Retrenchment: Agrarian Ideology and American Bankruptcy Law*, 54 Mo. L. Rev. 871 (1989).

[5] Katherine M. Porter, *Phantom Farmers: Chapter 12 of the Bankruptcy Code*, 79 Am. Bankr. L.J. 729, 733 (2005).

[6] *Id.* at 740. Bruce L. Dixon et al., *Factors Affecting State-Level Chapter 12 Filing Rates: A Panel Data Model*, 20 Emory Bankr. Dev. J. 401, 405 (2004).

only 723 Chapter 12 petitions were filed, a tiny percentage of the nearly 1.6 million bankruptcy petitions filed that year.[7] Supporters of Chapter 12 have argued that, despite the low numbers, the Chapter has been a success. There is evidence that the success rate for Chapter 12 proceedings is high relative to Chapter 11 and 13 cases.[8] In 2005, despite the relatively few number of Chapter 12 cases filed, it was made permanent. At the same time, its provisions were extended to cover family fishermen.[9]

Chapter 12 is limited and its goals are fairly narrow: to provide a reorganization alternative to family farmers and their close aquacultural cousins, family fishermen.[10] It differs from Chapter 13 in that it always involves a business. Although sole proprietors sometimes use Chapter 13 to reorganize their business as well as their personal affairs, Chapter 13 usually involves consumer debtors. It differs from at least the larger Chapter 11 cases in that it generally does not preserve the jobs and income of anyone other than a few family members who earn their income from the family farm. Fundamentally, its justification must rest on the belief that there is value to the preservation of family farming which merits special bankruptcy protection.

This chapter discusses the basic structure of Chapter 12, with special focus on provisions that are unique to it. It is relatively brief. Chapter 12 is usually given short shrift in bankruptcy courses because of the small number of Chapter 12 cases and because few of its provisions have been the subject of extensive litigation. There is good reason to believe that this lack of litigation indicates that the worst fears of the Chapter 12 critics have by no means come to pass.[11] While the propriety of a set of specialized rules for reorganizing family farms has been controversial,[12] Chapter 12 now seems likely to remain available to financially troubled family farmers and family-run commercial fishing operations for the foreseeable future.

---

[7] http://www.uscourts.gov/uscourts/Statistics/BankruptcyStatistics/BankruptcyFilings/2010/1210_f2.pdf (last viewed, May 28, 2012).

[8] *See* Jonathan K. Van Patten, *Chapter 12 In the Courts*, 38 S.D. L. Rev. 52 (1993) (indicating a confirmation rate of 60% and a confirmed plan completion rate of 90%). *See also* Bruce Dixon, *Factors Affecting State-Level Chapter 12 Filing Rates: A Panel Data Model*, 20 Bankr. Dev. J. 401 (2003-2004).

[9] For a detailed discussion of the rules regarding eligibility for relief under Chapter 12, see *supra* § 6.02[B][5] Eligibility for Relief in Chapter 12 — Family Farmers and Family Fishermen. *See generally* Mike Lowry, Note, *A New Paint Job on an '85 Yugo: BAPCPA Improves Chapter 12 but Will it Really Make a Difference?*, 12 Drake J. Agric. L. 231, 254 (2007).

[10] In 2005 eligibility was expanded to permit family fishermen to take advantage of Chapter 12. *See* § 6.02[B][5] Eligibility for Relief in Chapter 12 — Family Farmers and Family Fishermen, *supra*; Katherine M. Porter, *Phantom Farmers: Chapter 12 of the Bankruptcy Code*, 79 Am. Bankr. L.J. 729, 735 (2005).

[11] Jonathan K. Van Patten, *Chapter 12 in the Courts*, 38 S.D. L. Rev. 52 (1993).

[12] *See generally* Michael J. Herbert, *Once More Unto the Breach, Dear Friends: The 1986 Reforms of the Reformed Bankruptcy Reform Act*, 16 Cap. U. L. Rev. 325 (1987) (criticizing Chapter 12); Carol Ann Eiden, *The Courts' Rule in Preserving the Family Farm During Bankruptcy Proceedings involving FMHA Loans*, 11 Law & Ineq. 417 (1993); William W. Horlock, Jr., *Chapter 12: Relief for the Family Farmer*, 5 Bankr. Dev. J. 229 (1987); James J. White, *Taking From Farm Lenders and Farm Debtors: Chapter 12 of the Bankruptcy Code*, 13 J. Corp. L. 1, 2 (1987) ("Congress was wrong to enact a law that redistributes wealth from existing mortgagees to existing mortgagors . . . [and will diminish] . . . the farm debtor's power to mortgage his land").

§ 20.02 FILING, CONVERSION, AND DISMISSAL OF CHAPTER 12 CASES

[A] Chapter 12 Filing

Chapter 12 petitions can only be filed voluntarily.[13] Debtors are eligible for relief only if they are "a family farmer or family fisherman with regular annual income"[14] Both individual debtors, corporations, and partnerships may qualify, depending on whether more than 50% of the ownership interests are held by members of the same family and their relatives.[15] As with Chapter 13, debtors are eligible for relief if their secured and unsecured debts are below prescribed maximums, though the limits are somewhat different for family farmers than for family fishermen.[16] In addition, a specified portion of the debtor's income must be earned through the family farm or fishing operation.[17]

[B] Conversion and Dismissal

Chapter 12, like Chapter 13, is wholly voluntary; the debtor cannot be forced into it through an involuntary petition.[18] For the same reason, the debtor has an absolute right to convert a Chapter 12 case to a Chapter 7 case at any time.[19] This right to convert cannot be waived.[20]

This means that the Chapter 12 debtor who has come to the conclusion that the plan will not work or is too burdensome always has a ready exit. Any other party in interest, such as a creditor or the trustee, may request conversion of the case to Chapter 7 if the debtor has committed fraud in connection with the case.[21] Further, because farmers cannot be the targets of an involuntary petition, creditors cannot force the debtor into Chapter 7.[22]

Debtors also have a nearly absolute right to voluntarily dismiss their case.[23] There is one exception to the debtor's right to dismiss. If the debtor previously converted a Chapter 7 or 11 case to Chapter 12, the debtor merely has the right to request that the case be dismissed. Dismissal in this case is not available as a

---

[13] Bankruptcy Code §§ 301, 303. Section 303 does not permit involuntary Chapter 12 petitions.

[14] Bankruptcy Code § 109(f).

[15] Bankruptcy Code §§ 101(18)(B), 101(19A)(B).

[16] *See supra* § 6.02[B][5] Eligibility for Relief in Chapter 12 — Family Farmers and Family Fishermen.

[17] *See supra* § 6.02[B][5] Eligibility for Relief in Chapter 12 — Family Farmers and Family Fishermen.

[18] Bankruptcy Code § 303(a).

[19] Bankruptcy Code § 1208(a).

[20] Bankruptcy Code § 1208(a).

[21] Bankruptcy Code § 1208(d).

[22] *See supra* § 6.03[C] Persons Against Whom Involuntary Cases may be Filed.

[23] Bankruptcy Code § 1208(b).

matter of right.[24]

Any party in interest may request involuntary dismissal for cause, including such things as mismanagement, failure to file a plan, failure to commence payments under the plan, or termination of the plan according to its own terms.[25] In 2005, in an effort to provide additional protection for creditors who are owed support, the debtor's failure to pay a post-petition "domestic support obligation" was added as grounds to dismiss a case.[26] This gives children and former spouses protection against the interminable prolongation of a case in which there is no hope of success.

§ 20.03   ROLE OF THE PARTIES IN CHAPTER 12

The roles of the parties in family farmer and family fisherman reorganization cases are virtually identical to the roles of the parties in Chapter 13 cases. Creditors do not vote on the plan in either type of proceeding. This leaves cases largely under the control of the debtor and the standing trustee; creditors are relegated to a far more limited role.

[A]   Chapter 12 Debtor-in-Possession

In Chapter 12, as in chapters 11 and 13, the debtor remains in possession of estate property while the case is pending. In other words, the debtors get to keep their family farm while they try to reorganize. Likewise, family fishermen are permitted to keep their boats and operate their commercial fishing operation.[27] Subject to whatever limitations the court might impose, a Chapter 12 debtor-in-possession has nearly all of the ordinary rights, powers, and duties of a Chapter 11 trustee.[28]

[B]   Chapter 12 Trustees

Chapter 12, like Chapter 13, uses a standing trustee who is appointed to serve in all Chapter 12 cases in the district or division.[29] However, the Chapter 12 trustee plays a rather different and somewhat hybrid role. Like the Chapter 13 trustee, the Chapter 12 trustee is a party in interest and as such is entitled to be heard on most matters. He carries out many of the same functions as a Chapter 7 trustee. In Chapter 12, however, the trustee is not empowered to advise or assist the debtor. The Chapter 12 trustee also has the broad investigatory powers similar to those

---

[24]   Bankruptcy Code § 1208(b).

[25]   Bankruptcy Code § 1208(c).

[26]   Bankruptcy Code § 1208(c)(10).

[27]   Bankruptcy Code § 1208(c)(10).

[28]   Unlike a trustee, the debtor-in-possession does not have the right to compensation under § 330 for performance of his duties as the debtor-in-possession. Bankruptcy Code § 1203. Likewise, the debtor-in-possession, unlike a Chapter 11 trustee, is not required to investigate the operations of the debtor or to file reports concerning the results of its investigation. *See* Bankruptcy Code §§ 1203 & 1106(a)(3)-(4).

[29]   Bankruptcy Code § 1202(a).

given to a Chapter 11 trustee but not accorded to trustees in Chapter 13 cases.[30] In 2005, Chapter 12 was amended to make the trustee responsible for collecting and enforcing the debtor's domestic support obligations.[31]

The most significant potential difference between the role of a trustee in Chapter 12 and Chapter 13 lies in the fact that a Chapter 12 debtor-in-possession may under some circumstances be removed and replaced by the standing trustee. This cannot occur under Chapter 13.

In recognition of the fact that all Chapter 12 cases involve the operation of a business, Chapter 12 permits the court, upon request of a party in interest and after notice and a hearing, to replace the debtor-in-possession with the standing trustee.[32] This may only be done "for cause," which includes fraud, dishonesty, incompetence, or gross mismanagement on the basis of either the debtor's pre-petition or post-petition conduct.[33] A takeover of the estate is not necessarily permanent; the debtor-in-possession may be subsequently reinstated by the court.[34] The authority to replace the debtor-in-possession with a trustee has been invoked only rarely.[35]

[C] Creditors in Chapter 12 Cases

Just as in Chapter 13 cases, creditors in Chapter 12 cases play a limited role. Unlike in Chapter 11, creditors do not vote on the plan. Their main roles are to file claims, to seek relief from the automatic stay to recover their collateral, and to object to confirmation of debtors' plans.

Secured creditors' efforts to obtain relief from the automatic stay in order to permit foreclosure on the debtor's real estate are somewhat different in Chapter 12 than they are in either Chapter 11 or 13 because of the special "adequate protection" rule of § 1205(b)(3), which is different from those that apply in other chapters. It defines "adequate protection" to include payment of the customary rental value of the land.[36] Also unlike Chapters 11 and 13, Chapter 12 debtors are permitted to modify the rights of claims secured by their residence, in recognition that on many family farms in America, the debtor's residence is part of the farm.[37]

---

[30] Bankruptcy Code § 1202(b)(2).

[31] Bankruptcy Code § 1202(b)(6), (c).

[32] Bankruptcy Code §§ 1204, 1202(b)(5).

[33] Bankruptcy Code § 1204(a).

[34] Bankruptcy Code § 1204(b).

[35] In re Jessen, 82 B.R. 490 (Bankr. S.D. Iowa 1988).

[36] Bankruptcy Code § 1205(b)(3). In other respects, "adequate protection" has the same meaning as it does elsewhere in the Code. *Compare* Bankruptcy Code § 1305(b), *with* Bankruptcy Code § 361.

[37] Both parents of one of your co-authors grew up on farms during the Great Depression of the 1930s. Several of his aunts and uncles and many of his cousins are family farmers in western Ohio. He has visited the farms of these relatives many times and still does so for family gatherings. The hogs you might smell if you've ever stopped at the Interstate 70 rest area just inside the western border of Ohio belong to one of his uncles, whose farm was cut in half when the highway was built. This same co-author helped make hay one summer during college on one of his uncle's farms. This experience motivated him to study hard in school. The other co-author's grandmother spent the first six years of her life on a

Creditors with security interests in farm equipment, fishing gear, and other personal property may seek relief from the stay and object to plan confirmation according to the ordinary rules that apply elsewhere in the Code, with only minor variations. Further, the purchase money security interest rules in the hanging paragraph at the end of § 1325(a), which prevent Chapter 13 debtors from stripping down security interests on motor vehicles and other personal property,[38] have no corollary in Chapter 12.

§ 20.04 PROPERTY OF THE CHAPTER 12 ESTATE

The Chapter 12 estate encompasses more post-petition property than a Chapter 7 estate.[39] In this respect, Chapter 12 is similar to Chapters 11 and 13, where post-petition property is used to facilitate the debtor's rehabilitation. As in Chapter 13, "earnings from services performed by the debtor after the commencement of the case" are explicitly made a part of the debtor's Chapter 12 estate.[40] Making these earnings part of the debtor's estate ensures that they are protected by the automatic stay, and subjects the debtor's ability to use these funds to the restrictions imposed by § 363.[41]

§ 20.05 AUTOMATIC STAY — ADEQUATE PROTECTION

The automatic stay and adequate protection rules in Chapter 12 are different from their counterparts elsewhere in the Code. As explained in detail elsewhere,[42] the automatic stay prevents creditors from taking a wide variety of actions against the debtor, the debtor's property, or property of the estate, while a bankruptcy case is pending. Most importantly, it prevents secured creditors from taking possession of their collateral or taking any other action to foreclose their security interests or mortgages.[43]

However, secured creditors may obtain relief from the automatic stay and foreclose on their interests unless they are "adequately protected" against any deterioration of their property interests that might occur while the case is pending.[44] If a secured creditor obtains relief from the stay due to a lack of adequate protection, and forecloses on property the debtor needs to keep its business open, the debtor's effort to reorganize comes to rapid halt. Thus, disputes over whether secured creditors' property rights are adequately protected are, in reality, struggles over whether the debtor is able to reorganize at all.

---

homestead in the Dakotas. When that farm failed (long before the advent of Chapter 12), her family farmed on the outskirts of Chicago. This is the extent of our farm experience.

[38] *See supra* § 18.08[F][6] Certain Purchase Money Security Interests.

[39] Bankruptcy Code § 1207.

[40] Bankruptcy Code § 1207(b). *See supra* § 7.02[F] Post-Petition Earnings.

[41] *See supra* § 9.03 Use, Sale, or Lease of Estate Property.

[42] *See supra* Chapter 8 — The Automatic Stay.

[43] *See supra* § 8.02 Scope of the Automatic Stay.

[44] *Supra* § 8.06[B][1] for Cause: Lack of Adequate Protection.

[A] Adequate Protection in Chapter 12[45]

The first difference between Chapter 12 and its counterparts is a predicate to the second. Section 361, which provides the general definition of "adequate protection" for automatic stay and other purposes, does not apply in Chapter 12.[46] Instead, Chapter 12 contains its own somewhat broader definition of adequate protection. Under § 361, three types of protection are recognized: periodic payments, the grant of a lien on property, or any other means that provides the indubitable equivalent of the creditor's interest.[47] Section 1205 repeats those three methods of providing protection[48] and adds a fourth less demanding alterative: payment of the rental value of the farm. Section 1205(b)(3) thus provides that adequate protection can be provided to a secured creditor by "paying to such entity for the use of farmland the reasonable rent customary in the community where the property is located, based upon the rental value, net income, and earning capacity of the property."[49]

Secured lenders receive much less protection than they prefer under this provision, because it in effect freezes in place a single use of the property and gives protection for the value of that use alone. If the lender could seize the property, it might be able to put the property to a more economically valuable use, perhaps including selling it for residential or commercial purposes.[50] This issue has not created much of a stir, suggesting that it, like many of Chapter 12's perceived problems, has not caused much real world concern. In part this may be because farmland prices, which declined sharply in the early 1980s, have in more recent years been on the upswing, as farm commodity prices have risen. It also may be due to the fact that there are so few Chapter 12 cases, and not all of them generate adequate protection litigation. Indeed, to the extent land prices are stable or rising, there is no need to provide anything in the way of adequate protection. While there is some ambiguity in the statute, the generally accepted view is that, consistent with the Supreme Court's ruling in *Timbers of Inwood Forest*,[51] rent as adequate

---

[45] Nancy H. Kratzke & Thomas O. Depperschmidt, *"Reasonable Rent" and Opportunity Cost in the Family Farmer Bankruptcy Act*, 39 Drake L. Rev. 863 (1990).

[46] Bankruptcy Code § 1205(a).

[47] Bankruptcy Code § 361. *See supra* § 8.06[B][1] Relief for Cause: Lack of Adequate Protection.

[48] Bankruptcy Code § 1205(b)(1)-(4). Note two probably insignificant differences. Subsections (b)(1), (2), and (4) make it clear that co-owners, as well as creditors, are entitled to adequate protection; this is certainly true under § 361 as well. In addition, subsection (b)(4), the catchall provision, does not state that the relief granted must be the indubitable equivalent of the claimant's interest. Although this apparently permits somewhat broader forms of adequate protection than are allowed under § 361, there does not appear to be much practical significance to it.

[49] Bankruptcy Code § 1205(b)(3).

[50] In the view of one critic of Chapter 12, who was the author of the first edition of this book: "The borrower, by paying rent based on what may be a low economic value use of the property, would be able to keep the lender from foreclosing and converting it to what may be a higher economic value use." Michael J. Herbert, *Once More Unto the Breach, Dear Friends: The 1986 Reforms of the Reformed Bankruptcy Reform Act*, 16 Cap. U. L. Rev. 325, 345-46 (1987).

[51] United Sav. Assoc. of Tex. v. Timbers of Inwood Forest Assocs., Ltd. (In re Timbers of Inwood Forest Assocs., Ltd.), 484 U.S. 365 (1988). *See supra* § 8.06[B] Relief from Stay Upon Request of a Party, *supra*.

protection must be paid only when necessary to protect the creditor against a decline in the value of the property.[52] Thus, the issue may arise only rarely.

The addition of family fishermen to the scope of Chapter 12, on the other hand, increases the likelihood that adequate protection issues will become important in cases under Chapter 12. Debtors' principal asset in these cases are their boats. Fishing boats are far less likely to increase steadily in value than farm land. To the contrary, they are likely to depreciate in value, creating the same sort of adequate protection issues that arise in Chapter 11 cases. Here, however, the special adequate protection rule of § 1205(a)(3), which applies only to "farmland," has no effect.

[B] Chapter 12 Co-Debtor Stay

A second significant feature of the automatic stay in Chapter 12 that is borrowed from Chapter 13 is its co-debtor stay.[53] Section 1201(a) automatically stays all civil actions to collect consumer debts from co-debtors of the debtor.[54] The co-debtor stay is designed to protect the debtor from informal pressure from family members and friends who may have guaranteed one of the debtor's obligations. Thus, if the family farmer's parents guaranteed loans made to the debtor, the creditor may not put family pressure on the farmer by pursuing its claim against his parents.

However, the scope of the co-debtor stay is very limited. It does not apply if the debtor is a partnership or corporation, since a business entity has no consumer debts. Likewise, it does not apply to debts arising from the operation of the debtor's farm.[55] Not surprisingly, it does not apply if the co-debtor became liable as a commercial surety.[56] Further, the stay does not prevent the holder of a negotiable instrument that was signed by the co-debtor from presenting it and giving notice to the co-debtor of its dishonor,[57] which is a formal necessity to preserve the creditor's rights under Article 3 of the U.C.C.

The co-debtor stay, like the automatic stay of § 365, terminates when the case is closed, dismissed, or converted to Chapter 7.[58] However, relief from the stay can be obtained, upon request, when the debtor's plan does not provide for payment of the debt,[59] where the creditor's interest would be irreparably harmed by continuation of the stay,[60] or where the co-debtor protected by the stay is the one who received

---

[52] *E.g.*, Zink v. Vanmiddlesworth, 300 B.R. 394 (N.D.N.Y. 2003); In re Anderson, 88 Bankr. 877 (Bankr. N.D. Ind. 1988); In re Turner, 82 B.R. 465 (Bankr. W.D. Tenn. 1988). *See* Jonathan K. Van Patten, *Chapter 12 in the Courts*, 38 S.D. L. Rev. 52 (1993).

[53] *See supra* § 8.04 Co-Debtor Stays in Chapters 12 and 13.

[54] Bankruptcy Code § 1201(a).

[55] In re SFW, Inc., 83 B.R. 27 (Bankr. S.D. Cal. 1988).

[56] Bankruptcy Code § 1201(a)(1).

[57] Bankruptcy Code § 1201(b).

[58] Bankruptcy Code § 1201(a)(2).

[59] Bankruptcy Code § 1302(b)(2).

[60] Bankruptcy Code § 1302(b)(3).

the consideration for the claim held by the creditor.[61] Thus, relief from the co-debtor stay is quickly available where the debtor is liable only as a guarantor for a loan provided directly to someone else who is liable in his or her capacity as the principal obligor.

§ 20.06 USE, SALE, AND LEASE OF PROPERTY

Section 363 generally permits the trustee to use, sell, or lease estate property, other than "cash collateral" in the ordinary course, without court permission.[62] Use or sale of cash collateral or of other property outside the ordinary course requires court permission.[63] In some circumstances, property can be sold free and clear of any liens on the property.[64] A Chapter 12 debtor-in-possession generally has the same right to use, sell, or lease property as debtors-in-possession under other chapters.[65] Section 1206 seems to limit this right by giving the right to sell property free and clear of secured creditors' interests solely to the trustee. However, the few courts that have interpreted this language have permitted the debtor to conduct the sale provided that the sale is approved by the trustee.[66]

Thus, a Chapter 12 trustee is permitted to sell part or all of the debtor's farm, or the debtor's commercial fishing equipment, including any fishing boats it operates, free and clear of a creditor's mortgage or security interest, provided that the creditor receives a replacement lien on the proceeds received from the sale. The sale must be approved by the court after notice and a hearing, at which the principal issue is mostly whether the price is sufficient.

§ 20.07 CHAPTER 12 REORGANIZATION PLAN

As is true with any reorganization proceeding, the key to Chapter 12 is the debtor's plan. In this respect, Chapter 12 is nearly identical to Chapter 13.[67] Creditors have no right to vote on the plan, so there is little creditor participation in its formulation. Confirmation is based almost entirely on the debtor's ability to meet certain statutory mandates. As in Chapter 13, there is a time limit on the plan; a Chapter 12 plan may not extend for more than three years without court permission, and in no event may it extend for more than five years.[68]

---

[61] Bankruptcy Code § 1302(b)(1).

[62] Bankruptcy Code § 363(c).

[63] Bankruptcy Code § 363(b), (c)(1).

[64] Bankruptcy Code § 363(f).

[65] Bankruptcy Code § 1203.

[66] *E.g.,* In re Webb, 932 F.2d 155 (1st Cir. 1991); In re Brileya, 108 B.R. 444 (Bankr. D. Vt. 1989).

[67] *See supra* §§ 18.06 The Chapter 13 Plan — Required Provisions, *supra*; 18.07 Chapter 13 Plan — Permissive Provisions.

[68] Bankruptcy Code § 1222(c). There is a limited exception to this: payments on secured claims and certain long-term claims may be stretched beyond the three- to five-year period. Bankruptcy Code § 1222(c), (b)(5), (9). There is no requirement, however, that payments on secured claims be stretched beyond the plan period. Appeal of Freund (In re Fortney), 36 F.3d 701 (7th Cir. 1994).

[A]   Required Chapter 12 Plan Provisions

The provisions that are required to be included in Chapter 12 plans are virtually identical to those required to be included in Chapter 13 plans.[69] The plan must provide for submission of a sufficient amount of the debtor's future earnings to the trustee for execution of the plan;[70] it must provide for full payment of nearly all § 507 priority claims;[71] and, if it separates claims into different classes, it must provide for identical treatment of each claim within a class.[72]

[B]   Permissive Chapter 12 Plan Provisions

Additional provisions that are permitted to be included in a Chapter 12 plan are in most respects identical to those than can be included in a Chapter 13 plan.[73] The most significant difference is that a Chapter 12 plan may provide for the modification of a claim secured solely by the debtor's residence. Chapter 13 does not permit residential mortgages to be modified.[74] In addition, as noted above, there is nothing in Chapter 12 like the hanging paragraph at the end of § 1325(a)(9), and thus nothing in Chapter 12 prohibits bifurcation of partially secured liens on the debtor's personal property.[75]

Because of the limited duration of a Chapter 12 plan, which may never last longer than five years, § 1222(b)(5) and (9) permits the plan to cure any pre-petition defaults on long-term debts and to provide for the payment of any long-term secured claims over a period exceeding the duration of the plan.[76]

[C]   Duration of Chapter 12 Plans

In most cases a Chapter 12 plan must last a minimum of three years, and with court approval may be extended up to five years, for good cause. The rare Chapter 12 debtor who is able to pay his creditors' claims in full in less than three years, may obtain confirmation of a plan for whatever shorter period is necessary to fully satisfy his creditors' claims.[77] However, most Chapter 12 debtors are unable to pay their creditors in full in less then three years. These debtors must submit all of their projected disposable income for three years for payments to creditors under

---

[69] *See supra* § 18.06 The Chapter 13 Plan — Required Provisions.

[70] Bankruptcy Code § 1222(a)(1).

[71] Bankruptcy Code § 1222(a)(2). The 2005 Amendments added language that permits claims of governmental entities that arise from the sale of an asset used in the debtor's farming operations to be treated as non-priority claims.

[72] Bankruptcy Code § 1222(a)(3).

[73] *Compare* Bankruptcy Code § 1222(b), *with* Bankruptcy Code § 1322(b). *See supra* § 18.07 Chapter 13 Plan — Permissive Provisions.

[74] *See supra* § 18.07[B][2][a] Residential Real Estate Mortgages.

[75] *See supra* § 18.07[B][2][b] Certain Purchase Money Loans. *See, e.g.*, Harmon v. United States, 101 F.3d 574 (8th Cir. 1996); Zabel v. Schroeder Oil, Inc. (In re Zabel), 249 B.R. 764 (Bankr. E.D. Wis. 2000).

[76] Bankruptcy Code § 1222(b)(9).

[77] Bankruptcy Code § 1225(b)(1)(A).

the plan.[78]

Chapter 12 also permits payments to secured creditors to extend beyond the duration of the plan, and thus beyond the three or five-year limit, without any special court approval.[79] This permits family farmers and family fishermen to amortize secured claims over an extended period. This is particularly important with respect to real estate mortgages and claims secured by expensive farm implements. However, the proposed payment period may not be extended over such a long period that the creditor involved is left inadequately protected. If the useful economic life of the collateral is only seven years, extending the payment period for ten years, after the collateral is worthless, would deprive the creditor of its right to remain adequately protected.

[D]   Chapter 12 Treatment of Priority Claims

Like Chapter 13, Chapter 12 also requires full payment of priority claims.[80] One exception is made for governmental claims that arise as a result of the sale, transfer, exchange or other disposition of any of the debtor's farming assets.[81] This will have its biggest impact on § 507(a)(8) income tax claims that arise from the sale of farm commodities, which are no longer entitled to automatic priority in Chapter 12 and the requirement of full payment that accompanies it.[82] An additional exception was added, consistent with changes made to Chapter 13, for support claims that have previously been assigned to governmental agencies.[83] But this exception applies only if the plan provides for payment of all of the debtor's disposable income for five years.[84]

[E]   Chapter 12 Treatment of Unsecured Claims

Unsecured claims are given essentially the same treatment in Chapter 12 as they are in Chapter 13. The plan's treatment of unsecured claims is subject to two tests: the best interests of creditors test and the disposable income test.

[1]   Best Interests of Creditors

The "best interest of creditors" test requires that the plan payments, when reduced to their present value, must be at least equal the Chapter 7 liquidation value of the unsecured claims.[85] Thus, unsecured creditors must receive what they

---

[78] Bankruptcy Code § 1225(B)(1)(B).

[79] Bankruptcy Code § 1222(b)(9).

[80] Bankruptcy Code § 1222(a)(2).

[81] Bankruptcy Code § 1222(a)(2)(A). In 2011, the Supreme Court granted certiorari in *Hall v. United States*, 617 F.3d 1161 (9th Cir. 2010), *certiorari granted*, 121 S. Ct. 2989 (2011), to resolve the split between it and a contrary decision in *Knudesn v. IRS*, 581 F.3d 696 (8th Cir. 2009), regarding the priority treatment of capital gains tax on a post-petition sale of the debtor's farm.

[82] Neil E. Harl, *Major Developments in Chapter 12 Bankruptcy*, 16 Agric. L. Dig. 57, 58 (2005).

[83] Bankruptcy Code § 1322(a)(4).

[84] Bankruptcy Code § 1322(a)(4).

[85] Bankruptcy Code § 1225(a)(4).

would have received in a liquidation case, together with interest to compensate them for the delay in receiving payment under the plan. The best interests test thus operates the same way in Chapter 12 as it does in Chapters 11 and 13.[86]

The rate of interest that Chapter 12 debtors must pay to ensure that unsecured creditors receive the liquidation value of their claims is probably the same as that required to be paid in Chapter 13 cases. Some courts have relied on the Supreme Court's 2004 decision in *Till v. SCS Credit Corp.*,[87] regarding a similar issue on the appropriate rate of interest required to be paid to holders of secured claims under § 1325(a)(5).[88] If so, it must be based on the prime interest rate, together with whatever upward adjustment is necessary to reflect the creditor's risk of non-payment. However, a few courts have rejected the use of the *Till* standard with respect to the best interests test, based partially on *Till*'s status as a plurality decision, and its applicability to secured rather than unsecured claims. These courts continue to require the use of whatever method they deployed before *Till* to pick the appropriate rate of interest, usually based on the market rate that would apply to a similar loan.[89]

[2] Projected Disposable Income[90]

The second test is the "projected disposable income" test.[91] It applies only if the plan does not provide for full payment of claims of unsecured creditors.[92] But as a practical matter, full payment is usually not feasible, making it necessary for virtually all Chapter 12 plans to comply with the disposable income test.

Chapter 12's projected disposable income test is considerably different from the projected disposable income test applicable to many Chapter 13 debtors. In Chapter 13, debtors with household income above their state's median are required to submit the amount of their income that is available, after subtracting a set of presumed and actual expenses, to distribute to unsecured creditors.[93]

In Chapter 12, the amount required to be submitted for distribution to creditors depends on a calculation of the debtor's actual projected disposable income, based on whatever income the debtor has available after deducting amounts "reasonably

---

[86] *See supra* § 18.08[E][1] Best Interests of Creditors.

[87] Till v. SCS Credit Corp., 541 U.S. 465 (2004) (present value for secured claims under § 1325(a)(5)).

[88] *See, e.g.*, In re Bivens, 317 B.R. 755 (Bankr. N.D. Ill. 2004). *See* Carmen H. Lonstein & Steven A. Domanowski, *Payment of Post-petition Interest to Unsecured Creditors: Federal Judgment Rate Versus Contract Rate*, 12 Am. Bankr. Inst. L. Rev. 421 (2004). *See generally* § 18.08[F][4][b] Payments Equivalent to Amount of Secured Claim.

[89] In re Cook, 322 B.R. 336, 345 (Bankr. N.D. Ohio 2005) (coerced loan approach based on current market interest rates for loans in similar situations). *Cf.* In re Am. HomePatient, Inc., 420 F.3d 559 (6th Cir. 2005) (applying § 1129(a)(5)). *See generally supra* § 8.09[F][4][b] Payments Equivalent to Amount of Secured Claim.

[90] Melanie Fisher, Note, *Disposable Income Determination: Challenges in the Chapter 12 Family Farmer Context*, 18 J. Corp. L. 713 (1993).

[91] Bankruptcy Code § 1225(b)(1)(A).

[92] Bankruptcy Code § 1225(b)(1)(B).

[93] *See supra* § 18.08[E][2] Debtor's Projected Disposable Income.

necessary to be expended" for the support of the debtor and his dependents; amounts that must be paid to satisfy a domestic support obligation; and amounts that are necessary for the continuation, preservation, and operation of the debtor's farming or fishing business.[94] This is similar to the projected disposable income test that was used for all Chapter 13 debtors before the 2005 amendment's means testing rules were implemented, and the test that still applies to Chapter 13 debtors whose household income is below the applicable state median.[95]

Alternatively, the plan can be confirmed if "the value of the property to be distributed under the plan . . . is not less than the debtor's projected disposable income [for the duration of the plan]."[96] It is not entirely clear what this new language adds, other than perhaps to prevent the court from retroactively assessing the amount of the debtor's disposable income in cases where the "debtor's actual disposable income exceeds the projected disposable income on which the plan was based."[97]

[F] Secured Claims in Chapter 12[98]

Secured claims are given favorable treatment in other bankruptcy proceedings, and Chapter 12 is no exception. Secured claims are required to be paid in full, with compensation for any delay in receiving payment, to assure that the creditor receives the present value of its secured claim.[99] The interest rate required to be paid on secured claims is based on the same prime-plus formula adopted by the Supreme Court's plurality decision in *Till v. SCS Credit Corp.*[100] Liens on the debtor's property must remain in place until payments are completed.[101] The only exceptions are when the debtor surrenders the collateral to the secured creditor[102] or where the creditor acquiesces to the debtor's plan and accepts something less from the debtor.[103]

Chapter 12 differs from Chapter 13 by permitting secured claims to be paid beyond the three- to five-year duration of the plan.[104] Thus, the plan can provide

---

[94] Bankruptcy Code § 1225(b)(2).

[95] *See supra* § 18.08[E][2][b] Disposable Income for Debtors with Income Below the State Median.

[96] Bankruptcy Code § 1225(b)(1)(C).

[97] 8 Collier on Bankruptcy ¶ 1225.04, at 1225-26 to 30 (Alan A. Resnick & Henry J. Sommer eds., 15th rev. ed. 2006).

[98] William E. Callahan, Jr., Note, Dewsnup v. Timm *and* Nobelman v. American Savings Bank: *The Strip Down of Liens in Chapter 12 and Chapter 13 Bankruptcies*, 50 Wash. & Lee L. Rev. 405 (1993).

[99] Bankruptcy Code § 1225(a)(5)(B)(ii). *See* Thomas O. Depperschmidt & Nancy H. Kratzke, *The Search for the Proper Interest Rate Under Chapter 12 (Family Farmer Bankruptcy Act)*, 67 N.D. L. Rev. 455 (1991); Robert J. Kressel, *Calculating the Present Value of Deferred Payments Under a Chapter 12 Plan: A New Twist to an Old Problem*, 62 Am. Bankr. L.J. 313 (1988).

[100] 541 U.S. 465 (2004). *See* In re Torelli, 338 B.R. 390 (Bankr. E.D. Ark. 2006). *See generally* § 18.08[F][4][b] Payments Equivalent to Amount of Secured Claim.

[101] Bankruptcy Code § 1225(a)(5)(B)(i).

[102] Bankruptcy Code § 1225(a)(5)(C).

[103] Bankruptcy Code § 1225(a)(5)(A).

[104] Bankruptcy Code § 1222(b)(9). *See* In re Dunning, 77 B.R. 789 (Bankr. D. Mont. 1987); Travelers

for amortization of secured claims over long-term periods, provided the payments otherwise satisfy the cramdown standards of § 1225(a)(5)(B). For example, a claim secured by the debtor's combine[105] could be extended to be payable over seven years, even though the terms of the plan were to last only five years, and even though the contract with the creditor called for payments for only four more years.

§ 20.08   CONFIRMATION OF CHAPTER 12 PLANS

In addition to the basic requirements concerning payment of claims, Chapter 12 plans are subject to most of the same requirements as Chapter 13 plans. The plan must comply with the mandatory provisions of Chapter 12 and with other applicable provisions of the Bankruptcy Code.[106] The debtor must have paid the filing fee and any other fees required by law or by the plan.[107] This now explicitly includes any domestic support obligations that became payable after the debtor's petition was filed.[108] Thus, deadbeat moms and dads are unable to evade making support payments while their cases are pending. In addition, as with Chapter 13 plans, the plan must have been proposed in good faith and not by any means otherwise legally forbidden.[109]

The plan must also be feasible.[110] As with Chapter 13 plans involving individual debtors engaged in business, determining the feasibility of a Chapter 12 plan may be difficult. Plans based on unrealistic financial projections will not be confirmed.[111] The debtor must be able to supply the court with some reasonable assurances that the terms of the plan can be performed.[112] Likewise, plans based on unrealistic plans for the number of workers capable of operating the business, should not be confirmed.[113]

Ins. Co. v. Bullington, 89 B.R. 1010 (M.D. Ga. 1988), *aff'd*, 878 F.2d 354 (11th Cir. 1989).

[105] Farm combines are gigantic pieces of equipment. They sell for as much as $150,000.

[106] Bankruptcy Code § 1225(a)(1).

[107] Bankruptcy Code § 1225(a)(1).

[108] Bankruptcy Code § 1325(a)(7).

[109] Bankruptcy Code § 1225(a)(1).

[110] Bankruptcy Code § 1225(a)(1). *See* Janet A. Flaccus & Bruce L. Dixon, *New Bankruptcy Chapter 12: A Computer Analysis of If and When a Farmer Can Successfully Reorganize*, 41 Ark. L. Rev. 263 (1988).

[111] *E.g.*, In re Torelli, 338 B.R. 390 (Bankr. E.D. Ark. 2006).

[112] In re Ames, 973 F.2d 849 (10th Cir. 1992), *cert. denied* 507 U.S. 912 (1993); In re Clark, 288 B.R. 237 (Bankr. D. Kan. 2003).

[113] *E.g.*, In re Gough, 190 B.R. 455 (Bankr. M.D. Fla 1995) (financial projections based on tripling citrus crop yield on expanded acreage without increase in labor force).

§ 20.09 EFFECT OF CONFIRMATION OF CHAPTER 12 PLAN

Confirmation of a plan binds the debtor, each creditor, and any equity security holders or partners of the debtor who are provided for in the plan, regardless of whether they have objected to the plan, accepted the plan, or rejected the plan.[114] Thus, the plan has res judicata effect on the parties as to all matters that were litigated or that might have been litigated in connection with obtaining confirmation of the plan.

Unless the plan provides otherwise, confirmation of a plan operates to vest all of the estate's property back in the debtor.[115] Of course, confirmation requirements with respect to claims of secured creditors' rights are likely to require the plan to provide that secured creditors will retain their liens until full satisfaction of their secured claims.[116]

Like Chapter 13 plans, confirmation of a Chapter 12 plan does not automatically discharge the debtor. Instead, the debtor does not receive its discharge until completion of the terms of his plan.[117] Debtors who are unable to fulfill the terms of their plans due to circumstances beyond their control can receive a hardship discharge.[118] The availability of a hardship discharge is conditioned on the debtor's having already provided unsecured creditors with payments that are equivalent to what they would have received in a liquidation case, and upon the impracticability of modifying the plan.[119] The scope of a Chapter 12 discharge is discussed elsewhere.[120]

§ 20.10 MODIFICATION OF CHAPTER 12 PLANS

Debtors' plans are not set in stone. The debtor's proposed plan may always be modified prior to confirmation. After confirmation the plan may still be modified, but court confirmation is required before the proposed modification takes effect.

[A] Modification Prior to Confirmation

Occasionally, it becomes necessary to modify a proposed plan before it has been confirmed. This usually occurs in response to the court's refusal to confirm the plan or because of the debtor's recognition that the plan is unlikely to be confirmed. The debtor is given a virtually unlimited right to modify the plan, provided that the modification does not violate any of the requirements for a plan.[121]

---

[114] Bankruptcy Code § 1227(a).

[115] Bankruptcy Code § 1227(b).

[116] Bankruptcy Code § 1225(a)(5)(B)(i).

[117] Bankruptcy Code § 1228(a).

[118] Bankruptcy Code § 1228(b).

[119] Bankruptcy Code § 1228(b).

[120] *See supra* § 13.07 Chapter 12 Discharge.

[121] Bankruptcy Code § 1223(a).

Once modified, the modified plan becomes "the plan."[122] In other words, for purposes of confirmation and other matters, it is the final version of the plan that controls.

[B] Modification After Confirmation

The plan may also be modified after confirmation. The rules regarding modification of the plan after confirmation depart somewhat from the principle that Chapter 12 cases must be entirely voluntary. Chapter 12 cannot be commenced involuntarily by a creditor;[123] nor may a creditor file a plan.[124] However, unsecured creditors and the standing trustee have the right to propose modifications of the plan after confirmation.[125] To this rather limited extent, a Chapter 12 debtor may be forced into a plan he does not want — or, more precisely, a Chapter 12 debtor may be forced to choose between accepting and funding an unwanted plan, converting to Chapter 7, or dismissing the case altogether.[126]

A modification may be proposed by the debtor, an unsecured creditor, or the trustee at any time after confirmation but before completion of payments. The modification may (i) increase or decrease payments, (ii) extend or reduce the time for payments, or (iii) alter the distribution to a creditor to the extent necessary to take account of payments made outside the plan.[127]

To be confirmed, the plan must comply with the usual requirements.[128] However, because § 1229 conspicuously fails to refer to § 1225(b), a modified plans does not appear to be required to comply with the "disposable income" requirements of that section. Despite this, the 2005 Amendments specify that the plan may not be modified by a creditor or the trustee "based on an increase in the debtor's disposable income, to increase the amount of payments to unsecured creditors required for *a particular month* so that the aggregate of such payments exceeds the debtors's disposable income for such month."[129] Likewise, the 2005 Amendments prohibit creditors or the trustee from obtaining an amendment during the final year of the plan, if the amendment would leave the debtor with "insufficient funds to carry on the farming operation after the plan is completed."[130] These provisions prevent creditors, or the trustee, from taking opportunistic advantage of temporary fluctuations in the debtor's income which make it seem like an adjustment to the plan is appropriate.

---

[122] Bankruptcy Code § 1223(b).

[123] Bankruptcy Code § 303(a).

[124] Bankruptcy Code § 1221.

[125] Bankruptcy Code § 1229(a).

[126] The debtor always has the right to convert to Chapter 7 and nearly always has the right to voluntarily dismiss the case. Bankruptcy Code § 1208(a), (b).

[127] Bankruptcy Code § 1229(a).

[128] Bankruptcy Code § 1229(b), (c).

[129] Bankruptcy Code § 1229(d)(2).

[130] Bankruptcy Code § 1229(d)(3).

Any secured creditor who accepted or rejected the original plan is deemed to have accepted or rejected the modified plan, unless (i) the modification changes the creditor's rights, and (ii) the creditor changes its previous acceptance or rejection.[131] Since unsecured creditors do not vote on the plan, their view of the modified plan is irrelevant. The modified plan becomes "the plan," unless it is disapproved after notice and an opportunity for a hearing.[132]

§ 20.11   REVOCATION OF CHAPTER 12 PLAN CONFIRMATION

The rules regarding revocation of an order of confirmation must inevitably balance the interest of fairness to creditors with the interest of finality to the debtors and others. Thus, the timing and the substantive basis for revocation are both limited. Upon the request of a party in interest and after notice and an opportunity for a hearing, the court may revoke confirmation if it was procured by fraud. The request must be made within 180 days after the date the order of confirmation was entered.[133]

The potential grounds for revocation of confirmation are limited to proving that confirmation was procured through fraud.[134] Creditor confusion about the plan is not a sufficient basis to have confirmation revoked.[135]

If the order of confirmation is revoked, the court may either convert or dismiss the case under § 1207,[136] or if the debtor submits a modified plan, that modified plan may be confirmed.[137] If the modified plan is confirmed, the case continues under the new plan.

---

[131]   Bankruptcy Code § 1223(c).

[132]   Bankruptcy Code § 1229(b)(2).

[133]   Bankruptcy Code § 1230(a).

[134]   Bankruptcy Code § 1230(a).

[135]   In re Courson, 243 B.R. 288 (Bankr. E.D. Tex. 1999).

[136]   Bankruptcy Code § 1230(b).

[137]   Bankruptcy Code § 1230(b).

Chapter 21

ROLE OF PROFESSIONALS IN BANKRUPTCY PROCEEDINGS

§ 21.01 PROFESSIONALS IN BANKRUPTCY CASES[1]

Bankruptcy cases usually involve at least a few professional persons, such as lawyers, accountants, and appraisers. The simplest no-asset consumer case nearly always involves at least a lawyer for the debtor, even though a few hearty souls go into bankruptcy without one, possibly with the assistance of an unlicensed "petition preparer."[2] More complicated consumer cases involve a lawyer for the debtor, one for the trustee, one each for several secured creditors, and perhaps one for a creditor who is owed a non-dischargeable unsecured debt.

In complex business cases, there may be scores of lawyers for the debtor-in-possession, a creditors' committee, an equity security holders' committee, secured creditors, and unsecured creditors.[3] There may also be accountants, appraisers, auctioneers, investment bankers, real estate agents, and other professionals whose assistance is necessary or at least useful to the proceeding. Their assistance is rarely cheap.[4] It would be impossible to handle a complex business bankruptcy without people whose experience and expertise are sufficient to meet the challenges involved.

It is also necessary, when considering the proper role of a lawyer or other professional involved in a bankruptcy case, to deal with potential conflicts of interest that the professional may have. Especially given the fees demanded, it is imperative that the estate be provided with a full equivalent value in services. Part of that value is impartiality as between the various claimants against the estate. Ideally, a

---

[1] Stephen J. Lubben, *Choosing Corporate Bankruptcy Counsel*, 14 Am. Bankr. Inst. L.J. 391 (2006).

[2] Bankruptcy Code § 110(a)(1).

[3] *See generally* Susan M. Freeman, *Are DIP and Committee Counsel Fiduciaries for Their Clients' Constituents or the Bankruptcy Estate? What is a Fiduciary, Anyway?*, 17 Am. Bankr. Inst. L. Rev. 291 (2009).

[4] Alexander L. Paskay & Frances Pilaro Wolstenholme, *Chapter 11: A Growing Cash Cow, Some Thoughts on How To Rein in the System*, 1 Am. Bankr. Inst. L. Rev. 331 (1993); Robert M. Lawless & Stephen P. Ferris, *Professional Fees and Other Direct Costs in Chapter 7 Business Liquidations*, 75 Wash U. L.Q. 1207 (1997); Robert M. Lawless et al., *A Glimpse at Professional Fees and Other Direct Costs in Small Firm Bankruptcies*, 1994 U. Ill. L. Rev. 847. *See also* Daryl M. Guffey & William T. Moore, *Direct Bankruptcy Costs: Evidence from the Trucking Industry*, 26 Fin. Rev. 223 (1991); Michelle J. White, *Bankruptcy Costs and the New Bankruptcy Code*, 38 J. Fin. 477 (1983); Karen Hopper Wruck, *Financial Distress, Reorganization, and Organizational Efficiency*, 27 J. Fin Econ. 419 (1990); *see also* Elizabeth Warren & Jay Lawrence Westbrook, *Financial Characteristics of Businesses in Bankruptcy*, 73 Am. Bankr. L.J. 499 (1999).

professional who represents the estate should be wholly committed to pursuing the interests of the estate, and thus, indirectly, the interests of creditors as a whole. It is for this, as well as knowledge and experience, that the professional is being paid from funds that, after all, belong to the creditors.

For these reasons, the Bankruptcy Code regulates the employment of professionals whose fees are paid as administrative expenses from the debtor's estate. The bankruptcy court must approve the employment of any professional hired by the trustee, the debtor-in-possession, a creditors' committee, or an equity security holders' committee. Professionals with conflicts of interest are disqualified from serving in these roles. Moreover, the fees professionals charge must be approved by the court before they may be paid.

§ 21.02 EMPLOYMENT OF PROFESSIONALS

The Bankruptcy Code imposes restrictions on the employment of professional persons whose fees are paid by the debtor's estate. Because professional's fees are entitled to administrative expense priority, they reduce the amount that is otherwise available to pay pre-petition creditors. Sometimes, they can overwhelm the debtor's estate and transform Chapter 11 cases in particular into what one author characterized as a "feast for lawyers"[5] rather than a method of preserving the value of the debtor for the benefit of creditors.

Section 327 authorizes the trustee or debtor-in-possession to employ attorneys, accountants, appraisers, auctioneers, or other professional persons only after obtaining prior court approval.[6] Although the statute does not specify a standard, the test for whether the court should approve the estate's engagement of a professional is whether the person is "reasonably necessary" to assist the debtor or the trustee in administering the estate.[7] Further, professionals who are hired to provide services to the estate must not have conflicts of interest that would impair their ability to provide even-handed assistance to the estate for the benefit of all creditors.[8]

---

[5] Sol Stein, A Feast for Lawyers — Inside Chapter 11: An Exposé (1989).

[6] Bankruptcy Code § 327(a). Although the statutory language refers only to the trustee, it applies with equal force to professionals hired by a debtor-in-possession. *E.g.,*In re Prince, 40 F.3d 356, 360 & 360 n.2 (11th Cir. 1994).

[7] *E.g.,* In re Computer Learning Centers, Inc., 272 B.R. 897, 903 (Bankr. E.D. Va. 2001).

[8] Bankruptcy Code § 327(a). "Disinterested" means neutral; this differs from "uninterested" which means indifferent.

[A] Prior Court Approval[9]

Section 327 requires professionals to obtain prior bankruptcy court approval before they may be employed by the trustee or the debtor-in-possession.[10] Section 1103 similarly requires creditors' committees to obtain court approval to hire attorneys, accountants or other agents.[11] Bankruptcy Rule 2014 specifies the procedure for obtaining court approval to hire these professionals.[12] If a professional person is hired without prior court approval, she may lose her right to compensation for her services, and may be compelled to disgorge any fees she received.[13]

[1] Employment of Professionals Must be Reasonably Necessary

The court should approve employment of a professional person if that person's skills and expertise are reasonably necessary for the effective administration of the estate. In most cases, this is a fairly easy standard to meet. There is never any dispute over whether it is reasonably necessary for a Chapter 11 debtor to engage an attorney or an accountant to assist with the case, though in some cases the court might question whether the debtor needs professional assistance with the task involved and whether the task might be performed by other employees.

On rare occasions, the specific professional sought to be hired may be found unqualified to handle the matter.[14] Still, the trustee or debtor-in-possession must explain its reasons both for seeking to employ a professional for the task involved and for selecting the particular person she wishes to employ.[15]

One recurring point of contention is whether a trustee may employ a professional, such as an attorney, to perform tasks that might be an inherent part of the trustee's ministerial duties. For example, trustees are not usually permitted to employ an attorney or accountant to review the debtor's petition and schedules, unless the debtor's case is unusually complex. Nor may trustees employ profession-

---

[9] Anthony Collins, Jr., Comment, *A Change of Disposition: The Evolving Perception of Pre-approval Requirements under 11 U.S.C. 327*, 28 J. Legal Prof. 133 (2003).

[10] Bankruptcy Code § 327(a). *See* In re Singson, 41 F.3d 316, 319 (7th Cir. 1994); In re Albrecht, 245 B.R. 666 (B.A.P. 10th Cir. 2000); In re Anicom, Inc., 273 B.R. 756, 761 (Bankr. N.D. Ill. 2002).

[11] Bankruptcy Code § 1103(a).

[12] Fed. R. Bankr. P. 2014(a). Although the text of the rule refers only to the trustee and to a creditors' committee, a Chapter 11 debtor-in-possession has all of the rights, powers, and duties of a trustee. Bankruptcy Code § 1107(a).

[13] *E.g.*, In re Federated Dep't Stores, Inc., 44 F.3d 1310 (6th Cir. 1995); *see* Stephen R. Grensky, *The Problem Presented by Professionals Who Fail to Obtain Prior Court Approval of Their Employment or Nunc Pro Tunc Est Bunc*, 62 Am. Bankr. L.J. 185 (1988).

[14] *See* In re Crayton, 192 B.R. 970 (B.A.P. 9th Cir. 1996) (attorney who was unqualified and incompetent to represent a Chapter 11 debtor was disciplined and required to disgorge fees he had charged).

[15] Fed. R. Bankr. P. 2014(a). *See* In re Computer Learning Centers, Inc., 272 B.R. 897 (Bankr. E.D. Va. 2001).

als to prepare and distribute checks to creditors.[16] On the other hand, trustees are usually permitted to engage attorneys to pursue litigation to recover assets for the estate, to deny the debtor's discharge, or to litigate objections to claims, even though the trustee might herself be a licensed attorney and otherwise capable of performing these tasks.

The issue in these disputes is that the professional fees that are charged by the trustee's lawyer or accountant for her professional services transcend the compensation that otherwise is permitted to be paid to the trustee for her services as trustee. Permitting the trustee to hire a lawyer, sometimes an attorney in the trustee's own law firm, might permit the trustee to recover more fees than are otherwise permitted by § 326 for performing the trustee's routine duties.

The trustee's compensation as trustee is based on a percentage of the amount that the trustee distributes to creditors.[17] In Chapter 7 cases, the trustee can receive up to 25% of the first $5,000, 10% of amounts between $5,000 and $50,000, 5% of amounts between $50,000 and $1 million, and 3% of amounts in excess of $1 million of the amounts that she distributes to creditors.[18] Amounts paid to professionals are above these limits and might benefit the trustee if the trustee either wishes to act as her own lawyer in the case, or if she wishes to employ her own law firm as the attorney for the estate.

[2] Nunc Pro Tunc Approval

Even though prior approval is normally required, courts sometimes approve the employment of professionals "nunc pro tunc" (now for then) — after they have been employed and rendered services to the estate without receiving prior court approval. Although this practice undercuts the requirement of prior court approval, some courts find it difficult to turn their backs on attorneys and other professionals whose services benefit the estate.[19]

However, these courts may refuse to authorize employment nunc pro tunc and thus permit the professional to receive compensation unless the professional's failure to comply with § 327(a) was due to extraordinary circumstances.[20] In the view of some courts, mere negligence is not enough of an extraordinary circumstance to warrant nun pro tunc approval.[21] Other courts take a more flexible approach and approve late applications for approval even where the professional's failure to seek timely authorization to be hired was due to simple negligence.[22]

---

[16] *E.g.*, In re Guterl Special Steel Corp., 316 B.R. 843, 861 (Bankr. D. Pa. 2004).

[17] Bankruptcy Code § 326(a).

[18] Unlike many other dollar amounts in the Bankruptcy Code, these thresholds are not automatically adjusted every three years to keep up with inflation. Bankruptcy Code § 104.

[19] *See* In re Mehdipour, 202 B.R. 474 (B.A.P. 9th Cir. 1996).

[20] *See* In re THC Fin. Corp., 837 F.2d 389 (9th Cir. 1988).

[21] *E.g.*, In re Jarvis, 53 F.3d 416 (1st Cir. 1995). *See* Binswanger Cos. v. Merry-Go-Round Enters., 258 B.R. 608 (D. Md. 2001) (discussing conflicting authorities); *see also* In re Twinton Properties P'ship, 27 B.R. 817 (Bankr. M.D. Tenn. 1983), *aff'd*, 33 B.R. 111 (M.D. Tenn 1983).

[22] *E.g.*, In re Triangle Chems. Inc., 697 F.2d 1280 (5th Cir. 1983); In re THC Fin. Corp., 837 F.2d 389 (9th Cir. 1988).

Court approval of the professional's employment is not the same as court approval of the professional's fees. As explained below, §§ 328 and 330 impose further limits on the compensation of these professionals, whose fee applications must be approved separately.[23]

[B] Meaning of "Professional Persons"

Professionals whose employment must be approved by the court are those who take a central role in the administration of the estate and in the bankruptcy proceeding generally.[24] This includes attorneys for the trustee or the debtor-in-possession, as well as accountants, appraisers, and investment bankers engaged to assist with the reorganization process.

Other professionals, whose services would have been necessary even if a bankruptcy petition had not been filed, are not among those whose engagement must be approved.[25] Thus a Chapter 11 debtor-in-possession need not seek court approval to keep its in-house lawyers and accountants on the payroll. Section 327(b) makes this clear: "[I]f the debtor has regularly employed attorneys, accounts, or other professionals on salary, the trustee may retain or replace such professional persons if necessary in the operation of the business."[26] The Code does not contemplate court approval of these routine employment decisions that are made in the ordinary course of the debtor's operations.[27]

Despite this, anyone who might be regarded as a professional hired to assist with the reorganization should seek court approval before providing services to a trustee, a debtor-in-possession, or a creditors' committee, rather than run the risk that her engagement will later be challenged as one that should have been approved by the court. Failing to obtain approval in advance may lead the court to deny the professional the right to any fees and to require her to disgorge any fees that she had been paid without court approval.

[C] Conflicts of Interest[28]

Professionals hired by the trustee or a debtor-in-possession must have no conflict of interest with the interests of the estate. Section 327 requires that professionals neither hold or represent an interest adverse to the estate *and* that

---

[23] *See infra* § 21.03 Fees for Professionals.

[24] *E.g.*, In re D'Lites of America, 108 B.R. 352 (N.D. Ga. 1989).

[25] In re Johns-Manville Corp., 60 B.R. 612, 620-21 (Bankr. S.D.N.Y. 1986) (lobbyists hired in the ordinary course of the debtor's business).

[26] Bankruptcy Code § 327(b).

[27] *See generally* In re Yuba Westgold, Inc., 157 B.R. 869 (Bankr. N.D. Iowa 1993).

[28] John D. Ayer et al., *Ethics: Is Disinterestedness Still a Viable Concept? A Discussion*, 5 Am. Bankr. Inst. L. Rev. 201 (1997); A. Mechele Dickerson, *Privatizing Ethics in Corporate Reorganizations*, 93 Minn. L. Rev. 875 (2009); Kurt F. Gwynne, *Intra-committee Conflicts, Multiple Creditors' Committees, Altering Committee Membership and Other Alternatives for Ensuring Adequate Representation under Section 1102 of the Bankruptcy Code*, 14 Am. Bankr. Inst. L. Rev. 109 (2006); Nancy B. Rapoport, *Rethinking Professional Fees in Chapter 11 Cases*, 5 J. Bus. & Tech. L. 263 (2010); Nancy B. Rapoport, Enron *and the New Disinterestedness — The Foxes Are Guarding the Henhouse*, 13 Am. Bankr. Inst.

they be "disinterested."[29] Despite the statutory text, which plainly imposes a two-pronged standard, courts often regard the "no adverse interest" and the "disinterested" tests as overlapping, if not redundant.[30]

Section 101(14) defines a "disinterested person" as a person who:

(A) is not a creditor, an equity security holder, or an insider;

(B) is not and was not, within 2 years before the date of the filing of the petition, a director, officer, or employee of the debtor; and

(C) does not have an interest materially adverse to the interest of the estate or of any class of creditors or equity security holders, by reason of any direct or indirect relationship to, connection with, or interest in, the debtor, or for any other reason.[31]

Not surprisingly, creditors, owners, or their insiders may not be engaged as attorneys for the trustee or for the debtor-in-possession. This is frequently a problem in Chapter 11 cases when the law firm that seeks to represent the debtor-in-possession is the same firm that has represented the debtor prior to the case, either in connection with the debtor's efforts to negotiate a workout with its creditors or in connection with other matters. This law firm may be one of the debtor's creditors. The debtor may owe legal fees to the firm, or may have paid bills for services shortly before filing its petition, which are recoverable from the firm as an avoidable preference.[32] The debtor-in-possession has an interest in recovering that preference; its lawyers have an equal interest in leaving it be.[33] Thus, a law firm that represented the debtor before the petition is filed may find it necessary to waive any claim it has against the debtor, reimburse its client for any payment it has received for pre-petition services, or forego the opportunity to represent the debtor in the bankruptcy case.[34]

At first blush § 1107 appears to address this issue. It specifies that "a person is not disqualified for employment under section 327 . . . by a debtor in possession solely because of such person's employment by or representation of the debtor before the commencement of the case."[35] A court might use this language to permit

---

L. Rev. 521 (2005); Nancy B. Rapoport, *Turning and Turning in the Widening Gyre: The Problem of Potential Conflicts of Interest in Bankruptcy*, 26 Conn. L. Rev. 913 (1994); Nancy B. Rapoport, *The Intractable Problem of Bankruptcy Ethics: Square Peg, Round Hole*, 30 Hofstra L. Rev. 977 (2002).

[29] Bankruptcy Code § 327(a).

[30] *E.g.*, In re Martin, 817 F.2d 175, 179 n.40 (1st Cir. 1987); In re Vebeliunas, 231 B.R. 181, 189 (Bankr. S.D.N.Y. 1999).

[31] Bankruptcy Code § 101(14).

[32] Jay Lawrence Westbrook, *Fees and Inherent Conflicts of Interest*, 1 Am. Bankr. Inst. L. Rev. 287 (1993); Nancy B. Rapoport, *Turning and Turning in the Widening Gyre: The Problem of Potential Conflicts of Interest in Bankruptcy*, 26 Conn. L. Rev. 913, 928-30 (1994); *see generally* Chapter 15 — Preferences, *supra*.

[33] *See* In re First Jersey Securities, Inc., 180 F.3d 504 (3d Cir. 1999).

[34] *E.g.*, In re Project Orange Assocs., LLC, No. 10-12307 (MG), 431 B.R. 363 (Bankr. S.D.N.Y. 2010). *See generally* Patti Williams, Comment, *Bankruptcy Code Section 327(a) — New Interpretation Forces Attorneys to Waive Fees or Wave Good-bye to Clients*, 53 Mo. L. Rev. 309 (1988).

[35] Bankruptcy Code § 1107(b).

law firms to represent the debtor-in-possession even though they are owed fees for pre-petition services. However, the statutory language speaks only to the debtor's prior employment of the attorney or other professional. It does not address the effect of the professional's status as a creditor.[36] Courts that have carefully considered the relationship between §§ 327 and 1107 have adhered to the traditional view that an attorney who has a claim against the debtor may not serve as the debtor's counsel.[37]

Professionals are also disqualified if they represent an interest that is adverse to the estate.[38] This might suggest that an attorney (or a firm) that represents one of the debtor's creditors may not be employed as debtor's counsel or to serve as any other professional in the debtor's case. However § 327(c) provides that creditors' attorneys are not automatically disqualified from employment as a professional for the estate.[39] Creditors' attorneys are disqualified only if another creditor objects and if the court finds that "there is an actual conflict of interest."[40]

In some cases, the creditor's claim is so small compared to those of other more active creditors, that the attorney's representation of the debtor would not involve an actual conflict. If the creditor's claim is de minimis, or if the lawyer's firm represents the creditor in matters unrelated to the bankruptcy case, the court might find that there is no actual conflict. Where the proposed debtor's attorney represents a creditor in an unrelated matter, no actual conflict may occur, though the attorney must disclose the representation, and may find it necessary to obtain everyone's consent to, and the court's approval of the dual representation as a means of avoiding professional discipline.[41]

Another recurring issue is whether an attorney may represent multiple debtors in cases involving related entities. The most obvious example involves representing an individual debtor and a corporation the individual owns in simultaneous Chapter 11 reorganization proceedings involving both.[42] Thus, if Harland Wolff, the president and sole shareholder of Titanic Corporation, files his own Chapter 11 case while Titanic's separate Chapter 11 case is pending, it might appear to make sense for the same attorney to represent both Wolff and Titanic Corporation in their respective bankruptcy cases. A single attorney is likely to be familiar with the financial circumstances that led to the financial difficulties of both debtors, whose finances are likely to be intertwined with one another at least to some extent. Requiring these debtors to acquire separate counsel will likely lead to an expensive

---

[36] *E.g.,* In re Microwave Products of America, Inc., 94 B.R. 971, 974-75 (Bankr. W.D. Tenn. 1989); In re Viking Ranches, Inc., 89 B.R. 113, 115 (C.D. Cal. 1988).

[37] In re LKM Indus., Inc., 252 B.R. 589 (Bankr. D. Mass. 2000).

[38] Bankruptcy Code § 327(a).

[39] Bankruptcy Code § 327(c).

[40] Bankruptcy Code § 327(c).

[41] Regina S. Kelbon et al., *Conflicts, The Appointment of "Professionals," and Fiduciary Duties of Major Parties in Chapter 11,* 8 Bankr. Dev. J. 349 (1991); William I. Kohn & Michael P. Shuster, *Deciphering Conflicts of Interest in Bankruptcy Representation,* 98 Com. L.J. 127 (1993).

[42] *E.g.,* In re Lee, 94 B.R. 172 (Bankr. C.D. Cal. 1989). *See also* In re JMK Constr. Group, Ltd., 441 B.R. 222 (Bankr. S.D.N.Y. 2010).

duplication of efforts that will reduce the amount available to distribute to their creditors.

On the other hand, the corporation may have claims against Wolff, based on his mismanagement of the corporation, or on his receipt of preferential or other payments that Titanic might wish to recover.[43] Further, it may develop that a trustee should be appointed in the Titanic case, or that Titanic can only survive if Wolff's stock in the company is cancelled, and all of the value of the company is distributed to its creditors. These, and other potential conflicts of interest strongly suggest different counsel for each debtor.[44]

Here, it is critical for the attorney who seeks appointment as debtors' counsel to fully disclose all of the connections she and members of her firm have that might lead the court to conclude that an actual conflict exists.[45] As might be expected, the debtor's attorney is subject to especially strict scrutiny. Whether or not the debtor's attorney asks for compensation from the estate, the attorney must file with the court a statement regarding certain pre-petition transactions with the debtor. The statement must detail:

1. compensation paid during the year prior to the petition for services related to the case;

2. compensation promised during the year prior to the petition for services related to the case; and

3. the source of the compensation.[46]

If the compensation is found to be excessive, the court can order it to be returned.[47] Attorneys who fail to meet these obligations may find themselves obligated to return compensation received from their clients. For example, in *In re Dean*,[48] the bankruptcy court compelled a debtor's lawyer to return half of the $1875 he received in connection with the debtor's Chapter 7 case, when the debtor's failure to verify that a security interest in the debtor's mobile home had been perfected resulted in their loss of the asset to the bankruptcy trustee.

Moreover, an attorney or other professional who fails to reveal its conflict or to otherwise make an adequate disclosure may be denied fees or forced to disgorge fees it received before the information it should have disclosed came to light.[49] In the 1990s, a major New York law firm, with extensive experience in bankruptcy matters, was required to disgorge over $1 million in fees that it had received in the course of representing a debtor-in-possession, when the court held that it had not

---

[43] *E.g.*, In re Interwest Bus. Equip., 23 F.3d 311, 316 (10th Cir. 1994); In re Wheatfield Bus. Park, LLC, 286 B.R. 412, 418 (Bankr. D. Cal. 2002).

[44] *See, e.g.*, In re Lee, 94 B.R. 172 (Bankr. C.D. Cal. 1989).

[45] I.G. Petroleum, L.L.C. v. Fenasci (In re W. Delta Oil Co.), 432 F.3d 347 (5th Cir. 2005) (failure to disclose indirectly held ownership interest in the debtor).

[46] Bankruptcy Code § 329(a). *See* Fed. R. Bankr. P. 2017.

[47] Bankruptcy Code § 329(b).

[48] *In re Dean*, 401 B.R. 917 (Bankr. D. Idaho 2008).

[49] Atkins v. Wain, Samuel & Co. (In re Atkins), 69 F.3d 970 (9th Cir. 1995).

adequately disclosed its connections to the debtor in its initial application to be hired.[50]

[D]   Disclosure of Pre-Petition Fees

In most cases, attorneys seek compensation from their clients before filing bankruptcy petitions on their behalf. In Chapter 7 cases, where the debtor's attorney is not entitled to compensation from the estate, this is a virtual necessity. In Chapter 13 cases, it is a practical reality for lawyers who do not want to wait 3-5 years to be fully compensated. In Chapter 11 cases, the volume of work necessary to prepare a case to be filed, makes it likely that these pre-petition fees will be substantial.

These fees must be disclosed to the court.[51] If the amount of compensation is unreasonable, the court may require its disgorgement.[52] Attorneys who fail to make the necessary disclosure run the risk of disgorgement of all their fees,[53] and in egregious cases, disbarment.

§ 21.03   PROFESSIONALS' FEES[54]

The payment of professional fees from the estate has long been one of the most difficult problems in bankruptcy law. Because creditors are unlikely to be paid in full and may include those who have been gravely injured by the debtor's actions and some who have lost their jobs as a result of the debtor's financial trouble, it is sometimes uncomfortable to deal with demands from lawyers, accountants, and other professionals to be paid hundreds of dollars per hour for their work. On the other hand, the money wasted when a case is poorly administered may cost the creditors even more. Section 330 permits examiners, a Chapter 11 trustee, and professionals authorized to be hired under § 327, to receive "reasonable compensation for actual, necessary services rendered."[55] The court may also award them "reimbursement for actual, necessary expenses."[56] If approved, their fees are entitled to administrative priority expense under §§ 330(a), 503(b) and 507(a)(2).[57]

---

[50] In re The Leslie Fay Cos., 175 B.R. 525 (Bankr. S.D.N.Y. 1994).

[51] Bankruptcy Code § 329.

[52] Bankruptcy Code § 329.

[53] In re Jackson, 401 B.R. 333 (Bankr. N.D. Ill. 2009); Arnes v. Boughton (Matter of Prudhomme), 43 F.3d 1000 (5th Cir. 1995).

[54] Stephen J. Lubben, *The Direct Costs of Corporate Reorganization: An Empirical Examination of Professional Fees in Large Chapter 11 Cases*, 74 Am. Bankr. L.J. 509 (2000); Lynn M. LoPucki & Joseph W. Doherty, *Rise of the Financial Advisors: An Empirical Study of the Division of Professional Fees in Large Bankruptcies*, 82 Am. Bankr. L.J. 141 (2008); Lynn M. LoPucki & Joseph W. Doherty, *Routine Illegality in Bankruptcy Court, Big-Case Fee Practices*, 83 Am. Bankr. L.J. 423 (2009); Lynn M. LoPucki & Joseph W. Doherty, *The Determinants of Professional Fees in Large Bankruptcy Reorganization Cases*, 1 J. Empirical Legal Stud. 111, 140 (2004). *See generally* Lynn M. LoPucki, Courting Failure: How Competition for Big Cases Is Corrupting the Bankruptcy Courts (Univ. Mich. Press 2005).

[55] Bankruptcy Code § 330(a)(1); Fed. R. Bankr. P. 2016.

[56] Bankruptcy Code § 330(a)(2).

[57] *See supra* § 10.04[A][2] Administrative Expenses.

Before 1994, § 330(a) was clear that compensation could be awarded not just to the trustee, an examiner, or a professional person employed under § 327, but also to "the debtor's attorney." In 1994 the phrase referring to the debtor's attorney was eliminated from the statutory text. It was not until ten years later, in *Lamie v. United States Trustee* that the Supreme Court resolved the uncertainty created by this deletion, and ruled that a Chapter 7 debtor's attorney is not among those who are entitled to compensation from the estate.[58] The statute it seems, means what it says. Thus, Chapter 7 debtors' attorneys who expect to be paid must receive their fees in advance, as they will receive no compensation from the estate even in the few Chapter 7 cases in which assets are available to distribute to creditors.[59] The applicability of *Laime* to attorneys for debtors in Chapter 13 cases is not yet resolved. In Chapter 13, debtors' attorneys are usually compensated under § 330(a)(4)(B) rather than § 330(a)(1).[60] However, some courts have questioned whether *Laime* might be applied to prevent debtors' attorneys from recovering fees from the estate in Chapter 13.[61]

The Code's rules only apply to those who seek compensation from the estate. For example, a lawyer who is representing a creditor, and whose fees are not recoverable from the estate, may, within the normal rules governing professional conduct, charge whatever the client is willing to pay. A lawyer, accountant, or other professional who seeks compensation from the estate, and whose fee thus effectively comes out of the pockets of creditors generally, is subject to greater regulation. The usual rationale is the obvious one: Other creditors have not agreed to pay the lawyer anything, let alone what the lawyer is claiming. Even when there is a contract, however, such as an agreement with the trustee or the creditors' committee, the compensation provided for in that contract is subject to court review and the judge is not always obligated to award the amount provided for by the parties' agreement.

In reviewing professionals' fee applications, courts use a variety of approaches. Many use a test derived from a pre-Code bankruptcy case, *American Benefit Life Ins. Co. v. Baddock (In re First Colonial Corp. of America)*.[62] It requires the court to "ascertain the amount of time involved and the rate at which the services should be compensated."[63] Courts consider a wide variety of factors including:

(1) The time and labor required; (2) The novelty and difficulty of the questions; (3) The skill requisite to perform the legal service properly; (4) The preclusion of other employment by the attorney due to acceptance of the case; (5) The customary fee; (6) Whether the fee is fixed or contingent; (7) Time limitations imposed by the client or other circumstances; (8) The

---

[58]   Lamie v. United States Trustee, 540 U.S. 526 (2004).

[59]   *See* In re Mansfield, 394 B.R. 783 (Bankr. E.D. Pa. 2008) (debtor's attorney, who delayed receipt of half his fee for representing debtor in Chapter 7 case until after petition was filed, was entitled to retain the fee in this case, but in future, post-petition fees would be treated as discharged debts and would be subject to disgorgement by attorney if paid post-petition).

[60]   In re Lewis, 346 B.R. 89 (Bankr. E.D. Pa. 2006); Boone v. Burk (In re Eliapo), 468 F.3d 592 (9th Cir. 2006). *See* Lamie v. United States Trustee, 540 U.S. 526, 537 (2004).

[61]   *E.g.*, In re Moore, 312 B.R. 902 (Bankr. N.D. Ala. 2004).

[62]   544 F.2d 1291 (5th Cir. 1977).

[63]   544 F.2d at 1298-1299.

amount involved and the results obtained; (9) The experience, reputation, and ability of the attorneys; (10) The "undesirability" of the case; (11) The nature and length of the professional relationship with the client; and, (12) Awards in similar cases.[64]

Courts also use a "lodestar" approach that involves calculation not only of the ordinary market price for legal services, and the allowable number of hours, but also for the upward or downward revision of the amount derived if the services were exceptional or deficient.[65] Yet another method, derived from the treatment of attorney's fees in class action suits, focuses on the success of the lawyer's efforts — that is, how much property was obtained for the creditors.[66]

In some cases, compensation is awarded at or near the end of the proceeding or when a plan is confirmed. However, professionals frequently request interim compensation while the case is pending. In cases that extend over several years, interim compensation must be awarded to enable professionals to meet their own financial obligations. Requests for interim compensation may first be made 120 days after the order for relief, and each 120 days thereafter.[67] Still, professionals who are accustomed to billing their clients every thirty days may find that interim compensation every 120 days imposes a serious constraint on their cash flow.

Application of these apparently simple rules has generated considerable controversy. One issue of considerable debate has been the degree to which the Code's standard for determining compensation diverges from the long-standing tradition of insisting on "economy of the estate." Under the old Bankruptcy Act, the courts tended to demand what amounted to the lowest possible fee for the service, on the theory that this would preserve as much of the bankruptcy estate as possible for the creditors. Critics of this approach deemed it penny-wise but pound-foolish since it could deprive the proceeding of the best qualified (and thus best-paid) professionals. The legislative history to section 330 was quite specific:

> Attorneys' fees in bankruptcy cases can be quite large and should be closely examined by the court. However bankruptcy legal services are entitled to command the same competency of counsel as other cases. In that light, the policy of this section is to compensate attorneys and other professionals serving in a case under title 11 at the same rate as the attorney or other professional would be compensated for performing comparable services other than in a case under title 11 . . . . Notions of economy of the estate in fixing fees are outdated and have no place in a bankruptcy code.[68]

---

[64] 544 F.2d at 1298-1299.

[65] *See, e.g.,* In re UNR Industries, Inc., 986 F.2d 207 (7th Cir. 1993); Gerard Di Conza, Note, *Professional Fees in Bankruptcy: The Use of the Lodestar,* 1 Am. Bankr. Inst. L. Rev. 463 (1993).

[66] Christine Jagde & Mamie Stathatos, Note, *Professional Fees in Bankruptcy: Percentage-of-the-Recovery Method: A "Solvent" Response for Bankruptcy Proceedings?,* 1 Am. Bankr. Inst. L. Rev. 471 (1993).

[67] Bankruptcy Code § 331. The time period may be shortened by the court.

[68] 124 Cong. Rec. H1109 (daily ed. Sept 2, 1978) (statement of Rep. Edwards); 124 Cong. Rec. S17406 (Oct. 6, 1978) (statement of Sen. DeConcini). *See also* Mandy S. Cohen & Christopher C. Thomson, *Professional Compensation Reform: New Ideas or Old Failings?,* 1 Am. Bankr. Inst. L. Rev. 407 (1993).

The difficulty is determining what level of compensation is necessary to attract the most able lawyers, accountants, and others without in consequence turning the bankruptcy into a proceeding solely for their benefit.

In 1994, Congress expanded the statutory guidelines for awarding professional compensation. Under these guidelines, the court must consider various factors, including the time spent, the rates charged, the need for and benefits of the services, and whether the services were performed "within a reasonable amount of time commensurate with the complexity, importance, and nature of the problem, issue, or task addressed."[69] On the other hand, the Code explicitly prevents compensation for services that are unnecessarily duplicative, services that were not reasonably likely to benefit the estate, and services that were not necessary to the administration of the case.[70]

Section 330(a)(1)(B) also permits reimbursement for "actual, necessary expenses" of the employed professional.[71] To be eligible for reimbursement the expense must have actually been incurred and thus must not be based merely on "guesswork, formula or pro rata allocation."[72] and must have been "necessary," which usually means "properly required to accomplish the task for which the professional was employed." This permits professionals to recover for their out-of-pocket expenses, for items such as travel, rent, insurance, salaries, utilities, copying, and electronic legal research.[73]

§ 21.04 KEY EMPLOYEES

The Code imposes special restrictions on compensation paid to insider employees to induce them to remain with the debtor's business. Before 2005, "Key Employee Retention Plans" (KERPs) were subject to court approval under § 363(b)(1) as transactions outside the ordinary course of business.[74] Court approval depended primarily on whether the incentive program was fair and reasonable within the "business judgment" of the debtor.[75] However, these plans were sometimes used to inappropriately reward high-paid executives whose misconduct had led to the debtor's financial difficulties.[76] As a result, these employee retention plans are now subject to further limits.

---

[69] Bankruptcy Code § 330(a)(3)(A).

[70] Bankruptcy Code § 330(a)(4)(A).

[71] Bankruptcy Code § 330(a)(1)(B). *See* James Lockhart, *What Expenses Qualify for Reimbursement Under Bankruptcy Code Provision Allowing Reimbursement to Trustees, Examiners, and Professional Persons for Actual, Necessary Expenses*, 169 A.L.R. Fed. 197 (2001).

[72] In re Specialty Plywood, Inc., 160 B.R. 627, 632 (B.A.P. 9th Cir. 1993).

[73] *See* In re McKenzie, 460 B.R. 181 (Bankr. E.D. Tenn. 2011).

[74] Bankruptcy Code § 363(b)(1). *E.g.*, In re U.S. Airways, Inc., 329 B.R. 793, 797 (Bankr. E.D. Va. 2005). *See supra* § 9.03[C] Use, Sale, or Lease Outside the Ordinary Course.

[75] *E.g.*, In re Allied Holdings, Inc., 337 B.R. 617, 721 (Bankr. N.D. Ga. 2005); U.S. Airways, Inc., 329 B.R. 793, 797 (Bankr. E.D. Va. 2005).

[76] *See* In re U.S. Airways, Inc., 329 B.R. at 797.

New § 503(c)(1) permits transfers to "insiders" that are made "for the purpose of inducing such person to remain with the debtor's business" only if:

- the compensation is "essential" to retain the employee because she has a bona fide competitive job offer "at the same or greater rate of compensation";[77]

- the employee's services are "essential to the survival of the business"; and[78]

- the proposed compensation is not grossly disproportionate to other similar transfers made to "nonmanagement employees" under very specific statutory criteria.[79]

The Code also restricts "severance payments" to insiders unless the payments are generally available to "all full-time employees" and are not more than ten times the severance packages that were supplied to nonmanagement employees in the year before the payment is to be made.[80]

It also restrains other transfers or commitments outside the ordinary course that are "not justified by the facts and circumstances of the case."[81] This final restriction applies to "officers, managers, or consultants hired after the date of the filing of the petition" even if they are not subject to the rules for hiring "professionals" under §§ 327 and 328.

Debtors' efforts to sidestep these restrictions with compensation systems based on key employees' achievement of performance-based goals have been regarded with some skepticism by courts that have reviewed them. In *In re Dana Corp.*[82] Bankruptcy Judge Lifland[83] refused to approve what was characterized as a "performance bonus" that would have paid certain executives a sizeable portion of the bonus if the value of the debtor's business actually declined by almost 25%. This made the proposed compensation package appear to be the type of Key Employee Retention Plan that § 503(c)(1) was designed to prohibit.[84] Likewise, the court regarded payments to be made in exchange for these same employees agreeing to a "no-compete" agreement as severance packages that were subject to § 503(c)(2).[85] Subsequent revisions to the employee bonus plan, which eliminated their objectionable features, resulted in their approval.[86]

---

[77] Bankruptcy Code § 503(c)(1)(A).

[78] Bankruptcy Code § 503(c)(2).

[79] Bankruptcy Code § 503(c)(1)(C).

[80] Bankruptcy Code § 503(c)(2).

[81] Bankruptcy Code § 503(c)(3). *See* In re Pilgrim's Pride Corp., 401 B.R. 229 (Bankr. N.D. Tex. 2009) (standard for approval is higher than the business judgment test of § 363(b)(1)).

[82] 351 B.R. 96 (Bankr. S.D.N.Y. 2006).

[83] Judge Lifland is particularly well regarded judge who is active as a scholar and speaker on bankruptcy matters.

[84] 351 B.R. at 101-02.

[85] 351 B.R. at 102-03.

[86] In re Dana Corp., 358 B.R. 567 (Bankr. S.D.N.Y. 2006).

§ 21.05 REGULATION OF BANKRUPTCY LAWYERS AS "DEBT RELIEF AGENCIES"

Lawyers providing services to financially troubled consumer debtors are subject to additional regulations, that do not apply to lawyers generally. Those who provide bankruptcy assistance to consumer debtors with less than $175,750 in nonexempt assets — primarily consumer bankruptcy attorneys — are now regarded as "debt relief agencies" and subject to government regulation.[87]

[A] Debt Relief Agencies[88]

Sections 526, 527, and 528 regulate the activities and communications of "debt relief agencies." A debt relief agency is: "any person who provides any bankruptcy assistance to an assisted person in return for the payment of money or other valuable consideration, or who is a bankruptcy petition preparer."[89] An "assisted person" is "any person whose debts consist primarily of consumer debts and the value of whose nonexempt property is less than $175,750."[90] "Bankruptcy assistance" means:

> any goods or services sold or otherwise provided to an assisted person with the express or implied purpose of providing information, advice, counsel, document preparation, or filing, or attendance at a creditors' meeting or appearing in a case or proceeding on behalf of another or providing legal representation with respect to a case or proceeding under [the Bankruptcy Code].[91]

In other words, attorneys who used to think of themselves as consumer bankruptcy lawyers, are now "debt relief agencies."

The definition excludes any "author, publisher, distributor, or seller of works subject to copyright protection . . . when acting in such capacity." Nonprofit organizations exempt under § 501(c)(3) of the Internal Revenue Code are also exempt — this protects qualified credit counseling agencies and presumably most law school legal clinics from the regulations.[92] Exclusions are also available for creditors who are engaged in attempting to restructure debts owed to the creditor,

---

[87] *See* Bankruptcy Code § 101(3), (12A). The $175,750 threshold in § 101(3), like many dollar amounts in the Bankruptcy Code, is adjusted every three years. *Id.* § 104. It was last adjusted on April 1, 2010, and is set to be revised in 2013, 2016, and 2019.

[88] Henry J. Sommer, *Trying to Make Sense Out of Nonsense: Representing Consumers Under the "Bankruptcy Abuse Prevention and Consumer Protection Act of 2005,"* 79 Am. Bankr. L.J. 191 (2005); Robert Wann, Jr., *"Debt Relief Agencies:" Does the Bankruptcy Abuse Prevention and Consumer Protection Act of 2005 Violate Attorneys' First Amendment Rights?*, 14 Am. Bankr. Inst. L. Rev. 273 (2006).

[89] Bankruptcy Code § 101(12A).

[90] Bankruptcy Code § 101(3). This threshold, like many other dollar figures in the Bankruptcy Code, is subject to automatic adjustment every three years to keep up with inflation. *Id.* § 104. It was last set on April 1, 2010 and is scheduled to be adjusted in 2013, 2016, and 2019.

[91] Bankruptcy Code § 101(4A).

[92] Bankruptcy Code § 101(12A)(B).

banks, and officers, directors, employees, or agents of debt relief agencies.[93]

Thus, the Code's restrictions apply primarily to consumer bankruptcy lawyers[94] and to non-lawyer bankruptcy petition preparers and others who assist consumer debtors in seeking relief under the Bankruptcy Code. Early decisions holding that regularly licensed attorneys or those who are admitted pro hac vice are not debt relief agencies within the meaning of the term and are thus not governed by its regulatory provisions,[95] have since been overruled.[96]

[B]   Restrictions on Debt Relief Agencies[97]

Most of the regulations proscribe conduct that is already illegal, such as assisting debtors in submitting false or misleading documents in a bankruptcy case.[98] Not surprisingly, any attempted waiver of these prohibitions is void.[99] Moreover, the Code creates specific remedies for violations of these rules, permitting debtors to recover actual damages and attorneys' fees from debt relief agencies that violate the Code's regulations.[100] It also gives state attorneys general the right to enforce its provisions on debtors' behalf.[101]

Other portions of the regulations seem designed to impair the advice that attorneys might sensibly provide to their clients. For example, § 526(a)(4) prohibits a debt relief agency from advising a debtor "to incur more debt in contemplation of . . . filing a [bankruptcy] case," even though borrowing additional funds may be a way for the debtor to attempt to avoid bankruptcy.[102] Although several early decisions addressing the issue found § 526(a)(4) an unconstitutional restraint on speech, the Supreme Court in *Milavitz, Gallop & Pilavetz, P.A. v. United States* construed the statute narrowly and found it constitutionally valid. The Court held that the prohibition against advising debtors to incur more debt, was intended only to prohibit advising clients to "load up" on debt with the expectation of obtaining a discharge. Construed narrowly, it permits attorneys to engage in candid

---

[93]   Bankruptcy Code § 101(12A).

[94]   Hersh v. United States, 347 B.R. 19 (N.D. Tex. 2006); Olsen v. Gonzales 350 B.R. 906 (D. Or. 2006). *See* Gary Neustadter, *2005: A Consumer Bankruptcy Odyssey*, 39 Creighton L. Rev. 225, 314 (2006); Catherine E. Vance & Corinne Cooper, *Nine Traps and One Slap: Attorney Liability Under the New Bankruptcy Law*, 79 Am. Bankr. L.J. 283, 288-89 (2005).

[95]   In re Attorneys at Law and Debt Relief Agencies, 332 B.R. 66 (Bankr. S.D. Ga. 2005).

[96]   Milavetz, Gallop & Milavetz, P.A. v. United States, 130 S. Ct. 1324, 1331-1333 (2010).

[97]   Steven W. Rhodes, Thomas F. Waldron, Erwin Chemerinsky & Catherine E. Vance, *Ethics: New Challenges for Attorneys under the New Code*, 4 DePaul Bus. & Com. L.J. 567 (2006); George H. Singer, *The Year in Review: Case Developments under the Bankruptcy Abuse Prevention and Consumer Protection Act of 2005*, 82 N.D. L. Rev. 297, 306-10 (2006).

[98]   Bankruptcy Code § 526(c)(2); *see* Henry J. Sommer, *Trying to Make Sense Out of Nonsense: Representing Consumers Under the "Bankruptcy Abuse Prevention and Consumer Protection Act of 2005,"* 79 Am. Bankr. L.J. 191, 207-08 (2005).

[99]   Bankruptcy Code § 526(b).

[100]   Bankruptcy Code § 526(c). The Code expressly preserves any rights the debtor has under state law. Bankruptcy Code § 526(c)(3).

[101]   Bankruptcy Code § 526(c)(3).

[102]   Gary Neustadter, *2005: A Consumer Bankruptcy Odyseey*, 39 Creighton L. Rev. 225, 315 (2006).

discussions with their clients *about* incurring additional debt, for valid purposes.[103] Advising debtors to refinance a mortgage, or to purchase a reliable car, to permit the debtor to reduce her interest rate or to otherwise enhance her ability to repay her creditors is not prohibited by the Code's language. Thus, the Court's decision was consistent with the rulings of other courts that have construed § 526(a)(4) narrowly to avoid any unconstitutional effects.[104]

Debt relief agencies are also obligated to make an extensive set of disclosures to their clients (customers?), about their services and about bankruptcy and its alternatives.[105] Likewise, advertisements by those to whom the new moniker of "debt relief agency" is attached, are required to contain a set of very specific disclosures and detailed content, such as "We are a debt relief agency. We help people file for bankruptcy relief under the Bankruptcy Code."[106] Anyone who has exchanged email with a consumer bankruptcy lawyer has no doubt seen this disclosure included in the exchange. And, bankruptcy lawyers' phone answering systems make the disclosure, in an effort to ensure consistency and avoid the risk that a receptionist will fail to supply the required information.

In *Milavetz*, the Supreme Court confirmed that these provisions applied with equal force to attorneys and approved the required disclosures as constitutionally valid. The Court justified them as reasonably related to combating the problem of what otherwise might be inherently misleading commercial advertisements which carry the promise of relief from debt, without disclosing the inherent costs involved in filing for bankruptcy.[107] Subsequent lower court decisions have ruled that other features of these restrictions were similarly constitutional, if they were narrowly construed to refer to efforts to dishonestly manipulate the bankruptcy system.[108] Thus, § 526(a)(4)'s prohibition on bankruptcy lawyers and other debt relief agencies advising clients to incur additional debts in contemplation of bankruptcy is constitutional valid.[109] Likewise, the notices that "debt relief agencies" are required to supply to their clients,[110] the written contracts that they are required to obtain,[111] and the disclosures they are required to make,[112] do not offend the First Amendment.[113] Nor do they violate the Fourth Amendment's Due Process Clause.[114]

---

[103] 130 S. Ct. 1324 (2010).

[104] Hersh v. United States ex rel. Mukasky, 553 F.3d 743 (5th Cir. 2008).

[105] Gary Neustadter, *2005: A Consumer Bankruptcy Odyseey*, 39 Creighton L. Rev. 225 (2006).

[106] Bankruptcy Code § 528(a)(4), (b)(2).

[107] Milavetz, Gallop & Milavetz, P.A. v. United States, 130 S. Ct. 1324, 1331-1333 (2010).

[108] Conn. Bar Ass'n v. United States, 620 F.3d 81 (2d Cir. 2010).

[109] *Id.*

[110] Bankruptcy Code § 527.

[111] Bankruptcy Code § 528(a)(1)-(2).

[112] Bankruptcy Code § 528(a)(3)-(4).

[113] Conn. Bar Ass'n v. United States, 620 F.3d 81 (2d Cir. 2010).

[114] *Id.*

The Code also requires debt relief agencies to enter into written contracts with their clients.[115] Thus, consumer debtors' attorneys must enter into written fee arrangements with their clients that lay out the fees the client is responsible for in clear and conspicuous language.[116] This written contract must be executed within five business days after the "first date on which [the debt relief agency] provides any bankruptcy assistance services to [a debtor]."[117] The Code is unclear how this requirement is supposed to apply in connection with clients who, after consulting with a bankruptcy lawyer, decide to delay engaging the lawyer.

§ 21.06   BANKRUPTCY PETITION PREPARERS

The Bankruptcy Code restricts the activities of unlicensed "bankruptcy petition preparers" who may also be subject to sanction for the unauthorized practice of law. A bankruptcy petition preparer is a person who is not an attorney or an employee working under the direct supervision of an attorney "who prepares for compensation a . . . petition or any other document . . . for filing by a debtor in a . . . bankruptcy court."[118]

These individuals must sign, print their names on,[119] and attach their social security number,[120] to any such documents they prepare. They also must give their customers a disclosure, in the form prescribed by the Judicial Conference, that informs the debtor that the petition preparer is not an attorney and may not practice law or give legal advice.[121]

Petition preparers are precluded from supplying legal advice.[122] This specifically precludes petition preparers from advising the debtor:

- to file a petition;

- whether chapter 7, 11, 12, or 13 is appropriate for the debtor;

- whether the debtor's debts will be discharged in a bankruptcy case;

- whether the debtor will be able to retain her home, car, or other property,

- about the tax consequences of a bankruptcy case;

- how to characterize the debtor's property interests or debts;

- about bankruptcy rights and procedures.[123]

Similarly, bankruptcy petition preparers are precluded from using the word "legal"

---

[115] Bankruptcy Code § 528.

[116] Bankruptcy Code § 528(a)(1).

[117] Bankruptcy Code § 528(a)(1).

[118] Bankruptcy Code § 110(a).

[119] Bankruptcy Code § 110(b)(1).

[120] Bankruptcy Code § 110(c).

[121] Bankruptcy Code § 110(b)(2).

[122] Bankruptcy Code § 110(b)(2)(A).

[123] Bankruptcy Code § 110(e)(2)(B).

or similar words in their advertisements.[124]

In addition, the Code permits the Supreme Court to establish the maximum fees that a bankruptcy petition preparer may charge for her services[125] and requires petition preparers to provide the court with a statement of the fees that they charged in connection with a filed petition, signed under the penalty of perjury.[126]

Violation of these rules subjects a bankruptcy petition preparer to potential fines, penalties, and injunctions.[127] They also might run afoul of unauthorized practice rules of the state in which they ply their trade.[128]

---

[124] Bankruptcy Code § 110(f).

[125] Bankruptcy Code § 110(h)(1).

[126] Bankruptcy Code § 110(h)(2).

[127] Bankruptcy Code § 110(i), (j), (k). *See* In re Duran, 347 B.R. 760 (Bankr. D. Colo. 2006) (injunction, $2,000 fine to the United States Trustee, and $2,000 actual and statutory damages to the debtor); In re Reynoso, 477 F.3d 1117 (9th Cir. 2007) (penalties imposed on sellers of bankruptcy preparation software).

[128] In re Reynoso, 477 F.3d 1117 (9th Cir. 2007); Disciplinary Counsel v. Spates, 945 N.E.2d 1049 (Ohio 2011).

Chapter 22

TRANSNATIONAL BANKRUPTCY

§ 22.01 CROSS BORDER INSOLVENCY AND ITS THEORETICAL SOLUTIONS

[A] Issues in Cross Border Insolvency

Insolvency is a problem that is by no means limited to the United States. Businesses fail all over the world, and creditors and courts must deal with it.[1] The enactment of modern bankruptcy laws has been seen by banks and international institutions as a critical part of the financial development of countries' economies.[2] As one scholar put it: "Today even the leaders of the People's Republic of China agree with the Founders of the American Republic that a bankruptcy system is central to fundamental economic reform.[3]

In an era of international business and multi-national firms, failure inevitably requires application of overlapping legal rules and legal systems.[4] Because there is no overriding sovereignty to force any one nation's courts to defer to another's in either procedural or substantive matters, the resolution of these problems is left to

---

[1] European Bankruptcy Laws (David A. Botwinik & Kenneth W. Weinrib eds., 2d ed. 1986); Kevin P. Block, *Ukranian Bankruptcy Law*, 20 Loy. L.A. Int'l & Comp. L.J. 97 (1997); Shinichiro Abe, *Recent Developments of Insolvency Laws and Cross-Border Practices in the United States and Japan*, 10 Am. Bankr. Inst. L. Rev. 47 (2002); Samuel L. Bufford & Kazuhiro Yanagida, *Japan's Revised Laws on Business Reorganization: an Analysis*, 39 Cornell Int'l L.J. 1 (2006); Bruce G. Carruthers & Terence C. Halliday, *Negotiating Globalization: Global Scripts and Intermediation in the Construction of Asian Insolvency Regimes*, 31 Law & Soc. Inquiry 521 (2006); Juan M. Dobson, *Argentina's Bankruptcy Law of 1995*, 33 Tex. Int'l L.J. 101 (1998); Rafeal Efrat, *Global Trends in Personal Bankruptcy*, 76 Am. Bankr. L.J. 81 (2002); Klaus Kamlah, *The New German Insolvency Act: Insolvenzordnung*, 70 Am. Bankr. L.J. 417 (1996); Nathalie Martin, *The Role of History and Culture in Developing Bankruptcy and Insolvency Systems: The Perils of Legal Transplantation*, 28 B.C. Int'l & Comp. L. Rev. 1 (2005); Julia M. Metzger & Samuel L. Bufford, *Exporting United States Bankruptcy Law: The Hungarian Experience*, 21 Cal. Bankr. J. 153, 154 (1993); Pamela Bickford Sak & Tanya Senn, *The New Bankruptcy Law in Thailand*, 3 Asian Com. L. Rev. 50 (1998); Stacey Steele, *The New Law on Bankruptcy in Indonesia: Towards a Modern Corporate Bankruptcy Regime?*, 23 Melb. U. L. Rev. 144 (1999).

[2] *E.g.*, Angela C. Fleming, Comment, *Russia's Bid for Bankruptcy*, 5 J. Int'l Legal Stud. 145 (1999); Scott Horton, *The Death of Communism and Bankruptcy Reorganization*, 1994 Am. Bankr. Inst. J. 12; Henry N. Schiffman, *Bankruptcy Law Reform In Eastern Europe*, 28 Int'l Law. 927 (1994).

[3] Jay Lawrence Westbrook, *Universal Priorities*, 33 Tex. Int'l L.J. 27, 27-28 (1998).

[4] *See* Gabriel Moss, Ian F. Fletcher & Stuart Isaacs, The EC Regulation on Insolvency Proceedings: A Commentary and Annotated Guide (2002); Ian F. Fletcher, Insolvency in Private International Law (2d ed. 2005).

the vagaries of what is often referred to as "private international law."[5]

Since the 1990s, cross-border practice has emerged as an important branch of insolvency law, and efforts to harmonize and regularize the procedures to administer such cases have proliferated.[6] The Council of the European Community has promulgated a regulation on cross-border insolvency cases,[7] and the United Nations Commission on International Trade Law (UNCITRAL) has developed a Model Law (the "Model Law") to address the issues that arise in these cases.[8] The Model Law was adopted by the United States in 2005, as Chapter 15 of the Bankruptcy Code. In addition, the American Law Institute has developed a set of "Principles of Cooperation" for use by countries who are party to the North American Free Trade Agreement.[9]

Scholars and legal reformers have advocated a number of alternative approaches. The current default, defended by Lynn LoPucki, is territorialism. Under territorialism, local courts apply local law to assets within their jurisdiction, and distribute those assets according to local legal rules and procedures. The advantage of such an approach is that it does not actually require a cross border regime to wind up the affairs of a company. Where liquidations are involved, the value is distributed wherever it lands. Reorganizations, however, require cooperation and coordination. The problem with territoriality, however, is that multiple fora and multiple distributional schema make it devilishly difficult to reorganize an entity that does business in multiple countries.

Over the past two decades, Jay Westbrook, along with others, has proposed a more universal approach, with the goal of resolving the difficulties of a financially troubled international business under a unified international bankruptcy case in a single forum. UNCITRAL's Model Statute and Chapter 15 of the Bankruptcy Code focus on the "procedural" aspects of such a universal vision, creating a regime under which courts across jurisdictions would cooperate with the court at the debtor's center of main interest. The issues dealt with under the Model Law are quite limited. They include:

---

[5] Jay Lawrence Westbrook, *Theory and Pragmatism in Global Insolvencies: Choice of Law and Choice of Forum*, 65 Am. Bankr. L. J. 457 (1991).

[6] Jay Lawrence Westbrook, *Multinational Enterprises In General Default: Chapter 15, The ALI Principles, And The EU Insolvency Regulation*, 76 Am. Bankr. L.J. 1 (2002).

[7] This went into force as a "regulation" rather than a "convention." Council Regulation (EC) No 1346/2000 of 29 May 2000 on Insolvency Proceedings, available at http://eur-lex.europa.eu/LexUriServ/LexUriServ.do?uri=OJ:L:2000:160:0001:001:en:PDF (last visited, August 24, 2012); Samuel L. Bufford, *International Insolvency Case Venue in the European Union: the Parmalat and Daisytek Controversies*, 12 Colum. J. Eur. L. 429 (2006); Principles of European Insolvency Law (W.W. McBryde, A. Flessner and S.C.J.J. Kortmann, eds. 2003).

[8] U.N. Comm'n on Int'l Trade Law, Model Law on Cross-Border Insolvency with Guide to Enactment (1997) available at http://www.uncitral.org/pdf/english/texts/insolven/insolvency-e.pdf (last visited April 4, 2007); U.N. Comm'n on Int'l Trade Law, 30th Sess., at 3, U.N. Doc. A/CN.9/442 (1997) reprinted in 6 Tul. J. Int'l & Comp. L. 415 (1998); Cross-Border Insolvency: A Commentary on the UNCITRAL Model Law (Look Chan Ho, ed. 2006).

[9] *See generally* Am. L. Inst., Transnational Insolvency: Cooperation Among the NAFTA Countries: Principles of Cooperation Among the NAFTA Countries 9-10 (2003).

- procedures for recognition of foreign representatives of foreign insolvency proceedings;

- procedures for granting and coordinating stays in pending cases;

- definition of relief available to a foreign representative;

- definition of the "main" proceeding as the proceeding initiated at the center of main interest (COMI);

- mechanisms to permit communication;

- principles for coordinating pending proceedings; and

- a rule to prevent double dipping;

It leaves to further developments, the choice of law principles that will be applied in the various cases, as well as the substantive bankruptcy rules to be applied.

[B] Cooperative Territoriality[10]

In the absence of procedures for handling cross border cases, the default is that cases involving multi-national debtors will be handled through a territorial approach under which courts in each country seize the assets within their own borders to pay local creditors.[11] This has been referred to as the "grab rule."[12] Creditors grab whatever assets are within the jurisdiction of the local and administer them locally, applying local law (supplemented by choice of law rules). This results in piecemeal administration of a multinational corporation's property in multiple proceedings with duplicate expenses and unpredictable results.[13]

Assume, for example, that Globecom, Inc. is incorporated in the United States and has assets in both the United States and in Mexico. Under territorialism, the assets located in the United States would be administered in a bankruptcy proceeding in the United States according to U.S. law and the assets located in Mexico would be administered in Mexico. Creditors with claims against these assets would file claims in the respective cases, and would understand that those claims would be adjudicated under local law. Strict adherence to a territorial approach, however, creates a number of opportunities for abuse. The debtor, for example, might move assets from one country to the other in an effort to prefer particular creditors.[14] Sophisticated creditors might restrict the flow of assets within the country to protect their own distribution, while other, less sophisticated

---

[10] See Lynn M. LoPucki, Cooperation in International Bankruptcy: A Post-Universalist Approach, 84 Cornell L. Rev. 696 (1999).

[11] Lucian Arye Bebchuk & Andrew T. Guzman, An Economic Analysis of Transnational Bankruptcies, 42 J.L. & Econ. 775, 787 (1999); Ian F. Fletcher, Insolvency in Private International Law 12-14 (2d ed. 2005).

[12] Jay Lawrence Westbrook, Chapter 15 at Last, 79 Am. Bankr. L.J. 713, 716 (2005).

[13] Lucian Arye Bebchuk & Andrew T. Guzman, An Economic Analysis of Transnational Bankruptcies, 42 J.L. & Econ. 775 (1999); Jay Lawrence Westbrook, Theory and Pragmatism in Global Insolvencies: Choice of Law and Choice of Forum, 65 Am. Bankr. L.J. 457 (1991).

[14] Lynn M. LoPucki, The Case for Cooperative Territoriality in International Bankruptcy, 98 Mich. L. Rev. 2216, 2219 (2000).

creditors might be suprised to find that the debtor was virtually judgment proof in the relevant jursdiction. More importantly, though, governance and decisionmaking across borders is very difficult. Often asset values can best be maximized if business units are liquidated as a going concern, or decisions are made collectively. This is difficult where multiple judges have control over the debtor's assets.

Lynn Lopucki has been the principal advocate of "cooperative territoriality." Under that regime, parallel bankruptcy proceedings occur simultaneously in the affected countries, and the parties negotiate, and the courts cooperate with one another to find a solution to the debtor's problems that produces the highest recovery for all.[15] In many cases under current law, the parties and courts negotiate a framework for cooperation on a case by case basis. These frameworks are generally referred to as "protocols."[16] Creditors' negotiations over the terms of the protocol occur against the backdrop of the consequences of failing to agree with its threat of disorderly liquidation of the debtor's disparately located assets. The cooperation proposed by these scholars is delicate. A single judge, creditor, or administrator seeing advantage to non-cooperation can destroy any hope of a coordinated reorganization.[17]

Under cooperative territoriality, bankruptcy courts of separate countries still administer the assets of multinational debtors located in their own countries, as if they were part of a separate estate. According to its proponents, this eliminates most of the uncertainties about choice of law and limits the opportunities for debtors to engage in forum shopping. In this respect, it provides creditors with greater certainty about the consequences of the debtor's bankruptcy.[18]

[C]   Modified Universalism[19]

The alternative to territoriality is "universalism" in which a multinational entity is liquidated or reorganized in a single court, located at the debtor's "center of main interest" ("COMI"), with jurisdiction over all of the debtor's assets wherever they

---

[15] Lynn M. LoPucki, *The Case for Cooperative Territoriality In International Bankruptcy*, 98 Mich. L. Rev. 2216 (2000). *See also* David Costa Levenson, *Proposal for Reform of Choice of Avoidance Law in the Context of International Bankruptcies from a U.S. Perspective*, 10 Am. Bankr. Inst. L. Rev. 291 (2002).

[16] *E.g.*, Stonington Partners, Inc. v. Lernout & Hauspie Speech Products N.V., 310 F.3d 118 (3d Cir. 2002); Maxwell Communication Corp. v. Societe Generale (In re Maxwell Communication Corp.), 93 F.3d 1036 (2d Cir. 1996).

[17] *See* United States v. BCCI Holdings (Luxembourg), S.A., 48 F.3d 551 (D.C. Cir. 1995); Uunited States v. BCCI Holdings (Luxembourg), S.A., 46 F.3d 1185 (D.C. Cir. 1995); United States v. BCCI Holdings (Luxembourg), S.A., 73 F.3d 403 (D.C. Cir. 1996) (United States used its criminal law to advance the priority of its claims).

[18] Lynn M. LoPucki, *Cooperation in International Bankruptcy: A Post-Universalist Approach*, 84 Cornell L. Rev. 696, 751 (1999).

[19] Nigel John Howcroft, *Universal vs. Territorial Models for Cross-Border Insolvency: The Theory, the Practice, and the Reality that Universalism Prevails*, 8 U.C. Davis Bus. L.J. 366 (2008); Andrew T. Guzman, *International Bankruptcy: In Defense of Universalism*, 98 Mich. L. Rev. 2177 (2000); Jay Lawrence Westbrook, *Multinational Enterprises In General Default: Chapter 15, The ALI Principles, And The EU Insolvency Regulation*, 76 Am. Bankr. L.J. 1 (2002); Jay Lawrence Westbrook, *A Global*

are located.[20] In a bankruptcy system operating on a theory of "pure universalism," courts in other countries would be bound by international agreement to enforce the orders of the bankruptcy court in the debtor's home country, and distribute its assets according to that country's laws.[21]

However appealing this might seem, adoption of a system of pure universalism is viewed by most as politically unlikely to develop in the near future.[22] In order for it to develop, courts would have to be willing to cede authority to either an international court, or to a court in another jurisdiction. In the current world, such a widespread cession of sovereignty seems unlikely.[23]

An evolving model, embodied in the UNCITRAL Model Law and in efforts to harmonize national bankruptcy law, such as UNCITRAL's Legislative Guide for Insolvency Law,[24] is modified universalism.[25] Under this approach, assets are collected and distributed on a worldwide basis under the supervision of the court at the debtor's center of main interest (COMI). For this system to work, however, the "main proceeding" at the COMI must obtain the cooperation of the various courts which have jurisdiction over the debtor's assets. Chapter 15 of the Bankruptcy Code, which is based on UNCITRAL's Model Law on Cross Border Insolvency and which was adopted as part of the 2005 Amendments,[26] seeks to facilitate such an approach (without mandating it). Chapter 15 provides for the recognition of foreign representatives of foreign bankruptcy proceedings, and encourages the local court to cooperate and defer to the proceeding pending at the debtor's COMI.[27]

Critics of modified universalism agree that pure universalism is unlikely to find sufficient political support to become a reality. Further, they contend that the modified universalism of the sort represented by Chapter 15 and the UNCITRAL model on which it was based suffers from the difficulty in identifying the home country of a large multinational corporation which might be incorporated in one country, have its headquarters and run its financial affairs from another country,

---

Solution to Multinational Default, 98 Mich. L. Rev. 2276 (2000).

[20] Liza Perkins, *A Defense of Pure Universalism in Cross-Border Corporate Insolvencies,* 32 N.Y.U. J. Int'l L. & Pol. 787 (2000).

[21] Lynn M. LoPucki, *The Case for Cooperative Territoriality In International Bankruptcy,* 98 Mich. L. Rev. 2216, 2221 (2000); Jay Lawrence Westbrook, *A Global Solution to Multinational Default,* 98 Mich. L. Rev. 2276, 2309 (2000).

[22] Lynn M. LoPucki, *The Case for Cooperative Territoriality In International Bankruptcy,* 98 Mich. L. Rev. 2216, 2221 (2000).

[23] *See* Roper v. Simmons, 543 U.S. 551, 607, 622-28 (2005) (Scalia, J. dissenting).

[24] UNCITRAL Legislative Guide on Insolvency Law, available at http://www.uncitral.org/uncitral/en/uncitral_texts/insolvency/2004Guide.html (last viewed on May 30, 2012).

[25] *See* Jeremy Leong, *Is Chapter 15 Universalist or Territorialist? Empirical Evidence from United States Bankruptcy Court Cases,* 29 Wis. Int'l L.J. 110 (2011).

[26] *See infra* § 22.03 Chapter 15 of the Bankruptcy Code.

[27] Edward S. Adams & Jason K. Fincke, *Coordinating Cross-Border Bankruptcy: How Territorialism Saves Universalism,* 15 Colum. J. Eur. L. 43, 46 (2009); David Costa Levenson, *Proposal for Reform of Choice of Avoidance Law in the Context of International Bankruptcies from a U.S. Perspective,* 10 Am. Bankr. Inst. L. Rev. 291 (2002).

and have the lion's share of its assets in a third country.[28]

[D] Contractualism

Some scholars advance a third theory — "contractualism."[29] Under contractualism, the creditors would agree in advance to the bankruptcy regime that would govern in the event of default. There are a number of objections to contractualism. Some are procedural — how to ensure that a debtor chooses the same law to govern all of its contracts. Others run to the limits of contractualism itself. For example, not all of the creditors against a debtor are in a position to negotiate over the choice of insolvency law. These may include small claimants or employees, for example. Indeed, not all creditors choose to do business with the debtor at all. There is no reason to think that a tort claimant should be bound to a debtor's choice of insolvency law. The final objection is regulatory. Many jurisdictions view it as their prerogative to regulate assets located in their jurisdiction, and/or contracts entered into in their jurisdiction. Contractualism would enforce private agreements regarding the choice of bankruptcy law that would apply in the event of a debtor's insolvency. This would allow debtors to contract around the regulatory provisions of local law.[30]

[E] Universal Proceduralism

One of the authors of this treatise has argued for a hybrid approach that uses choice of law principles to narrow the distance between modified universalism and cooperative territorialism.[31] Territorialists assert that a serious weakness of both modified universalism and contractualism is the problem of forum shopping. Contractualism allows debtors and favored creditors to choose a favorable forum in advance, and the centralization associated with modified universalism has a similar effect, particularly when, as in the EU, there is a strong presumption that the debtor's center of main interest is the jurisdiction where they have incorporated. Universal proceduralism contemplates a "universal" bankruptcy case, administered from the debtor's center of main interest, but the centralization will be procedural only. The home court would apply a choice of law principle that would seek to mimic, as closely as possible, the distributions that would occur in a territorial case.[32]

---

[28] Lynn M. LoPucki, *The Case for Cooperative Territoriality In International Bankruptcy*, 98 Mich. L. Rev. 2216, 2221 (2000).

[29] Robert K. Rasmussen, *Resolving Transnational Insolvencies Through Private Ordering*, 98 Mich L. Rev. 2252 (2000); Robert K. Rasmussen, *A New Approach to Transnational Insolvencies*, 19 Mich. J. Int'l L. 1 (1997). *See* David Costa Levenson, *Proposal for Reform of Choice of Avoidance Law in the Context of International Bankruptcies from a U.S. Perspective*, 10 Am. Bankr. Inst. L. Rev. 291, 296 (2002).

[30] Robert K. Rasmussen, *A New Approach to Transnational Insolvencies*, 19 Mich. J. Int'l L. 1, 4-5 (1997).

[31] Edward J. Janger, *Virtual Territoriality*, 48 Colum. J. Transnat'l L. 401 (2010).

[32] Edward J. Janger, *Virtual Territoriality*, 48 Colum. J. Transnat'l L. 401 (2010); Edward J. Janger, *Universal Proceduralism*, 32 Brooklyn J. Int'l L. 819 (2007).

§ 22.02   ANCILLARY AND PARALLEL BANKRUPTCY PROCEEDINGS[33]

The UNCITRAL Model Law and EU Regulation draw a distinction between two types of cross-border insolvency proceedings: ancillary proceedings and plenary proceedings.[34] "Ancillary proceedings" (referred to in the EU Regulation as "secondary proceedings") refers to a special proceeding in which a domestic bankruptcy court gives assistance to a bankruptcy case pending in a foreign jurisdiction. Thus, an ancillary proceeding is not a regular bankruptcy case in which the debtor's assets are collected and distributed according to the usual priorities.[35] Instead, the purpose of an ancillary proceeding is to assist the debtor's main bankruptcy proceeding that is pending in another country where the debtor's "center of main interest" is located.

Former § 304 permitted bankruptcy courts in the United States to administer an ancillary proceeding to assist with the administration of a foreign bankruptcy case. Under former § 304, a representative appointed in a foreign insolvency proceeding could petition to begin an ancillary proceeding in an American bankruptcy court. The ancillary proceeding was not a full-blown bankruptcy case. Instead, it provided a means of facilitating the foreign court's proceeding.[36] Under § 304, the American bankruptcy court could enjoin the commencement or continuation of actions against the debtor's property or against the debtor regarding the property,[37] enjoin the commencement or continuation of the enforcement of any judgment against the debtor respecting the property, or any act or proceeding to create or enforce a lien against the property,[38] order the property or its proceeds to be turned over to the representative of the foreign case,[39] or order other appropriate relief.[40]

New Chapter 15, in 2005, also permits ancillary bankruptcy proceedings in the United States. It permits a bankruptcy court to recognize and cooperate with a "foreign main proceeding" involving a debtor who has interests or property in the United States.[41]

Alternatively, a debtor with a bankruptcy case pending in one country might initiate a full blown parallel bankruptcy case in a second country to administer the

---

[33] *See* Evelyn H. Biery, Jason L. Boland & John D. Cornwell, *A Look at Transnational Insolvencies and Chapter 15 of the Bankruptcy Abuse Prevention and Consumer Protection Act of 2005*, 47 B.C. L. Rev. 23, 31-32 (2005); Jay L. Westbrook, *A Global Solution to Multinational Default*, 98 Mich. L. Rev. 2276, 2300 (2000); Jay Lawrence Westbrook, *Multinational Enterprises In General Default: Chapter 15, The ALI Principles, And The EU Insolvency Regulation*, 76 Am. Bankr. L.J. 1, 10-12 (2002).

[34] Am. L. Inst., Transnational Insolvency: Cooperation Among the NAFTA Countries: Principles of Cooperation Among the NAFTA Countries 9-10 (2003). *See* Jay L. Westbrook & Jacob Ziegel, *The American Insolvency Law Institute NAFTA Insolvency Project*, 23 Brook. J. Int'l. L. 7, 8 (1997).

[35] *See supra* § 10.01 Meaning of Claims and Interests.

[36] *See, e.g.*, Interpool, Ltd. v. Certain Freights, 878 F.2d 111, 112 (3d Cir. 1989).

[37] Former Bankruptcy Code § 304(b)(1)(A).

[38] Former Bankruptcy Code § 304(b)(1)(B).

[39] Former Bankruptcy Code § 304(b)(2).

[40] Former Bankruptcy Code § 304(b)(3).

[41] Bankruptcy Code § 1517(b)(1).

assets that are within the jurisdictional control of that country.[42] A parallel proceeding is a full-blown bankruptcy case in which all of the usual rules and priorities apply. Judges in the parallel plenary cases usually attempt to coordinate their efforts seek to avoid inconsistent outcomes in the two cases. Chapter 15 also permits the opening of full parallel proceedings,[43] but requires U.S. bankruptcy courts to cooperate with a parallel proceeding pending in another country and to defer to the "main proceeding."[44]

§ 22.03　CHAPTER 15 OF THE BANKRUPTCY CODE[45]

The 2005 Amendments to the Bankruptcy Code included a major revision of the rules relating to transnational insolvency cases. New Chapter 15 is based on the United Nations Commission on International Trade Law's (UNCITRAL) Model Law on Cross-Border Insolvency.[46] UNCITRAL's model law has been adopted by nearly 20 other nations, including Australia (2008), Canada (2009), Greece (2010), Japan (2000), Mexico (2000), New Zealand (2006), Poland (2003), Romania (2003), South Korea (2006), South Africa (2000), Great Britain (2006), and the United States (2005).[47] Some of those jurisdictions are also members of the EU, and are therefore governed by the EC Regulation on Insolvency for cases involving other EU countries.[48]

The purposes of Chapter 15 and UNCITRAL's Model Law are "to provide effective mechanisms for dealing with cases of cross-border insolvency."[49] They attempt to:

---

[42] *See* Am. L. Inst. Transnational Insolvency Project, Court-to-Court Guidelines for Communications, available at http://www.iiiglobal.org/international/projects/ali.pdf (last visited Nov. 26, 2006); Jacob S. Ziegel, *Corporate Groups and Crossborder Insolvencies: A Canada-United States Perspective*, 7 Fordham J. Corp. & Fin. L. 367, 380 (2002).

[43] Bankruptcy Code § 1528.

[44] Bankruptcy Code § 1529.

[45] Evelyn H. Biery, Jason L. Boland, & John D. Cornwell, *A Look at Transnational Insolvencies and Chapter 15 of the Bankruptcy Abuse Prevention and Consumer Protection Act of 2005*, 47 B.C. L. Rev. 23 (2005); John J. Chung, *The New Chapter 15 of the Bankruptcy Code: A Step toward Erosion of National Sovereignty*, 27 Nw. J. Int'l L. & Bus. 89 (2006); Andrew B. Dawson, *Offshore Bankruptcies*, 88 Neb. L. Rev. 317 (2009); Jay Lawrence Westbrook, *Breaking Away: Local Priorities and Global Assets*, 46 Tex. Int'l L.J. 601 (2011).

[46] United Nations Commission on International Trade Law, Model Law on Cross-Border Insolvency, available at http://www.uncitral.org/uncitral/en/uncitral_texts/insolvency/1997Model.html (last viewed on May 30, 2012). *See* Cross-Border Insolvency: A Commentary on the UNCITRAL Model Law (Look Chan Ho ed., 2006); André J. Berends, *The UNCITRAL Model Law on Cross-Border Insolvency: A Comprehensive Overview*, 6 Tul. J. Int'l & Comp. L. 309 (1998).

[47] *See* http://www.uncitral.org/uncitral/en/uncitral_texts/insolvency/1997Model_status.html (last viewed on May 30, 2012).

[48] The European Union Regulation on Insolvency Proceedings appears at Council Regulation 1346/2000, 29 May 2000, on insolvency proceedings, 2000 O.J. (L160) 1-18 (effective May 30, 2001), as amended, available at http://eur-lex.europa.eu/LexUriServ/LexUriServ.do?uri=CELEX:32000R1346:EN:NOT (last viewed on May 30, 2012). It applies in twenty-four of the European Union's twenty-five countries. Denmark is the only country in the EU where it does not apply.

[49] Bankruptcy Code § 1501(a).

- promote cooperation between the courts and agencies of the United States and foreign countries involved in cross-border insolvency proceedings;[50]

- provide greater legal certainty for trade and investment;[51]

- promote fair and efficient administration of cross-border insolvencies that protects the interests of the debtor, creditors, and other interested persons;[52]

- facilitate the rescue of financially troubled businesses and thereby protect investment and preserve employment.[53]

The most significant features of Chapter 15 and the UNCITRAL model on which it is based are its provisions regarding "recognition" of a foreign bankruptcy proceeding by an American bankruptcy court, and those regarding the bankruptcy court's duties to cooperate with a foreign bankruptcy proceeding.

[A] Foreign Bankruptcy Proceedings: Main and Nonmain Proceedings

[1] Foreign Proceedings

Chapter 15 applies only in connection with a debtor who is the subject of a foreign proceeding.[54] A "foreign proceeding" is a:

collective judicial or administrative proceeding in a foreign country, including an interim proceeding, under a law relating to insolvency or adjustment of debt in which proceeding the assets and affairs of the debtor are subject to control or supervision by a foreign court, for the purpose of reorganization or liquidation.[55]

Thus, the mere fact that a lawsuit is pending against a debtor in a foreign country is not enough to trigger the Code's rules regarding cross border insolvency cases. The foreign case must be a collective proceeding in which all of the debtor's assets are under court supervision for the purpose of reorganizing or liquidating the debtor's financial affairs.

This is different in two respects from the definition of foreign proceeding that was used before the 2005 Amendments. First, the new language requires the foreign proceeding to be "collective." A single secured creditor's foreclosure action is not a foreign proceeding, even though it might result in liquidation of the debtor's assets, because it is not a "collective" proceeding. Second, unlike former § 101(23), the foreign proceeding need not be pending in the debtor's "home" country, where

---

[50] Bankruptcy Code § 1501(a)(1).

[51] Bankruptcy Code § 1501(a)(2).

[52] Bankruptcy Code § 1501(a)(4).

[53] Bankruptcy Code § 1501(a)(5).

[54] *See* Bankruptcy Code § 1502(1). For the purposes of Chapter 15, "debtor" means "an entity that is the subject of a foreign proceeding." Bankruptcy Code § 1502(1).

[55] Bankruptcy Code § 101(23).

its domicile, residence, principal place of business, or principal assets are located. Cases applying former § 304, which permitted ancillary proceedings to be initiated only if the foreign case was pending in the country of the debtor's main location, no longer control. However, to qualify as a foreign proceeding, the proceeding must be pending in a jurisdiction where the debtor has an "establishment."[56] An "establishment" is defined as "any place of operations where the debtor carries out a non-transitory economic activity."[57]

[2] Main Proceedings and Nonmain Proceedings

Chapter 15 distinguishes between two types of foreign bankruptcy proceedings: "foreign main proceedings" and "foreign nonmain proceedings." A "foreign main proceeding" is a foreign proceeding pending in the country where the debtor has the center of its main interests."[58] A "foreign nonmain proceeding" is a foreign proceeding pending in a country that is not the center of the debtor's interests.[59]

The Code treats foreign main proceedings differently from foreign nonmain proceedings. As explained below, "recognition" of a foreign main proceeding results in the immediate imposition of the automatic stay and enjoins nearly every type of action a creditor might take to recover from the debtor against assets located in the United States.[60] Recognition of a nonmain proceeding authorizes the court to enjoin creditors' collection efforts as necessary to protect the debtor's assets or the interests of creditors generally, but does not result in an automatic injunction against collection activities.[61] Recognition of a foreign main proceeding also affects the debtor's right to transfer its assets.

[3] Eligible Debtors

Chapter 15 imposes a few limits on who may be the subject of a Chapter 15 case. Chapter 15 does not apply to railroads, regulated financial institutions, and domestic insurance companies, who may not seek relief under Chapter 7.[62] Likewise, it excludes individual debtors (and their spouses) with debts below the limits imposed on debtors for relief under Chapter 13 who are either U.S. citizens or permanent residents.[63] Also excluded from eligibility are entities subject to the Securities Investor Protection Act of 1970, stockbrokers, and commodity brokers.[64]

---

[56] Bankruptcy Code § 1502(2), (4), (5).

[57] Bankruptcy Code § 1502(2).

[58] Bankruptcy Code § 1502(4).

[59] Bankruptcy Code § 1502(5).

[60] Bankruptcy Code § 1520(a)(1). *See supra* Chapter 8 — The Automatic Stay.

[61] Bankruptcy Code § 1521(a).

[62] Bankruptcy Code § 1501(c)(1). *See* Bankruptcy Code § 109(b). *See generally supra* § 6.02[B][2] Eligibility for Relief Under Chapter 7 — Liquidation.

[63] Bankruptcy Code § 1501(c)(2). *See* Bankruptcy Code § 109(c). *See generally supra* § 6.02[B][6][c] Chapter 13 Debt Limits.

[64] Bankruptcy Code § 1501(c)(3).

[B] "Recognition" of Foreign Bankruptcy Proceedings

Section 1509 permits the debtor's representative in a foreign bankruptcy proceeding to petition an American bankruptcy court for "recognition" of the foreign case.[65] Before recognition, the foreign representative does not have access to American courts. The petition must be accompanied by a certified copy of the decision that commenced the foreign case and appointed the foreign representative, a certificate from the foreign court in which the case is pending that affirms the existence of the foreign proceeding and of the appointment of the foreign representative, or some other evidence acceptable to the bankruptcy court that the foreign case is pending and that the applicant is the authorized foreign representative in the case.[66] The petition must also be accompanied by a statement that identifies all foreign proceedings with respect to the debtor that are known to the foreign representative.[67] This deals with the possibility that multiple cases are pending in several countries. If these original documents are not in English, they must be translated into English, along with any other documents the court requires.[68]

After notice and a hearing, the bankruptcy court is required to recognize the foreign proceeding if: (1) the foreign proceeding is either a foreign main proceeding or a foreign nonmain proceeding as those terms are defined in § 1502; (2) the foreign representative is an appropriate person or body; and (3) the petition is accompanied by the documents required by § 1515.[69]

This is considerably different from the application of former § 304. It permitted a bankruptcy court to grant relief, in the form of an ancillary bankruptcy proceeding, based on what would "best assure an economical and expeditious administration" of the debtor's estate consistent with six additional factors: (1) just treatment of holders of claims and interests; (2) protection of creditors in the United States against any prejudice and unfairness in the foreign proceeding; (3) prevention of preferential or fraudulent transfers of the debtor's property; (4) distribution of the estate's property in accordance with the bankruptcy code; (5) comity; and (6) providing the debtor with the opportunity for a fresh start.[70] Chapter 15 dispenses with this factor analysis, and requires the bankruptcy court to recognize most foreign proceedings, provided only that the application for recognition is legitimate.

The key exception to this is found in § 1506 which establishes a broad "public policy exception" to the rules in Chapter 15. It provides: "Nothing in this chapter prevents the court from refusing to take an action governed by this chapter if the action would be manifestly contrary to the public policy of the United States."[71]

---

[65] Bankruptcy Code § 1509(a).

[66] Bankruptcy Code § 1515(b).

[67] Bankruptcy Code § 1515(c).

[68] Bankruptcy Code § 1515(d).

[69] Bankruptcy Code § 1517; In re SphinX, Ltd., 351 B.R. 103 (Bankr. S.D.N.Y. 2006).

[70] Former Bankruptcy Code § 304(c)(1)-(6).

[71] Bankruptcy Code § 1506.

This is, however, a much more limited basis for refusing cooperation than the balancing test under former law.

While a petition for recognition is pending, the court may stay creditors' efforts to seize the debtor's assets and may entrust the administration of the debtor's assets to the foreign representative to preserve their value.[72] The court may also suspend the debtor's rights to transfer or encumber its assets, permit discovery, or grant nearly any relief that would be available to a bankruptcy trustee. However, this relief is not automatic — the foreign representative must apply for it in order to protect the debtor's assets and the interests of creditors.[73]

[C]   Effect of Recognition of Foreign Proceeding

[1]   Stay of Other Proceedings

Upon recognition of a foreign main proceeding, the automatic stay of § 362 goes into effect.[74] As explained elsewhere, this stays virtually every type of collection activity a creditor might engage in,[75] including administrative and judicial proceedings against the debtor,[76] efforts to obtain possession of the debtor's property,[77] and even informal collection efforts.[78] It does not stay criminal prosecutions or other proceedings that involve the enforcement of a governmental police or regulatory power.[79] None of these actions would be barred by § 362 either. More importantly, however, the stay under Chapter 15 is territorial, reaching only assets and creditors within the United States. Therefore, nothing in § 1520(a) prevents a creditor from commencing an action against the debtor in a foreign country "to the extent necessary to preserve a claim against the debtor."[80] Thus, if a creditor would lose its rights against the debtor under foreign law if it failed to initiate a claim against the debtor in that country, the creditor may do so. Likewise, of course, creditors may file claims in the case.[81] Apart from this, the court also has the discretionary authority to stay actions concerning the debtor's property or liabilities beyond the limits imposed by the automatic stay,[82] except with respect to criminal or regulatory enforcement proceedings, or to the extent that the extension would overlap with the stay granted by another proceeding.[83]

---

[72] Bankruptcy Code § 1519(a)(1), (2).

[73] Bankruptcy Code § 1519.

[74] Bankruptcy Code § 1520(a)(1).

[75] See supra § 8.02 Scope of the Automatic Stay.

[76] Bankruptcy Code § 362(a)(1).

[77] Bankruptcy Code § 362(a)(3).

[78] Bankruptcy Code § 362(a)(6).

[79] Bankruptcy Code § 362(b)(1), (4). See supra § 8.03 Exceptions to the Automatic Stay.

[80] Bankruptcy Code § 1520(b).

[81] Bankruptcy Code § 1520(c).

[82] Bankruptcy Code § 1521(a)(1), (2).

[83] Bankruptcy Code § 1521(d). The foreign representative might still seek discretionary relief from such proceedings under § 105. See supra § 8.05 Discretionary Stays.

Recognition of a foreign nonmain proceeding permits the bankruptcy court to stay any pending proceedings involving the debtor's assets and liabilities within the United States, but does not impose an automatic stay.[84] Whether the court should impose a stay to protect assets located within the scope of the bankruptcy court's authority depends on the extent to which this is "necessary to effectuate the purposes of [Chapter 15] and to protect the assets of the debtor or the interests of the creditors."[85]

[2]   Transfers of the Debtor's Property

Recognition of a foreign main proceeding invokes §§ 363, 549 and 552 all of which restrict a debtor's authority to freely transfer its property. As explained elsewhere, § 363 generally permits the debtor to use, sell, or lease its property in the ordinary course of business, but requires court authorization, consistent with principles of adequate protection of secured creditors under § 361, for the debtor to dispose of property outside the ordinary course or for the debtor to dispose of "cash collateral" even in the ordinary course of business.[86] Section 549 provides for the recovery of certain post-petition transfers.[87] Section 552 impairs the post-petition effect of security interests in after-acquired collateral.[88] These restrictions fall into place immediately upon recognition of the foreign case as a main case. Recognition also supplies the court with discretionary authority to suspend the transferability of the debtor's property beyond the limits imposed by these provisions.[89]

Recognition of a foreign nonmain proceeding gives the court discretionary authority to suspend the debtor's right to "transfer, encumber or otherwise dispose" of its assets.[90] However, the foreign representative of the nomain proceeding must seek this protection from the bankruptcy court in order to effectuate the purposes of Chapter 15 and to protect the debtor's assets and the interests of its creditors.[91]

[3]   Authority to Operate the Debtor's Business

Recognition of a foreign main proceeding gives the foreign representative the authority to operate the debtor's business and to exercise the same authority to use, sell, and lease estate property that is normally enjoyed by a bankruptcy trustee or a Chapter 11 debtor-in-possession.[92]

Recognition of a foreign nonmain proceeding does not instantly confer upon the foreign representative the right to operate the debtor's business, but it does permit

---

[84]   Bankruptcy Code § 1521(a)(1).

[85]   Bankruptcy Code § 1521(a).

[86]   Bankruptcy Code § 363(a)-(d). *See supra* § 9.03 Use, Sale, or Lease of Estate Property.

[87]   Bankruptcy Code § 549. *See supra* § 14.05 Post-Petition Transfers of Estate Property.

[88]   Bankruptcy Code § 552. *See supra* § 10.03[B][4] After-Acquired Collateral.

[89]   Bankruptcy Code § 1521(a)(3).

[90]   Bankruptcy Code § 1521(a)(3).

[91]   Bankruptcy Code § 1521(a).

[92]   Bankruptcy Code § 1520(a)(3).

the court to entrust "the administration or realization of all or part of the debtor's assets within the territorial jurisdiction of the United States to the foreign representative, or another person, including an examiner" as specified by the court.[93]

[4]   Distribution of Assets[94]

Recognition of either a foreign main or a nonmain proceeding permits the court to entrust the foreign representative with authority to distribute whatever of the debtor's assets are located in the United States.[95] The principle limitation on the court's authority in this regard, and perhaps a last vestige of § 304's multifactor test, is that the court must be "satisfied that the interests of creditors in the United States are sufficiently protected."[96]

[5]   Trustee's Powers

Recognition of either type of foreign proceeding also permits the court to grant the foreign representative any additional relief that is ordinarily available to a bankruptcy trustee or to a debtor-in-possession.[97] However, the foreign representative may not exercise the trustee's avoiding powers under §§ 522 (avoidance of security interests and liens in exempt property), 544 (strong-arm clause), 545 (statutory liens), 547 (preferences), 548 (fraudulent transfers), 550 (remedies for avoiding powers), or 724(a) (lien for non-compensatory penalties).[98] To take advantage of these avoiding powers, the foreign representative must initiate a parallel bankruptcy proceeding under the appropriate chapter of the Bankruptcy Code pursuant to its authority under § 1511.[99]

[6]   Additional Assistance

Bankruptcy courts are also authorized to provide "additional assistance" to a foreign representative, beyond the specific provisions contained in Chapter 15, so long as the court does not violate any specific limits it imposes.[100] In exercising discretion over whether to provide additional assistance, the court must consider the same factors that guided the court under former § 304.[101] This preserves some aspects of former § 304, the case law that developed under it, and the uncertainties with which it was associated, but it would appear to apply only where a court wishes

---

[93]   Bankruptcy Code § 1521(a)(5).

[94]   Edward J. Janger, *Virtual Territoriality*, 48 Colum. J. Transnat'l L. 401 (2010); Edward J. Janger, *Reciprocal Comity*, 46 Tex. Int'l L.J. 441 (2011).

[95]   Bankruptcy Code § 1521(b).

[96]   Bankruptcy Code § 1521(b).

[97]   Bankruptcy Code § 1521(a)(7).

[98]   Bankruptcy Code § 1521(a)(7).

[99]   Bankruptcy Code § 1511.

[100]   Bankruptcy Code § 1507(a).

[101]   Bankruptcy Code § 1507(b). *See supra* § 21.03[B] "Recognition" of Foreign Bankruptcy Proceedings.

to cooperate in a manner beyond that otherwise provided for by the statute.[102] The content of such additional relief is, however, difficult to conceive in the abstract.

[D]   Rights of Foreign Creditors

Chapter 15 gives foreign creditors the same rights regarding the commencement of and participation in a case under Chapter 15 as domestic creditors.[103] It requires that notification be given to foreign creditors whenever notice is to be given to creditors generally or is required to be given to a specific class or category of creditors.[104] Chapter 15 further provides for adjustment of the normal mechanisms and time limits for providing notice to foreign creditors as may be appropriate under the circumstances.[105]

Foreign creditors have the right to appear in the bankruptcy case to the same extent as domestic creditors.[106] Foreign creditors' priority rights are not to be altered because of their status as foreign creditors,[107] with two limited exceptions. First, it maintains the "foreign revenue rule" which prevents allowance of certain claims of foreign governments.[108] This primarily limits the enforceability of foreign tax claims.[109] Second, it also subjects the enforceability of such claims to any treaty that the United States might enter into with a foreign country.[110]

[E]   Commencement of a Parallel Proceeding

Recognition of a foreign main proceeding authorizes the foreign representative to commence a voluntary case involving the debtor under §§ 301 or 302.[111] Naturally, this is permitted only if "the debtor has assets in the United States."[112] Such petition would probably be under Chapter 11 where the foreign representative may or may not manage the affairs of the debtor. Of course, if a Chapter 7 petition were commenced, a trustee would be appointed. Nothing in Chapter 15 appears to prevent the foreign representative from being selected as the trustee. Chapter 15 requires the efforts in a domestic case to be limited to the debtor's assets that are within the territorial jurisdiction of the United States.[113]

---

[102] *See* Todd Kraft & Allison Aranson, *Transnational Bankruptcies: Section 304 and Beyond*, 1993 Colum Bus. L. Rev, 329, 339.

[103] Bankruptcy Code § 1513(a).

[104] Bankruptcy Code § 1514(a).

[105] Bankruptcy Code § 1514(d).

[106] Bankruptcy Code § 1513(a).

[107] Bankruptcy Code § 1513(b)(1).

[108] Bankruptcy Code § 1513(b)(2)(A).

[109] *See* Moore v. Mitchell, 30 F.2d 600 (2d Cir. 1929), *aff'd*, 281 U.S. 18 (1930); H.R. Rep. No. 109-31, at 111-112 (2005) *reprinted in* 2005 U.S.C.C.A.N. 88, 174.

[110] Bankruptcy Code § 1513(b)(2)(B).

[111] *See supra* § 6.02 Commencement of Voluntary Cases.

[112] Bankruptcy Code § 1528.

[113] Bankruptcy Code § 1528.

[F] Cooperation and Coordination with Foreign Courts and Foreign Representatives

A bankruptcy court in the United States must cooperate and coordinate its efforts with those of the foreign bankruptcy court in a foreign proceeding that the court has recognized[114] "to the maximum extent possible."[115] The court has express authority to "communicate directly with . . . a foreign court or a foreign representative, subject to the rights of a party in interest to notice and participation."[116] The trustee, debtor-in-possession, or examiner is similarly required to cooperate "to the maximum extent possible" with a foreign court or a foreign representative in a foreign case.[117]

This cooperation might be accomplished through a variety of means, including:

- appointment of a person to act at the direction of the court in connection with the cases;[118]

- communication "by any means . . . appropriate";[119]

- coordination of the administration and supervision of the debtor's assets and its operations;[120]

- approval or implementation of any agreement that might exist concerning coordination of the proceedings;[121] and

- coordination of concurrent proceedings involving the same debtor.[122]

A foreign representative of a foreign nonmain proceeding has standing to initiate an involuntary case under § 303.[123] However, an order for relief is granted under § 303 only if the petition is not controverted by the debtor, if the debtor is not paying its debts as they come due, or if a trustee, receiver, or other agent has been appointed in the past 120 days to take charge of substantially all of the debtor's assets.[124]

---

[114] Bankruptcy Code § 1528.

[115] Bankruptcy Code § 1525(a).

[116] Bankruptcy Code § 1525(b).

[117] Bankruptcy Code § 1526(a).

[118] Bankruptcy Code § 1527(1).

[119] Bankruptcy Code § 1527(2).

[120] Bankruptcy Code § 1527(3).

[121] Bankruptcy Code § 1527(4).

[122] Bankruptcy Code § 1527.

[123] *See supra* § 6.03 Commencement of Involuntary Cases.

[124] Bankruptcy Code § 303(h).

[G]   Concurrent Proceedings

Chapter 15 provides rules governing concurrent bankruptcy proceedings in more than one country.[125] As noted above, once a foreign main proceeding has been recognized, the foreign representative may commence a voluntary case involving the same debtor, provided that the debtor is otherwise eligible for relief under the Bankruptcy Code.[126] When concurrent proceedings are pending, the bankruptcy court "shall seek cooperation and coordination" with the foreign proceeding.[127] If the case in the United States is already pending when the foreign representative seeks recognition of a foreign proceeding, relief granted under §§ 1519 and 1521, restricting creditors' actions, must be consistent with whatever relief has previously been granted in the domestic case,[128] unless the foreign case is recognized as a foreign main proceeding.[129] If a foreign proceeding is recognized before a case is commenced in the United States, relief provided pursuant to recognition of the foreign case may be modified or terminated if it is inconsistent with relief in the domestic case.[130]

If more than one foreign case involving the same debtor is pending, which might easily occur with respect to financially troubled debtors with business activities in several countries, the court is similarly required to cooperate and coordinate with the foreign proceedings.[131] Proceedings in a domestic bankruptcy court must be consistent with proceedings in any foreign main proceeding that the bankruptcy court recognizes.[132]

---

[125] Bankruptcy Code § 1529.

[126] Bankruptcy Code § 1528.

[127] Bankruptcy Code § 1529.

[128] Bankruptcy Code § 1529(1)(a).

[129] Bankruptcy Code § 1529(1)(B).

[130] Bankruptcy Code § 1529(2)(A).

[131] Bankruptcy Code § 1530.

[132] Bankruptcy Code § 1530(1).

Chapter 23

SPECIAL USES OF BANKRUPTCY

§ 23.01 SPECIAL USES OF BANKRUPTCY

Bankruptcy can do more than discharge unpayable debt for those in financial difficulty. It can also be used as a tool to deal with many other difficult problems, particularly those faced by business entities that are looking for ways to deal with diverse creditors while continuing a business, or for ways to sell complicated types of assets. In this chapter, we discuss a few novel uses of Chapter 11. Some of these uses of bankruptcy are relatively new. Others, notably substantive consolidation, have a long history. Some are specifically provided for in the Code. Others raise thorny issues of statutory interpretation.

§ 23.02 MASS TORTS[1]

In modern industrial society, it is inevitable that some products will malfunction, workplace accidents will occur, and industrial processes will cause environmental harms. These mishaps may occur because of the bad luck, incompetence, or bad faith of an industrial enterprise. A sedative may have teratogenic properties that cause thousands of disabling birth defects. A commonly used mineral used to retard fires — and once used in baby powder — may cause a fatal lung disease. An intrauterine device may cause sterility. A commuter aircraft or jumbo jet may crash. Any of these disasters may result in a "mass tort" — a situation in which a single act, transaction, or product generates tens, hundreds or even thousands of personal injury lawsuits. And, although the mass tort liability of the Roman Catholic Church in America does not stem from a single product or incident, it raises many of the same issues that arise in other mass tort cases together with its own set of unusual questions related to the religious nature of the debtors involved in several diocesan bankruptcy reorganization cases.

Inside or outside of bankruptcy, mass torts have tested state and federal procedural rules' capacity to administer justice. Proposals for reform include massive consolidation of actions; unified discovery, pre-trial, and trial restrictions on the multiple awards of punitive damages; and review of attorneys' fees. All are controversial.

Almost by default, bankruptcy has become a battleground in the struggle over tort law. A bankruptcy is a collective proceeding; in most cases it provides the

---

[1] Alan N. Resnick, *Bankruptcy as a Vehicle for Resolving Enterprise-Threatening Mass Tort Liability*, 148 U. Pa. L. Rev. 2045 (2000); Mark J. Roe, *Bankruptcy and Mass Tort*, 84 Colum. L. Rev. 846 (1984).

debtor and creditors with a single forum in which all controversies can be decided before a single judge. True, that judge is generally unaided by a jury,[2] but the judge has the advantage of dealing with all matters concerning the debtor in a single setting. Moreover, the judge can provide for an equal distribution of available assets among all claimants, thus avoiding the possibility that those who sue early will collect in full while those who sue late will get little or nothing. There is nothing in the Bankruptcy Code that prevents a debtor from using it to attempt a global resolution of mass tort issues, and a number of companies have attempted exactly that. Cases involving asbestos claims, IUDs, breast implants, and commuter aircraft have found their way into Bankruptcy Court.[3]

[A] Future Claims[4]

One of the most difficult issues in many mass tort cases is how to deal with future claimants: those who have been exposed to the harmful effects of the debtor's conduct or product, but who have not yet discovered their injuries. In some cases, they have not manifested symptoms; in other cases they have not yet traced their illness or injuries to the debtor's product.[5] In some cases, they do not even know that they have been exposed to the source of the harm. Still others may not have yet been exposed to the defendant's product, but will be exposed to it and become ill or injured as a result of its defects weeks, months, and perhaps years after the bankruptcy case concludes.

Bankruptcy cases involving the harmful effects of asbestos raise most of these issues. If a construction worker who installed asbestos becomes ill and is diagnosed with asbestosis before the manufacturer of the asbestos insulation product she installed files a bankruptcy petition undoubtedly has a claim, because she had a right to payment and thus a "claim" before the bankruptcy case commenced.[6] However, one of this creditor's co-workers, who had contact with the debtor's product at the same time, might not develop symptoms of her disease until after the case is pending. This might be an unmatured claim at the time of commencement, or not a claim at all, depending on how claims are defined. Still others who occupy the building may not even be exposed to the harmful fibers until after the case is closed. Whether they should be permitted to participate in the case, through some representative, raises other difficulties.

---

[2] *See supra* § 5.02[E] Jury Trials in Bankruptcy Court.

[3] Kane v. Johns-Manville Corp., 843 F.2d 636 (2d Cir. 1988); Grady v. A.H. Robins, Co., 839 F.2d 198 (4th Cir. 1988); In re Owens Corning, Inc., 419 F.3d 195, 206 (3d Cir. 2005); In re Piper Aircraft Corp., 162 B.R. 619, 624 (Bankr. S.D. Fla.), *aff'd*, 168 B.R. 434 (S.D. Fla. 1994), *aff'd*, 58 F.3d 1573 (11th Cir. 1995).

[4] Larua Bartell, *Due Process for the Unknown Future Claim in Bankruptcy — Is this Notice Really Necessary?*, 78 Am. Bankr. L.J. 339 (2004); Ralph R. Mabey & Jamie Andra Gavrin, *Constitutional Limitations on the Discharge of Future Claims in Bankruptcy*, 44 S.C. L. Rev. 745 (1993); Sheldon S. Toll, *Bankruptcy and Mass Torts: The Commission's Proposal*, 5 Am. Bankr. Inst. L. Rev. 363 (1997); J. Maxwell Tucker, *The Clash of Successor Liability Principles, Reorganization Law, and the Just Demand That Relief be Afforded Unknown and Unknowable Claimants*, 12 Bankr. Dev. J. 1 (1995).

[5] *See, e.g.*, Grady v. A.H. Robins, Co., 839 F.2d 198 (4th Cir. 1988) (debtor did not discover that her injuries were related to the defendant's product until after the debtor's case was commenced).

[6] Bankruptcy Code § 101(5).

Whether these parties have claims is important in several key respects. First, only those with claims are entitled to participate in the debtor's bankruptcy case by voting on a plan and receiving a distribution of the debtor's assets.[7] If the creditor's rights attached after bankruptcy, the creditor cannot participate in the case. Second, the automatic stay has its biggest effect on those whose claims arose before commencement of the case.[8] Those whose claims arose later, may not be affected by the automatic stay.[9] Third, the debtor's liability on creditors' "claims" is discharged.[10] If the creditor's right to recover is not a claim, the debtor's liability is not discharged. On the one hand, the future claimant may prefer to allow his claim to "ride through" the bankruptcy, and assert it against the reorganized entity. On the other hand, it may not be assertable against the reorganized debtor, because it may not qualify as an administrative expense. Also, if the company is unable to reorganize, because of inability to resolve and contain its tort liability, the debtor may be forced to liquidate.[11] This may leave the future claimants with nothing.

Courts have developed several tests for determining whether future creditors hold claims.[12] One line of decisions focuses on the "right to payment" language in Section 101(3), and restricts creditors with claims to those whose right to sue the debtor accrued under state law before the case began. Under this test, future claimants would not have a claim in the bankruptcy, and their claims could not be resolved through reorganization. Other courts adopt a broader view of claims and apply a "conduct test" under which the determination of whether a creditor has a claim depends upon when the debtor's conduct, which gave rise to its liability to the creditor, occurred. If the conduct, such as manufacture of the defective product, occurred before the petition was filed, the creditor has a claim in the debtor's bankruptcy case even though the creditor's cause of action did not accrue under conventional state rules until after the petition is filed.[13] This test facilitates reorganization, but may deprive many claimants of their claims before they even know that they have them. A third test imposes a "due process" limitation on the "conduct" test. It treats the conduct as sufficient to give rise to the claim, but requires the creditor to have had some relationship with the defendant or its product before the case commenced for the creditor to have a cognizable claim in the debtor's bankruptcy case.[14] Under this test, those who are not exposed to the debtor's defective product until after the bankruptcy case is commenced, do not

---

[7] *See generally supra* § 10.02 Claims of Creditors.

[8] Bankruptcy Code § 362(a). *See supra* § 8.02 Scope of the Automatic Stay.

[9] *See* Grady v. A.H. Robins Co., 839 F.2d 198 (4th Cir. 1988).

[10] Bankruptcy Code § 524(a). *See supra* § 13.09 Effect of Discharge.

[11] *See* Schweitzer v. Consolidated Rail Corp., 758 F.2d 936 (3d Cir. 1985); Frederick Tung, *Taking Future Claims Seriously: Future Claims and Successor Liability in Bankruptcy*, 49 Case W. Res. L. Rev. 435 (1999).

[12] *See* In re Hoffinger Industries, Inc., 307 B.R. 112 (Bankr. E.D. Ark. 2004). Significantly, until recently, the Third Circuit followed the "right to payment test" articulated in *Avellino & Bienes v. M. Frenville Co. (In re M. Frenville Co.)*, 744 F.2d 332 (3d Cir. 1984). *Frenville* was recently overruled, en banc, by *Jeld-Wen, Inc. v. Van Brunt (In re Grossman's Inc.)*, 607 F.3d 114 (3d Cir. 2010).

[13] *See, e.g.*, Grady v. A.H. Robins Co. (In re A.H. Robins Co.), 839 F.2d 198 (4th Cir. 1988).

[14] In re Piper Aircraft Corp., 162 B.R. 619, 624 (Bankr. S.D. Fla.), *aff'd*, 168 B.R. 434 (S.D. Fla. 1994), *aff'd*, 58 F.3d 1573 (11th Cir. 1995).

have claims, and their claims are not, therefore, discharged.

[B]   Claims Trusts[15]

A key issue in many mass tort liability bankruptcy cases is how to handle the settlement of creditors' claims. Since its use in the Johns-Mansville bankruptcy,[16] cases involving mass tort claims have usually relied on a trust for the settlement of present and future claims.[17] The mechanism is now officially sanctioned by the Bankruptcy Code for use in cases involving liability related to exposure to asbestos.

Section 524(g) permits the court to create a qualified settlement trust funded by the debtor's assets and to issue a "channeling injunction" that requires present and future claimants to pursue their claims against the trust rather than against the reorganized debtor. By defining the precise scope of the debtor's liability to the trust, § 524(g) and similar channeling injunctions provide the assurance that prospective investors need to encourage them to supply the funds necessary to finance the debtor's reorganization.[18] Without this protection, investors would be reluctant to get involved with the reorganization, out of a fear that undeterminable future liabilities arising from the debtor's past would make further reorganization necessary. While 524(g) authorizes trusts and channeling injunctions for asbestos claims, it is not, by any means, clear that such channeling injunctions will work for cases not covered by that section.

[C]   Estimation of Future Claims[19]

Cases involving mass tort claims present difficult issues concerning the number and amount of valid claims against the estate. To avoid running the risk that the trust established to satisfy mass tort claims will turn out to be inadequate, it must be adequately funded. Otherwise, there is a risk that tort claimants will receive a disproportionally small portion of the debtor's residual value in violation of bankruptcy's core principal of equal treatment of creditors of the same class. Accordingly, the size and extent of tort victims' present and future claims must be estimated.

The Code explicitly provides for the estimation of creditors' future claims.

---

[15] Susan Power Johnston & Katherine Porter, *Extension of Section 524(g) of the Bankruptcy Code to Nondebtor Parents, Affiliates, and Transaction Parties*, 59 Bus. Law. 503 (2004); Linda J. Rusch, *Unintended Consequences of Unthinking Tinkering: The 1994 Amendments and the Chapter 11 Process*, 69 Am. Bankr. L.J. 349, 389-90 (1995) (explaining channeling injunctions under § 524(g)).

[16] Kane v. Johns-Manville Corp., 843 F.2d 636 (2d Cir. 1988); Marianna S. Smith, *Resolving Asbestos Claims: The Manville Personal Injury Settlement Trust*, 53 Law & Contemp. Probs 27 (1990).

[17] *See* Eric D. Green, James L. Patton, Jr., & Edwin J. Harron, *Future Claimant Trusts and "Channeling Injunctions" to Resolve Mass Tort Environmental Liability in Bankruptcy: The Met-Coil Model*, 22 Emory Bankr. Dev. J. 157 (2005).

[18] Sander L. Esserman & David J. Parsons, *The Case for Broad Access to 11 U.S.C. § 524(g) in Light of the Third Circuit's Ongoing Business Requirement Dicta in Combustion Engineering*, 62 N.Y.U. Ann. Surv. Am. L. 187 (2006).

[19] David S. Salsburg & Jack F. Williams, *A Statistical Approach to Claims Estimation in Bankruptcy*, 32 Wake Forest L. Rev. 1119 (1997).

Section 502(c) provides:

> (c) There shall be estimated for purpose of allowance under this section —
>
> > (1) any contingent or unliquidated claim, the fixing or liquidation of which, as the case may be, would unduly delay the administration of the case; or
> >
> > (2) any right to payment arising from a right to an equitable remedy for breach of performance.[20]

Bankruptcy Rule 3018(a) further provides that the court may temporarily allow claims for the purpose of permitting creditors to vote on a proposed plan. In addition, courts have utilized the estimation of claims for the purpose of determining the feasibility of plans[21] and for determining the amount of any distribution under a proposed plan.[22] Thus, the court may estimate the extent of mass tort claims as necessary for the purpose of permitting present and future creditors to vote on the debtor's plan.

Although § 502(c) permits and indeed requires the court to estimate creditors' claims, it is conspicuously silent about the appropriate method for doing so. This void has led courts and commentators to suggest a variety of methods.[23] The most common of these approaches is the "discounted value model"[24] in which the face amount of the claim is discounted by the probability of the claimant prevailing under applicable nonbankruptcy law.

In cases involving unspecified future claims, courts rely on expert testimony. In the A.H. Robins, Inc. Dalkon Shield bankruptcy case, the court relied on expert testimony to estimate the amount of existing and future tort claims at $4 billion.[25] When the trust established by the debtor's plan eventually shut down, it had paid out only 75% of that amount. By contrast, the Johns-Manville trust's initial funding proved inadequate to pay the unexpectedly large volume of claims that arose.[26]

[D] Bankruptcy of Religious Organizations[27]

Several American Diocese of the Roman Catholic Church have experienced financial difficulties arising from liabilities they faced in relationship to the child-abuse scandals that came to light in the late 1990s.[28] As of late 2012, this has led

---

[20] Bankruptcy Code § 502(c).

[21] *E.g.*, In re Farley, Inc., 146 B.R. 748 (Bankr. N.D. Ill. 1992).

[22] In re Rusty Jones, Inc., 143 B.R. 499, 505 (Bankr. N.D. Ill. 1992).

[23] David S. Salsburg & Jack F. Williams, *A Statistical Approach to Claims Estimation in Bankruptcy*, 32 Wake Forest L. Rev. 1119, 1130-52 (1997).

[24] *E.g.*, In re Farley, Inc., 146 B.R. 748, 753-54 (Bankr. N.D. Ill. 1992).

[25] Menard-Sanford v. Mabey (In re A.H. Robins Co.), 880 F.2d 694 (4th Cir. 1989).

[26] http://www.mantrust.org/history.htm (last viewed on June 1, 2012).

[27] Jonathan C. Lipson, *When Churches Fail: the Diocesan Debtor Dilemmas*, 79 S. Cal. L. Rev. 363 (2006); Felicia Anne Nadborny, Note, *"Leap of Faith" into Bankruptcy: An Examination of the Issues Surrounding the Valuation of a Catholic Diocese's Bankruptcy Estate*, 13 Am. Bankr. Inst. L. Rev. 839

eight of these diocese to file Chapter 11 petitions.[29] Along with the usual problems that arise in bankruptcies prompted by mass tort claims, diocesan bankruptcies raise numerous difficult management and property questions not usually encountered in bankruptcies of secular organizations.

Issues that have emerged in these cases that are peculiar to those in cases involving debtors with the unusual organizational structure of the Roman Catholic Church. Foremost among these are the constitutional implications of applying the Bankruptcy Code to bankruptcies of Catholic diocese in the normal fashion. Appointment of a trustee to take over the affairs of a diocese might violate the First Amendment's Free Exercise Clause.[30] At the same time, bankruptcy court involvement in the diocesan debtor's affairs could result in a constitutionally improper entanglement of the government into church matters, in violation of the principle of separation of church and state.[31]

Consider, for example, whether it would be appropriate for a trustee to take over the management of the diocese, either due to gross mismanagement or fraud on the part of the bishop[32] or because the Chapter 11 case is involuntarily converted to a liquidation cases under Chapter 7.[33] Although there is precedent for it,[34] appointment of a trustee to manage the affairs of a religious organization might violate the Free Expression Clause.[35]

Diocesan bankruptcy cases also give rise to difficult and perhaps unique property issues concerning ownership of parish property.[36] Catholic diocese are

---

(2005); Roundtable Discussion, *Religious Organizations Filing for Bankruptcy*, 13 Am. Bankr. Inst. L. Rev. 25 (2005).

[28] *See* http://www.bishop-accountability.org/resources/resource-files/timeline/2003-01-12-Goodstein-TrailOfPain.htm (last viewed, May 31, 2012).

[29] Petitions have been filed in Davenport, Fairbanks, Milwaukee, Tucson, San Diego, Spokane, Portland, and Wilmington. Information about these cases, including links to the diocesan webpages, is available at Bankruptcy Protection and the Sexual Abuse Crisis, http://www.bishop-accountability.org/bankrupt/ (last visited June 1, 2012). Other dioceses that have suggested the possibility of filing are Boston, MA, Los Angeles, CA, Covington, KY, and Belleville, IL.

[30] Ryan J. Donohue, Comment, *Thou Shalt Not Reorganize: Sacraments for Sale: First Amendment Prohibitions and Other Complications of Chapter 11 Reorganization for Religious Institutions*, 22 Emory Bankr. Dev. J. 293 (2005).

[31] Jonathan C. Lipson, *When Churches Fail: The Diocesan Debtor Dilemmas*, 79 S. Cal. L. Rev. 363, 365 (2006).

[32] Bankruptcy Code § 1104. *See supra* § 19.03[D] Appointment of Trustee or Examiner.

[33] Bankruptcy Code § 1112. *See supra* § 19.05[B] Involuntary Conversion or Dismissal.

[34] *E.g.*, In re United Church of the Minister of God, 74 B.R. 271, 280 (Bankr. E.D. Pa. 1987) (appointment of Chapter 11 trustee). *See also* Late Corp. of the Church of Jesus Christ of Latter-Day Saints v. United States, 136 U.S. 1 (1890) (receivership for church property).

[35] Lyman Johnson, *Debarring Faithless Corporate and Religious Fiduciaries in Bankruptcy*, 19 Am. Bankr. Inst. L. Rev. 523 (2011); Jonathan C. Lipson, *When Churches Fail: The Diocesan Debtor Dilemmas*, 79 S. Cal. L. Rev. 363, 400-03 (2006); Theresa J. Pulley Radwan, *Keeping the Faith: The Rights of Parishioners in Church Reorganizations*, 82 Wash. L. Rev. 75 (2007).

[36] Daniel J. Marcinak, Comment, *Separation of Church and Estate: On Excluding Parish Assets from the Bankruptcy Estate of a Diocese Organized as a Corporation Sole*, 55 Cath. U. L. Rev. 583 (2006); Allison Walsh Smith, Comment, *Chapter 11 Bankruptcy: A New Battleground in the Ongoing Conflict Between Catholic Dioceses and Sex-abuse Claimants*, 84 N.C. L. Rev. 282, 315-330 (2005).

divided up into numerous local parishes, each with its own church, school, and congregation.[37] If parish property is owned by the bankrupt diocese, the liquidation value of the debtor is considerable. If the only property the diocese owns is the land occupied by the diocesan cathedral, the bishop's residence, and his offices, its value may be meager, at least compared to the extent of claims against the diocese.[38] Moreover, resolution of these issues may necessitate an inquiry into the details of canon law that entangles the court into what otherwise might be viewed as purely church matters.[39]

§ 23.03 EMPLOYEES' RIGHTS: COLLECTIVE BARGAINING AGREEMENTS & RETIREMENT BENEFITS

[A] Rejection of Collective Bargaining Agreements[40]

For many companies, the liability that drives them into bankruptcy, or the cost that renders them unable to pay their debts is the employee payroll. In the U.S., airlines, steel manufacturers and other large companies have sought to use bankruptcy to renegotiate their obligations to unionized employees. Shortly after the Bankruptcy Code was amended in 1978, the Supreme Court held in the *NLRB v. Bildisco & Bildisco* case that a collective bargaining agreement was an executory contract that might be rejected under § 365.[41] If a collective bargaining agreement has no status apart from that as executory contract, then, like any executory contract, it can be rejected. There will, of course, be a claim for breach, but that claim is just another general unsecured claim, payable only in depreciated bankruptcy dollars.[42] If a debtor can cut its labor costs by $500,000,000, and is

---

[37] Joseph A. Rohner IV, Comment, *Catholic Diocese Sexual Abuse Suits, Bankruptcy, and Property of the Bankruptcy Estate: Is the "Pot of Gold" Really Empty?*, 84 Or. L. Rev. 1181 (2006).

[38] *Compare* Comm. of Tort Litigants v. Catholic Diocese of Spokane (In re Catholic Bishop), 329 B.R. 304, 318-20 (Bankr. E.D. Wash. 2005) (diocese estopped from asserting ownership right to parish property), *with* Munns v. Martin, 930 P.2d 318, 319-20 (Wash. 1997) (en banc) (diocese owns parish property).

See generally Christina M. Davitt, *Whose Steeple Is It? Defining the Limits of the Debtor's Estate in the Religious Bankruptcy Context*, 29 Seton Hall Legis. J. 531 (2005).

[39] Jonathan C. Lipson, *When Churches Fail: The Diocesan Debtor Dilemmas*, 79 S. Cal. L. Rev. 363, 385-90 (2006); Allison Walsh Smith, Comment, *Chapter 11 Bankruptcy: A New Battleground in the Ongoing Conflict Between Catholic Dioceses and Sex-abuse Claimants*, 84 N.C. L. Rev. 282, 315-330 (2005).

[40] Bill D. Bensinger, *Modification of Collective Bargaining Agreements: Does a Breach Bar Rejection?*, 13 Am. Bankr. Inst. L. Rev. 809 (2005); Babette a Ceccotti, *Lost in Transformation: The Disappearance of Labor Policies in Applying Section 1113 of the Bankruptcy Code*, 15 Am. Bankr. Inst. L. Rev. 415 (2007); Andrew B. Dawson, *Collective Bargaining Agreements in Corporate Reorganizations*, 84 Am. Bankr. L.J. 103 (2010). Daniel Keating, *The Continuing Puzzle of Collective Bargaining Agreements in Bankruptcy*, 35 Wm. & Mary L. Rev. 503, 526-34 (1994); Michael D. Sousa, *Reconciling the Otherwise Irreconcilable: The Rejection of Collective Bargaining Agreements Under Section § 1113 of the Bankruptcy Code*, 18 Lab. Law. 453, 469 (2003).

[41] 465 U.S. 513 (1984). *See supra* Chapter 11 — Executory Contracts and Unexpired Leases.

[42] *See supra* § 11.04 Rejection of Executory Contracts.

forced to pay only $50,000,000 to do so, it is still substantially ahead.

During the 1980s, this led a number of companies to file Chapter 11 with an eye toward rejecting their union contracts. This tactic aroused outrage, especially, but not exclusively, from organized labor. The Supreme Court, however, ruled that it was permissible; that nothing in the Bankruptcy Code or other federal law bestowed special bankruptcy privileges on union contracts.[43]

Congress quickly responded with a compromise. It accepted the basic principle that collective bargaining agreements could be rejected. However, it decided that these contracts should be given special status and special protection.

Congress' response to the collective bargaining agreement problem is embodied in § 1113.[44] It imposes special substantive and procedural rules for the rejection of collective bargaining contracts. The procedural requirements attempt to force both sides to attempt negotiation of a mutually satisfactory new deal. In this respect, it reinforces the bargain model of both Chapter 11 and of collective bargaining law. If the bargaining process fails, § 1113's substantive provisions require the court to determine whether a new deal is necessary to save the debtor. In this respect, section § 1113 models itself to a degree on Chapter 11's cramdown rules, but also on binding labor arbitration.

After the petition is filed, but before filing an application to reject a collective bargaining agreement, the debtor-in-possession[45] must make a proposal to the employee's representative — their union. This proposal must be based on the most complete and reliable information available; it must encompass those "necessary modifications" in the agreement as are "necessary to permit the reorganization."[46] The union must also be given all relevant information necessary to evaluate the proposal.[47] From that point on, § 1113 contemplates that the debtor-in-possession and the employees will negotiate with one another. In the somewhat rosy scenario of the Code, "the trustee shall meet, at reasonable times, with the authorized representative [of the employees] to confer in good faith in attempting to reach mutually satisfactory modifications of such agreement."[48]

If those negotiations fail, the debtor-in-possession may seek court authorization to modify the agreement unilaterally.[49] This requires court approval. The court

---

[43] NLRB v. Bildisco & Bildisco, 465 U.S. 513 (1984).

[44] Section 1114, enacted under the Retiree Benefits Bankruptcy Protection Act of 1988, has parallel provisions for dealing with the payment of insurance benefits to retired employees.

[45] Section 1113 refers to both the debtor-in-possession and the trustee. But, as a practical matter, § 1113 will most often be invoked by a debtor-in-possession. Section 1113 does not apply in Chapter 7 liquidation cases.

[46] Bankruptcy Code § 1113(b)(1)(A).

[47] Bankruptcy Code § 1113(b)(1)(B).

[48] Bankruptcy Code § 1113(b)(2); see, e.g., In re Delta Air Lines, 351 B.R. 67 (Bankr. S.D.N.Y. 2006) (debtor negotiated in good faith despite its refusal to agree to a "snapback" provision that would reinstate the terms of the original collective bargaining agreement upon recovery of the airline industry).

[49] See In re American Provision Co., 44 B.R. 907, 909 (Bankr. D. Minn. 1984) (establishing a widely cited nine-part test for when the debtor may reject a collective bargaining contract). See Jeffrey Berman, *Nobody Likes Rejection Unless You're a Debtor in Chapter 11: Rejection of Collective Bargaining*

approves only if (1) the requirements regarding the proposal and the negotiating process were met,[50] (2) the authorized representative of the employees has refused to accept the proposal without good cause,[51] and (3) the balance of equities "clearly" favors rejection of the agreement.[52]

This requires the court to find that the proposed modifications are necessary. But, courts have not agreed about what "necessary" means.[53] In *Wheeling-Pittsburgh Steel Corp. v. United Steelworkers of America*,[54] the Third Circuit held that necessary meant "essential."[55] Other courts, such as *Truck Drivers Local 807 v. Carey Transportation, Inc. (In re Carey Transportation, Inc)*,[56] take a more flexible approach that focuses on the debtor's long-term prospects rather than on whether the modifications are essential to prevent an immediate liquidation.[57] This more flexible standard is often paired with the requirement of § 1129(a)(11) that a plan of reorganization be confirmed only if confirmation is not likely to be followed by the liquidation of, or the need for further financial reorganization of the debtor.

Section 1113's requirement that the court determine that the balance of equities clearly favors rejection codifies the Court's *Bildisco* decision.[58] This standard, of course, is higher than the business judgment rule that governs whether other executory contracts can be rejected. In applying the standard, courts usually consider six factors:

Agreements Under 11 U.S.C. § 1113, 34 N.Y. L. Sch. L. Rev. 169, 173 (1989).

[50] Bankruptcy Code § 1113(c)(1).

[51] Bankruptcy Code § 1113(c)(2).

[52] Bankruptcy Code § 1113(c)(3).

[53] In re Family Snacks, Inc., 257 B.R. 884 (B.A.P. 8th Cir. 2001); Donald B. Smith & Richard A. Bales, *Reconciling Labor and Bankruptcy Law: The Application of 11 U.S.C. § 1113*, 2001 L. Rev. Mich. St. U. Det. C.L. 1145 (2001). *See generally* John F. Wagner Jr., Annotation, *Requirements for Obtaining Court Approval of Rejection of Collective Bargaining Agreement by Debtor in Possession or Trustee in Bankruptcy Under 11 U.S.C.A. §§ 1113(b) and (c)*, 89 A.L.R. Fed. 299 (1988).

[54] 791 F.2d 1074 (3d Cir. 1986).

[55] 791 F.2d at 1088-94. *See also* In re Royal Composing Room, Inc., 62 B.R. 403, 417-18 (Bankr. S.D.N.Y. 1986); In re Pierce Terminal Warehouse, Inc., 133 B.R. 639, 646-47 (Bankr. N.D. Iowa 1991). *See generally* David Keating, *The Continuing Puzzle of Collective Bargaining Agreements in Bankruptcy*, 35 Wm. & Mary L. Rev. 503, 527 (1994).

[56] 816 F.2d 82 (2d Cir. 1987). *See also* United Food and Commercial Workers Union, Local 328 v. Almac's, Inc. (In re Almac's, Inc.), 90 F.3d 1, 5-6 (1st Cir. 1996); Sheet Metal Workers' Int'l Assoc., Local 9 v. Mile Hi Metal Sys., Inc. (In re Mile Hi Metal Systems, Inc.), 899 F.2d 887, 22 C.B.C.2d 611 (10th Cir. 1990).

[57] Christopher D. Cameron, *How "Necessary" Became the Mother of Rejection: An Empirical Look at the Fate of Collective Bargaining Agreements on the Tenth Anniversary of Bankruptcy Code Section 1113*, 34 Santa Clara L. Rev. 841 (1994); Carlos J. Cuevas, *Necessary Modifications and Section 1113 of the Bankruptcy Code: A Search for the Substantive Standard for Modification of a Collective Bargaining Agreement in a Corporate Reorganization*, 64 Am. Bankr. L.J. 133 (1990); Daniel Keating, *The Continuing Puzzle of Collective Bargaining Agreements in Bankruptcy*, 35 Wm. & Mary L. Rev. 503, 526-34 (1994); Mitchell Rait, *Rejection of Collective Bargaining Agreements under Section 1113 of the Bankruptcy Code: The Second Circuit Enters the Arena*, 63 Am. Bankr. L.J. 355 (1989); Jay M. Rector, Comment, *Bankruptcy — How Necessary is 'Necessary' Under Section 1113?* Truck Drivers Local 807 v. Carey Transportation, 13 J. Corp. L. 941 (1988).

[58] *E.g.*, In re Century Brass Prods., Inc., 795 F.2d 265, 273 (2d Cir. 1986).

1. The likelihood and consequences of liquidation if rejection is not permitted;

2. The likely reduction in the creditors' claims if the agreement remains in effect;

3. The likelihood and consequences of a strike if the agreement is avoided;

4. The possibility and likely effect of employee claims for breach of contract if the agreement is avoided;

5. The cost-spreading abilities of the various parties, taking into account the number of employees covered by the agreement and how their wages and benefits compare with those of others in the industry; and

6. The good or bad faith of the parties in dealing with the debtor's financial problems.[59]

The degree to which this provision adequately addresses the problems of collective bargaining agreements is debatable. The power of the provision is undercut by the fact that labor claims receive no special priority in a Chapter 7 case. Therefore, if the debtor liquidates, § 1113 does nothing for the employees. On the other hand, the company cannot reorganize without its employees, and the employees cannot benefit from § 1113 unless the reorganization is successful. Employees' pension benefit plans are frequently part of the employer's collective bargaining contract with their employees.[60] Where employee's pension benefit plans are governed by collective bargaining agreements, § 1113 comes into play as well. However, an extra layer of complication is introduced here. Employee benefit plans, whether or not they are covered by a collective bargaining agreement, are also governed by ERISA, and many are guaranteed by the Pension Benefit Guarantee Corporation. As such, termination of employee benefit plans can be quite complicated.

[B] Retired Employees' Health Insurance Benefits[61]

Section 1114 provides special protection for insurance benefits of retired employees whose benefits are not covered by a collective bargaining contract governed by § 1113. Companies operating in Chapter 11 must meet the statutory standards of § 1114 to eliminate health insurance coverage provided to retired employees, even if the company could have terminated their coverage if it was not in Chapter 11. Section 1114 provides that a Chapter 11 debtor-in-possession "shall

---

[59] Truck Drivers Local 807 v. Carey Transp., Inc., 816 F.2d 82, 93 (2d Cir. 1987).

[60] Amy Lassiter, Note, *Mayday, Mayday!: How the Current Bankruptcy Code Fails to Protect the Pensions of Employees*, 93 Ky. L.J. 939 (2004-05).

[61] Daniel Keating, *Harsh Realities and Silver Linings for Retirees*, 15 Am. Bankr. Inst. L.J. 437 (2007); Daniel L. Keating, *Good Intentions, Bad Economics: Retiree Insurance Benefits in Bankruptcy*, 43 Vand. L. Rev. 161 (1990); Donald R. Korobkin. *Employee Interests in Bankruptcy*, 4 Am. Bankr. Inst L. Rev. 5 (1996); Susan J. Stabile, *Protecting Retiree Medical Benefits in Bankruptcy: The Scope of Section 1114 of the Bankruptcy Code*, 14 Cardozo L. Rev. 1911 (1993).

timely pay and shall not modify any retiree benefits."[62] Unpaid benefits are entitled to administrative expense priority under § 503.[63] Benefits may not be modified or eliminated unilaterally by the debtor. Instead, changes may be made only with the consent of the retired employees' representative[64] or approval by the court.[65]

In some cases, of course, modification may be necessary for the survival of the business. Modification or termination of retired employees' health benefits may be necessary to preserve the jobs of current employees. Employers may obtain court authorization for temporarily or permanently altering or eliminating health benefits for retired employees. Temporary modification of retired employees' health benefits is permitted if the court determines that such "interim modifications" are "essential to the continuation of the debtor's business or in order to avoid irreparable damage to the estate."[66]

Unilateral modification is permitted, but only after the debtor-in-possession has proposed adjustments "based on the most complete and reliable information available at the time . . . which provides for those necessary modifications . . . that are necessary to permit the reorganization of the debtor and assures that all creditors, the debtor, and all of the affected parties are treated fairly and equitably."[67] After such a proposal is made, the debtor-in-possession is admonished to "meet at reasonable times, with the [retired employees'] authorized representative to confer in good faith in attempting to reach mutually satisfactory modifications of such retiree benefits."[68] This duty to negotiate in good faith is based on the model established by § 1113 for modification of collective bargaining contracts, described above.

Additional protections were added in 2005 for retired employees whose benefits were modified in the six months before the debtor's bankruptcy petition. If the employer was insolvent at the time of the pre-bankruptcy modification the court may order the employer to reinstate the benefits to their original status, unless the court finds that the "balance of the equities clearly favors [the] modification."[69]

Section 1114 does not apply to benefits for current employees. Nor does it apply to well-compensated retired employees whose gross annual income in the twelve months before the debtor's petition was over $250,000, unless the retired employee demonstrates that she is unable to otherwise obtain medical insurance coverage.[70]

---

[62] Bankruptcy Code § 1114(e)(1). The rule applies with equal force to a Chapter 11 debtor under the management of a trustee.

[63] Bankruptcy Code § 1114(e)(2): *see supra* § 10.04[A][2] Administrative Expenses.

[64] Bankruptcy Code § 1114(e)(1)(B).

[65] Bankruptcy Code § 1114(e)(1)(A).

[66] Bankruptcy Code § 1114(h)(1).

[67] Bankruptcy Code § 1114(f)(1)(A).

[68] Bankruptcy Code § 1114(f)(2).

[69] Bankruptcy Code § 1114(l).

[70] Bankruptcy Code § 1114(m) (formerly located in § 1114(l)).

§ 23.04 "SINGLE ASSET" REAL ESTATE CASES[71]

Real estate booms are frequently followed by economic busts. The 1980s and early 1990s witnessed one of the most spectacular boom and bust cycles ever. Another bubble burst in 2008, in the wake of a more general financial crisis. Each time this happens, insolvent developers and developments reach for their lawyers in an effort to stave off foreclosure. In many of these cases, the debtor has only one major asset, a building, and only one major creditor, the financial institution from which it borrowed to build.

The paradigm usually involves a limited partnership that owns a single asset, usually an office building or an apartment complex. Section 101(51B) defines "single asset real estate" as

> real property constituting a single property or project, other than residential property with fewer than 4 residential units, which generates substantially all of the gross income of a debtor who is not a family farmer and on which no substantial business is being conducted by a debtor other than the business of operating the real property and activities incidental.[72]

This describes many real estate ventures.[73] Consider an example involving Downtown Realty Partners, Ltd., a limited partnership that owns a downtown office building, subject to a mortgage in favor of State Bank. Only a portion of the office space in the building is occupied and many of the tenants are behind on their rent. Other similar buildings in the same community face the same problems, driving down the rent that the partnership can charge from any new tenants that it attracts.

Vacant space, defaulting tenants, and low rents have left Downtown Realty Partners unable to make the regular monthly payments due to State Bank. As its financial circumstances worsened, Downtown Realty has not even been able to pay the interest that accumulates on the debt each month. In this worst case scenario, the total debt owed rises each month as the unpaid interest is added to the principal sum due to the bank. The bank is seriously dissatisfied with the situation, as it has its own cash-flow obligations to meet. Bank regulators are also likely to disapprove and may put pressure on State Bank to do something to correct the situation. Eventually, the Bank will seek to foreclose.

Faced with the prospect of losing its only asset and convinced that the economy will eventually improve, Downtown Realty is likely to respond by filing a Chapter 11 petition. This stops the foreclosure proceeding dead in its tracks. Indeed, if the property is worth less than the amount of the total debt owed to the bank, interest will not accrue on either the secured or unsecured claim.

Because the value of the land and building are based on the stream of revenue that they produce, the Downtown Realty's office building is likely to be worth

---

[71] Kenneth N. Klee, *One Size Fits Some: Single Asset Real Estate Bankruptcy Cases*, 87 Cornell L. Rev. 1285 (2002).

[72] Bankruptcy Code § 101(51B).

[73] Section 101(51B) aptly describes the 10 unit apartment building, in Portsmouth, Ohio, where one of your co-authors rents an apartment. His wife resides in it, during the week, to be close to her job as General Counsel of a small state university.

considerably less than the amount of the debt owed to State Bank. With a rising mortgage debt and a declining market value of the collateral, the bank is probably undersecured. The property, once worth $12 million, is now worth only $8 million. And the debt, once only $10 million, is now $15 million. Downtown Realty would like to write down the amount of the debt to the $8 million current market value of the collateral, and begin making payments based on its current financial capacity. State Bank prefers to get out from under the entire deal by foreclosing on the property. Single-asset real estate debtors in this situation usually have few other unsecured creditors. They may owe a few utility and maintenance bills, but these claims are likely to be small in comparison to the bank's large unsecured deficiency claim.

Here, Chapter 11 is not being used to preserve value. The building will remain an office building with tenants, no matter who owns it. The debtor is hoping that it might be able to either delay the foreclosure and negotiate with the bank to reduce the bank's claim on any guaranty or other recourse liability. Or the debtor may be hoping to take advantage of Chapter 11 cramdown to retain ownership of the asset by stripping the bank's lien down to the value of the collateral and making a negligible payment of the unsecured portion of the mortgagee's claims. Thus, the debtor's plan might call for paying the bank only $8 million, with interest, perhaps over a twenty to thirty year period, during which the bank might retain a mortgage on the land securing its $8 million claim. The $7 million unsecured balance would be classified separately from the claims of other unsecured creditors and receive only partial payment. Holders of other far smaller unsecured claims will be paid in full.

The bank is likely to vote against the plan, but as long as it is receiving the value of its secured and unsecured claims and provided that the equity interest holders are contributing new value to the plan and the property has been exposed to the market to ensure that the price being paid is fair, the court might confirm the plan.[74]

Here, the debtor and the bank are fighting over who will enjoy the benefit of any future increase in the value of the building. If the plan is confirmed, and the market improves, Downtown Realty's owners will reap the benefit of the appreciated value and the increased rental income received from new tenants. If State Bank is permitted to foreclose and keeps the building long enough for the building to appreciate in value, it will obtain the benefit of that appreciation. Of course, the bank might simply want to cut its losses. It may believe that the local economy will continue to decline and further reduce the value of its collateral. It may not want to keep the building, thus perhaps sending good money after bad, but if it gets the building it can at least sell it for its current value and obtain at least partial payment on what is at present a "non-performing" loan. This in turn may facilitate the bank's efforts to repair its own financial status and improve its capital position. Such improvements may get the bank out of hot water with the regulatory authorities and enable it to make new and it is to be hoped better loans.

Before 1994, the Code contained few provisions to deal with this problem. The most obvious provisions were § 1111(b) and the absolute priority rule of § 1129(b), which are discussed elsewhere.[75] However, § 1111(b) does not address the real

---

[74] *See supra* § 19.11 Confirmation over Objection of Impaired Class; Cramdown.

[75] Bankruptcy Code § 1111(b). *See supra* § 19.07[C][2] The 1111(b) Election.

desire of the creditor to terminate the bankruptcy, seize the collateral, and retain or resell it, and the absolute priority rule may or may not be subject to the "new value" exception. Creditors have taken several approaches in their efforts to prevent single-asset real estate debtors, like Downtown Realty Partners, to speculate on the real estate market at their creditors' potential expense.

Some have sought to have the stay lifted by arguing that the case was not filed in "good faith."[76] One court recently listed a multi-factor test for determining whether a case should be dismissed as filed in bad faith:

1. The debtor has only one asset;

2. The debtor has few unsecured creditors whose claims are relatively small compared to the claims of the secured creditors;

3. The debtor has no employees;

4. The debtor's one asset is the subject of a foreclosure action as a result of arrearages or default on the debt;

5. The debtor's financial condition is, in essence, a two-party dispute between the debtor and secured creditors, which can be resolved in the pending state foreclosure action;

6. The timing of the debtor's filing evidences an intent to delay or frustrate the legitimate efforts of the debtor's secured creditors to enforce their rights;

7. The debtor cannot meet current expenses including the payment of personal property and real estate taxes; and

8. The debtor has little or no cash flow.[77]

Another approach is to challenge the classification scheme of the debtor's plan which segregates the secured creditor's unsecured deficiency claim from the claims of other unsecured creditors.[78] Another approach has been to question the propriety of the new value exception to the absolute priority rule.[79] More central is an attack on the whole proceeding as lacking good faith because of the lack of any realistic chance for a successful reorganization.[80]

In 1994 and again in 2005, legislative changes to the Code added ammunition to the creditor's' arsenal. The Code now contains a special rule for relief from the automatic stay in "single asset real estate" cases. Relief from the stay is available to permit a mortgage foreclosure action ninety days after petition,[81] unless the debtor has either filed a plan that has a reasonable possibility of being confirmed

---

[76] In re Springs Hospitality, Inc., No. 06-13331, 2006 Bankr. LEXIS 1804 (Aug. 22, 2006, Bankr. D. Col.).

[77] Id.

[78] See supra § 19.08[D][2][c] Classification in Single-Asset Real Estate Cases; Kenneth N. Klee, *One Size Fits Some: Single Asset Real Estate Bankruptcy*, 87 Cornell L. Rev. 1285 (2002).

[79] See supra § 19.11[C] New Value Exception to Absolute Priority Rule.

[80] See supra § 19.10[B] Plan Proposed in Good Faith.

[81] Section 362(d)(3) specifies that the 90 days begins to run when an "order for relief" is entered. In voluntary cases, this is the date the petition is filed.

within a reasonable time or has commenced making monthly payments to keep up with regular interest that is accruing on the mortgage debt.[82] This puts considerable pressure on single asset real estate debtors who are not earning sufficient income from rent or other income to keep up with the interest that is accumulating on the debt while the case is pending.

§ 23.05 CONSOLIDATION OF CASES OF RELATED DEBTORS[83]

Except for spouses, who may file joint bankruptcy proceedings,[84] each individual or other entity in bankruptcy is treated separately. This is ordinarily true even if related debtors go into bankruptcy at the same time. For example, real estate developers commonly set up many related corporations and partnerships. Each development project involves different companies, although all of them are under the direct or indirect control of the same developer.[85] The developer's financial failure may result in the developer's personal bankruptcy as well as the bankruptcy of numerous related companies. In most cases, each of those bankruptcies will be dealt with separately, even though there is overlapping ownership, control, and debt among the various entities affected by the developer's collapse.

However, cases involving related debtors are sometimes handled differently, in one of two possible ways. First, it is common for the court to order "administrative consolidation" of cases involved related debtors. This is also sometimes referred to as "joint administration" or "procedural consolidation." In this type of purely administrative consolidation, the cases are handled together procedurally, but the various debtors' assets and debts are kept separate from one another just as they would have been if the cases were not jointly administered.[86] Far more rarely, bankruptcy courts exercise their plenary powers to order "substantive consolidation" of related debtors in which their assets are pooled together and creditor's claims are satisfied from the same consolidated fund.[87]

---

[82] Bankruptcy Code § 362(d)(3). *See supra* § 8.06[B][4] Single-Asset Real Estate Cases.

[83] Daniel J. Bussel, *Mutliple Claims, Ivanhoe and Substantive Consolidation*, 17 Am. Bankr. Inst. L. Rev. 217 (2009); Chauncey H. Levy, *Joint Administration and Consolidation*, 85 Com. L.J. 538 (1980); William H. Widen, *Report to The American Bankruptcy Institute: Prevalence of Substantive Consolidation in Large Public Company Bankruptcies from 2000 to 2005*, 16 Am. Bankr. Inst. L. Rev. 1 (2008).

[84] See *supra* § 6.02[D] Joint Petitions. Joint filing does not mean that the cases are substantively consolidated; substantive consolidation of joint husband-wife cases is analyzed in much the same way as substantive consolidation generally. *E.g.*, Reider v. Federal Deposit Insurance Corp. (In re Reider), 31 F.3d 1102 (11th Cir. 1994); Robert B. Chapman, *Coverture and Cooperation: The Firm, the Market, and the Substantive Consolidation of Married Debtors*, 17 Bankr. Dev. J. 105 (2000).

[85] One such case, conducted during the late 1980s & early 1990s, involved nearly 1000 separate limited partnerships. In re Cardinal Industries, Inc., 102 B.R. 991, 996 (Bankr. S.D. Ohio 1989). The bankruptcy judge involved, has never really recovered.

[86] *See generally* Gill v. Sierra Pacific Constr., Inc. (In re Parkway Calabasas Ltd.), 89 B.R. 832, 836 (Bankr. C.D. Cal. 1988).

[87] *See* William H. Widen, *Report to the American Bankruptcy Institute: Prevalence of Substantive Consolidation in Large Public Company Bankruptcies from 2000 to 2005*, 16 Am. Bankr. Inst. L. Rev. 1 (2008).

The purpose of joint administration is to make administration of related cases more efficient without affecting the substantive rights of creditors.[88] Substantive consolidation, on the other hand, vitally affects creditors' substantive rights. Accordingly, it is "to be used sparingly."[89]

[A] Joint Administration

Joint Administration, or "administrative consolidation" as it is sometimes called, is simply a method of simplifying procedures to increase convenience and reduce the costs of the bankruptcy case. Bankruptcy Rule 1015(b) specifically permits the court to order a joint administration of two or more estates if the petitions are pending in the same court and the petitioners are spouses; a partnership and at least one of its general partners; two or more general partners of the same partnership; or a debtor and an "affiliate."[90] Joint administration of cases involving married debtors is routine.

"Affiliate" is defined in several ways, but includes a variety of situations in which a person is likely to have effective control of a business entity by reason of equity or property ownership. The most common situation described in the rule is ownership of at least 20 percent of the voting equity of the debtor.[91] A corporation that is wholly owned by one individual is an affiliate of that individual. Likewise, a wholly owned subsidiary corporation is an affiliate of the parent corporation. Most closely held corporations, owed by family members or former business partners, are affiliates of their owners.

However, joint administration is very limited. It does not consolidate the debts or the assets of the debtors, which remain separate. It merely permits such things as the appointment of a single trustee, the use of "a single docket . . . including the listing of filed claims, the combining of notices to creditors of the different estates, and the joint handling of other purely administrative matters that may aid in expediting the cases and rendering the process less costly."[92] Even these actions are permitted only to the extent that they do not materially affect the interests of the creditors of the different estates. Rule 1015(c) specifies that "[p]rior to entering an order [for joint administration] the court shall give consideration to protecting creditors of different estates against potential conflicts of interest."[93] For example, in some cases, it might be necessary to have separate trustees because there are disputes between the debtors' estates. If a parent and subsidiary have both filed bankruptcy petitions, and the subsidiary has a claim against the parent, permitting

---

[88] In re Cooper, 147 B.R. 678, 682 (Bankr. D.N.J. 1992).

[89] Union Sav. Bank v. Augie/Restivo Baking Co. (In re Augie/Restivo Baking Co.), 860 F.2d 515, 518 (2d Cir. 1988) (quoting Flora Mir Candy Corp. v. R.S. Dickson & Co. (In re Flora Mir Candy Corp.), 432 F.2d 1060, 1062 (2d Cir. 1970), and Chemical Bank Trust Co. v. Kheel (In re Seatrade Corp.), 369 F.2d 845, 847 (2d Cir. 1966)). *See* William H. Thornton, *The Continuing Presumption Against Substantive Consolidation*, 105 Banking L.J. 448 (1988).

[90] Fed. R. Bankr. P. 1015(b).

[91] Bankruptcy Code § 101(2)(A).

[92] Fed. R. Bankr. P. 1015 advisory committee notes.

[93] Fed. R. Bankr. P. 1015(c).

the same person to serve as trustee in both debtors' cases would create an inappropriate conflict of interest for the trustee.

In short, administrative consolidation does not affect the fundamental legal distinction between the debtors. In the end, each debtor is liquidated or reorganized separately with each set of creditors receiving payment from the assets or future income of the debtor against whom their claims are made. In many of these cases, each debtor will owe money to a largely similar group of creditors, and in some cases, one debtor will be a co-obligor with another debtor, but the debts will be paid (or more likely not paid) by the debtor or debtors who actually owe them, not by the group as a whole.

[B]   Substantive Consolidation[94]

Substantive consolidation is the bankruptcy equivalent of piercing the corporate veil and removing the legal barrier between two entities that keeps their assets and debts separate from one another. The key difference between administrative and substantive consolidation is that in the former, each debtor's assets and liabilities are kept separate; when cases are substantively consolidated, the legal distinctions between the separate entities are eliminated.[95]

Substantive consolidation entails the elimination of legal distinctions between entities. If the bankruptcy cases of Titanic, Inc. and its sole shareholder, Harland Wolff are consolidated, their separate assets will be combined and their separate creditors will compete with one another to receive a distribution from the common fund. In substantive consolidation, there is a single liquidation or reorganization; all creditors of each entity are paid, if at all, from the property of the consolidated entity.

Sorting out the exact dimensions of the consolidated estate can be complicated. Consider for example a case in which the assets and debts of three separate corporations, Titanic, Inc., Olympic, Inc., and Britannic, Inc. are substantively consolidated. Suppose that Titanic has $10 million in debt and $4 million in assets, Olympic has $12 million in debt and $3 million in assets, and Britannic has $1 million in debt and only $100,000 in assets. Of Titanic's assets, $2 million is a debt owed to it by Olympic, and $500,000 is a debt owed to it by Britannic. Conversely, of Olympic's $12 million in debt, $2 million is its debt to Titanic and of Britannic's $1 million in debt, $500,000 is its obligation to Titanic. These are netted out upon consolidation, because an entity cannot owe money to itself. What remains are the group's "real" obligations — the debts it owes to outsiders; and its "real" assets — its tangible property plus claims it has against outsiders.

---

[94] Douglas G. Baird, *Substantive Consolidation Today*, 47 B.C. L. Rev. 5 (2005); Timothy E. Graulich, *Substantive Consolidation — A Post-Modern Trend*, 14 Am. Bankr. Inst. L. Rev. 527 (2006); J. Maxwell Tucker, *Substantive Consolidation: The Cacophony Continues*, 18 Am. Bankr. Inst. L. Rev. 89 (2010); William H. Widen, *Report to the American Bankruptcy Institute: Prevalence of Substantive Consolidation in Large Public Company Bankruptcies from 2000 to 2005*, 16 Am. Bankr. Inst. L. Rev. 1 (2008); William H. Widen, *Corporate Form and Substantive Consolidation*, 75 Geo. Wash. L. Rev. 237 (2007).

[95] *See* In re Las Torres Dev., LLC, 413 B.R. 687 (Bankr. S.D. Tex. 2009).

Netting out the intragroup transactions in this example, Titanic's assets drop to only $1.5 million, Olympic's debt drops to $10 million, and Britannic's debt drops to $500,000. After consolidation, the new entity has $20.5 million in debt owed to others and $4.6 million in assets available for distribution to its creditors.

Substantive consolidation, like piercing the corporate veil, makes shareholders liable for corporate debts.[96] Although many substantive consolidations involve corporations and their individual or corporate shareholders, many of them involve consolidating the estates of multiple subsidiaries of the same parent or other related entities. Moreover, many piercing cases merely involve giving creditors of the corporation access to the assets of the corporation's owner. Substantive consolidation gives creditors of all the consolidated entities access to the assets of all the consolidated entities. As such, it may significantly affect the distributions to creditors of the various debtors. For example, one debtor may be asset rich and debt poor (or even solvent), while other consolidated debtors may have considerable debt and few assets. Substantive consolidation will benefit the creditors of the asset-poor entity at the expense of the creditors of the asset-rich entity.

There is also a family resemblance between substantive consolidation and equitable subordination.[97] Under equitable subordination, creditors' claims are accorded a lower priority than they otherwise would be entitled to, usually because of the creditor's misconduct.[98] Equitable subordination is a less drastic remedy than substantive consolidation because it leaves intact the legal identity of those involved. It also focuses more precisely than substantive consolidation on redressing misconduct; one of the difficulties of substantive consolidation is that it can have a severe impact on the rights of third parties who were in no way involved in the misconduct that gave rise to the remedy.

Despite its long history,[99] substantive consolidation is not expressly authorized in the Code. Nor are there any guidelines for its application in the Code or the Rules. Instead, it is generally considered part of the court's generally equitable powers under § 105, which broadly permit the court to enter "any order, process, or judgment that is necessary or appropriate to carry out the provisions of [the Bankruptcy Code]."[100]

Substantive consolidation is arguably a remedy for dealing with several distinct problems. Sometimes substantive consolidation is in fact an extreme form of administrative consolidation that is used where it is simply not feasible to administer the estates separately. Sometimes it is a method of dealing with abuse

[96] *See* In re Owens Corning, Inc., 419 F.3d 195, 206 (3d Cir. 2005).

[97] Bankruptcy Code § 510(c)(1). *See supra* § 10.05[B] Equitable Subordination.

[98] *See* In re Owens Corning, Inc., 419 F.3d 195, 206 (3d Cir. 2005).

[99] *See* Reider v. FDIC (In re Reider), 31 F.3d 1102, 1105-08 (11th Cir. 1994); In re Bonham 229 F.3d 750 (9th Cir. 2000); Mary Elisabeth Kors, *Altered Egos: Deciphering Substantive Consolidation*, 59 U. Pitt. L .Rev. 381, 386-97 (1998).

[100] Bankruptcy Code § 105(a). J. Maxwell Tucker, *Substantive Consolidation: The Cacophony Continues*, 18 Am. Bankr. Inst. L. Rev. 89, 116 (2010) (contending that § 105 does not authorize a bankruptcy court to order the substantive consolidation).

or fraud. Still other times, it is voluntarily invoked by the debtor. Although there is a good deal of overlap in the facts examined and the rationales used in these various circumstances, they are to at least some degree analytically distinct.

Substantive consolidation because of administrative necessity arises when there is no feasible way to have a separate administration. Consider the practical difficulties that would arise if Titanic Corp., Olympic Corp., and Britannic Corp. are all engaged in the same business, all have an identical group of creditors, have never kept separate books and records, and are managed by the same people. Affiliated companies sometimes even use invoices and purchase orders interchangeably with one another, depending on whose stationary was most convenient. It may be impossible for them to determine which company owns what or owes what. In this situation, substantive consolidation may be a practical necessity. At best, it would be extravagantly expensive to sort this out, with little benefit for the creditors.[101] Whether the actions of the companies were fraudulent, abusive, or merely incompetent is not really relevant because there is no alternative other than to substantively consolidate the companies' estates into one.

However, most of the serious disputes over substantive consolidation involve situations in which it is possible to separately administer the debtors' cases. Consolidation is usually sought by creditors of at least one of the related entities (usually one with many debts and few assets), who contend that consolidation is the only way to save them from the effects of the various debtors' misconduct. Typically, these cases involve situations in which one or more of the debtors either (1) misled creditors about whom they were dealing with or (2) was grossly underfinanced by those in control of the debtor group. There are also cases in which there is outright fraud.

Creditors can be misled, intentionally or unintentionally, when the debtor group has failed to make clear to creditors which member of the group is obligated on its debts. If, for example, Titanic, Olympic, and Britannic are all subsidiaries of Ocean Group, Inc. and all use similar or identical stationary with the name of Ocean and its three subsidiaries on it for all documents, correspondence and payments, creditors might not be sure who they are dealing with in any single transaction.

Consolidation is also sometimes ordered when one or some of the affiliated debtors are seriously undercapitalized. Thus, HoldCo Inc. might operate as the parent of two companies: Franklin Fabrications Inc. and Franklin Sales, Inc. Franklin Fabrications manufactures items and sells them to HoldCo which resells them, in turn, to Franklin Sales, Inc. Franklin Sales, Inc. sells the goods on the open market. HoldCo has set the prices it pays Fabrications and the price that it charges to Sales so that HoldCo appears to make money, regardless of whether this causes the subsidiaries to make or lose money. In fact, the price it pays Fabrications is sometimes less than the cost to Fabrications of manufacturing the goods, and the price it receives from Franklin Sales is sometimes more than the items can be sold for on the market. As a result of these practices, when all three companies go into bankruptcy, all of the unencumbered assets are in HoldCo's

---

[101] *See, e.g.*, Chemical Bank v. Kheel, 369 F.2d 845 (2d Cir. 1966) (estimated cost of untangling the financial affairs of affiliates might exceed the entire value of the estate).

name. Neither Franklin Fabrications nor Franklin Sales have assets to distribute to their creditors. These creditors are likely to seek substantive consolidation, claiming that HoldCo's actions amount to a misuse of its subsidiaries to the detriment of their separate creditors.

Although situations of these two types are found in most substantive consolidation cases, courts have not developed specific rules that would indicate whether consolidation is necessary. Instead, they take a case-by-case approach which has resulted in a list of factors that are present in many cases where substantive consolidation has been ordered. An early substantive consolidation case, dealing with the consolidation of a parent and one of its subsidiaries, identified the following factors:

1. The parent owns or controls the sub,

2. The corporations have the same directors or officers,

3. The parent provides financing for the sub,

4. The parent created (incorporated) the sub,

5. The sub has grossly inadequate capitalization,

6. The parent pays salaries and expenses of the sub and subsidizes losses,

7. The sub conducts little or no business with any entity other than the parent,

8. The sub has few or no assets except those it received from the parent,

9. The parent refers to the sub as a department or division, rather than an separate corporation,

10. Directors and officers of the subsidiary act in the interests of the parent, and under the parent's orders,

11. Corporate formalities (such as separate books and records, shareholder and director meetings) are not maintained.[102]

Other cases have added to the list without necessarily increasing clarity. Additional factors identified include such things as fraudulent transfers between companies in the debtor group, intercorporate guarantees, the use of consolidated financial statements, commingled assets, and the difficulty of sorting out the property and debts of the various entities.[103]

Modern cases focus on a more narrow set of principles that encompass the factors that these traditional cases commonly articulate. In *In re Augie/Restivo Baking Co., Ltd.*,[104] the court said that these various factors are nothing more than variations on two more fundamental consideration: (i) whether creditors dealt with the entities as a single economic unit and did not rely on their separate identities in

---

[102] Fish v. East, 114 F.2d 177 (10th Cir. 1940).

[103] *See* In re Bonham, 226 B.R. 56 (Bankr. D. Alaska 1998).

[104] Union Sav. Bank v. Augie/Restivo Baking Co. (In re Augie/Restivo Baking Co., Ltd.), 860 F.2d 515 (2d Cir. 1988).

extending credit; and (ii) whether the affairs of the debtors are so entangled that consolidation will benefit all creditors.[105] Other cases have focused on the "substantial identity" of the affiliated debtors and whether the benefits of consolidation heavily outweigh the harm.[106]

The United States Supreme Court's 1999 decision in *Grupo Mexicano de Desarrollo, S.A. v. Alliance Bond Fund, Inc.*,[107] has led some to question the continued vitality of the doctrine of substantive consolidation, at least in the absence of express statutory authority for the bankruptcy court's authority to order it.[108] In *Grupo Mexicano*, the Court held that federal district courts lack the equitable power to enjoin prejudgment transfers of a debtor's assets, because such an equitable remedy did not exist when the federal courts were created under the Judiciary Act of 1789. Despite questions about the impact of *Grupo Mexicano* on the bankruptcy court's authority under § 105(a), courts have continued to regard it as a viable solution to the problems it addresses.[109]

---

[105] 860 F.2d at 518.

[106] In re Auto-Train Corp., 810 F.2d 270, 276 (D.C. Cir. 1987).

[107] 527 U.S. 308 (1999).

[108] Daniel B. Bogart, *Resisting the Expansion of Bankruptcy Court Power Under Section 105 of the Bankruptcy Code: The All Writs Act and an Admonition from Chief Justice Marshall*, 35 Ariz. St. L.J. 793, 810 (2003); J. Maxwell Tucker, Grupo Mexicano *and the Death of Substantive Consolidation*, 8 Am Bankr. Inst. L. Rev. 427 (2000).

[109] *See* In re Owens Corning, Inc., 419 F.3d 195, 208 n.14 (3d Cir. 2005); Douglas G. Baird, *Substantive Consolidation Today*, 47 B.C. L. Rev. 5, 20-21 (2005); J. Maxwell Tucker, *Substantive Consolidation: The Cacophony Continues*, 18 Am. Bankr. Inst. L. Rev. 89, 116 (2010).

TABLE OF CASES

[References are to pages]

[References are to pages]

[References are to pages]

[References are to pages]

[References are to pages]

[References are to pages]

[References are to pages]

H

[References are to pages]

[References are to pages]

M

[References are to pages]

[References are to pages]

N

O

[References are to pages]

[References are to pages]

[References are to pages]

[References are to pages]

[References are to pages]

TABLE OF STATUTES

[References are to pages]

[References are to pages]

[References are to pages]

[References are to pages]

[References are to pages]

[References are to pages]

[References are to pages]

[References are to pages]

[References are to pages]

[References are to pages]

[References are to pages]

[References are to pages]

[References are to pages]

[References are to pages]

[References are to pages]

[References are to pages]

[References are to pages]

[References are to pages]

[References are to pages]

[References are to pages]

[References are to pages]

[References are to pages]

[References are to pages]

[References are to pages]

[References are to pages]

[References are to pages]

TABLE OF STATUTES

[References are to pages]

[References are to pages]

INDEX

[References are to sections.]

A

ARBITRATION CLAUSES
Generally . . . 5.06

AUTOMATIC STAY
Co-debtor stays in Chapters 12 and 13 . . . 8.04
Discretionary stays . . . 8.05
Duration of automatic stay
  Generally . . . 8.06
  Automatic termination of stay
    Generally . . . 8.06[A]
    Conclusion of bankruptcy case
      . . . 8.06[A][2]
    Individual debtor's failure to file state-
      ment of intention . . . 8.06[A][5]
    Multiple prior petitions within one year
      . . . 8.06[A][4]
    Prior petition within one year
      . . . 8.06[A][3]
    Property no longer in estate
      . . . 8.06[A][1]
    Statement of intention, individual debt-
      or's failure to file . . . 8.06[A][5]
  Relief from stay upon request of party
    Generally . . . 8.06[B]
    Creditors, foreclosure in cases filed to
      delay, hinder or defraud
      . . . 8.06[B][5]
    Creditor standing . . . 8.06[B][7]
    Enforceability of pre-petition waivers
      . . . 8.06[B][6]
    Foreclosure in cases filed to delay, hinder
      or defraud creditors . . . 8.06[B][5]
    Form of . . . 8.06[C]
    Lack of adequate protection
      . . . 8.06[B][1]
    No equity and property not necessary for
      reorganization (See subhead: No equity
      and property not necessary for reorga-
      nization)
    Other than for lack of adequate protec-
      tion . . . 8.06[B][2]
    Pre-petition waivers, enforceability of
      . . . 8.06[B][6]
    Procedure for obtaining . . . 8.06[D]
    Single-asset real estate cases
      . . . 8.06[B][4]
    Stay, form of relief from . . . 8.06[C]
Enforcement of stay
  Actions in violation of stay are void
    . . . 8.07[A]
  Damages for violating stay . . . 8.07[B]
  Sovereign immunity . . . 8.07[C]
  Violation of stay are void, action in
    . . . 8.07[A]
Exceptions to
  Generally . . . 8.03

AUTOMATIC STAY—Cont.
Exceptions to—Cont.
  Governmental action (See Subhead: Public
    rights exceptions to stay)
  Private rights exceptions to stay
    Generally . . . 8.03[A]
    Commercial real estate leases
      . . . 8.03[A][3]
    Domestic obligations, family and
      . . . 8.03[A][1]
    Family and domestic obligations
      . . . 8.03[A][1]
    Negotiable instruments, presentment of
      . . . 8.03[A][4]
    Other private rights exceptions to auto-
      matic stay . . . 8.03[A][5]
    Pre-petition property interests, perfection
      of . . . 8.03[A][2]
    Presentment of negotiable instruments
      . . . 8.03[A][4]
  Public rights exceptions to stay
    Generally . . . 8.03[B]
    Criminal prosecutions . . . 8.03[B][1]
    Governmental pecuniary interests, spe-
      cific . . . 8.03[B][3]
    Regulatory enforcement . . . 8.03[B][2]
No equity and property not necessary for reorganiza-
tion
  Generally . . . 8.06[B][3]
  No equity in property . . . 8.06[B][3][a]
  Property not necessary for effective reorganiza-
    tion . . . 8.06[B][3][b]
Purpose of . . . 8.01
Scope of
  Generally . . . 8.02
  Acts
    Collect, to . . . 8.02[E]
    Perfect, create or enforce liens
      . . . 8.02[D]
    Possession or control of estate property,
      to obtain . . . 8.02[C]
  Administrative proceedings, judicial and
    . . . 8.02[A]
  Enforcement of judgments . . . 8.02[B]
  Estate property, acts to obtain possession or
    control of . . . 8.02[C]
  Judgments, enforcement of . . . 8.02[B]
  Judicial and administrative proceedings
    . . . 8.02[A]
  Liens, acts to create, perfect or enforce
    . . . 8.02[D]
  Setoff . . . 8.02[F]
  Tax court proceedings . . . 8.02[G]

AVOIDING POWERS
Involuntary gap transfers . . . 14.05[B]
Limitations on avoiding powers
  Generally . . . 14.08

I-1

[References are to sections.]

[References are to sections.]

[References are to sections.]

[References are to sections.]

[References are to sections.]

[References are to sections.]

[References are to sections.]

[References are to sections.]

[References are to sections.]

O

P

[References are to sections.]

R

[References are to sections.]

[References are to sections.]

[References are to sections.]